BIOLOGICAL SCIENCE **2**

Systems, Maintenance and Change

D.J. TAYLOR B.Sc., Ph.D., C.Biol., F.I.Biol.
Director of Continuing Education
Strode's Sixth Form College, Egham

N.P.O. GREEN B.Sc., C.Biol., M.I.Biol.
Headmaster
St George's College, Buenos Aires, Argentina

G.W. STOUT B.Sc., M.A., M.Ed., C.Biol., F.I.Biol.
Headmaster
International School of South Africa, Mafikeng, South Africa

Editor
R. SOPER B.Sc., C.Biol., F.I.Biol.
Formerly Vice-Principal and Head of Science
Collyers Sixth Form College, Horsham

CAMBRIDGE
UNIVERSITY PRESS

PUBLISHED BY THE PRESS SYNDICATE OF THE UNIVERSITY OF CAMBRIDGE
The Pitt Building, Trumpington Street, Cambridge CB2 1RP, United Kingdom

CAMBRIDGE UNIVERSITY PRESS
The Edinburgh Building, Cambridge CB2 2RU, United Kingdom
40 West 20th Street, New York, NY 10011-4211, USA
10 Stamford Road, Oakleigh, Melbourne 3166, Australia

First published 1984
Ninth printing 1987
Second edition 1990
Fourth printing 1995
Third edition 1997

Printed in the United Kingdom at the University Press, Cambridge

Typeset in Times 10/12 pt

A catalogue record for this book is available from the British Library

ISBN 0 521 56720 3 paperback

Contents

Preface to the first edition

The fundamental aim underlying the writing of *Biological Science* was the desire to emphasise the unifying scientific nature of biological systems despite the amazing diversity in structure and function seen at all levels of biological organisation.

Books 1 and 2 comprise a complete text for the A-level student, following all syllabuses in Biological Sciences and incorporating all the topic areas recommended by the GCE Interboard Working Party on the A-level common core in Biology (published 1983). The text will also be relevant to all first-year University and Further Education College students studying the Biological Sciences.

Each chapter is designed to provide comprehensive, up-to-date information on all topics in Biological Sciences, and the accuracy and relevance of this information has been checked by leading authorities in the appropriate fields and by practising teachers and examiners. The text includes:
– clearly written factual material,
– a carefully selected series of thoroughly pretested practical investigations relevant to the A-level course,
– a variety of types of question designed to stimulate an enquiring approach and answers to them.

Whilst it is recognised that the study of Biological Science follows no set pattern, the content of books 1 and 2 has been arranged so that each book contains material approximating to each year of a two-year course.

The appendices, which provide information and techniques vital to the study of Biological Science at this level, recognise that many students do not study Chemistry and Physics to the same level. Mathematical, physical and chemical concepts related to Biological Sciences are emphasised throughout the text, as appropriate.

Preface to the third edition

Since its publication in 1984, *Biological Science* has become established as one of the most comprehensive and authoritative A level Biology texts. It has remained one of our aims in writing the third edition to maintain its reputation as an up-to-date and comprehensive resource for current A level syllabuses.

In recent years there have been significant changes in content and format of syllabuses, with modular courses becoming important alternatives to 'linear' courses, and a new agreed subject core for Biology being established by SCAA in 1993, which has subsequently been revised in 1997. A typical modern syllabus is now composed of a core containing the agreed basis of the subject, with options that develop depth and range of experience in more specialist areas. Typically these options also emphasise the social, ethical and applied aspects of the subject, and emphasise the growing importance of biological sciences in the modern world.

The revision for the third edition has been far more comprehensive than that carried out for the second edition, with many substantial as well as more subtle changes to the text, diagrams, photographs and tables. Much new material has been written, and material which is no longer relevant has been removed. In addition, some of the material in the appendices has been removed and placed in the relevant chapters.

In recognition of the importance and popularity of certain topics, particularly in option areas, three completely new chapters have been added. These provide comprehensive coverage of Microbiology and biotechnology (chapter 12), Human health and disease (chapter 15) and Applied genetics (chapter 25). In addition, there is far more extensive coverage of human nutrition in chapter 10 and human reproduction in chapter 21 in line with present syllabuses. Where relevant, the ethical and social implications of these topics are also discussed. A wider range of topical issues is also included in the Ecology chapter (chapter 10).

In line with the changing emphasis of syllabuses, Variety of life has been condensed from three chapters into one (chapter 2), with examples relevant to current syllabuses being chosen. The chapter includes a new introductory discussion on classification and use of keys. Other chapters have been updated where necessary. Physiological topics throughout the book have, in particular, been modified in the light of new knowledge as well as to match syllabus requirements. The text also takes into account the trend towards a greater focus on higher plants and humans.

In addition to the changes described, a major effort has been made to make the text suitable for a wider range of students. Consideration has been given to reducing unnecessary complexity, especially in the use of language. Particular care has been taken with the introduction to each topic. Some sections have been reorganised, subheadings added, and greater use made of numbered lists and bulleted points. It is hoped that these changes will improve the readability whilst retaining the vigour and depth of the text.

Revision of this edition of the book has largely been carried out by Dennis Taylor during a sabbatical from Strode's College. As in the second edition, the ecology chapters (10 and 11) have been revised by Rosalind Taylor of Kingston University. The new chapter on Health and disease was mostly written by Roland Soper. Academic referees have checked new text with the aim of making it as factually correct as possible. Nevertheless, in an undertaking this large, errors and inaccuracies are difficult to avoid completely, and the authors are always grateful for notification of any that are spotted.

Acknowledgements

The authors and publisher would like to acknowledge the many friends, colleagues, students and advisers who have helped in the production of *Biological Science*.

In particular, we wish to thank:
Dr R. Batt, Dr I. Benton, Dr Claudia Berek, Professor R.J. Berry, Dr A.C. Blake, Dr John C. Bowman, Dr John Brookfield, Mr R. Brown, Dr Stuart Brown, Dr Fred Burke, Mr Richard Carter, Dr Norman R. Cohen, Dr I. Côte, Dr K.J.R. Edwards, Mr Malcolm Emery, Mr Nick Fagents, Dr James T. Fitzsimons, Dr John Gay, Dr Brij L. Gupta, Vivienne Hambleton, Dr David E. Hanke, Dr R.N. Hardy, Reverend J.R. Hargreaves, Dr S.A. Henderson, Mr Michael J. Hook, Mr Colin S. Hutchinson, Illustra Design Ltd, Dr Alick Jones, Mrs Sue Kearsey, Dr Simon P. Maddrell FRS, Professor Aubrey Manning, Dr Chris L. Mason, Mrs Ruth Miller, Dr David C. Moore, A.G. Morgan, Dr Rodney Mulvey, Dr David Secher, Dr John M. Squire, Professor James F. Sutcliffe, Stephen Tomkins, Dr Eric R. Turner, Dr Paul Wheater, Dr Brian E.J. Wheeler, Dr Michael Wheeler.

The authors are particularly indebted to Mrs Adrienne Oxley, who patiently and skilfully organised the pretesting of all the practical exercises. Her perseverance has produced exercises that teachers, pupils and laboratory technicians can depend upon.

However, the authors accept full responsibility for the final content of these books.

Finally, the authors wish to express their thanks to their wives and families for the constant support and encouragement shown throughout the preparation and publication of these books.

We also wish to thank the following for permission to use their illustrations, tables and questions.
Figures: 13.11, 13.14, 13.16b, 13.16c, 13.17b, 13.25a, 13.25b, 14.3b, 14.6, 14.7, 14.11, 14.14a, 14.16, 15.7, 17.14a, 17.56a, 17.56b, 18.16a, 18.16b, 19.11a, 19.20, 20.3, 20.15a, 20.15b, 20.15c, 20.24a, 20.24b, 21.1c, 21.23a, 21.23b, 21.29, 21.42, 21.50a, 21.50b, 21.50f, 22.25a, 22.25b, 22.29, 23.1, 23.3, 23.7a–f, 23.12a–j, 24.15, 25.27 Biophoto Associates; 13.12a Claus Meyer/Science Photo Library (SPL); 13.12b John Lee/Planet Earth Pictures; 13.16d, 22.16 Centre for Cell and Tissue Research, York; 13.22 Anderson & Cronshaw (1970) *Planta* **91**, 173–80; 13.25c Dr Martin Zimmermann, Harvard University; 13.27 Professor B.E.S. Gunning (1977) *Science Progress* **64**, 539–68, Blackwell Scientific Publications Ltd; 14.1a, 21.36 Dr Paul Wheater; 14.1b K.R. Porter/SPL; 14.3a Life Science Images; 14.4b Professors P.M. Motta & G. Macchiarelli/SPL; 14.4c, 14.4d, 15.19a, 15.19b SPL; 14.35 CNRI/SPL; 14.38b Ken Eward/SPL; 14.40a, 17.8 University of Zurich-Irchel/Nature & Science AG, FL-Vaduz; 14.40b BSIP PIR/SPL; 15.4 Unicef/Betty Press; 15.9 Andy Crump, TDR, WHO/SPL; 15.13 Vivien Fifield; 15.15c, 21.41 Biophoto Associates/SPL; 15.16, 21.52, 25.21 National Medical Slide Bank; 15.17 D. Phillips/SPL; 15.20a Philippe Plailly/SPL; 15.20b Scott Camazine/SPL; 15.23 National Institute of Health/SPL; 15.24 Dr Tony Brain/Spl; 15.25 Princess Margaret Rose Orthopaedic Hospital/SPL; 16.15 Dr B.E. Juniper; 16.17 T. Swarbrick, *Harnessing the hormone*, Grower Publications Ltd; 16.19 Long Ashton Research Station; 16.23 Centre Nationale de la Recherche Scientifique, *Regulateurs naturels de la croissance vegetale* (1964); 16.26 Dr Peter Evans, Southampton University; 16.32 Professor Anton Lang (1957) *Proc. Natl. Acad. Sci. USA* **43**, 709–17; 17.10, 17.14b Don Fawcett/SPL; 17.22, 17.33b, 20.17 Manfred Kage/SPL; 17.25, 21.50d Garry Watson/SPL; 17.27a, 17.27b Natural History Museum, London; 17.43 Profs. P.M. Motta & A. Caggiati/SPL; 17.56d Dr L. Orci, University of Geneva/SPL; 17.58 Daniel Heuchlin/NHPA; 17.61 Niall Rankin/FLPA; 17.68 Caroline E.G. Tutin; 18.18 P.G. Munro, Biopolymer Group, Imperial College; 18.19 A. Freundlich, Biopolymer Group, Imperial College; 18.24 Dr J. Squire, Biopolymer Group, Imperial College; 19.7 Dr R. Clark & M. Goff/SPL; 19.9 19.10 Michael & Patricia Fogden; 19.17a W. Higgs/ GSF Picture Library; 19.17b William S. Paton/Planet Earth Pictures; 19.17c Pete Oxford/Planet Earth Pictures; 20.2a E.H. Mercer (1959) *Proc. Roy. Soc. Lond. B* **150** 216–36; 20.31, 21.11a–f, GSF Picture Library; 21.10 Dr J. Gurdon (1977) *Proc. Roy. Soc. Lond. B* **198** 211–47; 21.13 Sinclair Stammers/SPL; 21.14 Horticultural Research Institute; 21.26 Hermann Eisenbeiss; 21.28 Howard Jones; 21.46a David Scharf/SPL; 21.46b Dr Everett Anderson/SPL; 21.50c, 21.50g, 21.50h Petit Format/Nestle/SPL; 21.50e Keith/Custom Medical Stock Photo/SPL; 22.29 Bettina Cirone/SPL; 23.8 M. Hirons/GSF Picture Library; 23.9, 24.26 ARC Poultry Research Centre; 23.13, 23.14 Dr S.A. Henderson, Department of Genetics, University of Cambridge; 23.28a O.L. Miller Jr & B.A. Hamkalo, Visualization of bacterial genes in action, *Science* **169** 392–5, 24 July 1970, copyright © 1970 by the American Association for the Advancement of Science; 24.30 John Birdsall Photography; 25.4 J.C. Revy/SPL; 25.10 British Diabetic Association; 25.12 John Frost Historical Newspaper Service; 25.13a, 25.14, 25.15, 26.9b Nigel Cattlin/Holt Studios International; 25.16 M. Baret, RAPHO/SPL; 25.17 Philippe Plailly/Eurelios/SPL; 25.18 PPL Pharmaceuticals; 25.20 British Union for the Abolition of Vivisection; 25.25 Cystic Fibrosis Trust; 25.28 Hattie Young/SPL; 25.32 Saturn Stills/SPL; 25.34 Klaus Gulbrandsen/SPL; 25.35 David Parker/SPL; 25.37 Cellmark Diagnostics; 26.3 D.R.B. Booth/GSF Picture Library; 26.7 Charles & Sandra Hood/Bruce Coleman Ltd; 26.8b Heather Angel; 26.9a Werner Layer/Bruce Coleman Ltd; 26.17 M.P.L. Fogden/Bruce Coleman Ltd; 27.5a, 27.5b AGPM; 27.6 Semences Nickerson, France; 27.7 D.F. Jones, Connecticut Agricultural Experiment Station; 27.9, 27.13 John Haywood; 27.10a S.E. Davis; 27.10b Kim Taylor/Bruce Coleman Ltd; 27.12 M.A. Tribe, I. Tallan & M.R. Erant (1978) *Case Studies in Genetics*, CUP.

Cover: Science Photo Library

Chapter Thirteen

Transport in plants

It was explained in section 5.9.8 that the exchange of substances between individual cells and their environments takes place by the passive processes of diffusion and osmosis, and the active processes of active transport and endocytosis or exocytosis. Within cells substances generally move by diffusion, but active processes, such as cytoplasmic streaming, can also occur. Over short distances these means of transport are rapid and efficient and in unicellular organisms, and multicellular organisms which have a large surface area to volume ratio, they are efficient enough for special transport systems to be unnecessary. For example, respiratory gases are exchanged by diffusion between the body surface and the environment in small organisms such as the earthworm.

In larger and more complex organisms, cells may be too widely separated from each other and from their external environments for these processes to be adequate. Specialised long-distance transport systems which can move substances more rapidly become necessary. Materials are generally moved by a mass flow system, **mass flow** being the bulk transport of materials from one point to another as a result of a pressure difference between the two points. With mass flow all the materials are swept along together at similar speeds, as in a river, whereas in diffusion molecules move independently of each other according to their own diffusion gradients. Some of the mass flow systems of plants and animals are summarised in table 13.1.

Note that animals are able to use the power of muscle contraction to force liquids or gases from one place to another, as when the heart pumps blood round the body. Plants on the other hand have to rely only on mechanisms such as evaporation, active transport and osmosis as will be seen later.

Both animals and plants have vascular systems. A **vascular system** is one which has tubes which are full of fluid being transported from one place to another. In animals the blood system is a vascular system. In plants the xylem and phloem form vascular systems. These systems require a source of energy to function. In the case of movement through xylem, the energy required comes directly from the Sun. Where mass flow occurs through specialised transport systems, such as phloem in plants and respiratory systems in animals, these systems are linked with specialised exchange systems whose function is to maintain concentration gradients between the transport system and the cells it serves.

Table 13.2 summarises the main groups of substances that move through plants and gives details of their movement.

The movement of substances through the conducting, or vascular, tissues of plants is called **translocation**. In vascular plants the vascular tissues are highly specialised and are called **xylem** and **phloem**. Xylem translocates mainly water and mineral salts (as well as some organic

Table 13.1 Some mass flow systems of animals and plants.

Mass flow system	Material(s) moved	Driving force
Plants		
vascular system:		
xylem (chapter 13)	mainly water and mineral salts	transpiration and root pressure
phloem (chapter 13)	mainly organic food, e.g. sucrose	active transport and osmosis
Animals		
alimentary system (chapter 8)	food and water	muscles of alimentary canal
respiratory system (chapter 9)	air or water	respiratory muscles
blood vascular system (chapter 14)	blood	heart or contractile blood vessels
lymphatic system (chapter 14)	lymph	general muscular activity in the body

Table 13.2 Movement of substances through plants.

	Uptake	*Transport*	*Elimination*
Water	osmosis into root	mass flow through xylem	diffusion (transpiration) through stomata (also small loss from cuticle and lenticels)
Solutes	diffusion or active transport into root	mass flow through xylem (mainly inorganic solutes) or phloem (mainly organic solutes)	shedding of leaves, bark, fruits and seeds; otherwise retained until death or passed to next generation in embryo of seed
Gases*	diffusion through stomata, lenticels, epidermis	diffusion through intercellular spaces and through cells	diffusion through stomata, lenticels, epidermis

* Movement of gases is considered in further detail in chapter 9.

nitrogen and hormones) from the roots to the aerial parts of the plant. Phloem translocates a variety of organic and inorganic solutes, mainly from the leaves or storage organs to other parts of the plant.

The study of translocation has important economic applications. For example, it is useful to know how herbicides, fungicides, growth regulators and nutrients enter plants, and the routes that they take through plants, in order to know how best to apply them and to judge possible effects that they might have. Also, plant pathogens such as fungi, bacteria and viruses are sometimes translocated, and such knowledge could influence treatment or preventive measures. In the 1960s, for example, a new group of fungicides was introduced which were described as **systemic** because they were translocated throughout plants. They provide longer-term, and more thorough, protection from important diseases like mildews.

13.1 Plant water relations

13.1.1 Osmosis

An understanding of plant water relations depends upon an understanding of osmosis and diffusion, which are explained in section 7.9.8. You should read this section if you have not already done so. It is pointed out in section 7.9.8 that osmosis can be regarded as a special kind of diffusion in which water molecules are the only molecules diffusing. This is due to the presence of a partially permeable membrane which does not allow the passage of solute particles. **Osmosis** is the movement of water molecules from a region of their high concentration (a dilute solution) to a region of their low concentration (a more concentrated solution) through a partially permeable membrane.

13.1.2 Terms used

In 1988 the Institute of Biology recommended the use of the term **water potential** to describe water movement through membranes. The two main factors affecting the water potential of plant cells are solute concentration and the pressure generated when water enters and inflates plant cells. These are expressed in the terms **solute potential** and **pressure potential** respectively. All of these terms are explained below.

13.1.3 Water potential (symbol ψ, the Greek letter psi)*

Water potential is a fundamental term derived from thermodynamics. Water molecules possess kinetic energy, which means that in liquid or gaseous form they move about rapidly and randomly from one location to another. The greater the concentration of water molecules in a system, the greater the total kinetic energy of water molecules in that system and the higher its so-called water potential. Pure water therefore has the highest water potential. If two systems containing water are in contact (such as soil and atmosphere, or cell and solution) the random movements of water molecules will result in the net movement of water molecules from the system with the higher water potential (higher energy) to the system with the lower water potential (lower energy) until the concentration of water molecules in both systems is equal. This is, in effect, diffusion involving water molecules.

Water potential is usually expressed in pressure units by biologists (such as pascals; 1 pascal = 1 newton per m^2).** Pure water has the highest water potential, and by convention this is set at zero.

---

* Technically, ψ means potential and water potential should be represented ψ_w. Since in living systems the solvent we are concerned with is always water, it is simpler to use ψ and assume the w.

** Pressure was formerly measured in atmospheres (atm), but now pascals are used (Pa).

1 Pa	=	1 N m^{-2}	(N = newton)		
1 bar	=	0.987 atm	=	10^5 Pa	=	100 kPa
1 atm	=	1.0132 bar	=	1.0132 × 10^5 Pa		
1000 kPa	=	1 MPa			

Note the following main points:

- pure water has the maximum water potential, which by definition is zero;
- water *always* moves from a region of higher ψ to one of lower ψ;
- all solutions have lower water potentials than pure water and therefore have negative values of ψ (at atmospheric pressure and a defined temperature);
- osmosis can be defined as the movement of water molecules from a region of higher water potential to a region of lower water potential through a partially permeable membrane.

Advantage of using water potential

Water potential can be regarded as the tendency of water molecules to move from one place to another. The higher (less negative) the water potential the greater tendency to leave a system. If two systems are in contact, water will move from the system with the higher water potential to the one with the lower water potential. The two systems do not necessarily have to be separated by a membrane.

Using the term water potential, the tendency for water to move between any two systems can therefore be measured, not just from cell to cell in a plant, but also, for example, from soil to root or from leaf to air. Water can be said to move through a plant down a gradient of water potential from soil to air. The steeper the gradient, the faster the flow of water along it.

13.1.4   Solute potential, ψ_s

The effect of dissolving solute molecules in pure water is to reduce the concentration of water molecules and hence to lower the water potential. All solutions therefore have lower water potentials than pure water. The amount of this lowering is known as the **solute potential**. In other words, solute potential is a measure of the change in water potential of a system due to the presence of solute molecules. ψ_s is always negative. The more solute molecules present, the lower (more negative) is ψ_s (see also section 7.9.8). For a solution, $\psi = \psi_s$.

13.1.5   Pressure potential, ψ_p

If pressure is applied to pure water or a solution, its water potential increases. This is because the pressure is tending to force the water from one place to another. Such a situation may occur in living cells. For example, when water enters plant cells by osmosis, pressure may build up inside the cell making the cell turgid and increasing the pressure potential (section 13.1.8). Also, water potential of blood plasma is raised to a positive value by the high blood pressure in the glomerulus of the kidney. Pressure potential is usually positive, but in certain circumstances, as in xylem when water is under tension (negative pressure) it may be negative.

Summary

Water potential is affected by both solute potential and pressure potential, and the following equation summarises the relationship between the two terms.

$$\underset{\text{water potential}}{\psi} = \underset{\substack{\text{solute}\\\text{potential}}}{\psi_s} + \underset{\substack{\text{pressure}\\\text{potential}}}{\psi_p}$$

Solute potential is negative and pressure potential is usually positive.

13.1.6   Movement of water between solutions by osmosis

The terms mentioned above can only be used with confidence if they are properly understood. Question 5.4 on page 145 in Book 1 can be a useful test of your understanding of ψ and ψ_s. ψ_p is dealt with below.

13.1.7   Osmosis and plant cells

The partially permeable membranes of importance in the water relations of plant cells are shown in fig 13.1. The cell wall is usually freely permeable to substances in solution, so is not important in osmosis. The cell contains a large central vacuole whose contents, the cell sap, contribute to the solute potential of the cell. The

Fig 13.1 *Partially permeable membranes of a typical plant cell. The cell surface membrane would normally be pressed tightly up against the cell wall*

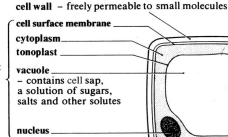

protoplast
– living part of cell

cell wall – freely permeable to small molecules
cell surface membrane
cytoplasm
tonoplast
vacuole
– contains cell sap, a solution of sugars, salts and other solutes
nucleus

cell surface membrane
– surrounds cytoplasm
tonoplast
– membrane surrounding vacuole
partially permeable membranes

two important membranes are the cell surface membrane and the tonoplast.

If a plant cell is in contact with a solution of lower water potential than its own contents (such as the concentrated sugar solution in Experiment 13.1 below), then water leaves the cell by osmosis through the cell surface membrane (fig 13.2). Water is lost first from the cytoplasm and then from the vacuole through the tonoplast. The protoplast, that is the living contents of the cell surrounded by the cell wall, shrinks and eventually pulls away from the cell wall. This process is called **plasmolysis**, and the cell is said to be **plasmolysed**. The point at which plasmolysis is just about to happen is called **incipient plasmolysis**. At incipient plasmolysis the protoplast has just ceased to exert any pressure against the cell wall, so the cell is **flaccid**. Water will continue to leave the protoplast until its contents have the same water potential as the external solution. No further shrinkage then occurs.

> **13.1** What occupies the space between the cell wall and the shrunken protoplast in plasmolysed cells?

The process of plasmolysis is usually reversible without permanent damage to the cell. If a plasmolysed cell is placed in pure water or a solution of higher water potential than the contents of the cell, water enters the cell by osmosis (fig 13.2). As the volume of the protoplast increases it begins to exert pressure against the cell wall and stretches it. The wall is strong and relatively rigid, so the pressure inside the cell rises rapidly. The pressure is called the **pressure potential** (ψ_p). As the pressure potential of the cell increases, due to water entering by

osmosis, the cell becomes **turgid**. Full turgidity, that is maximum ψ_p, is achieved when a cell is placed in pure water.

When the tendency for water to enter a cell is exactly balanced by pressure potential, the amount of water leaving the cell equals that entering the cell. There is no further net uptake of water and the cell is now in equilibrium with the surrounding solution. The contents of the cell are still likely to be of lower solute potential than the external solution because only a small amount of water is needed to raise the pressure potential to the equilibrium point, and this is not sufficient to dilute the cell contents significantly. Pressure potential therefore accounts for the fact that at equilibrium the solute potential of a plant cell can still be lower (its contents more concentrated) than that of the external solution.

Pressure potential is a real pressure rather than a potential one, and can only develop to any extent if a cell wall is present. Animal cells have no cell wall and the cell surface membrane is too delicate to prevent the cell expanding and bursting in a solution of higher water potential. Animal cells must therefore be protected by osmoregulation (chapter 20).

> **13.2** What is the ψ_p of a flaccid cell?
>
> **13.3** Which organisms, apart from plants, possess cell walls?

Experiment 13.1: To investigate osmosis in living plant cells

Materials

onion bulb or young rhubarb	distilled water
epidermis	1 M sucrose solution
microscope	2 teat pipettes
2 slides and cover-slips	filter paper
scalpel and forceps	

Method

Remove a strip of epidermis from the inner surface of one of the fleshy storage leaves of the onion bulb, or from the young rhubarb petiole. Rhubarb has the advantage of having coloured cell sap, but onion epidermis is easier to peel off. The epidermis can be removed by first slitting it with a scalpel, then lifting and tearing back the single layer of cells with fingers or forceps. Quickly transfer the epidermal strip to a slide and add two or three drops of distilled water. Carefully add a cover-slip and examine the cells with a microscope. Identify and draw a few epidermal cells. Repeat using another strip of epidermis and 1 M sucrose solution instead of distilled water. Observe the strip over a period of 15 min and draw any changes observed in one or more representative cells at high power. The

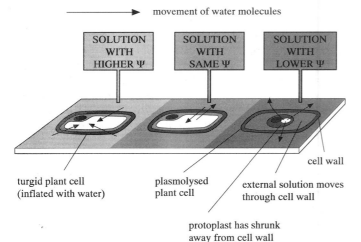

movement of water molecules

Fig 13.2 *Effect of different solutions on plant cells. In a solution with a higher water potential than the plant cell (a **hypotonic** solution), water enters the cell by osmosis and the cell becomes **turgid** (inflated with water). In a solution with a lower water potential (**hypertonic** solution), water leaves the cell by osmosis and the living part of the cell, the protoplast, shrinks. In a solution of equal water potential (**isotonic** solution), the cell remains normal.*

possibility of reversing the process observed can be investigated by irrigating with distilled water under the cover-slip to wash away the sucrose solution. Use filter paper to absorb any excess liquid.

Results

Fig 13.3 shows the appearance of onion epidermal cells left in 1 M sucrose solution for varying lengths of time.

13.1.8 Movement of water between cells by osmosis

Consider the situation in fig 13.4, in which two plant cells possessing different water potentials are in contact.

13.4 (*a*) Which cell has the higher (less negative) water potential?
(*b*) In which direction will water move by osmosis?
(*c*) At equilibrium the two cells will have the same water potential, which will be the average of the two, namely −1000 kPa. Assuming that ψ_s does not change significantly, what would be ψ_p at equilibrium in cell A and cell B?

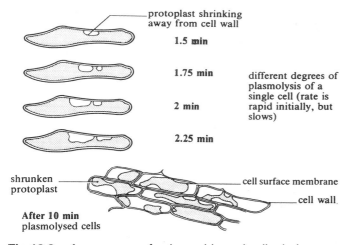

protoplast shrinking away from cell wall

1.5 min

1.75 min

2 min

2.25 min

different degrees of plasmolysis of a single cell (rate is rapid initially, but slows)

shrunken protoplast

cell surface membrane

cell wall

After 10 min plasmolysed cells

Fig 13.3 *Appearance of onion epidermal cells during plasmolysis. Strips of epidermal cells were left in 1 M sucrose solution for varying lengths of time.*

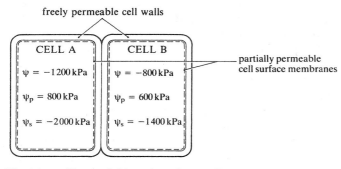

freely permeable cell walls

CELL A	CELL B
$\psi = -1200$ kPa	$\psi = -800$ kPa
$\psi_p = 800$ kPa	$\psi_p = 600$ kPa
$\psi_s = -2000$ kPa	$\psi_s = -1400$ kPa

partially permeable cell surface membranes

Fig 13.4 *Two neighbouring plant cells.*

13.1.9 Effect of heat and alcohol on membranes

The partial permeability of cell membranes can be destroyed by certain chemicals and treatments, such as ethanol and high temperatures. The membranes are still present but behave as if holes had been punched through them and they no longer provide a barrier to the passage of large molecules such as sucrose. High temperature and alcohols denature membrane proteins. Alcohols at high concentrations can also dissolve lipids.

Experiment 13.2: To determine the mean solute potential of the cell sap in a sample of plant cells using the method of incipient plasmolysis

There are several methods available for determining the solute potential of plant cells, but the most convenient is that of incipient plasmolysis. It makes use of the following relationships:

(1)　ψ of a cell = $\psi_s + \psi_p$; ψ of a solution = ψ_s.
(2)　$\psi^{cell} = \psi^{solution}$ when the two are in equilibrium.

Samples of the tissue being investigated are allowed to come to equilibrium in a range of solutions of different concentrations (water potentials) and the aim is to find which solution causes incipient plasmolysis, that is shrinkage of the protoplasts to the point where they just begin to pull away from the cell walls. At this point pressure potential is zero since no pressure is exerted by the protoplasts against the cell walls, so $\psi^{cell} = \psi_s^{cell} = \psi^{solution} = \psi_s^{solution}$ (from (1) and (2) above). In other words, the solution causing incipient plasmolysis has the same solute potential as the cell sap.

In practice, solute potential varies between cells in the same tissue and so some plasmolyse in more dilute solutions than others. Incipient plasmolysis is said to have been reached when 50% of the cells have plasmolysed. At this point 50% of the cells are unplasmolysed and the average cell can be said to be at incipient plasmolysis. The solute potential obtained is a mean value for the tissue.

Materials

onion bulb or rhubarb petiole
6 petri dishes
6 test-tubes
test-tube rack
labels or wax pencil
2×10 cm^3 or 25 cm^3 graduated pipettes
2×100 cm^3 beakers
brush (fine paintbrush)
distilled water
1 M sucrose solution
fine forceps
Pasteur pipettes

slides and cover-slips
microscope
graph paper
razor blade or sharp scalpel

Method

(An alternative method using beetroot is described after this first method.)

(1) Label six petri dishes and six test-tubes appropriately for each of the following sucrose solutions: 0.3 M, 0.35 M, 0.4 M, 0.45 M, 0.5 M and 0.6 M.

(2) Using a 10 cm^3 or 25 cm^3 graduated pipette, a beaker of distilled water and a beaker of 1 M sucrose solution, make up 20 cm^3 of sucrose solution of the required concentration in each test-tube. Table 13.3 shows the amounts used.

(3) Make sure that the solutions are mixed thoroughly by shaking. This is very important. Add the solutions to the appropriate petri dishes.

(4) **Onion**. Remove one of the fleshy storage leaves of an onion. While it is still attached to the leaf, cut the inner epidermis into six squares of approximately 5 mm side using a razor blade or scalpel. Remove each of the six squares using the fine forceps and immediately place one square of tissue into each petri dish. Agitate each dish gently to ensure that the tissue is completely immersed and washed with the sucrose solution. Leave for about 20 min.

   Rhubarb. Score the outer epidermis into six squares of approximately 5 mm side and remove the epidermis as described for onion.

(5) Remove the tissue from the 0.60 M solution and, using a brush, mount it on a slide in sucrose solution of the same concentration. Add a cover-slip and examine with a microscope.

(6) Select a suitable area of cells using lower power. Switch to a medium or high power objective and move the slide through the selected area, recording the state (plasmolysed or unplasmolysed) of the first 100 cells viewed. Cells in which there is any sign of the protoplast pulling away from the cell wall should be counted as plasmolysed.

(7) Repeat for all other squares of tissue, mounting them in their respective solution.

(8) From the total number of cells counted and number plasmolysed, determine the percentage of plasmolysed cells for each solution. Plot a graph of percentage of plasmolysed cells (vertical axis) against molarity of sucrose solution (horizontal axis).

(9) Read off from the graph the molarity of the sucrose solution which causes 50% of the cells to plasmolyse.

(10) Plot a graph of solute potential (vertical axis) against molarity of sucrose solution (horizontal axis) using the data provided in table 13.4.

Table 13.3 Sucrose dilution table for experiment 13.2.

Concentration of sucrose solution	Volume of distilled water/cm^3	Volume of 1 M sucrose solution/cm^3
0.30 M	14	6
0.35 M	13	7
0.40 M	12	8
0.45 M	11	9
0.50 M	10	10
0.60 M	8	12

Table 13.4 Solute potentials of given sucrose solutions at 20 °C.

Concentration of sucrose solution (molarity)	Solute potential/kPa	Solute potential/atm
0.05	−130	−1.3
0.10	−260	−2.6
0.15	−410	−4.0
0.20	−540	−5.3
0.25	−680	−6.7
0.30	−820	−8.1
0.35	−970	−9.6
0.40	−1 120	−11.1
0.45	−1 280	−12.6
0.50	−1 450	−14.3
0.55	−1 620	−16.0
0.60	−1 800	−17.8
0.65	−1 980	−19.5
0.70	−2 180	−21.5
0.75	−2 370	−23.3
0.80	−2 580	−25.5
0.85	−2 790	−27.5
0.90	−3 010	−29.7
0.95	−3 250	−32.1
1.00	−3 510	−34.6
1.50	−6 670	−65.8
2.00	−11 810	−116.6

(11) From this graph determine the solute potential of the solution which caused 50% plasmolysis. This is equal to the mean solute potential of the cell sap.

Results

A typical graph for onion epidermis is shown in fig 13.5. Similar results are obtained using rhubarb epidermis.

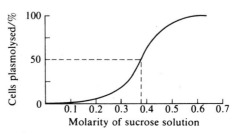

Fig 13.5 *Percentage of onion epidermal cells plasmolysed in different concentrations of sucrose solution.*

Use of beetroot tissue

Beetroot is a less convenient material to use, but a combination of this experiment with experiment 13.3 would enable an estimation of the pressure potential of beetroot cells to be made, although it should be pointed out that different beetroots may have different water potentials and solute potentials. Beetroots normally have a lower solute potential than onion or rhubarb because they have more sugar and inorganic salts in their vacuoles.

Modifications to the method are as follows:

(1)–(3)   As for onion and rhubarb experiment above, except use solutions of the following concentrations: 0.4 M, 0.45 M, 0.5 M, 0.55 M, 0.6 M and 0.7 M.

(4)   Cut a rectangular 'chip' of beetroot with square ends of approximately 5×5 mm. Thin sections (maximum 0.5 mm thick) should be cut from the end of this chip using a razor blade. The thinner the sections, the easier it is to count plasmolysed cells. The coloured sap enables easy detection of plasmolysis. The sections could be cut immediately before the practical class and kept in distilled water. Add several sections of beetroot tissue to each sucrose solution, and leave for about 30 min. Meanwhile examine similar sections, mounted in distilled water, with a microscope to become familiar with the appearance of the unplasmolysed cells. The margins of the sections are likely to be thinner and easier to examine. Some damaged cells may be colourless, and some small cells near vascular tissue may be seen. These can be ignored in subsequent counts.

(5)–(11)   As before, starting with tissue from 0.7 M solution.

Results

A set of results obtained for beetroot is given in table 13.5.

Table 13.5 Percentage of beetroot cells plasmolysed in different concentrations of sucrose solution.

Molarity of sucrose solution	Percentage of plasmolysed cells[*]
0.30	2.5
0.40	3.5
0.45	13.5
0.50	74.0
0.55	100.0
0.60	100.0

[*] Sample size 200 cells.

Experiment 13.3: To determine the water potential of a plant tissue

Water potential is a measure of the tendency of water molecules to pass from one place to another. The principle in this experiment is to discover a solution, of known water potential, in which the tissue being examined neither gains nor loses water. Samples of the tissue are allowed to come to equilibrium in a range of solutions of different concentrations and the solution which induces neither an increase nor a decrease in mass or volume of the tissue has the same water potential as the tissue. The method described below relies on volume rather than mass changes.

Materials

fresh potato tuber or fresh beetroot
6 petri dishes
5 test-tubes
test-tube rack
labels or wax pencil
2×10 cm^3 or 25 cm^3 graduated pipettes
tile
distilled water
1 M sucrose solution
scalpel or knife
2×100 cm^3 beakers
graph paper

Method

(1)   Label six petri dishes appropriately, one for each of the following: distilled water, 0.1 M, 0.25 M, 0.5 M, 0.75 M and 1.0 M sucrose solutions. Label five test-tubes appropriately, one for each of the sucrose solutions.

(2)   Using a graduated pipette, a beaker of distilled water and a beaker of 1 M sucrose solution, make up 20 cm^3 of sucrose solution of the required concentration in each test-tube. A dilution table is useful as described in experiment 13.2 (table 13.3).

(3)   Shake the tubes to mix the solutions thoroughly.

(4)   Pour the solutions into the appropriate petri dishes. Add 20 cm^3 of distilled water to the sixth petri dish.

(5) Place the petri dishes on graph paper, making sure their lower surfaces are dry.

(6) Using the knife or scalpel, cut 12 rectangular strips of tissue approximately 2 mm thick, 5 mm wide and as long as possible (about 5 cm) from a slice of tissue (2 mm thick) taken from the middle of a large beetroot or potato. It is important to work quickly to avoid loss of water through evaporation as this would lower the water potential of the tissue.

(7) Completely immerse at least two strips in each petri dish and immediately measure their lengths against the graph paper seen through the bottoms of the dishes. Agitate the contents of each dish to wash the strips.

(8) Leave in covered petri dishes for at least 1 h, preferably 24 h.

(9) Measure the lengths again, and calculate the mean percentage change in length. Plot a graph of the mean percentage change in length (vertical axis) against the molarity of the sucrose solution (horizontal axis). Changes in length are proportional to changes in volume.

(10) Read off from the graph the molarity of the sucrose solution which causes no change in length.

(11) Plot a graph of solute potential (vertical axis) against molarity of sucrose solution (horizontal axis) using the data provided in table 13.4.

(12) From this graph, determine the solute potential of the solution which caused no change in length. The water potential of the tissue is determined according to the following:

$$\psi^{cell} = \psi^{external\ solution} = \psi_s.$$

(13) If beetroot has been used and its solute potential determined from experiment 13.2, calculate the pressure potential from:

$$\psi = \psi_s + \psi_p.$$

Table 13.6 Lengths of beetroot strips left in distilled water or different concentrations of sucrose solution for 24 hours.

Molarity of sucrose solution	Length of beetroot strip at start/cm			Length of beetroot strip after 24 h/cm		
	1	2	3	1	2	3
0.00 (distilled water)	4.8	5.0	5.3	5.0	5.3	5.6
0.10	5.1	4.8	4.9	5.3	4.9	5.1
0.20	5.1	4.9	4.9	5.2	4.9	5.0
0.25	5.2	4.8	5.0	5.2	4.9	5.0
0.30	4.9	4.9	5.0	4.9	5.0	5.1
0.40	4.9	5.0	4.8	4.9	5.0	4.8
0.50	5.0	4.8	5.1	4.8	4.7	5.0
0.60	4.8	5.0	5.0	4.6	4.9	4.9
0.75	4.9	4.9	5.0	4.6	4.7	4.8
0.90	4.9	5.0	4.9	4.5	4.7	4.7
1.00	4.8	4.9	4.9	4.7	4.6	4.4
1.50	4.9	4.9	4.9	4.5	4.1	4.5

Results

More accurate results are likely to be obtained by pooling class results. See table 13.6 for specimen results.

13.7 What is the mean water potential of beetroot cells from the data in table 13.6? (You will need to determine mean percentage changes in length and draw graphs.)

13.8 Why are at least two strips of tissue added to each dish?

13.9 Why are the petri dishes covered when left?

13.10 If the solute potential of beetroot cells is −1400 kPa and their water potential is −950 kPa, what is their mean pressure potential?

13.11 Consider the experiment illustrated in fig 13.6 in which the hollow inflorescence stalk (scape) of a dandelion (*Taraxacum officinale*) is first cut longitudinally into four strips 3 cm long and the pieces then immersed in distilled water or sucrose solutions of different concentrations.

(a) Why did cutting the scape longitudinally result in immediate curling back of the cut strips?

(b) Why did scape B bend further outwards in distilled water?

(c) Why did scape C bend inwards in concentrated sucrose solution?

(d) Why did scape A retain the same curvature in dilute sucrose solution?

(e) Which of the following could be determined for scape cells using this method: solute potential, water potential or pressure potential? Design an experiment to determine the relevant value, giving full experimental details.

13.12 The red colour of beetroot is contained in the cell vacuoles. Using this information, design experiments to investigate the effects of heat and ethanol on the partial permeability of beetroot cell membranes.

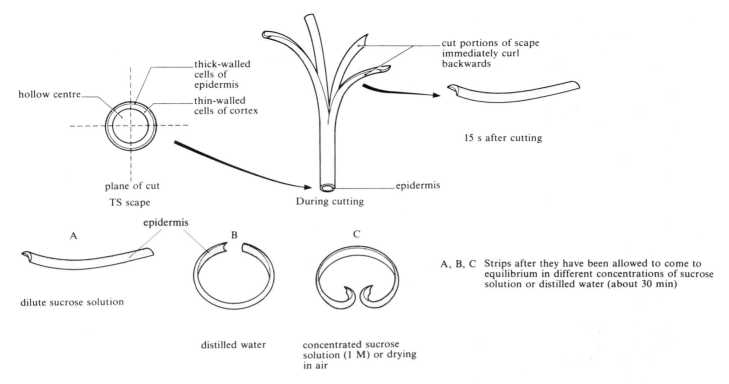

Fig 13.6 *Experiment on dandelion scapes. Investigation of the effects of distilled water and sucrose solutions on the curvature of strips of dandelion scape.*

13.2   Movement of water through the flowering plant

Water in the plant is in direct contact with water in the soil and with water vapour in the air around the plant. It has already been stated that water moves from higher to lower water potentials. Plant physiologists therefore think of water as moving through plants from a region of higher water potential in the soil to a region of lower water potential in the atmosphere, down a gradient of water potentials (fig 13.7). The water potential of moderately dry air is much lower than that of the plant so there is a great tendency for water to leave the plant.

Most of the water entering the plant does so through the root hairs. It travels across the root cortex to the xylem, ascends in the xylem to the leaves and is lost by evaporation from the surface of the mesophyll cells before diffusing out through the stomata. Loss of water from the surface of a plant is called **transpiration**, and the flow of water from the roots to the stomata forms the **transpiration stream**. It is estimated that more than 99% of the water absorbed by the average plant is lost.

13.3   Transpiration and movement of water through the leaf

Water normally leaves the plant as water vapour. The change from a liquid state to a vapour state requires the addition of energy which is provided by the Sun, and it is this energy that maintains the flow of water through the entire plant. Transpiration may occur from the following three sites.

- **Stomata:** by evaporation of water from cells and diffusion of the water vapour through stomata, the pores found in the epidermis of leaves and green stems. (About 90% of the water is lost this way.)
- **Cuticle:** by evaporation of water from the outer walls of epidermal cells through the waxy cuticle covering the epidermis of leaves and stems. (About 10% of the water lost, varying with thickness of cuticle.)
- **Lenticels:** by evaporation of water through lenticels. These are small slits in the stems and bark of trees for gas exchange. (Minute proportions, although this is the main method of water loss from deciduous trees after leaf fall.)

The quantities of water lost by transpiration can be very large. A herbaceous plant, such as cotton or sunflower, can lose between 1–2 dm^3 of water per day, and a large oak tree may lose more than 600 dm^3 per day.

Water is brought to the leaf in the xylem vessels. The structure of vessels is described in section 6.2.1. The xylem is part of the vascular bundles which spread to form a fine branching network throughout the leaf. The branches end in one or a few xylem vessels that possess little lignification. Water can therefore escape easily through their cellulose walls to the mesophyll cells of the leaf. Fig 13.8 shows the

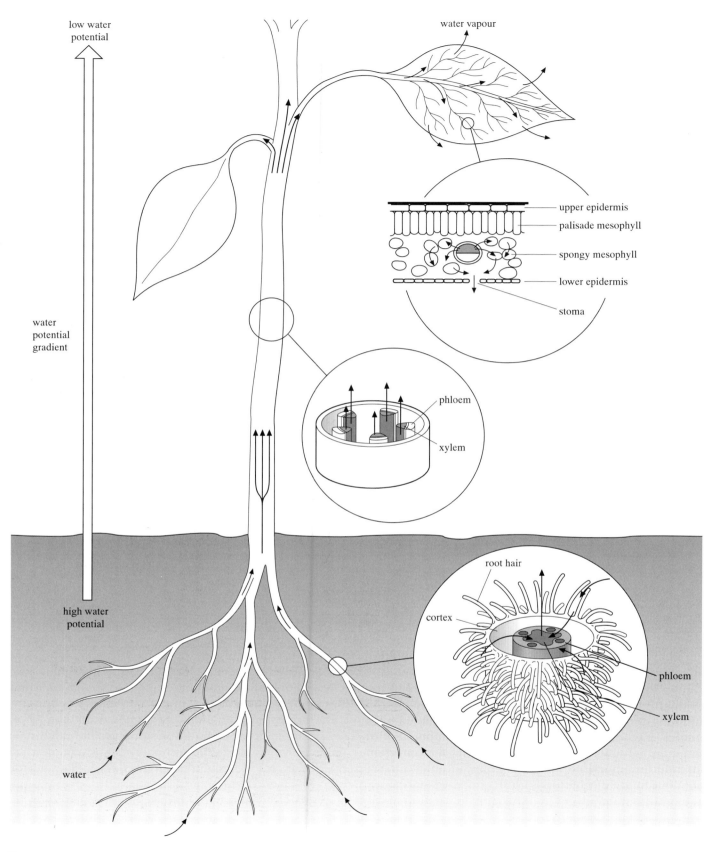

low water
potential

water vapour

water
potential
gradient

upper epidermis

palisade mesophyll

spongy mesophyll

lower epidermis

stoma

phloem

xylem

high water
potential

root hair

cortex

phloem

xylem

water

Fig 13.7 *Movement of water through a plant. Water in the soil is at a high water potential and water in the atmosphere is at a low water potential. Water moves from high to low potential down a gradient through the plant. The gradient is maintained by solar energy and evaporation of water from the surface of the plant (transpiration).*

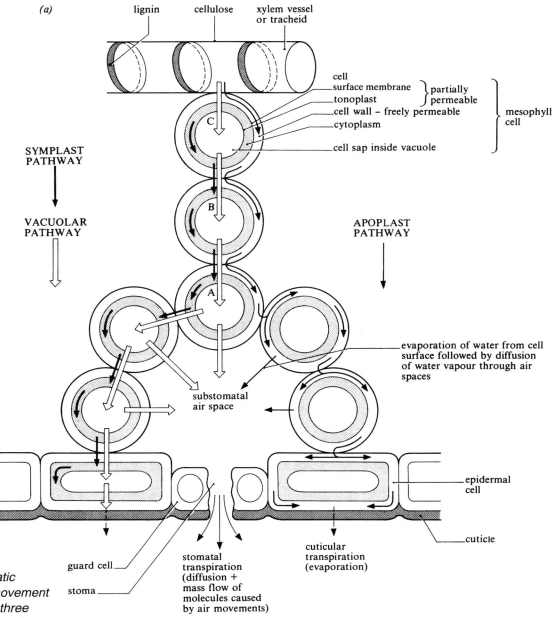

(a)

lignin   cellulose   xylem vessel
or tracheid

cell
surface membrane } partially
tonoplast   } permeable
cell wall – freely permeable
cytoplasm
cell sap inside vacuole

mesophyll
cell

SYMPLAST
PATHWAY

VACUOLAR
PATHWAY

APOPLAST
PATHWAY

evaporation of water from cell
surface followed by diffusion
of water vapour through air
spaces

substomatal
air space

epidermal
cell

cuticle

guard cell

stoma

stomatal
transpiration
(diffusion +
mass flow of
molecules caused
by air movements)

cuticular
transpiration
(evaporation)

Fig 13.8 *(a) Diagrammatic
representation of water movement
through a leaf. There are three
possible pathways: the symplast
and vacuolar pathways are shown
to the left, and the apoplast pathway
to the right. Cells A, B and C are referred
to in the text. Thickness of cell walls has
been exaggerated.
(b) Diagrammatic representation of a
group of cells summarising possible
pathways of water (and solute) movement.
More than one pathway may be used at
the same time. Such pathways may be
used across the leaf and across the root
cortex. Movement of ions by the vacuolar
pathway would involve active transport.
The apoplast pathway is the most
important, and the vacuolar pathway the
least important.*

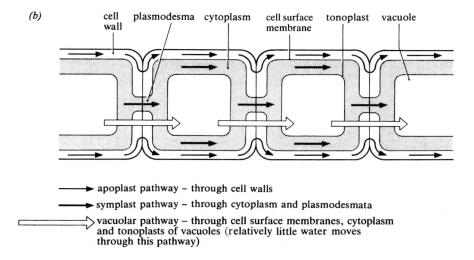

(b)   cell   plasmodesma cytoplasm   cell surface   tonoplast vacuole
       wall   membrane

⟶ apoplast pathway – through cell walls
⟹ symplast pathway – through cytoplasm and plasmodesmata
⟹ vacuolar pathway – through cell surface membranes, cytoplasm
and tonoplasts of vacuoles (relatively little water moves
through this pathway)

three pathways which water can then follow, namely the apoplast pathway (cell walls), the symplast pathway (cytoplasm and plasmodesmata) and the vacuolar pathway (from vacuole to vacuole).

> **13.13** Why does transpiration occur mainly through leaves and not so much through the cuticle and lenticels?

13.3.1 The apoplast pathway

The **apoplast** is the system of adjacent cell walls which is continuous throughout the plant. Up to 50% of a cellulose cell wall may be 'free space' which can be occupied by water. As water evaporates from the mesophyll cell walls into the intercellular air spaces, tension develops in the continuous stream of water in the apoplast, and water is drawn through the walls in a mass flow by the cohesion of water molecules (section 13.4). Water in the apoplast is supplied from the xylem.

13.3.2 The symplast pathway

The **symplast** is the system of interconnected protoplasts in the plant. The cytoplasm of neighbouring protoplasts is linked by the plasmodesmata, the cytoplasmic strands which extend through pores in adjacent cell walls (fig 13.8*b*). Once water, and any solutes it contains, is taken into the cytoplasm of one cell it can move through the symplast without having to cross further membranes. Movement might be aided by cytoplasmic streaming. The symplast is a more important pathway of water movement than the vacuolar pathway.

13.3.3 The vacuolar pathway

In the **vacuolar pathway** water moves from vacuole to vacuole through neighbouring cells, crossing the symplast and apoplast in the process and moving through membranes and tonoplasts by osmosis (fig 13.8*b*). The water potential gradient is set up as follows.

Water evaporates from the wet walls of the mesophyll cells into the intercellular air spaces, particularly into the larger substomatal air spaces. Taking cell A in fig 13.8*a* as an example, loss of water from the cell would result in a decrease in its pressure potential and its water potential. Cell B would then have a higher water potential than cell A (at equilibrium they would be equal). Water will therefore move from cell B to cell A, thus lowering the water potential of cell B relative to cell C. In this way a gradient of water potential is set up across the leaf from a higher potential in the xylem to a lower potential in the mesophyll cells. Water enters the mesophyll cells from the xylem by

osmosis. Although it is convenient to describe the movement of water in a step-by-step fashion, it should be stressed that the water potential gradient that develops across the leaf is a continuous one, and water moves smoothly down the gradient as a liquid would in moving along a wick.

It is sometimes imagined that water moves across the leaf in response to a gradient of solute potentials. However, although a water potential gradient exists, there is no evidence to suggest that solute potentials of the cells differ significantly from one another. Differences in water potential are due mainly to differences in pressure potential (remember that loss of a small amount of water from a cell has a much greater effect on pressure potential than on solute potential). The same applies to the root (section 13.5) where gradients of pressure potential and water potential, but not necessarily of solute potential, exist.

13.3.4 Exit of water through stomata

The three pathways described end with water evaporating into air spaces. From here water vapour diffuses through the stomata, from a high water potential inside the leaf to a much lower one outside the leaf. In dicotyledons, stomata are usually confined to, or are more numerous in, the lower epidermis. Control of stomatal opening is discussed in section 13.3.9.

Immediately next to the leaf is a layer of stationary air whose thickness depends on the dimensions and surface features of the leaf, such as hairiness, and also on wind speed. Water vapour must diffuse through this layer before being swept away by moving air (mass flow). The thinner the stationary layer, the faster is the rate of transpiration. There is a diffusion gradient from the stationary layer back to the mesophyll cells. Theoretically each stoma has a diffusion gradient, or 'diffusion shell' around it, as shown in fig 13.9. In practice the diffusion shells of neighbouring stomata overlap in still air to form one overall diffusion shell.

13.3.5 Measuring the rate of transpiration

Transpiration can easily be demonstrated by placing a bell jar over a potted plant with the pot enclosed in a plastic bag to prevent water loss from the soil. As transpiration occurs, a fluid collects on the inside of the bell jar which is shown to contain water when tested with cobalt(II) chloride paper (blue to pink in water) or anhydrous copper(II) sulphate crystals (white to blue in water).

Measuring rates of transpiration can be difficult, but satisfactory results, at least for the purposes of comparison, can be obtained by means of the two simple experiments described below.

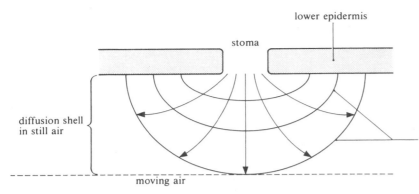

lower epidermis

stoma

diffusion shell
in still air

moving air

Arrows represent curved paths of diffusion
of water molecules

Lines represent contours of equal concentration
of water molecules (equal water potential); the
steeper the water potential gradient, the closer
together the contours and the faster the rate of
diffusion. The contours are closest at the edges of
the pores. The fastest rates are therefore from
the edges. This 'edge effect' means that water
loss and gaseous exchange are more rapid
through a large number of small holes than
through a smaller number of large holes with
the same total area

Fig 13.9 *Diffusion of water molecules from a stoma.*

Experiment 13.4: To investigate and measure factors affecting rate of transpiration using a potometer

A **potometer** is a piece of apparatus designed to measure the rate of water uptake by a cut shoot or young seedling. It does not measure transpiration directly, but since most of the water taken up is lost by transpiration, the two processes are closely related. Potometers are available commercially, but a simple version may be set up as shown in fig 13.10.

Materials

potometer (fig 13.10: conical filter flask, short rubber tubing, rubber bung with a single hole, hypodermic syringe and needle, graduated capillary tube)
large black polythene bag
large transparent polythene bag
small electric fan
retort stand and clamp
stop clock
thermometer
vaseline (petroleum jelly)
leafy shoot such as lilac
bucket

Method

(1) Select a suitable leafy plant, cut off the shoot and immerse the cut end immediately in a bucket of water to minimise the risk of air being drawn into the xylem. Immediately cut the shoot again under water, with a slanting cut, a few centimetres above the original cut. The stem must be thick enough to fit tightly into the bung of the potometer.

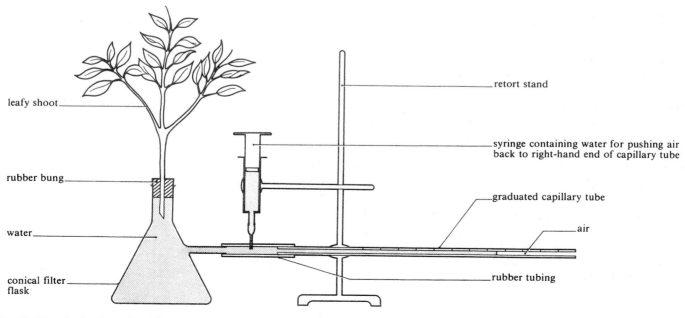

leafy shoot

rubber bung

water

conical filter flask

retort stand

syringe containing water for pushing air back to right-hand end of capillary tube

graduated capillary tube

air

rubber tubing

Fig 13.10 *A simple potometer.*

(2) Submerge a conical filter flask in a sink of water to fill it with water. Transfer the leafy shoot from bucket to sink and again immediately make a slanting cut a few centimetres above the last cut. Fit the shoot into the bung of the flask under water and push the bung in to make a tight fit.

(3) Submerge the graduated capillary tube, with rubber tubing attached, in the sink, fill it with water and attach it to the side arm of the filter flask.

(4) Remove the apparatus from the sink and set up the syringe with the needle pushed into the rubber tubing as shown in fig 13.10. The syringe can be clamped in a vertical position. The joint between shoot and bung should be smeared with vaseline to make certain it is airtight.

(5) As the shoot takes up water, the end of the water column in the capillary tube can be seen to move. It may be returned to the open end of the tube by pushing in water from the syringe. Allow the shoot to equilibrate for 5 min whilst regularly replacing the water taken up.

(6) Measure the time taken for the water column to move a given distance along the capillary tube and express the rate of water uptake in convenient units, such as $cm\,min^{-1}$. A number of readings should be taken, to ensure that the rate is fairly constant, and the mean result calculated. The temperature of the air around the plant should be noted.

(7) Each time the air bubble reaches the end of the graduated section of the tube return it to its original position with the syringe.

(8) The effects of some of the following factors on rate of uptake of water could be investigated:
   (a) wind – use a small electric fan (do not strongly buffet the leaves or the stomata will close);
   (b) humidity – enclose the shoot in a transparent plastic bag;
   (c) darkness – enclose the shoot in a black polythene bag;
   (d) removal of half the leaves – is the transpiration rate halved?
   (e) vaselining upper and/or lower epidermises of the leaves to prevent water loss.

In each case sufficient time should be allowed to ensure that the new rate has been attained. It is not always possible to change only one condition at a time; for example, enclosing the plant in a transparent bag will also lead to some reduction in light intensity.

Absolute rate of water uptake

Results can be converted to actual volume of water taken up per unit time, such as cm^3h^{-1}, if the volume of the graduated scale corresponding to each division is determined.

Most of the water taken up is lost through the leaves. An estimate of rate of water loss per unit leaf area can be obtained by measuring the volume of water lost as described above and then removing all the leaves and determining their surface area. The latter can be obtained by drawing the outlines of the leaves on graph paper and counting the enclosed squares. Using these data, results can be expressed as $cm^3h^{-1}m^{-2}$ leaf area.

Results

The effects of temperature, humidity, air movement and darkness are discussed in section 13.3.6.

13.3.6 Effects of environmental factors on transpiration

Plants show many features which enable them to reduce loss of water by transpiration in dry conditions. Such features are described as **xeromorphic**. Plants growing in dry habitats and subjected to drought are called **xerophytes** and possess many xeromorphic features which are described in more detail in chapter 20. Plants growing under conditions in which there is normally an adequate water supply are called **mesophytes**, but nevertheless can show some xeromorphic features.

Temperature

The external factor which has the greatest effect on transpiration is temperature. The higher the temperature, the greater the rate of evaporation of water from mesophyll cells and the greater the saturation of the leaf atmosphere with water vapour. At the same time, a rise in temperature lowers the relative humidity of the air outside the leaf. Both events result in a steeper concentration gradient of water molecules from leaf atmosphere to external atmosphere. The steeper this gradient, the faster is the rate of diffusion. Alternatively, it can be said that water potential increases inside the leaf while decreasing outside the leaf.

The temperature of the leaf is raised by solar radiation. Pale-coloured leaves reflect more of this radiation than normal leaves and therefore do not heat up as rapidly. The pale colour is usually due to a thick coat of epidermal hairs, waxy deposits or scales, and is a xeromorphic feature.

Humidity and vapour pressure

Low humidity outside the leaf favours transpiration because it makes the diffusion gradient of water vapour (or water potential gradient) from the moist leaf atmosphere to the external atmosphere steeper. As the concentration of water vapour in the external atmosphere, that is the humidity, rises, the diffusion gradient becomes less steep. Water potential of the atmosphere also decreases with altitude as atmospheric pressure decreases. High altitude plants therefore often show xeromorphic adaptations to reduce transpiration rates.

A xeromorphic feature of some leaves is the presence of sunken stomata, that is stomata in grooves or infoldings of the epidermis, around which a high humidity can build up and reduce transpiration losses. In some cases the whole leaf may roll up enclosing a humid atmosphere, such as in *Ammophila* (marram grass) (fig 13.11). A coat of epidermal hairs or scales will tend to trap a layer of still moist air next to the leaf, thus reducing transpiration.

Air movement

In still air a layer of highly saturated air builds up around the leaf, reducing the steepness of the diffusion gradient between the atmosphere inside the leaf and the external atmosphere. Any air movement will tend to sweep away this layer. Thus windy conditions result in increased transpiration rates, the increase being most pronounced at low wind speeds. High winds may result in closing of the stomata, stopping transpiration.

Hairs and scales trap still air as described above, tending to reduce transpiration rates.

Light

Light affects transpiration because stomata usually open in the light and close in darkness. At night, therefore, only small amounts of water are lost (through the cuticle or lenticels). As stomata open in the morning, transpiration rates increase.

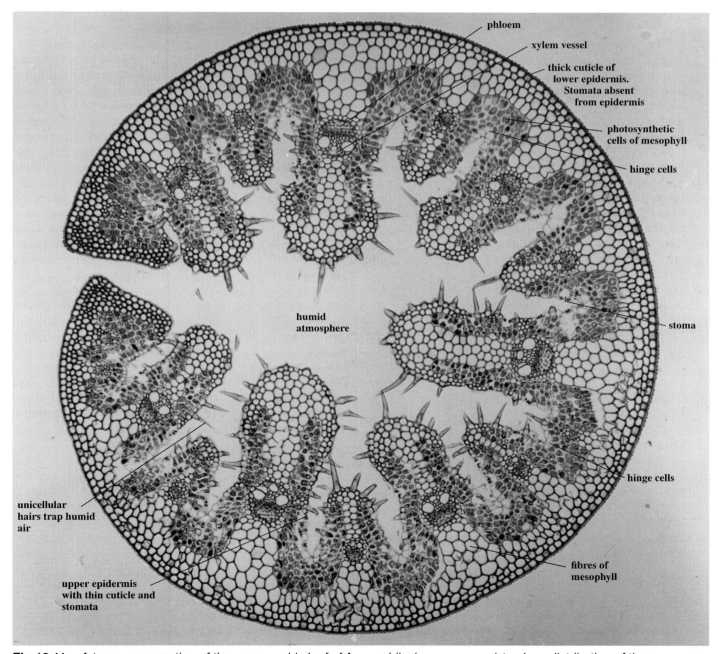

Fig 13.11 *A transverse section of the xeromorphic leaf of* Ammophila *(marram grass) to show distribution of tissues. The leaf is shown in the rolled condition.*

13.3.7 Effect of plant or internal factors on the rate of transpiration

The effects of some xeromorphic adaptations on transpiration rates have been considered above. Further examples of the ways in which such 'internal' as opposed to 'external' (environmental) factors can operate are given below.

Leaf surface area and surface area to volume ratio

Transpiration of a plant increases with its total leaf surface area, and with leaf surface area to volume ratio. Reduction of leaf surface is achieved when leaves are reduced to needles, such as in *Pinus* and other conifers, or to spines, as in cacti. There may also be a reduction in size in dry conditions. The shedding of leaves in dry or cold seasons by deciduous plants is a xeromorphic adaptation. In cold seasons water may be unavailable through being frozen in the soil.

Surface area to volume ratio can be reduced by using the stem as the main photosynthetic organ, as in cacti. Fig 13.12 shows the characteristic reduction in leaf surface area of succulents like cacti.

(a)

(b)

Fig 13.12 *(a) The cactus* Opuntia *has thick fleshy stems to conserve water, no leaves to reduce transpiration, and spines to protect it from grazing. (b)* Sempervivum *is a typical succulent with fleshy leaves for storing water.*

Cuticle

The cuticle is a layer which is secreted by the epidermis. It consists of a fatty substance called **cutin** which is relatively waterproof. In general, the thicker the cuticle the lower the rate of transpiration through it. Where it is thin, as in ferns, 30–45% of the transpiration losses can be through it.

The upper surfaces of dicotyledonous leaves, which are exposed to direct sunlight and are less protected from air currents than the lower surfaces, often possess thicker cuticles than the lower surfaces. Increased wax deposits on leaves can virtually eliminate cuticular transpiration. Also, waxy leaves are usually shiny and so reflect more solar radiation.

Stomata

In general, the greater the number of stomata per unit area, the greater is the rate of stomatal transpiration; however, their distribution is also important. For example, the lower surfaces of dicotyledonous leaves usually have more stomata than their upper surfaces (table 13.7), whereas monocotyledonous leaves, which are generally held vertically rather than horizontally, have similar upper and lower surfaces with similar stomatal distributions (see maize and oat, table 13.7). On average, fewer stomata occur in plants adapted to dry conditions. The number may vary within the same species as a result.

Experiment 13.5: To investigate stomatal distribution

Materials

    clear nail varnish
    slides and cover-slips
    fine forceps
    fresh fully expanded leaves
    microscope

Table 13.7 Stomatal densities in the leaves of some common plants.

	Number of stomata/cm^{-2}	
Plant	*upper epidermis*	*lower epidermis*
Monocotyledons		
maize (*Zea mais*)	5 200	6 800
oat (*Avena sativa*)	2 500	2 300
Dicotyledons		
apple (*Malus* spp.)	0	29 400
bean (*Phaseolus vulgaris*)	4 000	28 100
cabbage (*Brassica* spp.)	14 100	22 600
lucerne (*Medicago sativa*)	16 900	13 800
Nasturtium	0	13 000
oak (*Quercus* spp.)	0	45 000
potato (*Solanum tuberosum*)	5 100	16 100
tomato (*Lycopersicon esculentum*)	1 200	13 000

Based on Weier, T. E., Stocking, C. R. and Barbour, M. G. (1970) *Botany, an Introduction to Plant Biology*, 4th ed., John Wiley & Sons, p. 192.

Method

A convenient means of examining stomatal distribution is to make a replica of the leaf surface using clear nail varnish. Spread a thin layer of the nail varnish over the leaf using the brush in the bottle. Allow it to dry, then peel off the thin replica with fine forceps, lay it on a slide and add a cover-slip. It may be mounted in water for convenience. Examine with a microscope. Count the number of stomata in a given field of view and repeat several times in different areas. Obtain a mean value. Determine the area of the field of view of the microscope by measuring the diameter with a calibrated slide or transparent rule and using the formula πr^2 for the area, where r is the radius and π = 3.142. The number of stomata per square centimetre can then be calculated.

Compare the densities of stomata in upper and lower epidermises of the same leaf, and in different species. Is there any correlation between stomatal densities and the habitats of plants?

13.14 Examine fig 13.13. Describe and explain the relationships between the three variables shown.

13.3.8 Functions of transpiration

Transpiration has been described as a 'necessary evil' because it is inevitable, but potentially harmful. It happens because of the existence of wet cell walls from which evaporation occurs. Water vapour escapes mainly through the stomata which are needed for gaseous exchange between the plant and its environment. Gaseous exchange is essential to obtain the carbon dioxide needed for photosynthesis. (Because there is much more oxygen than carbon dioxide in the atmosphere, plants can get all the oxygen they need even with stomata shut. They therefore respire in the dark just as efficiently as they do in

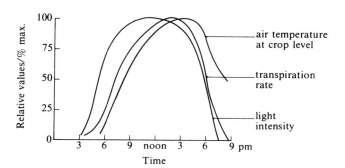

Fig 13.13 *Relationship between light intensity, air temperature and transpiration rate from lucerne leaves. (From data by L. J. Briggs & H. L. Shantz (1916)* J. Agr. Res., *5, 583–649; cited by A. C. Leopold (1964)* Plant growth and development, *p. 396. McGraw-Hill.)*

the light.) If there was no cuticle, stomata would be unnecessary and gaseous exchange would be even more efficient. However, loss of water could not then be controlled. The cuticle reduces water loss and further control is exercised by the stomata, which in most plants are highly sensitive to water stress and close under conditions of drought. They also usually close during the night when photosynthesis ceases. Loss of water can lead to wilting, serious desiccation, and often death of a plant. There is good evidence that even mild water stress results in reduced growth rate and causes economic losses in crops through reductions in yield.

Although it is inevitable, it is worth asking whether there might be some advantages associated with transpiration. Two possibilities are as follows.

- The evaporation of water from mesophyll cells that accompanies transpiration requires energy and therefore results in cooling of the leaves in the same way that sweating cools the skin of mammals. This is sometimes important in direct sunlight when leaves absorb large amounts of energy and experience rises in temperature which, under extreme conditions, can inhibit photosynthesis. However, it is unlikely that the cooling effect is of significance under normal conditions. Plants that live in hot climates usually have other means of avoiding heat stress.
- It has been suggested that the transpiration stream is necessary to distribute mineral salts throughout the plant, since these move with the water. Whilst this may be true, it seems probable that very low transpiration rates would be sufficient. For example, mineral salt supply to leaves is just as great at night, when transpiration is low, as during the day because the xylem sap is more concentrated at night. Uptake of mineral salts from the soil is largely independent of the transpiration stream.

13.3.9 Stomata – structure and mechanism of opening and closing

Stomata are pores in the epidermis through which gaseous exchange takes place. They are found mainly in leaves, but also in stems. Each stoma is surrounded by two guard cells which, unlike the other epidermal cells, possess chloroplasts. The guard cells control the size of the stoma by changes in their turgidity. The appearance of guard cells and stomata is well revealed by the scanning electron microscope, as shown in fig 13.14.

The appearance of epidermal cells, guard cells and stomata in surface view, as seen with the light microscope, is dealt with in section 6.1. Fig 13.15 is a diagram of section through a typical stoma, and shows that the guard cell walls are unevenly thickened. The wall furthest from the pore (called the dorsal wall) is thinner than the wall next to the pore (the ventral wall). Also, the cellulose

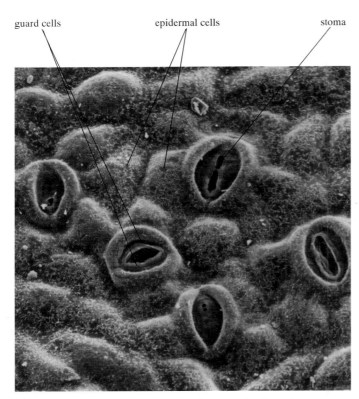

guard cells   epidermal cells   stoma

Fig 13.14 *Scanning electron micrograph of stomata on the lower surface of a leaf.*

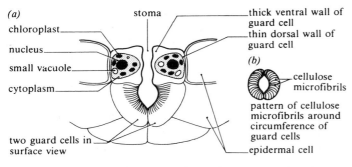

(a)
chloroplast
nucleus
small vacuole
cytoplasm
two guard cells in surface view

stoma
thick ventral wall of guard cell
thin dorsal wall of guard cell
(b)
cellulose microfibrils
pattern of cellulose microfibrils around circumference of guard cells
epidermal cell

Fig 13.15 *(a) Vertical section through a stoma, showing also part of the lower surface of the leaf. (b) Pattern of cellulose microfibrils in guard cell walls.*

microfibrils that make up the walls are arranged so that the ventral wall is less elastic than the dorsal wall. Some of the cellulose microfibrils form hoops around the sausage-shaped guard cells as shown in fig 13.15*b*. These hoops are inelastic. As the cells inflate with water, that is become turgid, the hoops tend to stop the cells increasing in diameter (getting fatter) so they can only expand by increasing in length. Because the ends of the guard cells are joined, and also because the thin dorsal walls stretch more easily than the thick ventral walls, each cell becomes semicircular in shape (fig 13.15). Thus a hole, the stoma, appears between the guard cells. The same effect can be obtained by inflating a sausage-shaped balloon which has had a piece of adhesive tape stuck along one side to mimic

the non-elastic ventral wall of the guard cell. The tape can also be wound loosely round the balloon to mimic the hoops.

When the guard cells lose water and turgidity, the pore closes. The question remains as to how the turgidity changes are brought about.

A traditional hypothesis, the 'starch–sugar hypothesis', suggested that an increase in sugar concentration in guard cells during the day led to their solute potential becoming more negative, resulting in entry of water by osmosis. However, sugar has never been shown to build up in guard cells to the extent necessary to cause the observed changes in solute potential. It has now been shown that potassium ions and associated negative ions accumulate in guard cells during the day in response to light and are sufficient to account for the observed changes. There is still doubt about which negative ions balance the potassium. In some species studied large quantities of organic acid ions accumulate, such as malate. At the same time the starch grains that appear in guard cell chloroplasts in darkness decrease in size. The reason is that starch is converted to malate and that this requires blue light. A possible route is:

$$PEP \underset{phosphoenolpyruvate}{} + CO_2 \xrightarrow[carboxylase]{PEP} oxaloacetate \xrightarrow[NADPH_2 \quad NADP]{malate\ dehydrogenase} malate$$

$$\uparrow \text{series of reactions}$$
$$\text{starch}$$

(Compare C_4 photosynthesis, section 7.9.)

Some plants, such as onion, have no starch in their guard cells. Here malate does not accumulate during stomatal opening and chloride ions (Cl^-), are taken up with the positive ions.

In darkness, potassium ions (K^+) move out of the guard cells into surrounding epidermal cells. The water potential of the guard cells increases as a result and water moves out of the cells. The loss of pressure makes the guard cells change shape again and the stoma closes.

Certain questions remain to be answered. For example, what causes the potassium ions to enter the guard cells in the light, and what function is served by the chloroplasts apart from storing starch? Potassium may enter in response to the switching on of an ATPase which is located in the cell surface membrane. Some evidence suggests that blue light may activate the ATPase. The ATPase may be needed to pump out hydrogen ions (H^+) and potassium ions may then enter to balance the charge (a similar pump occurs in phloem as discussed in section 13.8.4). The pH inside guard cells does decrease in the light, as this hypothesis would require. In 1979 it was shown that the enzymes of the Calvin cycle are absent from the chloroplasts of guard cells of broad bean (*Vicia faba*) and the thylakoid system is poorly developed, although chlorophyll is present. Normal C_3 photosynthesis therefore cannot occur and starch cannot be made by this route. This might explain why starch is made at night rather than during the day as in normal photosynthetic cells.

13.4   Ascent of water in the xylem

Xylem in flowering plants contains two types of water-transporting cell, the tracheid and the vessel, whose structures as seen in the light microscope are discussed in section 6.2.1 together with the appearance of vessels as seen with the scanning electron microscope (fig 6.12). The structure of the secondary xylem (wood) is dealt with in chapter 22. Xylem, together with phloem, forms the vascular or conducting tissue of higher plants. Vascular tissue consists of bundles of tubes called **vascular bundles** whose structure and arrangement in the primary stems of dicotyledonous plants (dicots) is shown in fig 13.16.

> **13.15** In the dicot stem, what is the overall shape of the following tissues in three dimensions: (*a*) epidermis, (*b*) xylem, (*c*) pericycle and (*d*) pith?

The fact that water can move up the xylem may be demonstrated by placing the cut end of a shoot in a dilute solution of a dye such as eosin. The dye rises in the xylem and spreads through the network of veins in the leaves. Sectioning and examination with a light microscope reveals the stain to be in the xylem.

Better evidence that xylem conducts water is given by 'ringing' experiments. These were among earlier experiments done before radioactive isotopes made the tracing of substances through living organisms much easier. In one type of ringing experiment an outer ring of bark, including phloem, is removed and, in the short term, this does not affect the upward movement of water. However, lifting a flap of bark, removing a section of xylem, and replacing the flap of bark leads to rapid wilting. Water therefore moves in the xylem.

Any theory for water movement up the xylem has to account for the following observations.

- Xylem vessels are narrow dead tubes ranging in diameter from 0.01 mm in 'summer wood' to about 0.2 mm in 'spring wood'.
- Large quantities of water are carried at relatively high speeds, up to $8\,m\,h^{-1}$ being recorded in tall trees and commonly in other plants at $1\,m\,h^{-1}$.
- To move water through such tubes to the height of a tall tree requires pressures of around 4000 kPa. The tallest trees, the giant sequoias or redwoods of California and *Eucalyptus* trees of Australia, can reach heights greater than 100 m. Water will rise in fine capillary tubes due to its high surface tension, a phenomenon called **capillarity**, but could rise only about 3 m in even the finest xylem vessels by this method.

The **cohesion–tension theory** of water movement adequately accounts for these observations. According to this theory, evaporation of water from the cells of a leaf is responsible for raising water from the roots. Evaporation results in a reduced water potential in the cells next to the xylem as described in section 13.3. Water therefore enters these cells from the xylem sap which has a higher water potential, passing through the moist cellulose cell walls of the xylem vessels at the ends of the veins, as shown in fig 13.8.

The xylem vessels are full of water and, as water leaves them, a tension is set up in the columns of water. This is transmitted back down the stem all the way to the root by **cohesion** of water molecules. Water molecules have high cohesion, that is they tend to 'stick' to each other, because, being polar, they are electrically attracted to each other and are held together by hydrogen bonding (section 3.1.2). They also tend to stick to the vessel walls, a force called **adhesion**. The high cohesion of water molecules means that a relatively large tension is required to break a column of water, that is a water column has a high tensile strength. The tension in the xylem vessels builds up to a force capable of pulling the whole column of water upwards by mass flow, and water enters the base of the columns in the roots from neighbouring root cells. It is essential that the xylem walls should be rigid if they are not to buckle inwards, as happens when sucking up a soggy straw. Lignin provides this rigidity. Evidence that the contents of xylem vessels are under high tension comes from measuring daily changes in the diameters of tree trunks using an instrument called a dendrogram. The minimum diameters are recorded during daylight hours when transpiration rates are highest. The minute shrinkage of each xylem vessel under tension combines to give a measurable shrinkage in diameter of the whole trunk.

Estimates of the tensile strength of a column of xylem sap vary from about 3000–30 000 kPa, the lower estimates being the more recent. Water potentials of the order required to generate enough tension to raise water, about –4000 kPa, have been recorded in leaves, and it seems likely that xylem sap has the required tensile strength to withstand this tension, though there may be a tendency for the columns to break, particularly in vessels of relatively large diameter.

Critics of the theory point to the fact that any break in a column of sap should stop its flow, the vessel tending to fill with air and water vapour, a process known as **cavitation**. Shaking, bending and shortage of water can all cause cavitation. It is well known that the water content of tree trunks gradually decreases during summer as the wood becomes filled with air. This is made use of in the lumber industry because such wood floats more easily. However, breaks in water columns do not greatly affect water flow rates. The explanation may be that water flows from one vessel to another, or by-passes air-locks by moving through neighbouring parenchyma cells and their walls. Also, it is calculated that only a small proportion of the vessels need be functional at any one time to account for the observed flow rates. In some trees and shrubs water moves only

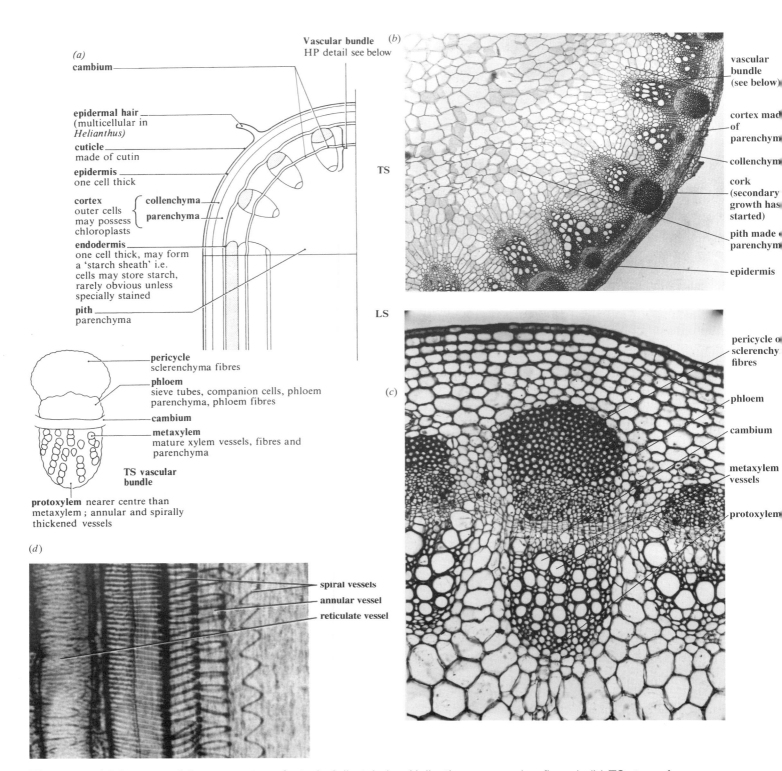

(a)

cambium

epidermal hair
(multicellular in
Helianthus)

cuticle
made of cutin

epidermis
one cell thick

cortex
outer cells
may possess
chloroplasts

{ collenchyma
  parenchyma

endodermis
one cell thick, may form
a 'starch sheath' i.e.
cells may store starch,
rarely obvious unless
specially stained

pith
parenchyma

Vascular bundle
HP detail see below

(b)

TS

LS

(c)

pericycle
sclerenchyma fibres

phloem
sieve tubes, companion cells, phloem
parenchyma, phloem fibres

cambium

metaxylem
mature xylem vessels, fibres and
parenchyma

TS vascular
bundle

protoxylem nearer centre than
metaxylem ; annular and spirally
thickened vessels

(d)

spiral vessels
annular vessel
reticulate vessel

vascular
bundle
(see below)

cortex made
of
parenchyma

collenchyma

cork
(secondary
growth has
started)

pith made of
parenchyma

epidermis

pericycle of
sclerenchyma
fibres

phloem

cambium

metaxylem
vessels

protoxylem

Fig 13.16 *(a) Anatomy of the young stem of a typical dicotyledon,* Helianthus annuus *(sunflower). (b) TS stem of*
Helianthus *as seen with low power of a light microscope. (c) High power view of a TS of a vascular bundle from a stem of*
Helianthus. *(d) LS of a stem of* Helianthus.

446

through the younger outer wood, which is therefore called **sapwood**. In oak and ash, for example, water moves mainly through the vessels of the current year, the rest of the sapwood acting as a water reserve. New vessels are added throughout the growing season, mostly early in the season when flow rates are higher.

A second force involved in water movement up the xylem is **root pressure**. This can be observed and measured when a freshly cut root stump continues to exude sap from its xylem vessels. The process is inhibited by respiratory inhibitors such as cyanide, lack of oxygen and low temperatures. The mechanism probably depends on active secretion of salts or other solutes into the xylem sap, thus lowering its water potential. Water then moves into the xylem by osmosis from neighbouring root cells.

The positive hydrostatic pressure of around 100–200 kPa (exceptionally 800 kPa) that is generated by root pressure is usually not sufficient alone to account for water movement up the xylem, but it is no doubt a contributing factor in many plants. It can be sufficient, however, in slowly transpiring herbaceous plants, when it can cause guttation. **Guttation** is the loss of water as drops of liquid from the surface of a plant (as opposed to vapour in transpiration). It is favoured by the same conditions that favour low transpiration rates, including dim light and high humidity. It is common in many rainforest species and is frequently seen at the tips of the leaves of young grass seedlings.

> **13.16** Summarise the properties of xylem which make it suitable for the long-distance transport of water and solutes.

13.5   Uptake of water by roots

The primary structure of a typical dicot root is shown in fig 13.17.

Water is absorbed mainly, but not exclusively, by the younger parts of roots in the regions of the root hairs. As a root grows through the soil, new root hairs develop a short distance behind the zone of elongation and older hairs die. These hairs are tubular extensions of epidermal cells (fig 13.17) and greatly increase the available surface area for uptake of water and mineral salts. They form a very intimate relationship with soil particles.

Fig 13.18*a* is a diagrammatic representation of the pathway taken by water across a root. A water potential gradient exists across the root from higher potential in the epidermis to lower potential in the cells adjacent to the xylem. This gradient is maintained in two ways:

- by water moving up the xylem, as described, setting up tension in the xylem and thus lowering the water potential of its sap;

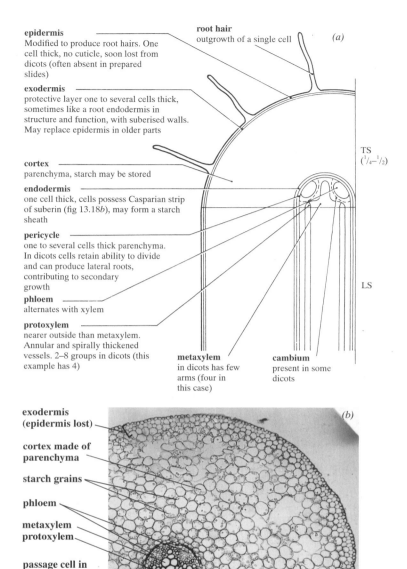

epidermis
Modified to produce root hairs. One cell thick, no cuticle, soon lost from dicots (often absent in prepared slides)

root hair
outgrowth of a single cell

(a)

exodermis
protective layer one to several cells thick, sometimes like a root endodermis in structure and function, with suberised walls. May replace epidermis in older parts

cortex
parenchyma, starch may be stored

endodermis
one cell thick, cells possess Casparian strip of suberin (fig 13.18*b*), may form a starch sheath

pericycle
one to several cells thick parenchyma. In dicots cells retain ability to divide and can produce lateral roots, contributing to secondary growth

phloem
alternates with xylem

protoxylem
nearer outside than metaxylem. Annular and spirally thickened vessels. 2–8 groups in dicots (this example has 4)

TS ($\frac{1}{4}$–$\frac{1}{2}$)

LS

metaxylem
in dicots has few arms (four in this case)

cambium
present in some dicots

exodermis (epidermis lost)

cortex made of parenchyma

starch grains

phloem

metaxylem

protoxylem

passage cell in endodermis

endodermis

pericycle made of parenchyma

(b)

Fig 13.17   *(a) Anatomy of a young root of a typical dicotyledon,* Ranunculus *(buttercup). (b) Low power view of a TS of the root of* Ranunculus *as seen with a light*

- the xylem sap has a more negative (lower) solute potential than the dilute soil solution.

Water moves across the root by pathways similar to those in the leaf, namely apoplast, symplast and vacuolar pathways.

13.5.1   Symplast and vacuolar pathways

As water moves up the xylem in the root, it is replaced by water from neighbouring parenchyma cells, such as cell A in fig 13.18*a*. As water leaves cell A, the

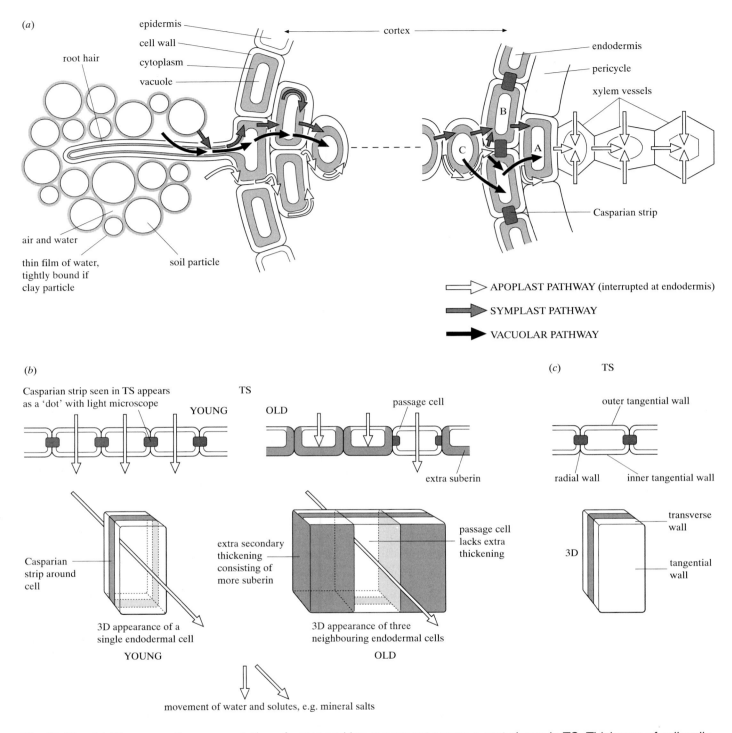

Fig 13.18 (a) *Diagrammatic representation of water and ion movement across a root shown in TS. Thickness of cell walls is exaggerated for clarity. Cells A, B and C are referred to in the text. The apoplast pathway is of greatest importance for both water and solutes. The symplast pathway is less important, except at the endodermis. Movement along the vacuolar pathway is negligible. (b) Structure and function of root endodermis showing Casparian strip in young endodermal cells and deposition of extra suberin in older endodermal cells, with exception of 'passage cells'. (c) Naming of walls. The transverse and radial walls are anticlinal (at right-angles to the surface of the root) and the tangential wall is periclinal (parallel).*

water potential of cell A decreases and water enters it from cell B by osmosis or through the symplast in exactly the same way as described for cells A and B in the leaf (section 13.3.2). Similarly the water potential of cell B then decreases and water enters it from cell C and so on across the root to the epidermis.

The soil solution has a higher water potential than cells of the epidermis including the root hairs. Water therefore enters the root from the soil by osmosis.

> **13.17** Arrange the following in order of ψ: soil solution, xylem sap, cell A, cell B, cell C, root hair cell. (Use the symbol > to mean greater than.)

13.5.2   Apoplast pathway

The apoplast pathway operates in much the same way as in the leaf (section 13.3.1). However, there is one important difference. When water moving through spaces in the cell walls reaches the endodermis its progress is stopped by a waterproof substance called **suberin** which is deposited in the cell walls in the form of bands called **Casparian strips** (fig 13.18b). Therefore water and solutes, particularly salts in the form of ions, must pass through the cell surface membrane and into the living part (cytoplasm) of the cells of the endodermis. In this way the cells of the endodermis can control and regulate the movement of solutes through to the xylem. Such control is necessary as a protective measure against the entry of toxic substances, harmful disease-causing bacteria and fungi, and so on. As roots get older the extent of suberin in the endodermis often increases, as shown in fig 13.18b. This blocks the normal exit of water and mineral salts from the cell (see fig 13.18b). However, plasmodesmata may stay as pores in the cell walls, and 'passage cells' in which no extra thickening occurs also remain to allow water and solutes to pass through to the xylem. The relative importance of apoplast, symplast and vacuolar pathways is not known.

13.6   Uptake of mineral salts and their transport across roots

As part of their nutrition, plants require certain mineral elements in addition to the carbohydrates made in photosynthesis. The uses of these elements are described in table 7.7. In plants, minerals are taken up from the soil or surrounding water by roots. Uptake is greatest in the region of the root hairs. The involvement of mycorrhizas is discussed in section 7.10.2.

In attempting to explain the uptake and movement of mineral ions, the following facts should be remembered.

- Mineral elements exist in the form of salts. Salts are made up of ions and in solution the ions can separate ('dissociate') and move about freely.

- Ions can cross membranes in a number of ways. One method is active transport. This requires energy in the form of ATP (made during respiration) and can lead to an accumulation of ions against a concentration gradient (section 5.9.8).

- There is a continuous system of cell walls, the apoplast, extending inwards from the epidermis of the root. Water, and any solutes it contains, enters the apoplast from the soil.

Fig 13.19 shows the uptake of potassium ions by young cereal roots which had previously been thoroughly washed in pure water. After 90 minutes the respiratory inhibitor potassium cyanide was added to the solutions.

> **13.18** (a) Describe the uptake of potassium ions at 0 °C and 25 °C.
> (b) Suggest why potassium cyanide (KCN) has the effects it does.
> (c) Suggest why the roots were thoroughly washed before placing them in a solution containing potassium ions.

Fig 13.19 shows that there are two distinct phases of uptake. The first phase lasts for about 10–20 minutes. Uptake during this phase is relatively rapid. Potassium ions come into contact with the epidermis of the root and start to move through the cell walls of the apoplast pathway, either by mass flow in the transpiration stream or by diffusion. The results show that this phase is more or less independent of temperature since it occurs just as rapidly at 0 °C. It is a passive process.

The second phase is temperature dependent and does not occur at 0 °C when the rate of metabolism and respiration is very low. Its inhibition by KCN shows that it is dependent on respiration. In fact, during this phase, the potassium ions are being taken into the cells of the roots across cell surface membranes by active transport.

Similar results to those in fig 13.19 can be obtained with isolated tissues. Those of storage organs, such as carrot, are commonly used. The data shown in fig 13.20 confirm the inhibition of respiration by potassium cyanide.

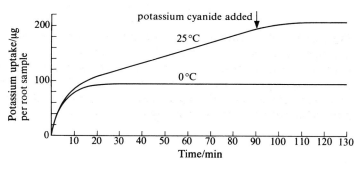

Fig 13.19 *Absorption of potassium ions by young cereal plants in an aerated solution.*

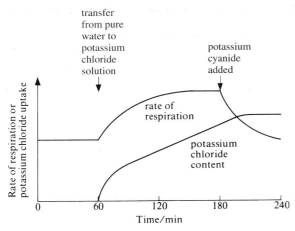

Fig 13.20 *Rate of respiration and uptake of potassium chloride by carrot discs. (Based on data by Robertson & Turner (1945).)*

To summarise so far, the uptake of ions by roots is a combination of:

- **passive uptake**, where ions move by mass flow and diffusion through the apoplast;
- **active uptake**, or **active transport**, in which ions can be taken up into cells against a concentration gradient using energy from respiration.

13.19 Fig 13.20 shows that the rate of respiration of carrot discs increases when they are transferred from pure water to potassium chloride solution. From the results shown, account for this increase.

13.20 Why does the rise in potassium chloride content stop when KCN is added?

13.21 In an experiment similar to that described in fig 13.19, but involving phosphate uptake, 16% of the phosphate taken up by barley roots over a short period could be washed out after transferring to pure water again. Explain.

13.22 Could ions reach the xylem entirely by means of the apoplast pathway?

Active transport is selective and dependent on respiration, whereas diffusion is non-selective and not dependent on respiration. Each cell of the root cortex is bathed in a solution similar in composition to that of the soil solution as a result of passive uptake. Thus there is a large surface area for ion uptake.

Ions moving in the apoplast can only reach the endodermis, where the Casparian strip prevents further progress as described in section 13.5.2. To cross the endodermis, ions must pass by diffusion or active transport through the cell surface membranes of endodermal cells, entering their cytoplasm and possibly their vacuoles. Thus the plant monitors and controls which types of ions eventually reach the xylem.

13.23 How could you demonstrate, using a radioactive ion and autoradiography, that the endodermis is a barrier to the movement of ions through cell walls?

Ions can also move through the symplast pathway. Once they are taken into the cytoplasm of one cell, they can move through the symplast without having to cross further membranes. The symplast extends from the epidermis right through to the xylem. Fig 13.18a summarises the possible ways in which ions can cross the root.

The final stage in the movement of mineral salts across the root is the release of ions into the xylem. To achieve this, ions must leave living cells at some stage, crossing back through a cell surface membrane. This could be by diffusion or active transport.

13.7 Translocation of mineral salts through plants

The pathway of mineral salts across the root to the xylem, described above, is the first stage in their translocation. Once in the xylem, they move by mass flow throughout the plant in the transpiration stream. Movement of mineral elements in the xylem can be demonstrated by ringing experiments like those already described, in which removal of tissues external to the xylem, such as phloem, has no effect on upward movement of ions. Analysis of the xylem sap also reveals that although some of the nitrogen travels as inorganic nitrate or ammonium ions, much of it is carried in the organic form of amino acids and related compounds. Some conversion of these ions to amino acids must therefore take place in the roots. Similarly, small amounts of phosphorus and sulphur are carried as organic compounds.

Thus, although xylem and phloem are traditionally regarded as conducting inorganic and organic materials respectively, the distinction is not clear-cut.

The chief **sinks**, that is regions of use, for mineral elements are the growing regions of the plant, such as the apical and lateral meristems, young leaves, developing fruits and flowers, and storage organs.

13.8 Translocation of organic solutes in phloem

Not all parts of a plant are photosynthetic. The main photosynthetic organs are the leaves. For those parts such as roots which are some distance from the sites of photosynthesis, there is a need for a transport system to circulate the products of photosynthesis. In vascular plants phloem is the tissue which carries products of photosynthesis away from the leaves to other parts. Fig

13.21 summarises the relationship between photosynthetic cells which produce organic food, and non-photosynthetic cells which receive the food. If you study fig 13.21 you will see that organic solutes must be able to move up and down in the same plant. This contrasts with movement in the xylem, which is only upwards. Note also that storage organs act either as sources (losing food) or as sinks (gaining food) at different times.

Typically, about 90% of the total solute carried in the phloem is the carbohydrate sucrose, a disaccharide. This is a relatively inactive and highly soluble sugar, playing little direct role in metabolism and so making an ideal transport sugar since it is unlikely to be used in transit. Once at its destination it can be converted back to the more active monosaccharides, glucose and fructose. Its high solubility means that it can be present in very high concentrations, up to 25% mass to volume in the phloem of plants such as sugarcane.

Phloem also carries certain mineral elements in various forms, particularly nitrogen and sulphur in the form of amino acids, phosphorus in the form of inorganic phosphate ions and sugar phosphates, and potassium ions. Small amounts of vitamins, growth substances such as auxins and gibberellins, viruses and other components may also be present.

Evidence for the circulation of carbon within the plant can be obtained by supplying leaves with carbon dioxide containing the radioactive isotope ^{14}C. Radioactive carbon dioxide is used in photosynthesis and ^{14}C passes into an organic compound such as sucrose. Its movement around the plant can then be traced by various techniques used to locate radioactive isotopes, such as autoradiography, holding a Geiger counter next to the plant surface, or extracting the isotope from different parts. Eventually, both phloem and xylem will be involved in the circulation of carbon. For example, carbon in the form of sucrose may reach the roots and be used in the manufacture of amino acids from nitrates. The amino acids, containing the carbon, can then travel up the shoots in the xylem.

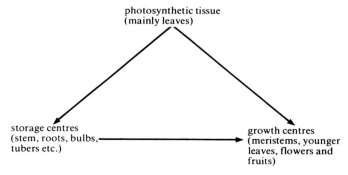

Fig 13.21 *Movement of organic solutes in a green plant.*

13.8.1   Features of phloem translocation

Before considering possible mechanisms for phloem translocation it is useful to list some outstanding facts which any hypothesis has to account for.

- **The quantity of material moved can be very large.** It is estimated, for example, that as much as 250 kg of sugar can be conducted down the trunk of a large tree during a growing season.
- **The rate of flow is high,** commonly 20–100 cm h^{-1}. Maximum rates in excess of 600 cm h^{-1} have been recorded.
- **The distances travelled can be very large.** The tallest trees, such as *Eucalyptus*, may be over 100 m tall. The leaves of *Eucalyptus* trees are located mainly near the top of the trunk, so assimilates must travel the length of the stem and often a considerable distance through the roots.
- **The amount of phloem is not great**. In a tree trunk, the functional phloem tissue is a layer only about the thickness of a postcard around the circumference. It forms the innermost layer of the bark of woody stems and roots. The older phloem, which is nearer to the outside, becomes stretched and dies as the plant grows and its circumference increases.
- **Movement is through tubes called sieve tubes which are very fine**, not more than 30 μm in diameter. This is comparable with a very fine human hair. At regular intervals the tubes are spanned by sieve plates with pores of even smaller diameter. The smaller the diameter of the tubes and pores, the greater is their resistance to the passage of fluid, and the greater the force required to move it. Pressure inside sieve tubes is high.
- Apart from sieve plates, sieve tubes have other structural features which must be taken into account (see next section).

> **13.24** How many sieve plates per metre would be encountered by a sucrose molecule moving through a sieve tube whose sieve tube elements were 400 μm long? (The sieve tube elements are the individual cells that make up the tube. They have sieve plates at each end.)

13.8.2   Structure of sieve tubes

The structure of phloem as seen with the light microscope is described in section 6.2.2. Phloem contains tubes called sieve tubes which are made from cells called sieve tube elements (or sieve elements). The elements are arranged end to end and fuse together to form the sieve tubes. Each element is separated from the next by a sieve plate, which contains pores to allow the flow of liquid from one element to the next.

In contrast to xylem vessels, which are dead empty tubes with few, if any, internal obstructions, phloem sieve tubes are living and do apparently contain obstructions to the flow of solution, namely the sieve plates and, to a lesser extent, the cytoplasm. Fig 13.22 is an electron micrograph of a mature sieve tube element, and fig 13.23 is a diagram showing the main features of sieve tube elements and their neighbouring companion cells.

During development of a sieve tube element its nucleus degenerates, making it an unusual example of a living cell with no nucleus; in this respect it is like mammalian red blood cells. At the same time many other important changes take place, the results of which are shown in fig 13.23. The cell walls at each end of the element develop into sieve plates. These are formed when the plasmodesmata of the end walls enlarge greatly to form sieve pores. A surface view of a sieve plate is shown in fig 6.13. The effect of all the changes is to leave a tube-like structure lined by a very narrow layer of living cytoplasm. This is surrounded by a cell surface membrane.

Closely associated with each sieve tube element are one or more companion cells. These come from the same parent cell as the neighbouring sieve tube element. Companion cells have dense cytoplasm with small vacuoles, and the usual cell organelles. They are metabolically very active, as indicated by their numerous mitochondria and ribosomes (fig 13.23). They have a very close relationship with sieve tube elements and are essential for their survival.

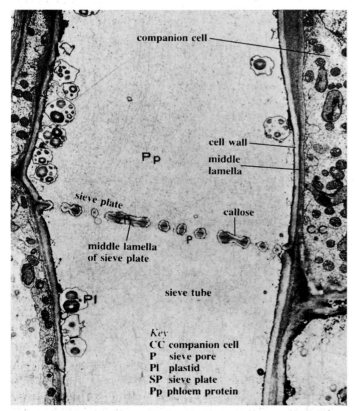

Fig 13.22 *Electron micrograph of a mature sieve tube element.*

In some plants sieve tube elements develop large quantities of a fibrous protein called **phloem protein** (P-protein). This sometimes forms deposits large enough to be seen with the light microscope. There has been much debate in the past about its function, but it is no longer believed to play a role in translocation.

13.8.3   Evidence for movement in phloem

It is important, especially in view of the discussion so far, to be certain that organic solutes really are carried in the phloem sieve tubes. Several types of experiment have been done, all of which support this belief.

- The earliest evidence for movement of sugars and other compounds in phloem came from ringing experiments, in which a ring of tissue containing phloem was removed from the outer region of the stem, leaving the xylem intact. Malpighi obtained evidence in 1675 for ascent of water in wood and descent of food in 'bark'. He removed rings of bark from trees (bark contains the phloem) and found that the leaves did not wilt, but that growth below the ring was greatly reduced. This is because he had stopped sugars moving down the plant without affecting passage of water upwards.

- Mason and Maskell, working with cotton plants in Trinidad during the 1920s and 1930s, did many ringing experiments, one of which is described in fig 13.24. From the results of the experiments shown in fig 13.24, Mason and Maskell concluded that some sideways exchange of sugars can take place between xylem and phloem when they are in contact and the phloem is interrupted (fig 13.24*a*) but that downward movement occurs in phloem (*b* and *c*).

- In 1945, a non-radioactive isotope of carbon, ^{13}C, was introduced into a plant as $^{13}CO_2$ and detected by mass spectrometry. A ring of phloem was killed with a fine jet of steam and translocation of ^{13}C-labelled sucrose through this section was shown to be prevented. Movement of mineral elements in the xylem is not affected by such treatment.

- Microautoradiography of stem sections from plants fed with $^{14}CO_2$ reveals radioactivity in the phloem. The introduction of radioactive isotopes in the 1930s and 1940s provided a tremendous boost to work on translocation.

- Confirmation that movement is through the sieve tubes comes from a neat type of experiment in which the ability of aphids to feed on translocating sugars is made use of. The aphid penetrates the plant tissues with its specially modified mouthparts; these include extremely fine, tube-like 'stylets', which are pushed slowly through the plant's tissues to the phloem. They can be shown to penetrate individual sieve tubes, as revealed by fig 13.25.

If the aphid is anaesthetised with carbon dioxide and the body removed, leaving the stylets in the plant, the

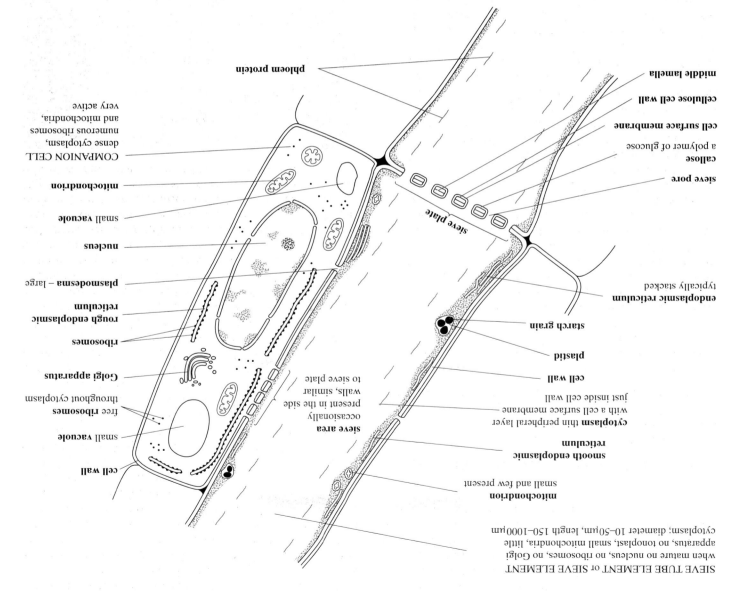

Fig 13.23 *Diagrammatic LS of sieve tube elements and a companion cell as seen with the electron microscope. If the sieve tube is damaged, for example by a grazing animal, more callose is rapidly deposited, blocking the sieve plate and preventing loss of valuable solutes from the sieve tube.*

SIEVE TUBE ELEMENT or SIEVE ELEMENT
when mature no nucleus, no ribosomes, no Golgi apparatus, no tonoplast, small mitochondria, little cytoplasm; diameter 10–50μm, length 150–1000μm

mitochondrion
small and few present

smooth endoplasmic reticulum

cytoplasm thin peripheral layer with a cell surface membrane just inside cell wall

cell wall

plastid

starch grain

endoplasmic reticulum typically stacked

sieve pore

callose a polymer of glucose

cell surface membrane

cellulose cell wall

middle lamella

sieve plate

sieve area occasionally present in the side walls, similar to sieve plate

COMPANION CELL dense cytoplasm, numerous ribosomes and mitochondria, very active

mitochondrion

small vacuole

nucleus

plasmodesma – large

rough endoplasmic reticulum

ribosomes

Golgi apparatus

free ribosomes throughout cytoplasm

small vacuole

cell wall

phloem protein

contents of the sieve tube will continue to be forced up the tube of the mouthparts by the high pressure in the sieve tube, and the oozing fluid can be collected by microcapillary tubes. This technique has found a number of useful applications, for example in estimating rate of flow through sieve tubes (rate of exudation from the tube) and in analysing their contents.

• Finally, improvements in the sensitivity of film used in microautoradiography have enabled precise location of the weakly emitting isotope of hydrogen, tritium (^{3}H), in sieve tubes rather than other phloem cells. The isotope is supplied as part of an amino acid or sucrose.

The facts which any hypothesis must account for are summarised in sections 13.8.1 and 13.8.2, that is large quantities of material move at relatively rapid speeds through very fine sieve tubes. Within the sieve tubes are apparent

13.8.4 Mechanism of translocation in phloem

Experiments have also established that different materials are carried up and down the phloem at the same time, although it is probable that this bidirectional movement is in neighbouring sieve tubes rather than in the same sieve tube.

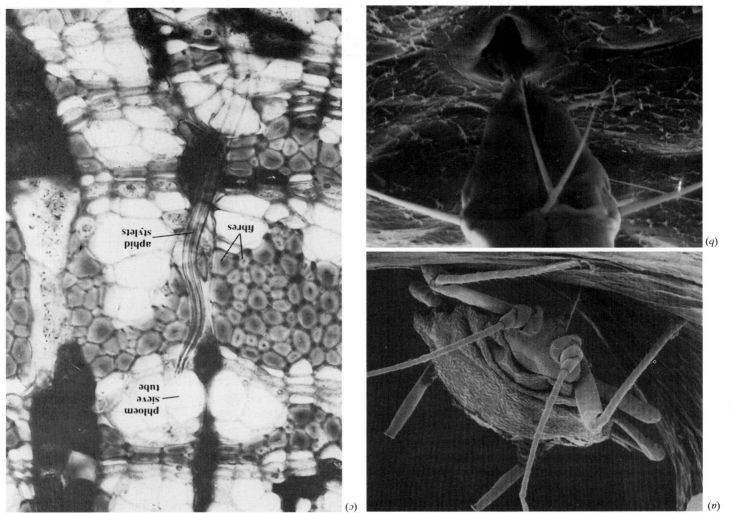

Fig 13.25 (a) and (b) An aphid with its feeding stylets inserted through a leaf epidermis. (c) Feeding stylets of an aphid inserted into a sieve tube.

Labels in (c): aphid stylets, fibres, phloem sieve tube

Fig 13.24 Ringing experiments on cotton plants carried out by Mason and Maskell.

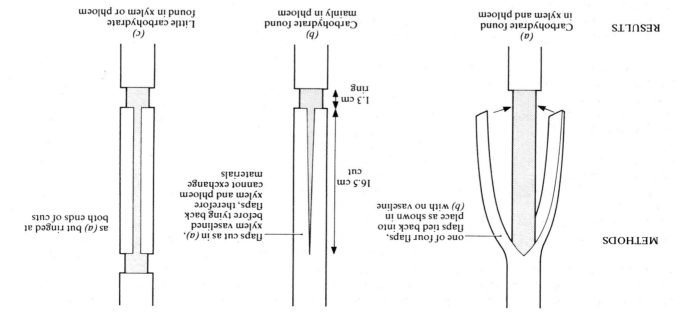

METHODS

(a) one of four flaps, flaps tied back into place as shown in (b) with no vaseline

(b) flaps cut as in (a), xylem vaselined before tying back therefore xylem and phloem cannot exchange materials

16.5 cm cut

1.3 cm ring

(c) as (a) but ringed at both ends of cuts

RESULTS

(a) Carbohydrate found in xylem and phloem

(b) Carbohydrate found mainly in phloem

(c) Little carbohydrate found in xylem or phloem

obstructions, the sieve plates, and other structural features such as phloem protein for which no certain roles have been found. Combine these facts with the fact that the system is delicate and easily damaged by interference, and it is not surprising that research workers have found it difficult to establish the mechanism of translocation through sieve tubes.

It is now believed that a mass flow of solution occurs through sieve tubes. Diffusion is far too slow to account for the rates observed. The evidence for mass flow through sieve tubes is summarised below.

● When phloem is cut, sap oozes out, apparently by mass flow. This is sometimes used commercially as a source of sugar by tapping trees. For example the sugar palm exudes 10 dm³ of sugar-rich sap per day.
● The prolonged exudation of sucrose solution from aphid stylets, as described in section 13.8.3, is evidence of hydrostatic pressure (pumping pressure) in sieve tubes.
● Certain viruses move in the phloem translocation stream, indicating mass flow rather than diffusion since the virus is incapable of locomotion. It cannot diffuse because it is not in solution.

Münch's mass flow and the pressure flow hypothesis

In 1930, Münch put forward a purely physical hypothesis to explain how mass flow might be brought about in sieve tubes. It can be illustrated by the model shown in fig 13.26.

In the model there is an initial tendency for water to pass by osmosis into A and C, but the tendency is greater for A because the solution in A is more concentrated than that in C. As water enters A, a pressure (hydrostatic pressure) builds up in the closed system A–B–C, forcing water out of C. Mass flow of solution occurs through B along the

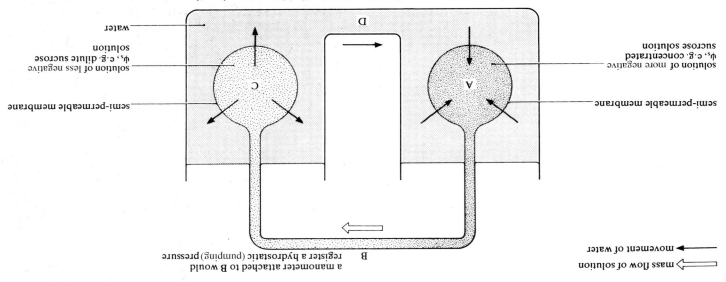

Fig 13.26 Physical model to illustrate Münch's mass flow hypothesis of phloem translocation. Equivalents in living plant: A: source, such as leaf; B: phloem; C: sink, such as roots, meristems, fruits; D: xylem, cell walls and intercellular spaces.

pressure gradient that is generated. There is also an osmotic gradient from A to C. Eventually the system comes into equilibrium as water dilutes the contents of A and solutes accumulate at C.

The model can be applied to living plants. The leaves are represented by A. They make sugar during photosynthesis, thus making the ψ_s of the leaf cells more negative. Water, brought to the leaf in xylem (D) enters the leaf cells by osmosis, raising their pressure potential (ψ_p). At the same time, sugars are used in the sinks, such as roots (C), for various purposes including respiration and synthesis of cellulose. This makes the ψ_s of these cells less negative (higher). A pressure gradient exists from leaves to roots, or, in more general terms, from sources to sinks, resulting in mass flow. In the living plant, equilibrium is not reached because solutes are constantly being used at the sinks (C) and made at the sources (A).

The Münch hypothesis is a purely physical explanation and so does not explain why sieve tubes must be living and metabolically active. It also does not explain the observation that leaf cells are capable of loading sieve tubes against a concentration gradient, that is the fact that the ψ_s of sieve tubes is more negative than that of the leaf cells. The hypothesis has therefore been modified to include an active loading mechanism of solutes into the sieve tubes. The osmotic and hydrostatic pressure gradient therefore starts in the tubes rather than in the photosynthetic cells. It is also believed that unloading at the sinks is an active process. The modern version of Münch's hypothesis is known as the **pressure flow hypothesis**.

Loading sieve tubes

It has been shown that the sucrose concentration in sieve tubes in leaves is commonly between 10 and 30%, whereas it forms only about a 0.5% solution in the photosynthetic

cells where it is produced. As stated above, loading of sieve tubes therefore takes place against a concentration gradient. The mechanism of loading has been the subject of much research in recent years. First the organic solutes have to move from the chloroplasts to the phloem tissue, a journey of 3 mm at most. Both symplast and apoplast routes are involved. The symplast route involves travelling through plasmodesmata and the apoplast route involves travelling by diffusion or mass flow in the transpiration stream through the cell walls.

In 1968 a modified type of companion cell, now known as a **transfer cell**, was reported by Gunning and fellow workers. The cells are found next to the sieve tubes as shown in fig 13.27. Transfer cells have numerous internal projections of the cell wall, a result of extra thickening of the wall. This results in an approximately tenfold increase in surface area of the cell surface membrane lining the wall. It is thought that such cells are thus modified for active uptake of solutes from neighbouring cells. Numerous mitochondria in their cytoplasm provide the energy for this. They are not found in all plants, but are common in the pea family and some other families. Even when transfer cells are absent, similar active transport processes are believed to occur.

Active loading of sucrose (and other substances such as amino acids, phosphates, potassium and ammonium ions) into companion cells is thought to be carried out by specific carrier protein molecules in the cell surface membranes of the companion cells. These carrier systems are thought to be similar to those in animal and bacterial cells in which transport of organic molecules is linked with transport of H^+ ions. H^+ ions are pumped out of the cell by a carrier which uses ATP as an energy source (fig 13.28). The H^+ ion gradient thus established represents potential energy. The H^+ ions diffuse rapidly back into the cell by way of specific carrier proteins that only function if they co-transport sucrose or other specific organic molecules. The active part of this process is therefore the establishment of a H^+ ion gradient across the membrane, with a lower pH (higher H^+ concentration) outside of the cell.

Active transport into the companion cells results in a very negative solute potential in them. As a result, water enters by *osmosis* and a mass flow of solution, including the sucrose, occurs into the sieve tubes through the numerous plasmodesmata that link the companion cells with the sieve tubes. The high pressures and mass flow thus predicted by the Münch hypothesis are thus generated in the sieve tubes (not in the mesophyll cells as imagined by Münch). Another possible mechanism is that active transport also takes place from the companion cell through the plasmodesmata into the sieve tube in the same way that sucrose enters the companion cell.

Unloading probably involves sucrose and other solutes leaving the sieve tubes through plasmodesmata into transfer cells at the sinks. This makes the ψ_s inside the sieve tube less negative, maintaining the pressure gradient between source, where sugar is loaded, and sink, where it is

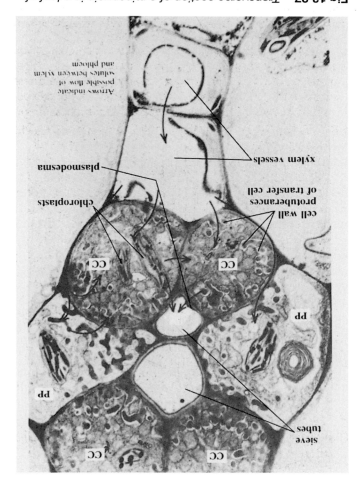

Fig 13.27 *Transverse section of a minor vein in a leaf of Senecio vulgaris. The phloem region, in the top half of the picture, shows six cells arranged around two sieve tubes. There are 4 companion cells (cc) modified as transfer cells. These have dense cytoplasm. There are phloem parenchyma cells (pp) to each side. These have less dense cytoplasm and wall ingrowths only on the sides facing the sieve elements. Plasmodesmata between sieve tubes and companion cells are common, but are very rare between sieve tubes and phloem parenchyma cells. In the lower half of the picture two xylem vessels occupy the centre, while to each side there are parts of two large bundle sheath cells. Arrows indicate some of the possible routes for movement of solutes into sieve tubes, including some solutes delivered to the apoplast by the xylem. Magnification ×6560.*

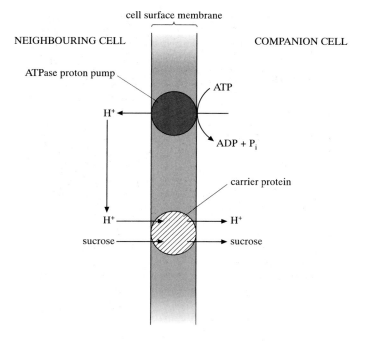

Fig 13.28 *Loading a companion cell with sucrose. H^+ ions are pumped out of the companion cell by a proton pump located in the cell surface membrane. This pump requires energy from ATP and has ATPase activity. Protons pass by facilitated diffusion back into the cell with sucrose through a combined hydrogen ion/sucrose carrier protein.*

unloaded. Unloading may also occur through the cell surface membrane of the sieve tube into the cell walls and into the apoplast.

Critical assessment of the pressure flow hypothesis

- The hypothesis predicts that mass flow will occur through sieve tubes and this seems to occur (the evidence has been given).
- The hypothesis requires the existence of an osmotic gradient and high pressure in the phloem. These have been demonstrated in a number of plants.

  The pressure gradients required to move solutes at the observed rates are relatively high. Assuming that the sieve pores are completely open, a *gradient* of 13 kPa per metre has been theoretically calculated as adequate and until recently it was doubted that such large gradients existed. Several attempts have been made to measure pressure in phloem directly, a very difficult task. Actual pressures varying from 1000–2000 kPa have been reliably recorded in recent years, and the gradient has been measured at 20 kPa per metre. It is therefore likely that the required pressure gradients *are* generated.

- Another criticism of the pressure flow hypothesis has been that it does not explain why sieve tubes should be living as opposed to the dead tubes of xylem. However, only living cells can maintain cell surface membranes, and these are required to prevent leakage of sucrose from the sieve tubes. Recent studies indicate that little metabolic energy is expended by living sieve tubes, suggesting that movement of solutes through them is passive, as predicted by the pressure flow hypothesis.
- Sieve plates are thought to be necessary, despite the resistance to flow which they create, to support the sieve tubes, preventing them from bulging and splitting or exploding outwards with the high internal pressures.
- Contents of the sieve tube are at a pH of about 7.5 to 8.0 (slightly alkaline). This would be expected if hydrogen ions were being pumped out as explained above. The pump would also explain the high concentrations of ATP found in sieve tubes. A summary of the movement of sucrose through the plant is given in fig 13.29.

13.8.5 First-aid mechanisms – a possible role for sieve plates, phloem protein and plastids

One danger faced by plants is damage from being eaten by animals. If sieve tubes are ruptured, leakage of high energy substances such as sucrose would be costly to the plant. Usually, damaged sieve tubes are sealed within minutes by deposition of callose across the sieve plates, blocking the sieve pores. This represents another possible role for sieve plates. It has been suggested that when phloem protein is present, it serves a first-aid function by blocking the sieve pores as soon as the tube is broken. When a sieve tube is cut, release of the pressure inside the tube causes a surge of its contents until they come up against a sieve plate and block it. This prevents escape of the contents of the sieve tube.

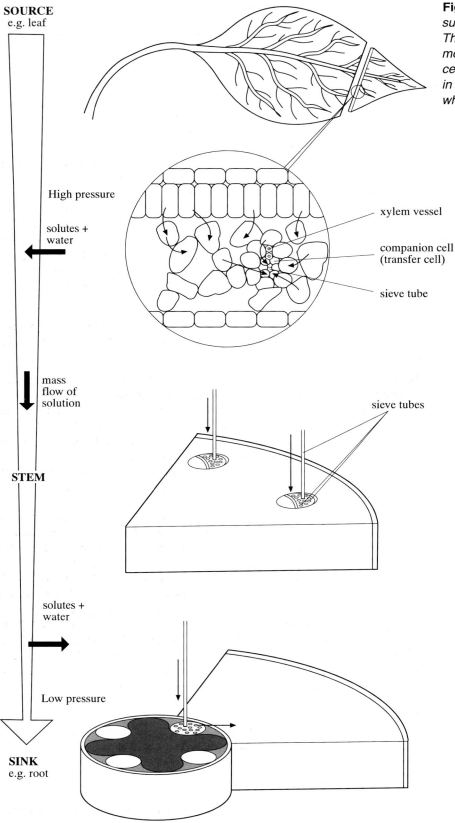

SOURCE
e.g. leaf

High pressure

solutes + water

mass flow of solution

STEM

solutes + water

Low pressure

SINK
e.g. root

xylem vessel

companion cell (transfer cell)

sieve tube

minor vein

sieve tubes

Fig 13.29 *Movement of solutes such as sucrose through the phloem of a plant. Three stages are involved, namely movement of solutes from photosynthetic cells to sieve tubes (loading), translocation in phloem and unloading at a 'sink' (a place where the solutes are used).*

Loading sieve tubes takes place here. Photosynthetic cells make sugars, particularly sucrose, and other organic solutes. Companion cells use energy to collect solutes by active transport. As solute concentration increases in the companion cells, water enters by osmosis. A pressure is created which pushes the solutes through plasmodesmata into the sieve tubes.

Translocation – Pressure inside sieve tubes is greatest at the source and lowest at the sink. Pressure pushes sucrose, etc. from source to sink.

Unloading of the sieve tubes takes place at the sinks. Solute is removed for use, thus maintaining the pressure gradient in the sieve tubes. Water follows.

Sinks are any region where solutes are being used, e.g. roots, fruits, storage organs and regions of growth.

In this section we shall look at the structure of blood and briefly consider its functions. In section 14.8 its functions will be examined in more detail.

14.3.1 Plasma

Plasma is a pale straw-coloured liquid. It consists of 90% water and 10% of a variety of substances in solution and suspension. The major components of blood plasma together with a summary of their functions are shown in table 14.1. The most abundant solute is sodium. The functions of plasma are dealt with in more detail in section 14.8.

14.3.2 Blood cells

Red blood cells (erythrocytes)

In humans red blood cells are small cells that lack nuclei when mature. They appear as circular, biconcave discs (table 14.2 and fig 14.1b). Their average diameter is 7–8 μm (an average animal cell is about 20 μm in diameter) and they are about 2.2 μm thick. Their particular shape results in a larger surface area to volume ratio than that of a sphere and therefore increases the area which can be used for gaseous exchange. Each cell is very thin, thus allowing efficient diffusion of gases across its surface. The shape makes it very flexible and this property allows it to squeeze through capillaries whose internal diameters are smaller than its own by bending into shapes like umbrella-tops. There are approximately five million red blood cells per mm^3 of blood (one drop of blood has a volume of about 50 mm^3). However this figure varies according to the age, sex and state of health of each individual. They make up about half the volume of blood, giving it an enormous oxygen-carrying capacity (about 20 cm^3 of oxygen per 100 cm^3 of blood).

Red blood cells are packed with **haemoglobin**, the oxygen-carrying protein pigment which gives blood its red colour. The lack of a nucleus makes more room for haemoglobin. (Red blood cells also lack mitochondria which makes more room and also means they have to respire anaerobically. Therefore they do not use up any of the oxygen they carry.) Haemoglobin combines reversibly with oxygen to form oxyhaemoglobin in areas of high oxygen concentration, and releases the oxygen in regions of low oxygen concentration. Red blood cells also contain the enzyme carbonic anhydrase which plays a role in carbon dioxide transport (section 14.8.4).

In the adult, each red blood cell has a relatively short life span of about three months (due to the lack of a nucleus to control repair processes) after which time it is destroyed in the spleen or liver. The protein portion of the red blood cell is broken down into amino acids. The iron of the haem

Table 14.1 Components of blood plasma and their functions.

Component	Function
Components maintained at a constant concentration	
Water	Major constituent of blood and lymph. Provides cells of the body with water. Transports many dissolved materials round the body. Regulation of water content helps to regulate blood pressure and blood volume.
Plasma proteins (7–9% of plasma)	
Serum albumins	Very abundant. Bind to and transport calcium. Produced by liver. Contribute to solute potential of the blood.
Serum globulins:	
α-globulins	Produced by liver. Bind and transport the hormone thyroxine, lipids and fat-soluble vitamins (A, D, E and K).
β-globulins	Produced by liver. Bind and transport iron, cholesterol and the fat-soluble vitamins (A, D, E and K).
γ-globulins	Antibodies. Produced by lymphocytes. Important in immune response.
Prothrombin	A protein involved in blood clotting.
Fibrinogen	Produced by liver. Takes part in blood clotting.
Enzymes	Take part in metabolic activities.
Mineral ions These include: Na^+, K^+, Ca^{2+}, Mg^{2+}, Cl^-, HCO_3^-, $H_2PO_4^-$, HPO_4^{2-}, PO_4^{3-}, SO_4^{2-}	All help collectively to regulate solute potential and pH levels in the blood. They also have a variety of other functions, e.g. Ca^{2+} may act as a clotting factor.
Components that occur in varying concentrations	
Products of digestion e.g. sugars, fatty acids, glycerol, amino acids. Vitamins Excretory products e.g. urea. Hormones e.g. insulin, sex hormones, growth hormone.	All are being constantly transported to and from cells within the body.

Table 14.2 Types of cell found in blood (diagrams not drawn to scale).

Component	Origin	Number of cells per mm^3	Function	Structure
Red blood cells	bone marrow	5 000 000	transport of oxygen and some carbon dioxide	
White blood cells	bone marrow			
(a) Granulocytes (72% of total white blood cell count) neutrophils (70%)		4 900	engulf bacteria	
eosinophils (1.5%)	bone marrow	105	allergic responses and anti-histamine properties	
basophils (0.5%)		35	produce histamine and heparin	
(b) Agranulocytes (28%) monocytes (4%)	bone marrow	280	engulf bacteria	
lymphocytes (24%)	bone marrow lymphoid tissue spleen	1 680	production of antibodies	
Platelets	bone marrow	250 000	start blood-clotting mechanism	

group is extracted and stored in the liver as ferritin (an iron-containing protein). It may be re-used later in the production of further red blood cells or as a component of cytochrome. The remainder of the haem molecule is broken down into two bile pigments, bilirubin (red) and biliverdin (green). These are later excreted by way of the bile into the gut.

Between 2–10 million red blood cells are destroyed and replaced each second in the human body. Each one contains about 250 million molecules of haemoglobin, a large protein, so the rate of protein synthesis is impressive. The rate of destruction and replacement is partly determined by the amount of oxygen in the atmosphere. If the quantity of oxygen being carried in the blood is low, the marrow is stimulated to produce more red blood cells than the liver destroys. This is one of the ways in which we acclimatise to lower oxygen levels at high altitudes, and is made use of by athletes in high altitude training. When the oxygen content of the blood is high, the situation is reversed.

14.2 List the main categories of substances transported by the blood.

White blood cells (leucocytes)

These cells are larger than red blood cells, and are present in much smaller numbers, there being about 7000 per mm^3 of blood. All have nuclei. They play an important role in the body's defence mechanisms against disease. Although they have nuclei, their life span in the bloodstream is normally only a few days. All are capable of a crawling movement known as **amoeboid movement**. This allows them to squeeze through pores in capillary walls to reach the tissues and sites of infection.

White blood cells can only be seen easily with a light microscope if they are stained. Staining shows that there are two main groups of white blood cell, the granulocytes and the agranulocytes, according to whether they show granules in their cytoplasm.

Granulocytes (polymorphonuclear leucocytes) (72%). These are made in the bone marrow but by cells different from those that make red blood cells. Granulocytes can be further subdivided into neutrophils, eosinophils and basophils.

- **Neutrophils** (phagocytes): These make up about 70% of the total number of white cells. They commonly squeeze between the cells of the capillary walls and wander through the intercellular spaces. From here they move to infected areas of the body. They are actively phagocytic and engulf and digest disease-causing bacteria (section 14.8.5).

- **Eosinophils**: These possess cytoplasmic granules which stain red when the dye eosin is applied to them. Generally they represent only 1.5% of the total number of white cells, but their population increases in people with allergic conditions such as asthma or hayfever. They possess anti-histamine properties. The number of eosinophils present in the bloodstream is under the control of hormones produced by the adrenal cortex in response to stress of various kinds.

- **Basophils**: These represent 0.5% of the white blood cell population. The granules in these cells stain blue with basic dyes such as methylene blue. The cells produce heparin, an anti-clotting protein and histamine, a chemical found in damaged tissues which is involved in inflammation. Inflammation stimulates repair of damaged tissues. Overproduction of histamine occurs in some allergies, such as hayfever.

Agranulocytes (mononuclear leucocytes) (28%). These cells possess non-granular cytoplasm and have either an oval or bean-shaped nucleus (fig 14.1a). Two main types exist.

- **Monocytes** (4%). These are formed in the bone marrow and have a bean-shaped nucleus. They spend only about 30–40 hours in the blood and then enter the tissues where they become macrophages. **Macrophages** are phagocytic and engulf bacteria and other large particles. They also play a role in the immune system by processing certain antigens, as explained in section 14.9. Together with neutrophils they form a system of phagocytes throughout the body which acts as a first line of defence against infection.

- **Lymphocytes** (24%). These are produced in the thymus gland and lymphoid tissues from cells which originate in the bone marrow. The cells are rounded and possess only a small quantity of cytoplasm. Amoeboid movement is limited. They are also found in lymph and the body tissues. Two types occur, T cells and B cells (section 14.9). They are involved in immune reactions (such as antibody production, graft rejection and in killing tumour cells). The life span of these particular cells can vary from a matter of days to up to ten years or more.

14.3.3 Platelets

Platelets are irregularly shaped, membrane-bound cell fragments, usually lacking nuclei, and are formed from special bone marrow cells. They are about one-quarter the size of red blood cells. They are responsible for starting the process of blood clotting. There are about 250 000 platelets per mm^3 of blood. They survive about 5–9 days before being destroyed by the spleen and liver.

14.4 The circulation

A general plan of the human circulation is shown in fig 14.2a. It shows the following features.

- It is a **double circulation**. This means that the blood passes through the heart twice for each circuit of the body. The advantage of this is that the blood can be sent to the lungs to pick up oxygen and then be returned to the heart to be pumped again before travelling round the body. Blood loses pressure going through the capillaries of the lungs, so the pressure is restored and boosted before the blood is circulated to the rest of the body. In vertebrates which have a single circulation this is not possible. In fish, for example, blood from the heart first goes to the gills to collect oxygen, but then continues round the whole body before returning to the heart. This is a **single circulation** (fig 14.2b). Only birds and mammals have true double circulations. It is probably no coincidence that only birds and mammals are warm blooded. Warm-bloodedness requires a high metabolic rate and this is only possible if a good supply of oxygen is available for high levels of aerobic respiration. Animals with a high metabolic rate can maintain higher levels of activity than other animals.

  Double circulation is made possible by the heart being divided into two. One half pumps deoxygenated blood to the lungs and the other half pumps oxygenated blood to the rest of the body. In effect we have two hearts which are stuck together and beat at the same time. The beginnings of a double circulation are seen in amphibians, and reptiles have an almost completely divided heart.

- The organs are arranged in parallel rather than in series (fig 14.2a). If they were arranged in series, blood would pass from organ A to B to C and so on, losing pressure, oxygen and nutrients at each stage. This would be extremely inefficient. Also, any damage done to a blood vessel linking two organs would interrupt the whole circulation.

- A portal vessel links the gut to the liver (fig 14.2a). A **portal vessel** is a blood vessel which links two organs, neither of which is the heart. (A similar system links the hypothalamus with the pituitary gland.) This means that the gut and liver are linked in series, not in parallel, a disadvantage as explained above. However, there is an overriding advantage: blood from the gut is very variable in composition, depending on whether or not it contains digested food products (or other substances such as alcohol). One of the functions of the liver is to monitor blood passing through it and help to maintain a relatively constant composition. For example, the liver can remove excess glucose from blood and store it as glycogen.

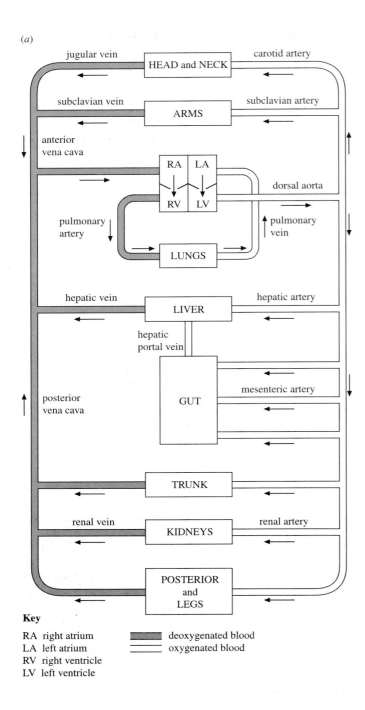

(a)

Key

RA right atrium
LA left atrium
RV right ventricle
LV left ventricle

▨ deoxygenated blood
▭ oxygenated blood

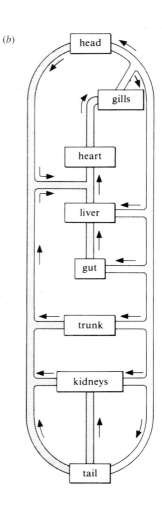

(b)

Fig 14.2 *(a) Double circulation of blood in the human body. The main blood vessels are shown. (b) Single circulation of blood in a fish.*

- the **tunica externa** ('external coat'), an external layer consisting mainly of inelastic white fibres (collagen fibres).

The structure of these vessels is shown and compared in table 14.3 and fig 14.3. Some of the tissues are also discussed in chapter 6 (see figs 6.14, 6.22 and 6.23).

14.5 Blood vessels

14.5.1 General structure

As blood circulates round the body it passes through a series of arteries, capillaries and veins. Basically each artery and vein consists of three layers:

- the **endothelium**, an inner lining of squamous epithelium;
- the **tunica media** ('middle coat'), a middle layer of smooth involuntary muscle and elastic fibres;

14.5.2 Arteries

The large arteries near the heart (that is the aorta, subclavians and carotids) must be able to withstand the high pressure of blood leaving the left ventricle of the heart. The walls of these arteries are thick and the middle layer is mainly composed of elastic fibres. This enables them to dilate (increase in diameter, or stretch) but not rupture when the heart contracts and forces blood into them at high pressure. Between heartbeats the arteries undergo elastic recoil and contract, tending to smooth out the flow of blood along their length (fig 14.4).

Table 14.3 Comparison of the structure and function of an artery, capillary and vein (diagrams are not drawn to scale).

Artery	Vein	Capillary
Transports blood away from the heart.	Transports blood towards the heart.	Link arteries to veins. Site of exchange of materials between blood and tissues.
Tunica media thick and composed of elastic and smooth muscle tissue.	Tunica media relatively thin and only slightly muscular. Few elastic fibres.	No tunica media. Only tissue present is squamous endothelium (section 6.3.1). No elastic fibres.
No semilunar valves (except where leave heart).	Semilunar valves at intervals along the length to prevent backflow of blood.	No semilunar valves.
Pressure of blood is high and has a pulse.	Pressure of blood low and no pulse detectable.	Pressure of blood falling and no pulse detectable.
Blood flow rapid.	Blood flow slow.	Blood flow slowing.
Low blood volume.	Much higher blood volume than capillaries or arteries.	High blood volume.
Blood oxygenated except in pulmonary artery.	Blood deoxygenated except in pulmonary vein.	Mixed oxygenated and deoxygenated blood.

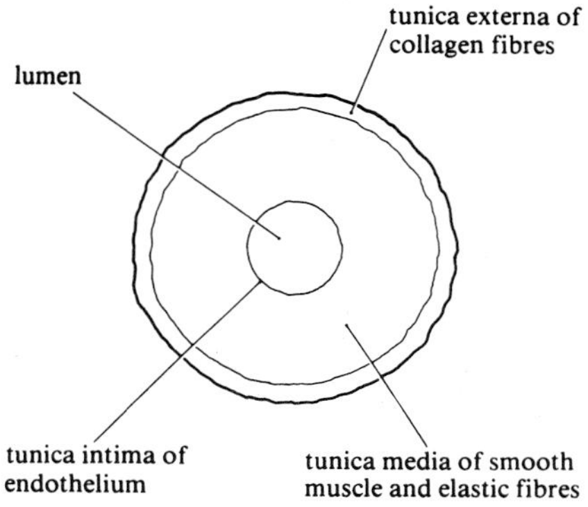

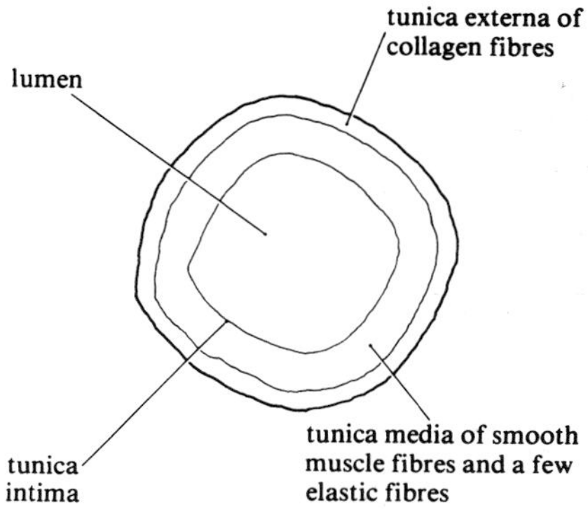

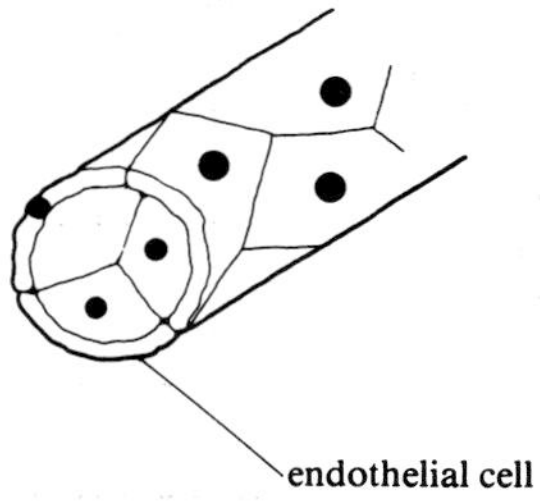

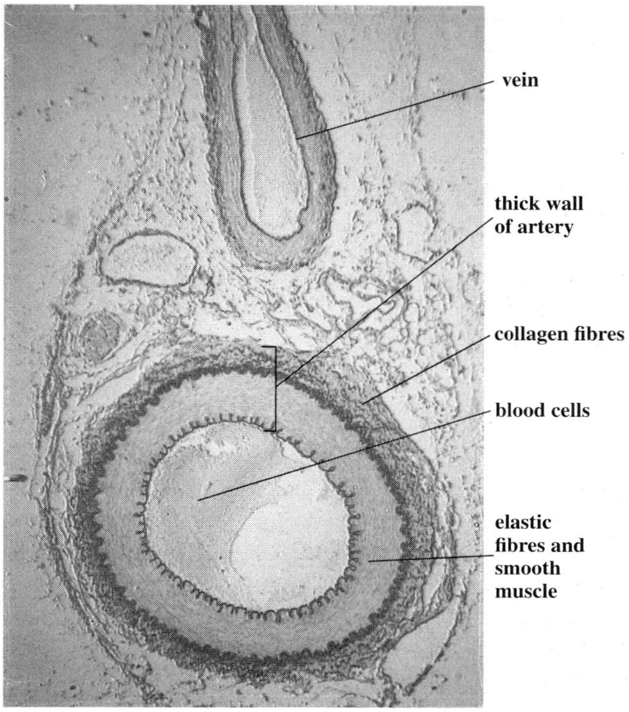

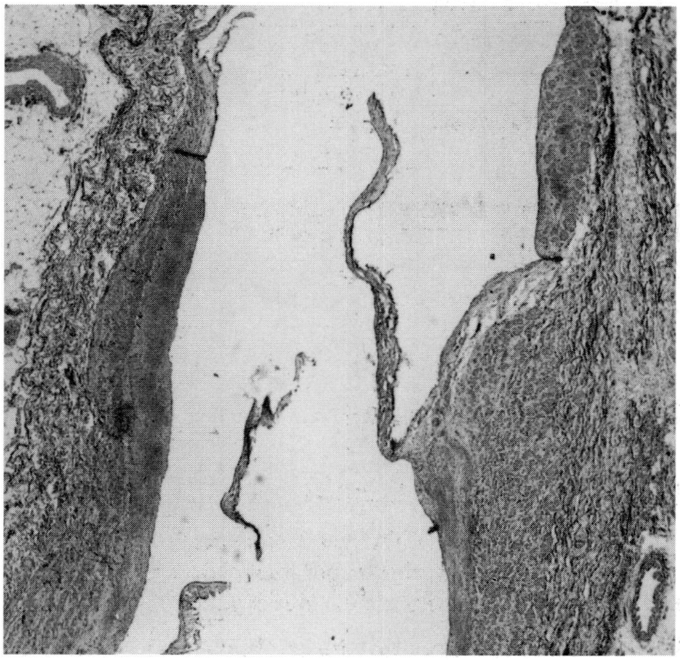

Fig 14.3 *(a) TS of an artery and a vein. (b) LS of a vein showing a valve.*

The arteries further away from the heart have a similar structure but possess relatively more smooth muscle fibres in the middle layer. They are supplied with neurones (nerve cells) from the sympathetic nervous system. Stimulation from this system regulates the diameter of these arteries and this is important in controlling the flow of blood to different parts of the body.

14.5.3 Arterioles

Blood passes from the arteries into small vessels called arterioles. These consist only of endothelium wrapped round by a few muscle fibres at intervals. Many arterioles possess 'sphincters' (fig 14.5) at the point where they enter the capillaries. These are circular muscle fibres which, when they contract, prevent blood from flowing into the capillary network. Also present in certain regions of the body are cross-connections, or 'shunt vessels', which act as short cuts between arterioles and venules (small veins) and serve to regulate the quantity of blood which flows through the capillary beds according to the needs of the body.

14.5.4 Capillaries

Blood passes from the arterioles into capillaries, the smallest blood vessels in the body (fig 14.6). They form a vast network of vessels penetrating all parts of the body, and are so numerous that no cell is more than 25 μm from any capillary. They are 4–10 μm in diameter and their walls, consisting only of endothelium, are permeable to water and dissolved substances. Red blood cells (diameter 7–8 μm) can only just squeeze through (fig 14.7).

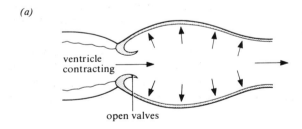

(a)

ventricle contracting

open valves

(b)

closed valves

ventricle relaxed

elastic recoil of vessel wall

Fig 14.4 *Diagram demonstrating how the arteries near the heart help in maintaining a continuous flow of blood in spite of a discontinuous flow received from the ventricles. (From Clegg & Clegg (2nd ed. 1963)* Biology of the mammal, *Heinemann Medical Books.)*

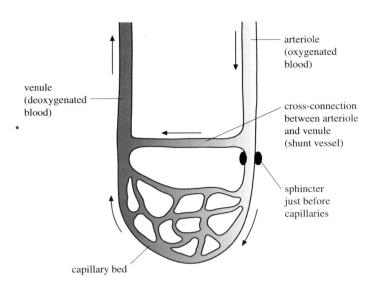

venule (deoxygenated blood)

arteriole (oxygenated blood)

cross-connection between arteriole and venule (shunt vessel)

sphincter just before capillaries

capillary bed

Fig 14.5 *The possible routes that blood may take between arteriole, capillary bed and venule.*

Fig 14.6 *Capillary bed showing arterioles and capillaries.*

It is in the capillaries that exchange of materials between the blood and body cells takes place. Where neighbouring endothelial cells join, a very small gap occurs which allows small soiute molecules and ions to leak out of the capillary. Larger molecules such as proteins stay in the blood. In the glomerulus of the kidney the walls of the capillaries also have pores (section 20.5). Blood flows slowly through the capillaries (less than 1 mm per second) because in total they have a very large cross-sectional area. This allows time for exchange.

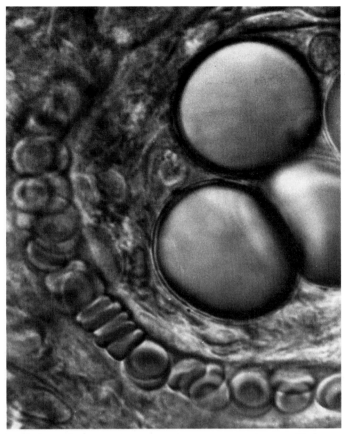

Fig 14.7 *Red blood cells squeezing through a capillary.*

14.5.5 Venules

Blood from the capillary beds drains into venules, whose walls consist of a thin layer of collagen fibres. These are tough and inelastic. They pass the blood into veins which eventually carry it back to the heart.

14.5.6 Veins

A vein possesses less muscle and elastic fibres in its middle layer than an artery and the diameter of its lumen is greater. Semi-lunar valves (fig 14.8) are present,

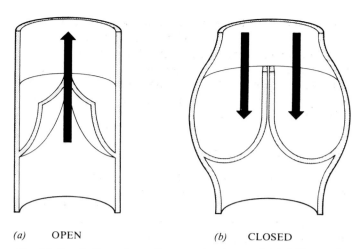

(a) OPEN   *(b)* CLOSED

Fig 14.8 *Action of semilunar valve in a vein. (a) Upward pressure of the blood forces the valve open and blood flows towards the heart. (b) Backflow of blood closes the valve, which resembles a pocket or cup when full of blood.*

which are formed from folds of the inner walls of the vein. They function to prevent backflow of blood, thereby maintaining a one-way flow of blood. A number of veins are located between the large muscles of the body (as in the arms and legs). When these muscles contract they exert pressure on the veins and squeeze them flat (fig 14.9). This helps the flow of blood to the heart.

14.6 Formation of tissue fluid

Tissue fluid is formed when blood passes through the capillaries. As mentioned, the capillary walls are permeable to small solute molecules and ions, but not to the red blood cells, platelets and plasma proteins. **Tissue fluid** is therefore a watery liquid which resembles plasma minus its proteins.

The solute potential exerted by solutes in the plasma is about $-3.5\,\text{kPa}$ and this is far more negative than the solute potential in the tissue fluid. Under these conditions one would normally expect water to flow from the tissue fluid

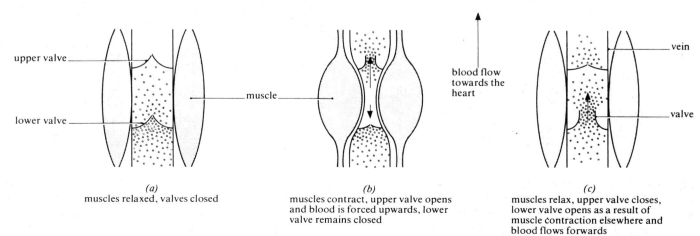

upper valve

lower valve

muscle

(a)
muscles relaxed, valves closed

(b)
muscles contract, upper valve opens and blood is forced upwards, lower valve remains closed

blood flow towards the heart

vein

valve

(c)
muscles relax, upper valve closes, lower valve opens as a result of muscle contraction elsewhere and blood flows forwards

Fig 14.9 *Diagram illustrating how muscle contraction around a vein helps one-way flow of blood towards the heart.*

into the blood plasma. However, the blood pressure at the arterial end of a capillary is about 5.2 kPa (fig 14.10). The forces of solute potential and blood pressure (hydrostatic pressure) work in opposite directions. The more negative the solute potential of the blood, the more water tends to *enter* it. The higher the blood pressure, the more water tends to *leave* it. The same is true of the tissue fluid, so solute potential and pressure of both blood and tissue fluid have to be considered when calculating which way water (and the solutes dissolved in it) will move. The figures in fig 14.10 show that in the first part of the capillary, fluid leaves the capillary. It enters the minute spaces between the cells to form the tissue fluid. It is through the tissue fluid

that exchange of materials between blood and tissues occurs.

The blood cannot afford to lose so much fluid constantly. Also, if tissue fluid continued to build up the tissue would swell, a condition called **oedema**. Therefore it is normally returned to the blood at the same rate that it is produced. This occurs in two ways.

- As tissue fluid is forming, protein molecules in solution stay behind in the blood. The blood therefore becomes more concentrated, in other words its solute potential becomes more negative. It also loses pressure as it passes through the narrow capillary, so by the time it

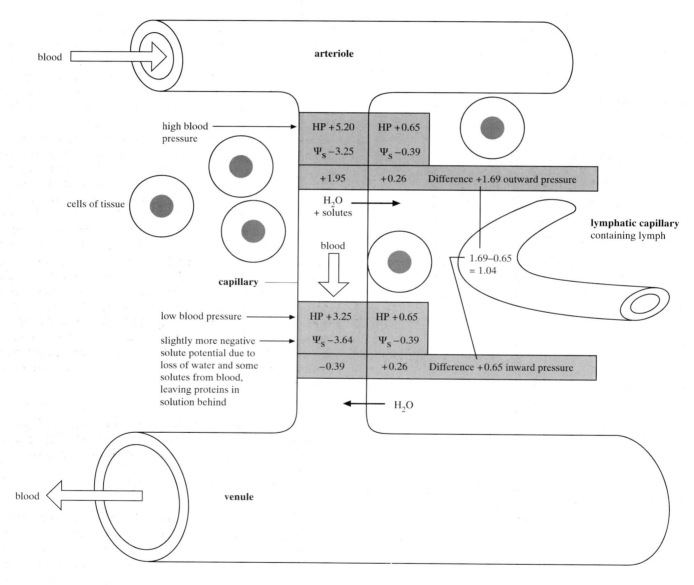

Fig 14.10 *Formation of tissue fluid and lymph. Tissue fluid is formed by filtration at the arteriole end of the capillary. Some of the fluid lost from the blood is replaced at the venule end of the capillary and some enters the lymphatic capillaries. Net movement of fluid is due to the balance between two forces, blood pressure (pumping or hydrostatic pressure, HP) due to the heart, and solute potential (ψ_s). The higher the solute concentration, the more negative the solute potential. Figures are in kPa. They are average values and do not apply to all capillaries.*

reaches the venule end of the capillary, fluid is tending to re-enter the blood capillary, as shown in fig 14.10.

- The rest of the tissue fluid drains into blindly ending lymphatic capillaries, and once inside these the fluid is termed **lymph**. The lymphatic capillaries join to form larger lymphatic vessels. The lymph is moved through the vessels by contraction of the muscles surrounding them, and backflow is prevented by valves present in the major vessels which act in a similar fashion to those found in veins (fig 14.11).

The lymphatic vessels of the body empty the lymph into the blood system at the subclavian veins just after they leave the arms and just before they reach the heart (fig 14.12).

Situated at intervals through the lymphatic system are **lymph glands** or nodes. Lymphocytes, in the course of circulation through the blood and lymph, accumulate in the lymph nodes. They produce antibodies and are an important part of the body's immune system. Phagocytes in the nodes also remove bacteria and foreign particles from the lymph.

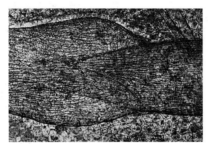

Fig 14.11 *LS through lymph vessel showing an internal valve.*

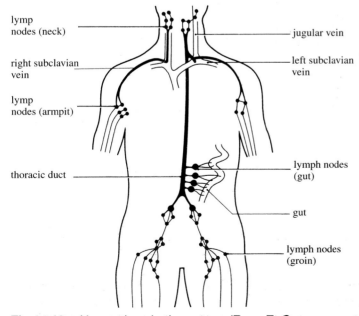

lymp nodes (neck)

jugular vein

right subclavian vein

left subclavian vein

lymp nodes (armpit)

thoracic duct

lymph nodes (gut)

gut

lymph nodes (groin)

Fig 14.12 *Human lymphatic system. (From E. G. Springthorpe (1973)* An introduction to functional systems in animals, *Longman.)*

14.7 The heart

14.7.1 Structure

The heart is situated between the two lungs and behind the sternum in the thorax. It is surrounded by a tough sac, the **pericardium**, the outer part of which consists of inelastic white fibrous tissue. The inner part is made up of two membranes. The inner membrane is attached to the heart and the outer one is attached to the fibrous tissue. Pericardial fluid is secreted between them and reduces the friction between the heart wall and surrounding tissues when the heart is beating. The inelastic nature of the pericardium as a whole prevents the heart from being overstretched or overfilled with blood.

There are four chambers in the heart, two upper thin-walled **atria** (singular **atrium**) and two lower thick-walled **ventricles** (fig 14.13). The atria receive blood from the veins and pump it to the ventricles which in turn pump it into arteries. The walls of the atria are thin because they only have to pump blood into the ventricles.

The right side of the heart is completely separated from the left. The right side deals with deoxygenated blood and the left side with oxygenated blood. The right atrium receives deoxygenated blood from the general circulation of the body whilst the left atrium receives oxygenated blood from the lungs. The muscular wall of the left ventricle is at least three times as thick as that of the right ventricle. This difference is due to the fact that the right ventricle only has to pump blood to the lungs, which are very near the heart in the thorax, whereas the left ventricle pumps blood all round the body. Therefore the blood entering the aorta from the left ventricle is at a much higher blood pressure (approximately 14.0 kPa) than the blood entering the pulmonary artery (2.1 kPa). The circulation to and from the lungs is called the **pulmonary circulation** and the circulation round the body is called the **systemic circulation**.

> **14.3** What other advantages are there in supplying the pulmonary circulation with blood at a lower pressure than that of the systemic circulation?

As the atria contract they force blood into the ventricles, and rings of muscle which surround the venae cavae and pulmonary veins at their point of entry into the atria contract and close off the veins. This prevents blood returning into the veins. The left atrium is separated from the left ventricle by a **bicuspid** (two-flapped) valve, whilst a **tricuspid** valve separates the right atrium from the right ventricle (fig 14.14*a*). Jointly, these are known as the **atrioventricular valves**. Attached to the ventricle side of the flaps are fibrous cords which in turn attach to conical-shaped papillary muscles which are extensions of the inner

(a)

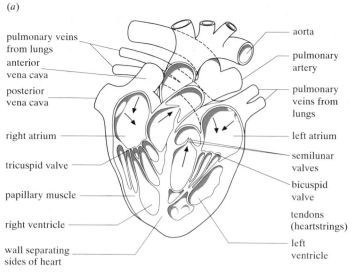

pulmonary veins from lungs
anterior vena cava
posterior vena cava
right atrium
tricuspid valve
papillary muscle
right ventricle
wall separating sides of heart

aorta
pulmonary artery
pulmonary veins from lungs
left atrium
semilunar valves
bicuspid valve
tendons (heartstrings)
left ventricle

(b)

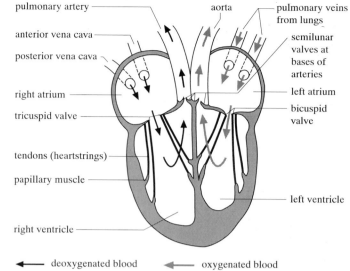

pulmonary artery
anterior vena cava
posterior vena cava
right atrium
tricuspid valve
tendons (heartstrings)
papillary muscle
right ventricle

aorta
pulmonary veins from lungs
semilunar valves at bases of arteries
left atrium
bicuspid valve
left ventricle

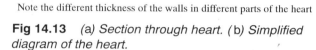
deoxygenated blood   oxygenated blood

Note the different thickness of the walls in different parts of the heart

Fig 14.13 *(a) Section through heart. (b) Simplified diagram of the heart.*

(a)

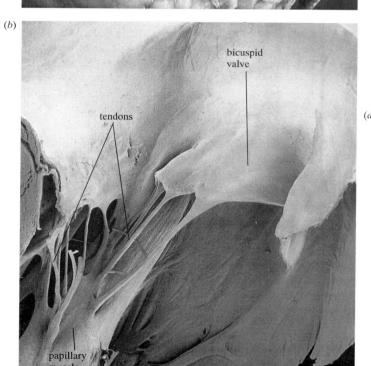

(b)

bicuspid valve
tendons
papillary muscle

(c)

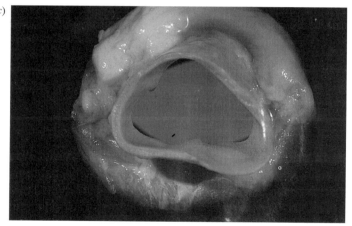

(d)

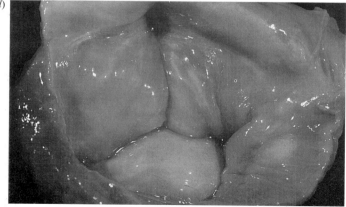

Fig 14.14 *(a) Tricuspid valves. (b) Bicuspid valve showing tendons which join the valve flaps to papillary muscle. (c) Open semilunar valve at the base of pulmonary artery. (d) Closed semilunar valve at the base of the pulmonary artery.*

wall of the ventricles. The atrioventricular valves are pushed open when the atria contract but, when the ventricles contract, the flaps of each valve press tightly closed so preventing return of blood to the atria. At the same time the papillary muscles contract so tightening the fibrous cords. This prevents the valves from being turned inside out. Semilunar valves (pocket valves) (fig 14.14b) are found at the points where the pulmonary artery and aorta leave the heart. These prevent blood from getting back into the ventricles.

Just beyond the aortic valve are the openings of the two coronary arteries. These are the only blood vessels which supply oxygenated blood to the walls of the heart.

Structure of cardiac muscle

The walls of the heart are composed of cardiac muscle fibres, connective tissue and tiny blood vessels. Each muscle fibre possesses one or two nuclei and many large mitochondria. Each fibre is made up of many myofibrils. These contain actin and myosin filaments which bring about contraction in the same way as skeletal muscle (section 18.4). They account for the striped appearance of the muscle fibres (striations in figs 14.15 and 14.16). The dark bands known as **intercalated discs** are cell surface membranes separating individual muscle cells. The structure of the membranes is modified to allow ions to

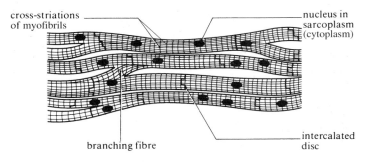

Fig 14.15 *Structure of cardiac muscle.*

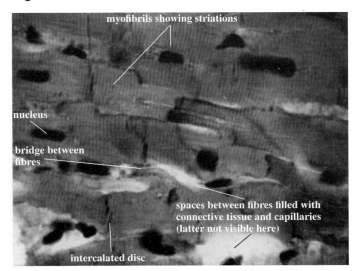

Fig 14.16 *Photograph of cardiac muscle.*

diffuse rapidly across them. This allows rapid spread of excitation (action potentials) through the muscle. When one cell becomes excited, the action potential spreads quickly to all the others, so that the whole mass of fibres behaves as one unit. The fibres branch and cross-connect with each other to form a complex net-like arrangement. Cardiac muscle contracts more slowly than skeletal muscle and does not fatigue as easily. No neurones are present in the wall of the heart.

14.7.2 The cardiac cycle

The cardiac cycle refers to the sequence of events which takes place during the completion of one heartbeat. It involves repeated contraction and relaxation of the heart muscle. Contraction is called **systole** and relaxation is called **diastole**. It occurs as follows.

- **Atrial diastole**. During the time when the atria and the ventricles are both relaxed, blood returning to the heart under low pressure in the veins enters the two atria. Oxygenated blood enters the left atrium and deoxygenated blood enters the right atrium. At first the bicuspid and tricuspid valves are closed (fig 14.17a) but, as the atria fill with blood, pressure in them rises (fig 14.18). Eventually it becomes greater than that in the relaxed ventricles and the valves are pushed open.
- **Atrial systole**. When atrial diastole ends, the two atria contract simultaneously. This is termed atrial systole and results in blood being pumped into the ventricles (fig 14.17b).
- **Ventricular systole**. Almost immediately (about 0.1 to 0.2 seconds later) the ventricles contract. This is called ventricular systole (fig 14.17c). When this occurs the pressure in the ventricles rises and closes the atrioventricular valves, preventing blood from returning to the atria. The pressure forces open the semi-lunar valves of the aorta and pulmonary artery and blood enters these vessels. The closing of the atrioventricular valves during ventricular systole produces the first heart sound, described as **'lub'**.
- **Ventricular diastole**. Ventricular systole ends and is followed by ventricular diastole (fig 14.17d). The high pressure developed in the aorta and pulmonary artery tends to force some blood back towards the ventricles and this closes the semi-lunar valves of the aorta and pulmonary artery. Hence backflow into the heart is prevented. The closing of the valves causes the second heart sound, **'dub'**. The two heart sounds are therefore:

  ventricular systole = 'lub'
  ventricular diastole = 'dub'

Ventricular systole, and the elastic recoil of the arteries as blood at high pressure is forced through them, causes a pulse. As blood gets further and further away from the heart, the pulse becomes less and less pronounced until, in the capillaries and veins, blood flows evenly (figs 14.19 and

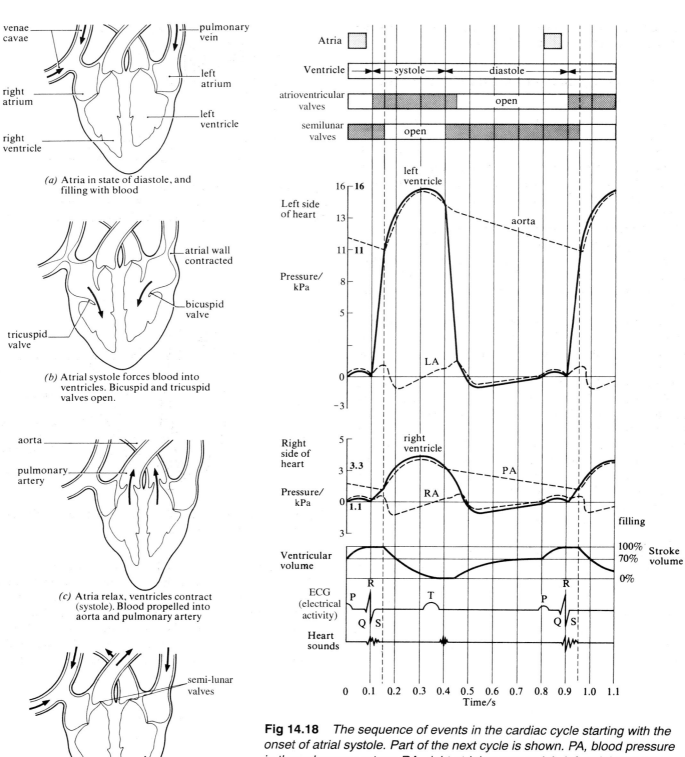

(a) Atria in state of diastole, and filling with blood

(b) Atrial systole forces blood into ventricles. Bicuspid and tricuspid valves open.

(c) Atria relax, ventricles contract (systole). Blood propelled into aorta and pulmonary artery

(d) Semi-lunar valves of aorta and pulmonary artery close. Atria begin to refill. Ventricles in state of diastole

Fig 14.18 *The sequence of events in the cardiac cycle starting with the onset of atrial systole. Part of the next cycle is shown. PA, blood pressure in the pulmonary artery; RA, right atrial pressure; LA, left atrial pressure. (From J. H. Green (1968)* An introduction to human physiology, *Oxford University Press.)*

Fig 14.17 *Sequence of heart actions involved in one complete heartbeat – the cardiac cycle.*

14.20). One complete heartbeat consists of one systole and one diastole and lasts for about 0.8 s (fig 14.18).

14.7.3 Myogenic stimulation of heart rate

When a heart is removed from a mammal and placed in a well-oxygenated salt solution at 37 °C it will continue to beat rhythmically for a considerable time, without stimuli from the nervous system or hormones. This demonstrates the **myogenic** nature of the stimulation of the heart, that is heart muscle has its own 'built-in' mechanism for bringing about its contraction (*myo*, muscle; *genic*, giving rise to).

The stimulus for contraction of the heart originates in a specific region of the right atrium called the **sino-atrial node** (or **SAN** for short). This is located near the opening of the venae cavae (fig 14.21). It consists of a small number of cardiac muscle fibres and a few nerve endings from the autonomic nervous system (the involuntary part of the nervous system – see next section). The SAN can stimulate the heartbeat on its own, but the rate at which it beats can be varied by stimulation from the autonomic nervous system.

The cells of the SAN slowly become depolarised during atrial diastole. This means that the charge across the membrane is gradually reduced. At a certain point an action potential (section 17.1.1) is set up in the cells (nerve impulses are started in the same way). A wave of excitation similar to a nerve impulse passes across the muscle fibres of the heart as the action potential spreads from the SAN. It causes the muscle fibres to contract. The SAN is known as the **pacemaker** because each wave of excitation begins here and acts as the stimulus for the next wave of excitation.

Once contraction has begun, it spreads through the walls of the atria through the network of cardiac muscle fibres at the rate of $1\,\mathrm{m\,s}^{-1}$. Both atria contract more or less simultaneously. The atrial muscle fibres are completely separated from those of the ventricles by a layer of connective tissue called the atrio-ventricular septum, except for a region in the right atrium called the **atrio-ventricular node** (AVN) (fig 14.21).

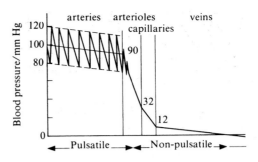

Fig 14.20 *Blood pressure throughout the human circulatory system. (From J. H. Green (1968) An introduction to human physiology, Oxford University Press.)*

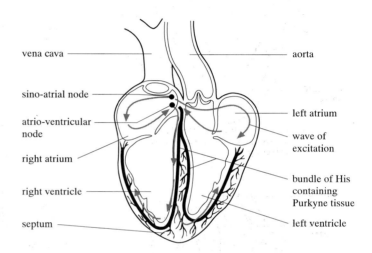

Fig 14.21 *Position of the sino-atrial and atrio-ventricular nodes, and the bundle of His.*

The structure of the AVN is similar to that of the SAN and is connected to a bundle of specialised muscle fibres, the **AV bundle**, which provides the only route for the transmission of the wave of excitation from the atria to the ventricles. There is a delay of approximately 0.15 s in conduction from the SAN to the AVN, which means that atrial systole is completed before ventricular systole begins.

	Volume/cm³	Pressure/kPa	Velocity/cm s⁻¹
aorta	100	13.3	40
arteries	300	13–5.3	40–10
arterioles	50	5–3.3	10–0.1
capillaries	250	3.3–1.6	< 0.1
venules	300	1.6–1.3	< 0.3
veins	2 200	1.3–0.7	0.3–5
vena cava	300	0.3	5–20

Fig 14.19 *Distribution of blood volume, pressure and velocity in the human vascular system. (From K. Schmidt-Nielsen (1980) Animal physiology, 2nd ed., Cambridge University Press.)*

The AV bundle is connected to the **bundle of His**, a strand of modified cardiac fibres which gives rise to finer branches known as **Purkyne tissue**. Impulses are conducted rapidly along the bundle at $5\,m\,s^{-1}$, and spread out from there to all parts of the ventricles. Both ventricles are stimulated to contract simultaneously. The wave of ventricular contraction begins at the bottom of the heart and spreads upwards, squeezing blood out of the ventricles towards the arteries which pass vertically upwards out of the heart (fig 14.21). The electrical activity that spreads through the heart during the cardiac cycle can be detected using electrodes placed on the skin and an instrument called an electrocardiogram (ECG). This has medical use since certain heart defects can be detected (fig 14.22).

Certain characteristics of cardiac muscle make it suited to its role of pumping blood round the body throughout the life of the mammal. Once muscle has begun to contract it cannot respond to a second stimulus until it begins to relax. The period during which it cannot respond at all is known as the **absolute refractory period** (fig 14.23). This period is longer in cardiac muscle than in other types of muscle, and enables it to recover fully without becoming fatigued, even when contracting vigorously and rapidly. It is thus impossible for the heart to develop a state of sustained contraction called **tetanus**, or to develop an oxygen debt. As muscle recovers it passes through a **relative refractory period** when it will respond only to a strong stimulus (fig 14.23).

14.7.4 Regulation of heart rate

The basic rate of the heartbeat is controlled by the activity of the SAN as described earlier. Even when removed from the body and placed into an artificial medium the heart will continue to beat rhythmically, although more slowly. In the body, however, the demands on the blood system are constantly changing and the heart rate has to be adjusted accordingly. This is achieved by control systems, one nervous and the other chemical. This is a **homeostatic response** whose overall function is to maintain constant conditions within the bloodstream even though conditions around it are constantly changing.

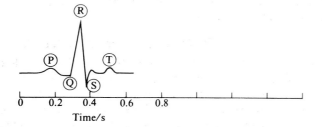

Fig 14.22 *An electrocardiogram (ECG) trace demonstrating the change in electrical potential across the heart during one cardiac cycle. P, atrial depolarisation over the atrial muscle and spread of excitation from the sino-atrial node during atrial systole; Q, R and S, ventricular systole; T, ventricular diastole begins.*

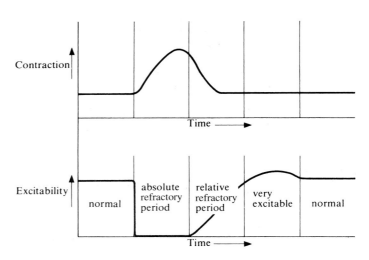

Fig 14.23 *The refractory period of cardiac muscle. The upper figure shows a record of the contraction of the muscle, the lower figure shows the varying excitability of the muscle to stimuli. (From Clegg & Clegg (2nd edition, 1963) Biology of the mammal, Heinemann Medical Books.)*

The amount of blood flowing from the heart over a given period of time is known as the **cardiac output** and depends upon the volume of blood pumped out of the heart at each beat, the **stroke volume**, and the **heart rate** (number of beats per minute):

cardiac output = stroke volume $\times$ heart rate

It is the cardiac output which is the important variable in supplying blood to the body. One way of controlling cardiac output is to control the heart rate.

Nervous control of heart rate

Overall nervous control of the cardiovascular system (heart and blood vessels) is located in a part of the hindbrain known as the **medulla**. Part of its function is to control heart rate. Certain nerves link the medulla with the heart, as shown in fig 14.24. The nervous system is divided into a voluntary nervous system and an autonomic nervous system which acts automatically and is not under voluntary control. The autonomic nervous system itself is divided into a sympathetic nervous system (SNS) and a parasympathetic nervous system (PNS). The SNS is generally associated with excitation of the body and preparing it for action, whereas the PNS has a relaxing influence. These are both involved in regulating the heart rate.

The medulla has two regions affecting heart rate, the **cardiac inhibitory centre** which reduces the heart rate, and the **cardiac accelerator centre** which stimulates the heart rate. Two parasympathetic nerves, called the **vagus nerves**, leave the inhibitory centre and run, one on either side of the trachea, to the heart (only one is shown in fig 14.24 for clarity). Here nerve fibres lead to the SAN, AVN and the bundle of His. Impulses passing along the vagus nerves reduce the heart rate. Other nerves, which are part of the sympathetic nervous system, have their origin in the cardiac

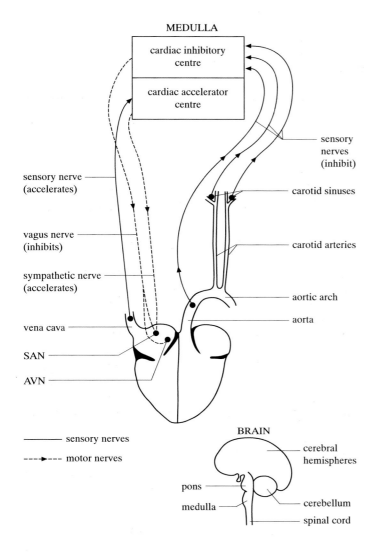

MEDULLA

cardiac inhibitory centre

cardiac accelerator centre

sensory nerves (inhibit)

sensory nerve (accelerates)

vagus nerve (inhibits)

sympathetic nerve (accelerates)

vena cava

SAN

AVN

carotid sinuses

carotid arteries

aortic arch

aorta

———— sensory nerves

---►--- motor nerves

BRAIN

cerebral hemispheres

pons

medulla

cerebellum

spinal cord

Fig 14.24 *Nervous control of the heart rate. Neurones connect the heart to the cardiac inhibitory and cardiac accelerator centres in the medulla of the hindbrain.*

accelerator region of the medulla. These run parallel to the spinal cord and enter the SAN. Stimulation by these nerves results in an increase in the heart rate. It is the coordinated activity of the inhibitory and accelerator centres in the medulla that controls the heart rate.

Sensory nerve fibres from stretch receptors within the walls of the aortic arch, the carotid sinuses and the vena cava run to the cardiac inhibitory centre in the medulla. Impulses received from the aorta and carotids decrease the heart rate, while those from the vena cava stimulate the accelerator centre which increases the heart rate. As the volume of blood passing to any of these vessels increases so does the stretching of the walls of these vessels. This stimulates the stretch receptors and increases the number of nerve impulses transmitted to the centres in the medulla.

For example, under conditions of intense activity body muscles contract strongly and this increases the rate at which venous blood returns to the heart. Consequently the walls of the vena cava are stretched by large quantities of blood and the heart rate is increased. At the same time the increased blood flow to the heart places the cardiac muscle of the heart under increased pressure. Cardiac muscle responds automatically (no nerves are involved) to this pressure by contracting more strongly during systole and pumping out an increased volume of blood. In other words stroke volume is increased. This relationship between the volume of blood returned to the heart and cardiac output was named after the English physiologist Starling and is known as **Starling's law**.

The increased stroke volume stretches the aorta and carotids which in turn, via stretch reflexes, signal the cardiac inhibitory centre to slow the heart rate. Therefore there is an automatic fail-safe mechanism which serves to prevent the heart from working too fast, and to enable it to adjust its activity in order to cope effectively with the volume of blood passing through it at any given time.

Hormonal control of heart rate

A number of hormones affect heart rate, either directly or indirectly. We shall consider those that have a direct effect first.

The most important of these is **adrenaline**. Adrenaline is secreted by the medulla (middle) of the adrenal glands. The adrenal medulla also secretes smaller amounts of the hormone noradrenaline which has similar effects to adrenaline. Both stimulate the heart, although adrenaline is more effective. Cardiac output and blood pressure are increased by increasing heart rate. The two hormones also have other effects on the body which prepare the body for action (the 'flight or fight' response) as described in section ~~17.1.2~~ 17.6.5.

Thyroxine, produced by the thyroid gland, raises basal metabolic rate (section 17.6.4). This in turn leads to greater metabolic activity, with greater demand for oxygen and production of more heat. As a result, vasodilation (dilation of the blood vessels) followed by increased blood flow occurs, and this leads in turn to increased cardiac output. Heart rate is also directly stimulated by thyroxine.

Other factors controlling heart rate

A number of other stimuli act directly on cardiac muscle or on the SAN. They are briefly summarised in table 14.4.

Many activities affect the cardiovascular centres in the medulla in some way or other, for example emotions, such as embarrassment, which causes blushing, or anger, which can make the skin turn white, sights and sounds. In such instances sensory impulses are transmitted to the brain where they pass to the cardiovascular centre in the medulla.

Table 14.4 Factors other than nervous and hormonal factors which affect heart rate.

Non-nervous stimulus	Effect on heart rate
high pH	decelerates
low pH (e.g. high CO_2 levels, as is the case during active exercise)	accelerates
low temperature	decelerates
high temperature	accelerates
mineral ions	the rate is affected directly or indirectly

14.7.5 Effects of exercise on the cardiovascular system

Short-term effects

During exercise the muscles need an increased blood supply so that oxygen and glucose can be provided for aerobic respiration and waste carbon dioxide and heat can be removed. Blood flow increases dramatically and this is achieved in a number of ways.

During periods of continuous heavy exercise the output of blood from the left ventricle of the heart may increase from the resting condition of 4–6 $dm^3 min^{-1}$ to 15 (untrained female) and 22 (untrained male) $dm^3 min^{-1}$, or even 30 $dm^3 min^{-1}$ for an athlete (this would fill an average bath in about two minutes). This is brought about both by an increased rate of contraction (heart rate) and a more complete emptying of the ventricles (stroke volume). It typically results in a rise in pressure of about 30% in the arteries. Roughly speaking, heart rate can triple and stroke volume can double in response to maximal exercise. In a trained athlete this, combined with vasodilation of blood vessels due to adrenaline and the sympathetic nervous system (see below), can result in a 25-fold increase in blood flow through the muscles about half of which is due to vasodilation and half due to increased blood pressure. Vasodilation also takes place in the heart's own blood vessels and in the lungs.

How is the increased cardiac output brought about? In anticipation of exercise, and during its early phase, the sympathetic nervous system and adrenaline stimulate an increased heart rate. However, during a period of prolonged exercise, the rate is maintained by further nervous and hormonal factors. For example, dilation of the veins in the muscles increases venous return to the heart, which results in increased cardiac output as discussed in section 14.7.4 (see also fig 14.24). Vasoconstriction of arterioles (section 14.7.7) occurs in tissues which are less in need of oxygen, particularly the gut, liver, kidneys and spleen. The effect of a rising carbon dioxide concentration due to exercise is discussed in section 14.7.7.

Eventually vasodilation of skin blood vessels occurs in response to a build-up of heat. The rising temperature of the blood is detected by the hypothalamus in the brain and this sends nerve impulses to the medulla which in turn will bring about vasodilation of arterioles in the skin. Capillary loops in the skin then open up, allowing loss of heat through the skin.

Fig 14.25 shows the effect of exercise on a marathon runner, and how cardiac output is increased from 5 to 30 $dm^3 min^{-1}$ by changes in the heart rate and stroke volume. Stroke volume increases about 50% whereas heart rate increases about 27%. Note that the stroke volume reaches its maximum long before heart rate does, but that stroke volume increases more rapidly at first. This is typical of a fit person. It is the greater cardiac output which is the biggest difference between a marathon runner and an untrained person (rather than differences in breathing capacity).

Long-term effects

The heart, like all muscles, gets stronger with exercise. Long-term training therefore results in a stronger heart and a higher cardiac output. As seen above, a 40% increase in cardiac output is typical in marathon runners compared with untrained people. The chambers of the heart get larger and the mass of muscle increases by 40% or more. All aspects of function improve, from an increase in blood vessels to greater numbers and size of mitochondria in the muscle fibres. Aerobic (endurance) exercise is necessary for these improvements, rather than short-burst anaerobic activity.

14.7.6 Measuring blood pressure

Blood pressure is the force developed by the blood pushing against the walls of the blood vessels. It is usually measured in the brachial artery in the arm by using

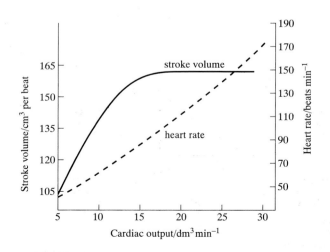

Fig 14.25 *Effects of exercise on a marathon runner. Stroke volume and heart rate at different levels of cardiac output are shown.*

a **sphygmomanometer**. The **systolic** pressure is produced by the contraction of the ventricles and the **diastolic** pressure is the pressure in the arteries when the ventricles relax. Blood pressure is affected by age, sex and state of health. The mean pressures for a healthy young person are about:

systolic: 16 kPa (120 mm Hg)
diastolic: 10 kPA (80 mm Hg).

This is expressed as 120 over 80.

Both pressures are affected by cardiac output and peripheral resistance (resistance to blood flow in the peripheral circulation) and indicate the general state of heart and blood vessels. Conditions which lead to narrowing and hardening of the arteries (**atherosclerosis**) or damage to the kidneys may increase the blood pressure, a condition known as **hypertension**, and impose a strain on the heart and blood vessels. This may lead to a weakening of artery walls and their rupture, or the clogging of narrowed vessels by blood clots (**thrombosis**). These are very serious if they affect the brain or the heart and lead to cerebral haemorrhage (stroke), cerebral thrombosis or coronary thrombosis (section 15.5).

14.7.7   Regulation of blood pressure

Blood pressure depends on several factors:

- heart rate;
- stroke volume;
- resistance to blood flow by the blood vessels (peripheral resistance);
- strength of heartbeat.

Heart rate and stroke volume have been discussed in the last section.

Resistance to blood flow is altered by contraction (**vasoconstriction**) or relaxation (**vasodilation**) of the smooth muscle in the blood vessel walls, especially those of the arterioles. This peripheral resistance is increased by vasoconstriction but decreased by vasodilation. Increased resistance leads to a rise in blood pressure, whereas a decrease produces a fall in blood pressure. All such activity is controlled by a **vasomotor centre** in the medulla of the hindbrain.

Nerve fibres run from the vasomotor centre to all arterioles in the body. Changes in the diameter of these blood vessels are produced mainly by variation in the activity of constrictor muscles. Dilator muscles play a less important role.

Vasomotor centre activity is regulated by impulses coming from pressure receptors (**baroreceptors**) located in the walls of the aorta and carotid sinuses in the carotid arteries (fig 14.26). Stimulation of parasympathetic nerves in these areas, caused by increased cardiac output, produces vasodilation throughout the body and consequent reduction in blood pressure as well as a slowing of the heart rate. The opposite occurs when blood pressure is low. In this case, a fall in blood pressure increases nerve impulse transmission along sympathetic nerves. This causes body-wide vasoconstriction and a rise in blood pressure.

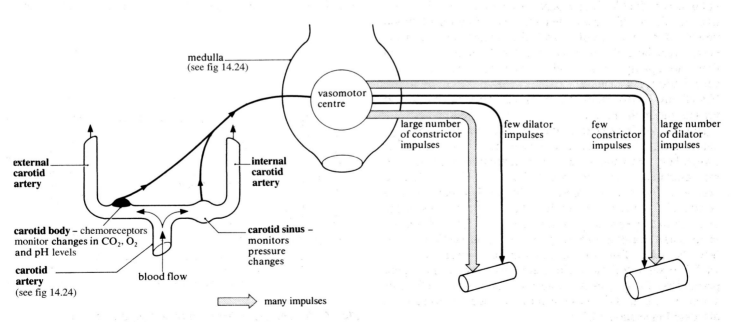

Fig 14.26   *Control of blood pressure. Relationships between the carotid body, carotid sinus, vasomotor centre and general circulatory system are shown.*

Chemical control of the vasomotor centre

Blood arriving at the carotid bodies carrying a high concentration of carbon dioxide stimulates chemoreceptors in these regions to transmit impulses to the vasomotor centre (fig 14.26). Nerve fibres leaving the chemoreceptors link with fibres from the carotid sinus by means of synapses before passing to the vasomotor centre. When the vasomotor centre is stimulated in this way it sends impulses to the blood vessels to vasoconstrict and therefore raises blood pressure. As increased carbon dioxide concentration in the body is usually brought about by increased activity by body tissues, the blood containing the carbon dioxide will be transported more rapidly to the lungs where removal of carbon dioxide in exchange for oxygen can take place more quickly.

Carbon dioxide can also directly affect the behaviour of the smooth muscle of the blood vessel itself. When a tissue suddenly becomes very active, producing a large quantity of carbon dioxide, the carbon dioxide acts directly on the blood vessels in the area and stimulates them to *dilate*. This increases their own blood supply thus allowing more oxygen and glucose to reach the active cells. It must be remembered, however, that when the carbon dioxide leaves this localised area it will have the effect of promoting vasoconstriction elsewhere via vasomotor activity. This is a good illustration of how dynamic and adjustable the control of blood pressure and therefore circulation and distribution of blood can be.

Other stimuli, such as types of emotional stress (for example excitement, pain and annoyance), increase sympathetic activity and therefore blood pressure. Also when the adrenal medulla is stimulated to produce adrenaline by impulses from higher nervous centres this again increases the rate of heartbeat, and therefore raises blood pressure. The significance of the control of heart rate and blood pressure is described further in section 19.1.

> **14.4** When an animal is wounded, its overall blood pressure rises, but the area in the vicinity of the wound swells as a result of local vasodilation. Suggest what the advantage of these changes might be.
>
> **14.5** Outline the main adjustments that occur to the heart rate and circulatory system just before, during and after a 100 m race.

14.7.8 Tachycardia and bradycardia

There are two major conditions of abnormal heart rate, tachycardia and bradycardia. **Tachycardia** (*tachys*, swift; *cardia*, heart) is a general term describing an increased heart rate. It may be caused by a variety of factors including emotional states, such as anxiety, anger and laughter, and overactivity of the thyroid gland. Severe tachycardia is often the result of changes in the electrical activity of the heart. Regions of the heart, other than the SAN, may also contribute to the stimulus for contraction in tachycardia.

A condition known as **bradycardia** (*bradys*, slow) occurs where the heart rate is reduced below the mean level. Long-term training, such as that carried out by athletes, results in an increase by as much as 40% in stroke volume because the heart gets stronger. Therefore, in order to maintain a constant cardiac output at all times, their resting heart rate is reduced.

Underactivity of the thyroid gland, and changes in the electrical activity of the SAN, can also give rise to bradycardia. The regulatory effects of the sympathetic and parasympathetic nervous systems on the SAN tend to counteract temporary conditions of tachycardia and bradycardia and restore normal heart rhythm.

14.8 Functions of mammalian blood

Blood performs many major functions. In the following list, the first four functions are carried out solely by the plasma.

- Transport of soluble organic compounds (digested food) from the small intestine to various parts of the body where they are stored or assimilated (used), and transport from storage areas to places where they are used, such as transport of glucose from the liver to the muscles when glycogen is converted to glucose.
- Transport of soluble excretory materials to organs of excretion. Urea is made in the liver and transported to the kidneys for excretion, and carbon dioxide is made by all cells and taken to the lungs to be excreted.
- Transport of hormones from the glands where they are produced to target organs, for example insulin from the pancreas to the liver. This allows communication within the body.
- Distribution of excess heat from the deeply seated organs. This helps to maintain a constant body temperature.
- Transport of oxygen from the lungs to all parts of the body, and transport of carbon dioxide produced by the tissues in the reverse direction. This involves red blood cells.
- Defence against disease. This is achieved in three ways:
  - (*a*) clotting of the blood by platelets and fibrinogen which prevents excessive blood loss and entry of pathogens;
  - (*b*) phagocytosis, performed by the neutrophils, monocytes and macrophages, which engulf and digest bacteria which find their way into the bloodstream and body tissues;
  - (*c*) immunity, achieved by antibodies and lymphocytes.

- Maintenance of a constant blood solute potential and pH as a result of plasma protein activity. As the plasma proteins and haemoglobin possess both acidic and basic amino acids, they can combine with or release hydrogen ions and so minimise pH changes over a wide range of pH values. In other words, they act as buffers.

14.8.1   Oxygen transport

Haemoglobin, found in the red blood cells, is responsible for the transport of oxygen round the body. Haemoglobin has four polypeptide chains and therefore has a quaternary structure (section 3.5.3). Each polypeptide chain possesses a globin polypeptide chain that is linked to a haem group, which is responsible for the characteristic red colour of the blood. An iron atom (Fe II) is located within each haem group, and each of these can combine with one molecule of oxygen (fig 14.27):

$$Hb + 4O_2 \underset{\text{low O}_2 \text{ concentration}}{\overset{\text{high O}_2 \text{ concentration}}{\rightleftharpoons}} HbO_8$$

whole haemoglobin molecule   oxyhaemoglobin

(Sometimes the biochemist's standard abbreviation HbO_2 is used to represent oxyhaemoglobin.)

Combination of oxygen with haemoglobin, to form oxyhaemoglobin, occurs under conditions when the concentration of oxygen is high, such as in the lung alveolar capillaries. When the concentration of oxygen is low, as in the capillaries of metabolically active tissues, the bonds holding oxygen to haemoglobin become unstable and oxygen is released. This diffuses in solution into the surrounding cells. Release of oxygen from haemoglobin is called **dissociation**.

The amount of oxygen that can combine with haemoglobin is determined by the oxygen concentration or **partial pressure**. (Partial pressure is a term which is used instead of concentration when referring to gases.) In a mixture of gases, the partial pressure of a given gas, such as oxygen, is that part of the total pressure which is due to that gas. Thus the more oxygen there is in the air, the greater its partial pressure. It is still measured in millimetres of mercury. For example, atmospheric pressure at sea level is 760 mm Hg. Approximately one-fifth of the atmosphere is oxygen, therefore the partial pressure of oxygen in the atmosphere at sea level is $^1/_5 \times 760 = 152$ mm Hg.

Dissociation curves

The greater the concentration, or partial pressure, of oxygen the more saturated haemoglobin becomes with oxygen. The degree to which the haemoglobin is saturated at different oxygen partial pressures can be measured. It might be imagined that a simple linear (straight line) relationship between degree of saturation and oxygen partial pressure will be obtained, but this is not the case, as fig 14.28 shows. The graph is not a straight line, but S-shaped, or **sigmoid**. This curve is called an **oxygen dissociation curve**.

The graph shows that at an oxygen partial pressure of approximately 30 mm Hg only 50% of the haemoglobin is present as oxyhaemoglobin, and at a partial pressure of zero no oxygen is attached to the haemoglobin molecule. 100% saturation is rarely achieved in natural conditions. The S shape of the curve is physiologically important. Over the steep part of the curve, a small *decrease* in the oxygen partial pressure of the environment will bring about a large fall in the percentage saturation of haemoglobin. The oxygen given up by the pigment in such a situation is available to the tissues. It is precisely those oxygen partial pressures which are likely to be found in tissues which bring about this large release of oxygen.

The Bohr effect

In regions with an increased partial pressure of carbon dioxide the oxygen dissociation curve is shifted to the right. This is known as the **Bohr effect** (fig 14.29). This shift is a physiological advantage. If you examine fig 14.29 you will see a vertical line at a partial pressure of about 29 mm Hg (the partial pressure which gives 50% saturation for the middle of the three curves). The three curves in fig 14.29 represent three different carbon dioxide concentrations or

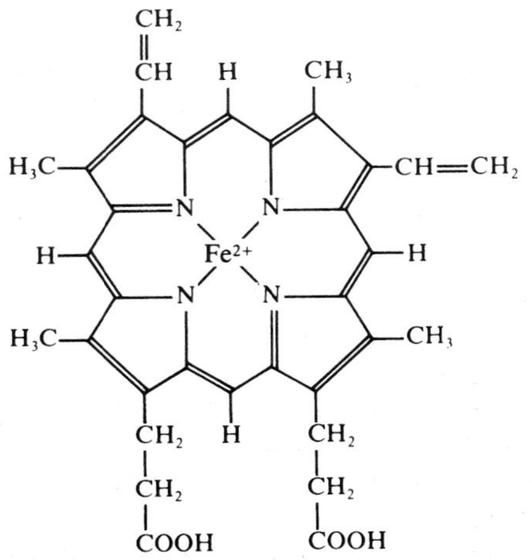

Fig 14.27 *A haem molecule.*

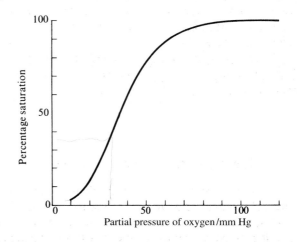

Fig 14.28 *Oxygen dissociation curve of haemoglobin.*

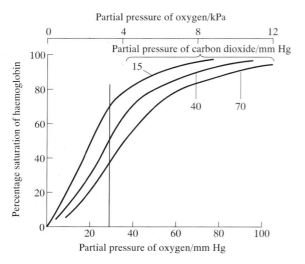

Fig 14.29 *Oxygen dissociation curves of haemoglobin at different partial pressures of carbon dioxide, showing the Bohr effect.*

14.6 (*a*) Temperature also affects the dissociation of haemoglobin. Bearing in mind the effect of carbon dioxide, suggest what the effect of a rise in temperature might be, and explain the physiological advantage of the change.

(*b*) The oxygen dissociation curve is not the same for all animals. For example, compared with humans, the curve for small mammals is displaced to the right. Suggest why this is the case.

14.7 Consider fig 14.30. The oxygen dissociation curve of the fetus is to the left of that of its mother. Suggest why this is so.

14.8 The oxygen dissociation curve of the South American llama, which lives in the High Andes at an altitude of about 5000 m above sea level, is located to the left of most other mammals (fig 14.31). Suggest why this is so.

partial pressures. The curve to the right represents a high partial pressure (70 mm Hg). Note from the vertical line that this results in a lower saturation of the haemoglobin at an oxygen partial pressure of 29 mm Hg. The curve to the left represents a low partial pressure of carbon dioxide (15 mm Hg) and at an oxygen partial pressure of 29 mm Hg this results in a higher saturation of the haemoglobin with oxygen. The effect of increased carbon dioxide is therefore to cause oxygen to be released from the haemoglobin molecule.

Carbon dioxide is a product of respiration. The faster respiration is occurring, the faster it is produced. High levels of respiration are therefore associated with high partial pressures of carbon dioxide. These are the conditions when oxygen is most needed, so it is an advantage that the carbon dioxide makes the haemoglobin release oxygen.

Carbon dioxide has this effect because when it dissolves it forms a weak acid:

$$H_2O + CO_2 \rightleftharpoons \underset{\text{carbonic acid}}{H_2CO_3} \rightleftharpoons H^+ + HCO_3^-$$

The hydrogen ions released combine with haemoglobin (as described in section 14.8.4) and make it less able to carry oxygen.

14.8.2 Myoglobin

Myoglobin is a red pigment very similar in structure to one of the polypeptide chains of haemoglobin. The two proteins have presumably evolved from a common ancestral molecule. It is found in skeletal muscles and is the main reason why meat appears red. It shows a great affinity for oxygen and its oxygen dissociation curve is displaced well to the left of haemoglobin (fig 14.32). In fact it only begins to release oxygen when the partial pressure of oxygen is below 20 mm Hg. In this way it acts as a store of oxygen in resting muscle, only releasing it when supplies of oxyhaemoglobin have been exhausted.

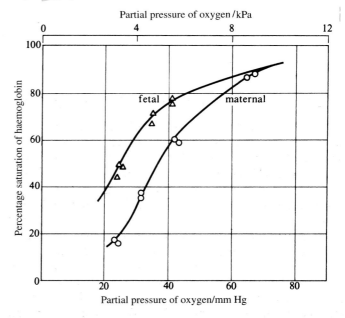

Fig 14.30 *Oxygen dissociation curves of fetal and maternal blood of a goat.*

Fig 14.31 *Oxygen dissociation curves of the llama and other mammals.*

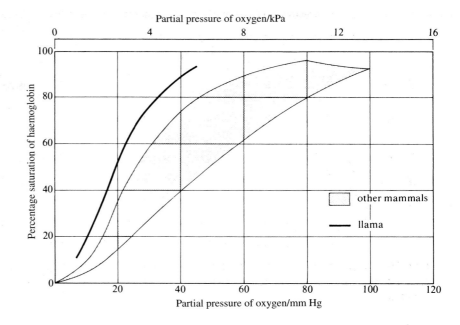

Fig 14.32 *Comparison of haemoglobin and myoglobin oxygen dissociation curves. Myoglobin remains 80% saturated with oxygen until the partial pressure of oxygen falls below 20 mm Hg. This means that myoglobin retains its oxygen in the resting cell but gives it up when vigorous muscle activity uses up the available oxygen supplied by haemoglobin.*

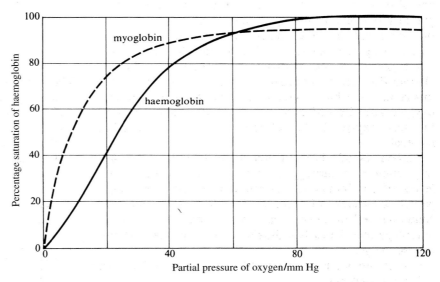

14.8.3 Carbon monoxide and haemoglobin

The affinity of the iron(II) in haemoglobin for carbon monoxide is about 250 times as great as it is for oxygen. Therefore haemoglobin will combine with any carbon monoxide available in preference to oxygen to form a relatively stable compound called **carboxyhaemoglobin**. If this happens oxygen is prevented from combining with haemoglobin, and therefore the transport of oxygen round the body by the blood is no longer possible. In humans collapse follows quickly after exposure to carbon monoxide and unless the victim is removed from the gas, asphyxiation is inevitable. A concentration of about 0.1% in air (about 0.6 mm Hg) can be lethal. Carboxyhaemoglobin is a cherry red colour and this may show in the skin colour of a victim. Removal from the gas must be followed by administering a mixture of almost pure oxygen that contains a small amount of carbon dioxide. The carbon dioxide stimulates the respiratory centre in the medulla. Faster breathing results, which helps to flush the carbon monoxide out of the lungs. Pure oxygen is used because the oxygen partial pressure in air is not sufficient to replace the carbon monoxide attached to the haemoglobin.

The two most common sources of carbon monoxide are car exhaust fumes and tobacco smoke.

14.8.4 Transport of carbon dioxide

Carbon dioxide is carried by the blood in three different ways. It must not be allowed to accumulate in the body because it forms an acid in solution and could lead to fatal changes in blood pH.

In solution (5%). Most of the carbon dioxide carried in this way is transported in physical solution. A very small amount is carried as carbonic acid (H_2CO_3).

Combined with protein (10–20%). Carbon dioxide combines with the amino group (NH_2) at the end of each polypeptide chain of haemoglobin to form a neutral carbamino-haemoglobin compound. The amount of carbon dioxide that is able to combine with haemoglobin depends on the amount of oxygen already being carried by the haemoglobin. The less oxygen being carried by the haemoglobin molecule, the more carbon dioxide that can be carried in this way:

$$HHbNH_2 \ + \ CO_2 \longrightarrow HHbN-C\overset{\displaystyle H}{\underset{\displaystyle OH}{}}\!\!\!\overset{O}{}$$

haemoglobin

carbamino-haemoglobin

As hydrogencarbonate (85%). Carbon dioxide produced by the tissues diffuses into the bloodstream and passes into the red blood cells where it combines with water to form carbonic acid. This process is catalysed by the enzyme carbonic anhydrase found in the red blood cells. It is an extremely efficient enzyme. Some of the carbonic acid then dissociates into hydrogen and hydrogencarbonate ions:

$$CO_2 + H_2O \rightleftharpoons H_2CO_3 \rightleftharpoons H^+ + HCO_3^-$$

The hydrogen ions tend to displace the oxygen from the haemoglobin as noted earlier. This is the basis of the Bohr effect. The deoxygenated haemoglobin accepts hydrogen ions from carbonic acid forming haemoglobinic acid (H.Hb). By accepting hydrogen ions, haemoglobin acts as a buffer molecule and so enables large quantities of carbonic acid to be carried to the lungs without any major change in blood pH.

The majority of hydrogencarbonate ions formed within the red blood cells diffuse out into the plasma along a concentration gradient and combine with sodium in the plasma to form sodium hydrogencarbonate. The loss of negatively charged hydrogencarbonate ions from the red blood cells leaves them with a more positive charge. This is balanced by chloride ions diffusing into the red blood cells from the plasma. This phenomenon is called the **'chloride shift'**.

When the red blood cells reach the lungs the reverse process occurs and carbon dioxide is released. The whole process is summarised in fig 14.33.

> **14.9** Summarise how carbon dioxide in the blood is expelled as gaseous carbon dioxide by the lungs.

14.8.5 Defensive functions of the blood

We are equipped with a complex system of defence mechanisms whose function is to enable us to withstand attacks by pathogens (disease-causing organisms), and to remove foreign materials from our bodies. Three important defensive mechanisms involving blood are:

(1) clotting of blood   } both contributing to
(2) phagocytosis   wound healing
(3) immune response to infection.

The first two are discussed here and the third in section 14.9.

Clotting

When a tissue is wounded, blood flows from it and coagulates to form a blood clot. This prevents further blood loss and entry of pathogenic microorganisms which is of clear survival value. It is just as important that blood in undamaged vessels does not clot. The highly complex series of reactions that takes place in order for coagulation to be achieved serves at the same time to prevent it from

Fig 14.33 *Carbon dioxide transport by the plasma and red blood cell.*

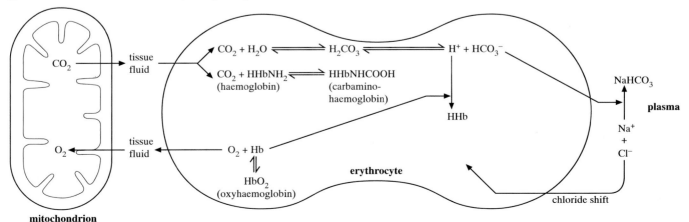

occurring unnecessarily. The whole clotting process depends on at least 12 clotting factors working in harmony with each other. Only the main clotting factors are described in this account. The process is summarised in fig 14.34.

Blood escaping from a skin wound is exposed to the air, and mixes with substances oozing from the damaged cells and ruptured platelets. Among these substances are:

- **thromboplastin**, a lipoprotein which is released from injured tissues;
- **clotting factors VII and X**, which are enzymes found in the plasma;
- **calcium ions**.

Together these substances catalyse the conversion of prothrombin to thrombin. **Prothrombin** is a protein found in the plasma. It is converted to an active enzyme, **thrombin**, which is a protease (a protein-digesting protein). Thrombin hydrolyses fibrinogen, another plasma protein, to **fibrin**. Fibrinogen is a large protein molecule which is soluble. Fibrin, however, is insoluble and fibrous in nature and forms very tangled needle-like fibres. Blood cells become trapped in the meshwork (fig 14.35) and a blood clot is formed. This dries to form a scab which acts to prevent further blood loss and as a mechanical barrier to the entry of the pathogens.

Because the clotting process is so elaborate, it means that the absence or low concentration of any of the essential clotting factors can produce excessive bleeding. For example, if an essential factor necessary for the action of thromboplastin is absent or only present in minute amounts, the individual will bleed profusely from any minor cut. One of the most common conditions associated with excessive bleeding is **haemophilia**. This is caused by a fault in one of two genes. One gene controls production of a protein called factor VIII; a fault in this protein is responsible for haemophilia A which accounts for 85% of haemophilia cases. The other gene controls production of the protein factor IX, a fault in which is responsible for haemophilia B which accounts for the remaining 15% of cases. Both genes are located on the X chromosome. The male carries only

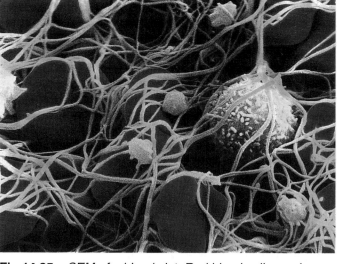

Fig 14.35 *SEM of a blood clot. Red blood cells can be seen trapped in a mesh of fibrous threads, as well as a white blood cell (large spiky cell) and some small platelets.*

one X chromosome, his other sex chromosome being a Y which carries no gene for blood clotting, so the condition is usually seen only in males, where only one faulty chromosome is needed to cause the condition. Two faulty X chromosomes would be needed to cause the condition in a woman. A female with one faulty chromosome will be a **carrier** since the faulty gene is recessive to the normal gene on the other X chromosome (section 24.6.1).

Clotting does not occur in undamaged blood vessels because the lining of the vessels is very smooth and does not promote platelet or cell rupture. Also present are substances which actively prevent clotting. One of these is **heparin**, which is present in low concentrations in the plasma and is produced by mast cells found in the connective tissues and the liver. It serves to prevent the conversion of prothrombin into thrombin, and fibrinogen to fibrin and is widely used clinically as an anticoagulant.

If a clot does form within the blood circulation it is called a **thrombus** and leads to a medical condition known as **thrombosis**. This may happen if the endothelium of a

Fig 14.34 *Major stages involved in blood clotting.*

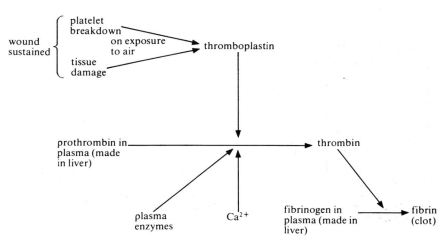

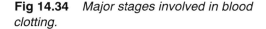

blood vessel is damaged and the roughness of the damaged area promotes platelet breakdown and sets in motion the clotting process. Coronary thrombosis, a thrombus developing in the coronary artery of the heart, is particularly dangerous and can lead to a swift death (section 15.5).

Phagocytosis

The main function of some of the white blood cells is the engulfing of invading microorganisms, and the clearing up of dead cells and debris, such as dust in the lungs. This process is called **phagocytosis** and the cells that carry it out are called **phagocytes**. Phagocytes form the body's first line of defence against attack by microorganisms.

Phagocytes show a kind of movement known as **amoeboid movement**, which means that they can crawl by a flowing movement of their cytoplasm. They are attracted to areas where cell and tissue damage has occurred. The stimulus for this attraction is the release of a variety of chemicals by the damaged blood cells, tissues, blood clotting products and bacteria. Movement towards a source of chemicals is called **chemotaxis**. They are able to recognise invading bacteria. Their ability to do this is enhanced by a group of about 20 proteins known collectively as **complement**. These proteins are also activated by bacterial infection. They have the following effects:

- some attract phagocytes by chemotaxis;
- some are involved in opsonisation (see below);
- some punch holes in the cell surface membranes of bacteria, causing the cells to swell and burst;
- some promote inflammation.

Opsonisation is the coating of bacteria with proteins called opsonins. The **opsonins** are usually a complement protein or an antibody. The process of opsonin recognition is shown in fig 14.36. Phagocytes have receptors in their cell surface membranes which match the opsonins and enable them to recognise, bind to and therefore engulf the bacteria. A phagocytic vacuole is formed (fig 14.37). Small lysosomes fuse with the phagocytic vacuole, forming a phagolysosome. Lysozyme and other hydrolytic enzymes, together with acid, are poured into the phagocytic vacuole from the lysosomes and the bacteria are digested. The soluble products of bacterial digestion are absorbed into the surrounding cytoplasm of the phagocyte.

The two types of phagocytic white blood cell are the **neutrophils** and the **monocytes** (table 14.2). Neutrophils are able to squeeze through the walls of blood capillaries and move about in the tissue spaces. Monocytes are larger cells and become **macrophages** (*macro* – large) which spend their lives patrolling tissues, particularly in the liver, spleen and lymph nodes. Some are stationary and line blood spaces in these organs. The role of macrophages is to engulf foreign particles as well as microorganisms. They can engulf much larger particles than can neutrophils, such as old red blood cells and malaria parasites, which are

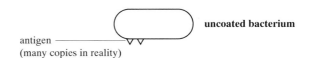

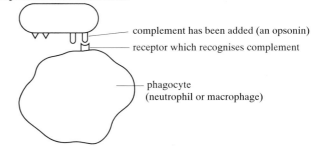

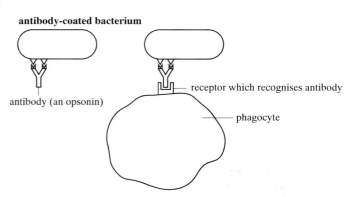

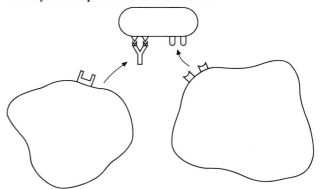

Fig 14.36 *The role of complement and antibodies (opsonins) in coating bacteria (opsonisation). Once coated, the bacteria are recognised by phagocytes and engulfed. (From the Greek word* opson, *meaning seasoning!)*

eukaryote cells and therefore much larger than bacteria which are prokaryotes. If the particles they ingest cannot be digested, they can retain them for long periods of time, often permanently. The macrophages together with the neutrophils form the body's **reticulo-endothelial system**.

Inflammation

When an area of the body is wounded or infected, the tissue surrounding the wound becomes swollen and painful. This is called **inflammation** and is due to the escape of chemicals, including histamine and 5-hydroxytryptamine,

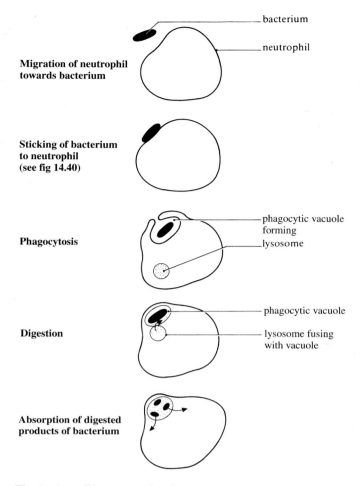

Migration of neutrophil towards bacterium

— bacterium
— neutrophil

Sticking of bacterium to neutrophil (see fig 14.40)

Phagocytosis

— phagocytic vacuole forming
— lysosome

Digestion

— phagocytic vacuole
— lysosome fusing with vacuole

Absorption of digested products of bacterium

Fig 14.37 *Phagocytosis of a bacterium by a phagocyte.*

from the damaged tissues. Collectively they cause local vasodilation of capillaries. This increases the amount of blood in the area and raises the temperature locally. Leakiness of the capillaries is also increased, permitting escape of plasma and white blood cells into the surrounding tissues and a consequent swelling of the area, a condition known as **oedema**. This plasma contains chemicals, which inhibit the growth of bacteria or kill them, and antibodies and phagocytes, all of which help to combat spread of infection. One of the chemicals is **interferon** which is secreted mainly by macrophages and some other white blood cells if they are exposed to foreign antigens. Interferon makes body cells resistant to infection by viruses. Phagocytes also engulf dead cell debris. Fibrinogen is also present to assist blood clotting if necessary, and the excess tissue fluid tends to dilute and reduce the effect of any potential toxic chemicals.

Wound healing

Towards the end of the inflammatory phase, cells called **fibroblasts** appear and secrete **collagen**. This is a fibrous protein and becomes linked to polysaccharide to form a meshwork of randomly arranged fibrous scar tissue. Vitamin C is important for collagen formation; without it

hydroxyl groups cannot be attached to the collagen molecule and so it remains incomplete. After about 14 days the disorganised mass of fibres is reorganised into bundles arranged along the lines of stress of the wound. Numerous small blood vessels begin to spread through the wound. They function to provide oxygen and nutrients for the cells involved in repairing and healing the wound.

Whilst these processes are going on within the wound, the epidermis around it is also engaged in repair and replacement activity. Some epidermal cells migrate into the wound and ingest much of the debris and fibrin of the blood clot which has formed over the wound. When the epidermal cells meet, they unite to form a continuous layer under the scar. When this is complete the scab sloughs off thus exposing the epidermis to the surrounding atmosphere.

Summary of events.

(1) Wound occurs, blood flows.
(2) Clotting process occurs.
(3) Inflammation occurs.
(4) White cells migrate into wound. They absorb foreign matter and bacteria, and remove cell debris.
(5) Fibroblasts enter the wound and synthesise collagen which is built up into scar tissue.
(6) Epidermal cells remove any final debris in the wound, and also begin to dismantle the scar.
(7) Epidermis creates a new skin surface in the area of the wound.
(8) Scab sloughs off.

If the wound is small, phagocytosis is usually sufficient to cope with any invasion by pathogens. However, if there is considerable damage, the immune response of the body is put into action.

14.9 The immune system

Immunity was defined by Sir Macfarlane Burnet as 'the capacity to recognise the intrusion of material foreign to the body and to mobilise cells and cell products to help remove that particular sort of foreign material with greater speed and effectiveness'.

In this section we shall be confining our attention to the **immune response**. This is the second line of defence after the phagocytes which, according to the definition above, are also part of the immune system. The immune response is the production of antibodies in response to antigens. Each antigen is recognised by a specific antibody.

14.9.1 Antibodies, antigens, B cells and T cells

An **antibody** is a molecule that is synthesised by an animal in response to the presence of foreign substances known as antigens. Each antibody is a protein molecule called an **immunoglobulin**. Its structure consists of two heavy chains (H-chains) and two light chains (L-chains) (fig 14.38). The antibody has a constant and variable part, the variable part acting something like a key which specifically fits into a lock. The human body can produce an estimated 100 million different antibodies, recognising all kinds of foreign substances, including many the body has never met. It does this by shuffling different sections of parts of the genes which produce the variable regions (like building different models from a basic set of shapes).

An **antigen** is a molecule which can cause antibody formation. All cells possess antigens in their cell surface membranes which act as markers, enabling cells to 'recognise' each other. Antigens are usually proteins or glycoproteins, that is proteins with a carbohydrate tail, although almost any complex molecule can be antigenic. The body can distinguish its own antigens ('self') from foreign antigens ('non-self') and normally only makes antibodies against non-self antigens. Microorganisms carry antigens on their surfaces.

Two systems of immunity have been developed by mammals, a **cell-mediated immune response** and a **humoral immune response**. The two systems involve the development of two types of lymphocyte, the T and B cells. Both types arise from precursor cells in the bone marrow.

The influence of the thymus gland is essential in the development of the T cells, hence the name T cells. B cells are named after the bursa, a branch of the gut in birds in which their B cells develop. The bursa is absent in mammals, although equivalent tissue exists. Each type of cell has an enormous capacity for recognising the millions of different antigens that exist. When an antibody–antigen reaction occurs it prevents, in a variety of ways, the antigen or antigen-possessing organism from acting upon the body in a harmful way.

Cell-mediated response

T cells attack the following:

- cells that have become infected by a microorganism, most commonly a virus;
- transplanted organs and tissues (see section 25.7.13);
- cancer-causing cells.

The whole cell is involved in the attack, so this type of immunity is described as cell-mediated immunity. T cells do not release antibodies.

Humoral response

B cells release antibodies into the blood plasma, tissue fluid and lymph. As the antibodies are released into fluids and

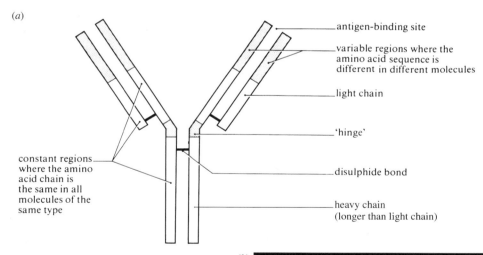

(a)

antigen-binding site

variable regions where the amino acid sequence is different in different molecules

light chain

'hinge'

disulphide bond

heavy chain (longer than light chain)

constant regions where the amino acid chain is the same in all molecules of the same type

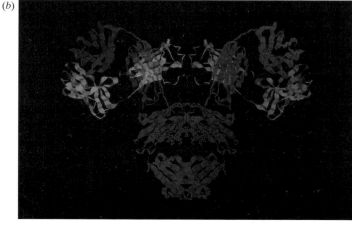

(b)

Fig 14.38 *Antibody molecule. (a) Diagram of the basic structure of an antibody molecule. The molecule is made up of four polypeptide chains, two heavy and two light chains. Antigens are bound between the light and heavy chains of the variable regions. (b) Computer-generated picture of antibody structure.*

the attack on the microorganisms takes place in the fluid, this type of immunity is described as humoral ('humor' means fluid). The antibodies of B cells attack bacteria and some viruses.

14.9.2 T cells and the cell-mediated response

The thymus gland is situated in the thorax just above the heart. It begins to function in the embryo and is at its most active at the time of, and just after, birth. After the period of weaning it decreases in size and soon ceases to function.

Evidence that the thymus gland is important in the development of the immune response can be demonstrated by the following experiments.

(1) Removal of the gland from a newborn mouse results in death from a deficiency of lymphocytes in its tissue fluid and blood.
(2) Tissue from an older mouse grafted onto an experimental newborn mouse with the gland removed is unable to recognise and react with antigens.
(3) If the thymus gland is removed from a much older mouse, this mouse suffers no adverse effects.

The stem cells of the bone marrow which give rise to T lymphocytes must pass through the tissue of the thymus gland before they can become fully functional. Here they develop into cells called **thymocytes**. At this stage any cells that recognise 'self' (the body's own antigens) are destroyed, so that the body does not attack itself later. Some of the thymocytes mature into T cells. They leave the thymus gland in the bloodstream. Some stay in the blood and some migrate to the tissue fluid, lymph nodes and other organs such as the spleen.

The cell surface membranes of T cells contain specific receptors with particular shapes, similar to antibodies. However, these receptors do not recognise *whole* antigen molecules, unlike antibodies. They bind only to *fragments* of antigens or other foreign molecules which are presented to them by other cells, often macrophages. Mature T cells possess a T4 molecule (**T4 cells**) or a T8 molecule (**T8 cells**) which give them different functions. T4 cells are known as **helper cells**. The HIV virus, which causes AIDS, infects mainly T-helper cells. There are two types of T8 cells, known as **suppressor cells** and **killer cells** (or cytotoxic cells). Each type of T cell produces a different type of lymphokine. **Lymphokines** are small peptide molecules with various functions which are described briefly below. They are also known as cytokines or interleukins.

T4 cells work in association with macrophages. The macrophage first captures an antigen-carrying organism. It then 'chops off' a piece of the antigen and presents it at its cell surface where it is recognised as a foreign peptide by a T4 cell (one with a matching receptor). The T4 cell then produces large amounts of lymphokines. These have various functions. In particular they:

- stimulate T cells to multiply;
- promote inflammation;
- stimulate B cells to make antibodies.

Killer cells (one type of T8 cell) produce smaller amounts of lymphokines, but kill body cells which have become infected by viruses, and cancer cells. This is done by a chemical attack or by 'punching' holes in the cells. They recognise foreign peptides which are *not* parts of antigens. They can recognise, for example, a stray part of a virus on the outside of an infected cell or a mutant protein produced by a cancer cell. They also attack and gradually destroy transplanted organs (see section 25.7.13).

The activity of all the different types of white blood cell, including phagocytes, is decreased by the lymphokines which are secreted by suppressor cells and stimulated by the lymphokines which are secreted by helper cells. The relative numbers of these two types of cells therefore regulates the whole immune response (fig 14.39).

14.9.3 B cells and the humoral response

The action of B cells is not as complicated. Each B cell has the function of recognising a particular antigen and producing antibodies that will bind to it. The cell surface membrane of B cells contains antigen receptors whose specific shape is identical to the antibodies that that cell can make. All the receptors in the membrane of one cell are identical, so a given cell can only recognise one type of antigen. When it binds to an antigen the cell is activated to clone itself, meaning that it multiplies to form many identical copies of itself. Activation requires the presence of lymphokines secreted by helper T cells as well as antigen, as described above and shown in fig 14.39. It is therefore slightly misleading to think in terms of separate cell-mediated and humoral responses because the two are dependent on each other.

Two types of B cell form, namely **memory cells** and **effector cells** (meaning they carry out the response). Effector cells are also known as plasma cells. These secrete huge numbers of antibody molecules into the blood, tissue fluid and lymph. Effector cells live for only a few days. The memory cells survive for long periods of time and enable a rapid response to be made to any future infection (see next section).

Once an antibody has reacted with an antigen, destruction of the antigen-bearing structure is brought about in a number of different ways. The most common method is to identify the antigen as a target for the action of phagocytes. Phagocytes have receptors that bind to the tail of the Y-shaped antibody (the opposite end to the variable regions).

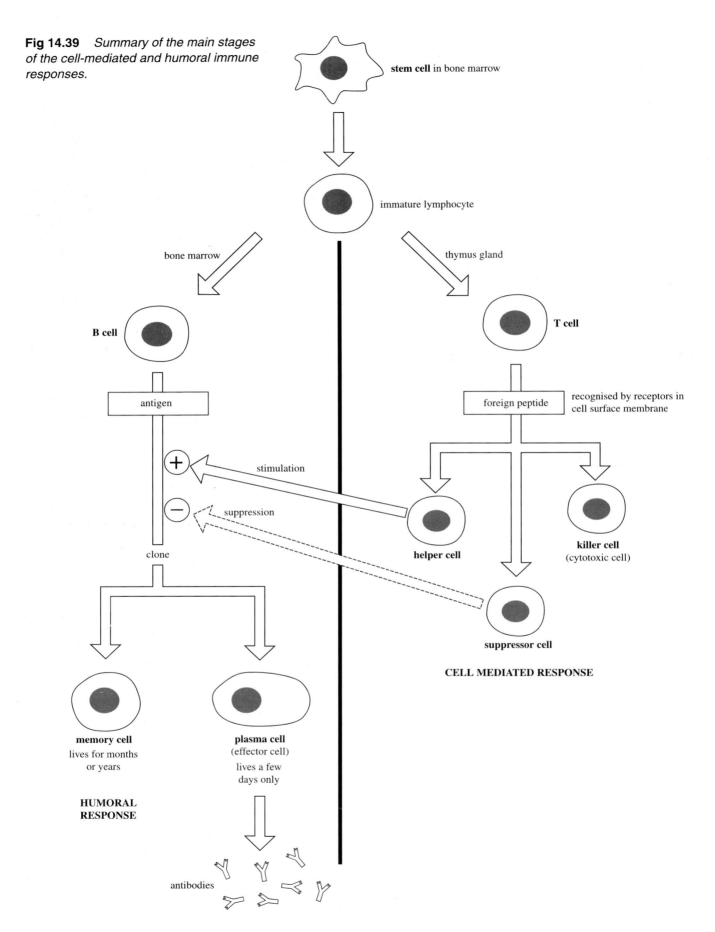

Fig 14.39 *Summary of the main stages of the cell-mediated and humoral immune responses.*

stem cell in bone marrow

immature lymphocyte

bone marrow

thymus gland

B cell

T cell

antigen

foreign peptide

recognised by receptors in cell surface membrane

+

stimulation

−

suppression

helper cell

killer cell (cytotoxic cell)

clone

suppressor cell

CELL MEDIATED RESPONSE

memory cell

lives for months or years

plasma cell (effector cell)

lives a few days only

HUMORAL RESPONSE

antibodies

(a)

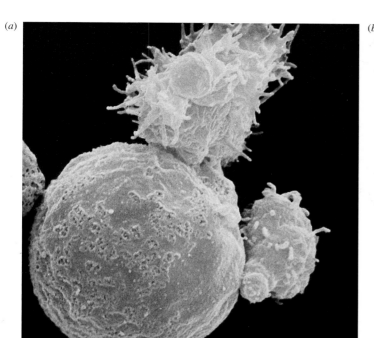

(b)

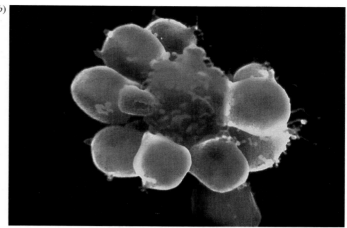

Fig 14.40 *(a) SEM of killer T cells (relatively small cells, top and right of picture) approaching a larger cell, which typically is a tumour cell, a virus-infected cell or a cell from a transplanted organ or tissue.*
(b) SEM of a killer T cell (relatively large cell in centre of picture) stuck to a cluster of foreign red blood cells which it is in the process of destroying.

14.9.4 The immune system has a memory

The memory cells mentioned in the previous section are important if a second infection of an antigen occurs. The population of memory cells is much larger than the original population of B cells from which they came. Therefore the response to the second infection, called the **secondary response**, is much more rapid and is also greater than the **primary response** to the original infection, as shown in fig 14.41. The primary response may not be rapid enough to prevent a person suffering from an infection, but if that person survives, they will rarely suffer

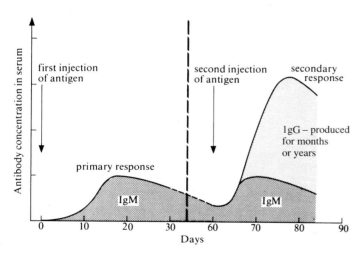

Fig 14.41 *Primary and secondary response to an initial and later dose of antigen. The secondary response is more rapid and intense than the first. IgM and IgG are two different types of antibody (immunoglobulins). IgM is responsible for the primary response. IgG starts the secondary response. (The heavy chain of the antibodies is different.)*

from it again because of the greater secondary response. With each exposure, the response gets more efficient. This is the basis of vaccination (and booster doses) (see next section).

14.9.5 Types of immunity

Immunity may be described as active or passive. Both types may be acquired naturally or artificially. Providing immunity artificially is called **immunisation**.

Natural active immunity

This is the kind of immunity which is obtained as a result of an infection. The body manufactures its own antibodies when exposed to an infectious agent. Because memory cells, produced on exposure to the first infection, are able to stimulate the production of massive quantities of antibody when exposed to the same antigen again, this type of immunity is most effective and generally persists for a long time, sometimes even for life.

Artificial active immunity (vaccination)

This is achieved by injecting (or less commonly administering orally) small amounts of antigen, called the **vaccine**, into the body of an individual. The process is called **vaccination**. If the whole organism is used as the vaccine, it is first made safe by being killed or attenuated (see below). The antigen stimulates the body to manufacture antibodies against the antigen. Often a second, booster injection is given and this stimulates a much quicker production of antibody which is longer lasting and which protects the individual from the disease for a considerable time. Several types of vaccine are currently in use.

- **Toxoids**. Toxins (poisons) produced by tetanus and diphtheria bacteria are detoxified with formaldehyde, yet their antigen properties remain. Therefore vaccination with the toxoid will stimulate antibody production without producing symptoms of the disease.
- **Killed organisms**. Some dead viruses and bacteria are able to provoke a normal antibody response and are used for immunisation purposes. An example is the flu vaccine which contains dead flu viruses.
- **Live vaccines (attenuated organisms)**. An attenuated organism is one which has been 'crippled' in some way so that it cannot cause disease. Often it can only grow and multiply slowly. Attenuation may be achieved by culturing the organisms at higher temperatures than normal, or by adding specific chemicals to the culture medium for long periods of time. Alternatively, the attenuated organism may be a mutant variety with the same antigens but lacking the ability to cause disease. Attenuated vaccines for the bacterial disease tuberculosis (TB), and for measles, mumps, rubella (german measles) and polio are in general use.
- With smallpox, which is now extinct, a live virus vaccine was used. However, the virus in the vaccine was not an attenuated virus but a closely related and harmless form.
- **New vaccines**. Vaccine development made little progress for many years, but new approaches to vaccine design are now possible using modern techniques of molecular biology and genetic engineering. Antigens are very often proteins and proteins are coded for by genes. If the gene for an antigen is transferred into a bacterium, using standard techniques described in chapter 12, the bacterium can be used as a 'factory' for producing large quantities of the antigen for use in vaccines. Cholera, typhoid and hepatitis B vaccines have been prepared in this way. Some vaccines can be made safer in this way, for example the whooping cough vaccine. An alternative approach is to synthesise antigens artificially from amino acids once their amino acid sequences are known.

Vaccination is a common experience in developed countries and is one of the weapons which have helped to reduce the incidence of infectious diseases so dramatically in those countries. Other weapons have been social and environmental improvements such as treatment to clean water for drinking, better nutrition and sewage treatment.

An example of the use of vaccination is the recommendation that all children in the UK should have the MMR vaccine at 2 years of age. This protects against measles, mumps and rubella. Also three doses of another triple vaccine, DTP (diphtheria, tetanus and pertussis (whooping cough)) are recommended at various ages. In some countries vaccination is a legal requirement. Smallpox has been made extinct by vaccination and some childhood diseases such as diphtheria, polio and measles have become extremely rare (fig 14.42). Polio may become

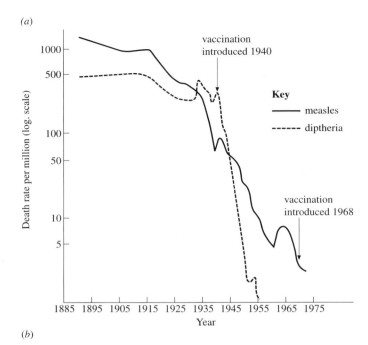

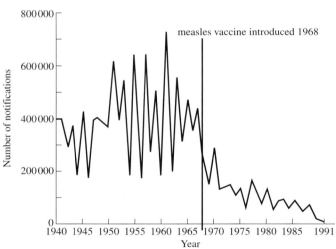

Fig 14.42 *The effect of vaccination on diphtheria and measles. (a) Death rate due to diphtheria and measles in children under the age of 15 years in England and Wales from the year 1885 to 1972. (Note that the vertical scale is logarithmic.) Vaccination for diphtheria was introduced in 1940. From being a feared killer of children, it was virtually eradicated within 15 years. (b) Measles notifications (reported cases) in England and Wales between the years 1950 and 1991. A measles vaccine was introduced in 1968. The graph shows that measles still tends to occur in minor epidemics in roughly two-year cycles.*
((a) From Registrar General's Statistical Review for England and Wales, *Part 1, Tables Medical, HMSO (1887–1974) HMSO. (b) From* The Health of The Nation and You, *Dept of Health, HMSO (1992) (Source OPCS).)*

extinct in the near future. The World Health Organisation, with support from various organisations like UNICEF and the World Bank, has targetted six major diseases in the developing world in its EPI programme (Expanded Programme on Immunisation). The diseases are diphtheria, whooping cough, tetanus, polio, measles and TB. Although not feared so much any more in developed countries, these are still killer diseases worldwide. Over 80% of children in developing countries now receive vaccination against these diseases. Hepatitis B is also being targetted.

Improvements to some vaccines, such as the flu vaccine, are still needed and there is still no vaccine against some diseases, notably cancers, leprosy, malaria and AIDS, despite intensive research.

Passive immunity

In passive immunity antibodies from one individual are passed into another individual. They give *immediate* protection, unlike active immunity which takes a few days or weeks to build up. However, it only provides protection against infection for a few weeks, for the antibodies are broken down by the body's natural processes, so their numbers slowly fall and protection is lost.

Natural passive immunity

Passive immunity may be gained naturally. For example, antibodies from a mother can cross the placenta and enter her fetus. In this way they provide protection for the baby until its own immune system is fully functional. Passive immunity may also be provided by colostrum, the first secretion of the mammary glands. The baby absorbs the antibodies through its gut.

Artificial passive immunity

Here antibodies which have been formed in one individual are extracted and then injected into the blood of another individual which may or may not be of the same species. They can be used for immediate protection if a person has been, or is likely to be, exposed to a particular disease. For example, specific antibodies used for combating tetanus and diphtheria used to be cultured in horses and injected into humans. Only antibodies of human origin are now used for humans. Antibodies against rabies and some snake venoms are also available. Antibodies against the human rhesus blood group antigen are used for some rhesus

negative mothers when carrying rhesus positive babies, as explained in section 14.9.8.

A summary of the different types of immunity is given in table 14.5.

14.9.6 Monoclonal antibodies

In the 1970s a technique was developed for isolating clones of B cells which produced only one type of antibody. For the first time it became possible to make large quantities of a single pure antibody. Antibodies produced in this way from single clones are called **monoclonal antibodies**. They have a number of important applications. Details of their production and applications are described in section 12.11.2.

14.9.7 Blood groups

When a patient receives a blood transfusion it is vital that they receive blood that is compatible with their own. If it is incompatible, a type of immune response occurs. This is because the donor's red cell membranes possess glycoproteins (known as **agglutinogens**) which act as antigens and react with antibodies (agglutinins) in the recipient's plasma. The result is that the donor's cells are agglutinated (in other words, the cells link or attach to each other when the antigens on their surfaces interact with the antibodies). Two antigens exist, named **A** and **B**. The complementary plasma antibodies are named **a** and **b**, and are present in the plasma all the time; they are not produced in response to the donor's antigen as is the case in the immune reactions already studied. A person with a specific antigen in the red cells does not possess the corresponding antibody in the plasma. For example, anyone with antigen **A** in the red cell membranes has no antibody **a** in the plasma and is classified as having blood group A. If only **B** antigens are present the blood group is B. If both antigens are present the blood group will be AB, and if no antigens are present the blood group is O (table 14.6).

When transfusion occurs it is important to know what will happen to the cells of the donor. If there is a likelihood of them being agglutinated by the recipient's plasma antibodies then transfusion should not take place.

Fig 14.43 indicates the consequences of mixing different blood groups together. Individuals with blood group O are termed **universal donors** because their blood can be given to people with other blood groups. It possesses cells which will not be agglutinated by the recipient's plasma antibodies. Although group O possesses **a** and **b** antibodies,

Table 14.5 Summary of different types of immunity.

	Active *antigens received*	**Passive** *antibodies received*
Natural	Natural active e.g. fighting infection, rejecting transplant	Natural passive from mother via milk or placenta
Artificial	Artificial active vaccination (injection of antigens)	Artificial passive injection of antibodies

Table 14.6 Blood groups.

Blood group	*O*	*A*	*B*	*AB*
percentage of population	46%	42%	9%	3%
antigen	–	A	B	A + B
antibody	a + b	b	a	–

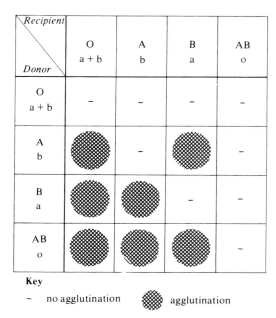

Recipient Donor	O a + b	A b	B a	AB o
O a + b	–	–	–	–
A b	●	–	●	–
B a	●	●	–	–
AB o	●	●	●	–

Key

– no agglutination   ● agglutination

Fig 14.43 *Interactions between human blood groups. Cell antigens are denoted by capital letters, antibodies by small letters.*

when the donated blood forms a relatively small proportion of the total blood volume, there will be very little agglutination of the recipient's cells because the donated plasma is diluted so much by the recipient's blood. However, in major transfusions the blood group must be matched more accurately. Individuals with group AB can receive blood from anyone and are called **universal recipients**. However, they can only donate to blood group AB.

The relationship between blood groups and the major histocompatibility complex (MHC) is discussed in section 25.7.13.

14.9.8   The rhesus factor

Of the total population, 85% possess red cells containing an antigen called the rhesus factor and are termed **rhesus positive**. The remainder of the population lack the rhesus antigen and are therefore described as **rhesus negative**. Rhesus negative blood does not usually contain rhesus antibodies in its plasma. However, if rhesus positive blood enters a rhesus negative individual the recipient responds by manufacturing rhesus antibodies.

The practical importance of this is made obvious when a rhesus negative mother bears a rhesus positive child. The rhesus factor is inherited. (Rhesus positive is dominant and rhesus negative recessive.) During the later stages of the pregnancy, fragments of the rhesus positive red blood cells of the fetus may enter the mother's circulation and cause the mother to produce rhesus antibodies. These can pass across the placenta to the fetus and destroy fetal red cells. Normally the antibodies are not formed in large enough quantities to affect the first-born child. However,

subsequent rhesus positive children can suffer destruction of their red cells. A rhesus baby is usually premature, anaemic and jaundiced, and its blood needs to be completely replaced by a transfusion of healthy blood. The condition is known as **haemolytic disease of the newborn**. It can be fatal, especially if the baby is born prematurely as often happens. Although a blood transfusion can now be undertaken whilst the baby is still in the womb, with modern screening methods the problem can be avoided, as explained below.

Protection against the rhesus reaction

(1) If an intravenous injection of anti-rhesus antibodies, called **anti-D**, is given to a rhesus negative mother within 72 hours of her giving birth, sensitisation of the rhesus negative mother by rhesus positive fetal cells is prevented. The anti-rhesus antibodies attach themselves to the rhesus antigens on the fetal cells which are in the mother's circulation and prevent them from being recognised by the mother's antibody forming cells. Hence the antibody process in the mother is not set in motion (fig 14.44). This means of prevention obviously depends on careful screening of all pregnant women. Testing blood groups is part of antenatal care in the UK.

(2) If a rhesus negative mother of blood group O is carrying a rhesus positive child of any blood group other than O, the problem will not arise. This is because if fetal cells enter the mother's circulation, the mother's **a** and **b** antibodies will destroy the blood cells before the mother has time to manufacture anti-rhesus antibodies.

14.9.9   Transplantation

Replacement of diseased tissue or organs by healthy ones is called transplantation and is a technique used increasingly in surgery today. However, when foreign tissue is inserted into or, in the case of skin, onto another individual it is usually rejected by the recipient because it acts as an antigen, stimulating the immune response in the recipient.

Types of transplant

The following terms are used for the different kinds of transplant.

Autograft – tissue grafted from one area to another on the same individual. Rejection is not a problem. This can be used in skin grafting.

Isograft – a graft between two genetically identical individuals such as identical twins. Again, rejection is not a problem.

Allograft – a tissue grafted from one individual to a genetically different individual of the same species.

Xenograft – a graft between individuals of different species such as from pig to human.

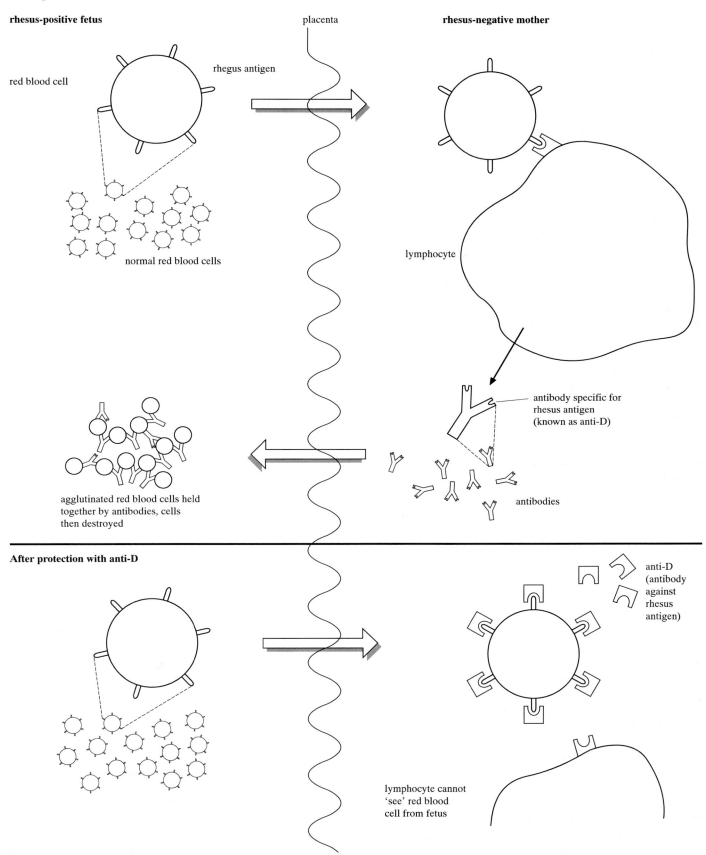

Before protection

rhesus-positive fetus

placenta

rhesus-negative mother

red blood cell

rhegus antigen

normal red blood cells

lymphocyte

antibody specific for rhesus antigen (known as anti-D)

agglutinated red blood cells held together by antibodies, cells then destroyed

antibodies

After protection with anti-D

anti-D (antibody against rhesus antigen)

lymphocyte cannot 'see' red blood cell from fetus

Fig 14.44 *Rhesus disease and its prevention.*

Rejection

Only allografting will be discussed here.

The simplest case is blood. Blood is technically a fluid tissue, so simple blood transfusion can be regarded as an allograft. Here rejection may occur and results in agglutination of the donor's red cells as discussed earlier. Finding a suitable donor for blood transfusion is relatively easy because there are only two antigens involved. However, all other cells in the body have many possible antigens as a result of a group of genes called the major histocompatibility complex (MHC). The problems of rejection that result are discussed in section 25.7.13.

Skin rejection can be used as an example of a typical rejection of a tissue. The following sequence of events takes place if skin is rejected.

(1) The skin allograft initially develops blood vessels in the first 2–3 days and generally looks healthy.
(2) During the next six days the number of blood vessels decreases, and a great number of killer T cells and macrophages gather in and around the graft.
(3) Two days later the graft cells begin to die and the graft is eventually cast off.

Prevention of graft rejection

There are several means of preventing graft rejection currently in use.

(1) Tissue matching – this is an obvious and necessary precaution to take before any surgery. The major histocompatibility complex is relevant here (section 25.7.13). Tissue matching is much more likely to occur between close relatives than between non-relatives.
(2) Exposure of bone marrow and lymph tissues to radiation by X-rays tends to inhibit production of white blood cells and therefore slows down rejection. Unpleasant side-effects occur and there is an increased risk of infection during the treatment.
(3) Immunosuppression – here the principle is to use chemicals which inhibit the entire activity of the immune system. When this occurs graft rejection is delayed, but the main problem with this technique is that the patient becomes susceptible to all kinds of infections. It has also been shown that immuno-suppression may make the patients more prone to develop cancer.
(4) One way of overcoming the problems of radiation and immunosuppression is to suppress only the cells responsible for rejection, namely the killer T cells. In this way the rest of the patient's immune system would continue to function normally. The most promising approach is to treat the patient (or their bone marrow) with monoclonal antibodies that recognise and destroy the killer T cells. A monoclonal antibody has been developed which is very effective at preventing rejection of transplanted kidneys, as described in section 12.11.2.

Chapter Fifteen

Health and disease

15.1 What is meant by health and disease?

The World Health Organisation has defined health as 'a state of complete physical, mental and social well-being and not merely the absence of disease or infirmity'. Note that there are three dimensions to this definition, namely physical, mental and social. Ill-health may not necessarily involve disease, and the term *disease* is rather more difficult to define than *health*. One possible definition is that it is a 'bodily disorder', or a 'disordered state of an organ or organism'. This may be suitable when describing a person with tuberculosis, a liver affected by alcohol, or a lung with a tumour, but what of a broken arm? The arm is certainly in a 'disordered state', but it would not normally be described as diseased. In fact, it is arguable that the term 'disorder' is sometimes to be preferred to disease, as perhaps in the case of genetic disorders/diseases. A better understanding of what we mean by disease can be obtained by considering how diseases may be classified.

Classification of disease

It is convenient to classify diseases into the following six main groups.

1 Diseases caused by other living organisms. Disease-causing organisms typically include viruses, bacteria, fungi, protozoans, flatworms and roundworms. These organisms live as parasites in or on the human body and interfere with its normal working. Diseases which are caused by bacteria, viruses and fungi are commonly referred to as **infectious diseases** or **communicable diseases**, such as cholera (caused by a bacterium) and measles (caused by a virus). Diseases caused by other organisms are more commonly referred to as **parasitic diseases**, such as malaria (caused by a protozoan).

2 Diseases that are 'human-induced' or 'self-inflicted'. These diseases are brought by humans on themselves, either as individuals or collectively as a society. They could also be described as **social diseases**. Many are particularly associated with modern industrialised societies and include coronary heart disease, alcoholism, drug abuse, lung cancer, domestic and industrial accidents, industrial diseases such as asbestosis, and pollution-related disorders. The latter include brain damage brought on by lead or mercury poisoning, some cases of asthma and possibly some cases of cancer found in people living near nuclear power stations.

3 Deficiency diseases. These are related to the absence of certain nutrients in the diet. They may be due to the absence of one of the main food groups such as protein which results in kwashiorkor and marasmus (chapter 9). The absence of specific vitamins may result in a number of diseases such as pellagra (vitamin B_1), scurvy (vitamin C) or rickets (vitamin D). Deficiency of minerals in the diet may also result in disease, such as calcium and phosphate deficiency causing rickets or lack of iodine causing thyroid goitre. Deficiency diseases are discussed in chapter 8.

4 Genetic and congenital (present at birth) disorders. These disorders are raising increasing concerns in the medical services and society in general. Examples of genetic disorders are cystic fibrosis, Huntington's disease and Down's syndrome. These and others are discussed in chapter 25. Advances in medical science ensure that many children who would in the past have died in infancy from such disorders are surviving and living to adulthood. This means that as a society we must provide means whereby adults with mental or physical handicaps, often severe, can lead fulfilling lives. On the other side of the coin, genetic screening can increasingly provide the information before birth whereby babies with genetic disorders can be aborted. This raises many social and ethical issues which provoke controversy in society. Some of these issues are discussed in chapters 21 and 25.

5 Ageing and degenerative diseases. Degeneration of the body tissues can also cause disease. For example, weakening of the eye muscles causes long-sightedness in many older people, and diseases of the circulatory system, such as arteriosclerosis (hardening of the arteries) result from ageing. Ageing of the joint and bone tissues often leads to arthritis.

6 Mental illness. Mental illness covers a wide variety of disorders. Examples are schizophrenia, senile dementia and depression. Certain drugs have been developed that control or reduce various forms of mental illness. The treatment of these illnesses changed dramatically during the twentieth century from life-long confinement in 'lunatic asylums' to 'care in the community'.

The six groups described above may also be grouped into the following categories.

- **Infectious or communicable disease.** Many diseases are passed on from one organism to another, that is they are transmitted and are thus said to be infectious, contagious, communicable or transmissible. Many of the diseases in group 1 above are infectious and are transmitted by way of droplets of liquid, in the air, food or water, by sexual intercourse or simply by touch. Many are transmitted by way of an intermediate organism called a **vector**, for example malaria by way of the mosquito (section 15.3.3), or bubonic plague by way of the rat flea.
- **Non-infectious disease.** Disease groups 2 to 6 above are described as non-infectious or non-transmissible. It could be argued that group 4 is a special case of transmission because genetic disorders are transmitted from parent to offspring due to the presence or absence of one or more inherited genes.

It is clear from the discussion above that there are no rigid boundaries between the disease categories. For example, many diseases involve a genetic predisposition and therefore an overlap between group 4 above and other categories, such as heart disease (group 2) and some mental illness (group 6). Like health, disease has physical, mental and social dimensions. Some diseases, for example, are associated with poverty, such as tuberculosis, and may therefore be described as having an important social dimension.

15.2   Global distribution of disease

When the distribution of disease worldwide is studied, the most striking feature to emerge is the difference between developed and developing countries. Fig 15.1 shows the number of deaths and the percentage of deaths due to different causes in developed (industrialised) countries and developing (Third World) countries. Infectious and parasitic diseases represent a relatively high proportion of disease in developing countries, whereas circulatory and degenerative diseases are, relatively speaking, the most important in developed countries. The infectious disease measles, for example, is still an important killer disease in many developing countries (table 15.1) although it is declining rapidly as a result of vaccination programmes (section 15.2.1). Measles is a more serious disease than most people think. It can cause pneumonia, blindness, deafness and inflammation of the brain (encephalitis) which in turn may cause brain damage (table 15.3, page 501). It used to be an important killer in developed countries (fig 15.2); 4188 people died of measles in England and Wales in 1930, but only 26 in 1980. Why have these changes come about and why are there such striking differences between developed and developing countries? The temptation is to suggest that medical intervention is responsible, but fig 14.42 shows that death rates from measles were declining rapidly in England

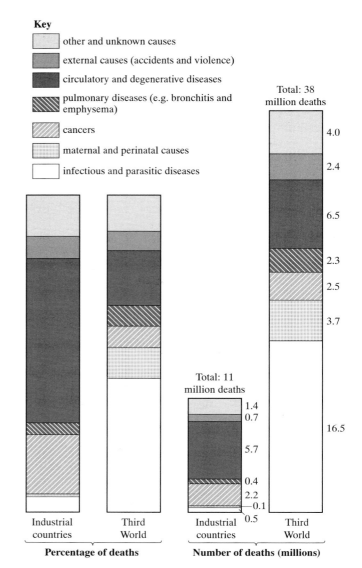

Fig 15.1 *Leading causes of death (mortality) in developed and developing countries in the year 1985. Percentage of deaths are shown to the left and numbers of deaths in millions are shown to the right. (Data from Lopez, A.D., 1993,* Causes of death in the industrialized and the developing countries: estimates for 1985' *in Jamison, D.T. and Mosley, H. (eds)* Disease Control Priorities In Developing Countries, *OUP).*

and Wales long before medical intervention. Vaccination against measles was not introduced in Britain until 1968. The same is true of some other infectious diseases which have been killers in the past, such as whooping cough and tuberculosis. The truth is that, in fighting disease, social and economic factors are just as important as medical intervention.

Some important infectious diseases are transmitted by faecal contamination of water and food. Examples are cholera, diarrhoea, typhoid and dysentery. These declined rapidly in England and Wales after the Public Health Act, 1875 which introduced public hygiene measures for the

Table 15.1 Mortality for selected infectious diseases – world estimates.

Disease	Deaths per year (mortality)
Respiratory disease (e.g. pneumonia, bronchitis, influenza, diphtheria)	10 000 000
Diarrhoea	4 300 000
Measles	2 000 000
Malaria	1 500 000
Tetanus	1 200 000
Tuberculosis (TB)	900 000
Hepatitis B	800 000
Pertussis (whooping cough)	600 000
Typhoid	600 000
Schistosomiasis (blood fluke)	250 000
HIV	200 000

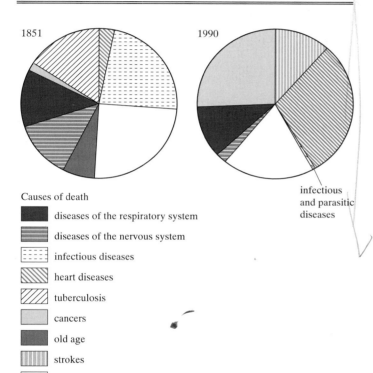

Causes of death

- diseases of the respiratory system
- diseases of the nervous system
- infectious diseases
- heart diseases
- tuberculosis
- cancers
- old age
- strokes
- all other causes

Fig 15.2 *Causes of death in England and Wales, 1851 and 1990. (Data for 1851 from Registrar-General, 1855,* England and Wales Report; *for 1990 from Registrar-General, 1992,* Annual Abstract of Statistics 1992, HMSO, London, Table 2.20, p37.)

proper disposal and treatment of sewage, and the purification of water. When considering infectious disease in general, improvements in living standards have been just as important. These increase *resistance* to disease. Particularly important are good nutrition and housing. Tuberculosis, a respiratory infection, began to decline as living standards improved since it is typically spread when people live in close contact, such as several people living in one room, and also when people are malnourished. Measles is a particularly important disease in developing countries because it tends to affect very young children, often under the age of one year before they have been vaccinated, and when the body is less able to fight infection. If the body is weakened by malnutrition, or by other infectious diseases or parasites, it makes measles and many other infectious diseases much more dangerous. Most measles deaths are caused by secondary infections.

To summarise, infectious diseases have been brought under control in the UK and other developed countries by improvements in hygiene, housing and nutrition as well as by direct medical intervention. The latter includes improvements in prevention, such as vaccination, and in treatment, such as the use of antibiotics (considered in more detail later). Overall social, economic and medical factors are all important and all interact in a complex way.

As vaccination programmes are extended to developing countries, so the incidence of infectious disease is declining in them. Measles is one of six major diseases targetted by the World Health Organisation (WHO) for prevention by means of vaccination in its Expanded Programme on Immunisation (section 15.2.1 and fig 15.3). The five others are tetanus, pertussis (whooping cough) and polio (fig 15.3), tuberculosis and diphtheria.

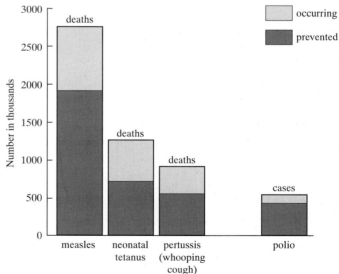

Fig 15.3 *Number of deaths due to measles, neonatal tetanus and pertussis (whooping cough), and number of polio cases occurring and prevented by vaccination in developing countries, 1990. (From* Work of WHO, Biennial Report 1992–3, *(1994), WHO, Geneva.)*

As infectious disease has been virtually eliminated as a major killer in developed countries, so other diseases have taken their place (figs 15.1 and 15.2). Notable among the circulatory diseases are coronary heart disease and strokes. The emergence of circulatory diseases and cancers as leading causes of death in developed countries is partly related to changes in lifestyle. Heart disease and strokes are discussed in section 15.5, and lung cancer has been discussed in section 7.9.5. These diseases are regarded as modern epidemics and will probably be brought under much greater control as societies develop strategies to tackle them. It can be argued that they are self-inflicted. Some major diseases of developed countries however are not related to lifestyle. They are due to an increasing length of life (longevity). As we age, so the body begins to degenerate. A whole range of degenerative diseases exists. Cancers, for example, become more common as we age.

Fig 15.2 compares causes of death in England and Wales for 1851 and 1990. Such data give an indication of the changes that can be expected as countries tackle infectious disease.

15.2.1   Vaccination

Role of vaccination

Over 10 million deaths worldwide per year are due to infectious diseases. To combat this terrible loss of life, vaccination is a powerful weapon and has been one of the great success stories of human medicine. Vaccination is the giving of antigens from a disease-causing organism, either by injection or orally, with the aim of causing the body's immune system to learn to make antibodies against the disease. The body should then be able to respond fast enough to infection by that disease to eliminate it before symptoms develop.

For vaccination to be successful as a strategy, it must be administered to as great a number of people as possible, and must continue to be used until the disease is eradicated. Vaccination is not compulsory in Britain because high enough uptakes can be achieved by government-backed education of the public. Providing a certain high percentage of the population are protected, epidemics can be prevented. Isolated cases can quickly be 'ring vaccinated' if necessary, whereby contacts and everyone in a given area around an outbreak of the disease can be vaccinated. However, it is important not to become complacent. Whooping cough began to increase in Britain again because many people stopped having their children vaccinated after scares about the safety of the vaccine (see safety and effectiveness of vaccines on page 500).

Another factor which must be taken into account is that diseases can spread across international boundaries, so it is important to have, in addition to national policies, a world-wide coordinated approach. This is one of the roles of the World Health Organisation.

The smallpox story

The most successful example of the effectiveness of vaccination is the elimination of smallpox. Up to the late 1960s a combined total of some 15 million cases of smallpox occurred annually in 33 different countries. The World Health Organisation started an eradication programme in 1956 and by 1977 the last case was reported in Somalia, and the disease was effectively extinct. The virus is still kept in secure laboratories in the USA and Russia, although there have been calls for the last samples to be destroyed.

Factors which contributed to the successful eradication of smallpox were:

Vaccination

- the virus did not keep changing its surface antigens, so the vaccine remained highly effective. Some organisms, such as those causing influenza and malaria, occasionally change their antigens by mutation, thus 'fooling' the immune systems of those who have developed antibodies against them as a result of infection or vaccination.
- a heat-stable vaccine was developed for work in tropical and sub-tropical climates.
- the vaccine was easy to administer by a scratch technique on the arm, so assistants could easily be trained.
- the vaccine was very reliable and effective.

Surveillance

- infected people were easily identified.
- rewards were offered to people who reported new cases.

Containment

- 'ring vaccination' was used in the final stages of eradication whereby everyone in the area around any site of infection was vaccinated.
- sufferers were kept in isolation until they were non-infectious.
- efforts were made to trace all contacts of those with the disease.
- international restrictions were made on the travel of those who had not been vaccinated.

All this required great international cooperation and financial support.

Vaccination programmes

Children in the UK can be given a series of vaccines to protect them against a range of diseases (table 15.2). In some countries vaccination is a legal requirement. Vaccination programmes have been particularly successful in virtually eliminating polio (poliomyelitis) and diphtheria (fig 14.42) in developed countries. Polio may soon become extinct

Table 15.2 Immunisation schedule offered to children in the UK. (From Department of Health, *Immunisation against Infectious Diseases* (1992) HMSO.)

	2 months	3 months	4 months	1 year	4 years	10–13 years	14 years	14–15 years
Diphtheria	✓	✓	✓	–	✓	–	–	–
Tetanus	✓	✓	✓	–	✓	–	–	✓
Polio	✓	✓	✓	–	✓	–	–	✓
Pertussis (whooping cough)	✓	✓	✓	–	–	–	–	–
Measles	–	–	–	✓1	–	–	–	–
Mumps	–	–	–	✓1	–	–	–	–
Rubella (German measles)	–	–	–	✓1	–	✓2	–	–
Haemophilus influenzae B (bacterium which may cause respiratory infection)	✓4	✓4	✓4	✓4	–	–	–	–
BCG (tuberculosis)	–	–	–	–	–	–	✓3	–

1 MMR vaccine (Measles, Mumps, Rubella) formerly given at 2 years of age, 2 females, 3 susceptibles, 4 one dose at 13 months to 4 years of age.

worldwide. Diphtheria is very rare in the UK, reduced to only 13 cases and no deaths between 1986 and 1991.

By 1984 the World Health Organisation's programme of vaccination, which is targetted against six major diseases (measles, pertussis [whooping cough], tetanus, polio, tuberculosis [TB], diphtheria), had immunised some 50% of the children in the world and this had risen to 80% by the mid-1990s. It has been estimated that this programme prevented more than one million deaths annually between 1974 and 1984. However, despite great progress, by 1990 about 3 million children were still dying each year from these diseases and about 4.6 million were still not fully vaccinated. Measles was killing 1.4 million annually (one every 20 seconds). Another 490 000 died of pertussis annually and 450 000 of TB. The annual cost, one-third of which is given in aid, is about US$ 1.5 thousand million.

The WHO Expanded Programme of Immunisation (EPI) aims to immunise more than 90% of the world's newborn against a number of viral and bacterial diseases by the year 2000. Hepatitis B is now also being targeted and it is hoped to eradicate polio by the year 2000.

There is still a need for new vaccines, for example against malaria, dengue fever, sleeping sickness, worm infections, HIV, leprosy and others. Not only are new vaccines required, but also more effective and safer vaccines than those in use at the present time are needed. For example the vaccine for cholera is only effective in 50% of patients and the duration of immunity is relatively short (see section 15.3.1). The flu vaccine also needs improvement to make it more effective.

Types of vaccine

The different types of vaccine are described in section 14.9.5. There has been much debate about the relative merits of live and killed vaccines. Generally speaking, live vaccines are more effective although in the past they have been more risky. Other factors such as cost, safety, politics and social acceptance can determine whether there is high uptake of a particular vaccine and whether it is successful.

There are many approaches to making and using a vaccine. For example in the UK three different vaccines have been licensed for typhoid vaccination:

(i) a killed whole cell vaccine (no longer available);
(ii) a polysaccharide extract from the capsule of the typhoid bacterium;
(iii) a live attenuated strain of the typhoid bacterium, *Salmonella typhi*.

The second one is the most recent, having been introduced in 1992. It requires the least number of doses and is the most preferred.

The most important issue for developed countries is the safety of the vaccine, whereas in a developing country the question of cost and how to deliver the vaccine are probably of greater importance.

A relatively recent development in the production of vaccines is that of using genetic engineering techniques. Many pathogens cannot be cultured outside their natural host. Thus the conventional approaches to vaccination cannot be used. For example, the microbe causing human syphilis (*Treponema pallidum*) and the bacterium that causes leprosy (*Mycobacterium leprae*) have never been grown in vitro (outside the body). Thus it is not possible to generate live attenuated or inactivated vaccines by culturing techniques. In these examples recombinant DNA technology offers an alternative approach, allowing genes for antigens to be transferred from these organisms to more useful hosts such as *E. coli*, yeast or mammalian cells. These can then be used to produce bulk quantities of antigens for vaccines. For example, the surface antigen gene of hepatitis is simple to identify, clone and express. However, not all protective antigens are as simple to develop.

Safety and effectiveness of vaccines

There is sometimes public controversy regarding the effectiveness of vaccines. Up to 1986, 160 million doses of measles vaccine (a live attenuated virus) had been administered in the UK, with an excellent record of protection. Of the children given vaccination, 5–15% developed fever on the fifth day, lasting several days. One recipient of vaccine in one million developed a disorder of the central nervous system known as **encephalitis**. This can cause extreme concern in parents when these facts appear in newspapers just as vaccination campaigns begin. The chances of this complication from measles vaccination is, in fact, less than the incidence of encephalitis from an unknown origin. Whooping cough (pertussis) vaccine, which contains dead bacteria, sometimes has a rare neurological adverse reaction resulting in convulsions and brain damage. This occurs once in about 100 000 doses and the possibility of permanent brain damage occurs once in 300 000 doses. Both measles and diphtheria vaccines can have local reactions of inflammation and laryngitis. However, deaths from these diseases still occur amongst unvaccinated children and parents must weigh up the information and take the responsibility of deciding whether or not to have their children vaccinated.

15.3   Infectious disease

Infectious diseases are those caused by other living organisms which invade the body and live parasitically. Such organisms are called **pathogens**. Some examples are given in tables 15.3–6. Further details of cholera, tuberculosis, malaria, AIDS, typhoid, paratyphoid and *Salmonella* food poisoning are given in the following sections.

The body's defence mechanisms against invading organisms are discussed in chapter 14 (see section 14.8.5 and 14.9 immune system).

The following technical terms are of use when discussing infectious disease.

aetiology – the study of the cause of disease
epidemiology – the study of all the factors that contribute to the appearance of a particular disease

causative agent – the organism which causes the disease
vector – an organism which carries a disease from one person to another or from an infected animal to a human, e.g. the mosquito is a vector for malaria (it is *not* the causative agent)
incubation period – the period of time between the original infection and the appearance of signs and symptoms
infective period – the time during which a person is capable of passing the disease on to another person
carrier – a person who has been infected but develops no signs or symptoms; the carrier can pass the disease on to another person
notifiable disease – a disease which must be reported by doctors to the health authorities due to its seriousness (e.g. cholera, TB, polio)
epidemic – situation in which a disease spreads rapidly through a large number of people and later 'disappears' again
pandemic – an epidemic which spreads across whole continents
endemic – describes a disease which is always present at a low level in a given population or region
signs – *visible* expression of the disease which can be found by examining a patient, e.g. a rash or a high temperature
symptoms – an indication of a disease which is not detectable by examination and can only be reported by the patient, e.g. a headache, nausea
prevention – measures taken to prevent a person from getting a disease, e.g. vaccination, sewage treatment, hygiene
treatment – measures taken to cure a disease or alleviate symptoms once a person has the disease, e.g. use of antibiotics

15.3.1   Cholera

Cholera is a good example of a waterborne disease. It is endemic in parts of Asia, particularly India. Epidemics occur from time to time in other countries, as in Peru in 1992 which was the first outbreak in South America of the twentieth century. In 1991 more than 16 000 people died worldwide from half a million cases of cholera. Improved treatment has reduced the death rate dramatically, but it is still a serious disease. Until it was discovered how to treat cholera the death toll was enormous. For example half a million New York residents were killed in one epidemic in 1832.

Transmission, signs and symptoms

The organism which causes cholera is a comma-shaped motile bacterium called *Vibrio cholerae*. The main source of infection is water contaminated by faeces from a sufferer of the disease or a 'carrier'. A carrier is an individual infected with vibrios who does not develop the typical symptoms of cholera. It is estimated that only about one

Table 15.3 Some common viral diseases of humans. Diseases are grouped according to method of spread.

Name of disease	Cause	Method of spread	Signs and symptoms	Type of vaccination
Influenza	Myxovirus (DNA virus); three types, A, B and C, of varying severity	Droplet infection	Sudden fever with headache, sore throat and muscular aches. Affects epithelia of respiratory passages, trachea and bronchi. Recovery within one week, but after-effects may last a month. Secondary infection of lung tissue by bacteria, leading to pneumonia may occur.	Killed virus: must be of right strain
Common cold	Large variety of viruses, most commonly rhino-virus (RNA virus)	Droplet infection	Nasal and bronchial irritation, resulting in sneezing and coughing. Usually only affects upper respiratory passages. Secondary bacterial infection may occur.	Living or inactivated virus given as intramuscular injection; not very effective because so many different strains of rhinovirus
Smallpox*	Variola virus (DNA virus), a pox virus	Droplet infection (contagion possible via wounds in skin, clothing, bedding, dressings)	High fever and generalised aching. Affects respiratory passages. Rash on the body two days later which spreads over body. Secondary infection by bacteria causes permanent scarring of the skin.	Living attenuated virus applied by scratching skin; no longer carried out because virus is extinct
Mumps	A paramyxovirus (RNA virus)	Droplet infection (or contagion via infected saliva to mouth)	Occurs mainly in children. Fever, followed by swelling of the parotid (salivary) glands on one or both sides, lasting about ten days. Testes, ovaries and pancreas are other organs that may be affected. Inflammation of the testes in male after puberty may cause sterility.	Living attenuated virus
Measles	A paramyxovirus (RNA virus)	Droplet infection	Occurs mainly in children. Sore throat, runny nose, watery eyes, cough and fever. Small, white spots (Koplik's spots) appear inside mouth on wall of cheek. Two days later reddish rash appears on neck at hair line – spreads over body. Recovery one week later, but virus can damage kidneys or brain. Secondary bacterial infections may occur.	Living attenuated virus
German measles (Rubella)	Rubella virus	· Droplet infection	Occurs mainly in older children and adults. Affects respiratory passages, lymph nodes in neck, eyes and skin. Slight fever, body rash which disappears after three days. Complications rare, except in women during first four months of pregnancy, when there is 20% chance of blindness, deafness or other serious defects of the baby.	Living attenuated virus; more essential for girls because disease causes complications in pregnancy
Poliomyelitis ('polio')	Poliovirus (a picornavirus) (RNA virus), three strains exist	Droplet infection or via human faeces	Fever, headache and feeling of stiffness in neck and other muscles. Nerve cells to muscles are destroyed causing paralysis and muscle wasting. When breathing muscles are paralysed, an 'iron lung' may be needed. Most cases of paralysis occur in children aged 4–12 years, but adults may also be affected.	Living attenuated virus given orally, usually on sugar lump
Yellow fever	An arbovirus, that is arthropod-borne virus (RNA virus)	Vector – arthropods, e.g. ticks, mosquitoes	Fever, headache, backache, nausea, tenderness in pit of stomach. Affects lining of blood vessels and liver. Fourth day vomit blood and bile (so-called 'black vomit'). Eyes become yellow. Faeces coloured black due to digested blood.	Living attenuated virus (control of vectors also important)
AIDS	HIV virus – a retrovirus (RNA virus)	Blood-borne. Can be spread by sexual intercourse – homo- and heterosexuals	Laboratory evidence of infection, i.e. antibodies to the virus, but few symptoms except swollen glands. AIDS-related complex (ARC) may develop in about 25% of people testing positive to AIDS virus. ARC includes loss of appetite, loss of weight, fevers, persistent dry cough, white spots due to thrush (*Candida albicans*), shingles, lymphoma (cancer of the lymphatic system), pneumonia, cryptosporidiosis (severe diarrhoea), tuberculosis and other diseases resulting from the breakdown of the immune system.	Not available
Hepatitis B	DNA virus	Blood-borne and can be spread by sexual intercourse	Incubation 6 weeks to 6 months. Infects liver. Flu-like symptoms. Jaundice, nausea and severe loss of appetitite	Genetically engineered

*Last recorded natural case in Somalia, October 1977; disease extinct, though virus kept in a few laboratories

Table 15.4 Some common bacterial diseases of humans. Diseases are grouped according to method of spread.

Name of disease	Cause	Method of spread	Signs and symptoms	Type of vaccination or antibiotic
Diphtheria	*Corynebacterium diphtheriae* (rod-shaped, Gram +)	Droplet infection	Bacteria grow on moist mucous membranes of upper respiratory tract. Toxin spread by blood to all parts of body. Slight fever, sore throat followed by severe damage to heart, nerve cells and adrenal glands.	Toxoid
Tuberculosis (TB)	*Mycobacterium tuberculosis* (rod-shaped, member of actinomycetes)	Droplet infection. Drinking milk from infected cattle.	Tubercle bacilli may infect many organs, but pulmonary TB of the lungs most common. General weight loss and cough. Sputum may contain blood.	BCG living attenuated bacteria. Must test first to see if already immune. Antibiotics, e.g. streptomycin.
Whooping cough (pertussis)	*Bordetella pertussis* (rod-shaped, Gram –)	Droplet infection	Mainly in young children. Severe coughing bouts, each cough followed by 'whoop' sound at expiration of air through narrowed passages.	Killed bacteria
Gonorrhoea	*Neisseria gonorrhoeae* (coccus, Gram –)	Contagion by sexual contact	Affects mainly mucous membranes of urinogenital tract. In male, burning feeling of discomfort on passing urine, after a yellow discharge. Accompanied by fever, headache and general feeling of illness. Can affect prostate gland or epididymis of testis. Untreated, disorders of joints may follow. In female, no symptoms in genital tract. Infection commonest in urethra and cervix of womb. Infection spreads from here to fallopian tubes which become filled with pus. Sterility results.	Antibiotics, e.g. penicillin, streptomycin
Syphilis	*Treponema pallidum* (a spirochaete)	Contagion by sexual contact	Chronic in nature and widespread in body tissues. Incubation 2–4 weeks. First show is sores or chancres (painless ulcer) on any part of body e.g. vagina, penis, lips, fingers, nipples. Sores heal in 3–8 weeks. Next phase 6–8 weeks later, includes fever, skin rashes. Patient highly infectious. Final phase patient non-infectious. Many tissues damaged e.g. heart disease, insanity, blindness.	Antibiotics, e.g. penicillin
Typhus	*Rickettsia*	Epidemic typhus: vector – louse. Endemic typhus: vector – rat flea. From rat to rat by flea and louse.	After 12–14 days headache, pain in back and limbs. Measles-like rash on armpits, hands and forearm. Delirium sets in, then coma. May affect linings of blood vessels causing clots. Death can result from toxaemia, heart or kidney failure.	Killed bacteria or living non-virulent strain. Antibiotics e.g. tetracyclines, chloramphenicol (control of vectors also important).
Tetanus	*Clostridium tetani* (rod-shaped Gram +)	Wound infection	Toxins cause muscular spasms in the region of mouth and neck. Extend throughout body. Convulsions become so severe patient dies through lack of oxygen.	Toxoid
Botulism	*Clostridium botulinum* In canned or smoked food etc. grows anaerobically.	Eating infected food.	Within 24 hours vomit, constipation, paralysis of muscles and intense thirst. 50% mortality.	Antitoxins can be used to neutralise toxins
Cholera	*Vibrio cholerae* (comma-shaped, Gram –)	Faecal contamination: (a) food- or water-borne material contaminated with faeces from infected person; (b) handling of contaminated objects; (c) vector, e.g. flies moving from human faeces to food.	Bacteria produce toxins causing inflammation of the gut and severe diarrhoea. Fluid loss so intense that diarrhoea is termed 'rice water'. Resulting dehydration and loss of mineral salts can cause death.	Killed bacteria: short-lived protection and not always effective. Genetically engineered vaccine now available. Antibiotics, e.g. tetracyclines, chloramphenicol.
Typhoid fever	*Salmonella typhi* (= *S. typhosa*) (rod-shaped, Gram –)	As cholera	Mild fever, slight abdominal pains. Affects alimentary canal, spreading to lymph and blood, lungs, bone marrow and spleen. Intensity of fever and pain increase and diarrhoea follows. Ulceration and rupture of intestine may follow. Infection spreads to other organs – lungs, bone marrow and spleen. Occurs 2 or 3 weeks after infection.	Polysaccharide extract from the bacterial capsule. Genetically engineered vaccine now available
Bacterial dysentery (bacillary dysentery)	*Shigella dysenteriae* (rod-shaped, Gram –)	As cholera	Bacteria produce toxins in the intestine causing abdominal pain with blood and mucus in diarrhoea. Comes on rapidly 2 or 3 days after swallowing an infecting dose of bacteria.	No vaccine. Antibiotic, e.g. tetracyclines.
Bacterial food poisoning (gastro-enteritis or salmonellosis)	*Salmonella* spp. (rod-shaped, Gram –)	Mainly foodborne – meat from infected animals, mainly poultry and pigs. Also via faecal contamination as with cholera.	Affects alimentary canal. Can be very brief, involving 'diarrhoea and vomiting' and develops in hours. Toxins develop rapidly in the gut and cause symptoms after an infected meal.	No vaccine. Antibiotics, e.g. tetracyclines; usually not necessary and not very effective.

Table 15.5 Diseases of humans caused by protozoa.

Cause	Disease	Transmission	Symptoms	Control and treatment
Plasmodium spp.	Malaria	*Anopheles* spp. mosquito bite	After ten days high fever develops. Fever may be continuous, irregular or twice daily.	Destruction of mosquito larvae with oil spray or insecticide. Drainage of breeding places of mosquitoes. Preventive drugs (prophylactics), e.g. chloroquine. Drugs to kill parasites in humans, e.g. primaquine.
Entamoeba histolytica	Amoebiasis (amoebic dysentery)	Uncooked food, unhygienic food preparation, 'carrier' handling food	Diarrhoea with loss of blood in stools, fever, nausea and vomiting. Can lead to death.	Hygienic food handling and preparation. Prevention of spread by flies. No acceptable chemical prophylaxis. Drugs to kill parasites in humans, e.g. metronidazole, diloxanide furoate.
Trypanosoma spp.	Trypanosomiasis (sleeping sickness) also disease of cattle (nagana), transferable between cattle and humans	Tsetse fly bite	Lymph glands enlarge, fever, enlargement of spleen and liver follow. Later parasite invades nervous system; results in sleepiness and muscular spasms.	Tsetse flies live in restricted areas – 'fly belts'. Fly screens on doors and windows, spraying of cattle, moving human settlements to areas cleared of flies. Drugs to kill parasites in humans, e.g. pentamidine.

Table 15.6 Diseases of humans caused by fungi.

Disease	Cause	Transmission	Symptoms	Control and treatment
Tinea pedis	'Athlete's foot'	Communal changing and bathing facilities with wet floors	Presence of sodden, peeling and cracked skin between toes. Often persistent in hot summer months.	Disinfection of communal bath and shower floors. Exclusion of infected individuals. Drugs: griseofulvin (antibiotic) taken by mouth.
Tinea capititis	Head ringworm	Highly contagious, direct contact by way of combs, brushes, caps, hats etc.	Small scaly spot with broken hairs. Spot increases in size, covered with greyish scales, thicker at edges forming a distinct margin.	Local application of fungicides as a variety of ointments. Drugs: griseofulvin (antibiotic) taken by mouth.
Candida albicans	Candidiasis (thrush)	Can occur in mouth, vagina, intestine, etc. Infection may arise due to loss of acidity in vagina, for example during pregnancy or as a result of diabetes in women. Infants can be infected in the mouth region at birth.	Local infection of yeast organisms forming fluffy white patches. Red inflamed skin under patch. Severe irritation.	Search for underlying predisposing factor. Drugs used locally as lotions, creams or pessaries (vaginal infection). Drugs: amphotericin.

infected person in 50 develops the disease, the rest being carriers. Thus the faeces containing vibrios are a considerable threat when the 'carriers' are free moving in a society. Drinking contaminated water, or washing food or utensils in it, is the most common means of transmission. Direct contamination of food with faeces as a result of poor hygiene is also possible.

Vibrio cholerae multiplies in the intestine, releasing a powerful toxin which results in violent inflammation of the intestine and production of a watery diarrhoea. The organisms can only multiply and flourish in the human intestine, although they can survive outside of the body.

The main sign of the disease is severe diarrhoea due to irritation of the bowel by toxins from the vibrios. The liquid of the faeces is so profuse and cloudy that it is called 'rice water'. Up to $15\,dm^3$ of fluid can be lost in a day. Abdominal pain and vomiting are also common. Fever is absent; in fact, the skin feels 'deathly' cold and often damp. Dehydration is rapid and quickly results in death unless rehydration treatment is given.

If the faeces are not collected or disposed of hygienically then one patient can infect a wide area of a community. Each cubic centimetre of diarrhoea will contain up to a thousand million vibrios. Thus a mild case of cholera or a carrier may create a great hazard as they move around.

Treatment and prevention

The prime cause of death from cholera is loss of water with its mineral salts, that is dehydration. Replacement of these is therefore the first task. Where there are epidemics, for example in refugee camps, cheap and immediate therapy is by oral rehydration, that is, by packs of water containing balanced mineral salts and sugar administered by mouth (fig 15.4). This replacement therapy must be 1.5 volumes to each volume of stool (faeces) lost. The fluid may also be administered by a drip feed into a vein.

Various antibiotics, such as tetracyclines and chloramphenicol, are effective at destroying the vibrios and decreasing the diarrhoea. Chloramphenicol is effective against tetracycline-resistant vibrios.

During a devastating epidemic in London in 1849 the physician John Snow demonstrated that cholera was transmitted by way of water by removing the handle of the Broad Street pump (now Broadwick Street). This had been the sole water supply for a poor slum community that was badly affected by cholera. The local epidemic ceased. Authorities were not convinced and in a second epidemic in 1854 Snow showed that cholera-ridden communities were drawing their water from the lower Thames. Populations drawing water from the upper, purer reaches of the Thames were almost cholera-free. In 1875 the Public Health Act was introduced which resulted in proper sewage treatment and water purification, and since 1893 any new cases in Britain have come in from abroad.

Improvements in basic human hygiene in all parts of the industrialising world, including better garbage and waste disposal, and in-house toilets with appropriate water flushing increased the cleanliness of cities. By 1900 life

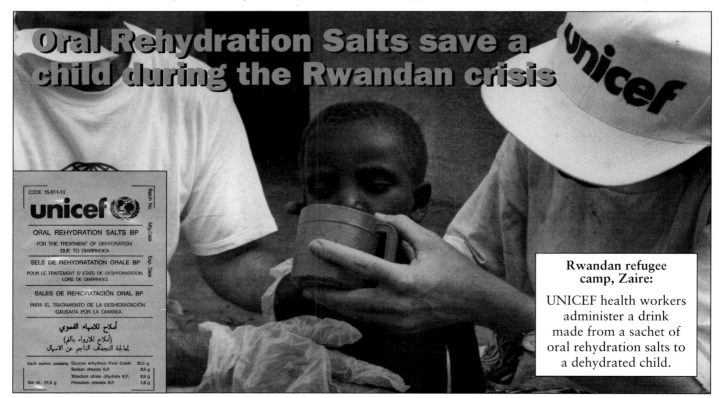

Rwandan refugee camp, Zaire:

UNICEF health workers administer a drink made from a sachet of oral rehydration salts to a dehydrated child.

Fig 15.4 *Leaflet from UNICEF which invites donations and points out that a small sachet of ready-mixed rehydration salts costs only 7p. These sachets can be used for a variety of diarrhoeal diseases, not just cholera.*

expectancy in Britain had improved markedly and nearly all infectious diseases were in decline, not just cholera.

Cholera is one of five epidemic diseases which must be notified to the World Health Organisation in Geneva. Reporting these diseases means that prompt international action can be taken to try to prevent their spread. This will include restrictions on travel into or out of the affected area.

The key measures in controlling cholera are:

- provision of clean drinking water.
- proper sewage treatment and sanitation.
- high standards of public and personal hygiene, particularly in relation to food (such as washing hands after defaecation).
- health education.
- **vaccination** – recommended for people visiting areas where cholera is endemic and for those living in such areas. The cholera vaccine contains heat-killed bacteria. It is only about 40–80% effective and protection only lasts for about 3–6 months. A second booster dose will bring a rapid response and will give immediate protection during an epidemic. Work is in progress on a genetically engineered vaccine. An important step has been the identification and cloning of the genes coding for the toxin and its production. One promising approach is to develop a live attenuated strain of the bacterium which has had one of the two toxin genes removed.
- control of flies which act as vectors in transferring faecal material to food.
- isolation of patients and hygienic disposal of faeces and vomit from patients.
- identification of carriers and prevention of their working in the food industry.
- immediate examination of diarrhoeal diseases for bacterial content and effective treatment supplied immediately.
- close contacts should be treated with drugs to kill any possible cholera bacteria, and people in the area should be vaccinated.

In the 1970s it was discovered that the tiny cholera vibrio could live inside algae, resting encysted in a dormant state for months and years. Since that time many new cholera epidemics in India, South America and southern Asian coastal regions have appeared. These have been traced to a new strain of *Vibrio cholerae* which first appeared in Indonesia in 1961. This new, more virulent strain, has been shown to be capable of surviving in sea water and may move around the world as a result, particularly when water is contaminated by sewage. Sewage tends to encourage the growth of algae because it contains nutrients, and resulting 'algal blooms' may also help to transmit the disease.

15.3.2   Tuberculosis (TB)

Historically TB has been one of the world's worst killer diseases. Traces of TB have been found in skeletons of the late Stone Age. Fig 15.5 shows the death rate from tuberculosis in England and Wales from 1838 to 1970. It was one of the world's great killer diseases in the nineteenth century and was the largest single cause of death in England and Wales during that time, accounting for one-fifth of all deaths. By 1990, the numbers of children dying from the disease had been reduced to less than 1 in 1 million in developed countries, but at least 30 million people worldwide still suffered symptoms, 95% of whom were living in developing countries. Up to 3 million a year are currently dying from TB, and up to one-third of the world's population carry the bacteria with no ill effects.

In the early 1990s the WHO declared the disease a global emergency as cases in the developed world, including Britain, began to increase again and resistance to drugs began to grow. In 1992 there were 5802 new cases in England. Worldwide, 8 million new cases are reported every year. In 1993, Dr Kochi, manager of the WHO's TB programme, said 'TB is out of control in many parts of the world. The disease, which is preventable and treatable, has been grossly neglected and no country is immune to it.' Its global distribution is indicated in fig 15.6.

The disease is caused by a fungus-like bacterium called *Mycobacterium tuberculosis*, first discovered by Robert Koch in 1882. It is sometimes referred to as the tubercle bacillus, bacilli being rod-shaped bacteria. The most common form in the UK is pulmonary TB which infects the lungs, although other organs may be affected. Two strains of the bacterium may cause the disease, the human and bovine forms. The latter can be present in cattle and can enter the milk of cows. It is very resistant and can remain

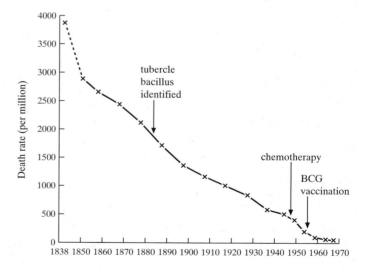

Fig 15.5   *Pulmonary tuberculosis: death rates in England and Wales from 1838 to 1970.*

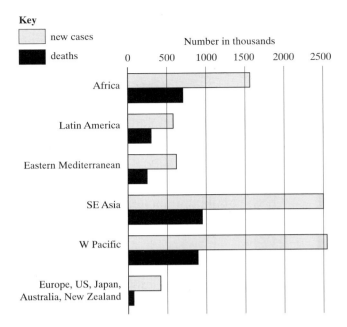

Key

new cases

deaths

Number in thousands

Fig 15.6 *New cases of TB and deaths from TB in different parts of the world in the late 1980s. (Source: World Health Organisation, 1989/90.)*

alive for long periods in milk products. It is a very serious disease of cattle and has also been responsible for a great deal of illness and death in humans in the past, particularly in children. Today, however, all milk in the UK is produced from cows that have been 'tuberculin tested', that is certified free of *Mycobacterium*. The milk also undergoes treatment at bottling plants where it is subjected to pasteurisation, sterilisation or ultra-high temperature. These processes destroy at least 99% of all bacteria, including all pathogens. Thus bovine tuberculosis is no longer of significance in humans.

Transmission, signs and symptoms

Transmission of pulmonary TB is by inhaling the bacteria into the lungs (droplet infection). It is much less infectious than the common cold, and requires prolonged contact between people. This accounts for the fact that it is associated with overcrowded living conditions, particularly where there is poor ventilation. The bacterium can also resist drying out and can survive in the air and in house dust for long periods. It is associated with poverty and bad housing where people sleep several to a room. Refugee camps, dormitories for the homeless, and prisoner of war camps are other situations in which it commonly spreads. In such conditions, malnutrition and other infections resulting in a weakened immune system can reduce resistance to the disease.

Tuberculosis can affect almost any tissue or organ in the body, but disease of the lung is by far the most frequent. It was commonly known as 'consumption' in the past because it consumed the body, causing it to waste away. The outcome of infection by tubercle bacilli depends on a

variety of factors. These include the age of the patient, the state of nutrition (which is usually related to social class) and the presence or absence of immunity. Immunity can be acquired by an individual as a result of a previous mild infection or by vaccination (see below).

The disease frequently shows itself by vague symptoms such as loss of appetite, loss of weight and excessive sweating. There are often no symptoms in early tuberculosis and the disease may only be accidentally discovered through a routine X-ray of the lungs (fig 15.7). The disease starts as an inflammation in one lung, which develops into a cavity. Then further cavities develop, spreading into both lungs. As progressive destruction of the lungs occurs the symptoms become more dramatic with coughing, appearance of blood in the sputum, chest pains, shortness of breath, fever and sweating, poor appetite and weight loss.

Treatment and prevention

Effective medical treatment only began in 1947 with the introduction of the antibiotic streptomycin. Mass vaccination did not begin in Britain until 1954. The decline up to this point must have been due mainly to improving social conditions, particularly improved housing. Vaccination accelerated the decline (fig 15.5) and by 1970 the annual death rate in Britain had fallen to 1526.

Vaccination. The development of an effective vaccine against the disease resulted from the work of two French scientists, Albert Calmette and Camille Guérin,

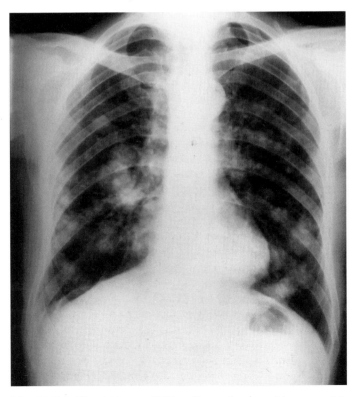

Fig 15.7 *Chest X-ray of TB sufferer. A normal lung would be uniformly dark. The clouded areas show areas of infection.*

hence the name of the vaccine Bacille Calmette-Guérin (BCG). As far back as 1921 they developed attenuated (less virulent) strains which were found to be effective for vaccination. Before treating any individual it is important to check if they are already suffering from TB or have recovered from it. The test is to puncture the skin with a special instrument which has a ring of six short needles (the Heaf test). This introduces a protein called tuberculin, purified from dead tubercle bacilli. In the absence of past or present TB the skin shows no reaction, but if an individual has the disease or has recovered, then the skin swells and reddens at the injection site. This indicates a substantial immunity and no vaccine is offered.

A detailed study of 50 000 healthy children, reported on in 1963, showed that the incidence of TB per 1000 children was 1.91 if unvaccinated, and 0.4 if vaccinated. The benefit of vaccination therefore lasts for a long period of time because the children still had immunity after more than ten years. Today children are vaccinated at age twelve to fourteen years (table 15.2). Tuberculin tests indicate that about 10% of children are positive at this age. These children are given a routine X-ray to ensure that no active pulmonary tuberculosis is present, and very few children have the disease.

Antibiotics. A cure for people already affected by TB did not come until 1943 when the antibiotic streptomycin was discovered. The number of cases started to fall more rapidly after this (fig 15.5) and continued to decline up to the mid-1980s, aided by the introduction of further antibiotics such as rifampicin, isoniazid and others. At that time in Western countries more than 80% of all active TB cases were of people over sixty years of age.

Resurgence of the disease

After 1980, the demographics of the disease shifted in that more and more young people between the ages of twenty five and thirty were developing the disease. Between 1980 and 1986 five different surveys in the USA showed a relationship between the rise of homelessness and surges of TB in young adult populations. It became clear by 1985 that new mutant strains of drug-resistant TB were also present in the population. In 1986 patients with strains of *Mycobacterium* resistant to both isoniazid and rifampicin numbered 0.5% of cases, by 1991 this had risen to 3% and to 6.9% in 1994. The main contributing factors were courses of treatment being too short to kill the bacteria and patients not completing the doses prescribed. The full course of treatment lasts 6–8 months and requires consumption of several tablets a day, every day. This gives a combination of at least three or four antibiotics to reduce the chance of a strain multiplying which is resistant to one of the antibiotics. The problem is made worse by the fact that the patient starts to feel well again after a few weeks. Supervision by health workers is difficult not only in developing countries, but also in large cities such as New York where many sufferers are homeless, and where TB has become a new epidemic.

From the beginning of the AIDS epidemic it was noted that HIV-positive members of the community developed a high rate of tuberculosis (section 15.3.4). Many developing countries took steps to heed a WHO warning regarding this relationship between HIV and TB. Doctors in the USA and most of Western Europe, however, took little notice of these facts for they tended to view the TB risk for HIV patients as a Third World problem. In Africa TB began to spread rapidly and HIV patients did not respond well to the two cheapest antituberculosis drugs, thiacetazone and streptomycin. By 1990 health experts in some African countries were predicting defeat in their efforts to control tuberculosis.

The new strains of drug-resistant bacteria spread rapidly and there were clear interconnections between these new strains and HIV. Patients with AIDS, with its immuno-deficiency, were very susceptible to infection, and death rates rose to 90–100% fatality. The percentage increases in TB for different European countries are shown in table 15.7. These are directly related to the increase in drug-resistant strains and HIV infection.

A report in 1996 on TB in Edinburgh during the period 1988–1992 showed the following:

4.1% increase in TB cases recorded among people over 65 years

12.6% increase in TB cases recorded in younger patients

In the elderly, most cases were the result of reactivation of TB caught in childhood or youth. The rise in both age groups was entirely due to the increased resistance to antibiotics of the tubercle bacilli.

Immigration is also associated with an increase in TB. For example areas in Britain with large immigrant populations have shown increases 25% higher than in the indigenous residents.

The World Health Organisation has started to achieve a more successful treatment of TB with its DOTS campaign (directly observed treatment under supervision). The patient is given pills under supervision and watched each time to check the pills are swallowed. This is done over a period of 6 to 8 months and results in a cure of over 85% of cases.

15.3.3　Malaria

Malaria has been one of the world's worst killer diseases throughout recorded human history. Despite attempts to eradicate it, it remains one of the worst diseases in terms of deaths annually, and has actually increased in incidence since the 1970s. About 200 to 300 million new cases occur worldwide each year, and about 1.5 million deaths, over two-thirds of which occur in Africa. It is particularly common in Africa south of the Sahara, and is widespread throughout Asia and Latin America (fig 15.8). It used to be common in Europe and North America. (Oliver Cromwell died of malaria and Sir Walter Raleigh suffered from it.)

Table 15.7 Percentage increase in tuberculosis cases in some European countries during the period 1987–91. (From World Health Organisation, *Press Release June 17*, 1992.) The US reported a 12% increase from 1986–91.

Country	Time period	% increase in TB
Switzerland	1986–90	33
Denmark	1984–90	31
Italy	1988–90	28
Norway	1988–91	21
Ireland	1988–90	18
Austria	1988–90	17
Finland	1988–90	17
Netherlands	1987–90	9.5
Sweden	1988–90	4.6
United Kingdom	1987–90	2.0
France, Germany, Belgium	1987–91	stable

Malaria provides a good example of how social, economic and biological factors are all important in controlling disease.

Transmission, signs and symptoms

The causative agent of malaria is the protozoan parasite *Plasmodium*. Four species cause malaria, but most cases are caused by one of two species: *Plasmodium vivax* is found in the subtropics; *Plasmodium falciparum* is more common and more lethal, and is found in both the tropics and subtropics. It is the largest single cause of death in Africa.

Malaria is transmitted by female mosquitoes of the genus *Anopheles*. This mosquito is itself a parasite, the females visiting humans for occasional meals of blood. During feeding, infected mosquitoes pass on the malaria parasite from their salivary glands. The mosquito is described as a **vector**.

An immature form of *Plasmodium* (the sporozoite) is injected into the blood of humans by the mosquito. This form disappears from the bloodstream as it enters various cells of the body, particularly the liver. Here it multiplies to produce large numbers of a form (the merozoite) which can infect other liver cells. Finally it leaves the liver and enters red blood cells. Each parasite cell in a red blood cell undergoes further division. The red cell bursts and the released parasite cells can enter other red blood cells. As a result of this extensive division, millions of these parasites can be present in the blood. Some of the parasites transform into male and female forms of the parasite (gametocytes).

If infected red blood cells are now sucked up by a mosquito the parasites survive digestion in the stomach of the mosquito and transform into male and female gametes. Fertilisation occurs and the zygote penetrates the wall of the stomach where it grows to produce a swelling containing immature parasites.

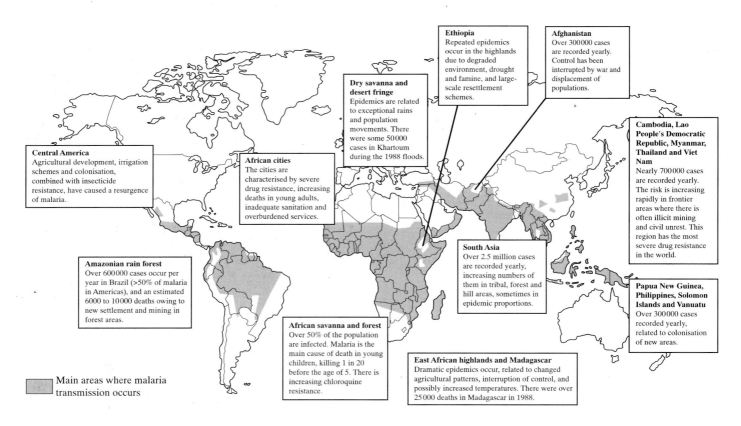

Fig 15.8 *Distribution of malaria worldwide. (Source: 'The Work of WHO' Biennial Report, 1992–93, fig 14.4, WHO, Geneva, (1994).)*

People who have been exposed to infection since birth and who have survived attacks of malaria develop a certain amount of tolerance to the disease. People with no history of previous infection will develop serious disease very rapidly. Ten days after infection a fever develops and the body temperature increases rapidly to 40.6–41.7 °C. The fever may last as long as 12 hours accompanied by headache, generalised aches and nausea. After the fever, sweating starts and then the temperature falls. The area of the abdomen over the spleen is tender.

The symptoms and fever coincide with the multiplication of the parasite when the red blood cells burst open and the parasites are released. The fevers occur every third day in *P. vivax* and *P. falciparum* malarias. The attacks can be complicated, however, as a result of successive infections by mosquitoes.

The infections by *P. falciparum* cause malignant malaria in which the fever is accompanied by other complications. The parasite tends to accumulate in blood vessels in the brain, causing convulsions or coma. Other common complications include kidney failure and pneumonia. Malaria caused by *P. falciparum* can be fatal within two or three days.

Prevention and treatment

Prophylaxis, that is the use of medicines (drugs) to prevent disease, can be used by people entering areas endemic for malaria. The usually accepted prevention is chloroquine or mefloquine which is taken weekly before and during a visit to endemic areas. The dose must also be taken for six weeks after leaving the area. Other synthetic drugs are proguanil hydrochloride and pyrimethamine. The effectiveness of these drugs has declined as the parasite developed resistance. *P. falciparum* is now resistant in most areas where malaria is endemic, such as Latin America, East Africa and S.E. Asia. New drugs are constantly being sought, but pharmaceuticals companies are tending to scale down work on antimalarial drugs because there is little profit to be made from developing countries.

A drug called Fansidar and another called Lariam (mefloquine) are effective against chloroquine-resistant *Plasmodium*. Mefloquine can cause unpleasant side effects such as nausea, dizziness, diarrhoea, vomiting, headache, abdominal pain and occasionally psychiatric disturbance. It was introduced in 1985 but already half the malaria cases in Thailand are resistant to it. A traditional drug, quinine, has come back into favour, but resistance is also growing to this.

Together with the use of drugs, other measures such as clothing (long sleeves and trousers) and mosquito nets at night should be used in mosquito areas (Fig 15.9). These are now often impregnated with new insecticides.

It may be necessary to administer drugs by injection. This then produces a high concentration of the chosen drug to kill the malaria organisms in the blood.

Eradication of malaria

In 1955 the World Health Organisation launched a programme designed to eradicate malaria from the world. Large sums of money were devoted to this project and the methods employed were as follows.

- **Drainage of stagnant water.** The larval stages of the mosquito live in stagnant water, so drainage removes breeding sites. This has had some success. However, the process is expensive and incomplete because rural populations must ensure that ponds, small ditches and even containers holding water are not allowed to provide breeding places for mosquitoes.

- **Destruction of the breeding stages of the mosquito.** The larvae and pupae of mosquitoes obtain their oxygen by means of small tubes which are pushed through the water surface film. Thus any method of blocking these tubes will result in the death of the intermediate life stages of the mosquito. The simplest method is a thin layer of oil spread over the water surface to block the breathing tubes. Petroleum oil sprayed from back packs is used. This method was used effectively in Brazil in 1938 and eliminated *Anopheles gambiae* by 1940.

- **Destruction of the adult mosquitoes.** This is aimed at killing the mosquitoes that enter houses. Thus the indoor surfaces are sprayed with a persistent insecticide. If dwellings are sprayed for three years, the cycle of man–mosquito–man can be disrupted because *P. vivax* and *P. falciparum* eventually die out in infected patients.

Fig 15.9 *This boy is sleeping under a mosquito net which has been sprayed with insecticide as a protective measure against mosquito bites.*

Such a programme requires tremendous resources in effort and money. In spite of this, very great efforts have eliminated malaria in many areas such as Chile, Europe (e.g. Cyprus, France, Italy, Netherlands), parts of Asia (e.g. Singapore) and N. America. In Africa it is still an important part of the public health programme, but the complete eradication of malaria in the world is still a very distant prospect.

Many factors work against anti-malaria programmes. For example, national boundaries are not barriers to mosquitoes and malaria can travel widely and rapidly. Political and financial difficulties in neighbouring countries, particularly in times of war, make it difficult to sustain a programme of preventive measures. In addition, migration of people into an area, for example looking for work or clearing and developing new land, can result in rapid infection of people not previously exposed to the disease and local epidemics (fig 15.8). This has happened as a result of the exploitation of the Amazon rainforest and in other areas including Madagascar, Ethiopia and Sri Lanka.

Another problem is that mosquitoes have become resistant to pesticides. In 1951 the first DDT-resistant strains of mosquitoes were reported from Greece, Panama and the USA. In many parts of the world spraying no longer prevents transmission of malaria. In addition, the passage of persistent insecticides such as DDT and dieldrin through the food chain became an increasing problem because birds and mammals at the top of the chain were found to have increasing amounts of the insecticides in their bodies (chapter 10). These effects have been found both on land and in the seas. DDT breaks down very slowly in soils and marshes and may be detected up to 30 years after spraying. Thus spraying with DDT and dieldrin has been suspended in many places.

Control of malaria has also been made more difficult because there is an enormous reservoir of the disease in monkeys, birds, rodents and reptiles which are also affected by it.

As a result of all these problems in trying to eradicate malaria, in 1969 WHO gave up the aim of trying to eradicate it and settled instead for a 'control' policy.

Vaccination. In the 1980s and 1990s there was a shift in emphasis to development of a vaccine against malaria. So far, despite intensive efforts, it has proved impossible, although it is a top priority of malaria research. It must be cheap as well as effective if it is to be afforded by developing countries.

The parasite is only vulnerable to attack by antibodies when not inside liver cells or red blood cells. Attempts have been made to develop vaccines against these vulnerable stages using dead or attenuated parasites, but without success. One possible reason is that the antigens of the parasite may change over time, so that antibodies against the original antigens fail to recognise the new antigens. There are also many different existing strains of malaria as well as different species. Genetic engineering to produce large quantities of relevant antigens has been attempted, as

well as other approaches. Mapping of the parasite's genes is underway with the 'Malaria Genome Project'. Work is also in progress on human genes responsible for the variable resistance shown to malaria.

A synthetic protein vaccine developed in Colombia started trials in Africa in 1994. It has been shown to be safe and to trigger a strong immune response. Trials are due to be completed in 1998.

15.3.4 AIDS – Acquired Immune Deficiency Syndrome

AIDS is thought to have originated in Central Africa. The HIV virus which causes it then appears to have migrated via Haiti to the USA, and has subsequently been identified in 71 other countries throughout the world. By late 1993 it had infected an estimated 14 million people, with over 3 million estimated cases of AIDS. By late 1995 an estimated 23 million people were infected (fig 15.10), and there were an estimated 3.1 million new infections and 1.5 million deaths. Half the new infections were of women and the majority were aged under 25. By the year 2000, around 40 million people may be infected by HIV. Fig 15.10 shows that the greatest problem is in sub-Saharan Africa, and this is where the greatest increases are being observed. The disease is also spreading rapidly in Asia (notably India, China, Vietnam and Cambodia), Central and E. Europe and the former Soviet Union.

AIDS is a disorder which damages the human body's immune system. It is caused by the HIV virus (Human Immunodeficiency Virus). This is an RNA virus and its structure is shown in fig 2.21 (see also figs 2.23 and 2.24). The virus replicates inside the T4 lymphocytes or 'helper' cells (see section 14.9.2). Thus these cells can no longer 'help' or induce other T cells, called killer cells, to fight invaders. The body's immune system breaks down, leaving the patient exposed to a variety of diseases (see later). It is important to realise, however, that infection with the HIV virus does not necessarily result in AIDS. As with other diseases, some people remain symptomless and are therefore termed 'carriers'.

Transmission, signs and symptoms

The HIV virus can only survive in body fluids and is transmitted by blood or semen. In 90% of cases the transmission is achieved by sexual contact. People can contract the disease as follows.

- **Intimate sexual contact.** The disease was first associated with homosexual communities, notably in American cities such as San Francisco, Los Angeles and Miami where there were high levels of promiscuity amongst homosexuals. Since then it has become clear that transmission can also take place between heterosexuals. It passes from the infected partner to his/her unaffected partner through vaginal or anal intercourse, or oral sex. The risk becomes propor-

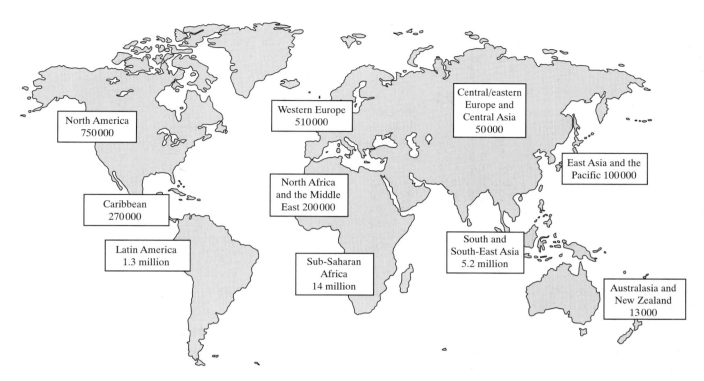

Fig 15.10 *Estimated total numbers of HIV infections in adults in different parts of the world, 1996. (Source: UNAIDS Geneva.)*

tionately greater amongst those who are promiscuous. In America and Europe the disease is still largely confined to homosexuals, but in Africa it is also present in the heterosexual community. There the most rapid spread is amongst prostitutes and this pattern may be occurring in the Western World. In October 1988 it was estimated that 50 000 people in the United Kingdom had the HIV virus in their blood and most of them were homosexuals (85%) who were expected to develop the fatal disease in the next 10–15 years.

- **Infected blood entering the bloodstream.** AIDS can be contracted by intravenous drug users practising self-injection by means of unsterilised needles and syringes. HIV has spread rapidly amongst intravenous drug users. Of the 250 000 heroin addicts in New York, it is officially estimated that 60% have already been infected by the virus. Once in the bloodstream of the drug addict, HIV can be passed on through sexual activity, to other drug users and to the general public.

Unfortunately the disease can be contracted after being given blood or blood products already infected with HIV. This has happened to some haemophiliacs who have been given factor VIII from infected blood. As a result of extensive screening programmes and other measures, which include heat treatment of blood products to inactivate the virus, the treatment of haemophilia has been prevented from being a means of HIV transmission in countries with adequate medical facilities.

Close contact between infected and non-infected people through cuts and open wounds has also been known to pass on the virus.

- **From mother to baby.** An infected pregnant woman can pass on the virus to her baby through the placenta, at birth or through breast milk during suckling. The chances of the infection being transmitted from the mother to her baby are currently estimated to be 25–50%.

The virus binds to receptors present in the surface of the T4 lymphocytes. From here it enters the lymphocytes by endocytosis or by fusing with the cell surface membrane and injecting its viral RNA directly into the cell (fig 2.23). The viral RNA is then copied into DNA by the activity of an enzyme called **reverse transcriptase** (section 2.4.5 and fig 2.23). The viral DNA enters the lymphocyte nucleus and becomes incorporated into the cell's own DNA. Thus it becomes a permanent part of the cells of an infected individual. Every time the human cell divides, so does the viral DNA, and thus spread of the viral genes is rapid.

The viral DNA may remain dormant for at least six years, the so-called **latency period**. However, suddenly, for some unknown reason, the lymphocyte begins to make copies of the viral genes in the form of messenger RNA. These then migrate from the nucleus into the lymphocyte cytoplasm and direct the synthesis of viral proteins and RNA. These assemble to form new HIV viruses which leave the lymphocyte by budding out from underneath the cell surface membrane (fig 2.24). The viruses spread and infect many other lymphocytes and brain cells. Eventually the cells in which the virus has multiplied are killed.

Current information suggests that 1–2% of HIV infected persons will develop AIDS each year, and that 5–10% of HIV infected persons will develop AIDS-related symptoms each year.

Four phases can be distinguished.

- During the first stage after infection the body produces HIV antibodies and there is a short flu-like illness. A skin rash is sometimes seen and there may be swollen lymph glands. Treatment of symptoms is possible and does not usually take place in hospital.

- The second phase is the antibody-positive phase (HIV-positive phase). It is the period between infection and the onset of clinical signs and may last from a few weeks to 13 or more years.

- The third phase is the **AIDS-related complex** (ARC) (fig 15.11). The individual may contract a variety of conditions. These are described as **opportunistic infections** and at this stage are not major, life-threatening infections. Common bacterial, viral and fungal infections occur and are often noted for their persistence and virulence. Oral and genital herpes or athlete's foot are common examples. If a person 'goes into' ARC the duration of this type of infection is lengthened, compared with that in a normal healthy person. Loss of weight may be seen at this stage (up to 10% body mass). A significant drop occurs in the number of T helper cells.

Appropriate nursing is required since this stage is the first real onset of the disease after diagnosis. An individual will have been dreading this development and often consider themselves in imminent danger of death.

- The fourth phase is noted for opportunistic infections, disease of body organs and the development of secondary cancers. HIV wasting syndrome is a condition which has been increasingly recognised in Africa where AIDS is called the 'slim disease'. In the West it is also recognised that some individuals become extremely ill, losing a great deal of weight. This causes weakness and loss of function without having one of the 'listed' conditions. This wasting may be due to cancer in the gut causing the patient to be starved of nutrients. It may also be caused by the body changing from normal anabolism to a catabolic crisis in which the body is 'burnt up' at a dangerous rate. Opportunistic infections occur which may be protozoal, viral, bacterial or fungal (table 15.8).

Test for the disease

A blood test is used to tell whether or not a person has been infected by the HIV virus. Under normal circumstances the immune system reacts to infection by producing antibodies, and when the HIV virus enters the body, anti-HIV antibodies are produced. The blood of the person being tested is added to HIV proteins which have been commercially prepared. If there are anti-HIV antibodies in the blood sample they will bind to the viral proteins and the person is then described as HIV positive. However, if the test proves negative that person may still be infected. This is because it takes up to three months or longer for HIV antibodies to be produced after infection.

Treatment and prevention

AIDS is caused by a virus and while bacteria can be controlled by antibiotics, these are not effective against viruses. Most treatments are therefore limited to relieving symptoms.

Present research on treatment and prevention is concentrating on three areas:

(1) restoring or improving the damaged immune system of victims.
(2) developing drugs that will stop the growth of the virus and also treat the other infections and symptoms that result from HIV infection.
(3) developing a vaccine against the virus.

These three methods are considered below.

Restoring the immune system. The strengthening of the immune system seems a logical step to take to help the body cells to combat the virus. Suppressor T-cells in cultures appear to be able to control the HIV virus. There are also individuals infected with the HIV virus who have no sign of the disease, nor any trace of the virus in the blood. They have in fact shown some

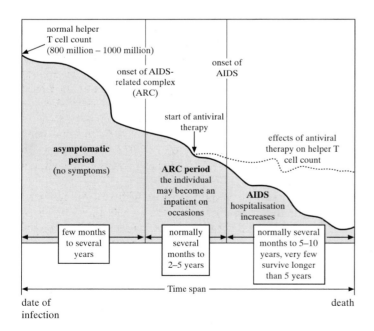

Fig 15.11 *Diagrammatic representation of the progress of HIV-related illness. Many people die when they get the first major opportunistic infection (onset of AIDS). It is very difficult to state when a person is going into the terminal stages of the disease. Many people make remarkable recoveries over a period of months or years.*

Table 15.8 Secondary infections associated with HIV infection.

Type of infection and cause	Signs and symptoms
Protozoal infections	
Pneumonia caused by *Pneumocystis carinii* (PCP or pneumocystosis)	About 60% of individuals contract pneumocystosis as the first AIDS-related infection and it is the most common cause of death in AIDS. Normally the immune system would keep this infection at bay, but in HIV patients life-threatening pneumonia develops. Treatment is by the drug co-trimoxazole.
Cryptosporidiosis caused by a small protozoan in the water supply	In patients whose immune system is damaged the population of protozoa in the gut rises to high levels and causes diarrhoea. There is great loss of fluid and intravenous fluid replacement is needed.
Toxoplasmosis caused by a protozoan (often associated with cats and raw meat)	Infection can cause lesions in the cerebrum of the brain. The patient lapses into paralysis and unconsciousness.
Viral infections (only most common shown)	
Herpes simplex virus	Also associated with ARC
Cytomegalovirus (CMV)	In HIV-related illness causes retinitis when the patient may rapidly become blind.
Bacterial infections	
Tuberculosis (TB)	See section 15.3.2
Salmonellosis	This infection is commonly associated with food poisoning, and is particularly dangerous to AIDS patients who should avoid undercooked foods, particularly eggs and poultry. (See section 15.3.6).
Fungal infections Candidiasis	This is a virulent infection in AIDS patients, and may extend from the mouth down the alimentary tract. (See table 15.6).
Secondary cancers (neoplasms)	Kaposi's sarcoma (KS) A purplish skin cancer was one of the first manifestations of AIDS in the western world. Not seen in all patients, but when present can be extremely disfiguring, especially if on the face. May develop internally and cause obstructions in the gut.
Non-Hodgkin's lymphomas	Seen in much higher numbers among patients with AIDS. Found in the central nervous system, the bone marrow and the gut. Often rapidly fatal.

improvement in their immune systems. In 1987 an experiment showed that blood samples from three individuals with antibodies to the virus in their blood, but no detectable virus, when taken and treated by removing T-suppressor cells began to grow the virus. When the cells were put back into the blood samples the virus was again suppressed. This showed that infection by the virus does not necessarily mean the disease will develop, and that AIDS is an opportunistic infection, causing disease only in someone whose immune system has been severely weakened.

Bone marrow transplants are a proven technique for the treatment of a form of cancer called leukaemia, the success of which depends on the genetic closeness of the donor and the recipient, with ideally identical twins or siblings being used. In theory a similar procedure should be applicable to AIDS patients and should provide the body with an immediate source of immune cells. Unfortunately to date there has been only one notable success using a combination of bone marrow transplant (from an identical twin), antiviral drugs and transfusions of lymphocyte blood cells.

Another line of attack is to use protein substances known as **lymphokines** (from lymphocytes and Greek *kinen* 'to move'). These are produced in small amounts by lymphocytes and move from cell to cell carrying a message through the immune system. The system can then deal with a threat from cancer cells or viruses. The best known is **interferon**, which can be produced by genetic engineering, and is now approved for use against cancer. A specific type of interferon called alpha-interferon has shown some success in causing the regression of Kaposi's sarcoma (a skin cancer associated with AIDS). Interleukin is another immune system activator which has shown some success against Kaposi's sarcoma.

Development of drugs.

- **Azidothymidine** (AZT) has received most attention in the media. Since 1986 there have been numerous trials with modest success and certainly life has been prolonged in a proportion of patients. It does have side-effects such as anaemia (requiring frequent blood transfusions) and there is the problem of supply in relation to an overwhelming demand from patients.
- **Zalcitabine** is a sister compound of AZT that has been shown to block replication of the HIV virus in laboratory cultures. Unfortunately trials have shown the drug to be highly toxic in humans.
- **Glycyrrhizin** is a component of licorice and has been used to treat hepatitis and various allergies. Japanese researchers have shown it to be capable of halting the growth of the HIV virus. No clinical trials have yet been conducted.
- **Ribavirin** has been used against influenza and other viruses in many countries, and against more viruses and in more animals than any other agent. In laboratory studies it has been found to inhibit replication of the AIDS virus and increase the number of T4 cells without damaging the infected cells.

There are a number of other drugs that are being developed and tested. However, in all the work on drug testing a very difficult issue is whether the use of a **placebo** (a comparable drug of useless effect) in drug trials for so lethal a disease as AIDS is proper. Should every AIDS patient who wants an experimental drug get it, even if it has not been proven in long-term trials? AIDS patients who are clamouring for a cure and have nothing to lose, argue that it is immoral and unfair to deny them such medication on demand. In terms of proper research and testing, however, scientists say that there is no other way than to give placebos to some patients and the real drug to the rest. Another factor is that of expense. Millions of pounds would be used up supplying a drug that may not work and in any case would never be useful for the majority of people.

Vaccine. In order to protect people not yet exposed to HIV the ideal solution would be to develop a vaccine. The most difficult part will be to overcome the ability of the virus to change its genetic structure and so alter the proteins on the surface of the virus which the antibodies recognise. Another problem in vaccine production is the matter of safety. Antiviral vaccines are generally made up of live viruses that have been attenuated (weakened), enabling them to protect against, but not cause a disease e.g. vaccines for measles, polio and rubella.

Researchers all over the world are striving to produce an effective vaccine, but as yet no product has been made ready for human trials. The best that vaccine researchers have been able to test so far, in laboratory animals, are a variety of protein antigens from the AIDS virus.

Simply developing a vaccine, even if it were possible, does not end the story, for how to test it safely and prove its effectiveness are formidable obstacles. Furthermore other difficult questions would be who gets it, and at what age? Should vaccination be a condition for employment, marriage, travel, insurance policies? Should it be voluntary or compulsory for high risk groups only, or for the general population? Should young people be allowed vaccination without parental approval? Should vaccination have to be revealed if so requested?

There are other obvious precautions which can be followed in trying to prevent the disease.

- The use of a barrier during intercourse can prevent the virus from infecting through blood or semen. Thus the use of a sheath or condom is recommended. This practice has been encouraged through many advertising campaigns throughout the world. There is evidence that this advice is beginning to be understood and used.
- Restriction to one sexual partner and the absence of promiscuity will also clearly reduce the risk of infection.
- A reduction in the spread of HIV can be brought about by the use of clean needles and syringes by drug addicts. Some health authorities in European countries, such as the Netherlands, provide free sterile needles and syringes for drug users.
- Since October 1985 all blood donated in Britain has been tested for the presence of antibodies to HIV which indicates whether or not the donor is infected. Blood containing these antibodies is not used.

- Education about the disease has an important part to play, particularly in reassuring the public about the real risks. There is no evidence that infection can occur by droplet infection through the nose or mouth, or by casual contact such as shaking hands. Healthcare staff who tend AIDS patients have never contracted the disease in this way.

15.3.5 Typhoid and paratyphoid fevers (*Salmonella typhi* and *S. paratyphi*)

Typhoid has been a great scourge of humans. It has typically been a disease of armies and over-crowded communities and is therefore associated with poverty, starvation and war. Before 1875 typhoid was a widespread disease in the UK, but the Public Health Act of that year brought about change. It led to improvements in sanitation and water supply both of which contributed to prevention of the spread of the disease.

In recent years some two hundred cases of typhoid have been notified to public health authorities in England and Wales, but most of these have been acquired abroad on holiday visits. Unfortunately, typhoid fever is always present in communities in the form of actual cases of the disease or in the form of carriers of the bacteria.

Typhoid and paratyphoid are caused by the bacteria *Salmonella typhi* and *Salmonella paratyphi* respectively. Paratyphoid is very similar to typhoid, but is usually milder in its symptoms.

Transmission, signs and symptoms

The bacteria are derived from the faeces of a sufferer from the disease or from a carrier. The disease is spread by water or from contaminated food. Typhoid spread needs only a small number of organisms, and is therefore described as having **high infectivity**. Paratyphoid, however, like food poisoning (salmonellosis) needs a larger dose of infecting organisms (**low infectivity**). Common sources of infection are listed below.

- Water supplies may be contaminated by human faeces through seepage of sewage into a reservoir, leakage from defective underground sewers or discharge of sewage into a river. Salmonella can live for about one week in sewage, or longer in water which has been diluted with sewage.
- Serious epidemics have also been traced to food. Milk can be contaminated by a carrier or from dirty equipment which has been washed with contaminated water. Outbreaks of typhoid in England, such as Epping, 1931 (260 cases, 8 deaths) and Bournemouth, 1938 (718 cases, 70 deaths) were caused by infected milk supplies. Aberdeen had an outbreak in 1964 caused by contaminated corned beef.
- Shellfish, oysters and mussels are often responsible for transmitting typhoid, due to their filter method of feeding whereby pathogenic organisms are extracted from the surrounding water.

When the infecting organisms have been swallowed they migrate to the lymph glands, where they multiply during a ten-day incubation period. After this time the organisms enter the bloodstream and the patient develops headache and muscular pains. A fever develops reaching its peak after about one week. A faint rash may appear. In the second week diarrhoea develops and the patient has mental confusion. The third week shows the peak of the illness and the patient deteriorates and may die. Other illnesses accompany these symptoms including bronchitis, pneumonia, meningitis and abscesses.

Since typhoid is a comparatively rare disease in the UK it may not be diagnosed readily. If there is a history of recent travel abroad, then any fever accompanied by other symptoms should be considered as a possible indication of typhoid. Blood samples will confirm, after culturing, the presence of antibodies against *S. typhi*.

Treatment and prevention

The disease had a 20% fatality rate before the use of antibiotics. Chloramphenicol and ampicillin are effective and reduce fatality rate to between 1 and 5%.

Any patient with typhoid requires the highest standards of nursing together with isolation and hygienic disposal of faeces. The two most important preventive measures are proper sewage treatment and purification of water supplies. Contamination of food can be reduced by personal hygiene, hygienic measures in the food trade and in the home, and control of flies, which can transfer faecal material to food (see also cholera, section 15.3.1).

Vaccination is effective by the injection of a suspension of the polysaccharide from the capsule of the bacteria. There is often a reaction to the injection with pain and swelling of the arm, and sometimes a fever. However, the vaccination is essential for travellers to parts of the world where sanitation is poor.

15.3.6   Salmonellosis – *Salmonella* and food poisoning

There are many cases of 'food poisoning' which develop within hours after infection. These illnesses are caused by salmonella organisms other than *S. typhi* or *S. paratyphi*, for example *Salmonella enteritidis*. They are referred to as **salmonellosis**. The economic and social costs of food poisoning can be very high. Salmonellosis in England and Wales was estimated to cost between £231 and £331 million in 1988 and 1989 in terms of lost production through sickness-related absence from work, investigation and treatment.

In contrast to typhoid, salmonellosis organisms have low infectivity, in other words large numbers of bacteria are required to cause infection. This is also in contrast to the high infectivity of *E. coli* 157, an increasingly important agent in food poisoning. Other bacteria may also cause food poisoning, for example *Listeria monocytogenes* which

is particularly associated with pâté and dairy products such as soft cheeses and causes **listeriosis**. *Staphylococcus aureus*, *Bacillus* and *Clostridium* species are also well-known causative agents which are beyond the scope of this book.

Salmonella enteritidis is particularly associated with eggs and meat from poultry. It was important in the rising incidence of salmonellosis from 1987 and accounted for 53% of salmonellosis in 1989 and 63% in 1991. At that time hen's eggs represented a newly recognised source of salmonellosis.

Fig 15.12 shows the number of cases in Britain of salmonellosis resulting from *Salmonella enteritidis* found in eggs. Despite environmental health regulations designed to eradicate the bacterium, the strain prevalent in poultry has increased since 1988.

Transmission, signs and symptoms

Salmonellosis is a classic foodborne disease. Table 15.9 shows the different types of food that were responsible for salmonella outbreaks during 1989–1991 and shows the

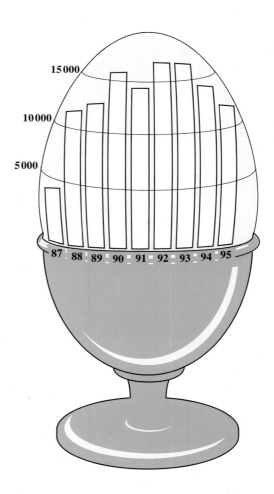

Fig 15.12 *Cases of food poisoning in Britain resulting from* Salmonella enteritidis *found in eggs, 1987–1995. (From* The Times, *23rd March 1996.)*

Table 15.9 Reported food sources in general outbreaks of salmonella infection 1989–91. (From *Communicable Disease Report* vol.3, Review no. 12, 5 Nov. 1993, Public Health Laboratories Service.)

Food	Number of outbreaks due to Salmonella enteritidis	Total number of salmonella outbreaks
chicken	16	23
turkey	5	21
beef	3	7
pork or ham	–	5
cold meats	2	7
other meats or pies	8	24
gravy or sauces	1	1
milk	–	3
other dairy products	–	1
eggs	45	50
vegetables or spices	–	1
bakery products	3	7
sweets or puddings	20	21
mixed foods	42	47
other/not stated*	114	174
total	**259**	**392**

*includes 12 outbreaks where infection was presumed to have been contracted abroad

relative importance of *S. enteritidis*. Salmonellosis not only infects humans but also many food animals such as poultry, pigs and cattle from which humans can be directly infected. The faeces of rats, mice and domestic pets may also contaminate human food.

Signs and symptoms of salmonella food poisoning appear suddenly, within 12 to 24 hours after eating contaminated food. Vomiting and diarrhoea occur, accompanied by a fever with a high temperature. Abdominal pain or discomfort, and headache, usually occur. Most people recover within a few days.

Dehydration is a risk, and may lead to complications such as low blood pressure and kidney failure. These complications are responsible for most of the deaths that occur. The elderly and the young, particularly babies, are most at risk. Accurate diagnosis requires a culture of the faeces to isolate the organisms.

Treatment and prevention

The treatment is to replace fluid and salt loss and to use drugs. Antibiotics are effective against salmonella organisms, and include tetracyclines and ampicillin, but they do not shorten the course of acute diarrhoea. Recently drug-resistant strains of *Salmonella* have begun to appear.

There are several methods of prevention.

- **Carriers** Symptomless carriers of the disease can retain the organisms in the faeces for some time and present a problem in society. About 2–5 people per thousand of the general population are thought to be carriers. Known carriers and people who have suffered the disease are not allowed to work in the food industry until samples of their faeces have been shown to be clear of the pathogenic organisms.
- **Hygiene in the home and food trade** Storage, preparation and cooking of food should all be carried out hygienically. Food should be stored cool or refrigerated to minimise bacterial growth. Great care should be taken in kitchens to separate the different preparatory processes, so that raw meat, particularly poultry and eggs do not cross-contaminate other foodstuffs. Cutting boards, dish cloths, dirty kitchen utensils and unwashed hands can all harbour salmonella and bring about transfer from food to food and place to place. Environmental Health Officers regularly inspect restaurants, shops and factories.
- **Thorough cooking** Cooking should be thorough enough to kill all bacteria. One of the greatest dangers is not thawing frozen food sufficiently. In addition, the Chief Medical Officer recommended in 1988 that raw eggs should be avoided and vulnerable groups such as the elderly, sick, babies and pregnant women should consume only eggs which have been cooked until the white and yolk are solid.
- **Meat inspection** by Environmental Health Officers is essential and any animals suffering from salmonellosis should not be used in the food industry. Low levels of salmonella contamination are regarded as inevitable amongst poultry, and only large outbreaks result in slaughter of the birds.
- Food poisoning is a **notifiable disease**. However, many mild cases go unreported. In 1995 food poisoning from all causes was at its highest level since records began in 1949: 80 000 cases were recorded in 1995 compared with 63 000 for 1992. Accurate monitoring of the incidence of food poisoning is essential in helping to decide what preventative measures to take.
- **Control of rodents** whose faeces may contain salmonella.
- **Proper sewage disposal** (see typhoid and cholera).
- **Control of flies** (see typhoid and cholera).
- **Government intervention** In 1989 the government took steps to control the rise in salmonella cases. Testing of poultry flocks became compulsory. More than three million infected laying hens were slaughtered and the Food Safety Act of 1990 raised standards in food production.

15.4 Disinfectants, sterilisation and antiseptics

As we have seen, microorganisms are extremely numerous and widespread and many have the ability to invade humans and other organisms and live parasitically and cause disease. It was not until their existence was established by Louis Pasteur in the nineteenth century that any effort could be directed to destroy them. Up to that time most surgical operations were followed by a period of pain and fever and diseases such as tetanus, septicaemia (blood poisoning) and gangrene. The deeper the surgeon operated into the body, the greater the risk of wound infection. Pasteur showed that microorganisms could be killed or removed by various techniques such as heat, chemicals or filtration.

Joseph Lister, who was appointed Professor of Surgery at the University of Glasgow in 1860, was greatly influenced by the findings of Pasteur and he began to develop chemical methods for the destruction of microorganisms. He began with carbolic acid (phenol) applied to surgical instruments, catgut used for sutures (stitches), ligatures and surgeons' hands to 'clean' whatever came in contact with the wounds of surgery (fig 15.13). He applied carbolic acid to the patient's skin before cutting and to wounds, and also sprayed the air of the operating theatre. His methods soon produced a reduction in infections following operations. The techniques that followed from his antiseptic work were designed to eliminate the microorganisms from the instruments and the body surface of the patient, rather than killing the organisms after they had been introduced.

Carbolic acid is an example of an antiseptic (see below). The concept of antisepsis was followed by asepsis or sterilisation. This involved sterilisation of the patient's skin before cutting and similar sterilisation of instruments, gowns, caps, masks, rubber gloves and catgut, in fact anything that came into contact with the patient during surgery.

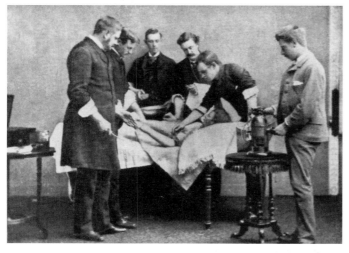

Fig 15.13 *Operation in Lister's day. The figure on the right holds a carbolic spray as pioneered by Lister.*

15.4.1 Antiseptics and disinfectants

Antiseptics and **disinfectants** are chemical substances that are used to destroy microorganisms in order to prevent infection. There are few that will destroy all microorganisms, but certain substances will destroy most of them.

The difference between an antiseptic and a disinfectant is that an antiseptic can be applied more or less safely directly to the human body, whereas disinfectants cannot. Antiseptics are used on living surfaces such as the skin. Disinfectants are used on substances such as working surfaces (kitchen tops, baths, sinks etc.), crockery, cutlery, operating theatres, drains, etc.

Antiseptics and disinfectants are generally prepared as liquids. Their effectiveness varies in that temperature, exposure time, concentration and the presence of organic matter can all limit their action.

The resistance of different microorganisms to given disinfectants or antiseptics varies considerably. For example the polio virus is very resistant, as is the tuberculosis bacterium (tubercle bacillus). Spore forms of bacteria and fungi are extremely resistant to changes in environmental conditions, so it is not surprising that they are also resistant to cold, chemical disinfectants.

There is a wide range of useful disinfectants.

- **Hypochlorites**, in the form of calcium hypochlorite and sodium hypochlorite, form hypochlorous acid and oxygen. The acid rapidly kills microorganisms. Domestos and Milton are commercial examples of this type of disinfectant.
- **Phenol** was one of the first disinfectants to be used by Lister although it is rarely used today. Phenol derivatives are used in combination with detergents for hospital cleaning purposes.
- The alcohols **ethanol** and **isopropanol** are often used as antiseptics, but they are also used as disinfectants for storing boiled syringes. 70% alcohol destroys tubercle bacilli and some viruses but not fungal or bacterial spores. The vapour is inflammable and so can be dangerous. The substances are also expensive.
- **Aldehydes**, in particular formaldehyde, can be used for disinfection and sterilisation of surfaces, but formaldehyde is too much of an irritant for skin use. Its power to destroy decay organisms led to its use as a preservative for dead organic material, although less harmful compounds are often used today.
- **Detergents** added to water increase the 'wettability' of the water and this helps to bring disinfectant molecules onto the surface. Additionally grease is removed and the cleansing action of the detergent removes bacteria and dust. Following with disinfectant allows greater penetration of the disinfectant.
- **Chlorxylenol** (marketed as Dettol) and iodine can be used as disinfectants as well as in more dilute form as antiseptics.

Useful antiseptics are shown in table 15.10.

15.4.2 Sterilisation

This process involves the removal of all life forms from any non-living object or material. Sterilisation is used in many ways to achieve an end result that cannot be obtained by disinfectants or antisepsis. For example liquids often require sterilisation, e.g. water for sterile processes, culture media for growing microorganisms. Solid materials such as instruments, clothing, even 'sterile' rooms and operating theatres all need to receive sterile treatment. There are a number of different methods which can be used.

- **Heat treatment** Usually heating in a dry oven or exposing to steam. Heat is one of the oldest ways of sterilising food in order to make it safe to eat. The amount of heat treatment that is used in commercial food processing depends on the kind of food and the microorganisms that may be found in the food. Only a very short time is required for 'pasteurising' milk

Table 15.10 Examples of antiseptics and their uses.

Antiseptic	Use
phenol (carbolic)	Used by Joseph Lister but is poisonous to humans and is no longer used as an antiseptic. Not as efficient as modern disinfectants.
chlorinated phenol derivatives, e.g. hexa-chlorophene, chlorxylenol ('Dettol')	Skin cleanser (about 100 times more effective than phenol). Not safe for babies. Hexachlorophene prepared in form of lotion or soap. Needs several days of washing with soap to be effective since the chemical accumulates in the skin. Widely used in soap by medical profession. Doctors, nurses and midwives use it for 'scrubbing up' before operations or the dressing of wounds and burns. Dettol can be used in preventing infection before and after childbirth. It has a powerful odour and therefore should not be used on cutlery and crockery.
soap	Skin. Not very powerful.
cetrimide – also a detergent (contains quaternary ammonium salts)	Cleaning minor wounds, and skin around major wounds. Virtually non-toxic to humans. Kills many bacteria as well as some fungi, e.g. *Candida* which causes thrush.
70% ethanol	Not a very good antiseptic but combines antiseptic properties with removal of grease and therefore good cleansing agent for skin.
iodine	Used as potassium iodide in 90% ethanol. Formerly used on wounds but can injure tissues. Still used on intact skin in preparation for surgery. Kills bacteria rapidly, including spores. Stains brown which limits its use.
hydrogen peroxide	An oxidising agent, decomposed by enzymes in blood to release oxygen. Can be used on skin or to clean wounds.
acridine dyes	Wounds
brilliant green, crystal violet	Ringworm

above 70 °C and thus eliminating the bacillus causing tuberculosis (section 15.3.2).

Tinned food is heat treated and may then be stored for long periods. To kill the spores of *Clostridium botulinum* (which causes botulism) requires some 200 minutes at 250 °C, compared with most bacterial spores which only require temperatures of around 120 °C and a much shorter treatment time.

- **Steam treatment** Using an autoclave, simply a steel chamber with a door for loading and unloading apparatus, cultures etc. Steam under pressure is fed into the chamber. The time of exposure to steam depends on the temperature and pressure in the autoclave. The temperature of 120 °C only requires about 12 minutes at a pressure of $150\,\mathrm{kN\,m^{-2}}$ for adequate sterilisation.

- **Radiation** Visible wavelengths have no effect on bacteria other than a warming effect. Shorter wavelengths, such as ultraviolet light, can result in death if the dosage is high enough. Most effective for this purpose are X-rays and γ (gamma) rays which can destroy microorganisms and so are useful for sterilisation. γ radiation from radio-isotopes allows simple and easily controlled sterilisation of disposable hypodermic syringes, scalpels, bandages etc. as well as some types of food.

15.4.3 Antibiotics

Antibiotics are chemicals produced by micro-organisms which are capable of destroying or inhibiting the growth of another microorganism (section 12.10.2). The microorganisms that produce antibiotics are mostly bacteria, but a few fungi also produce them. The definition of antibiotic has become looser with time. For example, as we have learned more about the chemical nature of antibiotics, scientists have begun to make more and more *synthetic* antibiotics. Also, chemicals which are active against microorganisms have been isolated from a variety of organisms such as plants, insects and amphibians. The treatment of disease with chemicals is called **chemotherapy**.

There are two types of antibiotic, biostatic and biocidal. **Biostatic** agents inhibit the growth and multiplication of susceptible microorganisms, e.g. chloramphenicol, erythromycin, sulphonamides and tetracyclines. The microorganisms can continue growth and multiplication if the agent is removed. **Biocidal** agents kill microorganisms, e.g. streptomycin, cephalosporins, penicillins and polymyxins. Biocidal antibiotics may become biostatic at lower concentrations. A biocide that kills bacteria is described as **bactericidal**. A biostat that acts on bacteria is described as **bacteriostatic**.

In 1928 Sir Alexander Fleming observed that a contaminating growth of fungus on an agar plate containing a growth of *Staphylococcus aureus* had apparently inhibited the growth of the bacteria. The commercial exploitation of this discovery was not achieved until 1941, when it played a considerable part in the Second World War in terms of the wounded and their infections (section 12.11.1).

The first bactericidal chemical (not strictly an antibiotic since it was synthetic) preceded the work of Fleming, because in 1935 it was announced in Germany that a red dye called prontosil could cure infections by certain bacteria (haemolytic streptococci). The active part of this dye was a substance called **sulphanilamide** and many derivatives of this compound, called **sulphonamides**, have been synthesised in succeeding years. They have been used in the treatment of bacterial infections such as streptococcal and some staphylococcal infections, meningitis, urinary infections and pneumonia. They also provided a means of combating sexually transmitted diseases such as gonorrhoea.

Sulphonamides are bacteriostatic drugs and therefore do not kill bacteria, but simply stop their growth and multiplication. They are competitive inhibitors of enzymes as described in section 4.4.1. The defence mechanisms of the body follow up the action of the drug and remove the bacteria. The bactericidal antibiotics that developed from Fleming's discovery are more powerful and rapid because they actively destroy bacteria. This action becomes extremely important in regions of the body where natural defence mechanisms are poor e.g. central nervous system and joint cavities.

Mechanism of action of antibiotics

Antibiotics are effective for a variety of reasons. Generally speaking they interfere with some aspect of metabolism of the microorganism which is not found in its host. Thus the microorganism suffers, but the host does not. Bacteria have a slightly different protein synthesising machinery and different cell walls to eukaryotes, and these are two obvious points of attack. Table 15.11 summarises some of the mechanisms by which antibiotics work.

Broad-spectrum antibiotics are effective against a broad range of different bacteria. For example, tetracyclines and chloramphenicols are highly active against almost all

Table 15.11 Most commonly used antibiotics.

Antibiotic	Targetted process	Original source	Mechanism of action and general points
penicillins cephalosporins	cell wall synthesis	*Penicillium notatum* (fungus) *Cephalosporin acremonium* (fungus)	In most Gram positive bacteria, inhibit formation of peptide links between molecules in cell wall. Wall bursts open (lysis). Effective only against growing bacteria. Widely used and well tolerated in the body, though some people are allergic.
vancomycin		*Streptomyces* (filamentous bacteria)	
rifampicin (synthetic form of rifamycin group)	transcription (RNA synthesis)	*Streptomyces*	Binds to RNA polymerase in bacteria but not mammals, prevents transcription.
streptomycin chloramphenicol erythromycin tetracyclines	translation (protein synthesis)	*Streptomyces*	Bind to bacterial (70S) ribosomes, not 80S eukaryote ribosomes. (Tetracycline can bind to 80S ribosomes but cannot enter mammalian cells.) Inhibit translation and protein synthesis. Streptomycin useful against *Staphylococcus aureus* (which causes spots and boils, blood poisoning or food poisoning, problems in hospitals especially drug-resistant form). Chloramphenicol only used for serious diseases, e.g. typhoid, or if no suitable alternative, as has serious and sometimes fatal effects on bone marrow. Erythromycin is useful alternative for patients allergic to penicillin.
anthracyclines	DNA replication		Anti-cancer drugs. Inhibit DNA synthesis in all cells but effect most marked in rapidly growing cancer cells.
amphotericin B nystatin	cell membrane function		Used mainly against fungi. Amphotericin binds to ergosterol (only found in fungal membranes) and distorts its shape, opening channels in membrane and affecting normal exchange of ions and molecules.
polymixin		*Bacillus polymixa*	Polymixin used against Gram negative bacteria, potentially dangerous to kidney and nervous system.
interferons	block protein synthesis and cell growth, only attach to cells infected by viruses, prevent modification of viruses inside cells	white blood cells	Active against viruses.

the common Gram positive and Gram negative pathogens. **Narrow-spectrum antibiotics** are effective against a narrow range of bacteria. Penicillins, for example, are ineffective against most Gram negative bacteria, which include some important pathogens such as the bacterium that causes tuberculosis.

Resistance

A major problem that is increasing is that many bacteria have been found to show resistance to antibiotics. The emergence of antibiotic-resistant bacteria is closely linked to the extent that antibiotics are used in humans and items of human diet. Resistant strains may appear rapidly or slowly, according to the amount or type of antibiotic used.

Resistance may occur through exclusion of the antibiotic. For example, Gram negative bacteria are naturally resistant to penicillins because their cell wall has a complex structure which excludes penicillins. In other cases entry of the antibiotic may be slowed down enough to enable the antibiotic to be broken down by enzymes as it arrives in the cell. A bacterium can achieve tetracycline resistance by making a protein which is inserted into the cell surface membrane and pumps out the antibiotic as soon as it enters.

Antibiotics may also be destroyed by enzymes inside the cells being targetted. A well-known and important example is the group of enzymes known as **penicillinases** which hydrolyses and destroys penicillins and cephalosporins. The bacterium therefore has resistance to these antibiotics. Some of the semi-synthetic penicillins are sufficiently different in structure to avoid hydrolysis.

Another problem is that, if the target of the antibiotic changes slightly, it may become inefficient. An example of this is resistance to streptomycin caused by a change in the structure of the ribosome, to which streptomycin normally binds. A change of only one amino acid in one of the ribosomal proteins as a result of random mutation can be sufficient.

An organism may acquire resistance in one of two ways:

- **Mutation** Spontaneous, random mutation can occur at any time. Microorganisms occur in such large numbers that there is a high chance of a resistant individual eventually appearing in the population. As soon as it does, use of the antibiotic to which it is resistant will give it a selective advantage over non-resistant types and it will multiply and eventually become the dominant type.

- **Transfer of resistance** Resistance can spread from one bacterium to another by transfer of the relevant genes. The most common mechanism is **conjugation**, a simple form of sexual reproduction described in section 2.3.3. The resistance genes are often on a plasmid (a small circular piece of DNA) which can replicate and send a copy into another bacterium by conjugation. Other methods of transferring genes also occur. Multiple resistance, that is resistance to two or more antibiotics, is commonly acquired using these methods

and this can also be transferred from one bacterial species to another. Multiple resistant *Staphylococcus aureus* (MRSA) is now a common problem in hospitals.

Antibiotics in human food

Concern has been growing about the use of antibiotics in farming. They have been used for the treatment of bovine mastitis or other infections in animals. Antibiotics are also used in feeding young farm stock to encourage growth, employed as food preservatives or to control disease in plants. As a consequence, these antibiotics occur as traces in human diets and then result in hazards to health. The hazards are direct toxic effects, hypersensitive reactions and the production of antibiotic resistance to pathogenic organisms transmissible to humans.

In order to ensure that there are no antibiotic residues in human food derived from animals, at least 48 hours should be allowed between last treatment and time of slaughter.

15.5 Cardiovascular disease

In the developed countries infectious diseases are no longer the major cause of death, as discussed in section 15.2. The average life expectancy is now about 76 years. As people age, however, they become prone to diseases of the heart and blood vessels, and cancers, and these two types of disease account for about two-thirds of all deaths in developed countries.

Cardiovascular disease (disease of the heart and blood vessels) is Britain's biggest killer, accounting for about 40% of all premature deaths. The two major cardiovascular diseases are **coronary heart disease**, which accounted for about 25% of all deaths in Britain in 1990 (30% for males and 23% for females), and **strokes**, responsible for about 10% of all deaths in Britain in 1990. Overall, this is between 300 and 400 people per day and represents about a five-fold increase since the Second World War. It is not surprising then that cardiovascular disease has been called the 'modern epidemic' as it is on a scale comparable to the major infectious diseases of the past.

Unfortunately Britain has one of the highest rates of cardiovascular disease in the world and in 1992 the Government set targets aimed at reducing its incidence (fig 15.14). The figures show targets for those aged under 65. Slightly less ambitious targets were set for the over-65s. The targets acknowledge the fact that, to a large extent, the deaths are avoidable and that it is important to understand their causes and to try to develop more effective strategies to reduce the numbers of deaths.

15.5.1 Atherosclerosis

By far the most common cause of cardiovascular disease is **atherosclerosis**. The process leading to atherosclerosis starts with the deposition of yellow fatty

streaks containing a high proportion of cholesterol in the inner coat of arteries. The deposits form beneath the lining known as the endothelium (fig 15.15). Later, fibres are deposited in the cholesterol and these often start to calcify and become hard, a process known as **arterio-sclerosis**. The deposits are referred to as **atheromatous plaques**. As a plaque increases in size it protrudes into the lumen of the artery and begins to block it. This commonly occurs in the aorta and coronary arteries which supply the muscle of the heart. If the plaque breaks through the smooth endothelium, its rough surface commonly causes a blood clot to develop. This is called a **thrombus** which may build up until it is large enough to block the artery. If the clot breaks away, it may block an artery at another location. A clot that breaks away like this is called an **embolus**.

The artery wall is made weaker by atheromatous plaques and may stretch as a result. Local stretching is called **aneurysm**. It may rupture, a process known as **haemorrhage**. This is more likely if arteriosclerosis has occurred. Once an artery is blocked, the tissue it supplies will suffer oxygen starvation and will be severely damaged or die. If thrombosis occurs in a coronary artery (**coronary thrombosis**), the heart is damaged and a 'heart attack' may occur. The medical term for a heart attack is **myocardial**

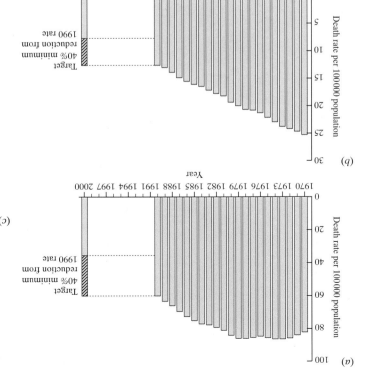

Fig 15.14 (a) Death rates for coronary heart disease in the UK for people aged under 65 and health target for the year 2000. (b) Death rates for stroke in the UK for people aged under 65 and health target for the year 2000. (From *The Health of the Nation (1992) HMSO.*)

infarction. (Myocardial refers to heart muscle; infarction means suffocation due to lack of oxygen.) If thrombosis occurs in the brain (**cerebral thrombosis**) a stroke may occur. Strokes are sometimes referred to as **cerebro-vascular accidents**. They are also caused by cerebral haemorrhage. They usually result in permanent damage to the cerebral hemispheres due to oxygen starvation. The cerebral hemispheres are the conscious part of the brain and control many functions such as speech and motor coordination (section 17.2.4). Both heart attacks and strokes may result in death.

A muscle that is exercised without an adequate blood supply will give rise to pain as a result of cramp. When the heart is involved, such pain is called **angina**. An angina attack may be brought on even by gentle exercise such as climbing stairs. The pain may spread out from the centre of the chest to the neck, jaws, arms and back.

Thus coronary heart disease has two main forms, angina and myocardial infarction (heart attack). A heart attack may be caused by a coronary thrombosis or simply by narrowing of the artery by atherosclerosis until the blood supply is sufficiently restricted. About half-a-million people a year in Britain have heart attacks and about one-third die as a result. Half of these die within one hour. There are now great efforts taken to try to avoid these deaths by carrying special equipment in ambulances and by suitable treatment

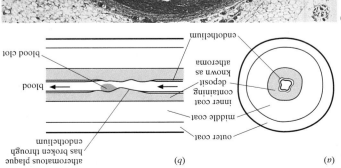

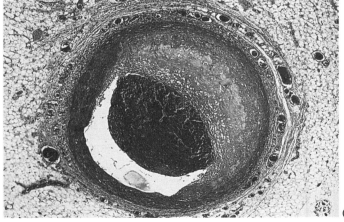

Fig 15.15 Narrowing of arteries caused by atherosclerosis. (a) TS artery narrowed by atheroma. (b) LS narrowed artery with blood clot forming. (c) Section through human coronary artery showing almost total obstruction by a haemorrhage developing into an atheromatous plaque. This obstruction of the coronary artery led to a heart attack.

in hospital casualty units. Drugs can be used to restore normal heart rhythms and a heart which has stopped beating can sometimes be restarted by administration of an electrical shock across the chest wall.

15.5.2 Possible causes of and methods for reducing atherosclerosis and cardiovascular disease

A number of factors are known or believed to be involved in development of atherosclerosis, and hence cardiovascular disease. Some are more important than others and usually several act together to bring it about. The three most important are diet, hypertension (high blood pressure) and smoking.

Diet. Atheroma contains fats and cholesterol, and it has been shown clearly that experimental animals fed on a high fat diet develop diseased arteries. In countries such as Greece and Japan where the average diet is relatively low in fat, cardiovascular disease is much less common. The main problem is caused by saturated fats (section 8.7.7) which cause a rise in blood cholesterol levels. In 1992 the UK government recommended that the average percentage of food energy derived by the population from saturated fatty acids should be reduced from 17% (proportion in 1990) to no more than 11% by 2005 (a 35% reduction). A 12% reduction in total fat was also proposed (from about 40% to 35% of food energy). On the other hand, polyunsaturated fatty acids, found in unsaturated fats, are thought to help reduce cholesterol levels in blood and are therefore beneficial to health.

Hypertension (high blood pressure). Raised blood pressure can considerably increase the chances of developing cardiovascular disease. It has been shown that men under the age of 50 years with a blood pressure of 170/100 are twice as likely to die of coronary heart disease as men with normal blood pressure of about 120/80. High blood pressure itself is associated with a number of different factors, including stress, obesity, smoking, drinking excessive amounts of alcohol and lack of exercise. There is also a genetic predisposition in some people. Some of these factors can obviously be avoided by changes in lifestyle.

Drugs known as β-blockers can be used to reduce hypertension. The hormone adrenaline has an excitatory effect on the body (section 17.6.5). It binds to specific receptors known as α- and β-receptors in its target organs. β-blockers block the β-receptors, thus inhibiting the action of adrenaline and reducing heart rate. The same drugs are used to treat angina because they reduce the need for oxygen in the heart muscle.

Smoking. Heavy smokers are more likely to develop cardiovascular disease. For example, people under the age of 45 years who smoke more than 25 cigarettes a day are 15 times more likely to die of heart disease than non-smokers. Nearly 40% of cardiovascular deaths are due to smoking. Smoking increases atherosclerosis and decreases the ability to remove blood clots that build up at atheromatous plaques.

The effects of smoking are many and complex.

- Carbon monoxide and nicotine are both toxic to the endothelium, the thin lining of the blood vessels, damaging the lining and making penetration by fats and cholesterol easier.
- Carbon monoxide combines with haemoglobin and reduces oxygen transport by about 15% in smokers. Oxygen deficiency is a cause of angina and may induce a heart attack.
- Nicotine increases blood pressure, heart rate and constriction of blood vessels.
- Cigarette smokers produce more fibrinogen, the blood clotting protein, and reduced levels of the enzymes involved in removing blood clots.
- Smoking greatly stimulates the sticking of blood platelets to the surface of the endothelium and these are involved in blood clotting.
- Nicotine has a direct effect on raising blood fat levels.

Smoking is the largest single cause of premature death in Britain. More than one-third of the extra deaths caused by smoking are due to cardiovascular disease. The effects of smoking on the lungs are discussed in chapter 9.

Physical exercise. Many studies have shown that the more a person is physically active at work or during their leisure time, the less chance they have of suffering from cardiovascular disease. The effects of exercise on the cardiovascular system are described in section 14.7.

Gender. Death rates from cardiovascular disease in women are less than half those for men, and women rarely suffer from it before the menopause. There is a protective effect from the female sex hormones and a harmful effect from the male hormone testosterone. After the menopause women show an increase in blood fats and a sharp increase in rates of cardiovascular disease.

Lipids are insoluble in plasma and are therefore carried in a combined form with other molecules. In particular they are commonly combined with proteins to form spherical particles called lipoproteins. The size and density of these particles varies. Two common types are the low density and high density lipoproteins (LDLs and HDLs respectively). HDLs contain 21% cholesterol while LDLs contain 55% cholesterol. Generally speaking, the higher the amount of HDLs and the lower the amount of LDLs in the blood, the better for health. LDLs tend to stick to artery walls and unload their fats, contributing to atheroma. In males, HDL levels tend to drop at puberty and LDL levels gradually increase with age. This is thought to be due to testosterone. Oestrogen on the other hand increases HDLs and therefore tends to protect women between puberty and menopause. They still get heart disease but on average about 10 years later than men.

Heredity. If one parent suffered from premature coronary heart disease then the risk of a man suffering a myocardial infarction is doubled. If both parents suffered, the risk is increased by a factor of five. This indicates that there could be a genetic predisposition to heart disease. It is anticipated that the genes responsible will be identified fairly soon and tests may become available to identify those at risk.

Stress. There is great difficulty in defining stress and quantifying it. However, there is general agreement that psychological and emotional stress is often an important factor in triggering attacks of angina or even a myocardial infarction.

Age. Arteriosclerosis appears to be an inevitable consequence of ageing and this increases the risk of cardiovascular disease (section 15.7).

15.5.3   Treatment of cardiovascular disease

Pacemakers

When there are problems with regularity of heartbeat an artificial pacemaker can be used to gain control over the electrical activity of the heart. A pacemaker has two basic components, a pulse generator containing a power source and one or two pacing leads, each with an electrode on its tip.

Pacemaking can be temporary or permanent. When long-term control of the heart is required, a permanent pacemaker is implanted under the skin. The two most common modes of pacing are

- **demand** this detects the heart's own rhythms and stimulates depolarisation of the heart muscle, and therefore contraction, as necessary; and

- **fixed rate** this fires at a predetermined rate, irrespective of the heart's own activity.

The pacemaker is a small, metal unit weighing between 30 and 130 g (fig 15.16). It is powered by a lithium battery with a life-span of up to 15 years. It is implanted in the chest under local anaesthetic.

Heart transplant surgery

In cases of heart disease where all other treatments are inadequate or inappropriate, a heart transplant may be advised. The first heart transplant was carried out in 1967 in South Africa. At first, survival rates were low, but great improvements in drugs used to prevent rejection have resulted in the majority of transplant patients surviving more than five years. The operation itself is relatively simple, with life being sustained by a heart–lung machine during the operation. The difficult task is caring for the patient afterwards, and relatively few institutions are equipped to do this. Although a relatively common procedure, demand greatly exceeds the supply of donor hearts. Attempts to develop artificial hearts have not been

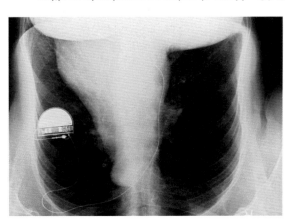

Fig 15.16   *X-ray showing pacemaker in position.*

successful. The latest proposal to meet the demand is to use hearts from pigs which have been genetically engineered to avoid the potential rejection problems. This not only raises animal rights issues but the possibility of transferring disease from one species to another. This is of serious concern, especially in the light of the transfer of BSE to humans from beef. Other ethical issues are raised by transplant surgery, particularly heart transplants. Choices have to be made about who to treat when there is a scarcity of organs. Should smokers be as entitled to treatment as non-smokers, for example? The high cost of transplant surgery also raises the question of how limited resources are best allocated within the National Health Service.

15.6   Cancer

Cancers caused about 25% of deaths in Britain in 1991 and are the most common cause of death after cardiovascular disease. This is typical of developed countries (section 15.2). Breast cancer is the most common cancer in women and lung cancer in men (table 15.12). Cancer is not a single disease; more than 200 types of cancer are known.

Cancers are a result of uncontrolled cell division. The type of nuclear division involved is mitosis. The problem is caused by mutations or abnormal activation of the genes which control cell division. When the genes are abnormal they are called **oncogenes** (*onkos* means tumour). About 100 of these have been discovered. A single faulty cell may divide to form a clone of identical cells. Eventually an irregular mass of relatively undifferentiated cells called a **tumour** is formed. Tumour cells (fig 15.17) can break away and spread to other parts of the body, particularly in the bloodstream or lymphatic system, causing **secondary tumours** or **metastasis**. This process is called **metastases.** Tumours that spread and eventually cause ill health and death are described as **malignant.** The majority of tumours, such as common warts, do not spread and are described as **benign.**

15.6.1 Causes of cancer

Changes in genes are called mutations and any factor bringing about a mutation is called a **mutagen**. An agent which causes cancer is called a **carcinogen**. Most mutated cells are either destroyed by the body's immune system or die with no ill-effect on the body. It is believed that development of a malignant cancer cell involves several steps and is usually caused by more than one factor operating over several years rather than a single factor. More than one mutation to the genes may occur. Up to 20% of the cancer worldwide may be caused by viruses.

Retroviruses. Evidence that cancers are genetic in origin was provided by work with retroviruses. Retroviruses are RNA viruses which, when they invade animal cells, use the enzyme reverse transcriptase (a viral coat protein) to make DNA copies of the viral RNA. The DNA is inserted into the host DNA where it may stay and be replicated for generations of cells. Some retroviruses are harmless. However, HIV is a harmful retrovirus and other retroviruses cause cancer. These contain a gene which alters host cell division genes, switching them on and causing the cell to become malignant. The genes become oncogenes. The advantage to the virus is that the cell makes many copies of itself and therefore of the virus.

DNA viruses. DNA viruses contain DNA as their hereditary material. Some contain their own oncogenes which can cause uncontrolled cell division of host cells. Examples which infect humans are the papilloma viruses which cause warts. Some papilloma viruses have been implicated in some forms of cervical cancer, making this a sexually transmitted disease. The Epstein–Barr virus may cause one form of Burkitt's lymphoma which is common in Africa.

Hereditary predisposition. About 5% of human cancers show a strong genetic predisposition, in other words they tend to run in families. More than 40 types of cancer, including cancer of the breast, ovary and colon, come into this category. The genes responsible may be oncogenes, or genes which lead to failure to kill cancer cells. In most cases other factors are required, but in a few cases, such as retinoblastoma, a single faulty gene is responsible. Retinoblastoma starts in the eye and spreads to the brain, causing death if untreated. It is caused by a dominant gene.

Two breast cancer genes have been identified and named BRCA1 and BRCA2. BRCA1 was cloned in 1994, and codes for a protein involved in transcription. A woman with one of these genes has about an 80% risk of developing breast cancer before the age of 70.

Ionising radiation. This includes X-rays, γ-rays and particles from the decay of radioactive elements. Cancers were caused in workers with X-rays at the beginning of the twentieth century and factory workers painting the dials of watches with a luminous paint containing radioactive radium and thorium. The radiation causes the formation of chemically active and damaging ions inside cells which can break DNA strands or cause mutations. The types of cancer linked with ionising radiation include skin cancer, bone marrow cancer, lung cancer and breast cancer. Medical and dental X-rays also expose patients to ionising radiation.

Ultraviolet light. This is the most common form of carcinogenic radiation and is non-ionising. DNA absorbs ultraviolet light and the energy is used in converting the bases into more reactive forms which react with surrounding molecules. Sunlight contains ultraviolet light and prolonged exposure to it can result in skin cancers, including melanoma which is highly malignant and commonly causes death through secondary brain

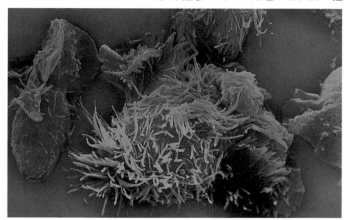

Fig 15.17 False colour SEM of human cancer cells. They are typically large in size and have a 'hairy' surface which is thought may increase mobility.

Table 15.12. The ten most common cancers in men and women in the UK. (From Cancer Research Campaign, Scientific Yearbook 1995–96.)

Men		Women	
Site in the body	% of all cancers	Site in the body	% of all cancers
Lung	21	Breast	19
Skin*	14	Skin*	11
Prostate	10	Lung	8
Bladder	6	Colon	6
Colon	6	Stomach	3
Stomach	5	Ovary	3
Rectum	5	Cervix	3
Lymph node**	3	Rectum	3
Oesophagus	2	Uterus	2
Pancreas	2	Bladder	2
Other cancers	26	Other cancers	40

*Non-melanoma, nearly always curable
**Non-Hodgkin's lymphoma

tumours. Depletion of the ozone layer results in a higher proportion of ultraviolet light reaching the Earth's surface. The brown skin pigment melanin offers some protection.

Radon gas. Radon gas is a natural source of radiation released from certain rocks such as granite. It may accumulate in houses in areas where these rocks are found. It has been linked to the development of leukaemia (cancer of white blood cells), lung, kidney and prostate cancers, although the evidence is inconclusive.

Chemical mutagens. Many chemicals are now recognised as causing cancer. The first example was described in 1775 as soot and coal tar, when chimney sweeps were discovered to develop cancer of the scrotum. Later mineral oils were also found to be carcinogenic, when shale oils were used as a lubricant in the cotton-spinning mills. The workers developed cancers of the abdominal wall where their clothes had been splashed. Workers in the synthetic dye industry in the late nineteenth century developed bladder cancer.

The list of chemical carcinogens has steadily lengthened over the last 90 years and now includes, in addition to the above, inorganic arsenic compounds which produce skin cancer and asbestos products which cause lung cancer. Some food additives (flavours, colourings and stabilisers) have been considered as possible carcinogens because they cause cancers in experimental animals. As a result a number have been withdrawn.

Tobacco smoke contains chemicals responsible for lung cancer (section 9.7). The most important of these are polycyclic hydrocarbons which are converted in the body to carcinogens. Many common foods contain carcinogenic chemicals (table 15.13) although the levels are mostly low.

15.6.2 Preventing and controlling cancer

There must be constant vigilance in the workplace regarding the possible dangers of exposure to carcinogens. The general public and workers should be made aware of any problems that may exist. Educational campaigns can encourage individuals to pay attention to early signs that may indicate the presence of cancer. Early diagnosis is important for increasing the chances of successful treatment.

Control should be considered as:

- prevention – protection against known carcinogens;
- early diagnosis – including screening programmes;
- treatment – urgent action once diagnosis is made.

Methods of prevention, diagnosis and treatment of cervical, breast and colon cancer are described below. Lung cancer is discussed in section 9.7.

Cervical cancer

England and Wales have one of the highest death rates from cervical cancer in the developed world (fig 15.18). Smoking

Table 15.13 Dietary carcinogens. (*From Molecular and Cell Biology*, Stephen L. Wolfe, Wadsworth, 1993).

Food	Active agent
alcohol	metabolised to acetaldehyde
basil	estragole
black pepper	safrole, piperine
celery, parsnips, parsley	furocoumarins
coffee, tea, chocolate	caffeine or theobromine*
common mushrooms	hydrazines
foods cooked in gas ovens	nitrosamines
grilled or barbecued beef, chicken, or pork	heterocyclic amines, nitropyrenes, nitrosamines
herbs, herbal teas	pyrrolizidine alkaloids
mould growth in peanut butter, grains, cheese, bread, fruits	aflatoxins and sterigmatocystin
mustard, mustard seed, horseradish	allylisothiocyanate
oil of sassafras	safrole
rhubarb	anthroquinone

*Not directly carcinogenic but promotes activity of carcinogen

doubles susceptibility to the disease. It is estimated that an effective screening programme should reduce deaths from the disease by over 80%. Deaths in England are falling gradually, but were still more than 1500 per year in the early 1990s. The Government's target is to reduce that by at least 20% by the year 2000.

The main method chosen to reduce the death rate was to set up an effective screening programme, because early diagnosis can be followed by effective treatment and cure. The screening test is known as the **cervical smear test** and was introduced in the 1960s. A national computerised system known as 'call and recall' was introduced in 1988. Women aged 20–64 are invited for cervical screening every 5 years. A few cells are gently scraped from the cervix and examined with a microscope for signs of abnormality which can lead to malignancy later (fig 15.19). Treatment at this stage is simple, free and can halt progress of the disease.

> **15.1** What information would you include in an education leaflet about cervical screening for the general public?

Breast cancer

Breast cancer is the commonest form of cancer among women in the developed world. Its incidence has increased slowly since the 1960s (table 15.12). It affects about one

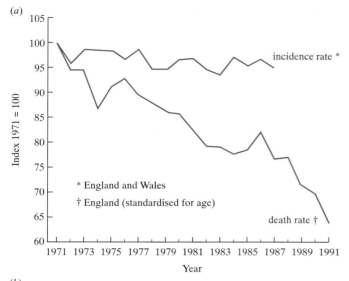

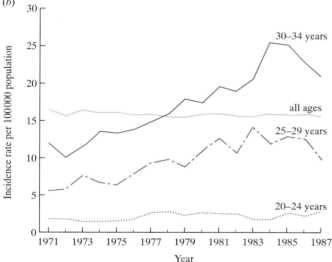

Fig 15.18 *(a) Incidence and death rates for cervical cancer from 1971–91. (b) Incidence rates for cervical cancer by age from 1971–87. (Source: OPCS (ICD 1 80), figs 3 and 4.)*

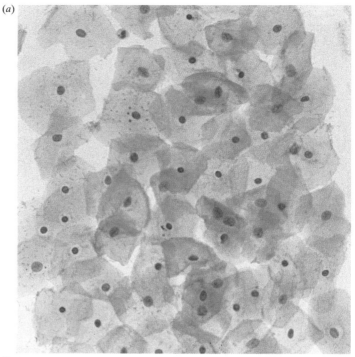

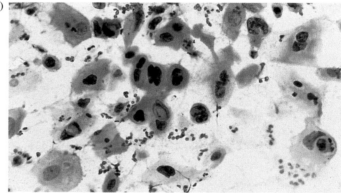

Fig 15.19 *Results of a cervical smear test. (a) Normal epithelial cells stained pink and blue. Note the small nuclei and large amounts of cytoplasm. (b) Malignant epithelial cells showing large, dark stained nuclei, indicating cell division, and very little cytoplasm.*

woman in twelve at some stage in their lives. In 1993 15 000 women died in England of breast cancer. About 90% were aged over 50. Once again, early diagnosis allows scope for effective treatment. A national breast cancer screening programme, using a computerised call and recall system, is used. Women aged 50–64 are invited to be screened every three years. Women of 65 or over may be screened on request. The screening technique is known as **mammography** and involves X-raying the breast (fig 15.20).

With both cervical and breast cancer screening, black and ethnic minority groups show a lower uptake of the service and attempts are being made by the UK Government to encourage more of these women to go for screening. The aim is to reduce deaths by 25% by the year 2000 compared with 1990, saving about 1250 lives per year.

Another method used for early diagnosis, which can be done by the woman herself, is to feel the breast for unusual lumps. Women can be educated for 'breast awareness' and should report any changes to their doctor without delay.

In 5% of cases of breast cancer there is a genetic predisposition. There is debate about the most appropriate response if genetic screening reveals a woman to be carrying the breast cancer genes BRCA1 or BRCA2. Trials with tamoxifen as a prophylactic (preventative measure) are underway and some at-risk women have opted to have their breasts removed surgically rather than risk developing the disease.

The main treatments for breast cancer are:

- surgery to remove the tumour;
- radiotherapy of the breast using X-rays to kill tumour cells;

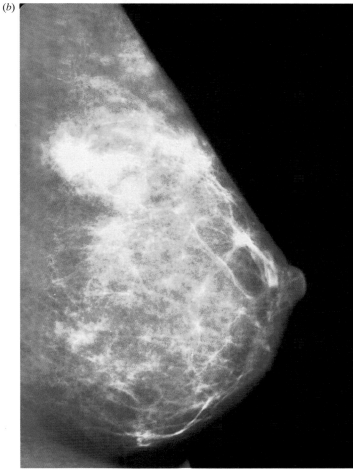

Fig 15.20 *(a) Woman undergoing mammography examination for the early detection of cancerous tumours in the breast. (b) Mammogram of breast in profile showing cancer tumours (bright areas).*

- chemotherapy of the whole body using chemicals which kill dividing cells (both normal and tumour cells);
- chemotherapy using tamoxifen, an anti-oestrogen hormone. Oestrogen can stimulate the growth of breast cancers, therefore growth can be controlled using tamoxifen.

The treatments may be used individually or in combination. The cancer may return some time after treatment. A woman whose breast cancer is diagnosed early has an 80% chance of surviving for 5 or more years after diagnosis.

Colon cancer

The colon is part of the large intestine. Cancer of the large intestine (bowel cancer) is the third most common form of cancer in Britain, accounting for about 14% of cancer deaths. About 1 person in 1200 is diagnosed each year. The condition may be symptomless in its early stages. Commonly though the tumour causes bleeding of the gut wall, leading to anaemia and traces of blood in the faeces. It may partially obstruct the colon affecting bowel movements, causing diarrhoea or constipation. Early diagnosis would therefore include being observant for these signs. The presence of the tumour can be revealed by means of a barium meal, which shows up an obstruction if the gut is X-rayed. Alternatively internal examination by endoscopy can be performed. The tumour can be removed surgically with an 80% chance of a complete cure if diagnosed early. The diseased section of bowel is removed and the two ends of the gut sewn together again.

There is growing evidence that diets relatively high in fat and meat may be associated with a higher occurrence of colon cancer, as well as some other forms of cancer. Reducing consumption of fatty foods and meat, and frequently eating fresh fruit and vegetables, and cereals with a high fibre content, can help to reduce the risk. There is also a genetic predisposition in some people. These people may be identifiable in future by genetic screening techniques and be able to take specific precautions, particularly regular check-ups. Early surgery to remove growths as they appear is relatively straightforward.

15.7   Ageing

After reaching maturity we enter a phase of gradual decline known as **ageing**. The body changes that lead to a decreasing life expectancy with age are known as **senescence**. Senescence is a characteristic of most living organisms. Despite advances in biology we still cannot fully explain the process, although there are many theories.

Humans have long cherished the idea that we may one day be able to prevent or slow down the process of ageing. But is death inevitable? To the biologist, ageing can be viewed as a kind of disease, a malfunctioning of the body systems. Biologists believe that they may be on the verge of being able to intervene in the human ageing process and the prospect of humans living for several hundred years is now being seriously considered. Needless to say, there would be many serious ethical arguments to resolve if this became possible.

Figs 15.21 and 15.22 summarise some of the changes associated with ageing.

15.7.1 Changes in the brain

Unlike most cells of the body, nerve cells either cannot regenerate themselves by dividing to replace dead cells, or do so very slowly. As a result, the number of nerve cells (neurones) in the brain declines with age. The average weight of the brain of a 90 year old is about 10% less than that of a 30 year old. In general, therefore, there is a decline in brain function with age. However, there is conflicting evidence about the degree and nature of decline in the absence of specific conditions such as Alzheimer's disease (see below). Intellectual skills and memory decline overall, but some types of problem solving which depend on experience or creative thinking may improve. Memory loss occurs, but this mainly affects rote learning and recall of specific facts, whereas recall of interconnected facts such as memory of current affairs or the plot of a novel may be unaffected. Accessing information rather than losing information from the brain seems to be the main problem. There is great individual variation.

Senile dementia

Dementia is mental deterioration as a result of physical changes within the brain. Certain intellectual functions, particularly memory, are progressively lost. **Senile dementia** is degeneration of brain cells as a result of the ageing process and typically occurs after the age of 65. Dementia before this age is sometimes referred to as presenile dementia.

Apart from the inability of neurones to replace themselves, another factor affecting the progress of senility is the supply of blood to the brain, which may be reduced as atherosclerosis or arteriosclerosis develops. A stroke or injury to the brain can cause dementia. Other possible causes of dementia-like symptoms are depression, chest infections, low blood sugar levels, hypothermia, alcohol abuse and hypothyroidism. It therefore has no single cause, and is simply the name given to a collection of symptoms rather than a single disease. Alzheimer's disease (see below) is by far the commonest cause of senile dementia, accounting for nearly 80% of cases. Creutzfeldt–Jakob disease ('mad cow disease') is another, rare, cause of dementia.

The earliest symptom of senile dementia is usually memory loss, particularly for recent events. Intellectual functions gradually decline, including understanding and powers of reasoning, resulting in confusion. The individual may lose concentration and interest in life generally and show lack of initiative. Personality may change. The person may often be irritable, emotionally unstable, with sudden extreme changes in mood, for example from tears to laughter. They may become embarrassingly uninhibited, abandon politeness, neglect personal hygiene or become antisocial. In the advanced stages, slowness, stiffness and awkwardness of movement can occur. Towards the end a person may cease to speak, think or move.

Risks increase with age. About 10% of over-65s suffer, and about 20% of over-80s.

Alzheimer's disease

Alzheimer's disease was first described by Alois Alzheimer in 1907. He examined brain tissue from patients dying with dementia. The tissue has a characteristic appearance under the microscope, with protein 'plaques' accumulating outside brain cells and tangled deposits of protein appearing inside the cells. Two key parts of the brain affected are the cortex of the cerebral hemispheres (the conscious part of the brain) and the hippocampus (involved with memory). Both plaques and tangles are caused by accumulation of abnormal proteins, amyloid β-protein in the case of plaques, and an abnormal form of tau protein which is overloaded with phosphate groups in the case of tangles. Normal tau protein is associated with microtubules in the elaborate cytoskeleton of neurones. The amyloid protein gene is found on chromosome 21 and the extra chromosome 21 in sufferers of Down's syndrome results in Alzheimer-like changes in their brains. The brains of Alzheimer's sufferers also shrink from loss of nerve cells (fig 15.23).

Alzheimer's disease is difficult to diagnose because its symptoms are similar to those of other diseases that cause dementia. It usually requires a post-mortem examination of brain tissue to confirm diagnosis. There is a genetic predisposition to the disease in some people, so it tends to run in families. There is also evidence that high levels of aluminium may contribute to the onset of the disease.

Nerve conduction velocity

Fig 15.22 shows a slight but steady decline in the speed of conduction of nerve impulses with age. Defects in synthesis of neurotransmitters may be one reason.

15.7.2 Changes in the locomotory system

The locomotory system includes joints, skeleton, muscles and tendons. Some of the changes in the system can be explained with reference to the fibrous protein collagen, a key constituent of bone and other connective tissues. Tendons are almost pure collagen. Muscle contains little collagen, but the amount increases with age as muscle fibres decline and are replaced by collagen (hence meat from older animals is tougher to eat). The structure of collagen also changes with age, with the fibres becoming thicker and less elastic. This would tend, for example, to make bone more brittle.

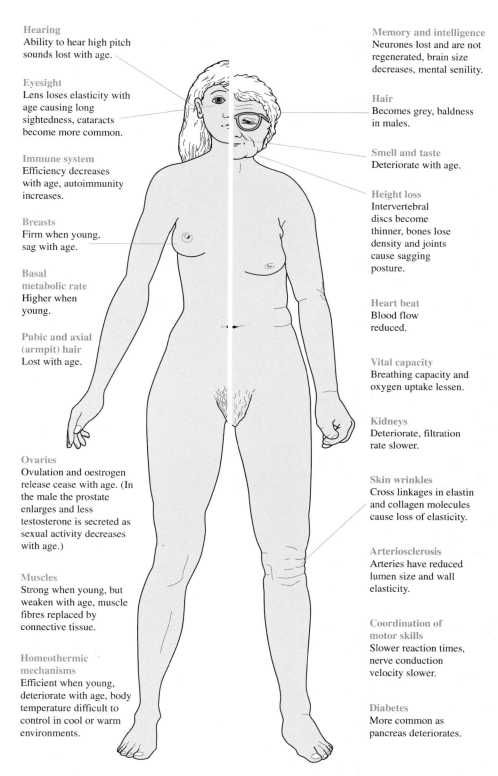

Hearing
Ability to hear high pitch sounds lost with age.

Eyesight
Lens loses elasticity with age causing long sightedness, cataracts become more common.

Immune system
Efficiency decreases with age, autoimmunity increases.

Breasts
Firm when young, sag with age.

Basal metabolic rate
Higher when young.

Pubic and axial (armpit) hair
Lost with age.

Ovaries
Ovulation and oestrogen release cease with age. (In the male the prostate enlarges and less testosterone is secreted as sexual activity decreases with age.)

Muscles
Strong when young, but weaken with age, muscle fibres replaced by connective tissue.

Homeothermic mechanisms
Efficient when young, deteriorate with age, body temperature difficult to control in cool or warm environments.

Memory and intelligence
Neurones lost and are not regenerated, brain size decreases, mental senility.

Hair
Becomes grey, baldness in males.

Smell and taste
Deteriorate with age.

Height loss
Intervertebral discs become thinner, bones lose density and joints cause sagging posture.

Heart beat
Blood flow reduced.

Vital capacity
Breathing capacity and oxygen uptake lessen.

Kidneys
Deteriorate, filtration rate slower.

Skin wrinkles
Cross linkages in elastin and collagen molecules cause loss of elasticity.

Arteriosclerosis
Arteries have reduced lumen size and wall elasticity.

Coordination of motor skills
Slower reaction times, nerve conduction velocity slower.

Diabetes
More common as pancreas deteriorates.

Fig 15.21 *Changes in the body that occur with ageing. (Based on fig 8.1, Philip Gadd (1983)* Individuals and populations, *Cambridge Social Biology Topics, CUP.)*

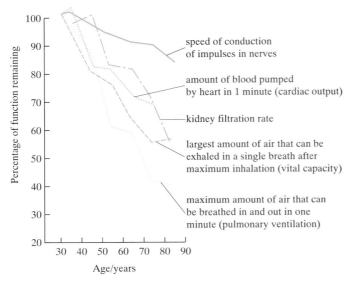

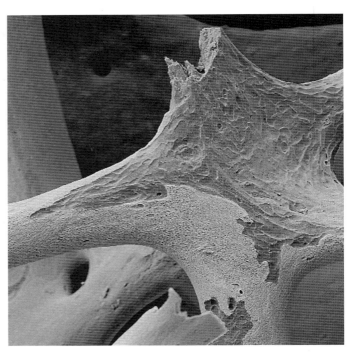

Fig 15.22 *Changes in the body with ageing. (From R. Passmore & J.S. Robson, A Companion to Medical Studies, vol 2, Blackwell Sci, 2nd ed., 1980.)*

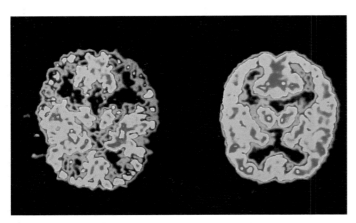

Fig 15.23 *Brain scans of (left) normal human brain and (right) brain of patient suffering from Alzheimer's disease. Areas of red and yellow show high brain activity, and blue and black show areas of low activity. The scan on the right shows reduction in function and blood flow in both sides of the brain which is often seen in Alzheimer's.*

Fig 15.24 *Scanning electron micrograph of the brittle and spongy fractured femur from a patient with osteoporosis. The dark areas show where bone mineral has been reabsorbed by the body, leaving the bone brittle and easy to fracture.*

Changes in bones

Bones become thinner, weaker and less flexible with ageing, partly because calcium starts to be lost faster than it is replaced from the age of about 35 years. This happens to everybody to some extent, but in some people it is particularly serious, leading to a condition known as **osteoporosis**.

Osteoporosis affects the whole skeleton but tends to affect the hips, wrists and vertebrae worst of all. Even a minor fall can result in broken bones. Apart from fractures, weakened bones in the spine result in compression of the bones and intervertebral discs and loss of height. The vertebrae may also collapse, causing curvature of the spine. Osteoporosis is most common in elderly women, affecting about 1 in 4 over the age of 60. Women are four times more vulnerable than men. This is because before menopause, which is the cessation of monthly periods, oestrogen helps to maintain bone strength. After menopause, levels of oestrogen decline. Oestrogen is antagonistic (has an opposite effect) to the hormone parathormone which stimulates the raising of blood calcium levels. Therefore in the absence of oestrogen, loss of calcium occurs from the bones, making the bones weaker and more easily fractured (fig 15.24).

Hormone replacement therapy (HRT) is recommended for most women after the menopause if they wish to avoid the problem. Oestrogen is taken either in pill form or by implants below the skin. It reduces the incidence of osteoporosis to the same level as in men. The undesirable side effects of long-term oestrogen treatment, such as an increased risk of blood clotting, can be reduced by adding progesterone to the oestrogen. A balanced diet rich in calcium, and regular exercise, also help to keep bones strong. Smoking and drinking alcohol increase the risk of osteoporosis.

Osteoporosis is an important disease in terms of the demands it makes on the health service. An estimated £640 million is spent each year in the UK on treating people with fractures, particularly hip fractures, due to osteoporosis. Only a quarter of those who break a hip stage a full recovery, and a quarter need to be placed permanently in nursing homes.

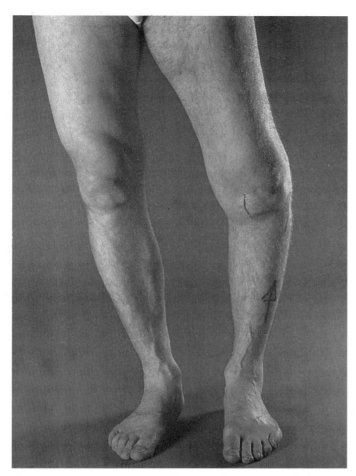

Fig 15.25 *A severe case of osteoarthrosis in the left knee of a man. The picture clearly shows the swelling and deformation of the joint which is associated with severe cases of the condition.*

Changes in joints and osteoarthrosis

The load-bearing joints such as the knees and hips are particularly subject to changes, as are the fingers. Joints in general tend to become stiffer and painful.

As ageing progresses, the smooth, tough cartilage which covers the ends of bones where they articulate with other bones becomes weaker and less extensive. It gradually breaks down. Eventually, in extreme cases, the ends of the bones may become exposed and start to grate against each other. They become thicker and denser and start to wear. This causes pain and stiffness, a condition which used to be known as **osteoarthritis** (fig 15.25). The more modern term is **osteoarthrosis**, because the term arthritis implies inflammation which does not occur.

A less frequent type of joint degeneration known as **rheumatoid arthritis** is commoner in older people than young people. It is an autoimmune disease, in which the body's immune system attacks its own tissues. Affected joints become hot and swollen during attacks. This is a genuine inflammatory response.

Changes in muscles

As a person gets older, muscle fibres tend to be replaced by connective tissue such as collagen, making the muscle weaker. This results in loss of body weight and body strength. Since the heart is a muscle it also becomes weaker.

15.7.3 Changes in the cardiovascular system

Fig 15.22 shows the decline with age in cardiac output (amount of blood pumped by the heart in one minute). By the age of 80 the cardiac output at rest has declined to about 70% of that of a 30-year old. Larger differences are noted after exercise. This could have effects on other body systems.

Two common causes of this decline are atherosclerosis and arteriosclerosis. Atherosclerosis (section 15.5.1) is not strictly speaking an inevitable consequence of ageing, although it takes many years to develop. Arteriosclerosis, however, does appear to be a consequence of ageing. It is commonly known as hardening of the arteries and is due to loss of elastic tissue in the artery walls as we age. Blood pressure rises as a result (hypertension), making haemorrhage (bursting of blood vessels) and thrombosis (blood clotting) more likely. The incidence of strokes is particularly associated with arteriosclerosis.

15.7.4 Changes in the respiratory system

Ageing is associated with a gradual loss of elastic tissue in the lungs and a decline in muscle power which affects the rate and extent of chest expansion. These and other degenerative changes bring about a decline in vital capacity and pulmonary ventilation (gas exchanged per minute) as shown in fig 15.22. This places limits on the amount of oxygen that can be made available to the body and hence the amount of work or exercise that can be carried out in a given time period.

15.8 Respiratory and genetic diseases

Respiratory disease (asthma, emphysema, bronchitis, lung cancer and the effects of smoking tobacco) is discussed in chapter 9. Genetic disease is discussed in chapter 25.

Chapter Sixteen

Coordination and control in plants

Plants, like animals, need some form of internal coordination if their growth and development is to proceed in an orderly fashion, with suitable response to their environment. Unlike animals, plants do not possess nervous systems and rely entirely on chemical coordination. Their responses are therefore slower and they often involve growth. Growth, in turn, can result in movement of an organ. In this chapter plant movements will be examined before studying the various ways in which plants coordinate their activities.

16.1 Plant movements

It is a characteristic of plants that they do not show locomotion (movement of the entire organism). However, movements of individual plant organs are possible and are modified by the sensitivity of the plant to external stimuli. Movements induced by external stimuli fall into two main categories: tropisms (tropic movements) and taxes (tactic movements).

> **16.1** What is the basic reason for the fact that animals show locomotion whereas plants do not?

16.1.1 Tropisms

A **tropism** is a movement of part of a plant in response to, and directed by, an external stimulus. The movement is almost always a growth movement. Tropic responses are described as positive or negative depending on whether growth is towards or away from the stimulus respectively. Some examples of tropisms are shown in table 16.1.

> **16.2** Complete a fourth column to table 16.1 to show for each response how it is advantageous to the plant involved.

Phototropism and geotropism will be discussed in more detail later in this chapter (sections 16.2.1 and 16.2.2).

Table 16.1 Examples of tropisms.

Stimulus	Type of tropism	Examples
light	phototropism	Shoots and coleoptiles positively phototropic. Some roots negatively phototropic, e.g. adventitious roots of climbers like ivy
gravity	geotropism	Shoots and coleoptiles negatively geotropic. Roots positively geotropic. Rhizomes, runners, dicotyledonous leaves **diageotropic***. Lateral roots, stem branches **plagiogeotropic***
chemical	chemotropism	Hyphae of some fungi positively chemotropic, e.g. *Mucor*. Pollen tubes positively chemotropic in response to chemical produced at micropyle of ovule
water	hydrotropism (special kind of chemotropism)	Roots and pollen tubes positively hydrotropic
solid surface or touch	haptotropism (thigmotropism)	Tendrils positively haptotropic, e.g. leaves of pea. Central tentacles of sundew, an insectivorous plant, positively haptotropic
air (oxygen)	aerotropism (special kind of chemotropism)	Pollen tubes negatively aerotropic

* diageotropism: growth at 90° to gravity, that is horizontal growth.
plagiogeotropism: growth at some other angle to gravity, that is not horizontal or directly towards or away from gravity.

16.1.2 Taxes

A **taxis** is a movement of an entire cell or organism (that is locomotion) in response to, and directed by, an external stimulus. As with tropisms they can be described as positive or negative, and can be further classified according to the nature of the stimulus. Note that this kind of movement occurs in a wide range of organisms, not just plants. Examples are given in table 16.2.

Table 16.2 Examples of taxes.

Stimulus	Taxis	Examples
light	phototaxis	**positive:** *Euglena*, a unicellular alga, swims towards light, chloroplasts move towards light, fruit flies fly towards light **negative:** earthworms, blowfly larvae, woodlice and cockroaches move away from light
chemical	chemotaxis	**positive:** sperms of liverworts, mosses and ferns swim towards substances released by the ovum; motile bacteria move towards various food substances **negative:** mosquitoes avoid insect repellent
air (oxygen)	aerotaxis (special kind of chemotaxis)	**positive:** motile aerobic bacteria move towards oxygen
gravity	geotaxis	**positive:** planula larvae of some cnidarians swim towards sea bed **negative:** ephyra larvae of some cnidarians swim away from sea bed
magnetic field	magnetotaxis	certain motile bacteria
resistance	rheotaxis	**positive:** *Planaria* move against water current, moths and butterflies fly into the wind

16.3 *Euglena* and *Chlamydomonas* are unicellular algae which swim by means of flagella. Both organisms are positively phototactic, meaning that they move towards light. This is an advantage since they are both photosynthetic. Design an experiment to demonstrate the preferred light intensity of *Euglena* or *Chlamydomonas* in phototaxis.

16.4 Fig 16.1 illustrates the distribution of motile bacteria 10 min after being placed under a cover-slip with a filament of a green alga, such as *Spirogyra*. (*a*) Put forward a hypothesis to account for the final distribution of the bacteria. (*b*) How could you check your hypothesis?

16.1.3 Kinesis

Another type of locomotory response is **kinesis**. Since this is virtually confined to the animal kingdom it is discussed in chapter 17 with animal behaviour.

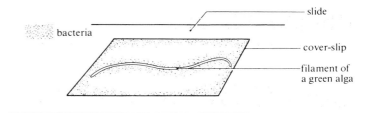

Fig 16.1 *Distribution of motile bacteria on a slide.*

16.2 Plant growth substances

Chemical coordination in animals is controlled by **hormones**. Hormones work at very low concentrations at sites some distance from where they are made. Plants are coordinated by chemicals which do not necessarily move from their sites of synthesis and hence, by definition, should not always be termed hormones. In view of this, and because their effects are usually on some aspect of growth, they are called **growth substances**. It is also important to realise that the precise mechanisms of action of plant growth substances are not yet clear and that they probably do not work in the same way as animal hormones. It should be borne in mind that growth can be divided into the three stages of cell division, cell enlargement and cell differentiation (specialisation), and that these stages have particular locations in plants (section 22.4). The action and distribution of different plant growth substances therefore reflects this. Five major types of growth substance are recognised:

- auxins, usually associated with cell enlargement and differentiation;
- gibberellins, also usually associated with cell enlargement and differentiation;
- cytokinins, associated with cell division;
- abscisic acid, usually associated with dormancy, as with buds;
- ethene (ethylene), often associated with ageing (senescence).

In this chapter, each type of growth substance will first be discussed separately, and then key stages in the life cycle of a plant will be discussed to emphasise the fact that growth substances often interact with each other to achieve their effects.

16.2.1 Auxins and phototropism

Discovery of auxins

The discovery of auxins was the result of investigations into phototropism that began with the experiments of Charles Darwin and his son Frances. Using oat coleoptiles as convenient material (fig 16.2), they showed that the growth of shoots towards light was the result of some 'influence' being transmitted from the shoot tip to the region of growth

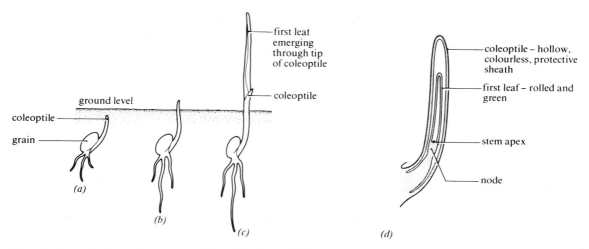

Fig 16.2 *Germination of a typical grass seedling: (a), (b) and (c) stages in germination, (d) section of coleoptile at stage (b).*

behind it. Some of their experiments are summarised in fig 16.3, the diagrams representing results obtained from many seedlings.

> **16.5** (a) List carefully the conclusions you could draw from experiments (a)–(d) in fig 16.3, given that the curvature was due to growth in the region behind the tip.
> (b) Why was experiment (c) necessary, bearing in mind the result from experiment (b)?

If the tropic response is analysed in terms of the following: stimulus → receptor → transmission → effector → response, then the largest gap in our knowledge remains the nature of the transmission. In 1913 the Danish plant physiologist Boysen-Jensen added to our knowledge. Fig 16.4 summarises some of his experiments.

> **16.6** What extra information is provided by Boysen-Jensen's experiments?
> **16.7** If these experiments were repeated in uniform light, draw diagrams to show what results you would expect. Give reasons for your answers.

In 1928 the Dutch plant physiologist Went finally proved the existence of a chemical transmitter. His aim had been to intercept and collect the chemical as it passed back from the tip and to demonstrate its effectiveness in a variety of tests. He reasoned that a small diffusing molecule should pass freely into a small block of agar jelly, whose structure is such that relatively large spaces exist between its molecules. Fig 16.5 illustrates some of his experiments.

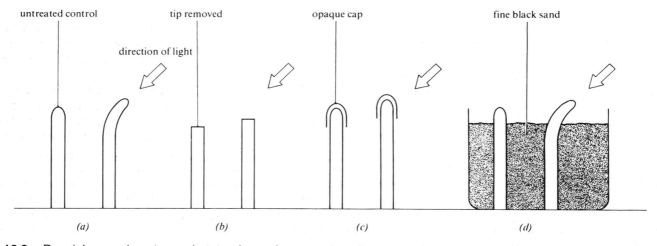

Fig 16.3 *Darwin's experiments on phototropism using oat coleoptiles. (a), (b), (c) and (d) are separate experiments showing treatment (left) and result (right).*

534

Fig 16.4 *Boysen-Jensen's experiments on phototropism using oat coleoptiles. (a), (b) and (c) are separate experiments showing treatment (left) and result (right).*

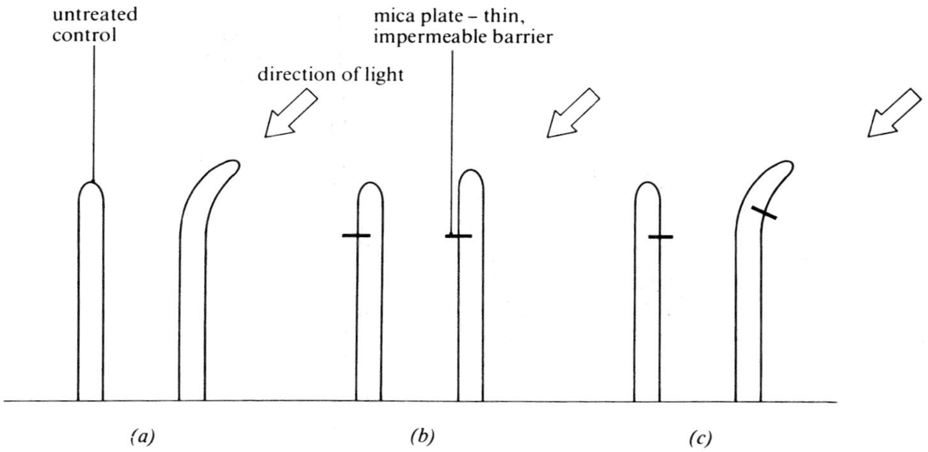

Fig 16.5 *(below) Went's experiments. (a) and (b) are separate experiments showing treatment (left) and result (right). Control experiments are shown alongside. All treatments were carried out in darkness or uniform light.*

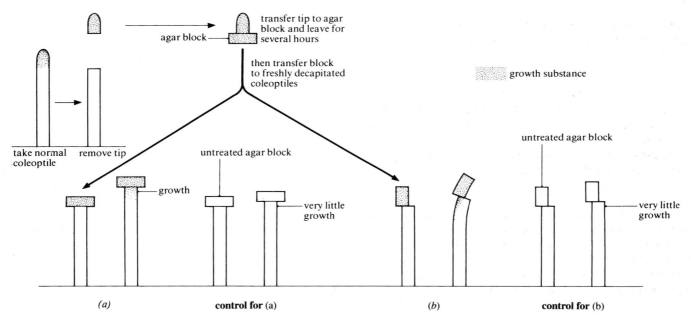

16.8 What would you conclude from the results shown in fig 16.5?

16.9 What result would you expect if the treated block had been placed on the right side of the decapitated coleoptile in experiment (b)?

A further experiment of note carried out by Went is illustrated in fig 16.6. In control experiments the tip was exposed to uniform light or darkness before transfer of agar blocks, and the degree of curvature induced by blocks **A** and **B** was the same. Unilateral illumination of the tip, however, resulted in unequal distribution of the chemical in blocks **A** and **B** (fig 16.6). Not only does this support the conclusions from Boysen-Jensen's experiments about the effect of light on the distribution of the chemical, but it shows how a test of measuring the amount of the chemical present, that is a bioassay, can be set up. A **bioassay** is an experiment in which the amount of a substance is found by

measuring its effects in a biological system. Went showed that the degree of curvature of oat coleoptiles was directly proportional to the concentration of the chemical (at normal physiological levels).

The chemical was subsequently named 'auxin' (from the Greek *auxein*, to increase). In 1934 it was identified as indoleacetic acid (IAA). IAA was soon found to be widely distributed in plants and to be intimately concerned with cell enlargement. Fig 16.7 summarises present beliefs concerning the movement of IAA during unilateral illumination of coleoptiles. It should be pointed out, however, that the coleoptile is the simplest system so far studied and that others appear to be more complex. Also, there is little evidence for the development of auxin gradients in the critical period before the response is measured.

Structure of IAA

The structure of IAA is shown in fig 16.8.

Other chemicals with similar structures and activity were

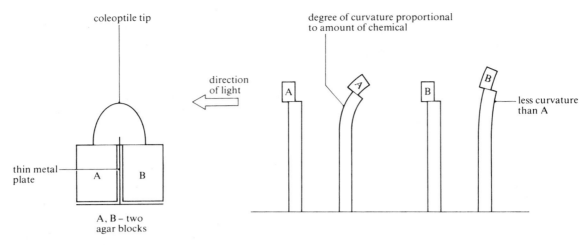

Fig 16.6 *Went's experiment showing effect of unilateral light on distribution of the chemical (auxin).*

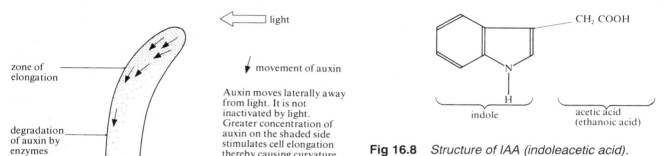

Fig 16.7 *Hypothesis for effect of unilateral illumination on distribution of auxin in a coleoptile.*

Fig 16.8 *Structure of IAA (indoleacetic acid).*

soon isolated, and similar substances have been synthesised, making a whole class of plant growth substances called auxins. Some of the commercial applications of these are discussed in section 16.2.5.

Synthesis and distribution of auxins

Auxins are made continuously in the shoot apex and young leaves. Movement away from the tip is described as basipetal (from apex to base of the organ) and polar (in one direction only). It moves, apparently by diffusion, from cell to cell and is eventually inactivated and degraded by enzymes. Long-distance transport can also occur via the vascular system (mainly phloem) from shoots to roots. A little auxin is probably made in roots. The effects of different auxin concentrations on shoot growth can be investigated by means of an experiment such as experiment 16.1.

Experiment 16.1: To investigate the effects of indoleacetic acid (IAA) on the growth of oat coleoptiles

The aim of the experiment is to investigate the effect of various concentrations of IAA on growth of oat coleoptiles. Growth is affected by white light and therefore cutting and transferring of coleoptiles during the experiment should be carried out under red light or in the minimum amount of light possible. Sucrose solution is used in the experiment as energy will be required for growth, and sucrose is an energy source. The apical tip (3 mm) of each coleoptile is removed in order to prevent natural auxins produced by the coleoptile from having an effect on growth.

Materials

germinating oat seedlings with coleoptiles at least 1.5 cm long (Soak 100 oat grains in water overnight, place the soaked seeds on damp paper towelling in a dish, cover the dish with aluminium foil and place in the dark to germinate (five days in an incubator at 20 °C). In order to obtain the 60 coleoptiles required for each experiment, at least 100 grains should be soaked to allow for germination failure.)
6 test-tubes in a test-tube rack
6 petri dishes + lids
$5 \times 5 \, \text{cm}^3$ graduated pipettes
$25 \, \text{cm}^3$ measuring cylinder or $10 \, \text{cm}^3$ graduated pipette
coleoptile cutter (fig 16.9)
paint brush
2% sucrose solution
distilled water
stock IAA solution $(1 \, \text{g} \, \text{dm}^{-3})$ IAA is not readily

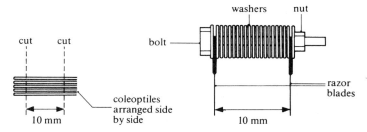

Fig 16.9 *Cutting 10 mm lengths of coleoptiles.*

soluble in water and is therefore first dissolved in ethanol: dissolve 1 g of IAA in 2 cm³ ethanol and dilute to 900 cm³ with distilled water. Warm the solution to 80 °C and keep at this temperature for 5 min. Make up to 1 dm³ with distilled water. Adjust quantities according to final volume required.

Method

(1) Take six test-tubes and six petri dishes and label them **A–F**.

(2) Add 18 cm³ of 2% sucrose solution to each test-tube.

(3) Using a clean 5 cm³ pipette, add 2 cm³ of IAA solution to tube **A** and mix the two solutions thoroughly.

(4) Using a fresh pipette transfer 2 cm³ of solution from tube **A** to tube **B** and mix the contents of tube **B** thoroughly.

(5) Using a fresh pipette each time, transfer 2 cm³ from tube **B** to tube **C**, mix, then transfer 2 cm³ from tube **C** to tube **D**, mix, then transfer 2 cm³ from tube **D** to tube **E**.

(6) Add 2 cm³ distilled water to tube **F**.

(7) Transfer the solutions from tubes **A–F** to petri dishes **A–F**.

(8) Take 60 germinated oat seedlings and cut 10 mm lengths of coleoptile, starting about 2 mm back from the tips. Use a double-bladed cutter with the blades held exactly 10 mm apart by a series of washers, two nuts and two bolts (see fig 16.9). If the tips of the coleoptiles are placed in a line, several lengths can be cut simultaneously.

(9) Using a paint brush, transfer 10 lengths of coleoptile to each dish, avoiding cross contamination of the solutions (the greater the number of coleoptiles used, the more statistically valid the results).

(10) Place a lid on each and incubate the dishes at 25 °C for three days in the dark.

(11) Remeasure the lengths of coleoptiles as accurately as possible.

(12) Ignoring the largest and smallest figures for each dish, calculate the mean (average) length.

(13) Plot a graph of mean length (vertical axis) against IAA concentration in parts per million (horizontal axis).

16.10 What is the concentration in parts per million (ppm) of IAA in each petri dish (1 g dm⁻³ = 1000 ppm)?

(14) Comment on the results and compare them with fig 16.10. More accurate results can be obtained by combining class results.

16.2.2 Auxins and geotropism

It is a common observation that roots are positively geotropic, that is grow downwards, and shoots are negatively geotropic, that is grow upwards. That gravity is the stimulus responsible can be demonstrated by using a piece of equipment called a **klinostat** (fig 16.11). As the chamber rotates, all parts of the seedling receive, in turn, equal stimulation from gravity. A speed of four revolutions per hour is sufficient to eliminate the one-sided effect of gravity and to cause straight shoot and root growth. A non-rotating control shows the normal response to gravity, with shoot growing up and root growing down. It is important to ensure even illumination during the experiment (or to carry it out in darkness) so that there can be no directional response to light.

The involvement of auxins in geotropism is demonstrated by the experiment shown in fig 16.12, which uses the techniques introduced by Went. Auxin moves out of the horizontally placed coleoptile tip but moves downwards as it does so. The greater auxin concentration on the lower surface of an intact coleoptile would stimulate greater cell elongation here, and hence upward growth.

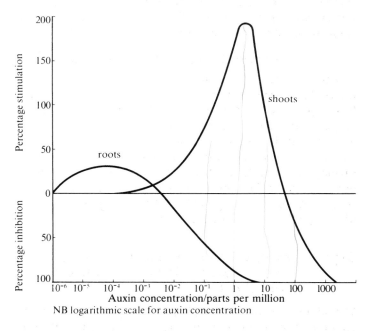

Fig 16.10 *Effect of auxin concentration on growth responses of roots and shoots. Note that concentrations of auxin which stimulate shoot growth inhibit root growth.*

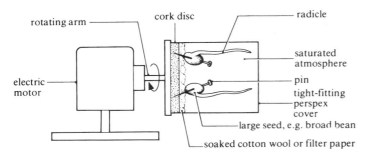

Fig 16.11 *Klinostat showing broad beans after several days growth with rotation.*

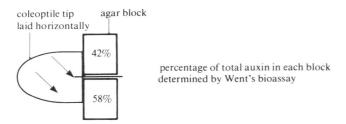

Fig 16.12 *Effect of gravity on distribution of auxin from a horizontal coleoptile tip.*

Decapitation of a root tip removes its sensitivity to gravity, but it is not so easy to demonstrate movement of auxins in roots because very low concentrations are present, and these do not give convincing results in the bioassay described. An interesting result though is obtained from the experiment shown in fig 16.13.

Observations of this type led to the hypothesis summarised in fig 16.14, which suggests that the opposite responses of roots and shoots are due to different sensitivities to auxin. Modifications of the hypothesis in the light of recent findings are discussed later in this section.

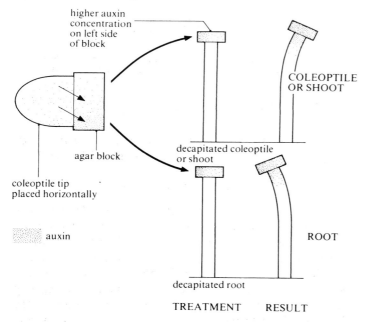

Fig 16.13 *Effect of uneven auxin distribution on growth of decapitated coleoptile and root.*

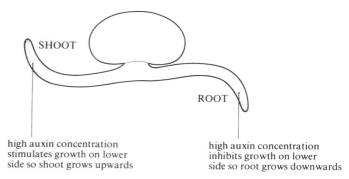

Fig 16.14 *Hypothesis for redistribution of auxin in a horizontally placed seedling.*

The different sensitivity of roots to auxin (fig 16.10) could also explain the negative phototropism shown by some; the higher accumulation of auxin on the shaded side would cause inhibition of growth with the result that cells on the light side would elongate faster and the root would grow away from light. An important aspect of plant growth regulation has thus been revealed. It is not only the nature of the growth substance which is relevant (qualitative control) but the amount of that substance (quantitative control).

The gravity-sensing mechanism

The question now arises as to how the gravity stimulus is detected. Darwin showed that removal of the root cap, the group of large parenchyma cells that protect the root tip as it grows through the soil abolishes the geotropic response. A section of the root cap reveals the presence of large starch grains contained in amyloplasts within the cells (fig 16.15).

It was suggested as long ago as 1900 that these cells act as **statocytes**, that is gravity receptors, and that the starch grains are **statoliths**, structures which move in response to gravity. The so-called **starch–statolith hypothesis** proposes that sedimentation of the starch grains through the cells occurs so that they come to rest on the lower sides of the cells with respect to gravity (fig 16.15). In some unknown way this affects the distribution of growth substances which are known to be produced sometimes in the root apex, sometimes in the root cap and sometimes in both. There is much evidence to support this hypothesis. All plant organs which are sensitive to gravity contain statocytes. They are found, for example, in the vascular bundle sheaths of shoots. Plants from which the starch grains have been removed by certain treatments lose their sensitivity to gravity, but regain it if allowed to make more starch.

> **16.11** How is this mechanism of gravity detection similar to that in animals?

538

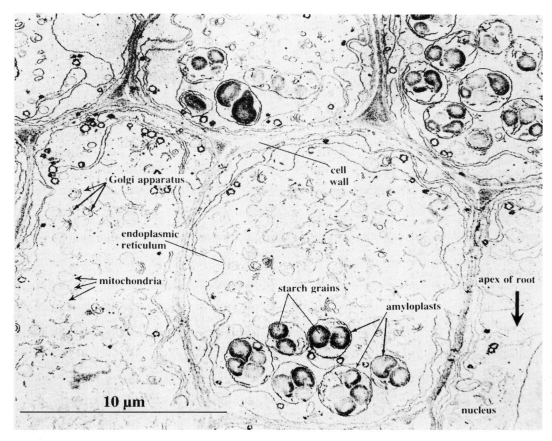

Golgi apparatus

cell wall

endoplasmic reticulum

mitochondria

starch grains

amyloplasts

apex of root

nucleus

10 μm

Fig 16.15 *Electron micrograph of section of root cap showing amyloplasts with starch grains located at the bottoms of the cells.*

Modern hypotheses on geotropism

In coleoptiles the gravity response seems to be mediated by auxins as described above, but with most shoots a geotropic response is still obtained if the tip is removed, and there is still doubt as to whether movement of auxin is involved. In roots, auxin redistribution does occur, but probably not dramatically enough to account for the observed changes in growth rates. Transmission of a growth inhibitor from the root cap to the zone of elongation has been shown, but this is not necessarily auxin. Several groups of workers have been unable to find auxin in the root caps of maize seedlings, a common experimental plant. Instead, abscisic acid, a well-known growth inhibitor, has been found. Ethene, another growth inhibitor, could also be involved. Finally, gibberellins (growth promoters) have been found in higher concentrations than normal in the rapidly growing sides of both shoots and roots when they are geotropically stimulated.

> **16.12** What can you conclude from the experiments shown in fig 16.16? Controls, using untreated agar, showed no curvature. When IAA was used instead of abscisic acid no significant curvature was obtained.

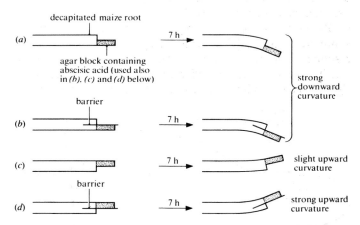

decapitated maize root

(a)

agar block containing abscisic acid (used also in (b), (c) and (d) below)

barrier

(b)

(c)

barrier

(d)

7 h

7 h

7 h

7 h

strong downward curvature

slight upward curvature

strong upward curvature

Fig 16.16 *Effect of abscisic acid on geotropic response to decapitated roots. (Based on experiments by Pilet, 1975.)*

16.2.3   Mode of action of auxins

The effect of auxins on cell enlargement is now reasonably well understood. During cell extension the rigid cellulose framework of the cell wall must be loosened. Extension then occurs by a combination of osmotic swelling as water enters the cell and by the laying down of new cell wall material. The orientation of the existing cellulose microfibrils probably helps to determine the direction of extension. 'Wall loosening' is induced by acid conditions, and by auxins. In 1973 four different groups of workers all demonstrated that, in the presence of auxins, hydrogen ion secretion out of the cells and into the cell walls is stimulated. This causes a lowering of pH outside the cell (increase in acidity) and hence wall loosening, possibly by an enzyme with a low pH optimum that breaks bonds in cell wall polysaccharides, thus allowing the walls to stretch more easily. The ability to maintain a low water potential inside the cell, and availability of water to enter the cell and generate a high pressure potential, are also necessary. More recent evidence suggests that acidification of the walls may not be the first effect of auxins. Instead, researchers are investigating the possibility that auxins bind to receptors in the cell surface membranes of epidermal cells and bring about changes in gene activity that result in production of new enzymes or other proteins concerned with growth.

16.2.4   Other effects of auxins

Apart from stimulating cell elongation and hence shoot growth, auxins have a number of other important roles in the plant which are summarised in table 16.4. Further details of their roles in differentiation, apical dominance, abscission and fruit growth are given later under the appropriate headings.

16.2.5   Commercial applications of auxins

Discovery of IAA led to the synthesis by chemists of a wide range of active compounds with similar structure.

Synthetic auxins have proved commercially useful in a variety of ways. They are cheaper than IAA to produce, and often more physiologically active because plants generally do not have the necessary enzymes to break them down. Table 16.3 gives some examples with their structures and summaries of their uses. Chlorine substitutions in the structures often increase activity.

Fruit setting.   Fig 16.17 shows the effect of treating tomatoes with a fruit-setting auxin. Fruit setting is the series of changes that takes place after fertilisation in the ovary which leads to the development of the young fruit. The fruits of some species, such as tomato, pepper, tobacco and figs, can be set by auxins.

Rooting hormones.   The synthetic auxins NAA (naphthalene acetic acid) and IBA (indolebutyric acid) are very effective at stimulating root development from stem cuttings. These compounds are the ones most commonly used in commercial rooting powders into which the cut ends of stems are dipped to stimulate rooting. Stem cuttings are used to produce some ornamental plants. This is a form of asexual reproduction and ensures genetic uniformity of the product.

Table 16.3 Commercial applications of auxins.

Type of auxin	Examples with structures	Uses
Indoles and naphthyls	NAA (naphthalene acetic acid) (compare with IAA, fig 16.8) IBA (indolebutyric acid)	**Fruiting** – help natural fruit set; sometimes cause fruit setting in absence of pollination (parthenocarpy) **Rooting hormone** – promote rooting of cuttings
Phenoxyacetic acids	2,4-D (2,4-dichlorophenoxyacetic acid) 2,4,5-T (2,4,5-trichlorophenoxyacetic acid) as above but extra chlorine atom in 5 position of ring MCPA (2-methyl-4-chlorophenoxyacetic acid) as 2,4-D but methyl group (CH₃) in 2 position of ring instead of chlorine	**Selective weedkillers** – kill broad-leaved species (dicotyledons). Used in cereal crops and on lawns. Also in conifer plantations for scrub clearance (conifers unaffected). 2,4-D/2,4,5-T mix used in Vietnam war by US as the defoliant 'Agent Orange' **Potato storage** – inhibit sprouting of potatoes **Fruiting** – prevent premature fruit drop (retard abscission)
Benzoic acids	2,3,6-trichlorobenzoic acid 2,4,6-trichlorobenzoic acid as above except chlorine atom in 4 position instead of 3 position of ring	Powerful **weedkillers**. Useful against deep-rooted weeds such as dandelion (*Taraxacum officinale*) and bindweed (*Convolvulus arvensis*)

Fig 16.17 *The three large trusses were set by spraying with beta naphthoxyacetic acid. The small one in the bottom left-hand corner was not sprayed and produced only one normal size tomato.*

Weedkillers. A group of auxins known as phenoxyacetic acids (see table 16.3) form effective herbicides. They are relatively cheap to manufacture and very effective. Their main attraction, though, is that they are selective. They affect broad-leaved plants (dicotyledonous plants or dicots) much more than monocotyledonous plants (monocots). Monocots include cereals and other grasses. 2,4-D will therefore kill dicot weeds in cereal crops and lawns. 2,4,5-T was particularly effective against woody perennials such as those found in rough pastureland. It has been banned, however, due to the presence of traces of a dioxin, an extremely toxic chemical which can cause fetal abnormalities, cancer and a particularly severe form of acne known as chloracne.

These weedkillers cause twisted growth and growth overall is reduced, eventually stopping. It is believed that the auxins interfere with the normal expression of genes and that the correct balance of enzymes needed for growth is not achieved. It is not known why they are more effective against dicots than monocots. It is not simply that higher quantities are absorbed by the broader dicot leaves.

Another group of auxins, the benzoic acids, are also useful weedkillers (table 16.3).

Plant growth regulators

It is important to distinguish between naturally occurring **plant growth substances** and synthetic **plant growth regulators** which are often based on the structure of the naturally occurring compounds but are more effective and less easily degraded by the plant and therefore tend to be used commercially, for example:

plant growth substance	auxin (indoleacetic acid)
plant growth regulators	phenoxyacetic acids (2,4-D)
	indolebutyric acid (IBA)
	indolepropionic acid (IPA)

16.2.6   Gibberellins

Discovery of gibberellins

During the 1920s a team of Japanese scientists at the University of Tokyo was investigating a particularly damaging worldwide disease of rice seedlings, caused by the fungus *Gibberella* (now called *Fusarium*). Infected seedlings became tall, spindly and pale and eventually died or gave poor yields. By 1926 a fungal extract had been isolated which induced these symptoms in rice plants. An active compound was crystallised by 1935 and a further two by 1938. These compounds were called **gibberellins**, after the fungus. Language barriers and then the Second World War delayed the initiation of work in the West, but immediately after the war there was competition between British and American groups to isolate these chemicals. In 1954 a British group isolated an active substance which they called **gibberellic acid**. This was the third, and most active, gibberellin (**GA₃**) isolated by the Japanese. Gibberellins were isolated from higher plants during the 1950s, but the chemical structure of GA₃ was not completely worked out until 1959 (fig 16.18). Now more than 50 naturally occurring gibberellins are known, all differing only slightly from GA₃.

Structure of gibberellins

All are **terpenes**, a complex group of plant chemicals related to lipids; all are weak acids and all contain the **gibbane** skeleton (fig 16.18).

gibbane skeleton

Fig 16.18
Structures of gibbane skeleton and gibberellic acid (GA₃).

gibberellic acid (GA₃)

541

Synthesis and distribution of gibberellins

Gibberellins are most abundant in young expanding organs, being synthesised particularly in young apical leaves (possibly in chloroplasts), buds, seed and root tips. They migrate after synthesis in a non-polar manner, that is up or down the plant from the leaves. They move in phloem and xylem.

Effects of gibberellins

Like the auxins, the main effect of gibberellins is on stem elongation, mainly by affecting cell elongation. Thus genetically dwarf varieties of peas and maize are restored to normal growth and dwarf beans can be converted into runner beans (fig 16.19). Stem growth of normal plants is promoted. Further information, relating to interaction with auxins, is given in section 16.3.

One of the classic effects of gibberellins, which has been much studied in an attempt to understand their mechanism of action, is the breaking of dormancy of certain seeds, notably of cereals. Germination is triggered by soaking the seed in water. After imbibing water the embryo secretes gibberellin which diffuses to the aleurone layer, stimulating synthesis of several enzymes including α-amylase (fig 16.20). These enzymes catalyse the breakdown of food reserve in the endosperm, and the products of digestion diffuse to the embryo, where they are used in growth.

16.13 (a) What is the substrate of α-amylase? (b) What is the product of the reaction it catalyses? (c) What other enzyme is required to complete digestion of its substrate? (d) Why is α-amylase so important in cereal seeds?

16.14 Explain the role of storage proteins in the aleurone layer by reference to fig 16.20.

Experiment 16.2: To test the following two hypotheses, (a) that gibberellin can stimulate breakdown of starch in germinating barley grains and (b) that gibberellin is produced in the embryo

The presence of amylase in barley seeds can be detected by placing a cut seed on the surface of agar containing starch. If the surface is moist, amylase will diffuse from the seed and catalyse digestion of the starch. Addition of iodine to the agar would stain remaining starch blue-black, revealing a clear 'halo' of digestion around the seed. The size of this circular zone gives a rough indication of how much amylase was present. In practice, sterile handling techniques are an important precaution because contaminating bacteria and fungi may also produce amylase.

Fig 16.19   *The influence of gibberellic acid (GA) on the growth of variety Meteor dwarf pea. The plant on the left received no GA and shows the typical dwarf habit. The remaining plants were treated with GA; the dose per plant in micrograms is shown. With doses up to 5 micrograms there is increased growth of the stems with increase in GA dosage. This is the principle of the dwarf pea assay of gibberellins.*

Fig 16.20 *Role of gibberellin in mobilising food reserves of barley grain during breaking of dormancy.*

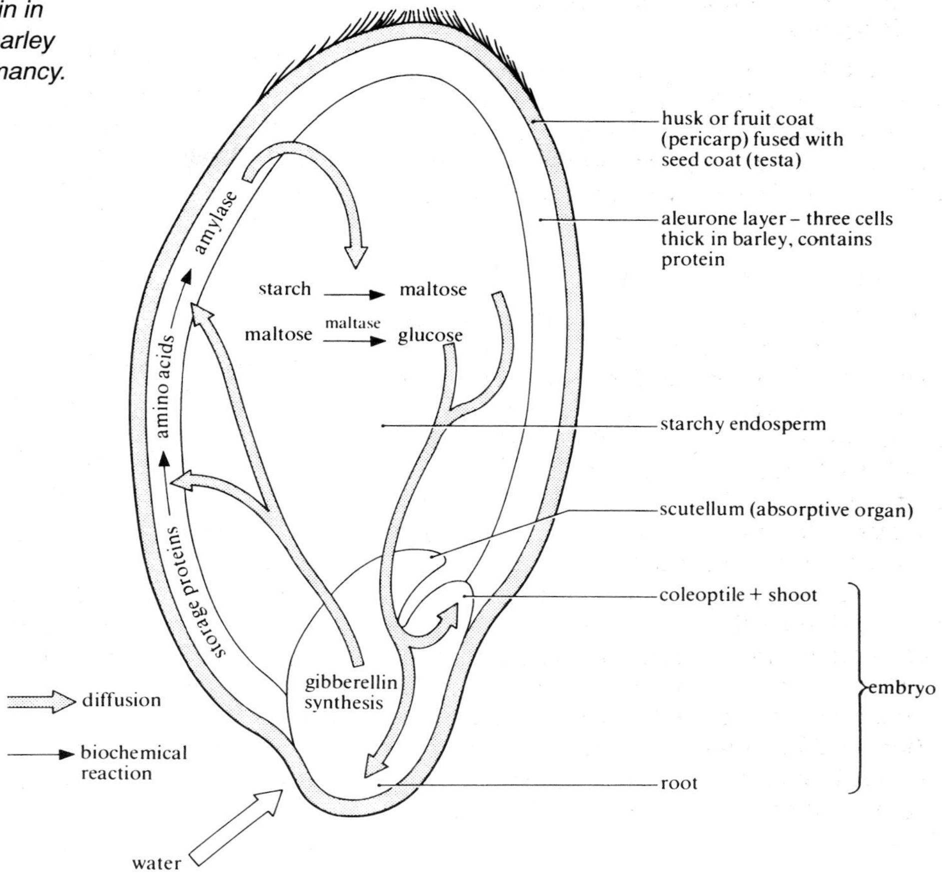

husk or fruit coat (pericarp) fused with seed coat (testa)

aleurone layer – three cells thick in barley, contains protein

starch ⟶ maltose

maltose ⟶ $\xrightarrow{\text{maltase}}$ glucose

amylase

amino acids

storage proteins

starchy endosperm

scutellum (absorptive organ)

coleoptile + shoot

gibberellin synthesis

embryo

root

⟹ diffusion

⟶ biochemical reaction

water

With careful experiment design, further hypotheses may be tested (see, for example, Coppage, J. & Hill, T. A. (1973) *J. Biol. Ed.* **7**, 11–18).

Materials (per student)

white tile
scalpel
forceps
50 cm^3 beaker
labels or chinagraph pencil
iodine/potassium iodide solution
sterile distilled water in sterile flasks ($\times 3$)
5% sodium hypochlorite solution or commercial sterilising fluid, e.g. Milton's or 70% alcohol
two starch agar plates (sterile): 1% agar containing 0.5% starch poured to a depth of about 0.25 cm in sterile petri dishes
two starch–gibberellin agar plates: as above but add gibberellin (GA$_3$) to the agar before autoclaving at the concentration of 1 cm^3 of 0.1% GA$_3$ solution per 100 cm^3 agar (final concentration 10 ppm GA$_3$) (Gibberellin does not dissolve readily in water and is best dissolved in ethanol; some of the GA$_3$ is destroyed during autoclaving but the seeds are sensitive to concentrations as low as 10^{-5} ppm GA$_3$.)
dehusked barley grains: to dehusk barley grains, soak them in 50% (v/v) aqueous sulphuric acid for 3–4 h and then wash thoroughly (about ten times) in

distilled water; violent shaking of the grains in a conical flask removes most of the husks; grains should be used immediately since soaking starts germination. Alternatively, 'embryo' and 'non-embryo' halves can be separated (see below) and stored under dry conditions in a fridge for a maximum of 2–3 days. Wheat grains are naked and do not need dehusking, and may be used as a substitute for barley.

Method

(1) Take two starch agar, and two starch–gibberellin agar plates appropriately labelled +GA or –GA. These have been sterilised. Label one of each type 'embryo' and the other 'non-embryo'.

(2) Cut at least two dry barley grains transversely in half (fig 16.21) on a tile, thus separating into 'embryo' and 'non-embryo' halves.

(3) Sterilise the halves in 5% sodium hypochlorite solution for 5 min. Then wash in three changes of sterile distilled water in sterile flasks.

(4) Using forceps sterilised by rinsing in 70% alcohol, place the halves immediately in the relevant dishes, cut face downwards, with minimal lifting of lids as follows:

–GA embryo half	+GA embryo half	–GA non-embryo half	+GA non-embryo half

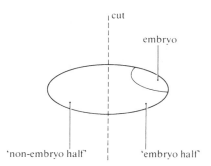

cut

embryo

'non-embryo half'   'embryo half'

Fig 16.21 *Cutting a barley grain for experiment 16.2.*

(5) Incubate for 24–28 h at 20–30 °C.
(6) Test for presence of starch in each dish by flooding the surface of the agar with I₂/KI solution. Draw the final appearance of each dish. Discuss the results.

> **16.15** Using starch agar it is often possible to demonstrate an association of amylase activity with fingerprints. Suggest reasons for this association.
>
> **16.16** What further experiment could you do, given the facilities, to prove that gibberellin causes synthesis of *new* amylase rather than activating pre-existing amylase?
>
> **16.17** How could you prove that amylase synthesis takes place in the aleurone layer?
>
> **16.18** How might the effect of gibberellin on barley seeds be used as a bioassay for gibberellin activity?

Other effects of gibberellins

Further effects of gibberellins on flowering, fruit growth and dormancy and their involvement in photoperiodism and vernalisation are discussed later under the appropriate headings. Their effects are summarised in table 16.4.

Mode of action of gibberellins

The mechanism of action of gibberellins remains unclear. In cereal grains GA₃ has been shown to stimulate synthesis of new protein, particularly α-amylase, and is effective in such low concentrations (as little as $10^{-5}\,\mu\text{g cm}^{-3}$) that it must be operating at a profound level in cell metabolism, such as the 'switching' on or off of genes which takes place during cell differentiation (section 23.9). No conclusive evidence that this is so has yet been obtained, and higher concentrations are required for its other effects. In cell elongation it is dependent on the presence of auxins.

Commercial applications of gibberellins

Gibberellins are produced commercially from fungal cultures.

- They promote fruit setting and are used for growing seedless grapes. The development of seedless fruits can sometimes occur if fertilisation does not take place and is known as **parthenocarpy**.
- GA₃ is used in the brewing industry to stimulate α-amylase production in barley, and hence promote 'malting'.
- A number of synthetic growth retardants act as 'anti-gibberellins', that is they inhibit the action of gibberellins. Application of these often results in short (dwarf), sturdy plants with deep green leaves and sometimes greater pest and disease resistance. They take up less space and may in the future lead to higher yields per acre; also they are less inclined to blow over.

Uses of plant growth regulators

Most plant growth regulators were discovered as a result of screening for herbicide activity. The rate and timing of the application of the regulator is of critical importance.

Plant regulators increasing yield.

- **Chlormequat chloride** to shorten and stiffen wheat straw to prevent lodging (that is, blowing over) allowing increased use of nitrogenous fertilisers.
- **Gibberellic acid** to increase fruit set of mandarins, clementines, tangerines and pears; to overcome losses of apple yield due to frost damage; to increase berry size in seedless grapes enabling the product to be sold fresh rather than dry as raisins; to overcome low temperature constraints to sugarcane growth in Hawaii.
- **Ethephon** (releases ethene) to increase latex flow in rubber.
- **Glysophosine** to ripen sugarcane.

Plant regulators improving quality.

- **Gibberellic acid** coupled with mechanical thinning to increase berry size of seedless grapes in California.
- **Ethene** to de-green citrus fruits.
- **Gibberellins** to delay ripening and improve storage life of bananas.

Plant regulators increasing the value of crops.

- **Gibberellic acid** to advance or retard maturity of globe artichokes to capture higher prices outside the main production season; to retard ripening of grapefruit to spread harvest and capture higher priced market; to force rhubarb for early production.
- **Maleic hydrazides** to extend storage life of bulbs and root crops.

Growth retardants.

- **Ethephon** (releases ethene) shortening stems of forced daffodils, retarding elongation and stimulating branching in tomatoes, geraniums and roses.

Table 16.4 Roles of plant growth substances in plant growth and development.

Process affected	Auxins	Gibberellins
Stem growth	**Promote cell enlargement in region behind apex.** Promote cell division in cambium.	**Promote cell enlargement in presence of auxin.** Also promote cell division in apical meristem and cambium. **Promote 'bolting' of some rosette plants.**
Root growth	**Promote at very low concentrations. Inhibitory at higher concentrations,** e.g. geotropism	Usually inactive
Root initiation	**Promote growth of roots from cuttings and calluses.**	Inhibitory
Bud (shoot) initiation	Promote in some calluses but sometimes antagonistic to cytokinins and inhibitory. Sometimes promote in intact plant if apical dominance broken (see below).	Promote in chrysanthemum callus. Sometimes promote in intact plant if apical dominance broken.
Leaf growth*	Inactive	Promote
Fruit growth	**Promote.** Can sometimes induce parthenocarpy.	**Promote.** Can sometimes induce parthenocarpy.
Apical dominance	**Promote, i.e. inhibit lateral bud growth.**	Enhance action of auxins.
Bud dormancy*	Inactive	**Break**
Seed dormancy*	Inactive	**Break,** e.g. cereals, ash
Flowering*	Usually inactive (promote in pineapple)	**Sometimes substitute for red light.** Therefore promote in long-day plants, inhibit in short-day plants.
Leaf senescence	Delay in a few species	Delay in a few species
Fruit ripening	–	–
Abscission	**Inhibit.** Sometimes promote once abscission starts or if applied to plant side of abscission layer.	Inactive
Stomatal mechanism	Inactive	Inactive

Process affected	Cytokinins	Abscisic acid	Ethene
Stem growth	**Promote cell division in apical meristem and cambium** Sometimes inhibit cell expansion	**Inhibitory, notably during physiological stress, e.g. drought, waterlogging**	**Inhibitory, notably during physiological stress**
Root growth	Inactive or inhibit primary root growth	Inhibitory, e.g. geotropism?	Inhibitory, e.g. geotropism?
Root initiation	Inactive or promote lateral root growth	–	–
Bud (shoot) initiation	Promote, e.g. in protonemata of mosses	–	–
Leaf growth*	Promote	–	–
Fruit growth	**Promote.** Can rarely induce parthenocarpy	–	–
Apical dominance	**Antagonistic to auxins, i.e. promote lateral bud growth**	–	–
Bud dormancy*	**Break**	**Promotes,** e.g. sycamore, birch	**Breaks**
Seed dormancy*	**Break**	**Promotes**	–
Flowering*	Usually inactive	Sometimes promote in short-day plants and inhibit in long-day plants (antagonistic to gibberellins)	Promotes in pineapple
Leaf senescence	**Delay**	Sometimes promotes	–
Fruit ripening	–	–	**Promotes**
Abscission	Inactive	**Promotes**	–
Stomatal mechanism	Promotes stomatal opening	**Promotes closing of stomata under conditions of water stress (wilting)**	Inactive?

* Light and temperature are also involved – see photoperiodism and vernalisation.
NB The information presented in this table is generalised. The growth substances do not necessarily always have the effects attributed to them and variation in response between different plants is common. It is best to pay closest attention to the positive effects. Those stressed in bold type are the most important for the A-level student.

- **Piproctanyl chloride**   dwarfing ornamentals, mainly chrysanthemums.
- **Dikegulac sodium**   retarding growth of hedges and woody ornamentals.

Other targets for plant growth regulators include:

- promotion of root initiation in plant propagation;
- breaking or enforcing dormancy in seed buds and storage organs;
- controlling development of lateral stems;
- increasing resistance to pests and adverse weather conditions, such as drought/pollution;
- controlling size, shape and colour of crops grown for the processed food market;
- suppressing unwanted vegetative growth;
- promoting or delaying flowering/controlling fruit set and ripening.

The benefit to cost ratio of using gibberellic acid to increase fruit setting in mandarin oranges has been reported as 9:1, for the production of seedless grapes 40:1, whilst the use of glysophosine has increased sucrose production in sugarcane by 10–15%. However the use of most plant growth regulators is restricted to commercially small and specialist crops with the exception of antilodging compounds. A number of regulators considered potentially useful during laboratory screening tests proved unreliable for commercial usage. Consequently the main thrust in this field centres on the development of herbicides and pesticides. Further manipulation of crops to human need will probably require a balanced mixture of several plant growth regulators.

16.2.7   Cytokinins

Discovery of cytokinins

During the 1940s and 1950s efforts were made to perfect techniques of plant tissue culture. Such techniques provide an opportunity to study development free from the influence of other parts of the organism, and to study effects of added chemicals. While it proved possible to keep cells alive, it was difficult to stimulate growth. During the period 1954–6 Skoog, working in the USA, found that coconut milk contained an ingredient that promoted cell division in tobacco pith cultures. Coconut milk is a liquid endosperm (food reserve) and evidence that it contained growth substances had already been obtained in the 1940s when it had been studied as a likely source of substances to promote embryo growth. In a search for other active substances a stale sample of DNA happened to show similar activity, although a fresh sample did not. However, autoclaving fresh DNA (heating it under pressure) produced the same effect and the active ingredient was shown to be chemically similar to the base adenine, a constituent of DNA (chapter 3). It was called **kinetin**. The term **kinin** was used by Skoog for substances concerned with the control of cell division. Later the term **cytokinin** was adopted, partly from cytokinesis, meaning cell division, and partly because kinin has an entirely different meaning in zoology (it is a blood polypeptide). The first naturally occurring cytokinin to be chemically identified was from young maize (*Zea mais*) grains in 1963 and hence was called **zeatin**. Note again the chemical similarity to adenine (fig 16.22).

Synthesis and distribution of cytokinins

Cytokinins are most abundant where rapid cell division is occurring, particularly in fruits and seeds where they are associated with embryo growth. Evidence suggests that in mature plants they are frequently made in the roots and move to the shoots in the transpiration stream (in xylem). Cytokinins may be re-exported from leaves via the phloem.

Effects of cytokinins

Cytokinins, by definition, promote cell division. They do so, however, only in the presence of auxins. Gibberellins may also play a role, as in the cambium. Their interaction with other growth substances is discussed later in section 16.3.2.

One of the intriguing properties of cytokinins is their ability to delay the normal process of ageing in leaves. If a leaf is detached from a plant it will normally senesce very rapidly, as indicated by its yellowing and loss of protein, RNA and DNA. However, addition of a spot of kinetin will result in a green island of active tissue in the midst of yellowing tissue. Nutrients are then observed to move to this green island from surrounding cells (fig 16.23).

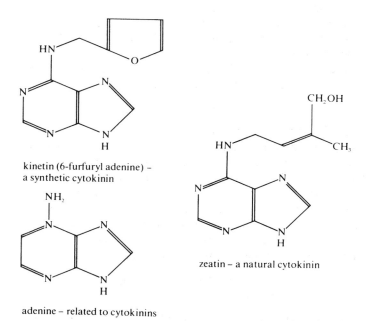

kinetin (6-furfuryl adenine) – a synthetic cytokinin

adenine – related to cytokinins

zeatin – a natural cytokinin

Fig 16.22   *Structures of kinetin, zeatin and adenine.*

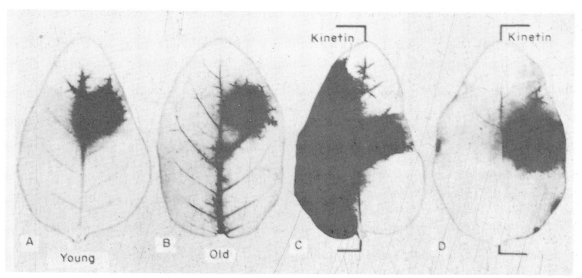

Fig 16.23 *Effect of kinetin upon translocation of an amino acid in tobacco leaves. Radioactive amino acid was supplied as indicated and after a period of translocation the leaves were exposed to photographic film. In the resulting autoradiographs, the areas containing the amino acid appear black.*

> **16.19** Study fig 16.23 and then answer the following.
> (a) What difference is there in the fate of applied amino acid between an old leaf and a young leaf?
> (b) Why should there be this difference?
> (c) What is the effect of kinetin on distribution of radioactive amino acid in old leaves?

Even when kinetin is applied to dying leaves on an intact plant a similar, though less dramatic, effect occurs. It has been shown that levels of natural cytokinins decrease in senescing leaves. A natural programme of senescence may therefore involve movement of cytokinins from older leaves to young leaves via the phloem.

Cytokinins are also implicated in many stages of plant growth and development (table 16.4 and section 16.3).

Mode of action of cytokinins

The similarity of cytokinins to the base adenine, a component of the nucleic acids RNA and DNA, suggests that they may have a fundamental role in nucleic acid metabolism. Some unusual bases, derived from transfer RNA molecules, have been shown to have cytokinin activity, raising the possibility that cytokinins are involved in transfer RNA synthesis. Whether this is true or not, it does not necessarily account for their role as growth substances, and further evidence is still being sought.

Commercial applications of cytokinins

Cytokinins prolong the life of fresh leaf crops such as cabbage and lettuce (delay of senescence) as well as keeping flowers fresh. They can also be used to break the dormancy of some seeds.

16.2.8 Abscisic acid

Discovery of abscisic acid

Plant physiologists have more recently obtained evidence that growth inhibitors, as well as growth promoters like auxins, gibberellins and cytokinins, are important in the normal regulation of growth. It had long been suspected that dormancy was caused by inhibitors when a group at the University of Aberystwyth, led by Wareing, set about trying to find them in the late 1950s. In 1963, an extract from birch leaves was shown to induce dormancy of birch buds. The leaves had been treated with short days to mimic approaching winter. Pure crystals of an active substance were isolated from sycamore leaves in 1964. The substance was called **dormin**. It turned out to be identical to a compound isolated by another group in 1963 from young cotton fruit. This accelerated abscission and was called **abscisin II** (**abscisin I** is a similarly acting, but chemically unrelated and less active compound). In 1967 it was agreed to call the substance **abscisic acid** (**ABA**). It has been found in all groups of plants from mosses upwards and a substance that plays a similar role, lunularic acid, has been found in algae and liverworts.

Structure of abscisic acid

Like the gibberellins, ABA is a terpenoid and has a complex structure (fig 16.24). It is the only growth substance in its class.

Synthesis and distribution of ABA

ABA is made in leaves, stems, fruits and seeds. The fact that isolated chloroplasts can synthesise it again suggests a link with the carotenoid pigments, which are also made in chloroplasts. Like the other growth substances, ABA moves in the vascular system, mainly in the phloem. It also moves from the root cap by diffusion (see geotropism).

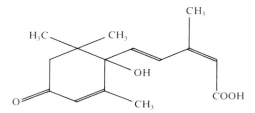

Fig 16.24 *Structure of abscisic acid.*

Effects of ABA

Table 16.4 summarises the effects of ABA on growth and development. It is a major inhibitor of growth in plants and is antagonistic to all three classes of growth promoters. Its classical effects are on bud dormancy (including apical dominance), seed dormancy and abscission (section 16.3.4) but it also has roles in wilting, flowering, leaf senescence and possibly geotropism. It is associated with stress, particularly drought. In wilting tomato leaves, for example, the ABA concentration is 50 times higher than normal and ABA is thought to bring about closure of stomata. High concentrations stop the plant growing altogether.

Mode of action of ABA

This is unknown.

Commercial applications of ABA

ABA can be sprayed on tree crops to regulate fruit drop at the end of the season. This removes the need for picking over a long time-span.

16.2.9   Ethene (ethylene)

Discovery of ethene as a growth substance

It was known in the early 1930s that ethene gas speeded up ripening of citrus fruits and affected plant growth in various ways. Later it was shown that certain ripe fruits, such as bananas, gave off a gas with similar effects. In 1934 yellowing apples were shown to emit ethene and it was subsequently shown to emanate from a wide variety of ripening fruits and other plant organs, particularly from wounded regions. Trace amounts are normal for any organ.

Structure of ethene

The structure of an ethene molecule is shown in fig 16.25.

Synthesis and distribution of ethene

As mentioned above, ethene is made by most or all plant organs. Despite being a gas, it does not generally move freely through the stem of air spaces in the plant because it tends to escape more easily from the plant surface. However, movement of the water-soluble precursor of ethene from waterlogged roots to shoots in the xylem has been demonstrated.

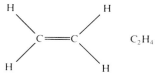

Fig 16.25 *Structure of ethene (ethylene).*

Effects of ethene

Ethene is known chiefly for its effects on fruit ripening and the accompanying rise in rate of respiration (the climacteric) which occurs in some plants (section 16.3.5). Like ABA it acts as a growth inhibitor in some circumstances and can promote abscission of fruits and leaves. Its effects are summarised in table 16.4.

Commercial applications of ethene

Ethene induces flowering in pineapple and stimulates ripening of tomatoes and citrus fruits. Fruits can often be prevented from ripening by storage in an atmosphere lacking oxygen; ripening can subsequently be regulated by application of ethene with oxygen. The commercial compound 'ethephon' breaks down to release ethene in plants and is applied to rubber trees to stimulate the flow of latex.

16.3   Synergism and antagonism

Having studied individual growth substances it has become clear that they generally work by interacting with one another, rather than each controlling its own specific aspect of growth. Two kinds of control emerge. In the first, two or more substances supplement each other's activities. It is often found that their combined effect is much greater than the sum of their separate effects. This is called **synergism** and the substances are said to be **synergistic**. The second kind of control occurs when two substances have opposite effects on the same process, one promoting and the other inhibiting. This is called **antagonism** and the substances are said to be **antagonistic**. Here the balance between the substances determines response.

Some of the better understood phases of plant growth and development can now be studied and the importance of synergism and antagonism demonstrated.

16.3.1   Shoot growth

The effect of gibberellins on elongation of stems, petioles, leaves and hypocotyls is dependent on the presence of auxins.

16.20   How could you demonstrate this experimentally?

16.3.2 Cell division and differentiation

Cytokinins promote cell division only in the presence of auxins. Gibberellins sometimes also play a role, as in the cambium when auxins and gibberellins come from nearby buds and leaves. The interaction of cytokinins with other growth substances was demonstrated in the classic experiments of Skoog in the 1950s, already mentioned. His team showed the effect of various concentrations of kinetin and auxin on growth of tobacco pith callus. A high auxin to cytokinin ratio promoted root formation whereas a high kinetin to auxin ratio promoted lateral buds which grew into leafy shoots. Undifferentiated growth would occur if the growth substances were in balance (fig 16.26).

16.3.3 Apical dominance

Apical dominance is the phenomenon whereby the presence of a growing apical bud inhibits growth of lateral buds. It also includes the suppression of later root growth by growth of the main root. Removal of a shoot apex results in lateral bud growth, that is branching. This is made use of in pruning when bushy rather than tall plants are required.

> **16.21** (*a*) What plant growth substance is made in the shoot apex? (*b*) Design an experiment to show whether it is responsible for apical dominance.

It is interesting to note that auxin levels at the lateral buds are often *not* high enough to cause inhibition of growth. Auxins exert their influence in an unknown way, possibly by somehow 'attracting' nutrients to the apex. In cocklebur it appears that the fall in auxin level in the stem after decapitation permits the lateral buds to inactivate the high levels of ABA that they contain. Gibberellins often enhance the response to IAA. Kinetin application to lateral buds, however, often breaks their dormancy, at least temporarily. Kinetin plus IAA causes complete breaking of dormancy. Cytokinins are usually made in the roots and move in the xylem to the shoots. Perhaps, therefore, they are normally transported to wherever auxin is being made, and they combine to promote bud growth.

Apical dominance is a classic example of one part of a plant controlling another via the influence of a growth substance. This is called **correlation** (fig 16.27).

16.3.4 Abscission

Abscission is the organised shedding of part of the plant, usually a leaf, unfertilised flower or fruit. At the base of the organ, in a region called the **abscission zone**, a layer of living cells separates by the breakdown of their middle lamellae, and sometimes breakdown of their cell walls. This forms the **abscission layer** (fig 16.28). Final shedding of the organ occurs when the vascular strands are broken mechanically, such as by the action of wind. A protective layer is formed beneath the abscission layer to prevent infection or desiccation of the scar, and the vascular strand is sealed. In woody species the protective layer is corky, being part of the tissue produced by the cork cambium, namely the periderm (section 22.4).

Abscission of leaves from deciduous trees and shrubs is usually associated with the onset of winter, but in the tropics it often occurs with the onset of a dry season. In both cases it affords protection against possible water

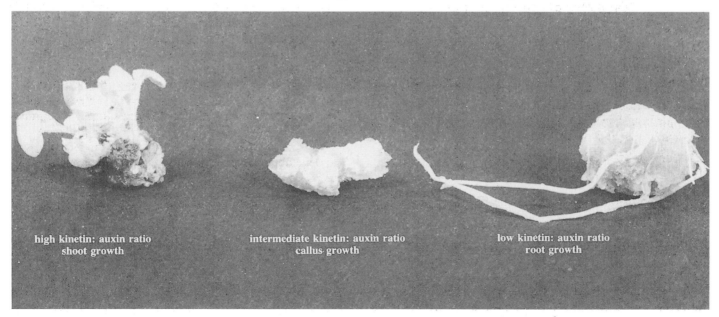

high kinetin: auxin ratio
shoot growth

intermediate kinetin: auxin ratio
callus growth

low kinetin: auxin ratio
root growth

Fig 16.26 *Cultures of tobacco callus. The culture medium in each case contains IAA (2 mg dm^{-3}). The culture 0.2 mg dm^{-3} kinetin (centre) continues growth as a callus; with a lower kinetin addition (0.02 mg dm^{-3}) it initiates roots and with a higher kinetin addition (0.5 mg dm^{-3}) it initiates shoots.*

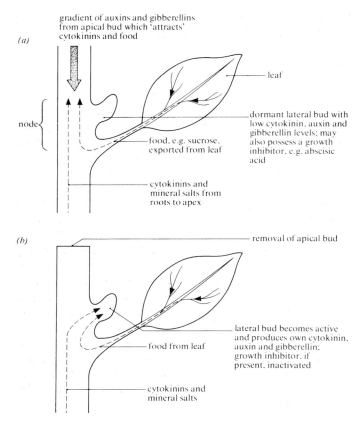

Fig 16.27 *Possible involvement of plant growth substances in apical dominance, (a) in presence of apical bud, (b) after removal of apical bud.*

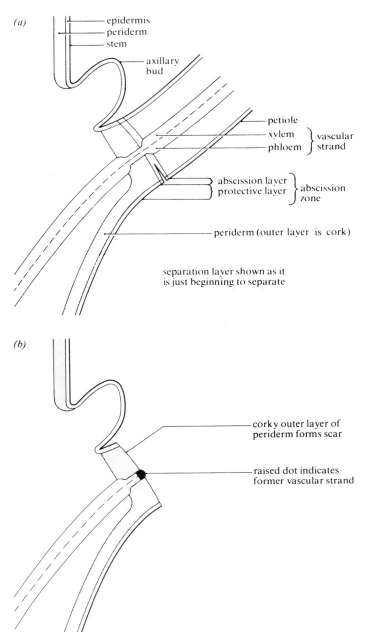

Fig 16.28 *Abscission zone of a leaf, (a) during abscission, (b) after abscission.*

shortage, leaves being the main organs through which water is lost by transpiration. In winter, for example, soil water may be unavailable through being frozen. In evergreen species, abscission is spread over the whole year and the leaves are usually modified to prevent water loss.

It has been shown that as a leaf approaches abscission, its output of auxin declines. Fig 16.29 summarises the effect of auxin on abscission. It is worth noting that once abscission has been triggered, auxins seem to accelerate the process.

Abscisic acid (ABA) acts antagonistically to auxin by promoting abscission in some fruits. Unripe seeds produce auxins, but during ripening auxin production declines and ABA production may rise. In developing cotton fruits, for example, two peaks of ABA occur. The first corresponds to the 'June drop' when self thinning of the plants occurs: only the aborted immature fruitlets have high ABA levels at this stage. The second corresponds with seed ripening.

There is some doubt as to whether ABA also affects leaf abscission. Applications of high concentrations are effective, but this could be a result of stimulating ethene production. Ethene is produced by senescing leaves and ripening fruits and always stimulates abscission when applied to mature organs. Some deciduous shrubs and trees produce ABA in their leaves just before winter (section 16.5.1) but this may be purely to induce bud dormancy.

Abscission is of immense horticultural significance because of its involvement in fruit drop. Commercial applications of auxins and ABA reflect this and have been discussed earlier in this chapter.

If flowers are not fertilised they are generally abscised (see 'fruit set' below).

16.3.5 Pollen tube growth, fruit set, fruit development and parthenocarpy

Germinating pollen grains are a rich source of auxins as well as commonly stimulating the tissues of the style and ovary to produce more auxin. This auxin is

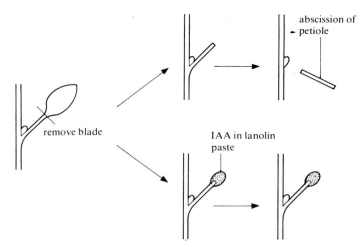

Fig 16.29 *Effect of auxin (IAA) on abscission of a leaf petiole. Removal of the leaf blade leads to abscission of the petiole. IAA substitutes for the presence of the leaf blade.*

necessary for 'fruit set', that is retention of the ovary which becomes the fruit after fertilisation. Without it abscission of the flower normally occurs. After fertilisation, the ovary and the ripe seeds continue to produce auxins which stimulate fruit development.

A few natural examples are known where fruit development proceeds without fertilisation, and therefore without seed development, for example banana, pineapple and some seedless varieties of oranges and grapes. Such development is called **parthenocarpy**. Unusually high auxin levels occur in these ovaries. Parthenocarpy can sometimes be artificially induced by adding auxins, as in tomato, squash and peppers. Seedless pea pods can just as easily be induced. Gibberellins have the same effect in some plants, such as the tomato, including some that are not affected by auxins, for example cherry, apricot and peach. Developing seeds are not only a rich source of auxins and gibberellins, but also of cytokinins (section 16.2.7). These growth substances are mainly associated with development of the embryo and accumulation of food reserves in the seed, and sometimes in the pericarp (fruit wall) from other parts of the plant.

Fruit ripening is really a process of senescence and is often accompanied by a burst of respiratory activity called the **climacteric**. This is associated with ethene production. The subsequent roles of ethene and ABA in fruit abscission were discussed in section 16.3.4.

16.4 Phytochrome and effects of light on plant development

The importance of environmental stimuli to the growth and orientation of plant organs has already been discussed with plant movements. The stimulus which has the widest influence on plant growth is light. Not only does it provide the energy for photosynthesis and influence plant movements, but it directly affects development. The effect of light upon development is called **photomorphogenesis**.

16.4.1 Etiolation

Perhaps the best way to demonstrate the importance of light is to grow a plant in the dark! Such a plant lacks chlorophyll (is chlorotic) and therefore appears white or pale yellow rather than green. The shoot internodes become elongated and thick and the plant is described as **etiolated**. In dicotyledonous plants, the epicotyl or hypocotyl (section 22.4.2) elongates in hypogeal or epigeal germination respectively and the plumule tip is hooked. Dioctyledonous leaves remain small and unexpanded. In monocotyledonous plants, the mesocotyl elongates during germination and the leaves may remain rolled up. In all leaves, chloroplasts fail to develop normal membrane systems and are called **etioplasts**. Plants make less supporting tissue and are fragile and collapse easily. Eventually they use up their food reserves and die unless light is reached for photosynthesis. Yet as soon as the plant is exposed to light, normal growth begins again. The significance of etiolation is that it allows maximum growth in length with minimum use of carbon reserves which, in the absence of light, the plant cannot obtain by photosynthesis.

> **16.22** How does the morphology (structure) of an etiolated plant suit it for growing through soil?

16.4.2 Discovery of phytochrome

The first stage in any process affected by light must be the absorption of light by a pigment, the so-called **photoreceptor**. The characteristic set of wavelengths of light it absorbs form its absorption spectrum (section 7.3.2); remaining wavelengths are reflected and give the substance a characteristic colour (chlorophyll, for example, absorbs red and blue light and reflects green light).

The seeds of many plants germinate only if exposed to light. In 1937 it was shown that, for lettuce seeds, red light promoted germination but far-red light (longer wavelength) inhibited germination. Borthwick and Hendrick, working at the US Department of Agriculture in the 1950s, plotted an **action spectrum** for the germination response (a spectrum of wavelengths showing their relative effectiveness at stimulating the process). Fig 16.30 shows that the wavelength most effective for germination was about 660 nm (red light) and for inhibition of germination about 730 nm (far-red light).

They also showed that only brief exposures of light were necessary and that the effects of red light were reversed by far-red light and vice versa. Thus the last treatment in an alternating sequence of red/far-red exposures would always

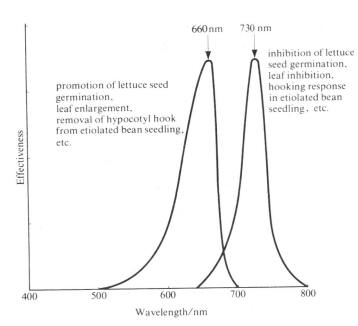

Fig 16.30 *Typical action spectra of a phytochrome-controlled response.*

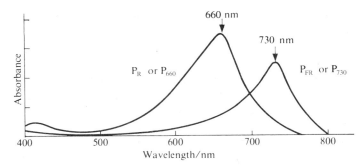

Fig 16.31 *Absorption spectra of the two forms of phytochrome.*

16.4.3   Photoperiodism and flowering

One of the important ways in which light exerts its influence on living organisms is through variations in daylength (**photoperiod**). The further from the equator, where days are almost a constant 12 hours, the greater the seasonal variation in daylength. Thus daylength is an important environmental signal in temperate latitudes where it varies between about 9 and 15 hours during the year. The effects of photoperiod on animals are discussed in section 17.8.5. In plants it is a matter of common observation that phenomena such as flowering, fruit and

be the effective one. The US team eventually isolated the pigment responsible in 1960 and called it **phytochrome**. Phytochrome, as they predicted, is a blue-green pigment existing in two interconvertible forms. One form, P_{FR} or P_{730} absorbs far-red light and the other, P_R or P_{660}, absorbs red light. Absorption of light by one form converts it rapidly and reversibly to the other form (within seconds or minutes depending on light intensity):

Normal sunlight contains more red than far-red light, so the P_{FR} form predominates during the day. This is the physiologically active form, but reverts slowly to the more stable, but inactive, P_R form at night. Phytochrome was shown to consist of a pigment portion attached to a protein. It is present in minute amounts throughout plants (hence it is not visible, despite its colour) but is particularly concentrated in the growing tips. Its absorption spectrum is shown in fig 16.31.

> **16.23**   What is the difference between an absorption spectrum and an action spectrum?

A number of developmental processes are mediated by low intensities of red light and reversed by far-red light or darkness, showing the involvement of phytochrome (fig 16.30 and table 16.5). The most significant of these is flowering, which is discussed later. The involvement of phytochrome in a process is shown by matching the action spectrum of the response with the absorption spectrum of phytochrome.

Table 16.5 Some phytochrome-controlled responses in plants.

General process affected	Red light promotes
Germination*	Germination of some seeds, e.g. some lettuce varieties
	Germination of fern spores
Photomorphogenesis (light-controlled development of form and structure)	Leaf expansion in dicotyledons. Leaf unrolling in grasses (monocotyledons). Chloroplast development (etioplasts converted to chloroplasts: see etiolation). Greening (protochlorophyll converted to chlorophyll). Inhibition of internode growth (including epicotyl, hypocotyl, mesocotyl), i.e. preventing of etiolation. Unhooking of plumule in dicotyledons
Photoperiodism	Stimulates flowering in long-day plants. Inhibits flowering in short-day plants. See flowering

* Experiments designed to investigate the effects of light on seed germination are described by J. W. Hannay in *J. Biol. Ed.* (1967) **1**, 65–73. The variety of lettuce suggested, 'Grand Rapids', is no longer available but some modern varieties could be screened for suitability. Such varieties currently available are 'Dandie', 'Kloek' and 'Kweik'. 'Dandie' is probably the most reliable but is fairly expensive because it is a winter-forcing variety. It is available from Suttons in small packets or from E. W. King & Co., Coggeshall, Essex in 10 g packets (enough for about 250 dishes of 50 seeds each). *Phacelia* seeds make an interesting contrast to lettuce.

NB In this experiment a green leaf can be used as a far-red filter.

seed production, bud and seed dormancy, leaf fall and germination are closely attuned to seasonal influences like daylength and temperature, and that survival of the plant depends on this.

The process involving the most profound change is flowering, when shoot meristems switch from producing leaves and lateral buds to producing flowers. The importance of photoperiod in flowering was discovered as early as 1910 but was first clearly described by Garner and Allard in 1920. They showed that tobacco plants would flower only after exposure to a series of short days. This occurred naturally in autumn, but could be induced by artificially short days of seven hours in a greenhouse in summer. As they examined other plants it became obvious that some required long days for flowering (**long-day plants**, LDPs) and some would flower whatever the photoperiod once mature (**day-neutral plants**).

Additional complications have since been found. For example, some plants are day-neutral at one temperature, but not at another; some require one daylength followed by another; in some, the appropriate daylength only accelerates flowering and is not an absolute requirement.

An important advance in our understanding came when it was shown that it is really the length of the dark period which is critical. Thus short-day plants (SDPs) are really long-night plants. If they are grown in short days, but the long night is interrupted by a short light period, flowering is prevented. Long-day plants will flower in short days if the long night period is interrupted. Short dark interruptions, however, do not cancel the effect of long days. Table 16.6 summarises the three main categories of plant.

Flowering in chrysanthemums

In the classical work of Garner and Allard, chrysanthemums were described as typical short-day plants. However it was later shown by Schwabe that, in addition, an exposure to cold temperatures (1–7 °C in a refrigerator for around three weeks) hastens flower bud formation in both long- and short-day conditions. In the absence of this cold temperature treatment, the plants may remain vegetative even in short days. For the rapid onset of flowering, short-day photoperiodic treatment and warm temperature are required following exposure to a lower temperature (vernalisation, see section 16.5). Evidence suggests that the vernalisation treatment is more effective if given during the dark period. The growing tip has been shown to be the seat of perception of the vernalisation stimulus. Flowering in chrysanthemums can be inhibited by:

- transfer to long-day treatment;
- transfer to low light intensity during short-day treatment;
- application of auxin paste suggesting that hormone balance may be important in inducing flowering.

Table 16.6 Classification of plants according to photoperiodic requirements for flowering.

Short-day plants (SDPs)	Long-day plants (LDPs)
e.g. cocklebur (*Xanthium pennsylvanicum*), chrysanthemum, soybean, tobacco, strawberry	e.g. henbane (*Hyoscyamus niger*), snapdragon, cabbage, spring wheat, spring barley
Flowering induced by dark periods longer than a critical length, e.g. cocklebur 8.5 h; tobacco 10–11 h (Under natural conditions equivalent to days shorter than a critical length, e.g. cocklebur 15.5 h; tobacco 13–14 h)	Flowering induced by dark periods shorter than a critical length, e.g. henbane 13 h (Under natural conditions equivalent to days longer than a critical length, e.g. henbane 11 h)

Day-neutral plants
e.g. cucumber, tomato, garden pea, maize, cotton Flowering independent of photoperiod

NB Tobacco (SDP) and henbane (LDP) both flower in 12–13 h daylength.

It is unusual for short-day plants to require vernalisation. Commercially, chrysanthemum propagation cuttings are taken during January–March when the vernalisation requirement will be met by the prevailing winter temperature.

16.4.4 Quality and quantity of light

The next step is to find the quality (colour) and quantity of light required. Remembering that the cocklebur (SDP) will not flower if its long night is interrupted, experiments revealed that red light was effective in preventing flowering but that far-red light reversed the effect of red light. Therefore phytochrome is the photoreceptor. These experiments were, in fact, part of the programme which led to the discovery of phytochrome. As would be expected, a LDP held in short days is stimulated to flower by a short exposure to red light during the long night. Again this is reversed by far-red light. The last light treatment always determines the response.

In some, though not all, cases low light intensities for a few minutes are effective, again typical of a phytochrome-controlled response. The higher the intensity used, the shorter the exposure time required.

16.4.5 Perception and transmission of the stimulus

It was shown in the mid-1930s that the light stimulus is perceived by the leaves and not the apex where the flowers are produced.

In addition to this, a cocklebur plant with just one induced leaf will flower even if the rest of the plant is under non-inductive conditions. This implies that some agent, that is a hormone, must pass from the leaf to the apex to bring about flowering. This concept is supported by the observation that the flowering stimulus can be passed from an induced plant to a non-induced plant by grafting, and that the stimulus is apparently the same for SDP, LDP and day-neutral plants because grafting between these is successful. The hypothetical flowering hormone has been called '**florigen**' but has never been isolated. Indeed, its existence is doubted by some plant physiologists.

Table 16.7 Effect of red/far-red light interruptions of long nights on flowering of cocklebur.

Red light		Two minutes red light followed by FR light	
Floral stage	Duration of red light/s	Floral stage	Duration of FR light/s
6.0	0	0.0	0
5.0	5	4.0	12
4.0	10	4.5	15
2.6	20	5.5	25
0.0	30	6.0	50

(After Downs, R. J. (1956) *Plant Physiol.* 31 279–84.)

16.4.6 Mode of action of phytochrome

How, then, does phytochrome exert its control? At the end of a light period it exists in the active P_{FR} form. At the end of a short night its slow transition back to the inactive P_R form, which takes place in darkness, may not be complete. It can be postulated, therefore, that in LDPs P_{FR} promotes flowering and in SDPs it inhibits flowering. Only long nights remove sufficient P_{FR} from the latter to allow flowering to occur. Unfortunately, short exposures to far-red light, which would have the same effect as a long night, cannot completely substitute for long nights, so the full explanation is more complex. Some time factor is also important.

We do know that gibberellins can mimic the effect of red light in some cases. Gibberellic acid (GA_3) promotes flowering in some LDPs, mainly rosette plants like henbane which bolt before flowering. (Bolting is a rapid increase in stem length.) GA_3 also inhibits flowering in some SDPs. Antigibberellins (growth retardants) nullify these effects.

So, does P_{FR} stimulate gibberellin production, and is this the flowering hormone? There are too many exceptions for this to be the case. Abscisic acid inhibits flowering in some LDPs, such as *Lolium*, but induces it in some SDPs, such as strawberry. In short, our understanding of the flowering process is still incomplete.

16.5 Vernalisation and flowering

Some plants, especially biennials and perennials, are stimulated to flower by exposure to low temperatures. This is called **vernalisation**. Here the stimulus is perceived by the mature stem apex, or by the embryo of the seed, but not by the leaves as in photoperiodism. As with photoperiod, vernalisation may be an absolute requirement (such as in henbane) or may simply hasten flowering (as in winter cereals).

Long-day plants (for example cabbage), short-day plants (such as chrysanthemum) and day-neutral plants (such as ragwort) can all require vernalisation. The length of chilling required varies from four days to three months, temperatures around $4\,°C$ generally being most effective. Like the photoperiodic stimulus, the vernalisation stimulus can be transmitted between plants by grafting. In this case the hypothetical hormone involved was called **vernalin**. It has subsequently been discovered that during vernalisation gibberellin levels increase, and application of gibberellins to unvernalised plants can substitute for vernalisation (fig 16.32). It is now believed that 'vernalin' is a gibberellin. It is clear now that photoperiodism and vernalisation serve to synchronise the reproductive behaviour of plants with their environments, ensuring reproduction at favourable times of the year. They also help to ensure that members of the same species flower at the same time and thus encourage cross-pollination and cross-fertilisation, with the attendant advantages of genetic variability.

Fig 16.32 *Carrot plants (var.* Early french forcing*). left: control; centre: maintained at 17 °C but supplied 10 mg of gibberellin daily for 4 weeks; right: plant given vernalising cold treatment (6 weeks). All photographed 8 weeks after completion of cold treatment.*

16.5.1 Photoperiodism and dormancy

The formation of winter buds in temperate trees and shrubs is usually a photoperiodic response to shortening days in the autumn, for example in birch, beech and sycamore. The stimulus is perceived by the leaves and, as mentioned before, abscisic acid (ABA) levels build up. ABA moves to the meristems and inhibits growth. Short days also induce leaf fall from deciduous trees (abscission). Often buds must be chilled before dormancy can be broken ('**bud-break**'). Similarly some seeds require a cold stimulus ('**stratification**') after imbibing water before they will germinate, thus preventing them from germinating prematurely once ripe. Gibberellins can substitute for the cold stimulus, and natural bud-break is accompanied by a rise in gibberellins as well as, in many cases, a fall in ABA. Breaking of bud dormancy in birch and poplar has been shown to coincide with a rise in cytokinins.

Apart from buds and seeds, storage organs are involved in dormancy and again photoperiod is important. For example, short days induce tuber formation in potatoes, whereas long days induce onion bulb formation.

> **16.26** Some buds remain dormant throughout the summer. What causes dormancy here?

Chapter Seventeen

Coordination and control in animals

Irritability or **sensitivity** is a characteristic feature of all living organisms and refers to their ability to respond to a stimulus. The stimulus is received by a **receptor**. It is transmitted by means of nerves or hormones, and an **effector** brings about a **response**.

Animals, unlike plants, have two different but related systems of coordination: the **nervous system** and the **endocrine system**. These are compared in table 17.1. A good case study of the difference between nervous and hormonal control is the control of digestive secretions in the gut. This is discussed in section 8.4. The two systems have developed in parallel in animals. Plants also have a chemical coordination system equivalent to hormones, so the extra possession of a nervous system in animals is probably related to their need to seek food. This requires sense organs and locomotion, which are controlled by a nervous system.

17.1 The nervous system

The nervous system is made up of highly specialised cells whose function is to

- receive **stimuli** from the environment. In multicellular organisms this is done by modified nerve cells called **receptors**. The structure and function of these is described in section 17.5.

Table 17.1 Comparison of nervous and hormonal control in animals.

Nervous control	Hormonal control
Electrical and chemical transmission (nerve impulses and chemicals across synapses)	Chemical transmission (hormones) through blood system
Rapid transmission and response	Slower transmission and relatively slow-acting (adrenaline an exception)
Often short-term changes	Often long-term changes
Pathway is specific (through nerve cells)	Pathway not specific (blood around whole body), target is specific
Response often very localised, e.g. one muscle	Response may be very widespread, e.g. growth

- convert the stimuli into the form of electrical impulses, a process called **transduction**.
- transmit them, often over considerable distances, to other specialised cells called **effectors** which are capable of producing an appropriate **response**. The structure and function of effectors is described briefly in section 17.5 and chapter 18.

Between the receptors and effectors are the conducting cells of the nervous system, the **neurones**. These are the basic structural and functional units of the nervous system and spread throughout the organism forming a complex communication network.

Types of nerve cell – a summary

The structure of the different types of nerve cell are shown and described in section 6.6. The three types described are **sensory neurones**, **motor neurones** and **interneurones** (fig 6.27). Each has a nerve cell body and a nerve fibre. The cell body contains the nucleus. The part of the fibre which conducts nerve impulses away from the cell body is the axon. Axons end in swellings called synaptic knobs. Leading towards the cell body is the part of the fibre known as the dendron which *receives* nerve impulses at fine branches called dendrites. Many nerve fibres are surrounded by a fatty myelin sheath and are said to be myelinated. In these neurones, the dendron and the axon form one fibre, with the cell body on a short branch to one side. Another type of neurone called a **bipolar neurone** will be described in this chapter. A bipolar neurone has two unconnected fibres, a dendron and an axon, which enter and leave at opposite sides of the cell body.

17.1.1 The nerve impulse

Measuring electrical activity in neurones

The fact that information can be transmitted along neurones as electrical impulses and bring about muscle contraction and secretion by glands has been known for over 200 years. Details of the mechanisms, however, were discovered only in the last 50 years, following the discovery of certain axons in squid which have a diameter of approximately 1 mm. These **giant axons** (which are involved in escape responses) have large enough diameters to allow electrodes to be inserted into them and experiments to be carried out.

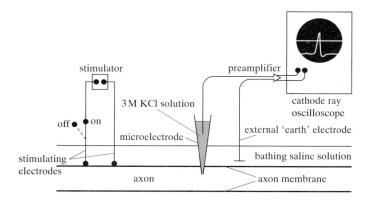

Fig 17.1 *The basic apparatus used to record electrical activity in the axon of an isolated neurone. The stimulator produces a current which generates an action potential in the axon and is detected and recorded using a microelectrode inserted into the axon. The signal is sent to a dual-beam cathode ray oscilloscope.*

Table 17.2 Ionic concentrations of extracellular and intracellular fluids in squid axon. (Values given are approximations in mmol kg^{-1} H$_2$O, data from Hodgkin, 1958.)

Ion	Extracellular concentration	Intracellular concentration
K$^+$	20	400
Na$^+$	460	50
Cl$^-$	560	100
A$^-$ (organic anions)	0	370

The apparatus now used to investigate electrical activity in neurones is shown in fig 17.1. The **microelectrode**, composed of a small glass tube drawn out to a fine point of 0.5 μm diameter, is filled with a solution capable of conducting an electric current such as 3 M potassium chloride. This is inserted into an axon and a second electrode, in the form of a small metal plate, is placed in the saline solution bathing the neurone that is being investigated. Both electrodes are connected by leads to a **preamplifier** to complete the circuit. The preamplifier increases the signal strength in the circuit approximately 1000 times and provides the input to a **dual-beam cathode ray oscilloscope**. All movements of the microelectrode are controlled by a **micromanipulator**, a device with adjusting knobs similar to those of a microscope, which enables delicate control over the position of the tip of the microelectrode.

When the tip of the microelectrode penetrates the axon cell surface membrane, the beams of the oscilloscope separate. The distance between the beams indicates the potential difference between the two electrodes of the circuit and can be measured. This value is called the **resting potential** of the axon (see below). In sensory cells, neurones and muscle cells this value changes with the activity of the cells and hence they are known as **excitable cells**. All other living cells show a similar potential difference across the membrane, known as the **membrane potential**, but in these cells this is constant and so they are known as **non-excitable cells**.

The resting potential

The potential difference (a charge) which exists across the cell surface membrane of all cells is usually, as in the case of nerve cells, negative inside the cell with respect to the outside. The membrane is said to be **polarised**. The potential difference across the membrane at rest is called the **resting potential** and this is about -70 mV (the negative sign indicates that the inside of the cell is negative with respect to the outside). The resting potential is maintained by active transport and passive diffusion of ions. This was discovered by Curtis and Cole in the USA, and Hodgkin and Huxley in England, in the late 1930s when they examined squid axons, as shown in table 17.2.

The cytoplasm inside the axon (known as **axoplasm**) has a high concentration of potassium (K$^+$) ions and a low concentration of sodium (Na$^+$) ions, in contrast to the fluid outside the axon which has a low concentration of potassium ions and a high concentration of sodium ions. (The distribution of chloride (Cl$^-$) and other ions is ignored in the following descriptions since it does not play a vital role in the process.) The gradients across the membrane are known as electrochemical gradients. The **electrochemical gradient** of an ion is due to its electrical and chemical properties. The electrical property of an ion is its charge – it will tend to be attracted to an opposite charge and repelled by a similar charge. Its movement is also affected by its concentration in a solution, a chemical property. It will tend to move from a high concentration to a low concentration. Predicting its movement is therefore difficult since it depends on a balance of both charge and concentration.

The resting potential is maintained by the active transport of ions *against* their electrochemical gradients by **sodium/ potassium pumps** (Na$^+$/K$^+$ pumps). These are carrier proteins located in the cell surface membrane (see section 5.9.8 active transport and fig 5.21). They are driven by energy supplied by ATP and couple the removal of three sodium ions from the axon with the uptake of two potassium ions as shown in fig 17.2.

The active movement of these ions is opposed by the *passive* diffusion of the ions which constantly pass down their electrochemical gradients through specific ion channel proteins as shown in fig 17.2. The rate of diffusion is determined by the permeability of the axon membrane to the ion. Potassium ions have a membrane permeability which is 20 times greater than that of sodium ions, for reasons explained below. Therefore potassium ion loss from

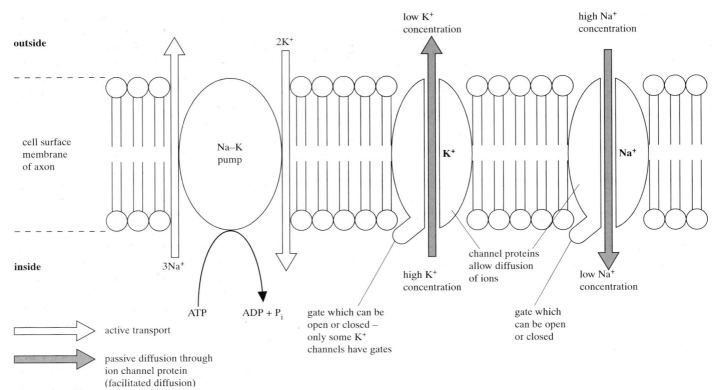

outside

cell surface
membrane
of axon

Na–K
pump

2K⁺

low K⁺
concentration

high Na⁺
concentration

K⁺

Na⁺

inside

3Na⁺

ATP   ADP + Pᵢ

high K⁺
concentration

channel proteins
allow diffusion
of ions

low Na⁺
concentration

gate which can be
open or closed –
only some K⁺
channels have gates

gate which
can be open
or closed

active transport

passive diffusion through
ion channel protein
(facilitated diffusion)

Fig 17.2 *Active and passive ion movements across the cell surface of an axon. The movements are responsible for the generation of a negative potential inside the axon. This is called the resting potential. Active transport takes place through the sodium/potassium pump. Ion channels (proteins) allow the passive movement of ions down their electrochemical gradients. The ion channels are gated, meaning they can be closed. They can be closed in response to a change in voltage across the membrane as happens during the propagation of a nerve impulse. Not all the gates shut at the same time.*

the axon is greater than sodium ion gain. This leads to a net loss of potassium ions from the axon, and the production of a *negative* charge within the axon. The value of the resting potential is largely determined by the potassium ion electrochemical gradient.

We can now turn our attention to how these cells generate nerve impulses. Basically, nerve impulses are due to changes in the permeability of the nerve cell membrane to potassium and sodium ions which lead to changes in the potential difference across the membrane and the formation of 'action potentials'.

The action potential

The experimental stimulation of an axon by an electrical impulse, as shown in fig 17.3, results in a change in the potential across the axon membrane from a negative inside value of about −70 mV to a positive inside value of about +40 mV. This polarity change is called an **action potential** and appears on the cathode ray oscilloscope as a spike, as shown in fig 17.3.

This is generated by a change in the sodium ion channel. This channel, and some of the potassium ion channels, are known as **gated channels**, meaning they can be opened or closed with polypeptide chains called gates. When the gate is closed, the membrane is not very permeable to the ion that normally passes through the gate. Opening the gate

increases permeability. Regulation is achieved mainly by the sodium gate which is closed in the resting cell. This helps to explain why the membrane is normally 20 times more permeable to potassium.

An action potential is generated by a sudden and brief opening of the sodium gates. This happens in response to a stimulus which brings about a slight depolarisation, or loss of charge, of the axon membrane. Opening the gates increases the permeability of the axon membrane to sodium ions which enter the axon by diffusion. This increases the number of positive ions inside the axon, which therefore becomes *further* **depolarised**. First the negative resting potential is cancelled out, at which point the membrane

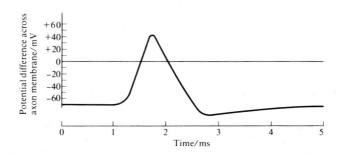

Fig 17.3 *A typical action potential in the axon of a squid.*

is completely depolarised, then it makes the potential difference across the membrane positive. Since the sodium gates are sensitive to depolarisation, the greater the depolarisation, the more gates open. This allows more sodium into the cell, causing greater depolarisation. The two processes therefore reinforce each other. This is called a positive feedback loop. It causes an explosive acceleration in the rate of entry of sodium. (Remember this is taking place within thousandths of a second.) The potential difference peaks at 40 mV, as shown in fig 17.4*a*. This peak corresponds to the maximum concentration of sodium inside the axon. The total depolarisation associated with the action potential has therefore been from −70 mV to +40 mV, a total of 110 mV. Calculations have revealed that relatively few sodium ions (about one-millionth of the internal sodium ions present, depending upon axon diameter) enter the axon and produce this depolarisation.

A fraction of a second after the sodium gates open, depolarisation of the axon membrane causes the potassium gates to open. Potassium therefore diffuses *out* of the cell (fig 17.4*b*). Since potassium is positively charged, this makes the inside of the cell less positive, or more negative, and starts the process of **repolarisation**, or return to the original resting potential.

At the peak of the action potential, the sodium gates start to close again. Sodium permeability therefore declines. The sodium–potassium pump continues to work during this time, so it gradually begins to restore the original resting potential. This repolarisation is shown by the falling phase of the action potential 'spike' (fig 17.4*a*) and results in the membrane potential returning to its original level. In fact, there is a slight overshoot into a more negative potential than the original resting potential. This is called **hyperpolarisation**. It is due to the slight delay in closing all the potassium gates compared with the sodium gates (the potassium graph starts to fall after the sodium graph in fig 17.4*b*). As potassium ions continue to return to the inside of the axon their positive charge restores the normal resting potential.

From the above account it can be seen that whilst the resting potential is determined largely by potassium ions, the action potential is determined largely by sodium ions (fig 17.4).

Nerve impulses travel as action potentials. A nerve impulse is an action potential which passes along an axon as a **wave of depolarisation**. The *outside surface* of the axon is negatively charged at the site of the action potential.

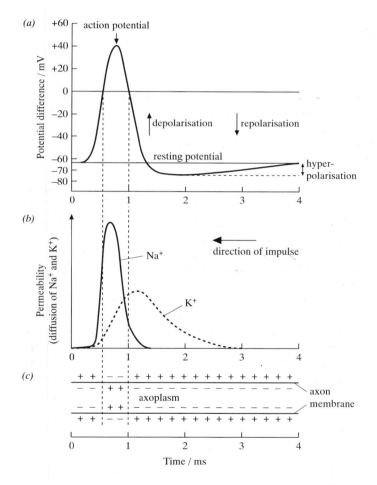

Fig 17.4 *Diagrams to show changes in the axon during the propagation of a nerve impulse: (a) the membrane potential, showing the electrical events associated with the nerve impulse, (b) change in permeability to ions, (c) the net charge across the axon membrane during production of an action potential.*

Features of action potentials

Propagation (conduction) of nerve impulses. A nerve impulse is a **wave of depolarisation** that moves

559

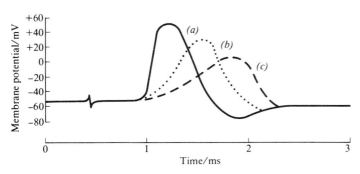

Fig 17.5 *Membrane potentials recorded from squid axons bathed in sea water containing different concentrations of sodium ions.*

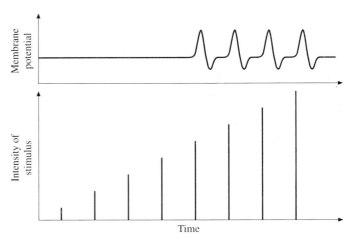

Fig 17.6 *The 'all-or-nothing' response. A certain 'threshold intensity' of stimulus must be reached before the nerve cell responds. It is also possible to see from the figure that the size of the action potential is always the same and is not affected by the intensity of the stimulus.*

along the surface of a nerve cell. Action potentials are **propagated**, that is self generated, along the axon by the effect of sodium ions entering the axon. This creates an area of positive charge, and a flow of current is set up in a **local circuit** between this active area and the negatively charged resting region immediately ahead. The current flow in the local circuit reduces the membrane potential in the resting region and this depolarisation produces an increase in sodium permeability and the development of an action potential in this region. Repeated depolarisations of immediately adjacent regions of the membrane result in the action potential being moved, or propagated, along the axon. Action potentials are capable, in theory, of being transmitted over an infinite distance, that is, they do not lose strength. The reason for this is that the production of an action potential at each point along the axon is a self-generating event resulting from a change in the local concentration of ions. So long as the outside and inside environments of the axon have the necessary differences in ionic concentrations, an action potential at one point will generate another action potential at the next point.

All-or-nothing law and coding for stimulus intensity. The body must have a way of distinguishing between weak and strong stimuli. One possibility would be to have a variable size of action potential depending on the size of the stimulus. In order to investigate whether this occurs, an experiment can be done in which stimuli of increasing intensity are given, and the size of the action potential measured. The results are shown in fig 17.6. They show that the size of the action potential is *not* affected by the size of the stimulus. This is known as the **all-or-nothing law** because the action potential either occurs or does not and its size is constant. In other words, there is a **threshold stimulus intensity** above which the action potential will be triggered whatever the strength of the stimulus.

It has also been shown that the *speed* at which the impulse is transmitted is not affected by the strength of the stimulus. So how *does* the body distinguish between weak and strong stimuli? The answer lies with the frequency of the action potentials (the number in a given time). The stronger the stimulus, within limits, the greater the frequency of action potentials set up. We can say that the frequency is a code for the intensity of a stimulus. Frequency is proportional to intensity. This is known as the **frequency code**.

Impulses at the frequency of 10 per nerve fibre per second keep the biceps muscle in tone (in a state of partial concentration ready for action). About 50 impulses per fibre per second are needed for steady contraction. Most nerve fibres can conduct impulses in the region of 10–100 per second, although some can conduct as many as 500 per second in natural situations (and more in experimental situations).

Speed of conduction. In vertebrates, the majority of neurones, particularly those of the spinal and cranial nerves, have an outer covering of myelin derived from the spirally wound Schwann cell (fig 6.30 and section 6.6.1). Myelin is a fatty material with a high electrical resistance and acts as an electrical insulator in the same way as the rubber and plastic covering of electrical wiring. The combined resistance of the axon membrane and myelin sheath is very high but, where breaks in the myelin sheath occur, as at the **nodes of Ranvier**, the resistance to current flow between the axoplasm and the fluid outside the cell is lower. It is only at these points that local circuits are set up and current flows across the axon membrane to generate the next action potential. This means, in effect, that the action potential 'jumps' from node to node and passes along the myelinated axon faster than the series of smaller local currents in a non-myelinated axon. This type of conduction is called **saltatory conduction** (*saltare*, to jump) and can lead to conduction speeds of up to $120\,m\,s^{-1}$ (fig 17.7).

In non-myelinated axons (axons lacking a myelin sheath) typical of those found in non-vertebrates, the speed of conduction of the action potential depends on the resistance of the axoplasm. This resistance, in turn, is related to the

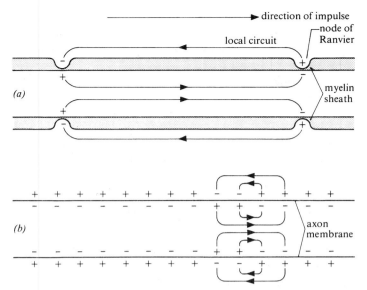

Fig 17.7 *Diagrams showing the difference in lengths of the local circuits produced (a) in a myelinated axon and (b) a non-myelinated axon. In (a) conduction is described as saltatory since the action potential effectively 'jumps' from node to node.*

diameter of the axon. The smaller the diameter, the greater is the resistance. In the case of fine axons (<0.1 mm) the high resistance of the axoplasm has an effect on the spread of current and reduces the length of the local circuits, so that only the region of the membrane immediately in front of the action potential is involved in the local circuit. These axons conduct impulses at about $0.5 \, \text{m s}^{-1}$. Giant axons, typical of many annelids, arthropods and molluscs, have a diameter of approximately 1 mm and conduct impulses at velocities up to $100 \, \text{m s}^{-1}$, which are ideal for conducting information vital for survival.

> **17.4** Explain, in terms of the resistance of the axoplasm and local circuits, why giant axons conduct impulses at greater velocities than fine axons.

Effect of temperature on speed of conduction. Temperature has an effect on the rate of conduction of nerve impulses and as temperature rises to about 40°C the rate of conduction increases.

> **17.5** Why do myelinated axons of frog having a diameter of $3.5 \, \mu\text{m}$ conduct impulses at $30 \, \text{m s}^{-1}$ whereas axons of the same diameter in cat conduct impulses at $90 \, \text{m s}^{-1}$?

17.1.2 The synapse

A synapse is the link between one neurone and another. There is no physical contact between one neurone

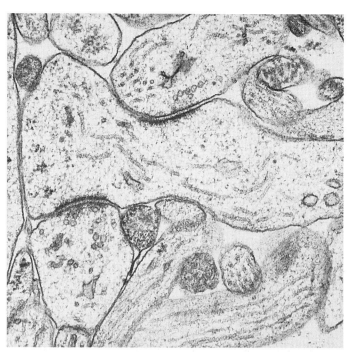

Fig 17.8 *Transmission electron micrograph of a motor neurone showing synapses. The synaptic cleft appears dark.*

and the next. Instead there is a tiny gap called the **synaptic cleft**. Synapses are usually found between the fine branches at the end of the axon of one neurone and the **dendrites** or **cell body** of another neurone. The number of synapses is usually very large, providing a large surface area for the transfer of information. For example, over 1000 synapses may be found on the dendrites and cell body of a single motor neurone in the spinal cord. Some cells in the brain may receive up to 10 000 synapses (fig 17.8).

Another type of synapse, with a similar function but a different structure, exists between the terminals of a motor neurone and the surface of a muscle fibre. This is called a **neuromuscular junction** and is described later in this section.

Structure of the synapse

The structure of a synapse is shown in figs 17.9 and 17.10. A synapse consists of a swelling at the end of a nerve fibre called a **synaptic knob** lying in close proximity to the membrane of a dendrite. The cytoplasm of the synaptic knob contains numerous mitochondria (for energy) and small **synaptic vesicles** (diameter 50 nm). Each vesicle contains a chemical called a **neurotransmitter** which is responsible for the transmission of the nerve impulse across the synapse. The membrane of the synaptic knob nearest the synapse is thickened and is called the **presynaptic membrane**. The membrane of the dendrite is also thickened and termed the **postsynaptic membrane**. These membranes are separated by a gap of about 20 nm, the **synaptic cleft**. The presynaptic membrane is modified for the attachment of synaptic vesicles and the release of

(a)

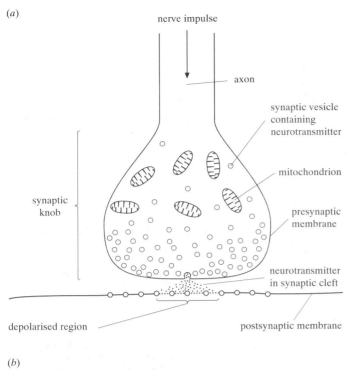

nerve impulse

axon

synaptic vesicle containing neurotransmitter

mitochondrion

presynaptic membrane

neurotransmitter in synaptic cleft

synaptic knob

depolarised region

postsynaptic membrane

(b)

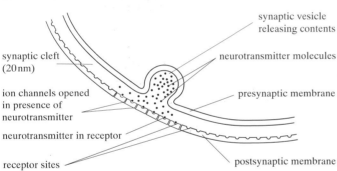

synaptic vesicle releasing contents

neurotransmitter molecules

presynaptic membrane

synaptic cleft (20 nm)

ion channels opened in presence of neurotransmitter

neurotransmitter in receptor

receptor sites

postsynaptic membrane

Fig 17.9 *Structure of a synapse.*

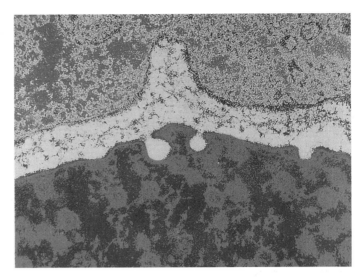

Fig 17.10 *Synapse as seen with an electron microscope.*

transmitter substance into the synaptic cleft. The postsynaptic membrane contains large protein molecules, which act as **receptor sites** for the transmitter substances, and numerous **channels** and **pores**, normally closed, for the movement of ions into the postsynaptic neurone (fig 17.11).

As stated, synaptic vesicles contain a neurotransmitter substance. This is produced either in the cell body of the neurone, from where it passes down the axon to the synaptic knob, or directly in the synaptic knob. In both cases, synthesis of transmitter substances requires enzymes produced by ribosomes in the cell body. In the synaptic knob the transmitter substance is 'packaged' into vesicles and stored ready for release. The two main transmitter substances in vertebrate nervous systems are **acetylcholine (ACh)** and **noradrenaline**, although other substances exist and are described at the end of this section. Acetylcholine is an ammonium compound. It was the first transmitter substance to be isolated (in 1920). Noradrenaline is described in section 17.6.5. Neurones releasing acetylcholine are described as **cholinergic neurones** and those releasing noradrenaline are described as **adrenergic neurones**. Noradrenaline is released by nerves in the sympathetic nervous system whereas acetylcholine is released by almost all other nerves (except some in the brain).

Mechanism of synaptic transmission

In the following account, the example of the neuro-transmitter acetylcholine will be used. The arrival of nerve impulses at the synaptic knob depolarises the presynaptic membrane, causing calcium channels to open, increasing the permeability of the membrane to calcium (Ca^{2+}) ions. As the calcium ions rush into the synaptic knob they cause the synaptic vesicles to fuse with the presynaptic membrane, releasing their contents into the synaptic cleft (**exocytosis**). The vesicles then return to the cytoplasm where they are refilled with transmitter substance. Each vesicle contains about 3000 molecules of acetylcholine.

Acetylcholine diffuses across the synaptic cleft, creating a delay of about 0.5 ms, and attaches to a specific receptor site (a protein) on the postsynaptic membrane that recognises the molecular structure of the acetylcholine molecule. The arrival of the acetylcholine causes a change in the shape of the receptor site which results in ion channels opening up in the postsynaptic membrane. Note that in the transmission of the nerve impulse along the axon, ion channels are opened in response to depolarisation, whereas in the postsynaptic membrane of the synapse it is in response to binding of neurotransmitter to receptor proteins.

Entry of sodium ions through the postsynaptic membrane causes **depolarisation** (fig 17.4a) of the membrane. This excites the cell, making it more likely to set up a nerve impulse (action potential). Having produced a change in the permeability of the postsynaptic membrane the acetyl-choline is immediately removed from the synaptic cleft, by

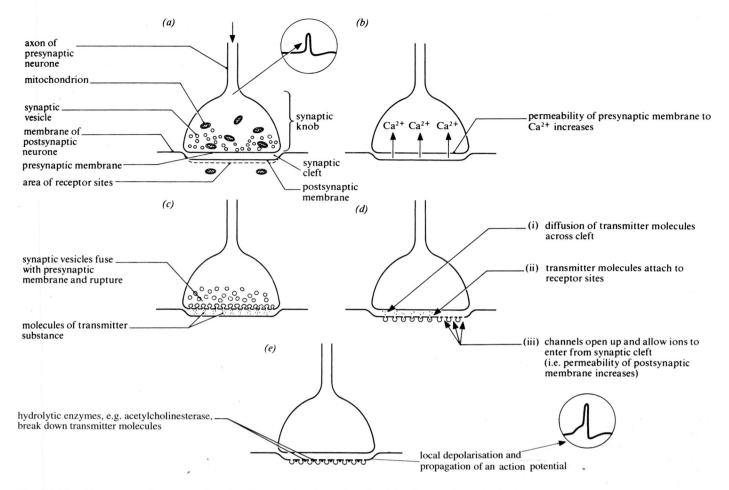

Fig 17.11 *Summary diagrams showing the mechanisms involved in chemical transmission at a synapse, (a) to (e) time sequence.*

the enzyme **acetylcholinesterase (AChE)**, also called **cholinesterase**. The enzyme is situated on the postsynaptic membrane and hydrolyses the acetylcholine to choline. The choline is reabsorbed into the synaptic knob to be recycled into acetylcholine by synthetic pathways in the vesicle (fig 17.11). Some nerve gases and insecticides work by inhibiting AChE as explained in section 4.4.3.

Other neurotransmitters

Some neurotransmitters are inhibitory in their effects. They cause **hyperpolarisation** rather than *depolarisation* of the postsynaptic membrane. Hyperpolarisation makes the inside of the cell even more negative, making it *less* likely to set up a nerve impulse.

There are three possible ways of removing neurotransmitters from the synaptic cleft:

- reabsorption by the presynaptic membrane;
- diffusion out of the cleft;
- hydrolysis by enzymes.

Roles of synapses

Excitatory synapses, spatial summation and temporal summation. At **excitatory** synapses ion-specific channels open up allowing sodium ions to enter and potassium ions to leave down their respective concentration gradients. This leads to a depolarisation in the postsynaptic membrane. The depolarising response is known as an **excitatory postsynaptic potential (epsp)** and the size of this potential is usually small but longer lasting than that of an action potential. The size of epsps fluctuates in steps, suggesting that transmitter substance is released in 'packets' rather than individual molecules. Each 'step' is thought to correspond to the release of transmitter substance from one synaptic vesicle. A single epsp is normally unable to produce sufficient depolarisation to reach the threshold required to propagate an action potential in the postsynaptic neurone. However, it does increase the chance of a further epsp generating an action potential, an effect called **facilitation**. The depolarising effect of several epsps is additive, a phenomenon known as **summation**. Two or

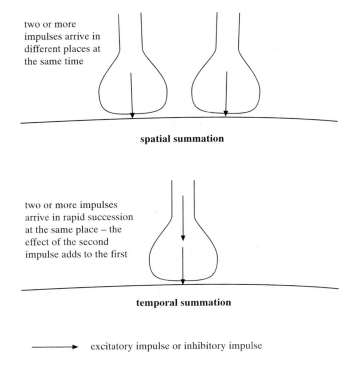

two or more impulses arrive in different places at the same time

spatial summation

two or more impulses arrive in rapid succession at the same place – the effect of the second impulse adds to the first

temporal summation

→ excitatory impulse or inhibitory impulse

Fig 17.12 *Spatial and temporal summation.*

more epsps arising simultaneously at different regions on the same neurone, usually from different neurones, may produce sufficient depolarisation to start an action potential in the postsynaptic neurone. This is **spatial summation** (related in space) (fig 17.12). The rapid repeated release of transmitter substance from several synaptic vesicles by the *same* synaptic knob, as a result of an intense stimulus, produces individual epsps which are so close together that they summate and give rise to an action potential in the postsynaptic neurone. This is **temporal summation** (summation through time) (fig 17.12). Therefore impulses can be set up in a single postsynaptic neurone as a result of either weak stimulation by several presynaptic neurones or repeated stimulation by one presynaptic neurone.

Inhibitory synapses. At inhibitory synapses the release of transmitter substance increases the permeability of the postsynaptic membrane by opening up ion-specific channels to chloride (Cl⁻) and potassium ions. As chloride ions rush in and potassium ions rush out down their concentration gradients, they produce a hyper-polarisation of the membrane known as an **inhibitory postsynaptic potential** (**ipsp**). In other words they make the inside of the neurone *more* negative, down to as low as $-90 \, mV$. This makes the neurone *less* likely to trigger an action potential.

Transmitter substances themselves are neither inherently excitatory nor inhibitory. For example, acetylcholine has an excitatory effect at most neuromuscular junctions and synapses, but has an inhibitory effect on neuromuscular junctions in cardiac muscle and gut muscle. These opposing effects are determined by events occurring at the postsynaptic membrane. The molecular properties of the receptor sites determine which ions enter the postsynaptic cell, which in turn determines the nature of the change in postsynaptic potentials as described above.

Neuromuscular junction. The neuro-muscular junction is a specialised form of synapse found between a motor neurone and skeletal muscle fibres. Each muscle fibre has a specialised region, the **motor end-plate**, where the axon of the motor neurone divides and forms fine branches ending in synaptic knobs. The branches lack a myelinated sheath. The neuromuscular junction includes both the motor end-plate and the synaptic knob. The fine branches run in shallow troughs on the cell surface membrane of the muscle fibre (fig 17.13*a*). This membrane is called the **sarcolemma** and has many deep folds in the troughs as shown in fig 17.13*b*. On stimulation, the synaptic knobs release acetylcholine by the same mechanisms as previously described. Changes in the structure of receptor sites on the folds of the sarcolemma (the postsynaptic membrane) increase the permeability of the sarcolemma to sodium and potassium ions and a local depolarisation known as an **end-plate potential** (**EPP**) is produced. This is sufficient to lead to an action potential passing along the sarcolemma and down into the muscle fibre through the **transverse tubule system** (**T-system**) (section 18.4.4). This action potential results in muscle contraction, as described in section 18.4.7. In most skeletal muscle there is one neuromuscular junction per fibre.

Functions of synapses

Since synapses have the effect of slowing down nerve impulses by about 0.5 ms per synapse, it can be assumed that their advantages outweigh this disadvantage. What are the advantages? They are summarised as follows.

- **Unidirectionality**. The release of transmitter substance at the presynaptic membrane, and the location of receptor sites on the postsynaptic membrane, ensure that nerve impulses can pass only in one direction along a given pathway. This gives *precision* to the nervous system, allowing nerve impulses to reach particular destinations.

- **Amplification**. Sufficient acetylcholine is released at a neuromuscular junction by each nerve impulse to excite the postsynaptic membrane to produce a response in the muscle fibre. Thus nerve impulses arriving at the neuromuscular junction, however weak, are adequate to produce a response from the effector, thereby increasing the *sensitivity* of the system.

- **Adaptation and fatigue**. The amount of transmitter substance released by a synapse steadily falls off in response to constant stimulation until the supply of transmitter substance is exhausted and the synapse is described as **fatigued**. Further passage of information along this pathway is not possible until after a period of recovery. The significance of fatigue is that it prevents

damage to an effector through overstimulation.

Adaptation also occurs at the level of the receptor and this is described in section 17.4.2.

- **Integration, convergence and spatial summation.** A postsynaptic neurone may receive impulses from a large number of excitatory and inhibitory presynaptic neurones. This is known as **convergence**, and the postsynaptic neurone is able to summate the stimuli from all the presynaptic neurones (a simple example is shown in fig 17.12). This spatial summation enables the synapse to act as a centre for the integration of stimuli from a variety of sources and the production of a coordinated response.

- **Facilitation.** This occurs at some synapses and involves each stimulus leaving the synapse more responsive to the next stimulus. The sensitivity of the synapse has therefore been increased, and subsequent weaker stimuli may cause a reponse. Facilitation is not temporal summation in that it is a chemically controlled response of the postsynaptic membrane and not an electrical summation of postsynaptic membrane potentials.

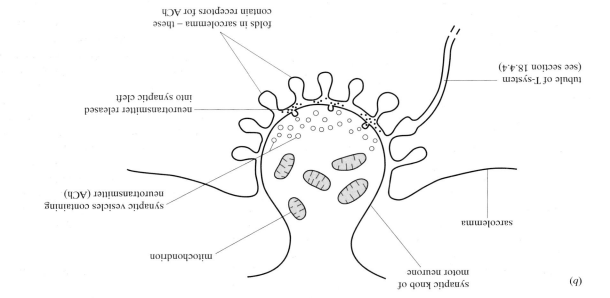

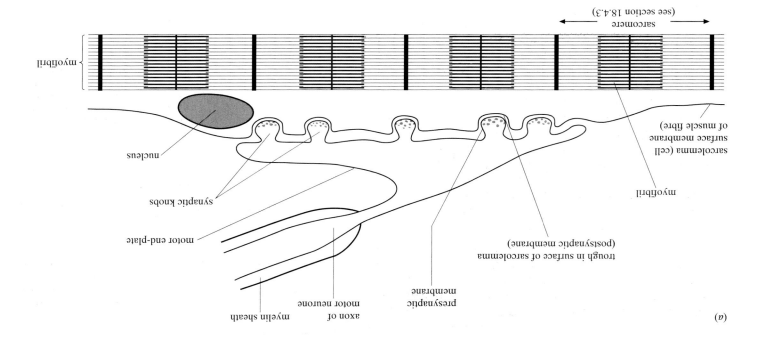

Fig 17.13 Structure of a neuromuscular junction: (a) detail visible with a light microscope. (b) detail visible with an electron microscope.

- **Discrimination and temporal summation.** Temporal summation at synapses enables weak background stimuli to be filtered out before they reach the brain. For example, receptors in the skin, the eyes and ears receive constant stimuli from the environment which have little immediate importance for the nervous system, such as background noise. Only *changes* in intensity of stimuli are significant to the nervous system. These increase the frequency of stimuli and pass across the synapse to cause a response.

- **Inhibition.** The transmission of information across synapses and neuromuscular junctions may be prevented at the postsynaptic membrane by the activity of certain neurotransmitters or drugs, as described in the next section. Presynaptic inhibition is also possible. It occurs at synaptic knobs that are in close contact with synaptic knobs from inhibitory synapses. Stimulation of these inhibitory synapses reduces the number of synaptic vesicles released by the inhibited synaptic knob. This arrangement enables a given nerve terminal to produce a variable response depending upon the activity of its excitatory and inhibitory synapses.

- Synapses allow control by a range of neurotransmitters in the brain. This chemical control increases the complexity and subtlety of the control of behaviour.

Drugs, neurotransmitters and synapses

Although acetylcholine and noradrenaline are the main neurotransmitters outside the brain, more than 50 natural neurotransmitters have been isolated from the brain, all associated with their own particular nervous pathways. In addition, many other chemicals affect synapses. These may affect the brain, and therefore behaviour, or other parts of the body such as the neuromuscular junction. Some of these substances and their functions are described in table 17.3 and below.

Amino acids. The major excitatory neurotransmitter in the brain is the amino acid **glutamate** (glutamic acid). A number of chemicals mimic glutamate

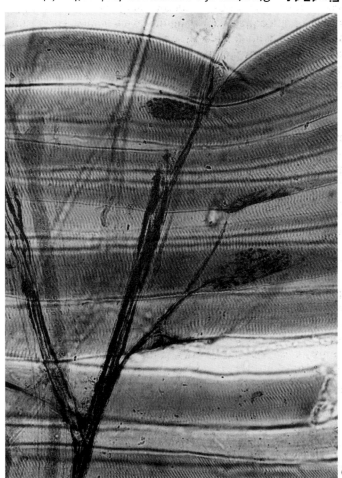
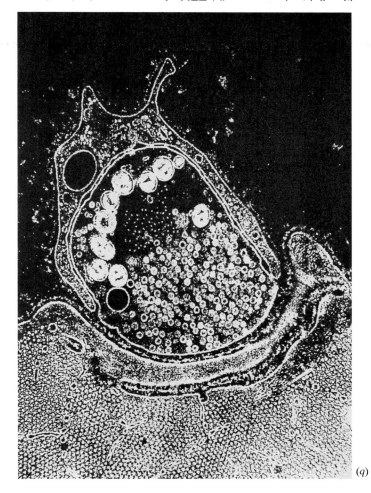

Fig 17.14 Structure of a neuromuscular junction (a) as seen with a light microscope. (b) TEM of neuromuscular junction. The end of the nerve (centre) is closely associated with the muscle fibre. Inside the nerve, clustered near to the muscle, are small vesicles containing neurotransmitter chemicals.

Table 17.3 Summary of chemical substances which affect the synapse and neuromuscular junction.

Substance	Site of action	Function/effect
acetylcholine	nervous system	excitation or inhibition
glutamic acid (amino acid)	brain	excitation
glycine (amino acid)	brain and spinal cord postsynaptic membrane	inhibition muscles relax
strychnine	brain and spinal cord postsynaptic membrane blocks glycine receptors	antagonistic to glycine muscles contract but will not relax
GABA (gamma aminobutyric acid) (amino acid)	brain	inhibition
β-endorphins enkephalins	brain opioid receptors in postsynaptic membrane	block 'pain pathways' and stimulate reward pathways
morphine **heroin**	brain opioid receptors in postsynaptic membrane	mimic endorphins and enkephalins
noradrenaline (monoamine)	brain and SNS	excitation
dopamine (monoamine)	brain	excitation, control of complex muscular movement, some emotional responses
serotonin	brain	excitation, control of mood, hallucinations
LSD (lysergic acid diethylamide) **mescaline**	brain	mimic serotonin? produce hallucinations
amphetamine	brain and SNS	inhibits monoamine oxidase so increases level of noradrenaline
cocaine	brain and SNS	as amphetamine above (and other effects)
Prozac	brain and SNS	blocks re-uptake of serotonin so increases effect
nicotine	postsynaptic membrane in SNS and PNS	mimics action of ACh on nicotinic receptors
muscarine	postsynaptic membrane in PNS	mimics action of ACh on muscarinic receptors
caffeine	brain	stimulates dopamine pathways
atropine	SNS and PNS	blocks action of ACh on muscarinic receptors
curare	SNS and PNS neuromuscular junction postsynaptic membrane	blocks action of ACh on nicotinic receptors
tetanus toxin	presynaptic membrane	prevents release of inhibiting transmitter substance
botulinum toxin	presynaptic membrane	prevents release of ACh
organophosphorous weedkillers and insecticides, some nerve gases	postsynaptic membrane	inactivates acetylcholine-esterase and prevents breakdown of ACh

Drugs are indicated in bold type.

and bind to glutamate receptors in the brain. One group of glutamate receptors are the major sites of action of the illicit drug known as **angel dust**. (An illicit drug is one which is illegal outside of medical use.)

The amino acid **glycine** is inhibitory, causing chloride channels to open in the postsynaptic membrane and resulting in hyperpolarisation (the contents of the cell become more negative). Glycine is important in the spinal cord where it helps control skeletal movements by making muscles relax (preventing their stimulation). Its importance is revealed by the effect of **strychnine** which blocks the glycine receptors and therefore inhibits the effects of glycine. The slightest stimulation then causes muscle contraction. Victims of strychnine poisoning suffocate through being unable to relax the diaphragm muscles.

The amino acid **GABA** is the most common neurotransmitter in the brain and is also inhibitory. It helps control muscle movement, for example by acting in the cerebellum (a part of the brain discussed in section 17.2.4). A deficiency of GABA produces the uncontrolled movements of Huntington's disease (section 25.7.5). It is the target of antianxiety drugs such as Valium, which enhance its activity.

Opioids, endorphins and enkephalins. Opioids are drugs which are derived from opium, that is obtained from the opium poppy. These drugs have been used for centuries as pain killers. **Morphine** and **heroin** are modern examples. In the brain there are naturally occurring substances which have similar effects, although they are 200 times stronger than morphine. These substances react with the opiate receptor in the brain (discovered in 1973) and are collectively called **endorphins** (meaning endogenously produced morphine-like compounds). Many have been identified and the best known are a group of small peptides known as **enkephalins**, for example **metenkephalin** and β-**endorphin**. The enkephalins are five amino acids long. They reduce pain, influence emotion and are involved with certain types of mental illness. Endorphins and enkephalins act at the postsynaptic membrane and suppress the synaptic activity which would normally lead to the sensation of pain. They are therefore natural pain killers. If used for medical purposes they are addictive and are only briefly effective. A burst of β-endorphin is released naturally during childbirth.

Opioids also produce pleasant sensations and may be associated with internal 'reward' pathways which reinforce certain types of behaviour. Since β-endorphin levels increase during exercise, this may help to explain the 'high' that joggers experience.

Research into these chemicals has opened up new ideas on brain functioning. It also helps to explain the control of pain and healing by such diverse activities as hypnosis, acupuncture and faith healing. Many more chemical substances of this type have yet to be isolated, identified and have their function determined.

Monoamines. **Noradrenaline**, another hormone secreted by the adrenal gland, is a monoamine and a neurotransmitter in the sympathetic nervous system which prepares the body for action (section 17.2.3). It also exists in the brain, increasing alertness and helping to maintain the state of arousal. It enhances our response to new stimuli. Pep pills containing **amphetamine** increase the level of noradrenaline in the brain by inhibiting the action of monoamine oxidase (MAO). This is the enzyme which under normal conditions removes noradrenaline once it has been reabsorbed at the synapses; MAO therefore prevents overstimulation. Another effect of amphetamine is to cause excess dopamine release and therefore stimulate reward pathways (see below). Amphetamine also stimulates the sympathetic nervous system indirectly by raising levels of noradrenaline at sympathetic nerve endings.

Some antidepressants are **monoamine oxidase inhibitors** and, presumably, are effective in treating depression by prolonging the effects of noradrenaline. Clinical depression is an illness which is characterised by fewer nerve impulses being transmitted through the brain. MAO inhibitors promote the activity of all the monoamines and can have undesirable side effects. A newer drug, **Prozac**, specifically blocks the re-uptake of serotonin into presynaptic axons and therefore promotes serotonin effects only (see below). It is now used widely for treatment of depression.

Dopamine, another monoamine, has a structure very similar to that of noradrenaline (fig 17.15). It is the natural neurotransmitter of 'dopamine pathways' in the brain. These are partly concerned with voluntary control of complex muscular movements. A deficiency of dopamine results in Parkinson's disease. Dopamine is also involved in emotional responses in the cerebral cortex and has been linked with schizophrenia. It can also stimulate the 'pleasure' centre of the hypothalamus. Amphetamines trigger the release of dopamine.

Serotonin is associated with control of moods, including depression, elation and mania. It is also involved in the onset of sleep, sensory perception and temperature regulation in the hypothalamus. Fig 17.15 shows that it has some similarity in structure to **LSD (lysergic acid diethylamide).** LSD is a hallucinogenic drug as is mescaline. They are thought to mimic some of the activities of serotonin. It is common to find similarities in structure between drugs that alter behaviour and neurotransmitters, suggesting that the drugs recognise the same receptors and either block or stimulate the natural effects.

Nicotine. Nicotine mimics the effect of the neurotransmitter acetylcholine (ACh) on certain receptors (not all those that acetylcholine binds to). The receptors concerned are called **nicotinic receptors** and are found in the membranes of postsynaptic cells. They are found in the sympathetic and parasympathetic nervous systems (section 17.2.3). Activation of the receptors leads to depolarisation and therefore excitation of the postsynaptic cell or effector.

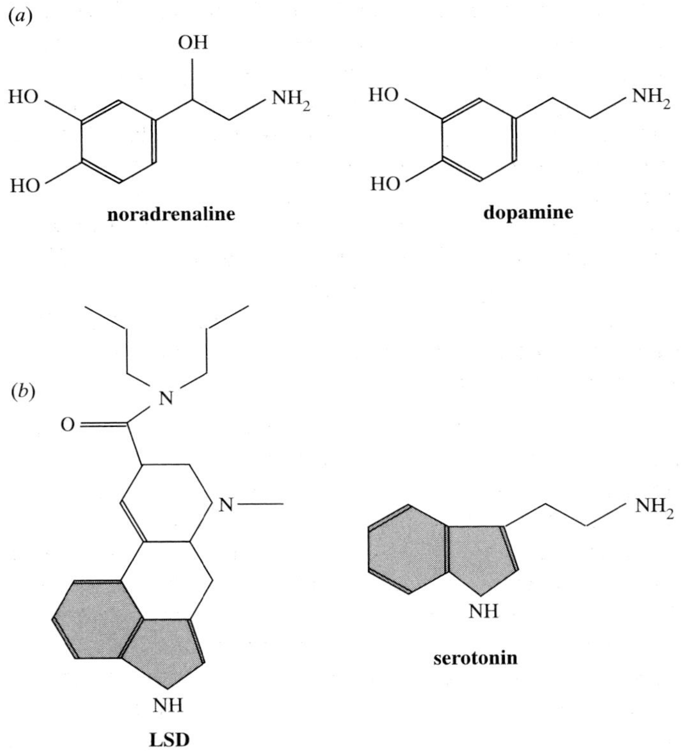

Nicotine causes strong sympathetic vasoconstriction in abdominal organs such as the gut, and in the limbs, but at the same time parasympathetic effects occur, such as increased gastrointestinal activity and, sometimes, slowing of the heart.

Nicotinic receptors are also found at neuromuscular junctions. If nicotine is applied directly to the junction it makes the muscle contract, mimicking acetylcholine. Nicotinic receptors are found in a few regions of the brain, but it is not understood how this relates to the psychological effects of the drug. Many of the receptors stimulate release of dopamine and therefore stimulate reward and pleasure pathways. However, the behavioural effects of nicotine are very subtle compared with some drugs.

Atropine. Cholinergic receptors, that is receptors stimulated by acetylcholine, are of two types, namely nicotinic receptors (mentioned above) and muscarinic receptors. (These receptors are named after the drug muscarine, a poison isolated from certain mushrooms. They are in the parasympathetic nervous system, for example in the heart and gut.) Atropine blocks the action of acetylcholine in the muscarinic receptors. Acetylcholine slows the heart and stimulates peristalsis in the gut, so atropine has the opposite effect because it blocks the receptors, preventing the binding of acetylcholine.

noradrenaline

dopamine

(a)

serotonin

LSD

(b)

Fig 17.15 Similarities in structure between (a) the two natural neurotransmitters noradrenaline and dopamine and (b) the drug LSD and the natural neurotransmitter serotonin. Many drugs that affect behaviour, such as LSD, resemble natural neurotransmitters.

Atropine is obtained from the deadly nightshade (*Atropa belladonna*). The use of the species name *belladonna*, meaning beautiful lady, refers to the use by women in the Middle Ages of a deadly nightshade extract, containing atropine, as eye drops to make the pupils dilate. This was thought to make women look more attractive to men. The drug inhibits parasympathetic stimulation of the iris, causing the circular muscles of the iris to relax. Today the drug is used for medical purposes. It can be used to dilate the pupils during an eye examination, before a general anaesthetic to inhibit mucous production in the respiratory tract, and to inhibit secretion of stomach acid in patients suffering from gastritis (overproduction of acid).

Curare. Curare specifically blocks the nicotinic receptors of acetylcholine. It therefore has opposite effects to acetylcholine and nicotine at these receptors. The effects of curare are particularly noticeable at neuromuscular junctions where it prevents muscle contraction, causing rapid paralysis throughout the body. The victim dies as a result of being unable to breathe. (Artificial respiration can save a victim if applied until the effect of the drug wears off.) This accounts for its use as a poison to tip arrows by some South American tribes when hunting; it prevents wounded animals escaping into thick undergrowth. Curare and related drugs can be used as a muscle relaxant on patients during surgical operations, which makes operating easier for the surgeon. Breathing is maintained artificially.

Caffeine. Like nicotine, caffeine is a stimulant, although a relatively weak one. It is thought to cause dopamine release in the brain and therefore stimulates reward pathways.

Cocaine. Cocaine is a stimulant, having very similar, though not identical, effects to amphetamine. Cocaine blocks the re-uptake of monoamines into the presynaptic axons. This results in overstimulation of dopamine pathways and other monoamine pathways. It occurs naturally in coca leaves, which are chewed by local people in the highlands of the Andes. Until about 1900 it was added to Coca Cola. As a drug of abuse it is used for the sense of euphoria it promotes, which helps in social situations. It can become addictive, particularly in its pure form **crack**. This leads to social withdrawal, depression and eventually heart and kidney disease. Cocaine has been used medically as a local anaesthetic for the eyes, nose, mouth (during dentistry) and throat, but non-medical use is illegal.

17.2 The parts of the nervous system

The nervous system can be divided into the central nervous system (brain and spinal cord) and the peripheral nervous system. The peripheral nervous system can be divided into the voluntary nervous system, which is under voluntary control from the brain, and the autonomic nervous system which operates automatically (involuntary). This system is divided into the sympathetic nervous system (SNS), which has a mainly excitatory effect on the body, and the parasympathetic nervous system (PNS), which acts antagonistically (oppositely) to the SNS and has a mainly calming influence. These subdivisions are summarised in fig 17.16.

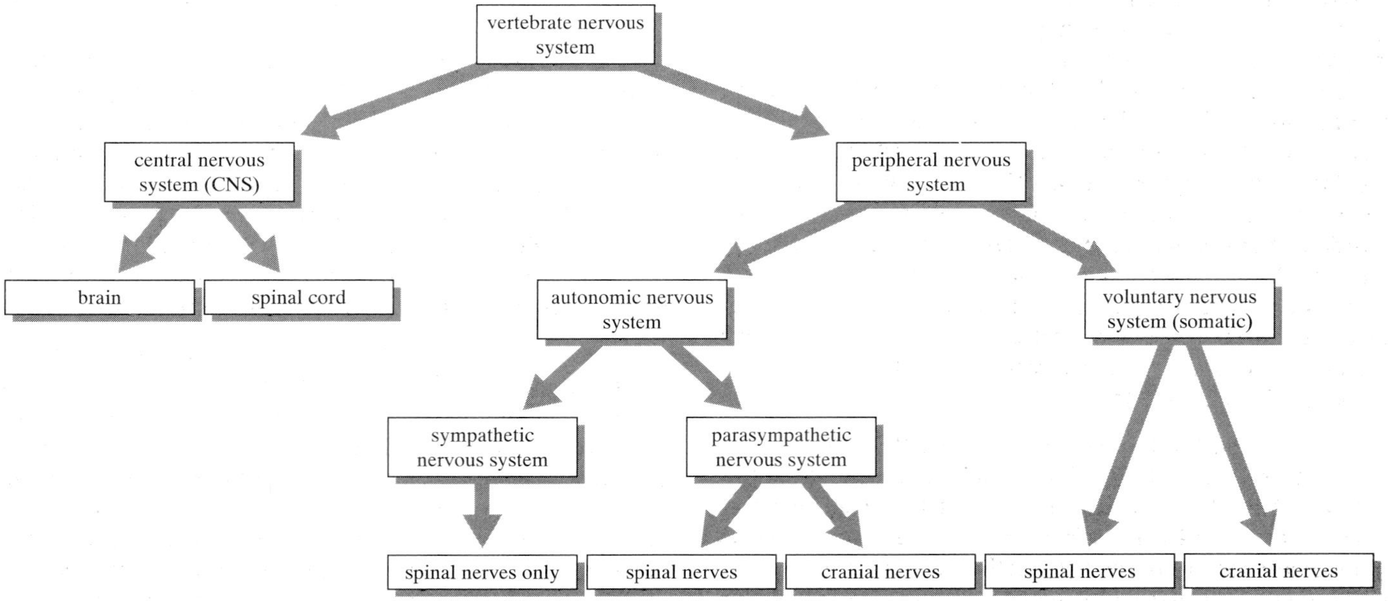

Fig 17.16 Outline classification of the vertebrate nervous system. (All spinal nerves and some cranial nerves have both sensory and motor neurones.)

- vertebrate nervous system
  - central nervous system (CNS)
    - brain
    - spinal cord
  - peripheral nervous system
    - autonomic nervous system
      - sympathetic nervous system
        - spinal nerves only
      - parasympathetic nervous system
        - spinal nerves
        - cranial nerves
    - voluntary nervous system (somatic)
      - spinal nerves
      - cranial nerves

17.2.1 The peripheral nervous system

All the nerves of the body together make up the peripheral nervous system. They all enter or leave the central nervous system, either the spinal cord in the case of **spinal nerves**, or the brain in the case of **cranial nerves**.

Spinal nerves arise from the spinal cord between the vertebrae along most of the length of the spinal cord. They all carry both sensory and motor neurones and are described as **mixed** nerves. Further details of spinal nerves and the spinal cord are given below. **Cranial nerves** arise from the brain and, with one exception (the vagus), supply receptors and effectors of the head. There are 12 pairs of cranial nerves in mammals, numbered I–XII in Roman numerals. Not all cranial nerves are mixed.

Three examples of cranial nerves are:

- *cranial nerve II* – **optic nerve** – this is a *sensory nerve* running from the retina to the brain;
- *cranial nerve III* – **oculomotor nerve** – this is a *motor nerve* running from the brain to the four eye muscles and helps control eye movements;
- *cranial nerve X* – **vagus nerve** – this is a *mixed nerve*. It runs between the brain and the heart, gut and part of the respiratory tract and decreases heart rate, stimulates peristalsis and is concerned with speech and swallowing. It includes an important motor nerve of the autonomic nervous system supplying the heart, bronchi and gut.

17.2.2 Reflex action and reflex arcs

The simplest form of response in the nervous system is **reflex action**. This is a rapid, automatic response to a stimulus which is not under the voluntary control of the brain. It is described as an **involuntary action**. The same stimulus produces the same response every time. The nervous pathway taken by nerve impulses in a reflex action is called the **reflex arc**.

The simplest reflex arcs in humans involve only two neurones, a sensory neurone and a motor neurone. The knee-jerk reflex is an example. Other reflex arcs involve three neurones: a sensory neurone, an interneurone and a motor neurone. One example is the withdrawal reflex associated with pricking a finger on a pin. This is a spinal reflex, meaning that the reflex arc passes through the spinal cord rather than the brain (these are called cranial reflexes). It is illustrated in fig 17.17. Note that there is a one-way system of nerve fibres through the spinal cord. Sensory neurones enter through the dorsal root (not route) and motor neurones emerge from the ventral root. All the nerve cell bodies are in the central nervous system (spinal cord). The nerve cell bodies of the sensory neurones are situated in the dorsal root, in a swelling called a ganglion. The nerve cell bodies of the interneurones and motor neurones are in the 'grey matter'. This appears grey because of the extra density of all the nuclei. The white matter around it contains only nerve fibres.

Importance of reflexes

Simple reflex arcs such as the one described allow the body to make automatic involuntary adjustments to changes in the external environment, such as the iris–pupil reflex and balance during locomotion. They also help control the internal environment, such as breathing rate and blood pressure, and prevent damage to the body as in cuts and burns. These help the body to maintain constant conditions, in other words they are involved in homeostasis.

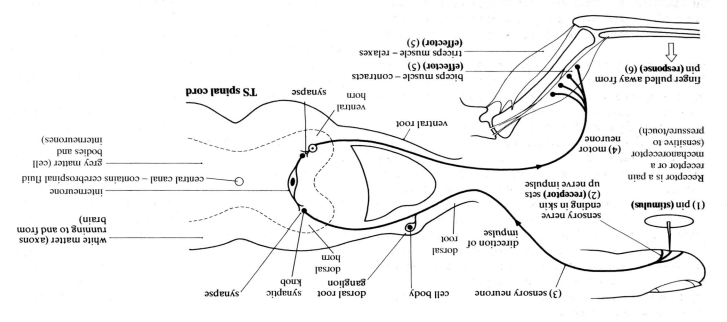

Fig 17.17 *A simplified example of reflex action and a reflex arc. The numbers in brackets refer to the basic structures in any reflex arc. Note the sequence: 1, stimulus; 2, receptor; 3, sensory neurone; 4, motor neurone; 5, effector; 6, response.*

More complex reflexes

In more complex reflexes, the sensory neurone synapses in the spinal cord with a secondary sensory neurone which passes to the brain. The brain identifies this sensory information and can store it for further use or send a motor nerve impulse down a motor neurone to synapse directly with spinal motor neurones and bring about a suitable response at an effector.

Conditioned reflexes

These are forms of reflex actions where the type of response is modified by past experience. These reflexes are coordinated by the brain. **Learning** forms the basis of all conditioned reflexes, such as in toilet training, salivation on the sight and smell of food, and awareness of danger (section 17.9). The first demonstration of conditioned reflexes is a classic example. Pavlov showed that dogs could learn a reflex by ringing a bell every time he gave them food. Eventually they would start to produce saliva when he rang the bell, even if no food was presented.

Many conditioned reflexes are modified versions of more simple reflexes. For example, if an empty metal baking tin is picked up and found to be extremely hot, burning the fingers, it will probably be dropped immediately, whereas a boiling hot, cooked casserole in an expensive dish, equally hot and painful, will probably be put down quickly but gently. The reason for the difference in the response reveals the involvement of conditioning and memory, followed by a conscious decision by the brain. The stimulus in both cases produces impulses passing to the brain in a sensory neurone. When the information reaches the brain it is interpreted and associated with information coming from other sense organs, for example the eyes, concerning the *cause* of the stimulus. The incoming information is compared with stored information concerning the nature and cause of the present stimulus and the likely outcome of allowing the spinal reflex to proceed. In the case of the metal tin, the brain works out that no further damage to either the body or the tin will occur if it is dropped and so initiates impulses in an excitatory motor neurone. This passes back down the spinal cord and synapses with the cell body of the motor neurone of the spinal reflex. Such is the speed of conduction through the pathway described that the impulses from the excitatory motor neurone reach the spinal motor neurone at the same time as impulses from the interneurone. The combined effect of these sends excitatory impulses to the effector muscle along the spinal motor neurone and the tin is dropped.

In the case of the casserole dish, the brain computes that dropping the casserole would probably scald the legs and feet, ruin the meal and break an expensive dish, whereas holding it until it could be put down safely would not cause much more damage to the fingers. If this decision is reached, impulses are initiated which pass down the spinal cord in an **inhibitory** motor neurone. These impulses arrive at the synapse with the spinal motor neurone at the same time as stimulatory impulses from the interneurone, and the latter are cancelled out. No impulses pass along the motor neurone to the muscle effector and the dish is held. Simultaneous brain activity would initiate an alternative muscle response which would result in the dish being put down quickly and safely.

The accounts of reflex arcs and reflex activity given above are, of necessity, simplified generalisations. The whole process of the coordination, integration and control of body functions is much more complex. For example, neurones connect different levels of the spinal cord together, controlling say the arms and legs, so that activity in one can be related to the other whilst at the same time other neurones from the brain achieve overall control.

Another reflex system exists for the control of activities which do not involve voluntary (skeletal) muscle. This is the autonomic nervous system.

17.2.3 The autonomic nervous system

The autonomic nervous system (*autos*, self; *nomos*, governing) is that part of the peripheral nervous system which controls activities inside the body that are normally involuntary, such as heart rate, peristalsis and sweating. It consists of motor neurones passing to the smooth muscles of internal organs. Smooth muscles are involuntary muscles. Most of the activity of the autonomic nervous system is controlled within the spinal cord or brain by reflexes known as **visceral reflexes** and does not involve the conscious control of higher centres of the brain. However, some activities, such as the control of the anal sphincter muscles which control defaecation, and bladder sphincter muscles which control urination (micturition), are also under the conscious control of the brain and control of these has to be learned. It is thought that many other autonomic activities may be able to be controlled by conscious effort and learning: many forms of meditation and relaxation have their roots in the control of autonomic activities, and considerable success has already been achieved in regulating heart rate and reducing blood pressure by conscious control or 'will power'. The overall control of the autonomic nervous system is maintained, however, by centres in the medulla (a part of the hind brain) and hypothalamus (also in the brain) (see section 17.2.4). These receive and integrate sensory information and coordinate this with information from other parts of the nervous system to produce the appropriate response.

The autonomic nervous system is composed of two types of neurone, a **preganglionic** neurone, which leaves the central nervous system in the ventral root before synapsing with several **postganglionic** neurones leading to effectors (fig 17.18).

There are two divisions of the autonomic nervous system: the **sympathetic** (SNS) and the **parasympathetic nervous systems** (PNS). The structure of the two systems differs mainly in the organisation of their neurones these differences are shown in fig 17.18.

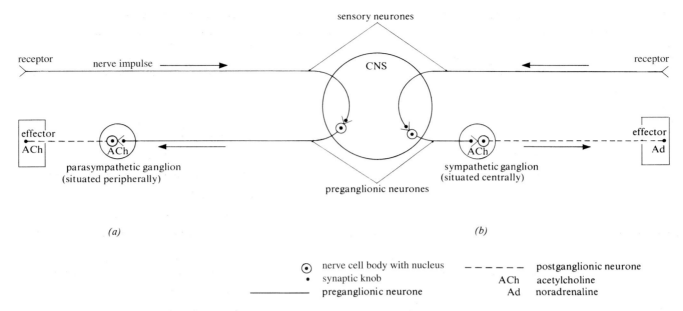

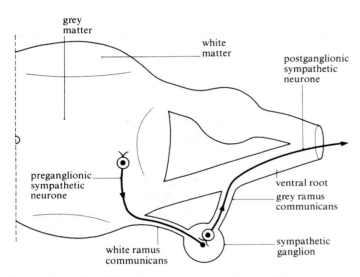

⊙	nerve cell body with nucleus
•	synaptic knob
———	preganglionic neurone
— — — — —	postganglionic neurone
ACh	acetylcholine
Ad	noradrenaline

Fig 17.18 *Simplified diagram showing the basic features of (a) the parasympathetic nervous system and (b) the sympathetic nervous system (the sensory neurones are not part of the autonomic nervous system).*

Fig 17.19 *Simplified diagram showing the position of a sympathetic ganglion and its relationship to the spinal cord and spinal nerve.*

In the sympathetic nervous system the synapses and cell bodies of the postganglionic neurones in the trunk region are situated in ganglia (swellings) close to the spinal cord. Each **sym   thetic ganglion** is connected to the spinal cord by   **mus communicans** and to the spinal nerve by   **communicans** as shown in fig 17.19. A   'ed sympathetic ganglia runs alongside the   ganglia of the parasympathetic nervous   ' close to, or within, the effector organ

              'etween the two systems include the   'transmitter substance released at the

postganglionic effector synapse, their general effects on the body and the conditions under which they are active. These differences are summarised in table 17.4.

The sympathetic and parasympathetic nervous systems generally have opposing (antagonistic) effects on organs they supply, and this enables the body to make rapid and precise adjustments of involuntary activities in order to maintain a steady state. For example, an increase in heart rate due to the release of noradrenaline by sympathetic neurones is compensated for by the release of acetylcholine by parasympathetic neurones. This action prevents heart rate becoming excessive and will eventually restore it to its normal level when secretion from both systems balances out. A summary of the antagonistic effects of these systems is shown in table 17.5. A careful study of this table will give you a good understanding of the functions of the two systems. A diagrammatic summary of the structure of the two systems is given in fig 17.20.

17.2.4   The central nervous system

The central nervous system consists of the brain and spinal cord. Like a telephone exchange with ingoing and outgoing wires, it is responsible for the coordination and control of the activity of the nervous system. It develops from an infolding of the outer layer of the embryo known as the ectoderm. This is immediately above the notochord, the long strengthening rod which becomes the backbone in vertebrates. The infolding ectoderm forms a dorsal, hollow neural tube running the length of the animal. The neural tube differentiates during development to form an expanded anterior (front) region, the **brain**, and a long cylindrical **spinal cord**.

Table 17.4 Summary of the differences between the sympathetic and parasympathetic nervous systems.

Feature	Sympathetic	Parasympathetic
Origin of neurones	Emerge from cranial, thoracic and lumbar regions of CNS	Emerge from cranial and sacral regions of CNS
Position of ganglion	Close to spinal cord	Close to effector
Length of fibres	Short preganglionic fibres Long postganglionic fibres	Long preganglionic fibres Short postganglionic fibres
Number of fibres	Numerous postganglionic fibres	Few postganglionic fibres
Distribution of fibres	Preganglionic fibres cover a wide area	Preganglionic fibres cover a restricted region
Area of influence	Effects diffuse	Effects localised
Transmitter substance	Noradrenaline released at effector	Acetylcholine released at effector
General effects	Increases metabolite levels, e.g. blood sugar Increases metabolic rate Increases rhythmic activities, e.g. heart rate Raises sensory awareness	Decreases metabolite levels, e.g. blood sugar None Decreases rhythmic activities, e.g. heart rate Restores sensory awareness to normal levels
Overall effect	Excitatory homeostatic effect	Inhibitory homeostatic effect
Conditions when active	Dominant during danger, stress and activity; controls reactions to stress	Dominant during rest Controls routine body activities

Table 17.5 Summary of the effects of the sympathetic and parasympathetic nervous systems on the body.

Region	Sympathetic	Parasympathetic
Head	Dilates pupils None Inhibits secretion of saliva	Constricts pupils Stimulates secretion of tears Stimulates secretion of saliva
Heart	Increases strength and rate of heart beat	Decreases strength and rate of heart beat
Lungs	Dilates bronchi and bronchioles Increases ventilation rate	Constricts bronchi and bronchioles Decreases ventilation rate
Gut	Inhibits peristalsis Inhibits secretion of alimentary juices Contracts anal sphincter muscle	Stimulates peristalsis Stimulates secretion of alimentary juices Inhibits contraction of anal sphincter muscle
Blood	Constricts arterioles to gut and smooth muscle Dilates arterioles to brain and skeletal muscle Increases blood pressure Increases blood volume by contraction of spleen	Maintains steady muscle tone in arterioles to gut, smooth muscle, brain and skeletal muscle, allowing normal blood flow Reduces blood pressure None
Skin	Contracts hair erector muscles (hair 'stands on end') Constricts arterioles in skin of limbs (skin whitens) Increases secretion of sweat	None Dilates arterioles in skin of face (skin reddens) None
Kidney	Decreases output of urine	None
Bladder	Contracts bladder sphincter muscle	Inhibits contraction of bladder sphincter muscles
Penis	Induces ejaculation	Stimulates erection
Glands	Releases adrenaline from adrenal medulla	None

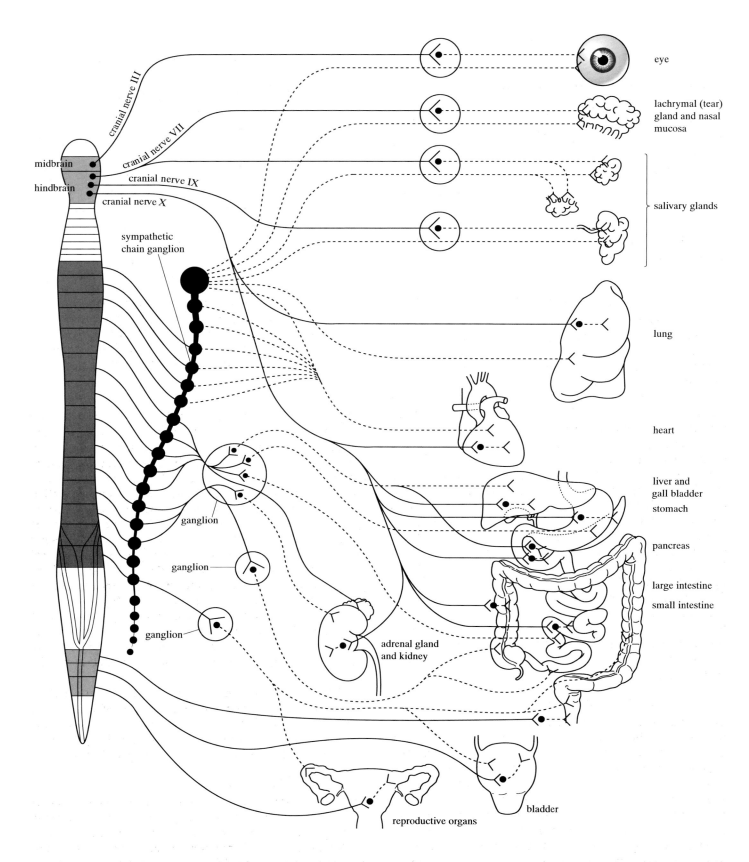

Fig 17.20 *Structure of the sympathetic and parasympathetic nervous systems. Together they form the autonomic nervous system which is the part of the nervous system responsible for involuntary (automatic or reflex) activity. The solid lines represent preganglionic fibres, and the dashed lines represent postganglionic fibres.*

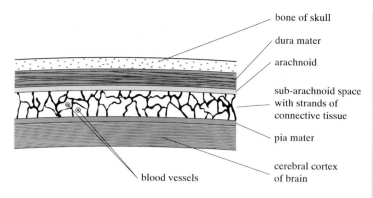

Fig 17.21 *The three meninges of the brain (dura mater, arachnoid and pia mater).*

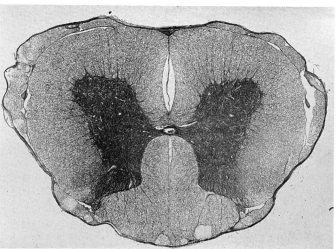

Fig 17.22 *Light micrograph of a cross-section of human spinal cord. The butterfly-shaped grey matter in the middle consists of nerve cells. The surrounding white matter is made up of myelinated nerve fibre bundles. Surrounding the cord are three layers of membranes (meninges).*

The meninges and cerebrospinal fluid

The central nervous system is surrounded by three layers or 'membranes' called **meninges** (fig 17.21) and is completely encased within the protective bones of the skull and vertebral column. The outer membrane forms the tough **dura mater** which is attached to the skull and vertebrae, and the inner membrane forms the thin **pia mater** which lies next to the nervous tissues. Between the two is the **arachnoid** 'membrane'. This includes a space, the **sub-arachnoid space**, strands of connective tissue, blood vessels and **cerebrospinal fluid (CSF)**. Most of this fluid is contained in the central canal of the spinal cord and continues forward to occupy four expanded cavities within the brain called the **ventricles**. The fluid therefore comes into contact with the outside and inside of the brain, and blood vessels lie within it for the supply of nutrients and oxygen to the nervous tissues and the removal of wastes (see fig 17.21). It also contains lymphocytes to protect against infection. Meningitis is caused by an infection of the meninges. About $100\,\text{cm}^3$ of fluid is present in the CNS and, apart from its nutritive, excretory and defensive functions, it supports the nervous tissues and protects them against mechanical shock. A continual circulation of fluid is maintained by ciliated cells lining the ventricles and central canal.

The spinal cord

The spinal cord (fig 17.22) is a cylinder of nervous tissue running from the base of the brain down the back. It is protected by the vertebrae of the backbone (vertebral column) and the meninges. It has a H-shaped central area of **grey matter**, composed of nerve cell bodies, dendrites and synapses surrounding a central canal which contains cerebrospinal fluid. Around the grey matter is an outer layer of **white matter**, containing nerve fibres whose fatty myelin sheaths give it its characteristic colour. There are 31 pairs of **spinal nerves** and these divide close to the spinal cord to form two branches called the **dorsal root** and **ventral root**. Sensory neurones enter the dorsal root and have their cell bodies in a swelling, the **dorsal root**

ganglion, close to the spinal cord. The sensory neurones then enter the **dorsal horn** of the grey matter where they synapse with interneurones. These, in turn, synapse with motor neurones in the **ventral horn** and leave the spinal cord via the ventral root (fig 17.17). Since there are many more interneurones than motor neurones, some integration must occur within the grey matter. Some sensory neurones synapse directly with motor neurones in the ventral horn, as in the familiar knee-jerk reflex. From the thorax region downwards, a **lateral horn** is present between the dorsal and ventral horns which contains the cell bodies of the preganglionic autonomic neurones. The white matter is composed of groups of nerve fibres, running between the grey matter and the brain and providing a means of communication between spinal nerves and the brain. **Ascending tracts** carry sensory information to the brain and **descending tracts** relay motor information to the spinal cord.

To summarise, the functions of the spinal cord include acting as a coordinating centre for simple spinal reflexes, such as the knee-jerk response, and autonomic reflexes, such as contraction of the bladder, and providing a means of communication between spinal nerves and the brain.

The brain

The human brain has been described as the most complex structure in the Universe. Although it has been compared to a computer, it is far superior to any computer yet built. Understanding how it functions remains one of the most challenging problems in biology. Nevertheless, progress has accelerated in recent years.

The brain contains an estimated 100 thousand million nerve cells with more than 1000 miles of nerve fibres per cubic centimetre of cerebral cortex, the thin outer layer of the forebrain in which our consciousness is located. Every nerve cell in the cortex receives, on average, about 1000 to 10 000 connections from other nerve cells, giving an astronomical number of combinations of nerve cells. Somehow, from this 'neural network', we achieve the process of conscious thought.

Although in the early twentieth century it was imagined that the functions of the brain were somehow vaguely distributed throughout its structure, we now know that different parts of the brain have very specific functions. Vision, for example, is located at the back of the cerebral cortex; heart rate is controlled from the medulla in the hindbrain. The cerebral cortex is conscious, but much of the activity of the brain is unconscious and not subject to voluntary control.

In this section we shall look at the main structures of the brain and their functions.

Origins of the brain

It helps to understand the structure of the brain if we examine its origins in simpler vertebrates and in the human embryo. Fig 17.23 shows the structure of a fish brain in section and from above. It shows that the brain is divided into three main regions, the forebrain, midbrain and hindbrain. These three divisions are seen just as clearly in the early embryonic development of the human brain. However, the story of evolution in the vertebrates includes a massive increase in the size of the brain in relation to the rest of the body. This increase in size is due mainly to an increase in size of the forebrain. Birds and mammals have larger forebrains than amphibians and reptiles, with the brains of mammals being largest. In mammals the forebrain has a folded surface and grows back over the midbrain and hindbrain so that, if the brain is viewed from above, the midbrain is no longer visible (fig 17.24*a*).

Of the mammals, primates have the largest forebrains of all relative to body size. Note that size alone is not the only indicator of quality. An average elephant's brain is four times heavier than an average human brain, and the average human male brain is larger than the average human female brain, a piece of evidence used by scientists in the nineteenth century to justify the assertion that men had superior brains (even though they ignored the fact that men generally have a larger body size too). Fig 17.24*b* shows a diagram of the main regions of the human brain as seen in section. Fig 17.25 shows a section through an actual human brain.

Fig 17.23 shows that vision in the fish is located in the midbrain. In humans, the eyes are still connected by the optic nerves to the midbrain, but most of the information continues forward to the forebrain where it is processed and converted to vision. The hindbrain in humans still more or less retains the same functions as in fish, and is divided into cerebellum, pons and medulla. It is with these 'older' parts that we shall start this brief tour of the brain's structure and function.

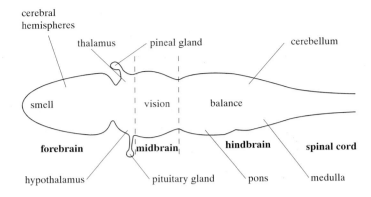

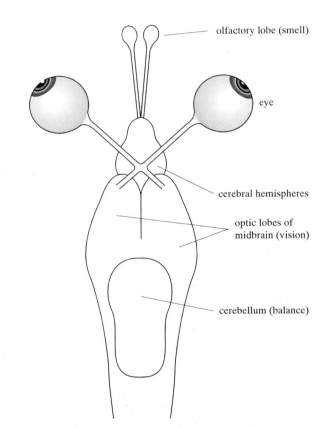

Fig 17.23 *Fish brain as seen from the side and from above.*

Hindbrain

Cerebellum. This is located at the back of the brain under the cerebral hemispheres. It is very folded and has an outer region, the cortex, which contains many nerve fibres and cell bodies. Like the cerebral cortex it appears greyish in colour. The cerebellum has been called the gyroscope of the body because it is concerned with balance. It receives information from the organs of balance in the ears and is concerned with the control and precision of all movements involving voluntary muscle.

Patients whose cerebellum has been damaged at first are not able to walk. They can learn to walk again, but do so

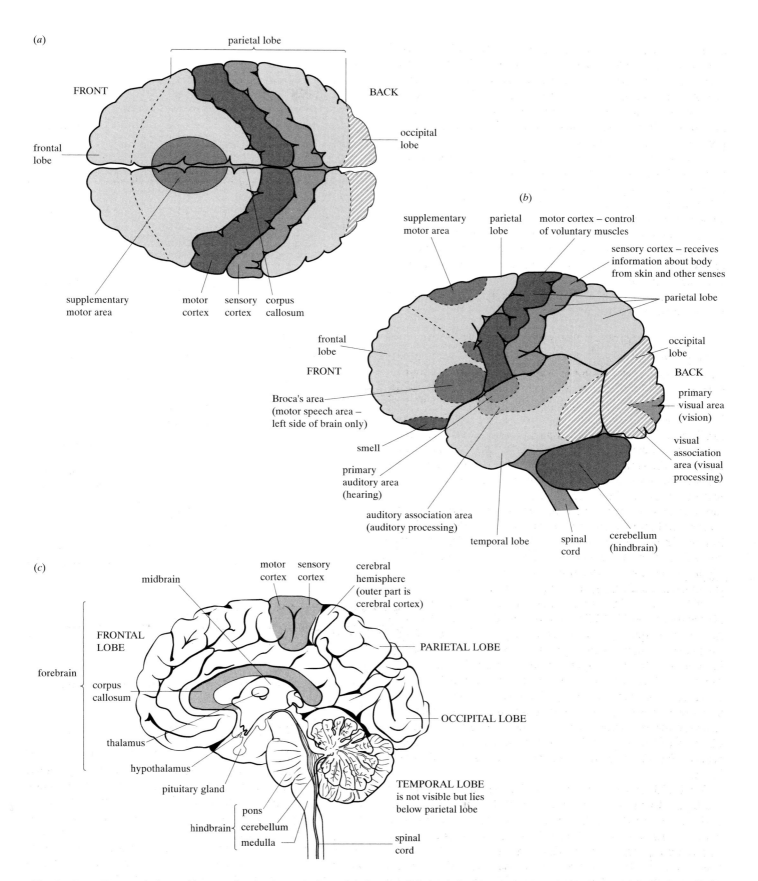

Fig 17.24 *External view of human brain as seen from (a) the top (b) the left side. A section through the brain is shown in (c).*

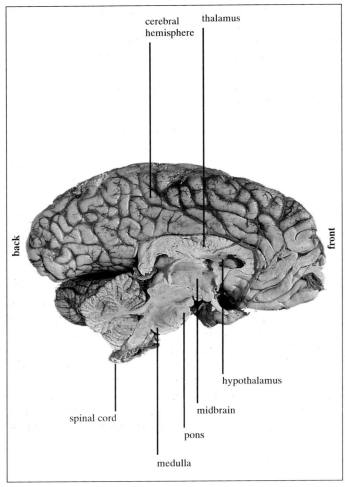

cerebral hemisphere
thalamus
back
front
spinal cord
hypothalamus
midbrain
pons
medulla

Fig 17.25 *Healthy human brain cut in half vertically through the middle (the left side is shown).*

awkwardly because walking is no longer 'automatically' controlled. It presumably requires some conscious effort. This is rather similar to toddlers learning to walk – they cannot think of much else while trying. Gradually the cerebellum learns the task so that it becomes a learned, unconscious activity. The cerebellum then merely needs the command from the conscious brain (the cerebral cortex) to walk and the cerebral cortex is then free to think about more important things. (If you think about walking it can be difficult!) Other activities such as swimming, riding a bike, driving a car, typing, balancing, maintaining posture, talking, running, can become automatic through the activity of the cerebellum. It is like an on-board computer which can take over from conscious control.

The cerebellum is also responsible for precision and fine control of voluntary movement. Try picking up a pencil. You can probably do this quite smoothly, even while still concentrating on what your teacher is saying. This is because the cerebellum is involved in the task. No machine has yet been made which can do this as smoothly or with as much versatility because it is an extremely difficult task. Once again, this is something that has to be learned by trial

and error, and conscious activity to begin with. Children learning to pick up objects show the difficulties of such tasks.

Pons. The pons is a relay station between the cerebellum, spinal cord and the rest of the brain (pons means bridge).

Medulla. The medulla is one of the best protected parts of the brain and one of the most vital. If the brain is cut above the medulla, basic heart rate and breathing rate can still be maintained, but damage to the medulla is fatal. It contains the cardiovascular centre, including a cardiac accelerator centre and cardiac inhibitory centre which regulate the rate and force of heart beat as described in section 14.7.4. It also controls blood pressure, vasoconstriction and vasodilation. The medulla also contains a breathing centre as described in section 9.5.5. It receives nerve impulses from other parts of the brain such as the cerebral cortex which can influence heart and breathing rates, particularly the latter. Nerves leaving the medulla are part of the autonomic nervous system and are therefore under reflex (involuntary) control. Sneezing, coughing, swallowing, salivation and vomiting are other activities controlled by the medulla.

Midbrain

As mentioned, the optic nerves enter the midbrain from the eyes, but in humans the original function of vision has been taken over by the forebrain. However, reflex movements of the eye muscles are still controlled from this part of the brain. Reflex movements of the head and neck and trunk in response to visual and auditory stimuli also originate from here, as well as changes in pupil size and lens shape in the eye.

Forebrain

Hypothalamus. The forebrain in humans is dominated by the cerebral hemispheres (see below) but it is also the region where the thalamus and hypothalamus are found (fig 17.24c). Although relatively small, the hypothalamus is one of the most interesting parts of the brain because it has so many functions. It is located just below the thalamus (hence its name), and is subdivided into at least a dozen separate areas, each with its own specific function. It is the main coordinating and control centre for the autonomic nervous system, and receives sensory neurones from all the receptors of that system and from taste and smell receptors. Information is relayed from here to effectors via the medulla and spinal cord, and is used in the regulation and control of heart rate, blood pressure, ventilation rate and peristalsis.

The hypothalamus is connected to, and controls, the pituitary gland. This 'axis' of hypothalamus and pituitary gland is important because it is the main link between the nervous system and the endocrine system and its hormones (see the example of ADH below, and section 17.6.2).

Within the hypothalamus are centres which control

various aspects of mood and emotions, such as aggression, rage, fear and pleasure. Artificial stimulation of these centres with electrodes provides some of the most convincing evidence of how localised brain function can be. For example, stimulation of the aggression centre in a cat makes its back arch, hair stand on end, tail lash, pupils dilate and it starts snarling. It will attack any suitable object, such as a rat or sometimes the experimenter. Interestingly, and probably no coincidence, this centre is close to the fear centre. Fear can easily turn to aggression.

Another centre is the pleasure centre. A rat given the choice of pressing a lever to obtain food or one to stimulate its pleasure centre starves to death for obvious reasons. While the notion of a pleasure centre is probably an oversimplification of what is a very complex area of behaviour. Other centres, however, do have very precise roles. For example, stimulation of the thirst centre will make an animal drink. There are also centres associated with hunger, satiety (a feeling of being 'full' or having eaten enough) and control of body temperature (section 19.5.4). The thirst centre, for example, helps to regulate the solute concentration of the blood and hence the osmotic properties of the blood. A high solute concentration (relatively low water concentration) results in the secretion of the hormone ADH (antidiuretic hormone) through nerve cells to the posterior lobe of the pituitary gland, from where it enters the blood. ADH decreases the volume of urine as explained in section 20.6.

All these centres monitor the blood with the overall purpose of maintaining homeostasis, or constant conditions, within the body. Relatively speaking the hypothalamus receives more blood than any other part of the brain. Using the information it receives, the hypothalamus, in association with the pituitary gland, is one of the major regulators of homeostasis.

Cerebral hemispheres

The outer 2–4 mm of the cerebral hemispheres (or cerebrum) is known as the **cerebral cortex**. It consists of 'grey matter' containing thousands of millions of nerve cells, including their cell bodies. Beneath the cortex is the 'white matter' (in contrast to the spinal cord where the grey matter is on the inside and the white matter on the outside).

The cerebral hemispheres are the site of consciousness, our sense of self, perhaps the most mysterious property of the brain. So far, the nature of consciousness is entirely unexplained. We are not even sure how many other animals show consciousness. Other rather vague properties such as intelligence, reasoning, personality, learning, emotions and the 'will' are located here, as well as some more specific functions, as shown in fig 17.26.

The right hemisphere controls the left side of the body and the left hemisphere controls the right side of the body.

Primary sensory areas receive sensory impulses from receptors in most parts of the body. The sensory areas form localised regions of the cortex associated with certain

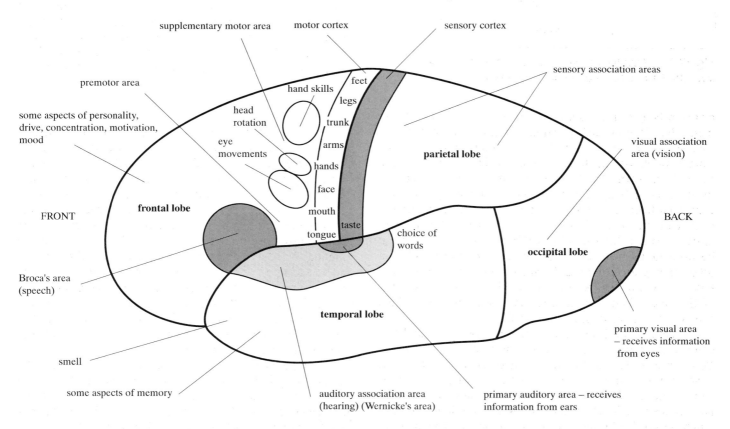

Fig 17.26 *Localisation of function in the cerebral hemispheres. Broca's area is in the left hemisphere in most people.*

senses as shown in fig 17.26. The size of the region is related to the number of receptors in the sensory structure.

Association areas are so named for several reasons. First, they associate incoming sensory information with information stored in the memory, so that the information is 'recognised'. Secondly, the information is associated with information arriving from other receptors. Thirdly, the information is 'interpreted' and given meaning within its present context and, if necessary, a decision is made about the most appropriate response. The association area passes instructions to its associated motor area. Association areas, therefore, are involved in memory, learning and reasoning, and the degree of success of the outcome may loosely be termed **intelligence**. Association areas are usually next to their related sensory area; for example, the **visual association area** is situated immediately next to the visual cortex in the **occipital lobe**. Some association areas may have a restricted function and are linked to other association centres that can further develop the activity. For example, the **auditory association area** only interprets sounds into broad categories which are relayed to more specialised association areas where 'sense' is made of the words.

Motor areas control movement of voluntary muscles, sending out nerve impulses in motor nerves.

The sensory and motor cortex. In the 1860s, a British neurologist, John Hughlings, discovered that when some of his epileptic patients had fits, the uncontrollable movements always started in one particular part of the body, for example the thumb on one hand. He suggested that the part of the brain controlling this part of the body was damaged and therefore the origin of the epilepsy. Hughlings' insight proved to be correct and, as we now know, the motor cortex must have been the part of the brain affected. In the 1940s and 1950s a Canadian neurosurgeon, Wilder Penfield, wishing to investigate the localisation of brain function more precisely, devised a method of stimulating the exposed surface of a human brain with weak electric currents. The patient was kept conscious during this procedure (there are no pain detectors in the cerebral cortex) so that they could report on any sensations. The technique proved very successful. Some parts of the brain, for example, released vivid but forgotten memories when stimulated.

Penfield discovered two strips of cortex at the top of the brain which were like maps of the body. One strip, the **sensory cortex**, dealt with sensory (incoming) information *from* the body. It receives impulses from receptors for touch in the skin and for position of muscles and joints. Just in front of this another strip, the **motor cortex**, sent motor nerve impulses out *to* different parts of the body, bringing about muscular movements that are normally voluntary. By stimulating different parts of these strips Penfield was able to map them and also to cause sensations or movements, like twitching the fingers, almost like working the strings of a puppet.

The maps are unusual in that they show us the body as the brain experiences it. Thus the lips, tongue and hands, which are very sensitive, and subject to very fine control of movement, 'occupy' relatively large areas of the strips, whereas the legs or trunk, for example, occupy relatively small areas. The tongue, for example, is involved in talking, and moves about very quickly and precisely during eating (if you think about it while eating you will bite your tongue). Motor control of the tongue is therefore complex and requires a relatively large part of the motor cortex. The tongue is also very sensitive, as you may have experienced in probing a huge cavern in a damaged tooth, only to discover that it is a very small hole. It therefore sends a relatively large amount of information to the brain, requiring a relatively large part of the sensory cortex.

The sensory and motor maps can each be illustrated graphically with a model called a **homunculus** (meaning 'little man'), as shown in fig 17.27. Fig 17.28 shows maps of the sensory and motor cortex.

Damage to the motor cortex, for example by a stroke, results in paralysis of the part of the body that the damaged part normally controls. Damage to the left hemisphere affects the right side of the body and vice versa. Damage to the sensory cortex results not only in loss of sensation from the relevant body part, but can also lead to loss of the knowledge of its existence and the person behaving as if it did not exist, even if that part can be operated by the motor cortex. For example, a man recovering from an accident complained that an arm had been sewn on to him as he tried to rationalise the experience of having an arm in bed with him that did not seem to belong to him. In such a situation the patient can be taught to use the arm, for example in dressing themselves.

Around the sensory and motor cortex strips are association areas which are involved in the processing of information relating to the activity of the strips. The **supplementary motor area** (fig 17.26) seems to be concerned with positional movements. The premotor area is involved in patterns of movement that involve groups of muscles, such as are used in swinging from branch to branch of a tree.

Language. The left hemisphere of the brain is concerned with language. The equivalent area in the right hemisphere is concerned with appreciation of music.

Information arrives from the ears through the auditory nerve to the primary auditory cortex in the temporal lobe (fig 17.27). From there it enters the association areas for analysis of its language content. Wernicke's area interprets the meaning of speech. Damage here affects both understanding and production of speech. The person can speak, but their sentences are ungrammatical and without meaning. For example, a man shown a bunch of keys, said 'indication of measurement of piece of apparatus or intimating the cost of apparatus in various forms'. Damage to the region between the parietal lobe and temporal lobe (see fig 17.26) can affect the ability to find the right word. Here word associations are common. For example, a man

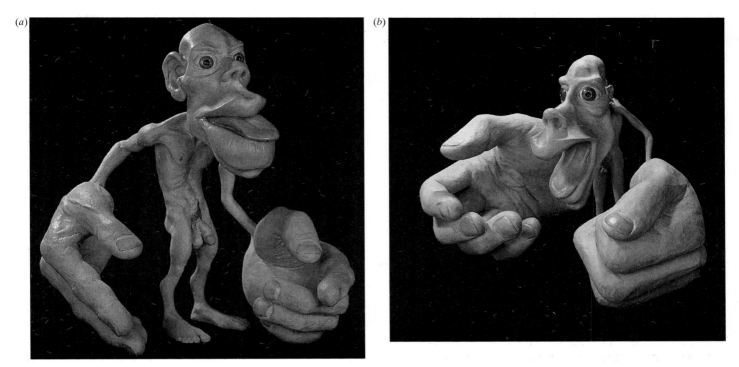

Fig 17.27 *(a) Sensory homunculus: this model shows what a man's body would look like if each part grew in proportion to the area of the cortex of the brain concerned with its sensory perception. (b) Motor homunculus: this model shows what a man's body would look like if each part grew in proportion to the area of the cortex of the brain concerned with its movement.*

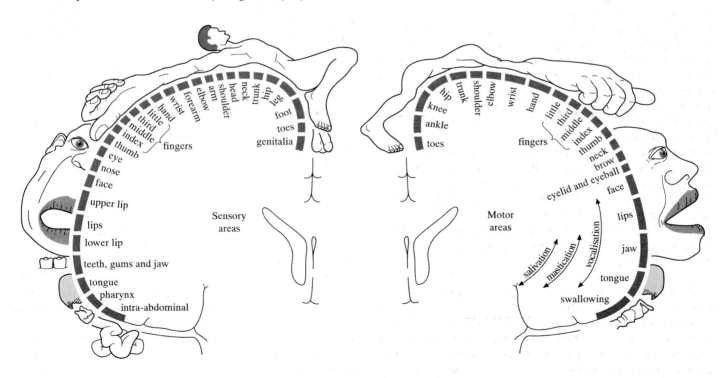

Fig 17.28 *Maps of the sensory and motor cortex.*

shown a nail file said it was a 'pair of scissors'. Dyslexia probably involves the occipital lobe (vision) and the temporal lobe (language).

A motor area associated with language is Broca's area in the frontal lobe, near the area of the motor cortex dealing with the mouth (lips and tongue) (fig 17.26). It is concerned with speech. Nerve impulses from here travel via the premotor area to the muscles of the tongue, pharynx and mouth. Breathing is also controlled during speech. Damage to Broca's area results in impaired speech, although the victim can understand speech perfectly well.

Vision. The primary visual area in the occipital lobe at the back of the head receives information from the eyes. Damage to this would result in blindness, even if the eyes were functioning perfectly. Damage to the association areas, however, affects the processing of vision. For example, a person might be able to see a friend but not recognise them if the program for constructing and recognising faces is damaged. Different association areas in the occipital lobe are concerned with analysis of features such as colour, movement, binocular vision, depth, shapes and features (such as edges and corners).

Corpus callosum

The right and left hemispheres are connected by a thick band of nerve fibres called the corpus callosum. When the function of a structure is unknown, one approach to discovering its function is to remove it and find out what happens. Roger Sperry, working at the University of Chicago in the 1950s cut through the corpus callosum of a cat and was surprised to discover that at first the cat behaved perfectly normally. He then showed that each hemisphere was functioning totally independently and could not communicate with the other. It seems that the corpus callosum almost literally lets the right hand know what the left hand is doing. The experiments were extended by Sperry to human patients. The object of the operation was to try to control grand mal epilepsy, a severe form of epilepsy which can result in major fits as often as every 30 minutes. It was hoped to stop the spread of the fit from the hemisphere where it started into the other. The operation was very successful, reducing both the severity and the frequency of the fits. The patient appeared normal after recovery. However, Sperry was able to show by carefully designed experiments that the two hemispheres were not communicating, as with the cat. One experiment is shown in fig 17.29. Further experiments confirmed that language is located in the left hemisphere.

Careful observation of such 'split brain' patients has revealed subtle changes in their behaviour. Because the left hemisphere tends to be dominant, the left side of the body (controlled by the right hemisphere) rarely shows spontaneous activity. The patient generally does not respond to stimulation of the left side. One man found that when he (or rather his left hemisphere) tried to read a paper, his left hand tried to throw it on the floor. The left

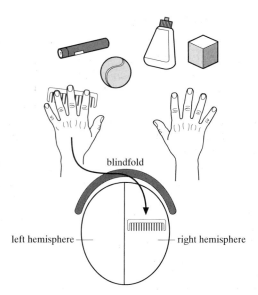

1 Subject is blindfolded.

2 Experimenter places the chosen object in the left hand. (No one must name the object or the right ear will hear and inform the left hemisphere.)

Left hand sends nerve impulses to right hemisphere.

Right hemisphere knows object is a comb.

3 Experimenter asks subject to find the object with the left hand in a mixture of objects.

Subject succeeds.

4 Experimenter asks subject to find th object with right hand (This is controlled by the left hemisphere.)

Subject fails.

5 Experimenter asks subject to say what the object was. Subject fails.

Only the left hemisphere can speak (language centre in left hemisphere)

Fig 17.29 *An experiment to investigate the effect of cutting the corpus callosum in a human patient.*

hand is controlled by the right hemisphere which was bored because it cannot read (language being in the left hemisphere). He found it easier to read sitting on his left hand.

How much we learn from split brain patients about normal behaviour is questionable. Such problems as those described should not affect anyone with an intact corpus callosum. Information can pass from one hemisphere to the other and tasks can be shared. However, the importance of the corpus callosum becomes clear, and it raises interesting questions about the nature of identity, especially when we are 'in two minds' about whether to do something.

17.3 Evolution of the nervous system

A study of animal evolution shows a progressive increase in complexity from cnidarians to mammals.

17.3.1 Cnidarians, e.g. *Hydra*

The development of multicellular organisation in the cnidarians led to a separation of stimulus and response, receptor and effector. Specialised cells, the nerve cells, evolved which link receptor to effector. The nervous system of primitive cnidarians, for example *Hydra*, is a **nerve net** or **plexus** composed of a single layer of short neurones in contact throughout the organism. Impulses spread out in all directions from the point of stimulation and at each synapse an impulse is lost. This impulse is used, effectively, to 'charge' the synapse so that subsequent impulses can cross the synapse. This process is called **facilitation** and, since an impulse is lost at each synapse in facilitating (making easier) the passage of the next impulse, the mechanism of conduction is called **decremental conduction**. Nervous conduction in this organism is therefore slow, due to the number of synapses to cross, and restricted because impulses die out as they progress outwards from the stimulus. The system is useful in producing localised responses, say within a tentacle, but of little value to the whole organism unless the stimulus is **intense** or **prolonged**. In most cnidarians, such as jellyfish and sea anemones, in addition to the nerve net there is a system of bipolar neurones arranged in tracts, called **through conduction tracts**, and able to transmit impulses rapidly over considerable distances and without apparent loss. This system enables the organism to make fairly rapid responses of the whole body to harmful stimuli, such as the withdrawal of tentacles, and this foreshadows the aggregation of neurones into nerves seen in higher organisms.

17.3.2 Annelids, e.g. earthworm

In the annelids neurones are associated into nerves. This has resulted in a nervous system with a single **ventral nerve cord** running the entire length of the organism. It consists of one pair of ganglia per segment joined by connecting neurones. Nerves to and from the tissues arise from the ganglia of each segment as shown in fig 18.26.

As a result of the unidirectional method of locomotion, annelids possess a head. This structure is specialised to assist with feeding and, since it is the first part of the body to come into contact with new environmental situations, it contains all the sensory structures necessary to detect stimuli associated with these situations. The increased input of sensory information from these receptors to the nervous system is dealt with by the enlarged anterior end of the nerve cord. This concentration of feeding apparatus, sense organs and nervous tissues into a 'head' region is called **cephalisation**. It should be emphasised though that the term applies to the development of *all* the features associated with the head and not just the nervous tissue.

The annelid nervous system shows all the basic features found in all other non-vertebrate groups. The enlarged anterior region of the nerve cord forms a pair of **cerebral ganglia** situated above the pharynx and linked to the ventral nerve cord around each side of the pharynx.

17.3.3 Arthropods, e.g. insects

In arthropods the basic organisation of the nervous system is almost identical to that of annelids except that the cerebral ganglia overlie the oesophagus. Cerebral ganglia are analogous to the vertebrate brain but do not possess the same degree of control over the entire nervous system seen in vertebrates. For example, removal of the head of a non-vertebrate has very little effect on movement, whereas in vertebrates the brain controls all movement of the body. Non-vertebrate cerebral ganglia, in fact, appear to act as relay centres between receptors and effectors and their role in integration and coordination is limited to a few responses involving hormones, such as the timing of reproductive activities in annelids and the control of moulting in arthropods (section 22.3.3).

17.4 Sensory receptors

The coordinated activity of an organism relies upon a continuous input of information from the internal and external environments. If this information leads to a change in activity or behaviour of the animals, it is a **stimulus**. The specialised region of the body detecting the stimulus is known as a **sensory receptor**.

The simplest and most primitive type of receptor consists of a single sensory neurone which is capable of detecting the stimulus and giving rise to a nerve impulse passing to the central nervous system, for example, skin mechanoreceptors such as the **Pacinian corpuscle** (section 17.5.1).

More complex receptors, known as sense cells, consist of modified epithelial cells able to detect stimuli. These form synaptic connections with their sensory neurones which transmit impulses to the CNS, for example mammalian taste buds.

The most complex receptors are **sense organs** such as the eye and ear. These are composed of a large number of sense cells, sensory neurones and associated accessory structures. In the eye there are two types of sense cells, rods and cones, many connecting neurones and many accessory structures such as the lens and iris.

A classification of receptors based on the type of stimulus detected is shown in table 17.6.

Animals only detect stimuli existing in one of the forms of energy shown in table 17.6. Structures transforming stimulus energy into electrical responses (nerve impulses) in axons are known as **transducers** and, in this respect, receptors act as **biological transducers**.

All receptors transform the energy of the stimulus into an electrical response which initiates nerve impulses in the neurone leaving the receptor. Thus receptors **encode** a variety of stimuli into nerve impulses which pass into the

Table 17.6 Types of receptors and the stimuli detected by them.

Type of receptor	Type of stimulus energy	Nature of stimulus
photoreceptor	electromagnetic	light
electroreceptor	electromagnetic	electricity
mechanoreceptor	mechanical	sound, touch, pressure, gravity
thermoreceptor	thermal	temperature change
chemoreceptor	chemical	humidity, smell, taste

central nervous system where they are decoded and used to produce the required responses.

17.4.1 The mechanism of transduction

Transduction is the name given to the process by which a receptor converts a stimulus into a nerve impulse. The stimulus may be light, electricity, touch, etc., as shown in table 17.6, but the nerve impulse is always the same in nature.

All sensory cells are excitable cells, and they share with nerve cells and muscle cells the ability to respond to an appropriate stimulus by producing a rapid change in their electrical properties. When not stimulated, sensory cells are able to maintain a resting potential as described in section 17.1.1. They respond to a stimulus by producing a change in membrane potential. Bernard Katz, in 1950, using a specialised stretch receptor known as a muscle spindle, was able to demonstrate the presence of a depolarisation in the immediate region of the sensory nerve ending in the muscle spindle. This localised depolarisation is found only in the sensory cell and is known as the **generator potential**. Subsequent investigations involving intracellular recordings, made by penetrating the membranes of receptor cells in muscle spindles and the mechanoreceptors of the skin (the Pacinian corpuscles), have revealed the following information about transduction:

- the generator potential results from the stimulus producing an increase in the permeability of the sensory cell membrane to sodium and potassium ions which flow down their electrochemical gradients;
- the magnitude of the generator potential varies with the intensity of the stimulus;
- when the generator potential reaches a certain threshold value it gives rise to an action potential (fig 17.30);
- the frequency of the nerve impulses in the sensory axon is directly related to the intensity of the stimulus.

17.4.2 Properties of receptors

There are various ways in which the effectiveness of receptors can be increased. Some of these are described below.

Sensory cells with various thresholds

Some sense organs, such as stretch receptors in muscle, are composed of many sense cells which have a range of thresholds. If a cell has a low threshold it responds to a weak stimulus. As the strength of the stimulus increases the cell can respond by producing an increasing number of impulses in the sensory neurone leaving the cell. However, at a given point saturation occurs, and the frequency of impulses in the neurone cannot be increased. A further increase in intensity of stimulus will then excite sense cells with higher thresholds, and these too will produce a frequency of nerve impulses which is proportional to the intensity of the stimulus. In this way the range of the receptor is extended (fig 17.31).

Adaptation

Most receptors initially respond to a strong constant stimulus by producing a high frequency of impulses in the sensory neurone. The frequency of these impulses gradually declines and this reduction in response, with time, is called **adaptation**. For example, on entering a room you may immediately notice a clock ticking but after a while become unaware of its presence. The rate and extent of adaptation in a receptor cell is related to its function and there are two types, rapidly and slowly adapting receptors.

Rapidly adapting receptors (phasic receptors) respond to changes in stimulus level by producing a high frequency of impulses at the moments when the stimulus is switched 'on' *or* 'off'. For example, the Pacinian corpuscle and other receptors concerned with touch and the detection of sudden changes act in this way. They register *change* in the stimulus.

Slowly adapting receptors (tonic receptors) register a constant stimulus with a slowly decreasing frequency of impulses.

Adaptation is thought to be related to a decrease in the permeability of the receptor membrane to ions due to sustained stimulation. This progressively reduces the size and duration of the generator potential and, when this falls below the threshold level, the sensory neurone ceases to fire.

The advantage of adaptation of sense cells is that it provides animals with precise information about *changes* in the environment. At other times the cells do not send signals, thus preventing overloading of the central nervous system with irrelevant and unmanageable information. This contributes to the overall efficiency and economy of the nervous system and enables it to ignore unchanging background information and to concentrate on monitoring aspects of the environment which have most survival value.

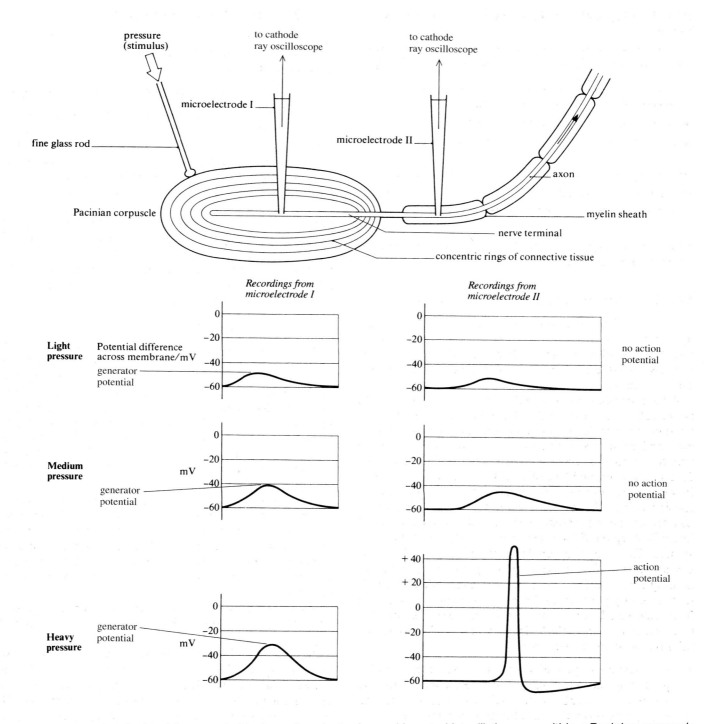

Fig 17.30 *The electrical activity recorded by two microelectrodes and inserted into (I) the axon within a Pacinian corpuscle and (II) the axon of the sensory neurone leaving the corpuscle. As the pressure on the fine glass rod (the stimulus) is increased, the size of the generator potential increases and at a certain threshold triggers an action potential in the sensory neurone.*

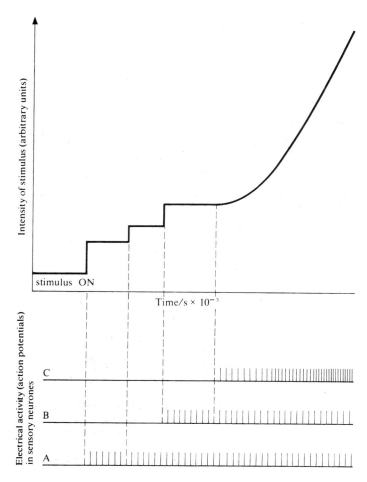

Fig 17.31 *The frequency of action potentials produced in sensory neurones leaving three sense cells, **A**, **B**, and **C**, each having different threshold levels. In the case of **B** and **C** the point at which the receptors become active coincides with the saturation point of the sense cell with the lower threshold.*

Convergence and summation

A high degree of sensitivity is achieved in many sense organs by an arrangement of sense cells and sensory neurones known as **convergence**. In such cases, several sense cells are connected to (converge on) a single sensory neurone. These cells are characteristically small, are found in large numbers and are extremely sensitive to stimuli. Whilst the effect of a stimulus on a single one of these cells would not produce a response in the sensory neurone, the combined effect of the simultaneous stimulation of several cells is cumulative. This cumulative stimulatory effect produced in the sensory neurone is known as **summation** and is similar in function to the summative effect described for synapses in section 17.1.2 and effectors in section 17.5.

A good example of convergence and summation is provided by rod cells of the retina in the eye. Some of these cells are capable of detecting a single quantum of light, but the generator potential produced is inadequate to produce an action potential in a neurone of the optic nerve.

However, several rods (ranging from two or three to several hundred) are connected to a single bipolar neurone and several of these are connected to a single optic nerve fibre. Stimulation of at least six rods is required to produce an impulse in an optic nerve fibre. The increased **visual sensitivity** produced by this arrangement of rods is highly adapted to dim-light vision and is well developed in nocturnal species such as owls, badgers and foxes. This high degree of sensitivity, however, is linked with a decrease in visual precision (acuity), as may be observed when attempting to read in poor light. In the human eye, and that of many other species which are active only during daylight, this problem is counteracted by the presence of cones which, with few exceptions, do not show convergence or summation. What cones lose in sensitivity they gain in acuity as described in section 17.5.3.

Spontaneous activity

Some receptors produce nerve impulses in sensory neurones in the absence of stimulation. This system is not as meaningless as it might at first seem as it has two important advantages.

- Firstly it increases the sensitivity of the receptor by enabling it to make a response to a stimulus that would normally be too small to produce a response in the sensory neurone. Any slight change in the intensity of the stimulus will now add to the existing potential in the receptor and produce a change in the frequency of impulses along the sensory neurone.
- Secondly the direction of the change in stimulus can be registered by this system as an increase or decrease in the frequency of the response in the sensory neurone. For example, infra-red receptors in pits in the face of the rattlesnake, which act as direction finders in locating prey and predators, show spontaneous activity and are able to discriminate increases or decreases in temperature of $0.1\,°C$.

Feedback control of receptors

The threshold of some sense organs can be raised or lowered by efferent (outward) impulses from the central nervous system. This 'resets' the sensitivity of the receptor to respond to different ranges of stimulus intensities. In many cases the mechanism of control involves feedback from the receptors, which produces changes in accessory structures enabling the receptor cells to function over a new range. This occurs, for example, in the iris of the eye.

17.5 Structure and function of receptors

17.5.1 Mechanoreceptors

Mechanoreceptors are considered the most primitive type of receptors and may respond to a range of mechanical stimuli such as touch, pressure, vibration and stretching.

Touch, pressure and vibration

The difference between touch and pressure is one of degree, and the detection of these stimuli depends on the position of the receptors within the skin. Touch receptors are also found in other regions of the body and account for the increased sensitivity in these regions. For example, two stimuli may be resolved by the tip of the tongue when 1 mm apart whereas this is only possible at a distance of 60 mm in the middle of the back.

Specialised sense organs known as **Meissner's corpuscles** are situated immediately beneath the epidermis in the skin and respond to touch (fig 17.32). They consist of a single twisted ending of a neurone enclosed within a fluid-filled capsule. Another type of receptor, the **Pacinian corpuscle** (fig 17.30), is found in the skin, joints, tendons, muscles and gut area, and consists of the ending of a single neurone surrounded by many layers of connective tissue. Pacinian corpuscles respond to pressure. Other mechano-receptors are also shown in fig 17.32.

All touch and pressure receptors are thought to produce a generator potential as a result of deformation of the receptor membrane leading to an increase in the permeability of the receptor cell to ions.

Muscle spindle

Proprioreceptors are stretch receptors, sensitive to the position and movement of parts of the body. They respond to changes in the state of contraction of muscles and act as stretch receptors in all activities associated with the control of muscular contraction. Specialised proprioceptors called muscle spindles have been found in the muscles of mammals and other animals. The muscle spindle has three main functions, one static and two dynamic:

- to provide information to the central nervous system on the state and position of muscles and structures attached to them (a static function);
- to initiate reflex contraction of the muscle and return it to its previous length when stimulated by a load (a dynamic function);
- to alter the state of tension in the muscle and reset it to maintain a new length (a dynamic function).

The structure and function of the muscle spindle is described in detail in section 18.4.4.

17.5.2 Thermoreceptors

The many free nerve endings in the skin are the major structures detecting temperature (fig 17.32). There are separate hot and cold receptors.

17.5.3 The eye

The eye is a sense organ which receives light of various wavelengths reflected from objects at varying

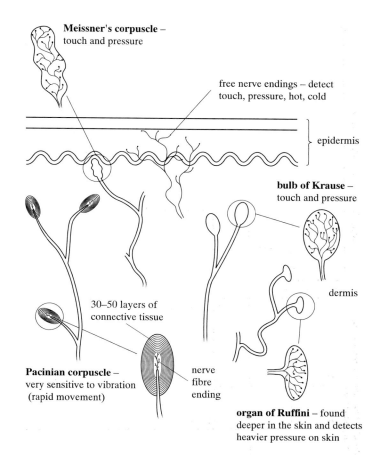

Fig 17.32 *Five types of touch receptor found in the skin.*

distances, the **visual field**, and converts it into electrical impulses. Optic nerves transmit these impulses to the brain where an image of remarkable precision is perceived.

Light travels as waves of electromagnetic radiation and the wavelengths perceived by the human eye occupy a narrow range, the **visible spectrum**, from 380–760 nm. Light is a form of energy and is emitted and absorbed in discrete packets called **quanta** or **photons**. The wavelengths of the visible spectrum carry sufficient energy in each quantum of radiation to produce a photochemical response in the sense cells of the eye.

The camera and the eye work on the same basic principles. These are:

- controlling the amount of light entering the structure;
- focusing images of the external world by means of a lens system;
- registering the image on a sensitive surface;
- processing the 'captured' images to produce a pattern which can be 'seen'.

Structure and function of the human eye

The eyes are held in protective bony sockets of the skull called **orbits** by four **rectus** muscles and two **oblique** muscles which control eye movement. Each human eyeball

(a)

upper eyelid

conjunctiva

cornea

aqueous humour

pupil

lens

iris

suspensory ligament

ciliary muscle

ciliary body

muscle

sclera

choroid

retina

vitreous hum

fovea

blind spot

optic nerve

muscle

Fig 17.33 *Structure of the human eye: (a) diagram of section through eye, (b) section.*

is about 24 mm in diameter and weighs 6–8 g. Most of the eye is composed of 'accessory structures' concerned with bringing light to the photoreceptor cells which are situated in the innermost layer of the eye, the **retina**. The eye is composed of three concentric layers: the sclera (sclerotic coat) and cornea; the choroid, ciliary body, lens and iris; and the retina (fig 17.33). The eye is supported by the hydrostatic pressure (3.3 kPa) of the aqueous and vitreous humours.

The structure of the human eye is shown in fig 17.33 and brief notes on the function of the various parts are given below.

Sclera – external covering of eye; very tough, containing collagen fibres, protects and maintains shape of eyeball.

Cornea – transparent front part of the sclera; the curved surface acts as the main structure refracting (bending) light towards the retina.

Conjunctiva – thin transparent layer of cells protecting the cornea and continuous with the epithelium of eyelids; the conjunctiva does not cover the part of the cornea over the iris.

Eyelid – protects the cornea from mechanical and chemical damage and the retina from bright light by reflex action.

Choroid – rich in blood vessels supplying the retina, and covered with black pigment cells to prevent reflection of light within the eye.

Ciliary body – at the junction of sclera and cornea; contains tissue, blood vessels and ciliary muscles.

Ciliary muscles – circular sheet of smooth muscle fibres that form bundles of circular and radial muscles which alter the shape of the lens during accommodation.

Suspensory ligament – attaches the ciliary body to the lens.

Lens – transparent, elastic biconvex structure; provides fine adjustment for focusing light on to the retina and separates the aqueous and vitreous humours.

Aqueous humour – clear solution of salts secreted by the ciliary body, finally draining into the blood through a canal.

Iris – circular, muscular diaphragm containing the pigment which gives the eye its colour; it controls the amount of light entering the eye.

Pupil – a hole in the iris; all light enters the eye through this.

Vitreous humour – clear semi-solid substance supporting the eyeball.

Retina – contains the photoreceptor cells, rods and cones, and cell bodies and axons of neurones supplying the optic nerve.

Fovea – most sensitive part of retina, contains cones only; most light rays are focused here. Less than 0.5 mm in diameter.

Optic nerve – bundle of nerve fibres carrying impulses from the retina to the brain.

Blind spot – point where the optic nerve leaves eye; there are no rods or cones here, therefore it is not light-sensitive.

> **17.6** List, in order, the structures through which light passes before striking the retina.

Accommodation

Accommodation is the reflex mechanism by which light rays from an object are brought to focus on the retina. It involves two processes and these will be considered separately.

Reflex adjustment of pupil size. In bright light the circular muscle of the iris diaphragm contracts, the radial muscle relaxes, the pupil becomes smaller and less light enters the eye, preventing damage to the retina (fig 17.34). In poor light the opposite muscular contractions and relaxations occur. The added advantage of reducing the pupil size is that this increases the **depth of focus** of the eye.

Refraction of light rays. Light rays from distant objects (more than about 6 m away) are parallel when they strike the eye. Light rays from near objects (less than 6 m away) are diverging (spreading out) when they strike the eye. In both cases the light rays must be **refracted** or bent to focus on the retina, though refraction must be greater for light from near objects. The normal eye is able to accommodate light from objects from about 25 cm to infinity. Refraction occurs when light passes from one medium into another with a different refractive index, and this occurs at the air–cornea surface and at the lens.

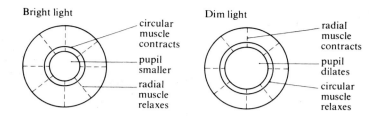

Fig 17.34 *The iris/pupil response to variations in light intensity.*

The degree of refraction at the corneal surface cannot be varied and depends on the angle at which the light strikes the cornea (which, in turn, depends upon the distance of the object from the cornea). Most refraction occurs here, and consequently the function of the lens is to produce the final refraction that brings light to a sharp focus on the retina; this is regulated by the ciliary muscles. The state of contraction of the ciliary muscles changes the tension on the suspensory ligaments. This acts on the natural elasticity of the lens which causes it to change its shape (radius of curvature) and thus the degree of refraction. As the radius of curvature of the lens decreases, it becomes thicker and the amount of refraction increases. The complete relationship between these three structures and refraction is shown in table 17.7. Fig 17.35 shows the changes occurring in the eye during accommodation to light from distant and near objects.

The image produced by the eye on the retina is inverted and reversed but the mental image is perceived in the correct position because the brain learns to accept an inverted reversed image as normal.

Structure of the retina

The photoreceptor cells of the retina face towards the choroid layer. The cells are therefore covered by the cell bodies and axons linking the photoreceptor cells to the brain as shown in fig 17.36.

The retina is composed of three layers of cells each containing a characteristic type of cell. First there is the **photoreceptor layer** (outermost layer) containing the photosensitive cells, the **rods** and **cones**, partially embedded in the pigmented epithelial cells of the choroid. Next is the **intermediate layer** containing bipolar neurones with synapses connecting the photoreceptor layer to the cells of the third layer. Cells called **horizontal** and **amacrine cells** found in this layer enable lateral inhibition to occur (see later). The third layer is the **internal surface layer** containing **ganglion cells** with dendrites in contact with bipolar neurones and axons of the optic nerve.

Structure and function of rods and cones

Rods and cones have an essentially similar structure as shown in fig 17.36, and their photosensitive pigments are attached to the outer surfaces of the membrane in the outer

Table 17.7 Relationship between structures changing the shape of the lens and the degree of refraction.

Ciliary muscle	Tension in suspensory ligament	Shape of lens	Refraction
contracted (near object)	no tension	more curved, thick	increased
relaxed (distant object)	taut	less curved, thin	decreased

segment. They have four similar regions whose structure and function are summarised below.

Outer segment. This is the photosensitive region where light energy is converted into a generator potential. The entire outer segment is composed of flattened membranous vesicles containing the photosensitive pigments. Rods contain 600–1000 of these vesicles stacked up like a pile of coins and they are enclosed by an outer membrane. Cones are so-called because their outer segments are essentially cone-shaped. These have fewer membranous vesicles which are formed by repeated infoldings of the outer membrane.

Constriction. The outer segment is almost separated from the inner segment by an infolding of the outer membrane. The two regions remain in contact by cytoplasm and a pair of cilia which pass between the two. These cilia consist of nine peripheral fibres only, the usual central two being absent. These no longer have a function.

Inner segment. This is an actively metabolic region. It is packed with mitochondria, which make energy available for visual processes, and polyribosomes for the synthesis of proteins involved in the production of the membranous vesicles and visual pigment. The nucleus is situated in this region.

Synaptic region. Here the cells form synapses with bipolar cells. Some bipolar cells may have synapses with several rods. This is called synaptic convergence, and whilst it lowers visual acuity it increases visual sensitivity. This is explained in section 17.4.2 under the heading 'Convergence and summation'. Other bipolar cells link *one* cone to *one* ganglion cell and this gives the cones greater visual acuity than rods. Horizontal cells and amacrine cells link certain numbers of rods together and cones together. This allows a certain amount of processing of visual information to occur before it leaves the retina. For example these cells are involved in lateral inhibition (see later).

Light from distant object

(a)

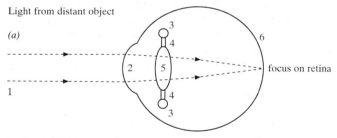

focus on retina

1   Parallel light rays reach eye   4   Suspensory ligament taut
2   Cornea refracts (bends) light rays   5   Lens pulled out thin
3   Circular ciliary muscle relaxed   6   Light focused on retina

(b)

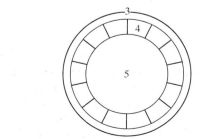

Light from near object

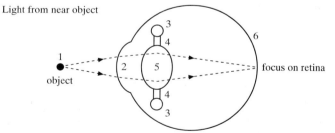

object   focus on retina

1   Diverging light rays reach eye   4   Suspensory ligament slack
2   Cornea refracts (bends) light rays   5   Elastic lens more convex
3   Circular ciliary muscle contracted   6   Light focused on retina

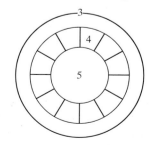

Fig 17.35 *Events occurring during accommodation of light rays from objects at various distances, (a) side views of eye, (b) front views of eye.*

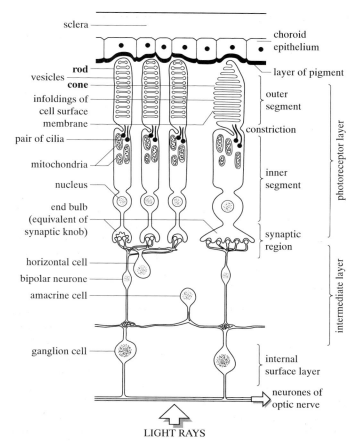

Labels on figure (top to bottom, left side):
sclera
rod — vesicles
cone
infoldings of cell surface membrane
pair of cilia
mitochondria
nucleus
end bulb (equivalent of synaptic knob)
horizontal cell
bipolar neurone
amacrine cell
ganglion cell

Labels on figure (right side):
choroid epithelium
layer of pigment
outer segment
constriction
inner segment
synaptic region
internal surface layer
neurones of optic nerve
photoreceptor layer
intermediate layer

LIGHT RAYS

Fig 17.36 *Diagrammatic section through the retina of the eye showing the ultrastructure of a rod and a cone. Connections between the sensory cells and the neurones of the optic nerve are shown in the inner segment. Light rays must pass through the ganglion cells and the intermediate layers before reaching the rods and cones.*

Differences between rods and cones

Rods are more numerous than cones, 120 million as opposed to 6 million, and have a different distribution. The rods are distributed uniformly throughout the retina except at the fovea, where the cones have their greatest concentration (50 000 per square millimetre). Since the cones are tightly packed together at the fovea, this gives them higher visual acuity (see below).

Rods are much more sensitive to light than cones and respond to lower light intensities. Rods only contain one visual pigment and, being unable to discriminate colour, are used principally for night vision. Each cone contains one of three visual pigments which enables them to differentiate colours. Cones are used mainly in daylight.

The rods have a lower visual acuity because they are less tightly packed together and they undergo synaptic convergence, but this latter point gives them increased collective sensitivity required for night vision (see below).

Sensitivity and acuity

Acuity refers to the precision, or sharpness, of the image we see. Thus if one part of the retina could distinguish between two separate, but closely placed points, and another part could not, the former part would have greater acuity. Acuity is greatest at the fovea, which is normally at the centre of our field of vision, and gradually decreases towards the edges of our field of vision. We move our eyes in order to maintain the image of what we are interested in on the fovea. The fovea contains only cones, and about 90% of the cones are located there. Many of the cones in the fovea synapse with only one bipolar neurone, as shown in fig 17.36, and the bipolar neurones synapse with only one ganglion cell. This 1:1 relationship provides maximum possible acuity because each part of the image is being detected by a different cell and there is no 'blurring' or combining of information. Acuity also increases as the number of cones in a given area increases (rather like a photograph where the closer the individual dots that make up the picture, the sharper the picture) so the fact that they are tightly packed together is an advantage. Cones further away from the fovea (and some in it) combine with two or more bipolar neurones, so some acuity is lost.

Overall there are about 120 million rods and 6 million cones in each retina, but only about 1.2 million ganglion cells. Thus convergence occurs (section 17.4.2) with about 105 photoreceptor cells to 1 ganglion cell. The degree of convergence is actually much greater for rods than cones, so they have much less acuity than cones. The greater the convergence, the lower the acuity. However, **sensitivity** to light increases with convergence (see question 17.7 below). Many rods synapse to a single bipolar cell and many bipolar cells synapse to one ganglion cell. In dim light, vision is poorest at the fovea, where most photoreceptor cells are cones, and best at the edges of the field of vision. You may have noticed that you can see more stars on a dark night out of the 'corners' of your eyes. In dim light only the rods are activated, so colour vision is lost as well as acuity.

17.7 Explain why synaptic convergence should increase visual sensitivity.

17.8 Explain in your own words why objects are seen more clearly at night by not looking directly at them.

The mechanism of photoreception

Rods contain the light-sensitive pigment **rhodopsin**, which is attached to the outer surface of the vesicles. Rhodopsin is a molecule formed by the combination of a protein called **scotopsin** with a small light-absorbing molecule called **retinene** (**retinal**). Retinene is a carotenoid molecule and is a derivative of vitamin A. It exists in two isomeric forms according to the light conditions as shown in fig 17.37.

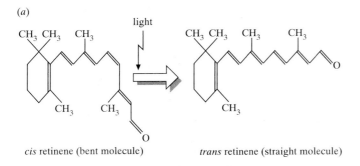

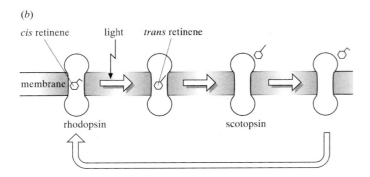

Fig 17.37 *(a) The action of light changes the structure of retinene from the* cis *isomer to the* trans *isomer (b) bleaching and regeneration of rhodopsin.*

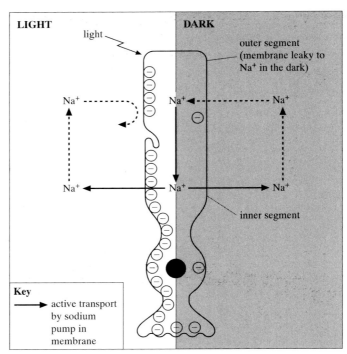

Fig 17.38 *Diagram of a rod showing the changes in sodium permeability of the outer segment produced in the presence of light. The negative charges ⊖ on the right side of the rod indicate the normal resting potential whereas those on the left indicate the hyperpolarisation.*

When a molecule of rhodopsin is exposed to light it is known that one photon of light will produce the above isomeric change. Once the change has happened the rhodopsin breaks down into retinene and scotopsin, a process known as **bleaching**.

$$\text{rhodopsin} \xrightarrow{\text{bleaching}} \text{retinene} + \text{scotopsin}$$

Rhodopsin is reformed immediately in the absence of further light stimulation (and therefore in the dark). *Trans* retinene is first converted into *cis* retinene and then recombined with scotopsin (fig 17.37*b*). This process is called **dark adaptation** and in total darkness it takes about 30 minutes for all rods to adapt and the eyes to achieve maximum sensitivity again.

How does the change in rhodopsin in rods in the light lead to production of an action potential? This involves changes in the outer segment and inner segment membranes of the rod (fig 17.38). In the inner segment of the rod is a sodium pump which continuously pumps out sodium ions. In the dark the outer segment membrane is leaky and allows the sodium back in again by diffusion, reducing the negative charge inside the cell ($-40\,\text{mV}$ instead of the normal $-70\,\text{mV}$ of most cells). In the light, however, the permeability of the outer segment membrane to sodium ions decreases whilst the inner segment continues to pump out sodium ions, thus making the inside

of the rod more negative (fig 17.38). This causes hyperpolarisation of the rod. This situation is exactly opposite to the effect normally found in sensory receptors where the stimulus produces a depolarisation and not a hyperpolarisation. The hyperpolarisation *reduces* the rate of release of excitatory transmitter substance from the rod which is released at its maximum rate during darkness. The bipolar neurone linked by synapses to the rod cell also responds by producing a hyperpolarisation, but the ganglion cells of the optic nerve supplied by the bipolar neurone respond to this by producing an action potential.

Role of horizontal cells and amacrine cells

Horizontal cells synapse with several bipolar neurones (fig 17.36). They are responsible for a phenomenon called **lateral inhibition**. This increases both sensitivity and acuity of vision. If the cells receive stimuli from two rods which are of equal intensity they cancel out (inhibit) the stimuli. They therefore enhance contrast between areas that are weakly stimulated and areas that are strongly stimulated. This makes features such as edges of objects stand out more clearly. Amacrine cells are stimulated by bipolar neurones and synapse with ganglion cells. They transmit information about changes in the level of illumination.

Table 17.8 Colours of the visible spectrum and approximate ranges of their wavelengths.

Colour	Wavelength/nm
red	above 620
orange	590–620
yellow	570–590
green	500–570
blue	440–500
violet	below 440

Colour vision

The human eye absorbs light from all wavelengths of the visible spectrum and perceives these as six colours broadly associated with particular wavelengths as shown in table 17.8. Colour as such does not exist, only different wavelengths of light. Colour is an 'invention' of the brain. There are three types of cone each possessing a different pigment which investigations have shown absorb light of different wavelengths. These are 'red', 'green' and 'blue' cones, which are most sensitive to red, green and blue light respectively. In laboratory tests it has been shown that all the different colours can be seen by using different combinations of pure red, green and blue light.

> **17.9** Using table 17.8 suggest what colour would be seen in the following situation. A person places a green filter (average wavelength 530 nm) over one eye and a red filter (average wavelength 620 nm) over the other eye and looks at an object.

The most generally accepted theory of colour vision is the **trichromacy theory**, which states that different colours are produced by the degree of stimulation of each type of cone. For example, equal stimulation of all cones produces the colour sensation of white. Fig 17.39 shows the sensitivity of the three types of cone to different colours of light. You can see that, although the cones are described as blue, green and red cones, this refers to their maximum sensitivity. They are also less sensitive to a limited range of other colours, and their sensitivities overlap. Different colours are therefore produced by different degrees of stimulation of the three cones. For example, orange light stimulates only green and red cones, blue light stimulates blue cones strongly and green cones weakly, and green light stimulates all three cones.

Although the trichromacy theory explains most of the experimental evidence obtained about colour vision, there are still a few facts that it does not explain. These are outside the scope of this book, but it is clear that further refinement of the theory is necessary.

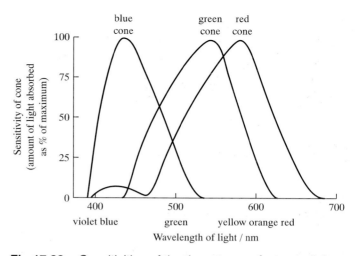

Fig 17.39 *Sensitivities of the three types of cone to light of different wavelengths (colours).*

The initial discrimination of colour occurs in the retina but the final colour perceived involves interpretation by the brain.

Colour-blindness. The complete absence of a particular type of cone or a shortage of one type can lead to various forms of colour-blindness or degrees of 'colour-weakness'. This is the inability to distinguish certain colours. For example, a person lacking red or green cones is 'red–green colour-blind' because they cannot distinguish between red and green, whereas a person with a reduced number of either cones will have difficulty in distinguishing a range of red–green shades. Colour-blindness, or its extent, is determined using test charts, such as the Ishihara test charts, composed of a series of dots of several colours. Some charts bear a number which a person with normal vision can perceive, whilst the colour-blind sufferer sees a different number or no number at all. Colour-blindness is a sex-linked recessive characteristic resulting in the absence of appropriate colour genes in the X chromosome. About 2% of men are red colour-blind, 6% are green colour-blind, but only 0.4% of women show any sign of colour-blindness.

Binocular vision and stereoscopic vision

Binocular vision occurs when the visual fields of both eyes overlap so that the fovea of both eyes are focused on the same object. It provides the basis of **stereoscopic vision**. Stereoscopic vision depends upon the two eyes producing slightly different images on the retina at the same time which the brain interprets as one image. The resolution of the two retinal images produced in stereoscopic vision occurs in the area of the brain called the **visual cortex**.

The more frontally the eyes are situated the greater the overlap between the eyes and the more that can be seen stereoscopically. For example, humans have a total visual field of 180° and a stereoscopic visual field of 140°. The

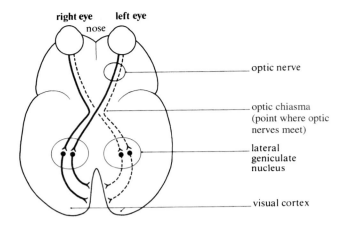

Fig 17.40 *Diagram of the human visual pathway as seen from the* underside *of the brain.*

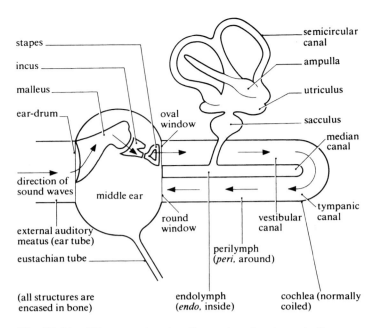

Fig 17.41 *Diagram showing the major structures in the mammalian ear involved in hearing and balance (not to scale).*

horse has laterally placed eyes with a limited forward stereoscopic visual field which it uses for viewing distant objects. For nearer objects the horse turns its head and uses monocular vision to examine details. Frontally placed eyes and centrally situated foveas, producing good visual acuity, are essential for good stereoscopic vision which provides an increased appreciation of size and perception of the depth and distance of objects. Stereoscopic vision is found mainly in predatory animals where it is vital when capturing prey by pouncing or swooping, as shown by members of the cat family, hawks and eagles. Animals which are hunted have laterally placed eyes giving wide visual fields but restricted stereoscopic vision. For instance the rabbit has a total binocular visual field of 360° and frontal stereoscopic vision of 26°.

The role of the brain

Nerve impulses generated in the retina are carried by the million or so neurones of the optic nerve to the primary visual area of the visual cortex, which is situated in the occipital lobe at the back of the brain (fig 17.26). Here each part of the retina, involving perhaps only a few rods and cones, is represented and it is here that the visual input is interpreted and we 'see'. However, what we see has meaning only after reference to other regions of the cortex and the temporal lobes, where previous visual information is stored and used in the analysis and identification of the present visual input (section 17.2.4). In humans, axons from the left side of the retina of both eyes, which see the right visual field, pass to the left visual cortex and axons from the right side of each retina, which see the left visual field, pass to the right visual cortex. The point where the

axons from those regions of the retina closest to the nose cross is called the **optic chiasma** and is included in the visual pathway shown in fig 17.40. About 20% of the optic neurones do not pass to the visual cortex but enter the midbrain, where they are involved in reflex control of pupil size and eye movements.

17.5.4   Mammalian ear

The mammalian ear is a sense organ containing receptors sensitive to gravity, movement and sound. Movements and positions of the head relative to gravity are detected by the vestibular apparatus which is composed of the **semicircular canals**, the **utricle** and the **saccule**. All other structures of the ear are involved in receiving, amplifying and transducing sound energy into electrical impulses and producing the sensation of hearing in the auditory regions of the brain.

Structure and function of the ear

The ear consists of three sections specialising in different functions (fig 17.41). The **outer ear** consists of the **pinna**, strengthened by elastic cartilage, which focuses and collects sound waves into the **ear tube** (external auditory meatus); the sound waves cause the **tympanic membrane** (eardrum) to vibrate. In the **middle ear**, vibrations of the tympanic membrane are transmitted across to the membranous **oval window** by movement of the three ear ossicles, the **malleus**, **incus** and **stapes** (hammer, anvil and stirrup). A lever system between these bones and the relative areas of contact of the malleus with the tympanic membrane ($60\,mm^2$) and the stapes with the oval window

($3.2\,mm^2$) amplifies the movement of the tympanic membrane 22 times. Damage to the tympanic membrane, due to atmospheric pressure changes, is prevented by a connection between the air-filled middle ear and the pharynx, the **Eustachian tube**. Finally there is the **inner ear** which consists of a complex system of canals and cavities within the skull bone which contain a fluid called **perilymph**. Within these canals are membranous sacs filled with **endolymph** and sensory receptors. Auditory receptors are found in the cochlea, and balance receptors are found in the utricle and saccule and the ampullae of the semicircular canals. The perilymph is enclosed by the membranes of the oval window and round window.

The nature of sound

Sound is produced by the vibration of particles within a medium. It travels as waves consisting of alternating regions of high and low pressure and will pass through liquids, solids and gases. The distance between two identical points on adjacent waves is the **wavelength** and this determines the **frequency** of **vibrations** or **pitch** (whether it sounds high or low). The human ear is sensitive to wavelengths between 40 and 20 000 Hz (cycles per second). The audible range of dogs reaches 40 000 Hz, and that of bats 100 000 Hz. Human speech frequencies vary between 500 and 3000 Hz, and sensitivity to high frequencies decreases with age.

Tone depends upon the number of different frequencies making up the sound. For example, a violin and trumpet playing the same note, say middle C, produce the same fundamental frequency of 256 Hz but sound different. This is due to overtones or harmonics produced by the instrument which give it its distinctive quality or **timbre**. The same principle applies to the human voice and gives it its characteristic sound.

The **intensity** (loudness) of a sound depends upon the amplitude of the sound waves produced at the source and is a measure of the energy they contain.

Cochlea and hearing

The cochlea is a spiral canal 35 mm long and subdivided longitudinally by a membranous triangle into three regions as shown in fig 17.42.

Both the vestibular and tympanic canals contain perilymph, and the two canals are connected at the extreme end of the cochlea via a small hole. The median canal contains endolymph. The **basilar membrane** separates the median and tympanic canals and supports sensory hair cells that can be brought into contact with the **tectorial membrane** above. This unit, consisting of basilar membrane, sensory cells and tectorial membrane, is called the **organ of Corti** and is the region where transduction of sound waves into electrical impulses occurs.

Sound waves transmitted from the ear tube to the oval window produce vibrations in the perilymph of the vestibular canal and these are transmitted via **Reissner's membrane** to the endolymph in the median canal. From

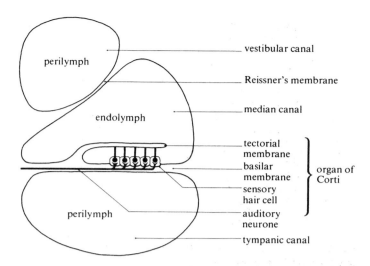

Fig 17.42 *Diagram of a TS cochlea showing the organ of Corti.*

there they are transferred to the basilar membrane and the perilymph in the tympanic canal, and are finally dissipated into the air of the middle ear as vibration of the round window.

The precise mechanism of transduction of pressure waves into nerve impulses is not known but is believed to involve relative movement of the basilar and tectorial membranes. Vibrations of the basilar membrane, induced by pressure waves, push the sensory hairs against the tectorial membrane and force the two membranes to slide past each other. The distortion produced in the sensory hairs due to the shearing forces causes a depolarisation of the sensory cells, the production of generator potentials and the initiation of action potentials in the axons of the auditory nerve.

Pitch and intensity discrimination

The ability to distinguish the pitch of a sound depends upon the frequency of the vibration-producing movement of the basilar membrane and stimulating sensory cells in a specific region of the organ of Corti. These cells supply a particular region of the auditory cortex of the brain where the sensation of pitch is perceived. The basilar membrane becomes broader and more flexible as it passes from the base of the cochlea to its apex and its sensitivity to vibration changes along its length so that only low-frequency sounds can pass to the apex. High-frequency (pitch) sounds stimulate the basilar membrane at the *base* of the cochlea and low frequency sounds stimulate it at the *apical end*. A pure sound, consisting of a single frequency, will only stimulate one small area of the basilar membrane whereas most sounds, containing several frequencies, simultaneously stimulate many regions of the basilar membrane. The auditory cortex integrates the stimuli from these various regions of the basilar membrane and a 'single' blended sound is perceived.

The intensity or loudness of the sound depends upon

each region of the basilar membrane containing a range of sensory cells that respond to different thresholds of vibration. For example, a quiet sound at a given frequency may only stimulate a few sensory cells, whereas a louder sound at the same frequency would stimulate several other sensory cells which have higher thresholds of vibration. This is an example of spatial summation.

Balance

Maintaining balance at rest and during movement of the body relies upon the brain receiving a continual input of sensory information concerning the position of various parts of the body. Information from proprioceptors in joints and muscles indicates the positions and state of the limbs, but vital information relating to position and movement of the head is provided by the **vestibular apparatus** of the ear, the **utricle**, **saccule** and **semicircular canals**.

The basic sensory receptors within these structures consist of cells which have hair-like extensions, **hair cells**, attached to dense structures supported in the **endolymph**.

Movement of the head results in deflection of the hairs and production of a generator potential in the hair cells.

Regions of the walls of the utricle and saccule, called **maculae**, contain receptor cells which have their hair-like processes embedded in a gelatinous mass that contains granules of calcium carbonate. This mass is called an **otoconium** (fig 17.43). Otoconia respond to the pull of gravity acting at right-angles to the Earth's surface and are mainly responsible for detecting the direction of movement of the head with respect to gravity.

The utricle responds to vertical movements of the head and the otoconia produce maximum stimulation when pulling the receptor hairs downwards, such as when the body is upside down (fig 17.44).

The saccule responds to lateral (sideways) movement of the head. The hair cells of the saccule are horizontal when the head is upright. Tilting of the head to the left produces a differential response from left and right saccules. The left receives increased stimulation as the otoconia pull downwards on the hairs whereas decreased stimulation

Fig 17.43 *Scanning electron micrograph of the inner ear showing part of the region of the saccule known as the macula. This forms the organ of balance and consists of supporting cells (general background) on which sensory ciliated cells (hair-like structures) are found. When the head tilts sideways, calcium carbonate crystals called otoconia (angular structure between ciliated cells at bottom) are moved by the endolymph and stimulate the ciliated cells.*

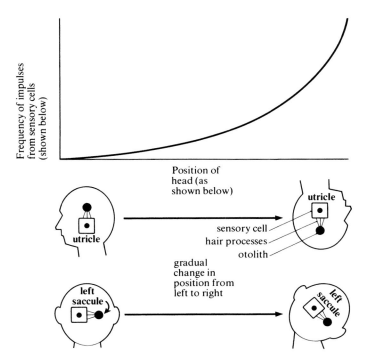

Fig 17.44 *Graph showing the effect of head position on the activity of receptor cells of the utricle and saccule.*

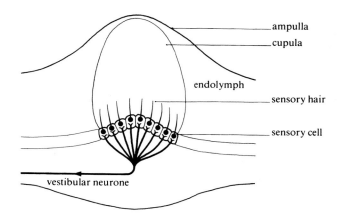

Fig 17.45 *Diagram showing a TS through the ampulla of a semicircular canal.*

occurs on the right. These displacements produce impulses passing to the cerebellum where the orientation of the head is perceived.

The three semicircular canals are arranged in three planes at right-angles to each other and detect the direction and rate of change of position of the head. At the base of each canal is a swelling, the **ampulla** containing a conical gelatinous structure, the **cupula**. This encloses the hair-like projections of the receptor cells. The cupula extends fully across the ampulla (fig 17.45). Rotational movement of the head, semicircular canals and cupula is resisted by the inertia of the endolymph which remains stationary. This produces a relative displacement of the cupula which is bent in the opposite direction to the head movement. The receptor cells respond by producing generator potentials leading to action potentials in the vestibular neurones. The direction and rate of displacement are both detected by the receptor cells. Linear acceleration is detected by both the maculae and cupulae.

17.6   The endocrine system

The endocrine system is made up of a number of glands called endocrine glands. A **gland** is a structure which secretes a specific chemical substance or substances. There are two types of gland in the body, exocrine glands and endocrine glands. An **exocrine gland** is one which secretes its product into a duct, for example the sweat gland which secretes sweat into tubes called sweat ducts that lead

to the surface of the skin. An **endocrine gland** has the following characteristics:

- it secretes chemicals called **hormones**;
- it has no duct (a **ductless gland**), instead, the hormone is secreted directly into the bloodstream;
- it has a rich supply of blood with a relatively large number of blood vessels.

Some glands have both endocrine and exocrine functions, such as the pancreas, which secretes the hormones insulin and glucagon, and also secretes pancreatic juice containing digestive enzymes into the pancreatic duct that leads to the gut.

A hormone is a **chemical messenger**. It has the following properties:

- it travels in the blood;
- it has its effect at a site different from the site where it is made, called the **target**, hence the term messenger;
- it fits precisely into receptor molecules in the target like a key in a lock – it is therefore **specific** for a particular target;
- it is a small soluble organic molecule;
- it is effective in low concentrations.

The endocrine and nervous systems function in a coordinated way to maintain a homeostatic state within the body. The two systems are compared in table 17.1. As we shall see, the hypothalamus in the brain is an important link between them (see also section 17.2.4). Despite their obvious differences, both systems share a common feature in the release of chemical substances as a means of communication between cells. It is believed that the two systems originated and developed side by side as the needs of communication became more complex due to the increase in the size and complexity of organisms. In both cases the principal role of the systems is the coordination and control of many of the major physiological activities of organisms.

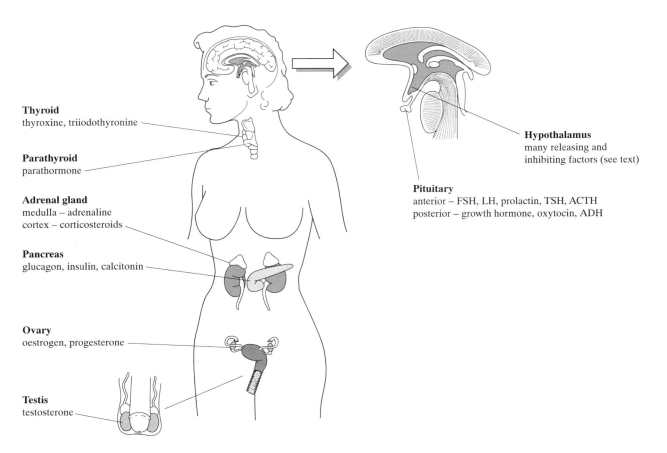

Thyroid
thyroxine, triiodothyronine

Parathyroid
parathormone

Adrenal gland
medulla – adrenaline
cortex – corticosteroids

Pancreas
glucagon, insulin, calcitonin

Ovary
oestrogen, progesterone

Testis
testosterone

Hypothalamus
many releasing and
inhibiting factors (see text)

Pituitary
anterior – FSH, LH, prolactin, TSH, ACTH
posterior – growth hormone, oxytocin, ADH

Fig 17.46 *Locations of the main endocrine organs in the human body.*

The major endocrine glands of the body are shown in fig 17.46 and their hormones and effects are summarised in table 17.9.

17.6.1 Mechanisms of hormone action

As summarised in table 17.10, all vertebrate hormones belong to one of four chemical groups:

- peptides and proteins;
- derivatives of amines, such as tyrosine;
- steroids;
- fatty acids.

Release of hormones

The mechanisms controlling the release of hormones by glands are as follows:

- presence of a specific metabolite in the blood, for example excess glucose in the blood causes the release of insulin from the pancreas which lowers the blood glucose level;
- presence of another hormone in the blood, for example many of the hormones released from the anterior pituitary gland are 'stimulating' hormones which cause the release of other hormones from other glands in the body;

- stimulation by neurones from the autonomic nervous system, for example adrenaline and noradrenaline are released from the cells of the adrenal medulla by the arrival of nerve impulses in situations of anxiety, stress and danger.

Negative feedback

In the first two cases above, the timing of hormone release and the amount of hormone released are regulated by feedback control. This is usually negative feedback control (rather than positive feedback control). A good example of negative feedback control is provided by thyroxine (see section 17.6.4).

The cascade effect

Hormones which are released by the presence of another circulating hormone are usually under the control of the hypothalamus and pituitary gland and the final response often involves the secretion of three separate hormones. A good example is the role of ACTH in cortisol production. This is shown in fig 17.47. The mechanism, known as the **cascade effect**, is significant because it enables the effect of the release of a small amount of initial hormone to become amplified (magnified) at each stage in the pathway. Cortisol, the final hormone released in the example in fig 17.47, is an anti-stress hormone secreted by the outer

Table 17.9 Summary of the major human endocrine glands, their functions and the control of their secretion.

Gland	Hormone	Functions	Secretion control mechanism
Hypothalamus	Releasing and inhibiting hormones and factors Posterior pituitary hormones produced here	Control of anterior pituitary hormones	Feedback mechanisms involving metabolite and hormone levels
Posterior pituitary gland	Receives hormones from hypothalamus – no hormones synthesised here Stores and secretes the following: Oxytocin Antidiuretic hormone (ADH) (vasopressin)	 Ejection of milk from mammary gland, contraction of uterus during birth Reduction of urine secretion by kidney	Feedback mechanisms involving hormones and nervous system Blood solute potential
Anterior pituitary gland	Follicle stimulating hormone (FSH) Luteinising hormone (LH) Prolactin Thyroid stimulating hormone (TSH) Adrenocorticotrophic hormone (ACTH or corticotrophin) Growth hormone (GH)	In male, stimulates spermatogenesis In female, growth of ovarian follicles In male, testosterone secretion In female, secretion of oestrogen and progesterone, ovulation and maintenance of corpus luteum Stimulates milk production and secretion Synthesis and secretion of thyroid hormones, growth of thyroid glands Synthesis and secretion of adrenal cortex hormones, growth of gland Protein synthesis, growth, especially of bones of limbs	Blood oestrogen and testosterone levels via hypothalamus and pituitary gland Blood testosterone levels via hypothalamus and pituitary gland Blood oestrogen levels via hypothalamus and pituitary gland Hypothalamus hormones Blood levels of thyroxine via hypothalamus and pituitary gland Blood ACTH via hypothalamus Hypothalamus hormones
Parathyroid gland	Parathormone	Increases blood calcium level Decreases blood phosphate level	Blood Ca^{2+} level, and blood PO_4^{3-} level
Thyroid gland	Triiodothyronine (T_3) and thyroxine (T_4) Calcitonin	Regulation of basal metabolic rate, growth and development Decreases blood calcium level	TSH Blood Ca^{2+} level
Adrenal cortex	Glucocorticoids (cortisol) Mineralocorticoids (aldosterone)	Protein breakdown, glucose/glycogen synthesis, adaptation to stress, anti-inflammatory/allergy effects Na^+ retention in kidney, Na^+ and K^+ ratios in extracellular and intracellular fluids, raises blood pressure	ACTH Blood Na^+ and K^+ levels and low blood pressure
Adrenal medulla	Adrenaline (epinephrine) Noradrenaline (norepinephrine)	Increases rate and force of heartbeat, constriction of skin and gut capillaries Dilation of arterioles of heart and skeletal muscles, raises blood glucose level General constriction of small arteries, raising of blood pressure	Sympathetic nervous system Nervous system
Islets of Langerhans	Insulin (beta cells) Glucagon (alpha cells)	Decreases blood glucose level, increases glucose and amino acid uptake and utilisation by cells Increases blood glucose level, breakdown of glycogen to glucose in liver	Blood glucose and amino acid levels Blood glucose level
Stomach	Gastrin	Secretion of gastric juices	Food in stomach
Duodenum	Secretin Cholecystokinin (pancreozymin)	Secretion of pancreatic juice Inhibits gastric secretion Emptying of gall bladder and release of pancreatic juice into duodenum	Acidic food in duodenum Fatty acids and amino acids in duodenum
Kidney	Renin	Conversion of angiotensinogen into angiotensin	Blood Na^+ level, decreased blood pressure
Ovary	Oestrogens (17β-oestradiol) Progesterone	Female secondary sex characteristics, oestrous cycle Gestation, inhibition of ovulation	FSH and LH LH
Corpus luteum	Progesterone and oestrogen Progesterone and oestrogen	Growth and development of uterus Fetal development	LH Developing fetus
Placenta	Chorionic gonadotrophin Human placental lactogen	Maintenance of corpus luteum Stimulates mammary growth	Developing fetus Developing fetus
Testis	Testosterone	Male secondary sexual characteristics	LH and FSH

Table 17.10 Summary table showing chemical nature of the major hormones of the body.

Chemical group	Hormone	Major source
Peptides and proteins	Growth hormone Oxytocin ADH (Vasopressin)	Posterior pituitary gland
	Parathormone	Parathyroid gland
	Calcitonin	Thyroid gland
	Insulin Glucagon	Islets of Langerhans (pancreas)
	Gastrin	Stomach mucosa
	Secretin	Duodenal mucosa
Amines	Adrenaline	Adrenal medulla
	Noradrenaline	Sympathetic nervous system and adrenal medulla
	Thyroxine Triiodothyronine	Thyroid gland
	Releasing and inhibiting hormones and factors of the hypothalamus	Hypothalamus
	Follicle stimulating hormone Luteinising hormone Prolactin Thyroid stimulating hormone Adrenocorticotrophic hormone	Anterior pituitary gland
Steroids	Testosterone	Testis
	Oestrogens Progesterone	Ovary and placenta
	Corticosteroids	Adrenal cortex
Fatty acids	Prostaglandins	Many tissues

region (cortex) of the adrenal glands. It belongs to a group of hormones known as glucocorticoids which help to regulate blood sugar levels at times of stress (see also section 17.6.5).

Effects on target cells

Hormones are very specific and only exert their effects on target cells which possess the particular protein receptors that recognise the hormone. Non-target cells lack these receptors and therefore do not respond to the circulating hormone. Once attached to a receptor, the hormone may exert its effect in a number of ways. Three of the most important are through effects on:

- the cell membrane;
- enzymes located in the cell membrane (second messenger mechanism);
- genes.

Examples of each of these follow.

Cell membrane. Insulin exerts one of its effects by increasing the uptake of glucose into cells. It binds with a receptor site and alters the permeability of the membrane to glucose. Adrenaline works on smooth muscle cells by opening or closing ion channels for sodium or potassium ions or both, changing membrane potentials and either stimulating or inhibiting contraction as a result.

Second messenger mechanism of hormone action. Adrenaline and many peptide hormones bind to receptor sites on the cell membrane but cannot enter the cells themselves. Instead they cause the release of a 'second messenger' which triggers a series of enzyme-controlled reactions. These eventually bring about the hormonal response. In many cases this 'second messenger' is the nucleotide **cyclic AMP** (cyclic adenosine monophosphate), as shown in fig 17.48. The figure also shows that when the hormone binds to the receptor site it activates the receptor protein to become the enzyme **adenyl cyclase**. This converts ATP to cyclic AMP. In general, cyclic AMP can

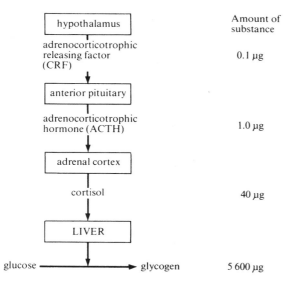

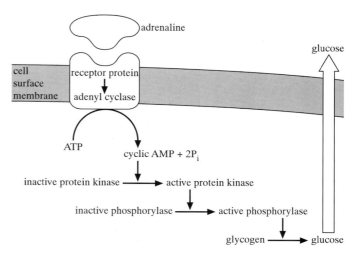

Fig 17.47 *An example of the 'cascade' effect in the control of the conversion of glucose to glycogen as a result of the release of adrenocorticotrophic releasing factor. The total amplification in this example is 56 000 times (data from Bradley, 1976).*

Fig 17.48 *Simplified diagram showing how adrenaline causes the release of glucose from a liver cell. The activation of membrane bound adenyl cyclase produces cyclic AMP which activates enzyme systems leading to the breakdown of glycogen to glucose. Glucose diffuses out of the cell into the bloodstream.*

trigger a wide variety of responses, depending on the particular cell stimulated.

In the case of adrenaline, cyclic AMP activates the enzyme protein kinase which in turn activates a phosphorylase enzyme which is needed to convert glycogen into glucose. The overall effect of adrenaline in this situation is therefore to release glucose. At each stage in the process an amplification occurs because only a few molecules of adenyl cyclase are needed to activate many molecules of protein kinase, and so on. This is the cascade effect.

Other hormones which use cyclic AMP as a second messenger include ADH (section 17.6.2 and 20.6), TSH (section 17.6.4), ACTH (section 17.6.5), glucagon (section 17.6.6), LH and FSH (section 21.6.6), and most releasing hormones from the hypothalamus.

Genes. Steroid hormones (the sex hormones and hormones secreted by the adrenal cortex) pass through the cell surface membrane and bind to a receptor protein in the cytoplasm. The complex formed passes to the cell nucleus where the hormones exert a direct effect upon the chromosomes by switching on genes and stimulating transcription (messenger RNA formation). The messenger RNA enters the cytoplasm and is translated into new proteins, such as enzymes, which carry out a particular function. For example, the hormone thyroxine passes through the cell surface membrane and binds directly to receptor proteins in the chromosomes, switching on certain genes.

In many cases of hormone action hormones appear to exert their effects by influencing enzymes associated with membranes or genetic systems.

17.6.2 The hypothalamus and pituitary gland

As stated earlier, much of the coordination of the body is achieved by the nervous and endocrine systems acting together. The major centres in the body for the coordination of the two systems of control are the hypothalamus and pituitary gland. The hypothalamus plays a dominant role in collecting information from other regions of the brain and from blood vessels passing through it. This information passes to the pituitary gland which, by its secretions, directly or indirectly regulates the activity of all other endocrine glands.

The hypothalamus

The hypothalamus is situated at the base of the forebrain immediately beneath the thalamus and above the pituitary gland (fig 17.24). It contains several distinct regions of nerve cells whose axons terminate on blood capillaries in the hypothalamus and posterior pituitary as shown in fig 17.49. (The pituitary gland can be divided into two parts, the anterior pituitary and the posterior pituitary.) Many physiological activities, such as hunger, thirst, sleep and temperature regulation, are regulated by nervous control through nerve impulses passing from the hypothalamus along neurones of the autonomic nervous system, giving involuntary (reflex) control of these processes. The control

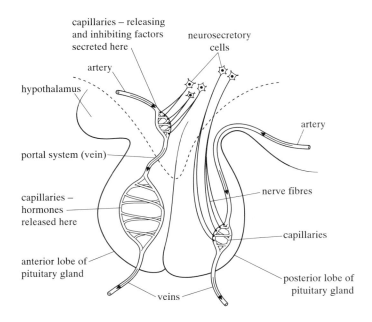

capillaries – releasing
and inhibiting factors
secreted here

neurosecretory
cells

artery

hypothalamus

portal system (vein)

capillaries –
hormones
released here

anterior lobe of
pituitary gland

veins

artery

nerve fibres

capillaries

posterior lobe of
pituitary gland

Fig 17.49 *Diagram showing the relationship between neurosecretory cells and blood vessels in the hypothalamus and pituitary gland.*

cells are nerve cells that have developed the secretory capacity to a high level. Chemical substances are produced in the cell bodies of these cells and packaged into granules or droplets before being transported down the axon by cytoplasmic streaming. At the end of the neurone these cells synapse with capillaries, and release their secretion into the blood when stimulated by nerve impulses passing down the axon.

The pituitary gland

The pituitary gland is a small red-grey gland, about the size of a pea, weighing about 0.5 g and hanging from the base of the brain by a short stalk (fig 17.24). It is divided into two lobes of different origin, the anterior pituitary and the posterior pituitary.

Anterior pituitary. This is connected to the hypothalamus by blood vessels which form a portal system. A **portal system** is one which connects two organs, neither of which is the heart. It has one capillary bed in the hypothalamus and a second in the anterior pituitary.

Nerve terminals from specialised neurosecretory cells release two groups of chemical substances, known as 'releasing factors' and 'inhibiting factors', into the blood capillaries at the hypothalamus end of the portal system. These pass to the pituitary end where they cause the release of six hormones known as **trophic hormones**. A trophic hormone is one which stimulates other endocrine glands to release their hormones. The trophic hormones are produced and stored by the anterior pituitary. These six hormones pass into the blood vessels that leave the pituitary and exert their effects on specific target organs throughout the body, as shown in table 17.11. Growth hormone is considered in more detail in section 22.5.

The release of growth hormone and prolactin (see table 17.11) can both be stimulated and inhibited by the hypothalamus, whereas the release of the other four shown in the table (FSH, LH, TSH and ACTH) is regulated by

by the hypothalamus of endocrine secretion, however, lies in the ability of the hypothalamus to monitor metabolite and hormone levels in the blood. A **metabolite** is any molecule that is taking part in metabolism, such as glucose. Information gathered in this way, together with information from almost all parts of the brain, then passes to the pituitary gland, either by the release of 'hormones' into blood vessels which supply the pituitary or by neurones. The information relayed by neurones passes through specialised neurones called **neurosecretory cells**.

All nerve cells release a chemical substance, a neurotransmitter, at their terminal synapse, but neurosecretory

Table 17.11 Summary table showing the main hormones of the hypothalamus, the anterior pituitary hormones influenced by them and their target organs.

Hypothalamus hormone	Anterior pituitary hormone and response	Site of action
Growth hormone releasing factor (GHRF) Growth hormone release-inhibiting hormone (GHRIH)* (somatostatin)	Growth hormone (GH) (see section 22.8.1)	Most tissues
Prolactin releasing factor (PRF) Prolactin inhibiting factor (PIF)	Prolactin Inhibition of prolactin secretion	Ovary and mammary gland
Luteinising hormone releasing hormone (LHRH)*	Follicle stimulating hormone (FSH) Luteinising hormone (LH)	Ovary and testis
Thyrotrophin releasing hormone (TRH)*	Thyroid stimulating hormone (TSH)	Thyroid gland
Adrenocorticotrophin releasing factor (CRF)	Adrenocorticotrophic hormone (ACTH)	Adrenal cortex

*Releasing factors with an established identity are known as 'hormones'. Luteinising hormone releasing hormone is able to stimulate the release of both FSH and LH.

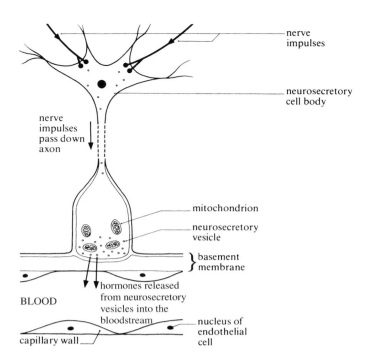

Fig 17.50 *Diagram showing a neurosecretory cell and its attachment to a blood capillary (not drawn to scale).*

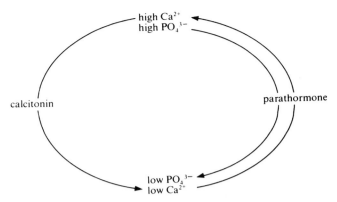

Fig 17.51 *Role of parathormone and calcitonin in the regulating of blood calcium level.*

negative feedback of hormones from the target glands acting on receptors in the hypothalamus and anterior pituitary. The six pituitary hormones stimulate the release of target gland hormones and, as the levels of these rise, they inhibit the secretion of the hypothalamus and pituitary hormones. When the blood levels of these target hormones fall below a certain level, hypothalamus and pituitary inhibition ceases allowing increased secretion from these glands. This is an example of negative feedback and is a control mechanism described in sections 19.5.4 and 20.6.

Posterior pituitary. This originates as an extension of the brain. It does not synthesise any hormones but stores and releases two hormones, **antidiuretic hormone (ADH** or **vasopressin)** and **oxytocin**. Antidiuretic hormone is released in response to a fall in the water content of blood plasma and leads to an increase in the permeability to water of the distal and collecting tubules of the nephron in the kidney so that water is retained in the blood plasma. A reduced volume of concentrated urine is excreted (section 20.6). Oxytocin causes contraction of the uterus during birth and the ejection of milk from the nipple (section 21.3.8).

ADH and oxytocin are produced by neurosecretory cell bodies lying in the hypothalamus and pass down the nerve fibres. These neurosecretory cells are much more specialised than those connected with the secretion of releasing factors and they form structures consisting of a swollen synapse attached to a capillary and surrounded by connective tissue (fig 17.50). Nerve impulses are relayed to the cell bodies of these neurosecretory cells from other regions of the brain and transmitted down the axons to the swollen ends of the axons where hormones stored in vesicles are released into the bloodstream and carried to target organs. Since the whole process involves both the nervous system and the endocrine system the response is known as a **neuroendocrine response**. Many neuro-endocrine responses result in a type of behaviour pattern known as a **neuroendocrine reflex** and many examples of these are associated with courtship and breeding activity.

17.6.3 Parathyroid glands

In humans there are four small parathyroid glands embedded in the thyroid gland. They produce only one hormone called **parathormone** which is a peptide composed of 84 amino acids. Parathormone and the thyroid hormone **calcitonin** (see below) work antagonistically (in opposite ways) to regulate the plasma calcium and phosphate levels. The release of parathormone increases the plasma calcium level to its normal level and decreases the plasma phosphate level. The activity of the parathyroid glands is controlled by the simple negative feedback mechanism shown in fig 17.51.

Overactivity of the gland reduces the level of calcium in the plasma and tissues due to calcium excretion in urine. This can lead to a state of tetany in which muscles remain contracted. Also the rate of excretion of phosphate is reduced and the level of phosphate ions in the plasma rises.

17.6.4 Thyroid gland

The thyroid gland produces three active hormones, **triiodothyronine (T$_3$)**, **thyroxine (T$_4$)** and **calcitonin**. T$_3$ and T$_4$ help to regulate metabolic rate, growth and development, whilst calcitonin is involved in the regulation of calcium levels in the blood. Calcitonin is referred to in section 17.6.3 above.

The structure of the thyroid gland

The thyroid gland is a bow-tie shaped structure found in the neck. It has lobes on each side of the trachea and larynx,

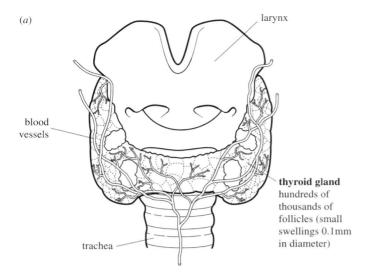

(a)

larynx

blood
vessels

thyroid gland
hundreds of
thousands of
follicles (small
swellings 0.1mm
in diameter)

trachea

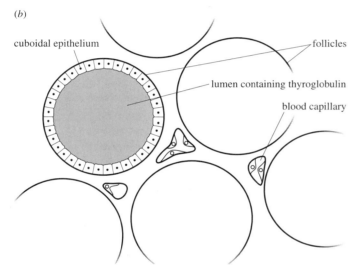

(b)

cuboidal epithelium

follicles

lumen containing thyroglobulin

blood capillary

Fig 17.52 *Structure of the thyroid gland: (a) bilobed appearance around the trachea, (b) section through a group of follicles.*

connected by a thin band of tissue (fig 17.52). It is made up of hundreds of thousands of tiny follicles which have a diameter of about 0.1 mm. Each follicle is a hollow sphere whose wall consists of a single layer of cuboidal epithelium. It is these cells that secrete thyroxine and T_3. They become columnar in shape and develop microvilli on their inner surface when the gland is activated by **thyroid stimulating hormone** (**TSH**) from the anterior pituitary gland.

The formation and release of T_3 and T_4

Triiodothyronine contains three iodine atoms in its structure and thyroxine contains four, hence the names T_3 and T_4 (fig 17.53). Iodine is taken up by active transport from the blood plasma in the numerous capillaries surrounding the follicles. It is taken up as iodine ions (I^-) and secreted into the lumen of the follicle. Here it is used to make T_3 and T_4 which are bound to a protein called thyroglobulin formed

3, 5, 3-triiodothyronine (T_3)

3, 5, 3, 5-tetraiodothyronine (T_4)
thyroxine

Fig 17.53 *Structural formulae of the main thyroid hormones T_3 and T_4.*

by the follicle cells. In order to obtain T_3 and T_4 for release into the blood, the epithelial cells take up thyroglobulin by pinocytosis and then remove the active hormone from the thyroglobulin. T_3 and T_4 have identical structures apart from the number of iodine atoms and both have the same effect on the body. Since T_4 (thyroxine) is secreted in much larger amounts, the following account will refer to thyroxine only.

The function of thyroxine (T_4)

The main effect of thyroxine is to control the basal metabolic rate (BMR). **Metabolism** is the term used to describe all the chemical reactions going on in the body. The **basal rate** is the rate at rest. Basal metabolic rate is therefore the rate at which oxygen and food are used to release energy and is directly related to the rate of cell respiration. The BMR in humans averages about $160 \, kJ \, h^{-1} \, m^{-2}$ body surface and is maintained at a steady state by the action of thyroxine. Thyroxine promotes the breakdown of glucose and fats to provide energy (section 19.5.2). Further effects which lead to an increase in energy release include increases in the uptake of oxygen by the body and the rate of cell respiration in the mitochondria. The number and size of mitochondria are also increased. The overall effect is to increase the rate of cell respiration and therefore the rate of ATP formation and heat production by the tissues. Increased heart rate and cardiac output also occur.

Thyroxine also has important influences on many other body processes. Thyroxine and growth hormone (GH) have a joint stimulatory effect on protein synthesis, leading to an increase in growth rate, particularly of the skeletal system. Unlike GH, thyroxine also stimulates brain development, so a deficiency in childhood can cause mental retardation (see later).

In many of the metabolic processes with which it is involved thyroxine appears to enhance the effects of other hormones such as insulin, adrenaline and glucocorticoids (section 19.5.2).

Control of thyroxine release

The effects of thyroxine are longer lasting than those of most other hormones and hence it is vital that large changes in its secretion are prevented. This is one of the reasons for the storage of T_4 within the gland so that it is readily available for release.

The level of T_4 circulating in the blood controls its release from the thyroid gland by negative feedback mechanisms involving the hypothalamus and anterior pituitary. Fig 17.54 shows that if excess T_4 is present in the blood it switches off its own production by switching off production of **TRH (thyrotrophin releasing hormone)** by the hypothalamus and **TSH (thyroid stimulating hormone)** by the anterior pituitary. This is negative feedback. The general principle is that the product of a series of reactions controls its own production by turning off the pathway when it reaches a certain level. This is comparable with a thermostat where the product, heat, switches off its own production when a certain temperature

is reached. If there is too little of the product, its production is switched on again because, in the case of thyroxine, inhibition of TRH and TSH is removed.

Superimposed on this feedback system are environmental factors, such as temperature, which influence higher centres of the brain. The temperature centre in the hypothalamus can also be stimulated directly. Prolonged exposure to cold, for example, causes the 'resetting' of the threshold in the pituitary for negative feedback so that release of TRH is stimulated (fig 17.54) and BMR and heat production are raised.

Overactivity of the thyroid gland (hyperthyroidism)

Both over- and underactivity of the thyroid gland can produce a swelling in the neck known as a **goitre**. Overactivity may be due to overproduction of thyroxine from an enlarged thyroid gland. The symptoms are increases in heart rate, ventilation rate and body temperature. The basal metabolic rate may increase by 50% with associated increases in oxygen consumption and heat production. Patients become very nervous and irritable and the hands shake when held out. Extreme hyperthyroidism is termed **thyrotoxicosis** and is associated with increased excitability of cardiac muscle which may lead to heart failure unless treated. This may involve the surgical removal of most of the gland or the destruction of the same amount by administering radioactive iodine.

Underactivity of the thyroid gland (hypothyroidism)

A lack of TSH production by the anterior pituitary, iodine deficiency in the diet or failure of enzyme systems involved in thyroxine production may result in hypothyroidism. If there is a deficiency of thyroxine at birth this will lead to poor growth and mental retardation, a condition known as **cretinism**. If the condition is diagnosed at an early stage thyroxine can be given to restore normal growth and development. Thyroxine deficiency in later life gives rise to a condition known as **myxoedema** and the symptoms are a reduction in metabolic rate accompanied by decreased oxygen consumption, ventilation, heart rate and body temperature. Mental activity and movement become slower and weight increases due to the formation and storage of a semi-fluid material under the skin. This causes the face and eyelids to become puffy, the tongue swells, the skin becomes rough and hair is lost from the scalp and eyebrows. All of these symptoms can be eliminated and the condition treated by taking thyroxine tablets.

17.6.5 Adrenal glands

There are a pair of adrenal (*ad*, to; *renes*, kidneys) glands located one just above each kidney (fig 17.46). Each gland is composed of two types of cells from different origins, and these cells function independently. The outer region is called the **cortex** and forms 80% of the

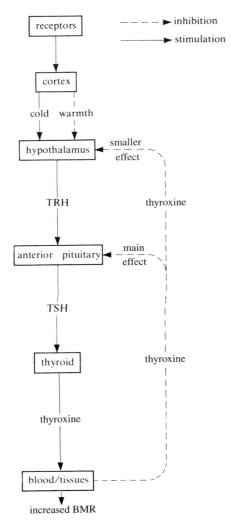

Fig 17.54 *Summary diagram showing the factors regulating thyroxine secretion and leading to homeostatic control of metabolic rate (BMR).*

gland. The inner region is called the **medulla** and is closely linked with the nervous system.

Adrenal cortex

The adrenal cortex produces steroid hormones of two types, as shown in table 17.12. All steroids are formed from a molecule called **cholesterol** which the cortex is able to synthesise and take up from the circulation following absorption from the diet. Steroids are lipid-soluble substances which diffuse through cell membranes and attach to cytoplasmic receptor proteins. The complexes formed then migrate into the nucleus where they attach to specific areas of the chromosome and switch on or off certain genes.

The size of the adrenal gland is closely linked to the output of ACTH and the ability to withstand stress. During long periods of stress the size of the gland increases. Investigations into the behaviour of organisms under stress have shown that the output of adrenal hormones increases with the rise in number in the population. In organisms where social hierarchies exist, there is a positive correlation between position in the hierarchy and increased size of the adrenal gland.

Control of cortical hormone release

Mineralocorticoid release is stimulated by the activity of **renin** and **angiotensin** as described in table 17.12. **Glucocorticoids** are secreted in response to **adrenocorticotrophic hormone (ACTH)**. An example of the role of ACTH in regulating the release of the glucocorticoid hormone cortisol is shown in fig 17.47. This is an example of the cascade effect which amplifies the amount of hormone produced.

ACTH is a protein molecule which contains 39 amino acids. It attaches to receptors on the surface of the cortical cells and activates adenyl cyclase to convert ATP to cyclic AMP (section 17.6.1). This activates enzymes known as **protein kinases** which stimulate the conversion of cholesterol to glucocorticoids.

Adrenal medulla

The adrenal medulla forms the centre of the adrenal gland. It is richly supplied with nerves as well as blood vessels. The cells of the medulla are modified neurones of the sympathetic nervous system. When stimulated they secrete adrenaline and noradrenaline in the ratio of 4:1 (section 17.6.1). Noradrenaline is also secreted as a neurotransmitter by synapses of the sympathetic nervous system. The adrenal medulla is not essential to life since its function is to boost the sympathetic nervous system. The actions of these hormones are widespread throughout the body and prepare the animal for action situations, often referred to as 'fight or flight' situations. They allow the body to respond to sudden demands imposed by stress such as exercise, pain, shock, cold, low blood sugar, low blood pressure, anger, passion and excitement. The sympathetic nervous system has a similar role.

Noradrenaline (also known as norepinephrine) and adrenaline (epinephrine) are formed from the amino acid tyrosine and belong to a group of biologically active

Table 17.12 Summary table showing the hormones secreted by the adrenal cortex and their functions.

Hormones	Function	Notes
Mineralocorticoids e.g. aldosterone	Control water and salt content of body by stimulating cation pumps in membranes to conserve Na^+ and Cl^- and remove K^+. Prevent excessive Na^+ loss in sweat, saliva and urine and maintain osmotic concentration of body fluids at a steady state	Renin released from juxtaglomerular apparatus in kidney produces angiotensin. This stimulates release of aldosterone which increases Na^+ uptake by kidney and leads to release of ADH which increases reabsorption of water by kidney tubules. Release is not stimulated by ACTH

Glucocorticoids e.g. cortisol	(A) Carbohydrate metabolism
	    (1) promote gluconeogenesis
	    (2) promote liver glycogen formation
	    (3) raise blood glucose level
	
	(B) Protein metabolism
	    (1) promote breakdown of plasma protein
	    (2) increase availability of amino acids for enzyme synthesis in the liver
	
	(C) Other roles
	    (1) prevent inflammatory and allergic reactions
	    (2) decrease antibody production
		Overactivity leads to Cushings' syndrome and patients show abdominal obesity, wasting of muscles, high blood pressure, diabetes and increased hair growth. Overproduction of ACTH by the anterior pituitary is Cushings' disease. Underactivity leads to Addison's disease as shown by muscular weakness, low blood pressure, decreased resistance to infection, fatigue and darkening of the skin

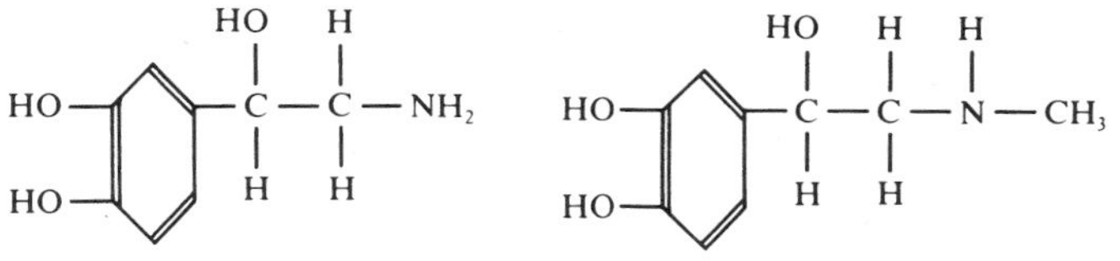

Fig 17.55 *Molecular structure of noradrenaline and adrenaline.*

molecules called **catecholamines** (fig 17.55). The effects of both hormones are basically identical as shown in table 17.13, but they differ in their effects on blood vessels. Noradrenaline causes vasoconstriction of all blood vessels whereas adrenaline causes *vasoconstriction* of blood vessels supplying the skin and gut and *vasodilation* of blood vessels to muscles and the brain. Both of these hormones activate two types of receptor sites on the target tissues known as α and β **adrenergic receptors**. These activate adenyl cyclase to make cyclic AMP and this leads to the specific tissue responses shown in table 17.13. Most organs have both α and β receptors with α receptors appearing to be more receptive to noradrenaline than adrenaline and vice versa in the case of β receptors.

17.6.6   Pancreas

Structure of the pancreas

Sections of the pancreas as seen at low power and high power with a light microscope are shown in fig 17.56a and b, and a diagrammatic interpretation of the structure is shown in fig 17.56c. The pancreas has both exocrine and endocrine functions. The bulk of the gland is made up of cells which surround the numerous branches of the pancreatic duct. Each branch is surrounded by a ring of cells (fig 17.56c) called an **acinus** (acinus means grape

Table 17.13 Physiological effects of noradrenaline and adrenaline.

Dilate pupils of eyes

Cause hair to stand on end

Relax bronchioles thus increasing air flow to lungs

Inhibit peristalsis

Inhibit digestion

Prevent bladder contraction

Increase force and rate of heartbeat

Cause almost general vasoconstriction

Increase blood pressure

Stimulate conversion of liver glycogen to glucose

Decrease sensory threshold

Increase mental awareness

pip). The acinar cells are exocrine cells. They secrete the enzymes of the pancreatic juice into the pancreatic duct in a way described in section 5.9.8 and shown in fig 5.23. The endocrine cells within the pancreas are described below.

Discovery of insulin

In this section we are concerned with the endocrine function of the pancreas. In 1868 Paul Langerhans, a German scientist who later became a Professor of Pathology, noticed tiny patches of cells about the size of a pinhead in the tissue of the pancreas. Examination with a microscope revealed that the cells were unlike most of the other cells of the pancreas and had a rich supply of blood vessels. They became known as islets (small islands) of Langerhans. Their structure is shown in fig 17.56c. They contain a small number of large cells, known as α **cells** (alpha cells), many smaller cells known as β **cells** (beta cells) and blood capillaries.

The function of the islets remained unknown until the twentieth century. Scientists discovered that removing the pancreas from an animal such as a dog resulted in a disease similar to the human disease sugar diabetes, and it was suspected that the pancreas produced a hormone which helped to regulate blood sugar. The hormone was named 'insulin', meaning island, even before its existence was confirmed. It was isolated by Banting, Best and Macleod in Canada in 1921. Injections of insulin into a dog from which the pancreas had been removed cured it of diabetes. They then succeeded in treating the condition in humans using insulin extracted from the pancreases of animals. Since then millions of lives have been saved worldwide and human insulin can now be prepared from genetically engineered bacteria as described in section 25.1.2.

Two hormones

It is now known that the islets of Langerhans secrete two hormones, insulin and **glucagon**. Both are proteins. Insulin is secreted by the β cells and glucagon by the α cells. These two hormones have antagonistic effects on the glucose level in the blood.

Insulin

Insulin is a small protein composed of 51 amino acids, whose primary structure (fig 5.27) was determined in 1950 by Fred Sanger in Cambridge. It is released in response to a rise in blood glucose level above $90\,mg$ per $100\,cm^3$ blood. It is carried in the blood plasma (the liquid part of blood) bound to β globulin and has an important effect on every organ of the body, although its main effect is on the liver and muscle. Receptor sites on cell surface membranes bind insulin, and this reaction leads to changes both in cell permeability and the activity of enzyme systems within the cell, the overall effect being to reduce blood sugar:

- increase in the rate of conversion of glucose to glycogen, called **glycogenesis** – this takes place mainly in the liver and muscle (glycogen granules can clearly be seen with an electron microscope, fig 5.12);

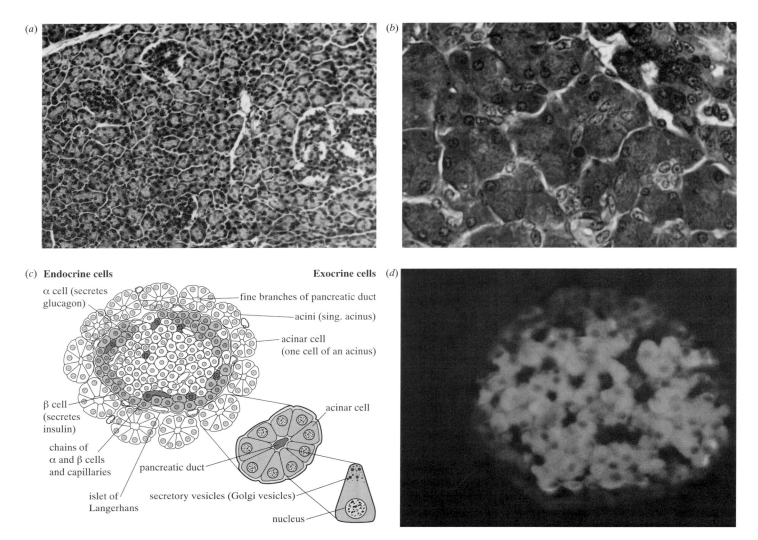

(a) Endocrine cells   Exocrine cells (d)

- α cell (secretes glucagon)
- fine branches of pancreatic duct
- acini (sing. acinus)
- acinar cell (one cell of an acinus)
- β cell (secretes insulin)
- chains of α and β cells and capillaries
- pancreatic duct
- acinar cell
- islet of Langerhans
- secretory vesicles (Golgi vesicles)
- nucleus

Fig 17.56 *Structure of the pancreas. (a) Low power light micrograph showing the islets of Langerhans surrounded by acinar cells. (b) High power light micrograph showing detail of one islet of Langerhans. (c) Diagram of islet of Langerhans and surrounding acinar cells. (d) Light micrograph of an islet of Langerhans showing central position of insulin-secreting cells (lighter) and the peripheral glucagon-secreting cells (darker).*

- increase in the rate of uptake of glucose by cells, especially skeletal muscle;
- increase in the use of glucose rather than other substances, such as fat, as a source of energy for cell respiration;
- increase in the conversion of glucose into fatty acids and fats, and fat deposition;
- increase in the rate of uptake of amino acids into cells and the rate of protein synthesis;
- decrease in gluconeogenesis (production of glucose).

Regulation of insulin production

Production of insulin is regulated by a negative feedback mechanism. A rise in blood sugar is detected by the β cells in the pancreas, which in response produce more insulin. As insulin levels rise, glucose is removed from the blood by the methods described and, as the blood glucose level gets lower, the β cells reduce output of insulin.

The secretion of insulin is vital to life since it is the only hormone which lowers the blood glucose level. A deficiency in insulin production leads to the metabolic disease known as **diabetes mellitus** in which the blood glucose reaches such a level that it exceeds that which the kidneys can reabsorb, and so is excreted in the urine.

The effects of insulin deficiency and excess are summarised in table 17.14.

Glucagon

Glucagon is a protein composed of 29 amino acids and is released, along with several other hormones, in response to a fall in blood glucose level below normal. This is usually the result of an increase in metabolic demand, for example as a result of exercise. Its role is to increase blood glucose level. Its main target is the liver. Glucagon stimulates the conversion of glycogen to glucose (**glycogenolysis**). It also stimulates the breakdown of proteins and fats to glucose

Table 17.14 Some of the effects of insulin deficiency and excess.

Deficiency	Excess
high blood glucose level (hyperglycaemia)	low blood glucose level (hypoglycaemia)
breakdown of muscle tissue	hunger
loss of weight	sweating
tiredness	irritability
	double vision

and conversion of lactic acid to glucose, processes known as **gluconeogenesis** (*gluco*, glucose; *neo*, new; *genesis*, giving rise to) (section 19.6.2).

Receptor sites in the liver cell membrane bind glucagon which activates adenyl cyclase to form cyclic AMP. The action of glucagon in bringing about an increase in glucose is similar to that of adrenaline and, in both cases, the cyclic AMP activates phosphorylase enzymes which stimulate the breakdown of glycogen to glucose as shown in fig 17.47. Glucagon has no effect on *muscle* glycogen. Regulation of glucagon secretion is similar to that of insulin in principle except that the α cells, not the β cells, are involved and they respond to falling blood glucose levels rather than rising levels.

Summary diagrams of the role of insulin and glucagon in controlling blood sugar level are shown in figs 19.4 and 19.22.

17.7   The study of behaviour (ethology)

Behaviour may be defined as the outwardly expressed course of action produced in organisms in response to stimuli from a given situation. The action modifies, in some way, the relationship between the organism and its environment and its adaptive significance is the perpetuation of the species. All living organisms exhibit a variety of forms of behavioural activity determined by the extent to which they are able to respond to stimuli. This varies from the relatively simple action of the growth of a plant stem towards a light source, to the complex sexual behaviour patterns of territory defence, courtship and mating seen in birds and mammals.

Plant behaviour is restricted to movements produced by growth or turgor changes and is stereotyped and predictable. The two main activities associated with plant behaviour are tropisms and taxes and details of these are described in section 16.1.

Animal behaviour is far more complex and diverse than plant behaviour and therefore it is extremely difficult to investigate and account for with any degree of scientific validity. The three main approaches to behavioural studies are the vitalistic, mechanistic and ethological approaches.

Vitalistic approach

This seeks to account for behavioural activities in terms of what animals are seen to do, and attempts to relate this to changes in the environment. It involves the total rejection of any study of the animal outside its natural environment. The technique has its foundations in natural history and has provided a wealth of valuable data, but it is essentially non-scientific since all the observations relate to past events which cannot be tested experimentally.

Mechanistic approach

This is an experimental approach and involves the study of particular aspects of behaviour under controlled conditions in a laboratory. It may be criticised on the grounds of the artificiality of the experimental situation, the nature of the behaviour activities and the way in which the results are interpreted. This technique is, however, used extensively in psychology and was pioneered by Pavlov.

Ethological approach

This is the contemporary approach to behavioural investigations and attempts to explain responses observed in the field in terms of the stimuli eliciting the behaviour. It involves both of the techniques outlined above and was pioneered by Lorenz, von Frisch and Tinbergen.

In all behavioural studies, great care has to be taken in interpreting the results of observations in order to eliminate subjectivity. For example, care must be taken to avoid putting oneself in the place of animal (**anthropocentrism**), or interpreting what is observed in terms of human experience (**anthropomorphism**) or interpreting the cause of the observation in terms of its outcome (**teleology**).

Recent advances in audio-visual technology have assisted the recording of behaviour activities. Infra-red photography has enabled animals to be filmed at night and time-lapse photography and slow-motion cinematography have enabled, respectively, slow-moving activities, such as moulting in insects, and fast-moving activities, such as bird flight, to be recorded and subsequently seen at speeds more suited to analysis by behaviouralists. The use of miniature cassette tape recorders for recording sounds and their subsequent analysis using sound spectrographs and computers has helped in the study of auditory communication between organisms. The movement of organisms is now studied either using implanted miniaturised signal generators, emitting signals that can be followed using direction-finding equipment, or by the use of tracking radar and satellite surveillance. These two techniques are employed successfully in following the migrations of mammals, birds and locusts.

Whatever the approach and techniques used in the investigation of behaviour, the fundamental explanation of behaviour activity must begin with a stimulus, end with a response and include all the stages occurring at various levels of oganisation within the body linking *cause* and *effect*.

Broadly speaking there are two forms of behaviour, **innate behaviour** and **learned behaviour**, but the distinction between the two is not clear-cut and the majority of behavioural responses in higher organisms undoubtedly contain components of both. However, for simplification in this elementary introduction to behaviour, the various aspects of behaviour are considered under these two headings in the next two sections.

17.8   Innate behaviour

Innate behaviour does not involve a single clear-cut category of behaviour, but rather a collection of responses that are predetermined by the inheritance of specific nerve or cytoplasmic pathways in multicellular or single-celled organisms. As a result of these 'built-in' pathways a given stimulus will produce, invariably, the same response. These behaviour patterns have developed and been refined over many generations (**selected**) and their primary adaptive significance lies in their survival value to the species. Another valuable feature of innate behaviour is the economy it places on nerve pathways within multicellular organisms, since it does not make enormous demands on the higher centres of the nervous system.

There is a gradation of complexity associated with patterns of innate behaviour which is related to the complexity of nerve pathways involved in their performance. Innate behaviour patterns include orientations (taxes and kineses), simple reflexes and instincts. The latter are extremely complex and include biological rhythms, territorial behaviour, courtship, mating, aggression, altruism, social hierarchies and social organisation. All plant behaviour is innate.

Taxes

A taxis or **taxic response** is a movement of the whole organism in response to an external directional stimulus. Taxic movements may be towards the stimulus (**positive**, +), away from the stimulus (**negative**, –), or at a particular angle to the stimulus, and are classified according to the nature of the stimulus. Some examples of types of taxes are shown in table 16.2. In some cases organisms are able to move by maintaining a fixed angle relative to the directional stimulus. For example, certain species of ants can follow a path back to their nest by setting a course relative to the Sun's direction. Other organisms orientate themselves so that, for example, their dorsal side is always uppermost. This is called the **dorsal light reaction** and is found in fish such as plaice which maintain their dorsal surface at right-angles to the sky.

Many organisms detect the direction of the stimulus by moving the head, which bears the major sensory receptors, from side to side. This is known as a **klinotaxic response** and enables symmetrically placed receptors on the head, such as photoreceptors, to detect the stimulus. If both receptors are equally stimulated, the organism will move forwards in approximately a straight line. This type of response is shown by *Planaria* moving towards a food source and by blowfly larvae moving away from a light source. In all cases of klinotaxis it is thought that successive stimulation of receptors on each side of the body is necessary in order to provide the 'brain' with a continuous supply of information since there is no long-term 'memory'.

Kineses

A **kinetic response** is a non-directional movement response in which the *rate* of movement is related to the *intensity* of the stimulus and not the *direction* of the stimulus. For example, the direction of movement of the tentacles of *Hydra* in search of food is random and slow, but if saliva, glutathione or water fleas are placed close to the *Hydra* the rate of movement of the tentacles increases.

Both kinetic and taxic responses can be observed through the use of woodlice in a **choice chamber** as described in experiment 17.1.

Experiment 17.1: To investigate orientation behaviour in woodlice by the use of a simple choice chamber.

Materials

old pair of tights	anhydrous calcium
bases of two petri dishes	chloride
Araldite	adhesive tape
hot metal rod	ten woodlice
cotton wool	plasticine

Method

(1) Cut a circle out of an old pair of tights 10 cm in diameter and stretch over the base of an 8.5 cm petri dish. Attach with Araldite, held in place by an elastic band until it sets.

(2) Burn out a 1.0 cm hole in the bottom of this petri dish using a hot metal rod.

(3) Divide the base of another petri dish in half using a plasticine strip 8.5 cm long, 1.4 cm deep and 0.5 cm wide.

(4) Place cotton wool soaked in water in one half of this petri dish and granules of anhydrous calcium chloride in the other half.

(5) Attach the petri dish base prepared in (1) above to the petri dish base prepared in (4) with adhesive tape as shown in fig 17.57.

(6) Introduce ten woodlice into the apparatus through the hole in the upper Petri dish and record the position and number active at 1 min intervals in a table such as table 17.15.

(7) After 20 min plot a graph of numbers present against time for each environment.

(8) Calculate the percentage number of woodlice active in the dry environment for each minute interval and plot on a graph against time.

(9) Explain the nature of the results obtained in terms of kineses and taxes.

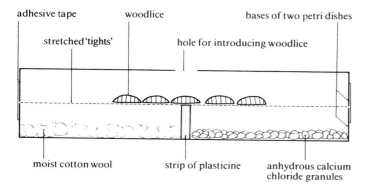

adhesive tape · woodlice · bases of two petri dishes

stretched 'tights' · hole for introducing woodlice

moist cotton wool · strip of plasticine · anhydrous calcium chloride granules

Fig 17.57 *Choice chamber apparatus for investigating orientation behaviour in woodlice.*

In simple experiments of this type the response of organisms to environments with extremes of a given variable can be investigated. Taxic responses are observed by the preference shown by the organisms for a particular environment. For example, woodlice exposed to areas of high and low humidity in a choice chamber congregate in larger numbers in the area of highest humidity, showing them to be **positively hydrotaxic**. More complex experiments can be devised using combinations of variables in order to determine which is strongest in eliciting a final response.

Kinetic responses are observed by recording the activity of woodlice at, say, 20 s intervals, in relation to their position in the choice chamber. Results of such investigations show that when first introduced into the choice chamber at the junction of two environments some woodlice move around whilst others remain stationary. After a short time all the woodlice begin moving and the speed of movement and rate of turning is always greatest in the drier side of the choice chamber than in the humid side. The increased, apparently random, moving and turning of the woodlice on the dry side is believed to indicate an attempt to find optimal conditions and, when these are found, the moving and turning response diminishes. These responses are examples of **orthokinesis**. The woodlice

move more slowly on the humid side and consequently usually congregate there. The preference shown for the humid side of the choice chamber indicates a positive taxic response to humidity.

Not all orientation behaviour patterns are rigid, and the response shown by an organism may vary depending upon other factors such as the degree of hunger, thirst, light, dark, heat, cold and humidity.

17.8.1 Simple reflexes in vertebrates

A simple reflex is an involuntary stereotyped response of part of an organism to a given stimulus. It is determined by the presence of an inherited pattern of neurones forming spinal and cranial reflex arcs, and the structure and function of these was described in section 17.2.

In terms of behaviour, simple spinal reflexes are either **flexion** responses, involving withdrawal of a limb from a painful stimulus, or **stretch** responses, involving the balance and posture of the organism. Both of these responses are primarily involuntary and most require no integration or coordination outside that found in the spinal cord. However both types of response may be modified by the brain according to circumstances and in the light of previous experience. When this happens innate and learned behaviour patterns overlap and the reflex action is now described as 'conditioned' as described in table 17.16. Many simple cranial reflexes too, may be conditioned, for example blinking in response to a sudden movement.

17.8.2 Instincts

Instincts are complex, inborn, stereotyped behaviour patterns of immediate adaptive survival value to the organism and are produced in response to sudden changes in the environment. They are unique to each species and differ from simple reflexes in their degree of complexity. Konrad Lorenz, a Nobel prize-winning ethologist, defined instincts as 'unlearned species-specific motor patterns'.

Table 17.15 Specimen arrangement of table of results.

| Time/min | Humid | | Dry | | |
	Number present	Number active	Number present	Number active	Percentage active dry side
0	4	1	6	4	40%
1	5	2	5	5	50%
2		etc.		etc.	
3					
–					
–					
–					
20					

Table 17.16 Summary of the major types of learned behaviour based on a classification proposed by Thorpe (1963).

Learned behaviour	Features of the learned behaviour
Habituation	Continuous repetition of a stimulus not associated with reward or punishment (reinforcement) extinguishes any response to the stimulus, e.g. birds **learn** to ignore a scarecrow. Important in development of behaviour in young animals in helping to understand neutral elements in the environment, such as movements due to wind, cloud-shadows, wave-action, etc. It is based in the nervous system and is not a form of sensory adaptation since the behaviour is permanent and no response is ever shown to the stimulus after the period of habituation.
Associative learning ⎧ Classical conditioning (conditioned reflex)	Based on the research of Pavlov on dogs. It involves the development of a conditioned salivary reflex in which animals **learn** to produce a **conditioned response** (salivation), not only to the natural **unconditioned stimulus** (sight of food) but also to a newly acquired **conditioned stimulus** (ticking of a metronome) which was presented to the dog along with the unconditioned stimulus. Animals learn to **associate** unconditioned stimuli with conditioned stimuli so either produces a response. For example, birds avoid eating black and orange cinnabar moth larvae because of bad taste and avoid all similarly coloured larvae even though they may be nutritious.
⎩ Operant conditioning (trial-and-error learning)	Based on the research of Skinner on pigeons. Trial motor activities give rise to responses which are reinforced either by rewarding (positive) or punishment (negative). The **association** of the outcome of a response in terms of reward or punishment increases or decreases respectively future responses. Associative learning efficiency is increased by repetition as shown in investigations carried out on learning in cuttlefish.
Latent learning (exploratory learning)	Not all behavioural activities are apparently directed to satisfying a need or obtaining a reward (i.e. appetitive behaviour). Animals explore new surroundings and **learn** information which may be useful at a later stage (hence latent) and mean the difference between life and death. For example in mice, knowledge of the immediate environment of its burrow may help it escape from a predator. At the time of acquiring this knowledge it had no apparent value. This appears to be the method by which chaffinches learn to sing, as described in section 17.8.2.
Insight learning	Probably the 'highest' form of learning. It does not result from immediate trial-and-error learning but may be based on information previously learned by other behavioural activities. Insight learning is based on advanced perceptual abilities such as thought and reasoning. Kohler's work on chimpanzees suggested 'insight learning': when presented with wooden boxes and bananas too high to reach the chimps stacked up the boxes beneath the bananas and climbed up to get them. Observations revealed that this response appeared to follow a period of 'apparent thought' (previous experience of playing with boxes [latent learning] may have increased the likelihood of the response).
Imprinting	A simple and specialised form of learning occurring during receptive periods in an animal's life. The learned behaviour becomes relatively fixed and resistant to change. Imprinting involves young animals becoming associated with, and identifying themselves with, another organism, usually a parent, or some large object. Lorenz found that goslings and ducklings deprived of their parents would follow him and use him as a substitute parent. 'Pet lambs', bottle-fed, show similar behaviour and this may have a profound and not always desirable effect later in life when the animal finds difficulty in forming normal relationships with others of the species. In the natural situation imprinting has obvious adaptive significance in enabling offspring to acquire rapidly skills possessed by the parents, e.g. learning to fly in birds, and features of the environment, e.g. the 'smell' of the stream in which migratory salmon were hatched and to which they return to spawn.

Instinctive behaviour is predominant in the lives of non-vertebrate animals where, in insects for example, short life cycles prevent modifications in behaviour occurring as a result of trial-and-error learning. Instinctive behaviour in insects and in vertebrates therefore is a 'neuronal economy measure' and provides the organism with a ready-made set of behaviour responses. These responses are handed down from generation to generation and, having successfully undergone the rigorous test of natural selection, clearly have important survival significance.

However, before concluding that instinctive behaviour patterns are completely inflexible as a result of their genetic origin, it must be stressed that this is not so. All aspects of the development of an organism, whether anatomical, biochemical, physiological, ecological or behavioural, are the result of the influence of constantly varying environmental factors acting on a genetic framework. In view of this, no behaviour pattern can be purely instinctive (that is genetic) or purely learned (that is environmental), and any subsequently described behaviour activity, whilst being either superficially instinctive or superficially learned, is influenced by both patterns. Some authorities prefer the terms **species-characteristic behaviour**, in preference to instinctive behaviour, and **individual-characteristic behaviour**, in preference to learned behaviour. But despite this terminology the same principle of genetic and environmental interaction applies. This point was demonstrated very clearly by Professor W. H. Thorpe in his investigations of chaffinch song. He found that chaffinches, whether reared by parent, reared in isolation, or deaf from the time of hatching, all produce sounds clearly identifiable to the human ear as those of a chaffinch. Sound spectrograms show, however, that these are only rudimentary songs, and that chaffinches reared by parents, listening to the songs of their parents and those of other chaffinches in the population, develop identical sound patterns to the older birds, characteristic of the local population. It was apparent that bird songs within a species have 'local dialects'. Songs of deaf birds or those in isolation remain rudimentary, thus demonstrating that the environment can significantly modify an instinctive pattern.

17.8.3　Motivation

The extent and nature of any behavioural response is modified by a variety of factors that are collectively known as **motivation**. For example, the *same* stimulus does not always evoke the *same* response in the *same* organism. The difference is always circumstantial and may be controlled by either internal or external factors. Presenting food to a starved animal will produce a different response from that shown by an animal that has been fed. In between the two extremes responses of varying strengths will be produced depending upon the degree of hunger experienced by the organism. However, if the act of feeding would place a hungry animal in danger of being attacked by a predator, the feeding response would be curbed until the danger passed.

Many behavioural responses associated with reproduction have a motivational element. For example, many female mammals are only receptive to mating attempts by males at certain times of the year. These times coincide with the period of oestrus and have the adaptive significance of ensuring that mating coincides with the optimum time for fertilisation and therefore the production of offspring at the most favourable time of the year. These behavioural patterns are known as **biological rhythms** and are described in section 17.8.5. In many species the degree of motivation, or 'drive', coincides in males and females, but in other species some system of communication between the sexes is essential to express the degree of motivation. In many primate species the timing of oestrus is signalled by a swelling and change of colour of the genital area of the female and this is displayed to the male (fig 17.58). Such behaviour reduces the likelihood of a male attempting to mate at a time when the female is not receptive. The signals used to bring about a change in behaviour are known as **sign stimuli** and, depending upon their origin or function, are classified as motivational, releasing or terminating stimuli.

Motivational stimuli

This type of stimulus may be **external**, for example increasing day length inducing territorial and courtship behaviour in birds, or **internal**, for example depleted food

Fig 17.58　*Female chimpanzee signalling to the male that she is sexually receptive.*

stores in the body during hibernation results in awakening and food seeking. Motivational stimuli provide the 'drive' or 'goal' preparing the organism for activity which may be triggered off by the second type of sign stimulus.

Releasing stimuli or 'releasers'

A releaser is either a simple stimulus or a sequence of stimuli produced by a member of a species which evokes a behavioural response in another member of the same species. The term 'releaser' was introduced by Lorenz and its role in behaviour was extensively studied by Tinbergen.

The effect of a releaser was demonstrated during an investigation into feeding in herring gulls. Young herring gulls normally peck at a red spot on the yellow lower mandible of the parent's bill to signal the parent to regurgitate fish which the young then swallow. In a series of controlled experiments, carried out by Tinbergen and Perdeck using cardboard models of adult gulls' heads, they found that the releaser of the begging response was the presence of a contrasting colour on the beak. Such was the strength of the releaser that a pointed stick with alternating coloured bands was able to elicit a greater response than the parent birds, as shown in fig 17.59.

Terminating stimuli

Terminating stimuli, as the name implies, complete the behavioural response and may be external or internal. For example, the external visual stimuli of a successfully completed nest will terminate nest building in birds, whereas the internal satisfaction or 'satiety' accompanying ejaculation in the male will terminate copulation and likewise a full stomach will terminate feeding.

Further examples of sign stimuli for a selection of behavioural mechanisms are discussed in sections 17.8.4–17.8.9.

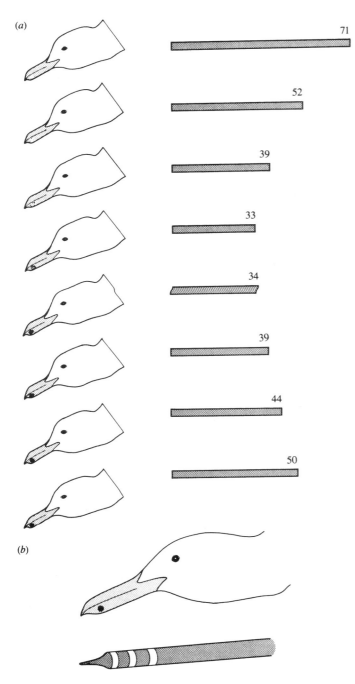

Fig 17.59 *(a) The horizontal bars indicate the number of pecking responses made by herring gull chicks to a series of cardboard models of adult herring gull heads having grey bills and spots of varying shade. (From Hinde, R. A. 1966, after Tinbergen, N., 1951.)*
(b) The artificial bill, coloured red with three white bars evoked 20% more pecks than an accurate three-dimensional model of an adult herring gull head and beak, coloured yellow with a red spot. (From Tinbergen and Perdeck, 1950, Behaviour, 3.1.)

17.8.4 Innate releasing mechanisms

Lorenz suggested that there must exist a means of filtering out stimuli which are irrelevant from those that are relevant to producing the correct behavioural response. Investigations suggest that this may occur peripherally at the receptors or centrally within the central nervous system. For example, Schneider found that the chemoreceptors on male moth antennae are only sensitive to the sex-attracting chemicals (**pheromones**) produced by the female of that species and not to those of other species. Modifications of Tinbergen and Perdeck's experiments on the herring gull have been carried out, and the results suggest, as Lorenz postulated, that centrally situated neurosecretory mechanisms control the response to sign stimuli.

17.8.5 Biological rhythms

Many behavioural activities occur at regular intervals and are known as biological rhythms or **biorhythms**. Well-known examples of these include the courtship displays and nesting behaviour of birds in the spring and the migration of certain bird species in autumn. The time interval between activities can vary from minutes to years depending on the nature of the activity and the species. For example, the polychaete lugworm *Arenicola marina* lives in a U-shaped burrow in sand or mud and carries out feeding movements every 6–7 min. This cyclical feeding pattern has no apparent external stimulus nor internal physiological motivational stimulus. It appears that the feeding pattern rhythm is regulated by a biological 'clock' mechanism dependent, in this case, on a 'pacemaker' originating in the pharynx and transmitted through the worm by the ventral nerve cord.

Rhythms involving an internal clock or pacemaker are known as **endogenous rhythms**, as opposed to **exogenous rhythms** which are controlled by external factors. Apart from examples such as the feeding behaviour of *Arenicola*, most biological rhythms are a blend of endogenous and exogenous rhythms.

In many cases the major external factor regulating the rhythmic activity is **photoperiod**, the relative lengths of day and night. This is the only factor which can provide a reliable indicator of time of year and is used to 'set the clock'. The exact nature of the clock is unknown but the clockwork mechanism is undoubtedly physiological and may involve both nervous and endocrine systems. The effect of photoperiod has been studied extensively in relation to behaviour in mammals, birds and insects and, whilst it is evidently important in activities such as preparation for hibernation in mammals, migration in birds and diapause in insects, it is not the only external factor regulating biological rhythms. Lunar rhythms, too, can influence activity in certain species, such as the palolo worm of Samoa. This polychaete worm swarms and mates through the whole South Pacific on one day of the year, the first day of the last lunar quarter of the year, on average the

2nd of November. The influence of lunar rhythms on tidal variations is well known, and these are two exogenous factors which have been shown to impose a rhythmic behaviour pattern on the midge *Clunio maritimus*. The larvae of *Clunio* feed on red algae growing at the extreme lower tidal limit, a point only uncovered by the tide twice each lunar month. Under natural conditions these larvae hatch, the adults mate and lay eggs in their two-hour-long life during which they are uncovered by the tide. In laboratory conditions of a constant 12 h light – 12 h dark photoperiod the larvae continued to hatch at about 15-day intervals, demonstrating the apparent existence of an endogenous clock programmed to an approximately semi-lunar rhythm coinciding with the 14.8-day tidal cycle.

The behaviour of many completely terrestrial insects appears to be controlled by endogenous rhythms related to periods of light and dark. For example, *Drosophila* emerge from pupae at dawn whereas cockroaches are most active at the onset of darkness and just before dawn. These regularly occurring biological rhythms, showing a periodicity of about 24 h, are known as **circadian** (*circa*, about; *dies*, day) rhythms or **diurnal** rhythms. In an investigation of the activity of a cockroach (*Periplaneta*) under two different light regimes (12 h light and 12 h darkness for 10 days followed by total darkness of 10 days), the cockroach restricted its activity in the latter regime to a time approximately related to the period of activity associated with the onset of darkness under the former light regime. The results of this investigation are shown in fig 17.60 and indicate that in the absence of an external time-cue the circadian rhythm persisted even though the onset of activity varied by a small amount each day. These results are consistent with the idea that circadian rhythms are controlled by an endogenous mechanism or 'clock', governed or 'set' by exogenous factors.

Circadian rhythms are believed to have many species-specific adaptive significances and one of these involves orientation. Animals such as fish, turtles, birds and some insects which migrate over long distances are believed to use the Sun and stars as a compass. Other animals, such as honeybees, ants and sandhoppers use the Sun as a compass in locating food and their homes. Compass orientation by Sun or Moon is only accurate if organisms using it possess some means of registering time so that allowances can be made for the daily movement of the Sun and Moon. The increasingly familiar concept of 'jetlag' is an example of a situation where the human internal physiological circadian rhythm is out of step with the day-and-night rhythm of the destination.

17.8.6 Territorial behaviour

A territory is an area held and defended by an organism or group of organisms against organisms of the same, or different, species. Territorial behaviour is common in all vertebrates except amphibia, but is rare in non-vertebrates. Research into the nature and function of

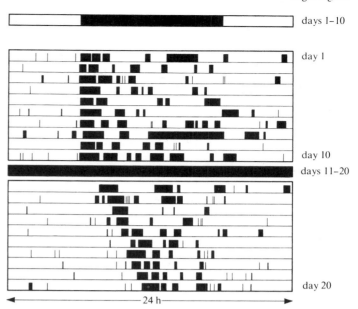

Light regime

days 1–10

day 1

day 10

days 11–20

day 20

←——————— 24 h ———————→

Fig 17.60 *Results of cockroach activity over a 20-day period. During days 1–10 the cockroach received a light regime of 12 hour light : 12 hour dark cycle and between days 11–20 the cockroach was kept in constant darkness as indicated in the figure. The black areas shown for each day represent the time and duration of each 'burst' of activity.*

territoriality has been carried out on birds and groups of primates. In the latter it forms an important part of their social behaviour.

The exact function of territory formation probably varies from species to species, but in all cases it ensures that each mating pair of organisms and their offspring are adequately spaced to receive a share of the available resources, such as food and breeding space. In this way the species achieves optimum utilisation of the habitat. The size of territories occupied by any particular species varies from season to season, according to the availability of environmental resources. Birds of prey and large carnivores have territories several square miles in area in order to provide all their food requirements. Herring gulls and penguins (fig 17.61), however, have territories of only a few square metres, since they move out of their territories to feed and use them for breeding purposes only.

Territories are found, prior to breeding, usually by males. Defence of the area is greatest at the time of breeding and fiercest between males of the same species. There are a variety of behavioural activities associated with territory formation and they involve threat displays between owners of adjacent territories. These threat displays involve certain stimuli which act as releasers. For example, Lack demonstrated that an adult male robin (*Erithacus rubecula*) would attack a stuffed adult male robin displaying a red breast, and a bunch of red breast feathers, but not a stuffed young male robin which did not have a red breast. The level

Fig 17.61 *Aerial photograph showing the territories occupied by penguins.*

of aggression shown by an organism increases towards the centre of the territory. The aggressiveness of males is determined partly by the level of testosterone in the body and this can affect territory size. For example, the territory size of a red grouse can be increased by injecting the bird with testosterone. Fig 17.62 shows the changes in territory size of three red grouse treated in this way. The boundary between adjacent territories represents the point where neighbouring animals show equally strong defence behaviour. Despite the apparent conflict and aggression associated with territory formation, actual fighting, which would be detrimental to the species, is rare and is replaced by threats, gestures and postures. Having obtained a territory, many species, particularly carnivores, proceed to mark out the boundary by leaving a scent trail. This may be done by urinating or rubbing glandular parts of the body against objects called **scent posts** along the boundary of the territory.

Although territorial behaviour involves the sharing of available resources amongst the population there are inevitably some organisms unable to secure and defend a territory. In many bird species, such as grouse, these weaker organisms are relegated to the edges of the habitat where they fail to mate. This appears to be one of the adaptive significances of territoriality as it ensures that only

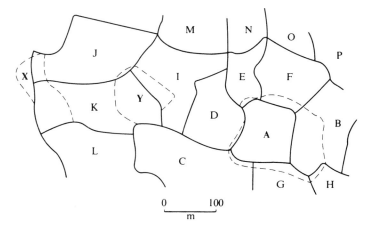

Fig 17.62 *The solid lines indicate the territories of a group of male red grouse. The dotted lines show changes which occurred after birds A, X and Y had received doses of testosterone. Birds X and Y had not previously held territories. (After Watson, A. (1970).* J. Reprod. Fert., *Suppl., 11.3.)*

616

the 'fittest' find a territory, breed and thus passes on their genes to the next generation. Thus a further function of territorial behaviour is associated with **intraspecific competition** and may act as a means of regulating population size.

17.8.7   Courtship and mating

There are many elaborate and ritualistic species-specific behaviour patterns associated with courtship and mating. In birds, mammals and some fish these two processes often follow the establishment of a territory by the male. Courtship is a complex behaviour pattern designed to stimulate organisms to sexual activity, and is associated with pair formation in those species where both sexes are involved in the rearing of offspring, as in thrushes, or in gregarious mixed-sex groups such as baboons. The majority of these species show rhythmic sexual activity of the type described in section 17.8.5.

Courtship behaviour is controlled primarily by motivational and releasing stimuli and leads to mating which is the culmination of courtship. During mating, the behavioural activities are initiated by releasing stimuli and ended by terminating stimuli associated with the release of gametes by the male.

The motivational stimuli for courtship in most species are external, such as photoperiod, and lead to rising levels of reproductive hormones and the maturation of the gonads. In most species this produces striking changes in the secondary sexual characteristics and other behavioural activities including colouration changes, as in the development of a red belly in male sticklebacks; increase in size of parts of the body, as in the plumage of birds of paradise; mating calls, as in nightingales; postural displays, as in grebes (fig 17.63) and the use of chemical sex attractants, as in butterflies and moths.

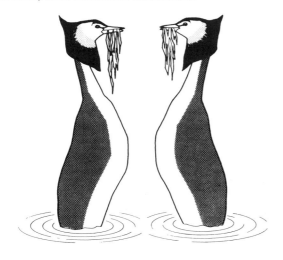

Fig 17.63   *A courtship behavioural activity in great crested grebes. Male and female grebes are shown here presenting nesting material to each other. (After Huxley, J. S. (1914). Proc. Zool. Soc. Lond., 1914 (2), 491–562.)*

Of the variety of signals used in the courtship to attract members of the opposite sex, sight, sound and smell play important roles. For example, the male fiddler crab, *Uca*, uses a visual display and attracts females by waving an enlarged chela in a bowing movement similar to that of a violinist. The vigour of the movement increases as a female is attracted to the male. Many insects, amphibia, birds and mammals use auditory signals in courtship. Some species of female mosquito attract males by the sounds produced by the frequencies of their wing beats, whilst grasshoppers, crickets and locusts **stridulate**. This involves either rubbing the hindlegs against each other or against the elytron (hardened wing case), or rubbing the elytra together to produce a 'chirping' sound which is species-specific and only produces a response from members of *that* species.

Some species of spiders employ a mechanical means of attracting the opposite sex; male spiders approach the web of a female sitting at the centre of the web and pluck a thread of the web at a species-specific frequency. The plucking 'serenades' the female and reduces her natural aggressive manner so enabling the male to approach and mate her. Unfortunately, if the male 'woos' a female of the wrong species or 'plays the wrong tune' he is attacked and killed!

The secretion and release by organisms of small amounts of chemical substances, leading to specific physiological or behaviour responses in other members of the same species, is used in courtship and mating and, as described later, the regulation of behaviour within social groups. These substances are called **pheromones** and are usually highly volatile compounds of low relative molecular mass. Many of these compounds function as natural sex attractants and the earliest to be identified were **civetone** from the civet cat and **muscone** from the musk deer. Both of these substances are secretions from the anal glands and are used commercially in the preparation of perfume. Mares, cows and bitches secrete pheromones whilst on 'heat'. This is undetectable by human olfactory epithelium but detectable by the males of the species concerned. **Bombykol**, a pheromone released by reversible glands at the tip of the abdomen of unfertilised adult female silk moths, is capable of attracting males of the same species from considerable distances. The olfactory receptors on the antennae of male moths detect the presence of the pheromone molecules in great dilutions and the males make a rheotactic response by flying upwind until they reach the female. Pheromones are used increasingly as a method of **biological control** in insect pest species such as the gypsy moth. In these cases the artificial release of the pheromone **gyplure** attracts males to the source of release where they can be captured and killed. This not only immediately reduces the number of male moths in the population but also, in preventing them from breeding, reduces the size of the next generation.

Pheromones are also used to induce mating as in the case of the queen butterfly *Danaus gilippus*. The pheromone is released by the male and brushed on to the female by a pair

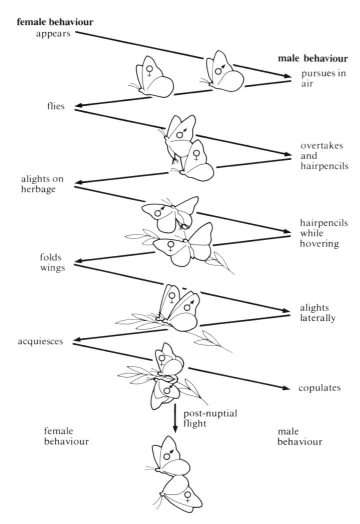

female behaviour
appears

male behaviour
pursues in air

flies

overtakes and hairpencils

alights on herbage

hairpencils while hovering

folds wings

alights laterally

acquiesces

copulates

post-nuptial flight

female behaviour

male behaviour

Fig 17.64 *Courtship and copulation in the queen butterfly. (The arrows indicate the stimuli and responses involved in the behavioural activities.) (From Brower, L. P., Brower, J. V. Z. and Cranston, F. P. (1965). Zoologica, 50, 18.)*

of brush-like structures, called hairpencils, everted from the tip of the abdomen. The entire courting and mating sequence is shown in fig 17.64.

Courtship in some species is accompanied by conflict behaviour on the part of one or both sexes. In species where individuals normally live a solitary existence, courtship conflict may be associated with changing attitudes to other members of the species as a result of increasing hormone levels. Other significances of this behaviour may be the tightening of the pair bond between the mating pair and the synchronisation of gonad development so that gametes mature at the same time. In certain species of spider, such as wolf spiders, conflict between male and female only diminishes for the act of copulation which culminates in the female killing the male.

17.8.8 Aggression (agonistic behaviour)

Aggression is a group of behavioural activities including threat postures, rituals and occasionally physical attacks on other organisms, other than those associated with predation. They are usually directed towards members of the same sex and species and have various functions, including the displacement of other animals from an area, usually a territory or a source of food, the defence of a mate or offspring and the establishment of rank in a social hierarchy.

The term 'aggression' is emotive and suggests an existence of unnecessary violence within animal groups; the alternative term **'agonistic'** is preferable. Agonistic behaviour has the adaptive significance of reducing intraspecific conflict and avoiding overt fighting which is not in the best interests of the species. Most species channel their 'aggression' into ritual contests of strength and threat postures which are universally recognised by the species. For example, horned animals such as deer, moose, ibex and chamois may resort to butting contests for which 'ground rules' exist. Only the horns are allowed to clash and they are not used on the exposed and vulnerable flank. Siamese fighting fish, *Betta splendens*, resort to threat postures involving increasing their apparent size as shown in fig 17.65.

The threats issued by two organisms in an agonistic conflict situation are settled invariably by one of the organisms, generally the weaker, backing down and withdrawing from the situation by exhibiting a posture of submission or appeasement. In dogs and wolves an appeasement posture may take the form of the animal lying down on its back or baring its throat to the victor.

Fig 17.65 *Stages in threat displays in Siamese fighting fish. (a) and (b) fish not showing threat displays, (c) and (d) operculum, o, and fins erected to increase their apparent size during threat displays. (From Hinde, R. A., 1970, after Simpson, 1968.)*

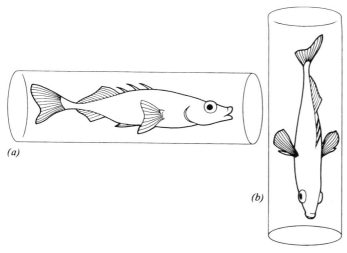

Fig 17.66 *(a) Full threat posture in male stickleback. (b) Reduced threat posture when contained in a tube held vertically. (After Tinbergen, N., 1951.)*

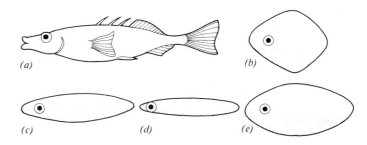

Fig 17.67 *Models used as releasers of aggressive behaviour in male sticklebacks holding a territory. (a) Accurate model not having a red belly does not elicit aggression from male stickleback. (b)–(c) are models of sticklebacks not having an accurate shape but having a red belly. All these models produced aggressive responses from male sticklebacks. (After Tinbergen, 1951.)*

During actual physical contact animals often refrain from using their most effective weapons on another member of the same species. For example, giraffes will fight each other using the short horns on their heads, but in defence against other animals they use their very powerful feet.

For agonistic behavioural activities to be most effective they must be stereotyped for any species and Tinbergen demonstrated several of these during investigations carried out on sticklebacks. In one series of experiments he demonstrated that the effectiveness of threat posture depended on the stickleback assuming a horizontal position with fins and spines outstretched. When trapped in a specimen tube and kept vertical a male stickleback does not have the same threat potential to ward off other sticklebacks as it has when free-swimming or held horizontally (fig 17.66).

In another series of experiments he demonstrated that agonistic behaviour in male sticklebacks defending a territory is triggered off by 'releasers' which can take the form of almost any object whose underside is coloured red. These objects act as mimics of male sticklebacks whose bellies turn red during the breeding season and who appear to the territory holder as a potential threat (fig 17.67).

At times of stress, for example during conflict situations or during courtship and mating, an organism may perform an action which is trivial and irrelevant to the situation. This is known as **displacement activity** and occurs when motivation is high but two conflicting 'releasers' present themselves. For example, one of a pair of birds involved in a territorial dispute may begin nest-building activities, such as pulling up grass, when presented with a choice between fighting or fleeing. Such displacement activities act as an outlet for pent-up activities. Many human activities may be considered displacement activities in certain circumstances, for example fist clenching, fist banging, nail biting, straightening clothes, finger drumming, etc. A similar form of behaviour is called **vacuum activity** which occurs when motivation is high and no releaser presents itself. In this case the normal response is produced but is not directed towards the normal object or situation, and so provides a means of reducing frustration; for example, showing irritation towards someone who is not the cause of the irritation but acts as a substitute.

17.8.9 Social hierarchies

Many species of insects and most vertebrates show a variety of group behavioural activities associated with numbers of individuals living together temporarily or permanently. This is known as **social behaviour** and the coherence and cooperation achieved has the adaptive significance of increasing the efficiency and effectiveness of the species over that of other species. In a social group of this kind a system of communication is essential, and the efficiency of the organisation is further increased by individuals carrying out particular roles within the society. One aspect of social behaviour arising out of these points is the existence of **social hierarchies** or **pecking orders**.

A pecking order is a **dominance hierarchy**. That is to say that animals within the group are arranged according to status. For example, in a group of hens sharing a hen-house a linear order is found in which hen A will peck any other hen in the group, hen B will peck all hens other than A and so on. Position in the hierarchy is usually decided by some agonistic form of behaviour other than fighting. Similar patterns of dominance have been observed in other species of birds and in mice, rats, cows and baboons. The institutional organisation of all human societies is based on a pattern of dominance hierarchy.

Pecking orders exist only where animals are able to

recognise each other as individuals and possess some ability to learn. The position of an animal within a pecking order usually depends on size, strength, fitness and aggressiveness and, within bird hierarchies, remains fairly stable during the lifetime of the individuals. Lower-order male members can be raised up the hierarchy by injection of testosterone which increase their levels of aggressiveness. The experimental removal of lower-order mice from a hierarchy and subsequent provision of unlimited food for them increases their mass, improves their vigour and can raise their position in the hierarchy when reintroduced to the group. Similarly placing lower-order mice into other groups where they are dominant appears to give them a degree of 'self-confidence' (to use an anthropomorphic term) which stays with them when reintroduced to their original groups and results in their rank increasing.

One advantage of pecking order is that it decreases the amount of individual aggression associated with feeding, mate selection and breeding-site selection. Similarly it avoids injury to the stronger animals which might occur if fighting was necessary to establish the hierarchy. Another advantage of pecking order is that it ensures that resources are shared out so that the fittest survive. For example, if a group of 100 hens is provided with sufficient food for only 50 hens, it is preferable, in terms of the species, for 50 hens to be adequately fed and the weaker 50 hens die than for them all to live and receive only half rations, as this might prevent successful breeding. In the short term, social hierarchies increase the genetic vigour of the group by ensuring that the strongest and genetically fittest animals have an advantage when it comes to reproducing.

Social organisation

When animals come together to form a cohesive social group individuals often assume specialised roles, which increases the overall efficiency of the group (fig 17.68). These roles include members specialised or designated for food-finding, reproduction, rearing and defence. Cooperation between members of a society sharing division of labour depends upon stereotyped patterns of behaviour and effective means of communication. These patterns of behaviour and methods of communication vary between species and are vastly different for primate and insect societies. Primate societies are flexible, in that roles are interchangeable between members of the group, whereas in insect societies differences in body structure and reproductive potential affect their role within the society, a feature called **polymorphism**.

Ants, termites and bees are social insects that live in colonies and have an organisation based on a **caste system**. In the honeybee colony there is a single fertile female queen, several thousand sterile female workers and a few hundred fertile male drones. Each type of honeybee has a specific series of roles determined primarily by whether it hatched from a fertilised or an unfertilised egg. Fertilised eggs are diploid and develop into females; unfertilised eggs

Fig 17.68 *Social grooming in adult chimpanzees provides a means of social cohesion within a group.*

are haploid and develop into males. Secondly, the type of food provided for female larvae determines whether they will become queens or workers. This food is called **royal jelly** and is one example of the importance of chemical substances in the organisation of the society. Information within the colony is transmitted either by chemical odours and pheromones during the many licking and grooming activities called **trophallaxes**, or by particular forms of visual orientation displays known as **dances**.

Karl von Frisch, a German zoologist and Nobel prize-winner, investigated the nature of these dances using marked worker bees in specially constructed observation hives. Worker bees 'forage' for sources of nectar and communicate the distance and direction of the source to other workers by the nature of a dance generally performed on a vertical comb in the hive. If the distance is less than about 90 m the worker performs a **round dance** as shown in fig 17.69a which intimates that the source is less than 90 m from the hive but gives no indication of direction. The **waggle dance** is performed if the source is greater than 90 m, and includes information about distance of source from the hive and its direction relative to the hive and the position of the Sun. The dance involves the worker walking in a figure-of-eight and waggling her abdomen during which, according to von Frisch, the speed of the dance is inversely related to the distance of the food from the hive; the angle made between the two loops of the figure-of-eight and the vertical equals the angle subtended at the hive by the Sun; and the food source and the intensity of the waggles is related to the amount of food at the source (fig 17.69b). It is thought that allowances for movement of the Sun are made by the use of an inbuilt 'biological clock' and that bees orientate on cloudy days by substituting polarised light from the Sun for the position of the Sun.

Recent evidence has suggested that bees may use high-frequency sound to communicate sources of food to other

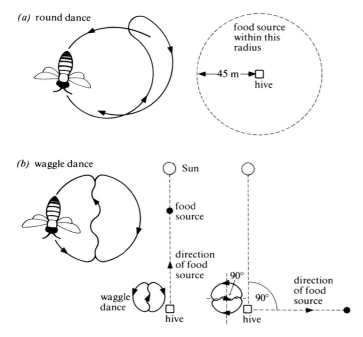

Fig 17.69 *Honeybee dances.*
(a) Round dance is performed when food is less than 90 metres from hive. (b) Waggle dance shows relation between hive, sun and direction of food source.

workers, but whether this is the main means of communication has yet to be demonstrated clearly. This does not, though, invalidate the data and interpretations of von Frisch and may be an associated communication system which augments the visual dance displays. The returning worker may also communicate the type of flower visited by feeding the other workers with some of the nectar collected.

17.8.10 Altruistic behaviour

One area of social behaviour which is not fully understood concerns the way in which certain organisms expend time and energy in caring for other members of the species. This phenomenon is called **altruism** and refers to a form of social behaviour whereby one organism puts itself either at risk or personal disadvantage for the good of other members of the species.

In the case of activities associated with mating and parental care, altruism is not so difficult to comprehend since the action is clearly in the interests of the parents, offspring and species. For example, the female baboon protects and cares for its offspring for almost six years whilst most bird species feed and protect their demanding offspring until they are capable of fending for themselves. What is not so clear is the reason why some organisms give support to organisms which are *not* their offspring, for example, birds and monkeys that call out warnings to others in danger and female monkeys who carry and care for the babies of other monkeys.

One insight into the mechanisms regulating this type of behaviour is seen in the **eusocial** insects such as honeybees, wasps and ants that have a caste system. Here the advantages to the species of division of labour based on a social hierarchy are apparent, but what is slightly obscure is the mechanism by which such behaviour arose.

Here the sterile female workers are prevented, by definition, from producing offspring, yet they spend their lives looking after their brothers and sisters. Investigation of the chromosome composition of the queen, drones and workers show that sisters (queen and workers) are more closely related to each other than mothers are to sons and daughters. This is because the fertile queen is diploid, the sterile worker is diploid and the drone (male) is haploid. Hence by helping their sister (queen) to reproduce they are effectively aiding in the production of queens, workers and drones with a genetic complement closer to their own than if they had offspring of their own. The conferring of a genetic advantage on closely related organisms forms the basis of altruistic behaviour.

Altruistic behaviour is very common amongst primates and varies from the extremes of social protection which exist between members of the same troop (monkeys), through acts of mutual grooming and food sharing (apes) to deliberate acts of self-sacrifice for family, God and country (humans). The extent of the altruistic behaviour appears to be related to close relatives (**kin**) such as offspring and **siblings** (brothers, sisters and cousins) with whom they share certain alleles. Thus the adaptive significance of altruistic behaviour is to increase the frequency of those alleles common both to the donor and recipient(s) of the altruistic behaviour. This behaviour is called **kin selected** and has led to the establishment of altruism because of the way it confers genetic advantages in kin by promoting survival and reproduction within the species.

In situations where the altruistic behaviour is directed generally towards members of the species rather than to close relatives, it is postulated that again the result of the behaviour will enable selection of those alleles responsible for the behaviour to be perpetuated within the benefiting group. This conclusion is backed up by observation which reveals that such general altruistic behaviour is much commoner in species such as the zebra, which live in coherent families, than in species such as the wildebeest where family groupings are uncommon.

Parallel examples of altruistic behaviour occur in humans too, where once again the intensity of the behaviour is related to kinship, and responses are strongest between family members sharing the same alleles.

17.9 Learned behaviour

17.9.1 Memory

Memory is the ability to store and recall the effects of experience and without it learning is not possible. Past experiences, in the form of stimuli and responses, are recorded as a 'memory trace' or **engram** and, since the extent of learning in mammals is proportional to the extent of the cerebral hemispheres, it would appear that these are the site of engram formation and storage.

The nature of the engram is not known and it exists only as a hypothetical concept backed up by conflicting data. Of the two broad areas of thought on the nature of the engram, one is based on changes in neuronal structure and organisation within the central nervous system and the other is based on permanent changes in brain biochemistry.

Histological examination of brain tissue shows the existence of neurones arranged in loops, and this has given rise to the concept of '**reverberating circuits**' as units of the engram. According to this view these circuits are continuously active carrying the memory information. It is doubtful if this activity could last for any length of time, and experiments suggest that memory has greater performance and stability than could be achieved by this mechanism alone. For example, cooling the brains of rats down to 0 °C causes all electrical activity in the nervous system to cease, but on restoring the rats to normal temperatures there is no impairment in memory. However, it is thought that such circuits may play a role in **short-term memory**, that is memory lasting at most for minutes, and in facilitating particular neural pathways. Events associated with short-term memory take longer to be recalled following concussion or amnesia and gradually disappear in old age. Long-term memory is more stable and suggests that some mechanism for permanent change exists in the brain.

Evidence based on the latter observation suggests that memory is a biochemical event involving the synthesis of substances within the brain. Extracts of the 'brains' of trained flatworms or rats injected into untrained flatworms or rats reduce the time taken by the latter organisms to learn the same task as compared with control groups. The active substance in all the experiments appears to be RNA.

Further evidence exists which suggests that the composition of the RNA of neurones changes during learning and that this may result in the synthesis of specific 'memory proteins' associated with the learned behaviour. Investigations have shown that injections of the protein-inhibiting drug, puromycin, also interfere with memory. For example, injecting puromycin into the brains of mice recently trained to choose one direction in a maze destroys their ability to retain this learning, whereas a control group, injected with saline, retained the learned behaviour. In conclusion, it would appear that the nature of memory is far from being clarified, but it seems probable that changes in electrical properties of neurones, the permeability of synaptic membranes, enzyme production associated with synapses and synaptic transmission are all concerned with formation of a 'memory trace'. Certainly it seems that memory is associated closely with events occurring at synapses.

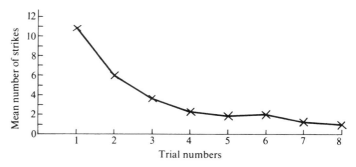

Fig 17.70 *The graph above shows a typical 'learning curve'. The graph shows the results of the number of times a cuttlefish strikes at a prawn kept in a glass tube. The prawn was presented to the cuttlefish on eight successive occasions lasting three minutes each time. As the cuttlefish unsuccessfully attacks the prawn the number of attacks decreases as the cuttlefish 'learns' that it cannot capture the prawn. (The results are based on data obtained from 40 cuttlefish, from Messenger, J. B. (1977),* Symp. Zoo. Soc. Lond., *38, 347–76.)*

17.9.2   Learning

Learning is an adaptive change in individual behaviour as a result of previous experience (fig 17.70). The degree of permanence of newly acquired learned behaviour patterns depends upon memory storing the information gained from the experience. In humans, acquiring or learning 'facts', for example for examinations, may be short-lived whereas the ability to carry out coordinated motor activities such as toilet training, riding a bicycle or swimming, lasts throughout life. Learning is generally thought of in terms of vertebrates, and mammals in particular, but has been demonstrated in all groups of animals except protozoans, cnidarians and echinoderms where neural organisation is absent or poorly developed. Psychologists have attempted to establish general 'laws of learning' but all attempts so far have failed. It would appear that learning is an individual event and occurs in different ways in different species and different contexts.

The classification and features of learned behaviour presented in this chapter are artificial and must be recognised as such. They do, however, cover the spectrum on current thinking on types of learning and are backed up by experimental evidence. A summary of the major types of learned behaviour is given in table 17.16 and is designed to provide only an introduction to the topic of learning.

Chapter Eighteen

Movement and support in animals

Movement and locomotion

Movement can occur at:

- cell level, for instance cytoplasmic streaming and swimming of gametes;
- organ level, such as heartbeat and movement of a limb;
- the level of the organism.

Movement of the whole organism from place to place is termed **locomotion**. Plants show cell and often organ movement, but they do not show locomotion, that is move from place to place in search of food or water. Plant movements are considered in chapter 16.

Whilst a few animals can survive successfully by remaining attached to one place (**sessile**), the vast majority have locomotory systems which presumably evolved to enable them to search for and acquire food. However, even sessile animals exhibit a great degree of mobility of their bodily parts.

Locomotion is used for:

- finding food;
- avoiding capture by predators;
- dispersal;
- finding new and favourable habitats;
- bringing together individuals for reproductive activity.

Locomotion involves coordination between the nervous, muscular and skeletal systems. Muscles used for locomotion are attached to the skeleton and are therefore called **skeletal muscles**. They act as machines, converting chemical energy into mechanical energy. They have the ability to contract and, when they do, they move systems of levers (bones) that make up part of the skeleton. Coordinated movement of the levers enables the animal to move about. The posture of the animal is also maintained by the musculo-skeletal system which is under the overall control of the central nervous system.

Other muscles within the body serve not to move the whole organism but to move materials from place to place within it. Cardiac muscle (section 6.5) of the heart pumps blood round the body, whilst smooth muscle located in the walls of various blood vessels constricts or dilates them to alter blood flow. Smooth muscle in the wall of the gut propels food along by means of peristalsis (section 8.3.5). These are just a few of many such activities which are constantly occurring within the body.

In this chapter we will be primarily concerned with locomotion, and two systems will be discussed in detail, namely the skeletal and muscle systems. This will be followed by a review of the types of locomotion that occur in a few representative organisms.

Support

As animals and plants increased in size through the process of evolution, the need for support became greater. This was particularly true once living organisms left water and colonised land. The skeleton in animals, and various mechanical tissues in plants, contribute to this support. In plants, the relevant mechanical tissues are collenchyma, sclerenchyma, and xylem. In addition, the turgid cells of the parenchyma are important for support. These tissues and their roles are discussed in chapters 6 and 22.

18.1 Skeletal systems

18.1.1 Functions of skeletons

The general functions of a skeleton are as follows.

- **Support.** The vast majority of animals possess some form of supportive structure. Structures of different design are needed for aquatic or terrestrial animals, animals with four legs or two legs, and for those that move over the ground or through the air. However, all skeletons provide a rigid framework for the body and are resistant to compression and tension (stretching) forces. They help to maintain the shape of the body. For terrestrial organisms the skeleton supports the weight of the body against gravitational force and in many cases raises it above the ground. This permits more efficient movement over the ground. Within the body, organs are attached to, and suspended from, the skeleton.
- **Protection.** The skeleton protects the delicate internal organs in those organisms with an exoskeleton (arthropods, section 18.1.3), and parts of the endoskeleton (section 18.1.4) are designed for a similar function. For example, in humans the cranium (skull) protects the brain and the sense organs of sight, smell, balance and hearing; the vertebral column protects the spinal cord, and the ribs and sternum protect the heart, lungs and large blood vessels.

- **Locomotion.** Skeletons composed of rigid material provide a means of attachment for the muscles of the body. Parts of the skeleton operate as levers on which the muscles can pull. When this occurs, movement takes place. Soft-bodied animals rely on muscles acting against body fluids to produce their form of locomotion (section 18.1.2).
- In addition the skeleton may have other functions, such as **making blood cells** and acting as a **store of calcium and phosphate** (see section 18.2.2).

Three major types of skeleton are generally recognised, namely the hydrostatic skeleton, exoskeleton and endoskeleton.

18.1.2   Hydrostatic skeleton

This is characteristic of soft-bodied animals. Here fluid is secreted within the body and surrounded by the muscles of the body wall. The fluid presses against the muscles which in turn are able to contract against the fluid. The muscles are not attached to any structures and thus they can only pull against each other. The combined effect of muscle contraction and fluid pressure serves to maintain the shape and form of the animal. Generally there are two muscle layers, one longitudinal and the other circular. When they act antagonistically against each other locomotion is achieved. If the body is segmented (as in the earthworm) then such pressure is localised and only certain segments will move or change shape. A detailed account of the function of the hydrostatic skeleton in locomotion is given for the earthworm in section 18.5.1.

18.1.3   Exoskeleton

This is a particular characteristic of the arthropods. Epidermal cells secrete a non-cellular exoskeleton, composed mainly of **chitin**. It acts as a hard outer covering to the animal and is made up of a series of plates or tubes covering or surrounding organs. Chitin is very tough, light and flexible. However, it can be strengthened by impregnation with 'tanned' (hardened) proteins, and, particularly in the aquatic crustaceans like crabs, by calcium carbonate. Where flexibility is required, as at the joints between plates or tubes, chitin remains unmodified. This combination of a system of plates and tubes joined together by flexible membranes provides both protection and mobility.

Arthropods are the only non-vertebrate group to possess jointed appendages. The joints are hinges, and the levers on either side are operated by flexor and extensor muscles which are attached to inward projections of the exoskeleton (fig 18.1). Chitin is permeable to water which could lead to desiccation of terrestrial animals like insects. This is prevented by the secretion of a thin waxy layer over the exoskeleton from gland cells in the epidermis. Therefore, the exoskeleton supports and protects the delicate inner parts of the animal and in addition prevents their drying up.

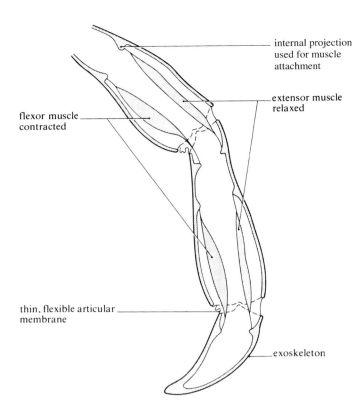

Fig 18.1   *Vertical section of an arthropod limb showing joints and muscles.*

The hollow tubular form of the exoskeleton is very efficient for support and locomotion in small animals, such as most arthropods, and can support a much greater weight without giving way than a solid cylindrical strut (like a bone) *of the same mass.* However, it loses this efficiency when organisms become bigger and their mass increases. As noted in section 2.8.6, as body size increases the surface area to volume ratio decreases. The extent of the exoskeleton depends on surface area. In large animals the exoskeleton would have to increase enormously in weight and thickness to do the same job just as efficiently. The end product would then be very heavy and cumbersome.

Growth takes place by **ecdysis** (moulting) in juvenile stages (larvae and nymphs) in insects and throughout adult life in crustaceans. This involves shedding the exoskeleton, thus exposing a new soft exoskeleton. Whilst still soft, growth takes place and the exoskeleton is extended and moulded into a larger form which often includes a change of shape. The new exoskeleton then hardens. The animal is vulnerable to predators whilst the new exoskeleton is hardening. At this stage the skeleton is unable to support the weight of the animal and movement is virtually impossible. This is less of a problem for aquatic species as their body weight is supported by the water, but aquatic and terrestrial organisms usually hide away during this time in an attempt to decrease their chances of being eaten by predators. Moulting is quite expensive in terms of the energy expenditure involved in building the exoskeleton in the first place and material loss when it is shed.

18.1.4 Endoskeleton

This is an internal skeleton and is the type which is typical of vertebrates (the only other animals with an internal skeleton being certain molluscs such as cuttlefish). In vertebrates the skeleton is:

- made either of cartilage or bone (unlike the chitin of exoskeletons);
- located inside the organism, with muscles 'outside' (in contrast to the exoskeleton where muscles are inside the skeleton);
- made of living tissue and so can grow steadily within the animal – this avoids the necessity for moulting which is typical of animals with exoskeletons;
- jointed, like the exoskeleton, although the joints are more complex. A number of different types of joint exist and bones that form them are maintained in their correct positions by ligaments.

Skeletal design in quadrupeds (four-legged animals) and bipeds (two-legged animals) is essentially the same, but there are slight differences at the shoulder and hip. This is associated with the type of locomotion shown by the animals concerned.

18.2 Skeletal tissues

The vertebrate skeleton is composed either of cartilage or bone. Both tissues provide an internal supporting framework for the body. Only cartilaginous fish (such as dogfish and sharks) possess a completely cartilaginous endoskeleton. All other vertebrates have a bony skeleton in their adult form, but with cartilage also present in certain regions, such as at the joints or between the vertebrae. In the embryo stage the skeleton of bony vertebrates is first laid down as hyaline cartilage (section 6.4.2). This is of great biological significance, as cartilage is capable of internal enlargement, and so different parts of the skeleton are able to grow in proportion to each other during the development of the organism. Bone is different from cartilage in this respect as it can grow only by addition of material to its outer surface.

18.2.1 Cartilage

Three types of cartilage are recognisable: **hyaline cartilage**, **white fibrous cartilage** and **yellow elastic cartilage**. A detailed account of their structure can be found in section 6.4.2. All types consist of a hard matrix penetrated by numerous connective tissue fibres. The matrix is secreted by living cells called **chondroblasts**. These later become enclosed in spaces (lacunae) scattered throughout the matrix. In this condition the cells are termed **chondrocytes**.

Hyaline cartilage is the most common type and is found particularly at the ends of bones articulating (meeting and moving relative to each other) to form joints. Its matrix of chondroitin sulphate is compressible and elastic, and is well able to withstand heavy weight and absorb sharp mechanical shocks such as might take place at joints. Embedded within the matrix are fine collagen fibres which provide resistance to tension (stretching). Dense connective tissue, called the perichondrium, surrounds the outer surface of this cartilage at all places except where it passes into the cavity of a joint.

White fibrous cartilage contains a dense meshwork of collagen fibres and is found as discs between vertebrae and as a component of tendons. It is very strong yet possesses a degree of flexibility. Yellow elastic cartilage possesses many yellow elastic fibres and is located in the external ear, epiglottis and pharynx.

18.2.2 Bone

Bone is a hard, tough connective tissue composed mainly of calcified material. Details of its structure can be found in section 6.4.2. It has a hard matrix (harder than cartilage) which contains living cells. The matrix is designed to resist both compression and tension. The mineral part of the matrix (about 70%) is a form of calcium phosphate and is very resistant to compression (high compressional strength). The organic part of the matrix (about 30%) includes many collagen fibres which are very resistant to tension (high tensile strength). These forces are discussed in more detail in section 18.2.3. The arrangement of the tissue into cylinders, which is described in section 6.4.2, also increases the strength of the whole bone.

When a vertical section of a long bone, such as a femur, is examined microscopically it is seen to be made up of several distinct components. It consists of a hollow shaft or **diaphysis**, with an expanded head or **epiphysis** at each end. Covering the entire bone is a sheath of tough connective tissue, the **periosteum**. The diaphysis is composed of compact bone whilst the epiphyses are composed of spongy bone covered by a thin layer of compact bone (section 6.4.2). The layout of the bony material is designed to withstand compression forces and to give maximum strength to the bone (fig 18.2).

Fatty yellow marrow occupies the marrow cavity of the diaphysis, whilst red marrow is present amongst the bony struts (**trabeculae**) of the epiphyses. Numerous small openings penetrate the surface of the bone, through which nerves and blood vessels cross into the bony tissue and marrow.

Apart from the functions listed at the beginning of section 18.1, a bony skeleton also produces red blood corpuscles and white blood cells. Also it takes part in the maintenance of constant calcium and phosphorus levels in

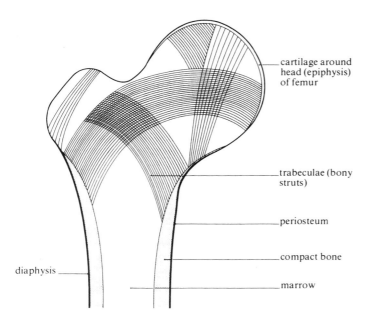

Fig 18.2 *Vertical section of the head of a femur showing arrangement of trabeculae (bony struts) in spongy bone.*

the bloodstream (see chapter 17) by providing a store of calcium and phosphate ions. These can be mobilised by the action of parathyroid and calcitonin hormones of the parathyroid and thyroid glands respectively.

18.2.3 Structure related to function

Using the femur (the thigh bone) as an example, we can now look at how the different tissues associated with a bone are adapted for the functions they perform. The femur is one of the 'long' bones of the body, which are involved in locomotion.

The femur is basically a hollow bone. When a compression force is exerted on one side of the bone, the other side is subjected to tension. Along the central axis of the bone the forces diminish and are neutralised. The material in the centre of the bone consequently does not need to contribute to its strength. Reduction in weight of the bone due to the absence of bone along its central axis is advantageous to the animal as it lightens the weight of the femur without reducing its mechanical efficiency. The perimeter of the femur is composed of compact bone which resists the tension and compressional forces (see section 8.4.4). Spongy bone at the head of the femur is a meshwork of interconnecting bony struts. They maintain the rigidity of the bone but with the minimum of weight.

Cartilage acts as a cushion between two articulating bones. Its matrix can be deformed by compression but will return to its original shape because it possesses good powers of elasticity (extensibility). The cartilage also reduces friction between the smooth, moving articular surfaces.

The tendons consist of inelastic white fibrous tissue and attach the muscles to the femur. The pull of the muscle is concentrated over a small area. Tendons also help to prevent muscle rupture if the muscle is suddenly subjected to a heavy load.

Ligaments are also composed of inelastic white fibrous tissue and connect the femur to other bones articulating with it at joints. They confine the movement of the structures at each joint to a specific direction and therefore promote the efficiency of its operation. Ligaments also strengthen the joint.

18.2.4 Support in vertebrates

Among the first animals to live on land were the amphibians. They evolved from fish and as they migrated from water to land they were faced with the problem of holding their bodies off the ground in the absence of any support by the air. As a consequence, evolution favoured the development of structures which linked together by interlocking projections. Collectively the vertebrae formed a strong but reasonably flexible girder that supported the weight of the body.

The legs of early amphibians splayed out from the sides of their bodies so that the animals were able to drag themselves over the ground. This type of stance and locomotion is also seen in primitive reptiles (fig 18.3*a*). When in motion, most of the muscular energy is used to hold the trunk off the ground. Such is the effort required to maintain this position that the animals spend the majority of their time whilst on land resting their bellies on the ground.

Later, the trend in evolution of the reptiles was towards bringing the limbs into a position beneath the body and raising the body well clear of the ground (fig 18.3*b*). This stance provides greater efficiency in locomotion and means that the weight of the body is transmitted through the four relatively straight limbs. This trend reaches its conclusion in the mammals (fig 18.3*c*).

Fig 18.3 *Types of stance in vertebrates:*
(a) a primitive amphibian stance – legs projected laterally from body and then down; (b) modern reptilian stance – intermediate between amphibian and mammals;
(c) mammalian stance – legs project straight down from beneath the body.

Some reptiles and mammals have evolved a **bipedal** gait, walking, running or hopping on their hindlimbs. This releases the forelimbs for developing manipulative skills such as feeding, building and cleaning. A special type of locomotion, called **brachiation** is typical of some monkeys and apes. These animals swing from tree to tree using their long arms and hands to grasp the branches. Other animals that climb and move about in trees are too small to brachiate; instead they jump from branch to branch. The most specialised form of aerial locomotion is true flight. This evolved simultaneously during the Jurassic period in the flying reptiles (pterodactyls) and in the first birds (which were descended from reptiles). The forelimbs were modified and adapted into wings. Flying reptiles eventually became extinct, but birds survived and evolved into many highly varied forms.

18.3 Anatomy of the skeleton of a mammal (the rabbit)

All mammalian skeletons can be divided into two main parts:

- the **axial skeleton**, which consists of the skull, vertebral column, ribs and sternum;

- the **appendicular skeleton**, which consists of two girdles, the pectoral and posterior pelvic girdle, attached to each of which is a pair of limbs.

18.3.1 The axial skeleton

The skull

The **skull** consists of the cranium to which the upper jaw is fused, and a lower jaw which articulates with the cranium. Muscles connect the lower jaw to the skull and cranium. The **cranium** is composed of a number of flattened bones tightly interlocking to form a series of **immovable joints**. Besides enclosing and protecting the brain, it protects the olfactory organs (organs of smell), middle and inner ear and the eyes. At the back end of the cranium are two smooth, rounded protuberances which articulate with the atlas vertebra to form a hinge joint that allows the nodding of the head.

The vertebral column

The vertebral column is the main axis of the body. It consists of a series of bones called **vertebrae**, placed end to end, and separated by **intervertebral discs** made of cartilage (fig 18.4). The vertebrae are held together by ligaments which prevent their dislocation, but permit a

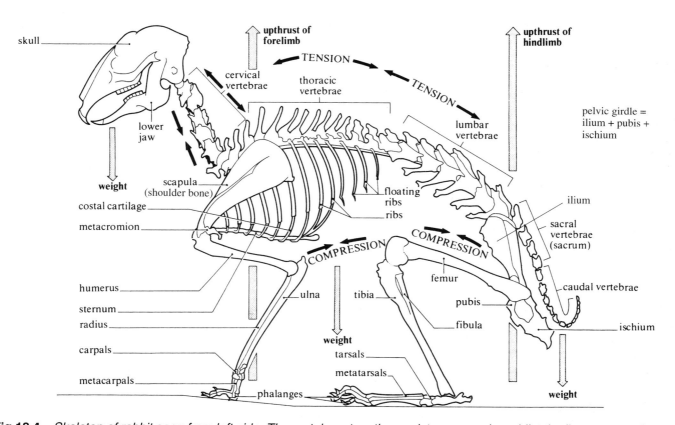

Fig 18.4 *Skeleton of rabbit seen from left side. The vertebrae together resist compression whilst the ligaments and muscles which link one vertebra to another resist tension. The abdominal muscles prevent the weight of the body from forcing the girdles apart.*

Table 18.1 Number and types of vertebrae in a range of mammals.

Types of vertebra	Region	Number of vertebrae				
		rat	rabbit	cat	cow	human
cervical	neck	7	7	7	7	7
thoracic	chest	13	12–13	13	13	12
lumbar	abdomen	6	6–7	7	6	5
sacral	hip	4	4	3	5	5
caudal	tail	30±	16	18–25	18–20	4

degree of movement, so that the vertebral column as a whole is flexible. The vertebral column also gives protection to the spinal cord. On the vertebrae are numerous projections for the attachment of muscles. When the muscles are active, they may bend the vertebral column ventrally, dorsally or from side to side.

The total number of vertebrae varies in different mammals. Nevertheless, in all mammals five regions of the vertebral column can be distinguished. The number and types of vertebrae in a variety of mammals are given in table 18.1.

Vertebrae from different regions of the vertebral column all have the same basic design. The structure of a typical vertebra is shown in fig 18.5. Note that two facets (articulating surfaces), called **prezygapophyses**, are present at the anterior (front) end of the vertebra, whilst two more, the **postzygapophyses** occur at the posterior (rear) end. An articulating surface is one where two bones meet and movement between the bones is possible. The prezygapophyses of one vertebra fit against the postzygapophyses of the vertebra immediately anterior to it. This arrangement enables the vertebrae to articulate with each other, as the smoothness of the articulating surfaces permits their slight movement over each other. This means the backbone is not completely rigid. Below each pre- and post-zygapophysis is a small notch. When adjacent vertebrae are fixed closely together the anterior notch of one vertebra is placed against the posterior notch of the vertebra immediately in front of it. This arrangement forms

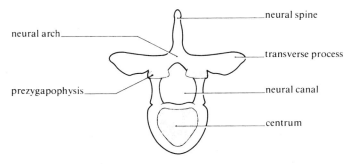

Fig 18.5 *Anterior (front) view of a typical mammalian vertebra.*

a hole through which a spinal nerve can pass. Other structures characteristic of all vertebrae are the **neural spine** and **transverse processes** for muscle attachment. The **centrum** forms a central rigid body to the vertebra over which the **neural arch** encloses the spinal cord.

Whilst there is a great degree of similarity between vertebrae, their design varies in different regions of the vertebral column. This is because of uneven distribution of body weight along the length of the column, and because the vertebrae are modified and adapted to perform those functions which are specific to each region.

When a rabbit stands up, its vertebral column is supported by the fore- and hindlimbs, with the bulk of the body weight suspended between them. The centra of the vertebrae withstand compression, whilst ligaments and muscles which overlay the dorsal parts of the vertebrae withstand tension (fig 18.4).

18.3.2 Structure and functions of the vertebrae of a rabbit

Cervical vertebrae

Cervicals 3–7 are very similar in structure (fig 18.6*a*). They possess a small centrum which is able to withstand compressional forces, and a short neural spine to which the neck muscles are attached. Some of these muscles run from the cervicals to the thoracic vertebrae and are used for holding up the neck, whilst others run to the back of the skull and serve to maintain the position of the head. On each side of the centrum is a single hole, the **vertebrarterial canal**, formed by fusion of a cervical rib with the transverse process. As its name implies, it serves as a channel for the vertebral artery to pass through to the brain. Thus this important blood vessel is protected as it crosses the vulnerable region of the neck.

The first two cervical vertebrae possess a quite different design and are modified to support the head and enable it to move in various directions. The first cervical vertebra is the **atlas** (fig 18.6*b*). Zygapophyses and a centrum are absent and the neural spine is very reduced. On its anterior surface are two concave depressions, the **articular facets** which articulate with the two processes from the skull to form a hinge joint. This supports the skull and permits it to be

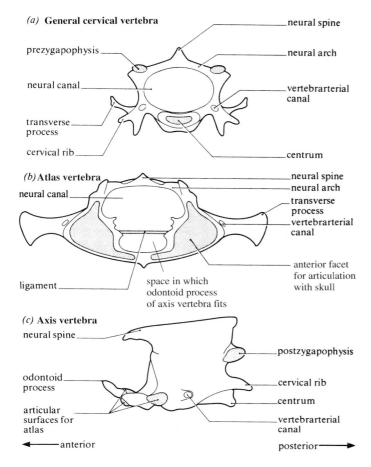

(a) **General cervical vertebra**

- neural spine
- neural arch
- vertebrarterial canal
- centrum
- prezygapophysis
- neural canal
- transverse process
- cervical rib

(b) **Atlas vertebra**

- neural spine
- neural arch
- transverse process
- vertebrarterial canal
- anterior facet for articulation with skull
- neural canal
- ligament
- space in which odontoid process of axis vertebra fits

(c) **Axis vertebra**

- neural spine
- postzygapophysis
- cervical rib
- centrum
- vertebrarterial canal
- odontoid process
- articular surfaces for atlas
- ←— anterior
- posterior —→

Fig 18.6 *(a) Fifth cervical vertebra of a rabbit, anterior view. Note the characteristic vertebrarterial canal. (b) Anterior view of atlas vertebra of a rabbit. Note absence of centrum and anterior facets. (c) Side view (left) of axis vertebra of a rabbit. Note odontoid process and forwardly projecting neural spine.*

nodded up and down. Wide, flattened transverse processes provide a large surface area for the attachment of those muscles that bring about the nodding action.

The second cervical vertebra is the **axis** (fig 18.6c). It possesses a peg-like structure called the **odontoid process** which projects forwards from the centrum. The process is formed by the fusion of the centrum of the atlas to that of the axis, and it fits into the cavity of the atlas below the ligament (fig 18.6b) so that it is separated from the neural canal. This arrangement gives a pivot joint which enables the head to be rotated from one side to the other (that is to be shaken). Such activity is brought about by muscles on the left and right sides of the neck. They run forwards from the neural spine of the axis to attach to the transverse processes of the atlas (fig 18.7). No prezygapophyses are present.

Thoracic vertebrae

These possess long, backwardly pointing neural spines and short transverse processes. Also present on the transverse

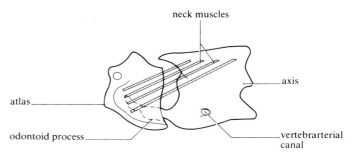

- neck muscles
- atlas
- odontoid process
- axis
- vertebrarterial canal

Fig 18.7 *The arrangement of the neck muscles between the atlas and axis vertebrae in rabbit.*

processes are small, rounded projections called **tubercular facets**. Anterior and posterior half or **demi-facets** are present on the sides of the centrum. Both types of facet are for articulation with the ribs (fig 18.8a). The end of the rib which joins to a thoracic vertebra branches into two projections, one being called the **capitulum** and the other the **tuberculum**. The tuberculum articulates with the facet of the transverse process whilst the capitulum articulates with two demi-facets of the centrum. Here the arrangement is quite complex. When two thoracic vertebrae are closely applied to each other, the anterior demi-facet of one vertebra fits closely to the posterior demi-facet of the vertebra in front of it to form a common depression. The capitulum of the rib fits into this depression thus effectively articulating with two vertebrae. As a result the thoracic vertebrae serve to support the ribs, but because of the complex arrangement between the vertebrae and ribs, movement between them is strictly limited. Some forward and sideways movement can occur, but in general the thoracic vertebrae are the least flexible of all.

Lumbar vertebrae

The vertebrae of this region are subject to the greatest stress in terms of gravity and locomotion. Not only must they provide rigidity for the body, but they must also permit bending, sideways movement and rotation of the trunk. Therefore, not surprisingly, this is the region where the large muscles of the back are attached and where there are many modifications of the vertebrae. The centrum and neural arch are massive, although the centrum is quite short. This arrangement provides greater flexibility between the lumbar vertebrae. The transverse processes are long and wide. They point forwards and downwards. Extra muscle bearing projections called meta-, ana-, and hypapophyses are present on the vertebrae (fig 18.8b). They also interlock with each other and keep the vertebrae in their correct positions relative to each other when this part of the vertebral column is placed under stress.

Sacral vertebrae (sacrum)

The four sacral vertebrae are fused together to form a broad structure, the **sacrum** (fig 18.8c). The most anterior sacral vertebrae possess well-developed transverse processes

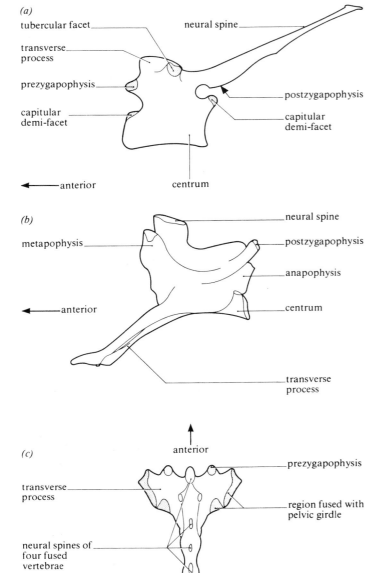

Fig 18.8 (a) *Left side view of thoracic vertebra of a rabbit. Note long neural spine and demi-facets.* (b) *Lumbar vertebra of a rabbit from left side. No hypapophysis is shown. Where it does occur (first and second lumbar vertebrae) it exists as a small projection from the ventral surface of the centrum.* (c) *Dorsal view of sacrum of a rabbit.*

which are fused to the pelvic girdle. It is through the sacrum that the weight of the body of a stationary animal is transmitted to the pelvic girdle and the legs. When an animal moves forwards, the thrust developed by the hindlimbs is transmitted via the pelvic girdle through the sacrum to the rest of the axial skeleton.

Caudal vertebrae

The number of caudal vertebrae varies greatly from one mammal to another (table 18.1) and is related to different

lengths of tails in such mammals. In general, as they pass towards the posterior end of the animal, transverse processes, neural arches and zygapophyses all become reduced in size and gradually disappear. This results in the terminal vertebrae only consisting of small centra. Humans possess four caudal vertebrae which are fused to form the **coccyx**. It is not visible externally.

Ribs and sternum

Each rib is a flattened, curved bone. Where it joins the backbone, it is forked into the **capitulum** and **tubercle** which provide points of articulation with the thoracic vertebrae. The joints formed permit movement of the ribs by the intercostal muscles during breathing. All of the ribs, thoracic vertebrae and the sternum form a thoracic cage which protects the heart, lungs and major blood vessels (fig 18.9).

In the rabbit the ventral ends of the first seven pairs of ribs, known as true ribs, are attached to the **sternum**, a flattened, kite-shaped bone, via **costal cartilages**. The next two pairs of ribs are also attached ventrally to the cartilage of the seventh ribs. The ventral ends of the remaining three or four pairs of ribs are unattached and are called floating ribs (fig 18.4).

18.3.3   The appendicular skeleton

Limb girdles

These provide a connection between the axial skeleton and the limbs. The width of the pectoral girdle separates the forelimbs, and that of the pelvic girdle the hindlimbs, and both contribute to the stability of the animal. A number of areas are modified for muscle attachment and articulation with the limb bones.

Pectoral girdle. This is composed of two separate halves. Each half consists of the scapula, coracoid process and clavicle. It is not fused to the axial skeleton but flexibly attached to it by ligaments and muscles. This arrangement enables the girdle and its associated limbs to

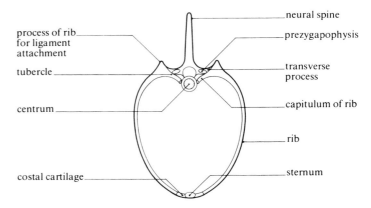

Fig 18.9 *Anterior view of thoracic vertebra of a rabbit attached to a pair of ribs.*

be moved through a great variety of planes of movement and angles. The girdle is strong enough to support the majority of the weight of a quadruped when it is stationary. It also acts as a shock absorber when the animal lands at the end of a jump.

The **scapula** is a flat, triangular-shaped bone which covers a number of the anterior ribs (figs 18.4 and 18.10*a*). At one end is a concave depression, the **glenoid cavity**, which articulates with the head of the humerus to form a ball-and-socket joint. A spine runs along the outer surface of the scapula and, at its free end, close to the glenoid cavity, are two projections, the **acromion** and **metacromion**, which are both used for muscle attachment. The **coracoid process** is all that remains of a small bone, the coracoid, which has fused with the scapula to form a projection above the glenoid cavity.

The **clavicle** is variable in size and shape in different mammals. In humans it is well developed, with one end articulating with the acromion process and the other with the sternum. It is used for muscle attachment and aiding the complex movements of the arms. It is sometimes referred to as the collar bone in humans. Its removal has no serious consequences. In quadrupeds it is much smaller and relatively less important. It forms the 'wishbone' in birds.

> **18.1** What advantages are there to mammals in possessing a flexible connection between the pectoral girdle and vertebral column?

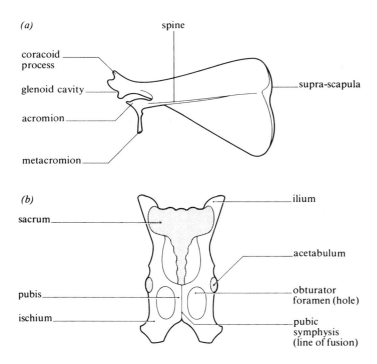

(a)

(b)

Fig 18.10 *(a) Left scapula of a rabbit. (b) Ventral view of the pelvic girdle of a rabbit. Note how the sacrum is fused to the ilium.*

Pelvic girdle. Like the pectoral girdle, this consists of two halves, each half comprising three bones, the ilium, ischium and pubis (fig 18.4). However, they are fused to each other to form a single structure. The ilium is fused to the sacrum of the vertebral column on each side. On the outer edge of each half is a depression, the **acetabulum**, which articulates with the head of the femur to form the ball-and-socket hip joint (fig 18.10*b*). The ilium is above the acetabulum. Dorsally it possesses a large crest to which the thigh muscles are attached.

Between the ischium and pubis is a large hole, the **obturator foramen**. Except for a small aperture through which blood vessels and nerves pass to the legs, it is covered by a sheet of tough inflexible connective tissue which provides yet another surface for muscle attachment. Such a design could be an adaptation to reduce the weight of the pelvic girdle and so lighten the load that has to be supported by the hind legs.

Ventrally a line of fusion can be seen where the two halves of the pelvic girdle meet. This is the **pubic symphysis**. Flexible cartilage in this region permits a widening of the female's girdle when giving birth.

Limbs

The limbs of all mammals are designed on the same basic plan, that of the **pentadactyl limb**, so named because each limb ends in five digits (fingers or toes) (fig 18.11). There are numerous variations of the general plan, which are adaptations to the different modes of life of different animals. In some cases the number of digits per limb has been reduced during evolution (section 26.7).

Forelimb. The upper part of the forelimb consists of a single bone, the **humerus**. At its upper end is the head which articulates with the glenoid cavity of the scapula. This forms a ball-and-socket joint at the shoulder which allows universal movement. Near the head are two roughened projections, between which is a groove, the

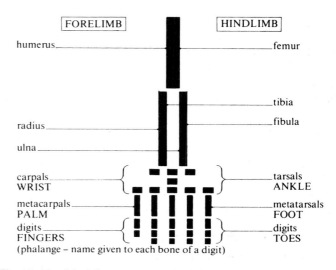

Fig 18.11 *Vertebrate pentadactyl limb.*

bicipital groove. It is along this groove that the tendon of the biceps muscle passes. At its lower end is the **trochlea** which articulates with the forearm to form a hinge joint at the elbow. A hole perforates the humerus just above the trochlea in the rabbit, but is absent in humans. Also visible is the characteristic **deltoid ridge** which runs anteriorly along the upper half of the humerus (fig 18.12*a*).

The lower part of the forelimb, the forearm, is composed of two bones, the **ulna** and **radius**. The ulna is the longer of the two. A notch, the **sigmoid notch**, at its upper end articulates with the trochlea of the humerus. Beyond the elbow joint is a projection, the **olecranon process**. This is an important structure, for when the arm is straightened it prevents any further backward movement of the forearm; hence dislocation does not occur. On the anterior surface of the humerus, above the trochlea, is a hollow into which the radius fits when the arm is bent (fig 18.12*b*).

The radius is a flattened, slightly curved bone which is relatively simple in design. In humans it is not firmly bound to the ulna; muscles are able to rotate the radius about the ulna so that the palm of the hand can be turned downwards or upwards, contributing to human manipulative skills. This freedom of movement is not present in the rabbit where both bones are tightly bound and the palm always faces downwards. However, this is not disadvantageous as the limb is in the best position for burrowing and running.

Distally (further from the main part of the body) the ulna and radius articulate with a number of small **carpal** bones which form the wrist. The carpals articulate with five long **metacarpals** which finally articulate with five **digits**. The first digit on the inside of the limb is composed of two **phalanges** whereas all the others contain three.

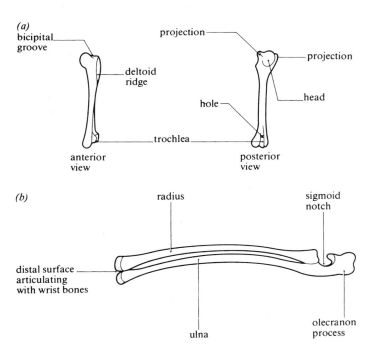

Fig 18.12 (a) Left humerus of a rabbit, anterior and posterior views. (b) Ulna and radius of a rabbit, side view.

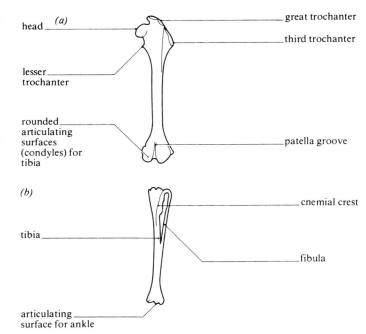

Fig 18.13 (a) Left femur of a rabbit, anterior view. (b) Anterior view of left tibia and fibula of a rabbit.

Hindlimb. The upper part of the hindlimb consists of a single bone, the **femur**. At its upper end is a large round head which articulates with the acetabulum of the pelvic girdle to form a ball-and-socket joint at the hip (fig 18.13*a*). Three processes called **trochanters** protrude below the head and provide points of attachment for the thigh muscles. The lower end of the femur has two curved convex surfaces, called **condyles**, which articulate with the tibia to form a hinge joint at the knee. A patella groove separates the two condyles. The **patella** bone (knee cap) is located here.

The **tibia** and **fibula** bones form the shank of the hindlimb. Two slight depressions at the upper end of the tibia represent the articular surfaces at the knee joint (fig 18.13*b*). The fibula is not part of this joint. It is a thin bone, and in the rabbit is fused to the tibia at its lower end. At the lower ends of the tibia and fibula are a number of **tarsal** bones. The two longest tarsals, one of which is the heel bone, articulate with the tibia and fibula to form the ankle joint. The tarsals articulate distally with long **metatarsal** bones to form the foot, whilst in turn the metatarsals articulate with digits composed of phalanges which form the toes. It is interesting to note that the rabbit hindlimb possesses only four digits.

18.3.4 Joints

In bony vertebrates, where a bone meets another bone, or bones, a joint is formed. Movement of parts of the skeleton over each other is only possible if there is a joint between them. A variety of different types of joint exist in the mammalian skeleton. They are summarised in table 18.2.

Table 18.2 A variety of joints in the endoskeleton of a mammal.

Type of joint	General characteristics	Examples	Function
Immovable/suture	A thin layer of fibrous connective tissue exists between the bones, holding them firmly in position	Between bones of skull; between sacrum and ilia of pelvic girdle; between bones of pelvic girdle	Provides strength and support for the body, or protection of delicate structures which cannot withstand any kind of deformation
Partially movable	Bones are separated from each other by cartilaginous pads		
(a) Gliding		Joints between vertebrae; wrist and ankle bones	Bones glide over each other to a limited extent. Collectively they provide a wide range of movement and confer strength on the limb.
(b) Swivel/rotating/ pivot		Joint between atlas and axis vertebrae	Permits shaking of head from side to side
Freely movable/synovial (fig 18.14)	Articulating bone surfaces are covered with cartilage and separated from each other by a synovial cavity containing synovial fluid		
(a) Hinge	Relatively few muscles operate this joint	Elbow, knee and finger joints	Permits movement in one plane. Capable of bearing heavy loads
(b) Ball and socket	Variety of muscles attached to the bones of the joint	Shoulder and hip joints	Permits movement in all planes, and some rotation. Unable to bear very heavy loads

Synovial joints (hinge joints and ball-and-socket joints) are similar to each other in design. The end surface of each articulating bone is covered by a smooth layer of hyaline cartilage. Though a living tissue, the cartilage contains no blood vessels or nerves. The nutrients and respiratory gases it requires diffuse from the synovial membrane and fluid. The cartilage serves to reduce friction between the bones during movement. Because of its elastic properties, the cartilage also acts as a shock absorber.

The bones of the joint are held in position by a number of ligaments which collectively form a strong fibrous 'capsule'. They run from one side of the joint to the other and are arranged in such a way as to cope effectively with the particular stresses suffered by the joint. The inner surface of the capsule is lined by a thin, cellular synovial membrane which secretes synovial fluid into the synovial cavity (fig 18.14). Synovial fluid contains mucin, a lubricant for the joint surfaces. The fluid serves to reduce friction between the joint surfaces. The synovial membrane acts as a waterproof seal preventing escape of synovial fluid. Therefore the joint effectively requires no maintenance.

18.4   The muscle system

Muscles are composed of many elongated cells called **muscle fibres** which are able to contract and relax. During relaxation muscles can be stretched, but they show elasticity which allows them to regain their original size and shape after being stretched. Muscles are well supplied with blood which brings nutrients and oxygen, and takes away metabolic waste products such as carbon dioxide. The amount of blood arriving at a muscle at any one time can be adjusted according to its need. Each muscle possesses its own nerve supply. Three distinct types of muscle can be identified.

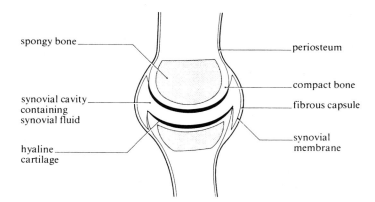

Fig 18.14 *Synovial joint of a mammal.*

spongy bone

periosteum

compact bone

synovial cavity containing synovial fluid

fibrous capsule

synovial membrane

hyaline cartilage

- **Skeletal muscle** (section 18.4.1) (also called striated, striped, voluntary). Muscle which is attached to bone. It is concerned with locomotion, contracts quickly and fatigues quickly. It receives nerves from the voluntary nervous system.
- **Smooth muscle** (also called unstriated, unstriped, involuntary). Muscle which is found in the walls of organs of the body such as the gut and bladder and is concerned with movement of materials through them. It contracts slowly and fatigues slowly. It receives nerves from the autonomic nervous system.
- **Cardiac muscle**. Muscle found only in the heart. It is self-stimulating and does not fatigue. It receives nerves from the autonomic nervous system. Its structure is described in chapter 14.

18.4.1 Skeletal muscles – gross structure

A skeletal muscle is attached to bone in at least two places, namely the **origin**, a fixed **non-movable** part of the skeleton, and the **insertion**, a movable part of the skeleton. Attachment is by means of tough, relatively inelastic tendons made up almost entirely of collagen (section 3.5). At one end a tendon is continuous with the outer covering of the muscle, while the other end combines with the outer layer of the bone (the periosteum) to form a very firm attachment (fig 18.15).

As muscles can only produce a shortening force (that is contract), it follows that at least two muscles or sets of muscles must be used to move a bone into one position and back again. Pairs of muscles acting in this way are termed **antagonistic** muscles. They may be classified according to the type of movement they bring about. For example, a **flexor** muscle bends a limb by pulling two parts of the skeleton towards each other, such as the biceps which flexes

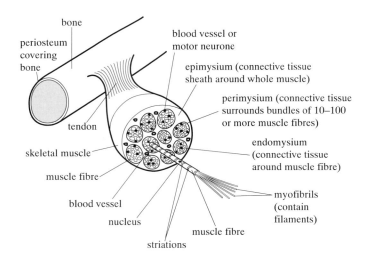

Fig 18.15 *A skeletal muscle showing the layers of connective tissue and other structures.*

the arm, causing the ulna and radius bones in the lower arm to be pulled upwards towards the humerus in the upper arm. An **extensor** is antagonistic to a flexor. The triceps muscle is antagonistic to the biceps and extends the lower arm. The activity of flexor and extensor muscles in the leg are examined in section 18.6.4.

It is rare that a movement will involve a single pair of antagonistic muscles. Generally, groups of muscles work together to produce a particular individual movement.

18.4.2 Striated muscle – histology

The structure of striated muscle as seen with a light microscope (its histology) is shown in fig 18.16. It is clear from the appearance of the muscle in longitudinal section (or in preparations of whole muscle fibres teased out from the muscle) why it is called striped or striated muscle. The reason for this appearance only becomes clear when an electron microscope is used, as described in the

(a)

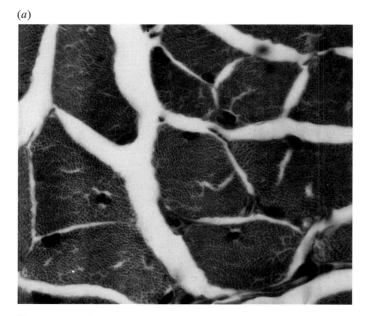

(b)

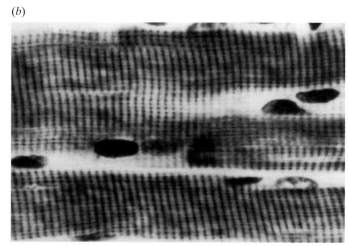

Fig 18.16 *Striated (voluntary or skeletal) muscle as seen with the light microscope: (a) TS, (b) LS.*

next section. The muscle is made up of many cells which are referred to as muscle fibres because they are so long. They can be several centimetres long and between 0.01 and 0.1 mm in diameter (an average cell is about 0.02 mm in diameter). They are cylindrical in shape and arranged parallel to each other. Each muscle fibre has many nuclei, a special arrangement not found in the other types of muscle. The nuclei are located near the surface of each fibre as can be seen in fig 18.16. Bundles of muscle fibres are surrounded by collagen fibres and connective tissue. Collagen also occurs between fibres. Each muscle fibre is surrounded by a cell surface membrane called the **sarcolemma** (*sarco-* means flesh and refers to muscle). This is very similar in structure to a typical cell surface membrane.

Inside the muscle fibres, it is just possible to see with a light microscope that there are numerous thin **myofibrils** (*myo-* also refers to muscle) which possess characteristic cross-striations. The myofibrils line up in parallel with their cross-striations next to each other, forming the stripes that are seen with the microscope.

18.4.3   Striated muscle – ultrastructure

It has only been possible to work out how muscle contracts by studying its ultrastructure (fine structure) with an electron microscope. In the electron microscope the myofibrils are clearly seen. They are about 1 μm across compared with the 100 μm (0.1 mm) of the whole fibre. The structure of a myofibril is shown in fig 18.17. It has a series of dark bands which line up with those of neighbouring myofibrils to form the striations seen in the whole fibre. Close examination of the myofibril shows that it is made up of two types of 'filaments' which run longitudinally. There are thin filaments and thick filaments. The thin filaments are made of a protein called **actin** and the thick filaments are made of a protein called **myosin**. In some places they overlap, like partly interlocking your fingers together. Where they do they produce a darker appearance (as your overlapping fingers would if you shone a light behind them). This explains the dark bands and striations previously mentioned (fig 18.16). The technical term for these bands is **A bands**. The light bands between the A bands are called **I bands**. Only actin filaments are present in the I bands. Closer examination shows another region in the A band where the filaments do not overlap and only myosin filaments are present. This is called the H zone. Finally, running through the middle of each light band is a line called the **Z line**. The overall structure is best described by means of diagrams such as fig 18.17.

It was soon realised that the distance between two Z lines represents the functional unit of muscle. This is the unit which is capable of contraction and is called a **sarcomere**. The myofibril, and therefore the muscle fibre, is made up of thousands of sarcomeres. If it is possible to understand how one sarcomere contracts, then it is possible to understand how the whole muscle contracts.

The banding pattern and the corresponding arrangement of actin and myosin filaments in a sarcomere is shown in fig 18.17. Figs 18.18 and 18.19 show the appearance as seen with an electron microscope.

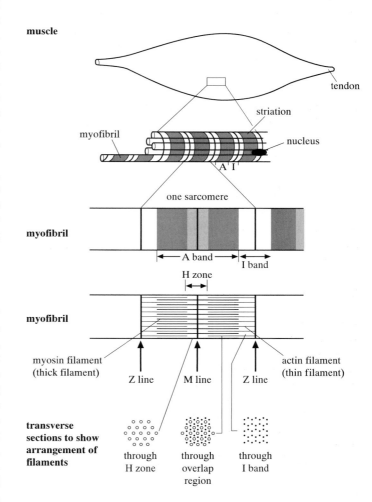

Fig 18.17   *Fine structure of skeletal muscle.*

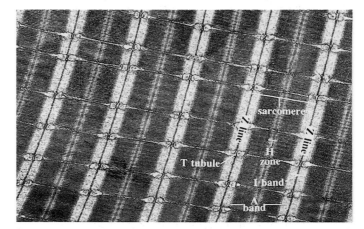

Fig 18.18   *Longitudinal section of fish muscle (roach). Note how the myofibrils, which run across the picture from left to right, are precisely lined up (× 7650).*

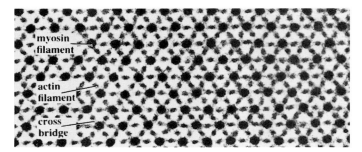

Fig 18.19 *Transverse section of insect flight muscle (giant water bug) in a contracted state. The appearance of cross bridges is explained later in the text. Note the regular arrangement of actin and myosin filaments. The thin actin filaments surround the thick myosin filaments in a hexagonal arrangement. In any row thick and thin filaments alternate as seen in the longitudinal sections in figs 18.17 and 18.18 (×137 000).*

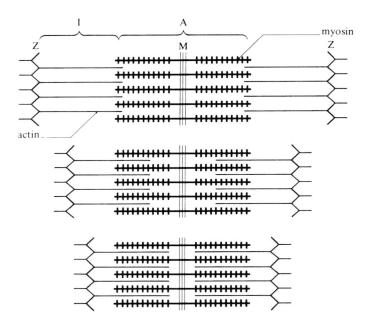

Fig 18.20 *Diagrammatic representation of how a sarcomere contracts by the actin filaments sliding between myosin filaments. Myosin is shown with its myosin heads. These are explained in the text.*

18.4.4   The sliding filament theory of muscle contraction

Once the structure was understood, it was proposed independently by two research teams that muscle contracts by the actin and myosin filaments sliding past each other (fig 18.20) (again, you can use interlocking fingers as an analogy – pushing them together shortens the distance they span, equivalent to muscle contraction by sliding filaments). Nothing actually contracts except the length of the sarcomeres and hence the whole muscle. The

two research teams who proposed the hypothesis in 1954 were H. E. Huxley and J. Hanson, and A. F. Huxley and R. Niedergerke. One piece of supporting evidence was the fact that, as muscle contracts, the dark bands (A bands) remain the same length and the light bands (I bands) and the H zones get shorter. This is explained by the hypothesis. Evidence has now confirmed the hypothesis which is known as the **sliding filament theory**.

We can now examine in more detail how the sliding is brought about. To do this, the structures of actin and myosin need to be examined in more detail.

Myosin (thick filaments)

A molecule of myosin consists of two distinct regions, a long rod-shaped region called a myosin rod, and a myosin head which consists of two similar globular parts (fig 18.21*a*). The globular heads appear at intervals along the myosin filaments, projecting from the sides of the filament. Where the actin and myosin filaments overlap, the myosin heads can attach to neighbouring actin filaments. The importance of this will become clear when we deal with the actual contraction mechanism of the sarcomere.

Actin (thin filaments)

Each actin filament is made up of two helical strands of globular actin molecules (G-actin) which twist round each other (fig 18.21*b*). The whole assembly of actin molecules is called F-actin (fibrous actin). It is thought that an ATP molecule is attached to each molecule of G-actin.

Contraction mechanism

An outline of the contraction mechanism is as follows. Where the actin and myosin filaments overlap the myosin heads can attach like 'hooks' to neighbouring actin filaments (F-actin), forming cross bridges. The bridges then move (each like a straight finger bending) to pull the actin filaments past the myosin filaments. Not all the bridges form at the same time (about half are attached at any given time which gives a smoother contraction). The energy for

(*a*) **myosin molecule**

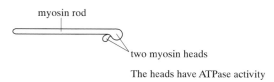

(*b*) **F-actin molecule** (fibrous actin)

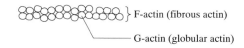

Fig 18.21 *(a) Structure of myosin showing its rod-like shape with two heads. (b) Structure of actin.*

this movement is provided by ATP. For ATP to release its energy it must be hydrolysed by the enzyme ATPase to ADP and phosphate. Each myosin head has ATPase activity. After sliding has occurred, the bridge detaches and changes back to its original shape (like the finger straightening) before re-forming again a little further along the actin filament. The sequence of events is shown in fig 18.22. It is sometimes described as a ratchet mechanism. The bridges form and re-form 50 to 100 times per second, using up ATP rapidly. This explains the need for numerous mitochondria in the muscle fibre, which can supply the ATP as a result of aerobic respiration. The sarcomere can shorten by as much as 30 to 60% of its length.

> **18.2** What happens to the length of the A band as the sarcomere contracts?

The question still remains as to how the whole process is started and stopped. Calcium ions activate the process (see roles of tropomyosin and troponin below). Calcium ions are located in the sarcoplasmic reticulum (the specialised endoplasmic reticulum of the muscle fibre) which forms swollen areas or vesicles at the Z lines of the sarcomeres, as shown in fig 18.23. Here the vesicles are in contact with tubes formed from the sarcolemma (the cell surface membrane which covers the muscle fibre). The sarcolemma

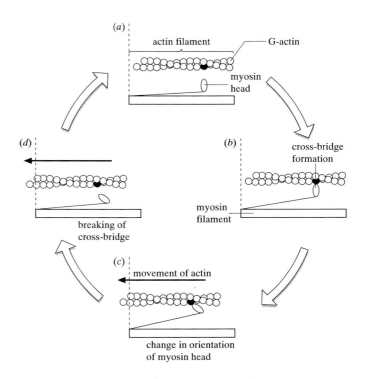

Fig 18.22 *Movement of actin by myosin during muscle contraction. By looking at the dashed line on the left of each diagram, you can see how the actin has moved in (c) and (d).*

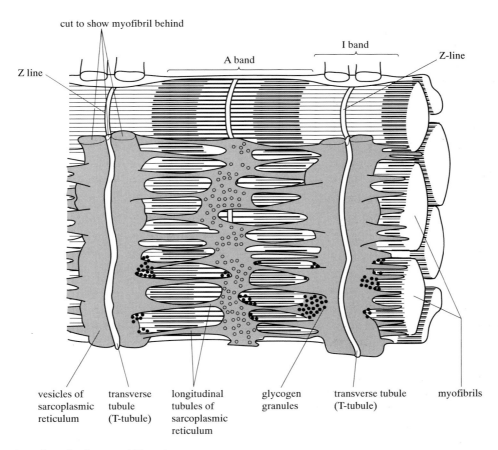

Fig 18.23 *Sarcoplasmic reticulum and T-system.*

folds inwards and forms a system of tubes which run through the sarcoplasm to the Z lines. This system of tubes is called the **T-system** (transverse tubules or T-tubules). This is shown in fig 18.23 and fig 18.18. When a nerve impulse arrives along a motor neurone at the neuromuscular junction at the surface of the muscle fibre, the depolarisation at the motor end plate is propagated through the T-system as a wave of depolarisation, or action potential. This causes the sarcoplasmic reticulum to release calcium ions.

Roles of tropomyosin and troponin

Actin filaments consist of F-actin together with two accessory proteins, **tropomyosin** and **troponin**. Tropomyosin forms two helical strands which are wrapped around the F-actin in a longitudinal fashion as shown in fig 18.24. Tropomyosin switches on or off the contraction mechanism. Troponin is a globular protein which binds to calcium ions and to tropomyosin.

When a muscle is at rest tropomyosin blocks the site to which myosin attaches (fig 18.24a). The actin is said to be in the 'off' position. When calcium ions are released from the sarcoplasmic reticulum they bind to troponin causing it, and the tropomyosin which is attached to it, to move away from the myosin binding site (fig 18.24b). The actin filament is now in the 'on' position and binds to myosin as shown in fig 18.22. When excitation of the muscle by nerve impulses ceases, calcium ions are pumped by active transport back into the sarcoplasmic reticulum by a calcium pump located in the membrane of the sarcoplasmic reticulum. This also requires ATP. The muscle then relaxes.

18.4.5 The energy supply

Within the body the source of energy for muscle contraction is usually glucose obtained from blood or from glycogen stored in the muscle, but may also be fatty acids. When these molecules are oxidised during respiration, ATP is generated.

Normally the oxygen used in aerobic respiration is supplied by haemoglobin. However muscles also have their own store of oxygen because they contain a protein similar to haemoglobin called **myoglobin** (section 14.8.2), which combines with oxygen and only releases it if the rate of its supply from haemoglobin cannot keep up with demand, as in strenuous exercise.

In resting muscle the level of ATP is low. It is soon used up when a muscle contracts, and has to be restored quickly by other processes until the rate of aerobic respiration adjusts to the activity.

One method is to use **phosphocreatine** to generate ATP under anaerobic conditions. This ensures that there is always a constant supply of ATP in the muscle which it can use for immediate contraction. There would only be sufficient phosphocreatine to supply total energy demand for about 5–10 s, and normally about 70% of the store is exhausted after 1 min of heavy exercise. It is therefore useful only for an explosive activity such as a sudden short sprint. At some stage, the phosphocreatine level has to be replenished. This is brought about by oxidation of fatty acids or glucose from glycogen.

When a muscle becomes very active its oxygen supply rapidly becomes insufficient to maintain adequate rates of aerobic respiration. Under these conditions anaerobic respiration occurs. An **oxygen debt** builds up as explained in section 9.3.7. The end-product of anaerobic respiration is lactic acid (lactate). As lactic acid builds up in the muscle, it causes muscular tiredness, pain and possibly contributes to muscle cramps. The time taken for lactate to be fully removed from the body after exercise represents the time it takes the body to repay the oxygen debt incurred during strenuous muscular activity. Training can increase the body's tolerance to lactic acid and increase the oxygen debt that it can build up.

18.4.6 Effects of exercise on muscles and muscle performance

Basic muscle size is inherited, but exercise can increase the size of muscles by up to 60%. This is mainly the result of an increase in the diameter of individual muscle fibres and an increase in their numbers. There is also an increase in the number of myofibrils within each muscle fibre.

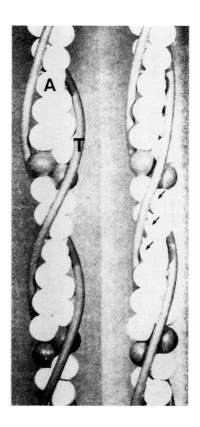

Fig 18.24 *Illustration of changes in actin filament structure (a) 'off' state – low Ca^{2+} level: tropomyosin blocks myosin attachment site. (b) 'on' state – high Ca^{2+} level: tropomyosin moves to expose attachment sites (arrows). A, actin; T, tropomyosin. Troponin is not shown (it lies near the grey balls).*

Long-term biochemical changes

The number and size of mitochondria increase within the fibres. Processes that take place in mitochondria such as the Krebs cycle, electron transport and oxidation of fatty acids all occur more rapidly.

Stamina training may double the ability of mitochondria to generate ATP. More phosophocreatine, glycogen and fat are stored and, as a result of the presence of more myoglobin, more oxygen is stored. The combined effect of these changes means that the athlete relies less on anaerobic respiration and therefore produces less lactate. There is greater ability to release fatty acids from fat stores for energy liberation. Hence fit people use up more fat during exercise than unfit people.

Long-term increase in muscle strength

Muscle strength is increased only if the muscle is working against a load (resistance) greater than that which it is normally used to. Either intensity or duration of exercise can be increased to achieve this. Muscles working at, or close to, their maximum force of contraction will increase in strength very quickly even if the daily exercise is a matter of minutes. Regular exercise is necessary to maintain strength of muscle. Without it they revert to their former state and become 'out of condition', losing both speed of contraction and strength.

Blood supply to muscles

Regular exercise results in an increase in the number of blood vessels supplying blood to the muscles. This serves to provide a more efficient system for glucose and oxygen transport, and for the removal of waste products of respiration.

During long-term exercise both circulatory and respiratory systems adapt so that any oxygen debt that builds up at the beginning of the bout of exercise can adequately be repaid during the exercise.

The ability to sustain exercise at a persistently high rate is generally dependent on the rate and efficiency at which oxygen can be taken up and used.

Coordination

Exercise improves coordination between pairs of antagonistic muscles, thus enabling more complex and skilful movement. Exercise also improves the speed at which muscles relax as well as contract. If a muscle does not relax rapidly enough, it may be torn by the pulling effect of the opposing muscle.

Muscles can be overstretched due to over-rigorous training, causing straining or tearing of muscle tissue. The likelihood of this happening can be reduced by the use of warming-up exercises. After strenuous exercise muscles are generally shorter and tighter and more prone to injury. Cooling-down exercises, concentrating on flexibility, can help prevent this by gently stretching the muscles.

18.4.7 Slow and fast muscle fibres

There are two major types of skeletal muscle fibre, namely **slow** or **tonic** fibres, and **fast**, **twitch**, or **fast-twitch** fibres. Table 18.3 indicates their structure, location and general properties. Some muscles contain purely slow fibres, some just fast fibres, and some contain mixtures of both.

Together the two types of fibre allow the organism to move about and to maintain posture. The fast fibres allow fast muscle contraction. Predators possess many fast fibres and use them for fast reactions to capture prey. On the other hand, prey species can also react quickly in order to avoid capture by predators. In both cases speed of body movement would influence the survival chances of the organism concerned.

When an animal is still it has to maintain a particular posture. This is achieved by contraction of the slow muscle fibres. They generate a slower, more sustained contraction, whilst at the same time consuming less fuel than the fast muscle fibres.

In humans both types of fibre occur in all muscles, but one or other usually predominates. The functional significance of this is that the predominantly slow muscles are suited to long-term slow contractions, and consequently are found in the extensor muscles, whilst fast muscle fibres dominate in the flexor muscles, which are designed to react at speed. Posture is maintained mainly by extensor muscles.

Fast muscle fibres are sometimes known as white muscle fibres. They contain relatively little of the red pigment myoglobin, which stores oxygen in muscle. Slow muscle fibres are sometimes known as red muscle fibres because they contain much more myoglobin.

18.5 Locomotion in selected non-vertebrates

18.5.1 Locomotion in the earthworm (*Lumbricus terrestris*)

Locomotion is not possible without a skeleton. The skeleton in segmented worms like the earthworm is the coelom, which is a hydrostatic skeleton. Its skeletal role is explained in section 18.1.2. The origin of the coelom is described in section 2.10.5. The coelom is surrounded by the body wall which contains two layers of antagonistic muscles (muscles that have opposite effects), an outer circular layer and an inner longitudinal layer. The circular muscle is divided into separate units along the length of the animal by septa (barriers) between the segments of the body, but the muscle fibres of the longitudinal layer generally extend over several segments. Locomotion is brought about by the coordinated activity of the two muscle layers and of the muscles that control the **chaetae**. These are bristle-like hairs which project from the lower surface of the worm.

Table 18.3 Structure, location and general properties of slow and fast skeletal muscle fibres.

	Slow/tonic muscle fibres	*Fast/twitch muscle fibres*
Structure	Many mitochondria Poorly developed sarcoplasmic reticulum Red – due to presence of myoglobin and cytochrome pigments Low in glycogen content Capillaries in close contact with fibres to allow fast exchange of materials	Few mitochondria Well-developed sarcoplasmic reticulum White – little or no myoglobin or cytochrome pigments Abundance of glycogen granules
Location	Deeply seated inside the limbs	Relatively close to the surface
Innervation	Associated with small nerve fibres (of $5\,\mu$m diameter). A number of end-plates are distributed along the length of the fibre. This is called multi-terminal innervation. Relatively slow conduction of action potential (2–$8\,\text{m s}^{-1}$)	Associated with large nerve fibres (of 10–$20\,\mu$m diameter). Usually one or possibly two end-plates per fibre Relatively fast conduction of action potential (8–$40\,\text{m s}^{-1}$)
Excitability	Membrane electrically inexcitable. Each impulse causes release of only small amount of acetylcholine. Therefore amount that membrane is depolarised depends on frequency of stimulation	Membrane electrically excitable
Response	Slow graded muscular contraction of long duration. Relaxation process slow (up to 100 times slower than twitch fibre)	Fast contraction (3 times faster than slow fibres) Fatigues quite quickly
Physiological activity	Depend on aerobic respiration for ATP production Many continue to function anaerobically if oxygen is in short supply in which case lactate is formed and an oxygen debt incurred Carbohydrate or fat store mobilised at same rate as respiratory substrate is oxidised Heat transported away from muscle as soon as it is produced Steady state between muscle activity and its needs is set up	Depend on the anaerobic process of glycolysis for ATP supply Oxygen debt quickly built up Glycogen used extensively as respiratory substrate Heat produced is absorbed by the fibres as the circulatory system does not immediately remove it Muscle contraction occurs during a period when the circulatory system has not had time to increase the oxygen supply to the muscle
Function	Enable sustained muscle contractions to occur. This is used for the maintenance of posture by the organism	Immediate, fast muscle contraction is permitted at a time when the circulatory system is still adjusting to the needs of the new level of muscle activity. Therefore of great importance during locomotion.

When an earthworm begins to move forward, contraction of the circular muscles begins at the anterior end of the body and continues, segment by segment, as a wave along the length of the body. This activity exerts pressure on the coelomic fluid in each segment, stretching the relaxed longitudinal muscle and changing the shape of the segments such that they become longer and thinner. This causes the anterior end of the worm to extend forwards. Chaetae, four pairs of which are present in all segments except the first and last, are retracted during the activity of the circular muscles and therefore do not slow down the forward movement (fig 18.25).

While the anterior end of the worm is moving forward, longitudinal muscle in more posterior segments contracts, causing this region of the worm to swell and press against the surrounding soil. Chaetae in this region are extended and help the worm to grip the soil. This is particularly useful during burrowing for the worm can exert a powerful thrust against the surrounding soil particles during forward locomotion.

Contraction of the circular muscle is quickly followed by contraction of the longitudinal muscles throughout the length of the body, and this means that different parts of the worm may either be moving forward (when the circular muscles contract) or static (when the longitudinal muscles contract) at any given movement. The net effect is a smooth

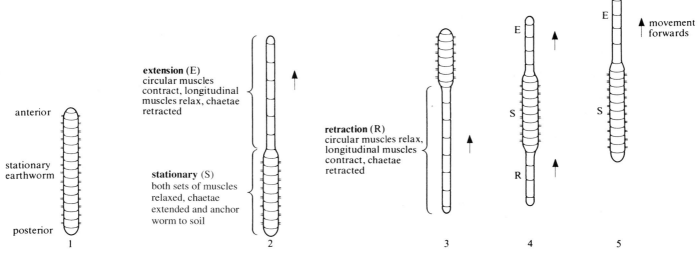

Fig 18.25 *Locomotion in the earthworm.*

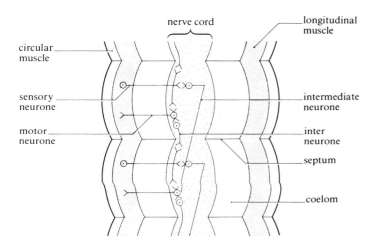

Fig 18.26 *Segmental nerves of longitudinal muscle in the earthworm (dorsal view). A similar arrangement is present in the circular muscle.*

peristaltic wave of activity moving along the length of the worm as it progresses forwards. The worm is also able to crawl backwards by reversing the direction of contraction of the muscles.

Control of muscle contraction is brought about by a complex network of neurones inside the segments. All segments are in contact with longitudinal nerve cord and also possess their own set of segmental nerves. This means that localised control of each segment is possible, as well as control of overall activity of the animal (fig 18.26).

The ventral nerve cord possesses a **giant axon** which runs along its length and conducts impulses along the body. When sensory receptors in the head are stimulated, impulses pass along the giant axon stimulating the longitudinal muscles to contract, thus causing the anterior end to be pulled back from the stimulus. Also present in the

nerve cord are two **lateral fibres** which run the length of the worm and carry impulses from the tail to the head. If the tail of the worm is stimulated, impulses pass along the lateral fibres from tail to head and cause the tail to be withdrawn. This is the basis of the worm's escape reaction.

18.5.2   Locomotion in insects

Insects have an exoskeleton. Its role in relation to muscles and locomotion is described in section 18.1.3.

Walking

This is achieved by the coordinated activity of three pairs of legs, one pair being attached to each of the three thoracic segments of the animal. Each leg consists of a series of hollow cylinders whose walls are composed of rigid exoskeletal material (see fig 18.1). The cylinders are linked together by joints and soft pliable membranes. Where the leg joins to the body, a form of ball-and-socket joint occurs, but all other joints in the leg are hinge joints. Bending and straightening of the legs is achieved by antagonistic flexor and extensor muscles attached to the inner surface of the exoskeleton on either side of a joint (fig 18.1).

When an insect begins to walk, three legs remain on the ground to support the animal whilst the other three move forward. The first leg on one side pulls the insect, whilst the third leg of the same side pushes. The second leg on the other side serves as a support for this activity. The process is then repeated but with the role of each trio of limbs reversed.

Many insects possess a pair of claws and a sticky pad at the ends of their legs. The pad consists of minute hollow tubes which secrete a sticky fluid that helps the insect to stick to smooth surfaces. Thus, these insects are able to walk up vertical surfaces as well as upside down.

Flight

The wings of insects are flattened extensions of the exoskeleton and are supported by an intricate system of

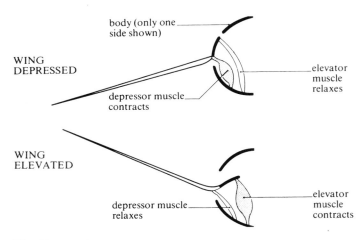

body (only one side shown)

WING DEPRESSED

elevator muscle relaxes

depressor muscle contracts

WING ELEVATED

depressor muscle relaxes

elevator muscle contracts

Fig 18.27 *Action of direct flight muscles in a large winged insect, such as a locust, butterfly or dragonfly.*

veins. Their movement is controlled by two main groups of muscles, **direct** and **indirect muscles**. In insects with large wings (such as locusts, butterflies and dragonflies) the muscles are actually attached to the bases of the wings (fig 18.27); these are the direct muscles. They raise and lower the wings as well as controlling the angle of the wing stroke during flight. When the angle of one wing is adjusted with respect to the other, the insect turns in the air. These muscles are also used to fold up the wings when the insect is stationary.

In large, winged insects such as the locust and butterfly the rate of wing beat is between 5–50 beats per second (table 18.4). Here the flight muscles contract each time as a result of a single nerve impulse. Hence impulses are generated at the same rate as the wings beat. Insect flight muscle which responds in this way is called **synchronous muscle**. In the housefly, which has a wing beat frequency of 120–200 beats per second, contraction of the flight muscles is much too fast to be triggered by individual nerve impulses. This muscle is termed **asynchronous** and receives roughly one impulse per 40 wing beats, which is necessary to maintain the muscle in an active state during flight. It can contract further and generate more power than synchronous muscle. Asynchronous muscle can also automatically contract in response to being stretched. This is called the **stretch reflex** and occurs faster than the speed of a nerve impulse.

> **18.3** The sarcoplasmic reticulum of insect flight muscle is modified to increase its surface area by being perforated at intervals. Can you suggest a reason for this?
>
> **18.4** Would synchronous or asynchronous muscle be expected to contain more sarcoplasmic reticulum? Give a reason for your answer.

Table 18.4 Wing speeds of a variety of insects.

	Wing speeds (times per second)	
large butterfly e.g. swallowtail	5	
locust	18	
hawkmoth	40	
housefly	120	at this speed a humming sound is heard
bee	180	
midge	700–1000	at this speed a high pitched whine is heard

In general, the smaller the insect the faster it beats its wings. NB Some insects have two pairs of wings (such as locusts and dragonflies). In some cases both pairs of wings beat together, as in bees; in others the back pair of wings beats slightly ahead of the front pair, for example locusts. Some insects have one pair of wings, such as flies and beetles. In houseflies the hindwings are reduced and modified to form a pair of club-shaped halteres which are sensory in function. They oscillate rapidly during flight, detect aerodynamic forces and provide information for the maintenance of stability in flight. Some insects (very few) have no wings, for example fleas.

18.6 Locomotion in vertebrates

18.6.1 Swimming in fish

Water, particularly sea water, has a high density, many hundreds of times greater than air. As such it represents a comparatively viscous medium to move through. However, its density is made use of by fish for support and to provide a medium against which the fish can thrust during swimming movements.

Any successful organism shows many adaptive features suited to the environment in which it lives and a fish is no exception. The body of most fish is highly streamlined, being tapered at both ends. This means that water flows readily over the body surface and that drag is reduced to a minimum. Apart from the fins, no other structures project from a fish, and it seems that the faster the fish, the more perfect is the streamlining. The scales of bony fish are moistened by slimy secretions from mucus or oil glands which considerably reduces friction between the fish and the water. The fins are also adaptations for moving efficiently through the water. The median fin (along the midline of the body) and the dorsal and ventral fins, which are unpaired, help to stabilise the fish. The paired pectoral and pelvic fins are used for steering and balancing the animal and the caudal, or tail, fin contributes to the forward movement of the fish through the water. Details of how the fins operate are discussed below.

18.6.2 Propulsion in fish

In animals like the earthworm and insects, whose locomotion was studied in previous sections, the body is clearly divided into segments. Although the vertebrate body is also built on a segmented plan, few systems still show it clearly. However, blocks of muscle, called **myotomes**, located on either side of the vertebral column in fish show a clear segmental pattern. These are responsible for movement of the fish. Each myotome has a zig-zag shape (which you may have noticed if you have eaten fish). The vertebral column is a long, flexible rod and, when myotomes on one side of it contract, it bends easily. It is part of the endoskeleton and is adapted for locomotion in its flexibility. The myotomes contract and relax alternately on each side of the vertebral column, beginning at the front end of the fish and travelling towards its tail. In other words, the blocks on opposite sides of the spinal cord are antagonistic. This activity bends the body of the fish into a series of waves, the number of bends increasing the longer and thinner the fish.

- Very compact fish such as the tunny show little evidence of this wave-like action, with as much as 80% of their forward thrust being achieved purely by the side-to-side lashing of the tail and caudal fin. This locomotion is called **ostraciform**.
- Longer fish, such as the dogfish and the majority of bony fish, exhibit **carangiform locomotion**. Here the posterior half of the fish is thrown into a series of waves.
- **Anguilliform locomotion**, as demonstrated by eels, is where the body is very long and thrown into many waves, so that different parts of the body are moving to the left or to the right at the same time.

These types of movement are shown in fig 18.28.

Forward propulsion is generally achieved by the side-to-side movement of the tail to which is attached the caudal fin. As the fish is thrust forward through the water, the side-to-side movement of the tail tends to make the head swing from side to side in a direction opposite to that of the tail. This is called **lateral drag**. Fortunately, it is not very pronounced because the water tends to resist the movement of the relatively large front end of the body (compared to the tail) and the large surface area of the dorsal median fin also resists sideways movement. Also it requires a much greater force to move the body sideways through the water than to propel it forwards. The magnitude of the force that the tail and caudal fin apply to the water depends on:

- their speed of action;
- their surface area:
- the angle at which they are held with respect to the direction of movement.

18.6.3 Locomotion in a bony fish, the herring

The external features of a herring are shown in fig 2.65. Bony fish possess a structure called the **swim bladder** or air bladder. The swim bladder is a sac that lies between the vertebral column and the gut and provides the fish with 'neutral buoyancy'. This means that the fish has a density equal to that of the surrounding water and therefore does not need to use energy to keep itself from sinking. It can concentrate its efforts on moving through the water.

With the development of a swim bladder, the paired fins could change from their original function of providing lift. In bony fish these fins are much smaller than in cartilaginous fish like sharks and dogfish, and are used instead as stabilisers or brakes, in the latter case being spread vertically at 90° to the body. Each pectoral fin may be used independent of the other pectoral fin, and in this way they act as pivots round which the fish can turn rapidly. When the fish is swimming in a straight line the paired fins are pressed firmly against the sides of the body, thus improving its streamlined shape. The symmetrical shape of the tail fin means that it transmits most of the force it develops against the water in a forward direction rather

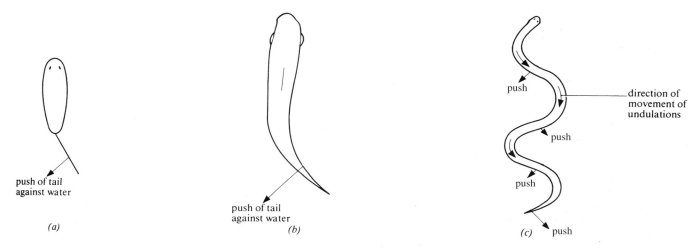

Fig 18.28 *Comparison of (a) ostraciform, (b) carangiform and (c) anguilliform locomotion.*

than up or down. The median fins resist the tendency of the head to swing from side to side in reaction to the tail as already described.

Two types of swim bladder exist.

- **Open swim bladder** (e.g. goldfish, herrings). The bladder is connected to the pharynx by a duct. Air is taken in or expelled from the bladder via the mouth and duct, thus decreasing or increasing the relative density of the fish respectively.
- **Closed swim bladder** (e.g. codfish). The bladder has completely lost its connection with the pharynx. By automatically increasing or decreasing the amount of gas in its bladder, the fish can match the density of the surrounding water and thus preserve 'neutral buoyancy'. Gas is extracted from, or returned to, the blood.

> **18.5** Summarise the adaptations that fish possess for efficient swimming.

18.6.4 Locomotion in quadrupeds, the dog

Walking

When a dog walks, its vertebral column remains rigid, and forward movement is achieved by the activity of the hindlimbs. They are moved forwards and backwards by alternative contraction of flexor and extensor muscles respectively.

When its extensor muscle contracts, each hindlimb, acting as a lever, extends and exerts a backward force against the ground, thrusting the animal forward and slightly upwards. When the flexor contracts, the limb is lifted clear of the ground and pulled forward. Only one limb is raised at any one time, the other three providing a tripod of support which balances the rest of the body. Beginning with the left forelimb in a stationary dog, the sequence of leg movement is as follows when it walks forward: left forelimb; right hindlimb; right forelimb; left hindlimb; and so on.

Running

As a dog begins to run, it loses its tripod means of support and develops a type of movement where the forelimbs move together, followed by the hindlimbs. The feet are in contact with the ground for much less time than in walking, and usually one forelimb touches the ground a split second before the other. This also occurs with the hindlimbs. Therefore the sequence of limbs touching the ground is: left forelimb; right forelimb; right hindlimb; left hindlimb.

As the dog reaches maximum speed, leg movement quickens even further, and as they extend, all four legs may be off the ground at the same time. The strong trunk muscles arch the flexible backbone upwards when all four limbs are underneath it, and downwards when the limbs are

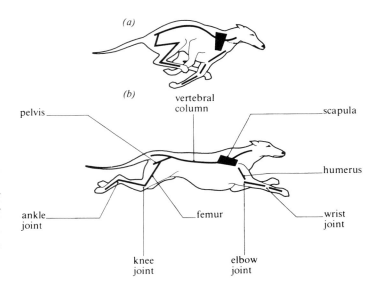

Fig 18.29 *Running sequence in a dog (such as a greyhound). (a) Backbone fully arched and feet immediately under the body. (b) Backbone fully extended and somewhat concave, limbs fully extended.*

fully extended. In this way the thrust of the limbs is increased and the stride of the dog considerably lengthened, both of which enable the dog to increase its speed (fig 18.29).

18.6.5 Walking in the human

Humans have a bipedal gait, meaning they walk on two legs. You will find it useful to refer to some of the terms introduced in section 18.4.1, namely origin and insertion, flexor and extensor, and antagonistic muscles.

Walking

In the standing position the weight of the body is balanced over two legs. When a stride is taken by the right limb the first thing to happen is that the right heel is raised by contraction of the calf muscle. This action serves to push the ball of the right foot against the ground and so exert a forward thrust. The right limb pushes further against the ground as it is pulled forwards, slightly bent at the knee (fig 18.30). As this occurs, the weight of the body is brought over the left foot which is still in contact with the ground and acting as a prop for the rest of the body. When the right limb extends, the heel is the first part of the foot to touch the ground. The weight of the body is gradually transferred from the left side to a position over the right heel and then, as the body continues to move forwards, over the right toe, backward pressure against the ground generally being exerted through the right big toe.

With the weight of the body now over the right leg, the left heel is raised and the whole sequence repeated.

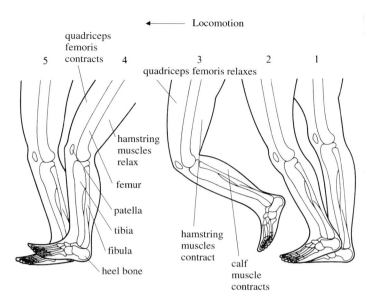

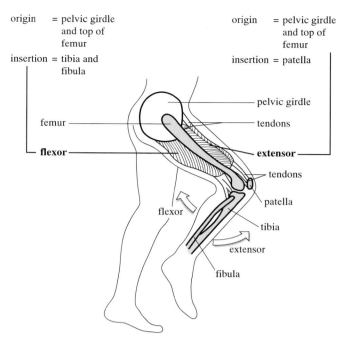

Fig 18.30 *Successive positions of the right leg during a single walking pace.*

Fig 18.31 *An example of a pair of antagonistic muscles involved in walking.*

Antagonistic muscles

The pattern of muscle activity involved in walking is complex, and involves sets of antagonistic muscles. However, the principles involved can be examined by using the flexing and extending of the leg at the knee as an example. The knee is a hinge joint. The flexors are the hamstring muscles at the back of the upper part of the leg (thigh). An example of one of these is the **biceps femoris**. (This also extends the thigh at the hip joint, which involves pulling it further away from the trunk.) The extensors are in the front of the thigh and the main one is the **quadriceps femoris**. This extends the leg at the knee joint (as well as flexing the thigh at the hip joint, which involves pulling the thigh closer to the trunk of the body). Origins and insertions are as follows and are shown in fig 18.31.

- Biceps femoris:
  origin = pelvic girdle and top of femur
  insertion = tops of fibula and tibia (bones of lower leg)
- Quadriceps femoris:
  origin = pelvic girdle and top of femur
  insertion = patella (knee-cap)

The two muscles work antagonistically so that as one contracts the other relaxes. In this way the movements indicated by arrows in fig 18.31 are brought about. The whole process is controlled by nerve impulses from motor neurones supplying the muscle fibres. These are carefully coordinated by reflexes as described below.

Inhibitory reflexes

For a limb, or part of a limb, to be moved backwards and forwards it must be operated by at least two opposing muscles or sets of muscles. When one contracts the other must relax. This is achieved by a simple inhibitory reflex mechanism. Normally, as a muscle begins to stretch, special receptors called **stretch receptors** (or muscle spindles or proprioreceptors) detect the stretching and send nerve impulses to the spinal cord which continue back to the muscle and make it contract sufficiently to resist the stretching. Imagine, for example, putting a weight in one hand: the arm would drop and the biceps muscle in your upper arm would stretch unless the biceps resisted the force by contracting. If its force of contraction exactly balances the effect of the weight, your hand will stay in the same place. This is under reflex control, although voluntary control can take over if necessary. If, however, the lower arm is being extended (moving away from the upper arm) the extensor muscle at the back of the arm is contracting and the biceps is being stretched (extended). It is important to inhibit the normal reflex which would make it contract in this situation.

The sensory neurone which leads from the stretch receptor to the spinal cord also synapses with interneurones in the grey matter of the spinal cord (fig 18.32). When suitably stimulated, these inhibit the motor neurones leading to the antagonistic muscle, which is therefore unable to contract and so remains relaxed.

A good example of this is the mechanism of walking.

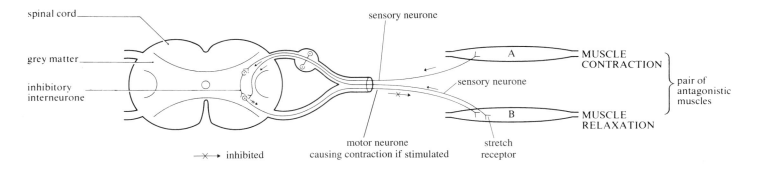

spinal cord

grey matter

inhibitory interneurone

sensory neurone

A — MUSCLE CONTRACTION

sensory neurone

B — MUSCLE RELAXATION

pair of antagonistic muscles

→×→ inhibited

motor neurone causing contraction if stimulated

stretch receptor

Fig 18.32 *Inhibitory reflex control of antagonistic muscles. When muscle A contracts (e.g. biceps femoris), impulses pass to the spinal cord where they meet an inhibitory interneurone. Contraction of muscle A requires muscle B (e.g. quadriceps femoris) to relax and be stretched. This stimulates stretch receptors in muscle B which send impulses to the spinal cord. If these were not inhibited they would pass on to muscle B and stop it from relaxing by causing it to contract. An opposite set of nerve cells makes muscle A relax when muscle B contracts ('reciprocal innervation').*

Initially the leg flexes at the knee in order to lift the foot off the ground. During flexing, the antagonistic extensor muscles are stretched but are reflexly inhibited from contracting. After flexion, the limb is straightened and the foot is again brought into contact with the ground. With the flexor muscles no longer contracting, inhibition of the extensor muscles ceases and the stretch reflex now operates, resulting in the contraction of the extensor muscles. When the limb is straight, no stretching in the extensor muscle stretch receptor is detected and the stretch reflex ceases. The whole process is then free to be repeated.

18.6 Why do sprinters generally run on their toes?

Chapter Nineteen

Homeostasis

An organism may be thought of as a complex system of chemical processes. These processes are self-regulating and tend to maintain a steady state within an external environment which is liable to change. The ability to maintain a steady state within a constantly changing environment is essential for the survival of living systems. In order to maintain this condition organisms from the simplest to the most complex have developed a variety of structural, physiological and behavioural mechanisms designed to achieve the same end, that is the preservation of a constant internal environment. The maintenance of a constant internal environment is called **homeostasis**. The advantage of a constant internal environment was first pointed out by the French physiologist Claude Bernard in 1857. Throughout his research he had been impressed by the way in which organisms were able to regulate physiological conditions, such as body temperature and water content, maintaining them within fairly narrow limits. This concept of self-regulation leading to physiological stability was summed up by Bernard in the now classic statement, 'La fixité du milieu interieur est la condition de la vie libre.' (The constancy of the internal environment is the condition of the free life.)

Bernard went on to distinguish between the **external environment** in which organisms live, and the **internal environment** in which individual cells live (in mammals, this is tissue fluid). He realised the importance of conditions in the latter being kept stable. For example, mammals are capable of maintaining a constant body temperature despite changes in the external temperature. If it is too cold the mammal may move to warmer or more sheltered conditions (a behavioural response); if this is not possible, self-regulating mechanisms operate to raise the body temperature and prevent further heat loss (a physiological response). All metabolic systems operate most efficiently if maintained within narrow limits close to optimum conditions. So the organism, as a whole, will function more efficiently if its cells are maintained at optimum conditions. Homeostatic mechanisms prevent large fluctuations from the optimum which are caused by changes in external and internal environments.

In 1932 the American physiologist Walter Cannon introduced the term **homeostasis** (*homoios*, same; *stasis*, standing) to describe how Bernard's 'constancy of the internal environment' is maintained. Homeostatic mechanisms maintain the stability of the cell environment and in this way provide the organism with a degree of independence of the environment. The more effective the mechanisms used, the more independent the organism is of the external environment. Independence of the environment can be used as a measure of the 'success' of an organism and, on this basis, more complex organisms such as mammals and flowering plants are seen as 'successful' since they are able to maintain relatively constant levels of activity despite fluctuations in environmental conditions. Such organisms are sometimes referred to as '**regulators**', meaning that they can regulate their own internal environments. They can typically exploit a wider range of environments and habitats than '**non-regulators**', which tend to be confined to environments which are more stable, such as oceans or lakes. Examples of non-regulators are cnidarians and algae, such as seaweeds and phytoplankton.

In order to achieve stability, the activities of organisms need to be regulated at all levels of biological organisation, from the molecular level to the level of the population. This means that organisms must use a range of structural, biochemical, physiological and behavioural mechanisms. In all these respects mammals are better equipped than simple animals like cnidarians to cope with changes in environmental conditions.

The mechanisms of regulation found in living organisms have many features in common with the mechanisms of regulation used in non-living systems, such as machines. The systems of both organisms and machines achieve stability by some form of control. In 1948, Wiener introduced the term **cybernetics** (*cybernos*, steersman) to mean the science of control mechanisms. This science is also commonly referred to as **control theory**. Plant and animal physiologists have used many of the very precise mathematical models of control theory to explain the functioning of biological control systems. Before studying some of the self-regulating mechanisms of living organisms, such as body temperature regulation and blood sugar levels, it is useful to have some understanding of the principles underlying control systems.

19.1 Control systems in biology

The application of control theory to biology has led to a clearer understanding of the different stages involved in the regulation of physiological processes. For example, living systems are now seen to be **open systems**;

Fig 19.1 *Basic components of a control system.*

that is they require a continuous exchange of matter between the environment and themselves. They are in a steady state with their environment but require a continuous input of energy in order to prevent them coming to equilibrium with the environment. A simple analogy is a fountain of water. It needs a constant input of material (new water) and can only be kept operating by a continuous input of energy. Yet it appears to remain constant, in other words in a steady state, with respect to its environment. The basic components of any control system are summarised in fig 19.1. Various terms may be used for each stage of the process and commonly used alternatives are shown in fig 19.1. The regulator in mammals is either an endocrine gland producing hormones, or part of the nervous system, often the brain or spinal cord.

The efficiency of the control system can be judged by:

- how little change there is from the reference point (or optimum level);
- the speed with which the level is restored after change.

Any change from the set-point activates the control systems and returns conditions towards their optimum level. As conditions return to the optimum, the corrective processes can be switched off, a process known as '**negative feedback**'. Feedback requires the action of the system to be related to a **reference point** or **set-point**, which is the optimum level of the variable being controlled (similar to the temperature set by a thermostat in a heating system). There are two forms of feedback, **negative** and **positive**. Negative feedback is more common.

Negative feedback

Negative feedback is associated with increasing the stability of systems (fig 19.2). If the system is disturbed, the disturbance sets in motion a sequence of events which tends to restore the system to its original state. The principle of negative feedback can be illustrated in terms of the regulation of oven temperature by the use of a thermostat. In the electric oven the control system includes an **effector**

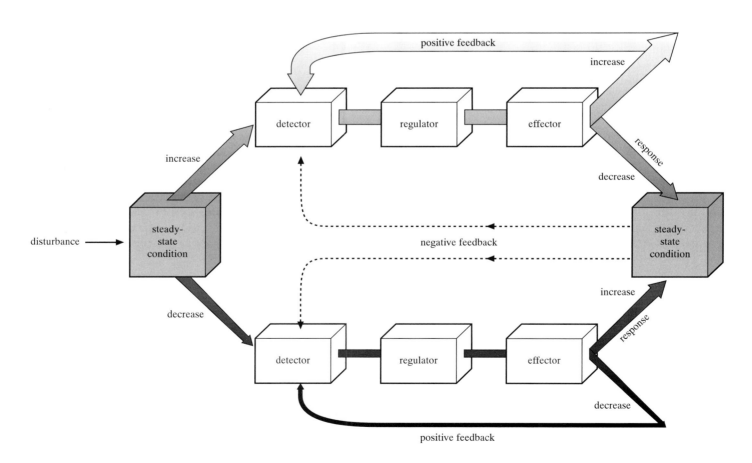

Fig 19.2 *A homeostatic control system. Negative feedback is shown by dotted lines. Negative feedback provides a means of switching off a process.*

(an element through which an electric current (an **input**) flows and which acts as a source of heat), an **output** (the oven temperature) and a thermostat which can be set to a desired level, the **set-point**. The thermostat acts as a **detector** (or **receptor**) and a **regulator**. The **stimulus** is heat. If the thermostat is set to read 150 °C, an electric current will provide a source of heat which will flow until the oven temperature passes the set-point of 150 °C, then the thermostat will cut out and no more heat will be supplied to the oven. When the oven temperature falls below 150 °C the thermostat will cut in again and the electric current will increase the temperature and restore the set-point. In this system the thermostat is functioning as an **error detector** where the error is the difference between the output and the set-point. The error is corrected by the effector (the heating element) being switched on or off. This is an example of a steady-state negative feedback system which is typical of many of the physiological control mechanisms found in organisms.

Examples of biological negative feedback mechanisms include the control of:

- oxygen and carbon dioxide levels in the blood by controlling rate and depth of breathing (section 9.5.5);
- heart rate (section 14.7.4);
- blood pressure (section 14.7.7);
- hormone levels, e.g. thyroxine (section 17.6.4 and fig 19.3), sex hormones (sections 21.6.4 and 21.6.6);
- metabolite levels, e.g. glucose (sections 17.6.6 and 19.2);
- water and ionic balances (section 20.3.5);
- the regulation of pH (section 20.8);
- body temperature (section 19.5).

Fig 19.3 illustrates the role of negative feedback in the control of thyroxine release by the thyroid gland. In this example the **detector** is the hypothalamus, the **regulator** is the pituitary gland and the **effector** is the thyroid gland.

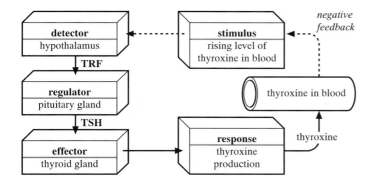

Fig 19.3 *The control of thyroxine production. This is a biological example of a simple control system. Thyroxine is a hormone produced by the thyroid gland.*
TRF, thyroid releasing factor; TSH, thyroid stimulating hormone; see section 17.6.4

Positive feedback

Positive feedback is rare in biological systems since it leads to an unstable situation and extreme states. In these situations a disturbance leads to events which increase the disturbance even further (fig 19.2). For example, during the propagation of a nerve impulse, depolarisation of the membrane of the neurone produces an increase in its sodium permeability. As sodium ions pass into the axon through the membrane they cause a further depolarisation which leads to even more sodium ions entering. The rate at which sodium ions enter therefore increases very rapidly and produces an action potential. In this case positive feedback acts as an amplifier of the *response* (depolarisation). Its extent is limited by other mechanisms as described in section 17.1.1. Positive feedback also occurs during labour when the hormone oxytocin stimulates muscular contractions of the uterus, which in turn stimulate the release of more oxytocin (section 21.7.12).

More complex mechanisms

There are several control mechanisms in the body which are more complex than those previously described. Broadly speaking they either involve the use of additional detectors (early-warning systems) or additional effectors ('fail-safe' systems). For example, temperature detectors situated externally and internally enable warm-blooded animals (homeotherms) to maintain an almost constant 'core' body temperature. Temperature receptors in the *skin* act as detectors of changes in the *external* environment. They send impulses to the hypothalamus which acts as a regulator and stimulates corrective measures before any change in *blood* temperature occurs. Other examples of this type of early-warning system include the control of ventilation during exercise, and control of appetite and thirst. Similarly multiple detectors and effectors provide fail-safe mechanisms for many vital processes, such as regulation of arterial blood pressure where stretch receptors in the carotid sinus and aorta, and baroreceptors in the medulla, respond to blood pressure changes and produce responses in various effectors including the heart, blood vessels and kidneys. Failure of any one of these is compensated for by the others.

19.2   Control of blood glucose levels

One of the most important metabolites in the blood is glucose. Its level must be controlled strictly. Glucose is the main respiratory substrate and must be supplied continuously to cells. The brain cells are especially dependent on glucose and are unable to use any other metabolites as an energy source. Lack of glucose results in fainting. The normal level of glucose in the blood is about 90 mg per 100 cm^3 blood, but may vary from 70 mg per 100 cm^3 blood during fasting up to 150 mg per 100 cm^3 blood following a meal. The sources of blood glucose and its relationships with other metabolites are described in section 19.6.2.

The control of blood glucose level is a good example of homeostasis and involves the secretion of at least six hormones and two negative feedback pathways. A rise in blood glucose level (**hyperglycaemia**) stimulates insulin secretion (section 17.6.6) whereas a fall in blood glucose level (**hypoglycaemia**) inhibits insulin secretion and stimulates the secretion of glucagon (section 17.6.6) and other hormones which raise blood glucose levels, such as adrenaline. The control mechanism is summarised in fig 19.4.

19.3   Temperature regulation

All living systems require a continuous supply of heat energy in order to survive.

The major source of heat for all living organisms is the Sun. Solar radiation is converted into heat energy whenever it strikes and is absorbed by a body. The extent of this solar radiation depends upon geographical location, and is a major factor in affecting the climate of a region. This, in turn, determines the presence and abundance of species. For example, organisms inhabit regions where the normal air temperatures vary from −40 °C, as in the Arctic, to 50 °C in desert regions. In some of the latter regions the surface temperature may rise as high as 80 °C. The majority of living organisms exist within confined limits of temperature, say 10–35 °C, but various organisms show adaptations enabling them to exploit habitats at both extremes of temperature (fig 19.5). This is not the only source of heat available to organisms. Solar radiation is used by photosynthetic organisms and this energy becomes locked up in the chemical bonds of organic molecules such as sugars. This provides an internal source of heat energy when released by the reactions of respiration.

Temperature indicates the amount of heat energy in a system and is a major factor determining the rate of chemical reactions in both living and non-living systems. Heat energy increases the rate at which atoms and molecules move and this increases the probability of reactions occurring between them.

19.3.1   The influence of temperature on the growth and distribution of plants

Temperature can act as a limiting factor in the growth and development of plants by influencing the rates of processes like cell division, photosynthesis and other

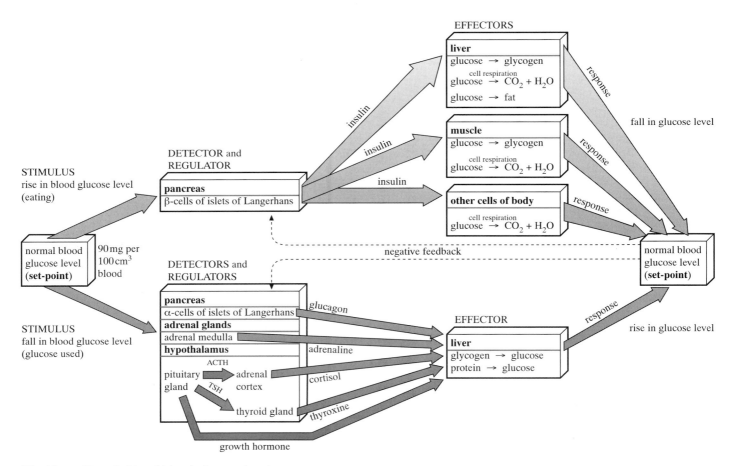

Fig 19.4 *Regulation of blood glucose level.*

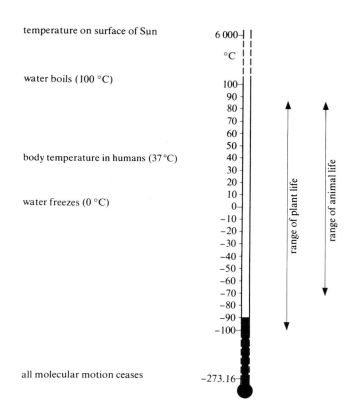

temperature on surface of Sun   6 000

°C

water boils (100 °C)   100
90
80
70
60
50

body temperature in humans (37 °C)   40
30
20
10

water freezes (0 °C)   0
−10
−20
−30
−40
−50
−60
−70
−80
−90
−100

all molecular motion ceases   −273.16

range of plant life

range of animal life

Fig 19.5 *Temperature reference points in living organisms and the ranges of temperature they are able to tolerate.*

metabolic processes. The light-independent reactions of photosynthesis are temperature dependent and lead to the various metabolic pathways described in chapter 7. The rates of photosynthesis, and the accumulation of sufficient food materials to enable the plant to complete its life cycle, are important factors in determining the geographical range of plants.

19.3.2   Adaptations of plants to low temperatures

The flora of northern temperate climates and the tundra show many adaptations that enable plants to take maximum advantage of the short warm summers. For example, the only plant species found are mosses, a few grasses and fast-growing annuals. Plants living in extreme northerly or southerly latitudes are subjected to long periods of adverse conditions, such as low light intensity, low temperatures and frozen soil. In order to survive in these conditions, plants show many structural, physiological and behavioural adaptations. For example, most temperate woody perennials are deciduous and lose their leaves, under the influence of the plant growth regulator substance abscisic acid (ABA), in order to prevent water loss by transpiration during periods when soil water uptake is limited by low temperatures (section 16.2.8). Wind and snow damage is also avoided by the shedding of leaves

during these periods, when the rate of photosynthesis would be severely limited by low light intensities, low temperatures and unavailability of water and salts. Throughout these periods the regions of next year's growth, the buds, are protected by scale leaves and are dormant. Their metabolic activity is inhibited by the presence of abscisic acid. Many coniferous species dominate the vegetation of the more temperate regions, particularly in northern latitudes. These species have needle-like leaves which reduce the amount of snow which can accumulate on them in winter and have a thick cuticle to prevent water loss in summer. Many species of annuals have short growing periods and survive the winter by producing resistant seeds or organs of perennation.

Low temperatures are required by many plant species in order to break dormancy. For example, lilac buds develop more quickly after being exposed to low temperatures than to high temperatures. Other examples of the effects of low temperature on plant growth are described in chapter 16 and section 22.4.

19.3.3   Adaptations of plants to high temperatures

In many regions of the world high temperatures are associated with water shortage, and many of the adaptations shown by plants in these regions are related to their ability to resist desiccation.

Plants are unable to escape high temperatures by moving to shaded areas and therefore they have to rely on structural and physiological adaptations to avoid overheating. It is the aerial parts of plants which are exposed to the heating effect of solar radiation, and the largest exposed surface is that of the leaves. Leaves characteristically are thin structures with a large surface area to volume ratio to allow gaseous exchange and absorption of light. This structure is also ideal for preventing damage by excessive heating. A thin leaf has a relatively low heat capacity and therefore will usually assume the temperature of the surroundings. In hot regions a shiny cuticle is secreted by the epidermis which reflects much of the incident light, thus preventing heat being absorbed and overheating the plant. The large surface area contains numerous stomatal openings which permit transpiration. As much as $0.5 \, kg \, m^{-2} \, h^{-1}$ of water may be lost from plants by transpiration in hot, dry weather, which would account for the loss of approximately $350 \, W \, m^{-2}$ in terms of heat energy. This is nearly half the total amount of energy being absorbed. As a result of these mechanisms plants are able to exercise a considerable degree of control over their temperature.

> **19.1** Why do plants suffer permanent physiological damage if exposed to temperatures in excess of 30 °C when the humidity is high?

During hot, sunny days many plants wilt. This occurs when the rate of transpiration is greater than the rate of water uptake. There is an overall loss of turgidity by cells such as parenchyma. **Wilting** may be observed in plants growing in greenhouses in response to the very high temperatures which develop in the leaves, even if adequately supplied with water. In such a situation it may therefore be a mechanism for preventing overheating by reducing the surface area of leaves exposed to direct sunlight. Wilting reduces the yield of plants. Once the temperature begins to fall, the plants recover very quickly even if the degree of wilting looks severe.

Plants living in dry conditions are called **xerophytes** and show many structural adaptations which enable them to survive (section 20.10). In most cases these adaptations are primarily concerned with regulating water loss, although the characteristic needle-shaped leaves permit maximum heat loss. The mechanisms for withstanding high temperatures, on the other hand, are mainly physiological. One physiological mechanism used by plants (not just xerophytes) to avoid wilting in dry conditions is to produce more abscisic acid. This causes stomata to close, thus reducing loss of water by transpiration.

19.3.4 The influence of temperature on the growth and distribution of animals

Temperature influences the metabolic activity of animals in a number of ways:

- the main effect is on the rate of enzyme activity and the rate of movement of atoms and molecules. This directly affects the rate of growth of animals (chapter 22).
- Temperature may also affect the geographical distribution of animals through its influence on plants as primary producers in the food chains. The ecological range of most animal species, with the exception of some insects, birds and mammals which are able to migrate, is determined by the local availability of food.

The variety of responses shown by animals to temperature depends upon:

- the degree of variation in temperature shown by the environment;
- the degree of control the organism has over its own body temperature.

Life is believed to have originated in the marine environment, the environment that poses the fewest temperature problems for living organisms because temperature fluctuations in aquatic environments are slight. The biological significance of this is that aquatic organisms have a relatively stable environment with regard to temperature and therefore do not need the same range of responses to temperature change that is shown by terrestrial animals. Most aquatic organisms, including non-vertebrates

and fish, have a body temperature which varies according to the temperature of the water, though some very active fish such as the tuna are able to maintain a body temperature higher than that of the water.

Another factor of importance in aquatic environments is that water has a maximum density at $4\,°C$ and consequently only the surface of the water freezes at $0\,°C$ as ice floats. Ice insulates the water below it. This enables many aquatic animals to continue to be active at times when most terrestrial organisms would be inactive due to sub-zero conditions.

Air temperature can fluctuate widely over a 24 h period (because air has a relatively low specific heat). One of the problems associated with the colonisation of land by animals was adapting to, or tolerating, these temperature fluctuations. This has produced many structural, physiological and behavioural responses, and is one of the major factors determining geographical distribution. The nature of the responses and examples are described in the following sections.

19.3.5 Gaining heat – ectothermy and endothermy

All animals gain heat from two sources:

- the external environment;
- the release of heat energy as a result of chemical reactions within their cells.

The extent to which different groups of animals are able to generate and conserve this heat is variable. All non-vertebrates, fish, amphibia and reptiles are unable to maintain their body temperature within narrow limits using *physiological* mechanisms, though many do so using behavioural mechanisms. Consequently these animals are described as **poikilothermic** (*poikilos*, various; *therme*, heat). Alternatively, because they rely more on heat derived from the environment than metabolic heat in order to raise their body temperature, they are termed **ectothermic** (*ecto*, outside). These animals used to be described as 'cold-blooded' but this is a misleading and inaccurate term.

Birds and mammals are able to maintain a fairly constant body temperature independently of the environmental temperature by using physiological mechanisms. They are described as **homeothermic** (or **homoiothermic** – *homoios*, like) or less correctly as 'warm-blooded'. Homeotherms are relatively independent of external sources of heat and rely on a high metabolic rate to generate heat which must be conserved. Since these animals rely on internal sources of heat they are described as **endothermic** (*endos*, inside). Some poikilotherms may, at times, have temperatures higher than those of homeotherms and, in order to prevent confusion, the terms ectotherm and endotherm are used throughout this text. Fig 19.6 shows the abilities of several vertebrates to regulate their body temperature in various external temperatures.

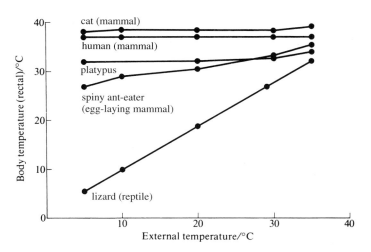

Fig 19.6 *The relationships between external (environmental) and internal (body) temperatures in vertebrates kept for 2 h at the external temperatures indicated.*

19.3.6 Losing heat

Whilst the main method of *gaining* heat differs between ectotherms and endotherms, the methods of heat loss to the environment are the same in both types of organism. These are radiation, convection, conduction and evaporation. In practice, heat can be transferred in either direction by the first three methods depending upon the **thermal gradient** (the direction of the temperature difference from hot to cold) but can only be *lost* from organisms by the latter method.

Radiation. Heat is transferred by infra-red radiation. Infra-red waves are part of the electromagnetic spectrum and are longer than the waves of the visible spectrum. They can be detected by special film sensitive to infra-red radiation, as shown in fig 19.7. Such photos show radiation of heat from the body. Heat loss (or gain) is proportional to the temperature difference between the body and its surroundings. Radiation accounts for about 50% of the total heat loss in humans and provides the main route for controlled heat loss in animals.

Convection. Heat is transferred between organisms and environment by convection currents in the air or water in contact with the surface of an organism. Convection currents are mass movements of air or water molecules. It is due to still air or water next to the skin being warmed, and rising as a result. The rate of heat transfer by this process is linked to the rate of air or water movement. It may be reduced by insulating materials such as feathers or hair in animals or clothing in humans.

Conduction. Conduction is the transfer of energy by physical contact between two bodies, for instance between the organism and the ground or the air. The molecules of the skin and anything it is in contact with

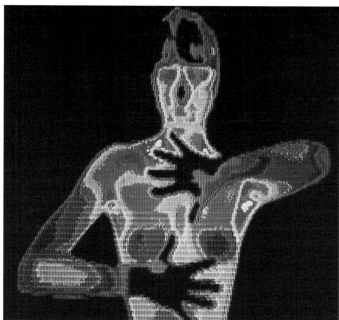

Fig 19.7 *Infra-red photo of a young woman with cold hands. The brighter areas of her body are warmer, whilst her hands show as dark areas.*

are in constant motion due to kinetic energy. The energy of this motion can be transferred from a region of higher temperature to a region of lower temperature. Heat exchange by this means is relatively insignificant for most terrestrial organisms, but may be considerable for aquatic and soil-dwelling organisms. Conduction to physical objects such as a chair is insignificant in humans (about 3%) but conduction to air is more significant, about 15% of heat loss in humans.

Evaporation. Heat is lost from the body surface during the conversion of water to water vapour. The evaporation of $1 \, cm^3$ of water (1 g) requires the loss of 2.45 kJ from the body. It is a limiting factor in the distribution of many plant and animal species. In humans water loss by evaporation takes place continuously through the skin even when a person is not sweating. It also occurs by evaporation from the lungs (lost in expired air). Neither of these can be controlled. However, partial control of heat loss is possible by regulating loss of water by sweating and panting.

19.3.7 Core temperature and surface temperature

When reference is made to body temperature in animal studies it usually refers to the **core temperature**. This is the temperature of the tissues below a level of 2.5 cm beneath the surface of the skin. This temperature is most easily measured by taking the temperature of the rectum (rectal temperature). Temperatures near the surface of the body can vary tremendously depending upon position and external temperature (fig 19.8).

653

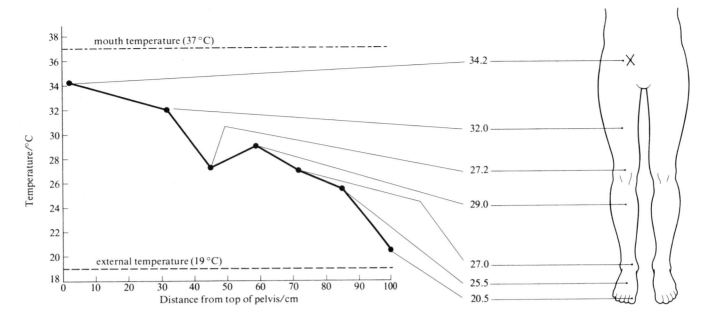

Fig 19.8 *Skin temperatures recorded at the pelvis and on the leg during a period of exposure to an external temperature of 19 °C. The low temperature at the knee cap probably reflects its poor blood supply.*

19.4 Ectothermic animals

The majority of animals are ectothermic, and their activity is determined by the environmental temperature. The metabolic rate of ectotherms is relatively low and they lack physiological mechanisms for conserving heat.

19.4.1 Temperature regulation in aquatic ectotherms

Aquatic ectotherms live within a restricted temperature range, determined by the size of the body of water in which they live. For example, the temperature of a pond can vary considerably throughout the year, whereas that of an ocean may change by only a few degrees. Despite this wide temperature fluctuation in small bodies of water, many insect species have aquatic stages in the life cycle (larvae, pupae or nymphs), since the aquatic temperatures are more stable and less extreme than terrestrial temperatures during the winter months. Mayflies, dragonflies, caddisflies, midges and mosquitoes all have an aquatic stage.

Aquatic non-vertebrates are able to tolerate greater temperature fluctuations than aquatic vertebrates due to their relatively simple physiology. Fish have a higher rate of metabolism than aquatic non-vertebrates but the majority of the extra heat produced as a result is rapidly spread around the body and lost to the environment by conduction through the gills and skin. Consequently, fish usually have a body temperature which is in equilibrium with that of the water. Fish cannot maintain a temperature below that of the water but may in some cases, as in the case of tuna fish, retain heat by means of a countercurrent heat exchange system. This can raise the temperature of the 'red' swimming muscle to about 12 °C above that of the sea water.

19.4.2 Temperature regulation in terrestrial ectotherms

Terrestrial (land-living) ectotherms have to cope with greater temperature fluctuations than those of aquatic ectotherms, but they have the benefit of living at higher environmental temperatures. This allows them to be more active. The relatively poor thermal conductivity of air reduces the rate of heat loss from the organisms whilst water loss by evaporation may be used to cool them. Many species are able to maintain temperatures slightly above or below air temperature and thereby avoid extremes.

Heat is gained and lost by terrestrial ectotherms by behavioural and physiological activities. The main sources of heat gain are the absorption of solar radiation and conduction from the air and the ground. The amount of heat absorbed depends upon:

- the colour of the organism;
- its surface area;
- its position relative to the Sun's rays.

Colour. A species of Australian grasshopper is dark in colour at low temperatures and absorbs solar radiation, thus heating up rapidly. As the temperature rises above a set point, further absorption is reduced by the exoskeleton becoming lighter in colour. This colour change is believed to be a direct response by pigment cells to body temperature. Such organisms are known as **basking heliotherms** (*helios*, sun).

Orientation. Changes in position of the organism relative to the Sun's rays vary the surface area exposed to heating. This practice is common in many terrestrial ectotherms including insects, arachnids, amphibia and reptiles. It is a form of *behavioural* thermoregulation. For example, the desert locust is relatively inactive at 17 °C but by aligning itself at right-angles to the Sun's rays it is able to absorb heat energy. As the air temperature rises to approximately 40 °C it re-orientates itself parallel to the Sun's rays to reduce the exposed surface area. Further increase in temperature, which may prove fatal, is prevented by raising the body off the ground or climbing up vegetation. Air temperature falls off rapidly over short distances above ground level, and these movements enable the locust to find a more favourable microclimate.

Reptiles

Crocodiles, too, regulate their body temperature on land by varying their position relative to the Sun's rays. They also open their mouths to increase heat loss by evaporation. If the temperature becomes too high, they move into the water which is relatively cooler. At night they retreat to water in order to avoid the low temperatures which would be experienced on land. Thermoregulation mechanisms have been studied most extensively in lizards.

Many different species of lizard have been studied and show a variety of responses to different temperatures. Lizards are terrestrial reptiles and exhibit many behavioural activities, as is typical of other ectotherms. Some species, however, use a number of physiological mechanisms to raise and maintain their body temperatures above that of the environment (fig 19.9). Other species are able to keep their body temperature within confined limits by varying their activity and taking advantage of shade or exposure. In both these respects lizards foreshadow many of the mechanisms of homeothermy shown by birds and mammals.

Surface temperatures in desert regions can rise to 70–80 °C during the day and fall to 4 °C at dawn. During the periods of extreme temperatures, most lizards seek refuge by living in burrows or beneath stones. This response and certain physiological responses are shown by the horned lizard (*Phrynosoma*) which inhabits the deserts of the south-west of the USA and Mexico. In addition to burrowing, the horned lizard is able to vary its orientation and colour, and as the temperature becomes high it can also reduce its body surface area by pulling back its ribs. Other responses to high temperatures involve panting, which removes heat by the evaporation of water from the mouth,

Fig 19.9 Varanus *rock monitor basking at its treehole in the sunlight to raise its body temperature.*

Fig 19.10 *Shovel-snouted lizard* (Aporosaura anchietae) *in the Namib desert. In the afternoon when the sand is hot, the lizard lifts opposite pairs of feet alternately so that they can cool in the air. This is known as thermal dancing.*

pharynx and lungs, eye bulging, thermal dancing (fig. 19.10) and the elimination of urine from the cloaca.

The marine iguana (*Amblyrhynchus*), a reptile, normally maintains a temperature of 37 °C as it basks on the rocky shore of the Galapagos Islands, but it needs to spend a considerable time in the sea feeding on seaweed at a temperature of approximately 25 °C. In order to avoid losing heat rapidly when immersed in water the iguana reduces the blood flow between surface and core tissues by slowing its heart rate (bradycardia).

Amphibians

The moist skin of amphibians provides an ideal mechanism to enable heat loss by evaporation. This water loss, however, cannot be regulated physiologically as in mammals. Amphibians lose water immediately on exposure to dry conditions and, whilst this helps heat loss, it leads to dehydration if the amphibian does not find moist shaded conditions where the rate of evaporation is reduced.

19.5 Endothermic animals

Birds and mammals are endothermic and their activity is largely independent of environmental temperature. In order to maintain a constant body temperature, which is normally higher than the air temperature, these organisms need to have a high metabolic rate and an efficient means of controlling heat loss from the body surface. The skin is the organ of the body in contact with the environment and therefore monitors the changing temperatures. The actual regulation of temperature by various metabolic processes is controlled by the hypothalamus of the brain.

19.5.1 Skin structure

The term 'skin' applies to the outer covering of vertebrate animals. The skin is the largest organ of the body and has many different functions. The structure of the skin varies in different vertebrate groups. The basic structure of human skin will be described here (fig 19.11).

The skin is composed of two main layers, the epidermis and dermis. These cover the underlying, or 'subcutaneous' tissue, which contains specialised fat-containing cells known as **adipose tissue**. The thickness of this layer varies according to the region of the body and from person to person.

Epidermis

The cells of this region are separated from the dermis by a basement membrane. The epidermis is composed of many layers of cells that form a stratified epithelium (section 6.3.2). The cells immediately above the basement membrane are cuboidal epithelial cells (section 6.3.1) and form a region known as the **Malpighian layer**. The cells in this layer are constantly dividing by mitosis and replace all the cells of the epidermis as they wear away. The Malpighian layer forms the lower region of the **stratum granulosum**, which is composed of living cells that become flatter as they approach the outer region of the epidermis, the **stratum corneum**. Cells in this region become progressively flattened and synthesise **keratin**, which is a fibrous protein which makes the cells waterproof. As the keratin content of the cells increases, they are said to become 'cornified'. Their nuclei disappear and the cells die. The thickness of the stratum corneum increases in parts of the body where there is considerable friction, such as the ball of the foot and the bases of the fingers. The outer covering of the skin forms a semi-transparent, thin, tough, flexible, waterproof covering pierced by the hair follicles and by pores, which are the openings of the sweat glands. The outermost squamous epithelial cells are continually being shed as a result of friction.

The stratum corneum has become modified in many vertebrates to produce nails, claws, hooves, horns, antlers, scales, feathers and hair. Keratin is the main component of all these structures.

Dermis

The dermis is a dense matrix composed of connective tissue rich in elastic fibres and contains blood capillaries, lymph vessels, muscle fibres, sensory cells, nerve fibres, pigment cells, sweat glands and hair follicles.

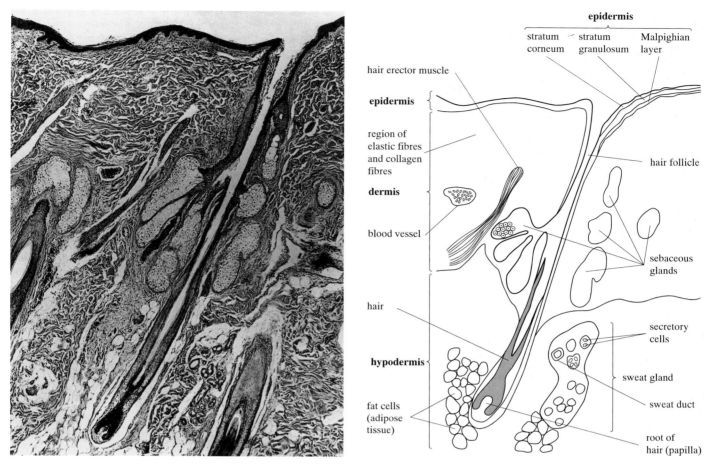

Fig 19.11 *(a) Vertical section through human skin. (b) Diagram of skin structure based on (a).*

Hair follicles are infoldings of the epidermis with a hair root, or **papilla**, at the base from which the hair develops. Hair is composed of cuboid epithelial cells which become cornified by impregnation with keratin. The outer region of the hair contains varying amounts of the pigment melanin which determines hair colour. The centre of the hair may contain air bubbles, and as the number increases with age, and melanin production falls off, the hair becomes white. Blood capillaries supply the growing hair with nourishment and remove waste substances. The upper part of the hair projects beyond the epidermis and is kept supple and waterproof by **sebum**, an oily secretion produced by **sebaceous glands** which open into the hair follicle. Sebum contains fatty acids, waxes and steroids, and spreads along the hair and onto the skin where it keeps the follicle free from dust and bacteria, as well as forming a thin waterproof layer over the skin. This not only prevents water loss from the skin but also prevents water entering the skin.

At the base of the follicle is a smooth muscle, the **hair erector muscle**, which has its origin on the basement membrane and its insertion on the hair follicle. Contraction of this muscle alters the angle between the hair and the skin which results in variation of the amount of air trapped above the skin. This is used as a means of thermoregulation and also as a behavioural response to danger in some vertebrates. When the hair 'stands on end' it increases the apparent size of the organism which may be sufficient to frighten off would-be attackers. The distribution of hair in humans is much more restricted than in other mammals.

Sweat glands are coiled tubular glands situated in the dermis and connected to a sweat duct which opens as a pore on the surface of the skin. They are found over the entire human body, but in some mammals are restricted to the pads of the feet. They are absent in birds. Water, salts and urea are brought to the glands by blood capillaries, and the secretory activity of the glands is controlled by the activity of the sympathetic nerve fibres. There are two types of sweat glands, **eccrine** and **apocrine**. Eccrine glands are the most common (approximately 2.5 million in humans), being found in most regions of the body. Apocrine glands are found in the armpits, around the nipples, the pubic region, hands, feet and anus. These release an odourless fluid which may later produce a strong odour due to bacterial activity in the fluid. Certain zinc and aluminium compounds can inhibit the activity of the glands and destroy bacteria. Most antiperspirants and deodorants contain these compounds.

Blood capillaries are numerous in the dermis and supply

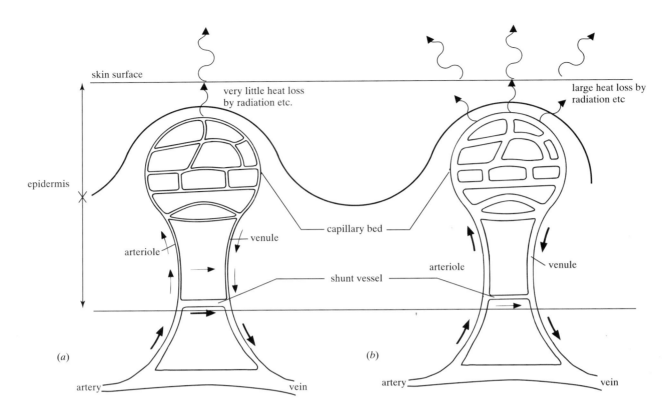

Fig 19.12 *Mechanism of regulation of blood flow through the skin. (a) Blood flow through the skin preventing heat loss. Constriction of the arteriole reduces blood flow through capillaries. Only sufficient blood passes into the skin to keep the tissues alive. Most of the blood flowing from the body bypasses the skin through the shunt vessels and reduces heat loss. (b) Blood flow through the skin increasing heat loss. Dilation of the arteriole increases blood flow through the capillaries. The capillaries dilate due to the rise in blood pressure within them. Heat is lost from the blood by radiation, convection and conduction and blood flow is increased to the sweat glands.*

the various structures already described. Many of the capillaries form loops and have shunts (fig 19.12) which enable the body to vary the amount of blood flowing through the capillaries. This is one of the many ways of regulating body temperature, as described in section 19.5.3.

Motor neurones run to the muscles and glands in the dermis whilst sensory neurones carry nerve impulses from the many sense cells situated in the dermis. These **sense cells** detect heat, cold, touch, pain and pressure. Some of the sense cells are simple and consist of free nerve endings, whereas others, such as the Pacinian corpuscle, are in capsules (fig 17.33).

19.5.2 Sources of heat

The major source of heat in endotherms is energy-releasing biochemical reactions which occur in living cells. The heat energy is released mainly by the breakdown of carbohydrates and fats taken in as part of the diet. Most of it comes from active tissues such as the liver and voluntary (skeletal) muscle. The rate of heat release in a resting organism is known as the **basal metabolic rate**

(BMR). This provides a 'base-line' for comparing the energy demands of various activities, and of different organisms (see section 9.5.8). The energy content of food required to meet the demands of the basal metabolic rate for an average-sized male human over a 24-hour period is approximately 8000 kJ. The exact amount per individual depends upon size, age and sex, being slightly higher in males.

The rate of energy release is regulated by factors such as environmental temperature and hormones. The hormone thyroxine, which is released from the thyroid gland, increases the metabolic rate and therefore heat production. Its effects are long term. The hormone adrenaline produces short-term increases in metabolic activity. Other sources of heat energy are initiated by nerve impulses. Repeated stimulation of voluntary muscle by motor neurones produces the shivering response which can increase heat production by up to five times the basal level. During shivering various groups of muscle fibres within a muscle contract and relax out of phase, so that the overall response is an uncoordinated movement. This response may be reinforced by other muscular activity such as rubbing the hands together, stamping the feet and limited forms of exercise. In many mammals there are areas near the thoracic blood vessels which are rich in brown fat cells; stimulation of these by sympathetic neurones causes the rapid oxidation of the numerous fat droplets in the cells in aerobic respiration. The resulting release of energy by the mitochondria in these cells is particularly important for hibernating animals since it helps to rapidly raise the core temperature during waking from hibernation. The hypothalamus is the centre controlling heat production for most of the mechanisms described above. Its role is discussed in more detail in section 19.5.4.

19.5.3 Loss of heat

Heat is lost from endotherms by the four mechanisms described in section 19.3.6, that is conduction, convection, radiation and evaporation. In all cases, the rate of loss depends upon the temperature differences between the body core and the skin, and the skin and the environment. The rate can be increased or decreased depending upon the rate of heat production and the environmental temperature.

There are three factors limiting heat loss, as described below.

The rate of blood flow between the body core and skin

The rate of heat loss from the skin by radiation, convection and conduction depends upon the amount of blood flowing through it. If the blood flow is low, the skin temperature approaches that of the environment whereas, if the flow is increased, the skin temperature then approaches core temperature. The skin of endotherms is rich in blood vessels and blood can flow through it by one of two routes:

- through capillary networks in the dermis;
- through shunt pathways deep in the dermis which link arterioles and venules.

Arterioles have relatively thick muscular walls which can contract or relax to alter the diameter of the vessels and the rate of blood flow through them. The degree of contraction is controlled by sympathetic nerves from the vasomotor centre in the medulla of the hindbrain. This in turn is controlled by nerve impulses received from the thermoregulatory centre in the hypothalamus. The rate of blood flow through the skin in humans can vary from less than $1\,cm^3$ per minute per $100\,g$ in cold conditions to $100\,cm^3$ per minute per $100\,g$ in hot conditions, and this can account for an increase in heat loss by a factor of five or six. Constriction of the arterioles forces blood through the low resistance shunt vessels from arteries to veins and the bulk of the blood by-passes the capillaries (fig 19.12). This is a typical response preventing heat loss. Dilation of the arterioles encourages blood flow through the capillary beds

and not through the shunt vessels. This increases blood flow through the skin and therefore heat is lost more rapidly.

The rate of sweat production and evaporation from the skin

Sweat is a watery fluid containing between 0.1 and 0.4% of sodium chloride, sodium lactate (from lactic acid) and urea. It is less concentrated than blood plasma and is secreted from tissue fluid by the activity of sweat glands under the control of neurones which are part of the sympathetic nervous system. These neurones come from the hypothalamus. Sweating begins whenever the body temperature rises above its mean value of $36.7\,°C$. Approximately 900 cm^3 of sweat are lost per day in a temperate climate, but the figure can rise as high as $12\,dm^3$ per day in very hot dry conditions, providing that there is adequate replacement of water and salts.

> **19.2** The latent heat of evaporation of sweat is $2.45\,kJ\,cm^{-3}$. Calculate the percentage of energy lost by sweating from a heavy manual worker who loses $4\,dm^3$ per day of sweat and has a daily energy intake of $50\,000\,kJ$.

When sweat evaporates from the skin surface, energy is lost from the body as latent heat of evaporation and this reduces body temperature. The rate of evaporation is reduced by low environmental temperatures, high humidity and lack of wind.

Many mammals have so much hair on their bodies that sweating is restricted to bare areas, for instance pads of the feet of dogs and cats, and the ears of rats. These mammals increase heat loss by licking their bodies and allowing moisture to evaporate, and by panting and losing heat from the moist nasal and buccal cavity. Humans, horses and pigs are able to sweat freely over the entire body surface.

Experiments have now confirmed that sweating only occurs as a result of a rise in core temperature. Experiments on humans and other animals have shown that lowering the core temperature, by swallowing ice water or cooling the carotid blood vessels with an ice pack around the neck, while at the same time exposing the skin to heat, results in a decrease in the rate of sweating. Opposite effects have been recorded by reversing the environmental conditions. Blood from the carotid vessels flows to the hypothalamus and these experiments have indicated its role in thermoregulation. Inserting a thermistor against the eardrum gives an acceptable measure of the temperature in the hypothalamus. The relation between changes in temperature in this region and the skin and rate of evaporation of sweat are shown in fig 19.13. The data come from an experiment carried out on a naked man in a heat-controlled chamber. Examine figure 19.13 and answer the following questions.

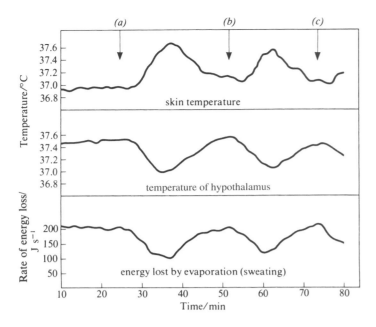

Fig 19.13 *Graphs showing the relation between skin temperature, temperature of the hypothalamus and rate of evaporation for a human in a warm chamber (45 °C). Iced water was swallowed at the points labelled (a), (b) and (c).*

19.3 Suggest why iced water was not given until 20 minutes after the start of the experiment.

19.4 Describe the relationship between the temperature of the hypothalamus and the rate of sweating.

19.5 Suggest why the skin temperature rises shortly after the ingestion of iced water.

The amount of insulation between the core and the environment

Insulation for the body is provided by air trapped outside the skin by hair and by fat in the dermis and just below the dermis (subcutaneous fat). In mammals, hair or clothes trap a layer of air, known as stagnant air, between the skin and the environment, and because air is a poor conductor of heat it reduces heat loss. Thick hair is known as fur. The amount of insulation provided by this means depends upon the thickness of the layer of trapped air. Reflex contractions of the hair erector muscles in response to decreasing temperatures increase the angle between the hair and the skin and so more air is trapped. The response is still present in humans but, as there is only a small amount of body hair, it only produces the effect known as 'goose-flesh' or 'goose-pimples'. Humans compensate for the lack of body hair by taking advantage of the insulating effects of clothing. The seasonal accumulation of a thick layer of subcutaneous fat is common in mammals, particularly in those species which do not hibernate and manage to withstand cold temperatures. Aquatic mammals, particularly those living in cold waters, such as the whale, sea-lion, walrus and seal, have a thick layer of fat known as blubber, which effectively insulates them against the cold.

19.5.4 Heat balance and the role of the hypothalamus

If the temperature of a body is to remain constant, then over a period of time the following equation must apply:

heat gained by body = heat lost by body

Endothermic animals are able to balance heat gain and heat loss by generating heat energy internally, and regulating the amount lost (fig 19.14). This is known as **homeothermy**. Any mechanism which has an input and an output and is capable of maintaining a constant value must be regulated by a control system as described earlier in this chapter (see fig 19.1).

Mammals have a well-developed control system involving receptors and effectors and an extremely sensitive control centre, the hypothalamus. The hypothalamus is located in the brain (fig 17.24). It monitors the temperature of the blood flowing through it. This blood is at core temperature (section 19.3.7). If the hypothalamus is to control a constant core temperature, as is the case with endotherms, it is vital that information regarding changes in the external temperature is also transmitted to the hypothalamus. Without such information the body would gain or lose a great deal of heat before changes in core temperature would activate the hypothalamus to take corrective measures. This problem is overcome by having thermoreceptors in the skin. These detect changes in the environmental temperature and send nerve impulses to the hypothalamus before changes in the core temperature take place. There are two types of thermoreceptors, hot and cold, which generate nerve impulses when suitably stimulated. Some pass to the hypothalamus and others to the sensory areas of the cortex, where the sensations associated with temperature (feeling hot or cold) are experienced according to the intensity of stimulation, the duration and the numbers of receptors stimulated. There are estimated to be 150 000 cold receptors and 16 000 heat receptors in humans. This enables the body to make rapid and precise adjustments to maintain a constant core temperature. In the context of control systems, the skin receptors act as disturbance detectors, responding before changes in body temperature take place. Factors bringing about changes in internal temperature, such as metabolic rate or disease, will immediately affect the core temperature and in these situations be detected by thermoreceptors in the hypothalamus. In most cases the activity of both skin and hypothalamus receptors combine to control body temperature.

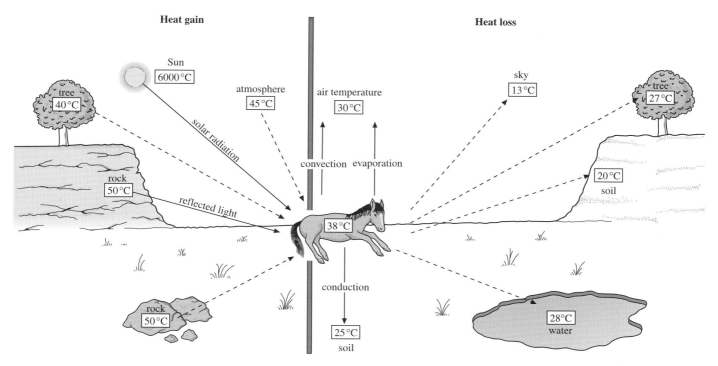

Fig 19.14 *Diagram showing the energy exchanges between a horse, with a body temperature of 38 °C, and the environment on a hot sunny day with an air temperature of 30 °C. The dotted lines represent radiation of heat.*

Heat gain centre and heat loss centre

Investigations into the activity of the hypothalamus have shown that there are two distinct centres concerned with temperature regulation, namely the **heat gain centre** and the **heat loss centre**. The functions of these centres are summarised in table 19.1. A summary of the control of temperature is shown in fig 19.15 and fig 19.16.

Fever

Some diseases produce an increase in core temperature known as **fever** as a result of the 'thermostat' in the hypothalamus being set at a higher temperature. It is believed that certain substances known as **pyrogens**, which may be toxins produced by pathogenic organisms or substances released by white blood cells known as neutrophils, directly affect the hypothalamus and increase the set-point. The raised body temperature stimulates the defence responses of the body and helps the destruction of pathogens. Antipyretic drugs such as aspirin and paracetamol lower the set-point and provide relief from the unpleasant symptoms of fever, but probably slow down the normal defence mechanisms. In cases of extremely high temperature these drugs are valuable in preventing irreversible damage to the brain.

Table 19.1 Functions of the heat loss and heat gain centres of the hypothalamus. These are situated in the anterior and posterior hypothalamus respectively and have antagonistic (opposite) effects.

Anterior hypothalamus *(heat loss centre)*	*Posterior hypothalamus* *(heat gain centre)*
Activated by increase in the temperature of the hypothalamus	Activated by nerve impulses from cold receptors in the skin or decrease in temperature of the hypothalamus
Increases vasodilation. Therefore increases heat loss from the skin by radiation, convection and conduction	Increases vasoconstriction. Therefore decreases heat loss from the skin by radiation, convection and conduction
Increases sweating and panting	Inhibits sweating and panting
Decreases metabolic activity	Increases metabolic activity through shivering and release of thyroxine and adrenaline
Decreases thickness of air layer by flattening hair (relaxing hair erector muscles)	Increases thickness of air layer by contraction of hair muscles, making hair stand on end

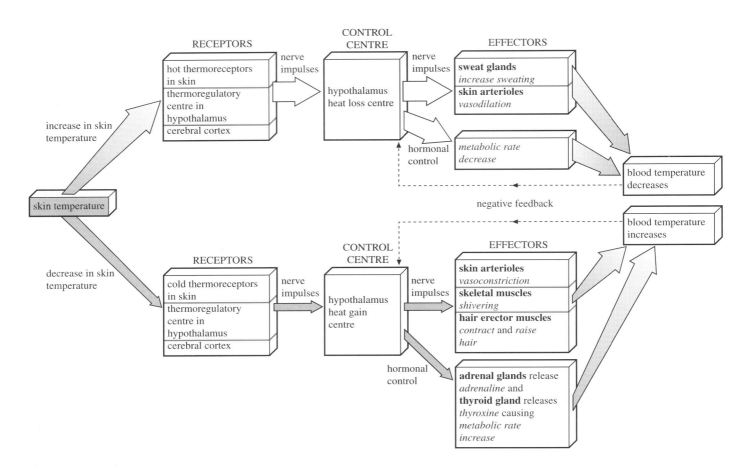

Fig 19.15 *Summary of reflex control of body temperature in a mammal involving the environment, hypothalamus, skin and blood temperature.*

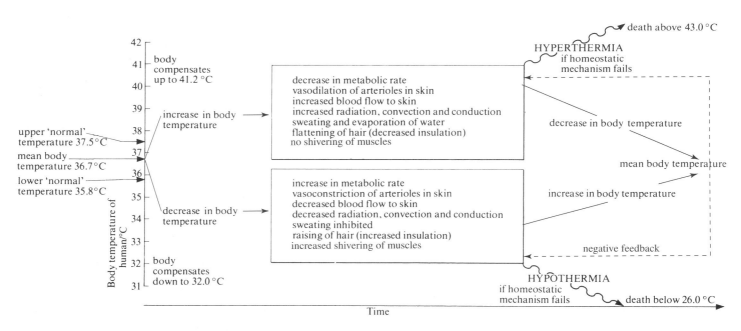

Fig 19.16 *Homeostatic control of human body temperature by physiological means. Behavioural changes also occur, for example adding or removing clothing, huddling in cold conditions to decrease surface area or stretching out in hot conditions to expose more skin.*

19.6 The onset of fever is often accompanied by shivering and a feeling of cold known as chill. Explain these symptoms in terms of the mechanism of control of body temperature.

19.5.5 Adaptations to extreme climates

Bergman's rule

The total heat production of endotherms depends upon the *volume* of the body whilst the rate of heat loss depends upon *surface area*. Volume increases more rapidly than surface area as the size of an animal increases. For this reason animals living in cold regions tend to be large, for example polar bears and whales, whilst animals living in hot climates are generally smaller, for instance insectivorous mammals. This phenomenon is known as **Bergman's rule** and is observed in many species, including the tiger, which decreases in size with distance from the Poles. There are exceptions to this rule, but the organisms concerned have adaptations favouring survival in these regions. For example, small mammals in temperate or arctic regions have a large appetite enabling them to maintain a high metabolic rate. They have small extremities, such as small ears, to reduce heat loss and are forced to hibernate in winter. Large mammals living in hot regions, such as the elephant and hippopotamus, have the opposite problems. The elephant has extremely large ears which are well supplied with blood, and flapping of these ears encourages heat loss by radiation and convection. The hippopotamus lacks sweat glands and adopts a similar behavioural response to temperature as the crocodile, in that it moves between land and water in an attempt to minimise the effects on its body of changes in temperature.

Allen's rule

Species living in colder climates have smaller extremities than related species in warmer climates. This is known as **Allen's rule** and may be seen in closely related species of, for instance, the fox (fig 19.17).

19.5.6 Adaptations to life at low temperatures

Dormancy

All ectotherms and many endotherms are unable to maintain a body temperature that allows normal activity during cold seasons, and they respond by showing some form of dormancy. Some of these responses are quite startling; for example, the larva of an insect parasite *Bracon*, which invades the Canadian wheat sawfly, is able to survive exposure to temperatures lower than −40 °C. This larva accumulates glycerol in its blood. The glycerol acts as an 'antifreeze' and is able to prevent the formation of ice crystals.

(a)

(b)

(c)

Fig 19.17 *Variation in ear length shown by three species of fox, each of which occupies a different geographical region. This is an example of Allen's rule. (a) The Arctic fox has the shortest ears, (b) the European fox, and (c) the Bat-eared fox from Botswana has the longest ears.*

Heat exchangers

Excessive heat loss to the environment from appendages is prevented in many organisms by the arrangement of blood vessels within the appendages. The arteries carrying blood towards the appendage are surrounded by veins carrying blood back to the body. The warm arterial blood from the body is cooled by the cold venous blood flowing towards the body. Similarly the cold venous blood from the appendage is warmed by the warm arterial blood flowing towards the appendage. Because the blood reaching the appendage is already cooled, the amount of heat lost is considerably reduced. This arrangement is known as a **countercurrent heat exchanger** and is found in the flippers and flukes of seals and whales, in the limbs of birds and mammals and in the blood supply to the testes in mammals (fig 19.18).

The countercurrent exchange principle is used for the transfer of materials other than heat, such as respiratory gases in fish gills and ions in the loop of Henle (sections 9.4.5 and 20.5.6).

Hypothermia

Hypothermia is a reduction in *core* temperature below about 32 °C. The technique of deliberately causing a state of hypothermia can be used in heart surgery since it allows the surgeon to carry out repairs to the heart without the risk of brain damage to the patient. By reducing the body temperature to 15 °C, the metabolic demands of the brain cells are so reduced that blood flow to the brain can be stopped, without any adverse effects, for up to one hour. For operations requiring a longer time than this, a heart–lung machine is used, in addition to hypothermia, to maintain blood circulation in the tissues.

19.5.7 Adaptations to life at high temperatures

Animals living in conditions where the air temperatures are higher than skin temperature gain heat, and the only means of reducing body temperature is by evaporation of water from the body surface. Hot regions may be, in addition, either particularly dry or humid, and this poses additional problems. In hot dry regions, although heat can be lost by the free evaporation of water, animals have the problem of finding adequate supplies of water to replace the water lost. In hot humid regions water is freely available but the humidity gradient between organisms and the environment often prevents evaporation. In this case behavioural mechanisms of temperature control often become more important. These involve taking advantage of the shade and breezes associated with humid forest and jungle habitats.

Bergman's rule

As noted in section 19.5.5, animals living in hot climates tend to be smaller than those living in cold climates. This can be explained by the fact that the amount of heat gained from the environment is approximately proportional to the body surface area. The majority of animals living in deserts, therefore, are small, such as the kangaroo rat (*Dipodomys*), and have fewer problems than larger animals, such as camels. In addition they are able to live in burrows in sand and soil where the microclimate poses fewer problems to life. Adaptations of the kangaroo rat for conserving water are discussed in section 20.3.1.

The camel – a case study

The camel is superbly adapted to a hot, dry climate in the following ways.

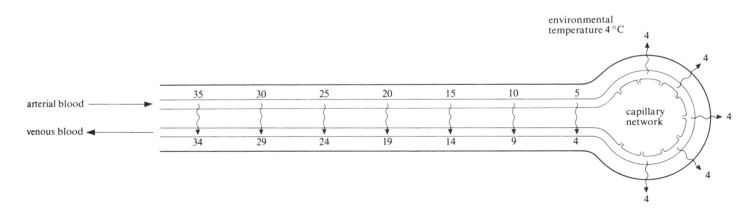

Fig 19.18 *Diagram showing the blood supply between the body of an endotherm with a stable temperature of 35 °C and an appendage such as a leg, in an environment at 4 °C. Heat flows from a warm body to a cool body and the rate of heat loss between the two bodies is proportional to the temperature difference between them. The countercurrent flow shown delivers blood to the capillary network at 5 °C and collects blood from it at 4 °C. The amount of heat lost to the environment is therefore proportional to the temperature difference of 1 °C. Likewise blood returning to the core of the body is only 1 °C cooler than the blood leaving the core. This mechanism prevents the excessive loss of metabolic energy and helps maintain the core temperature at 35 °C.*

- In hot dry conditions, with free access to water, it can regulate its body temperature between about 36 and 38 °C by losing heat through the evaporation of water from the body surface.

- If the camel is deprived of water, as say during a journey across the desert lasting several days, the difference in body temperature between morning and evening steadily increases according to the degree of dehydration. This daily fluctuation can be from 34 °C in the early morning to 41 °C in the late afternoon. By effectively being able to store up heat during the day the camel does not need to lose this heat by the evaporation of water. It functions, in fact, like a storage radiator. In a series of investigations carried out by Schmidt-Nielsen it was found that a 500 kg camel tolerating a 7 °C temperature rise stored approximately 12 000 kJ of heat energy. If this amount of heat were lost by the cooling effect of evaporation, in order to maintain a constant body temperature, it would require the loss of 5 dm³ of water. Instead the heat is lost by radiation, conduction and convection during the night.

- A second advantage of becoming 'partially ecto-thermic' during the day is that this reduces the temperature difference between the hot desert air and the camel, and therefore reduces the rate of heat gain.

- The fur of the camel acts as an efficient insulating barrier by reducing heat gain and water loss. In an experiment in which a camel was shorn like a sheep, the water loss increased by 50% over that of a control camel.

- The final significant advantage shown by the camel is its ability to tolerate dehydration. Most mammals cannot tolerate dehydration beyond a loss of body mass of 10–14%, but the camel can survive losses of up to 30%, because it is able to maintain its blood volume even when dehydrated. Heat death as a result of dehydration is due to a fall in volume of the blood. This results in the circulatory system being unable to transfer heat from the body core to the surface quickly enough to prevent overheating.

- Contrary to popular belief, the camel is unable to store water in advance of conditions of water shortage. It may be able to gain water from the oxidation of fat stored in the hump, but there is some doubt about the effectiveness of this.

- The camel is able to drink a vast volume of water in a short space of time to rehydrate the body tissues after a period of severe dehydration. For example, a 325 kg camel is known to have drunk 30 dm³ of water in less than ten minutes. This is roughly equivalent to a human of average build and weight drinking about 7 dm³ (12 pints) of water!

Fig 19.19 *(a) Diagram showing the blood supply to and from the liver and the positions of the bile duct and gut. (b) Map of the blood supply to and from the liver. Movement of bile is also shown.*

19.6 The liver

Apart from the skin, the liver is the largest visceral organ of the body. It is situated just below the diaphragm in the abdomen and makes up 3 to 5% of the body weight. It is basically an organ of homeostasis. It controls many metabolic activities essential for maintaining a constant blood composition. Many of its functions are associated with the metabolism of food brought from the gut. Because of its rich blood supply it also regulates many activities associated with blood and the circulatory system (fig 19.19). Despite the enormous variety of metabolic activities carried out by the liver its structure is relatively simple.

(a)

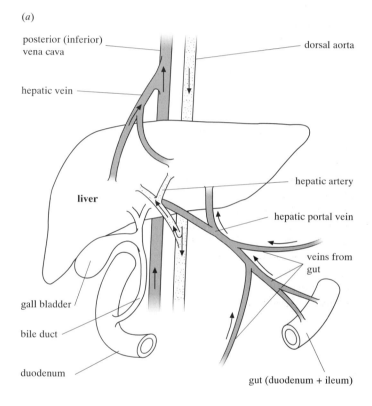

(b)

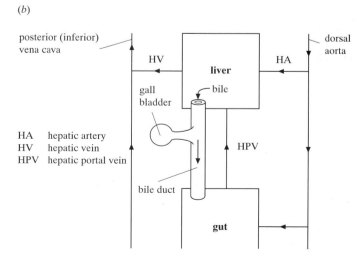

19.6.1 The position and structure of the liver

The liver is made up of several lobes and has a variable shape depending upon the amount of blood present within it. It is surrounded by a tough, fibrous capsule.

The cells of the liver are called **hepatocytes**. The only other cells found in the liver are nerve cells and cells associated with blood and lymph vessels. Hepatocytes have prominent nuclei and Golgi apparatus, many mitochondria and lysosomes, and are rich in glycogen granules and fat droplets. They are tightly packed together and, where their surface is in contact with blood vessels, there are microvilli which are used for the exchange of materials between the two.

The pig liver is convenient to study because the functional units of the liver, known as lobules, are more clearly defined than in other mammals. Each lobule has a diameter of about 1 mm (fig 19.20). Diagrams of the structure are shown in figs 19.21a and b. Between the lobules are branches of the hepatic artery, hepatic portal vein and bile duct. The hepatic portal vein carries absorbed food materials from the gut. The hepatic artery carries oxygenated blood. These blood vessels join to supply blood to the hepatocytes.

At the centre of each lobule is a branch of the hepatic vein. The hepatic vein is connected to the hepatic artery and hepatic portal vein by 'sinusoids'. These are blood spaces rather than blood vessels, but serve the same function. They radiate like the spokes of a wheel from the centre to the edges of the lobule. Blood flows slowly from the hepatic artery and hepatic portal vein to the hepatic vein past the hepatocytes, which also form rows across the lobule. As blood flows along the sinusoids, exchange of materials takes place between the blood and the hepatocytes, across the microvilli of the hepatocytes which touch the sinusoids. The sinusoids have a lining of thin endothelial cells containing pores with a diameter of up to 10 nm.

The sinusoids alternate with **bile canaliculi**. These are small canals which carry bile, made by the hepatocytes which line them, to the branches of the bile duct. Note that the bile flows in the opposite direction to the blood and does not mix with the blood (fig 19.21).

One other type of cell is found in the liver, known as the **Kupffer cell**. Kupffer cells are found attached to the walls of the sinusoids, but are now known to be macrophages (section 14.3.2). They are phagocytic and are involved in the breakdown of old red blood cells and the ingestion of potentially harmful bacteria.

19.6.2 Functions of the liver

It has been estimated that the liver carries out several hundred separate functions involving thousands of different chemical reactions. A vast amount of blood flows through it at any given time (approximately 20% of the total blood volume). The liver and the kidneys between them are the major organs responsible for maintaining the steady state of the blood. All food materials absorbed from the alimentary canal pass directly to the liver where they are stored or converted into some other form as required by the body at that time.

Carbohydrate metabolism

Role of insulin. Sugars such as glucose enter the liver from the gut by the hepatic portal vein, which is the only blood vessel in the body having an extremely variable sugar content. This gives a clue to the role of the liver in carbohydrate metabolism as the organ which maintains the blood glucose level at approximately 90 mg glucose per 100 cm^3 blood. The liver prevents blood glucose levels from varying up and down according to how recently food has been eaten. Low levels of glucose would be particularly damaging because some tissues cannot store glucose, such as the brain. All hexose sugars, including galactose and fructose, are converted to glucose by the liver and stored as the insoluble polysaccharide glycogen. Up to 100 g of glycogen are stored here but more is stored in muscle. The conversion of glucose to glycogen is known as **glycogenesis** and is stimulated by the presence of insulin. This is a hormone produced by the pancreas in response to high blood sugar levels (section 17.6):

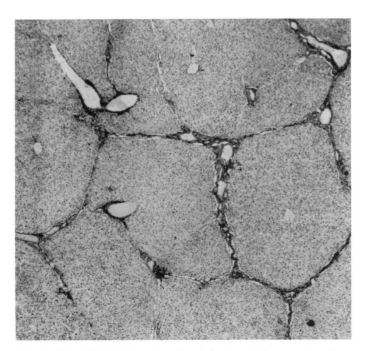

Fig 19.20 *TS pig liver showing lobules. In the centre of each lobule is a branch of the hepatic vein. Between the lobules (at the 'corners') are branches of the hepatic portal vein, hepatic artery and bile duct. The lobules are made up of rows of liver cells called hepatocytes with blood spaces and branches of the bile duct between.*

$$\text{glucose} \underset{\text{(phosphorylation)}}{\overset{\text{insulin}}{\rightleftharpoons}} \text{glucose phosphate} \rightleftharpoons \underset{\text{(condensation)}}{} \text{glycogen}$$

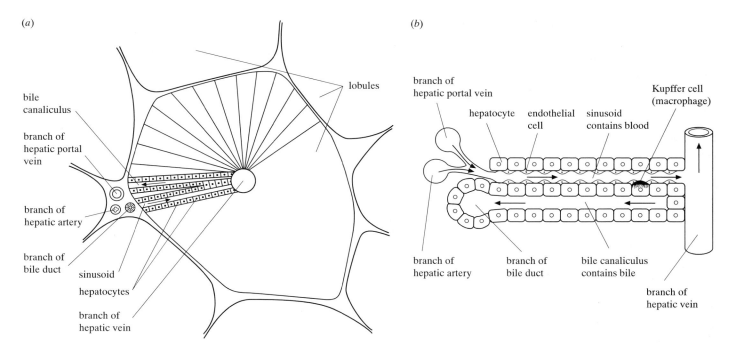

(a)

lobules

bile
canaliculus

branch of
hepatic portal
vein

branch of
hepatic artery

branch of
bile duct

sinusoid

hepatocytes

branch of
hepatic vein

(b)

branch of
hepatic portal vein

hepatocyte

endothelial
cell

sinusoid
contains blood

Kupffer cell
(macrophage)

branch of
hepatic artery

branch of
bile duct

bile canaliculus
contains bile

branch of
hepatic vein

Fig 19.21 *(a) Diagram of a transverse section of a liver lobule. (Arrows indicate flow of blood in sinusoids and flow of bile in canaliculi.) (b) A simplified diagram of part of a liver lobule.*

Role of glucagon. Glycogen is broken down to glucose to prevent the blood glucose level falling below $60\,mg$ per $100\,cm^3$ blood. This process is called **glycogenolysis** and involves the activation of a phosphorylase enzyme by the hormone glucagon. Glucagon is made in the pancreas and is released when blood sugar levels fall (section 17.6.6). In times of danger, stress or cold this activity is also stimulated by adrenaline, released by the adrenal medulla, and noradrenaline released both by the adrenal medulla and the endings of the sympathetic neurones (section 17.6.5):

$$\text{glycogen} \xrightleftharpoons{\text{phosphorylase}} \text{glucose phosphate} \rightleftharpoons \text{glucose}$$
$$\text{(store)} \qquad\qquad\qquad\qquad\qquad\qquad\qquad \text{(free)}$$

Lactic acid from anaerobic respiration. Muscle does not convert glycogen directly to glucose as shown above because it does not release glucose into the blood for the rest of the body, unlike the liver. Muscle only breaks down glycogen if it needs glucose for its own respiration, in which case the glycogen is converted to glucose phosphate (as above), but is then converted to pyruvate (glycolysis) which is used to produce ATP during aerobic or anaerobic respiration. Lactic acid (lactate) produced by anaerobic respiration in skeletal muscle can be converted later into glucose and hence glycogen in the liver:

$$\text{lactate} \longrightarrow \text{pyruvate} \longrightarrow \text{glucose} \longrightarrow \text{glycogen}$$

Gluconeogenesis. When the demand for glucose has exhausted the glycogen store in the liver,

glucose can be synthesised from non-carbohydrate sources. This is called **gluconeogenesis**. Low blood glucose levels (hypoglycaemia) stimulate the sympathetic nervous system to release adrenaline which helps satisfy immediate demand as described above. Low blood glucose levels also stimulate the hypothalamus to release CRF (section 17.6.5) which in turn releases adrenocorticotrophic hormone (ACTH) from the anterior pituitary gland. This leads to the synthesis and release of increasing amounts of the glucocorticoid hormones, particularly cortisol (also known as hydrocortisone). These stimulate the release of amino acids, glycerol and fatty acids, present in the tissues, into the blood and increase the rate of synthesis of enzymes in the liver which convert amino acids and glycerol into glucose. (Fatty acids are converted into acetyl coenzyme A and used directly in the Krebs cycle.)

Manufacture of fats. Carbohydrate in the body which cannot be used or stored as glycogen is converted into fats and stored.

A summary of carbohydrate metabolism involving the liver, muscles and tissues is shown in fig 19.22.

Protein metabolism

The liver plays an important role in protein metabolism which may be considered under the headings of:

- deamination;
- urea formation;
- transamination;
- plasma protein synthesis.

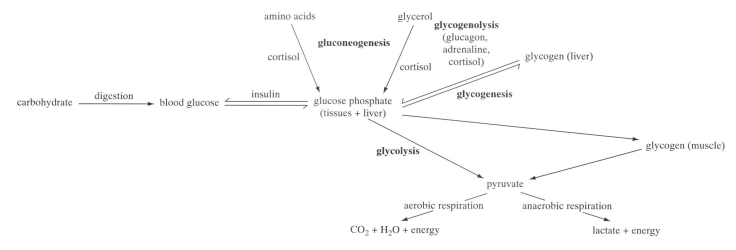

Fig 19.22 *Summary diagram of carbohydrate metabolism.*

Deamination. The body is unable to store excess amino acids taken up in the diet. Those not immediately required for protein synthesis or gluconeogenesis (making glucose) are deaminated in the liver. This process is described in section 20.4.

Transamination. This is the synthesis of amino acids by the transfer of the amino group from an amino acid to another organic acid. The general principle underlying these reactions is the exchange of chemical groups between the amino acid and the other organic acid:

NH₂ — C — COOH   +   O = C — COOH
(A) amino acid A   organic acid B

NH₂ — C — COOH   +   O = C — COOH
(B) amino acid B   organic acid A

For example, the amino acid, glutamic acid, could be synthesised by the following reactions:

NH₂ — C — COOH   +   O = C — COOH
CH₃ alanine   α-ketoglutaric acid

NH₂ — C — COOH   +   O = C — COOH
glutamic acid   pyruvic acid

Transamination is the means of producing amino acids which are deficient in the diet, and this is yet another of the liver's homeostatic mechanisms. The 'essential' amino acids, described in section 8.7.8, cannot be synthesised by transamination in the liver and must be obtained from the diet.

Plasma protein production. Plasma proteins are vital components of plasma and the majority of them are synthesised from amino acids in the liver.

- Albumin is the commonest protein and about 4 g per 100 cm³ is normally present in the blood. It plays an important part in exerting an osmotic potential which opposes the hydrostatic pressure developed in blood vessels. The antagonistic effects of these two factors maintain the balance of fluids inside and outside of blood vessels (section 14.6). Albumins also act as transport molecules within the blood, carrying substances such as calcium, bile, salts, and some steroid hormones.
- Globulins are very large molecules and blood carries about 3.4 g per 100 cm³. α- and β-globulins transport hormones (including thyroxine and insulin), cholesterol, lipids, iron and the vitamins B_{12}, A, D and K. γ-globulins are antibodies and are produced by lymphocytes and other cells of the immune system (not the liver). They are involved in the immune response (section 14.9). The other main plasma proteins are the blood-clotting factors prothrombin and fibrinogen, and their functions are described in section 14.8.5.

Fat metabolism

The liver is involved in the processing and transport of fats rather than their storage. Liver cells carry out the following functions:

- converting excess carbohydrates to fat;
- removing cholesterol from the blood and breaking it down or, when necessary, synthesising it;

- if glucose is in short supply, the liver can break down fats into fatty acids and glycerol for respiration. Fatty acids are converted to acetyl groups which combine with coenzyme A to form acetyl coenzyme A. This enters Krebs' cycle for oxidation as described in section 9.3.5. Fatty acids can also be exported from the liver after conversion to other chemicals. Glycerol can be converted to glucose as previously described under gluconeogenesis.

Vitamin storage

The main vitamins stored in the liver are the fat-soluble vitamins A, D, E and K. The livers of certain fish, such as cod and halibut, contain high concentrations of vitamins A and D. Vitamin K is a vital factor in blood clotting.

The liver also stores some of the water-soluble vitamins, namely vitamins B and C, especially those of the B group such as nicotinic acid, vitamin B_{12} and folic acid. Vitamin B_{12} and folic acid are required by the bone marrow for the formation of red blood cells and deficiency of these vitamins leads to various degrees of anaemia.

Mineral storage

Those elements required in small amounts such as copper, zinc, cobalt and molybdenum (trace elements) are stored in the liver along with iron and potassium (see breakdown of red blood cells below). Approximately one-thousandth of the dry mass of liver tissue in humans is iron. Most of this iron is temporary and comes from the breakdown of old red blood cells. It is stored here for later use in the manufacture of new red blood cells in the bone marrow.

Storage of blood

The blood vessels leaving the spleen and gut join to form the hepatic portal vein and, together with the blood vessels of the liver, they contain a large volume of blood which acts as a reservoir, although the blood is constantly moving through it. Sympathetic neurones and adrenaline from the adrenal medulla can constrict many of these hepatic vessels and make more blood available to the general circulation. If the blood volume increases, as for example during a blood transfusion, the hepatic veins along with other veins can dilate to take up the excess volume.

Making red blood cells

The liver of the fetus is responsible for red blood cell production but this function is gradually taken over by cells of the bone marrow (section 14.3.2). Once this process is established, the liver takes the opposite role and assists in breaking down red blood cells and haemoglobin.

Breakdown of haemoglobin

Red blood cells have a life-span of about 120 days. They are then broken down by the activity of phagocytic macrophage cells in the liver, spleen and bone marrow. The haemoglobin they contain is released and dissolves in the plasma. It is taken up from here by macrophages (special white blood cells) in the liver, spleen and lymph glands. The macrophages in the liver are called Kuppfer cells. Inside the macrophages haemoglobin is broken down into **haem** and **globin**. Globin is the protein part of the molecule and is broken down to its individual amino acids. These can be used according to demand. The iron is removed from haem and the remaining part of the molecule forms a green pigment called **biliverdin**. This is converted to **bilirubin**, which is yellow and a component of bile. The accumulation of bilirubin in the blood is a characteristic symptom of liver disease and produces a yellowing of the skin, a condition known as **jaundice**.

The iron is not wasted. In the blood it can combine with a plasma protein to form a complex called **transferrin**. The iron may then be re-used by cells in the bone marrow to make more haemoglobin. Alternatively it may be stored in the liver. In this case it is taken up by hepatocytes and stored as a compound called **ferritin**.

Bile production

Bile is a viscous, greenish yellow fluid secreted by hepatocytes. Between $500-1000 \, cm^3$ of bile are produced each day and stored and concentrated in the gall bladder. It is composed of about 98% water, 0.8% bile salts, 0.2% bile pigments, 0.7% inorganic salts and 0.6% cholesterol.

Bile is secreted into the duodenum where it is involved in digestion and the absorption of fats and is a means of excretion of bile pigments. The stimulus for its release into the duodenum is the presence of the hormone **cholecystokinin (CCK)**, also known as **pancreozymin** (section 8.4.3).

Bile salts are made from the steroid **cholesterol** which is synthesised in hepatocytes. The commonest bile salts are sodium glycocholate and sodium taurocholate. They are secreted with cholesterol and phospholipids in the form of large spherical particles called **micelles**. Molecules of bile salts resemble detergents in having a water-soluble (hydrophilic) end and a lipid-soluble (hydrophobic) end. The cholesterol and phospholipids hold the bile salt molecules together so that all the hydrophobic ends of the molecules point the same way. Inside the gut the hydrophobic ends attach to lipid droplets in the food whilst the other ends are attached to water. This decreases the surface tension of the lipid droplets and enables the lipid molecules to separate, forming an emulsion of smaller droplets. These have an increased surface area for attack by the enzyme pancreatic lipase which converts the lipids into glycerol and fatty acids so that they can then be absorbed from the gut. Bile salts also activate the enzyme lipase, but their action, in all cases, is purely physical. They are not enzymes. Too little bile salt in bile increases the concentration of cholesterol which may precipitate out in the gall bladder or bile duct as cholesterol gall stones. These can block the bile duct and cause severe discomfort.

Bile pigments have no function and are excretory products.

Cholesterol production

Cholesterol is produced by the liver and is used as the starting point for the synthesis of other steroid molecules. The major source of cholesterol is the diet, and many dairy products are rich in cholesterol or fatty acids from which cholesterol can be synthesised. Thyroxine both stimulates cholesterol formation in the liver and increases its rate of excretion in the bile. Excessive amounts of cholesterol in the blood can be harmful. It can be deposited in the walls of arteries, leading to **atherosclerosis** (narrowing of the arteries) and increased risk of the formation of a blood clot which may block blood vessels, a condition known as **thrombosis**. This is often fatal if it occurs in the coronary artery in the wall of the heart (coronary thrombosis or 'heart attack') or brain (cerebral thrombosis or 'stroke'). Although cholesterol is harmful in excess, it is essential to have some in the diet for the reasons stated.

Hormone breakdown

The liver destroys almost all hormones to various extents. Testosterone and aldosterone are rapidly destroyed, whereas insulin, glucagon and gut hormones, female sex hormones, adrenal hormones, ADH and thyroxine are destroyed less rapidly. In this way the liver has a homeostatic effect on the activities of these hormones.

Detoxification

Detoxification means the removal of toxins, or poisons. These are usually naturally occurring compounds which can be toxic if allowed to build up in the body. Detoxification is part of homeostasis and helps to maintain the composition of blood in a steady state. Bacteria and other pathogens are removed from the blood in the sinusoids by Kupffer cells, but the toxins they produce are dealt with by biochemical reactions in the hepatocytes.

Toxins are rendered harmless by one or more of the following reactions: oxidation, reduction, methylation (the addition of a $-CH_3$ group) or combination with another organic or inorganic molecule. Following detoxification these substances, now harmless, are excreted by the kidney. The major toxic substance in the blood, though, is ammonia, whose fate is described in section 20.4.

The detoxification process also removes harmful substances taken into the body such as alcohol and nicotine. Alcohol taken in excess over a period of time can result in liver breakdown, such as cirrhosis of the liver in alcoholics. It is removed by the enzyme alcohol dehydrogenase.

Some of the metabolic activities of the liver may be potentially harmful and evidence is growing that certain food additives may be converted into poisonous or carcinogenic (cancer-producing) substances by liver activity. Even the pain killer paracetamol, if taken in excess, is changed into a substance which affects enzyme systems and can cause liver, and other tissue, damage.

Heat production

Evidence is accumulating to show that the widespread belief that the metabolic activity of the liver results in it being a major source of heat production in the body of mammals may be false. Many of the liver's metabolic activities are endothermic and therefore require heat energy rather than release it. Under conditions of extreme cold the hypothalamus will increase the energy-releasing activity of the liver by stimulating the release of the hormones adrenaline and thyroxine. At 'normal' temperatures, however, the liver has been shown to be 'thermally neutral' but is usually 1–2 °C hotter than the rest of the body core.

Fig 19.23 summarises the functions of the liver.

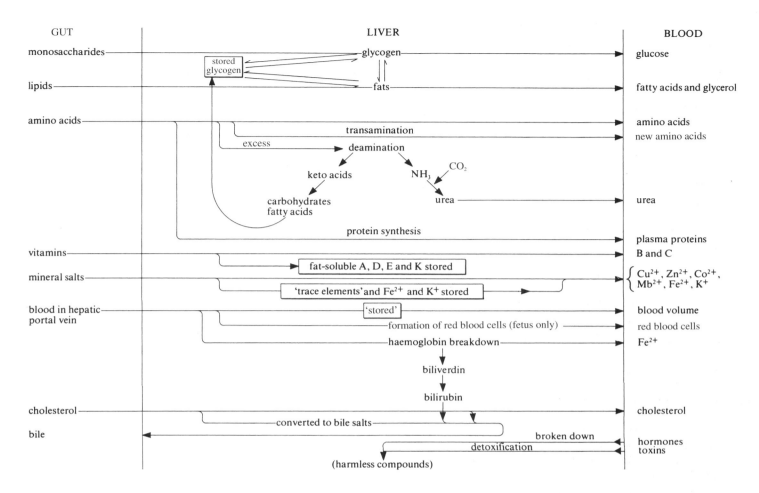

Fig 19.23 *Summary diagram of the functions of the liver.*

Chapter Twenty

Excretion and osmoregulation

Excretion and osmoregulation are two important homeostatic processes occurring in living organisms, helping them to maintain a constant internal environment, or steady state.

Excretion

Excretion is the removal from the body of waste products of metabolism. If allowed to accumulate these would prevent the maintenance of a steady state. Note that the definition states 'products of metabolism'. This means that the waste product has been made by the body itself. **Egestion** (or defaecation) is the removal of undigested food from the gut and is not regarded as excretion because the material taken into the gut through the mouth is not made by the body itself. The only excretory products in the faeces are bile pigments. These are breakdown products of the haem of haemoglobin. You should also be careful to distinguish between excretion and **secretion**. Secretion usually involves the release of useful substances such as hormones from cells (although a few waste products are secreted into the kidney tubules during excretion, as we shall see later).

Osmoregulation

Osmoregulation is the maintenance of constant osmotic conditions in the body. It involves regulation of the water content and solute concentration of body fluids, particularly of sodium, potassium and chloride ions. Body fluids include cell contents as well as fluids outside cells such as blood plasma, tissue fluid and lymph. It is vital that the composition of these fluids should remain constant in order for the cells to work efficiently.

20.1 The significance of excretion and osmoregulation

Excretion and osmoregulation have a number of functions which may be summarised as follows.

- **Removal of unwanted by-products of metabolic pathways**. This is necessary in order to prevent unbalancing the chemical equilibria of reactions. Many metabolic reactions are reversible and the direction of the reaction is determined by the relative concentrations of reactants and products. For example, in the enzyme-catalysed reaction:

$$A + B \rightleftharpoons C + D$$
$$\text{(reactants)} \qquad \text{(products)}$$

the continued production of C, a vital requirement of metabolism, is ensured by the removal of D, a waste product. This will ensure that the *equilibrium* of the reaction favours the reaction to proceed from left to right in the above equation.

- **Removal of toxic wastes**. This is the removal of waste products of metabolism which, if they accumulated, would affect the metabolic activity of the organism. Many of these substances are toxic, acting as inhibitors of enzymes involved in metabolic pathways.

- **Regulation of ionic concentration of body fluids**. Salts dissociate into ions in the aqueous conditions inside living organisms. For example, sodium chloride, taken in as part of the diet, exists in body fluids as sodium ions (Na^+) and chloride ions (Cl^-). If the balance of these and other ions is not carefully regulated within narrow limits, the efficiency of many cell activities is reduced; for instance a reduction in sodium ion concentration leads to a decrease in nervous coordination. Other important ions whose concentrations must be carefully regulated are K^+, Mg^{2+}, Ca^{2+}, Fe^{2+}, H^+, Cl^-, I^-, PO_4^{3-} and HCO_3^-, as they are vital for many metabolic activities including enzyme activity, protein synthesis, production of hormones and respiratory pigments, membrane permeability, electrical activity and muscle contraction. Their effects on water content, solute potential and pH of body fluids are described below.

- **Regulation of water content of body fluids**. The amount of water within the body fluids and its regulation is one of the major problems faced by organisms. The solutions to this problem have produced some of the most important structural and functional adaptations shown by organisms. The mechanisms of obtaining water, preventing water loss and eliminating water are varied, but they are of great importance in maintaining the solute potential and volume of body fluids at a steady state, as described later in this chapter. The solute potential of body fluids depends upon the relative amounts of solute and solvent (water) present. The mechanisms of regulation of solutes and water are known as **osmoregulation**.

- **Regulation of pH**. The nature of pH and methods of its measurement are described in appendix A1.1.5 but the mechanisms of excreting those ions which have a major influence on pH, such as hydrogen and hydrogencarbonate ions, are considered in this chapter. For example, the pH of urine may vary between 4.5 and 8 in order to maintain the pH of the body fluids at a fairly constant level.

20.1.1   Excretory products

The major excretory products of animals and plants, and their sources, are as follows.

- **Nitrogenous compounds such as urea, ammonia and uric acid**. These come from breakdown of proteins, nucleic acids or excess amino acids. They are discussed in more detail in section 20.2.
- **Oxygen from photosynthesis** in plants, algae and some bacteria. Some of this may be used in respiration.
- **Carbon dioxide from cell respiration**. In autotrophic organisms this may be used as a source of carbon.
- **Bile pigments** from the breakdown of haem in the liver.

20.1.2   Excretory structures

The following structures are used for excretion in different animals:

- the cell surface membrane of unicellular organisms;
- the Malpighian tubules and tracheae of arthropods;
- the kidneys, liver, gills and skin of fish and amphibia;
- the kidneys, liver, lungs and skin of vertebrates.

The cells of organisms having a relatively simple structure are usually in direct contact with the environment and their excretory products are immediately removed by diffusion. As organisms increase in complexity, excretory organs develop to remove excretory products from the body and pass them to the external environment. The most important excretory organs in vertebrates are the skin, lungs, liver and kidney. The roles of the first three only will be described at this stage.

Skin

Water, urea and salts are actively secreted from capillaries in the skin by the tubules of the sweat glands. Sweat is secreted onto the skin where the water evaporates. In this way heat is lost from the body and this helps to regulate the body temperature.

Lungs

Carbon dioxide and water vapour diffuse from the moist surfaces of the lungs, which in mammals are the only excretory organs for carbon dioxide. Some of the water released at the lung surface is metabolic, that is, produced as a waste product of respiration, but its exact origin is not really important in view of the large volume of water contained within the body.

Liver

Considering the many homeostatic roles of the liver described in section 19.6.2 it is not surprising that these include excretion. Bile pigments are excretory products from the breakdown of the haemoglobin of old red blood cells. They pass to the duodenum in the bile for removal from the body along with the faeces, for whose colour they are partly responsible. The most important excretory role of the liver is the formation of urea from excess amino acids (section 20.4).

20.1.3   Excretion in plants

Plants do not have as many problems regarding excretion as do animals. This is because of fundamental differences in physiology and mode of life between animals and plants. Plants are producers and they synthesise all their organic requirements according to demand. For example, plants manufacture only the amount of protein necessary to satisfy immediate demand. There is never an excess of protein and therefore very little excretion of nitrogenous waste substances. If proteins are broken down into amino acids, the latter can be recycled into new proteins. Three of the waste substances produced by certain metabolic activities in plants, that is oxygen, carbon dioxide and water, are raw materials (reactants) for other reactions, and excesses of carbon dioxide and water are used up in this way. Water is also a solvent. The only major gaseous excretory product of plants is oxygen. During light periods the rate of production of oxygen is far greater than the plant's demand for oxygen in respiration and this escapes from plants into the environment by diffusion.

Many organic waste products of plants are stored within dead permanent tissues such as the 'heartwood' or within leaves or bark which are removed periodically. The bulk of most perennial plants is composed of dead tissues into which excretory materials are passed. In this state they have no adverse effects upon the activities of the living tissues. Similarly, many mineral salts, taken up as ions, may accumulate. Organic acids, which might prove harmful to plants, often combine with excess cations and precipitate out as insoluble crystals which can be safely stored in plant cells. For example, calcium ions and sulphate ions are taken up together, but sulphate is used up immediately in amino acid synthesis leaving an excess of calcium ions. These combine with oxalic and pectic acids to form harmless insoluble products such as calcium oxalate and calcium pectate. Substances are not only eliminated through leaf loss but also through petals, fruits and seeds, although this excretory function is not the primary function of their dispersal. Aquatic plants lose most of their metabolic wastes by diffusion directly into the water surrounding them.

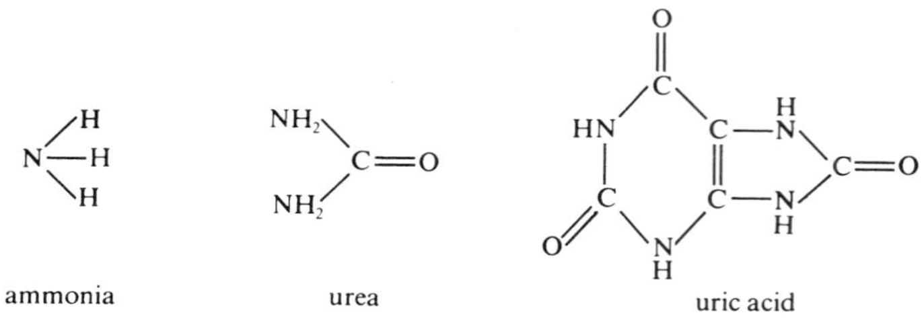

Fig 20.1 *Molecular structure of the three main nitrogenous excretory products.*

20.2 Nitrogenous excretory products and environment

Nitrogenous waste products are produced by the breakdown of proteins, nucleic acids and excess amino acids. The first product of the breakdown of excess amino acids is ammonia. It is produced by removal of the amino group from amino acids, a process called **deamination** (section 20.4). Ammonia may be excreted immediately or converted into the nitrogen-containing compounds urea or uric acid (fig 20.1). The exact nature of the excretory product is determined mainly by the availability of water to the organism (that is, its habitat), and the extent to which the organism controls water loss (table 20.1). The correlation with habitat may be summarised thus:

ammonia   aquatic (water conservation not a problem)
urea   aquatic/terrestrial
uric acid   terrestrial

20.2.1 Ammonia

The major source of ammonia is the deamination of excess amino acids. Ammonia is extremely toxic and must be eliminated. Being very soluble, it can be eliminated from the body rapidly and safely if diluted in a sufficient volume of water. This presents no real problems to organisms which have ready access to water but this applies only to those organisms living in freshwater. It is

Table 20.1 Summary of the relationship between excretory products and habitat of representative animal groups.

Animal	Excretory product	Habitat
protozoan	ammonia	aquatic
terrestrial insect	uric acid	terrestrial
freshwater bony fish	ammonia	aquatic
marine bony fish	urea, trimethylamine oxide	aquatic
bird	uric acid	terrestrial
mammal	urea	terrestrial

therefore excreted rapidly as ammonium ions (NH_4^+) in most aquatic organisms, from protozoa to amphibia, before it reaches concentrations which are toxic to the organism.

Marine and terrestrial organisms have an acute problem of gaining or conserving water respectively. Therefore very little is available for the elimination of nitrogenous waste. Table 20.1 reveals that organisms living in these environments have developed alternative means of nitrogen excretion. These involve the development of many anatomical, biochemical, physiological and behavioural mechanisms involving the elimination of nitrogenous waste whilst maintaining the composition of the body fluids at a steady state.

20.2.2 Urea

Urea is formed in the liver as described in section 20.4. It is much less toxic than ammonia and is the main nitrogenous excretory product in mammals. Its excretion is described in section 20.5.

20.2.3 Uric acid

Uric acid and its salts are ideal excretory products for terrestrial organisms and essential for organisms such as land-living insects and birds which produce shelled eggs. They combine a high nitrogen content with low toxicity and low solubility. They can be stored in cells, tissues and organs without producing any toxic or harmful osmoregulatory effects, and they require very little water for their excretion. As the concentration of uric acid in the tissue rises it settles out as a solid precipitate. The details of uric acid excretion are described in section 20.3.3. Humans excrete small quantities of uric acid but this is produced from the breakdown of nucleic acids and not from the breakdown of proteins. Approximately 1 g of uric acid is excreted in urine per day.

20.3 Nitrogenous excretion and osmoregulation in representative animals

Throughout this review it should be remembered that the environment influences the nature of the excretory product and the process of osmoregulation. The processes of nitrogenous excretion and osmoregulation involve the same body structures. This is because elimination of nitrogenous waste is usually associated with problems of gaining or losing water. The two processes will therefore be considered together.

20.3.1 The effect of environment on osmoregulation

The bodies of many aquatic organisms have a water potential which is higher than that of the environment (the body contents are less concentrated). The body therefore *loses* water by osmosis. The water loss is replaced in various ways, including drinking and eating. Organisms with bodies of lower water potential than the surrounding water (body contents more concentrated) *gain* water by osmosis. In order to minimise these exchanges the organisms often have an impermeable outer covering.

All terrestrial organisms face the problem of water loss from their body fluids to the environment. The body fluids of these organisms are maintained by specialised osmoregulatory/excretory organs, such as Malpighian tubules and kidneys. A balance must be achieved between the amount of water lost and gained. The problems of water balance are described in detail in section 20.6.

Osmoregulation also involves regulation of solute concentrations by the processes of diffusion and active transport.

Adaptations to severe drought

The kangaroo rat (*Dipodomys*) is remarkable among mammals in being able to tolerate drought conditions in the deserts of North America. It flourishes in these conditions by possessing a unique combination of structural, physiological and behavioural adaptations. Water loss by evaporation from the lungs is reduced by exhaling air at a temperature below body temperature. As air is inhaled it gains heat from the nasal passages which are cooled as a result. During exhalation water vapour in the warm air condenses on the nasal passages and is conserved. The kangaroo rat feeds on dry seeds and other dry plant material and does not drink. Water produced by the chemical reactions of respiration, and that present in minute amounts in its food, are its only sources of water. The classic investigations by Knut Schmidt-Nielsen (summarised in table 20.2) revealed the overall water metabolism balance for a kangaroo rat weighing 35 g metabolising 100 g of barley in experimental surroundings at 25 °C and a relative humidity of 20%. Throughout this period the only source of water was the barley grain.

Finally the kangaroo rat avoids excessive evaporative water losses in the wild by spending much of its time in the relatively humid atmosphere of its underground burrow.

Table 20.2 Water metabolism for a kangaroo rat under experimental conditions. The absorbed water was the water present in the food.

Water gains	cm^3	Water losses	cm^3
oxidation water from cell respiration	54.0	urine	13.5
absorbed water from food	6.0	faeces	2.6
		evaporation	43.9
Total water gain	60.0	Total water loss	60.0

The other spectacular example of water conservation is the camel, whose physiological adaptations are described in section 19.5.7.

20.3.2 Protozoans

Protozoans are single-celled organisms belonging to the Kingdom Protoctista (section 2.8.4). They are found in freshwater and marine habitats and provide an excellent example of the basic problems of osmoregulation faced by animal cells. An animal cell which is unprotected by any osmoregulatory mechanisms will die if its contents have a different water potential to their environment, as demonstrated by the red blood cell in fig 5.19. A single cell like a protozoan must therefore have an osmoregulatory mechanism. The cell contents are separated from the external environment only by a partially permeable cell surface membrane.

Excretion

Excretion of carbon dioxide and ammonia occurs by diffusion over the entire surface of the cell. This has a relatively large surface area to volume ratio which allows the efficient removal of waste substances.

Osmoregulation in freshwater species

Remember that the more concentrated a solution, the lower its water potential (and solute potential) (section 5.9.8 osmosis). When a cell is in a solution, water moves from the region of higher water potential to the region of lower water potential.

All freshwater species of protozoans have a lower water potential than their surroundings (more concentrated solution in their cells). There is therefore a constant tendency for water to enter the cell by osmosis through the cell surface membrane. The problem is overcome by the presence of organelles known as **contractile vacuoles**. These remove water which enters the cell by osmosis, therefore preventing the cell from increasing in size and bursting. The exact location and structure of the contractile vacuole is extremely variable. In *Amoeba* a contractile vacuole can form anywhere within the cell and release its fluid into the external environment at any point on its outer surface (fig 20.2). In *Paramecium* there are two contractile vacuoles with fixed positions (fig 20.3, see also fig 2.32). The method of functioning, however, appears to be the same in all species. Small vesicles (or canals in some species, such as *Paramecium*) in the cytoplasm fill with fluid from the cytoplasm. At first the fluid has the same composition, and therefore the same water potential, as the cytoplasm (fig 20.4). Most of the ions are then pumped out of the fluid by active transport, using energy in the form of ATP supplied by mitochondria that surround the vesicles. The remaining fluid in the vesicles is mostly water and is loaded into the contractile vacuole by the vesicle. The contractile vacuole gradually fills. Its membrane is almost

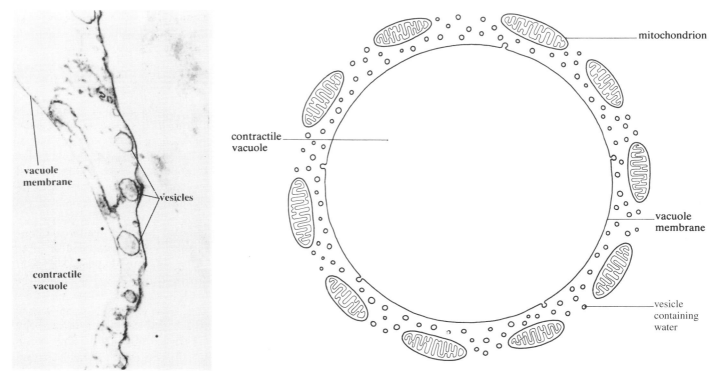

Fig 20.2 *Electron micrograph and diagram of contractile vacuole of* Amoeba. *The tiny vesicles fill with fluid from the cytoplasm. Ions in the fluid are then pumped back into the cytoplasm before the vesicles fuse with the membrane of the contractile vacuole, discharging water into the vacuole.*

completely impermeable to water so, despite its contents being very dilute (high water potential), water cannot escape back into the cytoplasm by osmosis. When it reaches a certain size, the contractile vacuole fuses with the cell surface membrane, contracts suddenly and releases its water.

Osmoregulation in marine species

Many of the marine protozoans do not have functional contractile vacuoles because their cell contents have the same water potential as sea water.

20.3.3   Insects

The great majority of insects are adapted for life on land. One of the major problems of life on land is the prevention of water loss. Adaptations for preventing water loss include:

- an almost impermeable waxy layer covering their exoskeletons which reduces water loss from the body surface;
- the only openings to the body for gaseous exchange are pairs of small holes in certain segments – these are called **spiracles**;
- there are valve-like structures in the spiracles to reduce water loss from the tubes that lead from the spiracles to the cells (the gaseous exchange system described in section 9.4.4);

- the excretory product is semi-solid, not liquid (see below);
- cleidoic eggs, meaning that the embryo develops inside an egg with a relatively impermeable shell that prevents water loss.

The strong exoskeleton is covered by a thin waterproof layer, the epicuticle ($0.3\,\mu$m thick). Water loss by evaporation is prevented by the way the molecules are organised. A highly organised single layer of lipid molecules is covered by several layers of irregularly arranged lipid molecules. If these wax or grease lipid layers are rubbed by sharp particles, such as sand, the structure is damaged, evaporation rate increases and the insect risks dehydration. Interestingly, as the air temperature around an insect is increased, there is a gradual increase in the rate of evaporation until a particular temperature is exceeded after which the evaporation rate increases rapidly. This point is known as the **transition temperature** (fig 20.5) and it marks the temperature at which the ordered orientation of the single layer of lipid molecules breaks down.

Some insects living on dry food in very dry habitats are able to take up water from the air providing that the relative humidity of the air is above a certain value, such as 90% for the mealworm (*Tenebrio*) and 70% for the house mite (*Dermatophagoides*).

The problem of preventing water loss by excretion is overcome by specialised excretory organs called

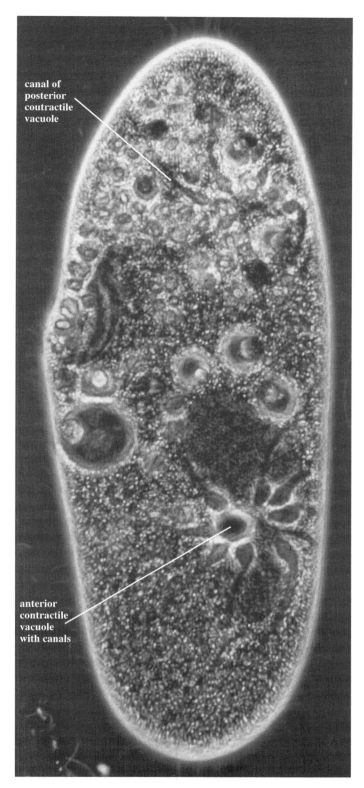

canal of posterior coutractile vacuole

anterior contractile vacuole with canals

Fig 20.3 *Photomicrograph of the fixed contractile vacuoles of* Paramecium. *A system of canals around each vacuole brings fluid from the cytoplasm to the vacuole. The vacuole itself swells and bursts at regular intervals, releasing water back into the environment each time it bursts. In the photograph, the anterior vacuole is full and the posterior vacuole has recently burst.*

Malpighian tubules which produce and excrete the almost insoluble waste substance **uric acid**.

Malpighian tubules are blind-ending extensions of the hindgut in insects. They lie in the abdomen and are bathed in blood. (The blood system of insects is open, meaning that the blood vessels empty blood into a cavity, the haemocoel, and do not have capillaries. The main organs are bathed in blood.) The number of tubules is variable in insects. Some have a pair and others may have several hundred. *Rhodnius*, a blood-sucking bug, has four tubules as shown in fig 20.6. The tubules of a wasp are shown in fig 20.7. In all cases they open into the hindgut at its junction with the midgut and may be long and slender or short and compact.

The tubule has two distinct regions, an **upper segment** (furthest from the gut), composed of a single layer of cells, and a **lower segment**. The upper segment absorbs fluid from the blood. As the fluid passes along the inside of the tubules, the cells of the lower segment, which have microvilli on their inner surfaces, absorb water and various salts. It is in the lower segment that the nitrogenous waste precipitates out of solution as solid crystals of uric acid. The concentrated contents of the tubule, still fluid, pass into the hindgut or rectum where they mix with waste materials from digestive processes. **Rectal glands** in the wall of the rectum absorb water from the faeces and uric acid suspension until the waste is dry enough for it to be eliminated from the body as pellets.

20.3.4 Freshwater fish

The excretory and osmoregulatory organs of the fish are the gills and kidneys. The gills are in contact with the external environment and are permeable to water, nitrogenous waste and ions. They have a large surface area for efficient exchange of respiratory gases, but this presents a problem when it comes to osmoregulation. This is particularly true when the fish lives in fresh water.

The internal body fluids of freshwater bony fish are more concentrated than their environment. Despite having a relatively impermeable outer covering of scales and mucus, there is a considerable movement of water by osmosis, and loss of ions by diffusion, through the highly permeable gills, which also serve as the organs of excretion for the waste nitrogenous substance ammonia. In order to maintain the body fluids at a steady state, freshwater fish have to lose a large volume of water continually (fig 20.8). They do this by producing a large volume of very dilute urine (of higher water potential than blood) which contains some ammonia and a number of solutes. Up to one-third of the body mass can be lost per day as urine. Ions which are lost from the body fluids are replaced by food and by active uptake from the external environment by special cells in the gills.

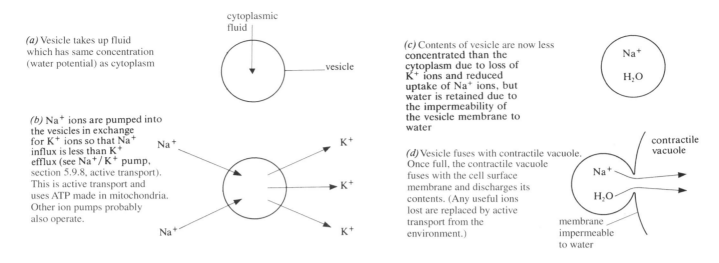

(a) Vesicle takes up fluid which has same concentration (water potential) as cytoplasm

cytoplasmic fluid

vesicle

(b) Na$^+$ ions are pumped into the vesicles in exchange for K$^+$ ions so that Na$^+$ influx is less than K$^+$ efflux (see Na$^+$/K$^+$ pump, section 5.9.8, active transport). This is active transport and uses ATP made in mitochondria. Other ion pumps probably also operate.

Na$^+$

K$^+$

Na$^+$

K$^+$

K$^+$

(c) Contents of vesicle are now less **concentrated than the cytoplasm due to loss of K$^+$ ions and reduced uptake of Na$^+$ ions, but water is retained due to the impermeability of the vesicle membrane to water**

Na$^+$

H$_2$O

(d) Vesicle fuses with contractile vacuole. Once full, the contractile vacuole fuses with the cell surface membrane and discharges its contents. (Any useful ions lost are replaced by active transport from the environment.)

contractile vacuole

Na$^+$

H$_2$O

membrane impermeable to water

Fig 20.4 *Diagrammatic explanation of a possible mechanism of water uptake by a contractile vacuole.*

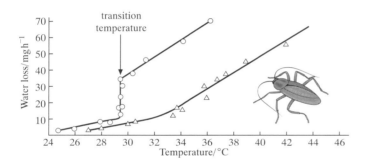

Fig 20.5 *Graph showing the water loss from the exoskeleton of a cockroach at various air temperatures (triangles). The circles indicate water loss plotted against the surface temperature of the exoskeleton. This shows the dramatic increase in water loss at about 29.5 °C, the* **transition temperature**.

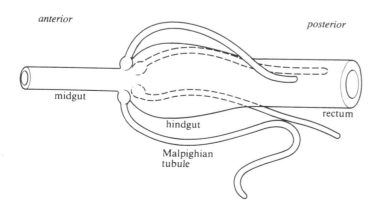

Fig 20.6 *Diagram showing the position of Malpighian tubules in relation to the gut of* Rhodnius, *a bug.*

20.3.5   Summary of water balance

The efficient functioning of animal cells relies on the maintenance of the steady state of the cell contents. Homeostatic exchange of water between cells, tissue fluid, lymph and blood plasma and the environment present problems for both aquatic and terrestrial forms of life. Aquatic organisms gain or lose water by osmosis through all permeable parts of the body surface depending on whether the environment is more dilute or more concentrated than their body. Terrestrial organisms have the problem of losing water and many mechanisms are used to maintain a steady-state water balance, as summarised for insects and mammals in table 20.3. This steady state is achieved by balancing loss and water gain, as shown in fig 20.9.

20.4   Formation of urea in humans

Urea is the nitrogenous waste product of humans and other land-living mammals. The advantages of using urea as a nitrogenous waste product are that it is:

* non-toxic – it can therefore be carried round the body in the blood from the liver where it is made until it is removed by the kidneys;
* very soluble – it does not require a great deal of water to get rid of it and it is easily transported;
* a small molecule – it is therefore easily filtered in the kidneys.

The body is unable to store excess amino acids taken in in the diet. Those not immediately needed for protein synthesis or making sugar must be got rid of. This takes place in the liver in two main stages:

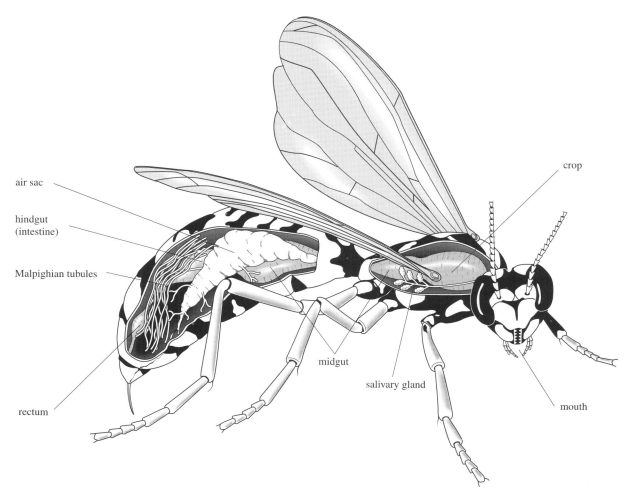

Fig 20.7 *Malpighian tubules of a wasp. The tubules are specialised excretory organs which are extensions of the hind gut.*

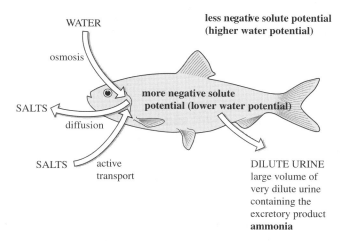

Fig 20.8 *Excretion and osmoregulation in a freshwater bony fish.*

- **deamination** – the amino group is removed from the amino acid and used to make ammonia;
- **detoxification** – ammonia is toxic (poisonous) and so is converted to a harmless product, urea, for transport to the kidneys.

Deamination

The amino acid is oxidised using oxygen. This results in removal of the amino group ($-NH_2$) and leaves an acid. The acid can enter the Krebs cycle and be used as a source of energy in cell respiration. The amino group is converted to ammonia (NH_3) during deamination.

Detoxification

Ammonia is converted into urea in the liver:

$$2NH_3 + CO_2 \longrightarrow \underset{NH_2}{\overset{NH_2}{>}}C=O + H_2O$$

ammonia   carbon dioxide   urea   water

This occurs by a cyclic reaction known as the **ornithine cycle** which is summarised in fig 20.10. If you start at

679

Table 20.3 Summary of water conservation mechanisms in two types of terrestrial animal, insects and mammals.

Organism	Water conservation mechanism
insect	impermeable cuticle spiracles with valves and hairs Malpighian tubules uric acid as nitrogenous waste cleidoic egg
mammal (including humans)	skin and hair are waterproof kidney produces urine containing urea more concentrated than blood viviparity (live birth) – developing embryo is not exposed to dry conditions behavioural response to heat restricted range of habitats some physiological tolerance to dehydration

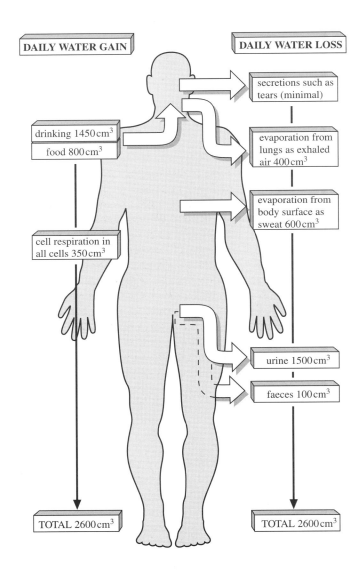

Fig 20.9 *Daily water loss and water gain by the human body.*

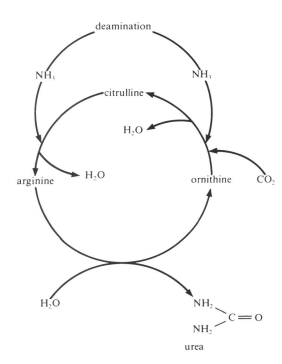

Fig 20.10 *Summary diagram of the ornithine cycle in the liver. Ornithine and citrulline are amino acids but are not obtained from the diet.*

ornithine in the cycle, you will see that overall two molecules of ammonia and one molecule of carbon dioxide are used, one molecule of water is made (two made, one used) and one molecule of urea. Ornithine is regenerated ready for the next cycle.

Urea is transported in the blood plasma from the liver to the kidneys.

> **20.1** List the blood vessels and organs, in sequence, through which urea must pass to reach the kidneys from the liver.

20.5   The human kidney

The kidney is the major excretory and osmoregulatory organ of mammals and has the following functions:

- removal of metabolic waste products;
- regulation of the water content of body fluids;
- regulation of the pH of body fluids;
- regulation of the chemical composition of body fluids by removal of substances which are in excess of immediate requirements.

The kidney has a rich blood supply and regulates the blood composition at a steady state. It therefore contributes to homeostasis. This ensures that the composition of the tissue fluid is maintained at an optimum level for the cells bathed by it and enables the cells to function efficiently at all times.

20.5.1   Position and structure of kidneys

There are a pair of kidneys in humans situated towards the back of the lower part of the abdominal cavity, on either side of the vertebral column. The left kidney lies slightly above the right.

The kidneys receive blood from the aorta via the **renal arteries**, and the **renal veins** return blood to the posterior (inferior) vena cava. Urine formed in the kidneys passes by a pair of **ureters** to the **bladder** where it is stored until it is released via the **urethra** (fig 20.11). Two muscle sphincters surround the urethra where it leaves the bladder, one of which is under voluntary control. These control release of urine, a process known as urination or micturition.

A transverse section of the kidney shows two distinct regions, an outer **cortex** and an inner **medulla** (fig 20.12). The cortex is covered by fibrous connective tissue, forming a tough capsule. The cortex contains glomeruli, which are just visible to the naked eye, renal corpuscles and parts of the nephrons (see below). The medulla is composed of tubular parts of the nephrons and blood vessels, which together form **renal pyramids**. The apex of each pyramid is called a **papilla**. All the pyramids project into the **pelvis** which leads into the ureter (fig 20.12). A large number of blood vessels run through the kidney and supply a vast network of blood capillaries.

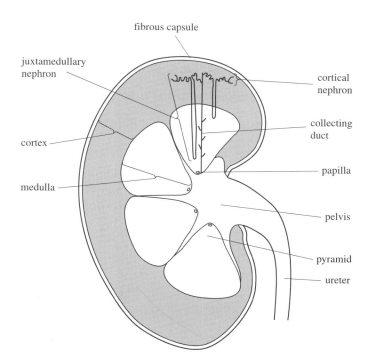

Fig 20.12   *TS through kidney showing the position of two nephrons.*

20.5.2   Nephron – overall structure and blood supply

The basic unit of structure and function of the kidney is the **nephron** (fig 20.13) and its associated blood supply. Each kidney, in a human, contains an estimated one million nephrons each having an approximate length of 3 cm. The total length of tubules in each kidney is about 120 km. This offers an enormous surface area for the exchange of materials. About one fifth of the blood passes through the kidneys for each circuit of the body and about 125 cm^3 of fluid is filtered out of the blood per minute. About 99% of the water is returned to the blood, so only about 1 cm^3 of urine is made per minute, although this varies with factors like drinking.

Each nephron is composed of six regions, each having its own particular structure and function:

(1) renal corpuscle (Malpighian body), composed of renal capsule and glomerulus (the renal capsule is also known as the Bowman's capsule);
(2) proximal convoluted tubule;
(3) descending limb of the loop of Henle;
(4) ascending limb of the loop of Henle;
(5) distal convoluted tubule;
(6) collecting duct.

These regions are shown in fig 20.13.

There are two types of nephrons, cortical nephrons and juxtamedullary nephrons, which differ in their positions in the kidney. **Cortical nephrons** are found in the cortex and have relatively short loops of Henle which just extend into

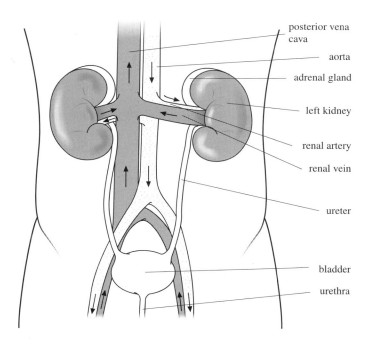

Fig 20.11   *Human excretory system. The size of the organs relative to the outline of the body is exaggerated for clarity.*

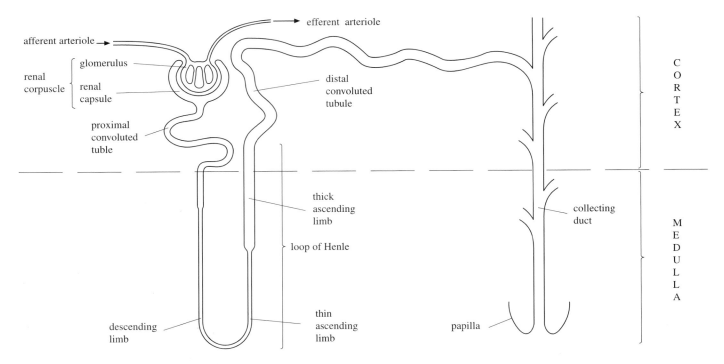

Fig 20.13 *Diagram showing the structure of a nephron. (Not to scale.)*

the medulla. **Juxtamedullary nephrons** have their renal corpuscle close to (= *juxta*) the junction of the cortex and medulla. They have long loops of Henle which extend deep into the medulla (fig 20.14*a*). The two types of nephrons have different uses. Under normal conditions of water availability the cortical nephrons deal with the control of blood volume, whereas, when water is in short supply, increased water retention occurs through the juxtamedullary nephrons.

Blood enters the kidney by the renal artery which branches into finer and finer arteries before entering the glomerulus of a renal corpuscle as an afferent arteriole. (Afferent means *to*, and efferent means *from*.) Filtered blood leaves the glomerulus by an efferent arteriole and flows through a network of capillaries in the cortex which surround the proximal and distal convoluted tubules and the loops of Henle in the medulla (fig 20.14*b*). The capillaries of the vasa recta run parallel to the loops of Henle and the collecting ducts in the medulla. These networks of blood vessels return blood, containing substances which are useful to the body, to the general circulation. Blood flow through the vasa recta is much less than through the capillaries around the proximal and distal convoluted tubules and this enables a water potential (solute potential) gradient to be maintained in the tissue of the medulla, as described later.

20.5.3 Histology of the kidney

Fig 20.15 shows the structure of the cortex and medulla regions of the kidney as seen with a light microscope.

20.5.4 Ultrafiltration

The first step in the formation of urine is ultrafiltration of the blood. This takes place in the renal capsule. **Ultrafiltration** is filtration under pressure. The pressure comes from the blood pressure and is known as hydrostatic pressure, or pumping pressure. Blood enters the glomerulus at high pressure direct from the heart via the dorsal aorta, renal artery and finally an arteriole (fig 20.11). The glomerulus is a knot of capillaries in the renal capsule (fig 20.15*d*). The diameter of the capillaries in the glomerulus is much less than that of the arteriole, so as the blood enters the narrow capillaries pressure rises. Water and small solute molecules are squeezed out of the capillaries through the epithelium of the renal capsule and into the interior of the capsule. Larger molecules like proteins, as well as red blood cells and platelets, are left behind in the blood. The structure of the glomerulus and renal capsule is specially adapted for filtration, as figs 20.16 to 20.19 show. Filtration takes place through three layers, which can be seen in transverse section in figs 20.16*b* and 20.19:

- **Endothelium of the blood capillary** This is very thin and is perforated with thousands of pores of about 10 nm diameter. They occupy up to 30% of the area of

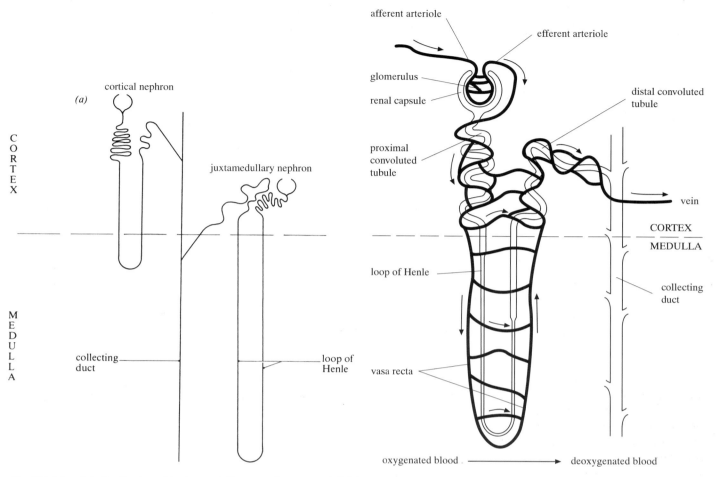

Fig 20.14 (a) *Cortical and juxtamedullary nephrons and* (b) *juxtamedullary nephron and its associated blood supply.*

the wall. The pores are not a barrier to plasma proteins because they are too large.

- **Basement membrane of the blood capillaries** All epithelial cells rest on a 'basement membrane'. It consists of a meshwork of fibres, including collagen fibres. Water and small solute molecules can pass through spaces between the fibres. Red blood cells and platelets are too large. Protein molecules are too large and are also repelled by negative electrical charges on the fibres.

- **Epithelium of the renal capsule** This is made of cells which are highly modified for filtration, called **podocytes** (pod meaning *foot*). Each cell has many foot-like extensions projecting from its surface. The extensions interlink with extensions from neighbouring cells as shown in figs 20.16a, 20.16b and 20.17. They fit together loosely, leaving slits called **slit pores** or **filtration slits** about 25 nm wide (fig 20.19). The filtered fluid can pass through these slits.

About 20% of the plasma is filtered into the capsule. Of the three layers, the basement membrane is the main filtration barrier. The filtered fluid in the capsule is called **glomerular filtrate** (**GF**). It has a chemical composition similar to that of blood plasma. It contains glucose, amino acids, vitamins, ions, nitrogenous waste (mainly urea, but also some uric acid and creatinine), some hormones and water.

Blood passing from the glomerulus has a lower water potential due to the increased concentration of plasma proteins and a reduced hydrostatic pressure.

Factors affecting the glomerular filtration rate (GFR)

The filtration pressure forcing fluid out of the glomerulus depends not only on the hydrostatic pressure of the blood, but also on the pressure of the glomerular filtrate (fig 20.20). If this equalled the hydrostatic pressure of the blood they would cancel each other out. In fact, the hydrostatic pressure of the glomerular filtrate is much lower than that of the blood, although not zero. Similarly the solute potential either side of the filtration barrier will affect the flow of fluid. Water tends to move from less negative solute potentials to more negative solute potentials (from less

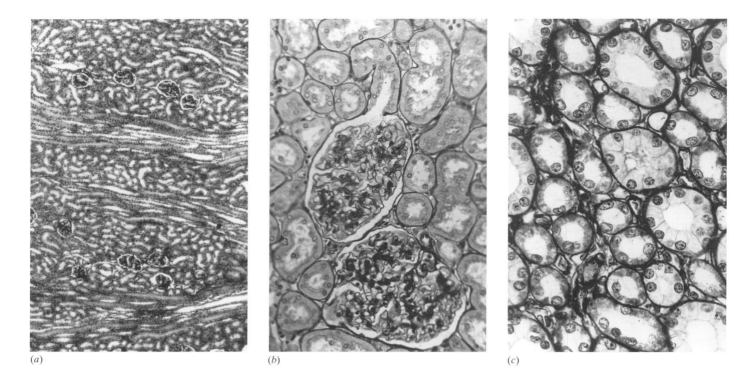

(a)   (b)   (c)

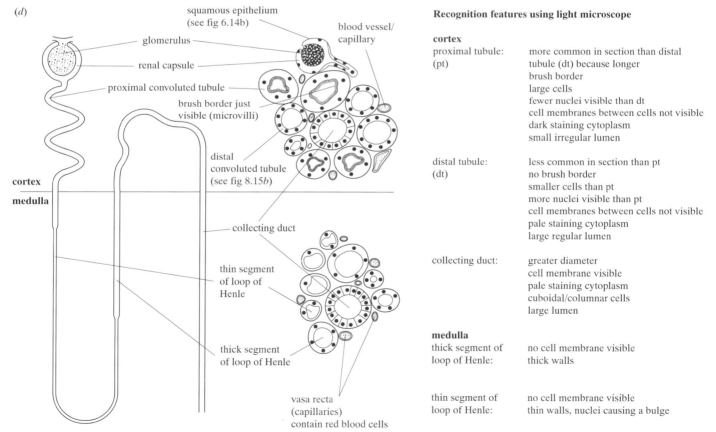

(d)

squamous epithelium
(see fig 6.14b)

glomerulus

renal capsule

blood vessel/
capillary

proximal convoluted tubule

brush border just
visible (microvilli)

distal
convoluted tubule
(see fig 8.15b)

cortex
medulla

collecting duct

thin segment
of loop of
Henle

thick segment
of loop of Henle

vasa recta
(capillaries)
contain red blood cells

Recognition features using light microscope

cortex

proximal tubule: (pt)	more common in section than distal tubule (dt) because longer
	brush border
	large cells
	fewer nuclei visible than dt
	cell membranes between cells not visible
	dark staining cytoplasm
	small irregular lumen
distal tubule: (dt)	less common in section than pt
	no brush border
	smaller cells than pt
	more nuclei visible than pt
	cell membranes between cells not visible
	pale staining cytoplasm
	large regular lumen
collecting duct:	greater diameter
	cell membrane visible
	pale staining cytoplasm
	cuboidal/columnar cells
	large lumen

medulla

thick segment of loop of Henle:	no cell membrane visible
	thick walls
thin segment of loop of Henle:	no cell membrane visible
	thin walls, nuclei causing a bulge

Fig 20.15   *Histology of the kidney. (a) Low power TS cortex showing sections through tubules and glomeruli. (b) High power TS cortex showing section through two glomeruli. (c) TS medulla showing sections through loops of Henle and collecting ducts. (d) Diagram interpreting sections through cortex and medulla.*

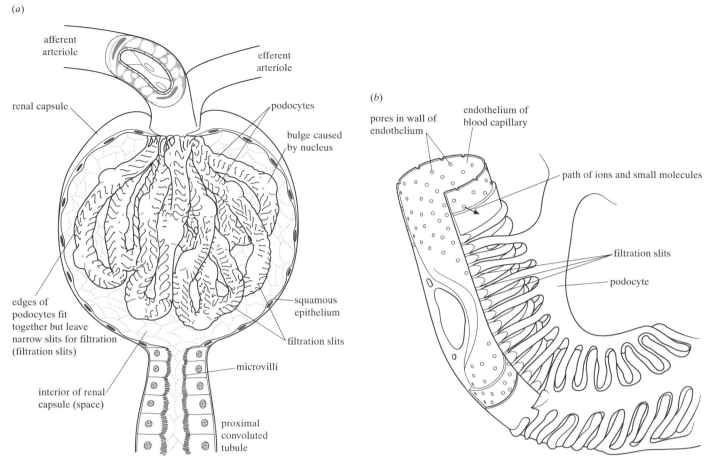

(a)

afferent
arteriole

efferent
arteriole

renal capsule

podocytes

bulge caused
by nucleus

(b)

pores in wall of
endothelium

endothelium of
blood capillary

path of ions and small molecules

filtration slits

podocyte

edges of
podocytes fit
together but leave
narrow slits for filtration
(filtration slits)

squamous
epithelium

filtration slits

interior of renal
capsule (space)

microvilli

proximal
convoluted
tubule

Fig 20.16 *(a) Structure of the renal corpuscle. The upper part shows afferent and efferent arterioles. Special epithelial cells called podocytes cover the outside surfaces of the capillaries of the glomerulus. The capillaries themselves are therefore hidden, although their outline is revealed. (Rather like a glove concealing fingers while revealing their shape. The glove is equivalent to the podocytes and the fingers are equivalent to the capillaries.) The lower part of the diagram shows the start of the proximal convoluted tubule, which has cuboidal epithelial cells with microvilli (a brush border). (Based on L. C. Junqueira & J. Carneiro (1980)* Basic Histology *3rd ed. Lange Medical Publications.) (b) Detailed view of podocytes and TS capillary. Note how the podocytes fit together like loosely interlocking fingers, leaving slits through which glomerular filtrate can pass on its way into the renal capsule.*

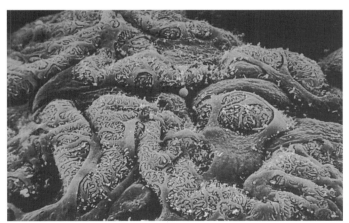

Fig 20.17 *Scanning electron micrograph of podocytes, ×900. The podocytes have a cell body with numerous braucle of varying size, which restrict the size of molecule able to pass across the membrane.*

concentrated to more concentrated solutions). As the blood flows from the afferent arteriole to the efferent arteriole through the glomerulus it loses water and small solute molecules, but the plasma proteins remain in the blood and increase in concentration by about 20% as a result of the loss of water. This makes the solute potential, and therefore the water potential, of the blood more negative and tends to decrease GFR. When all the forces are taken into account, the GFR is positive and fluid moves from the glomerulus to the renal capsule. The greater the water potential of the blood compared with the glomerular filtrate, the greater the filtration pressure and the GFR.

Filtration rate can be increased by raising blood pressure. It can also be raised by dilating the afferent arterioles (vasodilation) and therefore decreasing the resistance to the flow of blood into the glomerulus. A third regulatory mechanism is to increase the resistance in the efferent arterioles by constricting them (vasoconstriction).

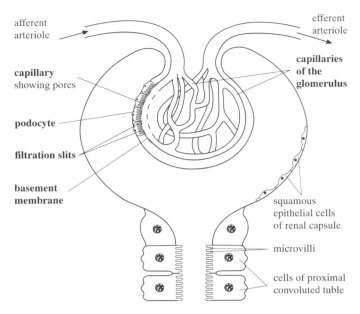

Fig 20.18 *Diagram of a renal corpuscle showing typical cells of the renal capsule.*

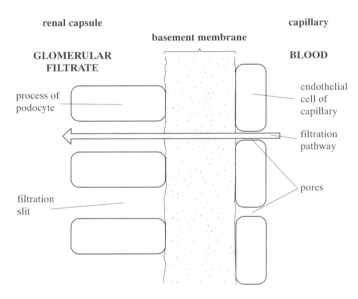

Fig 20.19 *Diagram showing the path taken by fluid (glomerular filtrate) as it passes from the plasma in a glomerular capillary to the lumen of a renal capsule.*

Vasodilation and vasoconstriction are under both nervous and hormonal control.

20.5.5 Selective reabsorption in the proximal convoluted tubule

Ultrafiltration produces about $125 \, cm^3$ of glomerular filtrate per minute in humans. This is equivalent to about $180 \, dm^3$ per day. Since only $1.5 \, dm^3$ of urine is produced each day, a great deal of reabsorption must occur. In fact, of the $125 \, cm^3$ of filtrate produced per minute

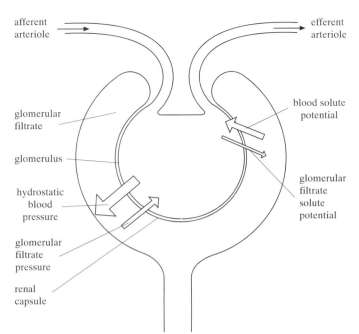

Fig 20.20 *The direction and magnitude of pressures influencing the filtration pressure in the glomerulus.*

$124 \, cm^3$ is reabsorbed on average, about 80% of it in the proximal convoluted tubule.

During ultrafiltration, substances which are useful and vital are lost from the plasma along with excretory substances. The function of the nephrons is to *selectively reabsorb* substances of further use to the body and those required to maintain the composition of the body fluids in a steady state. Further waste substances may be added to the tubules by active *secretion* from the blood capillaries surrounding the tubules.

Formation of urine therefore involves three key processes, namely ultrafiltration, selective reabsorption and secretion.

Analysis of fluid in the nephrons

By using extremely fine pipettes it has been possible to remove fluid from different parts of the nephron and to analyse its content in an attempt to find out what effect the different parts of the nephron have on the composition of the fluid. It is also possible to measure the rate of flow using the polysaccharide inulin as a tracer. It is injected into the blood from where it is filtered into the nephron. It is not reabsorbed from, or secreted into, the nephron so, as water is reabsorbed from the nephron, the concentration of inulin increases in proportion to the amount of water reabsorbed. As the amount of water decreases the flow rate of glomerular filtrate decreases.

In the example given in fig 20.21, the flow rate in the renal capsule is set at 100 arbitrary units. This is called the **flow rate index** (**FRI**). Flow rates at other points can be compared with this. FRI gives a measure of the amount of water. For example, if it changes from 100 to 40, 60% of the water must have been reabsorbed. Using the figures in

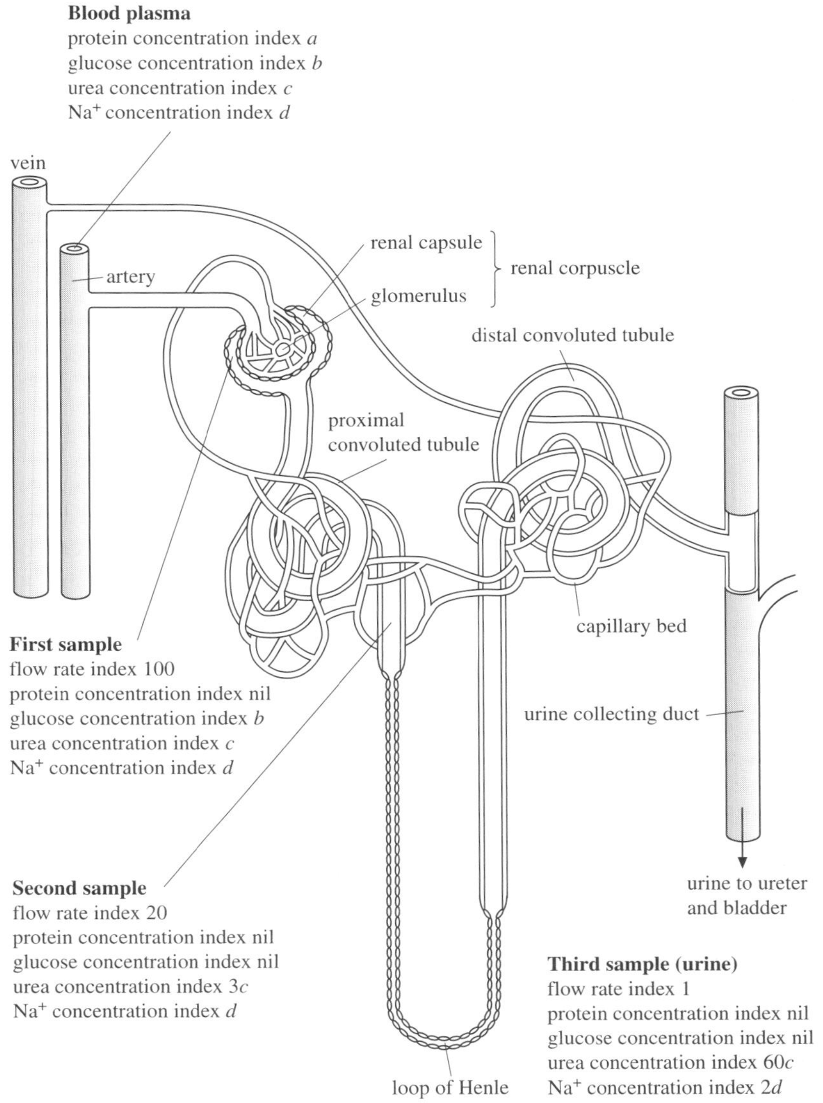

Fig 20.21 *Diagram of a single nephron and part of its blood supply. (Based on Nuffield Advanced Science (Biological Science) Study Guide, Penguin (1970) p.373.)*

fig 20.21, the amount of reabsorption of different solutes can be calculated as they move through the nephron. Try the following questions. If you cannot answer a question, look up the answer for an explanation and then try the next question before you look at further answers.

20.2 What happens to the concentration of solutes as fluid passes from the blood to the renal capsule? Explain.

20.3 In passing from the renal capsule to the end of the proximal convoluted tubule, the flow rate index changes from 100 to 20. What percentage of water has been reabsorbed back into the blood from the proximal convoluted tubule?

20.4 Only 20%, or one fifth, of the water remains at the end of the proximal con-

voluted tubule, so the concentration of all the solutes should have increased by 5 times, *unless* the proximal convoluted tubule has had an effect on the solute. Thus urea, for example, should have changed from a concentration index c to concentration index $5c$. However, it has changed to $3c$, only 3/5 or 60% of that predicted. This means that only 60% of the original urea remains and therefore 40% must have been reabsorbed. What percentage, if any, of the glucose and sodium ions were reabsorbed?

20.5 What changes, if any, took place in the amount of water, sodium ions and urea in the nephron between the end of the proximal convoluted tubule and the end of the collecting duct?

687

20.6 Overall, what percentage of the water and sodium ions were reabsorbed between the renal capsule and the end of the collecting duct?

Structure of the proximal convoluted tubule

The proximal convoluted tubule is the longest (14 mm) and widest (60 μm) part of the nephron and carries filtrate from the renal capsule to the loop of Henle. It is composed of a single layer of cuboidal epithelial cells with extensive microvilli forming a 'brush border' on the inside surface of the tubule (fig 20.22). At the opposite ends of the cells, their outer membranes rest on a basement membrane and are folded inwards to form a series of **basal channels**. These increase the surface area of the cells. Neighbouring cells are separated for most of their lengths by narrow spaces and fluid circulates through the basal channels and spaces. This fluid bathes the cells and is a link between them and the surrounding network of blood capillaries. The cells of the proximal convoluted tubules have numerous mitochondria concentrated near the basement membrane where they provide ATP for membrane-bound carrier molecules involved in active transport (fig 20.23). Electron micrographs of such cells are shown in fig 20.22.

Selective reabsorption in the proximal convoluted tubule

The proximal convoluted tubule cells are adapted for reabsorption as follows:

- large surface area due to microvilli and basal channels;
- numerous mitochondria;
- closeness of blood capillaries.

Over 80% of the glomerular filtrate is reabsorbed here, including all the glucose, amino acids, vitamins, hormones and about 80% of the sodium chloride and water. The mechanism of reabsorption is as follows.

- Glucose, amino acids and ions diffuse into the cells of the proximal convoluted tubule from the filtrate and are actively transported out of the cells into the spaces between them and the basal channels. This is done by carrier proteins in the cell surface membranes.
- Once in these spaces and channels they enter the extremely permeable blood capillaries by diffusion and are carried away from the nephron.
- The constant removal of these substances from the proximal convoluted tubule cells creates a diffusion gradient between the filtrate in the proximal tubule and the cells, down which further substances pass. Once inside the cells they are actively transported into the

(a)

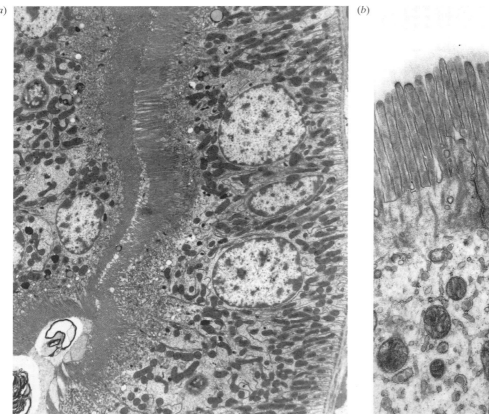

(b)

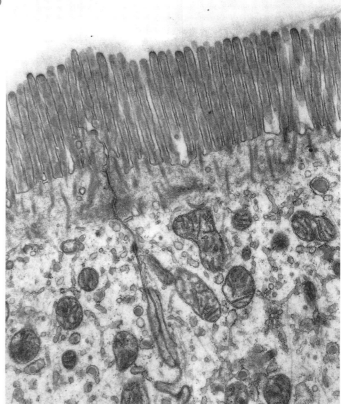

Fig 20.22 (a) Cuboidal epithelial cells of the proximal convoluted tubule as seen with an electron microscope, X7000. (b) Detail of microvilli (brush border) of epithelial cell of proximal convoluted tubule, x18 000.

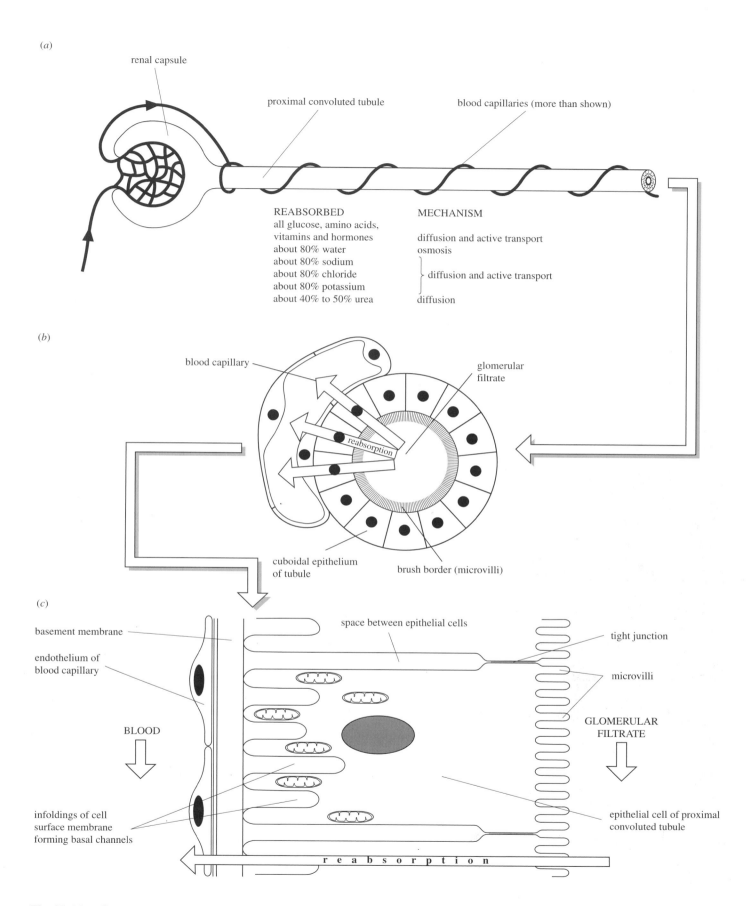

(a)

renal capsule

proximal convoluted tubule

blood capillaries (more than shown)

REABSORBED
all glucose, amino acids,
vitamins and hormones
about 80% water
about 80% sodium
about 80% chloride
about 80% potassium
about 40% to 50% urea

MECHANISM

diffusion and active transport
osmosis

} diffusion and active transport

diffusion

(b)

blood capillary

glomerular filtrate

reabsorption

cuboidal epithelium of tubule

brush border (microvilli)

(c)

basement membrane

endothelium of blood capillary

space between epithelial cells

tight junction

microvilli

BLOOD

GLOMERULAR FILTRATE

infoldings of cell surface membrane forming basal channels

epithelial cell of proximal convoluted tubule

r e a b s o r p t i o n

Fig 20.23 *Structure and function of the proximal convoluted tubule.*

(a)

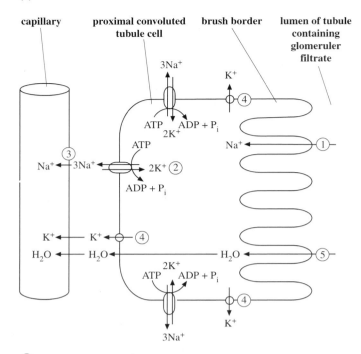

(b)

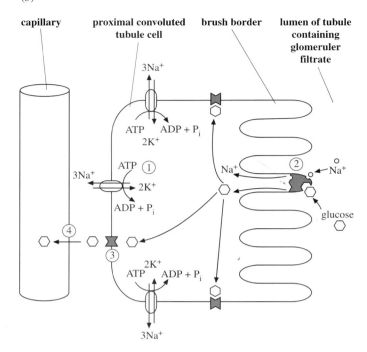

① Diffusion of Na^+ down its electrochemical gradient from higher concentration outside the cell to lower concentration inside and towards negatively charged interior of cell (all cells maintain a potential difference across their surface membranes, usually negative on the inside with respect to the outside). Na^+ enters through ion channels.

② Na^+/K^+ pumps in the base and sides of the cell pump out $3Na^+$ ions for every $2K^+$ ions pumped in, using ATP as an energy source (section 5.9.8). This maintains the Na^+ diffusion gradient into the cell. (6% of the total ATP used in the body is used in the kidneys by these pumps.)

③ Na^+ diffuses into the blood capillaries from the spaces around the tubule cells.

④ K^+ diffuses back out of the cell passively through K^+ ion channels.

⑤ Water always tends to follow Na^+ by osmosis. This occurs from the lumen of the tubule through the tubule cells and into the blood capillaries.

① Na^+/K^+ pump pumps out Na^+ and reduces concentration of Na^+ inside cell.

② A special transport protein reabsorbs both Na^+ and glucose. Such proteins are called symporters (the movement of the two molecules is linked). Na^+ and glucose are effectively moving down diffusion gradients, but this is only made possible by the active transport of the Na^+/K^+ pumps. The process is therefore sometimes referred to as secondary active transport.

③ Glucose leaves the cell by facilitated diffusion through a carrier protein (see fig 5.17).

④ Glucose diffuses into the blood capillary. Amino acids and some other nutrients follow the same type of route.

Fig 20.24 *(a) Selective reabsorption of sodium in the proximal convoluted tubule. (b) Selective reabsorption of glucose in the proximal convoluted tubule.*

spaces and channels and the cycle continues. Further details of the mechanisms involving sodium and glucose are shown in figs 20.24*a* and *b*.

The active uptake of sodium and other ions makes the solute potential in the tubular filtrate less negative (higher water potential) and an equivalent amount of water leaves the tubular filtrate and passes into the blood capillaries by osmosis. Most of the solutes and water are removed from the filtrate at a fairly constant rate. This produces a filtrate in the tubule which has the same water potential as the blood plasma in the capillaries.

About 40 to 50% of the urea from the filtrate is reabsorbed, by diffusion, into the blood capillaries and

passes back into the general circulation. Although this is not needed, it is harmless. The remainder is excreted in the urine.

Small proteins which pass into the tubule during ultrafiltration are removed by pinocytosis at the base of the microvilli. They are enclosed in pinocytotic vesicles to which lysosomes are attached. Hydrolytic enzymes in the lysosomes digest the proteins to amino acids which are either used by the tubule cells or passed on, by diffusion, to the blood capillaries.

Finally, active secretion of unwanted substances, such as creatinine and some urea, occurs out of the blood capillaries in this region. These substances are transported from the tissue fluid bathing the tubules into the tubular filtrate and eventually removed in the urine.

20.5.6   The loop of Henle

The function of the loop of Henle is to conserve water. The longer the loop of Henle, the more concentrated the urine that can be produced. This is a useful adaptation to life on land. Birds and mammals are the only vertebrates which can produce a urine which is more concentrated than the blood and they are the only vertebrates with loops of Henle. The urine of a human can be 4 to 5 times as concentrated as the blood. The drier the natural habitat of an animal, the longer its loop of Henle. For example, the beaver, a semi-aquatic mammal, has a short loop of Henle and produces a large volume of dilute urine, whereas the desert-dwelling kangaroo rat and the jerboa (hopping mouse) have long loops of Henle and produce small volumes of highly concentrated urine. Their urine is 6 to 7 times more concentrated than human urine and they do not need to drink water. They get enough from food and metabolic water produced during cell respiration.

The loop of Henle, together with the capillaries of the vasa recta and collecting duct, creates and maintains an osmotic gradient in the medulla which extends from the cortex to the tips of the pyramids (see fig 20.12).

The gradient extends across the medulla from a less concentrated salt solution at the cortex to a more concentrated salt solution at the tips of the pyramids. Water leaves the nephrons by osmosis in response to this gradient, as will be explained later, making the fluid inside the nephrons, which becomes the urine, more concentrated.

The loop of Henle has three distinct regions, each with its own function. These are:

- the **descending limb** which has thin walls;
- the **thin ascending limb** – this is the lower half of the ascending limb and has thin walls like the descending limb;
- the **thick ascending limb** – this is the upper half of the ascending limb and has thick walls.

The descending limb is highly permeable to water and permeable to most solutes. Its function is to allow substances to diffuse easily through its walls. Both parts of the ascending limb are almost totally impermeable to water. The cells in the thick part can actively reabsorb sodium, chloride, potassium and other ions from the tubule. Normally water would follow by osmosis the movement of these ions into the cells, but this cannot occur because the cells are impermeable to water as stated. The fluid in the ascending limb therefore becomes very dilute by the time it reaches the distal convoluted tubule.

The loop of Henle as a countercurrent multiplier

It has been noted that there is a gradient of salts across the medulla. The gradient is from about 300–1200 mOsm dm^{-3}, but for simplicity this will be referred to as 300 to 1200 units. We can now examine how this is achieved. It is best

to imagine a starting situation where the whole loop of Henle is filled with fluid at a concentration of 300 units (the normal concentration of tissue fluid and blood), and that this is in equilibrium with tissue fluid of the same concentration in the surrounding medulla. From this starting point a gradient has to be built up across the medulla. The process can be thought of as starting in the thick ascending limb. This carries out active transport of sodium ions out of the cells of the ascending limb into the tissue fluid of the medulla by means of a sodium–potassium pump (section 5.9.8, active transport). Sodium ions then diffuse from the fluid in the ascending limb into the cells of the ascending limb to replace the sodium ions lost. As they do they pass through a carrier protein which also accepts chloride and potassium ions. These are cotransported into the cells with sodium ions, against their concentration gradients, and diffuse out with sodium ions into the medulla. The whole process is driven by the sodium–potassium pump and results in sodium, potassium and chloride ions accumulating in the tissue fluid of the medulla. The concentration of these ions in the ascending limb *decreases* while the concentration in the medulla *increases* because water cannot leave the ascending limb by osmosis due to its impermeable wall. On the other hand, the descending limb is very permeable to water, and not very permeable to ions. A difference of about 200 units between the ascending limb and the medulla can be maintained by the pump, as shown in fig 20.25.

Box 20.1 The use of osmolarity

The concentrations of particles (ions or molecules) in solutions can be described in terms of solute potential or in terms of osmolarity. It is traditional in animal physiology to use osmolarity rather than solute potential. Because every particle (ion or molecule) in a solution contributes to the solute potential of that solution, osmolarity is used to refer to the total number of moles of all particles in 1 dm^3 of solution. One osmole is 1 mole of any combination of particles. For example, 1 mole of KCl produces a solution which has an osmolarity of 2 osmoles. This is because 1 mole of KCl will dissolve to produce 1 mole of K$^+$ ions and 1 mole of Cl$^-$ ions, that is 2 moles of particles are present.

Solutions with the same osmolarity have the same solute potential. Osmolarity is measured as osmoles per dm^3 or, more appropriately, as milliosmoles per dm^3 in the case of glomerular filtrate. This is written as mOsm dm^{-3}. Normal blood plasma and tissue fluid osmolarity is about 300 mOsm dm^{-3}. Normal urine is 300–1000 mOsm dm^{-3}. The osmolarity of the tissue fluid in the kidney medulla is about 1200 mOsm dm^{-3}. Seawater is about 1000 mOsm dm^{-3}.

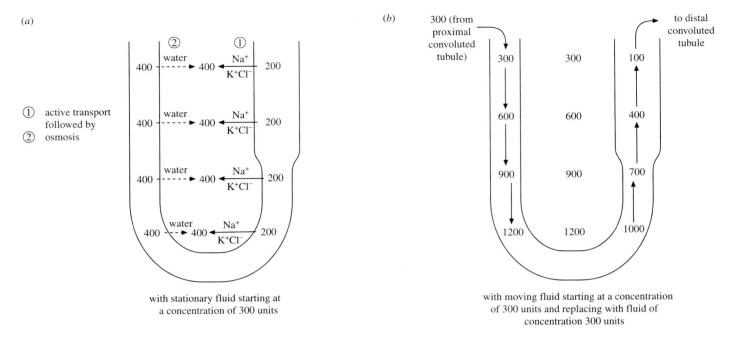

Fig 20.25 *Movement of ions and water from the loop of Henle into the medulla of the kidney. (a) The situation that would develop if the fluid in the loop of Henle were stationary. (b) The situation that develops in reality due to movement of fluid round the loop of Henle. Numbers refer to concentration of the fluid in milliosmoles per dm^3.*

The high concentration of salts in the medulla makes water leave the descending limb by osmosis, so the fluid in the descending limb gets more concentrated. If the fluid *did not move round* the loop of Henle the situation shown in fig 20.25a would develop. The pump cannot work fast enough to raise the concentration higher than 400 units because of leakage of ions back into the thick ascending limb. Now, imagine the real situation of fluid moving round the loop. The higher the fluid goes in the thick ascending limb the more sodium ions will have been removed, so the more dilute it gets. A gradient is established in the ascending limb. There is always a 200-unit difference between the ascending limb and the medulla due to the pump, so a similar gradient develops in the medulla. At the same time, more and more water is removed from the fluid as it passes down the descending limb, so the concentration of the fluid in the descending limb increases from top to bottom. The result of all this is the situation shown in fig 20.25b.

Some ions do move out of the descending limb, but water moves much more rapidly. The water does not dilute the medulla because it is carried away by the blood vessels of the vasa recta. The vasa recta follow the loops of Henle and the changes in the composition of the blood in the vasa recta are similar to those in the medulla. The flow of blood is slow, allowing it to come into equilibrium with the medulla at all levels. It does not therefore disrupt the gradient established in the medulla. The whole process is dynamic, meaning that it would soon be disrupted if the fluid stopped moving, or the pumps stopped working, or blood in the vasa recta stopped flowing.

The loop of Henle is known as a countercurrent multiplier. The term countercurrent refers to the fact that the fluid flows in opposite directions in the two sides of the loop, down one side and up the other. The multiplier effect is seen by comparing figs 20.25a and b. In fig 20.25b a gradient from 300 to 1200 units is created by a pump which is only capable of maintaining a difference of 200 units between one side of the loop of Henle and the other. The effect of the pump is multiplied by constant removal of sodium and other ions from the ascending side and their replacement from the proximal convoluted tubule on the descending side.

20.5.7 The distal convoluted tubule and collecting duct

In the last two regions of the nephron, the distal convoluted tubule and the collecting duct, fine tuning of the body fluid composition is achieved. The proximal convoluted tubule always functions in the same way, removing, for example, the same proportions of water and salts all the time as described in section 20.5.5. It functions as a coarse control, reabsorbing into the blood the bulk of the substances required.

Fine control of the precise amounts of water and salts reabsorbed is important in **osmoregulation**. This is one role of the distal convoluted tubule and collecting duct. They also control blood pH. These functions are described in more detail in sections 20.6 and 20.7.

The cells of the distal tubule have a similar structure to those of the proximal tubule, with microvilli lining the inner surface to increase the surface area for reabsorption, and numerous mitochondria to supply energy for active transport. The collecting duct carries fluid from the outer region of the medulla, next to the cortex, to the pyramids (fig 20.12). As the fluid moves down the collecting duct, the tissue fluid in the medulla surrounding the duct gets more and more concentrated, as noted above. Water therefore leaves the collecting duct by osmosis. The final concentration of the urine can be as high as the medulla, about 1200 units, although the actual amount of water lost is controlled by ADH as explained in section 20.6.

A comparison of the composition of plasma and urine is shown in table 20.4. It shows that the urine has a higher concentration of all solutes except sodium ions and normally lacks protein and glucose.

20.6 Osmoregulation, antidiuretic hormone (ADH) and the formation of a concentrated or dilute urine

The body maintains the solute potential of the blood at an approximately steady state by balancing water uptake from the diet with water lost in evaporation, sweating, egestion and urine, as shown in fig 20.9. The precise control of solute potential, however, is achieved primarily by the effect of a hormone called **antidiuretic hormone (ADH)**. Diuresis is the production of large amounts of dilute urine. Antidiuresis is therefore the opposite. ADH is antidiuretic in its effects, so has the effect of making urine more concentrated. ADH is a peptide (table 17.10). It is sometimes known as **vasopressin**.

ADH is made in the hypothalamus and passes the short distance to the posterior pituitary gland by a process called neurosecretion. This is explained in section 17.6.2.

When the blood becomes more concentrated (solute potential more negative), as in a situation where too little water has been drunk, excessive sweating has occurred or large amounts of salt have been eaten, osmoreceptors in the

hypothalamus detect a fall in blood solute potential. Osmoreceptors are special receptors which are extremely sensitive to changes in blood concentration. They set up nerve impulses which pass to the posterior pituitary gland where ADH is released. ADH travels in the blood to the kidney where it increases the permeability of the distal convoluted tubule and collecting duct to water. It does this by bringing about an increase in the number of water channels in the membranes lining the tubules. Water channels are proteins, like ion channels. They are manufactured inside the cell and 'stored' in the membranes of small Golgi vesicles which accumulate in the cytoplasm. When ADH binds to its specific receptors in the cell surface membrane it acts, via cyclic AMP (the second messenger system described in sections 17.6.1, 17.6.2 and 18), to stimulate the fusion of these vesicles to the cell surface membrane. When ADH secretion is stopped, the process goes into reverse, and by a process of endocytosis the vesicles are taken back into the cell ready for recycling next time ADH is secreted.

In the presence of ADH, the increased number of water channels allows water to move from the glomerular filtrate into the cortex and medulla by osmosis, reducing the volume of the urine and making it more concentrated (fig 20.26). The water is carried away in the blood.

ADH also increases the permeability of the collecting duct to urea, which diffuses out of the urine into the tissue fluid of the medulla. Here it increases the osmotic concentration, resulting in the removal of an increased volume of water from the thin descending limb.

The opposite occurs when there is a high intake of water. The solute potential of the blood begins to get less negative. ADH release is inhibited, the walls of the distal convoluted tubule and collecting duct become impermeable to water, less water is reabsorbed as the filtrate passes through the medulla and a large volume of dilute urine is excreted (fig 20.26).

Table 20.5 shows a summary of the events involved in regulating water balance, and the control mechanisms involved in regulating water balance are shown in fig 20.27. The hypothalamus also contains a 'thirst centre'. When blood solute potential is very negative, the thirst centre stimulates the sensation of thirst.

Failure to release sufficient ADH leads to a condition known as **diabetes insipidus** in which large quantities of dilute urine are produced (diuresis). The fluid lost in the urine has to be replaced by excessive drinking.

20.7 Control of blood sodium level

The maintenance of the plasma sodium level at a steady state is controlled by the steroid hormone **aldosterone** which also influences water reabsorption. It is secreted by the cortex (outer) region of the adrenal glands. A decrease in blood sodium leads to a decrease in blood volume because less water enters the blood by osmosis.

Table 20.4 The composition of plasma and urine and changes in concentration occurring during urine formation in humans.

	Plasma %	Urine %	Increase
water	90	95	–
protein	8	0	–
glucose	0.1	0	–
urea	0.03	2	67×
uric acid	0.004	0.05	12×
creatinine	0.001	0.075	75×
Na^+	0.32	0.35	1×
NH_4^+	0.0001	0.04	400×
K^+	0.02	0.15	7×
Mg^{2+}	0.0025	0.01	4×
Cl^-	0.37	0.60	2×
PO_4^{3-}	0.009	0.27	30×
SO_4^{2-}	0.002	0.18	90×

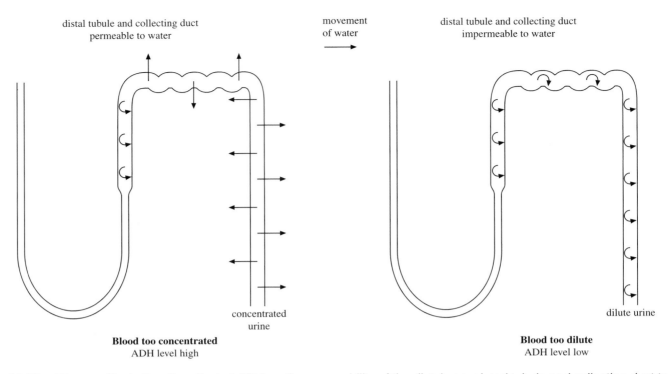

distal tubule and collecting duct
permeable to water

movement
of water
$\longrightarrow$

distal tubule and collecting duct
impermeable to water

concentrated
urine

dilute urine

Blood too concentrated
ADH level high

Blood too dilute
ADH level low

Fig 20.26 *Diagram illustrating the effect of ADH on the permeability of the distal convoluted tubule and collecting duct to water.*

Table 20.5 Summary of the changes produced in the distal convoluted tubule and collecting duct in response to ADH.

Blood concentration	Blood solute potential	ADH	Epithelium	Urine
rises	falls (more negative)	released	permeable	concentrated
falls	rises (less negative)	not released	impermeable	dilute

This in turn reduces blood pressure. This decrease in pressure and volume stimulates a group of secretory cells, the **juxtaglomerular complex**, situated between the distal convoluted tubule and the afferent arteriole (fig 20.28), to release an enzyme called **renin**. Renin activates a protein in the blood plasma, produced in the liver, to form the active hormone **angiotensin**, and this releases aldosterone from the adrenal cortex. Aldosterone travels in the blood to the distal convoluted tubule of the kidney. Here it stimulates the sodium–potassium pumps in the cells of the tubule, resulting in more sodium ions being pumped out of the distal convoluted tubule and into the blood capillaries around the tubule. Potassium moves in the opposite direction. This is an example of active transport.

Aldosterone also stimulates sodium absorption in the gut and decreases loss of sodium in sweat; both these effects tend to raise blood sodium levels. This in turn causes more water to enter the blood by osmosis, raising its volume and hence its pressure.

20.8 Control of blood pH

pH is a measure of hydrogen ion concentration. A neutral pH is 7.0, an acid pH is lower than 7 and a basic (or alkaline) pH is higher than 7. Some chemicals have the ability to resist pH changes in solution. These are called buffers. The normal pH of the blood plasma is 7.4. This must be kept to within very narrow limits. One reason is that enzymes and other proteins are easily denatured by changes in pH and this could prove fatal. Many other changes in body chemistry would also be affected by a large change in pH.

The body produces more acids than bases as a result of its chemistry, so the problem is usually one of reducing acidity. One factor which tends to increase acidity is production of carbon dioxide during cell respiration. This can dissolve to form a weak acid, carbonic acid, H_2CO_3. This dissociates into hydrogen ions, H^+, and hydrogen-carbonate ions, HCO_3^-. The hydrogen ions are buffered by haemoglobin as explained in section 14.8.3. A rise in carbon dioxide concentration brings about a reflex response which causes an increased breathing rate. This helps to get

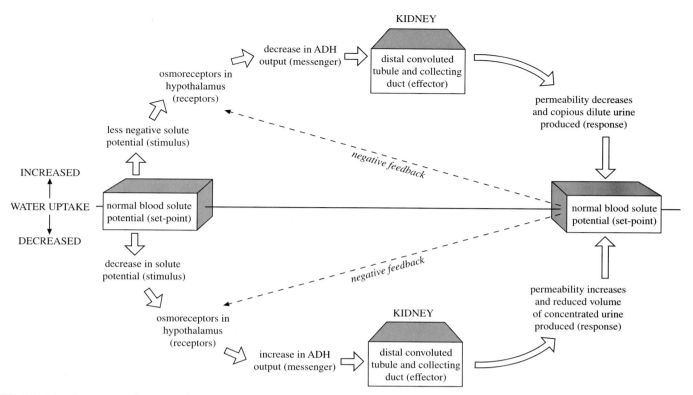

Fig 20.27 *Summary diagram of the control of blood solute potential.*

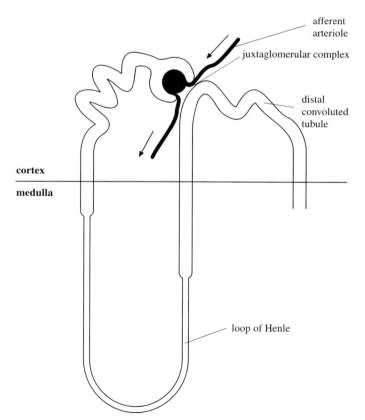

Fig 20.28 *Location of the juxtaglomerular cells in the kidney. The cells are found in the wall of the afferent arteriole and are sensitive to blood sodium level and blood pressure.*

rid of the excess carbon dioxide. The mechanism is explained in section 9.5.5. Hydrogencarbonate ions can also act as a buffer because at high concentrations of hydrogen ions, they combine with the hydrogen ions to form carbonic acid.

Hydrogencarbonate and phosphate buffers in the blood help to prevent excess hydrogen ions, produced by metabolic activities, from decreasing the pH of the blood. Changes in blood chemistry which would change the plasma pH from its normal level of 7.4 are also counteracted by the proximal and distal convoluted tubules, and the collecting duct, in two ways.

- If the blood starts to become too acidic, hydrogen ions are secreted by active transport across the cell surface membranes of the tubule or collecting duct cells from the blood into the tubules or collecting duct. If the source of hydrogen ions is carbon dioxide then the hydrogencarbonate ions also generated will return to the blood by diffusion. The reverse may happen if pH rises. The pH of the urine can vary from 4.5 to 8.5 as a result of these changes. (Note that a pH of 4.5 is 1000 times more acidic than a pH of 7.5 because the hydrogen ion concentration changes by a factor of 10 for each change in pH of 1 unit.)

- A fall in pH also stimulates the kidney cells to produce the base ion ammonium (NH_4^+) which combines with acids brought to the kidney and is then excreted as ammonium salts.

20.9   Kidney disease and its treatment

20.9.1   Kidney failure

The normal ageing process affects kidney function in various ways, particularly the efficiency of the filtering process. This gradually declines to about 50% by age 70. Some people, however, experience kidney disease, that is abnormal kidney functioning. A general term for a decline in kidney performance as a result of disease is **kidney failure**. It may be chronic or acute. **Chronic** kidney failure is progressive and takes place over a number of years. **Acute** kidney failure is when the kidney function stops, or almost completely stops, relatively suddenly. Some of the causes of these two types of failure are listed in table 20.6.

If kidney failure is not treated, death will result within a couple of weeks. This is often due to build up of potassium ions which causes heart failure. Kidney failure is a relatively common disease, affecting tens of thousands of people in the UK each year. If one kidney fails, it is possible to live, but if both fail medical intervention is vital.

20.9.2   Dialysis with a kidney machine – haemodialysis

There are two forms of dialysis. One uses an artificial membrane in a 'kidney machine' and is called haemodialysis. The other (section 20.9.3) uses a natural membrane in the patient's own body, the peritoneum, and is called **peritoneal dialysis**.

The first successful artificial kidney machines were being introduced by the early 1950s and now about 2500 people a year use them in the UK on a long-term basis, although sadly there are still insufficient to meet demand. Patients can learn to run a machine themselves and keep the machine at home, often connecting up to the machine in the late evening and detaching from the machine the next morning.

The artificial kidney works on the same principle as the real kidney. In summary, the blood is pumped out of the body, filtered to remove the waste materials, a process called **dialysis**, and then returned. Details are shown in fig 20.29.

The patient is connected to the machine by inserting a catheter (a hollow tube-like needle) into an artery, connecting this to a flexible tube leading to the machine and returning it to a vein. The lower part of the arm or leg may be used. When frequent use of the machine is required, the disconnected catheters may be left in place linked by a short tube.

The blood is pumped gently out of the artery and returned to the vein. Heparin is added to the blood to prevent clotting. The blood circulates slowly through dialysis tubing. This is an artificial partially permeable membrane which allows ions, very small molecules and

Table 20.6 Some common causes and characteristics of chronic and acute kidney failure.

Chronic kidney failure	*Acute kidney failure*
Causes	**Causes**
Bacterial infection of the pelvis and surrounding tissue	Decreased blood supply to the kidneys, possibly as a result of loss of blood through an accident, heart failure or toxic chemicals
Nephritis – inflammation of the glomeruli due to antibodies produced against certain bacterial infections such as throat infections	Severe bacterial infection or severe nephritis
Damage due to high blood pressure	Physical damage, e.g. in an accident
Damage due to obstruction in the ureters, bladder or urethra, e.g. by kidney stones (these may appear anywhere in the urinary tract but are most common in the pelvis)	Obstruction of the ureters, bladder or urethra, e.g. by kidney stones
Sugar diabetes	
Atherosclerosis (reduces blood supply)	
Characteristics	**Characteristics**
Progressive destruction of nephrons leading to:	
reduced quantity of urine	little or no urine produced
dilute urine	accumulation of nitrogenous waste in the blood
dehydration	salt imbalance
salt imbalance	pain
severe high blood pressure	
coma and convulsions	Often reversible if treated quickly

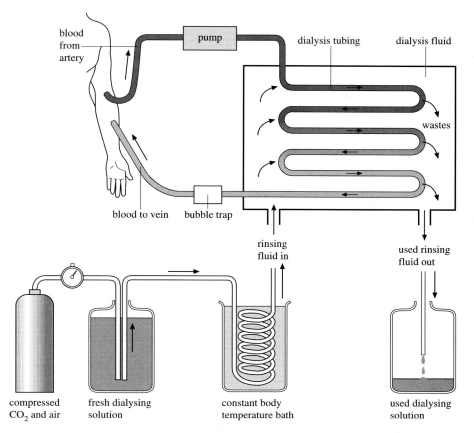

Fig 20.29 *Haemodialysis machine. Blood passes from an artery, through a coiled tube and back into a vein. The tube is a partially permeable membrane and is surrounded by dialysate. Waste products filter out into the dialysate.*

water to diffuse through it. Blood cells, platelets and protein molecules are too large to escape from the patient's blood. The tubing is bathed on the outside by a dialysing solution which has:

- the correct temperature;
- the correct ionic balance, particularly Na^+, K^+, Cl^-, Mg^{2+}, Ca^{2+}, and HCO_3^- (in the form of acetate, an organic anion);
- additional nutrients, such as glucose, which help to maintain the correct solute potential;
- the correct pH and buffering capacity.

Exchange between the blood and the dialysing solution (dialysate) takes place until an equilibrium is reached. Overall, unwanted substances are removed, particularly urea and excess sodium and potassium, and needed substances are kept. Note that the process is simpler than the real kidney because ultrafiltration does not occur and reabsorption of useful substances is not necessary.

The process takes 6 to 8 hours and is usually done at least twice a week. The solute potential of the dialysate is kept *less* negative (its water potential is higher) than that of the blood, despite the addition of glucose to the dialysate. Water would therefore tend to enter the blood. However, the blood pressure is raised to reverse this trend by squeezing the tube returning blood to the vein with a clip. The higher the pressure the greater the amount of water that will leave the blood. Regulation can therefore be achieved.

Acetate in the dialysate can be converted to hydrogen-carbonate ions in the body. This restores the body's own buffering capacity which tends to get used up during periods between treatments.

20.9.3 Peritoneal dialysis – use of the peritoneum, a natural membrane

This can be carried out in hospital. A thin plastic tube is inserted into the abdominal cavity through a small slit in the abdomen wall and can be left in permanently. The peritoneal membrane, or peritoneum, which lines the abdominal cavity is the dialysing membrane and is partially permeable. Dialysis fluid is added to the abdominal cavity down the tube and left for several hours before removal. Exchange takes place between the fluid and the tissue fluid in the rest of the abdomen. The fluid can be replaced regularly, 3 or 4 times a day. In between, the patient can be mobile and free to live a relatively normal life. For this reason it is described as **continuous ambulatory peritoneal dialysis**, or **CAPD** (ambulatory means moving about). Many patients prefer this to having to be connected to a kidney machine. The method is also simpler and less expensive. However, there is an increased risk of dangerous infections which can lead to peritonitis.

20.9.4   Kidney transplants

Kidney transplants were first performed in the UK in the 1960s and since then have become the most successful and most common form of organ transplantation. About 1800 are carried out each year in the UK, although this figure would be higher if sufficient donors were available. The UK has one of the lowest rates of kidney transplants in Europe. There is a high survival rate and problems of rejection have largely been overcome. A drug called cyclosporin A was commonly used to prevent rejection, but a new drug introduced in 1996 reduced acute rejection (rejection within 3 months) by a further 50%. Problems of rejection are discussed in section 25.7.13. The advantages of transplantation over dialysis treatment are that it is a lot cheaper and that the patient has a far better quality of life if the procedure is successful. The cost of dialysis was about £20 000 per year in the mid-1990s compared with £3000 per year for drug treatment after transplantation. The waiting list for transplants in the UK was 3700 in 1989.

Close living relatives are sometimes used as donors, since this greatly reduces the risk of rejection and a person can live normally with just one kidney. National and international systems for locating suitable donors have been set up. A patient is 'tissue typed' so that their antigens can be matched as closely as possible to those of the donor. If a recently deceased donor is to be used, tests for brain death of the donor are carried out and the kidneys are then removed and packed in ice. Meanwhile tissue typing and tests for hepatitis and HIV are carried out. The kidney is used as soon as possible, and must be used within 48 hours. The recipient may receive only a few hours notice of the operation.

Many moral and ethical issues are raised by kidney transplantation and dialysis. Some of the main ones are as follows.

- How much money? How much should we pay through taxes to the National Health Service?
- Sharing the money. How should existing resources be used? Should other branches of medicine receive more money, e.g. preventive medicine?
- Who? Who should be chosen for dialysis treatment and transplantation surgery when there are waiting lists? Should any people receive priority?
- Is it fair to ask a living relative to be a donor?
- Should more be done to promote the carrying of donor cards?
- How should the problem of getting permission from recently bereaved families for using someone's kidneys be handled?
- Should there be a market in kidneys for sale? In some countries there have been many cases of people selling a kidney to get out of debt. Is there anything wrong with this?
- Are tests for brain death of donors adequate? Is there a danger that judgements will be rushed because of the need for urgent action?

Some of these issues are addressed in *SATIS 16–19* unit 7, available through the Association for Science Education.

20.10   Water conservation in plants and algae

Plant tissue contains a higher proportion of water than animal tissue, and the efficient functioning of the plant cell and the whole plant depends upon maintaining the water content at a steady state. Plants do not have the same problems of osmoregulation as animals and they can be considered simply in relation to their environment. On this basis plants are classified as outlined below.

Hydrophytes

Freshwater aquatic plants such as Canadian pondweed (*Elodea canadensis*), water milfoil (*Myriophyllum*) and the water lily (*Nymphaea*) are classed as hydrophytes and have fewer osmoregulatory problems than any of the other plant types. Plant cells in fresh water are surrounded by a solution of higher water potential and water enters the cell by osmosis. The water passes through the freely permeable cell wall and the partially permeable cell surface and tonoplast membranes. As the volume of the vacuole increases due to water uptake, it generates a **turgor pressure** (pressure potential). The cell becomes turgid and a point is reached when the water potential has increased to equal that of the surrounding water (about zero) and no further water enters (see section 13.1.5).

Halophytes

Many algae live in sea water and they are the major autotrophic organisms of the seashore. The distribution of algal species down the shore is determined by many factors, including tolerance to wave action, desiccation when exposed by tides, and the nature of their photosynthetic pigments. In all cases these species can tolerate increases in salinity and their main osmoregulatory problem is the prevention of water loss by evaporation. Channel wrack (*Pelvetia canaliculata*) occupies the highest algal zone on sheltered rocky shores surrounding the British Isles, and its tolerance of dry conditions is aided by thick cell walls, a thick covering of mucilage and a stipe shaped as a channel. Fig 20.30 shows the rate of water loss and degree of tolerance of four common British species of seaweed which are zoned according to their ability to retain water when exposed to air.

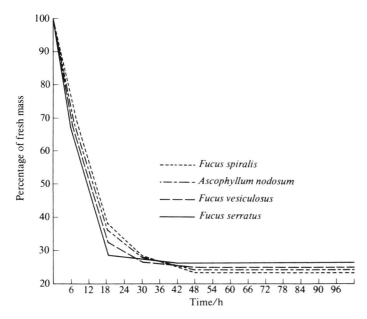

Fig 20.30 *Graph showing the comparative rates of water loss upon exposure to air for four species of algae found on the seashore. (From J. Zaneveld (1937) J. Ecol.,* **25**, *431–68.)*

Graph legend:
- - - - - - - *Fucus spiralis*
- · - · - · *Ascophyllum nodosum*
- – – – *Fucus vesiculosus*
──── *Fucus serratus*

Y-axis: Percentage of fresh mass (20 to 100)
X-axis: Time/h (6 to 96)

Halophytes, however, are defined as plants inhabiting areas of high salinity, such as those encountered in estuaries and salt marshes where salinity is constantly changing and may exceed that of sea water. Whilst the shoot system is not regularly exposed to high salinities, the root system must tolerate the increased salinities of the sand and mud which accompany hot windy periods when the tide is out. It was thought that these plants must tolerate periods of 'physiological drought' when water is unavailable to the tissues due to the low water potential of the environment of the roots. However, this does not seem to be the case and high transpiration rates and low water potential in root cells enable water to be taken up. Cord grass (*Spartina*) is a common halophyte found low down on estuaries and salt marshes; it has an extensive system of rhizomes for propagation, bearing adventitious roots for anchorage and purposes of water and ion uptake. Other halophytes of estuaries and salt marshes include smaller plants which store water when it is freely available. Common examples of these species are glasswort (*Salicornia*), seablite (*Suaeda maritima*) and sea purslane (*Halimione*). Some species, such as sea milkwort (*Glaux*) and *Spartina*, are able to regulate their salt content by excreting salt from glands at the margins of the leaves.

Mesophytes

The majority of angiosperm plant species are mesophytes, and they occupy habitats with adequate water supplies. They are faced with the problem of water loss by evaporation from all aerial parts. Features which help to reduce water loss are both structural (xeromorphic) and

physiological, and include the presence of a cuticle, protected stomata whose diameters can be regulated, a variable leaf shape, abscission (leaf fall) and an ecological distribution based upon tolerance to dehydration.

Xerophytes

Plants adapted to life in dry regions and able to survive long periods of drought are called xerophytes. These form the typical flora of desert and semi-desert regions and are common along the strand line of the seashore and in sand dunes. Some plants respond to extreme conditions by surviving in the seed or spore stage. These are known as **drought evaders** and can germinate following rainfall and grow, flower and complete seed formation in four weeks, for example the Californian poppy (*Escholtzia*). The seeds produced lie dormant until the next rainy spell.

Drought endurers, on the other hand, show many structural (xeromorphic) and physiological adaptations enabling them to survive in extremely dry conditions. Most of the xerophytic species of the British Isles are associated with the strand line and sand dunes, such as saltwort (*Salsola*) and sea sandwort (*Honkenya*) found growing in small mounds of sand on the shore. Sand couch grass (*Agropyron*) and marram grass (*Ammophila*) (fig 13.11) are dominant species of embryo dunes and have extensive rhizome systems with adventitious roots for obtaining water from well below sand level. *Agropyron* is able to tolerate salt concentrations in the sand up to 20 times that of sea water. Both *Ammophila* and *Agropyron* are important pioneer plants in the development of sand-dune systems.

Xerophytic plant species of desert regions show several adaptations to reducing water loss and obtaining and storing water. Some of these are summarised in table 20.7.

Fig 20.31 *The 'prickly pear' cactus,* Opuntia. *This desert plant is xerophytic, meaning it is adapted for dry conditions.*

Table 20.7 Summary of methods of conserving water shown by various plant species.

Mechanism of water conservation	Adaptation	Example
reduction in transpiration rate	waxy cuticle	prickly pear (*Opuntia*)
	few stomata	
	sunken stomata	pine (*Pinus*)
	stomata open at night	ice plant
	and closed by day	(*Mesembryanthemum*)
	surface covered with fine hairs	
	curled leaves	marram grass (*Ammophila*)
	fleshy succulent leaves	*Bryophyllum*
storage of water	fleshy succulent stems	candle plant (*Kleinia*)
	fleshy underground	*Raphionacme*
	tuber	
water uptake	deep root system	acacia
	below water table	oleander
	shallow root system	cactus
	absorbing surface moisture	

Chapter Twenty-one

Reproduction

Reproduction is the production of a new generation of individuals of the same species. It is one of the fundamental characteristics of living organisms. It involves the transmission of genetic material from one generation to the next, ensuring that the species survives over long periods of time, even though individual members of the species die.

Some members of a species will die before they reach reproductive age, due to factors such as predation, disease and accidental death, so that a species will only survive if each generation produces more offspring than the parental generation. Population sizes will vary according to the balance between rate of reproduction and rate of death of individuals. An increase in total numbers will occur where conditions are suitable. There are a number of different reproductive strategies, all with certain advantages and disadvantages which are described in this chapter.

A new individual normally has to go through a period of growth and development before it reaches the stage at which it can reproduce itself, and this is discussed in chapter 22.

Asexual and sexual reproduction

There are two basic types of reproduction, asexual and sexual. **Asexual reproduction** is reproduction by a single organism without production of gametes. It usually results in the production of genetically identical offspring, the only genetic variation arising as a result of random mutations among the individuals.

Sexual reproduction is the fusion of two gametes to form a zygote which develops into a new organism. It leads to genetic variation. Genetic variation is advantageous to a species because it provides the 'raw material' for natural selection, and hence evolution. Offspring showing most adaptations to the environment will have a competitive advantage over other members of the species and be more likely to survive and pass on their genes to the next generation. Over time, this process of natural selection can result in the species changing. Eventually new species may form, a process known as **speciation** (section 27.7). Increased variation can be achieved by the mixing of genes from two different individuals, a process known as genetic recombination. This is the essential feature of sexual reproduction. It occurs in almost all species, including in a primitive form in bacteria (section 2.3.3).

21.1   Asexual reproduction

Asexual reproduction is the production of offspring from a single organism without the production of gametes. The offspring are identical to the parent. Identical offspring from a single parent are referred to as a **clone**. Members of a clone only differ genetically as a result of random mutation. Most animal species do not naturally reproduce asexually, though successful attempts (section 21.1.4) have been made to clone certain species artificially.

There are several types of asexual reproduction. Examples from each of the five kingdoms of living organisms will be described below.

21.1.1   Kingdom: Prokaryotae (bacteria) and Kingdom: Protoctista

In unicellular organisms, such as bacteria and most protoctists, asexual reproduction occurs by a process called **fission**. This is the division of the cell into two or more daughter cells identical to the parent cell. The DNA replicates. In the case of protoctists, which are eukaryotes and therefore have nuclei, this is followed by nuclear division. In bacteria, and many protoctists such as *Amoeba* and *Paramecium*, two identical daughter cells are produced, a process called **binary fission** (section 2.3.3, figs 2.11 and 21.1). Under suitable conditions it results in rapid population growth, as described in section 2.3.5 for bacteria.

Multiple fission, in which repeated divisions of the parent nucleus are followed by division into many daughter cells, occurs in a group of protoctists which includes the malaria parasite *Plasmodium*. Here it occurs immediately after infection when the parasite enters the liver. About 1000 daughter cells are produced from one parent cell, each capable of invading a red blood cell and producing up to a further 24 daughter cells by multiple fission. Such enormous powers of reproduction compensate for the large losses associated with the difficulties of successful transfer from one human host to another by way of the vector organism, the mosquito.

21.1.2   Kingdom: Fungi

The typical body structure of fungi is a mass of fine tubes called **hyphae**. The whole mass of hyphae is called a **mycelium**. At the tips of the hyphae, spores can form, either enclosed in a special structure called the **sporangium**, or free. Spores are small structures containing a nucleus. They are produced in large numbers and are very light, being easily dispersed by air currents as well as by animals, particularly insects. Being small they usually have

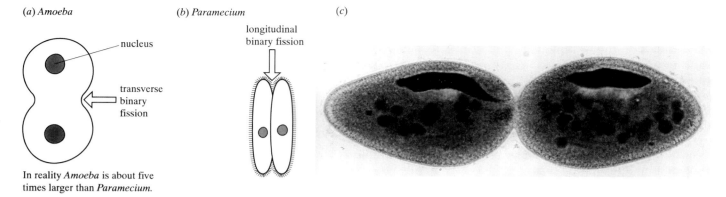

(a) *Amoeba*   (b) *Paramecium*   (c)

nucleus

transverse binary fission

longitudinal binary fission

In reality *Amoeba* is about five times larger than *Paramecium*.

Fig 21.1 *Asexual reproduction by binary fission. (a) Transverse binary fission in* Amoeba. *(b) Longitudinal binary fission in* Paramecium. *(c)* Amoeba *dividing by binary fission.*

small food stores and there is great wastage as many fail to find a suitable place for germination. However, they allow rapid multiplication and spread of fungi.

An example of a fungus that produces sporangia is *Mucor*. This is described in section 2.5.2 and fig 2.26. An example of a fungus that produces spores directly at the tips of its hyphae is *Penicillium*, as described in section 2.5.2 and fig 2.25. Yeasts are unusual fungi because they are unicellular and do not have hyphae. Yeast cells multiply rapidly in a form of asexual reproduction called budding (fig 2.27).

Budding is a form of asexual reproduction in which a new individual is produced as an outgrowth (bud) of the parent, and is later released as an independent, identical copy of the parent. It takes place in a number of other groups of organisms, notably the cnidarians, for example *Hydra* (see animals below).

21.1.3 Plant kingdom

The most common form of asexual reproduction in plants is called **vegetative propagation**. Vegetative propagation (or vegetative reproduction) is a form of asexual reproduction in which a bud grows and develops into a new plant. At some stage the new plant becomes detached from the parent plant and starts to lead an independent existence. Specialised organs of propagation often develop, but they must all have buds, and since buds only occur on stems, they must all contain at least a small part of a stem. Examples are bulbs, corms, rhizomes, stolons and tubers. Some of these also store food and are means of surviving adverse conditions, such as cold periods or drought. The food is used for growth when conditions become suitable. Plants possessing them can therefore survive from one year to the next. The structures are called **perennating organs**, and include bulbs, corms, rhizomes and tubers. In all cases the food stored comes mainly from photosynthesis of the current year's leaves.

Some of the organs of vegetative propagation and

perennation are described below. Artificial propagation is considered later in this chapter (section 21.3).

Bulb. A modified shoot, for example onion (*Allium*), daffodil (*Narcissus*) and tulip (*Tulipa*). An organ of perennation as well as vegetative propagation.

A bulb has a very short stem and fleshy storage leaves. It is surrounded by brown scaly leaves, the remains of the previous year's leaves after their food stores have been used. The bulb contains one or more buds. Each bud that grows forms a shoot which produces a new bulb at the end of the growing season. Roots are adventitious, that is they grow from the stem rather than from a main 'tap' root.

A typical bulb is illustrated in fig 21.2.

Corm. A short, swollen, vertical underground stem, as in *Crocus* and *Gladiolus*. An organ of perennation as well as vegetative propagation.

A corm consists of the swollen base of a stem surrounded by protective scale leaves; there are no fleshy leaves, unlike bulbs. Scale leaves are the remains of the previous season's foliage leaves. Roots are adventitious. At the end of the growing season contractile roots pull the new corm down into the soil. The corm contains one or more buds which may result in vegetative propagation (compare bulb).

A typical corm is illustrated in fig 21.3.

brown **scale leaf**, protective, foliage leaf of season before last

fleshy leaves storing food, swollen bases of last season's foliage leaves

apical bud next season's plant, contains embryo stem, foliage leaves and a flower

apical bud of next season's bulb

axillary bud, may also form a new plant

short, flattened **stem**

remains of last season's **adventitious roots**

Fig 21.2 *Diagrammatic section through a dormant bulb.*

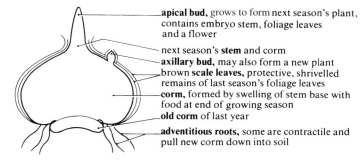

apical bud, grows to form next season's plant, contains embryo stem, foliage leaves and a flower

next season's stem and corm

axillary bud, may also form a new plant

brown **scale leaves,** protective, shrivelled remains of last season's foliage leaves

corm, formed by swelling of stem base with food at end of growing season

old corm of last year

adventitious roots, some are contractile and pull new corm down into soil

Fig 21.3 *Diagrammatic section through a dormant corm.*

Rhizome. A horizontally growing underground stem, such as in *Iris*, couch grass (*Agropyron repens*), mint (*Mentha*) and Michaelmas daisy (*Aster*). It is usually an organ of perennation as well as vegetative propagation.

A rhizome bears leaves, buds and adventitious roots. The leaves may be scale-like (small and thin, whitish or brownish in colour) as in couch grass or green foliage leaves as in *Iris*. An *Iris* rhizome is illustrated in fig 21.4.

Stolon. A creeping, horizontally growing stem that grows along the surface of the ground, for example blackberry (*Rubus*), gooseberry, blackcurrant and redcurrant (all *Ribes* spp.). It is not an organ of perennation.

Roots are adventitious, growing from nodes.

A plan of a typical stolon is illustrated in fig 21.5.

Runner. A type of stolon that elongates rapidly, as in strawberry (*Fragaria*) and creeping buttercup (*Ranunculus repens*).

A runner bears scale leaves with axillary buds and the buds give rise to adventitious roots and new plants. The runners eventually decay once the new plants are established. The runner may represent the main stem or grow from one of the lower axillary buds on the main stem, as illustrated in fig 21.6. In strawberry, scale leaves and axillary buds occur at every node, but roots and foliage leaves arise only at every other node. All axillary buds may give rise to new runners.

Tuber. A tuber is an underground storage organ formed from a stem or a root, swollen with food and capable of perennation. Tubers survive only one year, and shrivel as their contents are used during the growing season. New tubers are made at the end of the growing season, but do not arise from old tubers (in contrast to corms, which arise from old corms).

Stem tubers are stem structures produced at the tips of thin rhizomes, as in potato (*Solanum tuberosum*). Their stem structure is revealed by the presence of axillary buds in the axils of scale leaves (fig 21.7). Each bud may grow into a new plant during the next growing season. Bearing in

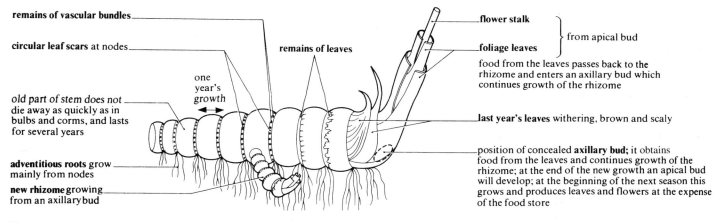

remains of vascular bundles

circular leaf scars at nodes

remains of leaves

flower stalk

foliage leaves

} from apical bud

food from the leaves passes back to the rhizome and enters an axillary bud which continues growth of the rhizome

one year's growth

old part of stem does not die away as quickly as in bulbs and corms, and lasts for several years

last year's leaves withering, brown and scaly

position of concealed **axillary bud;** it obtains food from the leaves and continues growth of the rhizome; at the end of the new growth an apical bud will develop; at the beginning of the next season this grows and produces leaves and flowers at the expense of the food store

adventitious roots grow mainly from nodes

new rhizome growing from an axillary bud

Fig 21.4 *Diagrammatic structure of an* Iris *rhizome.*

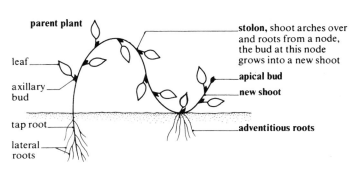

parent plant

leaf

axillary bud

tap root

lateral roots

stolon, shoot arches over and roots from a node, the bud at this node grows into a new shoot

apical bud

new shoot

adventitious roots

Fig 21.5 *Generalised plan of a stolon.*

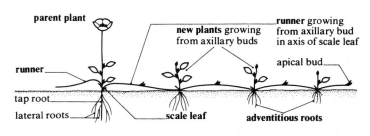

parent plant

runner

tap root

lateral roots

new plants growing from axillary buds

runner growing from axillary bud in axis of scale leaf

apical bud

scale leaf

adventitious roots

Fig 21.6 *Plan of a strawberry runner.*

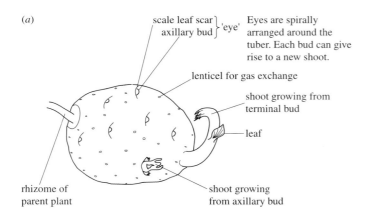

(a)

scale leaf scar ⎱ 'eye'
axillary bud ⎰

Eyes are spirally arranged around the tuber. Each bud can give rise to a new shoot.

lenticel for gas exchange

shoot growing from terminal bud

leaf

rhizome of parent plant

shoot growing from axillary bud

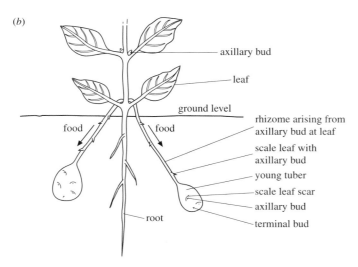

(b)

axillary bud

leaf

ground level

food   food

rhizome arising from axillary bud at leaf

scale leaf with axillary bud

young tuber

scale leaf scar

axillary bud

terminal bud

root

Fig 21.7 (a) Stem tuber of potato. (b) Potato plant early in the season.

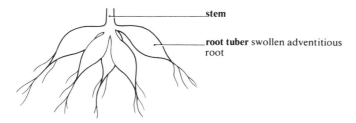

stem

root tuber swollen adventitious root

Fig 21.8 Root tubers of Dahlia.

mind that each plant produces more than one tuber and that each tuber has more than one bud, rapid multiplication is possible.

Root tubers are swollen adventitious roots, for example *Dahlia* (fig 21.8). New plants develop from axillary buds at the base of the old stem.

Swollen tap roots. A tap root is a main root that has developed from the radicle, the first root of the seedling. Tap roots are characteristic of dicotyledonous plants. Tap roots may become swollen with food-storing tissue, as in carrot (*Daucus*), parsnip (*Pastinaca*), swede

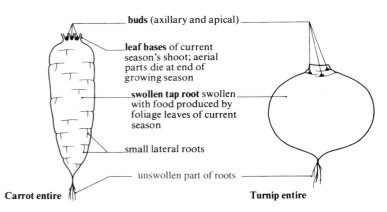

buds (axillary and apical)

leaf bases of current season's shoot; aerial parts die at end of growing season

swollen tap root swollen with food produced by foliage leaves of current season

small lateral roots

unswollen part of roots

Carrot entire   **Turnip entire**

Fig 21.9 Tap roots of carrot and turnip.

(*Brassica napus*), turnip (*Brassica rapa*) and radish (*Raphanus sativus*). Together with buds at the base of the old stem, just above the tap root, they form organs of perennation and vegetative propagation. Two types of swollen tap root are shown in fig 21.9.

Swollen tap roots are characteristic of biennial plants, plants that grow vegetatively during the first year of growth and survive winter by means of an underground storage organ. They produce flowers and seeds during the second year of growth, at the end of which they die.

Tillers. Before they flower, grass plants consist of a collection of shoots, also known as tillers (fig 2.41). Each tiller consists of a number of leaves, which arise from nodes on a very short stem at the base of the leaves. What looks like a stem in a non-flowering grass plant is mainly a series of leaf sheaths rolled into cylinders, one inside another. Where each leaf joins the stem, an axillary bud is located. This can grow into another tiller, depending partly on conditions such as availability of minerals and temperature. Each tiller is genetically and structurally identical to the original tiller. They normally all remain connected. Sometimes tillers emerge as stolons or rhizomes (as in couch grass) and give rise eventually to shoots or tillers which are independent of the main plant and are therefore a form of vegetative propagation. Normally though a collection of tillers is regarded as one plant.

21.1.4 Animal kingdom

Asexual reproduction occurs only in relatively unspecialised animals. Members of the animal phylum Cnidaria can undergo budding in which a new individual is produced as an outgrowth of the parent, as described for yeast (see Fungi above). An example is *Hydra* (fig 2.48a and g).

Another form of asexual reproduction is fragmentation. This is the breaking of an organism into two or more parts, each of which grows to form a new individual. Strong powers of regeneration are needed. The bodies of ribbon worms, a group of simple marine worms, break up easily into small pieces, each of which can regenerate a new individual. Starfish can regenerate if accidental fragmentation occurs.

Cloning of animals

Cloning is the production of many genetically identical copies of an individual by asexual reproduction. It may occur naturally, but techniques have been developed which allow the process to be carried out artificially. The first successful cloning of a vertebrate was carried out in the late 1960s by Dr J. Gurdon at Oxford University.

The process does not occur naturally among vertebrates but, by taking a cell from the intestine or skin of a frog and introducing its nucleus into an egg cell whose own nucleus had been destroyed by ultraviolet radiation, he was able to grow a tadpole, which in turn grew into a frog identical to the parent from which the nucleus was transplanted (fig 21.10).

Experiments like these showed that differentiated (specialised) cells still contain all the information needed to make the whole organism. They are said to be **totipotent**. They also suggested that similar techniques might successfully be used in cloning more advanced vertebrates. Research in Scotland in 1996 led to the successful cloning of a sheep (Dolly) from a cell taken from the parent's udder.

Cloning of a human embryo was carried out in the USA in 1993, although the clones were only grown to the stage of a few cells to demonstrate the possibility. (The process is banned on ethical grounds in the UK.) Cloning does find a use for other animal species however. It is possible to work on animal embryos at the stage of a few cells and to deliberately split the ball of cells into identical twins. This process can be repeated many times because the cells at this stage have not yet become irreversibly specialised. In this way many identical copies of a single useful animal can be created. The embryos can then be transferred to surrogate (recipient) mothers for further growth and eventual birth of the desired animals. Cloning embryos in this way is becoming increasingly important in animal breeding and has been used, for example, for cattle, sheep and goats. It speeds up the selective breeding of animals from desirable parents but raises many difficult issues (section 25.6).

Cells may also be cloned for special purposes. This technique is called **tissue culture**. Certain cells when placed in a suitable medium can be cultured indefinitely. The use of cloned cells allows a study of the action of such chemicals as hormones, drugs, antibiotics, cosmetics and pharmaceutical products to be made on cells. Such a technique is a useful substitute for laboratory animals such as rats, cats and dogs.

21.2 Advantages and disadvantages of natural asexual reproduction

Both asexual and sexual reproduction have advantages and both forms are used by many organisms. Some organisms such as humans and many other animals rely entirely on sexual reproduction. *Amoeba* apparently relies entirely on asexual reproduction. We cannot say that one form of reproduction is better than the other. They are both successful strategies in the right situation.

Advantages

During asexual reproduction parent cells divide into genetically identical daughter cells. In eukaryotes this involves mitosis. The advantages of this process are as follows.

- **Only one parent is required**. Where sexual reproduction involves two organisms, time and energy are used in finding a mate, or, in the case of non-motile organisms such as plants, special mechanisms such as pollination are required which may be wasteful of gametes. One solution to this problem is hermaphrodite organisms which produce both male and female sex organs.

- **Genetically identical offspring**. If the organism is well adapted to its environment, the fact that the offspring are genetically identical may be an advantage. Successful combinations of genes are preserved.

- **Dispersal and spread**. The methods of asexual reproduction often enable dispersal of a species. For example, *Penicillium* and *Mucor* are common moulds which spread rapidly by means of asexually produced spores which are light and easily dispersed by air currents. This enables the fungi to find fresh sources of food. Plants that produce rhizomes, such as sea couch grass in sand dunes, bracken, and *Spartina* (cord grass) in mud flats, spread rapidly by this means.

- **Rapid multiplication**. Bacteria can divide as often as once every 20 minutes allowing numbers to build up very rapidly. Many parasites rely on one or more asexual stages where rapid multiplication compensates for large losses at other stages in the life cycle. The malaria parasite, tapeworm and liver fluke are good examples.

Disadvantages

- No genetic variation occurs among the offspring. The advantages of variation are discussed with sexual reproduction (section 21.5).

- If spores are produced, many will fail to find a suitable place for germination and so energy and materials used in their manufacture are wasted.

- If an organism spreads in one area, it may result in overcrowding and exhaustion of nutrients.

21.3 Artificial propagation of plants – cloning

A number of methods of artificial propagation of plants are used in agriculture and horticulture. The first three methods discussed below, namely cuttings, grafting

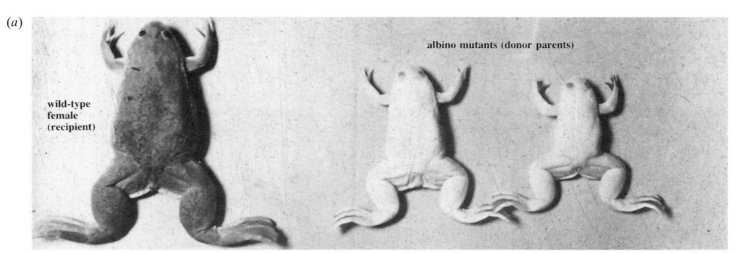

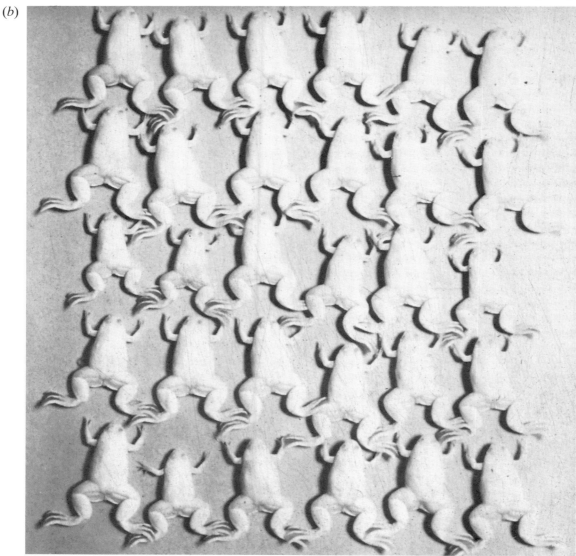

Fig 21.10 (a) *A clone of frogs* (Xenopus laevis) *produced by nuclear transplantation. An embryo was obtained from a cross between two albino mutants (donor parents). Its cells were separated and their nuclei transplanted into unfertilised eggs whose own nuclei had been destroyed with ultra-violet radiation. The eggs were from the wild-type female shown (the recipient). (b) The clones produced are all female and albino; this group of 30 were obtained from a total of 54 nuclear transfers.*

and layering, are traditional methods, but for commercial purposes they are gradually being replaced by modern methods involving tissue culture.

21.3.1 Cuttings

This is a simple procedure in which part of the plant is removed by cutting and placed in a suitable medium for growth. It produces roots and grows into a new plant. Rooting can be stimulated with a rooting hormone. The popular house plants *Geranium* and *Pelargonium* are commonly propagated in this way, using cuttings from their shoots. The African violet, another popular house plant, can be propagated from leaf cuttings. The process is used commercially for blackcurrant bushes in which cuttings from shoots are taken in the autumn. Chrysanthemums are also propagated by cuttings from shoots.

21.3.2 Grafting and budding

Grafting is the transfer of part of one plant, the **scion**, onto the lower part of another plant, the **stock**. This was originally done for apple trees because the plants could not be grown from cuttings, and seedlings showed too much variation because they are produced by sexual reproduction. It is now also used for some other fruit trees, such as plum and peach. The scion is chosen for its fruit and the stock for properties such as disease resistance and hardiness.

Most rose bushes are propagated by a variation of this method known as **budding** in which a bud is used as the scion rather than a shoot. New varieties are produced by *sexual* reproduction, but, like fruit trees, are not pure breeding. Artificial propagation therefore has an important role in preserving desired varieties.

21.3.3 Layering

Layering is used for plants that produce runners, such as strawberries. The runners are pegged out (layered) around the parent plant until they root, and are then cut to detach them from the parent plant.

21.3.4 Tissue culture, or micropropagation

Micropropagation is the propagation, or cloning, of plants by tissue culture. 'Micro' refers to the small size of the material used, usually isolated cells or small pieces of tissue. The material is grown in special culture solutions, so the process is also known as **tissue culture**. It developed from experiments which showed that plant tissues removed ('excised') from plants could be stimulated to grow in solution by the addition of nutrients and certain plant hormones, particularly auxins and cytokinins. The latter are needed for continued cell division. Tissue culture is now widely used for the rapid propagation of desired varieties (fig 21.11).

Totipotency

It was shown in the early 1960s that the nuclei of mature plant cells still contain all the information needed to code for the entire organism. Professor F. C. Steward of Cornell University, USA showed that mature cells removed from a carrot and placed in a suitable culture solution could be stimulated to start dividing again and to provide new carrot plants. The cells were described as **totipotent**, meaning that they retain the ability to grow into new plants in suitable conditions even when mature and specialised.

Why use tissue culture?

A summary of some of the important advantages of tissue culture is given below. Further details are given at the end of this section.

- Plants with desired characteristics can sometimes (though not always) be multiplied rapidly, producing many identical copies of the same plant. This is not easily done using conventional breeding methods which rely on sexual reproduction, particularly when plants are adapted for cross-pollination and outbreeding (see later). The technique is important for certain crops and other commercially important plants. New varieties obtained by plant breeding can be reproduced quickly. The technique therefore speeds up the development and introduction of new varieties.
- Cells can be genetically modified ('transformed') and grown into whole plants, known as **transgenic** plants, using tissue culture. Transgenic plants are discussed in section 25.2.1.
- Tissue cultures take up little space.
- Plants are grown in disease-free conditions. Viruses can be eliminated as described below.
- New methods of producing hybrids by fusing protoplasts, that is cells which have been released from their cell walls, have been developed. Hybrids between different species, such as potato and tomato, have been achieved in this way.
- The techniques may prove an efficient way of producing useful chemicals, such as pharmaceutical products, from plants.

Outline of the technique

The culture medium must contain the correct nutrients and hormones (plant growth substances, section 16.2). A typical medium will contain the inorganic ions needed for plant growth, such as a source of nitrogen, magnesium, iron and potassium (table 7.7). Also needed are sucrose as a source of energy, and vitamins. These chemicals are usually mixed with agar to form a jelly-like nutrient agar similar to that used for growing bacteria and fungi. Auxins and cytokinins are the two essential hormones. Auxins stimulate root growth and cell elongation and cytokinins stimulate shoot growth and cell division. Differences in the amount of auxin relative to cytokinin affect the way unspecialised cells develop. The tissue culture is grown on the surface of the agar in flasks or petri dishes.

Fig 21.11 *Tissue culture. (a) Auricula plant with well-developed leaves which can be cut into many small pieces for cloning. (b) Leaf fragments are transferred to agar under sterile conditions. (c) The leaf fragment has developed a callus and a new shoot. (d) The shoot has been removed from the leaf fragment and placed in deep agar to encourage roots to grow. (e) Young clones are then planted into light growing medium to strengthen root development. (f) Identical plants cloned from fragments of one leaf.*

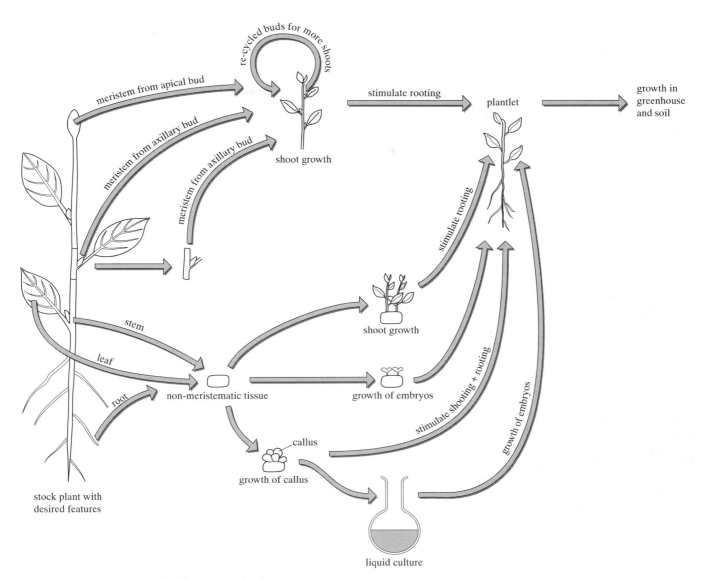

re-cycled buds for more shoots

meristem from apical bud

meristem from axillary bud

meristem from axillary bud

shoot growth

stem

leaf

root

stock plant with
desired features

non-meristematic tissue

growth of callus

callus

shoot growth

growth of embryos

stimulate shooting + rooting

liquid culture

growth of embryos

stimulate rooting

stimulate rooting

plantlet

growth in
greenhouse
and soil

Fig 21.12 *Methods for cloning from a stock plant.*

Temperature, light intensity, light quality, daylength and humidity are all controlled by growing the cultures in special growth rooms or cabinets. All procedures must be sterile because bacteria and fungi can also grow in the cultures and would grow faster and out-compete the plants in these conditions. The plant tissues themselves are surface sterilised in a dilute bleach solution, and other materials are also sterilised before use. All apparatus must be handled under sterile conditions, as in microbiological work (section 12.3).

Fig 21.12 summarises the main methods by which new plants can be grown using tissue culture. The pieces taken from the stock plant are known as **explants**. The most common method is to use meristematic tissue from apical or axillary buds. A **meristem** is a region where cell division is still taking place. In plants, growth is confined to such regions. Another method is to produce a callus from non-meristematic tissue (fig 21.13). A callus is an

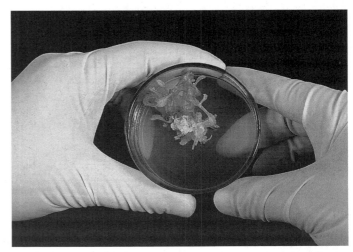

Fig 21.13 Nicotiana *plantlets growing from callus tissue culture on sterile agar.*

undifferentiated (unspecialised) mass of cells. Roots or shoots can be stimulated to grow from a callus or from non-meristematic tissue by adding auxins or cytokinins. Fig 21.13 shows young shoots arising from a callus. Sometimes embryos are produced rather than shoots and roots. Embryos can be placed in agar jelly to form artificial seed or grown into plantlets. Figs 21.11 shows further stages in the process.

Virus-free plants

Viruses can spread throughout plants and it is extremely difficult to prevent them from passing from one plant to another in traditional breeding programmes. However, viruses do not normally penetrate to the tips of meristems. It is therefore possible to use meristems for producing virus-free plants by cloning. Heat treatment of the meristems can increase certainty that they are virus-free. Stocks of virus-free meristems can be kept so that new plants can be produced as needed. This cuts the cost of setting up protected greenhouses and is a more reliable means of preventing spread of disease than traditional methods. Potatoes, fruit trees, some bulbs and ornamental plants are propagated in this way.

Production of potatoes – a case study

Micropropagation is used on a large scale for ornamental plants, fruit trees and plantation crops such as oil palm, date palm, sugar cane and banana, but so far has been used mainly on a small scale for agricultural crops. The only exception to this is the potato (table 21.1). One reason for using the technique with potatoes is the opportunity to produce virus-free plants. Large numbers of plantlets are produced by recycling meristematic tissue. The plantlets are then used to produce minitubers the size of peas (fig 21.14) which can be sown like seed. Over half a million minitubers can be produced per year from one original plant. Introduction of new varieties of potato with, for example, resistance to the serious virus disease potato leaf roll virus can be speeded up as a result.

Potatoes are an important crop worldwide, not just in Great Britain. The potato ranks fourth in the world in terms of agricultural production, behind the cereals rice, wheat and maize. Its popularity is increasing in Asian countries. Until recently new varieties could only be introduced by cross-breeding plants with desired features. However, there are several subspecies and not all of these will cross-breed. Of those that will cross-breed some produce only sterile hybrids. There is also the problem that it commonly takes about 10–15 years to produce a stable new variety by repeated genetic crossings.

Using tissue culture, wild relatives of the potato can be mass produced as well as the cultivated varieties. New varieties can now be 'instantly' created by transferring useful genes from, say, wild relatives of the cultivated varieties, or even from totally unrelated plants, into single cells using the standard techniques of genetic engineering. The most common technique uses the bacterium *Agrobacterium* as a vector (chapter 25). The 'transformed' cells can then be grown into plantlets by tissue culture and multiplied as described. In this way the gene for one of the coat proteins of the potato leaf roll virus has been introduced into the potato varieties Desiree and Pentland Squire. This is equivalent to vaccination against the virus. Although the potato may still get infected, the virus multiplies much more slowly than normal and the plant shows no, or few, signs of disease.

Another technique which has been successfully used with potatoes is to fuse two somatic (non-sex) cells from

Table 21.1 Comparison of traditional methods with tissue culture methods (micropropagation) for propagating potato tubers.

Traditional	Micropropagation
Year 1	
100 g tuber	100 g tuber
↓	↓
1 mature plant	one stock plant
	↓
	10 buds cultured
	↓
	shoot multiplication
	↓
1600 g tubers	65 000 minitubers each capable of producing 10 plants
Year 2	↓
16 mature plants	650 000 possible plants
	5% loss for establishment in soil
	617 500 mature plants
↓	↓
16 × 1600 g tubers = **25.6 kg**	617 500 × 500 g tubers = **308 750 kg**

(Based on table 12.3 *Molecular biotechnology*, 2nd ed., S.D. Primrose (1991), Blackwell, reproduced from Mantell *et al.* (1985).)

Fig 21.14 *Minitubers of potato look exactly like normal tubers but are only the size of peas.*

two different varieties. This involves first removing the cell walls to create naked protoplasts. The resulting **somatic hybrids** can be grown in tissue culture. Such hybrids can be made between two varieties which would not be able to be crossed using sexual reproduction due to incompatibility. Resistance to potato leaf roll virus and tolerance to cold have been bred into commercial varieties from wild potatoes in this way.

Advantages of micropropagation

- **Rapid multiplication**. When shoots are produced during cloning they produce buds in the normal way. These buds can be used to generate more shoots using the same tissue culture techniques. By constantly re-cycling buds in this way, the number of potential plants is multiplied at each stage. This can result in thousands or even millions of plants being produced from one shoot over a period of a year. This is much faster than traditional breeding methods, so new varieties can be introduced several years earlier than was possible by the old techniques.
- **Genetic uniformity**. Since plants produced are genetically identical, they all possess the desirable features of the stock plant. It is difficult to produce plants that breed true (are homozygous for the required features) when sexual reproduction is used.
- **Disease-free plants**. As explained, virus diseases can be eliminated by using meristematic tissue for propagation. Since the plants are prepared in sterile conditions they are also free from surface bacteria and fungi, some of which would cause disease.
- Tissue culture takes up relatively little space compared with growing plants in greenhouses or fields.
- Tissue culture can be carried out independently of seasonal changes in climate. One advantage of this is that plants can be produced out of season, when they can be sold for higher prices.
- Plant development is more closely controlled, guaranteeing product uniformity for customers.
- Some plants, such as banana, are sterile and have to be propagated asexually.
- The seeds of some plants, such as certain orchids, are difficult to germinate. The plants can be produced more reliably by asexual means.
- Micropropagation can be linked with genetic engineering to produce transgenic plants as described in section 25.4.
- Airfreighting is economic because the cultures are not bulky. This increases the possibility of international trade.

Disadvantages of micropropagation

- It is very labour intensive and not as convenient as sowing seed. The work is also skilled. Organisation and training of staff presents problems when carrying out procedures on a large scale. It also adds significantly to the cost of the operation. The process is normally only commercially viable for expensive products such as ornamental plants, and is not suitable for low-cost crops such as carrots.
- Sterile conditions must be maintained. This adds to the cost and makes operations much more demanding.
- Plants obtained from callus cultures sometimes undergo genetic changes. A small proportion of these changes may be commercially useful, but most are undesirable.
- Since the clones are genetically identical, crops are very susceptible to new diseases or changes in environmental conditions. Whole crops could be wiped out.

21.4 Sexual reproduction

Sexual reproduction is the production of offspring by the fusion of two **gametes** to form a diploid **zygote** which develops into the mature organism. The act of fusion is called **fertilisation**. At fertilisation the nuclei of the gametes fuse, bringing together two sets of chromosomes, one set from each parent. The presence of two sets of chromosomes is referred to as the diploid condition. Gametes are haploid, meaning that they carry one set of chromosomes.

Meiosis is an essential feature of life cycles in which sexual reproduction occurs because it provides a mechanism for reducing the amount of genetic material by half. This ensures that when gametes fuse, the diploid number of chromosomes is restored. If the chromosome number were not halved before production of gametes, the chromosome number would double with every generation (see fig 23.10).

During meiosis random segregation of chromosomes (**independent assortment**) and exchange of genetic material between homologous chromosomes (**crossing-over**) results in new combinations of genes being brought together in the gamete and this reshuffling increases genetic variation (section 23.4). The combination of two sets of chromosomes (**genetic recombination**), one set from each parent, in the zygote forms the basis of variation within species. The zygote grows and develops into the mature organism of the next generation.

Gametes are usually of two types, male and female, but in some primitive organisms they are of one type only. If the gametes are of two types, they may be produced by separate male and female parents or by a single parent bearing both male and female reproductive organs. Species that have separate male and female individuals are described as **unisexual**, such as humans and most other animals. Species capable of producing both male and female gametes within the same organism are described as **hermaphrodite**, or **bisexual**. Many protozoans, for example *Paramecium*, cnidarians such as *Obelia*, platyhelminths such as *Taenia* (tapeworm), oligochaetes such as *Lumbricus* (earthworm), crustacea such as *Balanus*

Table 21.2 Comparison of asexual reproduction with sexual reproduction (omitting bacteria).

Asexual reproduction	Sexual reproduction
One parent only	Usually two parents
No gametes are produced	Gametes are produced. These are haploid and nuclei of two gametes fuse (fertilisation) to form a diploid zygote
Depends on mitosis	Depends on meiosis being present at some stage in life cycle to prevent chromosome doubling in every generation
Offspring identical to parent	Offspring are *not* identical to parents. They show genetic variation as a result of genetic recombination
Commonly occurs in plants, simple animals and microorganisms Absent in more complex animals	Occurs in almost all plant and animal species
Often results in rapid production of large numbers of offspring	Less rapid increase in numbers

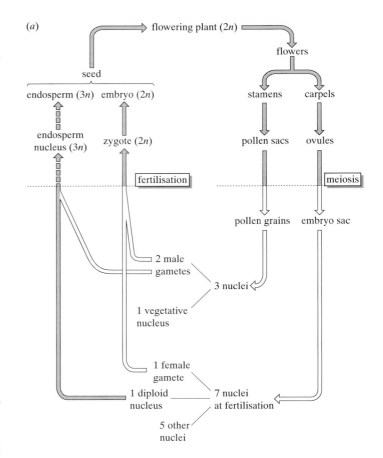

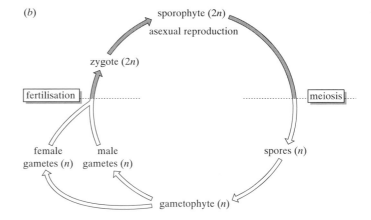

Fig 21.15 *(a) Life cycle of a flowering plant. (b) Life cycle showing alternation of generations. A diploid sporophyte generation alternates with a haploid gametophyte generation. The sporophyte generation reproduces asexually by means of spores, and the gametophyte generation reproduces sexually by means of gametes. All plants have this type of life cycle, although it is not very obvious in flowering plants.*

(barnacle), molluscs such as *Helix* (garden snail), some fish, lizards and birds, and most flowering plants are hermaphrodite.

A summary of some of the typical features of asexual and sexual reproduction is given in table 21.2.

21.5 Sexual reproduction in flowering plants

21.5.1 The life cycle of flowering plants

Flowering plants owe much of their success to the ways in which their sexual reproduction has been adapted to dry land. This has been discussed in section 2.7.7. The major adaptations are:

- the production of seeds and fruits to nourish and protect the embryo plants and to help in their dispersal.
- the absence of swimming male gametes. Male gametes are carried inside pollen grains to the female parts of the plant, a process called **pollination**. This is followed by the production of a pollen tube carrying male nuclei to the female gamete.
- the extreme reduction of the gametophyte generation, which is poorly adapted to life on land in simpler plants like bryophytes (see below).

An outline of the life cycle of flowering plants is given in fig 21.15a. If you are studying a range of plants, it would be useful to bear in mind that there is an alternation of generations in the life cycle, as is shown more simply in fig 21.15*b*. This is discussed in section 2.7.1. In flowering plants, the gametophyte generation is virtually non-existent and is not free-living. It would be difficult to realise that alternation of generations occurs if it were not for the comparison that can be made with more primitive ancestors.

21.5.2 The parts of a flower

The use of the term 'flowering plants' is a reference to the uniqueness of this group in producing flowers. Flowers are reproductive structures whose evolutionary origins are unclear, but which are sometimes regarded as collections of highly specialised leaves. A generalised flower is shown in fig 21.16, and some of the terms used to describe the flower parts are explained below. A collection of flowers borne on the same stalk is called an **inflorescence**. A collection of flowers may be more attractive to pollinating insects than a small solitary flower.

The **receptacle** is the top of the flower stalk (**pedicel**) from which the flower parts arise. The **perianth** consists of two whorls of structures called perianth segments. In monocotyledons the two whorls are usually similar, for instance daffodil, tulip and bluebell. In dicotyledons the two whorls are usually different, consisting of an outer whorl of **sepals** called the **calyx** and an inner whorl of **petals** called the **corolla**.

The **calyx** is the collection of sepals. Sepals are usually green and leaf-like structures that enclose and protect the flower buds. Occasionally they are brightly coloured and petal-like, serving to attract insects for pollination.

The **corolla** is the collection of petals. In insect-pollinated flowers the petals are usually large and brightly coloured, serving to attract insects. In wind-pollinated flowers the petals are usually reduced in size and green, or may be entirely absent.

The **androecium** is the collection of **stamens**, forming the male reproductive organs of the flower. Each stamen consists of an **anther** and a **filament**. The anther contains the **pollen sacs** in which **pollen** is made. The filament contains a vascular bundle that carries food and water to the anther.

The **gynoecium** is the collection of **carpels**, forming the female reproductive organs of the flower. A carpel consists of a **stigma**, **style** and **ovary**. The stigma receives the pollen grains during pollination and the style bears the stigma in a suitable position in the flower to receive the pollen. The ovary is the swollen, hollow base of the carpel and contains one or more ovules. **Ovules** are the structures in which the embryo sacs develop and which, after fertilisation, become seeds. Each is attached to the ovary wall by a short stalk called the funicle and the point of attachment is called the placenta.

The carpels of a flower may be separate and free, as in buttercup, or fused to form a single structure, as in white deadnettle. The styles of flowers with fused carpels may be fused or separate.

The receptacle and flower are described as **hypogynous** if the stamens and perianth are inserted below the gynoecium as in fig 21.16, **epigynous** if stamens and perianth are inserted above the ovary, and **perigynous** if the receptacle is flattened or cup-shaped with the gynoecium at the centre and the stamens and perianth attached round the rim. A **superior** ovary is an ovary located *above* the other flower parts on the receptacle, that is the ovary of a hypogynous flower. An **inferior** ovary is an ovary located *below* the other flower parts on the receptacle, that is the ovary of an epigynous flower.

The **nectaries** are glandular structures that secrete nectar, a sugary fluid that attracts animals for pollination, usually insects, but also birds and bats in the tropics.

The following terms are applied to whole plants and flowers.

- **hermaphrodite** (bisexual) plants – male and female sex organs borne on the same plant.
- **dioecious** (unisexual) plants – male and female sex organs borne on separate plants, that is the plants are either male or female, for example yew, willow, poplar and holly.
- **monoecious** plants – separate male and female flowers borne on the same plant, such as oak, hazel, beech and sycamore. Such plants are hermaphrodite.

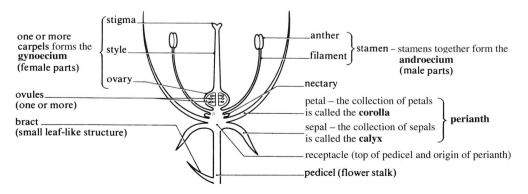

Fig 21.16 *Longitudinal section of a generalised flower.*

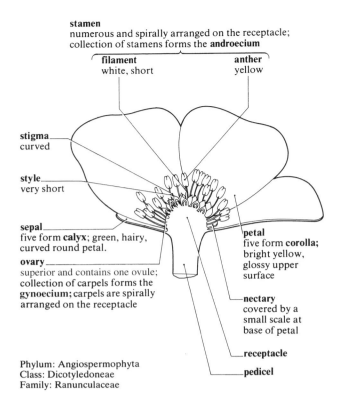

stamen
numerous and spirally arranged on the receptacle;
collection of stamens forms the **androecium**

filament
white, short

anther
yellow

stigma
curved

style
very short

sepal
five form **calyx**; green, hairy,
curved round petal.

ovary
superior and contains one ovule;
collection of carpels forms the
gynoecium; carpels are spirally
arranged on the receptacle

petal
five form **corolla**;
bright yellow,
glossy upper
surface

nectary
covered by a
small scale at
base of petal

receptacle

pedicel

Phylum: Angiospermophyta
Class: Dicotyledoneae
Family: Ranunculaceae

Representative flowers. Some representative insect-pollinated flowers are illustrated in figs 21.17–21.19. Fig 21.20 illustrates the structure of a typical grass flower, a wind-pollinated monocotyledon.

The structure of a flower is best illustrated by means of a half-flower, a view of the flower obtained by cutting the flower vertically down the middle into two equal halves and drawing one half, showing the cut surface as a continuous line.

21.5.3   Development of pollen grains

Each stamen consists of an **anther** and a **filament**. The anther contains four pollen sacs which produce pollen. The filament contains a vascular bundle supplying food and water to the anther. Fig 21.21 shows the

Fig 21.17   (left) *Half-flower of meadow buttercup* (Ranunculus acris), *a dicotyledon. It is a herbaceous perennial common in damp meadows and pastures. Flowers appear April to September. Pollination: insects such as flies and small bees. Fruit: each carpel contains one seed. No special dispersal mechanism.*

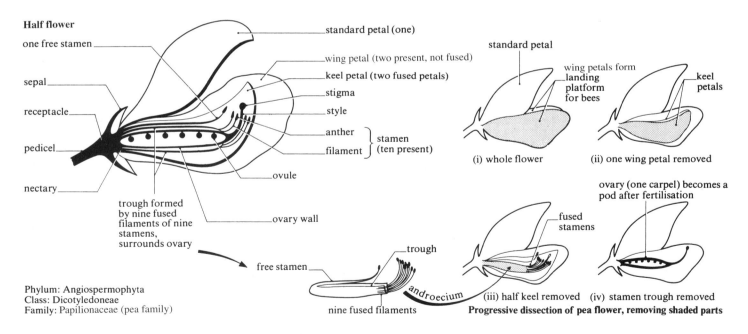

Half flower

one free stamen

sepal

receptacle

pedicel

nectary

trough formed
by nine fused
filaments of nine
stamens,
surrounds ovary

standard petal (one)

wing petal (two present, not fused)

keel petal (two fused petals)

stigma

style

anther
filament } stamen (ten present)

ovule

ovary wall

free stamen

nine fused filaments

Phylum: Angiospermophyta
Class: Dicotyledoneae
Family: Papilionaceae (pea family)

standard petal

wing petals form
landing
platform
for bees

keel
petals

(i) whole flower

(ii) one wing petal removed

ovary (one carpel) becomes a
pod after fertilisation

fused
stamens

trough

androecium

(iii) half keel removed

(iv) stamen trough removed

Progressive dissection of pea flower, removing shaded parts

Fig 21.18   *Structure of flower of sweet pea* (Lathyrus odoratus), *a dicotyledon belonging to the family Papilionaceae (pea family). Flowers appear in July. Calyx: five sepals. Corolla: five petals, one standard petal, two wing petals, two fused keel petals interlocking with wing petals. May be white or coloured. Pollination: bees are attracted by colour, scent and nectar. The standard petal is especially conspicuous. The two wing petals act as a landing platform. When a bee lands, its weight pulls them down together with the keel to which they are linked. The style and stigma emerge, striking the undersurface of the bee that may be carrying pollen from another flower. As the bee searches for nectar at the base of the ovary with its long proboscis, the anthers may rub pollen directly onto the undersurface of the style, from where it may be passed to the bee. Self-pollination may also occur. The garden pea (Pisum sativum) is similar, but more commonly self-pollinated. Fruit: a pod consisting of one carpel with many seeds.*

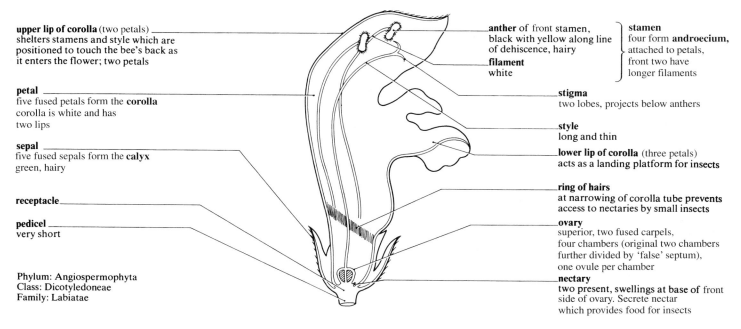

upper lip of corolla (two petals)
shelters stamens and style which are
positioned to touch the bee's back as
it enters the flower; two petals

petal
five fused petals form the **corolla**
corolla is white and has
two lips

sepal
five fused sepals form the **calyx**
green, hairy

receptacle

pedicel
very short

Phylum: Angiospermophyta
Class: Dicotyledoneae
Family: Labiatae

anther of front stamen,
black with yellow along line
of dehiscence, hairy

filament
white

stamen
four form **androecium**,
attached to petals,
front two have
longer filaments

stigma
two lobes, projects below anthers

style
long and thin

lower lip of corolla (three petals)
acts as a landing platform for insects

ring of hairs
at narrowing of corolla tube prevents
access to nectaries by small insects

ovary
superior, two fused carpels,
four chambers (original two chambers
further divided by 'false' septum),
one ovule per chamber

nectary
two present, swellings at base of front
side of ovary. Secrete nectar
which provides food for insects

Fig 21.19 *Half-flower of white deadnettle (*Lamium album*), a dicotyledon. The plant is a herbaceous perennial common in hedgerows and on waste ground. Flowers appear in April to June and autumn. Pollination: mainly bumblebees. A bee lands on the lower lip and as it enters the flower its back, which may be carrying pollen, touches the stigma first, thus favouring cross-pollination, although self-pollination is possible.*

internal structure of an anther, with its four pollen sacs containing pollen mother cells. Each pollen mother cell undergoes meiosis to form four pollen grains as shown in fig 21.22. The appearance as seen with a microscope is shown in fig 21.23.

Immediately after meiosis the young pollen grains are seen in groups of four called **tetrads**. Each grain develops a thick wall, often with an elaborate sculptured pattern characteristic of the species or genus. The outer wall, or **exine**, is made of a waterproof substance called sporopollenin. It is one of the most resistant and long-lasting substances in nature and allows grain coats to survive unchanged over long periods of time, sometimes millions of years. This fact, together with the ease of identifying the genus or species which produced the grain, has given rise to the science of palynology or pollen analysis. By studying pollen grains from a particular time and place it is possible to determine what plants were growing and thus to gain information about, for example, the ecosystems (including animals) and climate of that time. A particularly abundant source of pollen grains is peat, which accumulates to great depths over long periods of time in peat bogs.

> **21.1** How might pollen grains be useful as indicators of (*a*) past climate, (*b*) past human activities?

The pollen grain nucleus divides into two by mitosis to form a **generative nucleus** and a **pollen tube nucleus** (fig 21.22).

21.5.4 Development of the ovule

Each carpel consists of a stigma, style and ovary. Within the ovary one or more ovules develop. Each is attached to the ovary wall at a point called the **placenta** by a short stalk or **funicle** through which food and water pass to the developing ovule.

The main body of the ovule is called the **nucellus** and is enclosed and protected by two sheaths or **integuments**. A small pore is left in the integuments at one end of the ovule, the **micropyle**.

Inside the nucellus, at the end nearest the micropyle, one spore mother cell develops, known as the **embryo sac mother cell**. This diploid cell undergoes meiosis to produce four haploid cells, only one of which develops. This forms the **embryo sac** as shown in fig 21.24. The embryo sac grows and its nucleus undergoes repeated mitosis until eight nuclei are produced, four at each end of the embryo sac. One of these is the nucleus of the female gamete.

Two nuclei migrate to the centre of the embryo sac and fuse to become a single diploid nucleus. The remaining six nuclei, three at each end, become separated by thin cell walls and only one of these, the female gamete, appears to serve any further function. The rest disintegrate.

The final appearance of the mature carpel at fertilisation is shown in fig 21.25.

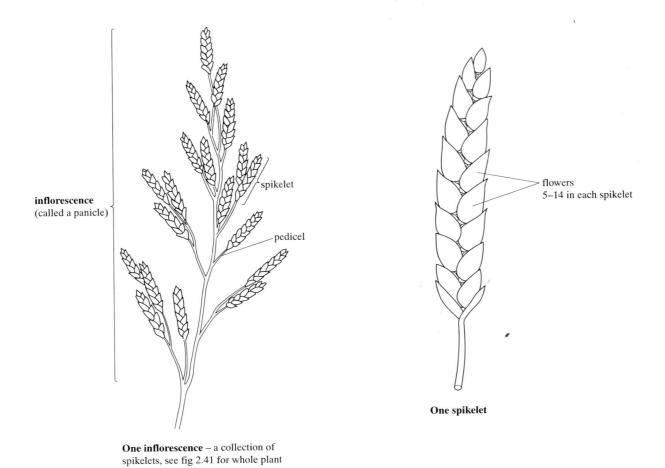

inflorescence
(called a panicle)

spikelet

pedicel

One inflorescence – a collection of
spikelets, see fig 2.41 for whole plant

flowers
5–14 in each spikelet

One spikelet

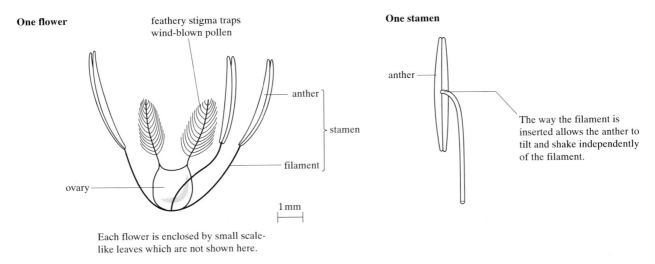

One flower

feathery stigma traps
wind-blown pollen

anther ⎫
      ⎬ stamen
filament ⎭

ovary

1 mm

Each flower is enclosed by small scale-
like leaves which are not shown here.

One stamen

anther

The way the filament is
inserted allows the anther to
tilt and shake independently
of the filament.

Fig 21.20 *Meadow fescue (Festuca pratensis), a wind-pollinated grass flower.*

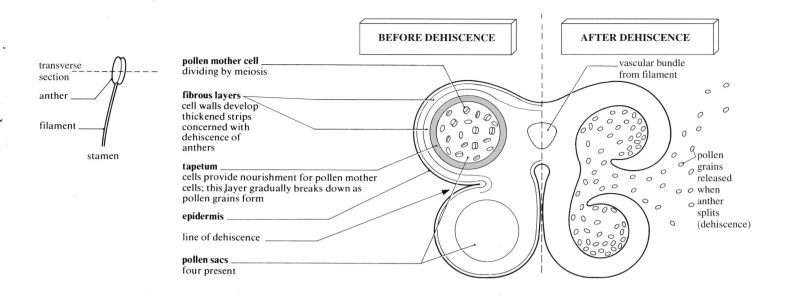

transverse section

anther

filament

stamen

BEFORE DEHISCENCE

AFTER DEHISCENCE

pollen mother cell dividing by meiosis

fibrous layers cell walls develop thickened strips concerned with dehiscence of anthers

tapetum cells provide nourishment for pollen mother cells; this layer gradually breaks down as pollen grains form

epidermis

line of dehiscence

pollen sacs four present

vascular bundle from filament

pollen grains released when anther splits (dehiscence)

Fig 21.21   *TS mature anther before and after dehiscence.*

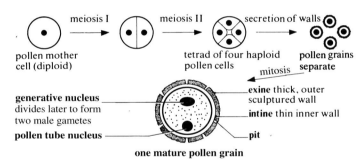

meiosis I

meiosis II

secretion of walls

pollen mother cell (diploid)

tetrad of four haploid pollen cells

mitosis

pollen grains separate

generative nucleus divides later to form two male gametes

pollen tube nucleus

exine thick, outer sculptured wall

intine thin inner wall

pit

one mature pollen grain

Fig 21.22   *Development of pollen grains.*

21.5.5   Pollination

After formation of pollen grains in the pollen sacs, the cells in the walls of the anther begin to dry and shrink, setting up tensions that eventually result in splitting (dehiscing) of the anther down the sides along two lines of weakness (fig 21.21). The pollen grains are thus released.

The transfer of pollen grains from an anther to a stigma is called **pollination**. (*Be careful not to confuse pollination with fertilisation.*) Pollination must be achieved if the male gametes, which develop inside the pollen grains, are to reach the female gamete. The male gametes are protected from drying out inside the pollen grain. Special mechanisms have evolved that increase the chances of successful pollination.

Transfer from an anther to a stigma of the same flower, or a flower on the same plant, is called **self-pollination**.

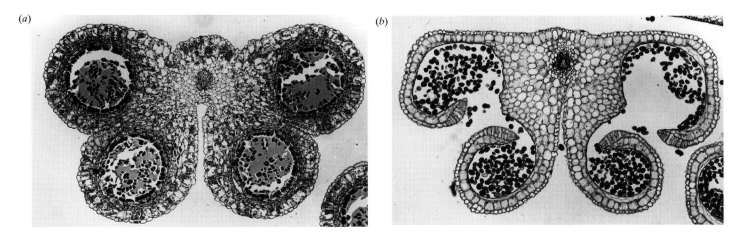

(a) *(b)*

Fig 21.23   *TS anther of* Lilium *(a) before dehiscence and (b) after dehiscence.*

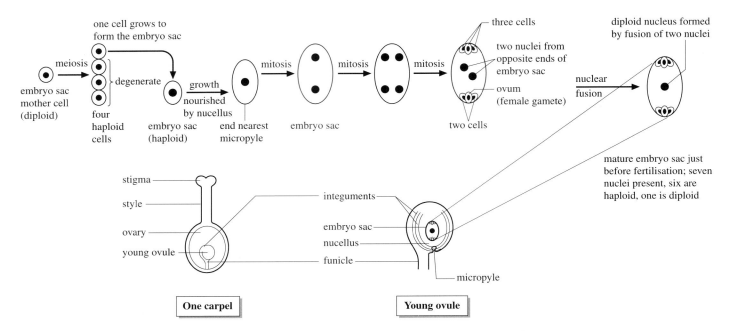

Fig 21.24 *Development of embryo sac and female gamete.*

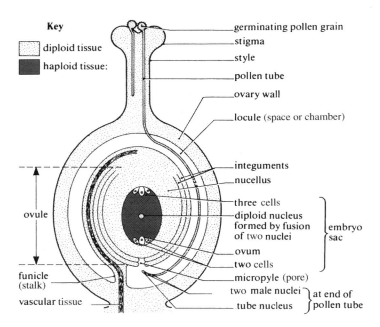

Fig 21.25 *LS carpel at fertilisation. Note that the ovule, which becomes the seed after fertilisation, contains both diploid parent tissue and haploid embryo sac tissue.*

Transfer of pollen from the anther of one plant to the stigma of another plant is called **cross-pollination**.

The relative merits of cross- and self-pollination

Cross-pollination leads to cross-fertilisation and has the advantage of increasing the amount of genetic variation. It is a form of 'outbreeding'. There are often special features to encourage it, some of which are described below. It is more wasteful of pollen, however.

Self-pollination leading to self-fertilisation has the advantage of greater reliability, particularly where members of the species are uncommon and are separated by large distances. This is because it is not dependent on an external factor, such as wind or insects, to deliver the pollen. It is also useful in harsh climates where insects are less common, such as high up on mountains. However, self-fertilisation is the extreme form of 'inbreeding' and can result in less vigorous offspring as a result (section 27.4.1). Examples of plants that rely on self-pollination are groundsel and chickweed. They produce no nectar or scent.

Both cross- and self-pollination have advantages and disadvantages and many plants balance the advantages by devices which favour cross-pollination but allow selfing to occur if crossing fails. For example, *some*, but not all, of the buds produced by violet and wood sorrel never open, so that self-pollination inside these is inevitable.

Mechanisms favouring cross-pollination

Dioecious and monoecious plants. Dioecious plant species have separate male and female plants. Self-pollination in dioecious plants is therefore impossible. Monoecious plants have separate male and female flowers on the same hermaphrodite plant. This also favours cross-pollination but selfing may also occur.

Protandry and protogyny. Sometimes anthers and stigmas mature at different times. If the anthers mature first, it is described as **protandry**; if the stigmas mature first it is **protogyny**. Protandrous flowers are much more common, for example white deadnettle, dandelion, and sage (*Salvia*) (fig 21.26). Protogyny occurs in bluebell and figwort (*Scrophularia*). In most cases of protandry and protogyny there is an overlapping period when both anthers and stigmas are ripe, thus allowing selfing if crossing has been unsuccessful.

Self-incompatibility (self-sterility). Even if self-pollination does occur, the pollen grain often does not develop, or develops very slowly, so preventing or reducing the chances of self-fertilisation. In all such cases there is a specific inhibition of pollen penetration of the stigma, or of pollen tube growth down the style, and this is genetically determined by 'self-incompatibility' genes.

When self-incompatibility occurs, some cross-pollinations are also incompatible. The most efficient use of the pollen will occur when a high proportion of cross-pollinations are compatible. An extreme example is clover, where all plants are self-incompatible, but cross-incompatibility occurs between less than one in 22 000 pairs.

Special floral structures. In most herma-phrodite flowers there are structural features that favour cross-pollination. In the case of insect-pollinated flowers the stigma is usually borne above the anthers, thus removing the possibility of pollen falling onto the stigma of the same flower. A visiting insect, possibly carrying pollen from another plant, will touch the stigma first as it enters the flower. Later, while the insect is seeking nectar, pollen is either brushed against it or falls onto it before it leaves the flower. This occurs in white deadnettle (fig 21.19). A more primitive mechanism may ensure that the stigma brushes against the insect as it lands, as in pea (see fig 21.18 for details). Such mechanisms are generally reinforced by protandry or protogyny and the flowers are often complex and irregular in shape, as in white deadnettle.

Flowers attract insects by providing a source of food (nectar or pollen) and stimulating the senses of sight and smell of the insects. The characteristics that enable flowers to do this are discussed below.

In the case of wind-pollinated flowers the stamens, the whole flower, or the inflorescence may hang downwards so that falling pollen will drop clear of the plant before being blown away, for example hazel catkins.

Although the variation in length of style described in question 21.5 and fig 21.27 apparently favours outbreeding, a much more important difference between pin-eyed and thrum-eyed primroses is a self-incompatibility mechanism which tends to restrict *cross-fertilisation* to pin-eye/thrum-eye crosses. The genes that control incompatibility, style length and anther height lie close together on the same chromosome and behave as a single inheritable unit.

Wind pollination and insect pollination

Pollen grains must be transferred to the female parts of flowers. The original agent of dispersal earlier in evolution was wind, but this is very inefficient because it relies solely on chance interception of the pollen grains by the flowers. Many flowering plants such as grasses, oak and hazel, still rely on wind, but they have to produce enormous quantities of pollen, a drain on the plant's materials and energy. Table 21.3 summarises the typical features of wind- and insect-pollinated flowers.

Insects specialised for flower-feeding appear in the fossil record at the same time as the flowering plants, and include bees, wasps, butterflies and moths. This suggests that once flowers evolved, insect pollination also rapidly evolved. The insect is a much more precise agent of dispersal than wind. It can carry a small amount of pollen from the anthers of one flower and deposit it precisely on the stigma of another flower. As a result, special relationships between flowers and insects have evolved. The reward the insects

Fig 21.26 *A bee entering a flower of meadow sage. The stamens are hinged to a plate and, as the head of the bee pushes against this, the stamens are lowered. This brushes pollen onto the bee's abdomen. The stigma of the flower increases in length as the flower ages. If a bee now enters an older flower, it will come into contact with the stigma and the pollen will be transferred from its abdomen to the stigma. This series of activities causes cross-pollination to take place.*

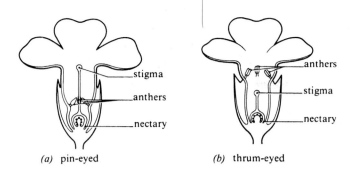

(a) pin-eyed   *(b)* thrum-eyed

Fig 21.27 *Variation in flower structure in primrose.*

receive from the flowers is food in the form of nectar or pollen. In a few special cases the insect and the plant it pollinates are so interdependent that neither species can survive without the other, such as one species of yucca plant and its associated moth.

Table 21.3 Summary of typical differences between wind-pollinated and insect-pollinated flowers.

Typical wind-pollinated flower	*Typical insect-pollinated flower*
Small petals not brightly coloured (usually green), or petals absent; flowers therefore inconspicuous	Large coloured petals; flowers therefore conspicuous. If flowers relatively inconspicuous they may be gathered together in inflorescences
Not scented	Scented
Nectaries absent	Nectaries present
Large branched and feathery stigma hanging outside flower to trap pollen	Small stigma, sticky to hold pollen and enclosed within flower
Stamens hanging outside flower to release pollen	Stamens enclosed within flower
Anthers attached only at midpoints to tip of filament so that they swing freely in air currents	Anthers fixed at their bases or fused along their backs to the filaments so that they are immovable
Large quantities of pollen owing to high wastage	Less pollen produced
Pollen grains relatively light and small; dry, often smooth, walls	Pollen grains relatively heavy and large. Spiny walls and stickiness help attachment to insect body (fig 21.29)
Flower structure relatively simple	Complex structural modifications for particular insects often occur
Flowers borne well above foliage on long stalks (e.g. grasses) or appear before leaves (e.g. many British trees)	Position and time of appearance variable in relation to foliage, though often borne above it for increased conspicuousness

Insect pollination has the important additional advantage that it encourages cross-pollination and hence cross-fertilisation, so the modifications of flowers to encourage insect pollination described below could be added to the list of features favouring cross-pollination.

In order to attract insects, flowers generally are large, with brightly coloured or white petals or, if small, are grouped into inflorescences. Often there are markings on the petals such as lines, spots or an increased intensity of colour that guide insects to the nectaries, as in violet, pansy, orchids and foxgloves. Insects can see ultraviolet wavelengths that are invisible to humans so many flowers have markings which reflect ultraviolet that are invisible to us. More specific than colours are the scents produced by flowers, some of which, like lavender and rose, are used by humans in perfumes. Smells of rotting flesh that attract carrion-eating insects are also produced by some plants, such as the arum lily which attracts dung flies. Recognition is also helped by flower shape.

One of the most complex and strange mechanisms for ensuring cross-pollination is the sexual impersonation of female wasps by certain orchids. The flower parts mimic the shape, colourings and even the odour of the female wasp, and the impersonation is so convincing that the male wasps attempt to copulate with the flower (fig 21.28). While doing so they deposit pollen and, on leaving the flower, collect fresh pollen to take to the next flower.

An example of a wind-pollinated flower is the grass, meadow fescue, shown in fig 21.20. Examples of insect-pollinated flowers are shown in figs 21.17 (buttercup), 21.18 (sweet pea) and 21.19 (white deadnettle).

21.5.6 Fertilisation

Once a pollen grain has landed on the stigma (fig 21.29) of a compatible species, it will germinate. A sucrose solution is secreted by the epidermal cells of the stigma. This stimulates germination of the grain and possibly supplies food. A **pollen tube** emerges from one of the pores (pits) in the wall of the pollen grain and grows rapidly down the style to the ovary. Its growth is controlled by the tube nucleus of the pollen grain, which is found at the growing tip of the tube. Growth is stimulated by auxins produced by the gynoecium, and the pollen tube is directed towards the ovary by certain chemicals, an example of chemotropism. It is probably also negatively aerotropic, that is it grows away from air. Growth depends on compatibility between the pollen and the style tissue as already described.

During growth of the pollen tube the **generative nucleus** of the pollen grain divides by mitosis to produce two male nuclei that represent the **male gametes** (fig 21.25). They cannot swim, unlike the sperm of lower plants, and depend on the pollen tube to reach the female gamete which is located in the embryo sac of the ovule. The pollen tube enters the ovule through the micropyle, the tube nucleus degenerates and the tip of the tube bursts, releasing the

Fig 21.28 *A digger wasp copulating with a fly orchid. The wasp is fooled into believing that the orchid is a female wasp.*

male gametes near the embryo sac, which they enter. One nucleus fuses with the female gamete, forming a diploid **zygote**, and the other fuses with the diploid nucleus forming a triploid nucleus known as the **primary endosperm nucleus**. This double fertilisation is unique to flowering plants. It leads eventually to the two structures found in the seed, namely the **embryo** and the **endosperm** (food store).

If, as is often the case, more than one ovule is present in the gynoecium, each must be fertilised by a separate pollen grain if it is to become a seed. Thus each seed may have been fertilised by a pollen grain from a different plant.

Experiment 21.1: To investigate the growth of pollen tubes

Stigmas secrete a solution containing sucrose ranging in concentration from about 2 to 45%. This helps to stick pollen grains to the stigma and to promote their germination. The addition of borate to the experimental solution helps to prevent osmotic bursting of pollen tube tips and stimulates growth.

Materials

microscope
cavity slide
flowers containing dehiscing anthers, such as deadnettle, wallflower, *Pelargonium* or *Impatiens*
10–20% (w/v) sucrose solution also containing sodium borate to a concentration of 0.01%
acetocarmine or neutral red

Method

Place a drop of sucrose solution in the central depression of a cavity slide and add pollen grains by touching the drop with the surface of a dehisced anther. Observe the slide at intervals over a period of 1–2 hours. The nuclei at the tip of growing tubes may be stained by irrigating with a drop of acetocarmine or neutral red.

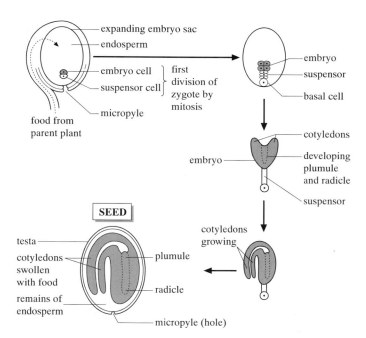

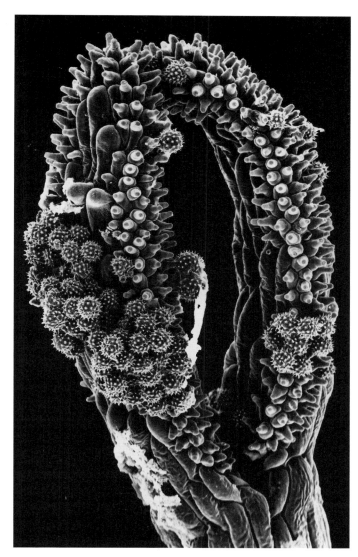

Fig 21.29 *Scanning electron micrograph of pollen grains on the stigma of a flower. The spiked surface of the grains is typical of insect-pollinated flowers.*

Fig 21.30 *Growth of an embryo in a non-endospermous dicotyledon seed, such as shepherd's purse (*Capsella bursa-pastoris*).*

21.5.7   Development of the seed and fruit

Immediately after fertilisation, the ovule becomes known as the **seed** and the ovary the **fruit**. The following changes take place. It will be useful to study figs 21.30 and 21.25 in order to understand these changes.

(1) The zygote grows by mitotic divisions to become a multicellular embryo which consists of a first shoot, the **plumule**, a first root, the **radicle**, and either one or two seed-leaves called **cotyledons** (one in monocotyledons and two in dicotyledons). These cotyledons are simpler in structure than the first true foliage leaves and may become swollen with food to act as storage tissue, as in the pea and broad bean. The plumule consists of a stem, the first pair of true foliage leaves and a terminal bud.

(2) The triploid primary endosperm nucleus undergoes repeated mitotic divisions to form the **endosperm**, a mass of triploid nuclei which are separated from one another by thin cell walls. In some seeds this remains as the food store, as in cereals such as wheat and maize.

(3) If the cotyledons act as a food store they grow at the expense of the endosperm, which may disappear altogether. Some seeds store food in both endosperm and cotyledons.

(4) As growth of the embryo and food store continues, the surrounding nucellus breaks down supplying nutrients for growth. Further nutrients are supplied by the vascular bundle in the stalk (funicle) of the ovule.

(5) The testa develops from the integument. It is a thin but tough protective layer.

(6) The micropyle remains a small pore in the testa through which oxygen and water will enter when the seed germinates.

(7) The final stages in development of the seed involve a reduction in the water content of the seed from the normal levels for plant tissues of about 90% by mass to about 10–15% by mass. This greatly reduces the potential for metabolic activity and is an essential step in ensuring seed dormancy.

(8) While the seeds develop, the ovary becomes a mature fruit, its wall being known as the **pericarp**. The changes that occur vary with species, but generally the fruit is adapted to protect the seeds and to help in their dispersal. The hormonal control of fruit development is discussed in section 16.3.5.

(9) The remaining flower parts wither and die and are lost in a controlled manner, just as leaves are in deciduous plants.

Some of the changes that occur after fertilisation are summarised in table 21.4.

Some stages in the development of the embryo are shown in fig 21.30. Germination is discussed in chapter 22.

21.5.8 Advantages and disadvantages of reproduction by seed

Advantages

- The plant is independent of water for sexual reproduction and therefore better adapted for a land environment.
- The seed protects the embryo.
- The seed contains food for the embryo (either in cotyledons or in the endosperm).
- The seed is usually adapted for dispersal.
- The seed can remain dormant and survive adverse conditions.
- The seed is physiologically sensitive to favourable conditions and sometimes must undergo a period of after-ripening so that it will not germinate immediately (chapter 16).

Disadvantages

- Seeds are relatively large structures because of the extensive food reserves. This makes dispersal more difficult than by spores.
- Seeds are often eaten by animals for their food reserves.
- There is a reliance on external agents such as wind, insects and water for pollination. This makes pollination (and hence fertilisation) more dependent on chance, particularly wind pollination.
- There is a large wastage of seeds because the chances of survival of a given seed are limited. The parent must therefore invest large quantities of material and energy in seed production to ensure success.
- The food supply in a seed is limited, whereas in vegetative reproduction food is available from the parent plant until the daughter plant is fully established.
- Two individuals are required in dioecious species, making the process more dependent on chance than reproduction in which only one parent is involved. However, dioecious plants are relatively rare.

The information provided above can be used to compare the advantages and disadvantages that seed-bearing plants have compared with non-seed-bearing plants, or to compare the relative merits of sexual reproduction and vegetative propagation within the seed-bearing plants.

21.6 Review of sexual reproduction in vertebrates

The evolution of the vertebrates shows a gradual adaptation to life on land. One of the major problems that had to be overcome in making the transition from an aquatic existence to a terrestrial existence involved reproduction.

Fish

The majority of fish shed their gametes directly into water. Fertilisation is external. Eggs contain a considerable amount of yolk, larval stages are common and any degree of parental care is rare.

Table 21.4 Summary of the changes that occur after fertilisation in flowering plants.

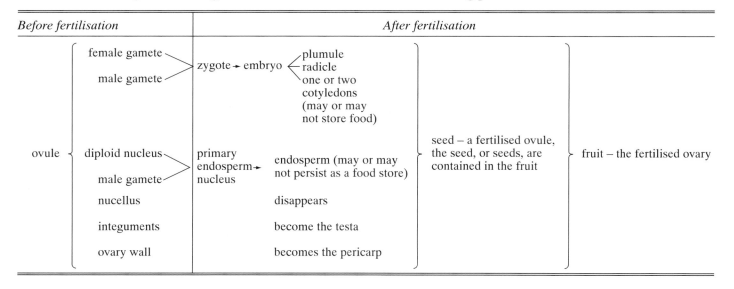

Before fertilisation			*After fertilisation*		
ovule	female gamete / male gamete → zygote → embryo	plumule, radicle, one or two cotyledons (may or may not store food)		seed – a fertilised ovule, the seed, or seeds, are contained in the fruit	fruit – the fertilised ovary
	diploid nucleus / male gamete → primary endosperm nucleus	endosperm (may or may not persist as a food store)			
	nucellus	disappears			
	integuments	become the testa			
	ovary wall	becomes the pericarp			

Amphibia

Amphibia have to return to water to mate, and the early stages of their development take place there also. There are, however, many amphibian species that show elaborate behavioural patterns associated with parental care. For example, the male *Pipa* toad spreads the fertilised eggs over the back of the female where they stick, become 'embedded' in the skin and develop into tadpoles. After about three weeks they escape from the mother's back and lead an independent existence.

Reptiles

Reptiles were the earliest group of vertebrates to overcome the problems of fertilisation and development on land. Release of gametes on to dry land would result in their drying up, so the first requirement of totally land-dwelling organisms must have been the introduction of male gametes into the female body, that is internal fertilisation. Internal fertilisation occurs in reptiles and the increased chances of fertilisation reduces the numbers of gametes which it is necessary to produce. Once fertilised, the zygote develops within a specialised structure, the **amniote (cleidoic) egg**, which provides the embryo with a fluid-filled cavity in which it can develop on land (fig 21.31). The outer shell provides protection from mechanical damage and surrounds the four membranes which develop from the embryo. These four extra-embryonic membranes, the yolk sac, amnion, chorion and allantois, provide the embryo with protection and are necessary for many of its metabolic activities including nutrition, respiration and excretion.

The **yolk sac** develops as an outgrowth of the embryonic gut and encloses the yolk, a food supply which is gradually absorbed by the blood vessels of the yolk sac. When the yolk has been used up the yolk sac is withdrawn into the gut.

The **amnion** completely encloses the embryo in the **amniotic cavity** which becomes filled with **amniotic fluid** secreted by the cells of the amnion. This provides the embryo with a fluid environment in which the embryo can develop. All reptiles, birds and mammals have an amnion and are called **amniotes**. As the embryo grows, the amnion is pushed out until it fuses with the third embryonic membrane, the **chorion**, which lies just inside the shell and prevents excessive water loss from the amnion.

The **allantois** is an outgrowth of the embryonic hindgut and rapidly expands, in reptiles and birds, to underlie the chorion. Here it functions primarily as a 'bladder' for storing excretory products and as the gaseous exchange organ of the embryo, facilitating the transfer of respiratory gases between the environmental atmosphere and the amniotic fluid via the porous shell.

Birds and egg-laying mammals

Birds and the early egg-laying mammals called monotremes, such as the duck-billed platypus, *Ornithorhyncus*, all produce an amniotic egg and, whilst the shell of the egg is lost in higher mammals, the four extra-embryonic membranes are retained; two of them, the chorion and allantois, give rise to the placenta in placental mammals (fig 21.49).

21.7 Human reproductive systems

21.7.1 The male reproductive system

The structure of the male reproductive system is shown in side view in fig 21.32a and more diagrammatically in front view in fig 21.32b. The excretory system is closely associated with the reproductive system and is also shown in the diagrams. The two systems together are traditionally known as the urinogenital system.

The main structures and their functions are listed below.

- **Testes** (singular testis). The two testes are the male **gonads**, that is the sites where the male gametes, or sperm, are made. They also produce the male sex hormone **testosterone**.
- **Scrotal sac.** The testes are situated outside the abdominal cavity in a sac of skin called the scrotal sac. As a result, the sperm develop at a temperature 2–3 °C lower than the main body temperature. This is the optimum temperature for sperm production. The life of sperm is greatly reduced if the temperature is higher.
- **Seminiferous tubules.** Inside each testis are about 1000 coiled seminiferous tubules (fig 21.33). Each tubule is about 50 cm long and 200 μm in diameter. The walls of the tubules produce the sperm (also known as spermatozoa), a process called **spermatogenesis**. **Leydig cells**, also known as **interstitial cells**, between the tubules produce the male sex hormone **testosterone**.
- **Vasa efferentia** (singular vas efferens). 10 to 20 vasa efferentia collect sperm from inside the testis and transfer them to the epididymis (fig 21.33).

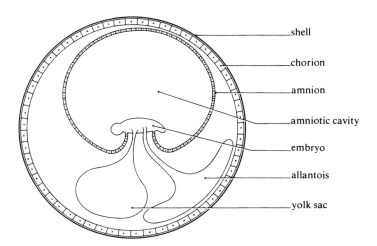

Fig 21.31 *Simplified diagram of the amniote egg.*

- shell
- chorion
- amnion
- amniotic cavity
- embryo
- allantois
- yolk sac

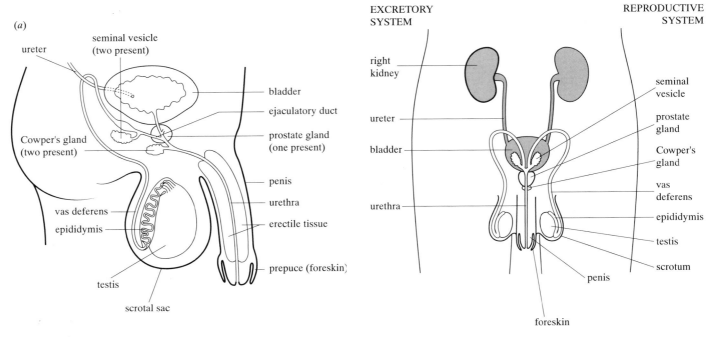

Fig 21.32 (a) Side view of the human male reproductive system. (b) Male reproductive system seen from the front. The shaded structures are the excretory system. The urethra is part of both systems, being also connected to the bladder. The two systems together are often referred to as the urinogenital system.

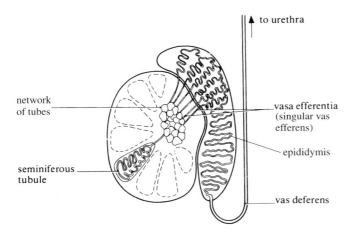

Fig 21.33 Simplified diagram showing the structure of the human testis and tubes carrying sperm from seminiferous tubules to the urethra.

- **Epididymis.** The epididymis is a very coiled tube, about 6 m long, pressed against the testis. Sperm take several days to pass through this tube. Sperm are concentrated here to about 5000 million per cm^3 by reabsorption of fluid secreted originally by the seminiferous tubule. They also develop the ability to swim, although they are inhibited from doing so until after ejaculation. Sperm pass to the base of the tube for a short period of storage before entering the vas deferens. Chemicals produced by the lining of the tube are essential for maturation of the sperm.

- **Vas deferens** (plural vasa deferentia). This is a straight tube about 40 cm long which carries sperm to the urethra. Most of the sperm are stored in the vas deferens.
- **Urethra.** This tube carries urine from the bladder, as well as sperm from the vasa deferentia, through the penis.
- **Penis.** The penis contains erectile tissue. When the male is sexually excited this tissue fills with blood, causing the penis to become erect. During sexual intercourse the erect penis is inserted into the vagina of the female before ejaculation of the semen.
- **Seminal vesicles.** The seminal vesicles secrete mucus and a watery alkaline fluid that contains nutrients, including the sugar fructose which is an energy source for the sperm. Each seminal vesicle empties its contents into the **ejaculatory duct** during the process of ejaculation of sperm, adding to the volume of the semen (sperm plus fluid). Further chemicals in the fluid may help sperm to penetrate the cervical mucus and may cause peristaltic movements of the lining of the uterus and fallopian tubes which help to carry the sperm towards the ovaries.
- **Prostate gland.** The prostate gland also secretes mucus and a slightly alkaline fluid which is released during ejaculation and helps to neutralise the acidity of the vagina, making the sperm more active.
- **Cowper's glands.** These secrete mucus and an alkaline fluid into the urethra. The alkaline fluid neutralises the acidity of any remaining urine.

726

21.7.2   The female reproductive system

The structure of the female reproductive system is shown in fig 21.34. The main structures and their functions are listed below. Note that, unlike the structures in the male, there are separate external openings to the excretory and reproductive systems.

- **Ovaries.**   The two ovaries are the female gonads, the sites where the female gametes are made. The gametes are known as **eggs** or **ova**. (Biologists and the medical profession usually refer to them as eggs.) The ovaries are almond-shaped, measure about 3–5 cm long, and 2–3 cm wide and also secrete the female sex hormones **oestrogen** and **progesterone**. Usually, one egg is produced every month during the fertile years of a woman. The outermost layer of cells of the ovary is composed of germinal epithelial cells from which gamete cells are produced. The outer region of the ovary is composed of developing follicles and the middle is composed of **stroma**, which contains connective tissue, blood vessels and mature follicles.
- **Oviducts or fallopian tubes.**   The tubes are about 12 cm long and carry eggs from the ovaries to the uterus. The ends of the tubes nearest the ovaries have feathery processes called **fimbriae**. They move closer to the ovaries at ovulation. Cilia lining the fimbriae

beat and cause a current which draws in the ovum or egg (more precisely the secondary oocyte) after it is released from the ovary. Cilia lining the oviduct beat and smooth muscle contracts causing peristaltic movements which move the egg down the oviduct to the uterus. If fertilisation takes place it occurs in the oviduct.

- **Uterus** (womb).   The uterus is about 7.5 cm long and 5 cm wide and is about the size and shape of an inverted pear. It lies behind the bladder. If fertilisation takes place, the embryo implants in the wall of the uterus and grows there until birth. The uterus grows much larger during pregnancy. The outer layer of the uterus wall, the **myometrium**, contains smooth muscle which contracts strongly during birth. The inner layer, the **endometrium**, contains glands and many blood vessels.
- **Cervix.**   This is the narrow entrance to the uterus from the vagina. It is normally blocked by a plug of mucus and a ring of muscle can close it.
- **Vagina.**   This is a muscular tube about 8–10 cm long whose walls contain elastic tissue. The lining is folded. It stretches during childbirth to allow passage of the baby, and during sexual intercourse when the penis is placed in it. The **clitoris** is a small structure which is equivalent to the male penis and like the penis can become erect.

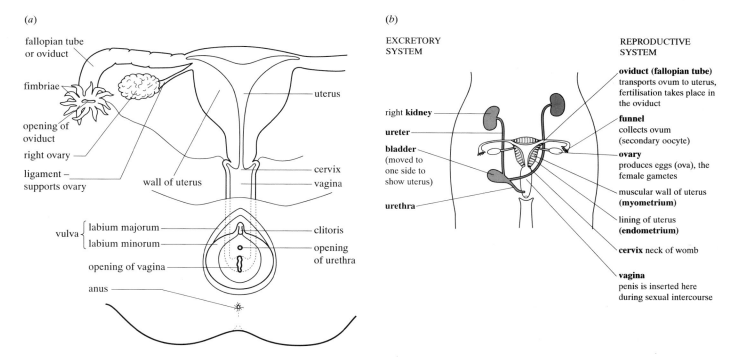

Fig 21.34   *(a) Diagram showing the human female reproductive system. The uterus and vagina are shown in section. The external genitalia and the openings of the urethra and anus are shown in surface view with the labia parted. (b) Female reproductive system seen from the front. The shaded structures are the excretory system. The two systems together are often referred to as the urinogenital system.*

21.7.3   Gametogenesis

There are three main stages to reproduction, namely gametogenesis, fertilisation and the development of the embryo. **Gametogenesis** is the production of gametes. Production of sperm is called **spermatogenesis** and production of eggs is called **oogenesis**. Both take place in the gonads, namely the testes in the male and the ovaries in the female. Both processes involve meiosis, the type of nuclear division which halves the number of chromosomes from two sets (diploid condition) to one set (haploid condition). The cells which undergo meiosis are called mother cells. Sperm mother cells are known as **spermatocytes** and egg mother cells as **oocytes**. Fig 21.35 is a diagrammatic summary of spermatogenesis and oogenesis which emphasises the main similarities and differences between the two processes. The processes are described in more detail in sections 21.7.4 and 21.7.5.

Note that both processes start with cells in the outer layer of the gonad, known as the **germinal epithelium**. In both males and females the process involves three stages, a multiplication stage, a growth stage and a maturation stage. The multiplication stage involves repeated mitotic divisions producing many spermatogonia and oogonia. Each then undergoes a period of growth in preparation for the first meiotic division and cell division. This marks the beginning of the maturation stage during which the first and second meiotic divisions occur followed by the formation of mature haploid gametes.

The gametes produced by a given individual will show variation as a result of independent assortment of chromosomes and crossing over during meiosis (section 23.4).

21.7.4   Spermatogenesis – development of sperm

Sperm are produced at the rate of about 120 million per day. Production of a given sperm takes about 70 days. The seminiferous tubule has a wall with an outer layer of **germinal epithelial cells** and about six layers of cells produced by repeated cell divisions of this layer (figs 21.36 and 21.37a and b). These represent successive stages in the development of sperm. The first divisions of the germinal epithelial cells give rise to many **spermatogonia** which increase in size to form **primary spermatocytes**.

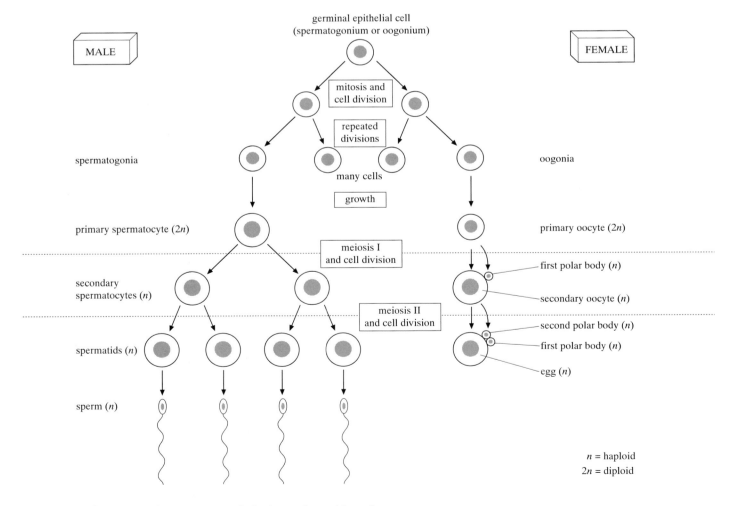

Fig 21.35   *Summary of gametogenesis in the male and female.*

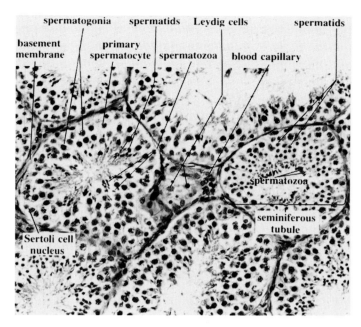

Fig 21.36 *Section through the human testis showing seminiferous tubules and Leydig (interstitial) cells.*

These undergo the first meiotic division to form haploid **secondary spermatocytes** and the second meiotic division to form **spermatids**. Between these rows of developing cells are large **Sertoli cells** stretching from the outer layer of the tubule to the lumen.

> **21.6** Sertoli cells contain abundant smooth endoplasmic reticulum, Golgi apparatus and many mitochondria and lysosomes. In view of the structure of these cells what can you suggest about their function?

Spermatocytes become embedded in the many infoldings of the cell surface membranes of the Sertoli cells and develop into spermatids before passing to the tops of the cells next to the lumen (central space) of the seminiferous tubule. Here they become mature **sperm**. The Sertoli cells carry out the remoulding of the spermatids to form sperm. Also all nutrients, oxygen and waste substances exchanged between the developing sperm and the blood vessels surrounding the tubules pass through the Sertoli cells. The fluid carrying sperm through the tubules is secreted by the Sertoli cells. The entire process from spermatogonia to sperm takes about two months.

Sperm

Sperm are extremely small cells, only $2.5\,\mu$m in diameter (compared with an average of $20\,\mu$m for animal cells) and about $50\,\mu$m long. The structure is shown in fig 21.38. The head contains the nucleus, which contains the haploid number of chromosomes (23 in humans). It also contains the **acrosome**, a large lysosome which contains hydrolytic enzymes which will be involved in the penetration of the layers of cells surrounding the egg immediately before fertilisation.

The short neck region of the sperm contains a pair of centrioles lying at right-angles to each other. The microtubules of one of the centrioles elongate during development of the sperm and run the entire length of the mature sperm forming the **axial filament** of the tail or flagellum.

The middle piece is the first part of the tail and is enlarged by the presence of many mitochondria arranged in a spiral around the axial filament. Mitochondria carry out aerobic respiration and produce ATP as a source of energy. The energy is used to bring about beating movements of the tail, allowing the sperm to swim at about $1-4$ mm per minute. In transverse section the tail shows the

(a)

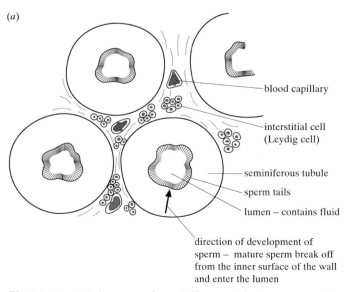

(b)

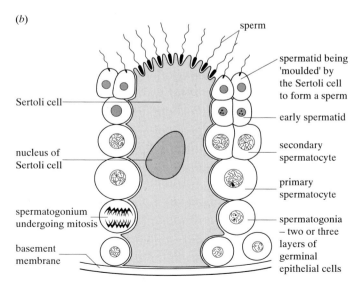

Fig 21.37 *(a) A group of seminiferous tubules seen in transverse section. (b) Diagram showing the structure of part of the wall of a seminiferous tubule. Cells in various stages of spermatogenesis are shown.*

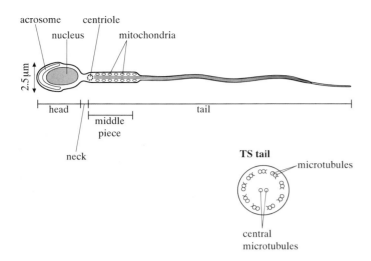

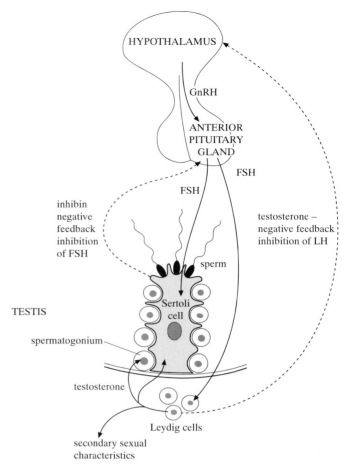

Fig 21.38 *Structure of a mature human sperm.*

characteristic arrangement found in flagella of nine pairs of peripheral microtubules surrounding a central pair of microtubules.

Activation of the tail takes place in the vagina. Movement of the tail is insufficient to cover the distance from the vagina to the site of fertilisation. However, its main function is to enable sperm to cluster around the oocyte, to orientate themselves and to help penetrate the oocyte.

Hormonal control of spermatogenesis

Spermatogenesis is controlled by the hypothalamus and anterior pituitary gland working together. The hypothalamus is part of the brain (fig 17.24) and the pituitary gland is found just below it. The hypothalamus secretes **gonadotrophin-releasing hormone (GnRH)** which travels in a small vein from the hypothalamus to the pituitary gland. GnRH in turn stimulates the anterior pituitary gland to secrete two hormones known as **gonadotrophins**. (A gonadotrophin is a hormone that stimulates a gonad, in this case the testis.) The two gonadotrophins are **follicle stimulating hormone (FSH)** and **luteinising hormone (LH)** (fig 21.39). The same two hormones are also secreted in the female (section 21.7.6). They are glycoproteins. FSH stimulates spermatogenesis by stimulating Sertoli cells to complete the development of spermatozoa from spermatids. LH stimulates the synthesis of the hormone **testosterone** by the **Leydig cells** (interstitial cells) of the testis. It is therefore also known as **interstitial cell stimulating hormone (ICSH)** in the male. Testosterone is a steroid hormone and is made from cholesterol. Testosterone stimulates growth and development of the germinal epithelial cells (spermatogonia) to form sperm, and also works with FSH to stimulate the Sertoli cells. A negative feedback mechanism operates whereby an increase in the level of testosterone results in a decrease in secretion of GnRH

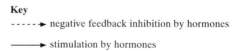

Key

----→ negative feedback inhibition by hormones

——→ stimulation by hormones

Fig 21.39 *Hormonal control of spermatogenesis. GnRH secreted by the hypothalamus stimulates the anterior pituitary gland to secrete FSH and LH. LH stimulates secretion of testosterone which stimulates sperm production but also acts as an inhibitor of the hypothalamus in a negative feedback system. FSH stimulates the Sertoli cells. Inhibin produced by the Sertoli cells forms a second feedback inhibition system, controlling FSH production by the anterior pituitary gland.*

from the hypothalamus, as shown in fig 21.39. This in turn results in declining levels of LH and FSH. Testosterone probably also acts directly on the anterior pituitary gland to reduce LH secretion, but this effect is weaker.

Role of inhibin

The Sertoli cells secrete another glycoprotein hormone called **inhibin** which is involved in the negative feedback control of sperm production. If spermatogenesis proceeds too rapidly, inhibin is released. Its target is the anterior pituitary gland where it reduces secretion of FSH (fig 21.39). It may also have a slight effect on the hypothalamus, reducing GnRH secretion. When the rate of spermatogenesis is low, inhibin is not secreted and FSH stimulates spermatogenesis.

Role of cyclic AMP

Both FSH and LH act by causing the release of cyclic AMP (adenosine monophosphate) within the cells they stimulate. Cyclic AMP is the 'second messenger' system discussed in section 17.6.1. It is released into the cytoplasm and then passes to the nucleus where it stimulates the synthesis of enzymes. In the case of LH, for example, the enzymes are involved in the synthesis of testosterone from cholesterol.

Secondary sexual characteristics

Testosterone is the main male sex hormone and it affects both primary and secondary sexual characteristics. Primary sexual characteristics are those present at birth, whereas secondary sexual characteristics are those that develop at puberty. Both testosterone and FSH are required for the successful production of sperm whereas testosterone alone controls the development of the secondary sexual characteristics during puberty and maintains these throughout adult life. These characteristics include:

- the development and enlargement of the testes, penis and glands of the reproductive tract;
- increased muscle development;
- enlargement of the larynx producing deepening of the voice;

- the growth of pubic hair and extra hair on the face, in the armpits and on the chest;
- changes in behaviour associated with courtship, mating and parental concern.

21.7.5   Oogenesis – development of eggs

Unlike the production of sperm in males, which only begins at puberty, the production of eggs in females begins before birth. An outline of the stages in oogenesis is shown in fig 21.35. During development of the fetus many oogonia are produced. These undergo mitosis and form **primary oocytes** which remain at prophase of meiosis I throughout childhood. Primary oocytes are enclosed by a single layer of cells, the **granulosa cells** (or follicle cells), and form structures known as **primordial follicles** (figs 21.40, 21.41 and 21.42). About two million of these follicles exist in the female just before birth, but only about 450 ever develop secondary oocytes which are released from the ovary during the menstrual cycle. During a woman's fertile years one primordial follicle per month develops into a mature follicle, known as a **Graafian follicle**. This is in response to the hormone FSH (follicle stimulating hormone). Within each developing follicle, a primary oocyte starts to develop into an egg. The primordial follicle first becomes a **primary follicle** as the granulosa cells multiply and form many layers of cells around the primary oocyte (figs 21.40, 21.41 and 21.42). In addition, cells from the stroma of the ovary form further layers outside these cells known collectively as the **theca**. The outer part of the theca contains blood vessels and merges with the stroma, the general 'background' material of the ovary. The inner part of the theca secretes female sex hormones, as do the granulosa cells.

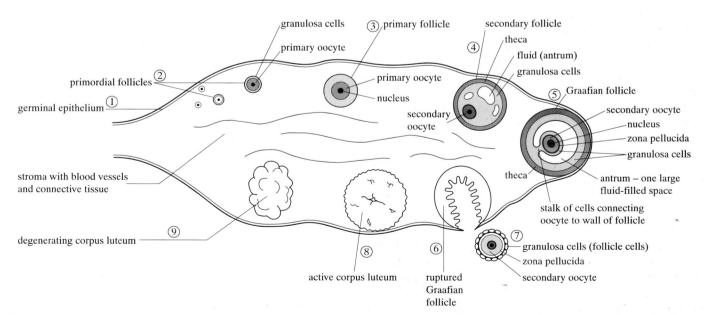

Fig 21.40   *Section through a human ovary showing the stages in the development of a Graafian follicle, ovulation and the formation and degeneration of the corpus luteum. Not all these stages would be seen together. The numbers indicate the sequence of the stages.*

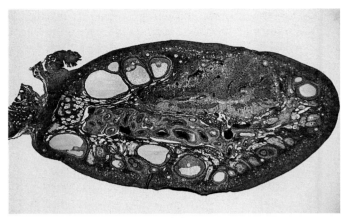

Fig 21.41 *LS human ovary showing developing follicles, X 7.*

As the primary follicle develops, a fluid is secreted by the granulosa cells which contains **oestrogen**, one of the female sex hormones. A fluid-filled space, the antrum, develops in the follicle. It is now referred to as a **secondary follicle**. Oestrogen stimulates growth of the follicle, which eventually becomes a mature follicle, also known as a **Graafian follicle**. It is about 1 cm in diameter. It contains a secondary oocyte and the first polar body, formed when the primary oocyte divides by meiosis I (fig 21.35). The secondary oocyte is haploid. The second meiotic division proceeds as far as metaphase but does not continue until a sperm fuses with the oocyte. At fertilisation the secondary oocyte undergoes the second meiotic division producing a large cell, the **ovum**, and a **second polar body**. All polar bodies are small cells. They have no role in oogenesis and they eventually degenerate. The structure of the secondary oocyte/ovum is shown in fig 21.43.

21.7 (*a*) In what important way is the structure of the egg similar to that of the sperm? (*b*) Summarise the important differences between sperm and eggs.

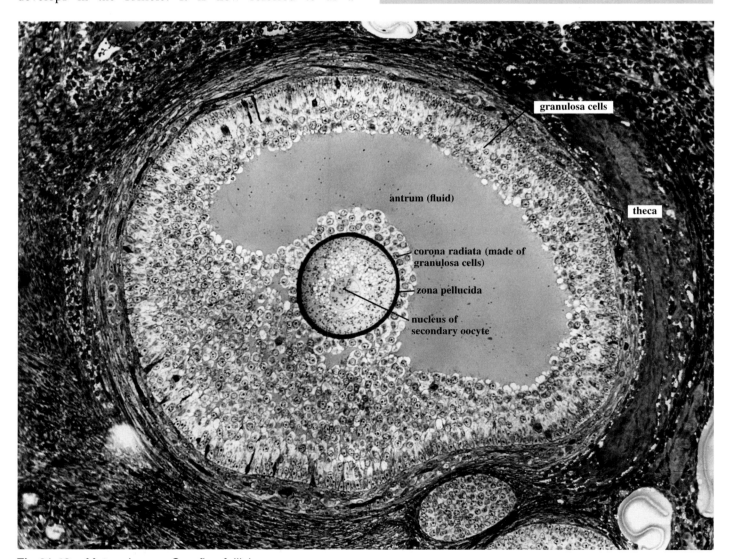

Fig 21.42 *Mature human Graafian follicle.*

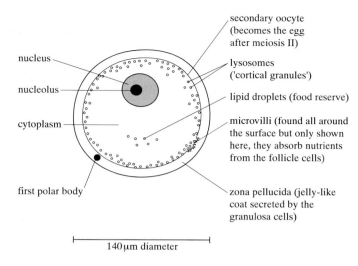

nucleus

nucleolus

cytoplasm

first polar body

secondary oocyte (becomes the egg after meiosis II)

lysosomes ('cortical granules')

lipid droplets (food reserve)

microvilli (found all around the surface but only shown here, they absorb nutrients from the follicle cells)

zona pellucida (jelly-like coat secreted by the granulosa cells)

140 μm diameter

Fig 21.43 *Structure of a secondary oocyte. The structure of the ovum or egg is identical except that one more polar body will be present as a result of division of the secondary oocyte. This division occurs at fertilisation. Granulosa (follicle) cells surround the zona pellucida but are not shown.*

21.7.6 Hormonal control of oogenesis and the menstrual cycle

As in the male, the control centres for producing gametes are the hypothalamus and the pituitary gland. The hypothalamus secretes GnRH which stimulates release of FSH and LH from the pituitary gland as in the male. As explained before, FSH and LH are referred to as gonadotrophic hormones because they stimulate the gonads, in this case the female gonads or ovaries. However, in the female, hormones are not secreted constantly but in cycles. Each cycle lasts about 28 days and is referred to as the **menstrual cycle**. Normally only one egg is produced per cycle. A new cycle begins on the first day of menstruation. A summary of the cycle is given below. Fig 21.44 shows the hormonal changes associated with the cycle, as well as the events occurring in the uterus and ovary at the same time.

(1) **GnRH** stimulates the anterior pituitary gland to secrete **FSH** (follicle stimulating hormone). FSH travels in the blood to its target, the ovaries.

(2) FSH molecules fit into receptor sites in the primordial follicles. They stimulate the development of several follicles, only one of which will complete development.

(3) The granulosa cells of the developing follicle start to produce the female sex hormone **oestrogen**. Oestrogen is a steroid hormone which is produced more and more rapidly in the first half of the cycle, corresponding to the growth of the follicle (fig 21.44). Oestrogen has two targets, the uterus and the anterior pituitary gland. In the uterus it stimulates repair and development of the lining of the uterus, the endometrium. This is in preparation for the possibility of pregnancy when an embryo will implant in the endometrium. In the anterior pituitary gland oestrogen inhibits the secretion of FSH. This is an example of negative feedback. It prevents the possibility of further follicles being stimulated so that only one egg is produced at a time. At the midpoint of the cycle oestrogen levels have built up to a high level which triggers the secretion of **LH** (luteinising hormone).

(4) LH and oestrogen are released in a surge (fig 21.44). The target of LH is the ovary where it causes ovulation. **Ovulation** is the release of the secondary oocyte from the Graafian follicle. The surge ensures precise timing of ovulation. At ovulation the secondary oocyte detaches from the wall of the follicle, is released into the body cavity and passes into the fallopian tube. Usually only one oocyte is released each month by one of the ovaries so that ovulation alternates between the pair of ovaries. The ovulated oocyte consists of a cell whose nucleus is in metaphase I of meiosis surrounded by a cell layer known as the **zona pellucida** and a layer of granulosa cells known as the **corona radiata** which protects the oocyte up to fertilisation.

The remaining part of the Graafian follicle is stimulated by LH to develop into the **corpus luteum** ('yellow body').

(5) The corpus luteum continues to secrete oestrogen, as well as another hormone, **progesterone**. Like oestrogen, progesterone has two targets, the uterus and the anterior pituitary gland. It stimulates the uterus to maintain its thickening and also stimulates glandular activity. In the anterior pituitary gland it inhibits release of LH, a second example of negative feedback. Like oestrogen, it also inhibits FSH. Release of progesterone is associated with a rise in body temperature of the female just after ovulation.

(6) If fertilisation does not occur, the corpus luteum starts to degenerate about 28 days into the cycle. The cause of this is not known, although it is suspected that it is due to chemicals secreted by the corpus luteum itself. Once it starts to degenerate, levels of oestrogen and progesterone decline, so inhibition of FSH is removed. Also, the endometrium breaks down, causing **menstruation** (the 'period'). This lasts for about five days into the next cycle.

A summary of the hormonal control of oogenesis is given in fig 21.45.

Role of hormones in premenstrual tension

Premenstrual tension (PMT) is the term used to describe the 'distressing psychological or physical symptoms' which some women experience regularly towards the end of each menstrual cycle and which 'significantly regress throughout the rest of the cycle'. Tension is not the only symptom; in fact more than 150 symptoms have been attributed to PMT

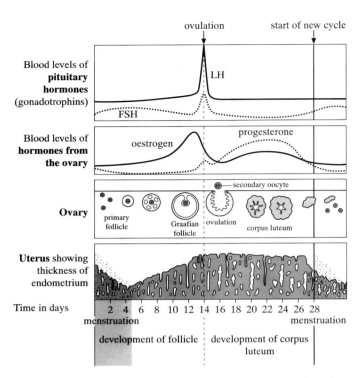

Fig 21.44 *Changes occurring during the menstrual cycle. Levels of the hormones FSH, LH, oestrogen and progesterone are shown, and the associated changes in the ovaries and uterus can be seen.*

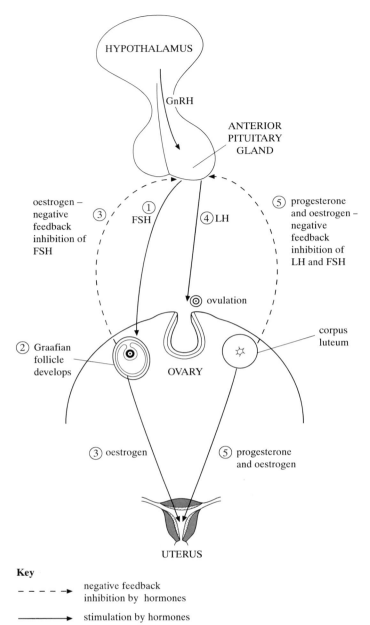

Key

- - - → negative feedback inhibition by hormones

——→ stimulation by hormones

Fig 21.45 *Hormonal control of oogenesis.*

at various times, and the term premenstrual syndrome (PMS) was introduced in 1953 to acknowledge this variety of effects. Some women who experience it describe the condition as devastating and about 75% of women are said to be affected in some way. The most common symptoms are depression, changes in mood, water retention and aches and pains. Little is known about the cause, but it is usually assumed to be hormonal in origin. Since it takes place in the few days before menstruation, it could be due to changes in the balance between progesterone and oestrogen which decline at different rates at this time. It may also be due to progesterone deficiency.

There is still debate as to whether the condition really exists. In 1993, certain psychologists (not all of them men) went so far as to suggest that it may not exist at all, that it was more of a 'social construct' than a medical condition, and that it was a way of 'legitimising and expressing distress'.

Menopause and hormone replacement therapy

Menopause is the cessation of monthly periods and marks the end of a woman's fertility. The average age of menopause in the UK is 51 years. Periods usually become irregular, before finally ceasing. The cause is the gradual failure of the ovaries. The number of follicles declines and they become less sensitive to FSH so that eggs are less and

less likely to be produced each month. Secretion of oestrogen declines and since oestrogen normally inhibits FSH by negative feedback, higher levels of FSH (and later LH) are typical of menopause. Many symptoms, both physical and psychological, are associated with menopause and these are mostly due to the reduced oestrogen levels (although progesterone levels also decline). The commonest symptoms are night sweats, random hot flushes during the day, and vaginal dryness. Other common symptoms are depression, irritability, fatigue, and softening of the bones due to loss of minerals, particularly calcium. Loss of calcium from the bones causes a condition known as **osteoporosis** (section 15.7.2). It is characterised by loss of bone mass; as a result the bones break more easily. It occurs because oestrogen is antagonistic to the hormone **parathormone**, which stimulates the raising of blood calcium levels. The symptoms can be prevented relatively easily by **hormone replacement therapy (HRT)**, in which oestrogen is taken either in pill form or by implants below the skin. HRT greatly reduces the rate at which calcium is lost from the bones, slowing it down to roughly the same rate as in men. 80% of female doctors in the relevant age group in the UK use HRT compared to 15% of the rest of the female population in this age group. Treatment can be short-term or continued for years, although in the long term, blood clotting and other undesirable side effects may occur. Some of these can be prevented by adding progesterone to the oestrogen.

It is important to realise that HRT is the *replacement* of *natural* hormones, unlike the Pill which adds synthetic hormones (section 21.9.1). Therefore the risks associated with taking the Pill, such as increased risk of thrombosis, are thought to be lower with HRT.

21.8   Sexual reproduction in humans

21.8.1   Sexual intercourse (copulation)

Internal fertilisation is an essential part of reproduction in terrestrial organisms. This is achieved in many organisms, including humans, by the development of a special organ, the penis, which is inserted into the vagina and releases gametes within the female reproductive tract.

Erection of the penis occurs as a result of an increase in blood content of spongy erectile tissue in the penis. Sexual stimulation involves stimulation of the parasympathetic nervous system. It results in vasoconstriction of the veins leading away from the penis and vasodilation of the arterioles entering the penis. As a result blood volume and pressure within the penis increase. In this erect state the penis can be inserted into the vagina where the friction, produced by the rhythmic movements of sexual intercourse, increases the stimulation of sensory cells at the tip of the penis. This activates neurones of the sympathetic nervous system which lead to closure of the internal sphincter of the bladder and contraction of the smooth muscle of the epididymis, vas deferens, and the male accessory glands, namely the seminal vesicles, prostate and Cowper's glands. This action releases sperm and seminal fluids into the top of the urethra where they mix to form **semen**. The increased pressure of these fluids in the urethra leads to reflex activity in the motor neurones supplying the muscles at the base of the penis. Rhythmic wave-like contractions of these muscles force semen out through the urethra during **ejaculation** which marks the climax of copulation. The other physiological and psychological sensations associated with this climax in both males and females are called **orgasm**.

Lubrication is provided during intercourse partly by a clear mucus secreted by the male Cowper's glands following erection but mainly by glands in the vagina and vulva of the female. Fluid from the blood also seeps through the vaginal epithelium.

Sexual excitement also causes the clitoris of the female to become erect. This is the female equivalent of the penis. The female orgasm involves muscular contractions of both the vagina and the uterus, and sensation can be centred on the clitoris, vagina or both.

The secretions of the male accessory glands are alkaline and decrease the normal acidity of the vagina to pH 6–6.5 which is the optimum pH for sperm motility following ejaculation. Approximately $3\,cm^3$ of semen is discharged during ejaculation of which only 10% is sperm. Semen contains about 100 million sperm per cm^3.

21.8.2   Passage of sperm to egg

Sperm are deposited at the top of the vagina close to the cervix. For fertilisation to take place, sperm have to travel from here through the cervix and uterus to the oviducts. The cervix is normally blocked by thick mucus. This mucus becomes thinner in the first part of the menstrual cycle, allowing the penetration of sperm to the uterus. Progesterone causes it to become thicker in the second half of the cycle.

Investigations have shown that some sperm pass from the vagina through the uterus and to the top of the oviducts within five minutes. This is faster than can be achieved by swimming and may be a result of contractions of the uterus and oviducts. These contractions could be caused by chemicals in the semen, including prostaglandins, and possibly by hormones such as oxytocin released by the female during sexual intercourse. It is more likely, however, to be due to the action of cilia which line the uterus and oviducts. It takes about 4–8 hours for most sperm to reach the oviducts. Sperm can survive in the female for 1–3 days but are only highly fertile for 12–24 h. Only a few thousand complete the journey from vagina to egg.

Capacitation

Sperm can only fertilise the secondary oocyte after spending several hours in the female genital tract, usually about seven hours, during which time they undergo an activating process known as **capacitation**. This involves a number of changes, including the removal of a layer of glycoprotein and plasma proteins from the outer surface of the sperm. Glycoprotein is originally added by the epididymis and plasma proteins from seminal fluid. They are removed by enzymes in the uterus. Cholesterol is also lost from the cell surface membrane around the sperm head, weakening the membrane. The membrane also becomes more permeable to calcium ions, which have the dual effect of increasing the beating activity of the sperm tail and promoting the acrosome reaction (see below).

During capacitation the acrosome membrane fuses with the cell surface membrane, a process which starts the release of acrosomal enzymes (see below).

Acrosome reaction

When a sperm reaches the secondary oocyte (fig 21.46), normally high up in the oviduct, the outer cell surface membrane of the sperm next to the acrosome, and the membrane of the acrosome, rupture. This enables hydrolytic (digestive) enzymes, such as **hyaluronidase** and **proteases**, stored in the acrosome to be rapidly released. These changes in the sperm head are known as the **acrosome reaction**.

21.8.3   Fertilisation

Fertilisation is the fusion of the sperm nucleus with the egg nucleus to form a diploid cell known as the zygote. It takes place in the following stages.

(1) The enzymes (particularly hyaluronidase) released by the acrosomes of the many sperm digest a path through the material that holds the granulosa (follicle) cells together.

(2) The sperm move by lashing their tails and reach the outer surface of the zona pellucida, a thick layer surrounding the secondary oocyte (see figs 21.42 and 21.43). The zona pellucida has special receptors to which the sperm heads can bind.

(3) Another acrosomal enzyme digests a path through the zona pellucida and the sperm moves through to the surface of the secondary oocyte.

(4) Here the head of a sperm will fuse with microvilli surrounding the secondary oocyte (fig 21.43) and penetrate its cytoplasm.

(5) Immediately the sperm has penetrated, the lysosomes in the outer region of the secondary oocyte, also known as **cortical granules**, release their enzymes which cause the zona pellucida to thicken and harden, forming the '**fertilisation membrane**'. This is called the **cortical reaction**. It prevents the entry of further sperm and therefore the possibility of more than one

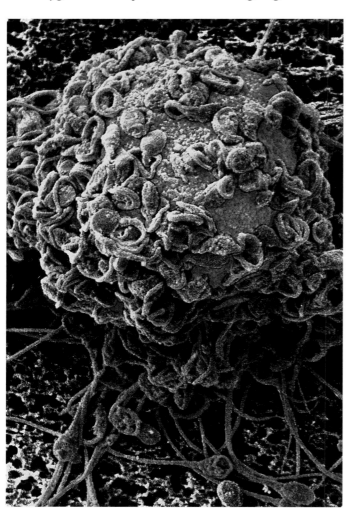

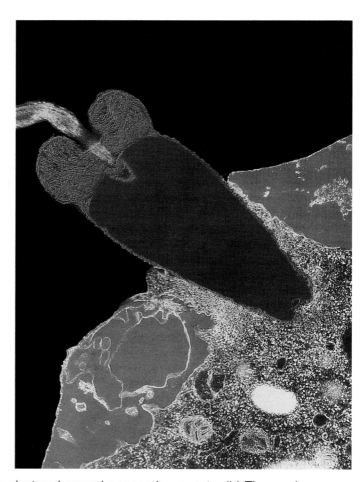

Fig 21.46 *(a) Scanning electron micrograph of human sperm clustered around a secondary oocyte. (b) The precise moment of fertilisation as a sperm penetrates the membrane of a sea urchin's egg. The dark wedge is the head of the sperm, which contains the genetic code. The grey shape behind it is the mitochondrion where energy is released that provides power for the tail. The sperm has digested the egg's surface coating of sugary protein and entered.*

sperm fertilising the same egg. The enzymes also destroy the sperm receptor sites, so sperm can no longer bind to the zona pellucida.

(6) The entry of a sperm acts as the stimulus for completion of the second meiotic division of the secondary oocyte which produces the ovum and the second polar body. The second polar body immediately degenerates and the tail of the sperm is lost within the cytoplasm of the ovum.

(7) The nucleus of the sperm swells as its chromatin becomes less tightly coiled. At this stage the nuclei of the sperm and secondary oocyte are called **pronuclei**.

(8) The male pronucleus fuses with the female pronucleus. This is the actual act of fertilisation. The new nucleus formed has two sets of chromosomes, one from the egg and one from the sperm. The cell is now diploid and is called the **zygote**. The new nucleus divides immediately by mitosis. The zygote then undergoes cytokinesis, or cell division, and produces two diploid cells.

21.8.4 The effect of fertilisation

If fertilisation occurs, the zygote develops into a ball of cells called the **blastocyst** which embeds itself into the wall of the uterus within eight days of ovulation. The outer cells of the blastocyst, the **trophoblastic cells**, then begin to secrete a hormone called **human chorionic gonadotrophin (HCG)**, which has a similar function to LH. This function includes prevention of the breakdown of the corpus luteum. The corpus luteum therefore continues to secrete progesterone and oestrogen and these bring about increased growth of the endometrium of the uterus. Loss of the lining of the endometrium is prevented and the absence of menstruation (the 'period') is the earliest sign of pregnancy. The placenta gradually takes over from the corpus luteum from about week 10 of pregnancy when it begins to secrete most of the progesterone and oestrogen essential for a normal pregnancy. Failure of the corpus luteum before the placenta is fully established is a common cause of miscarriage at about 10–12 weeks of pregnancy.

During pregnancy HCG may be detected in the urine and this forms the basis of pregnancy testing (section 12.11.2).

21.8.5 Implantation

As the zygote passes down the oviduct it divides by successive nuclear and cell divisions into a small ball of cells by a process called **cleavage**. Cleavage involves cell division without growth in size, because the cells continue to be retained within the zona pellucida. The cells just get smaller and smaller at this stage. Nuclear division is by mitosis. The cells formed are called **blastomeres** and they form a hollow ball of cells whose central cavity is called the **blastocoel**. This fills with liquid from the oviduct. The outer layer of blastomeres is called the **trophoblast** and this thickens at one point to form a

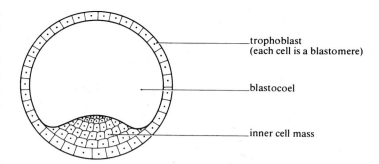

Fig 21.47 *Simplified diagram of a human blastocyst four days after fertilisation.*

mass of cells called the **inner cell mass**. This stage is called the **blastocyst** and is reached about 4–5 days after fertilisation. The structure of the blastocyst is shown in fig 21.47.

When the blastocyst arrives in the uterus the zona pellucida gradually disappears over about two days, allowing the cells of the trophoblast to make contact with the cells of the endometrium. The term 'tropho-' means 'feeding' and the trophoblast starts the process of invading the uterus wall and gaining nutrients from the endometrium. The trophoblast cells multiply in the presence of these nutrients and between the sixth and ninth days after fertilisation the blastocyst becomes embedded within the endometrium. This process is called **implantation**.

The cells of the trophoblast differentiate into an inner layer and an outer layer. The outer layer is called the **chorion**, and forms the **chorionic villi**, finger-like processes which grow into the endometrium (fig 21.48). The areas of the endometrium between these villi form interconnecting spaces which give this region of the endometrium a spongy appearance. Hydrolytic enzymes released by the trophoblast cause the arterial and venous blood vessels in the endometrium to break down and blood from them fills the spaces. In the early stages of development of the blastocyst, exchange of nutrients, oxygen and excretory materials between the cells of the blastocyst and the maternal blood in the uterus wall occurs through the chorionic villi. Later in development this function is taken over by the placenta.

21.8.6 Early embryonic development and development of extra-embryonic membranes

As stated, the outer cells of the blastocyst, the trophoblast, grow and develop into an outer layer or 'membrane' called the **chorion**. This plays a major role in nourishing and removing waste from the developing embryo. Meanwhile, two cavities appear within the inner cell mass (fig 21.47) and the cells lining these give rise to two further 'membranes', the **amnion** and the **yolk sac** (fig 21.48). As with the chorion, the use of the term

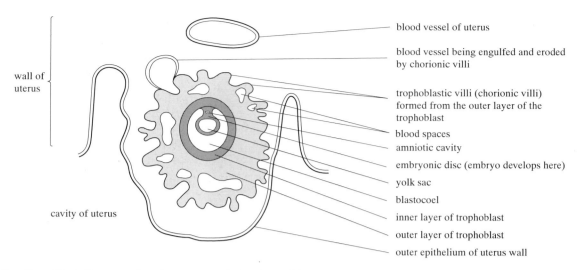

Labels (top to bottom, right side):
- blood vessel of uterus
- blood vessel being engulfed and eroded by chorionic villi
- trophoblastic villi (chorionic villi) formed from the outer layer of the trophoblast
- blood spaces
- amniotic cavity
- embryonic disc (embryo develops here)
- yolk sac
- blastocoel
- inner layer of trophoblast
- outer layer of trophoblast
- outer epithelium of uterus wall

Labels (left side):
- wall of uterus
- cavity of uterus

Fig 21.48 *Simplified diagram showing a recently implanted human blastocyst in the endometrium of the uterus. Enzymes produced by the outer layer of the trophoblast, the chorion, break down the blood vessels of the endometrium producing spaces containing blood which are used in the nourishment and excretion of the blastocyst.*

'membrane' here does not refer to membranes like those surrounding cells. The structures are called membranes because they are relatively thin, but they are made of cells.

The amnion is a thin membrane covering the embryo like an umbrella and has a protective function. Between the amnion and the embryo is the **amniotic fluid** which is secreted by the cells of the amnion and fills the amniotic cavity. As the embryo increases in size the amnion expands so that it is always pressed up against the uterus wall opposite the embryo. The amniotic fluid supports the embryo and protects it from mechanical shock.

The yolk sac has no significant function in humans but is important in reptiles and birds, where it absorbs food from the separate yolk and transfers food to the gut of the developing embryo.

The cells of the inner cell mass, between the early amnion and the yolk sac, form a structure called the **embryonic disc**, which gives rise to the embryo. The cells of the disc differentiate at an early stage (when the diameter is less than 2 mm) and form an outer layer of cells, the **ectoderm**, and an inner layer, the **endoderm**. At a later stage the **mesoderm** is formed and these three 'germ' layers give rise to all the tissues of the developing embryo. The development of three layers in this way is called **gastrulation** and occurs 10–11 days after fertilisation. The brain and spinal cord start to develop in the third week from a tube called the **neural tube** which arises in the ectoderm.

The tube starts as a groove in the ectoderm. Gradually the sides of the groove curve around to form a hollow tube which becomes swollen at one end to form the brain. This is the first organ to appear.

During the early stages of embryonic development exchange of materials between embryo and mother across the chorionic villi is adequate, but soon a fourth membrane, the **allantois**, develops from the embryonic hindgut. The chorion, amnion, yolk sac and allantois are called **extra-**

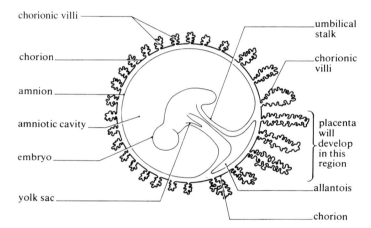

Labels (left side):
- chorionic villi
- chorion
- amnion
- amniotic cavity
- embryo
- yolk sac

Labels (right side):
- umbilical stalk
- chorionic villi
- placenta will develop in this region
- allantois
- chorion

Fig 21.49 *Simplified diagram showing the relationship between the human embryo and the four extra-embryonic membranes (amnion, chorion, allantois and yolk sac) about five weeks after fertilisation. The area where the allantois meets the chorion is called the allanto-chorion and becomes the placenta.*

embryonic membranes (fig 21.49). The allantois grows outwards until it comes into contact with the chorion where it forms a structure rich in blood vessels called the **allanto-chorion**. This contributes towards the development of a more efficient and effective exchange structure, the **placenta**.

21.8.7 Development of the embryo and fetus

Some of the early stages of embryo and fetal development are summarised in fig 21.50. Times are from conception, the time of fertilisation. After 6 weeks, the embryo is recognisably human and is called a fetus. Doctors and midwives date pregnancy from the last period,

Fig 21.50 *Diary of development of the human fetus.*

Week 1
Fertilisation. Cleavage to form a blastocyst 4–5 days after fertilisation. More than 100 cells. Implantation 6–9 days after fertilisation.

Week 2
The three basic layers of the embryo develop, namely ectoderm, mesoderm and endoderm. No research allowed on human embryos beyond this stage.

Week 3
Woman will not have a period. This may be the first sign that she is pregnant. Beginnings of the backbone. Neural tube develops, the beginning of the brain and spinal cord (first organs). Embryo about 2 mm long.

Week 4
Heart, blood vessels, blood and gut start forming. Umbilical cord developing. Embryo about 5 mm long.

Week 5
Brain developing. 'Limb buds', small swellings which are the beginnings of the arms and legs. Heart is a large tube and starts to beat, pumping blood. This can be seen on an ultrasound scan. Embryo about 8 mm long.

Week 6
Eyes and ears start to form.

Week 7
All major internal organs developing. Face forming. Eyes have some colour. Mouth and tongue. Beginnings of hands and feet. Fetus is 17 mm long.

By week 12
Fetus fully formed, with all organs, muscles, bones, toes and fingers. Sex organs well developed. Fetus is moving. For the rest of the gestation period, it is mainly growing in size. Fetus is 56 mm long from head to bottom. Pregnancy may be beginning to show.

By week 20
Hair beginning to grow, including eyebrows and eyelashes. Fingerprints developed. Fingernails and toenails growing. Firm hand grip. Between 16 and 20 weeks baby usually felt moving for first time. Baby is 160 mm long from head to bottom.

Week 24
Eyelids open. Legal limit for abortion in most circumstances.

By week 26
Has a good chance of survival if born prematurely.

By week 28
Baby moving vigorously. Responds to touch and loud noises. Swallowing amniotic fluid and urinating.

By week 30
Usually lying head down ready for birth. Baby is 240 mm from head to bottom.

40 weeks (9 months)
Birth.

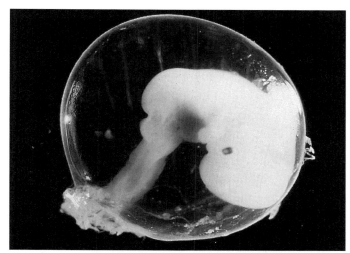

(a) Week 4: The heart is visible as the dark area near the middle of the embryo

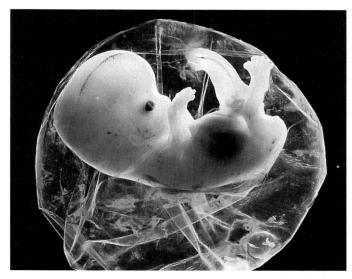

(b) Week 5–6: The arms and legs are developing.

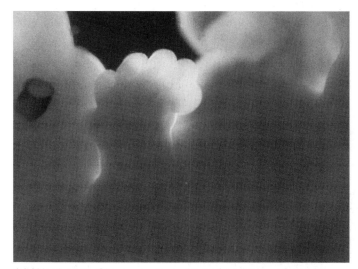

(c) Week 7–8: Close up view of hand and face showing early development of fingers and retina (dark area) of eye.

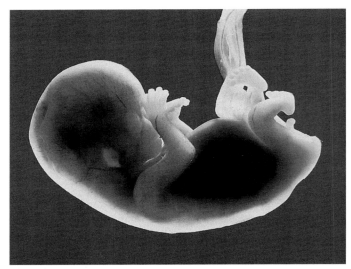

(d) *Week 11: Eyelids and ears have developed. The head is about half the total length*

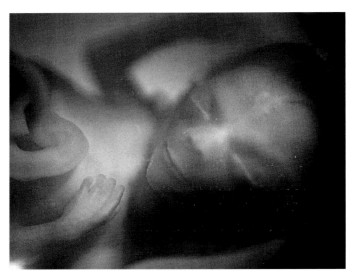

(e) *Week 12: The face looks more human with eyelids and lips visible.*

(f) *Week 20: Fetus inside embryonic membranes showing placenta in left half.*

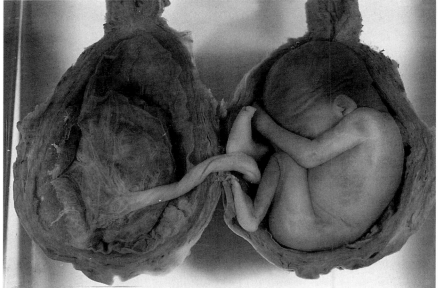

(g) *(bottom left) Week 20: close-up view showing development of hands and fingers. The fingers will close if the palm of the hand is touched.*

(h) *(below) Week 34: Nuclear magnetic resonance image of side view of women's abdomen. The fetus, on the right of the mother's spine, is in the normal position for birth with head down.*

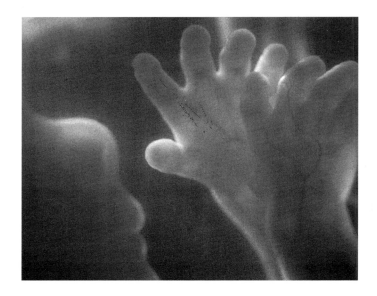

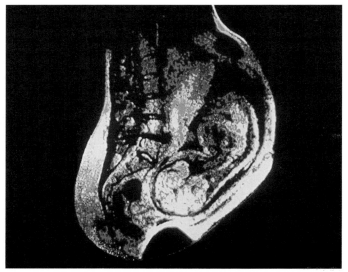

adding two weeks to the times given below. The fetus normally completes a total of about 38 weeks of development, the **gestation period**, before birth occurs. Most of the major organs are formed by the twelfth week of pregnancy, and the remainder of the gestation period is taken up by growth.

21.8.8   The placenta

The placenta is an organ found only in mammals and is the only organ in animals composed of cells derived from two different organisms, the fetus and the mother. Its function is to allow exchange of materials between mother and fetus. It takes over from the chorionic villi as the main site of exchange of materials after 12 weeks of pregnancy.

Structure of the placenta

The fetal part of the placenta consists of cells of the chorion which produce projections called **chorionic villi** (fig 21.51). These increase surface area for absorption. The chorionic villi become invaded by branches of two blood vessels of the fetus, the umbilical artery and the umbilical vein. They form capillary networks inside the villi. The

blood vessels run between the fetus and the uterus wall in the **umbilical cord** which is a tough structure about 40 cm long covered by cells derived from the amnion and chorion.

The maternal part of the placenta consists of projections from the endometrium. Between these and the chorionic villi are spaces supplied with arterial blood from arterioles in the uterus wall. Blood flows through the spaces from the arterioles to venules in the uterus wall. The placenta is a relatively large structure, weighing on average about 600 g when fully formed, and measuring 15–20 cm in diameter and 3 cm thick at the centre. About 10% of the mother's blood flows through it for each circuit of blood round the body. Because there is no direct contact between the mother's blood and the fetal circulation, the fetus is not exposed to the relatively high blood pressure of the maternal circulation. Another reason for preventing mixing of the blood is that mother and fetus may be of different ABO blood groups and their blood may not be compatible. Separation at birth would also be more difficult.

Mechanisms of uptake across the placenta

The cell surface membranes of the cells in the walls of the chorionic villi have microvilli, which increase their surface

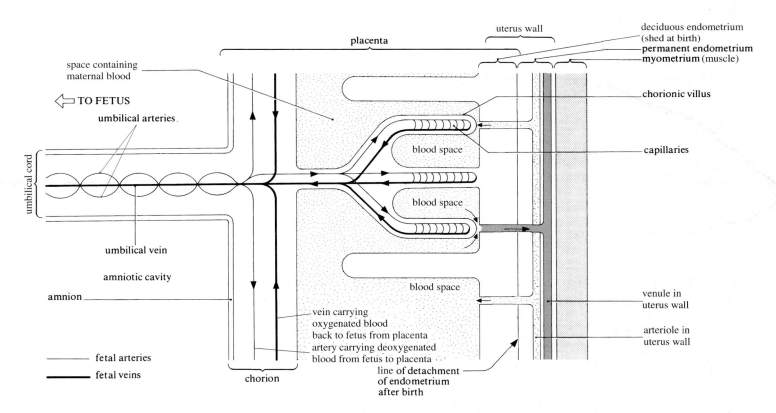

Fig 21.51   *The relationship between blood vessels in the umbilical cord, capillaries of the chorionic villi and the blood spaces of the human placenta. The placenta forms the link between the circulatory systems of the fetus and the mother.*

area for the exchange of substances by diffusion, facilitated diffusion, active transport and pinocytosis. Numerous mitochondria are found in these cells. They provide the energy for active transport and pinocytosis. The cell surface membranes contain carrier molecules used in the uptake of materials into the villi by active transport. Numerous small vesicles are found inside the cells of the villi as a result of materials being taken up from the blood by pinocytosis (section 5.9.8).

Examples of the different mechanisms of uptake are given in sections 21.8.9 and 21.8.10 below.

21.8.9 Exchange of useful substances between mother and fetus

Water. Water can cross the placenta by osmosis.

Nutrients. Glucose, amino acids, lipids, mineral salts and vitamins can all cross the placenta from the mother to the fetus. Glucose moves by facilitated diffusion through a special carrier protein as described in section 5.9.8. Ions, such as sodium, potassium and calcium, cross mainly by active transport, though some diffusion takes place. Amino acids, iron and vitamins cross by active transport. The importance of diet in pregnancy is discussed in chapter 8.

Respiratory gases. Oxygen is needed for aerobic respiration and diffuses from a region of high to low concentration from the mother's blood to the blood of the fetus. The haemoglobin of the fetus has a higher affinity for oxygen than that of adult haemoglobin and so the efficiency of exchange is increased. Carbon dioxide, a waste product of aerobic respiration, diffuses in the opposite direction.

Excretory products. Apart from carbon dioxide (see above) the fetus produces nitrogenous waste, mainly urea, which diffuses from fetus to mother across the placenta. It is removed by the mother's kidneys.

Antibodies. Antibodies can cross the placenta from mother to fetus. The fetus is therefore protected against the same diseases as the mother. This is known as **passive immunity**. It fades away gradually after birth because the immune system of the fetus has not learned to make the antibodies for itself (active immunity). Occasionally antibodies from the mother may be harmful to the fetus, as is sometimes the case with Rhesus antibodies (see below).

Endocrine organ. The placenta also functions as an endocrine organ. From the third month of pregnancy the placenta takes over completely from the corpus luteum as the main source of oestrogen and progesterone. The role of these hormones is summarised in table 21.5.

Throughout pregnancy oestrogen and progesterone are secreted in progressively greater amounts, first by the corpus luteum and then principally by the placenta. In the last three months of pregnancy oestrogen secretion increases faster than progesterone secretion and, immediately prior to birth, the progesterone level declines and the oestrogen level increases.

The placenta also secretes chorionic gonadotrophin and human placental lactogen whose functions are summarised in table 21.5. All these hormones are secreted by the chorion.

21.8.10 Harmful substances that may cross the placenta

Effect of cigarette smoking

The harmful constitutents of tobacco smoke are tars, irritants, carbon monoxide and nicotine. Of these, carbon monoxide and nicotine enter the mother's blood if she smokes and from there may cross the placenta into the baby's circulation. There has been much controversy over whether smoking affects the unborn child and if so, how serious the problem is.

Table 21.5 The hormones secreted by the placenta during pregnancy and their functions.

Oestrogen	*Progesterone*	*Human placental lactogen (HPL)*	*Chorionic gonadotrophin (CG)*
Stimulates development of duct system of breasts	Stimulates development of milk glands in breasts ready for lactation	Stimulates growth and development of breasts in preparation for lactation	Maintains activity of the corpus luteum up to 3 months of pregnancy until the placenta takes over, level then declines
Inhibits FSH release	Inhibits FSH release	Needed before oestrogen and progesterone can have their effects on the breasts (hence oestrogen and progesterone do not stimulate breast development during a normal menstrual cycle)	
Inhibits prolactin release and therefore inhibits lactation (see lactation)	Inhibits prolactin release and therefore inhibits lactation (see lactation)		
Stimulates growth of uterus, particularly muscle	Inhibits contraction of myometrium (relaxes muscle and helps to prevent miscarriage)		
Increases sensitivity of myometrium to oxytocin (see birth)	Maintains lining of uterus		

The most clearcut evidence concerns the effect on birthweight. Average birthweight is 3.40 kg (3400 g). The babies of mothers who smoke 10–20 cigarettes a day throughout pregnancy are on average 200 g (about 6%) lighter at birth. Smoking 30 cigarettes a day reduces birthweight by as much as 10%. This condition is described as **intra-uterine growth retardation (IUGR)**. IUGR can be a cause of premature birth. Babies born underweight or prematurely have a higher risk of complications if there are problems, resulting in higher rates of perinatal death (deaths just before or just after birth). Midwives and other members of the medical profession concerned with the care of new-born babies are very familiar with IUGR and claim that it is possible to tell from the umbilical cord and placenta whether the mother is a heavy smoker. This is because the blood vessels of the cord are noticeably narrower than normal and the placenta is smaller. Nicotine is known to cause vasoconstriction and therefore reduces blood flow through the placenta. Constant exposure to nicotine may therefore permanently affect development of the blood vessels in the umbilical cord and placenta. If blood flow to the fetus is restricted, oxygen and nutrients will be less freely available, possibly causing IUGR. Carbon monoxide may also have some effect since it reduces the oxygen carrying capacity of haemoglobin. There is no proof, however, that it is harmful to the fetus.

Other problems are associated with smoking in pregnancy. Premature birth, late miscarriages and perinatal deaths are all more common in smokers. A study in Great Britain of children followed from birth to age 7 years showed that children of smokers had a 30% greater chance of perinatal death and a 50% greater chance of heart abnormalities. At age 7 they were on average 6 months behind the children of non-smokers in reading age. These facts alone do not prove that smoking is the cause of all these problems. There could be some common factor. Smoking, for example, is more common among lower socioeconomic groups, where, for example, poverty and poor diet are also more common. However, carefully conducted investigations in which smokers are compared with control groups of non-smokers similar with respect to other important variables, such as weight, nutrition and socioeconomic group, show that smoking *can* probably cause effects such as premature birth and reduced birthweight.

Most women are well aware that smoking may harm the fetus, so why do some pregnant women smoke? Many women feel guilt or anxiety when they continue to smoke during pregnancy, but smoking may be physically or psychologically addictive, and it is difficult to give up if close friends or partners smoke, or if social circumstances are stressful. Sometimes women feel that if they give up smoking they will become so tense and irritable that other family members will suffer. In short, although smoking may be harmful it is not an easy issue to deal with.

Alcohol

Alcohol crosses the placenta easily. Again, there is controversy over exactly how harmful alcohol is to the fetus, and there are the same problems as with smoking over whether other factors associated with heavy drinking, such as poor diet, may also play a role.

Before considering the effects of alcohol, it is useful to be familiar with the units commonly used to measure alcohol consumption. Half a pint of beer or one glass of wine, sherry or spirit contains roughly one unit of pure alcohol (one unit is 8 g). A daily intake of this amount is estimated to increase the risk of developmental abnormalities by 1.7% and to reduce fetal growth by 1%. Women who drink more than 5 units a day are defined as heavy drinkers (7 units a day for men). It is estimated that an intake of 7.5 to 10 units a day is necessary for development of cirrhosis of the liver in the adult, a disease particularly associated with alcohol. This very high level of drinking in pregnancy can cause a condition known as **fetal alcohol syndrome (FAD)**. One or more of the following symptoms may then occur:

- mental retardation;
- microcephaly (small head/brain);
- behavioural problems such as hyperactivity and poor concentration;
- reduced growth rate, continuing after birth;
- poor muscle tone;
- flat face (poorly developed cheek bones), long thin upper lip, short upturned nose, sometimes a cleft palate.

The greatest harm is probably done during the early stages of pregnancy when the brain of the fetus is developing rapidly. Bearing in mind the particularly harmful effects on the brain, many doctors argue that, strictly speaking, there is no safe limit of alcohol consumption and recommend that women do not drink at all during pregnancy. On the other hand, it is probably more realistic to advise that the odd drink causes no harm, but that intake on any given occasion should be kept relatively low.

Apart from fetal alcohol syndrome, which is the third most common cause of mental retardation in the USA, studies from the USA indicate that drinking more than 100 g (12.5 units) of alcohol per week more than doubles the risk of delivering an underweight baby compared with women drinking less than 50 g (6.25 units) per week. Miscarriages are also more common. As mentioned, the effects of alcohol are difficult to disentangle from other sociological factors in such situations.

Drugs

The fetus is most sensitive to damage by any drugs during the phase of organ development which starts in the third week of pregnancy. At this stage the woman may only just be suspecting that she is pregnant. Pre-conceptual care and advice is therefore becoming more common, so that couples planning pregnancy can plan changes in lifestyle if necessary. Alcohol and nicotine are, strictly speaking, drugs but are described as 'socially acceptable' because they are legal. We can also consider illegal drugs and pharmaceutical products under the heading of drugs.

Illegal drugs. Of the illegal drugs, heroin and cocaine are probably of most concern. This is particularly true of the very pure form of cocaine, namely crack. If a woman is addicted to one of these drugs, her baby is also likely to become addicted and will usually have to undergo withdrawal symptoms after birth. Permanent brain damage of the fetus may occur during pregnancy, resulting in mental retardation or behavioural problems later in life. An addicted mother is less likely to maintain her own health and this in turn may result in premature birth with all the associated problems, including higher perinatal mortality. Statistics obtained in the USA show that among heroin-dependent mothers, perinatal mortality is 2.7 times higher than in control groups matched for social class and race. Babies had higher rates of jaundice (a liver problem), congenital (at birth) abnormalities, five times the risk of growth retardation, and twice the risk of being born prematurely. There were also more complications associated with birth. Both heroin and cocaine can damage the nervous system. In the USA about 300 000 babies are born each year addicted to crack.

Users of drugs that are injected are in general at more risk of catching HIV or hepatitis B through use of infected needles. LSD and marijuana may have harmful effects on the fetus. Marijuana appears to reduce the length of gestation by about 1 week.

Pharmaceutical products. Pharmaceutical products on general sale are carefully tested for harmful effects and are regarded as safe if instructions on doses are properly followed. Where possible, it is probably a wise precaution not to use drugs, especially early in pregnancy, since most will cross the placenta with ease and it is not really possible to prescribe safely in all situations.

The tragedy of the drug thalidomide resulted in increased precautions being introduced in the testing of drugs. Thalidomide was introduced in the early 1960s and prescribed to pregnant women who suffered particularly badly from 'morning sickness', a type of nausea which can become very intense in some women. An increase in numbers of deformed babies was soon traced back to the drug and it was banned. However, several thousand babies had already been affected. Deformities were characteristic. They often included missing or very stunted limbs. The bones of the limbs were much reduced or absent. The hands or feet often arose directly from the trunk of the body (fig 21.52). Either arms or legs, or sometimes both, were affected, depending on when the drug was taken during pregnancy. The drug also caused defects of the heart, gut, eyes and ears.

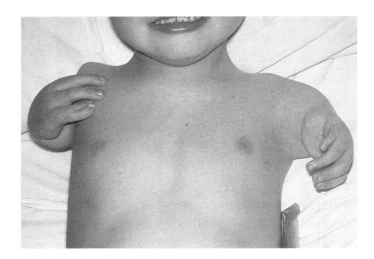

Fig 21.52 *Baby suffering from limb deformities caused by thalidomide.*

Viruses

Although most bacteria are too large to cross the placenta, most viruses are small enough to do so. If the mother catches a viral disease, she can therefore pass it to the fetus, where it may cause much greater damage, especially in the early stages of pregnancy when organs are still developing. Three examples which are of particular concern are Rubella (German measles), HIV and hepatitis B.

If the embryo or fetus is infected with Rubella it may cause miscarriage or congenital malformations. Common malformations are blindness, deafness and malformations of the heart and nervous system. Severe mental retardation may result. If contracted in the first month of pregnancy, as many as 50% of babies develop congenital malformations. A national vaccination programme, with particular care being taken to vaccinate females, has helped to reduce the risk of contracting German measles during pregnancy.

HIV and hepatitis B do not cause congenital malformations, but are life-threatening diseases.

Rhesus factor

The rhesus factor is an antigen found in the cell surface membranes of red blood cells. 84% of people possess the factor and are described as rhesus positive. Those who do not are described as rhesus negative. Presence of the rhesus antigen is genetically determined.

Red blood cells are too large to cross the placenta under normal circumstances. However, during birth, when the placenta is damaged, red blood cells of the fetus can reach the mother's blood.

A problem arises if the mother is rhesus negative and the baby is rhesus positive. If red blood cells from the fetus get into the mother's circulation, her body will recognise the rhesus (D) antigens as foreign, and make anti-rhesus (anti-D) antibodies against them. During a second pregnancy with a rhesus positive baby, the mother's immune system has already learned to make anti-D antibodies. Anti-D can cross the placenta into the blood of the fetus and cause problems which may prove fatal. A fuller discussion of the problems and how they can be prevented can be found in section 14.9.8.

> **21.8** Why should a Rh− woman who has not passed child-bearing age not be given Rh+ blood in a transfusion?
>
> **21.9** Why is there no problem if the baby is Rh− and the mother is Rh+?

21.8.11 Sex determination in the developing embryo

The sex of the embryo is determined by the sex chromosomes carried by the sperm, X in the case of a female and Y in the case of a male. All eggs carry one X chromosome. The resulting zygote therefore has the genotype XX (female) or XY (male) (section 24.6). In the early stages of embryonic development a pair of embryonic gonads, the **genital ridges**, develops, together with the beginnings of the female and male reproductive systems. Up to the sixth week of development, there is no structural difference between the male and the female. After that the sex chromosomes determine whether the system continues to develop as female or male.

The X chromosome carries a gene, the **Tfm gene (testicular feminisation gene)** which specifies the production of a particular protein molecule in the cell surface membranes of cells in the developing reproductive system. This protein acts as a testosterone receptor. Since both male and female embryos carry at least one X chromosome, this molecule is present in both sexes. The Y chromosome carries a gene called the **testis-determining gene**. This codes for the production of a protein molecule called the **H-Y antigen** which is found on the surface of all body cells of the male and is absent from the body cells of a female. It is responsible for cells of the undifferentiated genital ridges (gonads) differentiating into seminiferous tubules and interstitial cells. Without the H-Y antigen, the gonad becomes an ovary. Testosterone produced by the developing testes is released into the embryonic circulatory system and reacts with the testosterone receptor molecules in the target cells of the potential male reproductive system. The testosterone receptor/testosterone complex formed passes to the nuclei where it activates genes associated with the development of the tissues which give rise to the male reproductive system. Therefore an XY embryo will develop into a male fetus. The tissues of the potential female reproductive system are not activated and do not develop. In an XX embryo, the absence of testosterone allows the reproductive system to become female. A summary of these events is shown in fig 21.53.

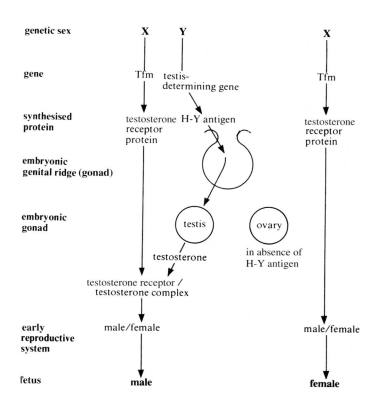

Fig 21.53 *The events involved in the differentiation of the early reproductive system of the embryo into a male or female system.*

The location of the testis-determining gene on the male chromosome has now been discovered. It is referred to as the **sex-determining region (SRY)** and is about 30 000 base pairs long (the total DNA in a human cell is about 3000 million base pairs).

21.8.12 Birth

During the final month of pregnancy the uterus becomes more and more sensitive to oxytocin. Oxytocin is a peptide hormone produced in the hypothalamus and released from the posterior pituitary gland. It causes contraction of the smooth muscle of the myometrium, the muscular lining of the uterus. The increased sensitivity is due partly to the synthesis of more and more oxytocin receptors in the myometrium, possibly a result of high levels of oestrogen. Oxytocin levels also rise as a result of the level of progesterone decreasing late in pregnancy. A third factor may be an influence of the fetus. The hypothalamus of the fetus releases ACTH from its pituitary gland. This stimulates the fetal adrenal gland to release corticosteroids which cross the placenta and enter the mother's circulation, causing a decrease in progesterone production and an increase in secretion of prostaglandins. Prostaglandins are secreted by the uterus and stimulate contraction of the uterus. The reduction in progesterone level also removes the inhibitory effect of progesterone on contraction of the myometrium. Oxytocin causes contraction of the smooth muscle of the myometrium, and prostaglandins increase the power of the contractions. The release of oxytocin occurs in 'waves' during labour. The muscular contractions it causes force the fetus out of the uterus. The onset of contractions of the myometrium marks the beginning of 'labour pains'. There are three stages to labour.

First stage

The cervix dilates during this stage. Labour starts with very mild contractions. Once they are coming regularly at 10–15 minute intervals it is recommended that the woman first contacts and then goes to the hospital if that is where she intends to give birth. The plug of mucus that blocks the cervix during pregnancy comes away and passes out of the vagina. This is called a 'show' and consists of a sticky pinkish mucus. At some stage during the first stage of labour the amnion bursts (the 'waters break'), releasing the amniotic fluid which runs out of the vagina, either slowly or in a gush. Also at some time during the first stage the woman will be taken to a delivery room if in hospital. Dilation of the cervix will be checked at intervals. A heartbeat monitor may be strapped around the upper part of the woman's abdomen to check the level of stress of the fetus. Alternatively, a stethoscope may be used.

The first stage of labour can be the painful stage and usually lasts 6–12 hours for first babies. Contractions gradually get stronger and more frequent due to positive feedback control of oxytocin production. The more the uterus contracts, the greater the stimulation of stretch receptors in the uterus and cervix. These send nerve impulses via the autonomic nervous system to the myometrium, which contracts even more, and so on. Other nerve impulses pass to the hypothalamus, stimulating the release of more oxytocin from the posterior pituitary gland. Contractions spread down the uterus and are strongest from top to bottom, thus pushing the baby downwards. Prostaglandins, hormones secreted by the uterus, also cause contraction. Throughout these contractions the cervix gradually dilates.

Pain relief is usually available in the form of 'gas and air' (a mixture of air and nitrogen(I) oxide), injections of pethidine or by means of an epidural. This is a local anaesthetic applied close to the spinal cord which removes feeling below about waist level and allows the woman to be conscious even if a Caesarean operation is necessary (surgical removal of the baby by opening the abdomen).

The cervix is fully dilated when it is about 10 cm wide, wide enough to allow the baby's head to pass through.

Second stage

In the second stage the baby is born. The baby is pushed out of the uterus and down the vagina, usually head first. Once the head is born the hard work is almost over because the rest of the body follows much more easily. As soon as the baby is breathing normally the umbilical cord is clamped at two places and cut between the clamps.

Third stage

This is the 'birth' of the placenta, caused by powerful contractions of the uterus. The placenta comes away from the wall of the uterus and passes out through the vagina. This stage happens quickly and easily. Bleeding is limited by contraction of muscle fibres around the blood vessels of the uterus which supply the placenta. Average blood loss is kept to about 350 cm^3.

21.8.13 Lactation

Lactation is the production of milk. The **mammary glands**, or breasts, contain milk glands. In the glands, special epithelial cells line small sacs called alveoli. These cells secrete milk. The alveoli are surrounded by a layer of tissue containing smooth muscle fibres. When the muscle contracts it causes milk to be released. Milk enters a series of ducts (tubes), and each duct has an expanded space called a sinus which stores milk (fig 21.54). The ducts eventually pass to separate openings in the nipple.

The breasts increase in size during pregnancy due to the development of the milk glands, controlled by progesterone, and ducts, controlled by oestrogen. **Human placental lactogen**, another hormone, is also involved, as shown in table 21.5. However, for milk to be produced, the hormone **prolactin** must be present. This is secreted by the anterior pituitary gland. Throughout pregnancy the presence of oestrogen and progesterone inhibits the secretion of prolactin and therefore the formation of milk. At birth, when the oestrogen and progesterone levels fall due to loss of the placenta, prolactin is no longer inhibited and it stimulates the alveoli to secrete milk.

Suckling reflex

The ejection of milk from the nipple involves a simple reflex action, the **milk ejection reflex** (fig 21.55). The

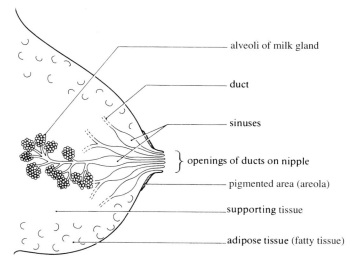

alveoli of milk gland

duct

sinuses

openings of ducts on nipple

pigmented area (areola)

supporting tissue

adipose tissue (fatty tissue)

Fig 21.54 *The human female breast showing the milk glands where milk is secreted and the ducts and sinuses carrying milk to the nipple.*

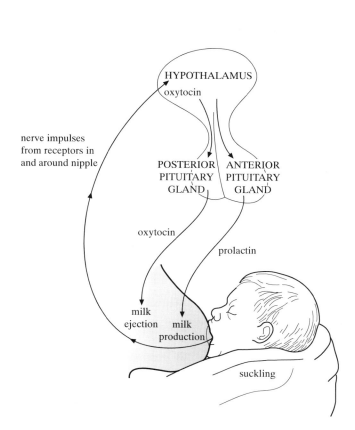

Fig 21.55 *Newborn infant suckling at the breast showing details of the suckling reflex. Lactation involves stimulation of milk secretion by prolactin and milk ejection by oxytocin.*

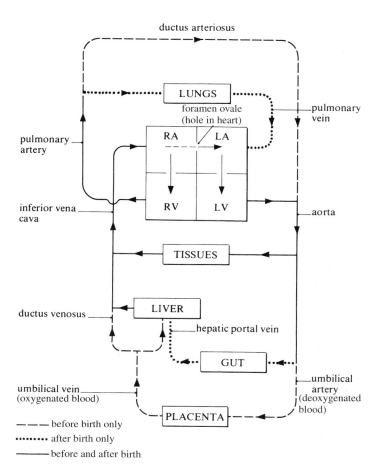

Fig 21.56 *Ante-natal (fetal) and post-natal circulatory systems. (The periods when the blood vessels are functional are indicated on the diagram.)*

sucking of the baby on the breast stimulates sensory receptors around and in the nipple. Nerve impulses pass from the receptors via the spinal cord to the hypothalamus which releases oxytocin from the posterior pituitary gland. This causes contraction of the smooth muscle fibres surrounding the alveoli and forces milk through the ducts and sinuses and out of the nipples. The stimulus of sucking also stimulates the release of prolactin by means of another reflex to the hypothalamus. Oxytocin also stimulates contraction of the muscle in the uterus, helping it to recover its normal tone after birth.

Colostrum

The first secretion of the breasts, following birth, is not milk but **colostrum**. This has a yellow colour and contains cells from the alveoli. It is rich in the protein globulin, but low in fat. It is believed to be a means of passing antibodies, particularly IgA (section 14.9.5), from mother to baby.

Milk as a food

Human milk contains fat, lactose (milk sugar) and the proteins lactalbumin and casein which are all easily digestible. The milk is made from nutrients circulating in the blood, such as lactose from glucose, protein from amino acids, and fats from fatty acids and glycerol. Milk alone is adequate to produce weight gains in the baby of 25–30 g per day.

In between breast feeds prolactin stimulates milk production for the next feed.

21.8.14 Changes in fetal circulation at birth

Throughout development in the uterus the fetal lungs and gut do not function since gaseous exchange and nutrition are provided by the mother via the placenta. Most of the oxygenated blood returning to the fetus via the umbilical vein by-passes its liver in a vessel, the **ductus venosus**, which shunts blood into the inferior vena cava and passes it to the right atrium (fig 21.56). Some blood from the umbilical vein flows directly to the liver; blood entering the right atrium, therefore, contains a mixture of oxygenated and deoxygenated blood. From here most of the blood passes through an opening in the wall separating the atria, the **foramen ovale**, into the left atrium. Some blood passes from the right atrium into the right ventricle and into the pulmonary artery but does not pass to the lungs. Instead it passes through the **ductus arteriosus** directly to the aorta, so by-passing the lungs, pulmonary vein and the atrium and ventricle of the left side of the heart. Blood from the left atrium passes into the left ventricle and into the aorta which supplies blood to the body and the umbilical artery. Pressure in the fetal circulatory system is greatest in the pulmonary artery and this determines the direction of blood flow through the fetus and placenta.

> **21.10** Describe a major change that would occur in the fetal circulation if blood pressure were highest in the aorta.

At birth the sudden inflation of the lungs reduces the resistance to blood flow through the pulmonary capillaries and blood flows through them in preference to the ductus arteriosus; this reduces the pressure in the pulmonary artery. At the same time the tying of the umbilical cord prevents blood from flowing through the placenta, and this increases the volume of blood flowing through the body of the baby and leads to a sudden increase in blood pressure in the aorta, left ventricle and left atrium. This pressure change causes the small valves guarding the foramen ovale, which open to the left atrium, to close, preventing the short-circuiting of blood from right to left atrium. Within a few months these valves fuse to the wall between the atria and close the foramen ovale completely. If this does not occur the baby is left with a 'hole in the heart' and will require surgery to correct the defect.

The increased pressure in the aorta and decreased pressure in the pulmonary artery force blood backwards along the ductus arteriosus into the pulmonary artery and hence to the lungs, thereby boosting its supply. After a few hours muscles in the wall of the ductus arteriosus constrict under the influence of the rising concentration of oxygen in the blood and close off this blood vessel. A similar mechanism of muscular contraction closes off the ductus venosus and increases blood flow through the liver. The mechanism of closing down the ductus venosus is not known but is essential in transforming the ante-natal (before birth) circulation into the post-natal (after birth) condition.

21.9 Human intervention in reproduction

Humans are increasingly able to intervene in their own reproduction as a result of advances in our understanding of reproductive physiology, genetics, molecular biology and improvements in medical technology. Some of the ways in which we do this are examined in this section, together with some of the social and ethical issues which are raised.

21.9.1 Contraception and birth control

Contraception is the prevention of conception, that is preventing the fusion of the male gamete with the female gamete. Both natural and artificial methods exist. **Birth control** includes contraception, but is broader in meaning because it also includes any measures taken after fertilisation which are designed to prevent birth. This includes measures which prevent implantation, such as the intra-uterine device (IUD or coil), and the 'morning-after pill' and abortion which are discussed in section 21.9.2.

Different methods of contraception and their relative advantages and disadvantages are summarised in table 21.6. Barrier methods block sperm from reaching the egg, either physically or chemically. Physical methods protect against sexually transmitted diseases such as HIV and have therefore become more popular. Natural methods have the advantage of having no physical side effects and of being accepted by Roman Catholics. Officially, the Roman Catholic church argues that the enjoyment of sex is a gift from God which should not be separated from the act of procreation. Some women will not use the IUD on the grounds that it prevents implantation and therefore results in the death of the blastocyst (young embryo). They argue that this can be regarded as unethical.

Introduction of the pill was controversial at the time (the early 1960s) because it was the first time that women could be virtually guaranteed that they would not get pregnant. This, it was argued, would lead to greater sexual permissiveness and contribute to a 'permissive society' with declining moral values. It can equally be argued that the easy availability of safe and effective contraception, together with education about its use, prevents many unwanted pregnancies and saves much emotional suffering. Some authorities argue that the relatively high level of unwanted pregnancies is evidence that there is still insufficient education about contraceptives and about the consequences of unwanted pregnancy, and that contraceptives should be more freely available. The problem is particularly acute in Britain compared with most other western European countries.

Termination of a pregnancy using a morning-after pill or, more controversially, abortion raises further issues. Use of the morning-after pill could be harmful to some women, although it is unlikely that the risks are greater than those of having a baby. Abortion is discussed more fully in section 21.9.2. It is widely used in some countries where contraceptives are not readily available as a form of birth control, as in Russia where the average woman has several abortions in her lifetime.

From a global point of view, contraception seems to be the only hope of restricting the growth of the human population. Strenuous efforts have been made to make contraception available in developing countries, with some success. For the first time it seems that we are in a position to be able to say that the total human population of the world will never again double. In developed countries

Table 21.6 Methods of contraception and birth control: their modes of action and relative advantages and disadvantages.

Method	Basis of action	Notes on use	Approximate failure rate*	Relative advantages	Relative disadvantages
Barrier methods					
Condom	A thin, strong rubber sheath. Prevents sperm entering the vagina.	Placed over erect penis just before sexual intercourse.	10% falling to 3% with experienced use.	Cheap, easy and convenient to use. Easily obtained. Gives some protection against sexually transmitted diseases such as HIV.	May disrupt act of love-making. Not as reliable as the Pill. Relies on male. May tear or slip off after climax.
Femidom	Female equivalent of the condom – a thin rubber or polyurethane tube with a closed end which fits inside vagina. Has two flexible rings, one each end, to keep it in place. The open end stays outside the vagina, flat against the vulva.	Inserted before intercourse and removed any time later.	Relatively new so no data. Probably similar to condom.	Gives woman some control. Other advantages as male condom.	
Diaphragm/cap	A flexible rubber dome which fits over the cervix and prevents entry of sperm to uterus. Used with a spermicidal cream or jelly (a spermicide is a chemical which kills sperm).	Inserted before intercourse. Must be left in place at least 6 hours after intercourse.	3–15%	Can be inserted a few hours before intercourse.	Must first be fitted by a doctor and training is required to fit. Occasionally causes abdominal pain. Check every 6 months that cap is right size.
Spermicide	Chemical kills sperm	Placed in vagina to cover lining of vagina and cervix. Effective for about 1 hour.	10–25%	Can be quite effective when used with condom or diaphragm.	High failure rate if used on its own.
Sponge	Polyurethane sponge impregnated with spermicide. Fits over cervix. Disposable.	Fit up to 24 hours before intercourse. Leave in place at least 6 hours after intercourse.	10–25%	Easier than cap because one size fits all and no fitting required.	High failure rate.
Hormonal methods					
'Pill'	Contains the female sex hormones oestrogen and progesterone. Prevents development of eggs and ovulation by inhibiting secretion of FSH.	One taken orally each day during first 3 weeks of cycle. After week 4 menstruation starts and the Pill is started again.	1%	Very reliable (almost 100% if properly used). Woman has control. No interference with lovemaking.	Short-term side effects may include nausea, fluid retention, and weight gain. Long-term side effects not fully understood, but increased risk of blood clotting may occur in some women. Not recommended for older women, or smokers over 35.
Minipill	Progesterone only. Ovulation may occur but cervical mucus is thickened, preventing entry of sperm.	Must be taken within 3 hours of same time every day.	2%	Very reliable. Lower dose of hormones than Pill. Therefore less risk to older women.	Breakthrough bleeding (light bleeding between periods) more common than with Pill. May cause headaches. Must be taken within 3 hours of same time each day.
Preventing implantation					
IUD (intra-uterine device) or coil	Small device made of copper, plastic or stainless steel. Inserted into uterus by a doctor and left in place. Prevents implantation.		3%	Can be left in place for long periods (up to 5 years). Suitable for women who have had children (easier to fit and larger uterus).	May cause bleeding and discomfort. IUD may come out.
Natural methods					
Abstinence	Avoid sexual intercourse.		0%	Effective.	Restricts emotional development of a relationship.
Rhythm method	Avoid sexual intercourse around the time of ovulation (total abstinence for about 7 days)		20%	Natural and acceptable to Roman Catholics.	High failure rate, even higher if periods are irregular. Requires good knowledge of body and good record-keeping. Requires a period of abstinence.
Temperature method	Note rise in temperature at ovulation and avoid sexual intercourse at these times.		up to 20%	Can increase reliability of rhythm method.	as above
Billings method	Note appearance of clear, thin, stretchy mucus in vaginal secretions at ovulation and avoid sexual intercourse at these times.		up to 20%		
Coitus interruptus (withdrawal)	Penis is withdrawn from vagina before ejaculation.		20%	Accepted by Roman Catholic church.	High failure rate. Requires much self-discipline. Penis may leak some sperm before ejaculation.
Sterilisation					
Vasectomy – male	Cut each vas deferens.		less than 1%	Very reliable. No side effects. Simple.	Very difficult to reverse.
Tying of oviducts – female	Cut both oviducts.		less than 1%	Very reliable.	Even more difficult to reverse than vasectomy.
Termination					
Morning-after Pill (section 21.9.2)	Contains RU486, an anti-progesterone.	Taken within 3 days of sexual intercourse.			For use only in emergencies. Long-term effects not known.
Abortion	Up to 24 weeks in UK	Premature termination of pregnancy by surgical intervention.		A measure of last resort.	Risk of infertility or other complications. Ethical, moral, religious issues raised. Emotionally difficult.

* % of pregnancies in first year of use.

contraception underpins our whole lifestyle and economy. It allows women to plan careers and couples to maintain a higher standard of living than would be possible with large families. It has allowed the populations of most developed countries to achieve stability. Some governments are now even concerned about declining populations, as in France.

21.9.2 Abortion

Abortion is the premature termination of a pregnancy. Medically speaking a miscarriage is a natural abortion, or **spontaneous abortion**. The theme of this section, though, is **induced abortion**, that is abortion which is deliberately brought about. The term abortion will therefore be used to mean induced abortion in this section.

Abortion is one of the most controversial issues associated with reproduction. It raises important ethical issues. There is an on-going debate within society, and in some countries such as Ireland and the USA it has become an important political issue. As in any debate, it is important not only to be able to express your own views clearly, but also to be willing to listen to and respect the views of others. People's opinions usually change slowly, after weighing up arguments over a period of time, and if you can put your own case well it will obviously have more influence on this process.

The law

Abortion was made legal in the UK by the Abortion Act, 1968. The Act was introduced because the number of illegal abortions being carried out was unacceptably high, and women's health was being put too much at risk. In the end, ethical arguments concerning the fetus played little part in the decision to legalise abortion. The Abortion Act was amended in 1991 so that at present:

- the legal age limit of the fetus for abortion is 24 weeks, the age at which a premature baby has a reasonable chance of survival using medical technology;
- in exceptional circumstances, when the fetus is shown to be suffering from severe handicap, abortions are allowed at any time up to birth (only 52 abortions were carried out on these grounds in 1991).

The grounds for abortion may be summarised as:

- risk to life, or grave permanent injury to physical or mental health, of the woman (any time);
- risk to the physical or mental health of the woman (up to 24 weeks) (these are the commonest grounds);
- risk to the physical or mental health of existing children (up to 24 weeks);
- substantial risk of the child being born seriously handicapped (any time).

Two medical practitioners must agree to the abortion and the father has no legal right to prevent an abortion.

During the 1990s, about 20% of all pregnancies in the UK were aborted.

Biological aspects of abortion

Four standard methods of abortion are described in table 21.7. The earlier the procedure is carried out, the easier and safer it is and there is a trend towards earlier abortions. Although no procedure is entirely without risk, an early abortion is in fact safer than allowing a pregnancy to proceed, so risk to the mother's health cannot be used as an argument against early abortion. Possible medical problems associated with abortion include the following.

- Occasionally infection occurs as a result of abortion. If this spreads through the uterus to the oviducts it may cause blockage of the oviducts and infertility. Such infections cause **pelvic inflammatory disease** whose symptoms include discomfort or pain in the pelvis region. About 5% of women who have abortions are made infertile as a result.
- The risk of a subsequent ectopic pregnancy is increased. This is implantation and development of the embryo in the oviducts.
- Damage to the cervix can occur which may affect the ability to carry another baby.
- Damage to the uterus may occur.
- The placenta may be retained, resulting in bleeding.
- An average of five women a year die from abortions in England and Wales.
- Emotional damage can occur. Counselling should be available after abortion as well as before. Feelings of guilt are common.

Ethical issues

The subject of abortion is a very emotional one and deserves careful consideration. Some of the commonly raised ethical issues are listed below.

- Abortion could be regarded as murder. Christians and Muslims believe that the soul is independent of the body and that it enters the body at the moment of conception. Many others also believe that from the moment of conception the new individual should have the same rights as anyone has after birth. However, the growing embryo can successfully split into identical twins at any time up to about 14 days, so it could be argued that it does not have an individual identity until at least that time.
- Even if abortion is accepted, is the scale of abortion too large? The rise in the number of abortions since it was legalised suggests that it has become more and more acceptable. Is the value of life being cheapened?
- Many abortions are being carried out on fetuses with disabilities such as Down's syndrome where the child could be expected to have a life of acceptable quality. Are we becoming intolerant of disability in general? Will this make us a less caring society and what would be the consequences? (This issue is also raised in section 25.7.)
- Many abortions are carried out beyond 12 weeks when either D and C or induced labour is necessary to

Table 21.7 Commonly used methods of abortion.

Technique	Stage of pregnancy	Summary of method	Further notes
Vacuum aspiration	Up to 12 weeks	Cervix is stretched and the contents of the uterus are gently sucked out using a flexible tube and a pump (aspirator). It takes about 30 minutes. Local anaesthetic used.	Most common method
Dilation and curettage (D and C)	12–16 weeks	Cervix is stretched and a curette, a spoon-shaped knife, is used to gently scrape the lining of the uterus. The contents can then be sucked out by vacuum aspiration. Local anaesthetic used.	
Prostaglandins or saline injection	16+ weeks	Prostaglandins are injected into the amniotic fluid, killing the fetus and causing contractions of the uterus. The fetus is born dead. Saline also kills the fetus and a hormone is added to cause contractions.	Fetus is too large to remove by earlier methods. More distressing than methods used at earlier stage.
RU486 (abortion pill)	Less than 10 weeks	Anti-progesterone. Embryo or fetus is rejected. Prostaglandin injection is given 1 or 2 days later to cause contractions and complete the abortion.	

achieve the abortion. All the major organs are developed by this stage. The fetus may therefore be able to feel pain. Abortion is allowed up to 24 weeks and there is evidence from hormonal changes that the fetus of 23 weeks can feel pain. We cannot know, though, the nature or extent of this pain since pain is a very subjective experience and is coloured by other feelings such as fear and anticipation.

- Is the legal limit of 24 weeks too late? Some 'Pro-Life' groups want the limit lowered, for example to 18 weeks, arguing that the fetus can feel pain at 24 weeks. The 24-week limit is based on the survival chances of the fetus if it is born prematurely. Should its life depend simply on the current state of medical technology? Some 'Pro-Life' groups are totally against abortion.
- If abortions were illegal, how should society deal with women who have become pregnant as a result of rape?
- The original argument for the legalisation of abortion is still a powerful one, namely that if it were not legal, many illegal abortions would be performed, resulting in financial exploitation of women, greater risk to health and the threat of being a social 'outcast'.
- Should the father have any right to prevent an abortion? Currently he does not.
- There is a worrying number of unwanted pregnancies among teenagers. If abortion were not available for these young women, it is likely that they would become trapped in relative poverty, unable to earn a living because of lack of child care facilities and a burden on the State through the need to claim benefits.
- 'Pro-Choice' groups, such as the National Abortion Campaign, argue that abortion should be available on demand, and therefore that there should be no legal restrictions. They also argue that there should be more National Health Service clinics carrying out the procedure rather than private practices, and that abortion should be allowed at any stage of pregnancy, otherwise women are being denied the freedom to control their 'own' bodies and futures.
- Extra children may impose severe financial stress on an existing family. Unwanted children are more likely to suffer from physical abuse, and are less likely to succeed in education, employment and marriage.

21.9.3 Infertility

Infertility cannot be defined precisely because there are varying degrees of infertility. For example, an average fertile couple have a 15% chance of conceiving each month if no contraception is used. A useful working definition is the failure to achieve pregnancy after one year of trying. In this situation the medical profession would recommend that investigations into the problem were justified.

The problem of infertility is surprisingly common. As many as 1 in 8 couples will experience problems in trying to conceive. Traditionally the finger of 'blame' tended to be pointed at the woman as the cause, but it is now known that the problem is almost as likely to be due to the man. Unfortunately, a lot less is known about male infertility because women have been studied in more detail, partly due to the traditional attitudes in medicine. For many people, having children is the most important aim in their lives, and is the thing that gives most purpose to their lives. To be deprived of the experience can cause great anguish and emotional pain. People will do almost anything to have children, and may pay large sums of money for treatment.

Those concerned with the treatment of infertile couples therefore have a great responsibility. Infertility treatment is not given high priority in the National Health Service (NHS) because it is not a life-threatening condition and because there is no shortage of people! In fact, IVF was withdrawn as a NHS treatment in 1996. However, affected couples are generally advised to visit their local GP first, and the NHS will carry out tests such as sperm counts in order to try to identify the cause of the problem. Couples will be referred to a hospital if necessary.

Some of the more common causes of infertility and their treatment are dealt with below.

Female infertility

Failure to ovulate. About 30% of female infertility is due to failure to ovulate. In 70% of such cases the cause is hormonal. Sometimes the hypothalamus or pituitary gland fail to produce hormones normally, with the result that either no follicles develop (lack of FSH) or egg release is affected (lack of LH). Alternatively, the ovaries may not be producing oestrogen and/or progesterone normally. In other cases there may be physical damage to the ovaries, they may be absent or not functioning normally, or very severe emotional upset or physical stress may prevent them from working normally.

Failure to ovulate can be cured in over 90% of cases. Hormone imbalance can be corrected using synthetic versions of natural hormones. The most commonly used drug is Clomiphene, a synthetic oestrogen-like drug which stimulates ovulation by bringing about the release of FSH from the pituitary gland. Tamoxifen is an alternative similar chemical. These drugs are taken as pills, usually for about five days soon after the menstrual cycle starts. If failure to *release* eggs is the problem, this may be overcome by using an injection of HCG (human chorionic gonadotrophin) which is chemically very similar to LH and acts as a substitute for LH. It is given at the time of the expected LH surge in the middle of the cycle. 'Fertility drugs' may also be used if other treatments fail since they are more powerful. They contain the pituitary hormones FSH and LH, or just FSH. They may, however, cause the release of several eggs in the same month and there is therefore a risk of multiple pregnancy. This risk can be reduced by checking for multiple ovulation using ultrasound, and by careful monitoring of hormone levels in the body.

An alternative strategy is to use injections of the hormone made by the hypothalamus, namely GnRH (gonadotrophin releasing hormone). This can be made artificially and administered in pulses using a small pump attached to the upper arm in order to mimic the natural activity of the hypothalamus.

Damage to the oviducts. About one-third of female infertility is due to tubal disease, that is damage to the oviducts. The tubes may be completely blocked, although this is not usually the problem. Infections may cause scarring, and hence partial or complete blockage or narrowing of the tubes, or damage the delicate linings of the oviducts. Another problem can be adhesions, where strands of tissue anchor the oviducts to other organs such as the uterus. This may be a result of the body repairing damage in that area, sometimes after operations. Adhesions can prevent the natural movements of the oviduct which are needed to collect and transport eggs.

If an infection is responsible, it is often pelvic inflammatory disease (PID) caused by bacteria which are normally harmless. PID is more common among women who have had a number of sexual partners and among women who use the coil (IUD). Other infections may occur after delivery of a baby or after a miscarriage or abortion. In a few rare cases women are born with blocked oviducts.

Endometriosis is another possible cause of damage to oviducts. In this condition, parts of the endometrium (the lining of the uterus) break away and grow elsewhere, for example in or around the ovaries or oviducts.

The best means of diagnosing this problem is to take an X-ray of the uterus and oviducts. A dye that is opaque to X-rays is injected into the uterus and will enter the tubes if they are not blocked. Laparoscopy (see IVF below) can be used to view the oviducts externally, and is particularly useful for examining adhesions.

The most common treatment is surgery. This is carried out with the aid of a microscope (microsurgery) because the tubes are extremely fine. Lasers have been used with some success. Sometimes the blocked portion of a tube is cut out and the tube rejoined. Adhesions can be removed relatively easily.

Uterus damage. About 5–10% of female infertility is caused by problems with the uterus. Here the problem is not one of getting pregnant, but of maintaining the pregnancy and preventing miscarriage. Implantation may be a problem, or problems may arise later. Occasionally the growth of fibroids, which are non-malignant tumours which grow from the walls of the uterus, can cause infertility. Similar, but smaller growths called polyps may have the same effect. Fibroids and polyps can be removed relatively easily by surgery. Adhesions within the uterus, sometimes the result of the scraping procedure of an abortion, can stick parts of the inside of the uterus together. It may be possible to remove these surgically. IUDs or infections can cause inflammation, in which case antibiotics can be prescribed. Less commonly there is a congenital abnormality (a problem already present when the woman was born), such as an absent, small or odd-shaped uterus.

Cervix damage. The cervix is the neck of the uterus. It may be damaged as a result of abortion or a difficult birth. Scar tissue may narrow it or it may stop producing the cervical mucus needed for the sperm to reach the uterus. Alternatively it may be widened, with the result that miscarriage is much more likely after 3 months of pregnancy. All these conditions can be treated by surgery.

Antibodies to sperm. In a few rare cases, women produce antibodies against their husband's sperm. These are found in the cervix, uterus and oviducts. This may be treated in various ways, including the use of drugs which suppress the immune system, but IVF is probably the best treatment (see below).

Male infertility

Absence of sperm. Absence of sperm in the semen is called **azoospermia**. About 5% of male infertility is a result of sperm not being produced at all, but even if they are produced they may not appear in the semen if the tubes between the testes and the seminal vesicles are blocked (fig 21.32). Blockage can be a result of scarring due to infection or injury. Gonorrhoea and TB (tuberculosis) are possible causes of infection. The blockage may be congenital.

Another cause of azoospermia can be a failure of the ejaculation mechanism. Retrograde ejaculation, in which sperm pass up the urethra to the bladder instead of down the urethra and out of the body, is possible for various reasons.

Failure to produce sperm may be a result of physical injury to the testes, or occasionally a result of infection by the mumps virus after puberty. Alternatively the problem may be hormonal, in which case it is very difficult to treat. Fig 21.57*a* summarises some of the causes of azoospermia.

Low sperm count. More than 90% of male infertility is due to low sperm counts. The cause is often unknown, but a number of factors have been shown to be possible causes. These are summarised in fig 21.57*b*.

Abnormal sperm. It is usual for a small proportion of sperm to be abnormal, for example having two tails, no tail, no head or abnormal shapes. However, if the proportion is high, fertility is reduced. The reasons for these abnormalities are usually not known, though they could be due to hormonal problems or infections in some cases.

Autoimmunity. About 5–10% of male infertility is probably due to an immune response by the male to his own sperm. Antibodies are made which attack the sperm and reduce the living sperm count. Reasons for this are unknown. The condition is difficult to treat; treatment with corticosteroids to reduce the immune response may result in unacceptable risk of infections. Alternatively, donor insemination may be recommended (see below).

Premature ejaculation. This is the situation where the man has an orgasm before penetration of the penis into the vagina. The problem is often overcome with experience.

Impotence. This is the inability to achieve or maintain an erection of the penis. The problem is usually psychological and counselling may help if it persists.

21.9.4 Treatment for infertility

Where environmental factors such as smoking, obesity, and stress are involved, treatment is aimed at removing or reducing the factor responsible. Surgical and hormone treatments are mentioned above where relevant and in fig 21.58. A number of other treatments are also available including in vitro fertilisation, donor insemination and artificial insemination.

In vitro fertilisation (IVF)

This is commonly known as the 'test-tube baby' technique. It was first devised by Patrick Steptoe and Robert Edwards in 1978 as a means of helping women with blocked oviducts. It is still mainly used for this problem and for patients with damaged oviducts which cannot be repaired surgically. However, it may be used where there are problems with endometriosis, low sperm counts or abnormal sperm (since fewer sperm are needed to fertilise eggs in vitro), and where the male or female are producing antibodies against the sperm. If the female cannot produce eggs it allows donor eggs to be used (see egg donation).

The technique involves fertilising one or more eggs outside the body, and then transferring the fertilised eggs, known as '**pre-embryos**', back into the uterus. This step is referred to as **embryo transfer**. The main stages of IVF are:

- stimulation of the ovaries with fertility drugs to produce several eggs;
- collecting the mature eggs;
- fertilising the eggs in the laboratory;
- culture of the pre-embryo;
- embryo transfer.

Stimulating the ovaries. The ovaries are stimulated with a fertility drug containing FSH in order to produce several eggs, thereby increasing the chances of successful egg collection and pregnancy later. Another drug, such as Clomiphene, may also be used to stimulate ovulation. The drugs are given early in the menstrual cycle. Growth of the follicles is monitored with ultrasound scans which allow the number and size of the follicles to be measured. Blood tests for oestrogen, progesterone and LH also help judge when ovulation is about to occur. An injection of LH in the form of HCG (a closely similar hormone) can help to control the timing of ovulation more precisely.

Collecting the eggs. Eggs can be collected from the follicles by laparoscopy. The laparoscope is a short telescope several centimetres long which is inserted into the abdomen, usually through the navel, in order to examine the pelvic region where the ovaries, oviducts and uterus are situated. Carbon dioxide gas is introduced to distend the abdominal cavity and separate the body wall from the gut. The procedure is carried out under general anaesthetic. A powerful light is shone down the telescope and enables the

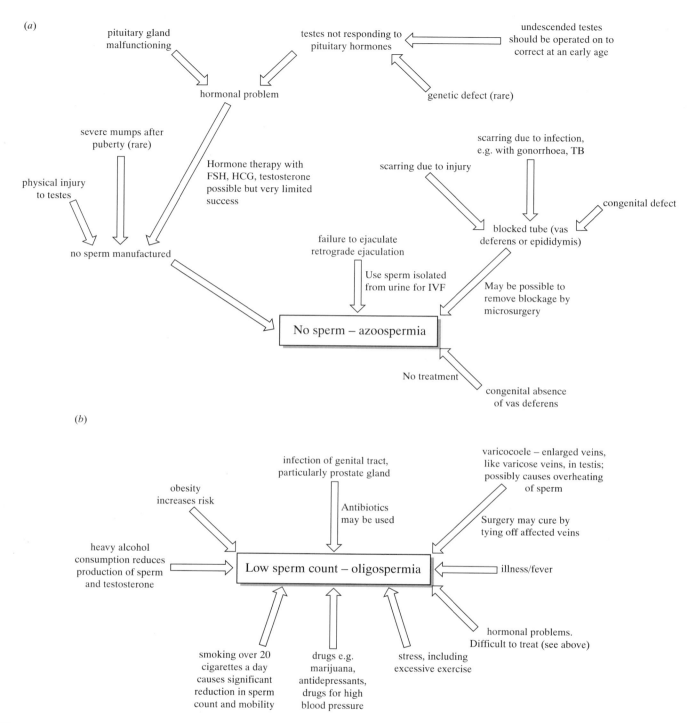

Fig 21.57 (a) *Some causes and treatments of azoospermia, the inability to produce semen containing sperm.* (b) *Some causes and treatments of low sperm counts (oligospermia).*

surgeon to view inside the body. Eggs are collected by sucking out the fluid contents of mature follicles with a fine hollow needle, also inserted through the abdominal wall. The fluid is immediately examined with a microscope for eggs and any eggs found are placed in a special culture medium in an incubator at body temperature. Between 5 and 15 eggs are usually collected.

An alternative way of collecting eggs is by using ultrasound as a guide and collecting through the vaginal route to the uterus and oviducts. This does not require a general anaesthetic, although pain relief and a sedative are given.

Fertilisation. Sperm are collected from the male partner and washed in a culture fluid to remove seminal fluid. About 100 000 healthy sperm are added to each egg about six hours after egg collection. This is done in a glass dish or tube. The fertilised eggs are grown for about two days, after which they are usually at the 2- to 8-cell stage. They are examined with a microscope to check suitability for embryo transfer into the woman's uterus. The larger the number transferred, the greater the chance of success, but this has to be balanced against the need to avoid multiple pregnancies, particularly of three or more fetuses. It is now recommended that a maximum of three pre-embryos are transferred. Spare pre-embryos can be frozen for further attempts if necessary. If three pre-embryos are transferred the risk of having twins if the woman gets pregnant is about 23% and the risk of triplets about 5%.

Embryo transfer. Embryos are transferred in a drop of culture fluid through the cervix and into the uterus using a fine plastic tube. A syringe gently squirts the fluid into the uterus. From 10 minutes to 4 hours later the woman can leave the hospital and resume normal life, although she is usually advised to 'take it easy' for a few days. A pregnancy test is usually performed 14 days after the procedure.

Success rate. The success rate if one pre-embryo is transferred is about 10%, for two pre-embryos about 14% and for three about 25%. There is a decline in success with age of the female from an average of 22% at age 28 years to 9.5% at age 40 years. Most clinics allow about three or four attempts, but the procedure is emotionally extremely demanding and some couples give up before this if they are not successful.

Ethical considerations. A number of fundamental ethical issues are raised by IVF, as well as more everyday social issues. These are summarised below but are worth discussing further.

- Some people would object on religious or moral grounds to any unnatural intervention into human reproduction, particularly to fertilisation outside the body.
- There is a serious ethical/moral problem over what to do with spare pre-embryos. The same arguments about

the right to life of embryos that have arisen in the discussion on abortion in section 21.9.2 can be raised. Should doctors have the right to dispose of spare pre-embryos? Should the parents have the right? It is estimated that at least half of all human embryos conceived naturally do not implant and are lost at the next period. Also, the embryo can split into identical twins at any point up to 14 days, making it possible to argue that there is no unique individual up to that point. Should research on spare pre-embryos be allowed? At present experiments can be carried out on pre-embryos up to 14 days after fertilisation because the nervous system does not start to form until that point and no organs have formed. Parents can opt to keep the pre-embryos frozen, possibly for later attempts at IVF or for embryo donation.

- Does the freezing of pre-embryos damage them in any way? So far there is no evidence that it does.
- Embryo research allows scientists to continue to perfect the techniques needed to improve IVF. Pre-embryos can also be used for research into infertility generally, contraception, cause of miscarriage and genetic diseases.
- Soon it will be possible to carry out extensive genetic screening of pre-embryos. Will this be a good thing, allowing us to reduce genetic disease, or will it encourage society to become less tolerant of genetic disease and disability? Will it encourage the selection of pre-embryos for particular characteristics such as sex?
- There is a possibility of multiple births, which increases the risk of miscarriage and perinatal mortality. It also increases the economic and care burden on a family.
- There is a higher risk of ectopic pregnancy with IVF (5% compared with 1% in the general population in the UK). This is linked with the fact that IVF is often used for women with damaged oviducts.
- An important problem with IVF is that it is extremely demanding emotionally and psychologically. There is a relatively high failure rate combined with desperate desire for success. Couples have to be counselled carefully before they undertake the procedure.
- The procedure is expensive, about £1000–£2000 in the UK in the early 1990s. Couples who are desperate for children may be tempted to make financial sacrifices they cannot really afford. It is sometimes difficult to judge whether the treatment should be recommended and clinics must guard against commercial exploitation of vulnerable people.
- There is no evidence that IVF babies have an increased risk of any abnormalities.

Gamete intra-fallopian transfer (GIFT)

GIFT is a variation of IVF which can be useful if the oviducts are not blocked. It is mainly used when there is no known cause for the infertility, or when the woman's cervical mucus is hostile to her partner's sperm, for example making antibodies. Sperm and eggs are added separately to the oviducts so that fertilisation takes place naturally in the woman's body rather than outside as in IVF. Laparoscopy or a more recent technique via the cervix is used. Pre-embryos move down the oviducts to the uterus where they may implant. The success rate is about 21%. Implantation is more likely to be successful with GIFT than with IVF.

Zygote intra-fallopian transfer (ZIFT)

This is another treatment for unexplained infertility. Pre-embryos (zygotes) are transferred into the oviducts rather than gametes as in GIFT. The advantage over GIFT is that fertilisation can be confirmed – with GIFT there is no means of knowing if fertilisation is taking place unless the woman becomes pregnant. The advantage over IVF is that the pre-embryos enter the uterus naturally by way of the oviducts. Greater success rates than with GIFT and IVF are anticipated.

Donor insemination (DI) or Artificial insemination by donor (AID)

If the male is infertile or has a very low sperm count, donor insemination is often a preferred option to adoption of a child. The technique may also be used by a fertile male if there is a risk of passing on an inherited disease. The technique is straightforward but requires careful counselling before being undertaken.

Potential donors are carefully screened for health, fertility and any history of genetic disease in their family. They are screened for HIV antibodies, hepatitis B and a few other diseases which may be transmitted in semen. Donors are matched to the male partner for race, height, skin, hair and eye colouring, body build and blood group. The Human Fertilisation and Embryology Act which came into force in 1991 makes it a requirement that information about donors and recipients is registered with the Human Fertilisation and Embryology Authority (HFEA). Eventually, it is planned that anyone over the age of 18 will be able to check whether they are DI offspring. However, the donor will remain legally anonymous.

In order to maximise the chances of success, the woman receiving the treatment is normally asked to keep a temperature chart to note when ovulation takes place. Clomiphene may be used to promote ovulation and to make its date more predictable. On the appropriate date the woman visits the clinic, the frozen sperm sample is selected and is gently released next to the opening of the cervix by means of a small plastic tube. The success rate is high – most women will fall pregnant within 6 months using this technique.

Ethical issues.

- The major issue is whether the child should be told the identity of the father. The genetic father (donor) is not the legal father since a change in the law in the late 1980s, so legally there are no problems with the relationship. Evidence suggests that children who are told are curious to know more about their genetic fathers but still maintain a loving relationship with the parents who have brought them up. If the child is not told, there is the risk that the information might be revealed at an inappropriate time. The father may feel very insecure about the child knowing since he will not wish to risk damaging their relationship.

- If the decision is made to tell the child, there follows the decision about when this should be done, and possibly whether family and friends should be told. Professional advice is that, on balance, the child is probably better told sooner rather than later, preferably before the teenage years.

- It may be imagined that because the legal father is not the genetic father, he may not have the same long-term commitment to the child. There is no evidence, however, that DI children are any less loved as a result of their origins. This is perhaps not surprising given the high motivation to have children needed to go through with the procedure and the counselling involved.

- Should the child have legal access to the identity of their genetic father and would this deter donors from coming forward?

- There is a slight risk that genetically related DI offspring might meet, enter a sexual relationship and have children. The number of successful donations from one donor is therefore legally restricted.

- There is some controversy over whether DI should be made available to unmarried couples, single women or lesbians. Where a stable home background is likely to be provided, some clinics consider such applicants. This is probably preferable to allowing people to select their own donors from among family, friends or acquaintances, which tends to happen if DI is denied.

- Some women and some men regard DI as a form of adultery, perhaps on religious grounds, and are therefore opposed to the method.

Artificial insemination by husband or partner (AIH)

AIH can be used in some cases of impotence and premature ejaculation. It has also been used in cases where the man is likely to face sterility as a result of surgery, for example for testicular cancer, or is living away from home for long periods of time. Some men give written consent for their widows to use their semen after their deaths. A man on active service in the forces, or someone diagnosed with a terminal illness, might do this for example. As a treatment for low sperm counts it is not very useful, although it is possible to enrich sperm samples for healthy sperm. IVF is a better option in this circumstance.

Egg donation

If the woman is unable to produce eggs, one solution is to use an egg donor. The techniques developed for IVF are followed to obtain the eggs, and after fertilisation with the male partner's sperm, the pre-embryos can be placed in the oviducts of the future mother. The technical difficulties of donating eggs are greater than donating sperm, and they cannot be successfully frozen. This makes HIV screening more difficult. One convenient source of eggs is spare eggs from women who are undergoing IVF or GIFT.

The ethical issues are similar to those for DI (see above).

Surrogacy

Surrogacy is a possibility when the woman cannot bear a child, for example through lack of a uterus. An agreement is reached with another woman to have the baby using sperm from the male partner. The egg may be supplied by the infertile woman if she can produce eggs. In this case the IVF or GIFT procedure is used and the pre-embryo replaced in the surrogate mother. Alternatively the egg of the surrogate mother can be used, in which case straightforward DI using the sperm of the male partner is possible.

Ethical issues.

- It is now illegal in the UK to enter into such an arrangement on a commercial 'Rent A Womb' basis. This is to avoid exploitation of infertile women.

- Probably the biggest potential problem is if the surrogate mother does not wish to hand over the baby at birth. It may be genetically hers. It is difficult to predict how a surrogate mother will react when the time comes to give up the baby.
- Should the child be told of its origins? (This question has already been discussed under DI.)
- If the surrogate mother suffers health damage or even death as a result of the pregnancy, what are the legal implications? Could the commissioning parties be sued? Who should decide if an abortion should take place if the child is going to be born disabled?
- If the child is born with a defect, particularly a genetic defect, the future mother may not wish to accept it.

Sub-zonal insemination (SUZI) or Micro-insemination sperm transfer (MIST)

SUZI is a newly developing technique whereby a few sperm are introduced directly next to the egg using a very fine probe while viewing with a microscope. The sperm are introduced below the zona pellucida, hence the term 'sub-zonal'. The eggs are obtained by the usual IVF procedure. The technique is not yet perfected nor widely available, but represents a promising line of research.

Chapter Twenty-two

Growth and development

22.1 What is growth?

Growth is a fundamental characteristic of all living organisms. It is often thought of simply as an **increase in size**, but if you think about this carefully you will realise that this is not an adequate definition. For example, the size of a plant cell may increase as it takes up water by osmosis, but this process may be reversible and cannot then be thought of as genuine growth. Also, when a zygote divides repeatedly to form a ball of cells, the early embryo, there is an increase in cell numbers without an increase in size (volume or mass). This is known as cleavage and is the result of cell division without subsequent increase in size of daughter cells. The process does involve development, so perhaps it should be regarded as growth despite the fact that no increase in size occurs.

The process of development is so closely linked with growth that the phrase 'growth and development' is commonly used to describe the processes which are normally thought of as growth. Development could be described as an **increase in complexity**.

Starting with an individual cell, growth of a multicellular organism can be divided into three phases:

- **cell division** – an increase in cell number as a result of mitosis and cell division;
- **cell enlargement** – an irreversible increase in cell size as a result of the uptake of water or the synthesis of living material;
- **cell differentiation** – the specialisation of cells; in its broad sense, growth also includes this phase of cell development.

However, each of these processes can occur at separate points in time. The example of cleavage has already been mentioned above. An increase in size without change in cell numbers may also occur, as in the region of cell elongation behind the root and shoot tips of plants. In the case of single-celled organisms, such as bacteria, cell division results in *reproduction* (not growth) of the individual and *growth* of the population.

It is therefore difficult to define growth. One acceptable definition is that growth is **an irreversible increase in dry mass of living material**. By specifying *dry* mass we can ignore the short-term fluctuations in water content that are particularly characteristic of plants. By specifying *living* material we can ignore non-living material such as inorganic limestone in corals.

All stages of growth involve biochemical activity. During growth the DNA message is translated and as a result specific proteins are made, including enzymes. Enzymes control cell activities. They bring about the changes which eventually result in a change in overall form and structure, both of individual organs and of the organism as a whole. This process is known as **morphogenesis** and is influenced by the environment as well as the genes.

Growth may be positive or negative. **Positive growth** occurs when synthesis of materials (anabolism) exceeds breakdown of materials (catabolism), whereas **negative growth** occurs when catabolism exceeds anabolism. For example, in the course of germination of a seed and the production of a seedling there is an increase in cell number, cell size, fresh mass, length, volume and complexity of form, while at the same time dry mass may actually *decrease* because reserves are being used up. From this definition, germination therefore includes a period of negative growth which only becomes positive when the seedling starts to photosynthesise and make its own 'food'.

22.2 Measuring growth

Fig 22.1 shows a variety of growth curves produced by plotting different parameters such as length, height, mass, surface area, volume and number against time. The shape of these curves is described as **sigmoid**, meaning S-shaped, and is typical of much growth.

A sigmoid curve can be divided into four parts as shown in fig 22.2.

- The first phase is the **lag phase** during which little growth occurs.
- This leads into the second phase, the **logarithmic** or **log phase**, during which growth proceeds exponentially. During this phase the rate of growth accelerates and at any point is proportional to the amount of material or number of cells already present. In all cases of growth the exponential increase eventually declines and the rate of growth begins to decrease. The point at which this occurs is known as the **inflexion point**. Rate of growth is at its maximum at the inflexion point (it is the point where the curve is steepest).
- The third phase is the **decelerating phase** during which growth becomes limited as a result of the effect

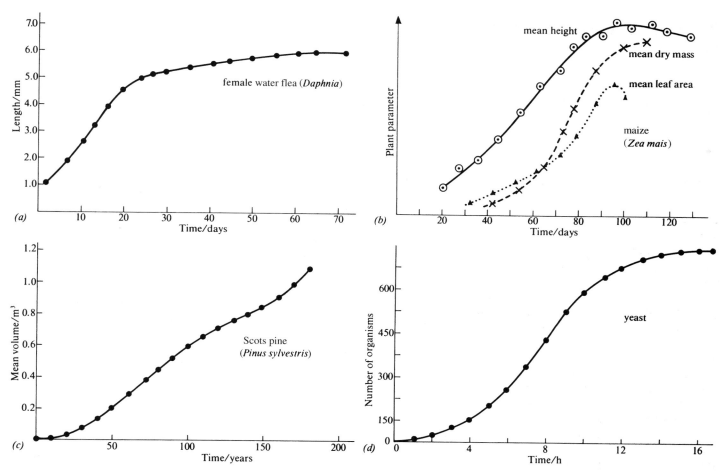

Fig 22.1 *Growth curves obtained using six different parameters and four different species. In all cases the curves are sigmoid.*

Fig 22.2 *A typical sigmoid growth curve showing the four characteristic growth phases and the inflexion point. The inflexion point is the point of maximum growth rate where the curve is steepest.*

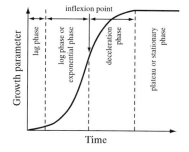

of some internal or external factor, or the interaction of both.

- The final phase is the **plateau phase** or **stationary phase**. This usually marks the period where overall growth has ceased and the parameter under consideration remains constant. The precise nature of the curve during this phase varies, depending on the species and what is being measured. In some cases the curve may continue to rise slightly until the organism

dies, as is the case with monocotyledonous leaves, many non-vertebrates, fish and certain reptiles. This indicates continuing **positive growth**. In the case of certain cnidarians the curve flattens out, indicating zero growth, whilst other growth curves may tail off, indicating a period of **negative growth**. The latter pattern is characteristic of many mammals, including humans, and is a sign of physical senescence associated with increasing age.

22.2.1 Methods of measuring growth

Growth can be measured at various levels of biological organisation, such as growth of a cell, organism or population. The numbers of organisms in a population at different times can be counted and plotted against time to produce a population growth curve as shown in fig 22.1*d*. At the level of the organism there are a variety of parameters which may be measured; length, area, volume and mass are commonly used. In plants, growth curves for roots, stems, internodes and leaves are often required, and length and area are the parameters commonly chosen. In the case of growth in animals and entire plants, **length** and **mass** are two commonly measured parameters. In humans, for example, changes in standing height and body mass are frequently used indicators of growth. With regard to mass there are two values that can be used, namely fresh (wet) mass and dry mass. Of the two, fresh mass is the easier to measure since it requires less preparation of the sample and has the advantage of not causing any injury to the organism, so that repeated measurements of the same organism may be taken over a period of time.

The major disadvantage of using fresh mass to measure growth is that it may give inconsistent readings due to fluctuations in water content. True growth is reflected by changes in the amounts of constituents other than water and the only valid way to measure these is to obtain the dry mass. This is done by killing the organism and placing it in an oven at 110 °C to drive off all the water. The specimen is cooled in a desiccator and weighed. This procedure is repeated until a constant mass is recorded. This is the dry mass. In all cases it is more accurate to obtain the dry mass of as large a number of specimens as is practicable and from this calculate the mean dry mass. This value will be more representative than that obtained from a single specimen.

22.2.2 Types of growth curve

Absolute growth curves

Plotting data such as length, height or mass against time produces a growth curve which is known as the **absolute growth curve** or **actual growth curve** (fig 22.3). The usefulness of this curve is that it shows the overall growth pattern and the extent of growth. Data from this graph enable the growth curves in figs 22.4 and 22.5 to be constructed.

Absolute growth rate

An **absolute growth rate** curve shows how the *rate* of growth changes with time (fig 22.4). The rate is measured as the change in a particular parameter, such as height or mass, in a particular time. For example, it could be the increase in height of a human over a period of a year. In particular it shows the period when growth is most rapid and this corresponds to the steepest part of the absolute growth curve. The peak of the absolute growth curve marks the point of inflexion on the sigmoid curve (fig 22.2) after which the rate of growth decreases as the adult size is attained. Overall a bell-shaped absolute growth rate curve is obtained from a sigmoid absolute growth curve.

Relative growth rate

A **relative growth rate** curve takes into account existing size (fig 22.5). Thus if a 5 year old and a 10 year old human both grew 10 cm in height in one year, their absolute growth rates would be the same, but the 5 year old would be growing relatively faster and have a greater relative growth rate. Existing size is taken into account by using the following calculation:

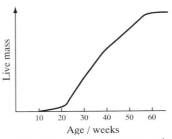

Fig 22.3 *Absolute growth curve or actual growth curve obtained by plotting live mass against age for sheep. (Data from L. R. Wallace (1948) J. Agric. Sci., **38**, 93 and H. Pálsson & J. B. Vergés (1952) J. Agric. Sci., **42**, 93.)*

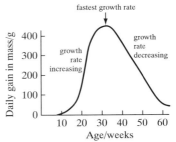

Fig 22.4 *Absolute growth rate curve plotted from data shown in fig 22.3. The graph shows how the daily gain in weight (growth rate) varies with age.*

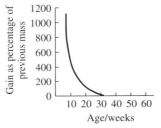

Fig 22.5 *Relative growth rate curve plotted from data shown in fig 22.3.*

$$\frac{\text{growth in given time period}}{\text{measurement at start of time period}} \quad \text{or} \quad \frac{\text{absolute growth rate}}{\text{original measurement}}$$

These calculations give the relative growth rate. Changes in relative growth rate with time can be shown on a **relative growth rate curve**, as in fig 22.5. This is a measure of the *efficiency* of growth, that is the rate of growth relative to the size of the organism.

A comparison of relative growth rate curves for organisms grown or reared under different conditions shows clearly the most favourable conditions for rapid growth and for growth over an extended period.

Growth in mammals, including humans

In the case of mammals the absolute growth curve is sigmoid but the exact shape of the curve appears to be related to the time taken to reach sexual maturity. In the rat the curve is steep and truly sigmoid since sexual maturity is reached quickly (within 12 months) whereas in humans the absolute growth curve shows four distinct phases of increased growth (fig 22.6). The absolute growth curve shows that maximum mass is achieved in adulthood. The absolute growth rate curve shows that rate of growth is greatest during infancy and adolescence, with a distinct adolescent spurt of growth being typical. The relative growth rate curve shows that relatively speaking, growth is greatest during embryological development.

22.3 Patterns of growth

Various patterns of growth occur among organisms.

22.3.1 Isometric and allometric growth

Isometric (*isos*, same; *metron*, measure) growth occurs when an organ grows at the same mean rate as the rest of the body. In this situation change in size of the organism is not accompanied by a change in shape of the organism. The relative proportions of the organs and the whole body remain the same. This type of growth pattern is seen in fish and certain insects, such as locusts (except for wings and genitalia) (fig 22.7). In such cases there is a simple relationship between linear dimension, area, volume and mass. The area increases as the square of linear dimension ($A \propto l^2$) whereas volume and mass increase as the cube of linear dimension ($V \propto l^3$ and $M \propto l^3$). An animal showing a small increase in overall dimensions with time therefore shows a marked increase in mass: for example, an increase in length of only 10% is accompanied by a 33% increase in mass.

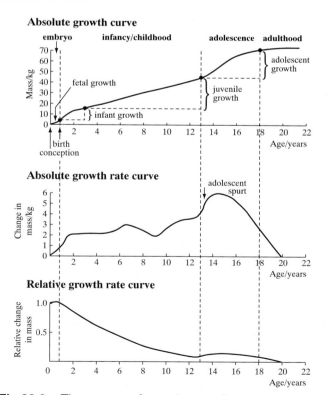

Fig 22.6 *Three types of growth curve for humans.*

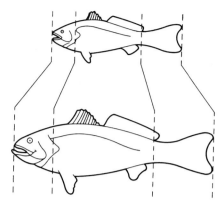

Fig 22.7 *Development in fish – an example of isometric growth. The external structures retain their shape and spatial relationships as a result of a proportional growth rate. (After Batt (1980) Influences on animal growth and development, Studies in Biology, No. 116, Arnold.)*

Allometric (*allos*, other; *metron*, measure) growth occurs when an organ grows at a different rate from the rest of the body. This produces a change in size of the organism which is accompanied by a change in shape of the organism. This pattern of growth is characteristic of mammals and illustrates the relationship between growth and development. Fig 22.8 shows how the relative proportions of various structures in humans change as a result of simultaneous changes in patterns of growth and development. In almost all animals the last organs to develop and differentiate are the reproductive organs. These show allometric growth and can be observed only in those organisms with external genital organs, hence they are not seen in many species of fish where growth appears to be purely isometric. Fig 22.9 shows the degree of variation in patterns of growth of different organs of a human. Again it can be seen that the last organs to develop are the reproductive organs.

The shapes of absolute growth curves for whole organisms as represented by length or mass show remarkable similarities and generally conform to the sigmoid shape described in section 22.2. However, several groups of organisms show variations on the general pattern which reflect adaptations to particular modes of life and environments as described in sections 22.3.2 and 22.3.3.

22.3.2 Limited and unlimited growth

Studies of the duration of growth in plants and animals show that there are two basic patterns. These are called **limited** (definite or determinate) growth and **unlimited** (indefinite or indeterminate) growth.

Growth in annual plants is limited and, after the plant matures and reproduces, there is a period of negative growth or senescence before the death of the plant. If the dry mass of the annual plant is plotted against time then an interesting variation on the sigmoid curve of fig 22.2 is seen, as shown in fig 22.10.

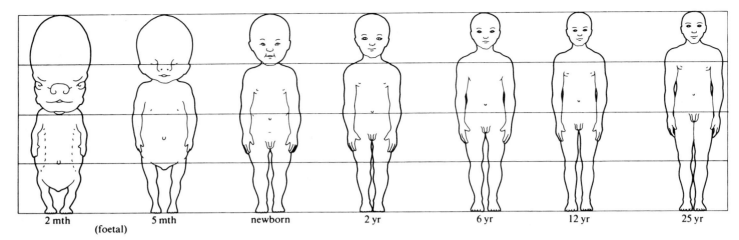

Fig 22.8 *Development in humans – an example of allometric growth. To show the relative rates of growth from the age of two months to 25 years each stage has been given a constant height. (After Stratz, cited in J. Hammond (ed.) (1955) Progress in the physiology of farm animals, 2, 431, Butterworths.)*

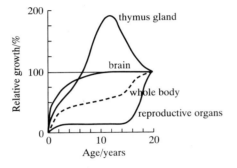

Fig 22.9 *Relative growth rates of the brain, thymus gland and reproductive organs of humans. The absolute growth curve of the whole body is also drawn for comparison. The thymus gland is involved in the early development of the immune system. (After Scammon.)*

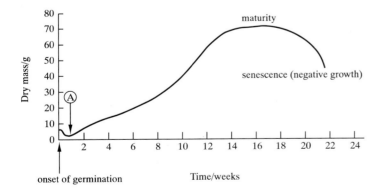

Fig 22.10 *Growth curve of a broad bean (Vicia faba) planted in March – an example of limited growth, where growth does not continue throughout life.*

22.1 Examine fig 22.10 and answer the following questions, based on your knowledge of the life cycle of an annual plant.
(a) Why is there negative growth initially during the germination of the seed?
(b) Describe the appearance of the seedling when positive growth occurs at A.
(c) What physiological process occurs here to account for positive growth?
(d) Why is the decrease in dry mass after 20 weeks very sudden?

Several plant organs show limited growth but do not undergo a period of negative growth, for example fruits, organs of vegetative propagation, dicotyledonous leaves and stem internodes. Animals showing limited growth include insects, birds and mammals, including humans.

Woody perennial plants on the other hand show unlimited growth and have a characteristic growth curve which is a cumulative series of sigmoid curves (fig 22.11), each of which represents one year's growth. With unlimited growth, some slight growth continues until death.

Other examples of unlimited growth are found among fungi, algae, and many animals, particularly non-vertebrates, fishes and reptiles. Monocotyledonous leaves show unlimited growth.

22.3.3 Growth in arthropods

A striking and characteristic growth pattern is associated with some arthropods, such as crustaceans and insects. Due to the inelastic nature of their exoskeletons they appear to grow only in spurts interrupted by a series of moults (**discontinuous growth**). An example is the typical growth pattern of an insect showing incomplete metamorphosis, as shown in fig 22.12. **Incomplete metamorphosis** occurs when there is a series of larval

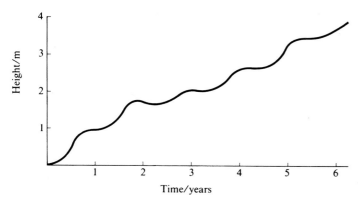

Fig 22.11 *Growth curve of a birch tree – a woody perennial. This is an example of unlimited growth, in which growth continues throughout life.*

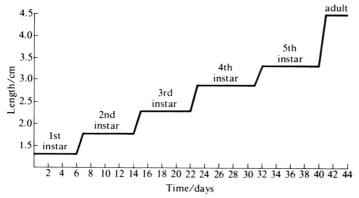

Fig 22.12 *Growth curve showing increase in length of the short-horned grasshopper. (After R. Soper & T. Smith (1979)* Modern Biology, *Macmillan.)*

stages, called instars, with each successive stage resembling the adult more closely. Moulting occurs between each stage, and growth in length is confined to the brief period before the new exoskeleton hardens. In such situations, growth curves based on length, such as that shown in fig 22.12, do not give a true reflection of growth. If a growth curve is plotted for the same insect, using dry mass as the growth parameter, a normal sigmoid curve is produced demonstrating that true growth, as represented by increase in living material, is continuous.

22.4   Growth and development in the flowering plant

22.4.1   Seed dormancy

Certain environmental conditions, namely availability of water, oxygen and a suitable temperature, must be present before the embryo of a seed will grow. However, in the presence of these factors, some seeds will not germinate and are described as **dormant**. They must undergo certain internal changes which can generally be described as **after-ripening** before they will germinate. These changes ensure that premature germination does not occur. For example, seedlings produced immediately from seeds shed in summer or autumn would probably not survive winter. In other words, mechanisms exist which ensure that germination is synchronised with the onset of a season favourable for growth. Some of the common mechanisms are discussed below.

Barrier methods

This mechanism often involves the outer layers of the seed being impervious to water or the passage of oxygen, or being physically strong enough to prevent growth of the embryo, as in many legumes. Sometimes physical damage (**scarification**) to the seed coat can remove this restriction. The process can be induced artificially by removing the testa or simply by pricking it with a pin. Under natural circumstances, bacteria or passage through the gut of an animal may have the same effect. The seeds of some species are stimulated to germinate by fire. More usually, however, the restriction is removed by some physiological change, involving the following factors.

Growth inhibitors. Many fruits or seeds contain chemical growth inhibitors which prevent germination. Abscisic acid often has this role, for instance in ash seeds. Thorough soaking of the seeds might remove the inhibitor or its effect may be overridden by an increase in a growth promoter such as gibberellin. Tomato seeds contain high levels of abscisic acid which prevent germination of the seeds inside the tomato fruit.

Light. The dormancy of some seeds is broken by light after water uptake, a phytochrome-controlled response. This stimulation of germination by light is associated with a rise in gibberellin levels within the seed. It occurs, for example, in some lettuce varieties. Less commonly, germination is inhibited by light, such as in *Phacelia* and *Nigella*. (For a relevant experiment, refer to the foot of table 16.5, section 16.4.2.) This may be an advantage if it ensures that the seed does not germinate until it is buried in a suitable medium such as soil.

Temperature. Seeds commonly require a cold period, a process known as **prechilling**, before germination will occur. This is common among cereals and members of the rose family (Rosaceae), such as plum, cherry and apple. It is associated with a rise in gibberellin activity and sometimes a reduction in growth inhibitors. It ensures that seeds must pass through a cold spell of a particular length before germination and are less likely to germinate during a warm spell in winter.

Exactly how light and cold treatments affect seeds is not clear, but increased permeability of the seed coat, as well as changes in levels of growth substances, may be involved.

22.2 Seeds which require a stimulus of light for germination are usually relatively small. What could be the significance of this?

22.3 The light which passes through leaves is enriched in green and far-red light relative to the light which strikes the leaf surface.
(a) Why is this?
(b) What ecological significance might this have in relation to seeds like lettuce, where germination is a phytochrome-controlled response? (Read section 16.4.2 if necessary.)

22.4.2   Germination

Germination is the onset of growth of the embryo, usually after a period of dormancy. The structure of the seed at germination has been described in section 21.5.

Environmental conditions needed for germination

Water. The initial uptake of water by a seed is by a process called **imbibition**. It takes place through the micropyle (a tiny hole in the testa, or seed coat) and testa and is purely a physical process caused by **adsorption** of water by substances within the seed. These include proteins, starch and cell wall materials such as hemicelluloses and pectic substances. The swelling of these substances can lead to strong imbibitional forces which are great enough to rupture the testa or pericarp (fruit coat) surrounding the seed. Water then moves from cell to cell by osmosis. Water is needed to activate the biochemical reactions associated with germination, because these take place in aqueous solution. Water is also an important reagent at this stage, being used in the hydrolysis (digestion) of food stores.

Minimum or optimum temperature. There is usually a characteristic temperature range outside which a given type of seed will not germinate. This will be related to the normal environment of the plant concerned and will be within the range 5–40 °C. Temperature influences the rate of enzyme-controlled reactions as described in section 4.3.3.

Oxygen. This is required for aerobic respiration, although such respiration can be supplemented with anaerobic respiration if necessary.

Physiology of germination

A typical seed stores carbohydrates, lipids and proteins, either in its endosperm or in the cotyledons of the embryo. Usually lipids in the form of oils form the major food reserves of the seed, though notable exceptions are the legume family (which includes peas and beans) and the grass family (which includes cereals) where starch is the major food reserve. These two groups form the principal crops of humans and we get the bulk of our carbohydrates from them. Legumes, particularly soya beans, are also especially rich in proteins; hence the use of soya beans as a source of protein in new foods. In addition, seeds contain high levels of minerals, notably phosphorus, as well as normal cytoplasmic constituents such as nucleic acids and vitamins.

As a result of imbibition and osmosis the embryo becomes hydrated, and this activates enzymes such as the enzymes of respiration. Other enzymes have to be newly synthesised, often using amino acids provided by the digestion of stored proteins.

Broadly speaking, there are two centres of activity in the germinating seed, the **storage centre** (food reserve) and the **growth centre** (embryo). The main events in the storage centre, with the exception of enzyme synthesis, are catabolic, that is concerned with breakdown.

Digestion of the food reserves proceeds mainly by hydrolysis as below:

$$\text{proteins} \xrightarrow{\text{proteases}} \text{amino acids}$$

$$\text{polysaccharides} \xrightarrow{\text{carbohydrases}} \text{sugars}$$

$$\text{for example starch} \xrightarrow{\text{amylase}} \text{maltose} \xrightarrow{\text{maltase}} \text{glucose}$$

$$\text{lipids} \xrightarrow{\text{lipases}} \text{fatty acids} + \text{glycerol}$$

The soluble products of digestion are then translocated to the growth regions of the embryo. The sugars, fatty acids and glycerol may be used to provide substrates for respiration in both the storage and the growth centres. They may also be used for anabolic reactions in the growth centre, that is, reactions concerned with synthesis. Of particular importance in these reactions are glucose and amino acids. A major use of glucose is for the synthesis of cellulose and other cell wall materials. Amino acids are used mainly for protein synthesis, proteins being important as enzymes and structural components of protoplasm. In addition, mineral salts are required for the many reasons given in tables 7.7 and 7.8.

Both storage and growth centres obtain the energy for their activities from respiration. This involves oxidation of a substrate, usually sugar, to carbon dioxide and water. A net loss in dry mass of the seed therefore occurs, since carbon dioxide is lost as a gas, and has a greater mass than the oxygen gas taken up in aerobic respiration. Water, another product of respiration, does not contribute to dry mass. This loss will continue until the seedling produces green leaves and starts to make its own food (fig 22.10).

A well-studied example of germination of a starchy seed is the barley grain, where it has been shown that the synthesis of α-amylase and other enzymes takes place in the outer layers of the endosperm in response to gibberellin secreted by the embryo. These outer layers contain stored protein which is the source of amino acids for protein synthesis. The process is described and experimentally investigated in section 16.2.6. Fig 16.20 shows an example of the role of hormones in early germination. The appearance of amylase in germinating barley grains can also be investigated by grinding them in water, filtering and centrifuging to obtain a clear extract and testing the activity of the extract on starch solution. By using samples of barley grains at different times from germination, the increase in amylase activity per grain over a period of a week can be determined.

22.4 Explain the results shown in fig 22.13.

Those seeds which store lipids convert them to fatty acids and glycerol. Each molecule of lipid yields three molecules of fatty acid and one of glycerol (section 3.3). Fatty acids are either oxidised directly in respiration or converted to sucrose, which is then translocated to the embryo.

22.5 (This question tests some basic knowledge of chemistry and of the chemistry of lipids. The latter is covered in section 3.3.)

Suppose 51.2 g dry mass of seeds, containing 50% fatty acid by mass, converted all the fatty acid to sugar in the following reaction:

$$C_{16}H_{32}O_2 + 11O_2 \longrightarrow C_{12}H_{22}O_{11} + 4CO_2 + 5H_2O + energy$$

fatty acid   sugar

(a) Assuming that no other changes occurred which might affect dry mass, calculate the gain or loss in dry mass of the seeds.
(Relative atomic masses: C = 12, H = 1, O = 16.)
(b) What other important change might affect dry mass?
(c) Calculate the volume of carbon dioxide evolved from the seeds at STP (standard temperature and pressure).
(1 mole of gas at STP occupies 22.4 dm³.)
(d) How can fatty acid be obtained from a lipid, and what would be the other component of the lipid?
(e) How many carbon atoms would one molecule of the parent lipid have contained if $C_{16}H_{32}O_2$ was the only fatty acid produced?
(f) What is the identity of the sugar formed in the reaction shown?
(g) How does the oxygen reach the storage tissue?

Respiration in germinating seeds

Rates of respiration in both storage tissues and embryo are high owing to the intense metabolic activity in both regions. Substrates for respiration may differ in each region and

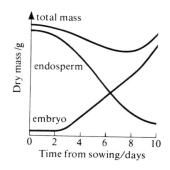

Fig 22.13 *Relative changes in dry mass of endosperm and embryo during germination of barley.*

may also change during germination. This is revealed by changes in the respiratory quotient (section 9.5.9).

22.6 When castor oil seeds were analysed for lipid and sugar content during germination in darkness, the results shown in fig 22.14 were obtained.

The RQ of the seedings was measured at day 5 and the embryo was found to have an RQ of about 1.0, while the remaining cotyledons had an RQ of about 0.4–0.5.
(a) Suggest as full an explanation of these results as you can (refer to section 22.4.2 for relevant information).
(b) What would you expect the RQ of the whole seedling to be on day 11? Explain very briefly.

22.7 The RQ of peas is normally between 2.8 and 4 during the first seven days of germination, but is 1.5–2.4 if the testas are removed. In both cases ethanol accumulates in the seeds, but in much smaller amounts when the testas are removed. Account for these observations.

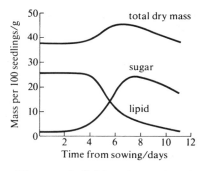

Fig 22.14 *Changes in lipid and sugar content of castor oil seeds during germination in the dark. (Based on data from R. Desveaux & M. Kogane-Charles (1952) Annls. Inst. natn. Rech. Agron., Paris, 3, 385–416; cited by H. S. Street & H. Opik (1976) The physiology of flowering plants 2nd ed., Arnold.)*

Growth of the embryo

Within the embryo growth occurs by cell division, enlargement and differentiation. Amounts of proteins, cellulose, nucleic acids and so on increase steadily in the growing regions while dry mass of the food store decreases. The first visible sign of growth is the emergence of the embryo root, the **radicle**. This is positively geotropic and will grow down and anchor the seed. Subsequently, the embryo shoot, the **plumule**, emerges and being negatively geotropic (and positively phototropic if above ground) will grow upwards.

There are two types of germination according to whether or not the cotyledons grow above ground or remain below it. In dicotyledons, if that part of the shoot axis, or internode, just below the cotyledons (the **hypocotyl**) elongates, then the cotyledons are carried above ground. This is **epigeal** germination. If the internode just above the cotyledons (the **epicotyl**) elongates, then the cotyledons remain below ground. This is **hypogeal** germination.

In epigeal germination, the hypocotyl remains hooked as it grows through the soil, as shown in fig 22.15*b*, thus meeting the resistance of the soil rather than the delicate plumule tip, which is further protected by being enclosed by the cotyledons. In hypogeal germination of dicotyledons the epicotyl is hooked, again protecting the plumule tip, as shown in fig 22.15*c*. In both cases the hooked structure immediately straightens on exposure to light, a phytochrome-controlled response.

In the grasses, which are monocotyledons, the plumule is protected by a sheath called the **coleoptile**, which is positively phototropic and negatively geotropic as described in section 16.1.1. The first leaf grows out through the coleoptile and unrolls in response to light.

On emerging into light a number of phytochrome-controlled responses rapidly occur in leaves, collectively known as photomorphogenesis. The overall effect is a change from etiolation (section 16.4.1) to normal growth. The major changes involved are summarised in table 16.5 and include expansion of the cotyledons or first true foliage leaves, as well as formation of chlorophyll ('greening'). At this point photosynthesis begins and net dry mass of the seedling starts to increase as it finally becomes independent of its food reserves. Once exposed to light, the shoot also shows phototropic responses although these are not phytochrome controlled.

22.4.3   Growth of the primary plant body

Meristems

In contrast to animals, growth in plants is confined to certain regions known as meristems. A **meristem** is a group of cells which retain the ability to divide by mitosis, producing daughter cells which grow and form the rest of the plant body. The daughter cells form the permanent tissue, that is, cells which have lost the ability to divide. There are three types of meristem, described in table 22.1. Two types of growth are mentioned in table 22.1, namely primary and secondary growth.

Primary growth is the first form of growth to occur. A whole plant can be built up by primary growth, and in most monocotyledonous plants and herbaceous dicotyledons it is the only type of growth. It is a result of the activity of the apical, and sometimes intercalary, meristems. The anatomy of mature primary roots and stems is dealt with in sections 13.4 and 13.5.

Some plants continue with **secondary growth** from lateral meristems. This is most notable in shrubs and trees. Plants which lack extensive secondary growth are called **herbaceous** plants or **herbs**. A few herbaceous plants show restricted amounts of secondary thickening, as in the development of additional vascular bundles in *Helianthus* (sunflower).

Apical meristems and primary growth

A typical apical meristem cell is relatively small, cuboid, with a thin cellulose cell wall and dense cytoplasmic

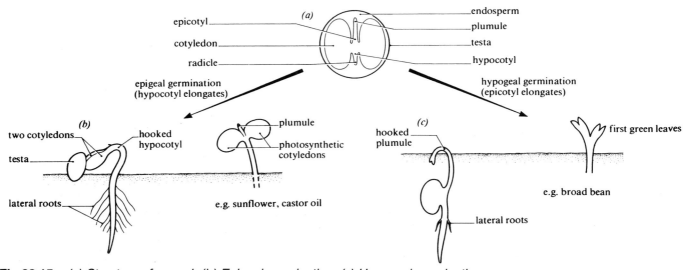

Fig 22.15   (a) *Structure of a seed. (b) Epigeal germination. (c) Hypogeal germination.*

Table 22.1 Types of meristem and their functions.

Type of meristem	Location	Role	Effect
Apical	Root and shoot apex	Responsible for primary growth, giving rise to primary plant body	Increase in length
Lateral (cambium)	Laterally situated in older parts of the plant parallel with the long axis of organs, e.g. the cork cambium (phellogen) and the vascular cambium	Responsible for secondary growth. The vascular cambium gives rise to secondary vascular tissue, including wood (secondary xylem); the cork cambium gives rise to the periderm, which replaces the epidermis and includes cork	Increase in girth
Intercalary	Between regions of permanent tissue, e.g. at nodes of many monocotyledons, such as bases of grass leaves	Allows growth in length to occur in regions other than tips. This is useful if the tips are susceptible to damage or destruction, e.g. eating by herbivores (grasses), wave action (kelps). Branching from the main axis is not then necessary	Increase in length

contents. It has a few small vacuoles rather than the large vacuoles characteristic of parenchyma cells, and the cytoplasm contains small, undifferentiated plastids called proplastids. Meristematic cells are packed tightly together with no obvious air spaces between the cells.

The cells are called **initials**. When they divide by mitosis one daughter cell remains in the meristem while the other increases in size and differentiates to become part of the permanent plant body.

22.4.4 Primary growth of the shoot

The structure of a typical apical shoot meristem is illustrated in figs 22.16 and 22.17. Fig 22.17 shows the approximate division of the shoot apex into regions of cell division, cell enlargement and cell differentiation. Passing back from the dome-shaped apical meristem, the cells get progressively older, so that different stages of growth can be observed simultaneously in the same shoot. Thus it is relatively easy to study developmental sequences of plant tissue.

Three basic types of meristematic tissue occur, namely the **protoderm**, which gives rise to the epidermis; the **procambium**, giving rise to the vascular tissues, including pericycle, phloem, vascular cambium and xylem; and the **ground meristem**, producing the parenchyma **ground tissues**, which in the dicotyledons are the cortex and pith. These meristematic types are produced by division of the meristematic cells (initials) in the apex. In the zone of enlargement, the daughter cells produced by the initials increase in size, mainly by osmotic uptake of water into the cytoplasm and then into the vacuoles. Increase in the length of stems and roots is mainly brought about by elongation of cells during this stage. The process is illustrated in fig 22.18.

The small vacuoles increase in size, eventually fusing to form a single large vacuole. The pressure potential developed inside the cells stretches their thin walls and the orientation of cellulose microfibrils in the walls helps to determine the final shape assumed by the cells. The final

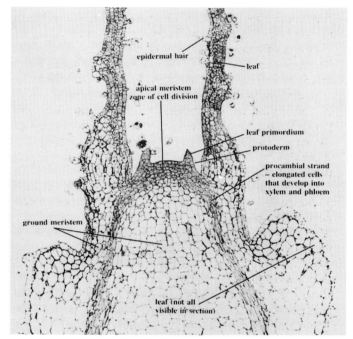

Fig 22.16 *The apical meristem of a shoot.*

Fig 22.17 *LS shoot tip of a dicotyledon showing apical meristem and regions of primary growth. For simplicity, vascular tissue to leaves and buds has been omitted.*

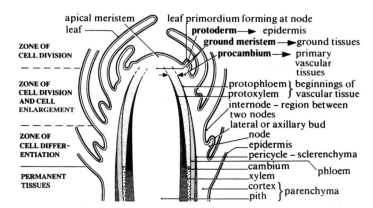

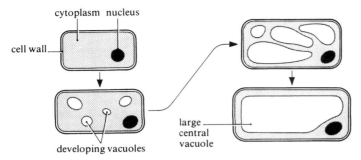

cytoplasm   nucleus

cell wall

developing vacuoles

large
central
vacuole

Fig 22.18 *Cell enlargement phase of growth of a meristematic cell.*

volume of cytoplasm may not be significantly greater than in the original meristematic cell, but is now confined to the cell periphery by the vacuole. As enlargement nears completion, many cells develop additional thickening of the cell walls, either of cellulose or lignin, depending on the type of cell being formed. This may restrict further expansion, but does not necessarily prevent it. Collenchyma cells in the cortex, for example, can continue elongating while extra cellulose is laid down in columns on the inside of the original walls. Thus they can give support to the plant while still growing. In contrast, developing sclerenchyma cells deposit thick layers of lignin on their walls and soon die. Thus their differentiation does not start until enlargement is virtually completed.

The procambium forms a series of longitudinally running strands whose cells are narrower and longer than those of the ground meristem. The first cells to differentiate in the procambium are those of the protoxylem to the inside, and protophloem to the outside. These are the parts of the primary xylem and phloem respectively, which form before elongation is complete. The protoxylem typically has only annular or spiral thickenings of lignin on tracheids (section 6.2.1). Since the lignin is not continuous, extension and stretching of the cellulose between the thickenings can occur as the surrounding tissue elongates. Both protoxylem and protophloem elements soon die and generally get crushed and stretched to the point of collapse as growth continues around them. Their function is taken over by later-developing xylem and phloem in the zone of differentiation.

In the zone of differentiation each cell becomes fully specialised for its own particular function, according to its position in the organ with respect to other cells. The greatest changes occur in the procambial strands, which differentiate into vascular bundles. This involves lignification of the walls of sclerenchyma fibres and xylem elements, as well as development of the tubes characteristic of xylem vessels and phloem sieve tubes. The final forms of these tissues are described in section 6.0. Sclerenchyma and xylem now add to the support previously given by collenchyma and turgid parenchyma. Between the xylem and phloem there are cells which retain the ability to divide. They form the vascular cambium, whose activities are described later with secondary thickening.

Leaf primordia and lateral buds

Development of the shoot also includes growth of leaves and lateral buds. Leaves arise as small swellings or ridges called leaf primordia, shown particularly clearly in fig 22.16. The swellings contain groups of meristematic cells and appear at regular intervals, their sites of origin being called **nodes** and the regions between **internodes**. The pattern of leaf arrangement on the stem varies and is called **phyllotaxis**. Leaves may arise in whorls with two or more leaves at each node, or singly, either in two opposite ranks or in a spiral pattern. Generally, however, they are arranged to minimise overlapping, and hence shading, when fully grown so that they form a **mosaic**.

The primordia elongate rapidly, so they soon enclose and protect the apical meristem, both physically and by the heat they generate in respiration. Later they grow and increase in area to form the blades. Cell division gradually ceases but may continue until they are about half their mature size.

Soon after the leaves start to grow, buds develop in the axils between them and the stem. These are small groups of meristematic cells which normally remain dormant, but retain the capacity to divide and grow at a later stage. They form branches or specialised structures such as flowers and underground structures such as rhizomes and tubers. They are thought to be under the control of the apical meristem (see Apical dominance, section 16.3.3).

22.4.5   Primary growth of the root

The structure of the typical apical root system is illustrated in fig 22.19.

At the very tip of the apical meristem is a **quiescent zone**, a group of **initials** (meristematic cells) from which all other cells in the root can be traced, but whose rate of cell division is much slower than their daughter cells in the apical meristem around them. To the outside, the cells of the **root cap** are formed. These become large parenchyma cells which protect the apical meristem as the root grows through the soil. They are constantly being worn away and replaced. They also have the important additional function of acting as gravity sensors, since they contain large starch grains which act as statoliths, sedimenting to the bottoms of cells in response to gravity. Their role is described in more detail in section 16.2.2.

Behind the quiescent centre, orderly rows of cells can be seen and the meristematic regions already described in the shoot, namely protoderm, ground meristem and procambium, can be distinguished (fig 22.19). In the root the term procambium is used to describe the whole central cylinder of the root, even though at maturity this contains the non-vascular tissues of the pericycle and the pith, if present.

The zone of cell division typically extends 1–2 mm back from the root tip, and overlaps slightly with the zone of cell elongation. Root tips are convenient material for observation of mitosis and a procedure for this is described

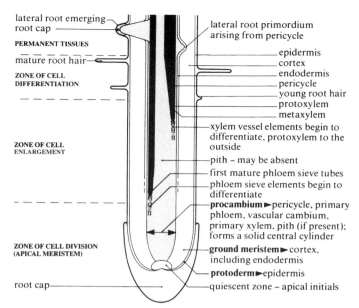

Fig 22.19 *LS apical meristem of a typical root. Xylem differentiation is shown to the right and phloem differentiation to the left. In reality xylem and phloem alternate round the root and would be on different radii. Also, in reality, the zone of enlargement would be longer.*

in section 23.0. Behind this zone, growth is mainly by cell enlargement, cells increasing in size in the manner described for the shoot and shown in fig 22.18. The zone of enlarging cells extends to a point about 10 mm behind the root tip and their increase in length forces the root tip down through the soil.

Some cell differentiation begins in the zone of cell division, with the development of the first phloem sieve tube elements (fig 22.19). In longitudinal sections, neat files of developing sieve tube elements can be seen, getting progressively more mature further back from the root tip, until they become mature sieve tubes. Development of phloem is from the outside inwards.

Further back in the zone of enlargement, the xylem vessels start to differentiate, also from the outside inwards (exarch xylem) in contrast to the stem (endarch xylem). The first-formed vessels are protoxylem vessels, as in the stem, and they show the same pattern of lignification and ability to stretch as cells around them grow. Their role is taken over by metaxylem, which develops later and matures in the zone of differentiation after enlargement has ceased. The xylem often spreads to the centre of the root, in which case no pith develops.

Development is easier to examine in roots than in shoots. In the latter, procambial strands to the leaves complicate the distribution of developing tissues. Development of xylem, in particular, is easily seen by squashing apical portions of fine roots such as those of cress seedlings and staining appropriately.

After all cells have stopped enlarging, further differentiation is completed. This includes the development of root hairs from the epidermis.

22.4.6 Lateral meristems and secondary growth

Secondary growth is that growth which occurs after primary growth as a result of the activity of lateral meristems. It results in an increase in girth. It is usually associated with deposition of large amounts of secondary xylem, called **wood**, which completely modifies the primary structure and is a characteristic feature of trees and shrubs.

There are two types of lateral meristem, the **vascular cambium** which gives rise to new vascular tissue, and the **cork cambium** or **phellogen**, which arises later to replace the ruptured epidermis of the expanding plant body.

Vascular cambium

There are two types of cell in the vascular cambium, the **fusiform initials** and the **ray initials**, illustrated in fig 22.20. Fusiform initials are narrow, elongated cells which divide by mitosis to form **secondary phloem** to the outside or **secondary xylem** to the inside. The amount of xylem produced normally exceeds the amount of phloem. Successive divisions are shown in fig 22.21. Secondary phloem contains sieve tubes, companion cells, sclerenchyma fibres and sclereids, and parenchyma.

Ray initials are almost spherical and divide by mitosis to form parenchyma cells which accumulate to form rays between the neighbouring xylem and phloem.

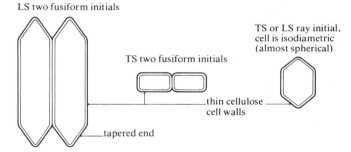

Fig 22.20 *Fusiform and ray initials.*

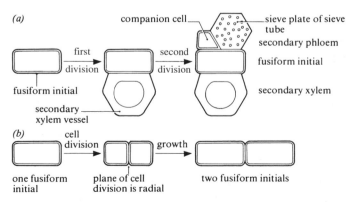

Fig 22.21 *(a) Two successive divisions of a fusiform initial to form xylem and phloem, seen in TS. In reality, differentiation of xylem and phloem to the stages shown would take some time, during which more cells would be produced. (b) Division of a fusiform initial to form a new fusiform initial, seen in TS.*

Secondary growth in woody dicotyledon stems

The vascular cambium is originally located between the primary xylem and primary phloem of the vascular bundles, its derivation from the apical meristem being shown in fig 22.17. It becomes active very soon after primary growth is complete. Fig 22.22 summarises the early stages in secondary thickening of a typical woody dicotyledon stem.

Fig 22.22*a* shows the original primary stem structure, omitting the pericycle for simplicity. Fig 22.22*b* shows the development of a complete cylinder of cambium. Fig 22.22*c* shows a complete ring of secondary thickening. Here, fusiform initials have produced large quantities of secondary xylem, and lesser quantities of secondary phloem, while the ray initials have produced rays of parenchyma. As the stem increases in thickness, so the

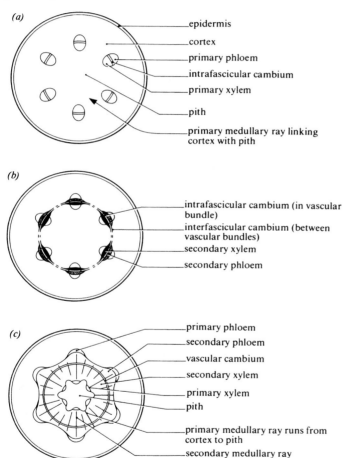

Fig 22.22 *Early stages in secondary thickening of a typical woody dicotyledon stem. (a) Primary structure of stem. (b) Cambium forms a complete cylinder as parenchyma cells in the medullary rays become meristematic, spreading outwards from the vascular bundles. Meanwhile secondary xylem and phloem are already being formed by the existing cambium. (c) A complete ring of secondary thickening has developed. Thickening is most advanced at the sites of the original vascular bundles where cambial activity first started.*

circumference of the cambium layers must increase. To achieve this, radial divisions of the cambial cells occur, as shown in fig 22.21. The original ray initials produce primary medullary rays which run all the way from pith to cortex, unlike the secondary medullary rays produced by later ray initials. The rays maintain a living link between the pith and cortex. They help to transmit water and mineral salts from the xylem, and food substances from the phloem, radially across the stem. Also, gaseous exchange can occur by diffusion through intercellular spaces.

The rays may also be used for food storage, an important function during periods of dormancy, as in winter. In three dimensions they appear as radially–longitudinally running sheets because the ray initials occur in stacks one above the other, as shown in fig 22.23. Fig 22.23 illustrates the appearance of wood (secondary xylem) and the rays it contains in the three planes TS, TLS and RLS.

Fig 22.24 shows part of the stem of a woody dicotyledon in its third year of growth, revealing the large amounts of secondary xylem produced. Fig 22.25 shows photographs of a three-year-old and a five-year-old stem of *Tilia*, the lime tree.

Annual rings

Each year in temperate climates, growth resumes in the spring. The first vessels formed are wide and thin-walled, being suitable for the conduction of large quantities of water. Water is required to initiate growth, particularly the expansion of new cells, as in developing leaves. Later in the year, fewer vessels are produced and they are narrower with thicker walls. During winter the cambium remains dormant. The autumn wood produced at the end of one year, as growth ceases, will therefore be immediately next to the spring wood of the following year and will differ markedly in appearance. This contrast is seen as the **annual ring** and is clearly visible in fig 22.25. Where vessels are concentrated in the early wood it is said to be **ring porous**, as opposed to **diffuse porous** wood, where they are evenly distributed, and where it is more difficult to see annual rings. In tropical climates, seasonal droughts may induce similar fluctuations in cambial activity.

The width of an annual ring will vary partly according to climate, a favourable climate resulting in production of more wood and hence a greater distance between rings. This has been used in two areas of science, namely dendroclimatology and dendrochronology. **Dendroclimatology** is the study of climate using tree ring data. Applications vary from correlation of recent climatic records with tree growth, of possible interest in a specific locality, to investigations of more distant climatic events several hundreds or even thousands of years in the past. The oldest-known living trees, the bristlecone pines, are about 5000 years old, and fossil wood of even greater age can be found.

Dendrochronology is the dating of wood by recognition of the pattern of annual rings. This pattern can act as a 'fingerprint', pinpointing the time during which the wood

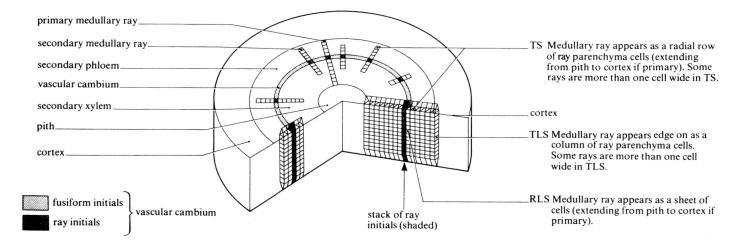

Fig 22.23 *Diagrammatic representation of primary and secondary medullary rays in a typical woody dicotyledon stem. A primary ray is shown to the right and a secondary ray to the left. (TLS, transverse longitudinal section; RLS, radial longitudinal section.)*

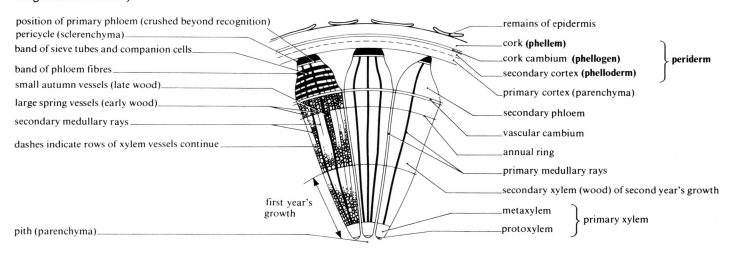

Fig 22.24 *TS of a typical woody dicotyledon stem in the third year of growth (age two years), such as* Tilia. *Details of secondary phloem, secondary xylem and secondary medullary rays are shown only in the left-hand sector.*

was growing. Dating of timbers at archaeological sites, in old buildings and ships and so on thus becomes feasible, provided enough data are available.

Heartwood and sapwood

As a tree ages, the wood at the centre may cease to serve a conducting function and become blocked with darkly staining deposits such as tannins. It is called **heartwood**, whereas the outer, wetter conducting wood is called **sapwood**.

Cork and lenticels

As the secondary xylem grows outwards, so the tissues outside it become increasingly compressed, as well as being stretched sideways by the increasing circumference. This affects the epidermis, cortex, primary phloem and all but the most recent secondary phloem. The epidermis eventually ruptures and is replaced by cork as the result of the activity of a second lateral meristem, the **cork cambium** or **phellogen**. It generally arises immediately

below the epidermis. **Cork** (or **phellem**) is produced to the outside of the cork cambium, while to the inside one or two layers of parenchyma are produced. These are indistinguishable from the primary cortex and form the **phelloderm** or secondary cortex. The phellogen, cork and phelloderm together comprise the periderm (fig 22.24).

As the cork cells mature, their walls become impregnated with a fatty substance called suberin which is impermeable to water and gases. The cells gradually die and lose their living contents, becoming filled either with air or with resin or tannins. The older, dead cork cells fit together around the stem, preventing desiccation, infection and mechanical injury. They become compressed as the stem increases in girth and may eventually be lost and replaced by younger cells from beneath. If the cork layer were complete, the respiratory gases oxygen and carbon dioxide could not be exchanged between the living cells of the stem and the environment, and the cells would die. At random intervals, however, slit-like openings, or **lenticels**, develop in the cork which contain a mass of loosely packed, thin-walled dead

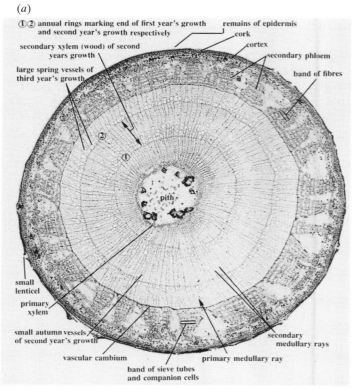

(a)

Fig 22.25 (a) TS of a two-year-old (third year) twig of Tilia vulgaris (×2.2). (b) Part of a TS of a five-year-old (sixth year) twig of Tilia vulgaris (×11.5).

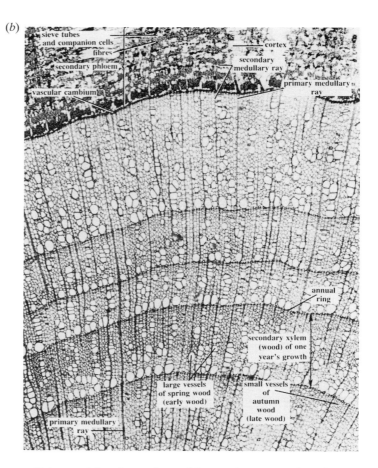

(b)

cells, lacking suberin. They are produced by the cork cambium and have large intercellular air spaces allowing gaseous exchange. Fig 22.26 shows a diagram of cork and lenticels.

Bark

Eventually a woody stem becomes covered with a layer commonly known as **bark**. The term bark is an imprecise one which is used to refer either to all the tissues outside the vascular system, or more strictly to those tissues outside the cork cambium. Peeling bark from a tree generally strips tissues down to the vascular cambium, a thin layer of cells which is easily ruptured.

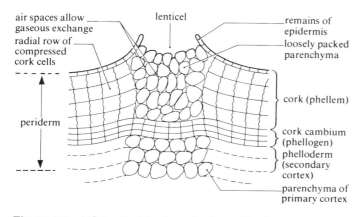

Fig 22.26 VS lenticel (cell contents omitted).

It is usual for the cork cambium to be renewed each year as the girth of the stem increases. Often a cork cambium arises in the secondary phloem, in which case the bark will, over a number of years, build up a layered appearance due to alternating layers of secondary phloem and bark.

22.5 Role of hormones in growth and development in humans

Human growth and development is controlled centrally by the hypothalamus and pituitary gland. The close association between these structures has already been noted in chapter 17 (section 17.6.2). The hypothalamus is the part of the brain immediately above the pituitary gland and receives information from the rest of the brain as well as from chemicals circulating in the blood. The hypothalamus controls the pituitary gland by secreting specific releasing and inhibitory factors which control the release of hormones from the pituitary gland. These in turn control other endocrine glands, which secrete hormones. In the case of growth and development these other glands include the thyroid gland, liver, adrenal cortex and gonads.

22.5.1 Pituitary gland and growth hormone

The most important hormone controlling growth and development is **growth hormone**, also known as **somatotrophin**, which is secreted by the anterior pituitary gland. It is a protein and was discovered during the early part of the twentieth century as a result of numerous experiments involving removal of the pituitary gland from animals. The rate and extent of growth in the experimental animals were greatly reduced. An extract from the pituitary gland was later isolated which, when injected into animals, caused an increase in body mass.

Secretion of human growth hormone (**hGH**) is controlled by the combined effects of two other hormones, produced by the hypothalamus (fig 22.27). These are **growth hormone releasing hormone (GHRH)**, also known as **somatocrinin**, and **growth hormone inhibitory hormone (GHIH)**, also known as **somatostatin**. Human growth hormone has a direct effect on all parts of the body, but particularly on growth of the skeleton and skeletal muscles. It also has an indirect effect by stimulating the release of small protein hormones called **somatomedins** from the liver. Somatomedins, also known as **insulin-like growth factors** or **IGFs** because they resemble insulin in structure and in some aspects of function, mediate or regulate some of the effects of human growth hormone. A summary of the regulation of the secretion of these hormones and their effects on the body is given in fig 22.27.

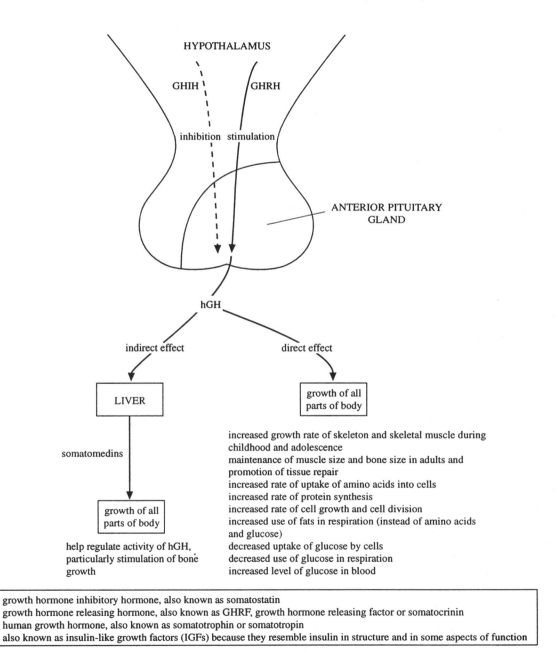

GHIH	growth hormone inhibitory hormone, also known as somatostatin
GHRH	growth hormone releasing hormone, also known as GHRF, growth hormone releasing factor or somatocrinin
hGH	human growth hormone, also known as somatotrophin or somatotropin
Somatomedins	also known as insulin-like growth factors (IGFs) because they resemble insulin in structure and in some aspects of function

Fig 22.27 *Regulation of the secretion of human growth hormone and somatomedins by the hypothalamus and anterior pituitary gland. The effects of these hormones on growth and development are also shown.*

Dwarfism

A deficiency of growth hormone results in dwarfism, more properly called pituitary dwarfism to distinguish it from other causes. Brain development and IQ are unaffected, unlike the situation with thyroid deficiency (section 17.6.4), and the body parts stay in proportion. The victim simply develops much more slowly. If the problem is due to growth hormone alone, then affected individuals do mature sexually. The dwarfism associated with African Pygmies has been discovered to be due to a deficiency of one of the somatomedins, indicating the additional importance of these growth factors.

In the past it was difficult to obtain sufficient human growth hormone to treat children with this condition (other animal growth hormones are ineffective), but human growth hormone can now be produced by bacteria as a result of genetic engineering, as described in section 25.2.2.

Gigantism

If over-production of human growth hormone occurs during childhood, when the bones are still capable of growth, the person becomes a 'giant', often reaching 8 feet in height (almost 2.5 metres) (fig 22.28). The usual cause is a tumour of the pituitary gland. The condition can be prevented if diagnosed early by removal or irradiation of part of the pituitary gland. If the condition occurs in adulthood, the bones are no longer capable of increasing in length, but can continue to grow in thickness, together with an increased growth of the soft tissues. This results in a condition called **acromegaly** (fig 22.29). The most distinctive feature of acromegaly is the enlarging of the hands, feet, skull, nose and jawbone.

22.5.2   Thyroid gland and growth

The thyroid gland secretes two hormones which influence growth and development, namely **thyroxine** (T_4) and **triiodothyronine** (T_3). They have similar effects, although thyroxine is far more abundant, accounting for about 90% of the total. They stimulate protein synthesis and, like human growth hormone, are particularly important in stimulating growth of the skeleton. The consequences of over- or under-secretion of the hormones is discussed in section 17.6.4.

22.5.3   Gonads and growth

The gonads are the gamete-producing organs, namely the ovaries in the female and the testes in the male. At the beginning of puberty they secrete sex hormones in response to signals from the pituitary gland and hypothalamus. The sex hormones are responsible for a fundamental change in growth and development and stimulate the development of secondary sexual characteristics. This is described in sections 21.6.4 and 21.6.6.

Fig 22.28 *Sandy Allen, the world's tallest woman, pictured with her family. Her abnormal growth started soon after her birth. It was diagnosed as being due to excessive production of the growth hormone somatotrophin, caused by a tumour of the anterior pituitary gland. In 1977 Allen underwent an operation to remove the gland and prevent further growth, by which time she had reached a height of 2.31 m (7'7") and a weight of 209 kg (nearly 33 stone).*

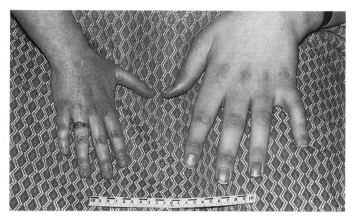

Fig 22.29 *Acromegaly – a woman's hand with a normal hand (left) for comparison. Acromegaly is a condition which results in an increase in the size of the hands, feet and face due to an excessive production of the growth hormone somatotrophin.*

22.5.4   **Adrenal cortex and growth**

The adrenal cortex is the outer region of each of the two adrenal glands and secretes steroid hormones. In both sexes, these include small amounts of both female and male sex hormones, oestrogens and androgens respectively. The androgens contribute to the adolescent growth spurt and development of pubic hair and underarm hair in both boys and girls. In the adult male, there is very little production of sex hormones by the adrenal glands, but small amounts of oestrogens and androgens continue to be made in females. The androgens may contribute to sexual behaviour, including sexual drive.

Chapter Twenty-three

Continuity of life

As noted at the beginning of chapter 5, one of the most important ideas in biology is the concept that the basic unit of structure and function of living organisms is the cell.

The cell theory was first proposed by Schleiden in 1838 and Schwann in 1839. Rudolph Virchow extended the theory in 1855 by declaring that new cells come only from pre-existing cells by cell division. Recognition of the continuity of life stimulated further workers throughout the later part of the nineteenth century to investigate the structure of the cell and the mechanisms involved in cell division. Improved techniques of staining and better microscopes revealed the importance of the nucleus, and in particular the chromosomes within it, as being the structures providing continuity between one generation of cells and the next. In 1879 Boveri and Flemming described the events occurring within the nucleus leading to the production of two identical cells, and in 1887 Weismann suggested that a specialised form of division occurred in the production of gametes. These two forms of division are called mitosis and meiosis respectively. It is useful to learn more about chromosomes before studying mitosis and meiosis.

23.1   Chromosomes

23.1.1   Chromosomes and karyotypes

The most important structures in the cell during division are the **chromosomes**. This is because they are responsible for the transmission of the hereditary information from one generation to the next. They do this because they contain DNA, the molecule of inheritance. Between divisions of the nucleus each chromosome contains one DNA molecule. Before the nucleus divides a copy of this DNA molecule is made so that at nuclear division the chromosome is a double structure, containing two identical DNA molecules. The two parts of the chromosome are referred to as **chromatids**. Each chromatid of a pair contains one of the two identical DNA molecules.

Although chromosomes stain intensely with certain dyes (stains), *individual* chromosomes cannot be seen very clearly in the period between divisions, known as interphase. This is because the chromosomes become very loosely coiled, long, thin threads spread throughout the nucleus. This material is referred to as **chromatin** (meaning

'coloured material'). Just before nuclear division, the chromosomes coil up into much more compact structures which are shorter, thicker and recognisable as separate structures which stain more intensely. Fig 23.1 shows a photograph of chromosomes in a human cell at this stage. You can see that each chromosome is made up of two chromatids. The chromatids are held together at a point called the **centromere** which may occur anywhere along the length of the chromosome (fig 23.2).

Each species has a characteristic number of chromosomes in each cell. In humans this is 46, as shown in fig 23.1. The number is very variable between species. For example, fruit flies have only eight chromosomes, whereas a small butterfly from Spain, *Lysandra*, has 380 chromosomes. Cats have 38 and dogs have 78. Most species have between 12 and 50 chromosomes per cell. The units of inheritance, the genes, are arranged along the chromosomes as indicated very diagrammatically in fig 23.2. In humans there are about 100 000 different genes.

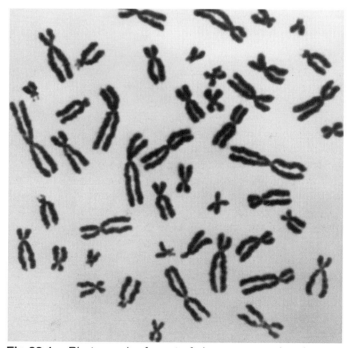

Fig 23.1   *Photograph of a set of chromosomes in a human male just before cell division. Each chromosome is made up of two chromatids held together at a point called the centromere. Forty-six chromosomes are present. Note their different sizes and positions of the centromeres.*

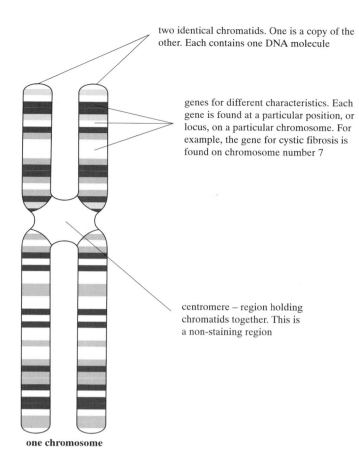

two identical chromatids. One is a copy of the other. Each contains one DNA molecule

genes for different characteristics. Each gene is found at a particular position, or locus, on a particular chromosome. For example, the gene for cystic fibrosis is found on chromosome number 7

centromere – region holding chromatids together. This is a non-staining region

one chromosome

Fig 23.2 *Simplified diagram of a chromosome. In reality there would be several hundred to several thousand genes. The number and size of genes is variable.*

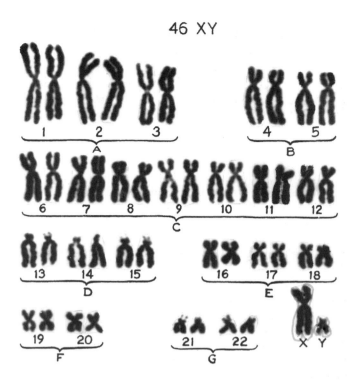

46 XY

Fig 23.3 *Karyogram of a human male, prepared from fig 23.1. Non-sex chromosomes (autosomes) are placed in groups of similar size (A to G). The sex chromosomes are placed separately. X, female, Y, male. Note there are 22 pairs of autosomes and one pair of sex chromosomes. Genes on the autosomes are described as autosomal. Genes on the sex chromosomes are described as sex-linked.*

If the chromosomes are cut out from a photograph such as fig 23.1 and lined up according to size it can be seen that there are in fact *pairs* of chromosomes. These are referred to as **homologous pairs** because they are similar in structure. A photograph of such an arrangement of human chromosomes is shown in fig 23.3. Such a photograph is called a **karyogram** and the set of chromosomes is called the **karyotype**. There are 23 pairs of chromosomes in fig 23.3. The reason that there are pairs of chromosomes is that one set comes from the female parent by way of the egg, and one set comes from the male parent by way of the sperm. When the sperm fuses with the egg at fertilisation, the resulting cell, the zygote, has two sets of chromosomes.

You will notice that there is an odd pair of chromosomes in fig 23.3, labelled X and Y. These are the sex chromosomes. The male, or Y, chromosome is shorter than the female, or X, chromosome, and lacks some of the genes found on the female chromosome, as explained in section 24.6. Normally, homologous pairs of chromosomes have genes for the same characteristics. The person whose karyotype is shown in fig 23.3 is a male (XY). A female would have two X chromosomes (XX). Chromosome mutations are sometimes visible in karyograms, as discussed in chapter 24.

23.1.2   Haploid and diploid cells

Species in which there are two sets of chromosomes as described above are referred to as **diploid**, given the symbol $2n$. The great majority of animal species and about half the plant species are diploid, with two sets of chromosomes per nucleus or cell. A few simple organisms have only one set of chromosomes and are referred to as **haploid** (symbol n) (see, for example, alternation of generations in chapter 2). In addition, gametes are haploid. Some organisms, including many plants, have three or more sets and are referred to as **polyploid**, but we shall ignore these in this chapter.

The advantages of possessing two sets of chromosomes are two-fold:

(1) Genetic variation is increased. Each individual will have a mixture of characteristics from both parents.
(2) If a gene on one chromosome of a pair is faulty, the second chromosome may provide a normal back-up.

23.1.3 Why have two types of nuclear division?

By the end of the nineteenth century it was known that two types of nuclear division occur. This is necessary if the organism has sexual reproduction in its life cycle, as can be explained by reference to fig 23.4.

All multicellular organisms grow from an original single cell which divides repeatedly to form the cells of the adult organism. Before each cell division the nucleus divides. If the number of chromosomes in the nucleus was halved every time a nucleus divided there would quickly be too few chromosomes in each cell. Instead, the daughter cells contain the same number of chromosomes as the parent cells, so that all the cells of the body contain the same number of chromosomes. This is achieved by the type of nuclear division known as **mitosis**.

Figure 23.4 shows however that in a life cycle involving sexual reproduction the zygote is formed by fusion of two cells, the male and female gametes. If these cells had two sets of chromosomes, the zygote and all subsequent cells would have four sets. The number of chromosomes would double every generation. Another type of nuclear division is therefore needed at some point in the life cycle to reduce the number of chromosomes. The diploid condition is then restored in the zygote. The type of nuclear division that reduces two sets of chromosomes to one set in the daughter cells is called **meiosis**. It is sometimes referred to as **reduction division**.

23.1.4 Summary

Mitosis is the process by which a cell nucleus divides to produce two daughter nuclei containing identical sets of chromosomes to the parent cell. It is usually followed immediately by division of the whole cell to form two daughter cells. This process is known as **cell division**.

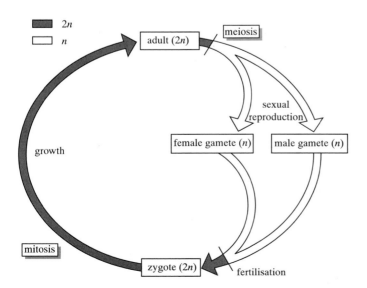

Fig 23.4 *Outline of the life cycle of an animal.*

Mitosis with cell division results in an increase in cell numbers and is the method by which growth, replacement and repair of cells occurs in eukaryotes. In unicellular eukaryotes, mitosis results in asexual reproduction leading to an increase in population size.

Meiosis is the process by which a cell nucleus divides to produce daughter nuclei each containing half the number of chromosomes of the original nucleus. An alternative name for meiosis is reduction division since it reduces the number of chromosomes in the cell from the diploid number ($2n$) to the haploid number (n). The significance of the process lies in the fact that it enables the chromosome number of a sexually reproducing species to be kept constant from generation to generation. Meiosis occurs during gamete formation in animals and during spore formation in plants. Haploid gametes fuse together during fertilisation to restore the diploid number of chromosomes.

23.2 The cell cycle

The sequence of events which occurs between one cell division and the next is called the **cell cycle**. It has three main stages.

(1) **Interphase.** This is a period of synthesis and growth. The cell produces many materials required for its own growth and for carrying out all its functions. DNA replication occurs during interphase.
(2) **Mitosis.** This is the process of nuclear division and is described later.
(3) **Cell division.** This is the process of division of the cytoplasm into two daughter cells.

The entire cycle is laid out in fig 23.5. The length of the cycle depends on the type of cell and external factors such as temperature, food and oxygen supplies. Bacteria may divide every 20 minutes, epithelial cells of the intestine wall every 8–10 hours, onion root-tip cells may take 20 hours whilst many cells of the nervous system never divide.

Experiment 23.1: To investigate the phases of mitosis using a root tip squash

Chromosomes can normally be observed only during nuclear division. The apical meristem of roots (root tips) of garlic ($2n = 16$), onion ($2n = 16$) and broad bean ($2n = 12$) provide suitable material for the experiment. The material is set up so that root development is stimulated. Later the root tips are removed, fixed, stained and macerated so that the chromosomes may be observed under the microscope.

Materials

pins	pair of fine needles
test-tube containing water	several sheets of
scalpel	blotting paper

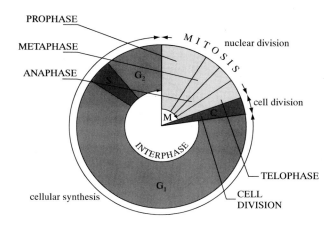

Phase	Events within cell
G_1	Intensive cellular synthesis, including new cell organelles. Cell metabolic rate high. Cell growth occurs. Substances produced to inhibit or stimulate onset of next phase as appropriate.
S	DNA replication occurs. Protein molecules called histones are synthesised and cover each DNA strand. Each chromosome becomes two chromatids. At this stage the cell is $4n$ (4 copies of each DNA molecule, 2 in each homologous chromosome).
G_2	Intensive cellular synthesis. Mitochondria and chloroplasts divide. Energy stores increase. Mitotic spindle begins to form.
M	Nuclear division occurs in four phases.
C	Equal distribution of organelles and cytoplasm into each daughter cell.

Fig 23.5 *The cell cycle.*

small corked tube
forceps
2 petri dishes
water bath and test-tube
microscope slide
cover-slip

clove of garlic
distilled water
acetic alcohol
molar hydrochloric acid
Feulgen stain

Method

(1) Place a pin through a clove of garlic and suspend in a test-tube full of water so that the base of the clove is covered with water. Leave for 3–4 days without any disturbance as this is likely to inhibit cell division temporarily.

(2) When several roots have grown 1–2 cm, remove the clove and cut off the terminal 1 cm of the roots.

(3) Transfer the roots to a small corked tube containing acetic alcohol and leave overnight at room temperature to fix the material.

(4) Remove the root tips with forceps by grasping the cut end of the root, transfer to a petri dish containing distilled water and wash for a few minutes to remove the fixative.

(5) Transfer the root tips to a test-tube containing molar hydrochloric acid which is maintained at 60 °C for 3 min (6–10 min for onion, peas and beans). This breaks down the middle lamellae holding the cells together and hydrolyses the DNA of the chromosomes to form deoxyribose aldehydes which will react with the stain.

(6) Pour the root tips and acid into a petri dish. Remove the roots into another petri dish containing distilled water and wash to remove the acid. Leave for 5 min.

(7) Transfer the roots to a small tube containing Feulgen stain and cork. Leave in a cool dark place (preferably a refrigerator) for a minimum of 2 h.

(8) Remove a root tip and place in a drop of acetic alcohol on a clean microscope slide.

(9) Cut off the terminal 1–2 mm of the root tip and discard the rest of the root.

(10) Tease out the root tip using a pair of fine needles and cover with a cover-slip. Place the slide on a flat surface, cover with several sheets of blotting paper and press down firmly over the cover-slip with the ball of the thumb. Do not allow the cover-slip to move sideways. The technique is called a 'squash'.

(11) Examine the slide under the low and high powers of the microscope and identify cells showing different phases of mitosis.

(12) Draw and label nuclei showing the various phases.

23.3 Mitosis

The events occurring within the nucleus during mitosis are usually observed in cells which have been fixed and stained. This in effect provides a series of 'snapshots' of the phases through which chromosomes pass during cell division. It must be remembered though that mitosis is a continuous process with no sharp distinction between the phases. The use of the phase-contrast microscope and time-lapse photography has enabled the events of nuclear division to be seen in the living cell as they happen. By speeding up the film, mitosis is seen as a continuous process. It can be divided for convenience into four stages. The changes occurring during these stages in an animal cell are described in fig 23.6. Photographs of mitosis in animal and plant cells are shown in figs 23.7 and 23.8.

23.3.1 Centrioles and spindle formation

Centrioles are organelles situated in the cytoplasm close to the nuclear envelope in animal and simpler plant cells. They occur in pairs and lie at right-angles to each other.

Each centriole is approximately 500 nm long and 200 nm in diameter and is composed of nine groups of microtubules arranged in triplets. Neighbouring triplets are attached to each other by fibrils (fig 23.9). **Microtubules**

Interphase

Variable duration depending on function of the cell. Just before nuclear division the DNA of each chromosome replicates. Each chromosome now exists as a pair of **chromatids** joined together by a **centromere**. At this stage the cell is 4n (4 copies of each DNA molecule, 2 in each chromosome of a homologous pair). During interphase chromosome material is in the form of very loosely coiled threads called **chromatin**. Centrioles have replicated.

Prophase

Usually the longest phase of division. Chromosomes shorten and thicken by coiling and tighter packaging of their components. Staining shows up the chromosomes clearly. Each chromosome is seen to consist of two chromatids held together by a centromere that does not stain. In animal cells the **centrioles** move to opposite poles of the cell. Short **microtubules** may be seen radiating from the centrioles. These are called **asters** (*astra*, a star). The **nucleoli** disappear as their DNA passes to certain chromosomes. At the end of prophase the nuclear envelope is no longer visible because it breaks up into small vesicles which disperse. A spindle is formed.

Metaphase

Chromosomes line up around the equator of the spindle, attached by their centromeres to the 'spindle fibres', which are microtubules.

Anaphase

This stage is very rapid. The centromeres split into two and the spindle fibres pull the daughter centromeres to opposite poles. The separated chromatids are pulled along behind the centromeres.

Telophase

The chromatids reach the poles of the cell, uncoil and lengthen to form chromatin again, losing the ability to be seen clearly. The spindle fibres disintegrate and the centrioles replicate. A nuclear envelope re-forms around the chromosomes at each pole and the nucleoli reappear. Telophase may lead straight into **cytokinesis** (cell division).

Fig 23.6 *Mitosis in an animal cell.*

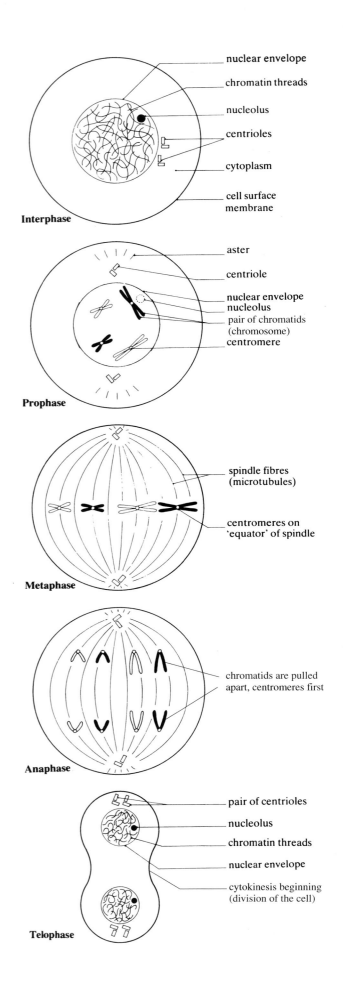

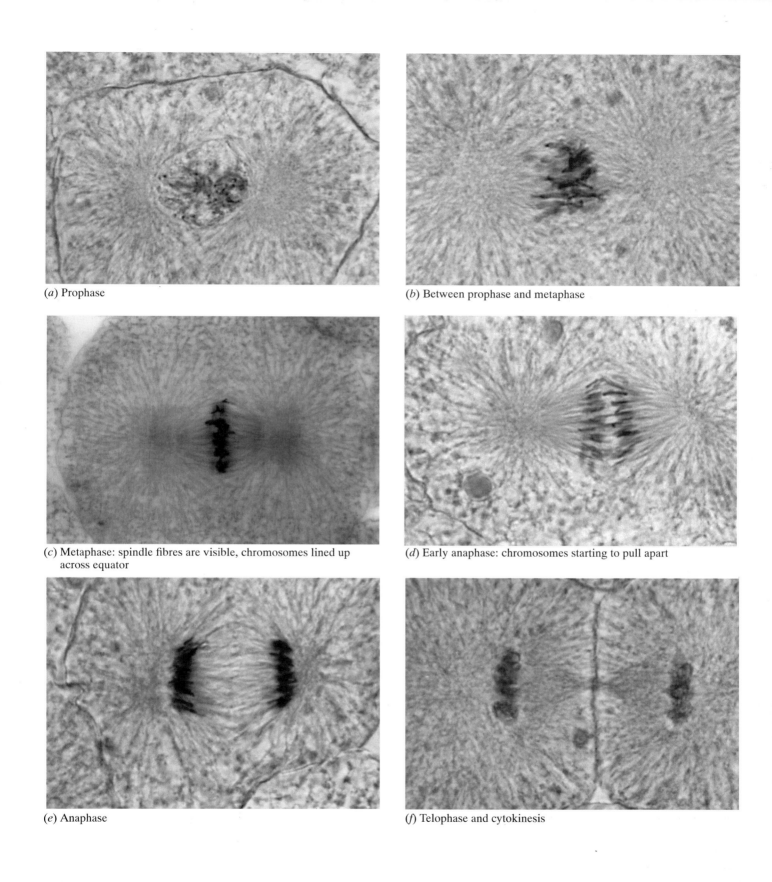

(*a*) Prophase

(*b*) Between prophase and metaphase

(*c*) Metaphase: spindle fibres are visible, chromosomes lined up across equator

(*d*) Early anaphase: chromosomes starting to pull apart

(*e*) Anaphase

(*f*) Telophase and cytokinesis

Fig 23.7 *Stages of mitosis and cell division in an animal cell.*

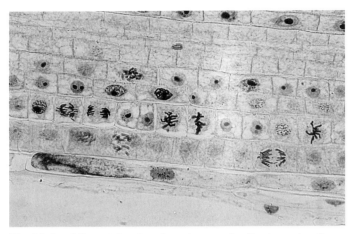

Fig 23.8 *LS root tip showing stages of mitosis and cell division typical of plant cells. Try to identify the stages based on information given in figure 23.7.*

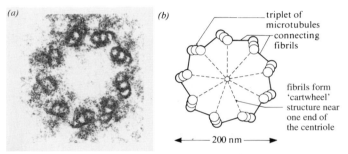

(a)   *(b)*

triplet of microtubules

connecting fibrils

fibrils form 'cartwheel' structure near one end of the centriole

← 200 nm →

Fig 23.9 *(a) Electron micrograph of a TS of a centriole from embryonic chick pancreas. (b) Diagram of TS through a centriole.*

are long hollow tubes about 25 nm in diameter and made of subunits of the protein tubulin as described in section 5.10.7.

In all cases centrioles lie in a material of poorly defined structure which initiates the development of microtubules. This region is called the **centrosome**. It is the centrosome and not the centriole which is responsible for making the spindle because the 'spindle fibres' are in fact microtubules. This explains how plants and fungi which lack centrioles also make spindles from microtubules. The function of the centrioles in nuclear division is not clear. They may be involved in orienting the spindle, thus helping to determine in which plane the cell divides. Some spindle fibres run from pole to pole, others run from the poles to the centromeres. The shortening of these spindle fibres by removal of the tubulin subunits accounts for the movement of chromosomes and chromatids during nuclear division. They are in effect 'reeled in' by the centrosomes.

The addition of the chemical colchicine to actively dividing cells inhibits spindle formation and the chromatid pairs remain in their metaphase positions. This technique enables the number and structure of chromosomes to be examined under the microscope.

Modified centrioles also occur at the bases of cilia and flagella, where they are known as **basal bodies**.

23.3.2   Cell division

Cytokinesis is the division of the cytoplasm. This stage normally follows telophase and leads into the G_1 phase of interphase. In preparation for division, the cell organelles become evenly distributed towards the two poles of the telophase cell along with the chromosomes. In animal cells the cell surface membrane begins to invaginate during telophase towards the region previously occupied by the spindle equator. Microfilaments in the region are thought to be responsible for drawing in the cell surface membrane to form a furrow around the outside surface of the cell. The cell surface membranes in the furrow eventually join up and completely separate the two cells.

In plant cells the spindle fibres begin to disappear during telophase everywhere except in the region of the equatorial plane. Here they move outwards in diameter and increase in number to form a barrel-shaped region known as the **phragmoplast**. Microtubules, ribosomes, mitochondria, endoplasmic reticulum and Golgi apparatus are attracted to this region and the Golgi apparatus produces a number of small fluid-filled vesicles. These appear first in the centre of the cell and, guided by microtubules, fuse to form a **cell plate** which grows across the equatorial plane (fig 5.30). The contents of the vesicles contribute to the new middle lamella and cell walls of the daughter cells, whilst their membranes form the new cell surface membranes. The spreading plate eventually fuses with the parent cell wall and separates the two daughter cells. The new cell walls are called **primary cell walls** and may be thickened at a later stage by the deposition of further cellulose and other substances such as lignin and suberin to produce a **secondary cell wall**. In certain areas the vesicles of the cell plate fail to fuse and the cytoplasm of neighbouring daughter cells remains in contact. These cytoplasmic channels are lined by the cell surface membrane and form structures known as **plasmodesmata**.

23.3.3   Comparison of mitosis in animal and plant cells

The most important event occurring during mitosis is the equal distribution of duplicate chromosomes between the two daughter cells. This process is almost identical in animal and plant cells but there are a number of differences, and these are summarised in table 23.1.

23.3.4   Summary of mitosis

As a result of mitosis a parent nucleus divides into two daughter nuclei, each with the same number of chromosomes as the parent nucleus. This is followed by division of the whole cell. In order to achieve this, chromosomes first replicate during interphase. The two replicate chromosomes are known as chromatids and separate during mitosis.

Table 23.1 Differences between mitosis in plant and animal cells.

Plant	Animal
No centriole present	Centrioles present
No aster forms	Asters form
Cell division involves formation of a cell plate	Cell division involves furrowing and cleavage of cytoplasm
Occurs mainly at meristems	Occurs in tissues throughout the body

23.3.5 Significance of mitosis

- **Genetic stability** Mitosis produces two nuclei which have the same number of chromosomes as the parent cell. Since these chromosomes were derived from parental chromosomes by the exact replication of their DNA, they will carry the same hereditary information in their genes. Daughter cells are genetically identical to the parent cell and no variation in genetic information can therefore be introduced during mitosis. This results in genetic stability within populations of cells derived from the same parental cells.
- **Growth** The number of cells within an organism increases by mitosis and this is the basis of growth in multicellular organisms (chapter 22).
- **Cell replacement** Replacement of cells and tissues also involves mitosis. Cells are constantly dying and being replaced, an obvious example being in the skin.
- **Regeneration** Some animals are able to regenerate whole parts of the body, such as legs in crustacea and arms in starfish. Production of the new cells involves mitosis.
- **Asexual reproduction** Mitosis is the basis of asexual reproduction, the production of new individuals of a species by one parent organism. Many species undergo asexual reproduction. The various methods are described more fully in chapter 21.

23.4 Meiosis

Meiosis (*meio*, to reduce) is a form of nuclear division in which the chromosome number is halved from the diploid number ($2n$) to the haploid number (n). Like mitosis, it involves DNA replication during interphase in the parent cell, but this is followed by *two* cycles of nuclear divisions and cell divisions, known as **meiosis I** (the **first meiotic division**) and **meiosis II** (the **second meiotic division**). Thus a single diploid cell gives rise to four haploid cells as shown in outline in fig 23.10.

Meiosis occurs during the formation of sperm and eggs (gametogenesis) in animals (chapter 21) and during spore formation in plants.

Like mitosis, meiosis is a continuous process but is conveniently divided into prophase, metaphase, anaphase and telophase. These stages occur in the first meiotic division and again in the second meiotic division. The behaviour of chromosomes during these stages is illustrated in fig 23.11, which shows a nucleus containing four chromosomes ($2n = 4$), that is two homologous pairs of chromosomes.

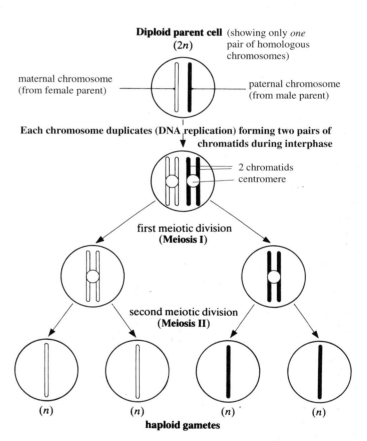

Fig 23.10 *The basic characteristics of meiosis showing one chromosome duplication followed by two nuclear and cell divisions. Note that, as for mitosis, chromosomes may be single or double structures. When double, the two parts are called chromatids.*

MEIOSIS I

Photographs of meiosis are shown in figs 23.12–14.

Prophase I

The longest phase.

(*a*) Chromosomes shorten and become visible as single structures.

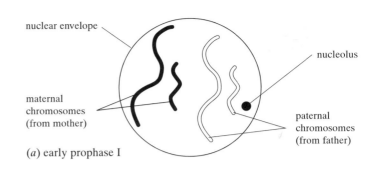

(*a*) early prophase I

(*b*) Homologous chromosomes pair up. This process is called **synapsis**. Each pair is called a **bivalent**. One of the pair comes from the male parent and one from the female parent. Each member of the pair is the same length, their centromeres are in the same positions and they usually have the same number of genes arranged in the same order. The bivalents shorten and thicken, partly by coiling. Each chromosome and its centromeres can now be seen clearly.

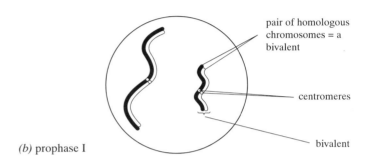

(*b*) prophase I

(*c*) The homologous chromosomes appear to repel each other and partially separate. Each chromosome is now seen to be composed of two **chromatids**. The two chromosomes are seen to be joined at several points along their length. These points are called **chiasmata** (*chiasma*, a cross). It can be seen that each chiasma is the site of an exchange between chromatids. It is produced by breakage and reunion between any two of the four strands present at each site. As a result, genes from one chromosome (e.g. paternal, **A, B, C**) may swap with genes from the other chromosome (maternal, **a, b, c**) leading to new gene combinations in the resulting chromatids. This is called **crossing over**.

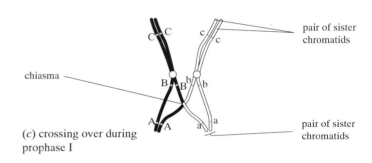

(*c*) crossing over during prophase I

(*d*) The chromatids of homologous chromosomes continue to repel each other and bivalents assume particular shapes depending upon the number of chiasmata. (Bivalents having a single chiasma appear as open crosses, two chiasmata produce a ring shape and three or more chiasmata produce loops lying at right-angles to each other.) By the end of prophase I:

- all chromosomes are fully contracted and deeply stained;
- the centrioles (if present) have migrated to the poles;
- the nucleoli and nuclear envelope have dispersed;
- lastly the spindle fibres form.

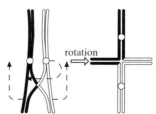

(*d*) bivalent with a single chiasma showing change in shape to an open cross as a result of rotation of the chromatids

Fig 23.11 *(a)–(k) Meiosis in an animal cell.*

Metaphase I

The bivalents become arranged around the equator of the spindle, attached by their centromeres.

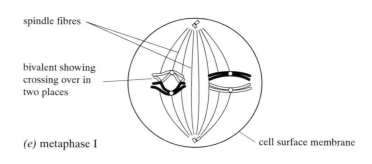

(e) metaphase I

Anaphase I

Spindle fibres pull homologous chromosomes, centromeres first, towards opposite poles of the spindle. This separates the chromosomes into two haploid sets, one set at each end of the spindle.

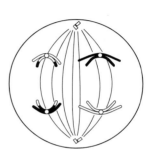

(f) anaphase I

Telophase I

The arrival of homologous chromosomes at opposite poles marks the end of meiosis I. Halving of chromosome number has occurred but the chromosomes are still composed of two chromatids.

If crossing over has occurred these chromatids are not genetically identical and must be separated in a second meiotic division. Spindles and spindle fibres usually disappear.

In animals and some plants the chromatids usually uncoil and a nuclear envelope re-forms at each pole and the nucleus enters interphase. Cleavage (animals) or cell wall formation (plants) then occurs as in mitosis. In many plants there is no telophase, cell wall formation or interphase and the cell passes straight from anaphase I into prophase of the second meiotic division.

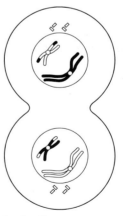

(g) telophase I in an animal cell

Interphase II

This stage is present usually only in animal cells and varies in length. No further DNA replication occurs.

Fig 23.11 *(continued)*

MEIOSIS II
Meiosis II is similar to mitosis.
Prophase II
This stage is absent if interphase II is absent. The nucleoli and nuclear envelopes disperse and the chromatids shorten and thicken. Centrioles, if present, move to opposite poles of the cells and at the end of prophase II new spindle fibres appear. They are arranged at right-angles to the spindle of meiosis I.

(h) prophase II

Metaphase II
Chromosomes line up separately around the equator of the spindle.

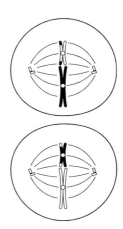

(i) metaphase II

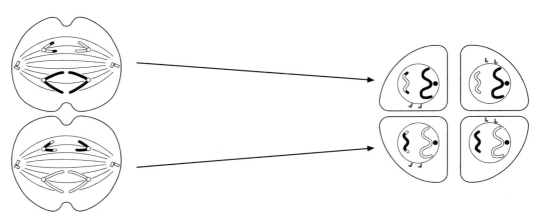

(j) anaphase II

(k) telophase II and cell cleavage in an animal cell

Anaphase II
The centromeres divide and the spindle fibres pull the chromatids to opposite poles, centromeres first.

Telophase II
As telophase in mitosis but four haploid daughter cells are formed. The chromosomes uncoil, lengthen and become very indistinct. The spindle fibres disappear and the centrioles replicate. Nuclear envelopes re-form around each nucleus which now possess half the number of chromosomes of the original parent cell (haploid). Subsequent cleavage (animals) or cell wall formation (plants) will produce four daughter cells from the original single parent cell.

Fig 23.11 (continued)

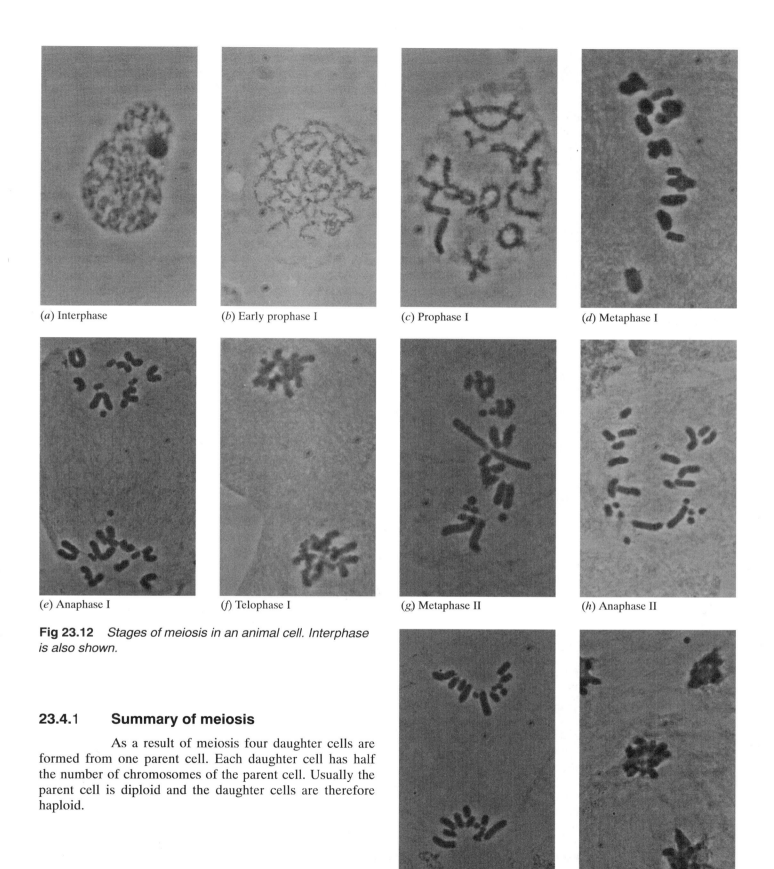

(a) Interphase (b) Early prophase I (c) Prophase I (d) Metaphase I

(e) Anaphase I (f) Telophase I (g) Metaphase II (h) Anaphase II

Fig 23.12 *Stages of meiosis in an animal cell. Interphase is also shown.*

23.4.1   Summary of meiosis

As a result of meiosis four daughter cells are formed from one parent cell. Each daughter cell has half the number of chromosomes of the parent cell. Usually the parent cell is diploid and the daughter cells are therefore haploid.

(i) Late anaphase II (j) Telophase II

Fig 23.13 *Crossing over in prophase I, showing chiasmata, in the locust Locusta migratoria. Eleven bivalents are present with one or two chiasmata each. Paternal and maternal chromosomes are represented by solid and dotted lines respectively in the drawing. At each chiasma a genetic exchange has occurred. The shape of the bivalent will vary from rod-shaped, to cross-shaped or ring-shaped, depending on the number and position of chiasmata. The unpaired X chromosome is deeply staining at this stage (Dr S. A. Henderson).*

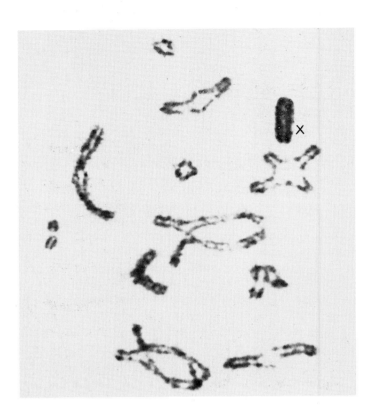

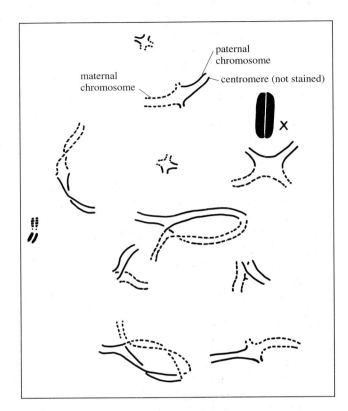

Fig 23.14 *Meiosis in living cells. Pairing and cell division at meiosis in living sperm mother cells (spermatocytes) of the locust Locusta migratoria. These preparations are photographed with an optical technique known as Nomarski interference contrast, which uses polarised light and produces images of remarkably 3D appearance in living, unstained cells. Two cells show chromosome pairing in early prophase I nuclei (arrowed). The two cells at top left are at the end of the first meiotic division. Groups of chromosomes have reached opposite poles of the spindle and cleavage of the cell has taken place. Two approximately equal daughter cells are produced. The fibrous structures stretching between the two groups of chromosomes are the microtubules of the spindle.*

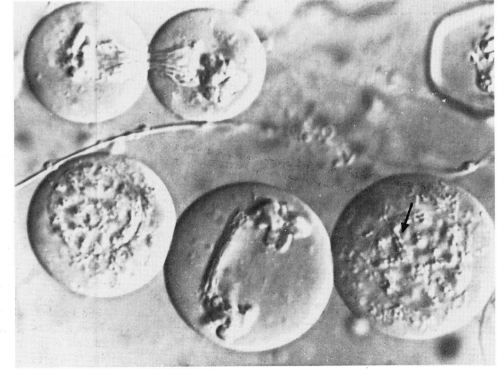

23.4.2   Significance of meiosis

- **Sexual reproduction**   Meiosis occurs in all organisms carrying out sexual reproduction. During fertilisation the nuclei of the two gamete cells fuse. Each gamete has one set of chromosomes (is haploid, *n*). The product of fusion is a zygote which has two sets of chromosomes (the diploid condition, *2n*). If meiosis did not occur fusion of gametes would result in a doubling of the chromosomes for each successive sexually reproduced generation. (An exception to this is shown in polyploidy which is described in section 24.9.) This situation is prevented in the life cycle of all sexually reproducing organisms by the occurrence, at some stage, of cell division involving a reduction in the diploid number of chromosomes (*2n*) to the haploid number (*n*).

> **23.1**   The amount of DNA present per cell during several nuclear divisions is represented diagrammatically in fig 23.15.
> (*a*) Which type of nuclear division is represented by fig 23.15?
> (*b*) What phases are represented by the dashed lines W, X and Y?
> (*c*) What type of cells are represented by the line Z?

- **Genetic variation**   Meiosis also provides opportunities for new combinations of genes to occur in the gametes. This leads to genetic variation in the offspring produced by fusion of the gametes. Meiosis does this in two ways, namely independent assortment of chromosomes and crossing over in meiosis I.

(1) *Independent assortment of chromosomes*   This is best explained by means of a diagram (fig 23.16). The orientations of bivalents at the equator of the spindle in metaphase I is random. Fig 23.16 shows a simple situation in which there are only two bivalents and therefore only two possible orientations (one in which the white chromosomes are alongside each other and one in which black and white are alongside). The more bivalents there are, the more variation is possible. Independent assortment refers to the fact that the bivalents line up independently and therefore the chromosomes in each bivalent separate (assort)

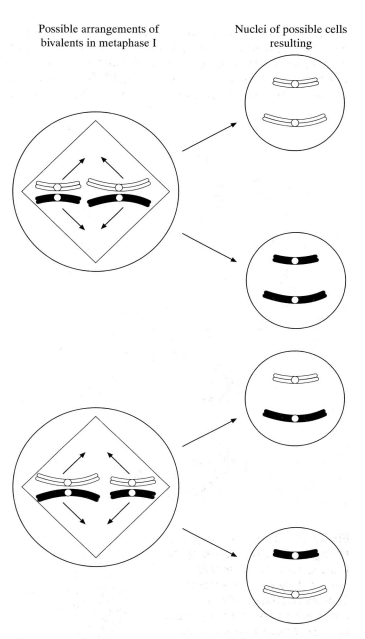

Possible arrangements of bivalents in metaphase I

Nuclei of possible cells resulting

Fig 23.16   *Independent assortment of chromosomes in meiosis. Two bivalents are shown. Each bivalent lines up on the equator independently of other bivalents, so that both possibilities shown in the diagram are equally likely. This increases the potential variation in the gametes, which are also shown.*

independently of those in other bivalents during anaphase I. The black and white chromosomes in fig 23.16 represent maternal and paternal chromosomes. Independent assortment is the basis of Mendel's second law (section 24.1.3).

(2) *Crossing over*   As a result of chiasmata, crossing over of segments of chromatids occurs between homologous chromosomes during prophase I, leading to the formation of new combinations of genes on the chromosomes of the gametes. This is shown in

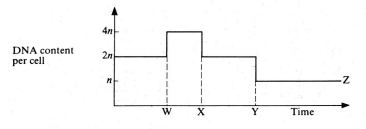

Fig 23.15   *Diagram for use in question 23.1.*

fig 23.11*k* where the four gametes produced as a result of meiosis are all different.

Variation is considered in more detail in section 24.8.4.

23.4.3 Comparison of mitosis and meiosis

The biologically significant differences between mitosis and meiosis are really between mitosis and meiosis I. Meiosis II is almost identical to mitosis. Therefore mitosis and meiosis I only are compared in table 23.2.

23.5 The structure of chromosomes

Analysis of chromosomes of eukaryotic cells has shown them to be composed of deoxyribonucleic acid (DNA) and protein, with small amounts of chromosomal RNA. (The 'chromosomes' of prokaryotic cells (bacteria) are composed of DNA only.) DNA has negative charges distributed along its length, and positively charged (basic) protein molecules called **histones** are bonded to it. This DNA–protein complex is called **chromatin**.

The large amount of DNA in cells means that there is a packaging problem. A human cell, for example, contains about 2.2 m of DNA distributed among 46 chromosomes. Each chromosome therefore contains about 4.8 cm (48 000 μm) of DNA. Human chromosomes are on average about 6 μm long, a packing ratio of 8000:1. In order to maintain a high degree of organisation when the DNA is folded, the histone proteins form a precise architectural 'scaffolding' for the DNA.

It has been shown that the DNA helix combines with groups of eight histone molecules to form structures known as **nucleosomes** having the appearance of 'beads on a string'. These nucleosomes, and the DNA strands linking them, are packed closely together to produce a 30 nm diameter helix with about six nucleosomes per turn. This is known as the 30 nm fibre, or the solenoid fibre. It has a packing ratio of about 40, that is 40 μm of DNA are packed into a 1 μm length of solenoid. The appearance of the solenoid fibres and the 'unpacked' solenoid ('beads on a string' form) are shown in fig 23.17.

Since the DNA must be even more tightly packed than this, the solenoids themselves must be folded or coiled in some way. How this is done is not yet known. The only clues at the moment come from a few examples of cells in which chromosomes have an unusual appearance. One example is in the amphibian oocyte (egg mother cell) which has 'lampbrush chromosomes', so-called because of their resemblance to brushes which were used to clean the glass of oil lamps. Electron micrographs of lampbrush chromosomes during metaphase show that each chromatid appears to be composed of a tightly coiled axis from which emerge several loops made up of a single DNA double helix (fig 23.18). These loops may represent the active DNA, that is DNA which has been exposed for the purpose of transcription (section 23.8.6).

The proposed structure of the chromosome is shown in fig 23.17.

Table 23.2 Comparison of mitosis and meiosis I.

	Mitosis	*Meiosis*
Prophase	Homologous chromosomes remain separate No formation of chiasmata No crossing over	Homologous chromosomes pair up Chiasmata form Crossing over may occur
Metaphase	Pairs of chromatids line up on the equator of the spindle	Pairs of chromosomes line up on the equator
Anaphase	Centromeres divide Chromatids separate Separating chromatids identical	Centromeres do not divide Whole chromosomes separate Separating chromosomes and their chromatids may not be identical due to crossing over
Telophase	Same number of chromosomes present in daughter cells as parent cells Both homologous chromosomes present in daughter cells if diploid	Half the number of chromosomes present in daughter cells Only one of each pair of homologous chromosomes present in daughter cells
Occurrence	May occur in haploid, diploid or polyploid cells Occurs during the formation of somatic (body) cells and some spores. Also occurs during the formation of gametes in plants	Only occurs in diploid or polyploid cells Occurs during formation of gametes or spores

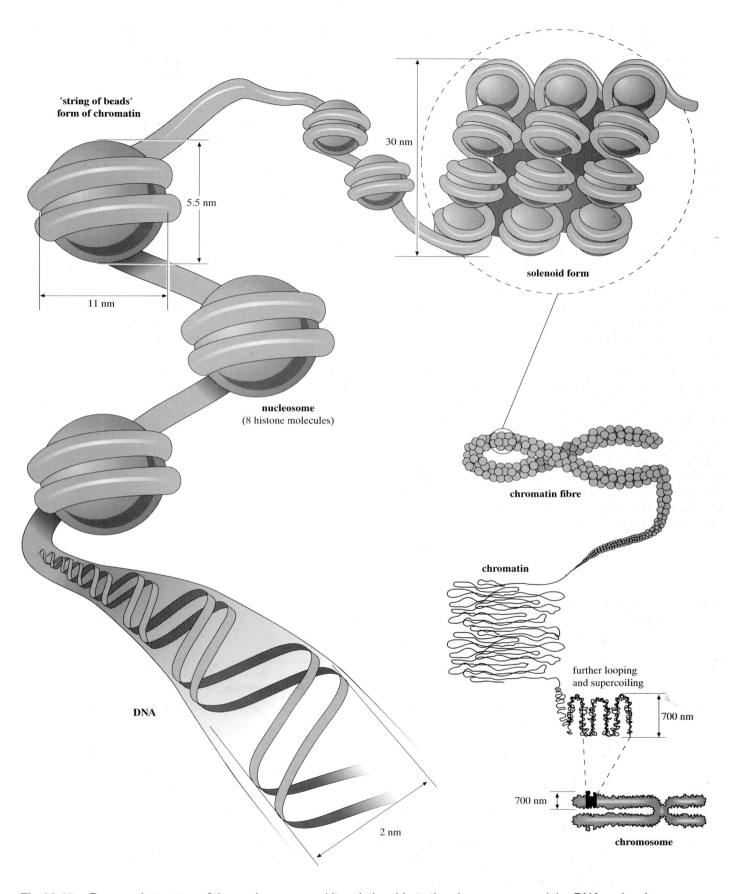

Fig 23.17 *Proposed structure of the nucleosome and its relationship to the chromosome and the DNA molecule.*

23.6 DNA

The structure of DNA has been described in section 3.6.3.

23.6.1 Evidence for the role of DNA in inheritance

It was proposed by Sutton and Boveri at the beginning of this century that chromosomes were the structures by which genetic information passed between generations. However, it took many years to clarify whether the genetic material was the DNA or the protein of the chromosomes. It was suspected that protein might be the only molecule with sufficient variety of structure to act as genetic material.

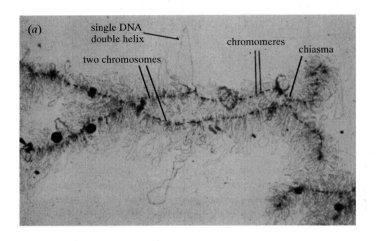

Evidence from bacteria

Frederick Griffith, an English bacteriologist, made an observation in 1928 which was later to prove significant in resolving the problem. In the days before the development of antibiotics, pneumonia was often a fatal disease. Griffith was interested in developing a vaccine against the bacterium *Pneumococcus* which causes one form of pneumonia. Two forms of *Pneumococcus* were known, one covered with a gelatinous capsule and virulent (disease-producing) and the other non-capsulated and non-virulent. The capsule protected the bacterium in some way from attack by the immune system of the host.

Griffith hoped that by injecting patients with either the non-capsulated, or the heat-killed capsulated forms, their bodies would produce antibodies which would give protection against pneumonia. In a series of experiments Griffith injected mice with both forms of *Pneumococcus* and obtained the results shown in table 23.3. Post mortems carried out on the dead mice always revealed the presence within their bodies of live capsulated forms. On the basis of these results Griffith concluded that something must be passing from the heat-killed capsulated forms to the live non-capsulated forms which caused them to develop capsules and become virulent. However, the nature of this **transforming principle**, as it was known, was not isolated and identified until 1944.

Table 23.3 Results of Griffith's experiments.

Injected form of Pneumococcus	*Effect*
live non-capsulated	mice live
live capsulated	mice die
heat-killed capsulated	mice live
heat-killed capsulated + live non-capsulated	mice die

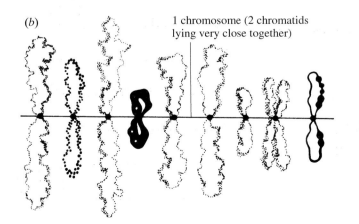

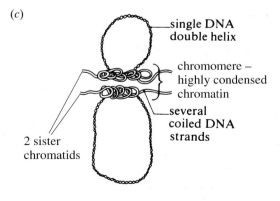

Fig 23.18 (a) A pair of lampbrush chromosomes in an amphibian oocyte. (b) and (c) The effects of stretching lampbrush chromosomes to show the central filament of DNA and the loops of DNA where mRNA synthesis takes place. The dense regions are known as chromomeres. Each chromomere and its associated loop is thought to be associated with a specific gene. (From H. G. Callan (1963) Int. Rev. Cytology, **15**, 1.)

For ten years Avery, McCarty and McCleod analysed and purified the constituent molecules of heat-killed capsulated pneumococcal cells and tested their ability to bring about transformation in live non-capsulated cells. Removal of the polysaccharide capsule and the protein fraction from the cell extracts had no effect on transformation, but the addition of the enzyme deoxyribonuclease (DNase), which breaks down (hydrolyses) DNA, prevented transformation. The ability of extremely purified extracts of DNA from capsulated cells to bring about transformation finally demonstrated that Griffith's 'transforming principle' was in fact DNA. Despite this evidence many scientists still refused to accept that DNA, not protein, was the genetic material. In the early 1950s a wealth of additional evidence, based upon the study of viruses, eventually demonstrated that DNA is indeed the carrier of hereditary information.

Evidence from viruses

Viruses became one of the major experimental materials in genetic research in the 1940s. Virus particles have an extremely simple structure consisting of a protein coat surrounding a molecule of nucleic acid, either DNA or RNA (section 2.4.2). As such they provided ideal research material to investigate whether protein or nucleic acid is the genetic material. In 1952 Hershey and Chase began a series of experiments involving a particular type of virus which specifically attacks bacterial cells and is called a **bacteriophage**. Bacteriophage T$_2$ attacks the bacterium *Escherichia coli* (*E. coli*) which lives in the human gut. The phage causes *E. coli* to produce large numbers of T$_2$-phage particles in a very short time.

The essence of Hershey and Chase's experiment involved growing T$_2$-phage particles in *E. coli* which had been grown on a medium containing radioactive isotopes of either sulphur (^{35}S) or phosphorus (^{32}P). The phage protein contains sulphur but not phosphorus, and the DNA contains phosphorus but not sulphur. Therefore the phage particles formed in *E. coli* labelled with radioactive sulphur had incorporated this into their protein coats, whereas those formed in phosphorus-labelled *E. coli* contained radioactively labelled ^{32}P DNA.

The labelled T$_2$-phage particles were allowed to infect non-radioactively labelled *E. coli* and after a few minutes the cells were agitated in a blender or liquidiser which stripped off the phage particles from the bacterial walls. The bacteria were then incubated and examined for radioactivity. The results are shown in fig 23.19.

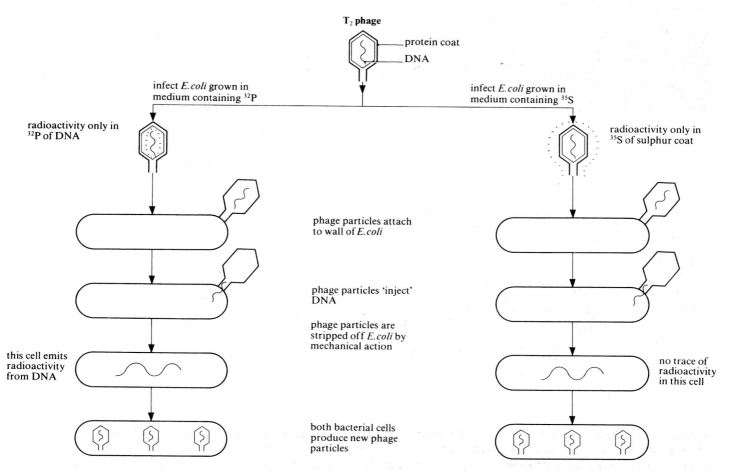

Fig 23.19 *Summary diagrams of Hershey and Chase's work on T$_2$ phage and E. coli.*

On the basis of these results Hershey and Chase concluded that it was the phage DNA and not the protein which entered the bacterial cell and gave rise to large numbers of phage progeny. These experiments demonstrated that DNA is the hereditary material. Confirmatory evidence that only the DNA contained within the phage is introduced into the bacterial cell has been provided by electron microscopy and increased knowledge of the life cycle of viruses. (The life cycle of virus and phage particles is described in sections 2.4.3 and 2.4.5.)

23.6.2 DNA replication

The double helical structure of DNA, as determined by Watson and Crick, is described in section 3.6.3. One of its most attractive features is that it immediately suggests a method by which replication could occur. Watson and Crick proposed that the two strands were capable of unwinding and separating, and acting as templates to which a complementary set of nucleotides would attach by base pairing. In this way each original DNA molecule would give rise to two copies with identical structures.

In 1956 Kornberg succeeded in demonstrating the synthesis of a DNA molecule in a test tube using a single strand of DNA as a template. Kornberg extracted and purified an enzyme from the bacterium *E. coli* which was capable of linking free DNA nucleotides, in the presence of ATP as an energy source, to form a complementary strand of DNA. This enzyme he named **DNA polymerase**. Later experiments showed that the nucleotides used naturally in cells have two extra phosphate groups attached. This activates the nucleotides. As each nucleotide links up to a growing DNA chain, the two extra phosphate groups are broken off. This releases energy which enables the remaining phosphate group of the nucleotide to form a bond with the sugar molecule of the neighbouring nucleotide. The process of replication is shown in fig 23.20.

It starts with the unwinding of the DNA double helix. This is controlled by the enzyme **helicase**. DNA polymerase then binds to the single stranded DNA that results and starts to move along the strand. Each time it meets the next base on the DNA, free nucleotides approach the DNA strand, and the one with the correct complementary base hydrogen-bonds to the base in the DNA. The free nucleotide is then held in place by the enzyme until it binds to the preceding nucleotide, thus extending the new strand of DNA. The enzyme continues to move along one base at a time with the new DNA strand growing as it does so. This movement can only happen in the $5' \longrightarrow 3'$ direction. If you look at fig 23.20 you will see that this means that only one strand (the top strand in the figure) can be copied continuously because the DNA polymerase is moving in the same direction as the unwinding enzyme. This is called **continuous replication**. The copying of the other strand (the bottom strand in the figure) has to keep being started again, because the DNA

polymerase has to move away from the unwinding enzyme in the $5' \longrightarrow 3'$ direction. This results in small gaps being left because the DNA polymerase cannot join the 3' end of one newly synthesised piece of DNA to the 5' end of the next. Another enzyme, **DNA ligase**, is needed to close the gaps. This is called **discontinuous replication**.

Proof of semi-conservative replication

The method of DNA replication proposed by Watson and Crick and shown in fig 23.20 is known as **semi-conservative replication** since each new double helix retains (conserves) one of the two strands of the original DNA double helix. The evidence for this mechanism was provided by a series of classic experiments carried out by Meselson and Stahl in 1958. *E. coli* has a single circular chromosome, and when cultures of these cells were grown for many generations in a medium containing the heavy isotope of nitrogen ^{15}N all the DNA became labelled with ^{15}N. The cells containing DNA labelled with ^{15}N were transferred to a culture medium containing the normal isotope of nitrogen (^{14}N) and allowed to grow. The cells were then left for periods of time corresponding to the generation time for *E. coli* (50 min at 36 °C), that is the time needed for the cells to divide once and therefore for the DNA to replicate once.

Samples were removed and the DNA extracted and centrifuged at 40 000 times gravity for 20 hours in a solution of caesium chloride (CsCl). During centrifugation the heavy caesium chloride molecules began to sediment to the bottom of the centrifuge tubes producing an increasing density gradient from the top of the tube to the bottom. The DNA settles out where its density equals that of the caesium chloride solution. When examined under ultraviolet light the DNA appeared in the centrifuge tube as a narrow band. The positions of the bands of DNA extracted from cells grown in ^{15}N and ^{14}N culture media and the interpretation of these positions are shown in fig 23.21. A diagram of semi-conservative replication is included in fig 23.22. These experiments conclusively demonstrated that DNA replication is semi-conservative.

23.2 There were three hypotheses suggested to explain the process of DNA replication. One of these is known as semi-conservative replication and is described above. The other hypotheses are known as conservative replication and dispersive replication. All three hypotheses are summarised in fig 23.22.

Draw diagrams to show the distribution of the different types of DNA in a density gradient which Meselson and Stahl would have found in the first two generations if the two latter hypotheses had been correct.

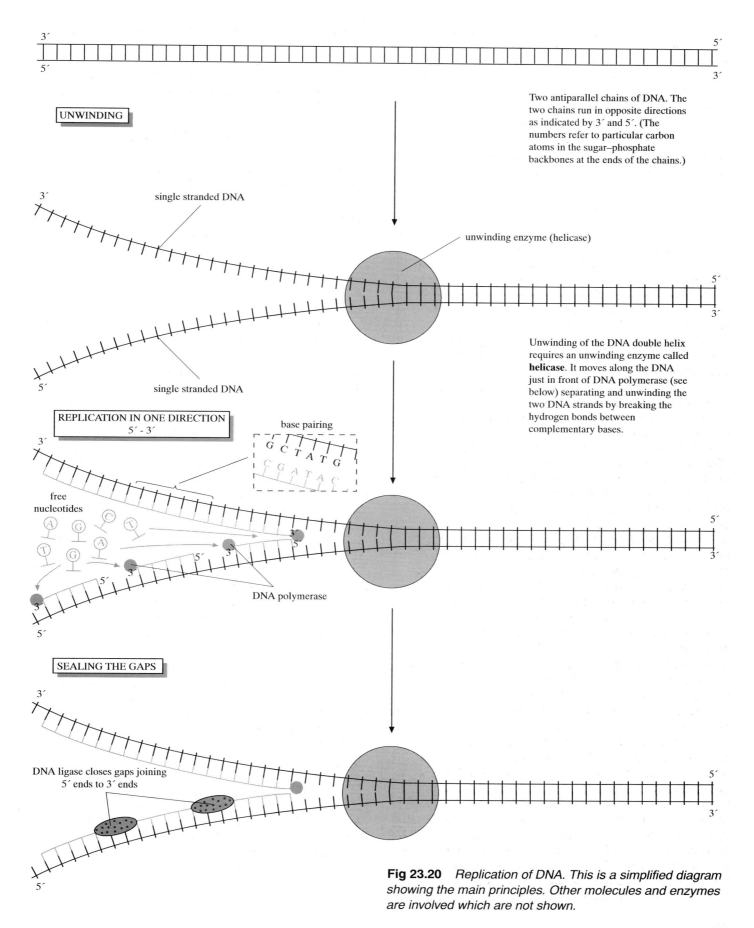

UNWINDING

Two antiparallel chains of DNA. The two chains run in opposite directions as indicated by 3´ and 5´. (The numbers refer to particular carbon atoms in the sugar–phosphate backbones at the ends of the chains.)

single stranded DNA

unwinding enzyme (helicase)

single stranded DNA

Unwinding of the DNA double helix requires an unwinding enzyme called **helicase**. It moves along the DNA just in front of DNA polymerase (see below) separating and unwinding the two DNA strands by breaking the hydrogen bonds between complementary bases.

REPLICATION IN ONE DIRECTION
5´ - 3´

base pairing

G C T A T G
C G A T A C

free nucleotides

DNA polymerase

SEALING THE GAPS

DNA ligase closes gaps joining 5´ ends to 3´ ends

Fig 23.20 *Replication of DNA. This is a simplified diagram showing the main principles. Other molecules and enzymes are involved which are not shown.*

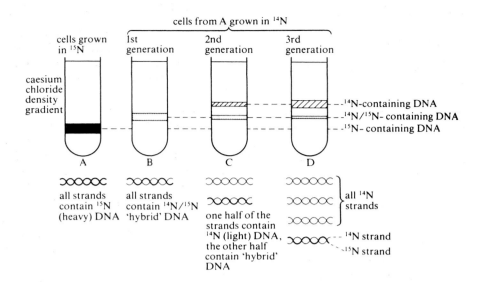

Fig 23.21 The results and interpretation of Meselson and Stahl's experiment into the process of DNA replication. The widths of the DNA bands in the centrifuge tubes reflect the amounts of the various types of DNA molecules. In tube C the ratio of the widths is 1:1 and in tube D the ratio is 3:1.

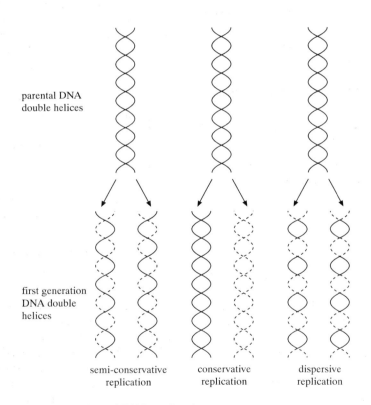

Fig 23.22 Diagrams explaining three theories of DNA replication.

23.7   The nature of genes

23.7.1   What are genes?

Mendel proposed in 1866 that the characteristics of organisms were determined by hereditary units which he called 'elementes'. These were later termed **genes** and shown to be located on chromosomes which transmitted them from generation to generation. Mendel would therefore have defined a gene as a **unit of inheritance**. This is a perfectly acceptable definition but it does not tell us anything about the physical nature of the gene.

Two possible ways of overcoming this objection are considered below.

A unit of recombination.   From his studies of chromosome mapping in *Drosophila* (section 24.2), Morgan postulated that a gene was **the shortest segment of a chromosome which could be separated from adjacent segments by crossing-over**. This definition regards the gene as a specific region of the chromosome determining a distinct characteristic in the organism.

A unit of function.   Since genes are known to determine the structural, physiological and biochemical characteristics of organisms it has been suggested that a gene can be defined in terms of its function. Originally it was proposed that a gene was **the shortest segment of a chromosome responsible for the production of a specific product**. We now know that genes are the codes for proteins. A gene could therefore be defined as **a piece of DNA which codes for a protein**. This definition can be made even more precise by stating that a gene is **the DNA code for a polypeptide** since some proteins are made up of more than one polypeptide chain and are therefore coded for by more than one gene.

23.7.2   The genetic code is a sequence of bases

When Watson and Crick proposed the double helical structure for DNA in 1953 they also suggested that the genetic information which passed from generation to generation, and which controlled the activities of the cell, might be stored in the form of the sequence of bases in the DNA molecule. Once it had been shown that DNA is a code for the production of protein molecules it became clear that the sequence of bases in the DNA must be a code for the sequence of amino acids in protein molecules. This relationship between bases and amino acids is known as the **genetic code**. The problems remaining in 1953 were to demonstrate that a base code existed, to break the code and to determine how the code is translated into the amino acid sequence of a protein molecule.

23.7.3   The code is a triplet code

There are four bases in the DNA molecule, **adenine** (A), **guanine** (G), **thymine** (T) and **cytosine** (C) (section 3.6). Each base is part of a nucleotide and the nucleotides are arranged as a polynucleotide strand. The sequence of bases in the strand can be indicated by the initial letters of the bases. This 'alphabet' of four letters is responsible for carrying the code that results in the synthesis of a potentially infinite number of different protein molecules. There are 20 common amino acids used to make proteins and that the bases in the DNA must code for. If one base determined the position of a single amino acid in the primary structure of a protein, the protein could only contain four different amino acids. If a combination of pairs of bases coded for each amino acid then 16 amino acids could be specified into the protein molecule.

> **23.3**   Using different pairs of the bases A, G, T and C list the 16 possible combinations of bases that can be produced.

Only a code composed of three bases could incorporate all 20 amino acids into the structure of protein molecules. Such a code would produce 64 combinations of bases, more than enough. Watson and Crick therefore predicted that the code would be a triplet code.

> **23.4**   If four bases used singly would code for four amino acids, pairs of bases code for 16 amino acids and triplets of bases code for 64 amino acids, deduce a mathematical expression to explain this.

It was later proved that the code is indeed a triplet code, meaning that three bases is the code for one amino acid.

Evidence for a triplet code

Evidence that the code is a triplet code was provided by Francis Crick in 1961. He produced mutations involving the addition or deletion of bases in T_4 phages. Adding or deleting a base changes the way in which the code is read after the point of addition or deletion, as explained in fig 23.23. The mutation is said to produce a 'frame-shift'. These frame-shifts produced base triplet sequences which failed to result in the synthesis of protein molecules with the original amino acid sequence. Only by adding a base and deleting a base at specific points could the original base sequence be restored. Restoring the original base sequence prevented the appearance of mutants in the experimental T_4 phages. Adding a single base is referred to as a (+) type mutation and deleting a base a (−) type. (+)(−) restores the

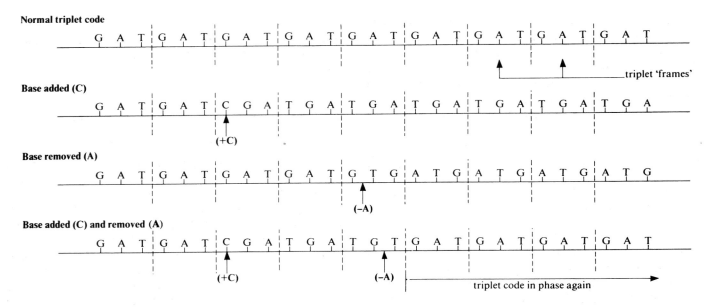

Normal triplet code

G A T | G A T | G A T | G A T | G A T | G A T | G A T | G A T | G A T

triplet 'frames'

Base added (C)

G A T | G A T | C G A | T G A | T G A | T G A | T G A | T G A | T G A

(+C)

Base removed (A)

G A T | G A T | G A T | G A T | G T G | A T G | A T G | A T G | A T G

(−A)

Base added (C) and removed (A)

G A T | G A T | C G A | T G A | T G T | G A T | G A T | G A T | G A T

(+C)   (−A)   triplet code in phase again

Fig 23.23 *Diagrammatic explanation of the effect of adding and deleting bases to the triplet code. The addition of the base C produces a frame-shift which makes the original message GAT, GAT, . . . read as TGA, TGA, . . . The deletion of the base A produces a frame shift changing the original message from GAT, GAT, . . . to ATG, ATG, . . . The addition of the base C at the point indicated and the deletion of the base A at the point indicated restores the original message GAT, GAT. (After F. H. C. Crick (1962) The genetic code I, Scientific American Offprint No. 123, Wm. Saunders & Co.)*

correct reading. The double mutants (++) or (−−) also produced frame-shifts which resulted in mutants which produced faulty proteins. However (+++) or (−−−) mutations usually had no effect on protein function. Crick argued that this is because such mutations do not cause frame-shifts, only the addition or deletion of one amino acid which often does not affect the performance of a protein. This implies that the code is read three bases at a time, that is in triplets.

These experiments also demonstrated that the code is **non-overlapping**, that is to say no base of a given triplet contributes to part of the code of the adjacent triplet (fig 23.24).

> **23.5** Using repeated sequences of the triplet GTA and the base C show that the sequence of triplets can only be restored by adding or deleting three bases. (Set out your answer as in fig 23.24.)

23.7.4 Breaking the code

Having established that the code was a triplet code, it remained to find out which triplets coded for which amino acids, in other words to break the code. In order to understand the experimental procedures used it is necessary to appreciate, in outline, the mechanism by which the triplet code is translated into a protein molecule.

Protein synthesis involves two types of nucleic acid, deoxyribonucleic acid, DNA and ribonucleic acid, RNA. There are three kinds of RNA: messenger RNA (**mRNA**),

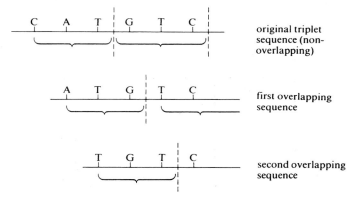

C   A   T | G   T   C

original triplet sequence (non-overlapping)

A   T   G | T   C

first overlapping sequence

T   G   T | C

second overlapping sequence

Fig 23.24 *Base sequences indicating non-overlapping and overlapping codes.*

ribosomal RNA (**rRNA**) and transfer RNA (**tRNA**). The DNA base sequence is copied (**transcribed**) on to strands of messenger RNA (mRNA) which leave the nucleus. These become attached to ribosomes in the cytoplasm where the base sequence of mRNA is **translated** into an amino acid sequence. Specific amino acids become attached to tRNA molecules which link up with complementary triplet bases on the mRNA. Adjacent amino acids brought together in this way react together to form a polypeptide chain. The process of protein synthesis, therefore, depends upon the presence of DNA, mRNA, ribosomes, tRNA, amino acids, ATP as an energy source and various enzymes and cofactors which catalyse each stage in the process.

Nirenberg used this information and various research techniques which had been developed during the late 1950s to design a series of experiments to break the code. The essence of his experiments involved using a known base sequence of mRNA as a coded message and analysing the amino acid sequence of the polypeptide chain produced from it. Nirenberg was able to synthesise a mRNA molecule that consisted of the same triplet (UUU) repeated many times. This was called **polyuridylic acid** (poly-U) and acted as a code. A series of 20 test-tubes was prepared, each containing cell-free extracts of *E. coli* including ribosomes, tRNA, ATP, enzymes and a different radioactive labelled amino acid. Poly-U was added to each test-tube and time was allowed for synthesis of polypeptides to occur. Analysis of the contents of the test-tubes showed that a polypeptide had been formed only in the test-tube containing the amino acid phenylalanine. Thus the genetic code had been partly solved. Nirenberg had shown that the base triplet of the mRNA, or **codon**, UUU determines the position of phenylalanine in a polypeptide chain. Nirenberg

and his co-workers then began preparing synthetic polynucleotide molecules of all 64 possible codons and by 1964 had translated the codes for all 20 amino acids (table 23.4).

23.7.5 Features of the genetic code

The code is a triplet code

As already stated, the genetic code is a triplet code, meaning that three bases in DNA code for one amino acid in a protein. The DNA code for a protein is first copied into messenger RNA (mRNA) before a protein is made. mRNA is complementary to the DNA. The complementary triplets in the mRNA are referred to as **codons**. Each codon is therefore three bases long and is the code for one amino acid. The DNA code for each amino acid can be obtained by converting the RNA codons back into their complementary DNA triplets of bases according to the rules shown in table 23.5.

Table 23.4 The base sequences of the triplet code and the amino acids for which they code.

NB these are **codons**, i.e. base sequences of mRNA and not DNA. The DNA genetic code would have complementary bases and T would replace U.

First base		Second base				Third base
	U	C	A	G	
U	UUU } phe UUC UUA } leu UUG	UCU UCC } ser UCA UCG	UAU } tyr UAC UAA c.t.* UAG c.t.*	UGU } cys UGC UGA c.t.* UGG trp	U C A G
C	CUU CUC } leu CUA CUG	CCU CCC } pro CCA CCG	CAU } his CAC CAA } gln CAG	CGU CGC } arg CGA CGG	U C A G
A	AUU AUC } ileu AUA AUG met	ACU ACC } thr ACA ACG	AAU } asn AAC AAA } lys AAG	AGU } ser AGC AGA } arg AGG	U C A G
G	GUU GUC } val GUA GUG	GCU GCC } ala GCA GCG	GAU } asp GAC GAA } glu GAG	GGU GGC } gly GGA GGG	U C A G

*c.t., chain termination codon, equivalent to a full stop in the message.

Table 23.5 The RNA bases which are complementary to those of DNA.

DNA bases	Complementary RNA bases
A (adenine)	U (uracil)
G (guanine)	C (cytosine)
T (thymine)	A (adenine)
C (cytosine)	G (guanine)

23.6 Write out the base sequence of mRNA formed from a DNA strand with the following sequence.

ATGTTCGAGTACCATGTAACG

The code is degenerate

Table 23.4 shows the genetic code in the form of codons. As can be seen from the table some amino acids are coded for by several codons. This type of code where the number of amino acids is less than the number of codons is termed **degenerate**. Analysis of the code also shows that for many amino acids only the first two letters appear to be significant.

The code is punctuated

Three of the codons shown in table 23.4 act as 'full stops' in determining the end of the code message. An example is UAA. They are sometimes described as 'nonsense codons' and do not code for amino acids. They presumably mark the end-point of a gene. They act as 'stop signals' for the termination of polypeptide chains during translation.

Certain codons act as 'start signals' for the initiation of polypeptide chains, such as AUG (methionine).

The code is universal

One of the remarkable features of the genetic code is that it is thought to be universal. All living organisms contain the same 20 common amino acids and the same five bases, A, G, T, C and U.

Advances in molecular biology have reached the point now where it is possible to determine the base sequences for whole genes and for whole organisms. The first organism whose complete genetic code was established was a virus, the phage ΦX174. The phage has only ten genes and its complete genetic code is 5386 bases long. The sequence was discovered by Fred Sanger, the man who first discovered the sequence of amino acids in a protein. He was awarded Nobel prizes for both these sequencing milestones. Whole genes can now be synthesised artificially, a practice which is of use in genetic engineering. Soon after the beginning of the twenty-first century it is anticipated that it will be possible to write out the entire genetic code of a human, an estimated 3000 million base pairs long, as a result of the Human Genome Project. (The genome is the total DNA in an organism.) Other organisms whose genomes are being sequenced are *E. coli*, yeast, the fruit fly *Drosophila*, a nematode worm and the laboratory mouse.

Summary

The main features of the genetic code are summarised below.

- A **triplet** of bases in the polynucleotide chain of DNA is the code for one amino acid in a polypeptide chain.
- It is **universal**: the same triplets code for the same amino acids in all organisms. (A few triplet codes in mitochondrial DNA and some ancient bacteria differ from the 'universal code'.)
- It is **degenerate**: a given amino acid may be coded for by more than one codon.
- It is **non-overlapping**: for example, an mRNA sequence beginning AUGAGCGCA is not read AUG/UGA/GAG … (an overlap of two bases) or AUG/GAG/GCG … (an overlap of one base). (However, overlapping of certain genes does occur in a few organisms such as the bacteriophage ΦX174. This seems likely to be exceptional and may be an economy measure when there are very few genes.)

23.8 Protein synthesis

'DNA makes RNA and RNA makes protein'

The information given so far in this chapter has shown that although DNA controls the activities of cells, the only molecules capable of being synthesised directly from DNA are proteins. These may have a structural role, such as keratin and collagen, or a functional role, such as insulin, fibrinogen and most importantly enzymes, which are responsible for controlling cell metabolism. It is the particular range of enzymes in the cell which determines what type of cell it becomes. This is the way in which DNA controls the activities of a cell.

The 'instructions' for the manufacture of enzymes and all other proteins are located in the DNA, which is found in the nucleus. However, it was shown in the early 1950s that the actual synthesis of proteins occurs in the cytoplasm at the ribosomes. Therefore a mechanism had to exist for carrying the genetic information from nucleus to cytoplasm. In 1961 two French biochemists, Jacob and Monod, suggested that the link was a specific form of RNA which they called **messenger RNA** (mRNA). This idea later proved to be correct. The sequence of events during protein synthesis was summarised by the slogan 'DNA makes RNA and RNA makes protein'.

23.8.1 The role of RNA

RNA exists as a single-stranded molecule in all living cells. It differs from DNA in possessing the pentose sugar ribose instead of deoxyribose and the pyrimidine uracil instead of thymine. Analysis of the RNA content of cells has shown the existence of three types of RNA which are all involved in the synthesis of protein molecules. These are messenger RNA (mRNA), transfer RNA (tRNA) and ribosomal RNA (rRNA). All three types are synthesised directly on DNA, and the amount of RNA in each cell is directly related to the amount of protein synthesis.

23.8.2 Messenger RNA

Analyses of cells have shown that 3–5% of the total RNA of the cell is mRNA. This is a single-stranded molecule formed on a single strand of DNA by a process known as **transcription**. In the formation of mRNA only one strand of the DNA molecule is copied. The synthesis of mRNA is described later. The base sequence of mRNA is a complementary copy of the DNA strand being copied and varies in length according to the length of the polypeptide chain for which it codes. Most mRNA exists within the cell for a short time. In the case of bacteria this may be a matter of minutes whereas in developing red blood cells the mRNA may continue to produce haemoglobin for several days.

23.8.3 Ribosomal RNA

Ribosomal RNA makes up approximately 80% of the total RNA of the cell. It is synthesised by genes present on the DNA of several chromosomes found within a region of the nucleolus known as the **nucleolar organiser**. The base sequence of rRNA is similar in all organisms from bacteria to higher plants and animals. It is found in the cytoplasm where it is associated with protein molecules which together form the cell organelles known as ribosomes (see section 5.10.4).

Ribosomes are the sites of protein synthesis. Here the mRNA 'code' is **translated** into a sequence of amino acids in a polypeptide chain.

23.8.4 Transfer RNA

The existence of transfer RNA (tRNA) was postulated by Crick and demonstrated by Hoagland in 1955. Each amino acid has its own family of tRNA molecules. tRNA transfers amino acids present in the cytoplasm to the ribosome. Consequently it acts as an intermediate molecule between the triplet code of mRNA and the amino acid sequence of the polypeptide chain. It makes up about 15% of the total RNA of the cell and, having on average 80 nucleotides per molecule, it is the smallest of all the RNAs. There are more than 20 different tRNA molecules in a given cell (60 have so far been identified) carrying specific amino acids. All tRNA molecules have the same basic structure (see fig 23.25).

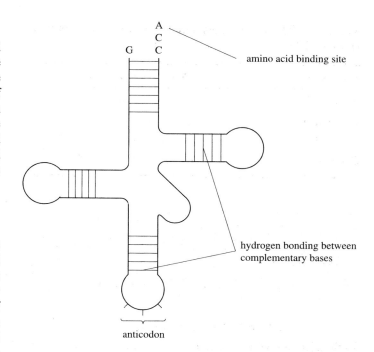

Fig 23.25 *A proposed model for the structure of transfer RNA (tRNA). The whole molecule is composed of about 80 nucleotides but only 21 show complementary base pairing.*

The 5'-end of the tRNA always ends in the base guanine whilst the 3'-end always ends in the base sequence of CCA. The base sequence of the rest of the molecule is variable and may include some 'unusual bases' such as inosine (I) and pseudouracil (y). The triplet base sequence at the anticodon (fig 23.25) is directly related to the amino acid carried by that tRNA molecule. Each amino acid is attached to its specific tRNA by its own form of the enzyme **aminoacyl–tRNA synthetase**. This produces an amino acid–tRNA complex known as **aminoacyl–tRNA** with sufficient energy in the bond between the final A nucleotide of CCA and the amino acid to later form a peptide bond with the adjacent amino acid. In this way a polypeptide chain is synthesised.

23.8.5 Summary of protein synthesis

Protein synthesis is a two-stage process, as summarised in fig 23.26:

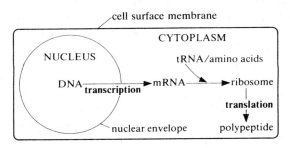

Fig 23.26 *Summary diagram of the main steps involved in protein synthesis.*

(1) transcription – this is the making of mRNA from DNA. A length of DNA (a gene) is copied into a mRNA molecule.

(2) translation – translating the base sequence in mRNA into an amino acid sequence in a protein.

23.8.6 Transcription

Transcription is the mechanism by which the base sequence of a section of DNA representing a gene is converted into the complementary base sequence of mRNA. The DNA double helix unwinds by breakage of the relatively weak hydrogen bonds between the bases of the two strands, exposing single strands of DNA. Only one of these strands can be selected as a **template** for the formation of a complementary single strand of mRNA. This molecule is formed by the linking of free nucleotides under the influence of RNA polymerase and according to the rules of base pairing between DNA and RNA (table 23.5 and fig 23.27).

The exact nature of the copying of DNA bases into RNA bases has been demonstrated using synthetic DNA composed solely of thymine nucleotides (TTT). When introduced into a cell-free system containing RNA polymerase and all four nucleotides (A, U, C and G) the messenger RNA formed was composed entirely of complementary adenine nucleotides.

When the mRNA molecules have been synthesised they leave the nucleus via the nuclear pores and carry the genetic code to the ribosomes. When sufficient numbers of mRNA molecules have been formed from the gene the RNA polymerase molecule leaves the DNA and the two strands 'zip up' again, re-forming the double helix.

23.8.7 Translation

Translation is the mechanism by which the sequence of bases in a mRNA molecule is converted into a sequence of amino acids in a polypeptide chain. It occurs on ribosomes. Several ribosomes may become attached to a molecule of mRNA like beads on a string and the whole structure is known as a polyribosome or **polysome**. These structures can be seen under the electron microscope (fig 23.28). The advantage of such an arrangement is that it allows several polypeptides to be synthesised at the same

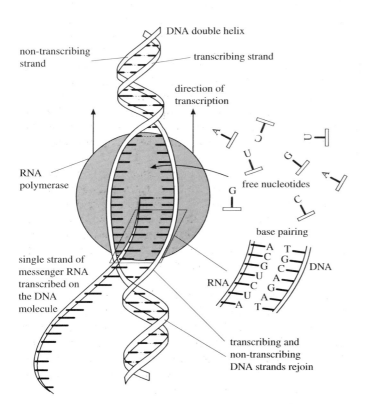

Fig 23.27 *Diagram showing the mechanism of transcription. In the presence of RNA polymerase the DNA double helix unwinds by breakage of the hydrogen bonds between complementary bases, and a polynucleotide strand of mRNA is formed from free RNA nucleotides. These line up opposite complementary DNA bases on the transcribing strand of template DNA. (Modified from E. J. Ambrose & D. M. Easty (1977)* Cell biology, *2nd ed., Nelson.)*

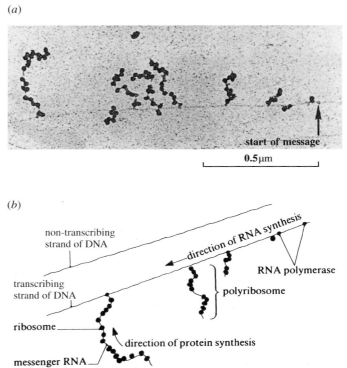

Fig 23.28 *Transcription and formation of a polysome in bacteria. Note that the mRNA does not need to leave the DNA in bacteria because there is no nucleus. (a) Electron micrograph of a piece of bacterial DNA showing stages in the development of mRNA and the attachment of ribosomes. (b) Diagrammatic representation of the structure shown in the electron micrograph in (a).*

time (section 23.8.3). Each ribosome is composed of a small and a large subunit, resembling a 'cottage loaf' (fig 5.27). The first two mRNA codons (a total of 6 bases) enter the ribosome as shown in fig 23.29a. The first codon binds the aminoacyl–tRNA molecule having the complementary anticodon and which is carrying the first amino acid (usually methionine) of the polypeptide being synthesised. The second codon then also attracts an aminoacyl–tRNA molecule showing the complementary anticodon (figs 23.29a and b). The function of the ribosome is to hold in position the mRNA, tRNA and the associated enzymes controlling the process until a peptide bond forms between the adjacent amino acids.

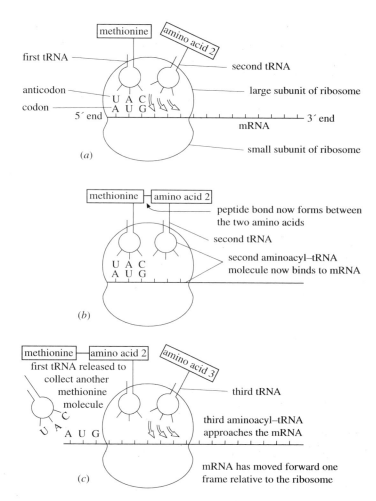

(a)

(b)

(c)

Fig 23.29 *(a) and (b) Stages in the attachment of aminoacyl–tRNA molecules by their anticodons to the codons on mRNA and the formation of a peptide bond between adjacent amino acids. (c) The relative movements of mRNA and ribosome exposing a new triplet (frame) for the attachment of the aminoacyl–tRNA molecule. The initial tRNA molecule is now released from the ribosome and cycles back into the cytoplasm to be reactivated by enzymes to form a new aminoacyl–tRNA molecule.*

Once the new amino acid has been added to the growing polypeptide chain the ribosome moves one codon along the mRNA. The tRNA molecule which was previously attached to the polypeptide chain now leaves the ribosome and passes back to the cytoplasm to be reconverted into a new aminoacyl–tRNA molecule (fig 23.29c).

This sequence of the ribosome 'reading' and 'translating' the mRNA code continues until it comes to a codon signalling 'stop'. These terminating codons are UAA, UAG and UGA. At this point the polypeptide chain, now with its primary structure as determined by the DNA, leaves the ribosome and translation is complete. The main steps involved in translation may be summarised under the following headings:

(1) binding of mRNA to ribosome,
(2) amino acid activation and attachment to tRNA,
(3) polypeptide chain initiation,
(4) chain elongation,
(5) chain termination,
(6) fate of mRNA,

and the process is summarised in fig 23.30.

As the polypeptide chains leave the ribosome they may immediately assume either secondary, tertiary or quaternary structures (section 3.5.3). If the ribosome is attached to ER (rough ER) the protein enters the ER to be transported. In such a situation the first part of the growing chain of amino acids consists of a 'signal sequence' of amino acids which fit a specific receptor in the ER membrane, thus binding the ribosome to the ER. The growing protein passes through the receptor into the ER as shown in fig 23.31. Once inside, the signal sequence is removed and the protein folds up into its final shape.

Evidence that it is the complementary base pairing between the mRNA codon and the tRNA anticodon which determines the incorporation of an amino acid into the polypeptide chain, and not the amino acid, was demonstrated by the following experiment. The tRNA–cysteine molecule normally pairs up, via its anticodon ACA, with the mRNA codon UGU. Exposure of this tRNA–cysteine molecule to a catalyst, Raney nickel, converted the cysteine to the amino acid alanine. When the new tRNA–alanine molecule (carrying the tRNA–cysteine anticodon) was placed in a cell-free system containing poly-UGU-mRNA the polypeptide chain formed contained only alanine. This experiment demonstrated the importance of the role of the mRNA–codon–tRNA–anticodon mechanism in translating the genetic code.

The whole sequence of protein synthesis occurs as a continuous process and is summarised in fig 23.32.

23.8.8   Non-coding DNA

Human DNA contains about 3000 million base pairs and an estimated 100 000 genes, although the number of genes can only be a rough guess at present. The problem

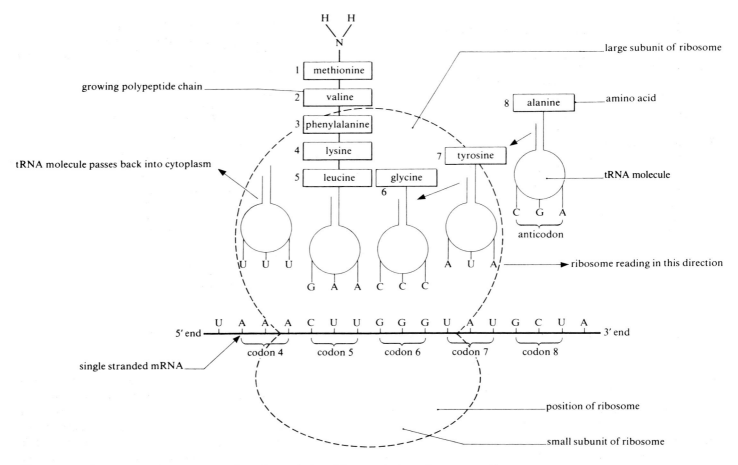

Fig 23.30 *Diagrammatic representation of translation. The anticodon of each specific aminoacyl–tRNA molecule pairs with its complementary bases of the mRNA codon in the ribosome. In the example above a peptide bond would next form between leucine and glycine and in this way an additional amino acid would be added to the growing polypeptide chain.*

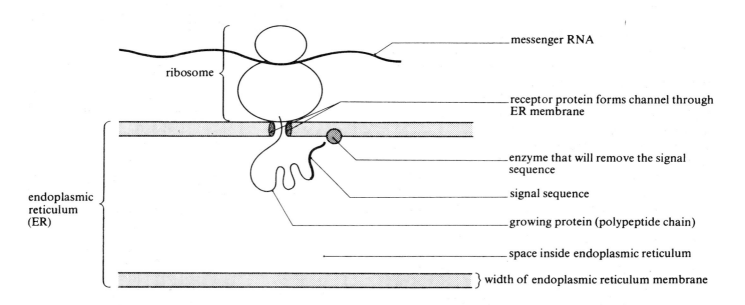

Fig 23.31 *Entry of newly synthesised protein into the endoplasmic reticulum.*

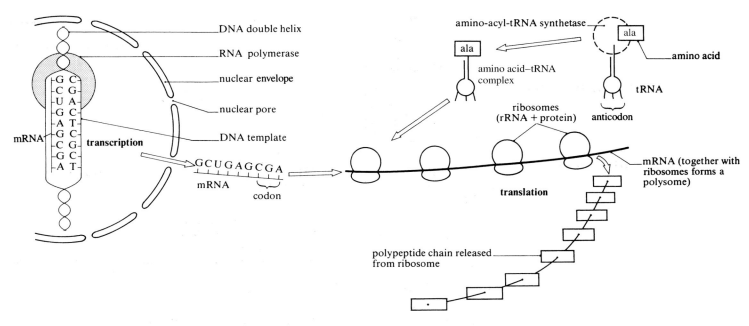

Fig 23.32 *Simplified summary diagram of the major structures and processes involved in protein synthesis in the cell.*

is that about 95% of the DNA appears to have no obvious function because it is non-coding. In other words it does not code for proteins or RNA. It has sometimes been referred to as 'junk DNA', although it is unwise to assume that something has no function just because its function is unknown. Some of it may be former genes which no longer serve any useful purpose. Some is probably structural, involved perhaps in packaging of chromosomes, for example. About 30–40% consists of short base sequences which are repeated many times. This includes the satellite DNA whose use in genetic fingerprinting is described in section 25.4.12. Some make up pieces of DNA called introns. These are discussed below.

Introns and exons

In 1977 biologists were surprised to discover that the DNA of a eukaryotic gene is longer than its corresponding mRNA. It should be the same length because the mRNA is a direct copy. It was discovered that immediately after the mRNA is made, certain sections of the molecule are cut out, before it is used in translation. The sections of the gene that code for these unused pieces of RNA are called **introns**. The remaining sections of the gene are the code for the protein and are called **exons** (fig 23.33). The size and arrangement of introns is very variable and characteristic for a particular gene. In prokaryotes there are no introns.

One possible function for introns has come with the discovery that the same mRNA may have different introns removed in different cells. The gene therefore has alternative introns and can code for different, though similar, proteins. This increases its potential use.

An example is the calcitonin gene. Two different forms of mRNA can be produced by this gene, depending on

which introns are removed. One is produced in the thyroid gland and codes for the protein calcitonin, which has 32 amino acids. Calcitonin is a hormone which acts to lower calcium levels in the blood. The other is produced in the hypothalamus and codes for a protein with 37 amino acids which is similar to calcitonin and is called CGRP (calcitonin gene-related peptide). This is a powerful vasodilatory agent. It is also released from nerve endings in some parts of the peripheral nervous system.

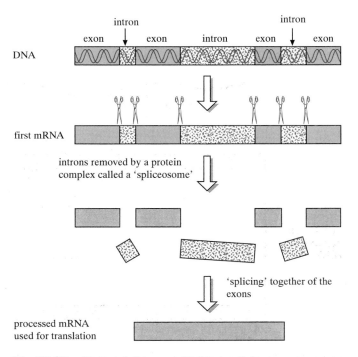

Fig 23.33 *Exons, introns and intron splicing.*

23.9 Gene control

Genetic research has come a long way since the discovery of the structure of DNA and the breaking of the genetic code. One of the areas that most concerns molecular geneticists is how gene activity is controlled so that an organised programme of development and cell activity is followed by each cell.

All somatic cells of an organism carry the same genes, that is they contain the same number of chromosomes carrying the same alleles. Despite this, cells in a multicellular organism show a wide variation in structure and function. Even within a single cell the rate at which certain protein molecules are synthesised varies according to circumstances and demand. Evidence for the mechanism by which genes are regulated within the cell was first obtained from studies into the control of enzyme synthesis in *E. coli*.

In 1961 Jacob and Monod carried out a series of experiments to investigate the nature of induction of enzyme synthesis in *E. coli*. Of the 800 enzymes thought to be synthesised by *E. coli* some are synthesised continuously and are called **constitutive enzymes**; others are synthesised only in the presence of an inducer compound, which may not be the substrate, and are called **inducible enzymes**. One of the latter enzymes is β-galactosidase.

E. coli will grow rapidly on a culture medium containing glucose. When transferred to a medium containing lactose instead of glucose it will not grow immediately but after a short delay begins to show the same growth rate as seen on a glucose medium. Investigations revealed that growth on the lactose medium required the presence of two substances not normally synthesised: β-galactosidase, which hydrolyses lactose to glucose and galactose, and **lactose permease**, which enables the cell to take up lactose. This is an example of where a change in environmental conditions (lactose instead of glucose) has induced the synthesis of a particular enzyme. Other experiments involving *E. coli* showed that high concentrations of the amino acid **tryptophan** in the culture medium suppressed the production of the enzyme **tryptophan synthetase** used to synthesise tryptophan. β-galactosidase synthesis is an example of **enzyme induction**, whereas the suppression of tryptophan synthetase is an example of **enzyme repression**. On the basis of these observations and experiments, Jacob and Monod proposed a mechanism to account for induction and repression, the mechanism by which genes are 'switched on and off'.

23.9.1 The Jacob–Monod hypothesis of gene control

The genes determining the amino acid sequences of the proteins described above are described as **structural genes**. Those for β-galactosidase and lactose permease are closely linked on the same chromosome. The activity of these genes is controlled by another gene called a **regulator gene** which is thought to prevent the structural genes from becoming active. This may be situated some distance from the structural genes. Evidence for the existence of a regulator gene comes from studies of mutant *E. coli* which lack this gene and as a consequence produce β-galactosidase continuously. The regulator gene carries the genetic code which results in the production of a **repressor molecule**. This prevents the structural genes from being active; it does not directly affect the structural genes but is thought to influence a gene immediately adjacent to the structural genes, the **operator gene**. The operator and structural genes are collectively known as the **operon** (fig 23.34).

The repressor molecule is thought to be a particular type of protein known as an **allosteric protein** which can either bind with the operator gene and suppress its activity ('switch it off') or not bind and permit the operator gene to become active ('switch it on'). When the operator gene is

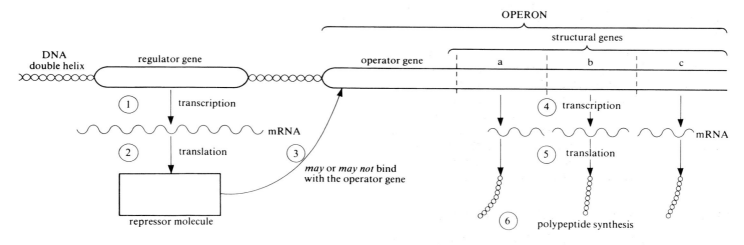

Fig 23.34 *The basic structures and processes involved in the control of protein synthesis according to the hypothesis produced by Jacob and Monod. The numbers indicate the sequence of events.*

'switched on' the structural genes carry out transcription and mRNA is formed which the ribosomes and tRNA translate into polypeptides. When the operator gene is 'switched off' no mRNA and no polypeptides are formed (fig 23.34).

The mechanism controlling whether or not the allosteric protein binds to the operator gene is simple, yet sensitive to varying intracellular conditions. It is thought that the repressor molecule has at least two active sites to which either an inducer molecule or a co-repressor molecule may become attached, depending upon their relative concentrations at any given time, as described in section 23.9.4.

23.9.2   Enzyme induction

The binding of an inducer molecule to its active site on the repressor molecule alters the tertiary structure of the repressor (allosteric effect) (section 4.4.4) so that it cannot bind with the operator gene and repress it. The operator gene becomes active and 'switches on' the structural genes.

In the case of *E. coli* grown on glucose medium, the regulator gene produces a repressor substance which combines with the operator gene and switches it 'off'. The structural genes are not activated and no β-galactosidase and lactose permease are produced. When transferred to a lactose medium the lactose is thought to act as an inducer of protein synthesis by combining with the repressor molecule and preventing it combining with the operator gene. The structural genes become active, mRNA is produced and proteins are synthesised. Lactose is thus an inducer of its own breakdown.

23.9.3   Enzyme repression

If a co-repressor molecule binds with its active site on the repressor molecule it reinforces the normal binding response of the repressor molecule with the operator gene. This inactivates the operator gene which, in effect, prevents the structural genes from being 'switched on'.

E. coli synthesises the amino acid tryptophan in the presence of the enzyme tryptophan synthetase. When the cell contains an excess of tryptophan some of it acts as a co-repressor of enzyme synthesis by combining with the repressor molecule. Co-repressor and repressor molecules combine with the operator gene and inhibit its activity. The structural genes are 'switched off', no mRNA is produced and no further tryptophan synthetase is synthesised. This is an example of feedback inhibition acting at the gene level.

23.9.4   Control of metabolic pathways

This dual mechanism of induction and repression enables the cytoplasm and nucleus to interact in a delicate control of cell metabolism. In the case of a simple metabolic pathway the initial substrate and final product can act as inducer and co-repressor respectively. This mechanism enables the cell to produce the amount of enzyme required at any given time to maintain the correct level of product. This method of metabolic control is highly economical. Negative feedback involving the inactivation of the initial enzyme by combination with the end-product would rapidly halt the pathway but would not prevent the continued synthesis of the other enzymes. In the system proposed by Jacob and Monod, the end-product, by combining with the repressor molecule to increase its repressive effect on the operator gene, would prevent the synthesis of all enzymes and halt the pathway.

23.9.5   Modification to the operon hypothesis

Since 1961, when Jacob and Monod suggested a mechanism by which genes are switched on and off, further evidence has accumulated which has helped to clarify aspects of the mechanism. Genetic evidence has suggested the existence of a **promoter gene** situated adjacent to the operator gene which acts between it and the regulator gene. It is thought to have two functions. First the promoter gene is the site to which RNA polymerase binds before moving along the DNA to begin the transcription of mRNA on the structural genes. This movement will, of course, depend upon whether the operator gene is 'operational' or not. Secondly, the base sequence of the promoter gene determines which strand of the DNA double helix attracts the RNA polymerase. In this way the promoter gene determines which strand of the DNA double helix acts as the template for mRNA transcription.

Chapter Twenty-four

Variation and genetics

Genetics may rightly be claimed to be one of the most important branches of biology. For thousands of years, humans have used the techniques of genetics in the improvement of domestic animals and crops without having any real knowledge of the mechanisms which underlie these practices. Various pieces of archaeological evidence dating back 6000 years suggest that humans understood that certain physical characteristics could be transmitted from one generation to another. By selecting particular organisms from wild stocks and interbreeding these, humans have been able to produce improved varieties of plants and animals to suit their needs.

It is only since the beginning of this century, though, that scientists have begun to appreciate fully the principles and mechanisms of heredity. Whilst advances in microscopy revealed that the sperm and the ova transmitted the hereditary characteristics from generation to generation, the problem nevertheless remained of how minute particles of biological matter could carry the vast number of characteristics that make up an individual organism.

The first really scientific advance in the study of inheritance was made by the Austrian monk Gregor Mendel who published a paper in 1866 which laid the foundations for the present-day science of genetics. He demonstrated that characteristics do not blend but pass from parents to offspring as discrete (separate) units. These units, which appear in the offspring in pairs, remain discrete and are passed on to subsequent generations by the male and female gametes which each contain a single unit. The Danish botanist Johannsen called these units **genes** in 1909, and the American geneticist Morgan, in 1912, demonstrated that they are carried on the chromosomes. Since the early 1900s the study of genetics has made great advances in explaining the nature of inheritance at both the level of the organism and at the level of the gene.

24.1 Mendel's work

Gregor Mendel was born in Moravia in 1822. In 1843 he joined an Augustinian monastery at Brünn in Austria (now Brno, in Czechoslovakia) where he took Holy Orders. From there he went to the University of Vienna where he spent two years studying natural history and mathematics before returning to the monastery in 1853. This choice of subjects undoubtedly had a significant influence on his subsequent work on inheritance in pea plants. Whilst in Vienna, Mendel had become interested in the process of hybridisation in plants and, in particular, the different forms in which hybrid offspring appear and the statistical relationships between them. This formed the basis of Mendel's scientific investigations on inheritance which he begin in the summer of 1856.

Mendel's success was due, in part, to his careful choice of experimental organism, the garden pea, *Pisum sativum*. He established that it had the following advantages over other species:

(1) There were several varieties available which had quite distinct characteristics.
(2) The plants were easy to cultivate.
(3) The reproductive structures were completely enclosed by the petals so that the plant was normally self-pollinating. This led to the varieties producing the same characteristics generation after generation, a phenomenon known as **pure breeding**.
(4) Artificial cross-breeding between varieties was possible and resulting hybrids were completely fertile. From the 34 varieties of garden pea, Mendel selected 22 varieties which showed clear-cut differences in characteristics and used these in his breeding experiments. The seven basic characteristics, or **traits**, that Mendel was interested in were length of stem, shape of seed, colour of seed, shape and colour of pod, position and colour of flower.

Many scientists before Mendel had performed similar experiments on plants but none had produced results which had the accuracy and detail of Mendel's, nor were they able to explain their results in terms of a mechanism of inheritance. The reasons for Mendel's success may be taken as a model of how to carry out a scientific investigation. They may be summarised as follows:

(1) Preliminary investigations were carried out to obtain familiarity with the experimental organism.
(2) All experiments were carefully planned so that attention was focused on only one variable at any time, thus simplifying the observations to be made.
(3) Meticulous care was taken in carrying out all techniques, thus preventing the introduction of other variables (see below for details).
(4) Accurate records were kept of all the experiments and the results obtained.
(5) Sufficient data were obtained to have statistical significance.

As Mendel stated,

'The value and utility of any experiment are determined by the fitness of the material to the purpose for which it is used.'

However, it is worth stating that there was an element of luck in Mendel's choice of experimental organism. The characters chosen by Mendel lacked many of the more complex genetic features which were later discovered, such as codominance (section 24.7.1), characteristics controlled by more than one pair of genes (section 24.7.6) and linkage (section 24.3).

24.1.1 Monohybrid inheritance and the principle of segregation

Mendel's earliest experiments involved selecting plants of two varieties which had clearly different characteristics, such as flowers distributed along the main stem (axial) or flowers at the tip of the stem (terminal). These plants, showing a single pair of contrasted characteristics, were grown for a number of generations. Seeds collected from axial plants always produced plants with axial flowers, whilst those from terminal plants always produced terminal flowers. This demonstrated to Mendel that he was using pure-breeding plants. With this information he was in a position to carry out hybridisation experiments (experimental crosses) using these plants. His experimental technique involved removing the anthers from a number of plants of one variety before self-fertilisation could have occurred. These he called 'female' plants. Pollen was then transferred, by means of a brush, from the anthers of another plant of the same variety to the stigmas of the 'female' plant. The experimental flowers were then enclosed in a small bag to prevent pollen from other plants reaching their stigmas. **Reciprocal crosses** were carried out by transferring pollen grains from axial plants to terminal plants and pollen grains from terminal plants to axial plants. In all cases the seeds subsequently collected from both sets of plants gave rise to plants with axial flowers. This characteristic, 'axial flower', shown by these first generation hybrid plants (subsequently called the **first filial generation** or **F_1 generation** by Bateson and Saunders in 1902) was termed **dominant** by Mendel. None of the F_1 plants produced terminal flowers.

The F_1 plants then had their flowers enclosed in bags (to prevent cross-pollination occurring) and were left to self-pollinate. The seeds collected from these F_1 plants were counted and planted the following spring to produce the **second filial generation** or **F_2 generation**. (An F_2 generation is always the result of allowing the F_1 generation to inbreed or, as in this case, to self-pollinate.) When these plants flowered, some bore axial flowers and others terminal flowers. In other words, the characteristic 'terminal flower', which was absent in the F_1 generation, had reappeared in the F_2 generation. Mendel reasoned that the terminal characteristic must have been present in the F_1 generation but as it failed to be expressed in this generation he termed it **recessive**. Of the 858 F_2 plants that Mendel obtained, 651 had axial flowers and 207 had terminal flowers. Mendel carried out a series of similar experiments involving in each case the inheritance of a single pair of contrasting characteristics. Seven pairs of contrasting characteristics were studied and the results of the experimental crosses are shown in table 24.1. In all cases the analyses of the results revealed that the ratios of dominant to recessive characteristics in the F_2 generation were approximately 3:1.

The example quoted above is typical of all Mendel's experiments involving the inheritance of a single characteristic (**monohybrid inheritance**) and may be summarised as follows.

Observations

Parents	axial flowers $\times$ terminal flowers		
F_1	all axial flowers		
F_2	651 axial flowers	207 terminal flowers	
F_2 ratio	3	:	1

On the basis of these, and similar results, Mendel drew the following conclusions.

(1) Since the original parental stocks were pure breeding, the axial variety must have possessed *two* axial factors and the terminal variety *two* terminal factors.

Table 24.1 The results of Mendel's experiments on the inheritance of seven pairs of contrasted characteristics. (The observed ratio of dominant to recessive characteristics approximates to the theoretical value of 3:1.)

Characteristic	Parental appearance		F_2 appearance		Ratio
	(dominant)	(recessive)	(dominant)	(recessive)	
length of stem	tall	dwarf	787	277	2.84:1
shape of seed	round	wrinkled	5 474	1 850	2.96:1
colour of seed	yellow	green	6 022	2 001	3.01:1
shape of pod	inflated	constricted	882	299	2.95:1
colour of pod	green	yellow	428	152	2.82:1
position of flower	axial	terminal	651	207	3.14:1
colour of flower	red	white	705	224	3.15:1
total			14 949	5 010	2.98:1

(2) The F_1 generation possessed *one* factor from *each* parent which were carried by the gametes.

(3) These factors do not blend in the F_1 generation but retain their individuality.

(4) The axial factor is dominant to the terminal factor, which is recessive.

The separation of the pair of parental factors, so that one factor is present in each gamete, became known as **Mendel's first law**, or the **principle of segregation**. This states that:

the characteristics of an organism are determined by internal factors which occur in pairs. Only one of a pair of such factors can be represented in a single gamete.

We now know that these factors determining characteristics, such as flower position, are regions of the chromosome known as **genes**.

The experimental procedure described above which was carried out by Mendel in the investigation of the inheritance of a *single* pair of contrasted characteristics is an example of a **monohybrid cross**. This may be represented in terms of symbols and placed in a modern context of gamete formation and fertilisation. By convention, the initial letter of the dominant characteristic is used as the symbol for the gene and its capital form (e.g. **A**) represents the dominant form of the gene (the dominant allele) while the lower case (e.g. **a**) represents the recessive allele. All of the terms and symbols described above are used in genetics and are summarised in table 24.2.

Fig 24.1 shows the correct way to describe a monohybrid cross or arrive at the solution to a genetics problem involving the inheritance of a single pair of contrasted characteristics.

Let:

A represent axial flower (dominant)
a represent terminal flower (recessive)

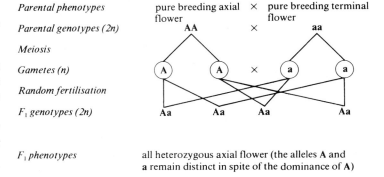

Parental phenotypes	pure breeding axial flower × pure breeding terminal flower
Parental genotypes (2n)	AA × aa
Meiosis	
Gametes (n)	A A × a a
Random fertilisation	
F_1 *genotypes (2n)*	Aa Aa Aa Aa
F_1 *phenotypes*	all heterozygous axial flower (the alleles **A** and **a** remain distinct in spite of the dominance of **A**)

The F_1 generation were self-pollinated

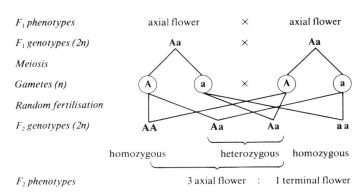

F_1 *phenotypes*	axial flower × axial flower
F_1 *genotypes (2n)*	Aa × Aa
Meiosis	
Gametes (n)	A a × A a
Random fertilisation	
F_2 *genotypes (2n)*	AA Aa Aa aa
	homozygous heterozygous homozygous
F_2 *phenotypes*	3 axial flower : 1 terminal flower

Fig 24.1 *Full genetic explanation of one of Mendel's monohybrid crosses. (2 n represents the diploid condition, n represents the haploid condition; see section 23.1.2.)*

Table 24.2 Glossary of common genetic terms with examples based on fig 24.1.

Genetic term	Explanation	Example
gene	The basic unit of inheritance for a given characteristic	flower position
allele	One of a number of alternative forms of the same gene responsible for determining contrasting characteristics	**A** or **a**
locus	Position of an allele within a DNA molecule	
homozygous	The diploid condition in which the alleles at a given locus are identical	**AA** or **aa**
heterozygous	The diploid condition in which the alleles at a given locus are different	**Aa**
phenotype	The observable characteristics of an individual usually resulting from the interaction between the genotype and the environment in which development occurs	axial, terminal
genotype	The genetic constitution of an organism with respect to the alleles under consideration	**AA, Aa, aa**
dominant	The allele which influences the appearance of the phenotype even in the presence of an alternative allele	**A**
recessive	The allele which influences the appearance of the phenotype only in the presence of another identical allele	**a**
F_1 generation	The generation produced by crossing homozygous parental stocks	
F_2 generation	The generation produced by crossing two F_1 organisms	

The ratio of dominant phenotypes to recessive phenotypes of 3:1 is called the **monohybrid ratio**. Mendel's conclusions regarding the transfer of a single characteristic by each gamete and the resulting genotypes can be demonstrated by mathematical probability. The probability of a gamete cell from a heterozygous F_1 parent containing either the dominant allele **A** or the recessive allele **a** is 50% or $\frac{1}{2}$. If each gamete is represented by $\frac{1}{2}$, the number of possible combinations of F_2 genotypes is represented by $\frac{1}{2} \times \frac{1}{2} = \frac{1}{4}$. Hence there are four possible F_2 genotypes. The statistical probability of the **A** and **a** containing gametes combining by random fertilisation is shown in fig 24.2. As a result of dominance the phenotypic appearance will be 3 dominant phenotypes : 1 recessive phenotype. The results of Mendel's breeding experiments bear out this theoretical ratio as shown in table 24.1.

24.1 If a pure strain of mice with brown-coloured fur are allowed to breed with a pure strain of mice with grey-coloured fur they produce offspring having brown-coloured fur. If the F_1 mice are allowed to interbreed they produce an F_2 generation with fur colour in the proportion of three brown-coloured to one grey.
(a) Explain these results fully.
(b) What would be the result of mating a brown-coloured heterozygote from the F_2 generation with the original grey-coloured parent?

24.1.2 Test cross

The genotype of an F_1 organism, produced by the breeding of homozygous dominant and homozygous recessive parents, is heterozygous but shows the dominant phenotype. An organism displaying the recessive phenotype must have a genotype which is homozygous for the recessive allele. In the case of F_2 organisms showing the dominant phenotype the genotype may be either homozygous or heterozygous. It may be of interest to a

Let the probability of the alleles **A** and **a** appearing in the heterozygote **(Aa)** = 1,
therefore $A = \frac{1}{2}$
$a = \frac{1}{2}$
Using these values the probability of each genotype and phenotype appearing in the F_2 generation can be demonstrated as shown below:

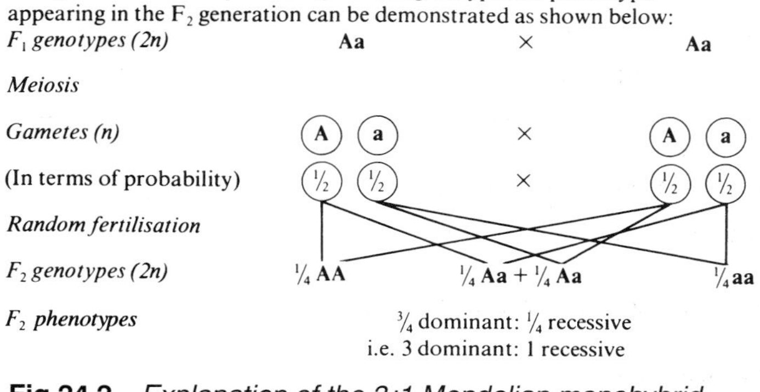

Fig 24.2 *Explanation of the 3:1 Mendelian monohybrid ratio in terms of probability.*

breeder to know the genotype and the only way in which it can be determined is to carry out a breeding experiment. This involves the use of a technique known as **test cross**. By crossing an organism having an unknown genotype with a homozygous recessive organism it is possible to determine an unknown genotype within one breeding generation. For example in the fruit fly, *Drosophila*, long wing is dominant to vestigial wing. The genotype of a long wing *Drosophila* may be homozygous (**LL**) or heterozygous (**Ll**). In order to establish which is the correct genotype the fly is test crossed with a double recessive (**ll**) vestigial wing fly. If the test cross offspring are all long wing the unknown genotype is homozygous dominant. A ratio of 1 long wing : 1 vestigial wing indicates that the unknown is heterozygous (fig 24.3).

24.2 Why is it not possible to use a homozygous dominant organism (such as **TT**) in a test cross experiment to determine the genotype of an organism showing the dominant phenotype? Illustrate your answer fully using appropriate genetic symbols.

24.1.3 Dihybrid inheritance and the principle of independent assortment

Having established that it was possible to predict the outcome of breeding crosses involving a single pair of contrasted characteristics, Mendel turned his attention to the inheritance of two pairs of contrasted characteristics. Since two pairs of alleles are found in the heterozygotes, this condition is known as **dihybrid inheritance**.

In one of his experiments Mendel used pea shape and pea cotyledon colour as the characteristics. Using the same techniques as described in section 24.1.1, he crossed pure-breeding (homozygous) plants having round and yellow peas with pure-breeding plants having wrinkled and green peas. The F_1 generation seeds were round and yellow. Mendel knew that these characteristics were dominant from earlier monohybrid breeding experiments but it was the nature and number of organisms of the F_2 generation produced from the self-pollination of the F_1 plants that now interested him. He collected a total of 556 F_2 seeds from the F_1 generation which showed the following characteristics:

315 round and yellow,
101 wrinkled and yellow,
108 round and green,
32 wrinkled and green.

The proportions of each phenotype approximated to a ratio of 9 : 3 : 3 : 1. This is known as the **dihybrid ratio**. Mendel made two deductions from these observations.

(1) Two new combinations of characteristics had appeared in the F_2 generation: wrinkled and yellow, and round and green.

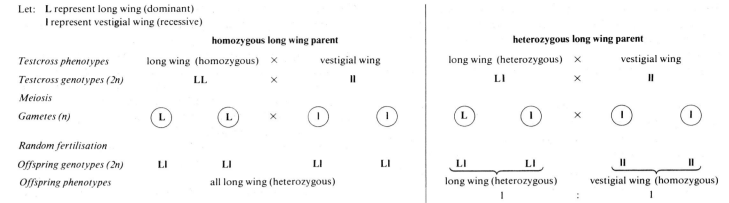

Fig 24.3 *A full genetic explanation of how to determine the genotype of an organism showing a dominant characteristic. This technique is known as a test cross, and produces offspring phenotypes as shown.*

(2) The ratios of each pair of **allelomorphic** characteristics (phenotypes determined by different alleles) appeared in the monohybrid ratio of 3:1, that is 423 round to 133 wrinkled, and 416 yellow to 140 green.

On the basis of these results Mendel was able to state that the two pairs of characteristics (seed shape and colour), whilst combining in the F_1 generation, separate and behave independently from one another in subsequent generations. This forms the basis of **Mendel's second law** or the **principle of independent assortment** which states that:

any one of a pair of characteristics may combine with either one of another pair.

The above experiment can be written out in terms of our present knowledge of genetics as shown in fig 24.4*a*. As a result of separation (segregation) of alleles (**R**, **r**, **Y** and **y**) and their independent assortment (rearrangement or **recombination**), four possible arrangements of alleles can be found in each of the male and female gametes. In order to demonstrate all the possible combinations of gametes that occur during random fertilisation a **Punnett square** is used. This is a grid named after the Cambridge geneticist R. C. Punnett and its value lies in minimising the errors which can occur when listing all possible combinations of gametes. It is advisable when filling in the Punnett square to enter all the 'male' gametes first in the vertical squares and then enter all the 'female' gametes in the horizontal squares. Likewise, when determining the F_2 phenotypes, it is advisable to mark off identical phenotypes in some easily identifiable way, as shown in fig 24.4*b*. From figs 24.4*a* and *b*, which are based on Mendel's first and second laws, it can

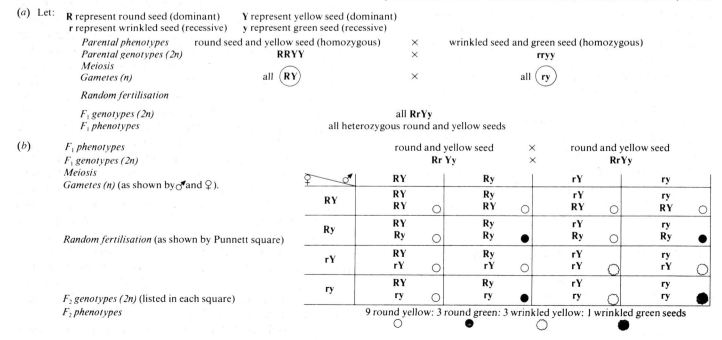

Fig 24.4 *(a) Stages in the formation of F_1 phenotypes from homozygous parents. This is an example of dihybrid cross since two characteristics are being considered. (b) Use of the Punnett square to show all possible combinations of gametes to form F_2 genotypes.*

be seen that each F_1 male and female genotype can give rise to gametes with the following combination of alleles:

R can only be present with **Y** or **y** (not **r**), that is **RY** or **Ry**,

r can only be present with **Y** or **y** (not **R**), that is **rY** or **ry**.

Thus there is a 1 in 4 chance of any gamete containing any of the four allele combinations shown above.

From a consideration of monohybrid inheritance, where $\frac{3}{4}$ of the F_2 phenotypes show the dominant allele and $\frac{1}{4}$ the recessive allele, the probability of the four alleles appearing in any F_2 phenotype is as follows:

round (dominant)	$\frac{3}{4}$
yellow (dominant)	$\frac{3}{4}$
wrinkled (recessive)	$\frac{1}{4}$
green (recessive)	$\frac{1}{4}$

Hence the probability of the following combinations of alleles appearing in the F_2 phenotypes is as follows:

round and yellow	=	$\frac{3}{4} \times \frac{3}{4}$	=	$\frac{9}{16}$
round and green	=	$\frac{3}{4} \times \frac{1}{4}$	=	$\frac{3}{16}$
wrinkled and yellow	=	$\frac{1}{4} \times \frac{3}{4}$	=	$\frac{3}{16}$
wrinkled and green	=	$\frac{1}{4} \times \frac{1}{4}$	=	$\frac{1}{16}$

The results of Mendel's breeding experiments with two pairs of contrasted characteristics approximated to the theoretical values shown above.

24.3 In the guinea pig (*Cavia*), there are two alleles for hair colour, black and white, and two alleles for hair length, short and long. In a breeding experiment all the F_1 phenotypes produced from a cross between pure-breeding, short black-haired and pure-breeding, long white-haired parents had short black hair. Explain (*a*) which alleles are dominant, and (*b*) the expected proportions of F_2 phenotypes.

24.4 Flower colour in sweet pea plants is determined by two allelomorphic pairs of genes (**R,r**, and **S,s**). If at least one dominant gene from each allelomorphic pair is present the flowers are purple. All other genotypes are white.

If two purple plants, each having the genotype **RrSs**, are crossed, what will be the phenotypic ratio of the offspring?

24.1.4 Summary of Mendel's hypotheses

The following summary includes terms taken from our present knowledge of the nature of genetics.

(1) Each characteristic of an organism is controlled by a pair of alleles.
(2) If an organism has two unlike alleles for a given characteristic, one may be expressed (the dominant allele) to the total exclusion of the other (the recessive allele).
(3) During meiosis each pair of alleles separates (segregates) and each gamete receives one of each pair of alleles (*the principle of segregation*).
(4) During gamete formation in each sex, either one of a pair of alleles may enter the same gamete cell (combine randomly) with either one of another pair (*the principle of independent assortment*).
(5) Each allele is transmitted from generation to generation as a discrete unchanging unit.
(6) Each organism inherits one allele (for each characteristic) from each parent.

NB The mechanism of dihybrid inheritance, the examples quoted in this section and the typical dihybrid ratio of $9:3:3:1$ only apply to characteristics controlled by genes on **different** chromosomes. Genes situated on the **same** chromosome may not show this pattern of independent assortment, as described in section 24.3.

24.2 The chromosomal basis of inheritance

Mendel published his results and hypotheses in 1866 in a journal, *The Proceedings of the Brünn Natural History Society*, which was sent to most of the learned scientific societies throughout the world. In all cases they failed to appreciate the importance of his findings, possibly because scientists at the time were unable to relate them to any physical structures in the gametes by which the hereditary factors might be transmitted from parent to offspring.

By 1900, as a result of improvements in the optical properties of microscopes and advances in cytological techniques, the behaviour of chromosomes in gametes and zygotes had been observed. In 1875 Hertwig noted that during the fertilisation of sea urchin eggs two nuclei, one from the sperm and one from the egg, fused together. Boverin, in 1902, demonstrated the importance of the nucleus in controlling the development of characteristics in organisms, and in 1882 Flemming clarified the chromosomal events involved in mitosis.

In 1900 the significance of Mendel's work was realised almost simultaneously by three scientists, de Vries, Correns and Tschermak. In fact, it was Correns who summarised Mendel's conclusions in the familiar form of two principles and coined the term '**factor**', Mendel having used the term '*elemente*' to describe the hereditary unit. It was an American, William Sutton, however, who noticed the striking similarities between the behaviour of chromosomes during gamete formation and fertilisation, and the transmission of Mendel's hereditary factors. These have been summarised in table 24.3.

On the basis of the evidence suggested above, Sutton and Boveri proposed that chromosomes were the carriers of Mendel's factors, the so-called **chromosome theory of heredity**. According to this theory, each

Table 24.3 A summary of the similarities between events occurring during meiosis and fertilisation and Mendel's hypotheses.

Meiosis and fertilisation	Mendel's hypotheses
Diploid cells contain *pairs* of chromosomes(homologous chromosomes)	Characteristics are controlled by *pairs* of factors
Homologous chromosomes *separate* during meiosis	Pairs of factors *separate* during gamete formation
One homologous chromosome passes into each gamete cell	Each gamete receives *one* factor
Only the *nucleus* of the male gamete fuses with the egg cell nucleus	Factors are transmitted from generation to generation as *discrete units*
Homologous pairs of chromosomes are restored at fertilisation, each gamete (♂ and ♀) contributing *one* homologous chromosome	Each organism inherits *one* factor from each parent

pair of factors is carried by a pair of homologous chromosomes, with each chromosome carrying one of the factors. Since the number of characteristics of any organism vastly outnumber the chromosomes, as revealed by microscopy, each chromosome must carry many factors.

The term **factor** as the basic unit of heredity was replaced by Johannsen, in 1909, with the term **gene**. Whilst gene is used to describe the unit of heredity, it is the alternative forms of the gene or **alleles** which influence phenotypic expression. Alleles are the alternative forms in which a gene may exist and they occupy the same **loci** (singular **locus**) on **homologous chromosomes**, as shown in fig 24.5.

Mendel's principle of segregation of factors could now be explained in terms of the separation (segregation) of homologous chromosomes which occurs during anaphase I of meiosis and the random distribution of alleles into gamete cells. These events are summarised in fig 24.6.

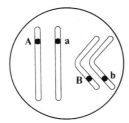

Fig 24.5 *A cell showing two pairs of homologous chromosomes. The positions of two different gene loci are indicated by circles. In this example two gene loci are shown situated on different pairs of homologous chromosomes and each gene is present as two alleles.*

24.2.1 Chromosomal explanation of independent assortment

Mendel's principle of independent assortment may also be explained in terms of the movement of chromosomes during meiosis. During gamete formation the distribution of each allele from a pair of homologous chromosomes is entirely independent of the distribution of alleles of other pairs. This situation is described in fig 24.7. It is the random alignment or assortment of homologous chromosomes on the equatorial spindle during metaphase I of meiosis, and their subsequent separation during metaphase I and anaphase I, that leads to the variety of allele recombinations in the gamete cells. It is possible to predict the number of allele combinations in either the male or female gamete using the general formula 2^n, where n = haploid number of chromosomes. In the case of humans, where $n = 23$, the possible number of different combinations is $2^{23} = 8\,388\,608$.

> **24.5** The deposition of starch in pollen grains in maize is controlled by the presence of one allele of a certain gene. The other allele of that gene results in no starch being deposited. Explain in terms of meiosis why half the pollen grains produced by a heterozygous maize plant contain starch.
>
> **24.6** Calculate the number of different combinations of chromosomes in the pollen grains of the crocus (*Crocus balansae*) which has a diploid number of six ($2n = 6$).

24.3 Linkage

All the situations and examples discussed so far in this chapter have dealt with the inheritance of genes situated on different chromosomes. Cytological studies have revealed that humans possess 46 chromosomes in all the somatic (body) cells. Since humans possess thousands of characteristics such as blood group, eye colour and the ability to secrete insulin, it follows that each chromosome must carry a large number of genes.

Genes situated on the same chromosome are said to be **linked**. All genes on a single chromosome form a **linkage group** and usually pass into the same gamete and are inherited together. As a result of this, genes belonging to the same linkage group usually do not show independent assortment. Since these genes do not conform to Mendel's principle of independent assortment they fail to produce the expected 9:3:3:1 ratio in a breeding situation involving the inheritance of two pairs of contrasted characteristics (dihybrid inheritance). In these situations a variety of ratios are produced which may be explained quite simply now that we possess a basic understanding of the mechanisms of inheritance as revealed by Mendel. (At this point it is worth

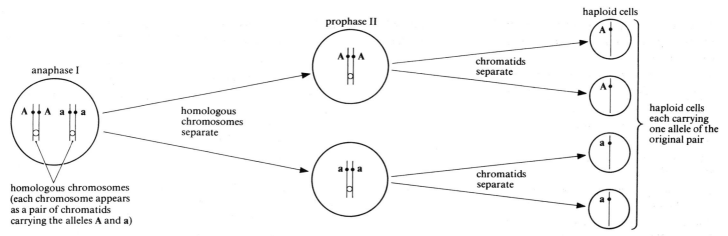

Fig 24.6 *Mendel's principle of segregation of factors (alleles)* **A** *and* **a** *described in terms of the separation of homologous chromosomes which occurs during meiosis.*

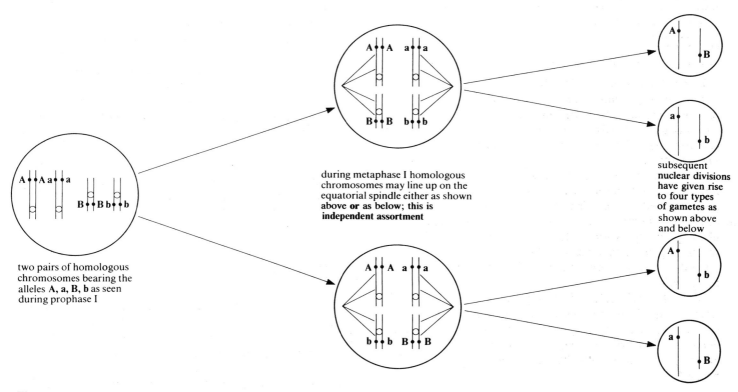

Fig 24.7 *Mendel's principle of independent assortment of factors (alleles)* **A**, **a**, **B**, **b**, *described in terms of the separation of homologous chromosomes which occurs during meiosis (compare fig 23.16).*

re-emphasising Mendel's good fortune in choosing to study the inheritance of pairs of characteristics located on *different* chromosomes.) In *Drosophila* the genes for body colour and wing length have the following **allelomorphs** (phenotypic characteristics determined by different alleles): grey and black body, and long and vestigial (short) wings. Grey body and long wing are dominant. If pure-breeding grey-bodied long-winged *Drosophila* are crossed with black-bodied vestigial-winged *Drosophila*, the expected F₂ phenotypic ratio would be 9:3:3:1. This would indicate a normal case of Mendelian dihybrid inheritance with random assortment resulting from the genes for body

colour and wing length being situated on non-homologous chromosomes. However this result is not obtained. Instead the F₂ show an approximately 3:1 ratio of parental phenotypes. This may be explained by assuming that the genes for body colour and wing length are found on the same chromosome, that is they are linked, as shown in fig 24.8.

In practice, though, this 3:1 ratio is never achieved and four phenotypes are invariably produced. This is because **total** linkage is rare. Most breeding experiments involving linkage produce approximately equal numbers of the parental phenotypes and a significantly smaller number of

Let:
    G represent grey body (dominant)
    g represent black body (recessive)
    L represent long wing (dominant)
    l represent vestigial wing (recessive)

Parental phenotypes   grey body, long wing   ×   black body, vestigial wing

Parental genotypes (2n)

Meiosis

Gametes (n)

Random fertilisation

F₁ genotypes (2n)

F₁ phenotypes   all heterozygous grey body, long-winged offspring

The F₁ generation was allowed to interbreed

F₁ phenotypes   grey body, long wing   ×   grey body, long wing

F₁ genotypes (2n)

Meiosis

Gametes (n)

Random fertilisation

F₂ genotypes (2n)

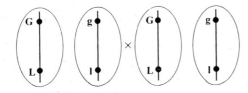

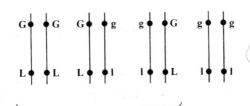

F₂ phenotypes   3 grey body, long wing: 1 black body, vestigial wing

phenotypes showing new combinations of characteristics, also in equal numbers. These latter phenotypes are described as **recombinants**. From this it is possible to produce the following definition of linkage:

> Two or more genes are said to be linked when phenotypes with new gene combinations (recombinants) occur less frequently than the parental phenotypes.

The events leading to the discovery of linkage by the American Thomas H. Morgan may be summarised in one of his experiments in which he predicted the results of a test cross between heterozygous grey-bodied, long-winged *Drosophila* (the F₁ generation of the experimental cross shown in fig 24.8) and homozygous recessive black-bodied vestigial-winged *Drosophila*. The two possible outcomes were predicted as follows:

(1) If the four alleles for grey and black body, and long and vestigal wings, were on different pairs of chromosomes (that is *not* linked) they should show independent assortment and produce the following phenotypic ratios:

     1 grey body, long wing : 1 grey body, vestigial wing;
     1 black body, long wing : 1 black body, vestigial wing.

(2) If the alleles for body colour and wing length were situated on the same pair of chromosomes (that is linked) the following phenotypic ratio would be produced:

     1 grey body, long wing : 1 black body, vestigial wing.
     An explanation of these predictions is given in fig 24.9.

Morgan carried out this test cross several times and never obtained either of the predicted outcomes. Each time, he obtained the following results:

     41.5%   grey body long wing
     41.5%   black body vestigial wing
     8.5%   grey body vestigial wing
     8.5%   black body long wing

On the basis of these results he postulated that:

(1) the genes were located on chromosomes;
(2) both the genes were situated on the same chromosome, that is linked;
(3) the alleles for each gene were on homologous chromosomes;
(4) alleles were exchanged between homologous chromosomes during meiosis.

The reappearance of recombinant alleles in 17% of the offspring was explained in terms of point (4). This is known as **crossing-over**.

Fig 24.8 *Genetic explanation of the 3 : 1 ratio produced in F₂ phenotypes as a result of linkage.*

(a) If the four alleles are situated on different pairs of chromosomes

Testcross phenotypes	grey body, long wing (heterozygous)	×	black body, vestigial wing (homozygous)

Testcross genotypes (2n) **GgLl** × **ggll**

Meiosis

Gametes (n)
(as shown by
♂ and ♀ in Punnett
square)

Random fertilisation
(as shown in Punnett
square)

♀ \ ♂	GL	Gl	gL	gl
gl	GL gl	Gl gl	gL gl	gl gl

Offspring genotypes (2n)
(listed in each square)

Offspring phenotypes 1 grey body, long wing: 1 grey body, vestigial wing:
1 black body, long wing: 1 black body, vestigial wing

(b) If the four alleles are situated on the same pair of chromosomes

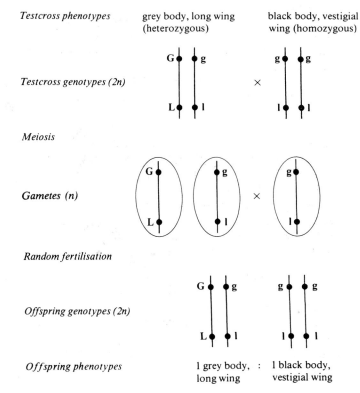

Testcross phenotypes grey body, long wing (heterozygous) black body, vestigial wing (homozygous)

Testcross genotypes (2n)

Meiosis

Gametes (n)

Random fertilisation

Offspring genotypes (2n)

Offspring phenotypes   1 grey body, long wing : 1 black body, vestigial wing

Fig 24.9 *(a) and (b) Genetic explanation of Morgan's predictions.*

24.7 A homozygous purple-flowered short-stemmed plant was crossed with a homozygous red-flowered long-stemmed plant and the F_1 phenotypes had purple flowers and short stems. When the F_1 generation was test crossed with a double homozygous recessive plant the following progeny were produced.

52 purple flower, short stem
47 purple flower, long stem
49 red flower, short stem
45 red flower, long stem
Explain these results fully.

24.3.1 Crossing-over and crossover values

In 1909 the Belgian cytologist Janssens observed **chiasmata formation** during prophase I of meiosis (section 23.4). The genetic significance of this process was clarified by Morgan who proposed that crossing-over of alleles occurred as a result of the breakage and recombination of homologous chromosomes during chiasmata. Subsequent research based on the microscopic examination of cells and recombinant phenotypic ratios has confirmed that crossover of genetic material occurs between virtually all homologous chromosomes during meiosis. The alleles of parental linkage groups separate and new associations of alleles are formed in the gamete cells, a process known as **genetic recombination**. Offspring formed from these gametes showing 'new' combinations of characteristics are known as **recombinants**. Thus crossing-over is a major source of observable genetic variation within populations.

The behaviour of a pair of homologous chromosomes in *Drosophila*, carrying the alleles grey body and long wing (both dominant) and black body and vestigial wing (both recessive), during formation of chiasmata may be used to illustrate the principle of crossing-over. A cross between a male heterozygous grey-bodied long-winged *Drosophila* and a female homozygous black-bodied vestigial-winged *Drosophila* produced heterozygous F_1 offspring with grey bodies and long wings as shown in fig 24.10.

Test crossing the F_1 generation flies with homozygous double recessive flies produced the following results.

Parental phenotypes	grey body, long wing	965
	black body, vestigial wing	944

Recombinant phenotypes	black body, long wing	206
	grey body, vestigial wing	185

These results indicate that the genes for body colour and wing length are linked. (Remember that a hybrid cross between an F_1 heterozygote and a double homozygous recessive would have produced a 1:1:1:1 phenotypic ratio if the genes had been situated on different chromosomes and therefore had undergone random assortment.) Using

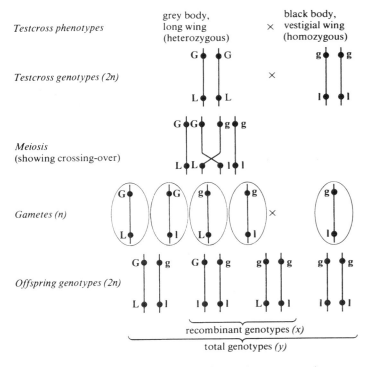

Fig 24.10 *Genetic explanation of crossing-over and the reappearance of recombinant genotypes. The recombination frequency can be calculated by counting the number of individuals showing recombination and the total number of individuals and applying the following formula: recombination frequency (%) = x/y × 100.*

the figures obtained from the above cross it is possible to calculate the recombination frequency of the genes for body colour and wing length.

The **recombination frequency** is calculated using the formula:

$$\frac{\text{number of individuals showing recombination}}{\text{number of offspring}} \times 100$$

From the example above the recombination frequency (%) is:

$$\frac{(206 + 185)}{(965 + 944) + (206 + 185)} \times 100$$

$$= \frac{391}{2300} \times 100$$

$$= 17\%$$

This value indicates the number of crossovers which have occurred during gamete formation. A. H. Sturtevant, a student of Morgan, postulated that the recombinant frequency or **crossover frequency (crossover value (COV))** demonstrated that genes are arranged linearly along the chromosome. More importantly, he suggested that the crossover frequency reflects the relative positions of genes on chromosomes because the further apart linked genes are on the chromosomes, the greater the possibility of crossing-over occurring between them, that is the greater the crossover frequency (fig 24.11).

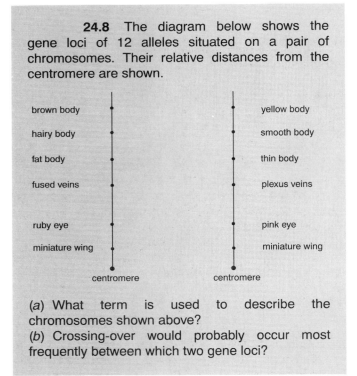

24.8 The diagram below shows the gene loci of 12 alleles situated on a pair of chromosomes. Their relative distances from the centromere are shown.

(a) What term is used to describe the chromosomes shown above?
(b) Crossing-over would probably occur most frequently between which two gene loci?

24.4   Gene mapping

The major significance of calculating crossover frequencies is that it enables geneticists to produce maps showing the relative positions of genes on chromosomes. Chromosome maps are constructed by directly converting the crossover frequency or value between genes into hypothetical distances along the chromosome. A crossover frequency or value (COV) of 4% between genes **A** and **B** means that those genes are situated 4 units apart on the same chromosome. A COV of 9% for a pair of genes **A** and **C** would indicate that they were 9 units apart, but it would not indicate the linear sequence of the genes, as shown in fig 24.12.

In practice it is usual to determine crossover values for at least three genes at once, as this **triangulation** process enables the sequence of the genes to be determined as well as the distance between them. Consider the following

Fig 24.11 *Three gene loci represented by A, B and C are shown on the chromosome. Crossing-over and separation of genes is more likely to occur between B and C or A and B since the frequency of crossing-over is related to the distance between the genes.*

Fig 24.12 *Possible gene loci of A, B and C on the basis of the data presented.*

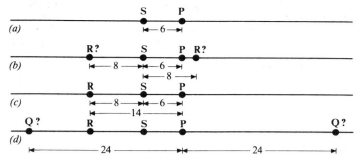

Fig 24.13 *Use of the triangulation process to establish the positions of genes P, Q, R and S on a chromosome.*

values as determined by a series of breeding experiments involving four genes **P**, **Q**, **R** and **S**:

$$P - Q = 24\%$$
$$R - P = 14\%$$
$$R - S = 8\%$$
$$S - P = 6\%$$

To calculate the sequence and distances apart of the genes, a line is drawn representing the chromosome and the following procedure carried out.

(1) Insert the positions of the genes with the least COV in the middle of the chromosome, that is $S - P = 6\%$ (fig 24.13*a*).

(2) Examine the next largest COV, that is $R - S = 8\%$, and insert both possible positions of **R** on the chromosome, relative to **S** (fig 24.13*b*).

(3) Repeat the procedure for the next largest COV, that is $R - P = 14\%$. This indicates that the right-hand position of **R** is incorrect (fig 24.13*c*).

(4) Repeat the procedure for the COV for $P - Q = 24\%$ (fig 24.13*d*). The position of **Q** cannot be ascertained without additional information. If, for example, the COV for $Q - R = 10\%$ this would confirm the left-hand position for gene **Q**.

A problem which arises in preparing chromosome maps is that of **double crossover**, particularly when considering genes which are widely separated, since the number of apparent crossovers will be less than the actual number. For example, if crossovers occur between alleles **A** and **B** and **B** and **C** in fig 24.14, **A** and **C** will still appear linked, but the chromosome will now carry the recessive allele **b**.

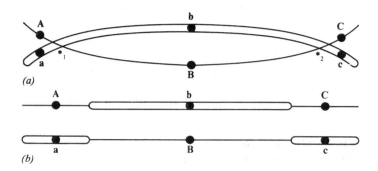

Fig 24.14 *(a) A pair of homologous chromatids, one carrying the dominant alleles A, B and C and the other carrying the recessive alleles a, b and c. Crossing-over occurs at two points $*_1$ and $*_2$. (b) The result of separation of the chromatids in which the sequences of alleles are different, although the sequences of gene loci and the distances between them remain the same.*

24.5 Linkage groups and chromosomes

Much of the evidence presented in this chapter so far has shown how our knowledge of the mechanics of inheritance has gradually increased. Most of the research into genetics in the early part of this century involved establishing the role of genes in inheritance. Morgan's research with the fruit fly (*Drosophila melanogaster*) established that the majority of phenotypic characteristics were transmitted together in four groups and these were called **linkage groups**. It was observed that the number of linkage groups corresponded to the number of pairs of chromosomes.

Studies on other organisms produced similar results. Breeding experiments using a variety of organisms revealed that some linkage groups were larger than others (that is they carried more genes). Examination of chromosomes in these organisms showed that they varied in length. Morgan demonstrated that there was a distinct relationship between these observations. This provided further confirmatory evidence that genes were located on chromosomes.

24.9 In maize the genes for coloured seed and full seed are dominant to the genes for colourless seed and shrunken seed. Pure-breeding strains of the double dominant variety were crossed with the double recessive variety and a test cross of the F_1 generation produced the following results.

coloured, full seed	380
colourless, shrunken seed	396
coloured, shrunken seed	14
colourless, full seed	10

Calculate the distance in units between the genes for coloured seed and seed shape on the chromosomes.

24.5.1 Giant chromosomes and genes

In 1913 Sturtevant began his work on mapping the positions of genes on the chromosomes of *Drosophila* but it was 21 years before there was a possibility of linking visible structures on chromosomes with genes. In 1934, it was observed that the chromosomes in the salivary gland cells of *Drosophila* were about 100 times larger than chromosomes from other body cells. For some reason these chromosomes duplicate without separating until there are several thousand lying side by side. When stained they can be seen with the light microscope and appear to be made up of alternating light and dark bands. Each chromosome has its own distinctive pattern of bands (fig 24.15). It was originally thought, or rather hoped, that these bands were genes, but this is not the case. Phenotypic abnormalities may be artificially induced in *Drosophila* and these correlate with changes in chromosomal banding patterns, as observed with the microscope. These phenotypic and chromosomal abnormalities in turn correlate with gene loci shown on chromosome maps which have been constructed on the basis of crossover values obtained from breeding experiments. Therefore it is possible to say that the bands on the chromosomes indicate the *positions* of genes but are not themselves genes.

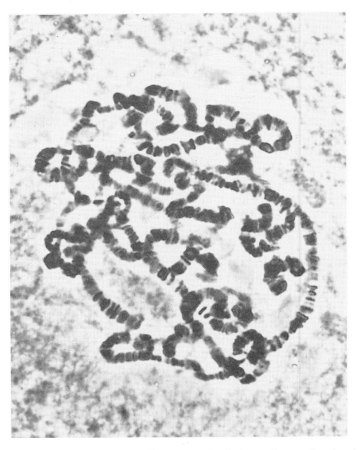

Fig 24.15 *Giant chromosomes from the salivary glands of* Drosophila melanogaster. *Four pairs of chromosomes are shown joined at their centromeres.*

24.6 Sex determination

The technique of relating phenotypic characteristics of organisms to the structure of their chromosomes, as described in earlier sections, is seen most clearly in the determination of sex. In *Drosophila* the observed phenotypic differences between the two sexes appear to be related to the differences in the size of their chromosomes, as shown in fig 24.16. Examination of the chromosome structure of a range of animals revealed that males and females showed certain chromosomal differences. Pairs of chromosomes (homologous chromosomes) are found in all cells, but one pair of chromosomes always shows differences between the sexes. These are the **sex chromosomes** or **heterosomes**. All other chromosomes are known as **autosomal chromosomes** or **autosomes**. As can be seen in fig 24.16, *Drosophila* has four pairs of chromosomes. Three pairs appear identical in both sexes (numbers II, III and IV), but the other pair, whilst appearing identical in the female, differ in the male. The chromosomes are known as X and Y chromosomes (see fig 24.17), and the genotype of the female is XX and that of the male is XY. These characteristic sex genotypes are found in most animals, including humans; but in the case of birds (including poultry), moths and butterflies the sex genotypes are reversed: the females are XY and the males are XX. In some insects, such as the grasshopper, the Y chromosome may be absent entirely and so the male has the genotype XO (see fig 23.13).

In the production of gametes the sex chromosomes segregate in typical Mendelian fashion. For example, in mammals each ovum contains an X chromosome; in males one half of the sperm contain an X chromosome and the

Fig 24.16 *Structure of chromosomes in male and female* Drosophila melanogaster. *Four pairs of chromosomes are shown. The sex chromosomes are numbered I.*

Fig 24.17 *Human sex chromosomes as they appear during metaphase of mitosis.*

other half contain a Y chromosome as shown in fig 24.18. The sex of the offspring depends upon which type of sperm fertilises the ovum. The sex having the XX genotype is described as **homogametic** as it produces gamete cells containing only X chromosomes. Organisms with the XY genotype are described as **heterogametic** since half their gametes contain the X chromosome and half the Y chromosome. In humans, the genotypic sex of an individual is determined by examining non-dividing cells. One X chromosome always appears in the active state, which has the normal appearance. If another is present, it is seen in a resting state as a tightly coiled dark-staining body called the **Barr body**. The number of Barr bodies is always one less than the number of X chromosomes present, that is male (XY) = 0, female (XX) = 1. The function of the Y chromosome appears to vary according to the species. In humans the presence of a Y chromosome controls the differentiation of the testes which subsequently influences the development of the genital organs and male characteristics (section 21.6.4). In some organisms, however, the Y chromosome does not carry genes concerned with sex. In fact it is described as genetically inert or genetically empty since it carries so few genes. In *Drosophila* it is thought that the genes determining male characteristics are carried on the autosomes and their phenotypic effects are masked by the presence of a pair of X chromosomes. Male characteristics, on the other hand, appear in the presence of a single X chromosome. This is an example of **sex-limited inheritance**, as opposed to sex-linked inheritance, and in humans is thought to cause suppression of the genes for the growth of a beard in females.

Morgan and his co-workers noticed that inheritance of eye colour in *Drosophila* was related to the sex of the parent flies. Red eye is dominant over white eye. A red-eyed male crossed with a white-eyed female produced equal numbers of F_1 red-eyed females and white-eyed males (fig 24.19a). A white-eyed male, however, crossed with a red-eyed female produced equal numbers of F_1 red-eyed males and females (fig 24.19b). Inbreeding these F_1 flies produced red-eyed females, red-eyed males and white-eyed males but *no* white-eyed females (fig 24.19c). The fact that male flies showed the recessive characteristic more frequently than female flies suggested that the white eye recessive allele was present on the X chromosome and that the Y chromosome lacked the eye colour gene. To test this hypothesis Morgan crossed the original white-eyed male with an F_1 red-eyed female (fig 24.19d). The offspring included red-eyed and white-eyed males and females. From this Morgan rightly concluded that only the X chromosome carries the gene for eye colour. There is no gene locus for eye colour on the Y chromosome. This phenomenon is known as **sex linkage**.

24.10 In *Drosophila* the genes for wing length and for eye colour are sex-linked. Normal wing and red eye are dominant to miniature wing and white eye.

(a) In a cross between a miniature wing, red-eyed male and a homozygous normal wing, white-eyed female, explain fully the appearance of (i) the F_1 and (ii) the F_2 generations.

(b) Crossing a female from the F_1 generation above with a miniature wing, white-eyed male gave the following results:

normal wing, white-eyed males and females	35
normal wing, red-eyed males and females	17
miniature wing, white-eyed males and females	18
miniature wing, red-eyed males and females	36

Account for the appearance and numbers of the phenotypes shown above.

24.6.1 Sex linkage

Genes carried on the sex chromosomes are said to be sex-linked. In the case of the heterogametic sex there is a portion of the X chromosome for which there is no homologous region of the Y chromosome (fig 24.20). Characteristics determined by genes carried on the non-homologous portion of the X chromosome therefore appear in males even if they are recessive. This special form of linkage explains the inheritance of **sex-linked traits** such as red–green colour blindness, premature balding and haemophilia. Haemophilia or 'bleeder's disease' is a sex-linked recessive condition which prevents the formation of factor VIII, an important factor in increasing the rate of blood clotting. The gene for factor VIII is carried on the non-homologous portion of the X chromosome and can appear in two allelomorphic forms: normal (dominant) and mutant (recessive). The following possible genotypes and phenotypes can occur:

genotype	phenotype
$X^H X^H$	normal female
$X^H X^h$	normal female (carrier)
$X^H Y$	normal male
$X^h Y$	haemophiliac male

In all sex-linked traits, females who are heterozygous are described as **carriers** of the trait. They are phenotypically

Parental phenotypes	female (♀)	×	male (♂)
Parental genotypes (2n)	XX	×	XY

Meiosis

Gametes (n)	Ⓧ Ⓧ	×	Ⓧ Ⓨ

Random fertilisation

Offspring genotypes (2n)	XX	XY		XX	XY
Offspring phenotypes	♀	♂		♀	♂

sex ratio 1 female : 1 male

Fig 24.18 *Genetic explanation of the sex ratio in humans.*

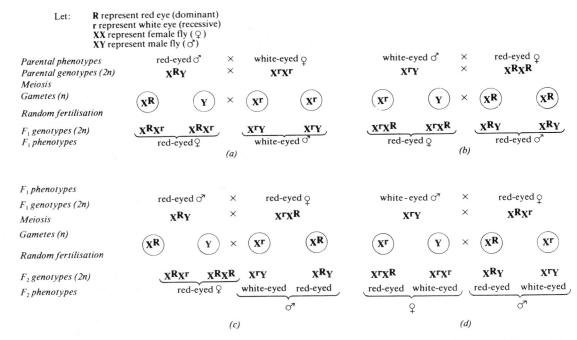

Let: **R** represent red eye (dominant)
  r represent white eye (recessive)
  XX represent female fly (♀)
  XY represent male fly (♂)

Parental phenotypes	red-eyed ♂	×	white-eyed ♀	white-eyed ♂	×	red-eyed ♀

(a) and *(b)*

(c) and *(d)*

Fig 24.19 *(a) and (b) Morgan's reciprocal experimental crosses between red-eyed and white-eyed* Drosophila. *Note the low frequency of appearance of white eyes. (c) Morgan's confirmatory inbreeding experimental cross between an F₁ red-eyed male and an F₁ (heterozygous) red-eyed female. (d) The experimental cross between a white-eyed male and an F₁ (heterozygous) red-eyed female. Note the appearance of the white-eye characteristic only in homozygous white-eyed female flies.*

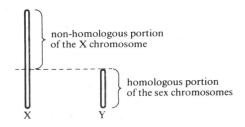

non-homologous portion of the X chromosome

homologous portion of the sex chromosomes

X   Y

Fig 24.20 *Homologous and non-homologous regions of the sex chromosomes.*

Let: **H** represent normal allele for blood clotting (dominant)
  h represent allele for haemophilia (recessive)
  XX represent female chromosomes
  XY represent male chromosomes

Parental phenotypes normal female (carrier) × normal male
Parental genotypes (2n) XᴴXʰ × XᴴY
Meiosis
Gametes (n) Xᴴ Xʰ × Xᴴ Y
Random fertilisation
Offspring genotypes (2n) XᴴXᴴ XᴴY XʰXᴴ XʰY
Offspring phenotypes normal female   normal male   normal female (carrier)   haemophiliac male

Fig 24.21 *Mechanism of inheritance of the sex-linked allele for haemophilia.*

normal but half their gametes carry the recessive gene. Despite the father having a normal gene there is a 50% probability (probability $\frac{1}{2}$) that sons of carrier females will show the trait. In the situation where a carrier haemophiliac female marries a normal male they may have children with phenotypes as shown in fig 24.21.

One of the best-documented examples of the inheritance of haemophilia is shown by the descendants of Queen Victoria. It is thought that the gene for haemophilia arose as a mutation in Queen Victoria or one of her parents. Fig 24.22 shows how the haemophilia gene was inherited by her descendants.

24.11 Body colour in cats and magpie moths is controlled by a sex-linked gene on the X chromosome. The following data were obtained in two breeding experiments where the homogametic sex was homozygous for body colour in the parental generation.

	Magpie moth (normal colour dominant to pale colour)	Cat (black colour dominant to yellow colour)
Parental phenotypes	pale male × normal female	black male × yellow female
Offspring phenotypes	1 normal male : 1 pale female	1 yellow male : 1 black female

Which is the heterogametic sex in each of these organisms?

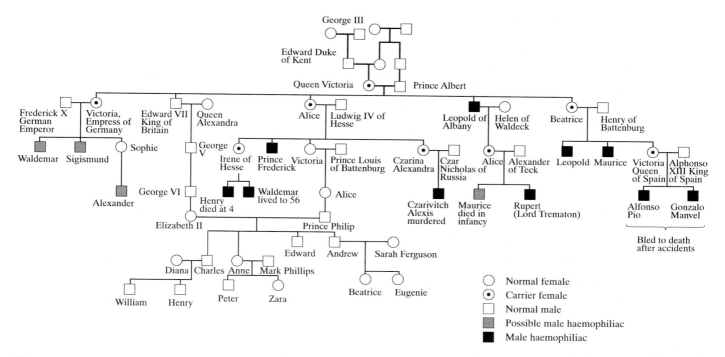

Fig 24.22 *Transmission of haemophilia in the descendants of Queen Victoria. In the diagram **only those descendants involved in the transmission and appearance of haemophilia have been shown.** The ancestry of the British Royal Family has also been given to show why haemophilia is absent from seven generations of Queen Victoria's descendants.*

24.7 Gene interactions

The topics in this chapter so far have represented the simpler aspects of genetics: dominance, monohybrid and dihybrid inheritance, linkage, sex determination and sex linkage. There are many situations in genetics where genes interact in ways other than those already described and it is probable that the majority of phenotypic characteristics in organisms result from these. Several types of gene interaction will now be considered.

24.7.1 Codominance

There are several conditions where two or more alleles do not show complete dominance or recessiveness due to the failure of any allele to be dominant in the heterozygous condition. This state of **codominance** is an exception to the situation described by Mendel in his monohybrid breeding experiments. It is fortunate that he did not select organisms which show this condition as it may have unnecessarily complicated his early work.

Codominance is found in both plants and animals. In most cases the heterozygote has a phenotype which is intermediate between the homozygous dominant and recessive conditions. An example is the production of blue Andalusian fowls by crossing pure-breeding black and splashed white parental stocks. The presence of black plumage is the result of the possession of an allele for the production of the black pigment melanin. The splashed

white stock lack this allele. The heterozygotes show a partial development of melanin which produces a blue sheen in the plumage.

As there are no accepted genotypic symbols for alleles showing codominance, the importance of specifying symbols in genetic explanations is apparent. For example, in the case of the Andalusian fowl, the following genotypic symbols may be used to illustrate the alleles: black – B; splashed white – b, W, B^W or B^{BW}. The results of a cross between black and splashed white homozygous fowl are shown in fig 24.23.

If the F_1 generation are allowed to interbreed, the F_2 generation shows a modification of the normal Mendelian phenotypic monohybrid ratio of $3:1$. In this case a phenotypic ratio of $1:2:1$ is produced where half the F_2 generation have the F_1 genotype (fig 24.24). This ratio of $1:2:1$ is characteristic of examples of codominance. Other examples are shown in table 24.4.

> **24.12** In cats, the genes controlling the coat colour are carried on the X chromosomes and are codominant. A black-coat female mated with a ginger-coat male produced a litter consisting of black male and tortoiseshell female kittens. What is the expected F_2 phenotypic ratio? Explain the results.

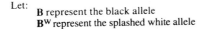

Let:
B represent the black allele
B^W represent the splashed white allele

Parental phenotypes	black (homozygous)	×	splashed white (homozygous)	
Parental genotypes (2n)	**BB**	×	**B^W B^W**	

Meiosis

Gametes (n) (B) (B) × (B^W) (B^W)

Random fertilisation

F₁ genotypes (2n) **BB^W** **BB^W** **BB^W** **BB^W**

F₁ phenotypes all 'blue' heterozygotes

Fig 24.23 *The production of F₁ hybrids of Andalusian fowl.*

F₁ phenotypes blue × blue

F₁ genotypes (2n) **BB^W** × **BB^W**

Meiosis

Gametes (n) (B) (B^W) × (B) (B^W)

Random fertilisation

F₂ genotypes (2n) **BB** **BB^W** **BB^W** **B^W B^W**

F₂ phenotypes black — blue — splashed white
1 : 2 : 1

Fig 24.24 *The production of F₂ hybrids of Andalusian fowl.*

Table 24.4 Examples of codominance.

Characteristic	*Alleles*	*Heterozygous phenotype*
Antirrhinum flower (snapdragon)	red × white	pink
Mirabilis flower (four-o'clock flower)	red × white	pink
Short-horn cattle	red × white	roan
Angora and rex rabbits	long hair and short hair	intermediate silky fur

24.7.2 Multiple alleles

In all the cases studied so far, each characteristic has been controlled by a gene which may have appeared in one of two forms or alleles. There are several conditions where a single characteristic may appear in several different forms controlled by three or more alleles, of which any two may occupy the same gene loci on homologous chromosomes. This is known as the **multiple allele** (or **multiple allelomorph**) condition and it controls such characteristics as coat colour in mice, eye colour in mice and blood group in humans.

Inheritance of blood groups

Blood group is controlled by an autosomal gene. The gene locus is represented by the symbol **I** (which stands for isohaemagglutinogen) and there are three alleles represented by the symbols **A**, **B** and **o**. The alleles **A** and **B** are equally dominant and **o** is recessive to both. The genotypes shown in table 24.5 determine the phenotypic appearance of blood groups. The presence of a single dominant allele results in the blood producing a substance called agglutinin which acts as an antibody. For example, the genotype **I^AI^o** would give rise to the agglutinogen **A** on the red blood cell membrane, and the plasma would contain the agglutinin **anti-B** (the blood group would be A). Blood grouping is described in section 14.9.7.

> **24.13** (*a*) Explain, using appropriate genetic symbols, the possible blood groups of children whose parents are both heterozygous, the father being blood group A and the mother B.
> (*b*) If these parents have non-identical twins, what is the probability that both twins will have blood group A?

24.7.3 Lethal genes

There are several examples of conditions where a single gene may affect several characteristics, including mortality. In the case of humans and other mammals a certain recessive gene may lead to internal adhesion of the lungs resulting in death at birth. Another example involving a single gene affects the formation of cartilage and produces congenital deformities leading to fetal and neonatal death.

In chickens which are homozygous for an allele controlling feather structure called 'frizzled', several phenotypic effects result from the incomplete development of the feathers. These chickens lack adequate feather insulation and suffer from heat loss. To compensate for this they exhibit a range of structural and physiological adaptations, but these are largely unsuccessful and there is a high mortality rate.

The effects of a lethal gene are clearly illustrated by the inheritance of fur colour in mice. Wild mice have grey-coloured fur, a condition known as agouti. Some mice have

Table 24.5 Human blood group genotypes.

Genotype	*Blood group (phenotype)*
I^AI^A	A
I^AI^o	A
I^BI^B	B
I^BI^o	B
I^AI^B	AB
I^oI^o	O

yellow fur. Cross-breeding yellow mice produces offspring in the ratio 2 yellow fur : 1 agouti fur. These results can only be explained on the basis that yellow is dominant to agouti and that all the yellow coat mice are heterozygous. The atypical Mendelian ratio is explained by the fetal death of *homozygous* yellow coat mice (fig 24.25). Examination of the uteri of pregnant yellow mice from the above crosses revealed dead yellow fetuses. Similar examination of the uteri of crosses between yellow fur and agouti fur mice revealed no dead yellow fetuses. The explanation is that this cross would not produce homozygous yellow (**YY**) mice.

24.7.4   Gene complex

The presence of a pair of alleles occupying a given gene locus and controlling the production of a single phenotypic characteristic is true in some cases only and exceptional in most organisms. Most characteristics are determined by the interaction of several genes which form a '**gene complex**'. For example, a single characteristic may be controlled by the interaction of two or more genes situated at different loci. In the case of the inheritance of the shape of the comb in domestic fowl there are genes at two loci situated on different chromosomes which interact and give rise to four distinct phenotypes, known as pea, rose, walnut and single combs (fig 24.26). The appearance of pea comb and rose comb are each determined by the presence of their respective dominant allele (**P** or **R**) and the absence of the other dominant allele. Walnut comb results from a modified form of codominance in which at least one dominant allele for pea comb and rose comb is present (that is **PR**). Single comb appears only in the homozygous double recessive condition (that is **pprr**). These phenotypes and genotypes are shown in table 24.6.

The F$_2$ genotypes and F$_2$ phenotypic ratios resulting from crossing a pure-breeding pea-comb hen with a pure-breeding rose-comb cock are shown in fig 24.27.

Let:
Y represent yellow fur (dominant)
y represent agouti fur (recessive)

Parental phenotypes	yellow fur	×	yellow fur
Parental genotypes (2n)	**Yy**	×	**Yy**
Meiosis			
Gametes (n)	Ⓨ ⓨ	×	Ⓨ ⓨ
Random fertilisation			
Offspring genotypes (2n)	YY Yy Yy		yy
Offspring phenotypes	1 yellow fur: 2 yellow fur : 1 agouti fur		
	die before birth		

Fig 24.25 *Genetic explanation of fur colour inheritance in mice showing the lethal genotype* **YY**.

24.14 In poultry, the allele for white feather (**W**) is dominant over the allele for black feather (**w**). The alleles for pea comb, **P**, and rose comb, **R**, produce the phenotypes stated. If these alleles are present together they produce a phenotype called walnut comb and if their recessive alleles are present in the homozygous condition they produce a phenotype called single comb.

A cross between a black rose-comb cock and a white walnut-comb hen produced the following phenotypes:

3 white walnut-comb, 3 black walnut-comb, 3 white rose-comb, 3 black rose-comb, 1 white pea-comb, 1 black pea-comb, 1 white single-comb and 1 black single-comb.

What are the parental genotypes? Show clearly how they give rise to the phenotypes described above?

24.7.5   Epistasis

A gene is said to be **epistatic** (*epi*, over) when its presence suppresses the effect of a gene at another locus. Epistatic genes are sometimes called '**inhibiting genes**' because of their effect on the other genes which are described as **hypostatic** (*hypo*, under).

Fur colour in mice is controlled by a pair of genes occupying different loci. The epistatic gene determines the presence of colour and has two alleles, coloured (dominant) and albino (white) (recessive). The hypostatic gene determines the nature of the colour and its alleles are agouti (grey) (dominant) and black (recessive). The mice may have agouti or black fur depending upon their genotypes, but this will only appear if accompanied by the allele for coloured fur. The albino condition appears in mice that are homozygous recessive for colour even if the alleles for agouti and black fur are present. Three possible phenotypes can occur and they are agouti, black and albino. A variety of phenotypic ratios can be obtained depending on the genotypes of the mating pair (fig 24.28 and table 24.7).

24.15 In White Leghorn fowl, plumage colour is controlled by two sets of genes, including the following:

W (white) dominant over **w** (colour)
B (black) dominant over **b** (brown).

The heterozygous F$_1$ genotype **WwBb** is white. Account for this type of gene interaction and show the phenotypic ratio of the F$_2$ generation.

Fig 24.26 *Variation in comb shape in domestic fowl (*top left*) single comb, (*top right*) pea comb, (*bottom left*) rose comb, (*bottom right*) strawberry comb.*

Table 24.6 Phenotypes and possible genotypes associated with comb shape in poultry.

Phenotype	*Possible genotypes*
pea	**PPrr, Pprr**
rose	**RRpp, Rrpp**
walnut	**PPRR, PpRR, PPRr, PpRr**
single	**pprr**

Fig 24.27 *Genetic explanation of comb inheritance in fowl.*

Let:
P represent presence of pea comb (dominant)
p represent absence of pea comb (recessive)
R represent presence of rose comb (dominant)
r represent absence of rose comb (recessive)

Parental phenotypes	pea comb	×	rose comb
Parental genotypes (2n)	**PPrr**	×	**RRpp**
Meiosis			
Gametes (n)	(**Pr**)	×	(**Rp**)
Random fertilisation			
F_1 genotypes (2n)		all **PpRr**	
F_1 phenotypes		all walnut comb	
F_1 phenotypes	walnut comb	×	walnut comb
F_1 genotypes (2n)	**PpRr**	×	**PpRr**
Meiosis			

Gametes (n) (as shown by ♂ and ♀)

Random fertilisation

F_2 genotypes (2n) (shown in Punnett square)

♀ \ ♂	**PR**	**Pr**	**pR**	**pr**
PR	**PR PR** ○	**Pr PR** ○	**pR PR** ○	**pr PR** ○
Pr	**PR Pr** ○	**Pr Pr** □	**pR Pr** ○	**pr Pr** □
pR	**PR pR** ○	**Pr pR** ○	**pR pR** △	**pr pR** △
pr	**PR pr** ○	**Pr pr** □	**pR pr** △	**pr pr** ◌

F_2 phenotypes 9 walnut comb : 3 pea comb : 3 rose comb : 1 single comb

Offspring symbols ○ □ △ ◌

Table 24.7 Some examples of the range of phenotypic ratios which can be produced as a result of epistatic gene interaction (see fig 24.28 for explanation of alleles).

Parental phenotypes	*Genotypes*	*Phenotypic ratios*
agouti × agouti	**AaCc** × **AaCc**	9 agouti : 3 black : 4 albino
agouti × black	**AaCc** × **aaCc**	3 agouti : 3 black : 2 albino
agouti × albino	**AaCc** × **Aacc**	3 agouti : 1 black : 4 albino
agouti × albino	**AaCc** × **aacc**	1 agouti : 1 black : 2 albino
agouti × albino	**AACc** × **aacc**	1 agouti : 1 albino
agouti × black	**AaCc** × **aaCC**	1 agouti : 1 black
albino × black	**AAcc** × **aaCC**	all agouti
albino × black	**AAcc** × **aaCc**	1 agouti : 1 albino

Fig 24.28 (below) *A genetic explanation of how unusual phenotypic ratios can be produced in the case of epistatic genes.*

Let: **A** represent agouti fur (dominant)
a represent black fur (recessive)
C represent coloured fur (dominant)
c represent albino fur (recessive)

Parental phenotypes	agouti	×	albino
Parental genotypes (2n)	**AaCc**	×	**Aacc**
Meiosis			

Gametes (n) (as shown by ♂ and ♀)

Random fertilisation

Offspring genotypes (2n) (as shown in Punnett square)

♀ \ ♂	**AC**	**Ac**	**aC**	**ac**
Ac	**AC Ac** ○	**Ac Ac** □	**aC Ac** ○	**ac Ac** □
ac	**AC ac** ○	**Ac ac** □	**aC ac** △	**ac ac** □

Offspring phenotypes 3 agouti : 4 albino : 1 black

Offspring symbols ○ □ △

24.7.6   Polygenic inheritance

Many of the obvious characteristics of organisms are produced by the combined effect of many different genes. These genes form a special gene complex known as a polygenic system. Whilst the effect of each gene alone is too small to make any significant impression on the phenotype, the almost infinite variety produced by the combined effect of these genes (**polygenes**) has been shown to form the genetic basis of **continuous variation**, which is described further in section 24.8.2.

24.8   Variation

The term variation describes the difference in characteristics shown by organisms belonging to the same natural population or species. It was the amazing diversity of structure within any species that caught the attention of Darwin and Wallace during their travels. The regularity and predictability with which these differences in characteristics were inherited formed the basis of Mendel's research. Whilst Darwin recognised that particular characteristics could be developed by selective breeding, as described in section 25.4.2, it was Mendel who explained the mechanism by which selected characteristics were passed on from generation to generation.

Mendel described how hereditary factors determine the genotype of an organism which in the course of development becomes expressed in the structural, physiological and biochemical characteristics of the phenotype. Whilst the phenotypic appearance of any characteristic is ultimately determined by the genes controlling that characteristic, the extent to which certain characteristics develop may be more influenced by the environment.

A study of the phenotypic differences in any large population shows that two forms of variation occur, discontinuous and continuous. Studies of variation in a character involve measuring the expression of that characteristic in a large number of organisms within the population, such as height in humans. The results are plotted as histograms or a graph which reveals the **frequency distribution** of the variations of that characteristic within the population. Typical results obtained from such studies are shown in fig 24.29 and they highlight the difference between the two forms of variation.

24.8.1   Discontinuous variation

There are certain characteristics within a population which exhibit a limited form of variation. Variation in this case produces individuals showing clear-cut differences with no intermediates between them, such as blood groups in humans, wing lengths in *Drosophila*, melanic and light forms in *Biston betularia*, style length in *Primula* and sex in animals and plants. Characteristics showing discontinuous variation are usually controlled by

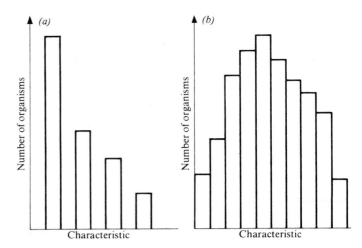

Fig 24.29 *Histograms representing frequency distribution in the case of (a) discontinuous variation and (b) continuous variation.*

one or two major genes which may have two or more allelic forms and their phenotypic expression is relatively unaffected by environmental conditions.

Since the phenotypic variation is restricted to certain clear-cut characteristics, this form of variation is alternatively known as **qualitative inheritance**, as opposed to **quantitative inheritance** which is characteristic of continuous variation.

24.8.2   Continuous variation

Many characteristics in a population show a complete gradation from one extreme to the other without any break. This is illustrated most clearly by characteristics such as mass, linear dimension, shape and colour of organs and organisms. The frequency distribution for a characteristic exhibiting continuous variation is a **normal distribution curve** (appendix section A2.3.3). Most of the organisms in the population fall in the middle of the range with approximately equal numbers showing the two extreme forms of the characteristic. Characteristics exhibiting continuous variation are produced by the combined effects of many genes (polygenes) and environmental factors.

Individually each of these genes has little effect on the phenotype but their combined effect is significant.

24.8.3   Influence of the environment

The ultimate factor determining a phenotypic characteristic is the genotype. At the moment of fertilisation the genotype of the organism is determined, but the subsequent degree of expression allowed to this genetic potential is influenced greatly by the action of environmental factors during the development of the organism. For example, Mendel's tall variety of garden pea normally attained a height of six feet. However, it would only do so if provided with adequate light, water and soil conditions. A reduction in the supply of any of these factors (**limiting factors**) would prevent the gene for height exerting its full effect. It was the Danish geneticist Johanssen who demonstrated the effect of the interaction of genotypic and environmental factors on phenotype. In a series of experiments on the mass of dwarf bean seeds he selected the heaviest and lightest seeds from each generation of self-pollinating dwarf bean plants and used these to produce the next generation. After repeating these experiments for several years he found only small differences in the mean mass of seeds from the same selected line, that is heavy or light, but large differences in mean mass of seeds from different selected lines, that is heavy and light. This suggested that both heredity and environment were influencing the phenotypic appearance of the characteristic. From these results it is possible to describe continuous phenotypic variation as being '**the cumulative effect of varying environmental factors acting on a variable genotype**'. The results also indicated that the extent to which a characteristic is inherited is determined primarily by the genotype. In the development of human characteristics such as personality, temperament and intelligence, there is evidence to suggest that both **nature** (hereditary factors) and **nurture** (environmental factors) interact to varying degrees in different individuals to influence the final appearance of the characteristic. It is these genetic and environmental differences which act to produce phenotypic differences between individuals. There is no firm evidence, as yet, to suggest that one factor is universally more influential than the other, but the environment can never increase the extent of the phenotype beyond that determined by the genotype (fig 24.30).

24.8.4 Sources of variation

It will be appreciated that, as a result of the interaction between discontinuous and continuous variations and the environment, no two organisms will possess identical phenotypes. Replication of DNA is so nearly perfect that there is little possibility of variation occurring in the genotypes of asexually reproducing organisms. Any apparent variation between these organisms is therefore almost certainly the result of environmental influences. In the case of sexually reproducing organisms there is ample opportunity for genetic variation to arise. Two processes occurring during meiosis, and the fusion of gametes during fertilisation, provide the means of introducing unlimited genetic variation into the population. These may be summarised as follows:

(1) *Crossing-over* – reciprocal crossing-over of genes between chromatids of homologous chromosomes may occur during prophase I of meiosis. This produces new linkage groups and so provides a major source of genetic recombination of alleles (sections 24.3 and 23.3).

(2) *Independent assortment* – the orientation of the chromatids of homologous chromosomes (bivalents) on

Fig 24.30 *Phenotypic variation in human height. All these children are the same age.*

the equatorial spindle during metaphase I of meiosis determines the direction in which the pairs of chromatids move during anaphase I. This orientation of the chromatids is random. During metaphase II the orientation of pairs of chromatids once more is random and determines which chromosomes migrate to opposite poles of the cell during anaphase II. These random orientations and the subsequent independent assortment (segregation) of the chromosomes give rise to a large calculable number of different chromosome combinations in the gametes (section 24.2.1).

(3) *Random fusion of gametes* – a third source of variation occurs during sexual reproduction as a result of the fact that the fusion of male and female gametes is completely random (at least in theory). Thus, any male gamete is potentially capable of fusing with any female gamete.

These sources of genetic variation account for the routine '**gene reshuffling**' which is the basis of continuous variation. The environment acts on the range of phenotypes produced and those best suited to it thrive. This leads to changes in allele and genotypic frequencies as described in chapter 27. However, these sources of variation do not generate the major changes in genotype which are necessary in order to give rise to new species as described by evolutionary theory. These changes are produced by mutations.

24.9　Mutation

A mutation is a change in the amount, arrangement or structure of the DNA of an organism. This produces a change in the genotype which may be inherited by cells derived by mitosis or meiosis from the mutant cell. A mutation may result in the change in appearance of a characteristic in a population. Mutations occurring in gamete cells are inherited, whereas those occurring in somatic cells can only be inherited by daughter cells produced by mitosis. The latter are known as **somatic mutations**.

A mutation resulting from a change in the amount or arrangement of DNA is known as **chromosomal mutation** or **chromosomal aberration**. Some forms of these affect the chromosomes to such an extent that they may be seen under the microscope. Increasingly the term mutation is being used only when describing a change in the structure of the DNA at a single locus and this is known as a **gene mutation** or **point mutation**.

The concept of mutation as the cause of the sudden appearance of a new characteristic was first proposed by the Dutch botanist Hugo de Vries in 1901, following his work on inheritance in the evening primrose *Oenothera lamarckiana*. Nine years later T. H. Morgan began a series of investigations into mutations in *Drosophila* and, with the assistance of geneticists throughout the world, identified over 500 mutations.

24.9.1　Mutation frequency and causes of mutation

Mutations occur randomly and spontaneously; that is to say any gene can undergo mutation at any time. The rates at which mutations occur vary between organisms.

As a result of the work of H. J. Muller in the 1920s it was observed that the frequency of mutation could be increased above the spontaneous level by the effects of X-rays. Since then it has been shown that the mutation rates can be significantly increased by the effects of high energy electromagnetic radiation such as ultra-violet light, X-rays and γ rays. High-energy particles, such as α and β particles, neutrons and cosmic radiation, are also **mutagenic**, that is cause mutations. A variety of chemical substances, including mustard gas, caffeine, formaldehyde, colchicine, certain constituents of tobacco and an increasing number of drugs, food preservatives and pesticides, have been shown to be mutagenic.

24.9.2　Chromosome mutations

Chromosomal mutations may be the result of changes in the number or structure of chromosomes. Certain forms of chromosomal mutation may affect several genes and have a more profound effect on the phenotype than gene mutations. Changes in the number of chromosomes are usually the result of errors occurring during meiosis but they can also occur during mitosis. These changes may involve the loss or gain of single chromosomes, a condition called **aneuploidy**, or the increase in entire haploid sets of chromosomes, a condition called **euploidy (polyploidy)**.

Aneuploidy

In this condition half the daughter cells produced have an extra chromosome $(n+1)$, $(2n+1)$ and so on, whilst the other half have a chromosome missing $(n-1)$, $(2n-1)$ and so on. Aneuploidy can arise from the failure of a pair, or pairs, of homologous chromosomes to separate during anaphase I of meiosis. If this occurs, both sets of chromosomes pass to the same pole of the cell and separation of the homologous chromosomes during anaphase II may lead to the formation of gamete cells containing either one or more chromosomes too many or too few as shown in fig 24.31. This is known as **non-disjunction**. Fusion of either of these gametes with a normal haploid gamete produces a zygote with an odd number of chromosomes.

Zygotes containing less than the diploid number of chromosomes usually fail to develop, but those with extra chromosomes may develop. In most cases where this occurs in animals it produces severe abnormalities. One of the commonest forms of chromosomal mutation in humans resulting from non-disjunction is a form of trisomy called Down's syndrome $(2n=47)$. The condition, which is named

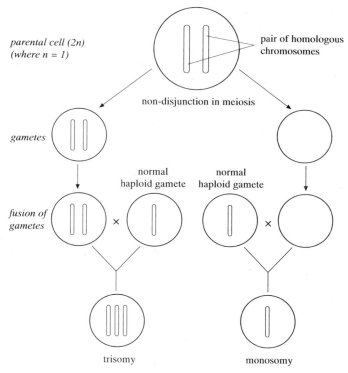

parental cell (2n)
(where n = 1)

pair of homologous chromosomes

non-disjunction in meiosis

gametes

normal haploid gamete

normal haploid gamete

fusion of gametes

×

×

trisomy

monosomy

Fig 24.31 *Non-disjunction in gamete cell formation and the results of fusion of these abnormal gametes with normal haploid cells. The resulting cells may show a form of polysomy where the chromosome number may be (2n + 1) trisomy, (2n + 2) tetrasomy, (2n + 3) pentasomy etc., or monosomy (2n − 1) depending upon the number of homologous chromosomes which fail to separate normally (see also fig 25.34).*

after the doctor who first described it in 1866, is due to the non-disjunction of the two chromosomes 21. It is described in section 25.7.6.

Non-disjunction of the male and female sex chromosomes may also occur and produce aneuploidy affecting secondary sexual characteristics, fertility and, in some cases, intelligence (sections 25.7.7 and 25.7.8).

Euploidy (polyploidy)

Gamete and somatic cells containing multiples of the haploid number of chromosomes are called **polyploids**, and the prefixes tri-, tetra-, and so on, indicate the extent of polyploidy, for example $3n$ is triploid, $4n$ is tetraploid, $5n$ is pentaploid and so on. Polyploidy is much more common in plants than in animals. For example, approximately half the 300 000 known species of angiosperms are polyploid. The relatively low occurrence in animals is explained by the fact that the increased number of chromosomes in polyploids makes normal gamete formation during meiosis much more prone to error. Since most plants are capable of propagating themselves vegetatively they are able to reproduce despite being polyploid. Polyploidy is often associated with advantageous features such as increased size, hardiness and resistance to disease. This is called **hybrid vigour** (section

27.4.2). Most of our domestic plants are polyploids producing large fruits, storage organs, flowers or leaves.

There are two forms of polyploidy, autopolyploidy and allopolyploidy.

Autopolyploidy. This condition may arise naturally or artificially as a result of an increase in number of chromosomes within the same species. For example, if chromosomes undergo replication (during interphase) and the chromatids separate normally (during anaphase) but the cytoplasm fails to cleave (during cytokinesis), a **tetraploid** ($4n$) cell with a large nucleus is produced. This cell will undergo division and produce tetraploid cells. The amount of cytoplasm in these cells increases to preserve the ratio of the volumes of nucleus : cytoplasm and leads to an increase in the size of the whole plant or some part of it. Autopolyploidy can be induced by the use of a drug called **colchicine** which is extracted from the corm of the autumn crocus (*Colchicum*). Concentrations of about 0.01% inhibit spindle formation by disrupting microtubules so that the chromatids fail to separate during anaphase. Colchicine and related drugs have been used in the breeding of certain varieties of economically important crops such as tobacco, tomatoes and sugarbeet. Autopolyploids can be as fertile as diploids if they have an even number of chromosomes sets.

A modified form of polyploidy can occur in animals and gives rise to cells and tissues which are polyploid. This process is called **endomitosis** and involves chromosome replication without cell division. The giant chromosomes in the salivary glands of *Drosophila* and tetraploid cells in the human liver are produced by endomitosis.

Allopolyploidy. This condition arises when the chromosome number in a sterile hybrid becomes doubled and produces fertile hybrids. F_1 hybrids produced from different species are usually sterile since their chromosomes cannot form homologous pairs during meiosis. This is called **hybrid sterility**. However, if multiples of the original haploid number of chromosomes, for example $2(n_1 + n_2)$, $3(n_1 + n_2)$ and so on (where n_1 and n_2 are the haploid numbers of the parent species) occur, a new species is produced which is fertile with polyploids like itself but infertile with both parental species.

Most allopolyploid species have a diploid chromosome number which is the sum of the diploid numbers of their parental species; for example rice grass, *Spartina anglica* ($2n = 122$), is a fertile allopolyploid hybrid produced from a cross between *Spartina maritima* (*stricta*) ($2n = 60$) and *Spartina alterniflora* ($2n = 62$). The F_1 hybrid formed from the latter two species is sterile and is called *Spartina townsendii* ($2n = 62$). Most allopolyploid plants have different characteristics from either parental species, and include many of our most economically important plants. For example, the species of wheat used to make bread, *Triticum aestivum* ($2n = 42$), has been selectively bred over a period of more than 5000 years. By crossing a wild variety of wheat, einkorn wheat ($2n = 14$), with 'wild grass' ($2n = 14$), a different species of wheat, emmer wheat

($2n = 28$), was produced. Emmer wheat was crossed with another species of wild grass ($2n = 14$) to produce *Triticum aestivum* ($2n = 42$) which actually represents the hexaploid condition ($6n$) of the original einkorn wheat. Another example of interspecific hybridisation involving crossing the radish and cabbage is described in section 27.9.

Allopolyploidy does not occur in animals because there are fewer instances of cross-breeding between species. Polyploidy does not add new genes to a gene pool (section 27.1.1) but gives rise to a new combination of genes.

Structural changes in chromosomes

Crossing-over during prophase I of meiosis involves the reciprocal transfer of genetic material between homologous chromosomes. This changes the allele sequence of parental linkage groups and produces recombinants, but no gene loci are lost. Similar effects to these are produced by the structural changes in chromosomes known as inversions and translocations. In other forms of change, such as deletions and duplications, the number of gene loci on chromosomes is changed, and this can have profound effects on the phenotypes. Structural changes in chromosomes resulting from inversion, deletion and duplication, and in some cases from translocation, may be observed under the microscope when homologous chromosomes attempt to pair during prophase I of meiosis. Homologous genes undergo synapsis (pairing) (section 23.3) and a loop or twist is formed in one of the homologous chromosomes as a result of the structural change. Which chromosome forms the loop and the arrangement of its genes depends upon the type of structural change.

Inversion occurs when a region of a chromosome breaks off and rotates through 180° before rejoining the chromosome. No change in genotype occurs as a result of inversion but phenotypic changes may be seen (fig 24.32).

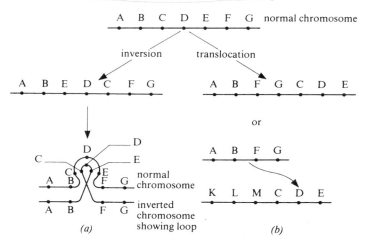

Fig 24.32 *Diagrammatic representation of inversion and translocation and their effects on the positions of genes A–G. (a) Looping in prophase due to inversion. (b) Part of the chromosome carrying genes C, D and E has broken off and become attached to the chromosome carrying genes K, L and M.*

This suggests that the order of gene loci on the chromosome is important, a phenomenon known as the **position effect**.

Translocation involves a region of a chromosome breaking off and rejoining either the other end of the same chromosome or another non-homologous chromosome (fig 24.31). The position effect may again be seen in the phenotype. Reciprocal translocation between non-homologous chromosomes can produce two new homologous pairs of chromosomes. In some cases of Down's syndrome, where the diploid number is normal, the effects are produced by the translocation of an extra chromosome number 21 onto a larger chromosome, usually number 15.

The simplest form of chromosomal mutation is **deletion**, which involves the loss of a region of a chromosome, either from the ends or internally. This results in a chromosome becoming deficient in certain genes (fig 24.33). Deletion can affect one of a homologous pair of chromosomes, in which case the alleles present on the non-deficient chromosome will be expressed even if recessive. If deletion affects the same gene loci on both homologous chromosomes the effect is usually lethal.

In some cases a region of a chromosome becomes duplicated so that an additional set of genes exists for the region of **duplication**. The additional region of genes may be incorporated within the chromosome or at one end of the chromosome, or become attached to another chromosome (fig 24.33).

24.9.3 Gene mutations

What is a gene mutation?

Sudden and spontaneous changes in phenotype, for which there are no conventional genetic explanations or any microscopic evidence of chromosomal mutation, can only be explained in terms of changes in gene structure. A **gene mutation** or **point mutation** (since it applies to a particular

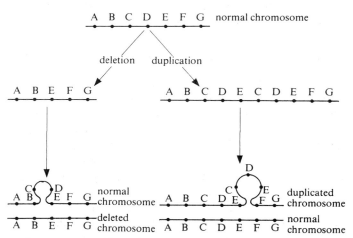

Fig 24.33 *Diagrammatic representations of deletion and duplication and their effects on the positions of genes A–G. In both cases looping can be seen.*

gene locus) is the result of a change in the nucleotide sequence of the DNA molecule in a particular region of the chromosome. Such a change in the base sequence of the gene is transmitted to mRNA during transcription and may result in a change in the amino acid sequence of the polypeptide chain produced from it during translation at the ribosomes.

Types of gene mutation

There are a variety of forms of gene mutation involving the addition, loss or rearrangement of bases in the gene. These mutations take the form of the **duplication**, **insertion**, **deletion**, **inversion** or **substitution** of bases. In all cases they change the nucleotide sequence and result in the formation of a modified polypeptide. For example, deletion causes a **frame-shift** and the implications of this are described in section 23.7.3.

Consequences of gene mutations

Gene mutations occurring during gamete formation are transmitted to all the cells of the offspring and may be significant for the future of the species. Somatic gene mutations which arise in the organism are inherited only by those cells derived from the mutant cells by mitosis. Whilst they may affect that organism, they are lost on the death of the organism. Somatic mutations are probably very common and go unnoticed, but in some cases they may produce cells with an increased rate of growth and division. These cells may give rise to a tumour which may be **benign** and not affect other tissues, or **malignant**, which live parasitically on healthy cells, a condition known as **cancer**.

The effects of gene mutation are extremely variable. Most minor gene mutations pass unnoticed in the phenotype since they are recessive, but there are several cases where a change in a single base in the genetic code can have a profound effect on the phenotype. **Sickle cell anaemia** in humans is an example of **base substitution** mutation affecting a base in one of the genes involved in the production of haemoglobin. This condition and its cause is described in more detail in section 25.7.2.

24.9.4 Implications of mutation

The effects of chromosome and gene mutations are very variable. In many cases the mutations are lethal and prevent development of the organism, for example in humans about 20% of pregnancies end in natural abortion before 12 weeks and of these about 50% exhibit a chromosome abnormality. Some forms of chromosome mutation may bring certain gene sequences together, and that combined effect may produce a 'beneficial' characteristic. Another significance of bringing certain genes closer together is that they are less likely to be separated by crossing-over and this is an advantage with beneficial genes.

Gene mutation may lead to several alleles occupying a specific locus. This increases both the heterozygosity and

size of the gene pool of the population and leads to an increase in variation within the population. Gene reshuffling as a result of crossing-over, independent assortment, random fertilisation and mutations, may increase the amount of continuous variation but the evolutionary implications of this are often short-lived since the changes produced may be rapidly diluted. Certain gene mutations, on the other hand, increase discontinuous variation and this has the more profound effect on changes in the population. Most gene mutations are recessive to the 'normal' allele which has come to form genetic equilibrium with the rest of the genotype and the environment as a result of successfully withstanding selection over many generations. Being recessive the mutant alleles may remain in the population for many generations until they come together in the homozygous condition and are expressed phenotypically. Occasionally a dominant mutant allele may arise in which case it will appear immediately in the phenotype (section 27.5, *Biston betularia*).

The information provided in this chapter accounts for the origins of variation within populations and the mechanism by which characteristics are inherited, but it does not explain how the amazing diversity of living organisms described in chapter 2 may have arisen. Possible answers to this problem form the basis of the next three chapters.

Chapter Twenty-five

Applied genetics

In the second half of the twentieth century, biology has entered what some scientists have referred to as its 'Golden Age'. From the discovery of the structure of DNA in 1953 to the ability to write the genetic code for a human being by the end of the century, the relatively new science of molecular biology has combined with genetics to give us a new and powerful biotechnology. It will have applications in industry, medicine and agriculture and many other fields. Its importance is reflected in the fact that the United States now spends about half its academic research budget on the life sciences. Like all new knowledge, it can be used for the benefit of humankind, but also presents new dangers. Physicists faced the same problem in the first half of the twentieth century when knowledge of the structure of the atom led to our ability to use nuclear power, with its potential for peaceful or destructive use. In fact, both Francis Crick and Maurice Wilkins, who with James Watson won the Nobel prize for their work in discovering the structure of DNA, had been physicists and had worked on weapons research during the Second World War before moving on to the science of life. Past experience has made scientists very aware of the social and ethical implications of their research and, as we shall see later, they even slowed down their work in the late 1970s while strict regulations and guidelines for genetic engineering were worked out. As a student of biology you will share in the responsibility for discussing the new issues that will certainly arise from our expanding knowledge of molecular genetics. The more informed our opinions are, and the more people are prepared to discuss the issues, the more likely we all are to benefit.

Genetic engineering

In the first part of this chapter we shall be looking at genetic engineering. This is the most powerful technique available in applied genetics and biotechnology. It gives us the power to study and to change the genetic instructions of an organism, including ourselves. Other living organisms can be changed for the benefit of humans, and we are even beginning to manipulate our own genes to cure genetic diseases ('gene therapy'). A brief summary of the history and applications of genetic engineering is given in table 25.1.

25.1   Genetic engineering of bacteria

The basic techniques of genetic engineering were worked out in the early 1970s. It usually involves inserting a new gene into an organism. The gene may be newly synthesised or transferred from another organism. In the case of bacteria, genetic engineering turns the bacterium into a living factory for the production of whatever protein the gene codes for. Examples we shall study later are the transfer of genes for human insulin, human growth hormone and bovine somatotrophin (BST) (sections 25.2.1–25.2.3).

25.1.1   Overview

It is now a routine process to be able to obtain copies of any gene. In some cases only a single original molecule is required. Making many identical copies of a molecule is called **cloning**. Traditionally it relies on the use of plasmids or bacteriophages. **Plasmids** are small circular pieces of DNA found in certain bacteria. They are separate from the bulk of the DNA and can replicate independently of the rest of the DNA (section 2.3.1). **Bacteriophages** (known as phages for short) are viruses which can 'inject' their DNA into bacteria for replication (fig 2.21). The piece of DNA to be cloned is combined with either a plasmid or the DNA of a phage. This modified plasmid or phage DNA is called recombinant DNA. **Recombinant DNA** is the name given to DNA formed after a piece from one organism is joined to a piece from another organism. If it is inserted into a bacterium, it will replicate (clone) itself and as the bacterium multiplies, so the recombinant DNA will multiply. If desired, the cloned DNA can be separated from the plasmid or phage DNA again. This allows, for example, its base sequence to be determined. While inside the bacterium the new gene may be active and used to make a useful protein, such as human insulin, which would not normally be made in that cell. The protein can later be extracted.

The plasmid or phage is known as the '**vector**' or '**cloning vector**', because it acts as a carrier for the DNA to be cloned. The process is summarised in fig 25.1 and described in more detail below. Inserting new genes into the

Table 25.1 A brief summary of the history and development of genetic engineering. (Based on table G7, p. 418, _The encyclopaedia of molecular biology_, ed. Sir John Kendrew (1994) Blackwell Science.)

1960s–1970s	Isolation of restriction enzymes and their use to analyse DNA structure.
1972–73	DNA cloning techniques involving recombinant DNA developed. First gene cloned (bacterial).
1974	First expression in a bacterium of a gene from a different species.
1977	First complete genetic code of an organism (base sequence of a complete genome). The organism was the phage ΦX 174 and its genetic code is 5375 bases long.
1978	Bacteria produce human somatostatin from a synthetic gene. Later the same year bacteria also produce human insulin from a synthetic gene.
1982	Insulin (Eli Lilly's Humulin) is the first product made by genetically engineered bacteria to be approved for use in Britain and the USA.
1981/82	First transgenic animals (mice) produced.
1983	First transgenic plants produced.
1985	First transgenic farm animals produced (rabbits, pigs and sheep).
1986	First controlled release of genetically engineered organisms into the environment.
1989	First patented transgenic animal, the oncomouse.
1990	Human genome project started. First successful gene therapy for SCID (section 25.7.11) in USA.
1990–92	First transgenic cereal plants (maize and wheat).
1992	Regulations for deliberate release of genetically engineered organisms established in the USA and EU. First complete base sequence of a chromosome (yeast chromosome III).
1993	First human gene therapy trial in UK. Gene therapy for cystic fibrosis and SCID begun in UK.
1994	Genetically engineered tomato marketed in the USA.
1996	Genetically engineered tomato marketed in Britain.
1997	First cloned mammal produced from a single cell. The sheep, Dolly, was developed from a single udder cell.

embryos of plants or animals to create what are known as **transgenic** organisms (organisms which can pass their genes on to their offspring) is more difficult and will be discussed in sections 25.3–25.5.

Genetic engineering in bacteria can be broken down into five stages.

- Stage 1: Obtain a copy of the required gene from among all the others in the DNA of the donor organism.
- Stage 2: Place the gene in a vector.
- Stage 3: Use the vector to introduce the gene into the host cell.
- Stage 4: Select the cells which have taken up the foreign DNA (the DNA of the donor).
- Stage 5: Clone the gene.

This is the simplest order of stages. However, they may not be carried out in this order, for example a group (or library) of genes may be inserted into a vector and cloned before it is possible to isolate the required gene.

25.1.2 Stage 1: Obtaining a copy of the gene required

This is the most difficult part of the process. For example, there are around 3000 million bases and 100 000 genes in the human genome (the total DNA in a human cell). A typical gene is several thousand base pairs long, so even to find a particular gene presents a difficult problem. Three methods are used to get a copy of a gene:

- make a copy of the gene from its mRNA, using reverse transcriptase;
- synthesise the gene artificially;
- use a 'shotgun' approach, which involves chopping up the DNA with 'restriction enzymes' and searching for the piece with the required gene.

The first two methods are the most straightforward and the technique of genetic engineering will be illustrated with these first. The third method will then be examined.

Using reverse transcriptase

Although there are only two copies of each gene in a diploid cell (one on a chromosome from the female parent and one on a chromosome from the male parent), if the gene is active it usually produces thousands of mRNA molecules which are complementary to the gene (section 23.8). It is often known in which cells the gene is active. For example, the gene for insulin is active in the β cells of the pancreas. Retroviruses contain an enzyme which can make a complementary DNA copy of an RNA molecule. (Making DNA from RNA is the opposite process to normal transcription where RNA is made from DNA.) The enzyme was therefore named **reverse transcriptase**. It has come to

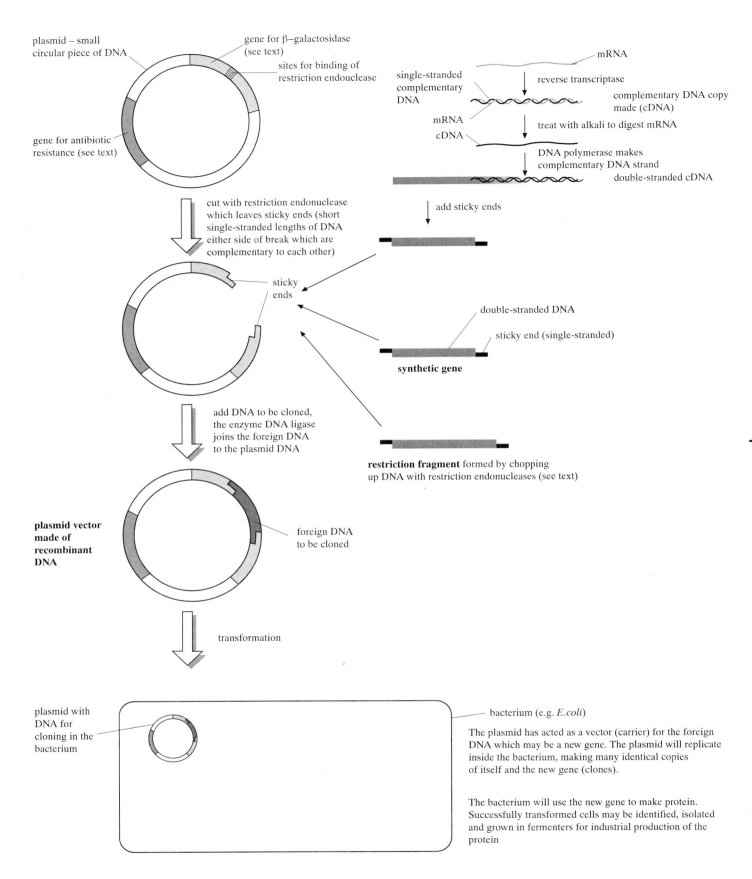

Fig 25.1 *Genetic engineering. Summary of a procedure designed to clone a gene. Details of the procedure are explained in the text.*

be a valuable tool in genetic engineering. (The virus uses it to turn its RNA genetic code into DNA so that it can infect new cells (section 2.4.5).) For some genes it is relatively easy to isolate the mRNA from that particular gene in a particular type of cell. Once this has been done, the procedure shown in fig 25.1 is used to make the gene coding for the required protein. The DNA formed in this way is called **complementary DNA**, or **cDNA**, whether it is single-stranded or double-stranded.

Synthesising a gene

The base sequence of a gene can be found directly, or a suitable base sequence can be worked out from the amino acid sequence of the protein it makes. A gene can then be constructed using nucleotides (remember each base is part of one nucleotide) and joining them together in the right order. This is only possible for short genes at present but, as techniques improve, this could become a routine possibility for any gene. It has been used for the synthesis of proinsulin and somatostatin genes. Somatostatin (otherwise known as growth hormone inhibitory hormone) is a protein hormone which contains only 14 amino acids.

The shotgun approach – using restriction enzymes

This was the original method for isolating genes and came with the discovery of enzymes called **restriction endonucleases** in the late 1960s and early 1970s. These enzymes are found in bacteria and they cut up DNA. Their function in bacteria is to cut up any invading virus DNA, thus *restricting* the multiplication of viruses in the cell. Different species of bacteria produce different restriction endonucleases. An endonuclease cuts (digests) a nucleic acid (hence 'nuclease') at specific points along the length of the molecule ('endo'- means internally, rather than attacking the molecule from the ends). The enzyme recognises a particular sequence of bases and cuts at these points. These cutting points are called **restriction sites**. Different enzymes attack different sequences. Well over 2000 different enzymes have now been isolated which attack 230 different sequences. The bacterium protects its own DNA by adding a methyl group to certain bases at the cutting sites.

Each enzyme is named after the bacterium from which it comes (fig 25.2). Note that the base sequence is often six bases long and palindromic, meaning that it reads the same in both directions. When studying fig 25.2 remember that the two complementary strands of DNA run in opposite directions. Some restriction enzymes leave a staggered cut with single-stranded ends (e.g. EcoRI, fig 25.2). These ends are described as '**sticky ends**' because they can be used to re-join fragments of DNA. They stick together by forming hydrogen bonds to complementary sticky ends from other DNA molecules cut by the same restriction enzyme (fig 25.1). For example, EcoRI produces the sticky end –TTAA. Some produce **blunt ends**, for example HindII in fig 25.2. In this way the DNA of any organism can be chopped up

into pieces of different size. The pieces are known as **restriction fragments**. The different lengths of these fragments depend on the restriction enzyme used, and on where the particular base sequences that the enzyme recognises are located (fig 25.3).

Each nucleotide in a piece of DNA carries a phosphate group which is negatively charged. Thus different lengths of DNA carry different total charges. These differences can be used to separate pieces of DNA of different length by placing them in an electrical field and allowing them to migrate to the positive electrode. This is done in a gel, and the technique is known as **gel electrophoresis** (fig 25.4). The gel is made of agarose (for very large fragments) or polyacrylamide (for smaller fragments). DNA is colourless, so its final position is revealed by staining or by using radioactive DNA and carrying out **autoradiography** which involves exposure of the gel to photographic film. The radiation blackens the film, showing the location of the DNA.

Having chopped up the DNA of the donor organism, one of the fragments will hopefully, by chance, contain an entire copy of the desired gene and not much else. This technique is sometimes referred to as the shotgun approach because it is not very specific and relies on chopping up all the DNA. It leaves the problem of finding the fragment with the desired gene which is discussed in section 25.1.3 below.

Split genes

Using reverse transcriptase or gene synthesis has an advantage over the shotgun approach in that the gene that is made is not a '**split gene**'. Split genes contain one or more sections of DNA called **introns** which are not part of the code for the final protein. The function of introns is still unclear, however if a eukaryote gene containing introns is placed in a bacterium, the bacterium does not have the necessary enzymes to remove the introns from the mRNA and a useless protein will therefore be made. Introns can be removed from the mRNA as shown in fig 25.5.

25.1.3 Stage 2: Putting genes into a vector

As explained earlier, the vectors most commonly used are plasmid DNA and phage DNA. The procedure for plasmid DNA will be described first, but is the same in principle to the procedure for phage DNA.

Plasmid DNA

The circular plasmid DNA molecules in bacteria are much smaller than those of the main chromosomal DNA and can easily be separated on the basis of size. The bacterial cells are broken open and chromosomal DNA is centrifuged down, leaving the plasmid DNA in the liquid (supernatant) above the pellet. The plasmids are then purified before cutting with a restriction enzyme (fig 25.1).

If a restriction enzyme has been used to isolate the donor DNA (i.e. the shotgun approach) the same restriction

Enzyme	Cuts DNA at	Origin of name

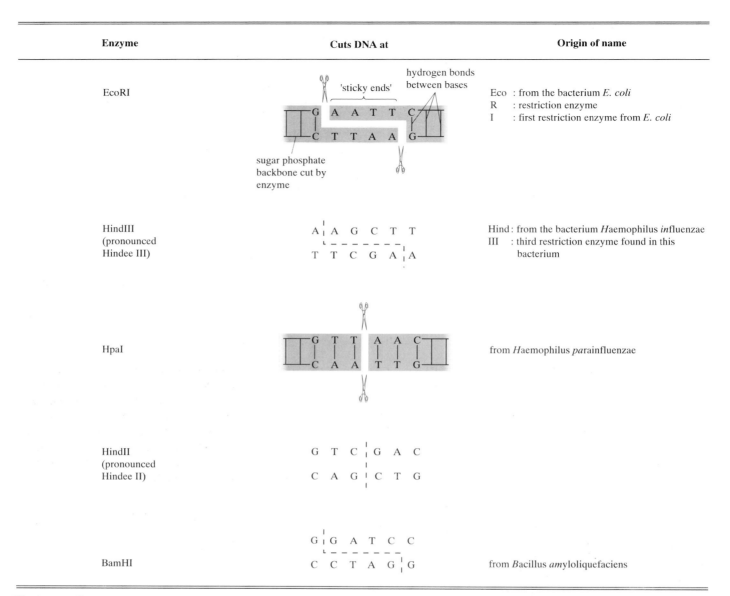

EcoRI

'sticky ends'

hydrogen bonds between bases

```
G A A T T C
C T T A A G
```

sugar phosphate backbone cut by enzyme

Eco : from the bacterium *E. coli*
R   : restriction enzyme
I   : first restriction enzyme from *E. coli*

HindIII
(pronounced
Hindee III)

```
A A G C T T
T T C G A A
```

Hind : from the bacterium *Haemophilus influenzae*
III   : third restriction enzyme found in this bacterium

HpaI

```
G T T A A C
C A A T T G
```

from *Haemophilus parainfluenzae*

HindII
(pronounced
Hindee II)

```
G T C G A C
C A G C T G
```

BamHI

```
G G A T C C
C C T A G G
```

from *Bacillus amyloliquefaciens*

Fig 25.2 *Some commonly used restriction enzymes. EcoRI, HindIII and BamHI make staggered cuts in the DNA leaving 'sticky ends'. A sticky end produced by, say, EcoRI can join to another sticky end produced by EcoRI. HindII and HpaI leave blunt ends. Diagrams of EcoRI and HpaI are shown in more detail.*

enzyme must be used for the plasmid DNA. The restriction fragments from the donor DNA, including those containing the wanted gene, are then mixed with the plasmid DNA and joined by their sticky ends. For example, the sticky end –AATT will bind to the complementary sticky end –TTAA. The initial attraction is due to hydrogen bonding, but the sugar–phosphate backbones are then joined using an enzyme called **DNA ligase**.

If the donor DNA is cDNA or a synthetic gene (from the first two methods above), or if the restriction enzyme in the shotgun method has produced blunt ends, then the procedure shown in fig 25.6 must be used.

Phage vector

Phages are useful as vectors for larger pieces of DNA than can reliably be carried by plasmids. One phage which is

commonly used is λ phage (fig 2.20). Part of the phage DNA is replaced with the DNA required for cloning. The part replaced is not needed for replication of the phage DNA inside the bacterial host cell, so cloning is unaffected. The procedure is summarised in fig 25.7. It is often used with the shotgun method of preparing DNA.

25.1.4   Stage 3: Introducing vector DNA into the host cell

The plasmid or phage vector must now be introduced into a bacterial cell which will allow the vector to multiply (clone itself and the foreign donor DNA it contains). The bacterium commonly used is *Escherichia coli*. *E. coli* is a normal inhabitant of the human gut and was chosen for this task because a great deal is known

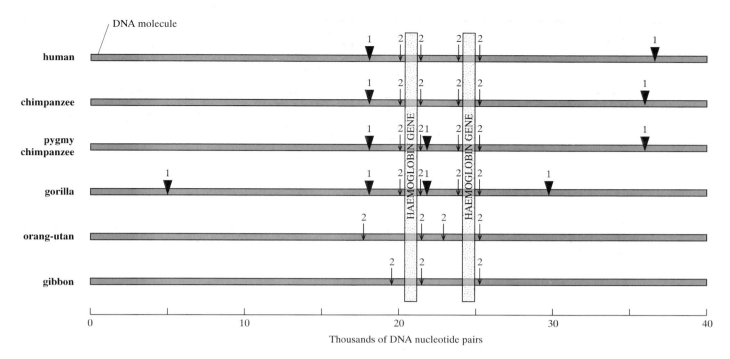

Fig 25.3 Use of restriction enzymes to chop up DNA and to produce restriction fragments of different length. In the example a part of the DNA which contains two haemoglobin genes from a range of primates has been chopped up by two restriction enzymes. Enzyme 1 is represented by ▼ and enzyme 2 is represented by ↓. Enzyme 1 will give two fragments with human DNA and enzyme 2 will give five fragments. The lengths of these fragments, and of those obtained if both enzymes are used together, would allow the positions of the cuts relative to each other to be worked out. This produces the 'restriction map' shown in the diagram. The more restriction enzymes used, the more detailed the map becomes. Note also that the more closely related the species, the more similar is their DNA and the more similar their restriction sites (cutting points). (Based on fig 7–4, p294, Molecular biology of the cell, 3rd ed., B. Alberts et al. (1994) Garland.)

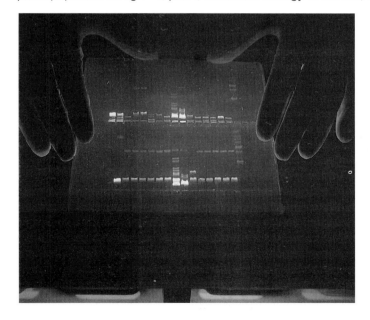

Fig 25.4 Gel electrophoresis to separate fragments of DNA of different length. The fragments are produced by chopping up the DNA with one or more restriction enzymes. The largest fragments are the slowest moving because they have more difficulty in moving through the pores in the gel. They are nearest the top of the gel in the photo.

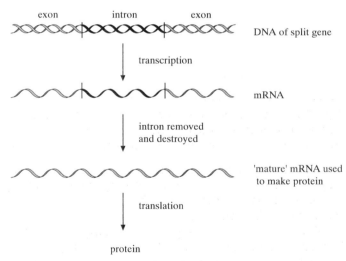

Fig 25.5 Transcription and translation of a gene containing an intron. The regions around introns are called exons. Genes may contain many introns. Only the exons code for protein.

839

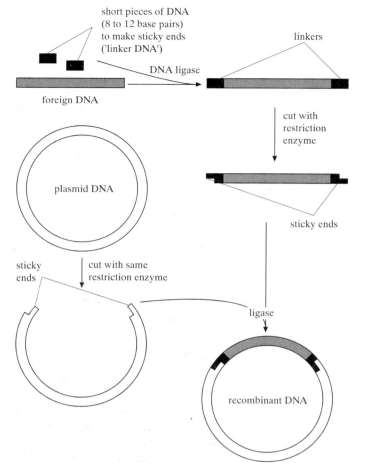

Fig 25.6 *Adding sticky ends to a blunt-ended DNA fragment, before adding the DNA to a vector to form a recombinant DNA molecule.*

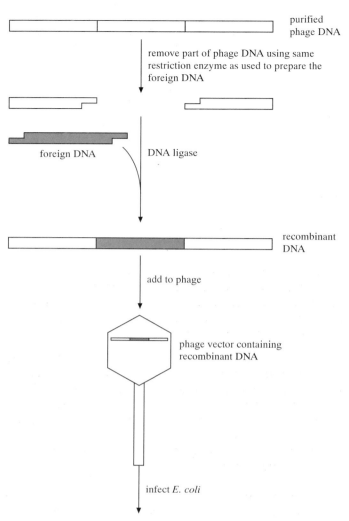

Fig 25.7 *Adding DNA to a phage vector.*

about its genetics and because it grows rapidly with a doubling time of 30 minutes. A mutant form of *E. coli* was specially developed for genetic engineering. This form can only survive in special laboratory conditions. Therefore if it escapes, with foreign genes inserted, it cannot infect humans.

If a plasmid vector is being used, it is added to a flask containing a culture of *E. coli*. Calcium ions, usually in the form of calcium chloride, are added to the flask, followed by a brief heat shock. This has the effect of making holes appear briefly in the cell surface membranes of the *E. coli*, making them permeable to DNA and allowing the plasmids to enter. The process of adding new DNA to a bacterial cell is called **transformation**

Phage vectors are introduced by infection of a bacterial lawn growing on an agar plate (section 12.8).

25.1.5   Stage 4: Cloning the DNA

A single phage containing one recombinant DNA molecule can produce more than 10^{12} identical copies of itself and the molecule in less than one day. *E. coli* cells containing plasmids are usually plated out onto nutrient agar in petri dishes. They can grow and divide once every 30 minutes, eventually forming visible colonies. This alone would produce at least as many copies of the required DNA as is obtained from phage vectors, but bacteria can also contain hundreds of copies of a plasmid and these will be copied each time the bacterium divides. Thus billions of clones are produced in a very short time with both techniques. The transformed bacteria must now be selected before further cloning.

Selecting the transformed bacteria

This will only be discussed for the situation in which plasmids have been used. When plasmid DNA is mixed with bacteria two problems arise. Firstly, not all the bacteria will be transformed (take up plasmids). Secondly, not all the plasmids will have taken up the foreign donor DNA. This problem is cleverly avoided by using plasmids which have two special features (fig 25.8):

- a gene for resistance to a particular antibiotic – if the bacteria are grown on a medium containing that

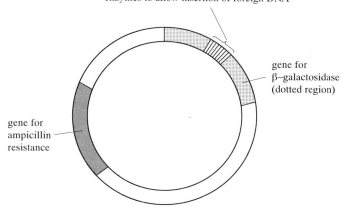

region containing restriction sites (indicated by lines) – these are the points which can be cut by restriction enzymes to allow insertion of foreign DNA

gene for β–galactosidase (dotted region)

gene for ampicillin resistance

Fig 25.8 *A plasmid vector containing a gene for resistance to the antibiotic ampicillin (a close relative of penicillin). This allows cells which are carrying the plasmid to be selected by treatment with ampicillin. Cells not carrying the plasmid will die.*

antibiotic, only the transformed cells (the ones containing plasmids) will survive and multiply to form colonies.

- a gene for the enzyme β-galactosidase which has had a group of restriction sites added – these restriction sites do not affect the performance of the gene. β-galactosidase is an enzyme which breaks down lactose to galactose and glucose (it breaks down any disaccharide containing galactose). It can also break down a colourless compound called X-gal to a blue compound. If foreign DNA is inserted at a restriction site in the gene, the gene will not work. Therefore if the bacteria that survive growing on the antibiotic are then grown on a medium containing X-gal, those colonies which lack the donor DNA will appear blue. Bacteria which form colourless colonies are the ones containing the donor DNA and can be isolated for further cloning.

25.1.6 Selecting bacteria with the required gene

If the shotgun method is used in Stage 1, the bacteria which are successful in cloning donor DNA are not necessarily all cloning the DNA containing the required gene. This is because the donor DNA was a mixture of a very large number of restriction fragments (up to a million in the case of human DNA). Only one or a few of these are likely to contain the piece of DNA or gene required for cloning, yet all will have been cloned. A mixture of clones like this is called a **library**. A library will also be produced by the reverse transcriptase method of Stage 1 if a mixture of mRNAs is used. This is sometimes necessary if the desired mRNA cannot be isolated in pure form. So after Stage 4, bacterial cultures have been isolated which are libraries unless a single gene was cloned, either by synthesis or from a single type of mRNA.

Using a gene probe

The required bacteria are selected using a **gene probe** as illustrated in fig 25.9. A gene probe can be used if some or all of the base sequence of the DNA being looked for is known. Alternatively the base sequence (or one very similar) can be predicted from a knowledge of the amino acid sequence of the protein it codes for, if this is known. The DNA or RNA probe that is made is a short sequence of nucleotides which is complementary to part of the required DNA and will therefore bind to it. For example, the probe AGTCCA would find and hydrogen bond to TCAGGT. Probes can be as short as 15 to 20 nucleotides, or much longer. The probe is usually made from radioactively labelled nucleotides using the radioactive element ^{32}P. When this binds to the DNA, the radioactivity acts as a marker which can be detected by autoradiography as shown in fig 25.9.

25.2 Applications of genetically engineered bacteria

25.2.1 Human insulin

Insulin is a protein hormone made in the pancreas which plays a vital role in the regulation of blood sugar levels (section 17.6.6). Its deficiency is one of the causes of the disease diabetes mellitus (sugar diabetes) where blood sugar levels become raised with harmful consequences. At least 3% of the population is affected by diabetes mellitus. This became a treatable disease from 1921 when two Canadian workers, Banting and Best, first isolated the hormone. Before that it resulted in terrible wasting symptoms (fig 25.10) and eventual death. Now more than 2 million people worldwide use insulin and the world market is worth several hundred million pounds a year.

Daily injections of insulin isolated from the pancreases of slaughtered pigs and cattle became the standard treatment. However, due to minor differences in the amino acid composition of insulin from species different to ourselves, and to traces of impurities, some patients were allergic to animal insulin and showed damaging side effects as a result of the injections. The ideal solution became possible with the introduction of genetic engineering. The gene for human insulin is inserted into a bacterium, and the bacterium is grown in a fermenter to make large quantities of the protein. An outline of the procedure currently used for human insulin is shown in fig 25.11.

A final problem which has not been discussed so far is how to switch the gene on in the bacterium. Not all the genes in a cell are switched on at any one time. Certain regions of DNA called **promoter regions** situated next door to the genes have to be activated before a gene is expressed. If the new gene is inserted in the middle of an existing gene, the switch for that gene may be used. The gene used in *E. coli* was for β-galactosidase (fig 25.8) but is

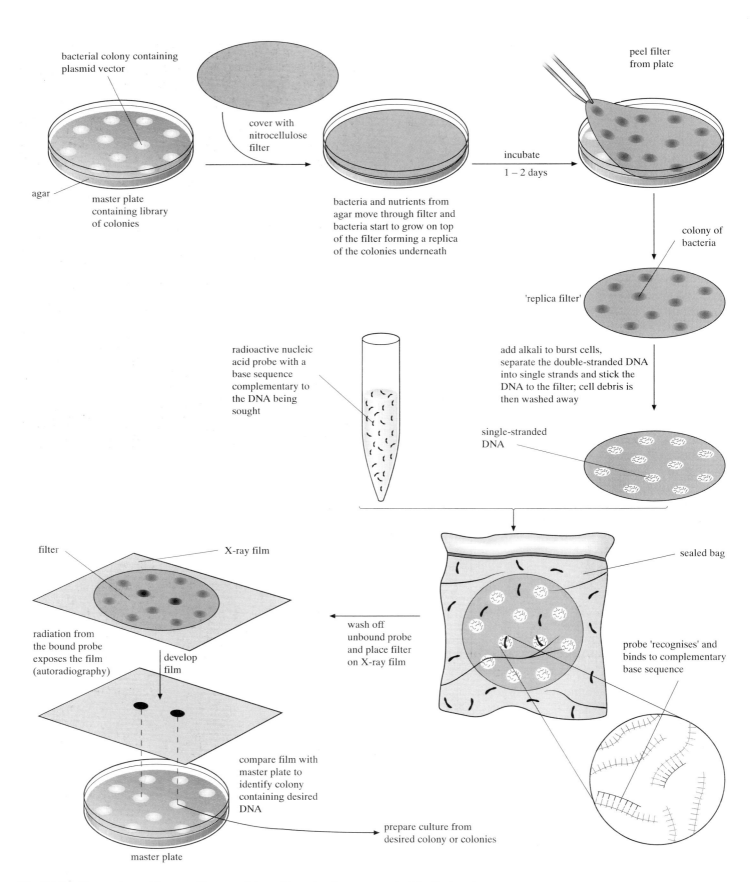

Fig 25.9 *Screening a library with a nucleic acid probe (a gene probe) to find a clone.*

Fig 25.10 *A young child who suffers from diabetes injecting herself with insulin.*

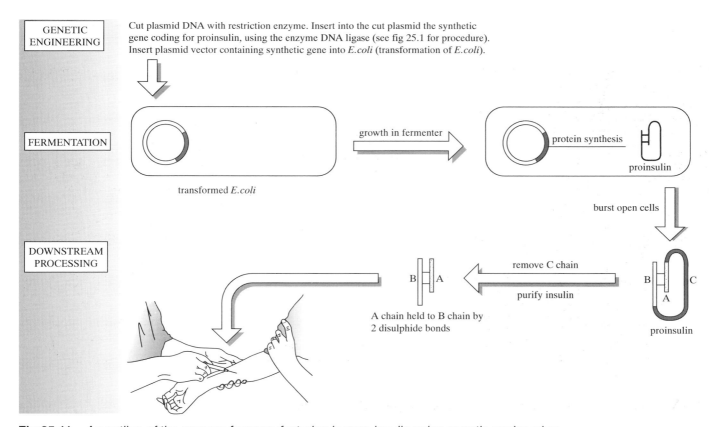

GENETIC ENGINEERING

Cut plasmid DNA with restriction enzyme. Insert into the cut plasmid the synthetic gene coding for proinsulin, using the enzyme DNA ligase (see fig 25.1 for procedure). Insert plasmid vector containing synthetic gene into *E.coli* (transformation of *E.coli*).

FERMENTATION

transformed *E.coli*

growth in fermenter

protein synthesis

proinsulin

burst open cells

DOWNSTREAM PROCESSING

B | A

A chain held to B chain by 2 disulphide bonds

remove C chain

purify insulin

B | C
A

proinsulin

Fig 25.11 *An outline of the process for manufacturing human insulin using genetic engineering.*

now tryptophan synthetase. Its promoter is switched on if *E. coli* is grown in a medium containing lactose.

The original technique was developed by Eli Lilly and Company and in 1982 human insulin, marketed as 'humulin', became the first genetically engineered pharmaceutical product to be approved for use.

25.2.2 Human growth hormone

Growth hormone is a small protein molecule produced in the pituitary gland. It affects all the tissues of the body, causing growth of almost all those that are capable of growing. Abnormally low levels of growth hormone in childhood result in dwarfism in which the body has normal proportions but is much smaller; intelligence is unaffected. Unlike the case with insulin, where insulin from slaughtered animals will function in humans, the growth hormones of different animals work only in the species of origin. Treatment of dwarfism has therefore relied on growth hormone extracted from the pituitary glands of dead humans, and the supply was not large enough to meet demand. Another problem was that extracts from pituitary glands were occasionally contaminated with the infectious protein that causes Creutzfeldt–Jakob disease (the same protein that may cause mad cow disease). After several fatalities among people who were treated in the 1970s the treatment was withdrawn. However, Genentech, a California-based company, have produced human growth hormone (hGH) from genetically engineered bacteria which contain the human gene for the hormone. It can be produced in much larger quantities and in a pure form. Regular injections of the hormone restore near-normal heights in children suffering from growth hormone deficiency.

The technique for producing the hormone is similar in principle to that shown for insulin in fig 25.11. The DNA code (gene) added to the bacterium is complementary DNA (cDNA), made from mRNA using reverse transcriptase as described in section 25.1.1. Before adding it to the vector, the cDNA has another piece of DNA added to it from the bacterium *E. coli*. This is the code for a 'signal sequence'. When translated, this becomes a sequence of amino acids which when added to the growth hormone acts like a key to allow it through the cell surface membrane of the bacterium and out of the cell. The hormone is therefore secreted from the bacterium into the surrounding medium after its manufacture, which makes purification a lot easier. The signal sequence is removed by a bacterial enzyme after its release, leaving the pure hormone.

25.2.3 Bovine somatotrophin, BST

As a result of genetic engineering, the gene for the hormone bovine somatotrophin, more commonly known as BST, has been added to bacteria and cloned in the same way as the genes for insulin and hGH. So it can now be produced in large quantities in a fermentation process.

BST is similar to human growth hormone. Like the latter, it is a small protein made in the pituitary gland and stimulates cell division, protein synthesis and growth in most parts of the body. It is particularly important for muscle and skeletal growth. If small doses are injected into cows every 1 to 2 weeks, it increases milk production by up to 25% (up to $5\,dm^3$ a day) and can result in a 10–15% increase in weight of beef cattle. Although the cattle consume more food, there is a net increase in profit. The dairy farmer can either sell more milk, or if restricted by milk quotas, can produce the same amount more cheaply (with fewer cows). Preliminary trials showed no change in behaviour, health or reproduction of the cattle, according to the manufacturers of BST, Monsanto of the USA. The cattle return to normal growth and milk production soon after the last injection.

During a trial programme with the hormone in the UK in 1985, the Ministry of Agriculture, Fisheries and Food (MAFF) allowed the milk from the cows to be mixed with that from other cows and sold to the public. This was despite protests from supermarkets and consumer groups. They also refused to identify the test herds. This produced great public alarm and protests. Use of BST has been banned in the EU. Some of the issues raised are summarised below and are worth discussing as an example of how science interacts with society and the importance of having informed opinions.

- Many people do not believe that use of BST would result in cheaper milk. They believe that only the manufacturers and farmers would benefit.
- There is concern about the long-term effects on human health. Since BST is very similar to human growth hormone, there is some concern that traces of the hormone in the milk might affect human growth. It could be argued that since the hormone is a protein, it would be digested before it could be absorbed, but there is no guarantee of this. It can also be argued that BST is a natural substance and that minute traces of it are already found in milk (about 2–10 parts per billion). No higher concentrations were found in the milk of BST-treated cows.
- There is already a surplus of milk and beef within the European Union.
- BST could help increase milk yields in August when there is a shortage of milk for cheese manufacture. This is because the autumn is a peak time for calving.
- Some evidence suggests that cows treated with BST are more susceptible to disease and may therefore need to be treated with other drugs to boost their immune systems. These might get into meat or milk. Cows producing high milk yields are more susceptible to mastitis, a disease of the udders. Recent research indicates that the incidence of mastitis may rise by up to 80% in BST-treated cows.
- BST has not been approved for use in the European Union and the Milk Marketing Board in the UK supports the ban on BST.

- Since the end of 1993 BST has been approved for use in the USA.
- Laboratory rats fed relatively high doses of BST showed no ill effects.
- Long-term trials on humans have not been carried out, nor have the effects on pregnant or lactating mothers been studied.

You can decide for yourself which arguments you find most persuasive. You might like to consider the issue from the point of view of (i) the manufacturer, (ii) the farmer and (iii) the consumer. Where should we go from here?

25.2.4 Cleaning up oil spills

Examples of how microorganisms can be used to clear up waste have already been met in chapter 12 in relation to treatment of sewage, recycling, biological mining and conversion of organic wastes into useful products such as sugar, alcohol and methane. Improvements in these will be possible with genetic engineering.

Another potentially important example is the attempt to produce genetically engineered bacteria capable of cleaning up oil spills. We still have no environmentally friendly method of doing this efficiently. Trials are underway with a genetically engineered strain of *Pseudomonas*, which can break down the four main groups of hydrocarbons present in oil (xylenes, naphthalenes, octanes and camphors) and can clean up oil in an oil–water mixture. The relevant genes occur on plasmids of naturally occurring *Pseudomonas* strains, but no single strain contains all four plasmids. All four types of gene have now been introduced into a single 'superbug'.

Such bacteria might be sprayed onto surfaces polluted with oil. The bacteria only work at the oil–water interface since they need oxygen. They are therefore better suited to cleaning up thin films of oil such as might cover rocks after a pollution incident, rather than thick slicks of oil. There is also the problem of releasing genetically engineered bacteria into the environment. At present the bacteria only work very slowly at low temperatures and would therefore not be very suitable for use in cold climates, as was needed when the oil tanker *Exxon Valdez* shed its oil in Alaskan waters in 1989.

25.3 Genetic engineering in eukaryotes

It is possible to genetically engineer eukaryotic organisms as well as bacteria. Organisms that have been genetically altered using the techniques of genetic engineering are generally referred to as **transgenic**.

Because transgenic organisms offer an alternative to traditional methods of animal and plant breeding, they offer an exciting new way forward in agriculture. Improving crops or domestic animals by traditional methods is a slow process which relies a lot on chance because of crossing over in meiosis and random segregation of chromosomes during sexual reproduction. For example, it takes 7–12 years to develop a new cereal variety. Genetic engineering offers the chance to add new genes directly, without relying on sexual reproduction. It opens up the possibility of 'designer' plants and animals with desirable properties such as disease resistance. Animals and plants can become 'living factories' for useful products other than food, just like bacteria in fermenters. The greatest challenge in agriculture is to improve food production in the developing countries and hopefully some of the new techniques will be applied to regions where food shortage is greatest. Ethical issues are raised, however, such as the well-being of animals and the fact that new genes are being released into the environment (fig 25.12).

Some key aims in plant and animal breeding which might be the subject of transgenics are:

- increased **yield**.
- improved **quality of food** from the point of view of health or digestibility, for example oil, fat, and protein.
- **resistance to pests and disease** – genes for resistance can be transferred from one species to another.
- increasing **tolerance of**, or **resistance to, environmental stress** such as drought, cold, heat or crowded conditions; for crops, tolerance to wind damage, acid or salty soils, waterlogged soils. Genes

Experts fear experiment brings fiction of the mad scientist one step closer to reality

Cloning breakthrough sounds ethical alarm

Scientists serve up vegetables that give cancer protection

Cloning humans would be genetic pornography says professor

Have they cloned the first human?

Scientists welcome move to clone sheep

Fig 25.12 *Newspaper headlines from the* Times, Sun *and* Evening Standard *relating to transgenic plants and animals.*

controlling stress responses can be isolated and moved from one organism to another.

- **rate of growth**, including time from birth, or planting, to maturity – the range of some crops might be extended by shortening their growing seasons.
- **herbicide resistance** (section 25.4.4).

The advantages of transgenics can be summarised as:

- a gene for a desirable characteristic can be identified and cloned;
- all the beneficial characteristics of an existing variety can be kept and just the desired new gene can be added;
- sexual reproduction is not necessary;
- transgenics is much faster than conventional breeding.

25.4 Transgenic plants

25.4.1 Getting new genes into plants

Using Agrobacterium

The most effective method of transferring genes into plants is to use the soil bacterium *Agrobacterium tumefaciens* as a vector. This bacterium contains a plasmid which can be used to carry the desired gene. It can infect, and therefore be used for, most dicotyledonous plants and causes **crown gall disease**. It enters through wounds and stimulates host cells to multiply rapidly, forming large lumps called **galls** which are really tumours (fig 25.13), masses of undifferentiated cells which grow independently of the rest of the plant like a cancer. Normally, wounded plant tissues release chemicals that stimulate cell division and the plant produces a group of cells called a **callus** which quickly covers the wound. Chemicals released by the wounded cells also stimulate *Agrobacterium* to infect the wound. Once it has infected the plant, the plasmid in *Agrobacterium* causes development of the gall. The plasmid, known as the T_i **plasmid** (tumour-inducing), contains a short piece of DNA called **T-DNA**. This leaves the bacterium and enters the plant cells where it is inserted into the plant's own DNA. Here it brings about the unregulated growth. The bacterium itself does not enter the cells, but can live between them, feeding on new products which the T-DNA directs the plant cells to make. The plant cells are said to be **transformed**.

The plasmid genes which control infection are different from those which cause unrestricted growth to form a tumour. The latter are on the T-DNA. It is therefore possible to remove the infection genes to make room for a new gene without affecting the ability of the T-DNA to transform plant cells. Also, the plasmid will no longer cause the crown gall disease.

Originally this technique could not be used for monocotyledonous plants which was a great disadvantage because monocots include the cereals, such as maize and wheat, which are the most important group of crops worldwide. However, this problem has now been overcome. The technique also works well for tomatoes, potatoes and many trees.

Whole plants can be grown from single transformed cells using the cloning techniques described in section 21.3. The first stage involves growing the cells in a liquid culture medium to produce an undifferentiated mass of cells called a callus. The callus can be plated out on to nutrient agar, and with the correct balance of hormones will produce shoots and roots and grow into a new plant. Another technique is to use *Agrobacterium* to infect the cut edges of discs punched out from leaves and to culture the discs on nutrient agar.

Using viruses

Phages (viruses that infect bacteria) can be used as vectors in the genetic engineering of bacteria, so viruses which attack plant cells should open up the possibility of doing the same in plants. The technique is still being developed.

Using guns

A surprisingly crude but effective method of introducing foreign DNA directly into plant cells is to use guns. The required DNA is coated onto the surface of 1 mm diameter gold or tungsten beads. These are placed next to the tip of a plastic bullet in the barrel of a specially designed gun. Originally the bullet was fired in the normal way with an explosive charge (and a fire-arms licence was needed) but pressurised gas is now used. The bullet is fired at a plate containing a microscopic hole. Some of the DNA-covered particles are sprayed through this hole into target cells or tissue held in a chamber just behind the hole. The barrel and the chamber are under vacuum during the firing process so that the particles do not slow down. Particles can be found in the cytoplasm of successfully transformed cells, so presumably the cell surface membranes heal themselves immediately after being shot.

25.4.2 Pest resistance – insecticides

Insects cause enormous crop losses in agriculture and some transmit diseases to farm animals. Since the Second World War many chemicals, starting with DDT, have been used as insecticides. Gradually we have come to understand the ecological damage that can be done (section 10.8.4) and are developing ways to reduce or avoid the problem. One strategy is to rely more on biological control.

The soil bacterium *Bacillus thuringiensis*, referred to by biologists as Bt, produces a powerful protein toxin which can be used against several species of insect pest. It is 80 000 times more powerful than the organophosphate insecticides commonly sprayed on crops and is fairly selective, killing only the larvae of certain species. Different strains of Bt kill different insects, mainly the larvae of moths and butterflies (caterpillars) and of some hemipterans, such as white flies (maggots), the larvae of flies, such as mosquitoes (aquatic larvae). Some kill nematode worms,

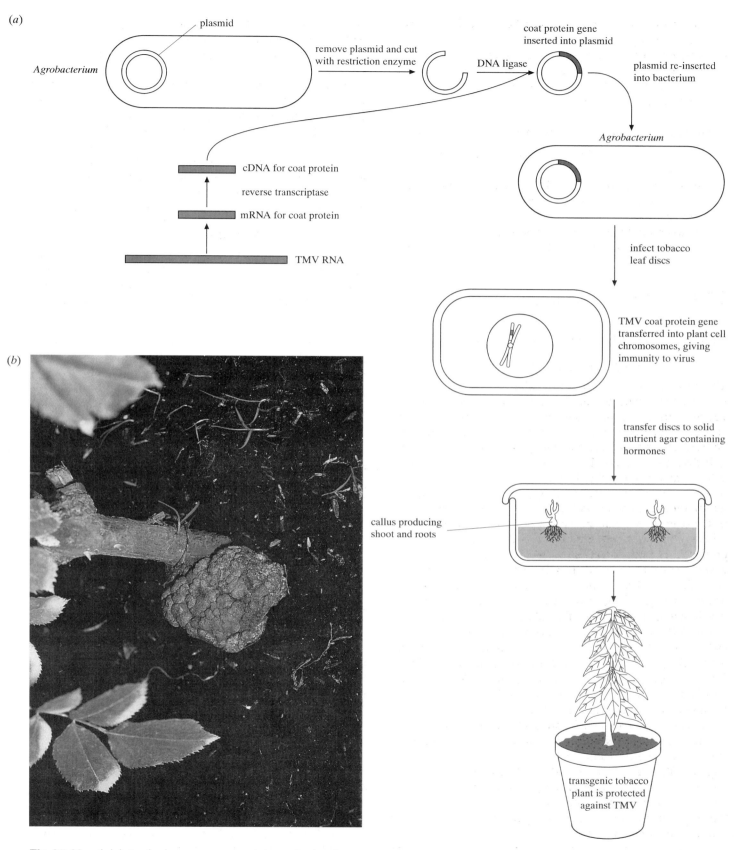

(a)

plasmid

Agrobacterium

remove plasmid and cut with restriction enzyme

DNA ligase

coat protein gene inserted into plasmid

plasmid re-inserted into bacterium

cDNA for coat protein

reverse transcriptase

mRNA for coat protein

TMV RNA

Agrobacterium

infect tobacco leaf discs

TMV coat protein gene transferred into plant cell chromosomes, giving immunity to virus

transfer discs to solid nutrient agar containing hormones

callus producing shoot and roots

transgenic tobacco plant is protected against TMV

(b)

Fig 25.13 *(a) Introducing a new gene into a plant cell using* Agrobacterium. *(b) Crown-gall tumour caused by* Agrobacterium *infection of a wound.*

which can also be pests. The toxin binds specifically to the inside of the insect's gut and damages the epithelium so that it cannot absorb digested food and starves to death (fig 25.14). The bacteria themselves can be applied to the crop as a form of biological control, but this is rather expensive because they quickly die, making regular spraying necessary. Attempts are being made to isolate the toxins and to stabilise them by protein engineering. A more cunning approach though is to take the gene responsible for the production of the toxin and to genetically engineer it into plants, giving them permanent protection. Caterpillars or other larvae eating their leaves would then die. This has been attempted and successfully achieved for some plants, for example maize. Maize is attacked by the European corn borer, an insect larva that tunnels into the plant from eggs laid on the undersides of leaves. In field trials normal and genetically engineered maize plants were deliberately infested with larvae and the results monitored over 6 weeks. The average length of the tunnels in the engineered plants was 6.3 cm and in the normal plants was 40.7 cm. The engineered plants also suffered less leaf damage. Rice,

Fig 25.14 *Cabbage white caterpillar six days after feeding on a plant treated with a Bt toxin. The caterpillar is dead and decomposing from the gut.*

cotton, potato, tomato and other crops have now all been genetically engineered in this way.

Another example which does not involve bacteria has also been successful. Several types of plant, particularly those of the legume family such as peas and beans, produce small polypeptides that inhibit proteinases in the insect gut. This reduces the ability of the insects to digest protein and prevents or slows down their growth. The genes responsible have been transferred to some other crops that lack them. This has proved particularly successful in giving seeds resistance to some beetle larvae that feed on them.

Many similar attempts involving genetic engineering are currently being made to protect plants against other pests such as fungi, bacteria and viruses. Genetically engineered pest resistance has three major advantages over other forms of pest control:

- pesticides are expensive and time consuming to apply;
- pesticides are rarely selective and kill harmless and useful organisms as well, such as pollinators;
- some pesticides accumulate in the environment and cause long-term changes in animals.

25.4.3 Pest resistance – viruses

Plant viruses are serious pests of crops. The first attempt to genetically engineer resistance to a virus was with tobacco plants. Tobacco is attacked by an RNA virus called tobacco mosaic virus (TMV – fig 2.18). TMV also attacks tomato plants, causing losses worth over 50 million dollars in the USA every year. *Agrobacterium* has been used to introduce a gene from TMV into tobacco plants. It codes for a virus coat protein. When deliberately infected with TMV these plants prove much more resistant than untreated control plants. Something rather similar to vaccination seems to take place (fig 25.15). Similar experiments have more recently been done to protect potato, tomato and alfalfa from virus attack.

25.4.4 Herbicide-resistant crops

An interesting application of genetic engineering in plants is the introduction of genes which give resistance to certain herbicides. The crop can then be sprayed with that herbicide and only the weeds will be killed. This solves the problem that weedkillers are not normally very selective. Weeds can reduce crop yields by over 10% even in developed countries where modern agricultural methods are used. It is estimated that genetically engineered herbicide resistance could double or even quadruple yields in some parts of Africa where serious weed problems are found. Particularly harmful are the parasitic weeds broomrape (*Orobanche*), found north of the Sahara, and witchweed (*Striga*), found in sub-Saharan Africa. They affect maize, millet, wheat, sorghum,

Fig 25.15 *Tobacco mosaic virus causes pale mottling on infected plants.*

make protein and other organic compounds. The process can be carried out only by certain bacteria. Some nitrogen-fixing species live in the root nodules of plants, particularly plants such as peas, beans, alfalfa and clover which are legumes. These plants benefit, but artificial nitrogen fertilisers have to be added to most crops if the soil is not to become deficient in nitrogen, especially where the same crop is grown year after year in the same soil as is often the case with cereals. Over 60 million tonnes of nitrogen fertiliser were used worldwide in 1987. If plants contained their own nitrogen-fixing genes, enormous savings could be made in the time, money and energy used in making, transporting and spraying the fertilisers.

Genetic engineering of nitrogen fixation is made difficult by the fact that nitrogen fixation is a complex process involving many enzymes. About 15 genes are involved (the Nif genes). Also, part of the process is anaerobic, requiring a means of excluding oxygen. Although a great deal of work has been done, it has so far proved impossible to make the genes function properly in eukaryotes.

25.4.6 Transgenic tomatoes

Soft fruits such as tomatoes, bananas and red peppers are usually picked green and ripened artificially using ethene gas in warehouses (section 16.2.9). This means they are still hard when picked, reducing bruising and enabling the fruit to be picked mechanically and tipped into containers. It also allows controlled ripening so that the fruit will have maximum appeal to the customer. However, much of the flavour of the fruit is lost during transport and shipping due to biochemical changes. A company called Calgene in the USA, and ICI Seeds in the UK, have produced a genetically engineered tomato in which the ripening process is slowed down. This means the fruit can be left on the plant for longer, giving both increased yields and a fuller development of flavour. There is therefore a twin advantage for farmer and customer. The tomatoes first went on sale in the USA in 1995 as 'Flavr Savr' tomatoes. They are expensive, but do taste better. They were first introduced in the UK by Sainsbury in 1996, initially in tomato paste. The issue of safety and genetically engineered foods, including Flavr Savr tomatoes, is discussed in section 25.6.

25.4.7 More examples of genetic engineering in plants

- New colours, patterns and shapes of flowers are being experimented with by the horticultural industry. For example, experiments are underway to produce blue roses.

sunflowers and legumes. Herbicide-resistant corn, wheat, sugar beet and oilseed rape have so far been produced by developed countries for their own use. These are resistant to the herbicide Basta.

25.4.5 Nitrogen fixation

A long-term goal in agriculture is to introduce the genes for nitrogen fixation into crop plants. Nitrogen fixation is the process by which atmospheric nitrogen gas is reduced to ammonia within cells so that it can be used to

- Use of crops to produce medical drugs instead of food. This should be cheaper than using cultures of mammalian cells as at present. For example, the human enkephalin gene has been expressed in plants.
- Use of plants to produce mouse monoclonal antibodies.
- Improve the poor bread-making quality of the high-yielding British wheats. Improving the quality of protein will improve the flour quality. At least 11% of the protein needs to be of the high quality required to produce the large volume and suitable texture of a good loaf.
- Improve the nutritional qualities of plant foods, for example increase the proportion of essential amino acids. Many legumes are deficient in sulphur-containing amino acids. Genes from the brazil nut may rectify this.

25.5 Transgenic animals

25.5.1 Getting new genes into animals

One of the earliest successes in creating transgenic animals was in a mouse. A growth hormone gene from a rat was inserted into the genome of a mouse. Attached to the growth hormone gene was a powerful promoter which was stimulated by the presence of heavy metals in the mouse's diet. When these heavy metals were included in the mouse's food, the growth hormone gene was almost continually 'switched on'. This made the mouse grow at 2–3 times faster than mice without the gene. The mouse with the growth gene also finished growth at about twice as large as normal. This was achieved through genetic engineering. There are five basic methods now used in the development of transgenic animals:

- microinjection of eggs;
- use of stem cells;
- virus vectors;
- direct uptake of DNA stimulated by calcium or an electric current ('transfection');
- use of liposomes.

Microinjection of eggs

If it is desired that all the cells of an animal should contain a new gene, it must be introduced into an egg cell. This is done by firstly giving a hormone fertility drug to a female to stimulate production of extra eggs by the ovary. Fertilisation is allowed to occur and then the fertilised eggs are collected. The donor DNA is then injected directly into one of the pronuclei of a fertilised egg using a very fine needle-like pipette while viewing under a microscope. The process is described in more detail in fig 25.16. In some, though not all, cases the DNA integrates into one or more of the chromosomes. The two pronuclei later fuse and the egg becomes the zygote. The fertilised eggs are transferred to one or more foster mothers (two offspring maximum per mother if sheep or cattle) and the offspring are later screened for the presence of the new gene. The best success rates achieved so far are about one transgenic animal for every 20 eggs treated (sheep) or 100 eggs (cows). Herds of animals must therefore be kept, making it an expensive process. The first experiments on farm animals were carried out on rabbits, pigs and sheep, and these have been followed by cattle and fish.

Use of stem cells

A process which gives more control than the method described above is becoming more popular. Here a few cells (known as 'stem cells') are taken from a young embryo. These cells can be cloned indefinitely in a test tube. The new gene can be introduced into the cells by various means, including microinjection. The advantage is that the cells that are expressing the new gene (transformed cells) can be identified before adding them to the foster mother. This saves producing many unwanted non-transgenic animals. It might also be possible to introduce

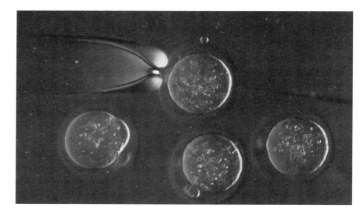

Fig 25.16 *Microinjection of DNA into an egg. The nuclei of the male and female gamete have not yet fused and at this stage are called pronuclei. They are visible at the centre of the egg. The DNA is injected into one of the pronuclei using the very fine needle-like pipette at the right of the photo. The egg cell is held steady by the larger pipette at the left. Several hundred copies of the DNA fragment are added.*

the gene into a specific region of a chromosome which may be necessary for normal expression of some genes. This ability would be particularly important if the technique is ever used with humans.

The successfully transformed cells are injected back into a normal embryo and become part of its normal development. The resulting animal is a mixture of two genetically different types of cell, some derived from the normal stem cells and some derived from the transformed stem cells. Such an animal is known as a **chimera** (after a mythological animal which had the head of a lion, the body of a goat and the tail of a serpent). The sex cells of the animal will also be mixed and some of its gametes will carry the new gene. These will give rise to completely transgenic animals in the next generation.

Virus vectors

This method is similar in principle to that used for phage vectors in bacteria. Plasmid vectors are not possible because animal cells do not contain plasmids. It is not used with egg cells but only when some of the body cells need to be transformed, as with gene therapy (section 25.7.11).

Direct uptake of DNA

Fragments of DNA can be taken up directly by phagocytosis under the right conditions. If DNA is prepared in the presence of calcium phosphate this process is stimulated, although it is not very efficient. It is best suited to gene therapy where only some of the cells in the body need to be modified. Alternatively a process called **electroporation** can be used in which the cells are stimulated with a brief shock from a weak electric current. This causes temporary holes to appear in the cell surface membrane, which becomes more permeable to DNA as a result.

Liposomes

Liposomes are small artificially created spheres (vesicles) surrounded by a phospholipid bilayer like a membrane. The required DNA is contained within the liposome. The liposomes fuse with and enter the cells (see also section 25.7.11).

25.5.2 Pharmaceutical proteins from milk

One use of transgenic animals is to produce relatively large quantities of rare and expensive proteins for use in medicine, a process sometimes referred to as 'pharming' of drugs. Such drugs cannot always be produced by bacteria in the way we have already seen for human insulin and hGH because bacteria do not always have the necessary machinery to process the proteins made. For example, the protein may have to be folded precisely or modified using mammalian cell machinery. Factor IX protein, for example, has to have a –COOH group added to some of its amino acids after production. Large-scale cell culture of the cells that produce these proteins is possible in theory but is very expensive and technically difficult.

The most successful approach so far has been to use the mammary glands to produce the protein so that it can be harvested by milking the animal. It is then relatively easy to purify it. A commercially successful example is the manufacture of **AAT (α-1-antitrypsin)** by PPL Pharmaceuticals, a company founded in 1987 and based in Edinburgh. They have several flocks of sheep, each producing different proteins. The first transgenic sheep to produce AAT was Tracy, although she herself is no longer used as a source of the protein. The offspring of transgenic animals continue to carry the gene, so whole flocks of transgenic sheep can eventually be built up (fig 25.17). Transgenic animals are seemingly perfectly normal, and no ill effects have been detected as a result of the treatment.

AAT is a naturally occurring protein found in human blood. A mutant form of the gene that codes for it causes a genetic disease which leads to emphysema (section 9.7.3) as a result of uninhibited elastase activity. Elastase is an enzyme produced by some white blood cells which destroys elastic fibres in the lungs as part of the normal turnover of elastic tissue. Its activity is normally regulated by AAT, which inhibits the enzyme. (Smoking is also thought to inhibit AAT, explaining one link between smoking and emphysema.) AAT is made in the liver and can be extracted from blood. However, more people need AAT than can be supplied by the usual means. The healthy human gene for AAT has now been added to sheep and the mammary gland of the sheep is used to express the gene. Sheep are used because they have a shorter generation time, lower cost and are easier to handle than cows.

The gene has a high degree of expression, meaning it is switched on most of the time. This results in nearly 50% of the milk protein being human AAT (fig 25.18). The sheep carries out the correct modification of the protein, including adding sugar to it to make it a glycoprotein. The procedure for making AAT is outlined in fig 25.19.

Fig 25.17 *Transgenic sheep awaiting milking. They have a human gene incorporated into their DNA which is responsible for production of the protein α-1-antitrypsin. This is produced in the mammary cells and excreted in the sheep's milk.*

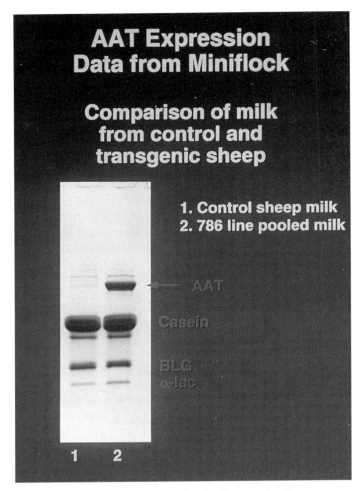

Fig 25.18 *Gel electrophoresis of milk proteins from a sheep. (1) Normal milk. (2) Milk from a transgenic sheep showing presence of a new band due to AAT.*

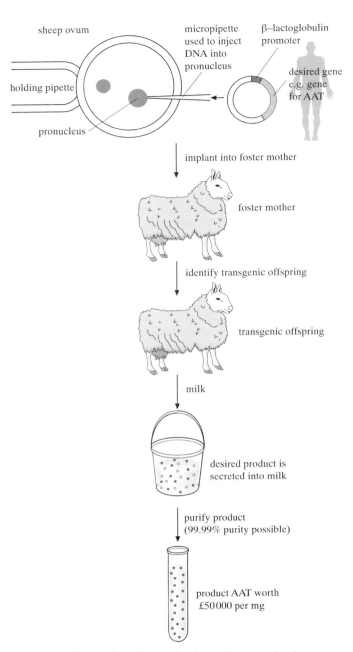

Fig 25.19 *Procedure for producing a transgenic sheep containing a human gene, e.g. the gene for AAT.*

All the cells of the sheep contain the same gene for AAT, so how do we ensure that only the cells of the mammary gland make it? The answer is to use the body's own regulatory system. Every cell in the body contains the entire genetic code, so every cell contains the genes for milk proteins (the same is true whether you are male or female). However, for the gene to be expressed the promoter, a piece of DNA next to the gene, must be switched on. By cloning one of the sheep's own milk protein promoters and attaching it to the human DNA, we can ensure that only mammary glands express that DNA. The promoter chosen is that for β-lactoglobulin, a protein present in high concentrations of milk.

Clinical trials with AAT will have to be completed before it is released, but it should be available within a few years.

Other examples of proteins produced in this way include factor IX, a blood-clotting protein whose absence causes one type of haemophilia (section 24.6.1). Another is **tPA (tissue plasminogen activator)** which is used to dissolve blood clots in patients suffering from heart disease. PPL Pharmaceuticals are now working on fibrinogen, the major

protein involved in blood clotting, which has a very complex secondary and tertiary structure. It would be used as a tissue glue after surgery; laid on a wound, it helps healing. It has already been purified from blood and used for this purpose in the USA.

25.5.3 Growth hormone

Growth hormone genes have already been discussed in sections 25.2.2 and 25.2.3 and the controversy over BST was discussed in section 25.2.3. Similar controversy arose over the introduction of human growth hormone genes into farm animals. When this was done the normal controls over production of the hormone were avoided. Transgenic sheep which overproduce growth hormone grow leaner and put on weight more quickly, making more efficient use of their food. However, they are more prone to infection, tend to die young and the females are infertile. Similarly, transgenic pigs grow leaner meat more efficiently. However, even more side effects were noted than with sheep, including arthritis, gastric ulcers, heart and kidney disease. Until ways are found of regulating the genes more precisely, the process will not be used commercially.

More recently scientists in Canada have added a gene from another fish (the ocean pout) to salmon which activates the salmon's own growth hormone gene. The salmon grow up to 30 times their normal weight and at 10 times the normal rate. Scottish fish farmers started breeding them on a trial basis in 1996.

25.5.4 Summary

Table 25.2 summarises some of the important examples of plant and animal transgenesis which had been achieved by the mid-1990s. Most new scientific and medical procedures are still tried first on mice because they breed so rapidly and are convenient to handle. The Home Office monitors experiments done in the UK. 181 000 procedures were carried out on mice in the UK in 1994 compared with 3000 on other transgenic animals. These are still relatively small numbers compared with what is expected in the future.

25.6 Benefits and hazards – the ethical and social implications of genetic engineering

From the earliest days of genetic engineering scientists have been very aware of the need to consider the potential hazards and ethical issues associated with this new branch of biology. Original concerns in 1971 focused on plans to clone cancer genes from viruses into *E. coli*. It was argued that if the genetically altered *E. coli* escaped from the laboratory, they might spread the gene into *E. coli* that live in the human gut by transferring the plasmids, for example by conjugation (section 2.3.3). It was also argued that human DNA, and the DNA of other mammals like mice, could contain cancer-causing genes (oncogenes) and that these might inadvertently get transmitted with neighbouring pieces of DNA being used for genetic engineering. In February 1975 a group of more than 100 internationally well-known molecular biologists met in California and decided that, until the risks could be more precisely estimated, certain restrictions should be placed on genetic engineering research. This was a remarkable self-imposed brake on scientific progress, not imposed by the Government but by the scientists themselves. Work on cancer viruses was stopped. Non-scientists who had been

part of the debate were invited to join the Advisory Committee that was set up by the American Government in 1976. Similar bodies were set up in Europe, including the Genetic Manipulation Advisory Group (GMAG) in the UK. After a two-year halt, during which safe procedures were established, research on cancer viruses and other work continued. Careful checks on the safety and implications of procedures remain to this day. Debate continues about how strict the rules and regulations should be. There has been more resistance to developments in Europe than in the USA.

In the 1980s an explosion of activity and interest was unleashed. Manufacturing companies quickly began investing billions of dollars into not just genetic engineering but all the 'biotechnologies' which were emerging from molecular biology. **Biotechnology**, a new industry, was born. We have examined some of the current applications of biotechnology in agriculture, medicine, industry and waste treatment in this chapter and in chapter 12, and further applications such as gene therapy and genetic fingerprinting will be discussed later in this chapter. What, then, are the major issues which face us now?

25.6.1 Human safety

The first food containing genetically engineered DNA to be approved for marketing was the 'Flavr Savr' tomato (section 25.4.6). This is a useful case study of concerns about the safety of foods.

One of the main concerns relates to the vectors used for transforming plant cells. These contain genes for antibiotic resistance, most frequently kanamycin resistance. These genes enter the transformed plants with the desired gene (fig 25.1). Flavr Savr tomatoes contain one of these antibiotic resistance genes. The concern is that when the tomato is eaten, the gene may pass from the tomato to the *E. coli* bacteria in the gut, making them resistant to kanamycin and related antibiotics. Since bacteria leave the gut in the faeces, the gene may spread to other potentially harmful bacteria in the environment which, if they infected humans, would be antibiotic resistant. In practice, the tomato gene, along with all the other DNA, would most likely be digested once eaten, and even if it were not, the chances of the gene passing through a series of organisms is extremely remote. Also, the kanamycin-resistance gene is already common in the environment. Nevertheless, scientists are trying to find ways to remove the marker genes after transformation.

In 1996 the European Union allowed genetically modified maize to be imported from the USA. The maize has a bacterial gene which increases its resistance to pests and disease, but also has a gene for resistance to the antibiotic ampicillin. Greenpeace is opposed to this introduction and is threatening legal action.

The public are extremely wary of genetically engineered products because of the publicity which has surrounded such issues as the use of growth hormones (see section

Table 25.2 Some plants and animals that have been genetically manipulated and some of the characteristics involved. (From Claire Pickering & John Beringer, *Modern Genetics*, *Biol. Sci.* Rev. 7, no. 4, March 1995, p. 34, Philip Allan.)

Examples of characteristics

Organism	Toxin for insect resistance	Herbicide tolerance	Antibiotic resistance	Change of flower colour	Virus resistance	Altered nutrients	Resistance to fungi	Production of pharmaceuticals	Resistance to bacteria	Prevention of ice crystal formation	Reduced accumulation of heavy metals in leaves	Delayed ripening	More rapid growth	Alterations for research on diseases	Tolerance to low temperatures	
Alleghenny serviceberry	•															Plants
Apple	•															
Cabbage		•														
Chicory			•													
Chrysanthemum				•												
Cotton	•	•														
Cucumber					•											
Eucalyptus			•													
Flax		•														
Lettuce					•											
Lucerne					•	•										
Maize	•	•			•	•										
Melon family					•											
Oilseed rape	•	•	•			•	•	•								
Papaya					•											
Peanut		•														
Petunia				•												
Plum					•											
Poplar	•															
Potato		•				•		•	•							
Rice	•		•			•										
Soybean		•				•										
Strawberry		•								•						
Sugar beet		•				•										
Sunflower						•										
Tobacco	•	•	•		•	•	•			•	•					
Tomato	•	•	•		•	•	•			•		•				
Walnut	•		•													
Wheat		•														
Carp													•			Animals
Catfish													•			
Cattle								•								
Goat								•								
Mice								•						•		
Pigs								•					•	•		
Rats								•						•		
Salmon													•			
Sea bass															•	
Sheep								•								
Trout													•			

25.2.3 for a discussion of the issue of BST). Companies that have invested millions of pounds in research and development cannot afford to make mistakes, and therefore have a strong vested interest in making sure their products are safe. For example, PPL who manufacture the anti-emphysema drug AAT imported all their sheep from New Zealand to ensure that they were scrapie-free. (Scrapie causes a disease in sheep similar to mad cow disease.) Transgenic goats being used by Genzyme Transgenics for the production of monoclonal antibodies in milk are fed only food free of pesticides and herbicides. Also, no protein or animal fat additives to their food are allowed so that any possibility of transfer of disease to humans from other animals is prevented. The products are probably safer than many traditional products which we are happy to accept.

25.6.2   Safety of the environment

In section 25.4.3 the possibility of producing virus-resistant crops was described. A fear which has been raised with the method used is that a different virus might infect the crop and have its genetic code (RNA or DNA) wrapped in the protein coat of TMV instead of its own normal protein coat. It might then be able to invade all the crops that TMV can invade. It is important that extensive trials are carried out in natural conditions in all cases of crop protection to be sure that incidents like this, or unthought-of problems, do not occur.

Both North America and Europe have very strict regulations controlling the release of genetically engineered organisms (GEOs) into the environment. In the European Union each member country has its own authority which oversees all releases of GEOs. In the UK the authority is jointly held by the Department of the Environment and the Ministry of Agriculture, Fisheries and Food (MAFF). One of the early controversies concerned genetically engineered 'ice-minus' bacteria. The original bacterium lives on many crop plants and makes them susceptible to frost damage because a protein it secretes helps the formation of ice crystals on the plants. The bacterium was genetically engineered to remove the gene coding for this protein, producing the so-called 'ice-minus' bacterium. The intention was to spray this on crops such as strawberries to make them more resistant to freezing. There was a passionate legal battle about the dangers of releasing GEOs into the environment, but permission was eventually given for release. After that the rules were made clearer and less restrictive.

The first approval for *unrestricted* release of a GEO in Britain was given by a Department of the Environment Advisory Committee in 1994. The organism was produced by the Belgian company 'Plant Genetic Systems' (PGS). It was a new type of oilseed rape which contains genes for resistance to the herbicide Basta (section 25.4.4). By that time over 60 small-scale field trials of GEOs had taken place in Britain and over 1000 in Europe and North America. There are far more potential dangers once unrestricted release is granted. Rapeseed, for example, can become a weed in hedgerows and would be impossible to control with Basta. It could cross-fertilise with relatives such as wild mustard, thus spreading the resistance to wild plants. PGS claim that the environmental risks with rapeseed are negligible.

Another concern is that developing herbicide-resistant plants may encourage the use of greater amounts of herbicides, particularly Basta, although the companies concerned argue that it may lead to less herbicide spraying because it will be more effective, and that older, more harmful herbicides will be phased out. Greenpeace were one organisation which opposed the release of the rapeseed.

Other crops that are resistant to disease, drought or other types of environmental stress, might similarly spread their resistance to weeds, producing weeds that might overrun agricultural areas very rapidly. There have been many hundreds of releases of transgenic plants elsewhere in the world. In China, for example, virus-resistant tobacco is being grown commercially. None of these releases has resulted in any known harmful environmental effects.

Genetically engineered fish, such as the giant salmon mentioned in section 25.5.3, pose a serious threat. The fish are contained so that in theory they should not escape. However, young, small fish have been known to be carried away by birds and dropped in local waters, and larger fish have been known to escape. There are many examples from the past of newly introduced animals causing great ecological damage, such as the rabbit in the UK and in Australia. If the Scottish salmon escape into the sea, where they migrate as adults, there are fears that they may affect the balance of the already endangered wild salmon populations. They might also affect food chains in unpredictable ways. Already more than 90% of the salmon in some Scottish streams are descended from salmon which have escaped from fish farms in Norway.

25.6.3   Animals and ethics

Humans often think of themselves as being superior to other animals (not to mention plants, fungi, bacteria and so on) and therefore having the 'right' to exploit other organisms for their own benefit. However there has been a growing trend in recent years to challenge the human-centred (anthropocentric) view of our relationship with other species. There is particular concern about the way we exploit animals for food and for development of medical products. One aim of genetic engineering is to increase the growth rate and yield of animals like cattle, pigs and poultry. The harmful effects of unregulated production of growth hormone on the health of pigs and sheep has been described in section 25.5.3. Use of BST in dairy cattle in the United States carries increased risk of mastitis (section 25.2.3). There appears to be little concern about whether the animals are biologically 'designed' to withstand the additional stress of increased production of milk, meat, eggs and other products. An interesting case study is Hermann, a transgenic bull born in

Holland in 1990. Hermann contains a gene which, if passed on to his female offspring, will enable them to produce a human milk protein (lactoferrin) in their milk. Environmental groups threatened to boycott companies that sponsored the work and this forced a Dutch producer of baby foods to withdraw from the project.

An important motive for producing modified animals for food is commercial profit. Where there is an additional motive, such as preventing or treating disease, the issues get even more complex because the well-being of the animal has to be balanced against the well-being of humans. Medical experiments may involve a certain amount of animal suffering. An example is provided by the oncomouse which was the first animal to be patented. The oncomouse is a transgenic mouse to which an oncogene has been added, a gene that causes cancer. The mice develop tumours much more frequently than normal and are used in cancer research. Some people argue that patenting animals is itself unethical because it reduces them to the level of objects. Others argue that experiments such as those with oncomice cause suffering and should therefore be banned. In January 1993 two UK animal rights groups, the British Union for the Abolition of Vivisection (BUAV) and Compassion in World Farming (CIWF) joined with other European groups to launch an appeal against the European patent for the oncomouse, which was granted in 1992. The European Patent Office held public hearings from November 1995 but ran out of time before a judgement could be made, leaving the issue unresolved. Patenting animals, it is argued, makes producing them more profitable, so by preventing patenting the animal welfare groups hope to reduce exploitation of animals. However, there is no guarantee that this would happen. In fact, some patents that have run out have been allowed to lapse. The Cancer Research Campaign (which has reduced its animal experimentation enormously in recent years) says its policy now is 'not to patent transgenic animals after consideration of the moral, scientific and utility issues'. The utility issues may include a growing feeling that it is not commercially worth patenting the animal. Public opinion may be part of the reason.

Fig 25.20 shows part of a letter sent by BUAV to its members in August 1995. Donald Crawford of BUAV says that transgenics 'causes pain and suffering to a large number of animals. We believe that the insertion of genes from other species into laboratory animals is an ethical minefield. The directions in which that approach to life can lead opens up a Pandora's box.' In response to BUAV's claims it can be argued that the research is contributing to our understanding of diseases like cystic fibrosis, heart disease, AIDS, multiple sclerosis and cancer for which

cures will only come about if their genetic basis is understood. Transgenic animals are protected by the same laws used for all laboratory animals. At the moment it seems likely that there will be a rise in the number of genetically engineered mice because of their help to us in understanding genetic disease.

At the other extreme of animal welfare are those animals that are used for pharmaceutical products such as AAT and factor IX which are probably the best cared-for farm animals in the world because they are the most valuable.

25.6.4   Patenting

Apart from the ethical aspects of patenting mentioned above there are other related issues. In 1992 an American company attempted to patent genetically engineered cotton and soya plants, however they were produced. Farmers would then have to pay royalties to sow the crop. Although the patents were granted, they have been challenged by the international community. The US National Institutes of Health tried to patent the human genome in 1991 but, after more international protest, they withdrew their application. However, the human breast cancer gene (BRCA1) was patented in the US once its base sequence had been determined and attempts are being made to patent the second breast cancer gene (BRCA2).

Some European companies tried to extend their patents on genetically engineered seed to preventing farmers from re-sowing seed from genetically engineered crops. They would therefore have had to buy new seed every year. Similarly they have tried to remove farmer's rights to breed

Our Ref: admin/masters/geneng

British Union for the
Abolition of Vivisection

16a Crane Grove,
London N7 8LB
Telephone 0171-700 4888
Fax 0171-700 0252

Dear Supporter,

Thank you for your enquiry about genetically engineered animals.

I am sending you our genetic engineering pack in which you will find detailed information about particular areas of concern, such as xenotransplantation (cross-species transplants) and animal patenting. I also enclose our general reading list which contains two books on the issue should you wish to pursue the topic further.

It is extremely worrying to note that, according to the most recent Home Office figures, the use of transgenic animals in research has increased by 33%, from 138,965 in 1993 to 184,188 in 1994 - a figure which does not include a further 202,311 animals deliberately created with a "harmful genetic defect". These statistics confirm that the genetic engineering of animals is _the_ growth area of the vivisection industry. This _must_ be challenged.

Fig 25.20   *Part of a letter sent by BUAV to its members in August 1995 as part of a campaign against patenting the oncomouse.*

from transgenic animals. The European Parliament and national governments have to try to balance the interests of all, including those of the farmers, the manufacturers and the consumers. In such circumstances ethical issues are not the only ones which are considered.

25.6.5 Insurance

A new UK Genetic Manipulatory Advisory Commission met for the first time in early 1997. On its first agenda was the issue of insurance companies. The insurance issue concerns how life insurance companies should use the results of genetic tests. Should they refuse insurance or raise premiums for people with an increased chance of dying from a particular disease, such as breast cancer or heart disease? Insurance companies are arguing that they *should* have access to the results of any genetic tests carried out on a person whose life is being insured.

25.6.6 Cloning

The cloning of the sheep, Dolly, in 1997 was an inevitable consequence of the progress being made in genetics and biotechnology (section 21.1.4). It raises the possibility of breeding many identical copies of animals, including transgenic animals, showing desirable features. One of the ethical concerns is that the techniques could be applied to humans, although such work is currently banned.

25.7 Human genetics

25.7.1 The scope of human genetics

About 1% of all live births produce children who suffer from some genetic disorder (more than 40 births per day in the UK). A high proportion of infant mortality is due to such disorders. Around 1 in 20 children admitted to hospital in the UK have a disorder which is entirely genetic in origin and 1 in 10 individuals will develop, sooner or later, some disorder that has been inherited. In addition, certain genes make certain diseases more likely in adulthood, in other words give a 'predisposition' to a disease. Examples are coronary heart disease, breast cancer and diabetes. Since any gene can undergo a mutation, and there are something like 100 000 human genes, there are theoretically thousands of possible genetic diseases. About 4000 have been recorded that are due to defects in single genes, but this number is increasing rapidly with modern genetic techniques. For 600 of these a known biochemical defect occurs. You yourself are probably a carrier of 4–8 different hereditary diseases which you may not suffer yourself, but which could be passed on to your children. Some mutations are fatal, some cause varying degrees of harm, generally referred to as genetic disease, and others are harmless. Some give both advantages and disadvantages,

such as the gene for sickle cell anaemia which we shall study later together with a number of other diseases.

So far genetic diseases are incurable, but the study of human genetics is reaching the point where cures for some will be possible, a topic we shall consider in section 25.7.11. As we learn more about genetic disease, so the need for more specialist clinics will grow, together with the need for more genetic counsellors who will have to help people to understand and cope with the decisions that will become more complex. Genetic counselling will be examined in sections 25.7.9 and 25.7.10.

As other diseases, particularly infectious diseases, have become successfully controlled, so the relative importance of genetic diseases has grown.

> **25.1** Give one economic and one social argument for research into genetic disease.

Although genetic disease is one of the main reasons for studying human genetics, there are other applications. Two of these, namely genetic fingerprinting and genetic compatibility in transplant surgery will also be studied (sections 25.7.12 and 25.7.13). Sometime near the beginning of the twenty-first century our knowledge of human genetics will be based on a knowledge of the entire base sequence of human DNA and the location of all the genes on our 46 chromosomes. This is currently being worked out by teams of scientists all over the world in a cooperative project called the Human Genome Project. It is impossible to predict the eventual value of this project but it cannot fail to be of fundamental importance to further understanding of human genetics.

The study of human genetics is raising some controversial issues which will have to be discussed by society as a whole, not just by geneticists and molecular biologists. You may already have read, for example, about genes for 'intelligence', 'criminal behaviour' or hetero- and homosexual behaviour. Some of the issues relating to genetic screening, gene therapy and genetic fingerprinting will be discussed in this chapter. In order to understand this chapter you will need to have an understanding of the basic laws of genetics and of the nature of gene and chromosome mutations.

Table 25.3 shows some of the genetic diseases we will be considering in the following sections, and the nature of these diseases.

25.7.2 Sickle cell anaemia

This disease is an excellent example of how a single mutation in a gene can have devastating consequences, and also of the role of natural selection in regulating how common a gene is in a population.

In 1904, a young Chicago doctor named James Herrick examined a 20-year-old black college student who had been admitted to hospital complaining of a variety of symptoms.

Table 25.3 Some common genetic diseases.

Genetic disease/disorder	Chromosome affected	Type of mutation	Expression of gene	Main symptoms	Defect	Frequency at birth
Gene mutations sickle cell anaemia	11	substitution	codominant (sometimes described as recessive) autosomal	anaemia and interference with circulation	abnormal haemoglobin molecule	1 in 1600 among black people
cystic fibrosis	7	in 70% of cases is a deletion of three bases	recessive autosomal	unusually thick mucus clogs lungs, liver and pancreas	failure of chloride ion transport mechanism in cell surface membranes of epithelial cells	1 in 1800 among white people
PKU (phenylketonuria)	12	substitution	recessive autosomal	brain fails to develop normally	enzyme phenylalanine hydroxylase defective	1 in 18 000
Huntington's chorea (disease)	4	a newly discovered type of mutation – the normal gene has 10–34 repeats of CAG at one end, the HC gene has 42–100 repeats of CAG	dominant autosomal	gradual deterioration of brain tissue starting on average in middle age	brain cell metabolism is inhibited	1 in 10 000 to 1 in 20 000 worldwide
haemophilia	X	substitution	recessive sex-linked	blood does not clot	factor VIII or IX protein defective	1 in 7000
Chromosome mutations Down's syndrome	21	extra chromosome 21 (trisomy 21)		reduced intelligence, characteristic facial features		1 in 750
Klinefelter's syndrome	sex	extra X chromosome in male (trisomy)		feminised male		1 in 500
Turner's syndrome	sex	missing X chromosome in female (monosomy)		sterile female		1 in 2500

autosomal – affecting non-sex chromosome (autosome)
monosomy – one chromosome missing ($2n - 1$)
trisomy – one extra chromosome ($2n + 1$)
monosomy and trisomy are examples of **aneuploidy**, where the total number of chromosomes is not an exact multiple of the haploid number

These included fever, headache, weakness, dizziness and a cough. Herrick discovered other problems. The patient's lymph nodes were enlarged, his heart was abnormally large and his urine revealed kidney damage. What was particularly striking though was the appearance of the patient's red blood cells under the microscope. Herrick described them as sickle-shaped (fig 25.21). The patient's haemoglobin level was about half normal, in other words he was suffering from anaemia (lack of haemoglobin). After resting for four weeks, the patient was discharged, but it was 6 years before Herrick published details of the case. Once he did, other cases were soon reported and the search began for the cause of the disease.

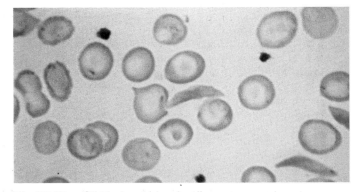

Fig 25.21   *Sickled red blood cells.*

The disease became known as **sickle cell anaemia** and was soon found to be associated with black people. Since the disease ran in families it was also soon realised that it is an inherited disease and that the gene causing it appeared to be recessive. A person is therefore only a sufferer if they have two copies of the gene, one inherited from the mother and one from the father. In other words, a sufferer is homozygous. Today about 1 in 400 black people in Britain and America suffers from the condition and about 1 in 10 is a carrier. A carrier is a person who has only one copy of the faulty gene, in other words is heterozygous. It is estimated that the disease causes about 100 000 deaths per year worldwide. It is not entirely confined to black people and is particularly common in Africa, Pakistan and India.

Symptoms

The major characteristics of the disease are anaemia and a tendency of the red blood cells to change shape (sickle) at low oxygen concentrations. The sickle cells are useless and have to be broken down. They tend to jam in capillaries and small blood vessels and prevent normal blood flow. A whole range of secondary symptoms is possible as a result (fig 25.22). The kidneys and joints are particularly affected. The blocking of blood vessels causes pain in the arms, legs, back and stomach which can be quite severe. Joints may become stiff and painful and hands and feet may swell. Affected individuals may show poor growth and development and are more prone to infections. If death occurs it usually follows an infection.

Children with sickle cell anaemia usually feel quite well for most of the time and can lead relatively normal lives. However, they will generally suffer occasional 'sickle cell crises' when a sudden worsening of pain, infection or anaemia may occur.

Cause

In 1949 a team of workers led by Linus Pauling showed that haemoglobin from sickle cell anaemia sufferers, HbS, is different from that of normal adult haemoglobin, HbA. Electrophoresis, a technique in which proteins are separated according to their overall charge, revealed that at pH 6.9 the overall charge on HbS is positive whereas it is negative on HbA. This was the first time that a disease had been shown to be caused by a faulty molecule. In 1956 Ingram showed that this difference was due to a single amino acid and since then the entire amino acid sequence of HbA and HbS has been determined. Haemoglobin is made of four polypeptide chains (fig 3.36), two α-chains which are 141 amino acids long and two β-chains which are 146 amino acids long. The fault occurs at the sixth amino acid in the β-chain. The amino acid should be glutamic acid. In HbS however it is replaced by valine. Using the codes for amino acids shown in table 23.4:

HbA	Val – His – Leu – Thr – Pro – **Glu** – Glu – Lys –
HbS	Val – His – Leu – Thr – Pro – **Val** – Glu – Lys –
amino acid	1 2 3 4 5 6 7 8

Glutamic acid carries a negative charge and is polar whereas valine is non-polar and hydrophobic. The presence of valine makes deoxygenated HbS less soluble. Therefore when HbS loses its oxygen the molecules come out of solution and crystallise into rigid rod-like fibres. These change the shape of the red cell, which is normally a flat circular disc. The reason for the changed amino acid is a change, or mutation, in the DNA coding for the amino acid. If you look at table 23.4 you should be able to make a prediction about what this change might have been. The possible mRNA codons for the two amino acids are as follows:

Glu: GAA GAG
Val: GUU GUC GUA GUG

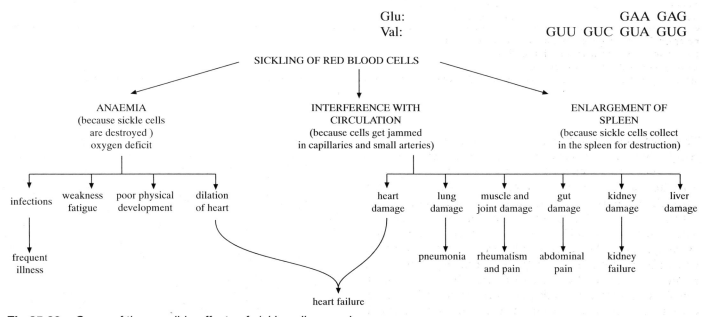

Fig 25.22 *Some of the possible effects of sickle cell anaemia.*

The complementary DNA triplet codes are therefore:

Glu: CTT CTC
Val: CAA CAG CAT CAC

To change the message from glu to val, T (thymine) must be replaced by A (adenine) in the second position of the triplet. Such a mutation is called a **substitution**. We now know that CTC is changed to CAC in the β-haemoglobin gene and that the gene is situated on chromosome 11.

What, then, happens in heterozygous individuals? Here, about half the molecules made are HbS and half are HbA. Strictly speaking therefore, the alleles HbA and HbS are co-dominant and the faulty gene is not recessive. Heterozygous people are unaffected except at unusually low oxygen concentrations, such as when flying in an unpressurised aircraft or climbing at high altitude. Then some of the cells sickle. The heterozygous condition is known as **sickle cell trait**.

Fig 25.23 shows that if two people suffering from sickle cell trait (carriers of sickle cell anaemia) have children, there is a 1 in 4 chance of any given child being a sufferer of sickle cell anaemia. Blood tests can be done to find out the phenotype of a given person so, if it runs in the family, people would be advised to have blood tests before having children. Prenatal diagnosis can be done using a HbS gene probe, or a particular restriction enzyme, on the DNA of the embryo or fetus. This is obtained from cells obtained by CVS or amniocentesis (section 25.7.9).

There is a final twist in this story. The faulty gene is a disadvantage and it is therefore surprising to find that it is so common. In such circumstances, geneticists suspect that the gene may also be an advantage in some circumstances. In the case of the sickle cell gene, an advantage has been found. Fig 25.24 shows the distribution of the gene worldwide and also shows the distribution of malaria. The distributions match quite closely, the gene becoming more common as malaria becomes more common. The frequency of the gene may reach 40% (40% HbS, 60% HbA genes in the population) in some parts of Africa. Malaria is a leading cause of death in areas where it occurs. Someone carrying the faulty gene is far less susceptible to malaria (the malaria

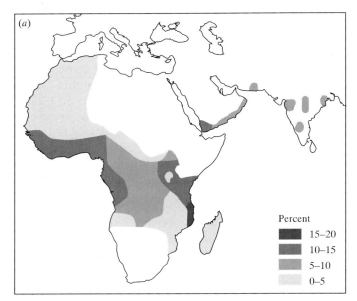

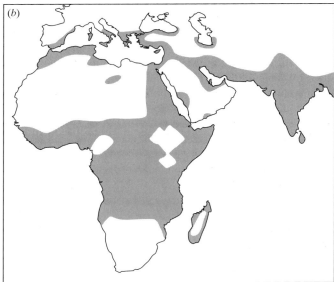

Fig 25.24 *Distribution of (a) the sickle cell gene and (b) malaria in Africa, the Middle East, India and southern Europe.*

parasite multiplies inside normal red blood cells). Although homozygous sufferers often die before reproductive age, heterozygous carriers have a **selective advantage** over non-carriers and so are more likely to survive and pass on their genes to the next generation. The final frequency of the gene in the population varies according to the amount of malaria. This is called **balanced polymorphism** (section 27.5).

25.7.3   Cystic fibrosis (CF)

Cystic fibrosis, or CF, is the most common genetic disease of northern Europeans and white North Americans. The gene responsible is autosomal (not associated with a sex chromosome) and recessive. About 1 in 20–25 of the population is a carrier and about 1 in 2000

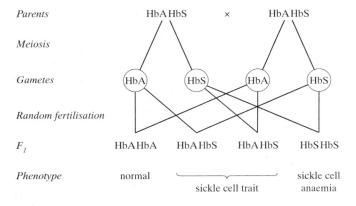

Fig 25.23 *Genetic diagram showing the possible children of two people suffering from sickle cell trait.*

860

is a sufferer. It occurs in fewer than 1 in 100 000 births among Africans and Asians. The disease gets its name from the fibrous cysts that appear in the pancreas. It is of particular interest, not just because it is so common, but because it is one of the first genetic diseases for which a cure has been attempted (section 25.7.11). As with sickle cell anaemia, the fact that it is so common suggests that carriers of the disease have an advantage over those with a normal genotype. It is unclear what this advantage is, but it may give increased resistance to cholera, a disease which was a common killer in Europe until the late nineteenth century.

Cause

The cause is a recessive mutation in a gene located on chromosome 7. The gene codes for a chloride channel (section 7.9.8) which is a protein, 1480 amino acids long, and known as **CFTR (cystic fibrosis transmembrane regulator)**. It allows diffusion of chloride ions into and out of epithelial cells and is located in the cell surface membranes of these cells. In CF sufferers it does not function. Since the gene is recessive, CF sufferers are homozygous and have two copies of the faulty gene.

The gene responsible for CF was cloned in 1989. This allowed the nature of the mutation to be discovered and also resulted in improved ability to detect carriers (section 25.7.9) using a simple mouthwash technique to obtain cells for DNA analysis. It also became possible to identify carriers or sufferers by prenatal diagnosis. In 70% of cases in central and western Europe the cause of the problem is the deletion of three base pairs from the gene; codon number 508 in the mRNA is therefore missing. As a result the amino acid phenylalanine (F) is missing at position 508 in the protein. The mutation is therefore called ΔF508 (Δ is the Greek letter delta, d, standing for deletion). More than 400 other mutations have been found in the same gene which also cause CF, but a further 15% of cases are caused by just five other mutations. Some result in mild forms of the disease. Some have been found in only one person.

Symptoms

One of the normal functions of the epithelial cells is to form mucus glands which secrete mucus. In CF patients this mucus becomes abnormally thick and sticky because the normal outward flow of chloride ions from the cells is prevented. Chloride ions are negatively charged, so in order to balance the negative charge which builds up in the cells more sodium ions enter. The high ion concentration inside the cell in turn prevents water from leaving the cell. The parts of the body most affected are the lungs, pancreas and liver. In the pancreas fibrous patches, called cysts, develop which give the disease its name. The thick mucus clogs up the airways of the lungs, and the branches of the pancreatic duct and the bile duct from the liver into the gut. Repeated lung infections are caused, as well as digestive problems, including poor release of pancreatic enzymes and poor absorption of digested food. The intestine may also become obstructed. In addition, males are almost always infertile and females are frequently infertile. Another characteristic symptom is that the sweat is saltier than usual because the sweat duct is relatively impermeable to chloride ions and once again sodium follows the chloride. This may explain an old saying: 'Woe is the child who tastes salty from a kiss on the brow for he is hexed and soon must die'. 95% of deaths are the result of lung complications. Average life expectancy has increased from 1 year to about 20–30 years with modern treatment methods, but about half the sufferers die by the age of 20.

Treatment

Treatment is concentrated on the lungs. It usually involves physiotherapy, possibly as much as five times a day, including slapping the back to dislodge mucus from the lungs (fig 25.25). Enzyme supplements can be given to improve food digestion and antibiotics to fight infection. In severe cases heart and lung transplants may be used. Much of the viscosity of the mucus is caused by DNA of dead infectious bacteria and dead white blood cells. Some success at reducing this has been achieved using the enzyme human DNase in the form of an aerosol to break down the DNA. The most desirable treatment though is gene therapy (section 25.7.11).

25.7.4 Phenylketonuria (PKU)

PKU occurs in about 1 in 10 000 live births among white Europeans and about 1 in 80 is a carrier. It is very rare in other races.

Cause

Like CF, PKU is a recessive, autosomal condition. It is a very distressing condition if not treated, but fortunately early diagnosis and treatment can prevent damage to health.

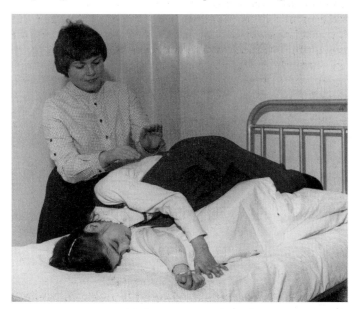

Fig 25.25 *Cystic fibrosis patient receiving physiotherapy.*

The disease is due to an inability to convert the amino acid phenylalanine to another amino acid, tyrosine:

$$\text{phenylalanine} \xrightarrow{\text{phenylalanine hydroxylase (PAH)}} \text{tyrosine}$$

The enzyme PAH is normally present in the liver, but is faulty in sufferers from PKU. The gene for this enzyme is on chromosome 12. As a result of faulty PAH, phenylalanine builds up in the body. The excess is converted to toxins which affect mental development. Affected children appear normal at birth because, while in their mother's uterus during pregnancy, excess phenylalanine moves across the placenta and is removed by the mother's liver. If not treated in infancy, harmful effects are soon noted. The most serious of these is severe mental retardation. Many untreated patients have IQs of less than 20. Before treatment became available more than 1% of all patients in mental hospitals were sufferers. Untreated sufferers rarely live beyond the age of 30. Other effects, which vary from patient to patient, include:

- hyperactive and irritable behaviour in children;
- awkward posture and walk;
- lighter skin pigmentation and fair hair (because tyrosine is normally used in the synthesis of the brown skin pigment melanin);
- dry, rough skin (eczema);
- repetitive movements of the fingers, hands or entire body;
- convulsions due to abnormal brain activity.

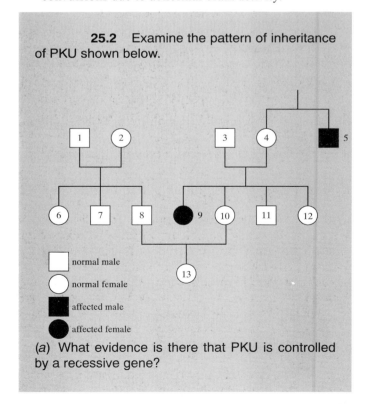

25.2 Examine the pattern of inheritance of PKU shown below.

☐ normal male
○ normal female
■ affected male
● affected female

(a) What evidence is there that PKU is controlled by a recessive gene?

(b) What evidence is there that PKU is *not* sex-linked?
(c) Which individuals are definitely carriers (heterozygous) based on the evidence available?
(d) Which other individuals *could* be carriers?
(e) In a real situation, the individuals numbered 10, 11 and 12 may well wish to know if they are carriers since their sister suffers from PKU. If one of them asked you what were their chances of being a carrier, what would you reply. Think carefully!

Identifying PKU in newborn babies

It is important to test for PKU in babies because there are no obvious symptoms for about the first six months, and by this time irreversible brain damage will have occurred if no action has been taken. A very sensitive blood test was developed in 1963 which detects the higher than normal levels of free phenylalanine in the blood of sufferers. Levels are commonly 30–50 times higher than normal. The test is now carried out on all babies four days after birth by pricking the heel for a blood sample.

25.3 Why is the baby not tested when it is first born?

Identifying carriers and prenatal diagnosis

Population screening is a possibility since 95% of all carriers can be detected using modern methods of DNA analysis. (Carriers used to be detected using a blood test.) Prenatal diagnosis of sufferers or carriers is also now possible, using chorionic villus sampling or amniocentesis, to sample cells followed by DNA analysis. It is not normally recommended because the disease is treatable. Prenatal diagnosis was not possible before because the excess phenylalanine was removed by the mother. Early experiments on gene transfer suggest that gene therapy may be possible in the future.

Treatment

The condition is managed by reducing the amount of phenylalanine in the diet to the minimum required. Phenylalanine is an essential amino acid (meaning that it cannot be made from other amino acids so some must be present in the diet for making proteins). Since sufferers cannot make tyrosine from phenylalanine (see above), tyrosine is also an essential amino acid needed in the diet of sufferers. Blood levels are monitored for the first few years of life to check that the correct balance is being maintained. Excess phenylalanine in adulthood is not damaging, presumably because brain development has ceased, so a normal diet can then be adopted. Suitable food is rather tasteless, but can be supplemented by small amounts of other foods such as meat and products low in phenylalanine. Sufferers must avoid gluten which means avoiding bread as well as some children's favourites such as sweets and some orange juices. This makes it difficult for young children. Children will feel ill if they do not stick to the diet.

25.7.5 Huntington's chorea (HC)

Huntington's chorea, or Huntington's disease, is caused by an autosomal mutation which is *dominant*, unlike the previous three examples. It affects about 1 in 10 000 people. In 1983 the gene was located on chromosome 4, but it took another 10 years of painstaking work to locate it precisely and to be able to clone it. The function of the protein it codes for is unknown, although it has been given a name, 'huntingtin'.

The disease was first described in 1872 by George Huntington. As an 8-year old boy he had witnessed the appalling consequences of the disease in two women: 'mother and daughter, both tall, thin, almost cadaverous, both bowing, twisting, grimacing.' The disease causes progressive deterioration of brain cells and gradual loss of motor control (control of voluntary muscle by motor nerves) resulting in uncontrollable shaking and dance-like movements. This accounts for the use of the term 'chorea', meaning dance, to describe the disease. Intellectual ability is lost, hallucinations, slurring of speech, mood changes, personality changes and memory loss (temporary or permanent) may all occur. The brain shrinks between 20–30% in size.

Two particularly difficult problems are associated with the disease.

- Firstly, symptoms do not usually start to appear until middle age (fig 25.26), by which time many sufferers will already have passed the disease on to their children. This is an additional source of distress for families. Life expectancy averages 15 years from the onset of symptoms and the slow decline can be emotionally very painful for close family members to witness.
- Secondly, because it is a dominant gene it will always be expressed, and on average 50% of the children will be sufferers if one parent is affected (there can be no 'carriers'). In the past, the children were unlikely to discover until they were young adults that a parent was

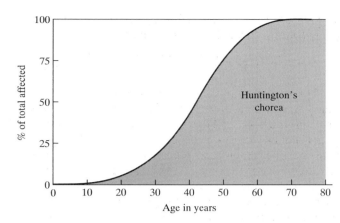

Fig 25.26 *Variation in the age of onset of Huntington's chorea.*

affected and that they had a 50% chance of going through what they observed happening to the parent.

Predictive diagnosis

Genetic counselling of families with a high risk of the disease is a clear need and, since the cloning of the gene in 1993, has been made easier by the introduction of highly reliable predictive DNA tests for the condition. These can tell a person if they will get the disease. There is now an internationally agreed code of practice for predictive testing, which includes counselling both before and after testing. Perhaps surprisingly, many children of affected parents who stand a 50% risk say that they would rather not know if they are going to develop the disease.

25.7.6 Down's syndrome

Chromosome mutations are discussed in section 24.9.2. They are a common cause of miscarriage, probably accounting for about 50 to 60% of all miscarriages. Three well-known examples in humans are discussed in the following sections. One affects autosomes (non-sex chromosomes), namely Down's syndrome, and two affect the sex chromosomes, namely Klinefelter's syndrome and Turner's syndrome. It will help if you revise your knowledge of meiosis (section 23.4) and karyograms (section 23.1.1).

Down's syndrome is named after the nineteenth century physician John Langdon Down who worked at an asylum in Surrey, England and who in 1866 was the first to describe the condition. It affects about 1 in 750 babies at birth, but over half of fetuses suffering from Down's syndrome abort spontaneously (miscarry). It was first shown to be due to an extra chromosome number 21 by the French physician Lejeune in 1959 using microscopy (fig 25.27) as techniques for staining human chromosomes were perfected for the first time in that year. Down's syndrome occurs in all races and a similar condition can even occur in chimpanzees and some other primates. The presence of three copies of a chromosome is known as **trisomy**, hence Down's syndrome is also known as **trisomy 21**.

Symptoms

Most children with Down's syndrome show typical facial features which include eyelids which apparently slant upwards due to a fold of skin over the inner corner of the eye. The face is typically flat and rounded (fig 25.28). Other characteristics include:

- mental retardation, often severe;
- short stature and relatively small skull due to poor skeletal development;
- heart defects occur in about one-quarter of Down's children;
- increased risk of infection, particularly respiratory and ear infections;
- coarse, straight hair;
- squat hands with a characteristic crease which runs all the way across the palm;
- intestinal problems and leukaemia are slightly more common than normal.

Affected children are characteristically very friendly, cheerful and often greatly enjoy music. It is important to understand that the condition ranges widely in degree and that jobs with limited responsibility can be successfully undertaken by many Down's sufferers, and many can live independent lives. Personality can equally vary widely. In other words they should be treated and thought of as people first and Down's sufferers second.

Explanation

In 96% of cases the cause of Down's syndrome is non-disjunction of chromosome 21 during anaphase of meiosis. This can take place during production of sperm, but is more common during production of eggs (see effect of maternal age below). About 70% of non-disjunctions occur in meiosis I and 30% in meiosis II. In meiosis I, it is caused by the failure of whole chromosomes to separate, whereas

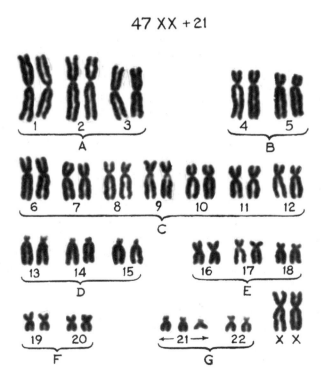

Fig 25.27 *The chromosomes of a female suffering from Down's syndrome. The non-disjunction of chromosomes 21 in one of the gametes has led to the presence of three chromosomes 21 in this female.*

Fig 25.28 *Young girl showing typical physical features characteristic of Down's Syndrome – slightly slanted eyes, round head and flat nasal bridge.*

864

in meiosis II chromatids fail to separate. The final effect is the same, with two chromosomes or two chromatids entering one daughter cell and none entering the other, instead of one entering each (fig 24.31). This should lead to an equal number of cases of monosomy 21 (only one chromosome 21), however this condition is fatal early in the development of the fetus like all cases of monosomy.

About 3–4% of Down's syndrome cases are due to a type of mutation known as a translocation (section 24.9.2). Chromosome 21 is translocated (moved) to chromosome 14 or, less commonly, to chromosome 22. An even less common cause is a 21 to 21 translocation.

Effect of mother's age

A correlation with the age of the mother has been shown for Down's syndrome (fig 25.29). There is no correlation with the age of the father. At age 20 the risk is 1 in 2000, at 30 it is 1 in 900, at 40 1 in 100 and at 44 1 in 40. The incidence therefore rises more and more steeply with age, shown by a straight line when a logarithmic scale is used as in fig 25.29. This is probably due to the fact that a woman's egg cells are produced while she is still an embryo. They are stored until stimulated to develop at the rate of one a month during her fertile years. Men, on the other hand, constantly produce new sperm from puberty until death.

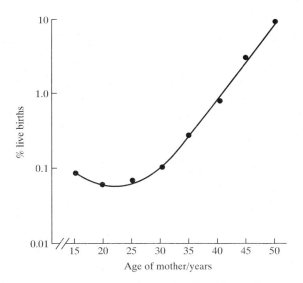

Fig 25.29 *Effect of maternal age on the incidence of Down's syndrome. Note that the vertical axis is logarithmic.*

Other trisomies involving autosomes

Most cases of trisomy involving autosomes are fatal and result in early miscarriage. Cases of trisomy involving some of the smallest chromosomes, namely chromosomes 13 and 18, sometimes survive to birth, but suffer many defects, including mental retardation. They usually die within three months because development cannot proceed normally. Other cases of trisomy surviving to birth are extremely rare.

25.7.7   Klinefelter's syndrome

In 1942, an American, Dr H. F. Klinefelter, studied nine male patients who could best be described as feminised males. Typical symptoms of these and similar patients are as follows:

- infertility – sperm are never produced, although erection and ejaculation are possible;
- usually taller than average;
- some breast development, although not necessarily very obvious;
- smaller testes than normal, although this is not necessarily obvious;
- higher than usual FSH secretion for males (FSH is follicle stimulating hormone and is produced by the pituitary gland in both men and women;
- trunk may show signs of obesity (eunuch-like appearance);
- little facial hair;
- voice pitched higher than normal;
- educational difficulties and behavioural problems are fairly common.

In 1959, it was discovered that Klinefelter's syndrome, as it became known, is due to an extra X chromosome. The genotype is therefore XXY instead of the normal XY and the sufferer has 47 chromosomes instead of 46. Like Down's syndrome, it is an example of trisomy. Fig 25.30 shows how the extra chromosome arises as a result of non-disjunction during meiosis. It may occur during spermatogenesis (sperm production) in the male parent or during oogenesis (egg production) in the female parent. The figure also shows that, as a result of non-disjunction in the male sex chromosomes, equal numbers of zygotes will contain only one X chromosome and no Y chromosome (represented as XO). This gives rise to Turner's syndrome, which is described in the next section. In the case of non-disjunction in the female, XXX and YO zygotes are also created. XXX does not produce a superwoman. In fact, there is no apparent physical difference between XXX women and XX women, apart from the fact that XXX women tend to be slightly taller. There is some evidence though that behavioural abnormalities and learning difficulties may occur more frequently in XXX women. YO zygotes do not develop because many vital genes are missing completely (remember the Y chromosome has missing genes compared with the X chromosome).

(a)

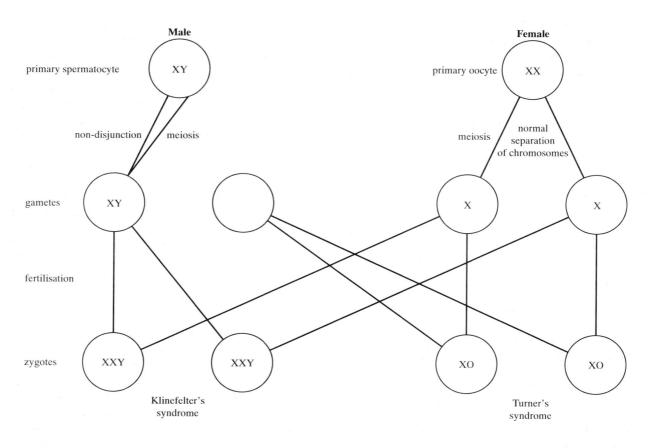

(b)

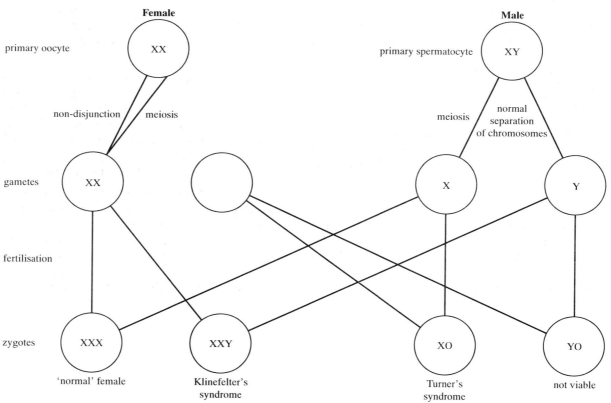

Fig 25.30 *Explanation of Klinefelter's syndrome and Turner's syndrome as a result of (a) non-disjunction of the father's sex hormones and (b) non-disjunction of the mother's sex chromosomes.*

Treatment

The condition is usually diagnosed only after puberty. Male hormones can be given. Breasts then return to normal size and a normal sex life can be led, even though sterility remains.

25.7.8 Turner's syndrome

This syndrome was first described by an American, Turner, in 1938. Patients can best be described as incompletely developed females, although there are often no obvious external differences compared with normal females. Typical symptoms are as follows:

- infertility – ovaries are absent (represented only as connective tissue);
- shortness of stature, averaging 1.5 m (less than 5 feet);
- small uterus;
- webbed neck may occur;
- puffy fingers with deep set finger nails which are more convex than normal;
- the hair line (line at which hair starts to grow) at the back of the head is lower than normal.

In 1959, Turner's syndrome was shown to be due to a missing X chromosome. The genotype is therefore XO instead of the normal XX and the sufferer has 45 chromosomes instead of 46. This is an example of monosomy. Fig 25.30 shows how Turner's syndrome can arise as a result of non-disjunction during meiosis and that it represents the 'flip-side' of Klinefelter's syndrome. In theory, equal numbers of Klinefelter's and Turner's syndrome individuals should be born. In reality, Turner's syndrome is significantly rarer, with about 1 in 2500 births compared with 1 in 500 births for Klinefelter's. This is because Turner's syndrome is far more likely to be fatal early in pregnancy. It is estimated that only about 2–3% of Turner's syndrome conceptions survive to birth. Interestingly, Turner's syndrome also seems to be responsible for a relatively high proportion of miscarriages, perhaps as great as 20%.

Treatment

From the age of puberty women can be given female sex hormones to make them develop breasts and have periods. This does not cure infertility but is done for social reasons to make the person feel more 'normal'. Growth can be stimulated with growth hormone.

Other combinations of sex chromosomes

Various other combinations of sex chromosomes are possible. Individuals with a Y chromosome are always male due to the presence of the SRY gene (sex-related Y gene), that is the gene for male sex development. Some XX males have been identified (1 in 20 000 births) but these have a piece of Y chromosome containing the SRY gene in one of their X chromosomes (a translocation mutation). They are physically like Klinefelter's patients. XXXY and XXXXY males occur and are mentally retarded. XXXX women are severely mentally retarded, although physically normal. The first XYY man was detected in 1961. Such men are usually normal and more research is needed to establish whether there are any consistent abnormal physical or mental characteristics. XXYY men have also been identified.

25.7.9 Genetic screening and prenatal diagnosis

In section 25.7.1 it was pointed out that everyone probably carries several genetic defects which can be referred to as genetic diseases or genetic disorders. More than 4000 such disorders have been identified, but with 100 000 different human genes there must be many more to find. Some common and important examples have already been discussed. Detecting mutant genes in an individual is known as **genetic screening**. Modern genetics is making this much easier than it was in the past. There are three situations where genetic screening is of particular relevance, namely prenatal diagnosis, carrier diagnosis and predictive diagnosis. These are explained below.

Prenatal diagnosis. This is the use of modern medical techniques to identify any health problems of the unborn baby. It includes the detection of genetic disease. If such a disease *is* detected, it is usually possible to provide counselling about the quality of life the child can expect and other potential problems. The parents are usually also given the option of an abortion.

Carrier diagnosis. This is the identification of people who carry a particular genetic disease, usually with no visible symptoms or harm to themselves. As stated already, we are all carriers of a few genetic diseases. Important examples are the genes for sickle cell anaemia, cystic fibrosis and PKU. Identification of carriers is becoming increasingly important and controversial as more and more genetic tests become available. There are obvious advantages. For example, if a couple considering having children both have a history of sickle cell anaemia in their families, they would be advised to be tested to discover if they were carriers. If they were, then it could be explained that they had a 1 in 4 chance of producing a child who would suffer from sickle cell anaemia. A genetic counsellor could then discuss the issues involved and possible options (section 25.7.10). As more tests become available, problems of economics arise. Can the Health Service afford mass screening programmes for cystic fibrosis, for example?

Predictive diagnosis. This is the prediction of a future disease which you are likely to suffer as a result of your genes but which has not yet produced any symptoms. The classic example of this 'genetic time bomb' is Huntington's chorea where the onset of the disease typically occurs in middle age. In this case, a single dominant gene is responsible and it is certain that if the person lives long enough they will get the disease. Many diseases are more complex than this. For example, people can be 'genetically predisposed' to suffer from heart disease, breast cancer and many other common diseases, but environmental factors, such as smoking, exercise and diet, also play a role. People can now be tested, if they wish, to find out if they have the Huntington's chorea gene, and fairly soon we may be able to carry out tests which estimate the risks of other diseases like heart disease. We therefore need to consider a number of related issues. For example,

should it be illegal for insurance companies to demand that genetic testing be done before offering life insurance and should they be allowed to penalise those who are at greater risk? Also, with more testing there would be a much greater demand for genetic counselling, with funding implications. These issues are discussed at the end of this section.

How, then, is genetic screening carried out. The four most important techniques are chorionic villus sampling, amniocentesis, pre-implantation diagnosis and gene probes.

Chorionic villus sampling (CVS)

The chorion is a 'membrane' (thin layer of cells) which grows from the embryo in the earliest stages of pregnancy. Its role is to invade the mother's uterus with small finger-like processes, the **chorionic villi**. These penetrate into blood spaces in the uterus lining and allow exchange of materials such as nutrients, oxygen and waste products between the mother and the embryo. The chorion later becomes part of the placenta. The technique was developed in China in the 1970s for withdrawing a small sample of the chorion for examination. The technique is shown in fig 25.31. The abdominal route is more common (fig 25.31a) and involves inserting a hollow needle through the body wall and uterus wall. A local anaesthetic is used. The cervical route (fig 25.31b) involves the use of a narrow, flexible tube called a catheter. No anaesthetic is needed. In both cases a syringe is attached to the tube or needle and is

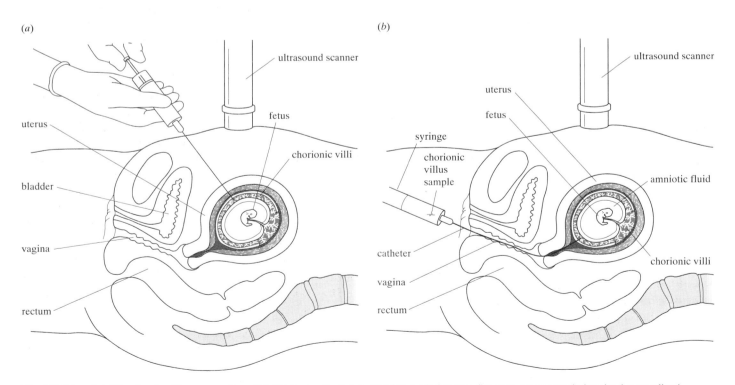

Fig 25.31 *(a) Chorionic villus sampling (CVS) through the wall of the abdomen (known as transabdominal sampling).*
(b) CVS through the vagina and cervix (known as transcervical sampling). The sample taken is a few millimetres across.

used to gently suck away a few fragments of chorionic villus material. Both methods are used in association with an ultrasound scanner which shows the contents of the uterus on a screen and helps to guide the tube into place. The fetus is checked before and after the procedure for signs of life.

The cells of the chorion are all derived from the zygote, like the embryo, and so are genetically identical to the embryo. The cell sample is relatively large compared with that obtained by amniocentesis (see below). Most of the cells are also actively dividing at this stage, so it is possible to examine cells immediately for their chromosome content (chromosomes are only visible when cells are dividing). A picture of the chromosomes can be used to make a karyogram and any chromosomal abnormalities can be identified, such as Down's, Klinefelter's or Turner's syndromes. This is known as **karyotype analysis**. The sex of the child can also be seen, which may be relevant if a sex-linked disease is suspected. The cells can also be cultured in a suitable medium in a laboratory so that further tests, such as DNA analysis, can be carried out. This could identify conditions such as cystic fibrosis, Huntington's chorea or thalassemia. The cells grow quickly and results can be obtained within 5–12 days. The great advantage of CVS is that it can be carried out early in pregnancy, between 8 to 12 weeks. It does, though, carry a slightly greater risk of miscarriage than amniocentesis. It is estimated that the risk of miscarriage is about 2% higher than the rate of natural miscarriage. If as a result of tests a decision is made to abort the fetus, the abortion is less difficult and risky, both physically and emotionally, than the later abortions carried out after amniocentesis.

Amniocentesis

Amniocentesis is a more widely available and older technique than CVS, introduced in 1967. It is usually performed at 15–16 weeks of pregnancy but can be done a few weeks earlier or up to 18 weeks. It cannot be done before there is sufficient amniotic fluid or cells to analyse. It is safer than CVS, causing an increased risk of miscarriage of about 0.5% (about 1 in 200). A hollow needle is inserted through the abdomen and uterus walls using ultrasound for guidance and a local anaesthetic (fig 25.32). About 20 cm^3 of amniotic fluid is sucked out of the amniotic sac which is tough and seals itself after removal of the needle. If possible, the placenta is avoided. The fluid is normally clear and yellow like urine. Amniotic fluid is constantly being swallowed by the baby and passes through its gut. It also contains urine from the baby. It therefore contains some living cells swept from inside the body as well as any living skin cells that may flake off. It may also contain cells from the amnion which, like the chorion, is derived from the zygote and is genetically identical to the fetus. The cells are spun down in a centrifuge and are cultured to increase their numbers and to obtain dividing cells. Results therefore take about 3–4 weeks to obtain, a regrettable delay if abortion is to be

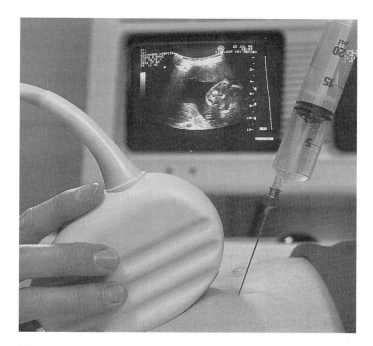

Fig 25.32 *A doctor is drawing in a sample of amniotic fluid from a pregnant woman. In the other hand the doctor holds an ultrasound transducer to detect the position of the fetus and placenta within the uterus. The image of the fetus is displayed on the screen in the background of the picture.*

carried out. The chromosomes of the dividing cells can be examined for abnormalities. The cells and the fluid from the sample can both be tested for products of faulty genes, such as α-**feto protein** (**AFP**), high levels of which indicate a higher than normal risk of certain birth defects such as spina bifida. Results from the fluid can be obtained within 7–10 days.

Pre-implantation diagnosis

This is a form of prenatal diagnosis which is carried out on the embryo before it implants in the uterus. It requires use of the test tube baby technique (IVF) (section 21.7.4). After fertilisation outside the body, a cell can be removed from the developing embryo at about the 8-cell stage without damaging its ability to continue to develop normally. After testing, only the healthy embryos need be replaced in the woman. This avoids the need for abortion. However, the low success rate and expense of IVF mean that this cannot be used as a routine procedure.

Gene probes and DNA analysis

Genetic screening by examining a person's DNA is known as **DNA analysis**. It involves the following stages and is illustrated in fig 25.33.

(1) The DNA is first **extracted** from cells. The cells may be obtained from a fetus by CVS or amniocentesis, or from a child or adult using, for example, a blood sample or a mouthwash.
(2) The DNA is then cut up into fragments of different length using **restriction enzymes**.

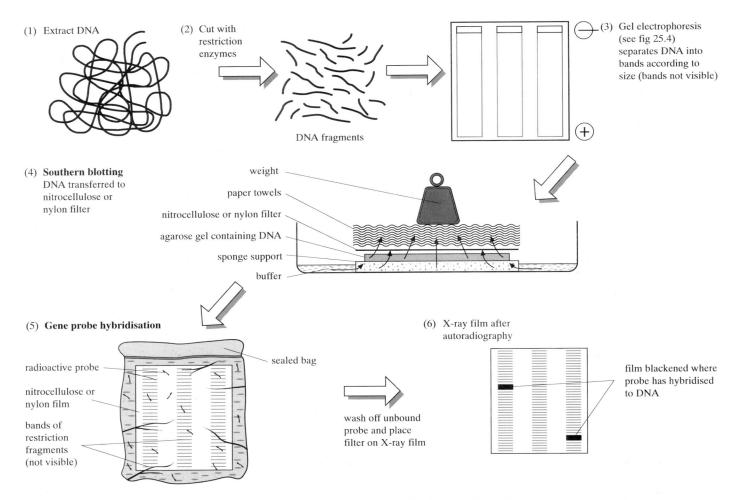

Fig 25.33 *Some stages in DNA analysis during genetic screening. During Southern blotting, denatured (single-stranded) DNA is transferred from an agarose gel to a nitrocellulose or nylon filter. Paper towels are no longer commonly used; techniques known as electroblotting or vacuum blotting are used instead.*

(3) The fragments are separated according to size using **gel electrophoresis** through an agarose gel as described earlier (fig 25.4). The smaller fragments move faster down the gel than the larger ones.

(4) The aim is now to find if a particular piece of mutant DNA is present in one of the fragments. It is looked for with a **gene probe**. The gene probe does not move very well through the gel, so a technique known as **Southern blotting** (after Edward Southern, who first developed the method in 1975) is used first. This is illustrated in fig 25.33 and is a commonly used technique in genetics (see also genetic fingerprinting, 25.7.12).

The DNA in the gel is first converted to the single-stranded form (denatured) by heating. It is then transferred to a nitrocellulose or nylon filter by a blotting action, making a precise replica of the original gel. The stack of paper towels acts as a wick which draws the buffer up through the sponge, the gel and the filter. The DNA sticks tightly to the filter.

(5) A **gene probe** is now used (section 25.1.6). This is a short, single-stranded piece of DNA whose base sequence is complementary to part of the gene being sought. Large quantities of the probe are made by cloning. It is made radioactive by labelling with ^{32}P and then added to a solution for hybridising (complementary binding) with the DNA on the nitrocellulose or nylon filter.

(6) **Autoradiography** is then carried out by placing the filter on an X-ray film. Radiation from any bands to which the probe has hybridised will blacken the film (fig 25.33). Many mutations are major chromosome deletions and so shorten the length of the restriction fragment. This makes the fragment more mobile in the gel so it will show up as a different band after radiography. One such example is the gene for sickle cell anaemia which can be detected in this way.

Other relevant techniques

Ultrasound scans can be used to detect a variety of conditions, some of which may be genetic in origin such as spina bifida.

Blood tests of the mother during pregnancy can detect raised levels of chemicals, such as AFP, associated with certain genetic conditions in the fetus.

Benefits of genetic screening

As already noted, despite the benefits of genetic screening, it also raises a number of problems. Both the possible benefits and the problems are considered below, but these are all points which need discussion.

- Genetic screening reduces suffering of both victims of genetic disease and their families. It could be argued that it is not morally right to bring a child into the world knowing it will suffer more than usual. Genetic screening gives couples a choice of whether to allow the birth of a child with a genetic defect.
- Genetic screening reduces the economic cost to the country. For example, it is estimated that it currently costs the NHS about £40 000 a year to keep alive a child who is suffering from cystic fibrosis.
- There is a public desire for tests. The cystic fibrosis test is not available on the NHS but 80–90% of people offered the test use it.
- If you know that you are genetically predisposed to a certain condition you may be able to change your lifestyle to reduce the possibility of it occurring. For example, a known predisposition to heart disease might make someone give up smoking.
- Screening programmes for diseases have been successful in reducing the incidence of the diseases when carried out with the understanding and approval of the communities involved. An example is screening for thalassemia in Cyprus. **Thalassemia** is similar to sickle cell anaemia in being a recessive gene which affects haemoglobin and gives resistance to malaria in the carrier state. It was common in Cyprus until a screening programme was introduced to identify mothers carrying affected fetuses and offer them abortions.
- Mothers over the age of 35 are usually offered free CVS or amniocentesis on the NHS because of the increased risk of Down's syndrome.

Problems associated with genetic screening

- Eventually we may be able to predict who is likely to suffer common diseases such as coronary heart disease and rheumatoid arthritis. Will insurance companies or employers demand genetic profiles of individuals and discriminate against them in some way, even though they may not even develop the disease? Will companies that do not use genetic testing be at a disadvantage? Should laws be passed which guarantee genetic privacy?

- Some genetic defects are not as serious as others. In fact, there is a continuous range of severity of disease. Who should decide then what is a severe abnormality? In the UK, abortion is allowed after the normal limit of 24 weeks for cases of 'severe abnormality'. Should abortion of an individual suffering from a treatable condition such as PKU be allowed or possibly encouraged by screening programmes?
- There is a risk that people who suffer from a genetic disease or condition will feel like social outcasts if more screening leads to fewer cases. Some genetically disabled people see the future as a nightmare. They do not necessarily view their impairment in the same way that non-sufferers do. Their values are often different and their opinions should be listened to and respected by non-disabled people. Do we have false values about what makes a life worthwhile? Should we accept that suffering is inevitable and learn the best way to cope with it?
- The eugenics movement at the beginning of the twentieth century showed the risks associated with genetic knowledge. Eugenics is the study of the possible improvement of the genetics of a species. Selective breeding is one method used. Negative eugenics is the removal of harmful genes; positive eugenics is the addition of beneficial genes. Attempts were made by the Nazis, for example, to justify the complete elimination of mentally and physically disabled people in the pursuit of a genetically 'pure' race. There have been various attempts to discriminate between races on the basis of genetics. If removal of harmful genes becomes common, will this lead to 'designer babies' with the addition of desirable genes for characteristics such as intelligence, musical ability, sports prowess, and height when techniques become available?
- Screening programmes which are designed to eliminate diseases can lead to social pressures on women or couples to have abortions when it may not be what they personally want. This has happened to some women in Cyprus as a result of the screening programme for thalassemia.
- If a disease is associated with one race, screening programmes may encourage discrimination. This happened with screening for sickle cell anaemia in the USA in the 1970s.
- What is now regarded as within the bounds of normal variation may come to be regarded as undesirable, for example low IQ.
- How accurate should tests be before they can be used? Is it acceptable, for example, to inform someone that there is an 80% probability that they will suffer a particular fatal disease?
- How should we handle the genetic counselling of people who are diagnosed as having a genetic disease, particularly one such as Huntington's chorea which carries a death sentence?

- If parents choose to go ahead with a pregnancy that they know will bring into the world a child who suffers from a genetic disease, should they have to pay the medical cost of treatment or should society pay? In 1963 Francis Crick suggested that the day might come when we should have a licence to have children. A law passed in China in 1995 requires parents to seek permission to have children if there is a significant risk of inherited defects. In the USA it has been suggested that couples should lose their medical insurance if they opt not to have a pregnancy terminated when the fetus is disabled.
- Will children sue their parents if they have allowed them to be born knowing that they will suffer? Successful lawsuits have been brought by children against their parents in the USA for other medical problems.
- Genes that cause harm later in life might be beneficial earlier in life.
- Techniques offer the possibility of selecting the sex of the baby, so that a baby of the undesired sex could be aborted.

25.7.10 Genetic counselling

Genetic counselling is the giving of information and advice about the risks of genetic disease and their outcome. Patients can be referred to genetic counsellors by their local doctors or other health professionals. Doctors have an important role to play in alerting patients to risks before problems arise. Genetic counselling is often carried out in special clinics in hospitals, and the counsellor is part of a team which includes specialist laboratory workers. Counsellors are usually doctors or paediatricians (specialists in childhood conditions) who have gone on to specialise. They must have a good understanding of medical genetics as well as being trained in sympathetic counselling techniques. It is particularly important during counselling not to try to impose one's own views on the people being counselled. By giving information and encouraging discussion people must be helped to make their own decisions.

Some of the issues which are commonly discussed are listed below.

Making a diagnosis. Making an accurate diagnosis of the problem is the first essential. This may involve a physical examination and laboratory tests. For example, a woman aged 20 who has not begun to menstruate and whose breasts have not developed could be suffering from Turner's syndrome, a hormone deficiency or simply delayed puberty. Chromosomal analysis could confirm whether or not Turner's syndrome is the cause.

Family history. Investigating the family history for previous cases of genetic diseases is commonly done. It is helped by drawing the family tree with the person being counselled.

Calculating risk. The genetic counsellor often has to calculate and explain the risk of having affected children. This is particularly likely when previous cases of genetic disease have occurred in the family. For example, if both members of a couple are carriers of a recessive gene, it can be explained that there is a 1 in 4 chance of any child being affected. This is not quite as straightforward as it sounds. One couple who had already had an affected child sued a doctor who gave this advice when later they had another affected child. They had assumed they could have three more children before another was affected. More complex situations such as sex linkage may have to be explained. Haemophilia is a sex-linked disease. Some diseases are controlled by many genes (polygenic) and here environmental factors also have an influence. Spina bifida, cleft lip and clubfoot belong in this category. Calculating risk becomes more difficult in such situations, and counsellors must rely on statistics. For example, cleft lip or cleft palate occurs in 1 in 1000 births in the general population, but is 40 times more common among the brothers and sisters of affected children. Older women may want to know the risks of having a Down's syndrome child, especially if they have already had one such child. It can be explained that chromosomal disorders have a low risk of recurrence in the same family because they are faults in cell division, not genetically inherited.

Explaining cause. The counsellor will normally try to explain the cause of any problem. For example, sickle cell anaemia is caused by sickling of red blood cells and it can be explained that this leads to anaemia and blockage of small blood vessels and that these in turn cause many other symptoms.

Quality of life. The quality and likely length of an affected child's life will also be relevant. Availability of treatment, support groups and financial help will need to be discussed. The likely effects on other members of the family if the affected child needs time-consuming and expensive care can be discussed. Many practical issues such as family holidays need to be considered.

Options. If a couple decides the risks are unacceptable, possible options must be explained. These include contraception or sterilisation, adoption, artificial insemination to avoid the husband's genes being passed on or IVF using a donor egg if the problem lies with the woman. Prenatal diagnosis is an option if the couple are willing to consider abortion of an affected fetus. CVS, amniocentesis and abortion itself must then be discussed. The reliability of any tests done, such as DNA analysis or ultra-sound scanning, must also be explained. If IVF (test tube baby technique) becomes more reliable in future, pre-implantation diagnosis (see above) may become possible. Gene therapy may also become possible (section 25.7.11).

Genetic screening. Part of the counsellor's job is to discuss the results of genetic screening with the person who has been tested. In section 25.7.9 three categories of screening were considered, namely prenatal diagnosis, carrier diagnosis, and predictive diagnosis. Genetic counselling after a positive diagnosis is very important. The possibility of receiving bad news from a test is difficult to prepare for and making decisions which have long-term consequences when one is feeling shocked and emotional is helped by the support of a counsellor. Some situations are particularly distressing, such as the case of a positive identification of Huntington's chorea. Counselling after screening is one of the most challenging tasks of a counsellor, and one which will become increasingly important as more genetic tests become available.

Responsibility. If one partner is responsible for transmission of a genetic defect, as in the case of dominant genes or sex-linked conditions, guilt and blame are common responses. The counsellor should try to emphasise sharing of responsibility and can point to the fact that we all carry some harmful genes, and in most cases we are lucky enough not to find out which ones.

25.7.11 Gene therapy

Although genetic disorders can often be prevented by genetic counselling and prenatal diagnosis, or treated with varying degrees of success, such as PKU, it has not yet been possible to cure genetic diseases. Advances in genetics have reached the point where this is beginning to be possible. The basic principle is to replace faulty genes with normal genes. An outline of the procedures used will be given in this section, together with discussion of the social and ethical issues raised.

Germ-line and somatic cell therapy

Successful experiments with mice have shown that gene therapy is possible. Genes were microinjected into fertilised eggs with a known genetic disorder and the corrected eggs were re-implanted into the mother. In this method all cells of the future mouse are normal because they are all derived from a corrected egg. This procedure is known as **germ-line therapy** and all descendants of the cured animal will be normal. At the moment such treatment is regarded as unethical in humans (see later) because the gene would be passed on to future generations. Treatment at the moment is focused on another technique called **somatic cell therapy**. This involves changing some, though not all, of the somatic cells which are the non-sex cells of the body. Changes in these cannot be inherited. The people treated will therefore be cured but they will still be able to pass the faulty gene on to their offspring.

Outline of procedure

In principle the procedure is to isolate the normal gene and clone it using methods discussed earlier in the chapter. A safe and efficient vector is then needed to introduce it into the chosen human cells. These cells may have to be isolated from the body first, corrected and then replaced. This would be relatively easy for blood diseases such as sickle cell anaemia because the cells that make blood cells can easily be removed from bone marrow and replaced. The final problem is to make sure the gene is expressed normally. If it is not switched on and off normally it could create more problems than it solves, for example by making too much product. The situation is more complex when a disease is caused by a dominant gene. Here the dominant gene must also be removed or made ineffective and techniques have not yet been developed for this.

Vectors which have been considered are:

- **viruses** – these are efficient at delivering DNA to the nucleus of the cell. The virus can be genetically engineered to remove the genes that allow it to multiply and cause disease. Retroviruses have been used successfully with mice, but it is not yet possible to control where the DNA is inserted and this can cause chromosome mutations.
- **liposomes** – their use is described below for cystic fibrosis therapy.
- **microinjection** and **electroporation** have been described in section 25.5.1. They are possible methods but are not as promising as viruses and liposomes.

Example of cystic fibrosis

Cystic fibrosis (CF) affects the epithelial cells of the body, but the life-threatening problems mainly affect the lungs. Lung and trachea epithelial cells are therefore the initial target for gene therapy. The aim is to get the gene, complete with its control sequences, into the cells so that it can make the normal protein, known as CFTR (section 25.7.3). Probably only about 10% of cells will need to be corrected to eliminate the problem.

Clinical trials have begun on human sufferers from CF using an aerosol inhaler to deliver the gene, like those used by asthmatics. The gene (a cDNA clone) is enclosed in a special liposome (section 25.5.1). Liposomes are specially designed to enter cells and release DNA into the cell so that it may bind with DNA in the nucleus. The technique was used successfully in mice in 1993. Trials with a virus vector have also begun. The virus chosen is adenovirus which normally attacks the respiratory tract. Unfortunately it does not insert its DNA into the host DNA. If the cell divides, the new DNA is not replicated at the same time so it eventually becomes diluted.

The treatment may only be effective for a few weeks until the epithelial cells die, but it will be easy to repeat the treatment at regular intervals. Hopefully a way will eventually be discovered of targetting the cells that make the epithelial cells so that a permanent cure can be given.

Example of SCID (severe combined immunodeficiency disease)

One form of this disease affects a gene coding for the enzyme ADA (adenosine deaminase). The mutant gene is recessive and makes no enzyme. Heterozygous children are unaffected because their one normal gene makes sufficient ADA. ADA is needed by the white blood cells (lymphocytes) responsible for immunity to infection. Without ADA they die, so sufferers of the disease have to live in a completely sterile environment, with no direct human contact, otherwise they normally die by the age of two (fig 25.34).

Two children, aged 4 and 9, were selected for gene therapy in the USA in 1990. Lymphocytes were isolated from the children, a normal gene introduced by means of a retrovirus vector, and the cells replaced. The treatment has to be repeated every 1 to 2 months. After a year they had shown significant improvement, were able to show an immune response and were able to start school.

Ethical issues

Few people would argue that somatic cell therapies present ethical problems, particularly those using simple techniques like the use of an inhaler. It is similar to using any other pharmaceutical product. Germline therapy, though, *is* controversial. It opens up the whole field of eugenics already discussed under genetic screening in the previous section. Exactly the same technique which can be used to cure a disease by replacing a faulty gene could be used for 'gene enhancement'. This is the addition of a desired characteristic. The American public has already demonstrated a desire for enhanced growth of normal children with demands for human growth hormone to be

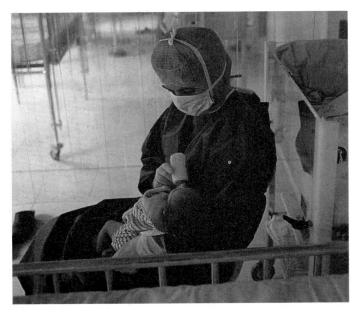

Fig 25.34 *Nurse bottle feeding a baby suffering from severe combined immunodeficiency disease (SCID). The nurse is wearing a full body gown with hair and face mask to prevent infecting the baby. Gene therapy for this condition involves inserting a gene for the enzyme into stem bone marrow cells and transplanting them into the baby where they may produce normal immune system blood cells.*

generally available. In countries like India and China the birth statistics have been distorted by abortion of girls because families want sons, although abortion on grounds of sex is now banned in India. If people are prepared to go to such lengths to select the sex of their children, why should they not make use of genetic engineering to select other inherited characteristics?

Germline therapy is also controversial because the change can be passed on to the children of the treated person and all subsequent generations. It can be argued that we should not have the right to affect future generations as well. Also, if there is even a slight possibility that the gene could be harmful in some circumstances the treatment should not be allowed. Strict regulatory procedures have to be gone through for any form of gene therapy and, on the recommendation of a Government committee in 1992, germline therapy has been made illegal for the time being in the UK.

25.7.12 Genetic fingerprinting and DNA profiling

Genetic fingerprinting was developed in 1984 by Alec Jeffreys and colleagues at the University of Leicester. A more recent and more sensitive version is known as DNA profiling. The technique has become well known to the general public through its use in criminal trials, such as the O.J. Simpson trial in the USA in 1995.

There are about 100 000 genes in the human genome (the genome being the total DNA in a cell). These code for proteins, but about 95% of the DNA is non-coding. Its function is still not clear, but some is probably structural. About 30–40% of this DNA consists of short sequences of bases which are repeated many times. Some of the repeat sequences are scattered throughout the DNA but some are found joined together in clusters, in other words in tandem. These 'tandem repeats' are known as **satellite DNA** (they were originally discovered as a separate fraction of DNA after centrifugation of the total DNA). Each cluster of repeated sequences is known as a **satellite**. Each sequence varies in the number of times it is repeated. Some satellites have only a small number of repeats and are known as **minisatellites**. It has been discovered that there is a great deal of variation between individuals in the number of repeats of these short sequences (they are 'hypervariable'). Minisatellites are therefore sometimes known as **VNTRs** (variable number tandem repeats). Each individual will have two allelic minisatellites at a particular locus, one inherited from the mother and one from the father. Genetic fingerprinting is a way of analysing the lengths of the minisatellites of a given individual.

Procedure

The DNA is extracted from cells and treated with a restriction enzyme. The enzyme chosen cuts either side of the minisatellites, leaving them intact so that their variable lengths are unaltered. Agarose gel electrophoresis is used to

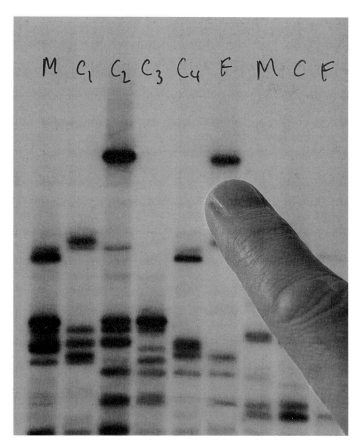

Fig 25.35 *Genetic fingerprints.*

separate the fragments, lining them up according to size as explained in section 25.1 and fig 25.4. From here the technique is as described for DNA analysis in section 25.7.9 and fig 25.33. Southern blotting is used to transfer the DNA to a nitrocellulose or nylon filter. A radioactive DNA probe with a base sequence which is complementary to part of the minisatellite repeat sequence is then hybridised to the DNA and its location found by autoradiography.

As stated, the minisatellites are different lengths in different individuals. The probe binds to the minisatellites which are found in different bands on the filter in different individuals because of their different lengths. The pattern for an individual is characteristic and therefore known as a fingerprint (fig 25.35). If the probe recognises and binds to several types of minisatellites throughout the genome it is called a **multi-locus probe** and will produce many bands on the autoradiograph. The more bands there are, the more unique the pattern. The probability of four bands matching by chance between two people is about 1 in about 250, whereas it is less than 1 in 1 million million for 20 bands (there are about 4.5 thousand million people in the world).

Multi-locus probes give best results with entire DNA. However, forensic scientists rarely work on good quality fresh material. Often it is dried samples contaminated with other materials like soil and bacteria. A more 'robust' method is often required. This can be achieved by using

single-locus probes. These can be used on smaller pieces of DNA (such as partially decomposed DNA) and also on smaller total amounts of DNA. They recognise just a single short repeating sequence which is unique to one minisatellite and therefore found only on one particular pair of homologous chromosomes. Restriction enzymes therefore produce two characteristic fragments per individual and only two bands eventually appear on the autoradiograph, one of maternal origin and one of paternal origin (fig 25.36). If two single-locus probes are used, four bands will appear, if three are used, six will appear, and so on. By using more probes greater validity in distinguishing between two individuals can be achieved if desired (see below). This technique is called **DNA profiling** and is now the most commonly used method in forensic work.

The technique can be made even more sensitive by using a method for amplifying the amount of DNA, known as the **polymerase chain reaction (PCR)**. This has meant that much smaller samples can be used for detection. This was demonstrated by a scientist who sent a piece of a licked stamp punched out with a hole punch to a laboratory for analysis. The saliva on the back of the stamp was diluted 200-fold and the sender was still correctly identified. (This technique is almost too sensitive for forensic work. For example, anyone who has shed dandruff or sneezed at the scene of the crime might become a suspect!)

Applications

Just as fingerprinting revolutionised forensic work in the early 1900s, so genetic fingerprinting is doing so now. DNA can be extracted from small samples of cells found at the scene of the crime, for example in traces of blood, hair roots or saliva. In cases of rape, semen may be used (fig 25.37). An even more common routine use of the technique is to settle paternity disputes. Fig 25.38 shows an example of the use of DNA profiling in such a dispute.

25.8 Look at fig 25.38. Which of the mother's children were fathered by F?

The first use of the technique for forensic work was in 1986 in the UK. In 1983 a schoolgirl had been found raped and murdered in a village near Leicester, and in 1986 a second girl was found. A man confessed to the second crime, but police believed he may also have been responsible for the 1983 crime. They asked Jeffreys at the University of Leicester to carry out DNA fingerprinting on semen samples from both crimes and on a blood sample from the suspect. These established that the man was innocent of both crimes! All the local men, a total of 1500, were then tested, but still with no positive result. The murderer was finally caught as a result of a conversation overheard by chance in a pub. DNA fingerprinting confirmed his guilt. In about 30% of the times that DNA fingerprinting is used, the person tested is shown not to match the scene-of-crime-DNA.

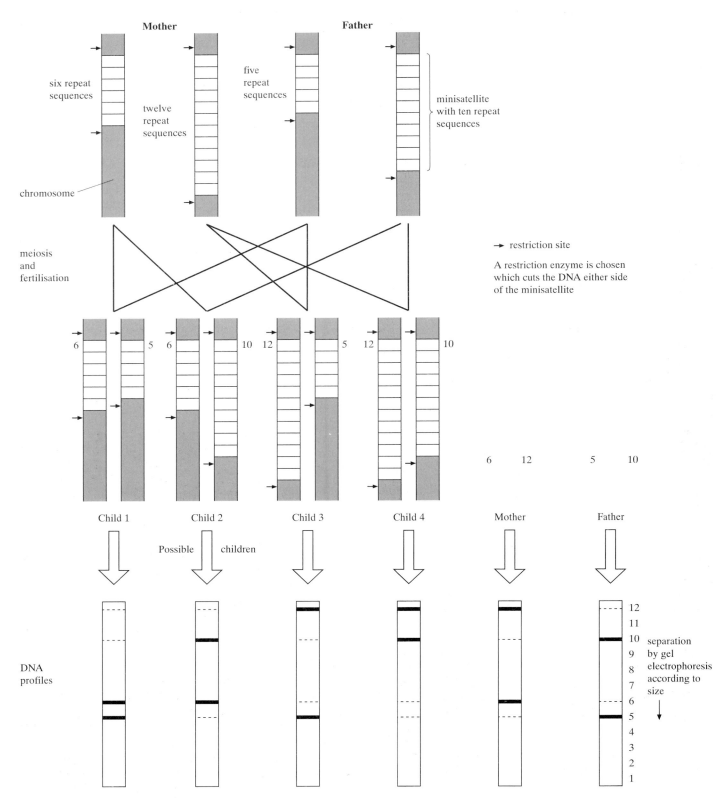

Fig 25.36 *Inheritance of minisatellites and variation in DNA profiles which result. In the population as a whole there is great variation in the lengths of the minisatellites, making the chances of two individuals producing the same DNA profile very small (see text).*

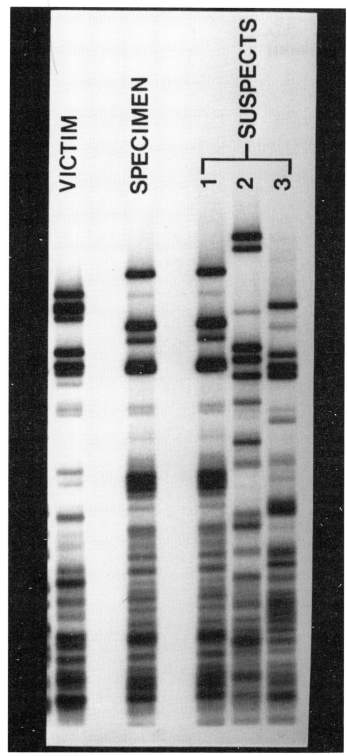

Fig 25.37 *Genetic fingerprint of a victim's blood, semen (specimen) and the blood of suspect rapists.*

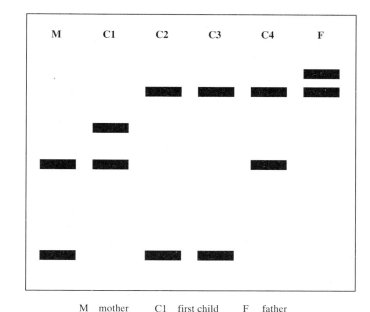

M mother   C1 first child   F father

Fig 25.38 *DNA profiles of people involved in a paternity dispute.*

Reliability and validity

Reliability is being able to get the same result each time a test is carried out. For example, would two different laboratories produce the same result with the same sample? Attempts are being made to standardise techniques throughout Europe to increase reliability. This is important for international crimes, such as terrorism and drug-rings.

Validity concerns whether or not the test is appropriate. The chief concern in forensic cases is the probability of one individual having the same profile or fingerprint as another. Courtroom battles over this issue have made headlines on a number of occasions. Jeffreys calculated that there was about a one in four chance of two people sharing a band if a multi-locus probe is used. Therefore there is a 1 in 4^n chance where n = number of bands. Thus there is a 1 in 256 chance of two people sharing four bands and less than 1 in 1 million million chance of sharing 20–30 bands (the number of bands in an average DNA fingerprint). Often though, forensic scientists are working with poor quality material and degraded DNA may only give a few bands. It cannot therefore always give a definite answer. Another complication is that the odds quoted apply only to the population as a whole. Relatives will show more similarities.

It is harder to make statistical calculations for single-locus probes because each band occurs with a different frequency in the population. On average, using one such probe the bands will match in 1 in 100 at most, with two probes 1 in 10 000 and with three probes 1 in 1 million. There is variation between different ethnic groups, so separate databases have been set up for different groups. It is easier to store the data digitally for single-locus probes than with multilocus probes.

The PCR method will probably become the standard method in the future. It is fast, could be automated, would be cheaper once set up, can use samples as small as a few cells and the data is easily stored. However, new databases will have to be set up.

Other examples of the use of the technique are:

- paternity cases involving pets, such as dogs, are sometimes brought, particularly to confirm pedigrees;
- whose baby? disputes – in 1993 there was confusion at a Southampton hospital over whether two newly born babies had accidentally been switched which was successfully resolved;
- prosecutions have been successfully brought against people who are caught in possession of endangered animals, particularly birds, but who have claimed that they have been bred from legally captive animals;
- zoos which are breeding endangered species try to maintain as much genetic diversity as possible – this can be monitored;
- relationships within families can be established; cases of incest can be identified;
- social behaviour in animals can be interpreted better if relationships between the animals are known – for example in prides of lions in Africa it has been shown that not all the males mate with the females; those who do not, though, are closely related to those who do, so their genes are still likely to be passed on;
- in immigration cases disputes over family relationships can be settled;
- unusual cases sometimes occur – for example a seed pod found in a truck matched an isolated tree where a corpse had been found; this helped to convict the owner of the truck.

25.7.13 Transplant surgery and the Major Histocompatibility Complex (MHC)

A familiar problem with transplant surgery is that of rejection of the transplanted organ. The body recognises the transplanted organ as 'foreign' and mounts an immune response against it which gradually destroys it. This is known as **rejection**. The immune system must also be able to recognise 'self', so that it does not attack and destroy its own body. (There are some diseases where this happens.) The body is able to label its own cells with marker proteins rather like flags, which enable different cells to recognise each other. This helps cells to 'know' where and what they are and is important, for example, in embryonic development when tissues and organs are forming. One set of marker proteins identifies 'self'. All cells except red blood cells have these 'self' markers. They are coded for by a set of genes on chromosome 6 known as the **major histocompatibility complex (MHC)**. There is more variation among these genes than for any others in human populations, so a vast range of markers is possible. The markers act as antigens, and are attacked by a particular type of white blood cell, the killer T cell, if they are foreign. T cells are a type of lymphocyte (section 14.9). The markers are in fact glycoproteins, that is proteins with a carbohydrate tail which sit in the cell surface membranes with the tail projecting outwards.

The MHC genes that produce these markers, or antigens, are arranged at three loci quite close together on chromosome 6. The genes are known as A, B and C, or HLA-A, HLA-B and HLA-C. (HLA stands for **human lymphocyte antigen**, because the antigens were first discovered on lymphocytes.) The three genes each have many different alleles (types), which accounts for the variety of 'self' antigens. The antigens are sometimes referred to as **transplantation antigens** because they are the antigens which get attacked in transplanted organs when rejection takes place.

Another part of chromosome 6 contains another group of genes, all of which are referred to as HLA-D genes. These are also involved in transplant rejection but in a different way. They also have many alleles and are needed for the functioning of another type of T cell known as a helper T cell (section 14.9). Every person has two copies of chromosome 6 (being diploid), and therefore two alleles each of genes A, B, C and the various D genes (probably three in total). (There are at least 40 common alleles of A, 59 of B and 12 of C). The particular combination of A, B, C and D antigens on one chromosome is called the **haplotype** (short for haploid genotype). Each person therefore has two MHC haplotypes, one on each chromosome 6. Because the genes in one haplotype are on the same chromosome and not very far apart, they tend to stay together during meiosis and be passed on as a unit from parent to child. There are millions of possible combinations of the alleles, but because of haplotypes, family members tend to have many more similarities than unrelated people. In addition, some haplotypes are much more common than others and some produce stronger immune responses than others.

The greater the difference between the alleles of the donor and the alleles of the recipient, the more likely the donor organ is to be rejected. However, the chances can be improved by matching the haplotypes that produce strong immune responses, and improved greatly if a relative can be used. This is sometimes possible for kidney transplants because a person can survive with one kidney. The perfect match is only likely to be found with an identical twin, since they are genetically identical.

ABO blood groups

Fortunately, human red blood cells do not show the same variation in MHC antigens that is shown by all other cells (unlike the red blood cells of some animals such as mice and chickens). If they did, it would be just as difficult to find a suitable blood donor as it is to find a suitable organ donor, and far more deaths would occur. A number of antigen systems occur in red blood cells, the most important of which is the ABO system. A, B, and O are alleles of one gene. The A and B alleles produce A and B antigens respectively, which are glycoproteins, but the protein produced by the O allele is non-functional. The function of the system is unknown. The consequences for blood transfusions are discussed in section 14.9.9. It is just as important to match blood groups when organs are being transplanted because the A and B antigens are present on the surfaces of many cells apart from red blood cells.

Chapter Twenty-six

Evolution – history of life

The word evolution means change over a period of time. It is one of the most powerful ideas in biology that living things may have evolved from relatively simple chemicals. The study of evolution provides a focus for investigations into the nature of life itself, the origins of life, the great diversity of living things and the underlying similarities in structure and function which they have.

This chapter attempts to describe and discuss the many theories concerning the origin of life and the possible ways in which species have originated. Traditionally the study of the history of life has been fraught with allegations of indoctrination. Indoctrination may be defined as a conscious effort to inculcate an unshakeable commitment to a belief or doctrine. Such an approach is not only anti-scientific but also intellectually dishonest, and efforts to avoid this have been made in this text.

A brief outline of the main theories concerning the origin of life is presented in this chapter so that students are aware that there is a range of opinions on the subject. Much of the evidence on which these theories are based is metaphysical, that is to say it is impossible to repeat the exact events of the origin of life in any demonstrable way. This is true of both scientific and religious (theological) accounts. However, one theory, evolution, is increasingly being seen not as a single theory but as a collection of individual scientific hypotheses each of which is capable of being tested, as described in appendix section A2.1.

In this chapter, and in chapter 27, scientific facts have been selected to produce an account of the processes underlying the origins and diversity of life. Because of the necessity to be selective this account lacks absolute objectivity; indeed, this is inevitably true of any account, be it historical, scientific or metaphysical. However, by stressing the limitations and assumptions associated with the evidence presented here, this account may have a degree of objectivity and tentativeness which characterises good scientific writing. It must be stressed that the evidence presented in this chapter, and the conclusions drawn from it, represent current views. These are constantly under review and their validity is limited by the knowledge available to us at any given time.

26.1   Theories of the origin of life

Theories concerned with the origin of the Earth, and indeed the Universe, are diverse and uncertain. It may have begun as a ball of particles, exploded in a 'big bang', emerged from one of several black holes, or be the design of a Creator. Science, contrary to popular belief, cannot contradict the idea of a divine origin for the early universe. Nor do theological views necessarily dismiss the scientific hypothesis that, during the origins of life, life acquired those characteristics which are explained by the natural laws of science.

The major theories accounting for the origin of life on Earth are:

(1) life was created by a supernatural being at a particular time (**special creation**);
(2) life arose from non-living matter on numerous occasions by a process of **spontaneous generation**;
(3) life has no origin (**steady-state**);
(4) life arrived on this planet from elsewhere (**cosmozoan**);
(5) life arose according to chemical and physical laws (**biochemical evolution**).

Each of these theories is dealt with in turn below.

26.1.1   Special creation

This theory is supported by most of the world's major religions and civilisations and attributes the origin of life to a supernatural event at a particular time in the past. Archbishop Ussher of Armagh calculated in 1650 AD that God created the world in October 4004 BC, beginning on October 1st and finishing with Man at 9.00 a.m. on the morning of October 23rd. He achieved this figure by adding up the ages of all the people in the biblical genealogies from Adam to Christ (the 'begats'). Whilst the arithmetic is sound, it places Adam as having lived at a time when archaeological evidence suggests that there was already a well-established urban civilisation in the Middle East.

The traditional Judaeo-Christian account of creation, given in Genesis 1:1–26, has attracted, and continues to attract, controversy. Whilst all Christians would agree that the Bible is God's word to Man, there are differences of interpretation concerning the length of the 'day' mentioned in Genesis. Some believe that the world and all species were created in six days of 24 hours' duration. They reject any other possible views and rely absolutely on inspiration, meditation and divine revelation. Other Christians do not regard the Bible as a scientific textbook and see the Genesis account as the theological revelation of the Creation of all living things through the power of God, described in terms understandable to humans in all ages. For them the Creation account is concerned with answering the question 'Why?' rather than 'How?'. Whilst science broadly relies on observation and experiment to seek truth, theology draws its insights from divine revelation and faith.

> 'Faith is the substance of things hoped for, the evidence of things not seen . . . by faith . . . we understand that the universe was created by God's word, so that what can be seen was made out of what cannot be seen.' (Hebrews 11 : 1, 3)

Faith accepts things for which there is no evidence in the scientific sense. This means that logically there can be no intellectual conflict between scientific and theological accounts of creation, since they are mutually exclusive realms of thought. Scientific truth to the scientist is tentative, but theological truth to the believer is absolute.

Since the process of special creation occurred only once and therefore cannot be observed, this is sufficient to put the concept of special creation outside the framework of scientific investigation. Science concerns itself only with observable phenomena and as such will never be able to prove or disprove special creation.

26.1.2   Spontaneous generation

This theory was prevalent in ancient Chinese, Babylonian and Egyptian thought as an alternative to special creation, with which it coexisted. Aristotle (384–322 BC), often hailed as the founder of biology, believed that life arose spontaneously. On the basis of his personal observations he developed this belief further in relating all organisms to a continuum, a *scala natura* (ladder of life).

> 'For nature passes from lifeless objects to animals in such unbroken sequence, interposing between them, beings which live and yet are not animals, that scarcely any difference seems to exist between neighbouring groups, owing to their close proximity.' (Aristotle)

In stating this he reinforced the previous speculations of Empedocles on organic evolution. Aristotle's hypothesis of spontaneous generation assumed that certain 'particles' of matter contained an 'active principle' which could produce a living organism when conditions were suitable. He was correct in assuming that the active principle was present in a fertilised egg, but incorrectly extended this to the belief that sunlight, mud and decaying meat also had the active principle.

> 'Such are the facts, everything comes into being not only from the mating of animals but from the decay of earth . . . . And among the plants the matter proceeds in the same way, some develop from seed, others, as it were, by spontaneous generation by natural forces; they arise from decaying earth or from certain parts of plants.' (Aristotle)

With the spread of Christianity, the spontaneous generation theory fell from favour, except among those who believed in magic and devil-worship, although it remained as a background idea for many more centuries.

Van Helmont (1557–1644), a much-acclaimed and successful scientist, described an experiment which gave rise to mice in three weeks. The raw materials for the experiment were a dirty shirt, a dark cupboard and a handful of wheat grains. The active principle in this process was thought to be human sweat.

> **26.1**   What did Van Helmont omit from his experiment?

In 1688 Francesco Redi, an Italian biologist and physician living in Florence, took a more rigorous approach to the problem of the origin of life and questioned the theory of spontaneous generation. Redi observed that the little white worms seen on decaying flesh were fly larvae. By a series of experiments he produced evidence to support the idea that life can arise only from pre-existing life, the concept of **biogenesis**.

> 'Belief would be vain without the confirmation of experiment, hence in the middle of July, I put a snake, some fish, some eels of the Arno and a slice of milk-fed veal in four large, wide-mouthed flasks; having well closed and sealed them, I then filled the same number of flasks in the same way, leaving only these open.' (Redi)

Redi reported his results as follows.

> 'It was not long before the meat and the fish, in these second vessels (the unsealed ones), became wormy and the flies were seen entering and leaving at will; but in the closed flasks I did not see a worm, though many days had passed since the dead fish had been put in them.'

> **26.2**   What do you consider was Redi's basic assumption?

These experiments, however, did not destroy the idea of spontaneous generation and, whilst the old theory took a set-back, it continued to be the dominant theory within the secular (non-religious) community.

Whilst Redi's experiments appeared to disprove the spontaneous generation of flies, the pioneer work in microscopy by Anton van Leeuwenhoeck appeared to reinforce the theory with regard to micro-organisms. Whilst not entering the debate between biogenesis and spontaneous generation, his observations with the microscope provided fuel for both theories and finally stimulated other scientists to design experiments to settle the question of the origin of life by spontaneous generation.

In 1765 Lazzaro Spallanzani boiled animal and vegetable broths for several hours and sealed them immediately. He then removed them from the source of heat. After being set aside for several days, none of them, on examination, showed any signs of life. He concluded from this that the high temperature had destroyed all forms of living organisms in his vessel and without their presence no life could appear.

> **26.3** Suggest another reason why Spallanzani's experiment might have prevented the growth of organisms.

In 1860 Louis Pasteur turned his attention to the problem of the origins of life. By this stage he had demonstrated the existence of bacteria and found solutions to the economic problems of the silk and wine industries. He had also shown that bacteria were ubiquitous (found in all environments) and that non-living matter could easily become contaminated by living matter if all materials were not adequately sterilised.

> **26.4** What were Pasteur's basic assumptions about the origins of life?

In a series of experiments based upon those of Spallanzani, Pasteur demonstrated the theory of biogenesis and finally disproved the theory of spontaneous generation.

The validation of biogenesis however raised another problem. Since it was now clear that a living organism was required in order to produce another living organism, where did the first living organism come from? The steady-state hypothesis has an answer for this but all the other theories imply a transition from non-living to living at some stage in the history of life. Was this a primeval spontaneous generation?

26.1.3 Steady-state theory

This theory asserts that the Earth had no origin, has always been able to support life, has changed remarkably little, if at all, and that species had no origin.

Estimates of the age of the Earth have varied greatly from the 4004 BC calculation of Archbishop Ussher to the present-day values of 5000 million years based on radioactive decay rates. Improved scientific dating techniques (appendix 4) have given increasing ages for the Earth, and extrapolation of this trend provides supporters of this theory with the hypothesis that the Earth had no origin. Whilst generally discrediting the value of geochronology in giving a precise age for the Earth, the steady-state theory uses this as a basis for supposing that the Earth has always existed. This theory proposes that species, too, never originated, they have always existed and that in the history of a species the only alternatives are for its numbers to vary, or for it to become extinct.

The theory does not accept the palaeontological evidence that presence or absence of a fossil indicates the origin or extinction of the species represented and quotes, as an example, the case of the coelacanth, *Latimeria*. Fossil evidence indicated that the coelacanths died out at the end of the Cretaceous period, 70 million years ago. The discovery of living specimens off the coast of Madagascar has altered this view. The steady-state theory claims that it is only by studying living species and comparing them with the fossil record that extinction can be assumed and then there is a high probability that this may be incorrect. The palaeontological evidence presented in support of the steady-state theory describes the fossil's appearance in ecological terms. For example, the sudden appearance of a fossil in a particular stratum would be associated with an increase in population size or movement of the organism into an area which favoured fossilisation.

26.1.4 Cosmozoan theory

This theory does not offer a mechanism to account for the origin of life but favours the idea that it could have had an extraterrestrial origin. It does not therefore, constitute a theory of origin as such, but merely shifts the problem to elsewhere in the Universe.

The theory states that life could have arisen once or several times in various parts of our Galaxy or the Universe. Its alternative name is the theory of **panspermia**. Repeated sightings of UFOs, cave drawings of rocket-like objects and 'spacemen' and reports of encounters with aliens provide the background evidence for this theory. Russian and American space probes have not yet succeeded in finding life within our Solar System but cannot comment on the nature of life outside our Solar System. Research into materials from meteorites and comets has revealed the presence of many organic molecules, such as cyanogen and hydrocyanic acid, which may have acted as 'seeds' falling on a barren Earth. There are several claims that objects bearing resemblance to primitive forms of life on Earth have been found in meteorites and in 1996 NASA scientists in the USA identified what they thought could be the remains of bacteria-like organisms in a rock from Mars (although they do not propose that life on Earth can be traced back to life on Mars). In all cases further evidence is needed.

26.1.5 Biochemical evolution

It is generally agreed by astronomers, geologists and biologists that the Earth is some 4.5–5.0 thousand million years old.

Many biologists believe that the original state of the Earth bore little resemblance to its present-day form and had the following probable appearance: it was hot (about 4000–8000 °C) and as it cooled carbon and the less volatile metals condensed and formed the Earth's core; the surface was probably barren and rugged as volcanic activity, continuous earth movements and contraction on cooling, folded and fractured the surface.

The atmosphere is believed to have been totally different in those days. The lighter gases hydrogen, helium, nitrogen, oxygen and argon would have escaped because the gravitational field of the partially condensed planet would not contain them. However, simple compounds containing these elements (amongst others) would have been retained, such as water, ammonia, carbon dioxide and methane, and until the earth cooled below 100 °C all water would have existed as vapour. The atmosphere would appear to have been a 'reducing atmosphere', as indicated by the presence of metals in their reduced form (such as iron(II)) in the oldest rocks of the Earth. More recent rocks contain metals in their oxidised form (for example iron(III)). The lack of oxygen in the atmosphere would probably be a necessity, since laboratory experiments have shown, paradoxically, that is far easier to generate organic molecules (the basis of living organisms) in a reducing atmosphere than in an oxygen-rich atmosphere.

In 1923 Alexander Oparin suggested that the atmosphere of the primeval Earth was not as we know it today but fitted the description given above. On theoretical grounds he argued that organic compounds, probably hydrocarbons, could have formed in the oceans from more simple compounds, the energy for these synthesis reactions probably being supplied from the strong solar radiation (mainly ultra-violet) which surrounded the Earth before the formation of the ozone layer, which now blocks much of it out. Oparin argued that if one considered the multitude of simple molecules present in the oceans, the surface area of the Earth, the energy available and the time scale, it was conceivable that oceans would gradually accumulate

organic molecules to produce a 'primeval soup', in which life could have arisen. This was not a new idea, indeed Darwin himself expressed a similar thought in a letter he wrote in 1871:

'It is often said that all the conditions for the first production of a living organism are now present, which could ever have been present. But if, (and oh what a big if) we could conceive of some warm little pond, with all sorts of ammonia and phosphoric salts, light, heat, electricity, etc. present that a protein compound was chemically formed ready to undergo still more complex changes, at the present day, such matter would be constantly devoured or absorbed, which could not have been the case before living creatures were formed.'

In 1953 Stanley Miller, in a series of experiments, simulated the proposed conditions on the primitive Earth. In his experimental high-energy chamber (fig 26.1) he successfully synthesised many substances of considerable biological importance, including amino acids, adenine and simple sugars such as ribose. More recently Orgel at the Salk Institute has succeeded in synthesising nucleotides six units long (a simple nucleic acid molecule) in a similar experiment.

It has since been suggested that carbon dioxide was present in relatively high concentrations in the primeval atmosphere. Recent experiments using Miller's apparatus but containing mixtures of carbon dioxide and water and only traces of other gases have produced similar results to

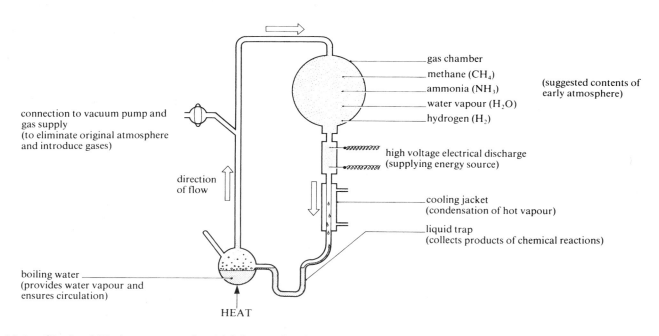

Fig 26.1 *Stanley Miller's apparatus in which he synthesised amino acids from gases under conditions thought to have been present in the primeval atmosphere. The gases and vapours were circulated under pressure and exposed to a high voltage for one week. At the end of the period the liquid products in the trap were analysed by paper chromatography. A total of 15 amino acids were isolated including glycine, alanine and aspartic acid.*

those of Miller. Oparin's theory has been widely accepted, but major problems remain in explaining the transition from complex organic molecules to living organisms. This is where the theory of a process of biochemical evolution offers a broad scheme which is acceptable to the majority of contemporary biologists. However, there is no agreement as to the precise mechanism by which it may have occurred.

Oparin considered that protein molecules were crucial to the transformation from inanimate to animate. Because of the zwitterionic nature of protein molecules they are able to form colloidal hydrophilic complexes which attract, and become surrounded by, envelopes of water molecules. These bodies may separate from the body of the liquid in which they are suspended (aqueous phase) and form a type of emulsion. Coalescence of these structures produces a separation of colloids from their aqueous phase, a process known as **coacervation** (*coacervus*, clump or heap). These colloid-rich coacervates may have been able to exchange substances with their environment and selectively concentrate compounds within them, particularly crystalloids. The colloid composition of a coacervate would depend on the composition of the medium. The varying composition of the 'soup' in different areas would lead to variation in the chemical composition of coacervates, producing the raw material for 'biochemical natural selection'.

It is suggested that substances within the coacervates may have undergone further chemical reactions and, by absorbing metal ions into the coacervates, formed enzymes. The alignment of lipid molecules (complex hydrocarbons) along the boundary between the coacervates and the external medium would have produced a primitive cell membrane which conferred stability on the coacervates. Thus the incorporation of a pre-existing molecule capable of self-replication into the coacervate, and an internal rearrangement of the lipid-coated coacervate, may have produced a primitive type of cell. Increase in size of coacervates and their fragmentation possibly led to the formation of identical coacervates which could absorb more of the medium and the cycle could continue. This possible sequence of events would have produced a primitive self-replicating heterotrophic organism feeding on an organic-rich primeval soup.

26.2 The nature of the earliest organisms

Current evidence suggests that the first organisms were heterotrophs as these were the only organisms capable of using the external supplies of available energy locked up within the complex of organic molecules present in the 'soup'. The chemical reactions involved in synthesising food substances appear to have been too complex to have arisen within the earliest forms of life.

As more complex organic molecules arose through 'biochemical evolution', it is assumed that some of these were able to harness solar radiation as an energy source and use it to synthesise new cellular materials. Incorporation of these molecules into pre-existing cells may have enabled the cells to synthesise new cellular materials without the need for them to absorb organic molecules, hence becoming autotrophic. Increasing numbers of heterotrophs would have reduced the available food resources in the primeval soup and this competition for resources would hasten the appearance of autotrophs.

The earliest photosynthetic organisms, whilst utilising solar radiation as their energy source, lacked the biochemical pathways to produce oxygen. At a later stage, it is believed that oxygen-evolving photosynthetic organisms developed, similar to existing blue-green bacteria (section 2.3), and this resulted in the gradual build-up of oxygen in the atmosphere. The increase in atmospheric oxygen and its ionisation to form the ozone layer would reduce the ultra-violet radiation striking the Earth. Whilst decreasing the rate of synthesis of new complex molecules, the decrease in radiation would confer some stability on successful forms of life. A study of the physiology of present-day organisms reveals a great diversity in biochemical pathways associated with energy capture and release, which may mirror many of Nature's early experiments with living organisms.

Despite the simplified account given above, the problem of the origin(s) of life remains. All that has been outlined is speculative and, despite tremendous advances in biochemistry, answers to the problem remain hypothetical. The above account is a simplified amalgam of present-day hypotheses. No 'ruling hypothesis' has yet achieved the status of an all-embracing theory (appendix section A2.1). Details of the transition from complex non-living materials to simple living organisms remain a mystery.

26.3 Summary of the 'theories' of the origin of life

Many of these 'theories' and the way they explain the existing diversity of species cover similar ground but with varying emphases. Scientific theories may be ultra-imaginative on the one hand and ultra-sceptical on the other. Theological considerations too, may fit into this framework, depending upon one's religious views. One of the major areas of controversy, even before the days of Darwin, was the relationship between scientific and theological views on the history of life.

Diagrams (*a*)–(*e*) in fig 26.2 represent straightforward descriptions of theories, hypotheses or beliefs on the history of life, whereas (*f*) and (*g*) represent an attempt to combine certain aspects of three theories, (*b*), (*c*) and (*d*), into an alternative acceptable to many people. The practices of science and religion are not, therefore, necessarily mutually exclusive, as witnessed by the number of scientists who hold religious beliefs.

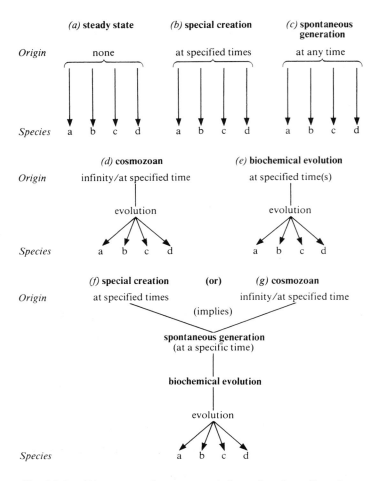

Fig 26.2 *Diagrammatic representation of various theories of the origin of life and the formation of species.*

26.4   The theory of evolution

The term 'evolution' has a special place in the study of the history of life. It has become the unifying concept which underpins the whole study of biology. Evolution implies an overall gradual development which is both ordered and sequential. In terms of living organisms it may be defined as **the development of differentiated organisms from pre-existing, less differentiated organisms over the course of time**.

The concept of evolution did not begin with Darwin and the publication of *On the Origin of Species*. Long before Darwin, attempts to explain the obvious diversity of living organisms which surround us had, paradoxically, led people to consider the basic structural and functional similarities which exist between organisms. Evolutionary hypotheses had been proposed to account for this and these ideas have themselves 'evolved' since the time of Darwin as knowledge has advanced.

The historical background to the development of the theory of evolution, as outlined in table 26.1, shows that the concept of continuity or gradual development of more complex species from pre-existing simpler forms had

occurred to several philosophers and natural historians before the formal declarations of evolutionary hypotheses were put forward in the early nineteenth century.

26.4.1   Lamarckian evolution

The French biologist Lamarck proposed, in 1809, a hypothesis to account for the mechanism of evolution based on two conditions: the use and disuse of parts, and the inheritance of acquired characteristics. Changes in the environment may lead to changed patterns of behaviour which can necessitate new or increased use (or disuse) of certain organs or structures. Extensive use would lead to increased size and/or efficiency whilst disuse would lead to degeneracy and atrophy. These traits acquired during the lifetime of the individual were believed to be heritable and thus transmitted to offspring.

According to Lamarckism, as the theory came to be known, the long neck and legs of the modern giraffe were the result of generations of short-necked and short-legged ancestors feeding on leaves at progressively higher levels of trees. The slightly longer necks and legs produced in each generation were passed on to the subsequent generation, until the size of the present-day giraffe was reached. The webbed feet of aquatic birds and the shape of flat fish could be explained similarly. In aquatic birds the constant spreading of the toe bones and the skin between them in order to swim to find food and escape predators gave rise to their webbed feet. Likewise adaptations resulting from fish lying on their sides in shallow water were proposed to explain the shape of flat fish. Whilst Lamarck's theory helped prepare the way for acceptance of the concept of evolution, his views on the mechanism of change were never widely accepted.

However, Lamarck's emphasis on the role of the environment in producing phenotypic changes in the individual was correct. For example, body-building exercises will increase the size of muscles, but these acquired traits, whilst affecting the phenotype, are non-genetic, and having no influence on the genotype cannot be inherited. To demonstrate this, Weismann cut off the tails of mice over many successive generations. According to Lamarckism, the enforced disuse of tails should have led to progeny with smaller tails. This was not the case. Weismann postulated that somatic (body)-acquired characteristics (resulting in phenotypic changes) did not directly affect the germ (gamete) cells which are the means by which characteristics are passed on to the next generation.

26.4.2   Darwin, Wallace and the origin of species by natural selection

Charles Darwin was born in 1809, the son of a wealthy doctor, and like many great people he had an undistinguished academic career. In 1831 he accepted an unpaid post as naturalist on the survey ship HMS *Beagle*,

Table 26.1 The history of evolutionary thought.

Ancient Chinese

Confucius	Life originated from a single source through a gradual unfolding and branching

Greek and Mediaeval period

Diogenes	All things are differentiations of the same thing and are the same thing
Empedocles	Air, earth, fire and water are the four roots of all things. Life arose by the action of the forces of attraction and repulsion on the four elements. Explained origin of Universe, plants, animals and humans (produced the germ of the idea of organic evolution)
Democritus	Living things arose by spontaneous generation from the slime of the Earth
Anaxogoras	Organisms sprang from atmospheric germs
Thales (640–546 BC)	All life came from water
Anaximander	Plants, then animals and finally humans arose from the mud of the emerging Earth
Aristotle (384–322 BC)	Proposed theory of continuous and gradual evolution from lifeless matter, based on his observations of animals. Recognised a 'scala natura' for animals
Dark Ages (400–1400 AD)	All theories based on those above or acceptance of special creation

Age of speculation (1400–1790)

John Ray (1627–1705)	Developed concept of species
Carl Linnaeus (1707–78)	Formalised 'binomial classification' system. Suggested genera were created separately and species were variants of them
Buffon (1707–88)	Suggested different types of animals had different origins at different times. Recognised influence of external environment. Believed in acquired inheritance
James Hutton (1726–97)	Theory of uniformatarianism. Gave age of Earth in millions of years

Age of formulation (1790–1900)

Erasmus Darwin (1731–1802)	Life arose from one single 'filament' made by God. Did not accept the preformation of humans. The filament evolved by acquired characteristics
Jean-Baptiste Lamarck (1744–1829)	Inheritance of acquired characteristics. Environment acts on organisms. Phenotype changes are passed on. Concept of use and disuse of organs
Georges Cuvier (1769–1832)	Established palaeontological evidence. Fossils the results of 'catastrophes' by which new species arose
William Smith (1769–1838)	Opposed Cuvier's theory of catastrophism on basis of continuity of similar species in related strata
Charles Lyell (1797–1875)	Demonstrated the progressive history of fossil evidence
Charles Darwin (1809–82)	Influenced by Lyell and Malthus. Established a theory of evolution by means of natural selection
Alfred Russel Wallace (1823–1913)	Similar theory to Darwin, but excepted humans from his theory
Hugo de Vries (1848–1935)	Recognised existence of mutations which were heritable as a basis for discontinuous variation and regarded species as arising by mutation
August Weismann (1834–1914)	Showed that the reproductive cells of animals are distinct and therefore unaffected by the influences acting on somatic tissues
Gregor Mendel (1822–84)	Work on genetics (published 1865) only came to light after 1900. Laws of inheritance

Developments in twentieth century (neo-Darwinism)

W. L. Johannsen	Phenotypic characteristics are determined by genotype and environmental factors
T. Henry Morgan	Developed chromosome theory of heredity on basis of cytological evidence
H. J. Muller (1927)	Genotype can be altered by X-rays; induced mutation
R. A. Fisher (1930)	No difference between change investigated by geneticists and change shown in the fossil record
G. W. Beadle and E. L. Tatum (1941)	Demonstrated the genetic basis of biochemical synthesis (following A. E. Garrod (1909) and J. B. S. Haldane (1935))
J. Lederberg and A. D. Hershey (1951)	Demonstrated value of using bacteria in studying changes in genotype
J. D. Watson and F. H. C. Crick (1953)	Proposed molecular structure of DNA and its mechanism of replication
F. Jacob and J. Monod (1961)	Proposed a mechanism for regulation of gene activity

which spent the next five years at sea charting the East Coast of South America. The *Beagle* returned to Falmouth in October 1836 via the coast of Chile, the Galapagos Islands, Tahiti, New Zealand, Tasmania and South Africa. For most of this time Darwin was concerned with studying geology, but during a five-week stay on the Galapagos Islands he was struck by the similarities shown by the flora and fauna of the islands and mainland. In particular he was intrigued by the characteristic distribution of species of tortoises and finches (section 26.7.2). He collected a great deal of biological data concerned with variation between organisms which convinced him that species were not unchangeable.

On his return home his work on the selective breeding of pigeons and other domestic animals gave him a clue to the concept of artificial selection, but he was unable to appreciate how this could operate in the wild. An earlier *Essay on the Principles of Population* by the Reverend Thomas Malthus, published in 1778, had highlighted the consequences of the reproductive potential of humans. Darwin applied this to other organisms and saw that despite this the numbers within populations remained relatively constant.

Having collated a vast amount of information he began to realise that under the intense competition of numbers in a population, any variation which favoured survival in a particular environment would increase that individual's ability to reproduce and leave fertile offspring. Less favourable variations would be at a disadvantage and organisms possessing them would therefore have their chances of successful reproduction decreased. These data provided Darwin with the framework to formulate, by 1839, a theory of evolution by natural selection, but he did not publish his findings at that time. Indeed Darwin's greatest contribution to science was not so much to show that evolution occurs but how it might occur.

In the meantime, another naturalist, Alfred Russel Wallace, who had travelled widely in South America, Malaya and the Eastern Indian archipelago, and also read Malthus, had come to the same conclusions as Darwin regarding natural selection.

In 1858, Wallace wrote a 20-page essay outlining his theory and sent it to Darwin. This stimulated and encouraged Darwin and in July 1858, Darwin and Wallace presented papers on their ideas at a meeting of the Linnean Society in London. Over a year later, in November 1859, Darwin published *On the Origin of Species by Means of Natural Selection*. All 1250 printed copies were sold on the day of publication and it is said that this book has been second only to the Bible in its impact on human thinking.

26.5 Natural selection

Darwin and Wallace proposed that natural selection is the mechanism by which new species arise from pre-existing species. This hypothesis/theory is based on three observations and two deductions which may be summarised as follows.

Observation 1: Individuals within a population produce on average more offspring than are needed to replace themselves.

Observation 2: The numbers of individuals in a population remain approximately constant.

Deduction 1: Many individuals fail to survive or reproduce. There is a 'struggle for existence' within a population.

Observation 3: Variation exists within all populations.

Deduction 2: In the 'struggle for existence' those individuals showing variations best adapted to their environment have a 'reproductive advantage' and produce more offspring than less well-adapted organisms.

Deduction 2 offers a hypothesis called natural selection which provides a mechanism accounting for evolution.

26.5.1 Evidence for natural selection

Observation 1: It was Malthus who highlighted the reproductive potential of humans and observed that human populations are able to increase exponentially (section 10.7). The capacity for reproduction is basic to all living organisms, and is a fundamental drive which ensures continuity of the species. This applies to other organisms as shown in table 26.2. If every female gamete was fertilised and developed to maturity, the Earth would be totally overcrowded in a matter of days.

Observation 2: All population sizes are limited by various environmental factors, such as food availability, space and light. Populations tend to increase in size until the environment supports no further increase and an equilibrium is reached. The population fluctuates around this equilibrium, as discussed in section 10.7.3 Hence population sizes generally remain approximately constant over a period of time related to the length of the organism's life cycle.

Deduction 1: The continuous competition between individuals for environmental resources creates a 'struggle for existence'. Whether this competition occurs within a species (**intraspecific competition**) or between members of different species (**interspecific competition**) may be irrelevant in affecting the size of the individual population (section 10.7), but it will still imply that certain organisms will fail to survive or reproduce.

Table 26.2 Reproductive potential of selected species.

Crassostrea virginica	American oyster	1.0 million eggs per season
Lycoperdon sp.	giant puff ball	7.0×10^{11} spores
Papaver rhoeas	poppy capsule	6000 seeds
Carcinus maenas	shore crab	4.0 million eggs per season

Observation 3: Darwin's study of beetles whilst an undergraduate at Cambridge, his subsequent journey in the *Beagle* and his knowledge gained through the selective breeding of certain characteristics in pigeons convinced him of the importance of variation within a species. Likewise the adaptive significance of the interspecific variation seen in Galapagos finches gave Darwin a clue to his second deduction. Data collected by Wallace in the Malayan archipelago provided further evidence of variation between populations. Darwin and Wallace, however, were unable to account for the sources of the variation. This was not to be clarified until Mendel's work on the particulate nature of inheritance.

Deduction 2: Since all individuals within a population show variation and a 'struggle for existence' has been clearly established, it follows that some individuals possessing particular variations will be more suited to survive and reproduce. The key factor in determining survival is adaptation to the environment. Any variation, however slight, be it physical, physiological or behavioural, which gives one organism an advantage over another organism will act as a **selective advantage** in the 'struggle for existence'. (The term 'selective advantage' is less emotive than that coined by the social philosopher, Herbert Spencer, who described natural selection as 'survival of the fittest'. Spencer did not mean fit in the usual sense of the word. He used 'fit' to mean well adapted to the environment. The phrase 'survival of the fittest' is often misunderstood. There is not some kind of physical contest going on between members of a species, the 'nature red in tooth and claw' spoken of by the Victorians. The phrase 'survival of the fittest' is therefore probably best not used.)

Favourable variations will be inherited by the next generation. Unfavourable variations are 'selected out' or 'selected against', their presence conferring a **selective disadvantage** on that organism. In this way natural selection leads to increased vigour within the species and ensures the survival of that species. The whole of Darwin's and Wallace's hypothesis of natural selection is summed up most succinctly in Darwin's own words:

'As many more individuals of each species are born than can possibly survive, and as, consequently, there is a frequently recurring struggle for existence, it follows that any being, if it vary however slightly in any manner profitable to itself, under the complex and sometimes varying conditions of life, will have a better chance of surviving and thus be naturally selected. From the strong principle of inheritance, any selected variety will tend to propagate its new and modified form.' (Darwin, 1859)

Many misconceptions have grown up around the theory of evolution as outlined by Darwin and they may be summarised as follows.

(1) Darwin made no attempt to describe how life originated on the Earth: his concern was with how new species might arise from pre-existing species.

(2) Natural selection is not simply a negative, destructive force, but can be a positive mechanism of change within a population (section 27.5). The 'struggle for existence' described by Darwin was popularised by the coiling of unfortunate terms such as 'survival of the fittest' and 'elimination of the unfit' by the philosopher Herbert Spencer and the Press of the day.

(3) The misconception that humans were 'descended from the apes' by some process of linear progression was over-sensationalised by the Press and offended both the religious and secular communities. The former saw this as an insult to their belief that 'Man' was created in the 'image of God', whilst the latter were outraged by the apparent undermining of the 'superior position' of humans within the animal kingdom.

(4) The apparent contradiction between the Genesis six-day Creation account and that of a progressive origin for species was highlighted by the meeting of the British Association for the Advancement of Science in June 1860. Bishop Samuel Wilberforce of Oxford vehemently attacked the conclusions of Darwin as outlined in *On the Origin of Species* but not being a biologist his address lacked accuracy. In concluding, he turned to Professor Thomas Henry Huxley, a supporter of Darwin's theory, and asked whether he claimed his descent from a monkey through his grandfather or grandmother. Huxley replied by explaining the more important ideas of Darwin and correcting the misconceptions of Bishop Wilberforce. In conclusion he implied that he would prefer to have a monkey for an ancestor than 'to be connected with a man who used great gifts to obscure the truth'. This unfortunate controversy has continued as the Genesis versus Evolution debate. Professor R. J. Berry has summarised the extremes of the debate as:

(a) those who are awed by scientists and believe that the Bible has been disproved;

(b) those who cling to the inspiration of Scripture and their interpretations of it, and shut their eyes to the fact that God's work can be studied by scientific methods.

26.6 Modern views on evolution

The theory of evolution as proposed by Darwin and Wallace has been modified in the light of modern evidence from genetics, molecular biology, palaeontology, ecology and ethology (the study of behaviour) and is known as **neo-Darwinism** (*neo*, new) This may be defined as *the theory of organic evolution by the natural selection of inherited characteristics*.

Different types of evidence support different aspects of the theory. In order to accept neo-Darwinian evolutionary theory it is necessary to:

(1) establish the fact that evolution (change) has taken place in the past (**past evolution**);

(2) demonstrate a mechanism which results in evolution (**natural selection of genes**);

(3) observe evolution happening today ('**evolution in action**').

Evidence for past evolution comes from many sources based on geology, such as fossils and stratigraphy (the study of the order and ages of rock formations). Evidence for a mechanism is found in the experimental and observational data of the natural selection of characteristics that are inherited, such as the selection of shell colour in the snail *Cepaea* (section 27.5.1), and the mechanism of inheritance demonstrated by Mendelian genetics, as in Mendel's work on peas. Finally, evidence for the action of these processes occurring today is provided by studies of present populations, such as speciation in the herring gull (section 27.8.4), and the results of artificial selection and genetic engineering, as in the cultivation of wheat and the synthesis of genes.

There are no laws of evolution, only well-supported hypotheses which add together to form a convincing theory. However, we must guard against accepting current ideas as proven fact because that would stifle intellectual growth and the search for truth. The uncritical acceptance of evolutionary theory is a case in point. Some of the events presented as evidence for evolutionary theory can be reproduced under laboratory conditions, but that does not prove that they did take place in the past; it merely indicates the possibility that these events occurred. The debate these days is not so much about whether evolution takes place but about how it takes place, in particular whether it always takes place by natural selection of randomly generated mutations.

26.7 Evidence for the theory of evolution

Evidence of relevance to the theory of evolution is provided from many sources, the main ones being:

- palaeontology
- geographical distribution
- classification
- plant and animal breeding
- comparative anatomy
- adaptive radiation
- comparative embryology
- comparative biochemistry

These are all discussed below.

Much of the evidence presented in this chapter was unavailable to Darwin and Wallace at the time of publication of their papers on the origin of species by natural selection, although this did not prevent Darwin from

using his intuition, as is typical of great scientists. This is shown by his statement:

'In October 1838, that is, 15 months after I had begun my systematic enquiry, I happened to read, for amusement, Malthus on Population, and being well prepared to appreciate the struggle for existence which everywhere goes on from long-continued observation of the habits of animals and plants, it at once struck me that under these circumstances favourable variations would tend to be preserved, and unfavourable ones to be destroyed. The result of this would be the formation of new species. Here, then, I had at last got a theory by which to work.'

The evidence presented here largely supports the theory of evolution by natural selection as outlined in section 26.5, although remember it does not provide proof, nor does it prove that no other mechanisms are involved. It draws on data obtained from many sources, and in all cases is interpreted in terms that assume that evolution does occur. Circular arguments and exceptions to the evidence are common and alternative interpretations can be found, but the broad concept of evolution is backed up by a wealth of scientific evidence. When reading the following sections try to judge for yourself the evidence available and decide whether the conclusions drawn are justified. Try to distinguish between what is evidence for evolution, and what is evidence for natural selection being the mechanism. In the remainder of this chapter we are mainly concerned with evidence for evolution, while in chapter 27 evidence for natural selection is presented.

26.7.1 Palaeontology

Palaeontology is the study of fossils. Fossils are any form of preserved remains thought to be derived from a living organism. They may include the following: entire organisms, hard skeletal structures, moulds and casts, petrifications, impressions, imprints and coprolites (fossilised faecal pellets) (table 26.3).

Fossil evidence alone is not sufficient to prove that evolution has occurred, but it supports a theory of progressive increase in complexity of organisms. Fossils were well known before evolution was generally accepted. They were interpreted either as the remains of former creations or as artefacts inserted into the rocks by God. Most of the remains found so far can be classified into the same taxonomic groups (phyla and classes) as living species, but whether they represent the ancestors of present-day forms can only be debated, not proved.

The oldest fossil-bearing rocks contain very few types of fossilised organisms and these all have a simple structure. Younger rocks contain a greater variety of fossils with increasingly complex structures. Throughout the fossil record many species which appear at an early stratigraphic level (their level in the rock deposits) disappear at a later level. This is interpreted in evolutionary terms as

Table 26.3 Types of fossils, their formation and examples.

Fossil	Fossilisation process	Examples
Entire organism	Frozen into ice during glaciation	Woolly mammoths found in Siberian permafrost
" "	Encased in the hardened resin (amber) of coniferous trees	Insect exoskeletons found in Oligocene rocks in Baltic coast
" "	Encased in tar	'Mummies' found in asphalt lakes of California
" "	Trapped in acidic bogs: lack of bacterial and fungal activity prevents total decomposition	'Mummies' found in bogs and peat in Scandinavia
Hard skeletal materials	Trapped by sedimentary sand and clay which form sedimentary rocks, e.g. limestone, sandstone and silt	Bones, shells and teeth (very common in British Isles)
Moulds and casts	Hard materials trapped as above. Sediments harden to rock. The skeleton dissolves leaving its impression as a mould of the organism. This can be infilled with fine materials which harden to form a cast. Great detail is thus preserved	Gastropods from Portland Stone, Jurassic. Casts of giant horsetails (*Calamites*) of Carboniferous forests. Internal casts of mollusc shells showing muscle attachment points
Petrifaction	Gradual replacement by water-carried mineral deposits, such as silica, pyrites, calcium carbonate or carbon. Slow infilling as organism decomposes producing fine detail	Silica replacements of the echinoderm *Micraster*
Impressions	Impressions of remains of organisms in fine-grained sediments on which they died	Feathers of *Archaeopteryx* in Upper Jurassic. Jellyfish in Cambrian found in British Columbia. Carboniferous leaf impressions
Imprints	Footprints, trails, tracks and tunnels of various organisms made in mud are rapidly baked and filled in with sand and covered by further sediments	Dinosaur footprints and tail scrapings indicate size and posture of organisms
Coprolites	Faecal pellets prevented from decomposing, later compressed in sedimentary rock. Often contain evidence of food eaten, e.g. teeth and scales	Cenozoic mammalian remains

indicating the times at which species originated and became extinct.

Evidence suggests that geographical regions and climatic conditions have varied throughout the Earth's history. Since organisms are adapted to particular environments, the constantly changing conditions may have favoured a mechanism for evolutionary change that accounts for the progressive changes in the structures of organisms as shown by the fossil record. Ecological considerations also fit in with the fossil evidence. For example, plants appeared on land before animals, and insects appeared before insect-pollinated flowers.

One of the major criticisms of using fossil evidence in support of an evolutionary theory is the lack of a continuous fossil record. Gaps in the fossil record ('missing links') are taken as strong evidence against a theory of descent by modification. However, there are several explanations for the incompleteness of the fossil record. These include the facts that:

- dead organisms decompose rapidly;
- dead organisms are eaten by scavengers;
- soft-bodied organisms do not fossilise easily;
- only a small fraction of living organisms will have died in conditions favourable for fossilisation;
- only a fraction of fossils have been discovered.

Fig 26.3 *Photograph of trilobite fossil in Cambrian rocks.*

Support for an evolutionary process increases as more and more possible 'missing links' are discovered, either as fossils, such as *Seymouria* (amphibian/reptile), *Archaeopteryx* (reptile/bird) and *Cynognathus* (reptile/mammal), or as living organisms representing groups with close structural similarities, such as *Peripatus* (fig 26.17) and *Latimeria*.

Alternatively, there exists the possibility that new species appeared so suddenly that intermediate forms in the lineage do not exist. Eldredge and Gould have proposed a process called '**punctuated equilibria**' which accounts for the sudden appearance of new species. According to this proposal species remain unchanged for long periods of time before giving rise to new species in comparatively short periods of time. This presumably would be the result of a relatively sudden and important change in environmental conditions. This process depends on the fact that evolutionary rates can vary and that some new species arise rapidly, making the fossil record appear incomplete. These apparent 'jumps' in the evolutionary sequence have given rise to the term '**saltatory evolution**' (*saltare*, to jump). Darwin himself considered this possibility and stated as much in the *Origin of Species*:

'I do not suppose that the process (speciation) . . . goes on continuously; it is far more probable that each form remains for long periods unaltered, and then again undergoes modification.'

Evolution, then, does not always have to be gradual.

The fossil history of the horse

The horse provides one of the best examples of evolutionary history (phylogeny) based on an almost complete fossil record found in North American sedimentary deposits from the early Eocene to the present.

The earliest recognisable odd-toed, hoofed mammals (perissodactyls) appeared about 54 million years ago and present-day perissodactyls include horses, tapirs and rhinoceroses. The oldest recognisable horse-like fossils belong to a genus called *Hyracotherium* which was widely distributed throughout North America and Europe during the early Eocene. By the beginning of the Oligocene it was extinct everywhere except North America. It was a small animal, lightly built and adapted for running. The limbs were short and slender and the feet elongated so that the digits were almost vertical. There were four digits in the forelimbs and three digits in the hindlimb. The incisors were small and the molars had low crowns with rounded cusps covered in enamel.

The probable course of development of horses from *Hyracotherium* to *Equus* involved at least twelve genera and several hundred species. The major trends seen in the development of the horse were connected with locomotion and feeding. They represent adaptations to changing environmental conditions and may be summarised as follows:

- increase in size,
- lengthening of limbs and feet,
- reduction of lateral digits,
- increase in length and thickness of the third digit,
- straightening and stiffening of the back,
- better-developed sense organs,
- increase in size and complexity of the brain associated with development of sense organs,
- increase in width of incisors,
- replacement of premolars by molars,
- increase in tooth length,
- increase in crown height of molars,
- increased lateral support of teeth by cement,
- increased surface areas of cusps by exposure of enamel ridges.

A dominant genus from each geological period of the Cenozoic has been selected to show the progressive development of the horse in fig 26.4. However, it is important to note that there is no evidence that the forms illustrated are direct relatives of each other.

The significance of the fossil sequence shown in fig 26.4 is that it supports a theory of progressive change based on homologous structures such as limbs and teeth. **Homologous structures** are structures found in different species which are believed to have a common evolutionary origin. Each of the species shown in fig 26.4 represents a stage of development which was successful for several million years (as judged by the abundance of fossils) before becoming extinct. The extinction of a species did not, however, represent the disappearance of the family line. The fossil evidence reveals that another closely related species always 'took over' after its extinction. As all the species in the sequence show structural and ecological similarities, this gives support to a theory of descent with modification. Other fossils found in the same rock strata suggest changing climatic conditions which, together with other evidence, indicates that each species was adapted to prevailing conditions.

The history of the horse does not show a gradual transition regularly spaced in time and locality, and neither is the fossil record totally complete. It would appear that several offshoots occurred from the line represented in fig 26.4, but they all became extinct. All modern horses appear to be descended from *Pliohippus*. The modern genus *Equus* arose in North America during the Pleistocene and migrated into Eurasia and Africa where it gave rise to zebras and asses as well as the modern horse. Paradoxically, having survived in North America for millions of years, the horse became extinct there several thousand years ago, at a time which coincided with the arrival of humans. Cave-paintings from other parts of the world suggest that the earliest use for the horse was as a source of food. The horse was absent from North America until its reintroduction by the Spaniards almost 500 years ago.

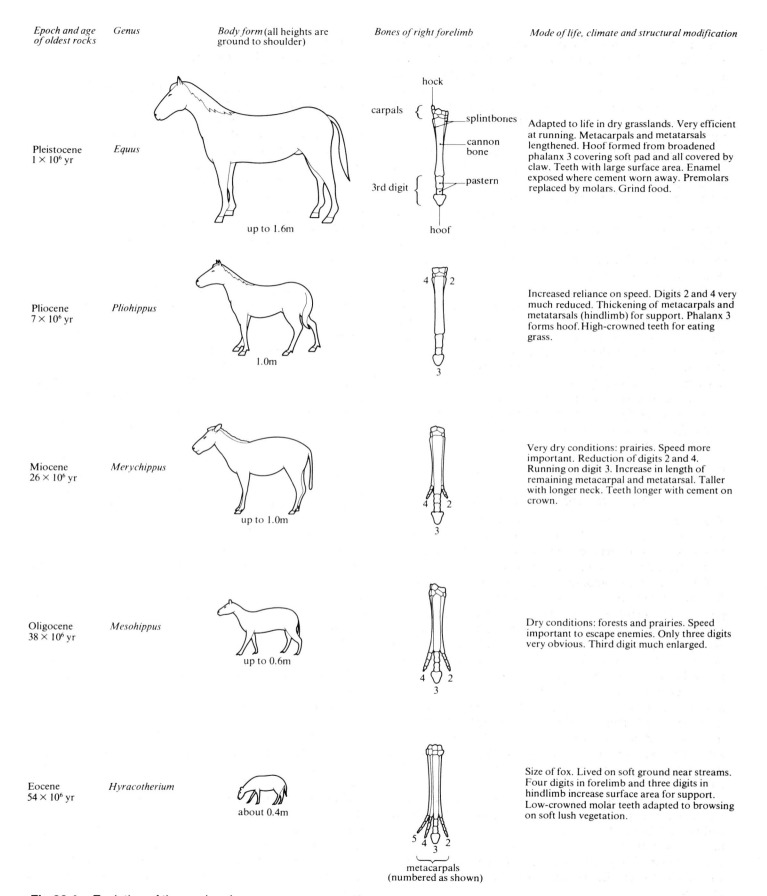

Epoch and age of oldest rocks	Genus	Body form (all heights are ground to shoulder)	Bones of right forelimb	Mode of life, climate and structural modification
Pleistocene 1 × 10⁶ yr	*Equus*	up to 1.6m	hock, carpals, splintbones, cannon bone, pastern, 3rd digit, hoof	Adapted to life in dry grasslands. Very efficient at running. Metacarpals and metatarsals lengthened. Hoof formed from broadened phalanx 3 covering soft pad and all covered by claw. Teeth with large surface area. Enamel exposed where cement worn away. Premolars replaced by molars. Grind food.
Pliocene 7 × 10⁶ yr	*Pliohippus*	1.0m	4 2 3	Increased reliance on speed. Digits 2 and 4 very much reduced. Thickening of metacarpals and metatarsals (hindlimb) for support. Phalanx 3 forms hoof. High-crowned teeth for eating grass.
Miocene 26 × 10⁶ yr	*Merychippus*	up to 1.0m	4 2 3	Very dry conditions: prairies. Speed more important. Reduction of digits 2 and 4. Running on digit 3. Increase in length of remaining metacarpal and metatarsal. Taller with longer neck. Teeth longer with cement on crown.
Oligocene 38 × 10⁶ yr	*Mesohippus*	up to 0.6m	4 2 3	Dry conditions: forests and prairies. Speed important to escape enemies. Only three digits very obvious. Third digit much enlarged.
Eocene 54 × 10⁶ yr	*Hyracotherium*	about 0.4m	5 4 3 2 metacarpals (numbered as shown)	Size of fox. Lived on soft ground near streams. Four digits in forelimb and three digits in hindlimb increase surface area for support. Low-crowned molar teeth adapted to browsing on soft lush vegetation.

Fig 26.4 *Evolution of the modern horse.*

26.7.2   Geographical distribution

All organisms are adapted to their environment to a greater or lesser extent. If the abiotic and biotic factors within a habitat are capable of supporting a particular species in one geographical area, then one might assume that the same species would be found in a similar habitat in a similar geographical area, for example lions in the savannah of Africa and the pampas of South America. This is not the case. Plant and animal species are discontinuously distributed throughout the world. Ecological factors often account for this discontinuous distribution, but evidence from the successful colonisation of habitats by plant and animal species introduced there by humans suggests that factors other than those of ecological adaptation are involved. Rabbits are not endemic (naturally occurring) species in Australia, yet their rapid increase in numbers following their introduction by humans indicates the suitability of the Australian habitat. Similar examples of this principle are illustrated by the spread of domestic animals and plants by humans, such as sheep, corn, potatoes and wheat. An explanation for the discontinuous distribution of organisms is based on the concept of species originating in a given area and then spreading (dispersing) outwards from that point. The extent of the dispersal will depend upon the success of the organisms, the efficiency of the dispersal mechanism and the existence of natural barriers such as oceans, mountain ranges and deserts. Wind-blown spores and seeds and flying animals would appear to have the best adaptations for dispersal over land and sea.

In contrast to, and despite the general principle of organisms being naturally confined to certain parts of the world, many related forms are found in widely separated regions, for example the three remaining species of lungfish are found separately in tropical areas of South America (*Lepidosiren*), Africa (*Protopterus*) and Australia (*Neoceratodus*); camels and llamas are distributed in North Africa, Asia and South America; and racoons are widely found in North and South America and a small area of south-east Asia. Fossil evidence indicates that the distribution of these organisms was not always as seen today and that in the past they were more widely distributed.

Whilst none of this evidence has any immediate significance for evolutionary theory, it does point to the fact that the distribution of land masses was not always as it is today, as explained below.

It used to be believed that the world had always been as it now is and that the present continents and oceans had never changed positions. Early geologists, such as Hutton and Lyell (table 26.1), accounted for the existence of sedimentary rocks in terms of the periodic rise and fall of the sea. Later it was suggested that there were once two large continental masses, one in the Northern Hemisphere called Laurasia and one in the Southern Hemisphere called Gondwanaland, linked by extensive land bridges across which animals and plants could migrate and disperse. Subsequent geological research has modified this idea and favours the hypothesis of **continental drift**, based on the concept of **plate tetonics**. The hypothesis of continental drift was first proposed by Snider in 1858 but developed by Taylor in America and Wegener in Germany in the late 1800s. Wegener proposed that, during Carboniferous times, Laurasia and Gondwanaland formed one large land mass called Pangaea (Greek, all earth) which floated on the denser molten core of the Earth. It is now believed, though, that continents have drifted apart as a result of convection currents within the Earth spreading upwards and outwards, dragging plates on which the continents float. This hypothesis would account for the continuous movements of land masses and the present distribution of species such as that of the lungfish (fig 26.5).

In the case of the camels and llamas (family Camelidae) it is believed that they arose from a common ancestor which fossil evidence suggests had its origin in North America. During the Pleistocene this ancestor spread southwards into South America via the Isthmus of Panana, and northwards into Asia before changes in sea level separated it from North America (fig 26.6). Throughout this time it is thought that progressive changes within the Camelidae occurred, producing the two genera *Camelus* and *Lama* at the extremes of their Pleistocene migration.

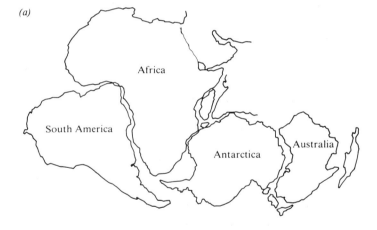

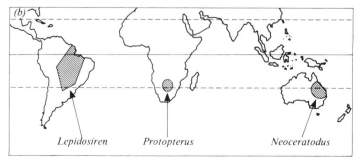

Fig 26.5   (a) *Relative positions of South America, Africa and Australia during early stages of continental drift, indicating proximity of areas where lungfish may have originated.*
(b) *Present distribution of species of lungfish.*

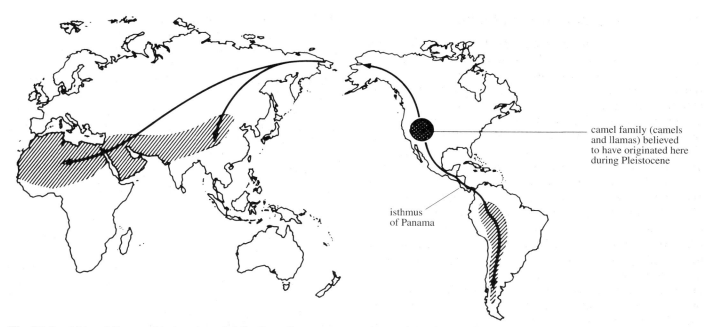

Fig 26.6 *Map of the world showing distribution of present members of the family Camelidae, the camels in North Africa and Asia and the llamas in South America. During Pleistocene times the camel family was distributed throughout North and South America and much of Asia and North Africa. This distribution is based on fossil evidence. Solid black lines indicate possible migration routes. (Based on Matthews (1939)* Climate of evolution, *Vol. 1, 2nd ed., NY Acad. of Sci.)*

Forms intermediate between the present camels and llamas exist in the fossil record throughout North America, Asia and North Africa. The fossil record indicates that other animals of the camel family in other parts of the world became extinct at the close of the last Ice Age.

Another example of discontinuous distribution as a result of geographical isolation is provided by the monotremes and marsupials of Australasia. Australasia is believed to have broken away from the other land masses during the late Jurassic, just after the appearance of primitive mammals. The mammals are divided into three orders: monotremes, marsupials and eutherians. In Australasia only the monotremes and marsupials developed. Here they coexisted and underwent adaptive radiation (modification of the same basic structures for different functions) to produce the characteristic Australasian fauna represented by the monotremes *Tachyglossus* and *Zaglossus* (the spiny anteaters) and the duck-billed platypus (*Ornithorhynchus*), and 45 genera of marsupials. Elsewhere in the world the more advanced eutherian (placental) mammals also developed. As they spread out over the continents it is believed that they ousted the more primitive monotremes and marsupials from their ecological niches, except where geographical barriers disrupted their dispersal, as into Australasia.

These points may be summarised as:

- species originated in a particular area;
- species dispersed outwards from that area;
- dispersal could only occur for most species where land masses were close enough together to permit dispersal;
- the absence of more advanced organisms from a region

usually indicates the prior separation of that region from the area of origin of those organisms.

Whilst none of the evidence presented above indicates the mechanism by which species are thought to have originated, it does suggest that various groups have originated at various times and in various regions. Fossil evidence reveals the ways in which these organisms have undergone gradual modification (evolution), but again no indication of the possible mechanism.

Evidence for a possible mechanism of the origin of species by natural selection is supplied by the distribution of plants and animals on oceanic islands. Both Wallace and Darwin were struck by the amazing diversity of species found on islands such as the Hawaiian and the Galapagos groups. Geological evidence indicates that these islands were formed by oceanic volcanic activity which thrust them up above sea level, so that they have never had any direct geographical links with any land mass. Plant species must have arrived on the islands by wind dispersal as spores and seeds, or water dispersal as floating seeds and masses of vegetation. Aquatic and semi-aquatic organisms are believed to have been carried there by ocean currents, whilst terrestrial organisms may have been carried clinging to logs or floating masses of vegetation. Birds, bats and flying insects would have fewer problems of dispersal to these islands.

The Galapagos Islands are situated in the Pacific Ocean on the equator almost 1200 km west of Ecuador and form an archipelago described further in section 27.8.3. When Darwin visited the islands in 1853, he noticed the similarity of the species found there to those on the nearest mainland, a fact he had also observed on the Cape Verde Islands off the coast of West Africa. However, the plant and animal species on oceanic islands were noticeably larger in most cases. This may be accounted for by the lack of competition from larger, and more dominant, advanced species which were absent from the islands, but which co-habited with smaller related species on the mainland. For example, the giant tortoise (*Geochelone elephantopus*), nearly 2 m long and weighing 260 kg, feeding on the plentiful vegetation found on the islands presumably attained this size due to the absence of competition from various mammalian species which existed on the mainland. Darwin noticed too that iguana lizards on the Galapagos Islands were abundant and again much larger than related mainland species. Lizards are terrestrial reptiles, but on the Galapagos Islands, where two species were found, one was aquatic. The aquatic form, *Amblyrhyncus cristatus*, fed on marine algae and showed adaptations for locomotion in water such as a laterally flattened tail and well-developed webs of skin between the toes of all four limbs (fig 26.7). Competition for food, space and a mate within the terrestrial form is thought to have exerted a selection pressure on the lizards and favoured those showing variations with aquatic adaptations. This mechanism of environmental factors operating on a variable genotype is called **natural selection** and is described above. It could have been the process which gradually gave rise to the aquatic species. It was, however, the diversity of adaptive structures shown by the 13 species of finches found within the archipelago which had the greatest influence on Darwin's thinking on the mechanism of the origin of species. Only one type of finch existed on the mainland of Ecuador and its beak was adapted to crushing seeds. On the Galapagos Islands, six major beak types were found, each adapted to a particular method of feeding. The various

Fig 26.7 *Giant aquatic lizard of the Galapagos Islands underwater.*

types, their feeding methods and number of species are summarised in fig 26.8.

Darwin postulated that a group of finches from the mainland colonised the islands. Here they flourished, and the inevitable competition produced by increase in numbers, and the availability of vacant ecological niches, favoured occupation of niches by those organisms showing the appropriate adaptive variations. Differences between species relate to small differences in body size, feather colour and beak shape. Several species of finch are found on all the bigger islands. The ground and warbler finches, thought to be the oldest types, are found on most islands. The tree and vegetarian/tree finches are missing from the outlying islands, and the woodpecker finches are confined to the central group of islands. The actual species distribution is interesting and has been explained by Lack on the basis of adaptive radiation and geographical isolation. For example, on the central islands there are many species of several different types of finch, such as ground, tree warbler and woodpecker, rather than several species of the same type. Even where several species of only one type of finch are present, as on the outlying islands, each species differs in its ecological requirements. This fits in with the Gaussian exclusion principle (section 10.7.5) which states that two or more closely related species will not occupy the same area unless they differ in their ecological requirements.

26.7.3 Classification

The system of classification described in chapter 2 was proposed by Linnaeus before the time of Darwin and Wallace, but has implications for the origin of species and evolutionary theory. Whilst it is possible to conceive that all species, both living and extinct, were created separately at a specific time or had no origin, the structural similarity between organisms, which forms the basis of a natural system of **phylogenetic classification**, suggests the existence of an evolutionary process. These similarities and differences between organisms may be explained as the result of progressive adaptation by organisms within each taxonomic group to particular environmental conditions over a period of time.

Numerical taxonomists, working mainly from comparative phenotypic characters have found it possible to construct a phenetic classification system which is consistent, to the extent of present knowledge, with the concept of evolution. These systems of classification are capable of standing in their own right as a basis for biological organisation, but they also strongly suggest that an evolutionary process has occurred.

26.7.4 Plant and animal breeding

One of the earliest features of human civilisation was the cultivation of plants and domestic animals from ancestral wild stocks. By selecting those

Types of finch	Beak shape	Food source	Habitat	Number of species
large ground finch (ancestral)	typical main land type: short and straight	crushing seed	coastal	1
ground finches	various, but short and straight as above	seeds/insects	coast/lowlands	3
cactus ground finches	long slightly curved, split-tongue	nectar of prickly-pear cactus	lowland	2
insectivorous tree finches	parrot-like	seeds/insects	forest	3
vegetarian tree finch	curved, parrot-like	fruit/buds/soft fruit	forest	1
warbler finch	slender	insects in flight	forest	1
woodpecker finches	large, straight, (uses cactus spine or stick to poke insects out of holes in wood)	larvae insect	forest	2

members of the species which showed a favourable variation, such as increased size or improved flavour, and artificially breeding them by selective mating, selective propagation or selective pollination, the desired characteristics were perpetuated. Continued selective breeding by humans has produced the varieties of domestic animals and plants of agricultural importance seen today. It is known from archaeological remains that early humans were successful in rearing cattle, pigs and fowl, and cultivating cereal crops and certain vegetables. Until Mendel's work on genetics was revealed, the theoretical basis of inheritance and breeding was not clear, but this has not stopped humans carrying out practical breeding programmes. In terms of genetics, humans are preserving those animal or plant genes which are considered desirable and eliminating those which are undesirable for their purposes. This selection uses naturally occurring gene variation, together with any fortuitous mutations which occur from time to time.

Whilst varieties of dogs, cats, birds, fish and flowers have been produced for sporting or decorative purposes, it is economically important varieties of animals and plants that have been studied most by plant and animal breeders (fig 26.9). Some specific examples of phenotypic characteristics which have been artificially selected are shown in table 26.4. A recently developed form of artificial selection is the selection for resistance to antibiotics, pesticides and

Fig 26.8 (a) Adaptive radiation of Darwin's finches. (After Lack.) (b) A male cactus finch (Geospiza scandens).

(b)

895

(a)

(b)

Fig 26.9 *The result of selective breeding. The wild pig (a) is native to Europe, Asia and Africa but has been selectively bred to produce a variety of breeds, of which the English Large White (b) with its high quality of meat yield, is an example.*

herbicides shown respectively by pathogens, pests and weeds. A vicious circle is produced as new strains of organisms become immune to the ever-increasing number of chemical substances produced to contain and control them.

Since characteristics can be 'produced' by our ability to selectively breed, as in the case of breeds of dogs or pigeons, Darwin used this as evidence for a mechanism by which species might arise naturally. In the case of *natural* selection the environment rather than humans was believed to act as the agent of selection. Artificially selected forms

Table 26.4 Selected phenotypic characteristics and examples of them.

Phenotypic characteristic	Example
Hardiness	Sweetcorn grown in England
Size	Potato, cabbage
Increased yield	Milk, eggs, wool, fruit
Earlier maturity	Cereal crops (two per season)
Lengthened season	Strawberries
Taste/eating quality	Apples, seedless grapes
Harvesting ease	Peas
Length of storage	Beans/peas for freezing
Increased ecological efficiency	Protein from plants, e.g. soyabean
Resistance to disease	Rust and mildew (fungi)-resistant wheat

probably would not have arisen in the wild; in most cases they are unable to compete successfully with closely related non-domesticated forms.

26.7.5 Comparative anatomy

Comparative study of the anatomy of groups of animals or plants reveals that certain structural features are basically similar. For example, the basic structure of all flowers consists of sepals, petals, stamens, stigma, style and ovary; yet the size, colour, number of parts and specific structure are different for each individual species. Similarly, the limb-bone pattern of all tetrapods (animals with four legs) from amphibia to mammals has the same structural plan: it is called the **pentadactyl limb** (fig 18.11). This basic structure has been modified in several ways as illustrated in fig 26.10. In each case, the particular structure is adapted to a certain method of locomotion in a particular environment.

Organs from different species having a similar basic form, microscopic structure, body position, and embryonic development are said to be **homologous**, a term introduced in 1843 by Richard Owen.

Homologous structures showing adaptations to different environmental conditions and modes of life are examples of adaptive radiation. The ecological significance of these processes is considered in section 26.7.6. The specific functions that these structures carry out may vary in different organisms. These differences reflect the particular ways the organisms are adapted to their environments and modes of life. Other examples of homology are given below.

Branchial arches/Ear bones. Certain bones of the jaw in fish can be traced through other vertebrates, where they are involved in jaw suspension, to mammals where they appear as the ear bones: the malleus, incus and stapes (fig 26.11).

Halteres. The hind pair of wings typical of most insects have been modified in the Diptera into little rods, the halteres, which serve as gyroscopic organs helping to maintain balance in flight.

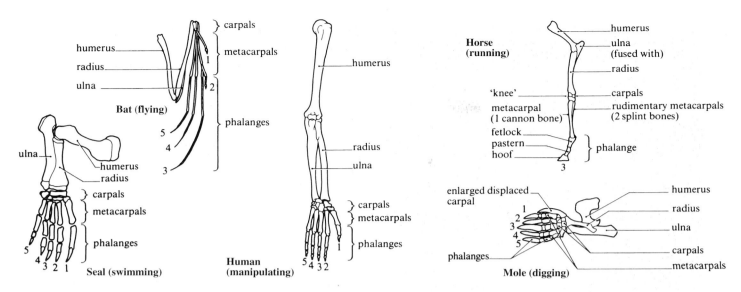

Fig 26.10 (above)   *Adaptations of the pentadactyl limb shown by mammals.*

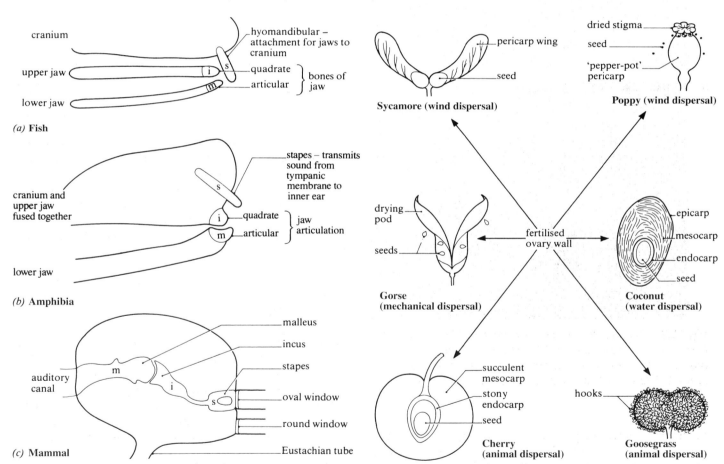

Fig 26.11   *Relative positions and functions of bones of the mammalian ear as seen in fish and amphibia.*

Fig 26.12   *Variation in pericarp (fertilised ovary wall) structure for different methods of seed dispersal.*

Pericarp. The ovary wall in flowering plants becomes modified, following fertilisation of the ovules, in a variety of ways to aid seed dispersal (fig 26.12).

Whilst homology does not prove that evolution has occurred, the existence of homology within a group of organisms is interpreted as evidence of their descent from a common ancestor and indicates close phylogenetic relationships.

Linnaeus used homology as the basis of his system of classification. The more exclusive the shared homologies, the closer two organisms are related. For example, butterflies and moths belong to the same order (Lepidoptera) whereas wasps and bees belong to another order (Hymenoptera).

Certain homologous structures in some species have no apparent function and are described as **vestigial organs**. The human appendix, although not concerned with digestion, is homologous with the functional appendix of herbivorous mammals. Likewise, certain apparently non-functional bones in snakes and whales are thought to be homologous with the hip bones and hindlimbs of quadruped vertebrates. The vertebrae of the human coccyx are thought to represent vestigial structures of the tail possessed by our ancestors and embryos. It would be very difficult to explain the occurrence of vestigial organs without reference to some process of evolution.

26.7.6   Adaptive radiation

Homologous structures and divergent evolution

When a group of organisms share a homologous structure which is specialised to perform a variety of different functions, it illustrates a principle known as **adaptive radiation**. For instance, the mouthparts of insects consist of the same basic structures: a labrum (upper lip), a pair of mandibles, a hypopharynx (floor of mouth), a pair of maxillae and a labium (fused second pair of mandibles, lower lip). Insects are able to exploit a variety of food materials, as shown in fig 26.13, because some of the above structures are enlarged and modified, others reduced and lost. This produces a variety of feeding structures.

The relatively high degree of adaptive radiation shown by insects reflects the adaptability of the basic features of the group. It is this 'evolutionary plasticity' which has permitted them to occupy such a wide range of ecological niches.

The presence of a structure or physiological process in an ancestral organism, which has become greatly modified in more specialised, apparently related organisms, may be interpreted as indicating a process of descent by modification. This is the basis of evolutionary theory as defined in section 26.4.2. The significance of adaptive radiation is that it suggests the existence of divergent evolution based on modification of homologous structures.

Analogous structures and convergent evolution

Similar structures, physiological processes or modes of life in organisms apparently bearing no close phylogenetic links but showing adaptations to perform the same functions are described as **analogous**. Examples of analogous structures include the eyes of vertebrates and cephalopod molluscs (squids and octopuses), the wings of insects and bats, the jointed legs of insects and vertebrates, the presence of thorns on plant stems and spines on animals, and the existence of vertebrate neuroendocrines, such as

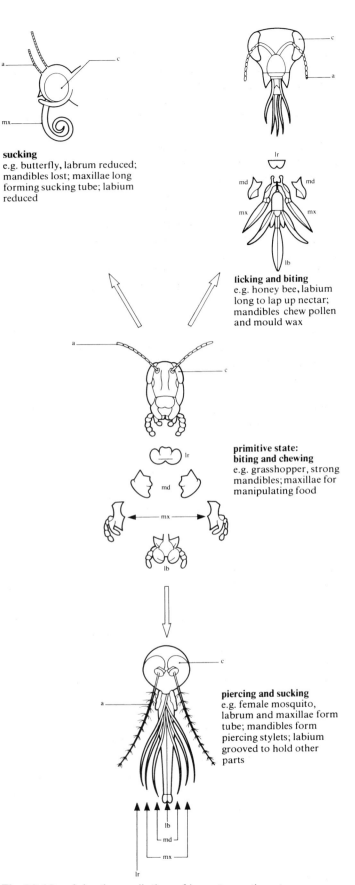

sucking
e.g. butterfly, labrum reduced; mandibles lost; maxillae long forming sucking tube; labium reduced

licking and biting
e.g. honey bee, labium long to lap up nectar; mandibles chew pollen and mould wax

primitive state: biting and chewing
e.g. grasshopper, strong mandibles; maxillae for manipulating food

piercing and sucking
e.g. female mosquito, labrum and maxillae form tube; mandibles form piercing stylets; labium grooved to hold other parts

Fig 26.13 *Adaptive radiation of insect mouthparts; a, antennae; c, compound eye; lb, labium; lr, labrum; md, mandibles; mx, maxillae.*

acetylcholine, 5-hydroxytryptamine and histamine, in nettle stings. Analogous structures only bear superficial similarities. For example, the wings of insects are supported by toughened veins composed of cuticle, whereas both bats and birds have hollow bones for support. Likewise the embryological development of the cephalopod and vertebrate eye is different. The former produces an erect retina with photoreceptors facing the incoming light, whereas the latter has an inverted retina with photoreceptors separated from incoming light by their connecting neurones (fig 17.36). Thus the vertebrate eye has a blind spot which is absent in cephalopods.

The existence of analogous structures suggest the occurrence of **convergent evolution**. Convergent evolution may be explained in terms of the environment, acting through the agency of natural selection, favouring those variations which confer increased survival and reproductive potential on those organisms possessing them.

The significance of divergent evolution, suggesting an evolutionary process, and convergent evolution, suggesting an evolutionary mechanism, is highlighted by the **parallel evolution** of marsupial and placental mammals. Both groups are thought to have undergone convergent evolution and come to occupy identical ecological niches in different parts of the world (fig 26.14 and table 26.5).

26.7.7   Comparative embryology

A study of the embryonic development of the vertebrate groups by Von Baer (1792–1867) revealed striking structural similarities occurring in all the groups, particularly during cleavage, gastrulation and the early stages of differentiation. Haeckel (1834–1919) suggested that this had an evolutionary significance. He formulated the principle that 'ontogeny recapitulates phylogeny', that is the developmental stages through which an organism passes repeat the evolutionary history of the group to which it belongs. Whilst this principle over-generalises the situation, it is attractive and there is some evidence to support it. If just the embryos and fetal stages of all the vertebrate groups are examined it is impossible to identify the group to which they belong.

Fig 26.15 shows that it is only in the later stages of development that they begin to assume some similarity to their adult form. At comparable stages the vertebrate embryos all possess the following:

(1) External branchial grooves (visceral clefts) in the pharyngeal region and a series of internal paired gill pouches. These join up in fishes to form the gill slits involved in gaseous exchange. In the other vertebrate groups the only perforation that develops becomes in adults the Eustachian tube and auditory canal involved in hearing.
(2) Segmental myotomes (muscle blocks), which are evident in the tail-like structure. These are retained only in certain species.

(3) A single circulation which includes a two-chambered heart showing no separation into right and left halves, a situation retained completely only in fishes.

As development proceeds in the vertebrate embryo, changes occur which produce the characteristics of fish, amphibian, reptile, bird or mammal depending upon the embryo's parentage. The interpretation placed on these observations is that these embryos, and hence the groups to which they belong, had a common ancestor. There seems little point in an organism having developmental structures which are apparently non-functional in the adult unless they are the remaining stages of ancestral structures. However the principle of recapitulation cannot be accepted entirely since no living organisms can show all the features of their proposed evolutionary ancestors. What appears to be probable is that organisms retain the inherited development mechanisms of their ancestors. Hence at various stages in development it is likely that an organism will show structural similarities to the embryos of its ancestors. Subsequent adaptations to different environmental conditions and modes of life will modify later stages of the developmental process. Observation reveals that the closer the organisms are classified on the basis of common adult homologous structures the longer their embryological development will remain similar. Organisms showing adaptations to certain modes of life and environments not typical of the major group to which they belong show fewer similarities to other members of the group during their embryonic development. This is clearly seen in the development of the parasitic flatworms *Fasciola* and *Taenia*, where a series of larval stages showing adaptations to secondary hosts exist which do not appear in the development of the free-living flatworms, such as *Planaria*. Similarly, the terrestrial earthworm *Lumbricus* does not possess the ciliated trochopore larva which is typical of more ancestral annelids. This evidence highlights the limitations of Haeckel's principle of recapitulation.

Study of the embryological development of major groups of organisms reveals structural similarities in the embryonic and larval stages which are not apparent in the adult stages. These observations are interpreted as suggesting phylogenetic relationships between various groups of organisms and the implication underlying this is that an evolutionary process exists. On the basis of the cleavage patterns of the zygote and the fate of the blastopore, triploblastic animals may be divided into two groups, the protostomes and deuterostomes. **Protostomes** show spiral cleavage and their blastopore becomes the mouth of the adult. This pattern of development is seen in the annelids, molluscs and arthropods. **Deuterostomes** show radial cleavage and their blastopore becomes the anus of the adult. The echinoderms and chordates show this pattern of development. These differences are shown in fig 26.16. It is evidence such as this which has helped to clarify problems of the phylogenetic affinities of the echinoderms. The adult structure of echinoderms suggests that they are a

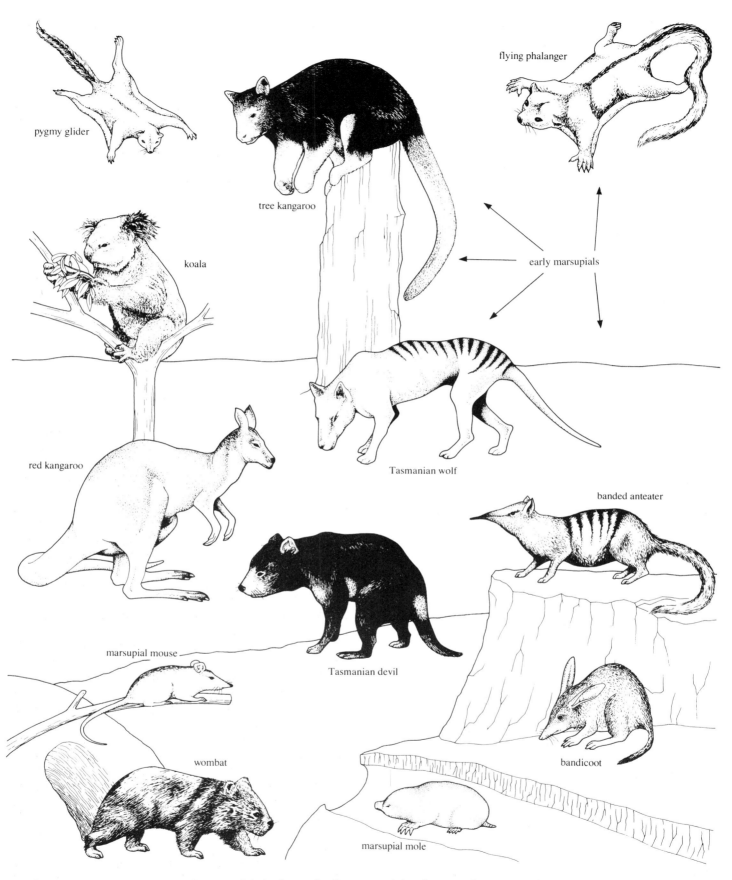

Fig 26.14 *Adaptive radiation of marsupials in Australia (from a variety of sources).*

Table 26.5 Examples of parallel evolution shown by marsupial and placental mammals.

Marsupial mammals (Australasia)	Placental mammals (elsewhere)
Marsupial mole	Mole
Marsupial mouse	Mouse
Banded anteater	Anteater
Wombat	Prairie dog
Kangaroo	Antelope
Bandicoot	Rabbit
Flying phalanger	Flying squirrel
Koala	Sloth
Tasmanian wolf	Hyena

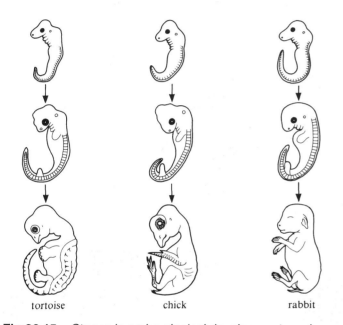

tortoise   chick   rabbit

Fig 26.15 *Stages in embryological development as shown by examples from three vertebrate classes.*

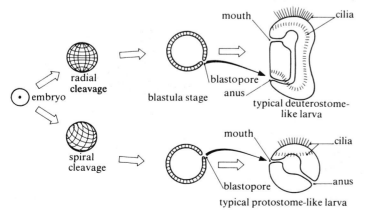

Fig 26.16 *Early development stages of deuterostomes and protostomes.*

non-vertebrate phylum, but their deuterostomic embryological development confirms their affinity with the chordate line of development. This example illustrates the principle that phylogenetic relationships should not be decided purely on the evidence of adult homologous structures.

Evidence of the progressive development of various groups on the basis of their embryology can be seen within the plant kingdom, but examples are less well documented than for the animal kingdom. The early gametophyte of mosses and ferns, as represented by the protonema produced by germination of the spores, has a similar structure, physiology and pattern of growth to the filamentous green algae from which it is therefore thought to have developed. The existence of alternation of generations in plant life cycles, and the various forms the generations take (which are adaptations to various environmental conditions) may be interpreted as examples of homology and therefore provide further evidence for evolutionary relationships between plant groups.

The cone-bearing plants represent a group which show features intermediate between those plants adapted to a terrestrial existence and those plants which still require water for the transfer of gametes. In the cone-bearing cycads the male gametophyte resembles the light dry microspore (pollen grain) of the flowering plants in that it is distributed by wind. As the male gametophyte develops, a pollen tube is formed as in flowering plants, but instead of carrying a non-motile male gamete to the archegonium, two flagellated sperm are produced in the tube which swim to the ovule to bring about fertilisation. The cycads therefore appear to represent an intermediate group between non-vascular plants and flowering plants and this suggests that a phylogenetic continuum exists within the plant kingdom.

The existence of a group of organisms possessing features common to two other groups showing different levels of complexity, or adapted to different environments, may be interpreted as suggesting phylogenetic continuity between the three organisms based on the descent of one group (such as the flowering plants) from another (the non-vascular plants) via the intermediate form (the cycads). Many of these intermediate forms are extinct and it is only by studying the fossil record that a progressive developmental sequence can be deduced. In many cases intermediate forms have not been found. These are equivalent to the 'missing links' (gaps) in the fossil record. It may be that these links do not exist, according to the hypothesis of punctuated equilibria (section 26.7.1). However, their absence may be explained by the possibility that they do not fossilise or have not yet been found. In the case of the phylogenetic link between the annelids and the arthropods there is one group of organisms, of which *Peripatus* is typical, which has features of both annelids and arthropods (fig 26.17). The annelid features include a body wall containing circular and longitudinal muscles, non-jointed parapodia-like limbs, segmental excretory tubules and a double ventral nerve chord. The arthropod features include a chitinous cuticle, spiracles and tracheae

Fig 26.17 *The primitive arthropod* Peripatus.

and an open blood system. Another 'living fossil' intermediate form is represented by the lungfish, which suggests a link between fish and amphibians.

Whilst much of this evidence suggests that some form of evolutionary process has occurred, it must be appreciated that there is no conclusive proof that it did occur.

26.7.8 Comparative biochemistry

As techniques of biochemical analysis have become more precise, this field of research has shed new light on evolutionary ideas. The occurrence of similar molecules in a complete range of organisms suggests the existence of biochemical homology in a similar way to the anatomical homology shown by organs and tissues. Again, this evidence for an evolutionary theory is supportive of other evidence rather than confirmatory in its own right. Most of the research which has been carried out on comparative biochemistry has involved analysis of the primary structure of widely distributed protein molecules, such as cytochrome *c* and haemoglobin, and more recently of nucleid acid molecules, particularly ribosomal RNA. Slight changes in the genetic code as a result of gene mutation produce subtle variations in the overall structure of a given protein or nucleic acid. This forms a basis for determining phylogenetic relationships if the following assumption is made: the fewer the differences in the molecular structure, the fewer the mutations which have occurred and the more closely related in an evolutionary sense are the organisms containing the molecule. Large differences in the molecular structure represent large differences in the DNA. Predictably, this situation exists in organisms showing fewer anatomical homologies.

Cytochromes are respiratory proteins situated in the mitochondria of cells and are responsible for the transfer of electrons along the respiratory pathway (section 9.3.5). Cytochrome *c* is one such protein from the pathway. It has an iron-containing prosthetic group surrounded by a polypeptide chain containing between 104 and 112 amino acids, depending upon the species. Modern techniques of computerised mass spectrometry have enabled the primary structure of the cytochrome *c* polypeptide chain to be worked out for a range of organisms, including bacteria, fungi, wheat, screwworm fly, silkworm, tuna, penguin, kangaroo and primates. The similarity in the cytochrome *c* amino acid sequence between 21 organisms studied in this way is surprisingly high. In 20 out of 21 organisms studied, ranging from the athlete's-foot fungus to humans, the amino acids in positions 78–88 were identical (table 26.6). The amino acid sequence for cytochrome *c* of humans and chimpanzees is identical and differs from the rhesus monkey by only one amino acid. The computer studies, based on amino acid sequences of cytochrome *c*, have produced plant and animal phylogenetic trees which show close agreement with phylogenetic trees based on anatomical homologies.

Similar results have been obtained from the study of the globin proteins, haemoglobin and myoglobin, involved in oxygen transport and storage. The similarities and differences between the haemoglobin molecule of four primate species are shown in table 26.7. The relationships between the various globins, based on amino acid sequences, and their occurrence in organisms are shown in fig 26.18. Variations in the amino acid sequence of cytochrome *c* and the globins are thought to have arisen by mutations of ancestral genes.

Immunological research has also produced evidence of phylogenetic links between organisms. Protein molecules, present in serum, act as antigens when injected into the bloodstream of animals that lack these proteins. This causes the animal to produce antibodies against them which results in an antigen/antibody interaction. This immune reaction depends upon the host animal recognising the presence of foreign protein structures in the serum. Human serum injected into rabbits sensitises them to human serum and causes them to produce antibodies against human serum proteins. After a period of time, if human serum is added to a sample of sensitised rabbit serum, antigen/antibody complexes form which settle out as a precipitate that can be measured. Adding serum from a variety of animals to samples of rabbit serum containing antibodies against human serum produces varying amounts of precipitate. Assuming that the amounts of precipitate are directly related to the amounts of 'foreign' protein present, this method can be used to establish affinities between animal groups as shown in table 26.8.

This technique of comparative serology has been used extensively to check phylogenetic links. For example, zoologists were uncertain as to the classification of the king crab (*Limulus*). When various arthropod antigens were added to *Limulus* serum the greatest amount of precipitate was produced by arachnid antigens. Arachnids include spiders and scorpions. This evidence reinforced morphological evidence, and *Limulus* is now firmly established in the class Arachnida. Similar work has clarified many phylogenetic uncertainties amongst the mammals.

Table 26.6 Cytochrome *c* amino acid sequences for 21 species.

Species	*Amino acid sequence* 70										80										90					
	0	1	2	3	4	5	6	7	8	9	0	1	2	3	4	5	6	7	8	9	0	1	2	3	4	5
Human	D	T	L	M	E	Y	L	E	N	P	K	K	Y	I	P	G	T	K	M	I	F	V	G	I	K	K
Rhesus monkey	D	T	L	M	E	Y	L	E	N	P	K	K	Y	I	P	G	T	K	M	I	F	V	G	I	K	K
Horse	E	T	L	M	E	Y	L	E	N	P	K	K	Y	I	P	G	T	K	M	I	F	A	G	I	K	K
Pig, bovine, sheep	E	T	L	M	E	Y	L	E	N	P	K	K	Y	I	P	G	T	K	M	I	F	A	G	I	K	K
Dog	E	T	L	M	E	Y	L	E	N	P	K	K	Y	I	P	G	T	K	M	I	F	A	G	I	K	K
Grey whale	E	T	L	M	E	Y	L	E	N	P	K	K	Y	I	P	G	T	K	M	I	F	A	G	I	K	K
Rabbit	D	T	L	M	E	Y	L	E	N	P	K	K	Y	I	P	G	T	K	M	I	F	A	G	I	K	K
Kangaroo	D	T	L	M	E	Y	L	E	N	P	K	K	Y	I	P	G	T	K	M	I	F	A	G	I	K	K
Chicken, turkey	D	T	L	M	E	Y	L	E	N	P	K	K	Y	I	P	G	T	K	M	I	F	A	G	I	K	K
Penguin	D	T	L	M	E	Y	L	E	N	P	K	K	Y	I	P	G	T	K	M	I	F	A	G	I	K	K
Pekin duck	D	T	L	M	E	Y	L	E	N	P	K	K	Y	I	P	G	T	K	M	I	F	A	G	I	K	K
Snapping turtle	E	T	L	M	E	Y	L	E	N	P	K	K	Y	I	P	G	T	K	M	I	F	A	G	I	K	K
Bullfrog	D	T	L	M	E	Y	L	E	N	P	K	K	Y	I	P	G	T	K	M	I	F	A	G	I	K	K
Tuna	D	T	L	M	E	Y	L	E	N	P	K	K	Y	I	P	G	T	K	M	I	F	A	G	I	K	K
Screwworm fly	D	T	L	F	E	Y	L	E	N	P	K	K	Y	I	P	G	T	K	M	I	F	A	G	I	K	K
Silkworm moth	D	T	L	F	E	Y	L	E	N	P	K	K	Y	I	P	G	T	K	M	I	F	A	G	L	K	K
Wheat	N	T	L	Y	D	Y	L	L	N	P	K	K	Y	I	P	G	T	K	M	V	F	A	G	L	K	K
Fungus (*Neurospora*)	N	T	L	F	E	Y	L	E	N	P	K	K	Y	I	P	G	T	K	M	V	F	P	G	L	K	K
Fungus (*baker's yeast*)	N	N	M	S	E	Y	L	T	N	P	K	K	Y	I	P	G	T	K	M	A	F	G	G	L	K	K
Fungus (*Candida*)	P	T	M	S	D	Y	L	E	N	P	K	K	Y	I	P	G	T	K	M	A	F	G	G	L	K	K
Bacterium (*Rhodospirillum*)	A	N	L	A	A	Y	V	K	N	P	K	A	F	V	L	E	S	K	M	T	F	K	–	L	T	K

Key to amino acids

A	alanine	F	phenylalanine	K	lysine	P	proline	T	threonine
C	cysteine	G	glycine	L	leucine	Q	glutamine	V	valine
D	aspartic acid	H	histidine	M	methionine	R	arginine	W	tryptophan
E	glutamic acid	I	isoleucine	N	asparagine	S	serine	Y	tyrosine

After Dayhoff, M. O. and Eck, R. V. (1967–8) *Atlas of protein sequence and structure*, National Biomedical Research Foundation, Silver Spring, Md.

Table 26.7 Similarities and differences between the polypeptide chains of haemoglobin in four primate species.

Species	*Polypeptide chains* α-*haemoglobin (141 amino acids)*	β-*haemoglobin (146 amino acids)*	γ-*haemoglobin*
Human	+	+	+
Chimpanzee	+	+	1
Gorilla	1	1	1
Gibbon	3	3	2

Haemoglobin is composed of four polypeptide chains, made up of α, β, and γ polypeptides. + indicates no difference in amino acid sequence from that of human, figures indicate number of amino acid differences.

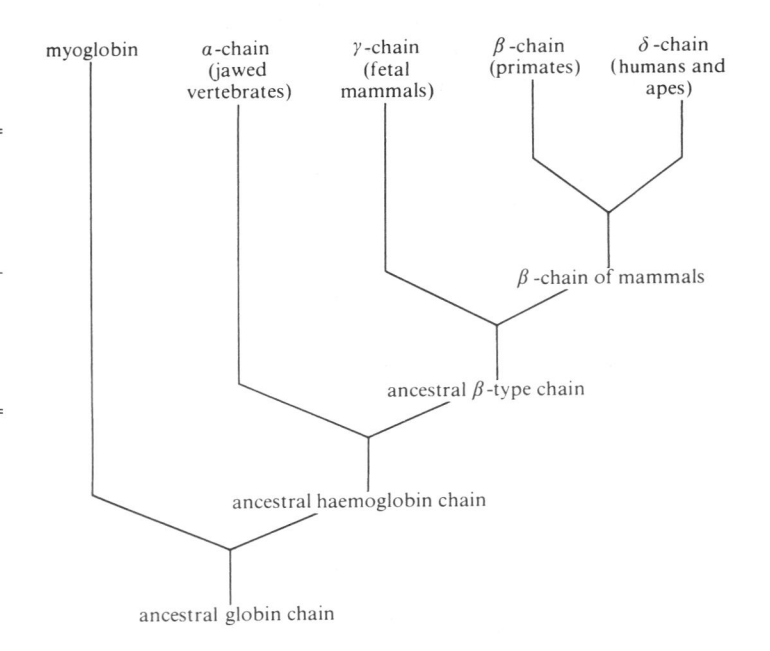

Fig 26.18 *Supposed origins of myoglobin and vertebrate globin polypeptide chains. All five types are found in humans. (After V. M. Ingram, (1963)* Haemoglobins in genetics and evolution, *Columbia University Press.)*

refining the theory and its application to all observed circumstances.

All scientific accounts, hypotheses and theories of the history of life are tentative and, as long as we remain objective in our search for truth, will remain so.

Since evolution forms a focal point within the study of biology it would be remiss to conclude this chapter without relating evolution to the perspective of the natural world. To do this it is fitting to quote from Darwin's final paragraph in the *Origin of Species*,

'There is a grandeur in this view of life, with its several powers, having been originally breathed by the Creator into a few forms or into one; and that, whilst this planet has gone cycling on according to the fixed law of gravity, from so simple a beginning endless forms most beautiful and most wonderful have been and are evolving.'

26.8   Human evolution

The course of human evolution has been followed mainly by means of the fossil record which is itself incomplete. However, the fragmentary fossil evidence recovered has enabled **palaeoanthropologists** to begin to piece together a phylogeny (evolutionary history) for primates.

The early stages of human evolution are studied by means of the comparative anatomy of fossils and the evidence of the comparison of many features, from biochemistry to behaviour, of present-day humans with other mammalian species. Later stages of human evolution are studied using the additional evidence from archaeological investigations. The existence of **artefacts** (objects made by humans) such as stone tools, pottery and fire hearths, provide us with an insight into the ways in which modern humans have developed culturally as well as biologically.

Undoubtedly the greatest problem in studying human phylogeny is finding adequate fossil remains. Some excellent remains have been found, for example those in the sediments of the **Olduvai Gorge** in northern Tanzania by Louis, Mary and Richard Leakey, but usually these consist of the skull and teeth only. These structures persist due to their extreme thickness and great hardness (fig 26.19).

Initially fossils are dated with respect to the age of the strata (layers) of rocks in which they are found and the ages of those above and below. This gives a **relative dating** for the fossils. **Absolute dating** is achieved by radioactive dating techniques as described in appendix 4. Age estimates based upon both techniques are usually preferable to either in isolation.

Whatever conclusions we reach regarding humans and their probable ancestors must be tentative and open to revision in the light of new discoveries. Despite this caution, there is a generally accepted view of human phylogeny which is presented below.

Table 26.8 Amounts of precipitate produced by adding serum from the following mammals to rabbit serum containing anti-human antibodies against human serum (amount of precipitate produced with human serum taken as 100%).

Human	100%
Chimpanzee	97%
Gorilla	92%
Gibbon	79%
Baboon	75%
Spider monkey	58%
Lemur	37%
Hedgehog	17%
Pig	8%

The separation of animal phyla into protostomes and deuterostomes on the basis of embryological development has been reinforced by analysis of the phosphate-containing storage molecules found in muscle and used in the synthesis of ATP. Protostomes, represented by annelids, molluscs and arthropods, contain arginine phosphate, whilst deuterostomes, represented by echinoderms and chordates, contain creatine phosphate.

A final example of biochemical homology is provided by the presence of similar or even identical hormones in vertebrates, where they carry out a range of different functions. For example, a hormone similar to mammalian prolactin occurs in all vertebrate groups where it is produced by the pituitary gland. Although it has been reported that there may be 90 distinct effects of prolactin, these can be arranged under two broad headings, reproduction and osmoregulation (table 26.9).

26.7.9   Conclusion

Neo-Darwinian evolutionary theory is based on evidence from a broad range of sources and supported by a mass of otherwise unrelated observations. This constitutes to the scientist the strongest type of evidence for the 'validity' of the theory. Evolution is widely accepted amongst scientists but there is still much work to be done in

Table 26.9 Action of prolactin in vertebrates.

Group	Reproduction	Osmoregulation
Bony fish	Secretion of skin mucus	Increases urine production
Amphibia	Secretion of 'egg jelly'	Increases skin permeability to water
Reptiles	Suppresses egg production	Stimulates water loss in turtles
Birds	Production of 'crop milk'	Increases water uptake
Mammals	Mammary development and lactation	ADH-like activity

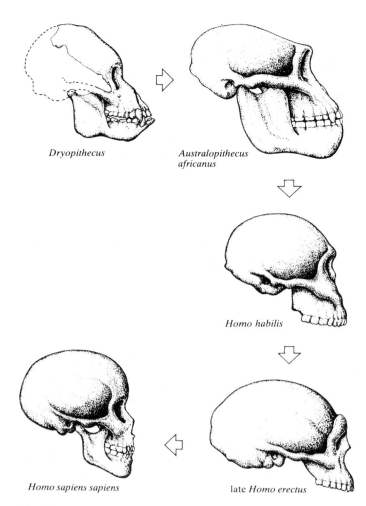

Dryopithecus

Australopithecus africanus

Homo habilis

late *Homo erectus*

Homo sapiens sapiens

Fig 26.19 *Representative skulls showing the transition from* Dryopithecus *to* Homo sapiens.

26.8.1 Human phylogeny

Humans belong to an order of mammals called **primates** which also includes tarsiers, lorises, lemurs, monkeys and apes (see table 26.10). Many of the characteristics of this order are adaptations to life in a forest environment, and it was these requirements for an aboreal (tree-dwelling) existence which were essential for the later evolutionary development of our ancestors. They enabled them to exploit the new ecological niches which appeared as the lush forests of the Miocene period gave way to the drier grassland savannahs of the Pliocene period.

Within the order Primates are three groups of animals called **anthropoids**. These include the **New World monkeys** (marmosets and spider monkeys), the **Old World monkeys** (baboons and proboscis monkeys) and **hominoids** (apes and humans). Humans and their ancestors are more closely related to apes than any other anthropoid, and apes, in turn, are closer in phylogeny to Old World monkeys than to New World monkeys (see table 26.8).

It is generally accepted that the ape/human stock probably diverged from that of monkeys about 25–30 million years ago, during the Oligocene period, and the

Table 26.10 Characteristics of the order Primates.

Grasping limbs	opposable thumb with grip for power and precision
Rotating forelimb	hand can rotate through 180°
Stereoscopic vision	eyes close together on face with parallel optical axes
Visual acuity	increased numbers of rods/cones with own nerve cells
Reduced olfaction	reduced snout allowing flatter face
Enlarged skull	expanded area for cerebrum, ventral foramen magnum
Large brain	increased sensory/motor areas, deeply fissured
Few offspring	longer gestation period, increased parental care
Social dependency	corporate activities, group cohesion

subsequent separation of apes and human ancestors occurred between 5 and 10 million years ago in the middle of the Miocene period. From that time onwards, the family **Pongidae** (fossil forms and present-day gibbons, orangutans, gorillas and chimpanzees) and the family **Hominidae** (fossil forms and modern humans) have evolved along different lines. Recent evidence, based on comparative biochemistry (section 26.7.8), has suggested that gorillas and chimpanzees may have diverged from human stock as recently as 5 million years ago. No supporting fossil evidence for this exists as yet.

Various fossil forms of relevance to human ancestry are represented in table 26.11. Four genera and six species are included. They show a transition in biological features such as skull appearance, tooth structure, brain size, upright posture and diet.

Of particular significance in the evolution of humans was the development of an upright posture (bipedalism) and the increase in brain size.

The transition from walking on four legs to walking on two legs (**bipedalism**) had implications far beyond those affecting the skeleton and muscles. It is now believed that the acquisition of an upright posture and the accompanying changes in the nervous system allowed the subsequent enlargement of the cerebral hemispheres. The common ancestors of humans and apes are likely to have used all four limbs for movement, something like chimpanzees, but with the appearance of *Ramapithecus* more time was spent in an upright posture. By about 4 million years ago our hominid ancestors were bipedal and fully erect.

Freedom of the hands from locomotion enabled them to be used for carrying objects and manipulating the environment, all vital activities preadapting hominids for later dextrous activities associated with their cultural evolution. In addition, an upright posture gave the hominids increased height and range of vision which would have had advantages for them living, as they did, in the open savannah.

Table 26.11 Summary of the main features associated with human phylogeny.

Genus	Age of appearance/ million years ago	Skull	Brain capacity/cm^3	Teeth	Diet	Posture	Significance
Dryopithecus (earliest fossil ape)	25 (Miocene)	large muzzle	?	large canines, incisors, molars square	soft fruit, leaves	knuckle walker	earliest fossil ape, persisted until 10 million years ago
Ramapithecus	15 (Miocene)	deeper jaw	?	small canines, flattened molars, thicker enamel	seeds, nuts	partially upright	earliest hominid ground-dwelling in savannah
Australopithecus afarensis ('Lucy')	4.0 (Pliocene)	large jaws	450	small canines, small incisors	herbivorous	fully erect	still at home in trees but savannah dwellers
A. africanus	2.5	ventral foramen	450	small canines	carnivorous	fully erect	small game hunter, many variant forms
Homo habilis	2.0 (Pleistocene)	lighter jaw	700	small canines	carnivorous	fully erect	earliest stone tools, began hunting for meat, major increase in brain size foreshadowing social attributes
Homo erectus ('Peking Man')	1.5	thick, low forehead brow ridges	880	small canines	omnivorous	5–6 feet tall	beginning of cultural evolution, stone tools, cooperative hunting in bands, rudimentary language, used fire
Homo sapiens	0.25			small canines	omnivorous	5–6 feet tall	
(Swanscombe)	0.25	heavy jaw	1200				cave-dweller
(Neanderthal)	0.08	face long and narrow, brow ridges, enlarged nasal cavity	1500	heavier than modern teeth, wisdom teeth	omnivorous	5–6 feet tall	buried their dead, flint flake tools
(Cro-Magnon, modern man)	0.03	vaulted cranium, shorter skull, reduced jaws	1400	teeth closer together, wisdom teeth	omnivorous	5–6 feet tall	polyphyletic origin giving rise to geographical races, cave-painting

Along with the advantages of bipedalism was the **increasing brain size** as recorded by cranial capacities. Table 26.11 shows that the cranial capacities of hominids increased from about 450 cm^3 to about 1400 cm^3. However, sheer volume alone does not give a complete picture of the brain potential which developed during human evolution. The complex infolding of the outer cortical tissue increased the surface area to give a much greater working area for the brain. This increase in effective area enabled control and coordination to be exercised over the newly developing behavioural activities such as tool-making, hunting and speech.

The course of human evolution is remarkable in that the gradual transitions in physical features (skeleton, movement, diet) were paralleled by an accelerating development in social behaviour. The process of becoming human is called **hominisation** and it is believed to have been influenced by:

- the development of *manipulative skills* and *speech;*
- changes in sexual behaviour allowing *pair bonding* and increased *parental supervision* of children;
- the establishment of *communal organisation* and *social responsibility*, arising from the principle of *food sharing.*

These biological and social changes were accompanied by changes which were transmitted from person to person by communication rather than inherited genetically. They signalled the development of *culture* which is defined as 'a store of information and set of behaviour patterns, transmitted, not by genetical inheritance, but by learning by imitation, by instruction or by example.'* Culture embraces many different aspects of the life of people including customs, rituals, shared knowledge, language, beliefs, laws, religion, food and employment. Our knowledge of early human cultural evolution is limited to artefacts which archaeologists have recovered. Most of these are stone tools but their study gives useful insights into early human activities.

*Stephen Tomkins (1984), *The Origins of Mankind*, CUP.

26.8.2 Stone tools

The increased brain size of *Homo habilis*, the dissociation of the hands from locomotion and the ability of the hands to achieve both power and precision grips led to the development of **stone tools**. *Homo habilis* (literally 'handy man') at first probably used pebble tools and sticks in much the same way as present-day chimpanzees and gorillas. Chimpanzees strip leaves from twigs before inserting the twig into termite holes. When the termites climb onto the twig it is withdrawn and the termites eaten. The earliest human artefacts were made by *Homo habilis* (2 million years ago) and these were *chopping tools*, *hammer stones*, and *percussion flakes* made from lava or quartz and used for scraping. Later artefacts produced by *Homo erectus* (1.5 million years ago) required greater skill in manufacture and included *hand-held axes* with two cutting edges leading to a point. Sophisticated tools made from flint, bone and wood, however, did not appear until the Upper Palaeolithic, 35 000 years ago. The physical ability to make tools requires sophisticated coordination of the hands and eyes. Such biological activity must be associated with the knowledge required to select materials, impart the skills to others and use these tools, the so-called cultural components of human development (fig 26.20).

The rate of progress in design, manufacture and use of hand tools from the pebbles of 2.5 million years ago to the hand-axes of 0.2 million years ago seems incredibly slow when compared to human technological achievements of the last 100 years. Since 1890 we have witnessed the origin of aircraft and sent people to the Moon, conquered most infectious diseases with vaccinations and antibiotics, transplanted organs and created artificial limbs and organs, developed computing to a sophisticated level, extended our senses with electron microscopes and radio telescopes, harnessed nuclear energy and exploited the potentials of biotechnology. This rapid increase in technology is not associated with increasing brain size but results from advances in research and development based on knowledge and skills transmitted from the previous generation. A child brought up by animals in total isolation from other humans (as in the case of the fabled Tarzan) would have no greater technological expertise than our hominid ancestors. It is through education alone, that is the transmission of culture, that humans are capable of the exponential technological advancement witnessed in the last 100 years.

26.8.3 Language

Oral communication is not unique to humans. Birds sing, porpoises 'beep', bats 'chirp' and monkeys and apes chatter, grunt and howl. Humans alone have developed spoken and written languages which are used to communicate information not just about the physical world but to formulate abstract concepts of art, science, philosophy and religion. We do not know when speech began but whatever its origins, the basic anatomical

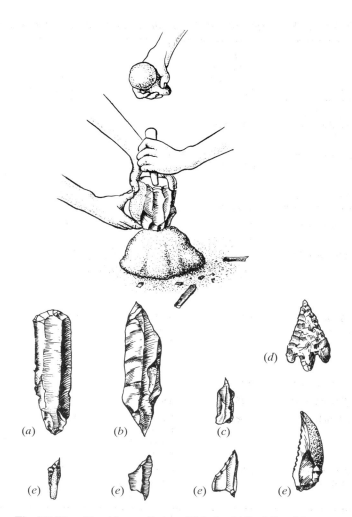

Fig 26.20 *The Upper Palaeolithic tool kit of Cro-Magnon man. Using a hammer stone and antler tine punch, long-bladed flakes were struck from a flint core placed on a stone anvil. Flakes were then retouched to make such things as (a) end scraper, (b) burin chisel, (c) microburin drill, (d) arrowhead, (e) microliths (barbs). (After S. Tomkins (1984)* The Origins of Mankind, *Cambridge University Press.)*

structures associated with speech had to be present in our ancestors. These include the lips, tongue and larynx and three areas of the brain, the speech motor cortical area (controlling the delivery of speech) and two further areas also on the left side of the cerebrum. One of these areas stores auditory, visual and verbal information, and the other is involved in formulating statements and response, that is putting words together. Studies of imprints of blood vessels and brain convolutions present in fossil skulls (**endocasts**) show that there was a substantial development of these areas in both *Australopithecus africanus* and *Homo habilis*.

26.8.4 Social behaviour in humans

Social behaviour is developed to a greater extent in humans than in any other species and extends beyond pair formation and family life to the establishment of communities at the level of bands, tribes, chiefdoms and nation states.

The course of the evolution of human social behaviour was intimately linked with the development of culture and both were categorised by:

- establishment of the family (one partner or many wives);
- prolonged childhood during which time children could acquire the prevailing culture;
- increased use of speech for communication;
- development of the concepts of a home base and food sharing;
- increased cooperation in food-gathering enterprises;
- division of labour by age and sex, with older males hunting in bands to increase efficiency of hunting and women staying together to 'educate' children and gain protection from danger;
- stabilisation of a broader social structure where the dominance hierarchy was replaced by kinship and prohibition of incest;
- extension of geographical range by tolerance of less optimal environments;
- use of simple tools and eventually the manufacture of complex tools;
- use of fire for cracking rocks, hardening wood, cooking food and defence against animals;
- development of folk wisdom, art, religion, philosophy, science and technology.

Thus we see the basic biological needs of food, sex and safety were satisfied more efficiently by the development of group activities based on a common economic–political–sexual structure enriched and supported by the rapid development of culture.

Indeed it can be said that current human evolution is based more on cultural development than on social behaviour.

26.8.5 Art and religion

Whilst humans share many aspects of behaviour with other primates and non-primates, there are some which are unique to the species and these include art, religion and free-will.

The earliest examples of representations of animals and humans come from the Upper Palaeolithic (30 000 years ago). Some are carved in wood or ivory and some are carved on cave walls. The significance of this early art is not known, but we do know that such activities require tools, skill, observation, thought, motivation and possibly leisure. Most of the best-known *cave paintings*, such as those at Lascaux in France, are no older than 20 000 years and used earth pigments, soot and burnt animal residues. What is interesting about these paintings is the variety of abstractions and techniques which are employed and the significance of work. Were they connected with rituals, religious beliefs, simply 'art for art's sake' or an early attempt at graffiti?

In some cases the art forms depicted animals and sex and these were often associated with death and birth respectively. Whether they had religious significance is not clear, but current opinion suggests they were not associated with religious figures as we know them today. *Religion* is believed to have developed at about the same time as cave painting as evidenced by the form of burials found in various parts of the world. In many cases the dead were buried along with offerings such as food, tools and decorative ornaments. It is believed that this symbolism indicates established religious practices. Such a development requires the involvement of conscious intelligent thought, one of the most sophisticated aspects of cultural development. Religion as it is perceived today is fairly recent, the earliest shrines and temples and their accompanying artefacts being less than 10 000 years old.

Chapter Twenty-seven

Mechanisms of speciation

The previous chapter described how Darwin came to appreciate that inherited variation occurs in natural populations as well as in artificial breeding situations. He realised that this variation was significant in the process of evolution by natural selection, but could not explain the mechanism by which variations could appear. It was only with the reappearance of the work of Mendel on inheritance, and the appreciation of its importance in the understanding of evolution, that scientists began to get a deeper understanding of the mechanism. Modern explanations of variation between organisms are a blend of evolutionary theory based on the work of Darwin and Wallace and genetic theory based on principles established by Mendel. Variation, inheritance and evolutionary theory may now be studied using evidence from a branch of biology known as **population genetics**.

27.1 Population genetics

A population is a group of organisms of the same species usually found in a clearly defined geographical area. Following the rediscovery of Mendel's demonstration of the particulate nature of inheritance, the study of genes became important in the study of variation, inheritance and evolutionary change. Bateson, the scientist who introduced the term 'genetics' in 1905, saw genetics as

'the elucidation of the phenomena of heredity and variation'.

It is the study of population genetics which forms the basis of modern views of evolutionary theory, a theory referred to as **neo-Darwinism**.

Genes, sometimes working together with environmental factors, determine the phenotypes of organisms and are responsible for variation within populations. The theory of natural selection suggests that phenotypes adapted to the environmental conditions are '**selected for**' whereas non-adapted phenotypes are '**selected against**' and eventually eliminated. Whilst natural selection operates on *individual* organisms of a species, it is the collective genetic response of the *whole population* that determines not only the survival of the species but also the formation of new species. Only those organisms which successfully reproduce before dying contribute to the future of the species. The fate of an individual organism is relatively insignificant in the history of a species. In other words, the

long-term effects of natural selection are at the level of the gene and the population rather than the individual because members of the population can interbreed, exchange genes and thereby pass on genes to the next generation and there is therefore a flow of genes between members of a population. Natural selection of the 'fittest' genes takes place.

27.1.1 Gene pool

A gene pool is the **total variety of genes and alleles present in a sexually reproducing population**. In any given population the composition of the gene pool may be constantly changing from generation to generation. New combinations of genes produce unique genotypes which, when expressed in physical terms as phenotypes, undergo environmental selection pressures which continually select and determine which genes pass on to the next generation.

A population whose gene pool shows consistent change from generation to generation is undergoing evolutionary change. A static gene pool represents a situation where genetic variation between members of the species is inadequate to bring about evolutionary change.

27.1.2 Allele frequency

The appearance of any physical characteristic, for example coat colour in mice, is determined by one or more genes. Several forms of each gene may exist and these are called alleles (table 24.2). The number of organisms in a population carrying a particular allele determines the **allele frequency** (which is sometimes, incorrectly, referred to as the gene frequency). For example, in humans the frequency of the dominant allele for the production of pigment in the skin, hair and eyes is 99%. The recessive allele, which is responsible for the lack of pigment, a condition known as **albinism**, has a frequency of 1%. This means that of the total number of alleles controlling production of the pigment, 1% result in a lack of pigment and 99% result in its presence. It is usual in studies of population genetic studies to represent gene or allele frequencies as decimals rather than percentages or fractions. Hence this dominant allele frequency is 0.99 and the recessive albino allele frequency is 0.01. Since the total population represents 100% or 1.0

it can be seen that:

dominant allele frequency	+	recessive allele frequency	=	1
0.99	+	0.01	=	1

In terms of Mendelian genetics the dominant allele would be represented by a letter, say **N** (for normal pigmentation), and the recessive allele would be represented by **n** (the albino condition). In the example above, $\mathbf{N} = 0.99$ and $\mathbf{n} = 0.01$.

Population genetics has borrowed two symbols from the mathematics of probability, p and q, to express the frequency with which a pair of dominant and recessive alleles appear in the gene pool of the population. Therefore,

$$p + q = 1$$

where p = dominant allele frequency, and q = recessive allele frequency.

In the case of pigmentation in humans, $p = 0.99$ and $q = 0.01$, since

$$p + q = 1$$
$$0.99 + 0.01 = 1$$

The value of the above equation lies in the fact that if the frequency of either allele is known, the frequency of the other may be determined. For example, if the frequency of the recessive allele is 25% then $q = 25\%$ or 0.25.
Since
$$p + q = 1$$
$$p + 0.25 = 1$$
$$p = 1 - 0.25$$
$$p = 0.75$$

That is, the frequency of the dominant allele is 0.75 or 75%.

27.1.3 Genotype frequencies

The frequencies of particular alleles in the gene pool are of importance in calculating genetic changes in the population and in determining the frequency of genotypes. Since the genotype of an organism is the major factor determining its phenotype, calculations of genotype frequency are used in predicting possible outcomes of particular matings or crosses. This has great significance in horticulture, agriculture and medicine.

The mathematical relationship between the frequencies of alleles and genotypes in populations was developed independently in 1908 by an English mathematician G. H. Hardy and a German physician W. Weinberg. The relationship, known as the **Hardy–Weinberg equilibrium**, is based upon a principle which states that

'the frequency of dominant and recessive alleles in a population will remain constant from generation to generation provided certain conditions exist.'

These conditions are:

(1) the population is large;
(2) mating is random;
(3) no mutations occur;

(4) all genotypes are equally fertile, so that no selection occurs;
(5) generations do not overlap;
(6) there is no emigration or immigration from or into the population, that is, there is no gene flow between populations.

Any changes in allele or genotype frequencies must therefore result from the introduction of one or more of the conditions above. These are the factors that are significant in producing evolutionary change, and when changes occur the **Hardy–Weinberg equation** provides a means of studying the change and of measuring its rate.

27.1.4 The Hardy–Weinberg equation

Whilst the Hardy–Weinberg equation provides a simple mathematical model of how genetic equilibrium can be maintained in a gene pool, its major application in population genetics is in calculating allele and genotype frequencies.

Starting with two homozygous organisms, one dominant for allele **A** and one recessive for allele **a**, it can be seen that all offspring will be heterozygous (**Aa**).

Let	$\mathbf{A}$ = dominant allele		
	$\mathbf{a}$ = recessive allele		
Parental phenotypes	homozygous dominant	×	homozygous recessive
Parental genotypes (2n)	$\mathbf{AA}$	×	$\mathbf{aa}$
Meiosis			
Gametes (n)	Ⓐ Ⓐ	×	ⓐ ⓐ
Random fertilisation			
F_1 *genotypes (2n)*	$\mathbf{Aa}$ $\mathbf{Aa}$		$\mathbf{Aa}$ $\mathbf{Aa}$
F_1 *phenotypes*	all heterozygous		

If the presence of the dominant allele **A** is represented by the symbol p and the recessive allele **a** by the symbol q, the nature and frequency of the genotypes produced by crossing the F_1 genotypes above are seen to be:

F_1 *phenotypes*	heterozygous	×	heterozygous
F_1 *genotypes (2n)*	$\mathbf{Aa}$	×	$\mathbf{Aa}$
Meiosis			
Gametes (n)	Ⓐ ⓐ	×	Ⓐ ⓐ

Random fertilisation		$\mathbf{A}$ (p)	$\mathbf{a}$ (q)
	$\mathbf{A}$ (p)	$\mathbf{AA}$ (p^2)	$\mathbf{Aa}$ (pq)
	$\mathbf{a}$ (q)	$\mathbf{Aa}$ (pq)	$\mathbf{aa}$ (q^2)

F_2 *genotypes (2n)*	$\mathbf{AA}$ (p^2)	$\mathbf{2Aa}$ ($2pq$)	$\mathbf{aa}$ (q^2)
F_2 *phenotypes*	homozygous dominant	heterozygous	homozygous recessive

Since **A** is dominant, the ratio of dominant to recessive genotypes will be 3:1, the Mendelian monohybrid cross ratio. From the cross shown above it can be seen that the following genotypes can be described in terms of the symbols p and q:

p^2 = homozygous dominant
$2pq$ = heterozygous
q^2 = homozygous recessive

The distribution of possible genotypes is statistical and based on probability. Of the three possible genotypes resulting from such a cross it can be seen that they are represented in the following frequencies:

AA   **2Aa**   **aa**
$\frac{1}{4}$ $\frac{1}{2}$ $\frac{1}{4}$

In terms of genotype frequency the sum of the three genotypes presented in the above population equal one, or, expressed in terms of the symbols p and q, it can be seen that the genotypic probabilities are:

$$p^2 + 2pq + q^2 = 1$$

(In mathematical terms $p+q=1$ is the mathematical equation of probability and $p^2 + 2pq + q^2 = 1$ is the binomial expansion of that equation (that is $(p+q)^2$)).

To summarise, since

p = dominant allele frequency
q = recessive allele frequency
p^2 = homozygous dominant genotype
$2pq$ = heterozygous genotype
q^2 = homozygous recessive genotype

it is possible to calculate all allele and genotype frequencies using the expressions:

allele frequency $\quad p+q \quad = 1$, and
genotype frequency $p^2 + 2pq + q^2 \quad = 1$.

However, in most populations it is only possible to estimate the frequency of the two alleles from the proportion of homozygous recessives, as this is the only genotype that can be identified directly from its phenotype.

For example, one person in 10 000 is albino, that is to say that the albino genotype frequency is 1 in 10 000. Since the albino condition is recessive, that person must possess the homozygous recessive genotype and in terms of probability it can be seen that

$$q^2 = \frac{1}{10\,000}$$
$$= 0.0001$$

Knowing that $q^2 = 0.0001$ the frequencies of the albino allele (q), the dominant pigmented allele (p), the homozygous dominant genotype (p^2) and the heterozygous genotype ($2pq$) may be determined in the following manner.

Since
$$q^2 = 0.0001$$
$$q = \sqrt{0.0001}$$
$$= 0.01,$$

the frequency of the albino allele in the population is 0.01 or 1%.

Since
$$p + q = 1$$
$$p = 1 - q$$
$$= 1 - 0.01$$
$$= 0.99,$$

the frequency of the dominant allele in the population is 0.99 or 99%.

Since
$$p = 0.99$$
$$p^2 = (0.99)^2$$
$$= 0.9801,$$

the frequency of the homozygous dominant genotype in the population is 0.9801, or approximately 98%.

Since
$$p = 0.99 \text{ and } q = 0.01,$$
$$2pq = 2 \times (0.99) \times (0.01)$$
$$= 0.0198,$$

the frequency of the heterozygous genotype is 0.0198, or approximately 2% of the population carry the albino allele either as heterozygotes or albino homozygotes.

These calculations reveal a surprisingly high value for the frequency of the recessive allele in the population considering the low number of individuals showing the homozygous recessive genotype.

Heterozygous individuals showing normal phenotypic characteristics but possessing a recessive gene capable of producing some form of metabolic disorder when present in homozygous recessives are described as **carriers**. Calculations based on the Hardy–Weinberg equation show that the frequency of carriers in a population is always higher than would be expected from estimates of the occurrence of the disorder in the phenotype. This is shown in table 27.1.

27.1 Cystic fibrosis occurs in the population with a frequency of 1 in 2200. Calculate the frequency of the carrier genotype.

27.1.5 Implications of the Hardy–Weinberg equation

The Hardy–Weinberg equation shows that a large proportion of the recessive alleles in a population exist in carrier heterozygotes. In fact, the heterozygous genotypes maintain a substantial potential source of genetic variability. As a result of this, very few of the recessive alleles can be eliminated from the population in each generation. Only the alleles present in the homozygous recessive organism will be expressed in the phenotype and so be exposed to environmental selection and possible elimination.

Many recessive alleles are eliminated because they confer disadvantages on the phenotype. This may result

Table 27.1 Some metabolic disorders and the frequencies of homozygous recessive and heterozygous genotypes.

Metabolic disorder	Approximate frequency of homozygous recessive genotype (q^2)	Frequency of 'carrier' heterozygous genotype ($2pq$)
albinism (lack of pigmentation in body)	1 in 10 000 (in Europe)	1 in 50
alkaptonuria (urine turns black upon exposure to air)	1 in 1 000 000	1 in 503
amaurotic family idiocy (leads to blindness and death)	1 in 40 000	1 in 100
diabetes mellitus (failure to secrete insulin)	1 in 200	1 in 7.7
phenylketonuria (may lead to mental retardation if not diagnosed)	1 in 10 000 (in Europe)	1 in 50

from the death of the organism prior to breeding or **genetic death**, that is the failure to reproduce. Not all recessive alleles, however, are disadvantageous to the population. For example, in human blood groups the commonest phenotypic characteristic in the population is blood group O, the homozygous recessive condition. This phenomenon is also clearly illustrated in the case of sickle-cell anaemia. This is a genetic disease of the blood common in certain populations in Africa, India, certain Mediterranean countries and amongst black North Americans. Homozygous recessive individuals usually die before reaching adulthood thereby eliminating two recessive alleles from the populations. Heterozygotes, on the other hand, do not suffer the same fate. Studies have revealed that the sickle-cell allele frequency has remained relatively stable in many parts of the world. In some African tribes the genotype frequency is as high as 40%, and it was thought that this figure was maintained by the appearance of new mutants. Investigations have revealed that this is not the case, and in many parts of Africa where malaria is a major source of illness and death, individuals possessing a single sickle-cell allele have increased resistance to malaria. In malaria regions of Central America the selective advantage of the heterozygous genotype maintains the sickle-cell allele in the population at frequencies between 10 and 20%.

The maintenance of a fairly constant frequency for a recessive allele which may be potentially harmful is known as **heterozygote advantage**. In the case of black North Americans who have not been exposed to the selection effect of malaria for 200–300 years the frequency of the sickle-cell allele has fallen to 5%. Some of this loss may be accounted for by increased gene flow resulting from black–white marriages, but an important factor is the removal of the selection pressure for the heterozygote due to the absence of malaria in North America. As a result of this the recessive allele is slowly being eliminated from the population. This is an example of evolutionary change in action. It clearly shows the influence of an environmental selection mechanism on changes in allele frequency, a mechanism which disrupts the genetic equilibrium predicted by the Hardy–Weinberg principle. It is mechanisms such as these that bring about the changes in populations which lead to evolutionary change.

27.2 Factors producing changes in populations

The Hardy–Weinberg principle states that given certain conditions the allele frequencies remain constant from generation to generation. Under these conditions a population will be in genetic equilibrium and there will be no evolutionary change. However the Hardy–Weinberg principle is purely theoretical. Few, if any, natural populations show the conditions necessary for equilibrium to exist (section 27.1.3).

The four major sources of genetic variation within a gene pool were described in detail in section 24.8.4, and they are crossing-over during meiosis, independent segregation during meiosis, random fertilisation and mutation. The first three sources of variation are often collectively referred to as **sexual recombination**, and they account for **gene reshuffling**. These processes however, whilst producing new genotypes and altering genotype frequencies, do not produce any changes in the existing alleles, hence the allele frequencies within the population remain constant. Many evolutionary changes, however, usually occur following the appearance of new alleles and the source of this is mutation.

Other situations in which the conditions for the Hardy–Weinberg principle do not exist are when:

- there is non-random breeding;
- the population is small and leads to genetic drift;
- genotypes are not equally fertile so there is genetic load;
- gene flow occurs between populations.

These situations are discussed below.

27.2.1 Non-random breeding

Mating in most natural populations is non-random. Sexual selection occurs whenever the presence of one or more inherited characteristics increases the likelihood of bringing about successful fertilisation of gametes. There are many structural and behavioural mechanisms in both plants and animals which prevent mating from being random. For example, flowers possessing increased size of petals and amounts of nectar are likely to attract more insects and increase the likelihood of pollination. Colour patterns in insects, fishes and birds, and behavioural patterns involving nest-building, territory possession and courtship, all increase the selective nature of breeding.

An experimental investigation with *Drosophila* illustrated the effect of non-random mating on genotype and allele frequencies. A culture of fruit flies containing equal numbers of red-eyed and white-eyed males and females was set up and within 25 generations all white-eyed fruit flies were eliminated from the population. Observation revealed that both red-eyed and white-eyed females preferred mating with red-eyed males. Thus sexual selection, as a mechanism of non-random mating, ensures that certain individuals within the population have an increased reproductive potential so their alleles are more likely to be passed on to the next generation. Organisms with less favourable characteristics have a decreased reproductive potential and the frequency of their alleles being passed on to subsequent generations is reduced.

27.2.2 Genetic drift

This refers to the fact that variation in gene frequencies within populations can occur by chance rather than by natural selection. Random genetic drift or the **Sewall Wright effect** (named after the American geneticist who realised its evolutionary significance) may be an important mechanism in evolutionary change in small or isolated populations. In a small population not all the alleles which are representative of that species may be present. Chance events such as the premature accidental death prior to mating of an organism which is the sole possessor of a particular allele would result in the elimination of that allele from the population. For example, if an allele has a frequency of 1% (that is $q = 0.01$) in a population of 1 000 000 then 10 000 individuals will possess that allele. In a population of 100 only one individual will possess that allele so the probability of losing the allele from a small population by chance is much greater.

Just as it is possible for an allele to disappear from a population, it is equally possible for it to drift to a higher frequency simply by chance. Random genetic drift, as its name implies, is unpredictable. In a small population it can lead to the extinction of the population or result in the population becoming even better adapted to the environment or more widely divergent from the parental population. In due course this may lead to the origin of a new species by natural selection. Genetic drift is thought to have been a significant factor in the origin of new species on islands and in other reproductively isolated populations.

A phenomenon associated with genetic drift is the **founder principle**. This refers to the fact that when a small population becomes split off from the parent population it may not be truly representative, in terms of alleles, of the parent population. Some alleles may be absent and others may be disproportionally represented. Continuous breeding within the **pioneer** population will produce a gene pool with allele frequencies different from that of the original parent population. Genetic drift tends to reduce the amount of genetic variation within the population, mainly as a result of the loss of those alleles which have a low frequency. Continual mating within a small population decreases the proportion of heterozygotes and increases the number of homozygotes. Examples of the founder principle were shown by studies carried out on the small populations of religious sects in America who emigrated from Germany in the eighteenth century. Some of these sects have married almost exclusively amongst their own members. In these cases they show allele frequencies which are uncharacteristic of either the German or American populations. In the case of the Dunkers, a religious sect in Pennsylvania, each community studied was made up of about 100 families, a population so small as to be likely to lead to genetic drift. Blood group analyses produced the following results:

	Blood group A
indigenous Pennsylvanian population	42%
indigenous West German population	45%
Dunker population	60%

These values would appear to be the result of genetic drift occurring within small populations.

Whilst genetic drift may lead to a reduction in variation within a population it can increase variation within the species as a whole. Small isolated populations may develop characteristics atypical of the main population which may have a selective advantage if the environment changes. In this way genetic drift can contribute to the process of speciation (evolution of new species).

27.2.3 Genetic load

The existence within the population of disadvantageous alleles in heterozygous genotypes is known as **genetic load**. As mentioned in section 27.1.5, some recessive alleles which are disadvantageous in the homozygous genotype may be carried in the heterozygous genotype and confer a selective advantage on the phenotype in certain environmental conditions, such as the sickle-cell trait in regions where malaria is endemic. Any increase in recessive alleles in a population as a result of harmful mutations will increase the genetic load of the population.

27.2.4 Gene flow

Within the gene pool of a given breeding population there is a continual interchange of alleles between organisms. Providing there are no changes in allele frequency as a result of mutation, gene reshuffling will confer genetic stability or equilibrium on the gene pool. If a mutant allele should arise, it will be distributed throughout the gene pool by random fertilisation.

Gene flow is often used loosely to describe the movement of alleles within a population as described above, but strictly speaking it refers to the movement of alleles from one population to another as a result of interbreeding between members of the two populations. The random introduction of new alleles into the **recipient** population and their removal from the **donor** population affects the allele frequency of both populations and leads to increased genetic variation. Despite introducing genetic variation into populations, gene flow has a conservative effect in terms of evolutionary change. By distributing mutant alleles throughout all populations, gene flow ensures that all populations of a given species share a common gene pool, that is it reduces differences between populations. The interruption of gene flow between populations is therefore a prerequisite for the formation of new species.

The frequency of gene flow between populations depends upon their geographical proximity, and the ease with which organisms or gametes can pass between the two populations. For example, two populations may be situated so close together that interbreeding is continuous and they may be considered in genetic terms as being one population since they share a common gene pool, such as two snail populations in adjacent gardens separated by a privet hedge.

It is relatively easy for flying animals and pollen grains to be actively or passively dispersed into new environments. Here they may interbreed or cross with the resident population, thereby introducing genetic variation into that population.

27.3   Selection

This is a mechanism that can be thought of as operating at two interrelated levels, at the level of the organism and at the level of the alleles.

Selection is the process by which those organisms which appear physically, physiologically and behaviourally better adapted to the environment survive and reproduce; those organisms not so well adapted either fail to reproduce or die. The former organisms pass on their successful characteristics to the next generation, whereas the latter do not. Selection depends upon the existence of phenotypic variation within the population and is part of the mechanism by which a species adapts to its environment.

When a population increases in size, certain environmental factors become limiting, such as food availability in animals and light in the case of plants. This produces competition for resources between members of the population. Those organisms exhibiting characteristics which give them a competitive advantage will obtain the resource, survive and reproduce. Organisms without those characteristics are at a disadvantage and may die before reproducing. Both the environment and population size operate together to produce a **selection pressure** which can vary in intensity.

Therefore, selection is the process determining which alleles are passed on to the next generation by virtue of the relative advantages they show when expressed as phenotypes. Selection pressure can then be seen as a means of increasing or decreasing the spread of an allele within the gene pool and these changes in allele frequency can lead to evolutionary change.

Major changes in genotype arise from the spread of mutant alleles through the gene pool. The extent of selection and the time it takes will depend upon the nature of the mutant allele and the degree of effect it has upon the phenotype. If the allele is dominant, it will appear in the phenotype more frequently and be selected for or against more rapidly. If the allele is recessive and has no effect in the heterozygous state, as is the case with most mutants, it will not undergo selection until it appears in the homozygous state. The chances of this occurring immediately are slight and the allele may be 'lost' from the gene pool before appearing in the homozygous condition. An allele which is recessive in a given environment may persist until changes in the environment occur where it may have an advantage. These effects would probably appear first in the heterozygote and selection would favour its spread throughout the population, as in the case of sickle-cell anaemia.

A recessive mutant allele may spread rapidly through a population if it occupies a position (locus) on a chromosome very close (linked) to a functionally important dominant allele which is strongly selected for. In this 'linked' condition the chances of the mutant allele combining with another mutant allele to produce the homozygous condition are increased (fig 27.1).

The influence of a given mutant allele can vary. Those mutations affecting alleles controlling important functions are likely to be lethal and removed from the population immediately. Evolutionary change is generally brought about by the gradual appearance of many mutant alleles which exert small progressive changes in phenotypic characteristics.

There are three types of selection process occurring in natural and artificial populations and they are described as stabilising, directional and disruptive. They may be best explained in terms of the normal distribution curve associated with the continuous phenotypic variation found in natural populations (fig 27.2).

27.3.1   Stabilising selection

This operates when phenotypic features coincide with optimal environmental conditions and competition is not severe. It occurs in all populations and

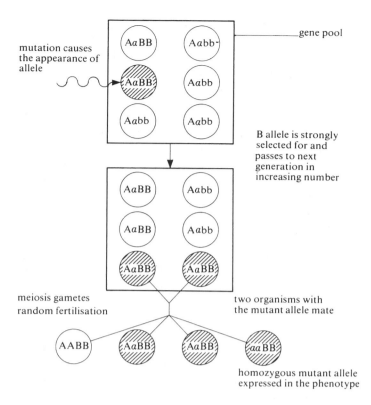

tends to eliminate extremes from the population. For example, there is an optimum wing length for a hawk of a particular size with a certain mode of life in a given environment. Stabilising selection, operating through differences in breeding potential, will eliminate those hawks with wing spans larger or smaller than this optimum length.

Karn and Penrose carried out a study on the correlation between birth weight and post-natal mortality on 13 730 babies born in London between 1935 and 1946. Of these 614 were still-born or died within one month of birth. Fig 27.3 shows that there is an optimum birth weight of about 3.6 kg (about 8 lb). Babies heavier or lighter than this are at a selective disadvantage and have a slightly increased rate of mortality. From these results it is possible to calculate the intensity of selection pressure.

If 614 babies died at birth or within one month this represents a mortality of 4.5%. Even at the optimum birth weight 1.8% of babies died. Hence the selection pressure for weight at birth for babies of 3.6 kg is 4.5% − 1.8% = 2.7% or 0.027. At a birth weight of 1.8 kg there is a 34% mortality giving an intensity of selection pressure at this weight of approximately 30% or 0.3. It should be pointed out, however, that advances in paediatric medicine have considerably reduced post-natal mortality since 1946.

Stabilising selection pressures do not promote evolutionary change but tend to maintain phenotypic stability within the population from generation to generation.

Fig 27.1 *Diagram showing the increased rate of spreading of a mutant allele (α) through a population if linked to a dominant allele (B) which is strongly selected for.*

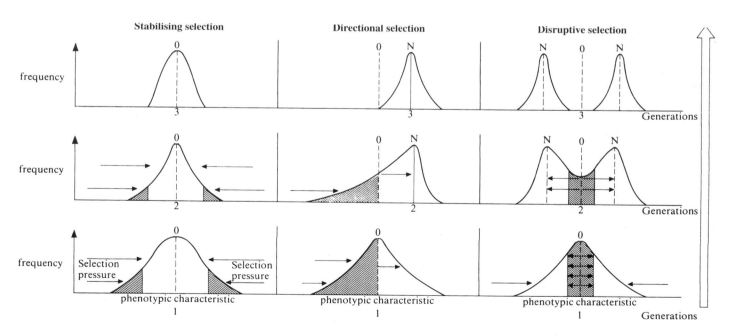

Fig 27.2 *Diagrams showing the three types of selection operating within populations. 0 indicates the original coincidence between optimum phenotype and optimum environmental conditions; N indicates the new position of coincidence of optimum phenotype and optimum environmental conditions. Organisms possessing characteristics in the shaded portions of the normal distribution are at a selective disadvantage and are eliminated by selection pressure. (The numbers 1–3 indicate the order of generations.)*

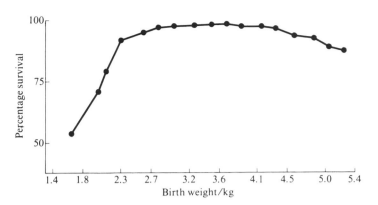

Fig 27.3 *The relationship between percentage survival and birth weight in human babies. (After M. N. Karn & L. S. Penrose (1951)* Ann. Eugen., London, **16** *147–64.)*

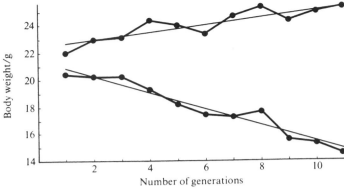

Fig 27.4 *Changes in weight in two mouse populations in successive generations undergoing selection for body weight. (After D. S. Falconer (1953)* J. Genetics, **51** *470–501.)*

27.3.2   Directional selection

This form of selection operates in response to gradual changes in environmental conditions. It operates on the range of phenotypes existing within the population and exerts selection pressure which moves the mean phenotype towards one phenotypic extreme. Once the mean phenotype coincides with the new optimum environmental conditions, stabilising selection will take over.

This kind of selection brings about evolutionary change by producing a selection pressure which favours the increase in frequency of new alleles within the population. Directional selection forms the basis of artificial selection where the selective breeding of phenotypes showing desirable traits increases the frequency of those phenotypes within the population (section 27.4). In a series of experiments, D. S. Falconer selected the heaviest mice from a population at six weeks and let them inbreed. He also selected the lightest mice and allowed them to inbreed. This selective breeding according to mass resulted in the production of two populations, one increasing in mass and the other decreasing (fig 27.4). After termination of selective breeding neither group returned to the original population mass of approximately 22 g. This suggested that the artificial selection of phenotypic characteristics led to some genotypic selection and some loss of alleles from each population. Many classic examples of natural directional selection can be seen in evidence today and they are discussed in section 27.5.

27.3.3   Disruptive selection

This is probably the rarest form of selection but can be very important in bringing about evolutionary change. Fluctuating conditions within an environment, say associated with season and climate, may favour the presence of more than one phenotype within a population. Selection pressures acting from within the population as a result of increased competition may push the phenotypes away from the population mean towards the extremes of

the population. This can split a population into two subpopulations. If gene flow between the subpopulations is prevented, each population may give rise to a new species. In some cases this form of selection can give rise to the appearance of different phenotypes within a population, a phenomenon known as **polymorphism** (*poly*, many; *morphos*, form), and is discussed in section 27.5.1. Within a species organisms with different phenotypes, or **ecotypes**, may show adaptations to particular environmental conditions (section 27.6.2). When a species occupies an extremely large geographical range, organisms distributed along it may show local changes in phenotypic characteristics which are intermediate between those at the extremes of the range. This continuous gradation of characteristics along a geographical range is usually a phenotypic response to climate and/or edaphic (soil) variables and is known as a **cline** (section 27.6.3).

27.3.4   Intensity of selection pressure

The intensity of selection pressure within a population varies at different times and in different places and may be determined by changes in external or internal factors. External factors may include an increase in numbers of predators or pathogens or competition from other species (**interspecific competition**) for food and breeding space in the case of animals, and light, water and mineral salts in the case of plants. Changes in climatic conditions or the state of the habitat in which organisms live may exert new selection pressures. Internal factors such as a rapid increase in the size of the population can result in increased competition for environmental resources (**intraspecific competition**). As the population size increases, so do the numbers of parasites and predators. Pathogens, too, are more easily transmitted from organism to organism as the host population rises and diseases spread very rapidly. All of these factors may not only affect the intensity of the selection pressure but also the direction of the pressure. 'New' phenotypes (and genotypes) are selected for, and poorly adapted organisms are eliminated from the population. The organisms to be eliminated first are those at the non-adaptive extremes of the phenotypic range.

One result of increased selection pressure is that it may cause organisms to become **specialised** to certain modes of life or narrower environmental conditions. This may be a disadvantage for the future of that species. Increased uniformity and dependency by a species increases the likelihood of that species becoming extinct should environmental conditions change. The fossil record contains many extinct organisms that were bizarre and overspecialised.

> **27.2** How might a knowledge of selection pressure and mode of life be useful in the eradication of a **named** parasite?

From what has been said it can be seen that increased selection pressure is a conservative mechanism selecting for the phenotype best adapted to the prevailing environmental condition (the optimum phenotype).

A reduction in the intensity of selection pressure usually has the opposite effects to those described above. It may be produced by an absence of predators, pathogens, parasites and competing species or an increase in optimum environmental conditions. These conditions are usually found when an organism is introduced into a new environment. It is conditions such as these which are believed to have favoured the diversity of finch species found on the Galapagos Islands.

27.4 Artificial selection

Humans have practised artificial selection in the form of the domestication of animals and plants since the earliest times of civilisation. Darwin used evidence from artificial selection to account for the mechanism whereby changes in species could arise in natural populations, that is natural selection. The basis of artificial selection is the isolation of natural populations and the selective breeding of organisms showing characteristics or traits which have some usefulness to humans. In the case of cattle, the Hereford and Aberdeen Angus breeds have been selected for the quality and quantity of their meat, whereas Jersey and Guernsey cows are favoured for their milk yield. Hampshire and Suffolk sheep mature early and produce a good quality meat but lack the hardiness and foraging ability of the Cheviot and Scotch Blackface. The latter examples show that no single breed has all the characteristics necessary for the best economic yield under all conditions and therefore a planned programme of selective breeding is often practised to increase the quality of the breed and the yield.

In artificial selection humans are exerting a directional selection pressure which leads to changes in allele and genotype frequencies within the population. This is an evolutionary mechanism which gives rise to new breeds, strains, varieties, races and subspecies. In all cases these groups have isolated gene pools, but they have retained the basic gene and chromosomal structure which is characteristic of the species to which they still belong.

27.4.1 Inbreeding

This involves selective reproduction between closely related organisms, for example between offspring produced by the same parents, in order to propagate particularly desirable characteristics. Inbreeding is a particularly common practice in the breeding of 'show' animals such as cats and dogs. It was used by livestock breeders to produce cattle, pigs, poultry and sheep with high yields of milk, meat, eggs and wool respectively, but for reasons stated below inbreeding is not now widely practised.

Prolonged inbreeding can lead to a reduction in fertility and this is a particular problem in the breeding of livestock. Intensive breeding reduces the variability of the genome (the sum of all the alleles of an individual) by increasing the number of homozygous genotypes at the expense of the number of heterozygous genotypes. In order to overcome these problems breeders resort to outbreeding after several generations of inbreeding. For example, a dairy farmer may use his own bull and successive generations of his own cows to produce cows with a high milk yield. Before the cattle begin to show signs of decreased resistance to disease and reduced fertility, the farmer will use another bull or artificially inseminate his breeding cows with semen acquired from a cattle-breeding centre. This introduces new alleles into the herd, thereby increasing the heterozygosity of the breeding population.

27.4.2 Outbreeding

This is particularly useful in plant breeding, but is being used increasingly in the commercial production of meat, eggs and wool. It involves crossing individuals from genetically distinct populations. Outbreeding usually takes place between members of different varieties or strains, and in certain plants between closely related species. The progeny are known as **hybrids**, and have phenotypes showing characteristics which are superior to either of the parental stock. This phenomenon is known as **hybrid vigour** or **heterosis**. Hybrids produced from crossing homozygous parental stocks from different populations are called F_1 hybrids and show advantages such as increased fruit size and number, increased resistance to disease and earlier maturity. In maize (sweet corn), hybridisation has increased the grain yield of the F_1 hybrids by 250% over the parental stocks (fig 27.5). In the case of double-cross hybridisation, the hybrids produced by

(a)   (b)

Fig 27.5 *An example of hybrid vigour. Photograph (a) shows two parental maize varieties which when interbred produce the hybrid shown in the centre of the photograph. The ear shown in the centre of the photograph (b) was produced by hybridisation of parental stocks with ears A and B as shown on the left and right of the photograph. (Photograph by D. F. Jones, Connecticut Agricultural Experiment Station.)*

crossing two inbred strains are themselves crossed. The resulting hybrid produces ears having the quality and yield which more than covers the costs involved in a two-year breeding programme (fig 27.6).

Increased vigour results from the increased heterozygosity which arises from gene mixing. For example, whilst each homozygous parent may possess some, but not all, of the dominant alleles for vigorous growth, the heterozygote produced will carry all the dominant alleles, as shown in fig 27.7.

Increased vigour in certain varieties may not result simply from the increased prominence of dominant alleles, but also from some form of interaction between particular combinations of alleles in the heterozygote.

If F_1 phenotypes are continually inbred the vigour will decrease as the proportion of homozygotes increases (fig 27.8).

Selective hybridisation can induce changes in chromosome number (chromosomal mutation), a phenomenon known as **polyploidy**, which can lead to the production of new species. An example of this is described in section 24.9.2.

27.4.3   Artificial selection in humans

Recent advances in human knowledge of the structure of the gene, the genetic code, the mechanisms of heredity and the prenatal diagnosis of genetic defects, have opened up the possibilities of selecting or eliminating certain characteristics in humans. The science of **eugenics** is concerned with the possibilities of 'improving' the 'quality' of the human race by the selective mating of certain individuals. This is a very emotive topic and raises all sorts of objections. Aldous Huxley in his book *Brave New World*, published in 1932, fictionalised the day when eugenics would be taken to its extreme possibilities and particular types of individuals would be produced according to the needs of society at that time. Whilst these ideas are repugnant to societies in which the freedom and rights of the individual are paramount, there are strong arguments for the exercise of limited forms of eugenic practice. In medicine, **genetic counselling** is becoming more acceptable as a means of informing couples with family histories of genetic abnormalities about the possible risks involved in having children. By applying the Hardy–Weinberg equation it is possible to calculate the number of carriers of metabolic disorders such as phenylketonuria or abnormalities of the blood, such as thalassaemia, sickle-cell anaemia or haemophilia. Known carriers can be advised as to the likelihood of marrying another carrier and the possibilities of producing offspring affected by the disorder. Such forms of preventive medicine offer advice rather than dictate policy. Any scientific advances which reduce suffering must receive sympathetic appreciation. The dangers of eugenics lie in their possible abuse.

Fig 27.6 *The phenotypes produced by double-cross hybridisation in maize. The maize crop on the right was produced by crossing the hybrids of the inbred strain (shown on the left).*

Parental genotypes (2n)	**FFgghhIIjj × FFGGHHiiJJ**
Meiosis	
Gametes (n)	(F g h I J) × (F GH i J)
Random fertilisation	
F₁ genotypes (2n)	**FfGgHhIiJj**
F₁ phenotypes	This carries a dominant allele for each gene

Fig 27.7 *A simple genetic explanation of increased vigour in F₁ hybrids.*

Fig 27.8 *Maize stalks of eight generations. The seven stalks on the right demonstrate loss of hybrid vigour as a result of inbreeding from the hybrid shown on the left. The last three generations show reduced loss of vigour as a result of their becoming homozygous. (Photograph by D. F. Jones, Connecticut Agricultural Experiment Station.)*

27.5   Natural selection

Natural selection, as postulated by Darwin and Wallace, represented a hypothesis based on historical evidence. For Darwin, the time span involved in the evolutionary change of a population was such that it could not be observed directly. Recent changes accompanying the industrial, technological and medical revolutions have produced such strong directional and disruptive pressures that we can now observe the results of dramatic changes in genotypic and phenotypic characteristics of populations within days. The introduction of antibiotics in the 1940s provided a strong selection pressure for strains of bacteria that have the genetic capability of being resistant to the effects of the antibiotics. Bacteria reproduce very rapidly, producing many generations and millions of individuals each day. Random mutation may produce a resistant organism in the population which will thrive in the absence of competition from other bacteria which have been eliminated by the antibiotic. As a result, new antibiotics have to be developed to eliminate the resistant bacteria, and so the cycle continues. Other examples of the effects of chemicals in producing selection pressure have been seen with DDT on body-lice and mosquitoes and the effect of the anticoagulant warfarin on rats. Following the development of resistant strains they spread very rapidly throughout the population.

Perhaps the classic example of evolutionary change is provided by the response of moth species to the directional selection pressure produced by the atmospheric pollution which accompanied the industrial revolution. Within the last 100 years darkened forms of about 80 species of moths have appeared in varying frequencies throughout the United Kingdom. This is a phenomenon known as **industrial melanism**. Up to 1848 all reported forms of the peppered moth (*Biston betularia*) appeared creamy-white with black dots and darkly shaded areas (fig 27.9). In 1848 a black form of the moth was recorded in Manchester, and by 1895, 98% of the peppered moth population in Manchester was black. This black 'melanic' form arose by a recurring random mutation, but its phenotypic appearance had a strong selective advantage in industrial areas for reasons put forward and tested by Dr H. B. D. Kettlewell.

The moths fly by night and during the day they rest on the trunks of trees. The normal form of the moth is extremely well camouflaged as its colouration merges with that of the lichens growing on the trunks. With the spread of the industrial revolution sulphur dioxide pollution from the burning of coal killed off the lichens growing on trees in industrial areas, exposing the darker bark, which was further darkened by soot deposits (fig 27.10).

In the 1950s Kettlewell released known numbers of marked light and dark forms into two areas, one a polluted area near Birmingham where 90% of the population was the black form, and the other an unpolluted area in Dorset where the dark form was rarely found. On recapturing the moths using a light trap he obtained the following results:

Fig 27.9 *Polymorphic forms of peppered moth,* Biston betularia. *(a) The normal form,* Biston betularia typica; *(b) the melanic form,* Biston betularia carbonaria. *(From E. B. Ford (1973)* Evolution studied by observation and experiment, Oxford Biology Readers, **55**, *Oxford University Press.)*

	Birmingham	Dorset
Percentage marked dark form	34.1	6.3
Percentage marked light form	15.9	12.5

Kettlewell demonstrated using cine-film that robins and thrushes feed on the moths. This is a form of natural selection known as **selective predation**, and it acts as a selection pressure on the distribution of the melanic and non-melanic forms.

The results show that the melanic form of the moth, *Biston betularia carbonaria*, has a selective advantage in industrial areas over the lighter form, *Biston betularia typica*, whereas the lighter form has the selective advantage in non-polluted areas.

Subsequent research has demonstrated that the colouration of the dark form is due to the presence of a dominant melanic allele. Fig 27.11 shows the distribution of the two forms in the British Isles in 1958.

The presence of melanic forms in non-industrial areas of the east of England is explained by the distribution of melanic forms by prevailing westerly winds. Since the introduction of the Clean Air Act in 1956 the proportion of non-melanic forms has increased to much higher levels again as the selection pressure on these forms has been reduced in industrial areas.

(a)

(b)

Fig 27.11 *The distribution of melanic and non-melanic forms of* Biston betularia *in the British Isles in 1958. (After H. B. D. Kettlewell (1978)* Heredity, **12**, *51–72.)*

Fig 27.10 *Melanic and non-melanic forms of* Biston betularia *on tree trunks in (a) an area near Birmingham, and (b) an area in Dorset. (Courtesy of Dr H. B. D. Kettlewell, Department of Zoology, University of Oxford.)*

27.5.1 Polymorphism

Polymorphism plays a significant role in the process of natural selection. It is defined as the existence of two or more forms of the same species within the same population, and can apply to biochemical, morphological and behavioural characteristics. There are two forms of polymorphism, **transient polymorphism,** and **balanced**, or **stable, polymorphism**.

Balanced polymorphism

This occurs when different forms coexist in the same population in a stable environment. It is illustrated most clearly by the existence of the two sexes in animals and plants. The genotypic frequencies of the various forms exhibit equilibrium since each form has a selective advantage of equal intensity. In humans, the existence of

the A, B, AB and O blood groups are examples of balanced polymorphism. Whilst the genotypic frequencies within different populations may vary, they remain constant from generation to generation within that population. This is because none of them have a selective advantage over the other. Statistics reveal that white men of blood group O have a greater life expectancy than those of other blood groups, but, interestingly, they also have an increased risk of developing a duodenal ulcer which may perforate and lead to death. Red–green colour blindness in humans is another example of polymorphism, as is the existence of workers, drones and queens in social insects and pin-eyed and thrum-eyed forms in primroses.

A classic quantitative study of balanced polymorphism was carried out by Cain, Currey and Shepherd on the common land snail *Cepaea nemoralis*. The shells of this species may be yellow (and appear green with the living snail inside), brown, or various shades including pale fawn, pink, orange and red. The lip of the shell may be dark brown, pink or white and the whole shell may have up to five dark brown bands following the contours of the shell (fig 27.12). Both colouration and banding pattern are determined genetically. The colours are determined by multiple alleles with brown being dominant to pink and both being dominant to yellow. Banding is recessive.

Studies have revealed that the snails are predated upon by thrushes which carry the snails to a nearby stone which they use as an 'anvil' to crack open the shell; the snail inside is then eaten. By studying the proportion of types of shell found near an anvil with those in the immediate

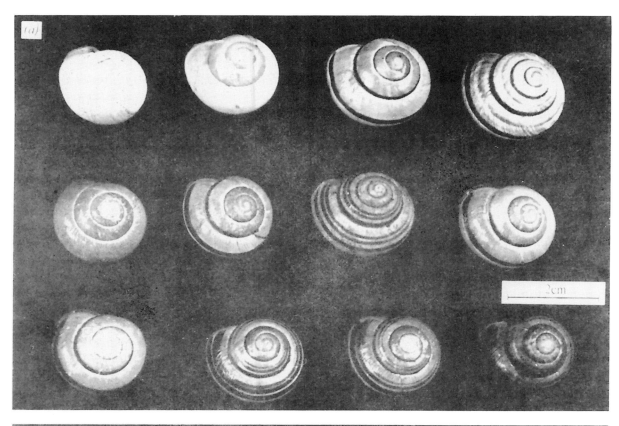

Fig 27.12 *Colour and banding pattern variation in the shells of* Cepaea nemoralis. *The extremes of colour and banding are shown as a progression from yellow unbanded (top left) to brown banded (bottom right). Photographs (a) and (b) show top and side views of the same shells. (After Tribe, Tallan & Erant (1978)* Basic Biology Course, *Book 12, Cambridge University Press.)*

Fig 27.13 *Unbanded shells of* Cepaea nemoralis *against a background of leaf litter. The shell on the extreme right is yellow, the shell at the top of the photograph is pink and the two shells on the left are brown. (After E. B. Ford (1973)* Evolution studied by observation and experiment, *Oxford Biology Reader,* **55**, *Oxford University Press.)*

habitat, Cain, Currey and Shepherd demonstrated that selective forces were at work within the population. In areas where the background was fairly uniform, such as grass and woodland litter, the yellow and brown unbanded shells had a selective advantage as fewer of these shells were found near the anvil (fig 27.13). In areas where the ground cover was tangled and mottled, as in rough pasture or hedgerows, the darker banded shells had a selective advantage. The forms suffering the greatest predation in any area were those which were visually conspicuous to the thrushes. A large population of polymorphic snails may include several areas with a range of backgrounds. Seasonal effects also produce changes in background colour and pattern. Although predation of conspicuous forms is continuous there is no overall selective advantage for any form, hence the numbers of each form within a population remain fairly constant from year to year.

The balance in numbers of each form may not be determined purely by colour and banding pattern. There is evidence to suggest that physiological effects may help to maintain the polymorphic equilibrium. In some areas where the soil is calcareous and dry and the background cover is light, the dominant forms are not always those with the least conspicuous colour and banding pattern. The genetic basis

for the polymorphism shown by *Cepaea* is thought to rely on the existence of a special form of gene linkage. The genes for colour and banding pattern are linked and form a **super-gene** which acts as a single genetic unit and is inherited as such. These genes determine characteristics which have such a selective advantage that they are maintained within the population. It is the variety of allelic forms of these genes maintained by the heterozygotes which forms the basis of the polymorphism. The added linkage of genes controlling certain physiological effects is also thought to contribute to the maintenance of the balanced polymorphism. The existence of a number of distinct inherited varieties coexisting in the same population at frequencies too great to be explained by recurrent mutations, as in the case of *Cepaea*, is called **genetic polymorphism**.

Transient polymorphism

This arises when different forms, or **morphs**, exist in a population undergoing a strong selection pressure. The frequency of the phenotypic appearance of each form is determined by the intensity of the selection pressure, such as the melanic and non-melanic forms of the peppered moth. Transient polymorphism usually applies in situations where one form is gradually being replaced by another.

27.6   The concept of species

A species represents the lowest taxonomic group which is capable of being defined with any degree of precision. It may be defined in a variety of ways and some of these are summarised in table 27.2.

Organisms belonging to a given species rarely exist naturally as a single large population. It is usual for a species to exist as small interbreeding populations, called **demes**, each with its own gene pool. These populations may occupy adjacent or widely dispersed geographical areas. Spatial separation of populations means that the species may encounter a variety of environmental conditions and degree of selection pressure. Mutation and selection within the isolated populations may produce the following degrees of phenotypic variation within the species.

27.6.1   Geographical races

Populations which are distributed over a wide geographical range or have occupied well-separated geographical habitats for a long period of time may show considerable phenotypic differences. These are usually based on adaptations to climatic factors. For example, the gypsy moth (*Hymantria dispar*) is distributed throughout the Japanese islands and eastern Asia. Over this range a variety of climatic conditions is encountered, ranging from subarctic to subtropical. Ten geographical races have been recognised which differ from each other with regard to the timing of hatching of their eggs. The northern races hatch later than the southern races. The phenotypic variations shown by the 10 races are thought to be the result of climatic factors producing changes in gene frequencies within their gene pools. The evidence that these variations are genetically controlled is shown by the fact that under identical environmental conditions the different races still hatch at different times.

Table 27.2 Alternative ways of defining a species.

Biological aspect	Definition
Breeding	A group of organisms capable of interbreeding and producing fertile offspring
Ecological	A group of organisms sharing the same ecological niche; no two species can share the same ecological niche
Genetic	A group of organisms showing close similarity in genetic karyotype
Evolutionary	A group of organisms sharing a unique collection of structural and functional characteristics

27.6.2   Ecological races (ecotypes)

Populations adapted to ecologically dissimilar habitats may occupy adjacent geographical areas; for example the plant species *Gilia achilleaefolia* occurs as two races along the coast of California. One race, the 'sun' race, is found on exposed southerly facing grassy slopes, whilst the 'shade' race is found in shaded oak woodlands and redwood groves. These races differ in the size of their petals, a characteristic which is determined genetically.

27.6.3   Clines

A species exhibiting a gradual change in phenotypic characteristics throughout its geographical range is referred to as a **cline**. More than one cline may be exhibited by a species and they may run in opposite directions as shown by fig 27.14.

Species exhibiting marked phenotypic variation within a population according to their degree of geographical isolation are known as **polytypic species**. One classic form of a polytypic species is illustrated by gulls belonging to the genus *Larus* (section 27.8.4).

All cases of phenotypic variation described above represent varying degrees of genetic dissimilarity which may interfere with the breeding potential of members of the populations if brought together.

27.7   Speciation

This is the process by which one or more species arise from previously existing species. A single species may give rise to new species (**intraspecific speciation**), or, as is common in many flowering plants, two different species may give rise to a new species (**interspecific hybridisation**). If intraspecific speciation occurs whilst the populations are separated it is termed **allopatric speciation**. If the process occurs whilst the populations are occupying the same geographical area it is called **sympatric speciation**.

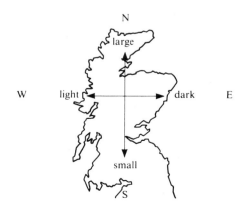

Fig 27.14   *Phenotypic variation in size and fur colour shown by the wood mouse* (Apodemus) *in Scotland.*

27.8   Intraspecific speciation

There are several factors involved in intraspecific speciation, but in all cases gene flow within populations must be interrupted. As a result of this each subpopulation becomes genetically isolated. Changes in allele and genotype frequencies within the populations, as a result of the effects of natural selection on the range of phenotypes produced by mutation and sexual recombination, lead to the formation of races and subspecies. If the genetic isolation persists over a prolonged period of time and the subspecies then come together to occupy the same area they may or may not interbreed. If the breeding is successful they may still be considered to belong to the same species. If the breeding is unsuccessful, then speciation has occurred and the subspecies may now be considered to be a separate species. This is the way in which it is believed evolutionary change can be brought about.

An initial factor in the process of speciation may be the reduction in the intensity of selection pressure within the population. This may lead to increased intraspecific variability. These new phenotypes may enable the population to increase its geographical range if the phenotypes show adaptations to environmental conditions found at the extremes of the range. Providing there is no reduction in gene flow throughout the population, the species, whilst exhibiting the localised phenotypic variation (ecotypes), will share the same gene pool and continue to exist as a single species. This is the situation found in a cline.

Speciation will only occur as a result of the formation of barriers which lead to reproductive isolation between members of the population. Reproductive isolation is brought about by some form of what the geneticist Theodosius Dobzhansky called **isolating mechanisms**.

27.8.1   Isolating mechanisms

An isolating mechanism is a means of producing and maintaining reproductive isolation within a population. This can be brought about by mechanisms acting before or after fertilisation. Dobzhansky suggested a classification of isolating mechanisms which has been modified and is shown in table 27.3.

27.8.2   Allopatric speciation

Allopatric (*allos*, other; *patria*, native land) speciation is characterised by the occurrence, at some stage, of spatial separation. Geographical barriers such as mountain ranges, seas or rivers, or habitat preferences, may produce a barrier to gene flow because of spatial separation. This inability of organisms or their gametes to meet leads to reproductive isolation. Adaptations to new conditions or random genetic drift in small populations lead to changes in

Table 27.3 Isolating mechanisms (after Dobzhansky).

Prezygotic mechanisms (barriers to the formation of hybrids)

Seasonal isolation	Occurs where two species mate or flower at different times of the year; for example in California *Pinus radiata* flowers in February whereas *Pinus attenuata* flowers in April
Ecological isolation	Occurs where two species inhabit similar regions but have different habitat preferences; for example *Viola arvensis* grows on calcareous soils whereas *Viola tricolor* prefers acid soils
Behavioural isolation	Occurs where animals exhibit courtship patterns, mating only results if the courtship display by one sex results in acceptance by the other sex; for example certain fish, bird and insect species
Mechanical isolation	Occurs in animals where differences in genitalia prevent successful copulation and in plants where related species of flowers are pollinated by different animals

Postzygotic mechanisms (barriers affecting hybrids)

Hybrid inviability	Hybrids are produced but fail to develop to maturity; for example hybrids formed between northern and southern races of the leopard frog (*Rana pipiens*) in North America
Hybrid sterility	Hybrids fail to produce functional gametes; for example the mule ($2n = 63$) results from the cross between the horse (*Equus equus*, $2n = 60$) and the ass (*Equus hemionus*, $2n = 66$)
Hybrid breakdown	F_1 hybrids are fertile but the F_2 generation and backcrosses between F_1 hybrids and parental stocks fail to develop or are infertile, for example hybrids formed between species of cotton (genus *Gossypium*)

allele and genotype frequencies. Prolonged separation of populations may result in them becoming genetically isolated even if brought together. In this way new species may arise. For example, the variety and distribution of the finch species belonging to the family Geospizidae on the islands of the Galapagos archipelago are thought to be the result of allopatric speciation.

David Lack suggested that an original stock of finches reached the Galapagos Islands from the mainland of South America and, in the absence of competition from endemic species (representing relaxed selection pressure), adaptive radiation occurred to produce a variety of species adapted to particular ecological niches. The various species are believed to have evolved in geographical isolation to the point that when dispersal brought them together on certain islands they were able to coexist as separate species.

27.8.3 Sympatric speciation

Genetic differences may accumulate allopatrically in populations which have been geographically isolated for a much shorter period of time. If these populations are brought together, hybrids may form where these overlap. For example, both the carrion crow (*Corvus corone*) and the hooded crow (*Corvus corone cornix*) are found in the British Isles. The carrion crow is completely black and is common in England and southern Scotland. The hooded crow is black with a grey back and belly and is found in the north of Scotland. Hybrids formed from the mating of carrion and hooded crows occupying a narrow region extending across central Scotland (fig 27.15). These hybrids have reduced fertility and serve as an efficient reproductive barrier to gene flow between the populations of the carrion and hooded crows.

In time, selection against cross-breeding may occur, leading to speciation. Since such speciation occurs finally in the same geographical area, this is called **sympatric** (*sym*, together; *patria*, native land) **speciation**.

Sympatric speciation does not involve geographical separation of populations at the time at which genetic isolation occurs. It requires the development of some form of reproductive isolating mechanism which has arisen by selection within a geographically confined area. This may be structural, physiological, behavioural or genetic.

Sympatric speciation is more commonly thought of as providing an explanatory mechanism of how closely related species, which probably arose from a common ancestor by temporary isolation, can coexist as separate species within the same geographical area. For example, in the Galapagos archipelago the finch *Camarhynchus pauper* is found only on Charles Island, where it coexists with a related form *C. psittacula* which is widely distributed throughout the

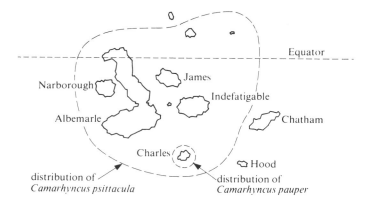

Fig 27.16 *The Galapagos Islands and the distribution of two species of finch illustrating coexistence following allopatric speciation.*

central islands (fig 27.16). The finch species appear to choose their mates on the basis of beak size. The range of beak sizes of *C. pauper* on Charles Island and *C. psittacula* on Albemarle Island are approximately equal, but on Charles Island *C. psittacula* has a longer beak. This difference is significant enough to ensure that the two species, which feed on different foods, appear unattractive to each other during the breeding season. In this way the species remain distinct and are able to coexist.

27.8.4 Ring species

This is a special form of sympatric speciation which occurs at the point where two populations at the extremes of a cline meet up and inhabit the same area, thus 'closing' the ring. For example, gulls of the genus *Larus* form a continuous population between latitudes 50–80 °N, encircling the North Pole. A ring of ten recognisable races or subspecies exist which principally differ in size and in the colour of their legs, backs and wings. Gene flow occurs freely between all races except at the point where the 'ends of the ring' meet at the British Isles. Here, at the extremes of the geographical range, the gulls behave as distinct species, that is the herring gull (*Larus argentatus*) and the lesser black-backed gull (*L. fuscus*). These have a different appearance, different tone of call, different migratory patterns and rarely interbreed. Selection against cross-breeding is said to occur sympatrically.

Sympatric speciation without geographical isolation in sexually reproducing species is unlikely. However, in asexually reproducing organisms, including vegetatively propagated angiosperms, a single mutant so different from its parent population as to be genetically isolated could give rise to a new species sympatrically. An example is polyploidy in *Spartina* (section 24.9.2).

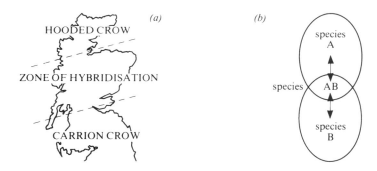

Fig 27.15 *Hybrid barrier as a means of preventing gene flow between two populations. The maintenance of the two crow species is shown to be due to the existence of a zone of hybridisation extending across Scotland as shown in (a). The existence of hybrid barriers between adjacent populations is common and functions as follows. Where the geographical ranges of A and B overlap, mating produces a hybrid with lowered fertility. A will interbreed freely with AB and AB with B but the existence of AB prevents free interbreeding of A and B populations.*

27.3 Ten subspecies of the *Larus argentatus–fuscus* population form a continuous ring extending from the British Isles through Scandinavia, Russia, Siberia, across the Bering Straits, through Alaska and Canada and back to the British Isles. If the subspecies inhabiting the Bering Straits and Alaska was eliminated what predicted effects might this have on the population?

27.9   Interspecific hybridisation

This is a form of sympatric speciation which occurs when a new species is produced by the crossing of individuals from two unrelated species. Fertile hybrids usually appear only in cases of interspecific hybridisation as a result of a form of chromosome mutation known as **allopolyploidy** (section 24.9.2). An example of this was demonstrated by Kapechenko in the case of hybrids formed between the cabbage and the radish. The genetic changes involved in this hybridisation are shown in fig 27.17.

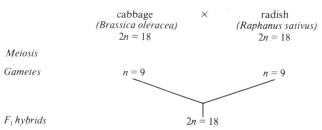

During meiosis in the F_1 hybrids chromosomes from each parent cannot pair together to form homologous chromosomes. The F_1 hybrids are therefore sterile. Occasionally non-disjunction of the F_1 hybrids produces gametes with the diploid set of chromosomes ($2n = 18$).

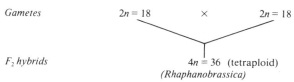

The F_2 hybrids are fertile. Homologous pairing can occur in meiosis as two sets of parental chromosomes are present. Diploid gametes ($2n = 18$), are produced which possess 9 chromosomes from the parental cabbage and 9 chromosomes from the parental radish.

Fig 27.17 *Stages involved in the hybridisation of the cabbage and the radish.*

Answers and discussion

Chapter 13

13.1 The external solution. Remember that the cell wall is freely permeable to solutions (fig 13.2).

13.2 Zero. The protoplast is not exerting pressure against the cell wall.

13.3 Prokaryotes, fungi and some protoctists such as algae. These organisms are also protected against bursting in solutions with higher water potential, or in pure water.

13.4 (*a*) Cell B to (*b*) From cell B to A

(*c*) Cell A at equilibrium: $\psi_P = \psi - \psi_s$
$$= -1000\,\text{kPA} - -2000\,\text{kPa}$$
$$= 1000\,\text{kPA}$$
Cell B at equilibrium: $\psi_P = \psi - \psi_s$
$$= -1000\,\text{kPa} - -1400\,\text{kPa}$$
$$= 400\,\text{kPa}$$

13.5 $-1060\,\text{kPa}$. For intermediate values between those shown in table 13.4, plot a graph of molarity of sucrose solution against solute potential.

13.6 Average ψ_s of beetroot cells is about $-1400\,\text{kPa}$.

13.7 ψ beetroot is about $-940\,\text{kPa}$.

13.8 A more accurate result can be obtained by taking the mean value of two or more replicates. Some indication of the variation that can be expected between strips is given in table 13.6.

13.9 To prevent evaporation of water, with subsequent increase in concentration of sucrose solutions, and possible drying up of beetroot strips.

13.10 $\psi_P = \psi - \psi_s$
$$= -950\,\text{kPa} - -1400\,\text{kPa}$$
$$= 450\,\text{kPa}.$$
Note that different beetroots may have different values of ψ_s and ψ.

13.11 (*a*) The cells of the intact scape are turgid and their walls are therefore tending to expand as pressure potential increases. The thick walls of the epidermal cells are less capable of stretching than the thin walls of the cortex cells and therefore exert a restraining influence on expansion of the cortical cells. The latter are under compression. Cutting the epidermis removes the restraint, each cortical cell expands slightly and there is an overall increase in volume of the cortex which causes the strip to curve outwards.

(*b*) Distilled water has a higher water potential than the scape cells. Water therefore enters the tissue from the distilled water by osmosis, inflating the cortical cells even further and causing outward curvature.

(*c*) The concentrated sucrose solution has a lower water potential than the scape cells. Water therefore leaves the tissue by osmosis, causing greater shrinkage of the cortical cells than the epidermal cells and a bending inwards of the tissue.

(*d*) The dilute sucrose solution must have the same water potential as the scape cells. There is therefore no net gain or loss of water by solution or tissue.

(*e*) Water potential. An outline of the experiment is as follows.
Prepare a dilution series of sucrose solutions from 1 M to distilled water (such as distilled water, 0.2 M, 0.4 M, 0.6 M, 0.8 M and 1.0 M). The typical curvature of freshly cut dandelion scapes

should be recorded by drawing and then two pieces of scape placed in each solution in separate labelled petri dishes (two pieces are preferred so that an average can be obtained). Observe and accurately record curvatures (such as by drawing) after equilibrium has been reached (about 30 min). The solution which induces no change in curvature has the same ψ as the average dandelion scape cell immediately after the cut was made.

13.12 Outlines of two suitable experiments are as follows.
Effect of temperature. Cut cubes of fresh beetroot, wash to remove the red pigment from broken cells, and place in beakers of water at different temperatures over a range, say, from 20–100°C. The appearance of red pigment in the water would indicate destruction of the partial permeability of the tonoplast (vacuole membrane) and cell surface membrane, attended by diffusion of the pigment from the cell sap to the water. The time taken for the appearance of a standard amount of pigment would give an indication of the rapidity of breakdown of membrane structure. The colour could be measured in a colorimeter or simply by eye.
Effect of ethanol. Method as above, using a range of ethanol concentrations instead of a range of temperatures.

13.13 (*a*) Leaves contain a very large number of stomata for gaseous exchange and there is little resistance to movement of water vapour through these pores.
(*b*) Leaves have a large surface area (for trapping sunlight and exchanging gases). The greater the surface area, the greater will be the loss of water by transpiration.

13.14 Light intensity increases as the Sun rises, reaching a maximum at midday when the Sun attains its highest point in the sky. Air temperature rises similarly, but it takes about two hours for the heating effect of the Sun to be reflected in a rise in air temperature (mainly because the soil has to heat up first and then radiate heat to the air). The initial rise in transpiration rate between 3 a.m. and 6 a.m., before air temperature rises is due to opening of the stomata in the light. From 6 a.m. onwards transpiration rate is closely correlated with temperature for reasons explained in the text. It is not closely correlated with light intensity, presumably because the stomata are now fully open and any further increase in light intensity has no effect.

During the afternoon, light intensity decreases as the Sun sinks, followed by a drop in temperature with the same lag of about two hours. Transpiration rate decreases both as a result of decreasing temperature and decreasing light intensity, but it is much more closely correlated with a decrease in the latter, probably because this causes stomatal closure. By about 7.30 p.m. it is dark and the stomata are probably closed. Any remaining transpiration is probably cuticular and still influenced by temperature.

13.15 (*a*) Hollow cylinder
(*b*) Solid rod/cylinder providing support
(*c*) Solid rod/cylinder providing support
(*d*) Solid cylinder

13.16 (1) Long tubes formed by fusion of neighbouring cells, with breakdown of cross-walls between them.

(2) No living contents, so less resistance to flow.

(3) Tubes are rigid so do not collapse.

(4) Fine tubes are necessary to prevent water columns from collapsing.

13.17 ψ soil solution > root hair cell > cell C > cell B > cell A > xylem sap

13.18 (*a*) There is a rapid initial uptake of potassium (K^+) at both temperatures (during the first 10–20 min). After 20 min there is a continuous gradual uptake of K^+ at 25 °C but no further uptake at 0 °C. Uptake at 25 °C is inhibited by KCN.

(*b*) The inhibition by KCN indicates that it is dependent on respiration. The uptake at this time is therefore probably by active transport across cell surface membranes into cells.

(*c*) To flush out any existing K^+ ions from the root.

13.19 Rise in respiratory rate is accompanied by a rise in KCl uptake. Once KCl is available, it is therefore apparently taken up by active transport, the energy being supplied by an increased respiratory rate.

13.20 KCN inhibits respiration and therefore inhibits active transport of KCl into the carrot discs.

13.21 Much of the phosphate inside the root was in the apoplast and could therefore diffuse out to the water outside, reversing passive uptake.

13.22 No. The endodermis is a barrier to movement of water and solutes through the apoplast pathway (see section 13.5.2).

13.23 Autoradiography reveals the location of the ion in thin sections. Treat one plant with an inhibitor of active transport (such as low temperature or KCN) and have an untreated control plant: allow them both to take up the radioactive ion. In the treated plant ions will move only passively by way of the cell walls. Autoradiography should show that the radioactive ion tends to penetrate the root only as far as the endodermis, whereas the control should show much greater movement of ions to the tissue inside the endodermis.

13.24 2500 sieve plates per metre:

$$1 \text{ m} = 10^6 \, \mu\text{m}.$$
$$400 \, \mu\text{m} = 4 \times 10^2 \, \mu\text{m}$$
$$10^6/(4 \times 10^2) = 10^4/4 = 2500$$

Chapter 14

14.1 The majority of the pellet consists of red blood cells.

14.2 Solutes, such as Na^+ and K^+ ions, products of digestion etc., plasma proteins, gases (O_2 in red blood cells, CO_2 in rbcs and plasma).

14.3 The oxygenated blood of the systemic circulation reaches the body capillaries at a much higher pressure. This is essential for the efficient function of organs and tissue fluid formation and permits a high metabolic rate and a high body temperature to be maintained. It is essential that a much lower pressure is developed in the pulmonary artery in order to prevent rupture of the delicate pulmonary capillaries.

14.4 Local vasodilation in the wounded area enables more blood carrying oxygen and nutrients to arrive there and speed up the process of repair and replacement. Increased body blood pressure prepares the body of the animal to respond to any further stress more readily and efficiently.

14.5 **Before the race.** Adrenaline is secreted in anticipation of the race. This stimulates vasoconstriction throughout the body in all but the most vital organs. Hence blood pressure is raised. Heart rate is also increased. (Extra blood is also passed to the general circulation from the spleen.)

During the race. Increased metabolic activity takes place during the race, especially in the skeletal muscles. Increased carbon dioxide levels in these regions promote local vasodilation. The increased body temperature further enhances vasodilation. However the general increase in carbon dioxide level in blood is noted by the chemoreceptors of the aorta and carotid bodies which in turn stimulate the vasomotor centre to promote vasoconstriction. This increases blood pressure and therefore speeds up blood flow. Heart rate is also increased and a more complete emptying of the ventricles occurs. Towards the end of the race the muscles will be respiring anaerobically and producing lactic acid (section 9.3.8). Strong contractions of the muscles squeeze the veins and promote faster venous return to the heart.

Recovery. The oxygen debt is paid off and lactic acid removed from the blood system. Tissues subside in activity and the carbon dioxide level decreases. Consequently there is a return to normal of heartbeat and blood pressure.

14.6 (*a*) Increased metabolic activity increases the temperature in a part of the body. This produces a reduction in the affinity of oxygen for haemoglobin and an increased dissociation of oxygen. Thus the dissociation curve is shifted to the right. This is physiologically advantageous as more oxygen is delivered to the active regions.

(*b*) Small mammals possess a much higher metabolic rate than humans and therefore it is appropriate that oxygen should be released much more readily.

14.7 The position of the curve of the fetus relative to that of its mother means that its blood has a greater affinity for oxygen than the maternal blood. This has to be so, as the fetus must obtain all of its oxygen from its mother's blood at the placenta. So, at any given partial pressure of oxygen the fetal blood will take up oxygen from the maternal blood and will always be more saturated with oxygen than the maternal blood. This is just as true for the human fetus.

14.8 This means that the blood has a high affinity for oxygen and that it is able to combine with it at the low oxygen tensions experienced at high altitude. This is another good example of physiological adaptation.

14.9 (1) Carboxyhaemoglobin reaches the lungs and takes up oxygen and forms oxyhaemoglobin.

(2) Oxyhaemoglobin has a lower affinity for H^+ ions than haemoglobin and releases H^+ ions.

(3) H^+ ions combine with hydrogencarbonate ions in the red blood cell so forming carbonic acid.

(4) Carbonic acid dissociates into carbon dioxide and water, catalysed by the enzyme carbonic anhydrase.

(5) As a result of the loss of hydrogencarbonate ions from the red blood cell, further hydrogencarbonate ions diffuse into the red blood cell from the plasma.

(6) More carbonic acid is formed which dissociates into more carbon dioxide and water.

(7) Carbon dioxide diffuses out of the red blood cell and is eventually excreted from the body via the lungs.

Chapter 15

15.1 Some suggestions are:
- reason for test;
- recall interval;
- relevant age group;
- particular groups at risk (older women and those who have had several sexual partners are more at risk);
- cost (free);
- location of cervix;

- test procedure (internal examination involved, with possibility of slight discomfort or pain/embarrassment);
- incidence of positive results;
- treatment of test is positive;
- how to obtain further information.

15.2 Some suggestions are:
- male doctor;
- knowing the GP;
- embarrassment;
- fear of pain/discomfort;
- fear of result.

Chapter 16

16.1 Locomotion is primarily associated with the need to search for food (and is closely associated with the development of a nervous system). Plants are autotrophic, that is make their own organic requirements, so do not need to search for food.

16.2 See table 16.2(ans).

16.3 Various methods are possible. A simple experiment is illustrated in fig 16.3(ans).

16.4 (a) The bacteria are aerobic and positively aerotactic. Therefore they swim towards oxygen along a gradient from low oxygen concentration to high oxygen concentration. The highest oxygen concentrations are around the edges of the cover-slip, where

Table 16.2(ans).

Example	Advantage
Shoots and coleoptiles positively phototropic	Leaves exposed to the light which is the source of energy for photosynthesis
Roots negatively phototropic	Exposed roots more likely to grow towards soil or equivalent suitable substrate
Shoots and coleoptiles negatively geotropic	Shoots of germinating seeds will grow upwards through soil towards light
Roots positively geotropic	Roots penetrate soil
Rhizomes, runners diageotropic	Helps plants colonise new areas of soil
Dicotyledonous leaves diageotropic	Flat surface of leaf will gain maximum exposure to sunlight (at right-angles to incident radiation)
Lateral roots plagiogeotropic	Large volume of soil exploited and the arrangement of roots provide support (similar to guy-ropes supporting a tent)
Branches plagiogeotropic	Larger volume of space occupied for exploitation of light
Hyphae positively chemotropic	Grow towards food
Pollen tubes positively chemotropic	Grow towards ovule, where fertilisation takes place
Roots and pollen tubes positively hydrotropic	Water essential for all living processes
Tendrils positively haptotropic	Essential for their function of support
Sundew tentacles positively haptotropic	Enables plants to imprison insects which walk over the tentacles
Pollen tubes negatively aerotropic	Another mechanism ensuring that initial growth of the pollen tube is towards the issue of the style (away from air)

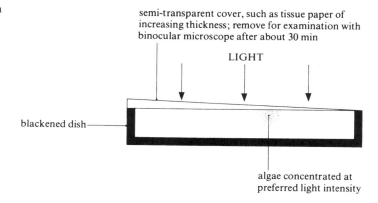

Fig 16.3(ans) *Experiment to demonstrate preferred light intensity of* Euglena *or* Chlamydomonas.

oxygen is diffusing into the water from the atmosphere, and adjacent to the algal filament where oxygen is being released as a waste product of photosynthesis.

(b) Leave the slide in the dark for about 30 minutes and re-examine. All the bacteria should now be around the edges of the cover-slip because the alga cannot photosynthesise in the dark.

16.5 (a) The stimulus of light is detected by the coleoptile tip. Some kind of signal is transmitted from the tip (the receptor) to the region behind the tip (the effector).

(b) Experiment c was a check on the result from experiment b which could have been the result of injury to the coleoptile.

16.6 Further evidence of the existence of a signal, presumably a chemical transmitter substance (hormone), has been obtained. It cannot pass through an impermeable barrier. It moves mainly down the shaded side of the coleoptile. In experiment b mica prevented this movement. Light therefore either inhibits production of the hormone, causes its inactivation (stimulates its breakdown) or causes it to be redistributed laterally.

16.7 See fig 16.7(ans).

16.8 The coleoptile tip produces a chemical which diffuses into the agar. It can stimulate growth in the region behind the tip and restores normal growth (experiment a). There is little or no lateral transmission of the chemical (experiment b) under conditions of uniform illumination or darkness.

16.9 The coleoptile would have grown to the left.

16.10 A 100 ppm   B 10 ppm   C 1 ppm   D 0.1 ppm   E 0.01 ppm   F zero

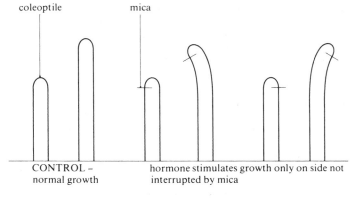

Fig 16.7(ans) *Repetition of Boysen-Jensen's experiments in uniform light. Three experiments are shown; treatment left, result right, in each case.*

16.11 See section 17.5.4.

16.12 (*a*) Abscisic acid can be transported away from root tips, undergo lateral transport in root tissues in response to gravity, and inhibit growth.

(*b*) IAA is probably not involved in the geotropic response of maize since it is apparently not transported away from the root tip.

16.13 (*a*) Starch

(*b*) Maltose

(*c*) Maltase

(*d*) The main food reserve of cereal seeds is starch, stored in the endosperm.

16.14 Storage proteins are digested (hydrolysed) to provide amino acids, the basic units of proteins. These are reassembled to produce enzymes (which are always proteins), such as α-amylase, which are then used to digest the food stores of the endosperm.

16.15 The amylase activity could be associated with micro-organisms present on the fingers or with saliva which has been transferred from mouth to fingers. Note the importance, therefore, of not handling the seeds after their surface sterilisation in this kind of experiment.

16.16 Incubate seeds with radioactive (^{14}C-labelled) amino acids. This results in production of labelled amylases. Alternatively, incubation of seeds with inhibitors of protein synthesis (such as cycloheximide) prevents synthesis of amylase and no amylase activity is then recorded.

16.17 Dissection of the seeds into aleurone and non-aleurone portions should show that the initial appearance of labelled amylase is in the aleurone layer. Alternatively, separate incubation of endosperm with aleurone layers and endosperm without aleurone layer, with starch–gibberellin agar would result in amylase production only in the former (difficult to do in practice).

16.18 One of the best bioassays for gibberellin (quick, reliable and sensitive) involves incubating embryo halves of barley grains with the substance being assayed. After two days the amount of reducing sugar present is proportional to the amount of gibberellin present.

16.19 (*a*) The amino acid is retained by the young leaf and does not move very far from the point of application. In the old leaf some of it is exported via the veins and midrib.

(*b*) The young leaf would use the amino acid to make protein in growth. The old leaf is no longer growing and so is exporting nutrients to other parts of the plant such as roots and young leaves.

(*c*) Amino acids are retained by, or move towards, tissues treated with kinetin. (The reasons for this are unknown, but presumably connected with the maintenance or stimulation of normal cell activity by kinetin.)

16.20 One solution would be to take a plant where applied gibberellin is known to affect stem growth and remove its source of auxin by removing the shoot apex. Gibberellin should then prove ineffective. It is important to demonstrate that the response can be restored by addition of auxin (such as IAA in lanolin paste) as injury might be the reason for lack of response to gibberellins, or another chemical might be involved. Such experiments do demonstrate a total dependence on auxin.

16.21 (*a*) Auxin (IAA)

(*b*) See fig 16.21(ans).

16.22 Small leaves offer less resistance to passage through the soil (leaves of grasses remain inside the coleoptile). The hooked plumule of dicotyledonous plants protects the delicate apical meristem from soil particles. Elongated internodes ensure the maximum chance of reaching light.

16.23 See chapter 7.

16.24 The graph is shown in fig 16.24(ans).

The opposite effects of red and far-red light are demonstrated. Red light exposure of 30 s, at the intensity used in the experiment, completely nullifies the inductive effect of a long night. The effectiveness of red light increases with time of exposure up to 30 s. The red light is reversed by far-red light, although a longer exposure (50 s) was needed to completely reverse the effect. These results suggest that phytochrome is the photoreceptor involved.

16.25 There are several possible methods. Fig 16.25(ans) illustrates one simple solution. Boxes represent light-proof covers, used as appropriate to give short days.

16.26 Lateral bud inhibition or apical dominance is largely controlled by auxins. (See apical dominance, section 16.3.3.)

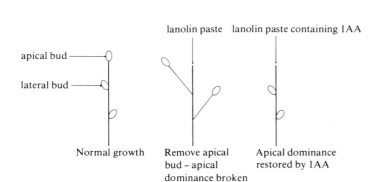

Fig 16.21(ans) *Experiment to show the role of IAA in apical dominance.*

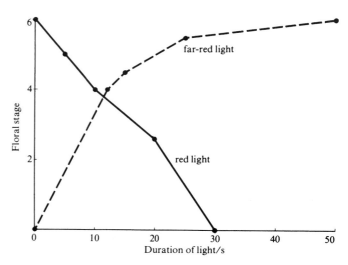

Fig 16.24(ans) *Effects of red light and red/far-red light interruption of long night on flowering of cocklebur.*

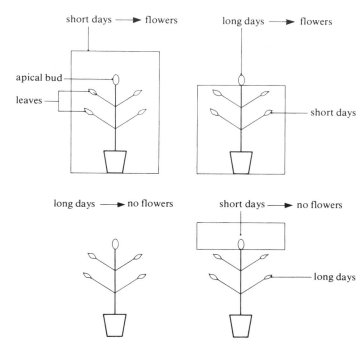

Fig 16.25(ans) *Experiment to determine whether leaves or floral apex are sensitive to the photoperiod that stimulates flowering.*

Chapter 17

17.1 (*a*) A steep concentration gradient of Na^+ ions exists between the outside and inside of the axon and Na^+ ions rapidly diffuse down this gradient.

(*b*) The relatively high negative potential within the axon encourages the inward movement of the positively charged Na^+ ions.

17.2 If the outflow of positive K^+ ions from the axon balanced the inflow of positive Na^+ ions into the axon there would be no change, or perhaps only a slight decrease, in the resting potential. Such a slight change would be insufficient to reach the threshold required to produce an action potential.

17.3 (*a*) Normal sea water

(*b*) One-half sea water

(*c*) One-third sea water

The size of the membrane potential spikes is determined by the number of Na^+ ions entering the axon from the extracellular fluid. The solutions in which (*a*), (*b*) and (*c*) were recorded contained progressively fewer Na^+ ions.

17.4 The resistance of axoplasm decreases with increasing diameter of the axon. As the resistance decreases, the length of the membrane influenced by the local circuit increases and this lengthens the distance between adjacent depolarisations and leads to an increase in conduction velocity.

17.5 The frog is a cold-blooded (poikilothermic) organism, active within the temperature range 4–25°C, whereas the cat, being warm-blooded (homeothermic), maintains a constant temperature of 35 °C. This increase in temperature increases the speed of conduction of the nerve impulses by a factor of three.

17.6 The path taken by light as it passes through the eye is as follows:
conjunctiva $\longrightarrow$ cornea $\longrightarrow$ aqueous humour $\longrightarrow$ lens $\longrightarrow$ vitreous humour $\longrightarrow$ retina.

17.7 Light from an object falling onto several rods which are linked to the brain by separate neurones may not have sufficient energy to produce a propagated action potential in each neurone and therefore the light may not be detected. If, however, the same light falls on three rods which are linked to the same neurone supplying the brain, the separate generator potentials produced by the rods would summate and produce an action potential which would be registered in the brain as light.

17.8 When looking directly at an object, light reflected from it passes along the optical axis of the eye and strikes the retina at the fovea which contains cones only. During daylight this will produce a detailed image in the brain due to the high light intensity activating the cones. At night the light intensity would be too low to activate the cones. By looking slightly to one side of the object the reflected light from it will not strike the fovea but a point on the retina to the side of it where there are rods. At night these will be activated by the low light intensity and an image will be produced in the brain.

17.9 The object will appear yellow. Each retina will distinguish one colour only. In one eye, green cones will be stimulated by light of 530 nm and, in the other, red cones will be stimulated by light of 620 nm. Mixing will occur in the brain due to equal stimulation by these colours and the object will appear to be the colour of the average of the combined wavelengths, that is $\frac{530 + 620}{2}$ nm = 575 nm, which corresponds to yellow.

Note that mixing light does not produce the same results as mixing pigments like paints. Blue and yellow light does not, for example, produce the sensation of green (you can work out from table 17.8 what it does produce). Failure to realise this held up theories on colour vision for a long time.

Chapter 18

18.1 (*a*) It allows free movement of the rib cage of the mammal.

(*b*) The flexible suspension enables the animal to withstand the shock sustained by the forelimbs when it lands at the end of a jump.

(*c*) The forelimbs possess a wide range of movement, which is useful for such activities as climbing, cleaning the face, manipulating food and digging.

18.2 A band remains the same length.

18.3 It allows greater movement of Ca^{2+} ions needed for muscle contraction.

18.4 Synchronous. This type of muscle has much more sarcoplasmic reticulum because it requires more nervous impulses to operate it, and each nerve impulse depends on the release of Ca^{2+} ions by the sarcoplasmic reticulum.

18.5 (*a*) Streamlined shape.

(*b*) Smooth surface
  – scales overlap each other in an appropriate direction.
  – mucus/oily covering thus reducing friction.

(*c*) Various types of fin to promote forward propulsion and stability during swimming.

(*d*) Highly muscular body.

(*e*) Swim bladder in bony fishes.

(*f*) Highly coordinated neuromuscular activity with segmental muscle blocks along the back.

18.6 This position increases the effective length of their limbs. Consequently each stride taken is longer and so propels the body forward over a greater distance. Assuming that the speed of movement of the limbs remains the same, the sprinter will therefore move forward at a faster pace.

Chapter 19

19.1 Rate of transpiration gets lower as atmospheric humidity increases. When humidity is high, the rate of transpiration is low and the plant cannot lose heat and reduce its temperature.

19.2 4 dm^3 sweat lost per day = 4000 cm^3
2.45 kJ of energy is lost per cm^3 of sweat.
Therefore energy lost = 4000 × 2.45 = 9800 kJ
9800/50 000 × 100 = 19.6%

19.3 During this period the subject was allowed to equilibrate with his surroundings.

19.4 There is a direct relationship between these two variables which suggests that the rate of sweating is controlled by activity of the hypothalamus.

19.5 The direct relationship between skin temperature and evaporation during the first 20 min established that an equilibrium exists between the two. As the evaporation rate falls, due to the action of the hypothalamus in response to the ingestion of iced water, latent heat of evaporation is not being lost from the skin and this accounts for the observed rise in skin temperature.

19.6 'Fever' is due to the resetting of the 'thermostat' at a higher temperature. Until the core temperature rises to that temperature, the 'normal' body temperature is too low and the body reacts as if it has been cooled. In these conditions the body responds by shivering and the body continues to *feel* cold until the core temperature reaches the temperature of the thermostat in the hypothalamus.

Chapter 20

20.1 Hepatic vein, posterior vena cava, right atrium of heart, right ventricle, pulmonary artery, lungs, pulmonary vein, left atrium of heart, left ventricle, dorsal aorta, renal artery, kidney.

20.2 Protein has 'disappeared' between blood and renal capsule. This is because these molecules are too large to be filtered into the capsule. All the other solutes pass through into the renal capsule in solution and their concentration remains unaffected.

20.3 80%. 20% remains in the tubule.

20.4 All the glucose was reabsorbed. Na$^+$ stayed at d, therefore 80% was reabsorbed (1/5 or 20% remains).

20.5 Flow rate index changed from 20 to 1. Therefore 19/20 or 95% of the remaining was reabsorbed. Therefore concentration of solutes should have increased by a factor of 20. Na$^+$ concentration increased from d to $2d$, $20d - 2d = 18/20$ reabsorbed = 90% remaining Na$^+$ reabsorbed. Urea concentration increased from $3c$ to $60c$ which is a 20-fold increase, therefore there was no change in the *amount* of urea in the nephron.

20.6 99% of water was reabsorbed (FRI changed from 100 to 1). 98% of the Na$^+$ was reabsorbed.

Chapter 21

21.1 (*a*) If the parent plants that produced the pollen grains can be identified, then certain deductions can be made about the climate that such plants would have grown in.
(*b*) Any human interference with the natural vegetation would be reflected in the pollen record. For example, pollen of weed species and agricultural plants, such as wheat, would indicate clearance of natural vegetation for agriculture. Similarly, absence of pollen from trees in some areas would indicate forest clearance.

21.2 If a plant species is dioecious, half of its individuals do not produce seeds. Also, there is a large wastage of pollen which is a disadvantage in terms of material and energy resources.

21.3 Separate sexes is more economical in animals than in plants because the males and females can move about. There is therefore less wastage of gametes.

21.4 (50%). Remembering that the pollen grain is haploid:

Parent plant genotype	*Possible pollen genotypes*
S_1S_2	S_1 ⎫ in equal numbers
	S_2 ⎭

S_1 pollen grains would be compatible with S_2S_3 style tissue
S_2 pollen grains would be incompatible with S_2S_3 style tissue
Note that neither S_1 nor S_2 pollen grains would be compatible with the style of the parent plant (S_1S_2), so that self-fertilisation is impossible.

21.5 (*a*) The part of the bee's body receiving most pollen will be that which brushes against the anthers while the bee is taking nectar. Thus pollination will generally occur between anthers and stigmas at the same height within the flower, that is between pin-eyed and thrum-eyed flowers.
(*b*) It encourages outbreeding (the opposite of inbreeding).

21.6 The functions of the cell organelles suggest that the cells manufacture materials for use within the cell. The raw materials for these processes come from the breakdown of materials entering the cell, using enzymes stored in the lysosomes. The synthesised products are packaged by the Golgi apparatus and stored for subsequent usage. Smooth ER is used to produce testosterone, a steroid. Mitochondria supply energy in the form of ATP.

21.7 (*a*) Both are haploid.
(*b*) Sperm: motile, small (2.5 μm diameter), no food store, produced continuously.
Egg: stationary, large (140 μm diameter), some food store, produced once per month in cycles.

21.8 The Rh antigens in the donor's blood would stimulate the mother's immune system to make Rh antibodies. These would not harm the mother, but it would then be impossible to prevent haemolytic disease of the newborn if she had a Rh$^+$ baby.

21.9 The baby's immune system does not start to function until after birth. Even if it did, it would not have time to react and produce antibodies to cross the placenta into the mother during the period immediately before birth when the placenta is damaged.

21.10 Blood would flow in the reverse direction along the ductus arteriosus.

Chapter 22

22.1 (*a*) There is loss of mass due to respiration of food reserves in the seed.
(*b*) Green leaves have grown and opened above the ground.
(*c*) Photosynthesis. Its rate must now be greater than respiration.
(*d*) This is due to dispersal of fruits and seeds.

22.2 Small seeds have relatively small food reserves; it is therefore important that the growing shoot reaches light quickly so that photosynthesis can start before the reserves are exhausted.

22.3 (*a*) Chlorophyll strongly absorbs red and blue light, but not green and far-red light (see chlorophyll absorption spectrum fig 7.11).

(b) Red light stimulates lettuce seed germination, but far-red light inhibits it (section 16.4.2). Seeds under a leaf canopy, where the light will be enriched in far-red, might therefore be inhibited from germinating until a break in the canopy ensures that they will not be too shaded for efficient photosynthesis and growth.

22.4 At the onset of germination, food reserves in the barley grain, principally starch, with some protein, are mobilised. Starch is converted to sugars, and proteins to amino acids, and these are translocated to the embryo for use in growth. Therefore, endosperm dry mass decreases while embryo dry mass increases.

At the same time there is an overall loss in dry mass during the first week. This is due to aerobic respiration, which consumes sugar, in both endosperm and embryo (though to a greater extent in the latter). At about day 7 the first leaf emerges and starts to photosynthesise. The resulting increase in dry mass more than compensates for respiration losses so that a net increase in dry mass is observed. At the same time the rate of growth of the embryo, now a seedling, increases.

22.5 (a) There is a gain in dry mass of 8.6 g, calculated as follows.
Mass of seeds = 51.2 g
Mass of fatty acid = 51.2/2 = 25.6 g
M_r fatty acid = 256
Therefore 1 mole = 256 g, so 25.6 g = 0.1 mole
From the equation,
0.1 mole fatty acid ⟶ 0.1 mole sugar + 0.5 mole water + 0.4 mole carbon dioxide
M_r sugar = 342
Therefore 25.6 g fatty acid ⟶ 34.2 g sugar + water + carbon dioxide
Water is not included in the dry mass and carbon dioxide is lost as a gas, therefore the gain in dry mass = (34.2 − 25.6) g = 8.6 g.
(b) Respiration would result in a decrease in dry mass. In reality there would still be an increase in dry mass.
(c) Volume of carbon dioxide evolved from the seeds = 8.96 dm³ at STP, calculated as follows:
from the equation, 0.1 mole fatty acid ⟶ 0.4 mole carbon dioxide. 0.4 mole carbon dioxide occupies 0.4 × 22.4 dm³ at STP = 8.96 dm³.
(d) By hydrolysis, catalysed by a lipase. The other component of the lipid is glycerol.
(e) 51 carbon atoms (the lipid would be tripalmitin: the fatty acid is palmitic acid). Each lipid molecule comprises three fatty acid molecules, each with 16 carbon atoms, plus one glycerol molecule with three carbon atoms.
(f) Sucrose or maltose.
(g) Oxygen reaches the storage tissue by diffusion through the testa and micropyle.

22.6 (a) The dominant food store is lipid, which comprises about 70% of the dry mass of the seeds before germination. By day 4 the mass of lipid is starting to decrease and the mass of sugar begins to rise. Lipid is therefore being converted to sugar and translocated to the embryo. Note that no sugars can be formed by photosynthesis since germination occurs in darkness. At day 5 the RQ of the embryo = 1, indicating that the embryo is respiring the sugar derived from the lipids. At the same time, the cotyledons (RQ = 0.4−0.5) are gaining energy from the conversation of lipid to sugar, and possibly from oxidation of sugar and fatty acids.
$C_{18}H_{34}O_3 + 13O_2 \longrightarrow C_{12}H_{22}O_{11} + 6CO_2 + 6H_2O + energy$
ricinoleic   sucrose
acid (fatty
acid derived
from a lipid)
RQ = 6/13 = 0.46
Conversion of lipid to sugar takes place with an increase in dry mass, so total dry mass of the seedlings increases up to 6 or 7 days. Beyond this point, the lipid reserves are running low, so rate of use of sugar starts to exceed the rate of production. Net mass of sugar, and total mass of seedlings, then starts to decrease. Sugar is used in respiration and in anaerobic reactions.
(b) At day 11, the RQ of the whole seedlings would probably be slightly less than 1.0. It is a combination of two reactions: the main one is the oxidation of sugar in respiration, RQ = 1, but there would probably still be a small contribution from the conversion of lipid to sugar, RQ 0.4−0.5.

22.7 Normally insufficient oxygen is able to penetrate the testa to allow exclusively aerobic respiration: the RQ is a combination of the RQ for aerobic respiration (probably about 1.0) and that for anaerobic respiration, which is infinity (∞). Removal of the testa allows more rapid penetration of oxygen by diffusion, with a consequent increase in aerobic respiration and decrease in RQ. Ethanol is a product of anaerobic respiration so less accumulates when the testas are removed.

Chapter 23

23.1 (a) Meiosis
(b) W – interphase
X – telophase I
Y – telophase II
(c) Gamete cells

23.2 See fig 23.2(ans).

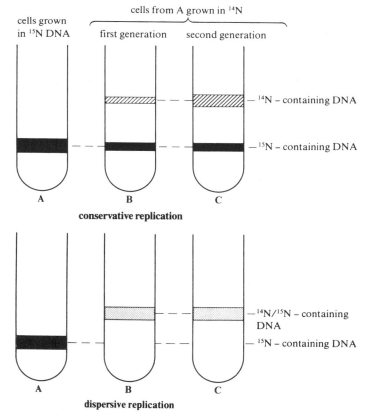

Fig 23.2(ans) Diagrams explaining two further theories of DNA replication. The appearance of DNA in a caesium chloride density gradient according to the theories presented in fig 23.22.

23.3

Bases	A	G	T	C
A	AA	AG	AT	AC
G	GA	GG	GT	GC
T	TA	TG	TT	TC
C	CA	CG	CT	CC

23.4 4 bases used once = $4 \times 1 = 4^1 = 4$
4 bases used twice = $4 \times 4 = 4^2 = 16$
4 bases used three times = $4 \times 4 \times 4 = 4^3 = 64$
therefore the mathematical expression is x^y where x = number of bases and y = number of bases used.

23.5 See fig 23.5(ans).

23.6 UAC AAG CUC AUG GUA CAU UGC

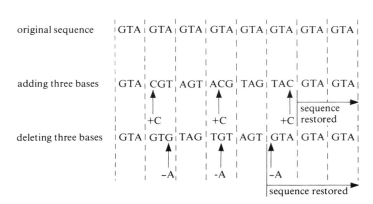

Fig 23.5(ans) *Answer to question shown diagrammatically. The general principle behind restoring the normal triplet sequence by the addition or deletion of three bases is to add or delete the three bases at any position along the length of the polynucleotide code.*

Chapter 24

24.1

(a) Let: **B** represent brown fur (dominant)
b represent grey fur (recessive)

Parental phenotypes	brown fur	×	grey fur
Parent genotypes (2n)	**BB**	×	**bb**

Meiosis

Gametes (n) Ⓑ Ⓑ × ⓑ ⓑ

Random fertilisation
F₁ genotypes (2n) **Bb**   **Bb**   **Bb**   **Bb**
F₁ phenotypes all brown fur

F₁ phenotypes	brown fur	×	brown fur
F₁ genotypes (2n)	**Bb**		**Bb**

Meiosis

Gametes (n) Ⓑ ⓑ × Ⓑ ⓑ

Random fertilisation
F₂ genotypes (2n) **BB** **Bb** **Bb** **bb**
F₂ phenotypes 3 brown fur : 1 grey fur

(b)

Experimental phenotypes	brown fur	×		grey fur
Experimental genotypes (2n)	**Bb**	×	**bb**	

Meiosis

Gametes (n) Ⓑ ⓑ × ⓑ ⓑ

Random fertilisation
Offspring genotypes (2n) **Bb** **Bb** **bb** **bb**
Offspring phenotypes 1 brown fur : 1 grey fur

In the case of monohybrid inheritance, the offspring from a heterozygous genotype crossed with a homozygous recessive genotype produce equal numbers of offspring showing each phenotype: in this case 50% brown fur and 50% grey fur.

24.2 If an organism having an unknown genotype is testcrossed with a homozygous dominant organism, all the offspring will show the dominant characteristics in the phenotype, as shown below.

Let: **T** represent a dominant allele
t represent a recessive allele

	homozygous × homozygous	heterozygous × homozygous
Testcross phenotypes		
Testcross genotypes (2n)	**TT** × **TT**	**Tt** × **TT**
Meiosis		
Gametes (n)	Ⓣ Ⓣ × Ⓣ Ⓣ	Ⓣ ⓣ × Ⓣ Ⓣ
Random fertilisation		
Offspring genotypes (2n)	**TT TT TT TT**	**TT TT Tt Tt**
Offspring phenotypes	all tall (homozygous)	all tall (½ homozygous, ½ heterozygous)

24.3 *(a)* If short black hair appeared in the F₁ phenotypes, then short hair must be dominant to long hair and black hair must be dominant to white.

(b) Let: **B** represent black hair
b represent white hair
S represent short hair
s represent long hair

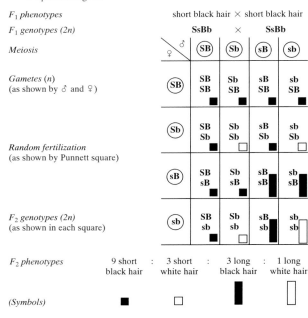

F₁ phenotypes	short black hair × short black hair
F₁ genotypes (2n)	**SsBb** × **SsBb**

F₂ phenotypes 9 short black hair : 3 short white hair : 3 long black hair : 1 long white hair

(Symbols) ■ □ ▮ ▯

24.4 Let:

R, r and S, s represent two allelomorphic pairs of genes controlling flower colour

Parental phenotypes purple × purple

Parental genotypes (2n) RrSs × RrSs
Meiosis

♀ \ ♂	RS	Rs	rS	rs
Gametes (n) (as shown by ♂ and ♀) **RS**	RS RS ●	Rs RS ●	rS RS ●	rs RS ●
Random fertilization (as shown by Punnett square) **Rs**	RS Rs ●	Rs Rs ○	rS Rs ●	rs Rs ○
F₂ genotypes (2n) (as shown in each square) **rS**	RS rS ●	Rs rS ●	rS rS ○	rs rS ○
rs	RS rs ●	Rs rs ○	rS rs ○	rs rs ○

Offspring phenotypic ratio 9 purple : 7 white
(Symbols) ● ○

24.5 The two alleles segregate during metaphase I and anaphase I.

24.6 The number of different combinations of chromosomes in the pollen gamete cells is calculated using the formula 2^n, where *n* is the haploid number of chromosomes.

In crocus, since $2n = 6$, $n = 3$.

Therefore, combinations $= 2^3 = 8$.

24.7 The F_1 phenotypes show that purple flower and short stem are dominant and red flower and long stem are recessive. The approximate ratio of 1:1:1:1 in a dihybrid cross suggests that the two genes controlling the characteristics of flower colour and stem length are not linked and the four alleles are situated on different pairs of chromosomes (see below).

Let:
P represent purple flower
p represent red flower
S represent short stem
s represent long stem

Since the parental stocks were both homozygous for both characters the F_1 genotypes must be **PpSs**.

Testcross phenotypes purple flower, short stem × red flower, long stem:

Testcross genotypes (2n) **PpSs** × **ppss**
Meiosis
Gametes (n) (as shown by ♂ and ♀)

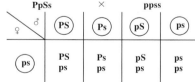

♀ \ ♂	PS	Ps	pS	ps
Random fertilisation (as shown in Punnett square) **ps**	PS ps	Ps ps	pS ps	ps ps

Offspring genotypes (2n) (listed in each square)

Offspring phenotypes 1 purple flower, short stem: 1 purple flower, long stem: 1 red flower, short stem: 1 red flower, long stem

24.8 (*a*) Homologous chromosomes
(*b*) Body colour and wing length

24.9 Out of the 800 seeds produced, only 24 show the results of crossing-over between the genes for seed colour and seed shape. In the other 776, the alleles for seed colour and seed shape have remained linked as shown by their approximate 1:1 ratio.

Hence the crossover value is $(24/800) \times 100 = 3\%$. Therefore the distance between the genes for seed colour and seed shape is 3 units.

24.10 (*a*) Let:

N represent normal wing (dominant)
n represent miniature wing (recessive)
R represent red eye (dominant)
r represent white eye (recessive)
XX represent female fly (♀)
XY represent male fly (♂)

(i) *Parental phenotypes* miniature wing, red eye ♂ × normal wing, white eye ♀

Parental phenotypes (2n) $X^{nR}Y$ × $X^{Nr}X^{Nr}$
Meiosis

Gametes (n) X^{nR} Y X^{Nr} X^{Nr}

Random fertilisation
F_1 genotypes (2n) $\underline{X^{nR}X^{Nr}\quad X^{nR}X^{Nr}}$ $\underline{X^{Nr}Y\quad X^{Nr}Y}$

F_1 phenotypes normal wing, red eye ♀ normal wing, white eye ♂

(ii) Assuming no crossing-over between the genes for wing length and eye colour in the female, the following results are likely to appear:

F_1 phenotypes normal wing, white eye ♂ × normal wing, red eye ♀
F_1 genotypes (2n) $X^{Nr}Y$ × $X^{nr}X^{nR}$
Meiosis

Gametes (n) X^{NR} Y × X^{nR} X^{Nr}

Random fertilisation
F_2 genotypes (2n) $X^{Nr}X^{nR}$ $X^{Nr}X^{Nr}$ $X^{nR}Y$ $X^{Nr}Y$

F_2 phenotypes normal wing, red eye ♀ normal wing, white eye ♀ miniature wing, red eye ♂ normal wing, white eye ♂

(*b*) The lack of a 1:1:1:1 ratio of phenotypes resulting from this cross indicates crossing-over between the genes for wing length and eye colour in the female

Testcross phenotypes normal wing, red eye ♀ × miniature wing, white eye ♂

Testcross genotypes (2n) $X^{nR}X^{Nr} \times X^{nR}Y$

Meiosis

♂ \ ♀	X^{nR}	X^{Nr}	X^{nr}	X^{NR}
Gametes (n) (as shown by ♀ and ♂) *Random fertilization* (as shown in Punnett square) **X^{nr}**	$X^{nR}X^{nr}$ ♀	$X^{Nr}X^{nr}$ ♀	$X^{nr}X^{nr}$ ♀	$X^{NR}X^{nr}$ ♀
Offspring genotypes (2n) (as listed in squares) **Y**	$X^{nR}Y$ ♂	$X^{Nr}Y$ ♂	$X^{nr}Y$ ♂	$X^{NR}Y$ ♂

Offspring phenotypes	wing: eye:	miniature red	normal white	miniature white	normal red
Experimental results		36	35	18	17

The alleles for wing length and eye colour are shown on the two F_1 female (X) chromosomes in the explanation above. Crossing-over between the alleles will give the recombinant genotypes shown above. Out of 106 flies, 35 show recombination of alleles (18 + 17), therefore the crossover value is 35/106 = approximately 30%.

24.11 Magpie moth

Let: **N** represent normal colour (dominant)
n represent pale colour (recessive)

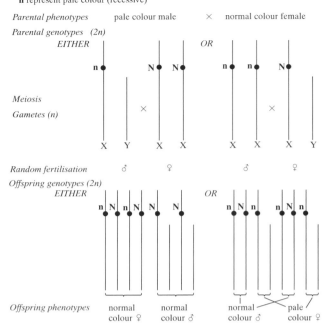

Parental phenotypes   pale colour male   ×   normal colour female
Parental genotypes (2n)
EITHER   *OR*

Meiosis
Gametes (n)

Random fertilisation
Offspring genotypes (2n)
EITHER   *OR*

Offspring phenotypes   normal   normal   normal   pale
colour ♀   colour ♂   colour ♂   colour ♀

From the results for the offspring phenotypes it is seen that the heterogametic sex in the magpie moth is the female.

Cat

Let: **B** represent black colour (dominant)
n represent yellow colour (recessive)

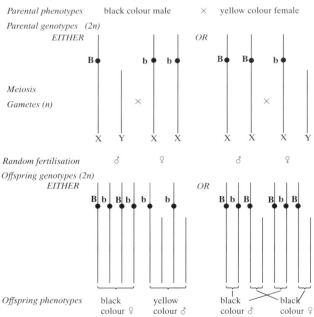

Parental phenotypes   black colour male   ×   yellow colour female
Parental genotypes (2n)
EITHER   *OR*

Meiosis
Gametes (n)

Random fertilisation
Offspring genotypes (2n)
EITHER   *OR*

Offspring phenotypes   black   yellow   black   black
colour ♀   colour ♂   colour ♂   colour ♀

From the results for the offspring phenotypes it is seen that the heterogametic sex in the cat is the male.

24.12 Let:

B represent black coat colour
G represent ginger coat colour
XX represent female cat
XY represent male cat

Parental phenotypes   ginger-coat male   ×   black-coat female
Parental genotypes (2n) X^GY × X^BX^B
Meiosis

Gametes (n) $\boxed{X^G}$ $\boxed{Y}$ × $\boxed{X^B}$ $\boxed{X^B}$

Random fertilisation
F_1 genotypes (2n) X^GX^B X^GX^B X^BY X^BY

F_1 phenotypes   tortoiseshell-   black coat colour ♀
coat colour ♀

(The parental female must be homozygous for black-coat colour since this is the only condition to produce a black-coat phenotype).

F_1 phenotypes   black-coat male   ×   tortoiseshell-coat female
F_1 genotypes (2n) X^BY × X^GX^B
Meiosis

Gametes (n) $\boxed{X^B}$ $\boxed{Y}$ × $\boxed{X^G}$ $\boxed{X^B}$

Random fertilisation
F_1 genotypes (2n) X^BX^G X^BX^B X^GY X^BY

F_2 phenotypes   tortoiseshell-   black coat   ginger coat   black coat
coat colour ♀   colour ♀   colour ♂   colour ♂

24.13 (a)

Let:
I represent the gene for blood group
A represent the allele A ⎫
B represent the allele B ⎬ (equally dominant)
o represent the allele O (recessive)

Parental phenotypes   blood group A   ×   blood group B
Parental genotypes (2n) I^AI^o × I^BI^o
Meiosis

Gametes (n) $\boxed{I^A}$ $\boxed{I^o}$ × $\boxed{I^B}$ $\boxed{I^o}$

Random fertilisation
Offspring genotypes (2n) I^AI^B I^AI^o I^oI^B I^oI^o

Offspring phenotypes blood groups AB   A   B   O

(b) There is a probability of $\frac{1}{4}$ (25%) that each child will have blood group A. So the probability that both will have blood group A is $\frac{1}{4} \times \frac{1}{4} = 1/16$ (6.25%).

24.14 Let:

    P represent pea comb
    R represent rose comb
    a single **P** allele and a single **R** allele occurring together produce walnut comb
    a double homozygous recessive genotype produces single comb
    W represent white feathers (dominant)
    w represent black feathers (recessive)

If eight different phenotypes are produced from the cross, each parent must possess as many heterozygous allelles as possible. Hence the genotypes are as shown below:

Parental phenotypes	black, rose-comb cock	×	white, walnut-comb hen
Parental genotypes (2n)	**wwRrpp**	×	**WwRrPp**

Meiosis

Gametes (n)
(as shown by ♀ and ♂)

Random fertilisation
(as shown in Punnett square)

Offspring genotypes (2n)
(as shown in squares)

♀ \ ♂	WRP	WRp	WrP	Wrp	wRP	wRp	wrP	wrp
wRp	WRP wRp ○	WRp wRp △	WrP wRp ○	Wrp wRp △	wRP wRp ●	wRp wRp ▲	wrP wRp ●	wrp wRp ▲
wrp	WRP wrp ○	WRp wrp △	WrP wrp □	Wrp wrp ◌	wRP wrp ●	wRp wrp ▲	wrP wrp ■	wrp wrp ◉

Offspring phenotypes
(Symbols)

3 white, walnut-comb: 3 black, walnut-comb: 3 white, rose-comb: 3 black, rose-comb: 1 white, pea-comb:
    ○   ●   △   ▲   □

1 black, pea-comb: 1 white, single-comb: 1 black, single-comb
    ■   ◌   ◉

24.15 Since both dominant allelles, **W**, white, and **B**, black, are present in the heterozygous F_1 genotype, and the phenotype is white, it may be concluded that the alleles show an epistatic interaction where the white allele represents the epistatic gene. The F_2 generation is shown below.

Using the symbols given in the question

F_1 phenotypes	White cock	×	white hen
F_1 genotypes (2n)	**WwBb**	×	**WwBb**

Meiosis

Gametes (n)
(as shown by ♂ and ♀)

Random fertilisation
(as listed in Punnett square)

F_2 genotypes (2n)
(as listed in the squares)

♀ \ ♂	WB	Wb	wB	wb
WB	WB WB ○	Wb WB ○	wB WB ○	wb WB ○
Wb	WB Wb ○	Wb wB ○	wB Wb ○	wb Wb ○
wB	WB wB ○	Wb wB ○	wB wB ●	wb wB ●
wb	WB wb ○	Wb wb ○	wB wb ●	wb wb ▨

F_2 genotypes
(Symbols)

12 white colour: 3 black colour: 1 brown colour
    ○   ●   ▨

Chapter 25

25.1 Economic: relieve economic burden of (i) individual families who have to care for sufferers, and (ii) the community which has to bear the cost of treatment on the National Health Service.
Social: relieve suffering of (i) individuals affected, and (ii) their families.

25.2 (*a*) Couple 3 and 4 are phenotypically normal but have an affected daughter. If the gene were dominant, at least one of the parents would be affected. The gene is unlikely to have arisen as a spontaneous mutation because it is already in the family (individual 5).
(*b*) Individual 9 is an affected woman born to phenotypically normal parents. Given that the gene is recessive, both parents must have a copy of the gene. If it were sex-linked, the father would show the symptoms of PKU because the Y chromosome only carries genes for sex.
(*c*) Individuals 3 and 4 are definitely carriers.
(*d*) Individuals 1, 2, 6, 7, 8, 10, 11, 12 and 13 *could* all be carriers. It is impossible to prove a person is not a carrier on the basis of normal breeding patterns. A biochemical test would be needed.
(*e*) A common answer to this question is 1 in 2 (or 50%) since a 1 : 2 : 1 ratio of affected : carrier : normal would be expected among the children of individuals 3 and 4. However, individuals 10, 11 and 12 know they are not PKU sufferers and so are either carriers or normal. In this situation there is a 2 in 3 chance of being a carrier (66.7%). Your advice might also include visiting a GP to enquire about the possibility of genetic counselling and being tested for being a carrier.

25.3 Its excess phenylalanine is removed by the mother while it is in the uterus. It takes a few days for the levels of phenylalanine to build up.

25.4 If it were not essential, it might be manufactured in the body. A phenylalanine-restricted diet would then be useless for controlling the condition.

25.5 A high level of phenylalanine in the mother's blood would cross the placenta and lead to restricted brain development in the fetus.

25.6 (*a*) End uncertainty/plan for future/may affect decision on whether to have children.
(*b*) Possible death sentence/would keep wondering if symptoms had started, e.g. if you forgot something/still don't know when symptoms will start even if you know you have the disease/no treatment available.

25.7 Age of onset is after it is passed on to children.

25.8 C2, C3 and C4

Chapter 26

26.1 A control experiment in which each variable was systematically eliminated.

26.2 Redi's basic assumption was that the presence of 'worms' was due to the entry of the flies through the open flasks.

26.3 Sealing the broths would prevent the entry of organisms to the vessels. Lack of air within the vessels may have deprived organisms of oxygen for respiration.

26.4 Pasteur's basic assumptions were that each generation of organisms develops from the previous generation and not spontaneously.

Chapter 27

27.1 The carrier genotype is the heterozygous genotype. The Hardy–Weinberg equation is used to calculate genotype frequencies. The equation may be represented as

$$p^2 + 2pq + q^2 = 1$$

where

p^2 = frequency of homozygous dominant genotype,
$2pq$ = frequency of heterozygous genotype,
q^2 = frequency of homozygous recessive genotype.
The incidence of cystic fibrosis in the population appears in individuals with the homozygous recessive genotype, hence q^2 is 1 in 2000 or $1/2000 = 0.0005$.

$$
\begin{aligned}
\text{Therefore } q &= \sqrt{0.005} \\
&= 0.0224.
\end{aligned}
$$

$$
\begin{aligned}
\text{Since } p + q &= 1 \\
p &= 1 - q \\
&= 1 - 0.0224 \\
&= 0.9776.
\end{aligned}
$$

The frequency of the heterozygous genotype ($2pq$) is therefore

$$
\begin{aligned}
2 \times (0.9776) \times (0.0224) \\
&= 0.044 \\
&\quad 1 \text{ in } 23 \\
&\approx 5\%
\end{aligned}
$$

Approximately 5% of the population are carriers of the recessive gene for cystic fibrosis.

27.2 *Fasciola hepatica*, the liver fluke, is a parasite which infests sheep. It has an intermediate host, the snail *Limnaea truncatula*, which lives in fresh water and damp pastures. Draining ponds and wet areas would bring about a change in environmental conditions which would exert a selection pressure tending to eliminate *Limnaea*. As the numbers of the snail fall this would reduce the numbers of available hosts which would lead to a decrease in the numbers of the parasite, *Fasciola*.

27.3 Reduced selection pressure at the extremes of each new population would favour increased variability. New phenotypes may show adaptations to the areas previously occupied by the eliminated subspecies and spread inwards to occupy the vacated ecological niche. The initial geographical separation of the cline may have initiated allopatric speciation. If the ring was reformed, gene flow may be impossible due to genetic isolation and each subpopulation would diverge genetically even further to form distinct species, as is the present case in the British Isles where the species exist sympatrically. If the genetic isolation between the two subpopulations was not too great, hybrids may form when the subpopulations were reunited. This zone of hybridisation may act as a reproductive barrier as is the case with the carrion and hooded crows.

Appendix 1
Biological chemistry

A1.1 Elementary chemistry

An **atom** is the smallest part of an element that can take part in a chemical change. An **element** is a substance which cannot be split into simpler substances by chemical means, for example the elements carbon, oxygen and nitrogen. A **compound** is a substance which contains two or more elements chemically combined, as shown below.

Compounds	*Elements*
water	hydrogen and oxygen
glucose	carbon, hydrogen and oxygen
sodium chloride	sodium and chlorine

A **molecule** is the smallest part of an element or compound which can exist alone under normal conditions, such as H_2, O_2, CO_2 and H_2O.

A1.1.1 Structure of the atom

All elements are made up of atoms. The word 'atom' comes from the Greek word *atomos* meaning indivisible.

The particles which make up atoms are protons, neutrons and electrons, details of which are given in table A1.1. Protons and neutrons have equal mass, and together make up the mass of the nucleus. The electrons have very much lower mass than the protons or neutrons and, when the mass of an atom is being considered, usually only the mass of the nucleus is taken into account.

A neutron is composed of a proton and an electron bound together, so that its charge is neutral.

Atoms are electrically neutral because the number of protons in a nucleus equals the number of electrons orbiting around it.

The number of protons in the nucleus of an atom is called the **atomic number** of that element. It also equals the number of electrons in an atom. For an individual atom,

Table A1.1 The locations, masses and charges of protons, neutrons and electrons.

Particle	*Location*	*Mass*	*Charge*
proton	the dense central core of the atom, forming the nucleus which has a diameter about 1/100 000 that of the atom	1 unit $(1.7 \times 10^{-24}\text{g})$	positive (+1)
neutron		1 unit	neutral (0)
electron	in 'orbits' around the nucleus	1/1870 unit $(9.1 \times 10^{-28}\text{g})$	netative (−1)

the number of protons plus the number of neutrons equals the **mass number**.

The atoms of some elements exist in different forms called **isotopes** which have different mass numbers (section A1.3). The average mass of an atom is the **relative atomic mass** (A_r) and is usually an average value for a natural mixture of the isotopes. For example, chlorine is made up of a mixture of isotopes of mass numbers 35 and 37; the proportions of the isotopes are such that naturally occurring chlorine has a relative atomic mass of 35.5.

The known elements, of which there are over 100, can be listed in order of ascending atomic number as shown in table A1.2. As indicated in the table the electrons are arranged in successive shells around the nucleus. The first shell can hold up to two electrons (being nearest the nucleus it is the smallest), the second shell can hold up to eight electrons, the third shell can hold up to 18 electrons and the fourth shell can hold up to 32 electrons.

Table A1.2 The first 20 elements in order of ascending atomic number.

Atomic number	*Mass number*	*Relative atomic mass**	*Element*	*Symbol*	*Arrangement of electrons*
1	1	1.0	hydrogen	H	1
2	4	4.0	helium	He	2
3	7	6.9	lithium	Li	2,1
4	9	9.0	beryllium	Be	2,2
5	11	10.8	boron	B	2,3
6	12	12.0	carbon	C	2,4
7	14	14.0	nitrogen	N	2,5
8	16	16.0	oxygen	O	2,6
9	19	19.0	fluorine	F	2,7
10	20	20.2	neon	Ne	2,8
11	23	23.0	sodium	Na	2,8,1
12	24	24.3	magnesium	Mg	2,8,2
13	27	27.0	aluminium	Al	2,8,3
14	28	28.1	silicon	Si	2,8,4
15	31	31.0	phosphorus	P	2,8,5
16	32	32.1	sulphur	S	2,8,6
17	35	35.5	chlorine	Cl	2,8,7
18	40	39.9	argon	Ar	2,8,8
19	39	39.1	potassium	K	2,8,8,1
20	40	40.1	calcium	Ca	2,8,8,2

*Relative atomic mass (A_r) was formerly atomic weight.
Figures for A_r are given to the nearest decimal place.
The symbols for some common elements are, in ascending order of atomic number, chromium (Cr), manganese (Mn), iron (Fe), cobalt (Co), nickel (Ni), copper (Cu), zinc (Zn), arsenic (As), bromine (Br), molybdenum (Mo), silver (Ag), cadmium (Cd), iodine (I), barium (Ba), platinum (Pt), mercury (Hg), lead (Pb), radium (Ra), uranium (U), plutonium (Pu).

There are also further shells in the larger atoms, but these need not be considered here. The arrangements of electrons in shells for the first 12 elements are shown in fig A1.1.

Any element with an electronic configuration in which the outermost shell is full is particularly unreactive. Hence helium and neon (table A1.2) are so unreactive that they seldom form compounds with other atoms. Thus they are called noble gases.

The tendency of all other elements is to attain full electron shells through reaction with other elements. When two atoms react to form a compound there are basically two types of bond that can form between them, ionic and covalent bonds.

A1.1.2   Ionic bonding

This is a process in which electrons are transferred from one atom to another. Consider sodium reacting with chlorine (fig A1.2a). The sodium atom loses an electron and therefore has an overall positive charge of +1 (its nucleus contains 11 positively charged protons and is surrounded by 10 negatively charged electrons). Similarly the chlorine atom has gained an electron and now has an overall negative charge of −1. Both have full, and therefore stable, electron shells.

These charged particles are no longer true atoms and instead are called **ions**. Hence the sodium ion is represented as Na^+ and the chloride ion as Cl^-. Positively charged ions are called **cations**, and negatively charged ions **anions**. The resulting compound is sodium chloride (formula NaCl) but no molecules of NaCl exist. Instead there is an association of sodium and chloride ions in equal numbers (ionic formula Na^+Cl^-). Compounds like this which are formed by

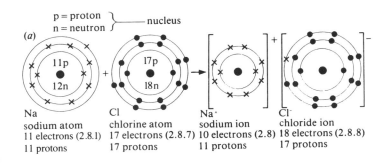

(a)
p = proton ⎫ nucleus
n = neutron ⎭

Na
sodium atom
11 electrons (2.8.1)
11 protons

Cl
chlorine atom
17 electrons (2.8.7)
17 protons

Na⁺
sodium ion
10 electrons (2.8)
11 protons

Cl⁻
chloride ion
18 electrons (2.8.8)
17 protons

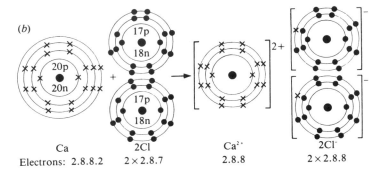

(b)

Ca
Electrons: 2.8.8.2

2Cl
2 × 2.8.7

Ca²⁺
2.8.8

2Cl⁻
2 × 2.8.8

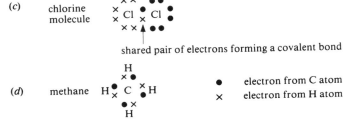

(c)   chlorine molecule

shared pair of electrons forming a covalent bond

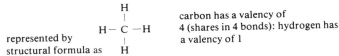

(d)   methane

represented by structural formula as

● electron from C atom
× electron from H atom

carbon has a valency of 4 (shares in 4 bonds): hydrogen has a valency of 1

(e) In ethene (ethylene), C_2H_4, there are two pairs of shared electrons between carbon atoms:

ethene

● × electrons from C atom
○ electron from H atom

The two pairs of shared electrons are represented by a double bond, thus

C = C

Fig A1.2 (a) Formation of sodium chloride. (b) Formation of calcium chloride. (c) Formation of the covalent chlorine molecule. (d) Formula of methane. (e) Formula of ethene. For clarity, electrons from different atoms have been given different symbols (x, • or o). In reality, all electrons are indistinguishable. Only the outer shells of electrons are shown in (c), (d), and (e).

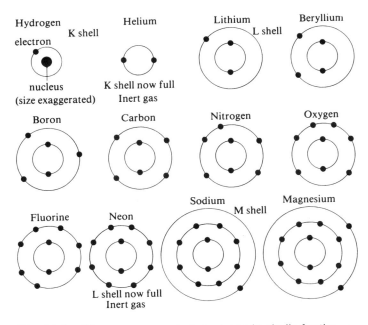

Hydrogen
K shell
electron
nucleus
(size exaggerated)

Helium
K shell now full
Inert gas

Lithium
L shell

Beryllium

Boron

Carbon

Nitrogen

Oxygen

Fluorine

Neon
L shell now full
Inert gas

Sodium
M shell

Magnesium

Fig A1.1 The arrangement of electrons in shells for the first 12 elements. (The nucleus is omitted from all except hydrogen.)

the transfer of electrons are called **ionic compounds**. They are usually formed when metals react with non-metals. The metal produces a cation and the non-metal an anion. Salts are all ionic compounds.

Another typical example is calcium chloride (formula $CaCl_2$) (fig A1.2b). Here two electrons are lost from the calcium atom, and one gained by each chlorine atom. Therefore the calcium ion is represented as Ca^{++} or Ca^{2+}.

The number of electrons transferred (lost or gained) is the **valency**, sometimes called the **combining power**. Therefore sodium and chlorine have a valency of one and calcium has a valency of two. The number of plus or minus signs shown for an ion is therefore equal to its valency; for example, potassium and hydroxyl ions have a valency of one and so are written as K^+ and OH^-, magnesium and sulphate ions have a valency of two and so are written as Mg^{2+} and SO_4^{2-}, and aluminium has a valency of three and so is written as Al^{3+}.

Ionic formulae

Ionic compounds do not exist as molecules but as collections of ions. The ionic formula shows the ratio in which elements are combined in an ionic compound; for example, the formula for the compound aluminium oxide is Al_2O_3, meaning that Al^{3+} and O^{2-} ions are in the ratio of $2:3$. If an ion with more than one atom is present, such as in SO_4^{2-} (sulphate), the number of that ion present, if more than one, is indicated by using brackets, for example $Al_2(SO_4)_3$; but Na_2SO_4 needs no brackets as only one sulphate ion is involved.

A1.1.3   Covalent bonding

In this type of bonding electrons are not donated or received by the atoms concerned; instead, they are shared. Consider two chlorine atoms; each has seven electrons in its outer shell (electron configuration 2, 8, 7). In covalency, two chlorine atoms contribute one electron each to a shared pair of electrons, making a chlorine molecule, formula Cl_2. In this way both atoms obtain an approximation to the noble gas configuration and molecules are produced, not ions (fig A1.2c). The shared pair of electrons is conventionally written as a single bond thus $Cl-Cl$. Chlorine is said to have a covalency of one (it shares one of its electrons). Another example is methane, CH_4. Carbon has an atomic number of six with four electrons in its outer shell (2, 4); hydrogen has an atomic number of one and has only one electron (fig A1.2d).

In ethene (ethylene), C_2H_4, there are two pairs of shared electrons between carbon atoms, and the two pairs are represented by a double bond (fig A1.2e). In some compounds there are three pairs of shared electrons, a triple bond, such as in ethyne (acetylene), C_2H_2.

Covalent compounds are far more common than ionic compounds in biological systems.

The valencies of some common elements and the charges on common ions are given in table A1.3.

Table A1.3 Valencies of some elements and charges of some ions.

(a) Valencies of some elements.

1	2	3	4
F	O	N	C
Cl	S	P	Si

(b) Charges of some ions of single elements

−2	−1	+1	+2	+3
O^{2-}	F^-	H^+	Mg^{2+}	Al^{3+}
	Cl^-	Na^+	Ca^{2+}	
	Br^-	K^+	Zn^{2+}	
			Ba^{2+}	
	I^-	Cu^+ copper (I)	Cu^{2+} copper (II)	
			Fe^{2+} iron (II)	Fe^{3+} iron (III)
			Pb^{2+} lead (II)	

(c) Charges of some ions of more than one element

−3	−2	−1	+1
PO_4^{3-} phosphate (V)	SO_4^{2-} sulphate	NO_3^- nitrate	NH_4^+
	CO_3^{2-} carbonate	NO_2^- nitrite	ammonium
		OH^- hydroxyl or hydroxide	
		HCO_3^- hydrogen carbonate (formerly bicarbonate)	

Formulae of covalent compounds

For simple covalent compounds the formula represents the number of each type of atom present in one molecule; for example CO_2 (carbon dioxide) means that one atom of carbon is combined with two atoms of oxygen.

A1.1.4   Chemical equations

When chemical equations are written, not only must the correct formulae for the chemicals be used but also the equations must be balanced, that is there must be the same number of atoms of each element on the right-hand side of the equation as on the left. This can be done in the following way.

(1) Write a word equation, for example

   methane + oxygen $\longrightarrow$ carbon dioxide + water

(2) Write the correct formulae.

   $CH_4 + O_2 \longrightarrow CO_2 + H_2O$

(3) Check if the equation balances. The equation in (2) does not, as there are three oxygen atoms on the right side and only two on the left; also there are four hydrogen atoms on the left and two on the right.

(4) Balance the equation, if necessary, using large numbers in front of the relevant formulae and remembering that the formulae cannot be altered.

$$CH_4 + 2O_2 \longrightarrow CO_2 + 2H_2O$$

($2O_2$ means two molecules of oxygen (4 atoms of oxygen); $2H_2O$ means two molecules of water (4 atoms of hydrogen, 2 atoms of oxygen).)

Ionic equations

Equations for reactions between ionic compounds can be written simply as ionic equations. Consider the following reaction:

$$2NaOH + H_2SO_4 \longrightarrow Na_2SO_4 + 2H_2O$$
sodium   sulphuric   sodium   water
hydroxide   acid   sulphate

(All three compounds are aqueous.)
The equation can be rewritten to show the ions present:

$$2Na^+ + 2OH^- + 2H^+ + SO_4^{2-} \longrightarrow 2Na^+ + SO_4^{2-} + 2H_2O$$

Removing ions common to both sides of the equation (not involved in the reaction) gives the ionic equation:

$$2OH^- + 2H^+ \longrightarrow 2H_2O$$

This is the only reaction which has taken place.

A1.1.5 Acids, bases, salts, pH and buffers

A hydrogen atom consists of one electron and one proton. If the electron is lost it leaves a proton, and a proton may therefore be regarded as a hydrogen ion, usually written H^+. An **acid** is a substance which can act as a **proton donor** and this is a substance which can ionise to form H^+ as the cation. For the purpose of this book an acid will be defined as a substance which ionises in water to give H^+ ions as the cation. A **strong** acid, such as hydrochloric acid, is one which undergoes almost complete **dissociation** (separation of its constituent ions). It is therefore a more efficient proton donor than a **weak** acid, such as ethanoic acid or carbonic acid, in which only a small proportion of the acid molecules dissociate to give hydrogen ions:

$$HCl \rightleftharpoons H^+ + Cl^- \quad CH_3COOH \rightleftharpoons CH_3COO^- + H^+$$
hydrochloric acid   ethanoic acid

Typical properties of acids are as follows.

- Many acids react with the more reactive metals such as magnesium or zinc to produce hydrogen.
- Acids are neutralised by bases to give salts and water only.
- Almost all acids react with carbonate to give carbon dioxide.
- Acids have a sour taste in dilute solution, for example ethanoic acid (vinegar).
- Solutions of acids give a characteristic colour with **indicators**; for example, they turn blue litmus red.

A **base** is a substance which reacts with an acid to form a salt and water only (otherwise defined as a **proton acceptor**). Most bases are insoluble in water. Those that are soluble in water form solutions called **alkalis**, such as sodium hydroxide, calcium hydroxide and ammonia solutions. Other typical properties are as follows.

- Bases usually have little action on metals.
- Bases react with aqueous solutions of the salts of most metals to precipitate an insoluble hydroxide.
- Reactions with ammonium salts gives ammonia.
- Solutions of alkalis give a characteristic colour with indicators; for example, they turn red litmus blue.

A **salt** is a compound in which the replaceable hydrogen of an acid has been partly or wholly replaced by a metal. An example is sodium chloride where the hydrogen atom of hydrochloric acid has been replaced by an atom of sodium. When a salt dissolves in water its constituent ions dissociate, that is they become free ions separated from one another by water molecules.

The pH scale

The acidity or alkalinity of a solution is related to the concentration of hydrogen ions in the solution. This is expressed as its pH (p represents a mathematical operation, H represents hydrogen). The pH is defined as the logarithm to the base of 10 of the reciprocal of the hydrogen ion concentration. Pure water contains 1×10^{-7} moles of hydrogen ions per decimetre cubed (litre). The pH of water is therefore $\log(1/10^7) = 7$.

A pH of 7.0 represents a neutral solution (at room temperature). A pH of less than 7.0 represents an acidic solution, and a pH of more than 7.0 represents an alkaline solution.

The pH scale ranges from about −1 to about 15 (usually 0–14). The scale is logarithmic, so a change in pH of one unit represents a ten-fold change in hydrogen ion concentration.

Cells and tissues normally require a pH value close to 7 and fluctuations of more than one or two units from this usually cannot be tolerated. Mechanisms therefore exist to keep the pH of body fluids as constant as possible. This is partly achieved by buffers.

Buffers

A **buffer solution** is a solution containing a mixture of a weak acid and its soluble salt. It acts to resist changes in pH. Such changes can be brought about by dilution, or by addition of acid or alkali.

As acidity (hydrogen ion concentration) increases, the free anion from the salt combines more readily with free hydrogen ions, removing them from solution. As acidity decreases, the tendency to release hydrogen ions increases. Thus the buffer solution tends to maintain a constant, balanced hydrogen ion concentration. For example

$$HPO_4^{2-} + H^+ \underset{\text{high pH}}{\overset{\text{low pH}}{\rightleftharpoons}} H_2PO_4^-$$
$$\text{hydrogen} \qquad \text{dihydrogen}$$
$$\text{phosphate} \qquad \text{phosphate}$$

Some organic compounds, notably proteins, can function as buffers and they are particularly important in blood.

A1.2 Oxidation and reduction

All biological processes require energy to drive them and the biologist must be aware of the various reactions that make energy available for such processes. Chemical reactions which liberate energy are termed **exothermic** or **exergonic**, whilst those that use energy are **endothermic** or **endergonic**. Synthetic (anabolic) processes are endergonic (such as photosynthesis), whilst breakdown (catabolic) processes are exergonic (such as respiration). The sum of the catabolic and anabolic reactions of the cell occurring at any one moment represents its metabolism.

A cell obtains the majority of its energy by oxidising food molecules during the process of respiration. **Oxidation** is defined as the loss of electrons. The opposite process, in which electrons are gained, is called **reduction**. The two always occur together, electrons being transferred from the **electron donor**, which is thereby oxidised, to the **electron acceptor**, which is thereby reduced. Such reactions are called **redox** reactions, and they are widespread in the chemical processes of biological systems. Several mechanisms of oxidation and reduction exist, as described in the following sections.

A1.2.1 Oxidation

Oxidation may occur directly by the addition of molecular oxygen to a substance, which is then said to be oxidised.

$$A + O_2 \rightarrow AO_2$$

However, the most common form of biological oxidation is when hydrogen is removed from a substance (**dehydrogenation**).

$$AH_2 + B \xrightarrow[\text{dehydrogenase}]{\text{dehydrogenation}} A + BH_2$$

A has been oxidised and *B* reduced.

A cell possesses a number of substances called **hydrogen carriers** which act like B in the equation above. Each dehydrogenation is catalysed by a specific dehydrogenase enzyme and the carriers are arranged in a linear order such that their level of potential energy (section A1.6.2) decreases from one end of the line (which is where the hydrogen atoms enter) to the other. This means that each time hydrogen atoms are transferred from one carrier to another of lower potential energy, a small quantity of energy is liberated. In some cases this can be incorporated into ATP.

In some reactions, each atom of hydrogen (which can be regarded as a hydrogen ion or proton, H^+, plus one negatively charged electron, e^-) is not transferred as a whole. Here the process only involves the transfer of electrons. For example

$$2FeCl_2 + Cl_2 \rightleftharpoons 2FeCl_3$$
$$\text{iron(II)} \qquad \text{iron(III)}$$
$$\text{chloride} \qquad \text{chloride}$$

Iron(II) ions are oxidised to iron(III) ions by the loss of one electron per ion, or

$$Fe^{2+} \rightleftharpoons Fe^{3+} + e^-$$
$$\text{reduced} \qquad \text{oxidised}$$

The electrons are transferred to the chlorine molecule which is thereby reduced and forms two chloride ions. So the complete ionic equation is

$$2Fe^{2+} + Cl_2 \rightleftharpoons 2Fe^{3+} + 2Cl^-$$
$$\text{reduced} \quad \text{oxidised} \qquad \text{oxidised} \quad \text{reduced}$$

Cytochromes, which contain iron, work in mitochondria and convey electrons (derived from hydrogen atoms which have split into hydrogen ions and electrons) along an electron transport chain. Here the electrons are passed from less electronegative atoms to more electronegative ones. The products of such reactions possess less potential energy than the reactants and the difference is liberated as energy which is utilised in one form or another. At the end of the chain is a cytochrome that also contains copper. This copper transfers its electrons directly to atmospheric oxygen and is thereby oxidised itself.

$$2Cu^+ - 2e^- \rightleftharpoons 2Cu^{2+}$$
$$2H^+ + 2e^- + \tfrac{1}{2}O_2 \rightleftharpoons H_2O$$
$$\overline{2H^+ + 2Cu^+ + \tfrac{1}{2}O_2 \rightleftharpoons Cu^{2+} + H_2O}$$

A1.2.2 Reduction

Reduction occurs when molecular oxygen is removed from a substance, or hydrogen atoms are gained by a substance, or when an electron is gained by a substance.

A1.3 Isotopes

Atoms of some elements exist in more than one form, the different forms being called **isotopes** (*iso*, same; *topos*, place; same position in the periodic table of elements). All the isotopes of a given element have the same number of protons and electrons (same atomic number) and therefore have identical chemical properties. However, they differ in the neutron content of their nuclei and therefore have different masses. To distinguish between isotopes, mass number is added to the symbol of the element; for example oxygen has three naturally occurring isotopes, ^{16}O, ^{17}O and ^{18}O. One isotope is usually much commoner than the others; for example the ratio of presence of $^{16}O : ^{17}O : ^{18}O$ is 99.759% : 0.037% : 0.204%.

Some combinations of protons and neutrons give nuclei which can exist without change for a long time. These nuclei are said to be stable. Other combinations give unstable nuclei, that is they tend to break up or decay, emitting particles and radiation. Such nuclei are said to be radioactive and can easily be detected using various instruments such as Geiger–Müller tubes and counters, scintillation counters and so on. As the atomic number of the nucleus increases, so the relative number of neutrons needed for stability increases. For example, the 92 protons of uranium need 138 neutrons to be stable. Isotopes of uranium with larger numbers of neutrons are radioactive, their nuclei being unstable.

The rate of decay is often expressed as the **half-life**. This is the time during which, on average, half the atoms present will decay. For example, ^{14}C has a half-life of 5570 years.

Radioactive isotopes can emit 'rays' of particles and radiation of three kinds.

(1) α **particles**. These are identical to helium nuclei, that is they consist of two protons plus two neutrons. They have two positive charges.

An example of α particle emission is given below (see also fig A4.1). (The upper number on the left-hand side of each element's symbol is the mass number and the lower is the atomic number.)

$$^{238}_{92}U \longrightarrow \,^{234}_{90}Th + \,^{4}_{2}He$$

The ^{238}U nucleus ejects an α particle, thus losing four units of mass and two of charge and becoming an isotope of thorium.

(2) β **particles**. These are fast-moving electrons derived from the nucleus when a neutron changes to a proton. β particles have a single negative charge (see also fig A4.1).

An example of β particle emission is

$$^{234}_{90}Th \longrightarrow \,^{234}_{91}Pa + \beta(e^-)$$

The thorium nucleus ejects an electron; one of its neutrons therefore becomes a proton. Its atomic mass is unchanged, but its atomic number (number of protons) is increased by one, and it becomes an isotope of protactinium.

(3) γ **rays**. These are very short wavelength electromagnetic waves associated with α and β decay. They have a high energy and are very difficult to stop, passing, for example, through thick sheets of lead.

α particles are easily stopped, for example by air or by a thin sheet of paper. β particles have a greater penetrating power but are stopped by a thick sheet of aluminium or a thin sheet of lead. The particles and the radiation can be harmful to living organisms if they are in close enough proximity to cells.

A1.4   Solutions and the colloidal state

Solutions have at least two parts or phases: the **continuous** (**dispersion**) phase or **solvent**, in which the **disperse** phase or **solute** is supported or dissolved.

In 1861 Graham distinguished between two types of solute which he called **crystalloids** and **colloids**. These he differentiated according to whether the solute molecules were capable of passing through a parchment (partially permeable) membrane. In fact, in biological systems there is no clear distinction between them since the biological solvent is always water and the properties of any water-based solution depend upon the size of the solute molecule and the effect of gravity. Three types of solution may be identified.

(1) **True solution**.   In this, solute particles are small and comparable in size to the solvent molecules, forming a homogeneous system, and the particles do not separate out under the influence of gravity; for example salt solution and sucrose solution. Such solutions are regarded by chemists as forming one phase.

(2) **Colloidal solution**.   The solute particles are large by comparison with those of the solvent, forming a heterogeneous system, but the particles still do not separate out under gravity; for example clay in water.

(3) **Suspension** or **emulsion**.   The solute particles are so large that they cannot remain dispersed against gravitational force unless the suspension is stirred continuously. A suspension has solid particles whereas an emulsion has liquid particles in the disperse phase, for example a silt suspension.

The three systems above can be described as **dispersion systems** because the particles are dispersed through a medium. Dispersion systems can involve all three states of matter, namely solid, liquid and gas; for example gas in water (soda water), sodium chloride in water (salt solution) and solid in solid (copper in zinc as brass). All can be called solutions, but generally this term refers to those systems that have a liquid solvent.

Many biological systems exist as colloidal solutions which are either hydrophobic or hydrophilic: a **hydrophobic sol** is water-hating, such as clay or charcoal in water, and a **hydrophilic sol** is water-loving, such as starch, table jelly, gelatin and agar-agar. Most of the colloidal solutions occurring in organisms, such as protein solutions, are hydrophobic sols. The viscosity of a hydrophilic sol, such as table jelly, can be increased by making it more concentrated or by lowering the temperature. As viscosity increases, the sol may set and is then called a **gel**. A gel is a more or less rigid colloidal system, although there is no sharp distinction between sol and gel. Ionic composition, pH and pressure are other factors which can affect sol–gel transformations and all may be important in living cells under certain circumstances. Characteristics of the colloidal state are shown in table A1.4.

Table A1.4 Characteristics of the colloidal state.

Phenomenon	Physical properties	Biological properties
Dialysis (the separation of particles by partially permeable membranes)	Colloids cannot pass through such membranes	Colloidal cytoplasm is retained within the cell surface membrane. Large molecules cannot pass through and therefore must be changed to smaller molecules such as starch to glucose
Brownian movement	Very small particles viewed under a microscope vibrate without changing position. This movement is due to the continuous bombardment of the molecules by the solvent molecules, for example Indian ink in water	All living cytoplasm is colloidal and minute particles in the cell can be seen to exhibit Brownian movement
Filtration	The movement of particles during this process depends on the size of the molecule. The actual size of the particles can be measured by varying the size of the filter pores	
Solute potential (osmotic potential)	Hydrophobic colloids develop extremely small solute potentials in solution. Hydrophilic colloids develop small but measurable solute potentials in solution	
Precipitation	Hydrophobic colloids can be precipitated (coagulation). A positively charged colloid will precipitate a negatively charged colloid. Electrolytes have the same effect	Dilute acids or rennet coagulate casein of milk, as in cheese-making. Precipitation of pectin from cell walls occurs during jam-making. Heat irreversibly coagulates egg albumen
Surface properties	Colloidal particles present an enormous surface area to the surrounding solvent. The surface energy is considerable here and this energy can cause molecules to aggregate at the surface interface. This is called **adsorption**. For example, charcoal is used to adsorb gases in respirators, or dyes from solution. This phenomenon can be used for stabilising colloidal sols, such as in the addition of egg to mayonnaise, or soap to oil-based insecticides	Adsorption of molecules occurs in the cell colloids particularly in cells near to, or concerned in the uptake of, ions, such as cortical cells of the root
Gel to sol and reverse changes	The sol state is fluid and the gel state is solid; for example, starch in hot water is a colloidal sol but when cooled it becomes a colloidal gel. Change of pH, temperature, pressure and the presence of metallic ions can also be equally effective	Clotting of blood is a sol to gel change with the gelation of the protein fibrinogen. Heat changes egg albumen from sol to gel
Imbibition	The absorption of fluid by colloids is called **imbibition**; for example gelatin taking in water	The testa of a dry seed or cellulose in cell walls take up water by imbibition. The release of gametes from sex organs, such as antheridia, is due to imbibitional swelling

A1.5 Diffusion and osmosis

Molecules and ions in solution can move passively and spontaneously in a particular direction as a result of diffusion. Osmosis is a special type of diffusion. It is discussed in detail in section 5.9.8. Such movements in living organisms do not require the expenditure of energy, unlike active transport. Another type of movement, namely mass flow, is considered in chapter 13.

A1.5.1 Diffusion

Diffusion involves the random and spontaneous movement of individual molecules and ions. For example, if a bottle of concentrated ammonia solution is left on a bench and the stopper removed, the smell of ammonia soon penetrates the room. The process by which the ammonia molecules spread is diffusion, and although individual molecules may move in any direction, the net direction is outwards from the concentrated source to areas of lower concentration. Thus diffusion may be described as the *movement of molecules or ions from a region of their high concentration to a region of their low concentration down a concentration gradient*. In contrast to mass flow it is possible for the net diffusion of different types of molecule or ion to be in different directions at the same time, each type moving down its own concentration gradient. Thus in the lungs, oxygen diffuses into the blood at the same time as carbon dioxide diffuses out into the alveoli; mass flow of blood through the lungs, however, can be in one direction only. Also, smaller molecules and ions diffuse faster than larger ones, assuming equal concentration gradients. There is a modified form of diffusion called facilitated diffusion which is described in section 5.9.8.

A1.6 Laws of thermodynamics

All chemical changes are governed by the laws of thermodynamics. The first law, called the **law of conservation of energy**, states that for any chemical process the total energy of the system and its surroundings always remains constant. This means that energy is neither created nor destroyed, and that if the chemical system gains energy then that quantity of energy must have been provided by the surroundings of the system, and vice versa. Therefore energy may be redistributed, converted into another form or both, but never lost.

The second law states that when left to themselves, systems and their surroundings usually approach a state of maximum disorder (**entropy**). This implies that highly ordered systems will readily deteriorate unless energy is used to maintain their order. All biological processes obey, and are governed by, these two laws of thermodynamics.

A1.6.1 Energy relations in living systems

Consider the decomposition of hydrogen peroxide into water and oxygen:

$$2H_2O_2 \rightleftharpoons 2H_2 + O_2$$

Generally, pure hydrogen peroxide will persist for a long time with no significant decomposition. For decomposition to occur, molecues must, on collision, have energy greater than a certain level, called the **activation energy**, E_a. Once this energy is reached, changes in the bonding pattern of the molecules occur and the reaction may generate enough energy to proceed spontaneously. The activation energy required varies with different reactants.

Addition of heat energy is the most common way in which activation energy is reached, and most reactants require quantities far greater than that provided by normal temperatures. For example, it is only when hydrogen peroxide is heated to $150\,°C$ that it decomposes rapidly enough to cause an explosive reaction. Water and oxygen are produced and energy is liberated. The overall energy change which occurs in this reaction is called the **free energy change** (ΔG). As the reaction is very rapid, and the products water and oxygen generally do not re-unite to form hydrogen peroxide, the energy liberated is lost from the chemical system to the environment. Therefore ΔG is negative (fig A1.3).

Obviously high temperatures would be lethal to biological systems and so enzymes are used instead. Acting as catalysts, they reduce the activation energy required by the reactants and therefore increase the rates of chemical reactions without addition of energy, such as a rise in temperature, to the system. Catalase is the enzyme that promotes rapid decomposition of aqueous solutions of hydrogen peroxide in living systems.

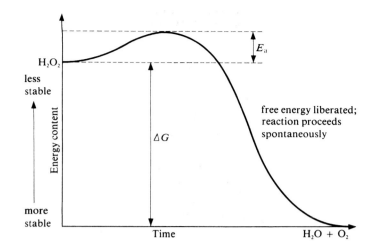

Fig A1.3 *Activation energy.*

A1.6.2 Potential energy

This is defined as the energy which a system possesses because of its position and condition. Consider a stationary ball at the top of a slope (fig A1.4). The ball possesses an amount of gravitational potential energy equal to the work done to place it there originally. When it rolls down the slope some of the potential energy of the ball is converted into kinetic energy. When the ball comes to rest at the bottom of the slope it possesses less potential energy than it had at the top. In order to restore the ball's potential energy to its original value, energy from the environment must be used to raise it once more to the top of the slope.

Potential energy for biological systems is built up by green plants during the production of sugar when photosynthesis occurs (fig A1.5). During this process, solar energy boosts certain electrons from their orbits with the result that they acquire potential energy. When oxidation of the sugar takes place during respiration, the potential energy of the electrons is used in various forms by living systems.

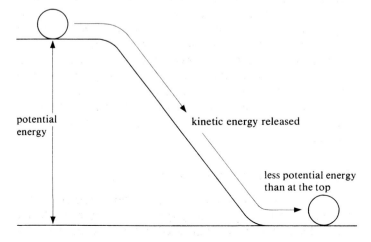

Fig A1.4 *Potential and kinetic energy.*

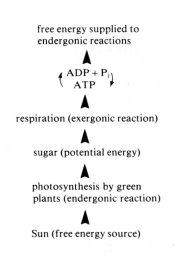

free energy supplied to
endergonic reactions

$$\left\{\begin{matrix} ADP + P_i \\ ATP \end{matrix}\right.$$

respiration (exergonic reaction)

sugar (potential energy)

photosynthesis by green
plants (endergonic reaction)

Sun (free energy source)

Fig A1.5 *Movement of energy through biological systems.*

A1.7   Chromatography

Chromatography is a technique used for the separating of mixtures into their components. The technique depends upon the differential movement of each component through a stationary medium under the influence of a moving solvent. For example, the green pigment in plants, when dissolved in a suitable solvent and allowed to pass through a stationary medium such as powdered chalk, separates into a number of different coloured pigments. A similar experiment is described in experiment A1.3.

There are three basic types of chromatography, depending on the nature of the stationary medium: **paper chromatography**, **adsorption column chromatography** and **thin-layer chromatography**. Paper chromatography is used in experiments A1.1–1.3 and is also described further in section 7.6.3. The various techniques of chromatography are now widely used in chemistry, biology, biochemistry and such specialist sciences as forensic medicine.

Electrophoresis

Electrophoresis is a modified form of chromatography used to separate charged molecules. An electric current is applied across a chromatographic medium such that one end has a positive charge and the other a negative charge. Individual molecules in the mixture move outwards through the medium towards the ends depending on their relative masses and charges. Electrophoresis is commonly used in the isolation and identification of amino acids, where the technique is improved further by adjusting the pH of the medium.

A1.7.1   The concept of R_f values

The movement of the solute relative to the solvent front on a chromatographic system is constant for that solute. This can be expressed in the term R_f as shown below.

$$R_f = \frac{\text{distance moved by solute}}{\text{distance moved by solvent front}}$$

If the solvent front goes off the end of the paper then it is possible to express the movement of a particular solute in comparison with the movement of another standard solute.

$$\text{Thus } R_x = \frac{\text{distance moved by solute}}{\text{distance moved by standard solute } x}$$

See fig A1.6c.

A1.7.2   Two-dimensional paper chromatography

Complex mixtures of solutes cannot always be separated efficiently by chromatography in one direction only. Thus a further separation must be carried out using a second solvent at right-angles to the first for a better separation of the spots (fig A1.6d). A square sheet of paper

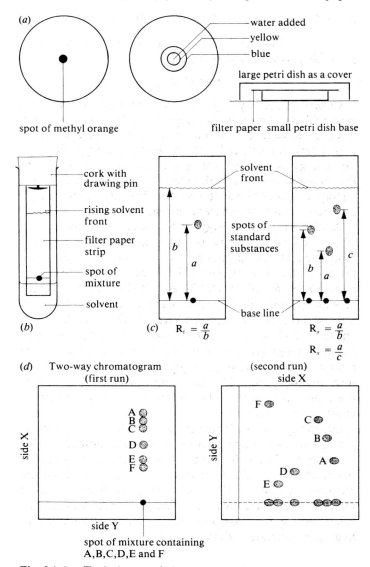

Fig A1.6   *Techniques of chromatography.*

is used. The test solution is applied to the base line near one end and the first separation is carried out. The paper is removed, dried and turned through 90° and a further chromatographic run is made with a different solvent. As a result the partially separated solutes of the first run are further separated in the second solvent which has different characteristics from the first. The paper is removed, dried, and the solutes located with a suitable reagent. The identification of a given compound can be made by comparison of its position with that of known standard compounds. This was the technique used by Calvin during his experiments to identify the initial products of the photosynthetic process (section 7.6.3).

Before running chromatograms of biological interest, it is helpful to practise the technique using coloured inks or indicators. The following experiments will show that the smaller, that is the more concentrated, the spot of origin, the better the separation. They also show that the longer the chromatogram runs, the better the separation of the samples.

Experiment A1.1: Separation of indicators

Materials

Whatman no. 1 or no. 3 filter paper petri dish
methyl orange (screened) pipette
bottle of 880 ammonia

Method

Place a drop of screened methyl orange in the centre of the filter paper. Wave the paper in the air to dry it, hold it over an open bottle of 880 ammonia for a short while and then place the paper over a petri dish (fig A1.6a). Add one drop of water to the spot of the indicator.

Observations

The two indicators present in the methyl orange move outwards at different rates, the blue ring moving faster than the yellow ring. The blue ring is the indicator bromothymol blue and the yellow is methyl orange.

Experiment A1.2: Separation of coloured inks into their various components

Materials

boiling tube   drawing pin
cork   water-soluble felt-tip pens
filter paper   distilled water

Method

(1) Obtain a boiling tube and cork as shown in fig A1.6b. Pin a rectangle of filter paper to the underside of the cork by means of a drawing pin. Draw a pencil line across the free end of the filter paper about 1 cm up from the end.
(2) Mark crosses at equal intervals across the paper on the origin line, one cross for each ink being tested.
(3) Using water-soluble felt-tip pens of different colours, spot a sample ink on each cross and label the spot in pencil below the origin. The spot should be no larger than 2 mm. Allow the spots to dry.
(4) Suspend the paper in the boiling tube so that the origin is close to the surface of the solvent with the end of the paper just immersed. The solvent is distilled water.
(5) Allow the chromatogram to run until the solvent front is 1 cm from the top of the paper. Remove the chromatogram and allow to dry, having marked the end of the solvent front in pencil.
(6) If larger scale chromatography tanks are available these can be used for either ascending or descending runs.

Experiment A1.3: To separate plant pigments by paper chromatography

Materials

leaves of nettle or   Buchner funnel
spinach   separating funnel
blender or knife   light petroleum (BP
90% propanone (acetone)   37.8–48.9 °C)
mortar and pestle   boiling tube and cork
small piece of capillary   filter paper
  tube   drawing pin

Method

Mince some leaves of nettle (*Urtica dioica*) or spinach in a blender (or simply cut them up into small pieces by chopping with a knife). Grind up the leaves with 90% propanone (acetone) in a mortar. Filter the extract through a Buchner funnel into a separating funnel. Add an equal volume of light petroleum. Shake the mixture thoroughly. Wash through with water several times and each time discard the water layer with its contents. The solvent for running the chromatogram is 100 parts of light petroleum : 12 parts of 90% propanone. Use a boiling tube and filter paper as described in the previous experiment. In the same manner rule a pencil line about 1 cm from the bottom of the filter paper. By means of a small piece of capillary tube, spot the mixture of pigments in the centre of the pencil line. Pour the solvent into the boiling tube to a depth of about 2 cm and then fix the cork and paper into the tube. The solvent should be allowed to run until it is just below the cork. This should take about 1–2 h. The tube should be placed in dim light.

Results

The following colour bands should be shown

Colour of spot	R_f value	Pigments present
yellow	0.95	carotene
yellow-grey	0.83	phaeophytin
yellow-brown	0.71	xanthophyll (often differentiates into two spots)
blue-green	0.65	chlorophyll *a*
green	0.45	chlorophyll *b*

Appendix 2
Biological techniques

A2.1　Scientific method

Science may be defined in terms of either knowledge or method. Scientific **knowledge** is the total body of factual material which has been accumulated (by scientific **method**) relating to the events of the material world.

'Science is almost wholly the outgrowth of pleasurable intellectual curiosity.'
A. N. Whitehead

In order to satisfy their curiosity, scientists must continually pose questions about the world. The secret of success in science is to ask the right questions.

'The formulation of a problem is often more essential than its solution, which may be mainly a matter of mathematical or experimental skill. To raise new questions, new possibilities, to regard old problems from a new angle, requires creative imagination and marks real advance in science.' Albert Einstein

Scientific investigations may begin in response to observations made by scientists or in response to some internal 'inductive' process on the part of scientists. Those aspects of knowledge which are described as scientific must, as the contemporary philosopher of science Karl Popper has stated, be capable of 'refutation'. This means that the facts of scientific knowledge must be testable and repeatable by other scientists. Thus it is essential that all scientific investigations are described fully and clearly as described in section A2.2. If investigations yield identical results under identical conditions, then the results may be accepted as valid. Knowledge which cannot be investigated as described above is not scientific and is described as 'metaphysical'.

Facts are based on **observations** obtained directly or indirectly by the senses or instruments, such as light or radio telescopes, light or electron microscope and cathode ray oscilloscopes, which act as extensions of our senses.

All the facts related to a particular problem are called **data**. Observations may be **qualitative** (that is describe colour, shape, taste, presence and so on) or **quantitative**. The latter is a more precise form of observation and involves the measurement of an amount or quantity which may have been demonstrated qualitatively.

Observations provide the raw material which leads to the formulation of a hypothesis (fig A2.1). A **hypothesis** is an assumption or question based on the observations, that may provide a valid explanation of the observations. Einstein stated that a hypothesis has two functions.

(1) It should account for all the observed facts relevant to that problem.
(2) It should lead to the prediction of new information. New observations (facts, data) which support the hypothesis will strengthen it. New observations which contradict the hypothesis must result in it being modified or even rejected.

In order to assess the validity of a hypothesis it is necessary to design a series of experiments aimed at producing new observations which will support or contradict the hypothesis. In most hypotheses there are a number of factors which may influence the observation; these are called **variables**. Hypotheses are objectively tested by a series of experiments in which each one of the hypothetical variables influencing the observations is

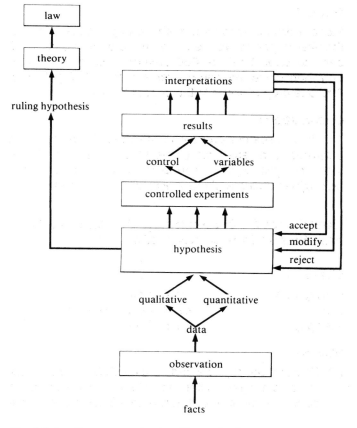

Fig A2.1　*Summary of scientific method.*

951

systematically eliminated. The experimental series is said to be **controlled** and this ensures that only one variable of the problem is tested at a given time.

The most successful hypothesis becomes a **ruling hypothesis**, and if it withstands attempts at falsification and continues to be successful in predicting previously unexplained facts and relationships it may become a **theory**.

The trend throughout scientific study is to achieve higher levels of predictability (probability). When a theory has proved invariable under all circumstances, or such variations as occur are systematic and predictable, then it may be accepted as a **law**.

As knowledge increases and techniques of investigation improve, hypotheses and even well-established theories may be challenged, modified and even rejected. Science is dynamic and controversial and the objective methods of science are always exposed to challenge.

A2.2 Laboratory work and writing up an experiment

Before beginning any experimental investigation, the aim of the experiment should be made clear. This may involve the testing of a hypothesis, such as 'The germination of seeds requires the presence of water, oxygen and an optimum temperature', or a more open-ended investigation, such as 'What is the effect of light on the behaviour of woodlice?'. In both cases the experiment must be designed so that it can be performed, and the data produced should be reliable, relevant to the aim and hopefully used in producing a conclusion.

All experiments should follow a logical progression in the reporting or writing up of the experiment.

(1) **Title**. This should be a clear statement outlining the problem to be investigated. For example *'Experiment to investigate the effect of pH on enzyme activity'*. It should be a broad statement of intent which is made specific by the hypothesis or aim.

(2) **Hypothesis or aim**. This is a statement of the problem or the posing of a question. It may include an indication of the variables under examination and the possible outcome of the investigation. For example *'To investigate the effect of solutions of pH 2–10 on the rate of digestion of the protein albumin by the enzyme pepsin and to determine the optimum pH of the reaction'*.

(3) **Method or procedure**. This is an account of the activities carried out during the performance of the experiment. It should be concise, precise and presented logically in the order in which the apparatus was set up and the activities performed during the experiment. It should be written in the past tense and not in the first person. Using the information given, another scientist should be able to repeat the experiment.

(4) **Results and observations**. These may be qualitative or quantitative and should be presented as clearly as possible in some appropriate form or forms, such as verbal description, tables of data, graphs, histograms, bar charts, kite diagrams and so on. If several numerical values are obtained for repeated measurements of one variable, the mean (x) of these values should be calculated and recorded.

(5) **Discussion**. This should be brief and take the form of the answer(s) to possible questions posed by the hypothesis, or confirmation of the aim. The discussion should not be a verbal repetition of the results, but an attempt to relate theoretical knowledge of the experimental variables to the results obtained.

A **conclusion** may be included if there is clear-cut verification of the stated aim. For example, for the aim given in (2) above a conclusion could state that there is 'a relationship between pH and enzyme activity and for this reaction the optimum pH is x'. The discussion of the results of this same experiment should include such theoretical aspects as the nature of the reaction and the possible chemical and physical aspects of the effects of pH on the three-dimensional structure of enzyme molecules.

A2.3 Presenting data

As a result of qualitative and quantitative investigations, observations are made and numerical data obtained. In order for the maximum amount of information to be gained from investigations, they must be planned carefully and the data must be presented comprehensively and analysed thoroughly.

A2.3.1 Tabulations

Tables form the simplest way of presenting data and consist of columns displaying the values for two or more related variables. This method gives neither an immediate nor clear indication of the relationships between the variables, but is often the first step in recording information and forms the basis for selecting some subsequent form of graphical representation.

A2.3.2 Graphical representation

A graph is a two-dimensional plot of two or more measured variables. In its simplest form a graph consists of two axes. The vertical y axis bears values called **ordinates** which show the magnitude of the **dependent** variable. This is the 'unknown quantity', that is the variable whose value is not chosen by the experimenter. The horizontal x axis bears values called **abscissae** which show the magnitude of the **independent** variable, which is the known quantity, that is the variable whose value is chosen by the experimenter.

The following stages are used in constructing a graph.

(1) The scale and intervals for each axis should match the magnitude of the variables being plotted and fill the graph paper as completely as possible.

(2) Each axis should begin at 0, but if all the values for one variable are clustered together, such as ten points lying between 6.12 and 6.68, a large scale will be required to cover these points. In this case, still begin with the axis at 0 but mark a break in the axis, marked as ─/ /─, just beyond.

(3) Each axis must be labelled fully in terms of the variable, for example 'temperature/°C', and have equally spaced intervals covering the range of the interval, such as 0–60 at 12 five-unit intervals.

(4) The points plotted on the graph are called **coordinates** and represent the corresponding values of the two variables, such as when $x = a$ and $y = b$.

(5) Actual points should be marked by an **X** or ⊙ and never by a dot only.

(6) The points marked on the graph are the record of the actual observations made and may be joined by a series of straight line segments drawn with a ruler, by a smooth curve or, in some cases, a regression line (a line of best fit) (section A2.4.3). These graphs are called **line graphs**. Straight line segments and smooth curves are preferable to a regression line.

(7) The graph should have a full title, such as 'Graph showing the relationship between . . .'.

(8) Only the points on the graph represent actual data, but estimates of other values can be obtained from reading off coordinates at any point on the line. This is called **interpolation**. Similarly, coordinates outside the range of the graph may be determined by extending the line of the graph, a technique known as **extrapolation**. In both cases it must be stressed that these values are only estimates.

In graphs where the x axis is 'time', the steepness of the curve or **gradient** at any point can be calculated and this gives a measure of the rate of change of the variable under investigation. For example, in the graph shown in fig A2.2 the rate of growth is calculated by drawing a tangent to the curve at the desired point and completing a triangle with the tangent at the hypotenuse, as shown in fig A2.3. The value of the y interval is then divided by the value of the x interval and this gives the rate of change in terms of the units used in labelling the graph.

A2.3.3   Frequency distributions

Many relationships exist where each value of the dependent variable, corresponding to the independent variable, represents the number of times the latter value occurs, that is its frequency. Such relationships form a **frequency distribution** or **distribution**, for example lengths of earthworms in a population.

(a)

Time/days	0	2	4	6	8	10	12	14	16	18	20	22	24	26
Mean height/mm	1	2	4	11	24	43	73	92	105	112	117	122	124	126

(b)

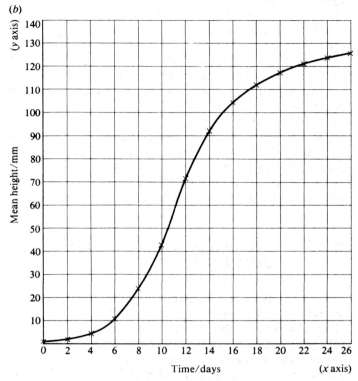

Fig A2.2   (a) Two sets of data relating to mean heights of oat seedlings and time. (b) Graph showing the relationship between mean heights of oat seedlings and time.

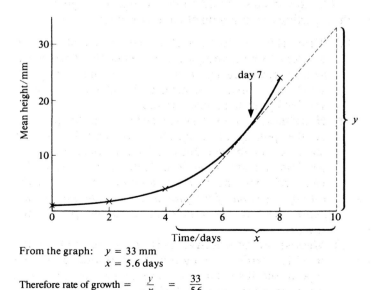

From the graph: $y = 33$ mm
$x = 5.6$ days

Therefore rate of growth $= \dfrac{y}{x} = \dfrac{33}{5.6}$

$= 5.9$ mm day^{-1}

Fig A2.3   Method of calculating rate of change at a given point, for example day 7.

If the value of the independent variable can assume any value within a given range, its frequency distribution can be represented by a conventional graph as described above. These graphs are called **frequency curves** and may take one of the following forms depending upon how the data are presented. If the data are presented as numbers of individuals within defined intervals as shown in fig A2.4a, the distribution is known as a **continuous distribution** and the total area beneath the curve represents the total frequency.

(1) **Normal distribution curve**. Here the frequency distribution is symmetrical about a central value and examples include physical parameters such as height and mass of biological structure. This type of distribution is shown in fig A2.4.

(2) **Positive skew**. Here the curve is asymmetrical, with the highest frequencies of the independent variable corresponding to its lower values and with a 'tail off' towards the higher values as shown in fig A2.5a. Examples include number of children per family, clutch size in birds and density of phytoplankton with depth.

(3) **Negative skew**. Here the highest frequencies of the independent variable correspond to the higher values and 'tail off' towards the lower values, as shown in fig 2.5b. This form of distribution is rarer than positive skew and represents a distribution showing some form of bias. Examples include optimum temperature for enzyme-controlled reactions and the output of thyroid-stimulating hormone in response to thyroxine.

(4) **Bimodal distribution**. Here there are two peaks (or modes), and it usually indicates the presence of two populations each exhibiting a partial normal distribution.

(a)

Mass class/kg	50-52	52-54	54-56	56-58	58-60	60-62	62-64	64-66	66-68	68-70	70-72
Frequency	4	7	11	16	24	29	26	16	8	4	2

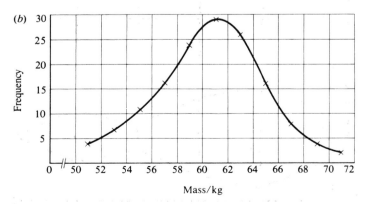

Fig A2.4 (a) Number of 18-year-old males falling into 2 kg mass classes and represented as a table. (b) The graph representing the data from (a) forms a normal distribution curve.

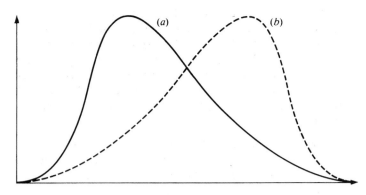

Fig A2.5 (a) Positive skewed distribution. (b) Negative skewed distribution.

(5) **Cumulative frequency distribution**. The data presented in fig A2.4 may be presented as in fig A2.6, where the cumulative number of individuals below certain arbitrary class boundaries are shown. Where these data are presented graphically a cumulative frequency curve is produced.

(a)

Mass/kg	50	52	54	56	58	60	62	64	66	68	70	72
Cumulative frequency	0	4	11	22	38	62	91	117	133	141	145	147

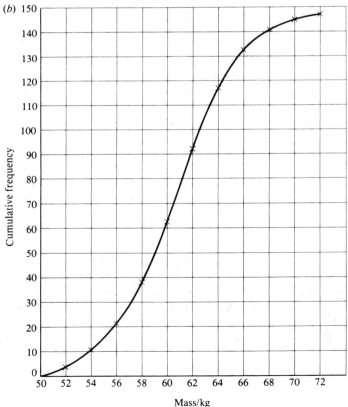

Fig A2.6 Data (a) and graph (b) based upon fig A2.8a showing the cumulative frequency distribution of mass in 18-year-old males.

If the values of the independent variable assume discrete values, that is whole numbers such as 3 and 5 (as in the numbers of petals of a dicotyledon), or represent physical traits such as blood groups, they exist as only discrete values and the distribution is described as **discontinuous**. In these cases it is inappropriate to plot a continuous graph and other forms of graphical representation are used as described below.

(1) **Column graph**. This shows the frequency with which distinct characteristics occur within a population, such as human blood groups (see fig A2.7a).

(2) **Histogram**. This represents continuous values of the independent variable which have been grouped into classes of equal widths. Where classes of equal width are chosen, for example 0–5, 5–10, 10–15, and so on, the limits of the interval are conventionally represented by the lower integer, that is 0–4.99, 5–9.99, 10–14.99 and so on. This is a useful way of representing data from a small sample and superficially resembles a column graph (fig A2.7b).

(3) **Bar graph**. This is a modified form of histogram usually representing the relationship between a continuous dependent variable, such as energy content, and a non-numerical independent variable, for example various foods (fig A2.7c). A modified form of bar graph is used in presenting ecological data and this is called a **presence–absence graph**. An example of this is shown in fig 11.22.

(4) **Kite diagram**. This is a special type of bar graph that provides an extremely clear visual display of the change in frequency of non-numerical variables which are continuously distributed within an area. A kite diagram is constructed by plotting the frequencies of each variable as a line symmetrically placed astride the x axis as shown in fig A2.8a. Once all of the frequencies have been plotted along the x axis, the adjacent limits of the lines are joined together by straight lines, as in a line graph, as shown in fig A2.8b. The enclosed area is usually shaded to present a clearer visual display. The use of kite diagrams is described in section 11.4.3.

Each one of the methods of presenting data described above is applicable to different biological situations, and all are represented in the chapters in these books. All methods have their relative merits, and the choice of which to use should be made on the basis of which will accurately and efficiently reveal relationships and patterns between variables.

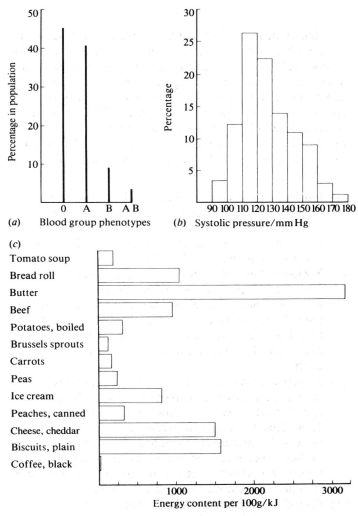

Fig A2.7 *Methods of presenting data. (a) Column graph showing frequency of blood group phenotypes in the population. (b) Histogram showing systolic blood pressure frequencies in women aged 30–9 years. (c) Bar chart showing energy content of foods in a three-course meal.*

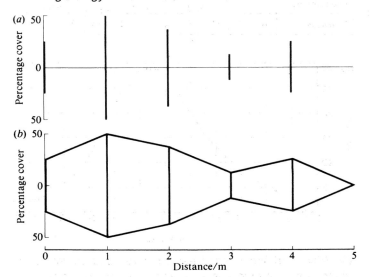

Fig A2.8 *(a) and (b) method of constructing a kite diagram.*

A2.4 Elementary statistical methods in biology

When data are recorded as a series of values representing variables, such as heights or heart rate, it is useful to know both the average value and the spread of values. Estimates of the average value are called 'measures of central tendency' and these include the mean, the median and the mode. Estimates of the spread of values are called 'measures of dispersion' and they include variance and standard deviation.

A2.4.1 Measures of central tendency

Mean (arithmetic mean)

This is the 'average' of a group of values and is obtained by adding the values together and dividing the total by the number of individual values. For example, the mean ($\bar{x}$) for values $x_1, x_2, x_3, x_4, ... x_n$ is given by

$$\bar{x} = \frac{x_1 + x_2 + x_3 ...... + x_n}{n}$$

$$\text{or } x = \frac{\Sigma x}{n}$$

where Σ = sum or total of, x = individual values and n = number of individual values.

If the same value of x occurs more than once, the mean ($\bar{x}$) can be calculated using the expression

$$\bar{x} = \frac{\Sigma fx}{\Sigma f}$$

where Σf = sum of the frequencies of x, or simply n.

Median

This represents the middle or central value of a set of values. For example, if five values of x are arranged in ascending order as x_1, x_2, x_3, x_4 and x_5, the median value would be x_3 since there are as many values above it as below it. If there are an even number of values of x, for example x_1 to x_6, the median is represented as the mean of the two middle values (($x_3 + x_4$)/2).

Mode

This is the most frequently occurring value of a set of values. For example if the numbers of children in 10 families is 1, 1, 1, 2, 2, 2, 2, 2, 3, 4, the mode or modal value is 2.

Each of the three values described above has its relative advantages, disadvantages and applicability. One example of the use of mean and mode is illustrated by reference to the number of children per family. The mean number of children per family is 2.4, but as children are discrete beings it is more usual to describe the number of children per family in whole numbers, thus using the modal value which is 2.

In a normal frequency distribution the values of the mean, the median and the mode coincide as shown in fig A2.9a, whereas in cases where the frequency distribution is skewed, these values do not coincide as shown in fig A2.9b.

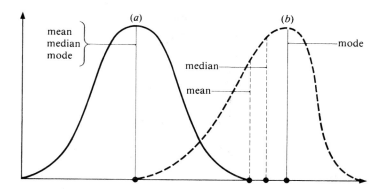

Fig A2.9 *Distributions of mean, median and mode in (a) a normal distribution and (b) a skewed distribution.*

A2.4.2 Measures of dispersion

Measures of dispersion are used in conjunction with measures of central tendency to give an indication of the extent to which values are 'spread' or 'clustered' around the 'average'. This is illustrated with respect to a normal distribution by the curves shown in fig A2.10. In statistical analysis, one of the most useful measures of dispersion is the root mean square deviation or standard deviation, since it may be applied both to predicting the distribution of values about the average and to determining whether two sets of data are significantly different from one another and the degree of difference between them.

Standard deviation

The standard deviation (s) of a set of values is a measure of the variation from the arithmetical mean of these values and is calculated using the expression

$$s = \sqrt{\left(\frac{\Sigma fx^2}{\Sigma f} - \bar{x}^2 \right)}$$

where Σ = sum of, f = frequency of occurrence of, x = specific values, and $\bar{x}$ = mean of the specific values.

For example, a sample of ten common limpet shells (*Patella vulgaris*) from a rocky shore have the following maximum basal diameters in millimetres: 36, 34, 41, 39, 37, 43, 36, 37, 41, 39. In order to calculate the mean maximum basal diameter and the standard deviation it is necessary to calculate f, fx^2 and x^2 as shown in the following table:

x	f	fx	fx^2
34	1	34	1 156
36	2	72	2 592
37	2	74	2 738
39	2	78	3 042
41	2	82	3 362
43	1	43	1 849
	$\Sigma f = 10$	$\Sigma fx = 383$	$\Sigma fx^2 = 14\ 739$

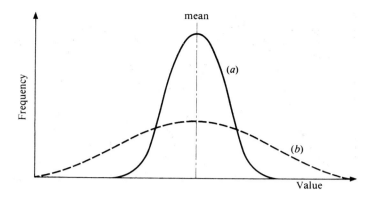

Fig A2.10 *Two normal distribution curves showing the distribution of two sets of data (possibly populations) with identical total frequencies (that is the areas under the curves are equal). Curve (a) has a restricted range and is clustered around the mean. Curve (b) represents a wider range and is not clustered around the mean.*

Therefore $\bar{x} = 38.3$ and $\bar{x}^2 = 1\,466.9$.

$$s = \sqrt{\left(\frac{\Sigma fx^2}{\Sigma f} - \bar{x}^2 \right)}$$

$$s = \sqrt{\left(\frac{14\,739}{10} - 1466.9 \right)}$$

$$= \sqrt{\left(1473.9 - 1466.9 \right)}$$

$$= \sqrt{7}$$

Therefore $s = 2.65$.

In this population of the common limpet the mean maximum basal diameter of the shell is 38.3 mm, with a standard deviation of 2.7 mm (correct to one decimal place). If these values are applied to a larger population of the common limpet then it may be assumed, on statistical grounds, that approximately 68% of the population will have a basal diameter of the shell of 38.3 mm plus and minus one standard deviation (2.7 mm), that is they will lie within a range 35.6–41.0 mm; approximately 95% of the population will have a basal diameter of the shell of 38.3 plus and minus two standard deviations (5.4 mm), that is they will lie within the range 32.9–43.7 mm, and practically 100% will lie within plus and minus three standard deviations. The value of calculating the standard deviation is that it gives a measure of the spread of values from the mean. A small standard deviation indicates that there is little dispersion or variation from the mean and that the population is fairly homogeneous, as shown by curve (a) in fig A2.10. As the value of the standard deviation increases, the degree of variation within the population increases as shown by curve (b) in fig A2.10.

Variance

The **variance** is the square of the standard deviation and the variance for a set of numbers is calculated using the expression:

$$\text{variance } (s^2) = \frac{\Sigma fx^2}{\Sigma f} - \bar{x}^2$$

where f is the number of values in the set.

Variance is useful in ecological investigations involving, nutrition, reproduction and behaviour since it gives an indication of how organisms are dispersed within the population. Populations may be:

* randomly dispersed,
* aggregated into clusters, or
* regularly dispersed.

To determine the type of population dispersion within an area, the area is divided up into a number of equal-sized quadrats (section 11.2) and the number of individuals within the population, per quadrat, is counted. From these data the mean and variance are calculated using the expressions:

$$\text{mean } (\bar{x}) = \frac{\Sigma fx}{f} \qquad \text{variance } (s^2) = \frac{\Sigma fx^2}{\Sigma f} - \bar{x}^2$$

where f is the number of quadrats containing x individuals. Using the following expression:

$$\text{population dispersion} = \frac{\text{variance}}{\text{mean}}$$

the three types of dispersion can be determined as shown in fig A2.11.

A2.4.3   Relationships between variables

Data should always be presented in such a way as to reveal relationships between two or more sets of data. The simplest way of doing this is to plot a graph showing the relationship between variables, but this is only valuable if one of the variables (the independent variable) is under the control of the experimenter, as for example in the case of data shown in fig A2.2.

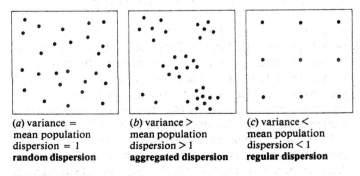

(a) variance = mean population dispersion = 1 **random dispersion**

(b) variance > mean population dispersion > 1 **aggregated dispersion**

(c) variance < mean population dispersion < 1 **regular dispersion**

Fig A2.11 *Types of dispersion.*

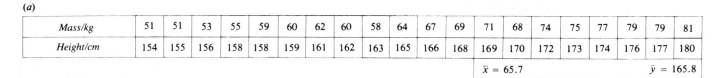

(a)

Mass/kg	51	51	53	55	59	60	62	60	58	64	67	69	71	68	74	75	77	79	79	81
Height/cm	154	155	156	158	158	159	161	162	163	165	166	168	169	170	172	173	174	176	177	180

$\bar{x} = 65.7$ $\bar{y} = 165.8$

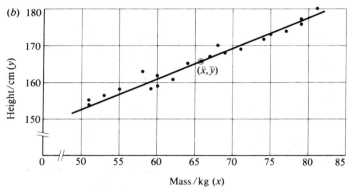

Fig A2.12 *Data showing mass and corresponding heights of 20 16-year-old male students, represented as a table (a) and a scatter diagram (b). The regression line is drawn.*

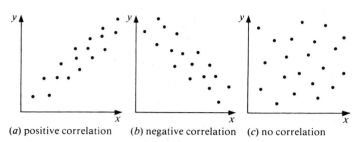

(a) positive correlation   (b) negative correlation   (c) no correlation

Fig A2.13 *Patterns of correlation; (a) positive correlation; (b) negative correlation; (c) no correlation.*

In other cases, where both variables are dependent, the value of one variable is plotted against the corresponding value of the other variable as, for example, in the case of heights and masses of 20 sixth-form students given in fig A2.12a. These values are plotted and shown in fig A2.12b, which is called a **scatter diagram**. Visual inspection shows that there is some form of relationship between the two variables but this cannot be described more accurately until a relationship, presented by a straight line, can be drawn through the points.

This single line is called a **'line of best fit'** or a **regression line** and the proximity of the points to the line gives an indication of the degree of correlation between the two variables. The position of the line of best fit should pass through the point representing the mean values of mass and height ($\bar{x} = 65.7$ kg and $\bar{y} = 165.8$ cm) and the distribution of points above and below the line should be approximately equal. From this line the predicted values of height corresponding to mass can be calculated.

Correlation

The relationship between the two variables, x and y, described above may be represented by a term called **correlation**. Varying degrees of correlation may exist between x and y as shown by the scatter diagrams in fig A2.13.

Presenting data in the form of a scatter diagram is not a reliable way of demonstrating the significance of the correlation since it is subjective. It is possible to represent correlation in terms of a statistical measure called the **correlation coefficient**. This can vary between −1 and +1; −1 represents a perfect negative correlation, such as oxygen tension in the atmosphere and rate of spiracle opening in insects; 0 represents no correlation, such as size of tomato fruits and number of seeds; +1 represents a perfect positive correlation, such as age and body length in the locust.

Appendix 3
Nomenclature and units

A3.1   Alphabetical list of common current names of chemicals

Old name	New name (nc = no change)
acetaldehyde	ethanal
acetamide	ethanamide or nc
acetic acid	ethanoic acid or nc
acetoacetic acid	3-oxobutanoic acid
acetone	propanone
acetylene	ethyne
adenine	nc
adenosine	nc
adipic acid	hexanedioic acid
alanine	2-aminopropanoic acid
alcohol (ethyl)	ethanol
alcohol (wood)	methanol
aldehyde	nc
aldol	3-hydroxybutanal
aliphatic	nc
alkyl	nc
ammonium hydroxide	ammonia solution
p-amino benzoic acid	{ (4-aminobenzoic acid (4-aminobenzenecarboxylic acid
aspartic acid	aminobutanedoic acid
benzaldehyde	benzenecarbaldehyde or nc
benzene	nc
benzoic acid	benzenecarboxylic acid or nc
bicarbonate	hydrogencarbonate
butyric acid	butanoic acid
camphor	nc
cane sugar	sucrose
carbon tetrachloride	tetrachloromethane
carboxylic acids	nc
chloroform	trichloromethane

citric acid	2-hydroxypropane-1,2,3-tricarboxylic acid
cobalt chloride	cobalt(II) chloride
dextrose	(+) glucose
ethyl acetate	ethyl ethanoate or nc
ethyl alcohol	ethanol
ethylene	ethene
ferric	iron(III)
ferrous	iron(II)
formaldehyde	methanal
fructose	nc
fumaric acid	*trans*-butanedioic acid
glucose	nc
glutamic acid	2-aminopentanedioic acid
glycerine/glycerol	propane-1,2,3-triol
glycine	aminoethanoic acid / aminoacetic acid
glycolic acid	hydroxyethanoic acid / hydroxyacetic acid
glyoxyllic acid	oxoethanoic acid / oxoacetic acid
indoleacetic acid (IAA)	indolylethanoic acid
isopropyl alcohol	propan-2-ol
lactic acid	2-hydroxypropanoic acid
lactose	nc
malic acid	2-hydroxybutanedioic acid
malonic acid	propanedioic acid
maltose	nc
nitric acid	nc
oleic acid	*cis*-octadec-9-enoic acid
oxalic acid	ethanedioic acid
palmitic acid	hexadecanoic acid
phenol	nc
phosphate	phosphate(V)
phosphoric acid	phosphoric(V) acid
phosphorous acid	phosphoric acid
potassium permanganate	potassium manganate(VII)
pyridine	nc
pyrogallol	benzene-1,2,3-triol
pyruvic acid	2-oxopropanoic acid
quinol	benzene-1,4-diol
stearic acid	octadecanoic acid
succinic acid	butanedoic acid
sucrose	nc
1-tartaric acid	(-) 2,3-dihydroxybutanedioic acid
thiourea	thiocarbamide or nc
toluene	methylbenzene
urea	carbamide or nc
n-valeric acid	pentanoic acid
xylene	dimethylbenzene

A3.2 Units, symbols, abbreviations and conventional terms

absolute	abs.
adenosine 5'-pyrophosphate	ADP *use* adenosine diphosphate
adenosine 5'-triphosphate	ATP *use* adenosine triphosphate
adrenocorticotrophic hormone	ACTH
angstrom	Å *preferably* use SI units $10\ \text{Å} = 1\ \text{nm}$
anterior	ant.
antidiuretic hormone	ADH
approximately equal	$\approx$
basal metabolic rate	b.m.r. or BMR
calciferol	vitamin D_2 preferred for biological activity (vitamin D is the generic term)
calorie	cal *use* SI unit joule $1\ \text{cal} = 4.2\ \text{J}$
Centigrade	*use* Celsius (°C)
central nervous system	CNS
cerebrospinal fluid	c.s.f. or CSF
chi-squared	χ^2
coenzyme A	CoA
degree Celsius	°C
deoxyribonucleic acid	DNA
endoplasmic reticulum	ER
extracellular fluid	e.c.f. or ECF
figure (diagram)	fig
Geiger–Müller tube	GM
gram	g (gramme is continental spelling)
growth hormone	GH
haemoglobin	Hb
joule	J
kilo ($10^3 \times$)	k
Krebs cycle	or tricarboxylic acid cycle
luteinising hormone	LH
mass	m
maximum	max.
mean value of x (statistics)	$\bar{x}$
minimum	min.
minute	min
molar (concentration)	M (mol dm^{-3}) molar means 'divided by amount of substance'
mole (unit of amount of substance)	mol replaces gram-molecule, gram-ion, gram-atom etc.
negative logarithm of hydrogen ion concentration	pH, plural – pH values
newton	N
normal saline	avoid *use* isosmotic saline
number of observations	n (or f)
parts per million	ppm
petroleum ether	avoid *use* light petroleum
pressure	p
red blood corpuscle	r.b.c. or RBC
respiratory quotient	r.q. or RQ
ribonucleic acid	RNA
solidus	/ expressed in units of
solution	soln.
species	sp. (singular), spp. (plural)
standard deviation (of hypothetical population)	s
(of observed sample)	S or s.d.
sum (statistics) (of hypothetical population)	Σ
(of observed sample)	S or Σ
temperature (quantity)	T (absolute) / t (other scales)
thyroid stimulating hormone	TSH
time	t
variety (biology)	var.
volume	vol.
white blood corpuscle	w.b.c. or WBC

A3.3   SI units

A3.3.1   Names and symbols for SI units

Physical quantity	Name of SI unit	Symbol
length	metre	m
mass	kilogram	kg
time	second	s
electric current	ampere	A
thermodynamic temperature	kelvin	K
luminous intensity	candela	cd
amount of substance	mole	mol
solid angle	steradian	sr

A3.3.2   Derived units from SI units

Quantity	SI unit	Symbol	Expressed in terms of SI units
work, energy, quantity of heat	joule	J	$kg\ m^2\ s^{-2}$; $1\ J = 1\ N\ m$
force	newton	N	$kg\ m\ s^{-2}$; $= J\ m^{-1}$
power	watt	W	$kg\ m^2\ s^{-3}$; $= J\ s^{-1}$
quantity of electricity	coulomb	C	$A\ s$
electrical potential	volt	V	$kg\ m^2\ s^{-3}\ A^{-1}$; $W\ A$
luminous flux	lumen	lm	$cd\ sr$
illumination	lux	lx	$cd\ sr\ m^{-2}$ or $lm\ m^{-2}$
area	square metre		m^2
volume	cubic metre		m^3
density	kilogram per cubic metre		$kg\ m^{-3}$

A3.3.3   Special units still in use (should be progressively abandoned)

Quantity	Unit name and symbol		Conversion factor to SI
length	angstrom	Å	$10^{-10}\ m = 0.1\ nm$
length	micron	μm	$10^{-6}\ m = 10^{-3}\ mm = 1\ \mu m$
volume	litre	l	$10^{-3}\ m^3 = 1\ dm^3$
mass	tonne	t	$10^3\ kg = Mg$
pressure	millimetres of mercury	mmHg	$10^2\ mmHg = 13.3\ kPa$

A3.3.4   Prefixes for SI units

These are used to indicate decimal fractions of the basic or derived SI units.

Multiplication factor	Prefix	Symbol
$0.000\ 000\ 000\ 001 = 10^{-12}$	pico	p
$0.000\ 000\ 001 = 10^{-9}$	nano	n
$0.000\ 001 = 10^{-6}$	micro	μ
$0.001 = 10^{-3}$	milli	m
$1000 = 10^3$	kilo	k
$1\ 000\ 000 = 10^6$	mega	M
$1\ 000\ 000\ 000 = 10^9$	giga	G
$1\ 000\ 000\ 000\ 000 = 10^{12}$	tera	T

Thus 1 nanometre (nm) $= 1 \times 10^{-9}$ m,
also 1 centimetre (cm) $= 1 \times 10^{-2}$ m.
Note that the kilogram is somewhat out of place in the above table since it is a basic SI unit. In the school laboratory the most convenient units are grams (g) and cubic centimetres (cm^3). Where possible the basic SI units should be used.

A3.3.5   Rules for writing SI units

- The symbol is not an abbreviation and thus a full stop is not written after the symbol except at the end of a sentence.
- There is no plural form of a unit; thus 20 kg or 30 m, not 20 kgs or 30 ms.
- Capital initial letters are never used for units except when named after famous scientists, such as N (Newton), W (Watt) and J (Joule).
- Symbols combined in a quotient can be written as, for example, metre per second or $m\ s^{-1}$. The use of the solidus (stroke, /) is restricted to indicating the unit of a variable, such as temperature /°C.
- The raised decimal point is not correct. The internationally accepted decimal sign is placed level with the feet of the numerals, for example 3.142. The comma is no longer used to separate groups of three digits but a space is left instead so that figures appear 493 645 189 not as 493,645,189.

Appendix 4
The geological time scale

The history of the Earth is divided for convenience into a series of four geological **eras** and eleven periods. The two most recent periods are further divided into seven systems or **epochs**.

The rocks of the Earth's crust are stratified, that is they lie layer upon layer. Unless disrupted by earth movements, the rocks get progressively younger towards the top of a series of layers (strata). William Smith in the eighteenth century noticed an association between fossil groups and particular strata. The sequence of fossils revealed a gradual increase in complexity of organisms from the lower strata to the highest, indicating that over geological periods of time some organisms have advanced in complexity.

Radioactive dating has established an approximate age for the oldest rocks belonging to each period. The geological time scale and the distinctive biological events associated with each period, as revealed by fossil evidence, are shown in table A4.1.

A4.1　The age of the Earth

Current estimates are that the planet Earth is about $4.6-4.9 \times 10^9$ years old. These estimates are based mainly on the dating of rocks (**geochronology**) by radioactive dating techniques.

In section A1.3 it was explained that atoms of some elements exist in a number of forms called isotopes, some of which are radioactive. Radioactive elements 'decay' at a constant rate which is independent of temperature, gravity, magnetism or any other force. The rate is measured in terms of the 'half-life'.

Three principal methods of radioactive dating are currently used, as shown in fig A4.1. Methods (1) and (2) are used for determining the ages of rocks in the Earth's crust, whereas the third method, radiocarbon dating, is used for dating fossils and has direct relevance in discussions of the history of life.

Radiocarbon dating

The normal non-radioactive isotope of carbon is ^{12}C. The radioactive isotope, ^{14}C, occurs in minute quantities (<0.1%) in air, surface waters and living organisms. It is continually being produced in the atmosphere by the action

Table A4.1 Geological time scale and history of life (age = years $\times 10^6$).

Era	Period	Epoch	Age	Animal groups	Plant groups
CENOZOIC (*cenos*, recent)	Quaternary	Recent (Holocene)	0.01	Dominance of humans	
		Glacial (Pleistocene)	2	Origin of humans	
	Tertiary	Pliocene	7	Adaptive radiation of mammals	Adaptive radiation of flowering plants, especially herbaceous types
		Miocene	26		
		Oligocene	38	Dogs and bears appeared	
		Eocene	54	Apes and pigs appeared	
		Palaeocene	65	Horses, cattle and elephants	
MESOZOIC (*mesos*, middle)	Cretaceous		135	Extinction of ammonites and dinosaurs; origin of modern fish and placental mammals	Dominance of flowering plants
	Jurassic		195	Dinosaurs dominant; origin of birds and mammals; insects abundant	Origin of flowering plants
	Triassic		225	Dinosaurs appear; adaptive radiation of reptiles	Abundance of cycads and conifers
PALAEOZOIC (*palaeos*, ancient)	Permian		280	Adaptive radiation of reptiles; beetles appear; extinction of trilobites	Origin of conifers
	Carboniferous		350	Origin of reptiles and insects; adaptive radiation of amphibia	Abundance of tree-like ferns, e.g. *Lepidodendron*, forming 'coal forests'
	Devonian		400	Origin of amphibia and ammonites; spiders appear; adaptive radiation of fish (cartilaginous and bony)	Earliest mosses and ferns
	Silurian		440	Origin of jawed fish; earliest coral reefs	Earliest spore-bearing, vascular plants
	Ordovician		500	Origin of vertebrates, jawless fish; trilobites, molluscs and crustacea abundant	
	Cambrian		570	Origin of all non-vertebrate phyla and echinoderms	
ARCHEOZOIC	Pre-Cambrian		1 000	*Selected organisms* primitive metazoans	
			2 000	primitive eukaryotes	
			3 000	blue-green bacteria (prokaryotes), bacteria	
			3 500?	origins of life?	
			5 000?	origin of Earth?	

(1) Uranium/thorium methods
Uranium and thorium are generally found occurring together in the same rocks

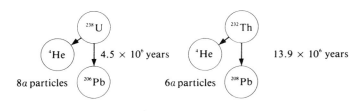

(2) Potassium/argon methods

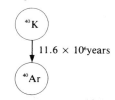

(3) Radiocarbon dating methods

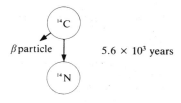

Fig A4.1 *Radiometric dating techniques.*

of cosmic rays on nitrogen and oxygen nuclei, and there is good evidence to suggest that the rate of ^{14}C production has been constant for several thousand years. An equilibrium has been set up whereby production of ^{14}C balances ^{14}C loss by radioactive decay. ^{14}C is found occurring freely as $^{14}CO_2$ and the ratio of $^{14}C : {}^{12}C$ compounds remains theoretically constant. Living organisms absorb ^{14}C either as carbon dioxide or as organic molecules throughout life. At death no more carbon is taken in and the ^{14}C continues to decay according to the rate shown by the half-life. By calculating the amount of ^{14}C in the dead organism and comparing it with the amount of ^{14}C in a living organism, the age of the dead organism can be estimated. For example, if the amount of ^{14}C in a fossil mammalian bone was found to be one-quarter that in the same bone from a recently killed mammal and the half-life is 5.6×10^3 years, the estimated age of the fossil bone would theoretically be 11.2×10^3 years. Using this technique, organic remains can be dated back, fairly accurately, for up to 10.0×10^4 years.

There are many sources of error involved in radiometric dating, so ages determined by these methods are only approximate. However, these methods have proved to be of great value in extending our knowledge of the Earth.

Index

References to figures are underlined; to tables are *underlined italics*

reticulo-endothelial system 484; *see also* macro-phage *and* neutrophil *under* white blood cells
retina 588, 589
    convergence 590, 591
    photoreception mechanism 591–2
    see also cones; rods
retinal structure 589, *591*
retinine 591
retrovirus 524; *see also* HIV
reverse transcriptase
    for gene copying 835, *836*, 837
    HIV replication by 511
rhesus factor 492, *493*, 744–5
rheumatoid arthritis 531
rhizome 703
ribosomes
    binding to ER 803
    role in protein synthesis 802–3, *804*
    70S, as antibiotic binding site *519*
ribs *627*, 629, 630
ring species 926
ringing experiments 445, 452, *454*
risk assessment, in genetic disease 872
RNA 798
    as chromosome component 790
    role of 801
RNA polymerase 802
mRNA 798, 799, *802*, *804*, *805*, *836*
    complementary bases *800*
    DNA strand selection 807
    function of 800, 801
rRNA 798, 801
tRNA 798, 801, *804*, *805*
    synthesis of, and cytokines 546
rods 589–91
    convergence and summation 586
    photoreception mechanism 591–2
    synaptic convergence 590, 591
root
    anatomy of dicot *447*
    cell differentiation in 769
    effect of auxin concentration *537*, 538
    mineral uptake *448*, 449–50
    primary growth 768–9
    radicle 723, 766
    tap root 704
    water uptake by 447–9
root cap 768, *769*
root pressure, and water movement 447
rubella *499*, *501*, 744
runner 703

sacral vertebrae *627*, *628*, 629–30
sacrum 629–30
saltatory conduction 560
saltatory evolution 890
SAN (sino-atrial node) 473, 474, 475
sapwood 771
sarcolemma 564, *565*, 637–8
sarcomere 635, 636–8
sarcoplasmic reticulum *637*
satellite 874
saturation of receptors 584, *586*
scapula *627*, 631
sclera 588
scientific investigation method 808
sebum 657
second messenger mechanism 600–1, 731
secondary sexual characteristics 771, 774
secondary thickening 770, *771*
secretin *599*
seed
    development of 723–4
    dormancy 763
    embryo growth 766
    reproduction strategy assessment 724

seed food reserve 702–4, 764
    mobilisation of 542, *543*
seedless fruit development 544, 551
segregation 809–11, *815*
selection: *see* artificial *and* natural selection
selection pressure 914, 916–17, 920
selective advantage 887
self-sterility 719
semi-conservative replication 794, *795*, *796*
semicircular canals *594*, 596–7
seminal vesicles 726
seminiferous tubules 725, *726*, *729*
senescence: *see* ageing
senile dementia 528
sensitivity
    of animals 556
    visual 586, 590, 591
sensory areas of brain 579–80
    cortex *579*, 580, *581*
sensory cells
    adaptation of 584
    as excitable cells 584
    thresholds of 584, *585*, *586*
sensory neurones, spinal cord connection 575
sensory receptor 583–6
    convergence of 586
    feedback control system 586
    spontaneous activity 586
    summation of 586
    mechanoreceptors 586–7
    thermoreceptors 587
    see also ear; eye; transduction
sepals 713, *715*
serotonin *567*, 568
Sertoli cells 729, 730–1
serum 460
serum globulins *461*
severe combined immunodeficiency disease (SCID) 873–4
sewage disposal 496–7, 515
sex attractants 617
sex chromosomes 745, 820–2, *823*
    (non-)homologous regions *822*
sex determination, fetal 869, 874
sex genotypes 820
sex hormones
    and cardiovascular disease 522
    and growth 774
    see also follicle stimulating hormone; gonadotrophin releasing hormone; human chorionic gonadotropin; inhibin; luteinising hormone; oestrogen; testosterone
sex-limited inheritance 821
sex-linked syndromes 821–2
    colour-blindness 593
    Klinefelter's *858*, 865, *866*, 867
    Turner's *858*, 866, 867
    see also haemophilia
sexual behaviour, and androgens 775
sexual reproduction 711–12
    adaptation to land 712–13
    of amphibia 725
    of birds 725
    comparison with asexual reproduction *712*
    of fish 724
    and meiosis 778
    reproductive organs, development pattern 761
    of reptiles 725
sexual reproduction, flowering plants 712–24
    anatomy of flower 713–14
    assessment of 724
    fertilisation 721–2
    ovule development 715, *718*
    pollen grain development 714–15, *717*

seed and fruit development 723–4
    see also embryo, development of; ovary; pollination
sexual reproduction, human
    fertilisation 736–7
    intercourse 735
    movement of sperm 735–6
    see also birth; birth control; embryo, development of; infertility; ovary; pregnancy
shivering 658–9
shoot, effect of auxin concentration *537*, 538
shoot growth
    cell differentiation during 768
    plant growth substance interrelations 548
    primary 767–8
shunt vessels 466, 658, 659
sickle-cell anaemia 833, 857–60, 912
sieve plate 451, *452*, *453*, 457
sieve pore *453*
sieve tube
    development in root 769
    development in shoot 768
    loading of 455–6, *458*
    structure of 451–2, *453*, *456*
    as translocation element 452–3, *454*
    unloading 456–7, *458*
sieve tube element 452
sign stimuli 613, 614
single-locus probe 875, 877
sino-atrial node 473, 474, 475
sinusoids 666
skeleton
    exoskeleton 624–5, 676
    function of 623–3
    hydrostatic 624, 639–41
skeleton (mammalian)
    anatomy of 627–33
    axial 627–8
    limb girdles 630–2
    limbs 631–2
    ribs *627*, 629, 630
    vertebrae 628–30
skin
    autonomic nervous system effect *573*
    as excretory structure 673
    thermoregulation by 658, 659
    structure of 656–8
skull, anatomy of 627
slit pores 683, *685*
smallpox 498, *501*
smoking-related disease
    cancer 525
    heart disease 522
    osteoporosis 530
smooth muscle: *see* muscle, smooth
social behaviour, human 907–8
social disease 495
social hierarchies 619–21
social organisation 620–1
sodium absorption, effect of aldosterone 694
sodium blood level control 693–4
sodium gate 558
sodium–potassium pump
    ATP usage 557, *558*
    effect of aldosterone 694
    in loop of Henle 691
    in neurone 557
    of proximal tubule *690*
sodium reabsorption
    in loop of Henle 691
    by nephron *689*, *690*
solenoid fibre 790, *791*
solute potential
    of blood, control mechanism 693, *695*
    definition of 429

Chapter Fourteen

Transport in animals

The simpler animals such as cnidarians and platyhelminths lack specialised systems for the transport and distribution of materials. The organisms in these groups possess a large surface area to volume ratio, and diffusion of gases over the whole body surface is sufficient for their needs. Internally the distance that materials have to travel is again small enough for them to move by diffusion or cytoplasmic streaming (sections 5.9.8 and 5.10.2).

As organisms increase in size and complexity so the quantity of materials moving in and out of the body increases. The distance that materials have to travel within the body also increases, so that diffusion becomes inadequate as a means for their distribution. Some other method of conveying materials from one part of the organism to another is therefore necessary. This generally takes the form of a mass flow system, as described at the beginning of chapter 13 (see also table 13.1). There are two circulatory systems which rely on mass flow in animals, namely the blood vascular system and the lymphatic system. A vascular system is one which contains fluid-filled vessels involved in transport.

14.1 General characteristics of a blood vascular system

The purpose of a blood vascular system (or blood system for short) is to provide rapid mass flow of materials from one part of the body to another over distances where diffusion would be too slow. On reaching their destination the materials must be able to pass through the walls of the circulatory system into the organs or tissues. Likewise, materials produced by these structures must also be able to enter the circulatory system. In other words, exchange systems are linked to mass flow systems.

Every blood system possesses three distinct characteristics:

* a circulatory fluid, the blood;
* a contractile, pumping device to propel the fluid around the body – this may either be a modified blood vessel or a heart;
* tubes through which the fluid can circulate, the blood vessels.

Two distinct types of blood system are found in animals. They are the open and closed blood systems.

The open blood system (most arthropods, some cephalopod molluscs). Blood is pumped by the heart into an aorta which branches into a number of arteries. These open into a series of blood spaces collectively called the **haemocoel**. In other words, blood does not stay in the blood vessels, hence the term 'open'. Blood under low pressure moves slowly between the tissues, gradually percolating back into the heart through open-ended veins. Distribution of blood to the tissues is poorly controlled.

The closed blood system (echinoderms, most cephalopod molluscs, annelids, vertebrates including humans).

* Blood stays in the blood vessels. It does not come into direct contact with the body tissues.
* Blood is pumped by the heart rapidly around the body under high pressure and back to the heart.
* Distribution of blood to different tissues can be adjusted, depending on demand.
* The only entry and exit to the system is through the walls of the blood vessels.

Blood vessels are named according to their structure and function. Vessels conveying blood away from the heart are called **arteries**. These branch into smaller arteries called **arterioles**. The arterioles divide many times into microscopic **capillaries** which are located between the cells of nearly all the body tissues. It is here that exchange of materials between blood and tissues takes place.

Within the organ or tissue the capillaries reunite to form **venules** which begin the process of returning blood to the heart. The venules join to form **veins**. Veins carry blood back to the heart. The structure of each type of blood vessel is discussed in detail later in section 14.5.

14.2 The development of blood systems in animals

14.2.1 Annelids

Annelids are coelomate animals. The presence of a coelom separates the body wall from the internal organs and gives the advantage of independence of movement of internal structures such as the gut. However, this means there is a need for some form of transport system in the body. A blood system has evolved which connects gut and body wall. The earthworm, for example, has a well-developed blood system in which blood circulates around the body through a system of blood vessels.

Two main blood vessels run the length of the body, one dorsal and one ventral. They are connected by blood vessels in each segment. Near the front of the animal, five pairs of these connecting vessels are contractile and act as pumps. The main blood vessels can also pump blood.

The blood contains haemoglobin dissolved in the plasma rather than being carried in red blood cells. Haemoglobin transports oxygen around the body.

14.2.2 Arthropods

Arthropods have an open blood system (see above). The coelom is drastically reduced and its place taken by the haemocoel. This is a network of blood-filled spaces called **sinuses** in which the internal organs are suspended. Gaseous exchange in most arthropods is achieved by the tracheal system (section 2.8.6), and the blood vascular system is not used for transporting respiratory gases. Arthropod blood is colourless and contains no haemoglobin.

14.2.3 Vertebrates

The blood systems of all vertebrates possess a muscular heart, lying in a ventral position near the front of the animal. The heart is responsible for pumping blood rapidly to all parts of the body. Arteries carry blood away from the heart, and veins carry blood from the body back to the heart. Oxygen is carried by haemoglobin in red blood cells. The human blood system will be studied in detail as an example of both a vertebrate and a mammal. The lymphatic system will also be examined briefly where its functions overlap with those of the blood system.

14.3 Composition of blood

The average adult has about $5\,dm^3$ of blood. Technically speaking blood is a liquid tissue. It is made up of several types of cell which are found bathed in a fluid matrix called **plasma**. The different types of blood cell can be seen in a blood smear (fig 14.1a). The cells make up about 45% by volume of the blood. The other 55% is plasma. If blood is centrifuged, the cells (and platelets, which are really cell fragments) form a red pellet at the bottom of the tube, with the straw-coloured plasma above.

14.1 Why is the pellet red?

Plasma from which the clotting protein fibrinogen has been removed is called **serum**. The pH of the blood is kept between 7.35 and 7.45.

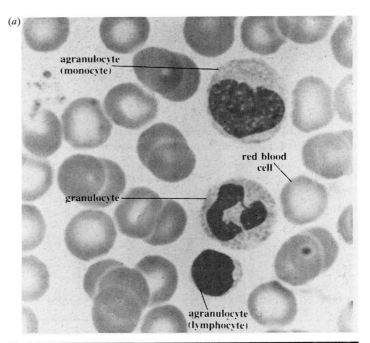

(a)

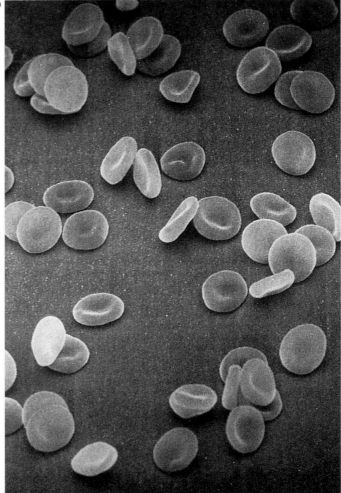

(b)

Fig 14.1 (a) A blood smear showing red blood cells and three types of white cell. (b) A scanning electron micrograph of red blood cells of a mammal.